Vol 6

£15
Ripley
HT
9/35

A SHAKESPEARE BIBLIOGRAPHY

The Catalogue of the Birmingham Shakespeare Library

BIRMINGHAM PUBLIC LIBRARIES

PART TWO: ACCESSIONS POST-1931

VOLUME VI

English Shakespeariana
Nash-Zukofsky

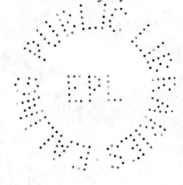

MANSELL 1971

© 1971 Birmingham Public Library and Mansell Information/ Publishing Ltd

Published by Mansell Information/Publishing Ltd
3 Bloomsbury Place, London WC1A 2QA, England

The paper on which this catalogue has been printed is based on require-
ments established by the late William J. Barrow for a permanent/durable
book paper. It is laboratory certified to meet or exceed the following values:
Substance 89 gsm
pH cold extract 9·4
Fold endurance (MIT $\frac{1}{2}$ kg tension) 1200
Tear resistance (Elmendorf) 73 (or 67 x 3)
Opacity 90·3%

SBN 7201 0135 2 (Volume I)
7201 0136 0 (Volume II)
7201 0137 9 (Volume III)
7201 0138 7 (Volume IV)
7201 0139 5 (Volume V)
7201 0140 9 (Volume VI)
7201 0140 7 (Volume VII)

Printed and bound in England

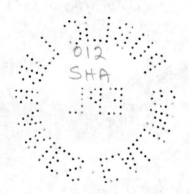

Nash, Thomas *works relating to*

—— ASHE (G.)
Hamlet and Pyrrhus [: comparison
between Hamlet and the Marlowe-Nashe
play Dido and Aeneas].   FROM [Notes
and Queries, Vol. 192].   [1947].

587301

—— CUNLIFFE (J. W.)
Nash and the earlier Hamlet.
IN Publications of the Modern
Language Association of America,
Vol. 21.   (Baltimore)   1906.

428341

—— SCHRICKX (W.)
Shakespeare's early contemporaries:
the background of the Harvey-Nashe
polemic and "Love's labour's lost".
(Antwerpen)
bibliog.   1956.

665395

—— STALKER (A.)
Shakespeare and Tom Nashe [: imaginary
conversations between Coleridge and
Lamb.]   (Stirling)   1935.

435912

—— STALKER (A.)
Shakespeare, Marlowe and Nashe
[: critical examinations of
Richard III, Henry V etc.]
(Stirling)   1936.

462712

—— TANNENBAUM (S. A.)
Thomas Nashe (a concise bibliography).
[With references to Shakespeare.]
pp. viii, [ii] 31.   (New York)
1941.
Elizabethan Bibliographies.
Edn. limited to 300 copies.

527144

see also MOORE (W. H.) Baconian Studies.

Nash, Thomas Shakespeare's grandson *works relating to*

—— RATCLIFF (S. C.) and JOHNSON (H. C.) eds.
Warwick County Records, vol. 1:
Quarter Sessions Order Book, Easter,
1625 to Trinity, 1637 [including
entries relating to Thomas Nash.]
Edited [with introduction] by S. C.
Ratcliff and H. C. Johnson.   With a
foreword by Lord Hanworth.   (Warwick:
Warwickshire County Council, Records
Committee)
ports. illus.   1935.

436276

NATHAN, GEORGE JEAN
The Avon flows

For editions of this play see under
English Editions: Othello:
Alterations &c.

NATHAN (G. J.)
Materia critica [: a critic's notes
on dramatic criticism and the
theatre in general.   With references
to Shakespeare.]   (New York) 1924.

544438

Nathan, George Jean *works relating to*

—— FRICK (CONSTANCE)
The Dramatic criticism of George Jean
Nathan.   [With a foreword by G. J.
Nathan, a list of his books, biblio-
graphical notes and references to
Shakespeare.]   (Ithaca, N.Y.)
port.   1943.

542792

NATHAN (N.)
Is Shylock Philip Henslowe?
FROM Notes and Queries [Vol. 193].
pp. 163-166.   1948.

596207

NATHAN, NORMAN
Leontes' provocation.
IN SHAKESPEARE QUARTERLY XIX: 1.
pp. 19-24.   (New York)
1968.

605711

NATHAN (NORMAN)
The Marriage of Duke Vincentio and
Isabella.
IN SHAKESPEARE QUARTERLY VII.
pp. 43-45.
(New York)   1956.

605711

NATHAN (NORMAN)
Shylock, Jacob, and God's judgment.
IN SHAKESPEARE QUARTERLY I: 4.
pp. 255-259.
(New York)   1950.

605711

Nathaniel (Sir)[pseud.] Shakspeare
and the stage: a vexed question.
[With bibliographical notes.] From
[The New Monthly Magazine, Vol.130].

[1864.]

579655

NATIONAL BOOK COUNCIL, afterwards
NATIONAL BOOK LEAGUE
Book Lists, Second Series [No. 11]:
Shakespeare.   pp. 32.   [1952.]

655367

NATIONAL BOOK COUNCIL, afterwards
NATIONAL BOOK LEAGUE
  A History of Shakespearean production
  [: an exhibition of pictures, play-
  bills, books, etc.] arranged by the
  Arts Council of Great Britain and the
  Society for Cultural Relations with
  the U.S.S.R., Jan. 15-Feb. 28, 1948.
  [Catalogue, poster, etc.]   pp. 36.
                                  1948.

                               588769

[NATIONAL BOOK COUNCIL, afterwards]
NATIONAL BOOK LEAGUE
  Some editions of Shakespeare's plays,
  exhibited at 7, Albemarle Street,
  Jan. and Feb., 1948.   pp. 8. [1948.]

                               588768

NATIONAL BOOK LEAGUE
  Shakespeare and his times [: catalogue
  of an exhibition to mark the four-
  hundredth anniversary of Shakespeare's
  birth].   1964.

                               667953

National Character

—— CLARK (CUMBERLAND)
  Shakespeare and national character:
  a study of Shakespeare's knowledge
  and dramatic use of the distinctive
  racial characteristics of different
  peoples of the world.
    illus.   bibliog.   1932.   398517
    ———— Another edn.   1934.   416880

—— HERTZ (F. [O.])
  Humanism and nationality in England:
  Bacon, Shakespeare.   IN Hertz (F. [O.])
  Nationality in history and politics: a
  study of the psychology and sociology of
  national sentiment and character. [With
  bibliographical notes.]
                                   1944.
  (International Library of Sociology and
  Social Reconstruction)

                               548300

—— MITCHELL (A.)
  Shakspeare's nationalities.   FROM
  [Charing Cross], Vol. 6.
                                [1878.]

                               554165

National Junior Shakespeare Club <u>see</u>
Societies and Clubs.

NATIONAL LIBRARY OF SCOTLAND, EDINBURGH
and EDINBURGH UNIVERSITY LIBRARY
  Shakespeare: an exhibition of printed
  books to mark the Quater-centenary
  of his birth.   Drawn form the resources
  of the National Library of Scotland
  and the Library of the University of
  Edinburgh.   (Edibburgh)   1964.

                               668235

NATIONAL PORTRAIT GALLERY
  O sweet Mr. Shakespeare, I'll have his
  picture: the changing image of
  Shakespeare's person, 1600-1800.
                                   1964.

    illus.   668095

National Shakespearian Fund established
by J. O. Halliwell in 1861 [for the
purchase of New Place Gardens, Anne
Hathaway's Cottage, etc., and erection
of a library and museum at Stratford-
on-Avon].   Vellum sheets headed
"Shakespearian Census" intended for
the recording of subscriptions.
                                [1861]

                               472927

National Socialist Party *see* Germany

National Theatre Company

—— Production of Othello, the Moor of
  Venice.   [Script]   (British Home
  Entertainments Ltd.)   [1965]

                               752259

—— TYNAN, KENNETH PEACOCK, ed.
  Othello: the National Theatre
  production.   1966.

    illus.   753063

National Theatre Project

—— CARRIC (A.)
Shakespeare Memorial: a National
Theatre.   IN The Mask, Vol. 1.
1909.

460751

—— Donald ([Sir]R.) The Press and the
theatre. In The Worlds Work, Vol.17.

1910-11.

231462

—— JACKSON (Sir B. [V.])
The Problem of Stratford-on-Avon.
IN ANDREWS (J.) and TRILLING (OSSIA)
eds., International theatre. 1949.

597571

—— Littlewood (S.R.) Shakespeare in the
Cromwell Road: a personal view
of the "National Theatre". Port.
In The Sphere, Vol. 153.

1938.

485156

—— Littlewood (S.R.) Shakespeare - the
critics' target [: a problem for the
new National Theatre.] Illus.
In The Sphere, Vol. 154.

1938.

492638

—— LYTTLETON (Mrs. [EDITH S.])
The National Memorial Theatre: the
work of the Shakespeare Memorial
Committee.   IN The World's Work,
Vol. 17.   1910-11.

231462

—— A Masque setting forth the true hon-
ouring of our rare and precious poet,
William Shakespeare.   pp. 45.
[1916.]
"Shakespeare Memorial National
Theatre, 1916", printed on cover.

494451

—— THE NATIONAL THEATRE
founded in Shakespeare's name: its
purpose, scope and meaning. pp. 16.
illus.   [1938.]

619322

—— Pratt (T.) The Shakespeare Memorial
National Theatre. In Manchester
Literary Club. Papers, Vol.37.

(Manchester)   1911.

518393

—— ROSE (Mrs. [CONSTANCE])
"Plain Mrs. Rose" [: reminiscences,
with references to the Shakespeare
Memorial Theatre].   (Cheltenham)
ports.   1936.

452685

—— [SHAKESPEARE MEMORIAL NATIONAL THEATRE
COMMITTEE]
Theatre Royal, Drury Lane; Shakespeare
matinée, Nov. 26, 1935, in aid of the
National Theatre Appeal. [Programme.]
pp. 28.   1935.

444823

Nationality *see* National Character

Natural History
see also Flowers and Plants

—— BALDWIN, THOMAS WHITFIELD
The Pedigree of Theseus' pups.
Midsummer-Night's Dream, IV, 1, 123-130.
IN DEUTSCHE SHAKESPEARE-GESELLSCHAFT
WEST, JAHRBUCH 1968.   pp. 109-120.
(Heidelberg)

754129

—— B[LACKBURN] ([Mrs.] J[ANE])
The Crows of Shakespeare [: sketches
of scenes from Shakespeare] by J. B.
(Edinburgh)   1899.   527552
_____ Another copy, with original
boards.   668394

—— BLYTON (W. J.)
English cavalcade [: England as
depicted by poets and novelists.
Including a chapter on Shakespeare
entitled "Nature magic".]
illus.   map.   1937.

463625

—— Brown (C.) Shakespeare and the horse.
Reprinted from 'The Library', April,
1912. pp.31.

1912.

468014

—— [BYRNE (MURIEL ST. C.) ed.]
The Elizabethan zoo: a book of beasts
both fabulous and authentic.   [Selected
from P. Holland's Translation of
Pliny, 1601, and E. Topsell's "Historie
of foure-footed beastes", 1607, & his
"Historie of serpents", 1608.]
illus.   1926.
The Haslewood Books.

517671

—— CHUBB (P.)
Shakespeare's joy in nature.   FROM
The Standard, Vol. 17.   (New York)
1930.

441355

CORDLEY (C.)
Shakespeare's dogs.   IN The Gentleman's
Magazine, Vol. 290.   1901.

157420

Dewar (G.A.B.) Shakespeare's Nature.
In The New Liberal Review, Vol.6.

1904.

180054

HARRIS (C. A.)
Did Shakespeare keep bees?   FROM The
Month, February, 1934.   pp. [8.]
1934.

416888

Harris (D.F.F.) Biology in Shakespeare.
pp.[15]. From The Scientific Monthly,
Jan. 1932.
(New York)   1932.

444388

HARRISON (THOMAS PERRIN)

Shakespeare's birds. Reprinted from
Tennessee Studies in Literature, Vol.3.
pp.[10]. (Knoxville, Tenn.)
1958.

666908

Harrison, Thomas Perrin
Shakespeare's rural muse. IN

CORDER, JIM W., ed.
Shakespeare 1964 [: a record of the
celebrations of the Shakespeare
Quatercentenary at Texas Christian
University]. (Fort Worth, Tex.)
1965.

illus.   745402

Harry (J.E.) Dog and dogs: the story
of man's constant companion. [With
a chapter on Shakespeare's dogs.]
2nd edn.

(New York)   1936.

460785

HARTING, JAMES EDMUND
The Birds of Shakespeare, or the
ornithology of Shakespeare critically
examined, explained and illustrated.
Including "Of men and birds: prolegomena
to the 'Birds of Shakespeare'" by G.
Steiner. (Chicago: Argonaut Inc.)
1965.

753996

HOPE (CONSTANCE)
Shakespeare and the song of a lark.
IN The Month, Vol. 94.   1899.

150079

Hulme (F.E.) Natural history lore and
legend: examples of quaint and bygone beliefs gathered in from divers
authorities, ancient and mediaeval,
of varying degrees of reliability.
[With references to Shakespeare.]
Illus.

1895.

528991

KEEPER OF THE BEES [pseud.]
Shakespeare and the honey comb.
IN British Bee Journal, March 1934.
1934.

428639

KIRKMAN (J.)
Animal nature versus human nature in
King Lear.
IN Transactions of the New Shakespeare
Society, Series 1.   Nos. 6-7.
pp. 385-408.   1877-9.

11987

KIRMSE ([Miss] PERSIS)
Shakespeare and the birds [: drawings
illustrating quotations from Shakespeare].
pp.57.   1938.

487928

KIRMSE ([Miss] PERSIS)
Shakespeare at the kennels: drawings
from quotations of Shakespeare's
plays.   pp. 64.   1934.

428120

KIRMSE ([Miss] PERSIS)
Shakespeare at the Zoo [: a book of
drawings].   pp. 55.   1936.

458245

KIRMSE ([Miss] PERSIS)
Shakespeare with the pets: a book of
drawings [illuminated with quotations
from Shakespeare's plays.]   pp. 55.
1935.

441578

KNIGHT (GEORGE WILSON)
The Shakespearian tempest.   [With
an appendix, The Shakespearian aviary:
bird-life in Shakespeare.]
1932.   399670
_____ Another edn.   The Oxford
Bookshelf.   (Oxford)
1940.   520941

LUCE (M.)
Man and nature; or, Essays and sketches:
[prose and verse.   Containing essays on
Shakespeare, especially as a poet of
nature].

1935.

435959

MASSINGHAM (HAROLD JOHN)
The Tree of life.   [With chapters on
Shakespeare, dealing with his study
of nature, philosophy and religion].
1943.

543975

MATTHISON (KAILA M.)
Shakespeare and sheep-shearing.   IN
Matthison (A. L.) Nothing about paint
[: essays].   (Birmimgham)
1944.   547270
Another copy.   546854

——Maxwell (J.C.) Animal imagery in
  Coriolanus.[With bibliographical
  notes.]In The Modern Language
  Review, Vol.42.

      (Cambridge)   1947.

         266816/42

——[Miller (T.)] Shakspere and sheep-
  shearing. Illus. From [Miller (T.)
  Pictures from country life.]

      [1848.]

         518327

—— MURRY (J. M.)
  Shakespeare and the cuckoo.
  IN Murry (J. M.) Katherine Mansfield
  and other literary portraits. 1949.

         598951

——PHIPSON (EMMA)
  The Natural history similes in Henry VI.
  IN Transactions of the New Shakespeare
  Society, Series 1. Nos. 6-7.
  pp. 354-384.   1877-9.

         11987

——PUMPHREY (MARY E.)
  Shakespeare's birds. FROM Friends
  Quarterly Examiner, Jan. and April,
  1931. pp. [24].   1931.

         439152

—— RAGG (L.)
  Trees and gardens in Shakespeare's
  plays. IN The Tree lover, Vol. 3.
        1939-41.

         574705

——Rohde (Eleanour S.) Shakespeare's
  wild flowers: fairy lore, gardens,
  herbs, gatherers of simples and bee
  lore. Illus.

        1935.

(Medici Society.)

         443234

——SEAGER (H. W.)
  Natural history in Shakespeare's time.
        1896.
    Large paper edition.

         471781

——Shakspere as a naturalist. From
  The Sphinx, Vol. 4.

      (Manchester)   1871.

         527622

——Shakspearean dogs. FROM Once a week
  [New Series, Vol. 10].   1872.

         554168

——STOCKELBACH (Mrs. LAVONIA)
  The Birds of Shakespeare. pp. 52.
  [Verona, N.J.]
  illus.   1940. 525216
  Privately printed. Signed by author.
  ———— Another edn. 30 plates.
        [1954.] 642669

—— Sullivan ([Sir] E.) What Shakespeare
  saw in nature. In The Nineteenth
  century and after, Vol. 73.

      1913.

         243292

——Westacott (C.A.) The Compassionate
  onlooker, William Shakespeare 1564-
  1616 [: quotations from Shakespeare's
  works interspersed with notes by
  the compiler, showing Shakespeare's
  attitude to animals]. pp.8.

      [1941.]

(United Humanitarian League and the World
League against Vivisection and for the Protection of Animals.)

         530215

——WESTACOTT (C. A.)
  Shakespeare and the animals.
  pp. 47.   (Letchworth)
  port.   [1949.]

         603147

——YODER (AUDREY)
  Animal analogy in Shakespeare's
  character portrayal. [With a bibliography and bibliographical notes.]
  (New York)   1947.

         590617

Nature *see* Man and Nature; Natural History; Flowers and Plants; Tempests

NAUCLERUS [J.]
Chronici Commentarii, 1516, Vol. 1
[: extract relating to the Lear
legend]. IN KIRBY (T. A.) and
WOOLF (H. B.) eds., Philologica.
(Baltimore)   1949.

        610545

NAUMAN, JANET
  Henry IV part one. A scene-by-scene
  analysis with critical commentary.
  (New York)   1964.

    Study master series. 746819

Navarro (Mme. Marie Antoinette de)
    formerly Mary Anderson

see: Anderson (Mary)

Navy *see* **Sailors and the Sea**

Naylor (E.W.) ed., It was a lover and
   his lass. (Duet). [Words by]
   Shakespeare [from As You Like It].
   pp. 4.

[c.1925.]

516976

NAYLOR (EDWARD WOODALL) ed.
   Peg-a-Ramsey: traditional [song in
   "Twelfth Night"] arranged and edited
   with words by E. W. Naylor.   pp. 8.
                                    [1926.]

542322

NAYLOR (EDWARD WOODALL) ed.
   Two Ophelia songs [from Shakespeare's
   "Hamlet": 1. How should I your true
   love know?   2. And will he not come
   again?]   Arranged for chorus or
   mixed voices (S.C.Bar.) unaccompanied,
   by B. Naylor, from E. W. Naylor's
   "Shakespeare Music" Curwen Edition.
   pp. 8.   1933.

542328

Nazis *see* **Germany**

NEALE (Sir JOHN ERNEST)
   England's Elizabeth: a lecture
   delivered at the Folger Shakespeare
   Library on November 17, 1958, the
   fourth centenary of the accession of
   Queen Elizabeth I.   pp. [4], 20.
   (Washington)
     port.   1958.   666451
   _____ IN Life and letters in Tudor
   and Stuart England.   (Folger
   Shakespeare Library)   (Ithaca, N.Y.)
                          1962.   667762

NEALE (JOHN PRESTON) and LE KEUX (JOHN
HENRY)
   Views of the ancient church of the
   Holy Trinity, Stratford upon Avon.
   With an historical and architectural
   description.   pp. 16.
                   1825.   467246
   _____ Large paper edn.
                   1825.   508332

NEARING (HOMER)
   Julius Caesar and the Tower of London.
   [With bibliographical notes.]   IN
   Modern Language Notes, Vol. 63.
   (Baltimore, Md.)   1948.

439157/63

NEARING (HOMER)
   A Note on King John, V, vii, 112-114.
   IN Notes and Queries, Vol. 192.
                     1947.

588005

NEARING (HOMER)
   The Penaltie of Adam [: criticism of
   As you like it.   With bibliographical
   notes].   IN Modern Language Notes,
   Vol. 62.   (Baltimore, Md.)   1947.

439157/62

NEARING (HOMER)
   Shakespeare as a nondramatic poet:
   Sonnet XXIX.
   IN SHAKESPEARE QUARTERLY XIII: 1.
   pp. 15-20.
   (New York) 1962.

605711

NEARING (H.)
   A Three-way pun in Richard II.
   IN Modern Language Notes, Vol. 62.
   (Baltimore, Md.)
   bibliog.   1947.

439157/62

Needham (F.) Note [with references to
   A Winter's Tale and Much Ado about
   Nothing.] In Newcastle (W.Cavendish,
   [1st] Duke of) A Pleasante & merrye
   humor off a roge. pp.[46].

(Bungay)   1933.

(Welbeck Miscellany, No.1.)

431337

Needleman (M.H.) and Otis (W.B.)
   An Outline-history of English
   literature to Dryden. [With a
   chapter on Shakespeare and bibliographical notes.] Revised edn.

(New York)   1937.

(College Outline Series)

506389

Neel ([L.]B.) Music for Shakespeare,
   No.2 : A Midsummer Night's
   Dream. [Broadcast] April 22nd,
   1950. ff.6. Typescript.

1950.

60906C

NEEL (LOUIS BOYD)

see also DAVIES (ROBERTSON) and others.

Neil (S.) A Documentary biography of
   William Shakespeare. *From* The
   Birmingham Morning News, April 26th,
   May 10th and 13th, 1872.

(Birmingham)   1872.

446499

NEIL (SAMUEL)
   The Home of Shakespeare, described by
   S. Neil and illustrated in thirty-
   three engravings by F. W. Fairholt.
   [With An Architectural account of the
   collegiate church of the Holy Trinity
   by E. H. Knowles].   pp. 80.   (Warwick)
                           [?1871]   394908
   _____ 2nd edn.   [1878]   508515
   _____ 11th edn.   With forty-eight
   engravings.   [c.1898] 467567

NEILL (KERBY)
More ado about Claudio: an acquittal
for the slandered groom.
IN SHAKESPEARE QUARTERLY III: 2.
pp. 91-107.
(New York) 1952.

605711

NEILL (WILLIAM ALEXANDER) [pseud.
A. Cantab]
Othello: a tale of a Moor and an
Amour, by A. Cantab. pp. 12.
(Liverpool) 1856.

665103

NEILSON (FRANCIS)
Hamlet and Shakespeare. pp. 86.
(New York) 1950.

645894

NEILSON (FRANCIS)
Shakespeare and The Tempest. (Rindge,
N.H.) 1956.

665315

NEILSON (FRANCIS)
A Study of Macbeth for the stage.
(New York) 1952.

667773

Neilson, Francis *works relating to*

— IN MEMORIAM: Francis Neilson,
1867-1961 [: Shakespearean scholar].
Illus. FROM The American Journal of
Economics and Sociology, Vol.20, No.4.
(New York) 1961.

667774

Neilson, Harold V. *works relating to*

— Mr. Harold V. Neilson's Shakespeare
Memorial Theatre, 1919-1933 [a
selection of press opinions]. pp.
23. [Loughborough] [c.1935.]

649960

NEILSON (WILLIAM ALLAN)
The Variorum Twelfth Night, [by
H. H. Furness. A review]. IN
The Atlantic Monthly, Vol. 89.
(Cambridge, Mass.) 1902.

170922

NEILSON (WILLIAM ALLAN) ed.
The Chief Elizabethan dramatists,
excluding Shakespeare. Selected
plays by Lyly, Peele, Greene, Marlowe,
Kyd, Chapman, Jonson, Dekker, Marston,
Heywood, Beaumont, Fletcher, Webster,
Middleton, Massinger, Ford, Shirley.
Edited from the original quartos and
folios with notes, biographies, and
bibliographies by W. A. Neilson.
ports. [1911.]

483542

NEILSON (WILLIAM ALLAN) and THORNDIKE
(ASHLEY HORACE)
The Facts about Shakespeare.
Revised edn. (New York)
illus. plan. tables. bibliog.
1961.

666823

NEJGEBAUER (A.)
Twentieth-century studies in
Shakespeare's Songs, Sonnets, and Poems.
2: The Sonnets. IN SHAKESPEARE
SURVEY 15. (Cambridge) 1962.

667174

NELSON (ALEC)
The Home of Grandfather Shakespeare.
FROM Home Chimes, New Series. Vol.13.
pp.[13.] 1892.

667273

NELSON (ROBERT JAMES)
Shakespeare. The play as mirror.
IN Nelson (R. J.) Play within a play:
the dramatist's conception of his art;
Shakespeare to Anouilh. (New Haven,
[Conn.]) 1958.
Yale Romanic Studies: Second Series, 5.

731490

[NELSON (S.) ed.]
Ariel's song, composed by [T. A.]
Arne, arranged by S. Nelson.
[Words from] the Tempest. pp. [ii] 5.
[c.1840.]
Standard Songs, No. 1.

600317

[NELSON (S.) ed.]
Come unto these yellow sands, by H.
Purcell, arranged by S. Nelson. [Words
from] The Tempest [by Shakespeare].
pp. [ii] 5.
[c.1840.]
(Standard Songs, No. 2)

600319

[NELSON (S.) ed.]
"O! bid your faithful Ariel fly" by
[T.] Linley, arranged by S. Nelson.
[Words adapted from] The Tempest
[by Shakespeare]. pp. [ii] 7.
[c.1840.]
Standard Songs.

600318

Nelson Classics
LAMB (CHARLES and MARY [A.])
Tales from Shakespeare.
frontis. [c.1915.]

545578

Nelson's Famous Books
LAMB (CHARLES and MARY [A.])
Tales from Shakespeare. With a
frontispiece by N. M. Price and line
drawings by F. G. Moorsom.   [1933.]

406059

Nelson's Famous Books
LAMB (CHARLES and MARY [A.])
Tales from Shakespeare. With a
frontispiece by N. M. Price and 16
line drawings by F. G. Moorsom.
[1937.]

467563

Nelson's Winchester Classics
LAMB (CHARLES and MARY [A.])
Tales from Shakespeare.
ports.   [1932.]

392828

NEMEROY (HOWARD)
The Marriage of Theseus and Hippolyta.
IN The Kenyon Review, Vol. 18.
(Gambier, Ohio)   1956.

594031/18

Németh (A.) The Cult of the Shakespearean drama in Hungary. From
Danubian Review, Vol. 5.

([Budapest])   1937.

512777

Nesbit (E[dith]) The Children's Shakespeare. Illustrated by R. Klep.

(New York)   1938.

496765

NESBIT (E[DITH])
Twenty beautiful stories from
Shakespeare. Official text for
members of the National Junior
Shakespeare Club. Illustrated by
M. Bihn. Edited and arranged, [with
a preface], by E. T. Roe. (Chicago)
1926.

422519

NESBIT (EDITH) and CHESSON (HUGH)

The Merchant of Venice and other stories.
Illustrated by F. Brundage and M.Bowley.
pp.64. Illus.   [c.1920.]

667236

NESBITT (GEORGE LYMAN)
Benthamite reviewing: the first twelve
years of the Westminster Review, 1824-
1836 [containing references to criticism of Shakespeare's works. With
a bibliography.] (New York) 1934.
Columbia University Studies in English
and Comparative Literature.

434098

NESS (FREDERIC WILLIAM)
The Use of rhyme in Shakespeare's plays.
[With a bibliography and bibliographical
notes.] (New Haven, [Conn.])
1941.

544711

Ness, Frederic William *works relating to*

— LANDIS (P.)
[Review of] The Use of rhyme in
Shakespeare's plays, by F. W. Ness.
FROM Journal of English and Germanic
Philology, Vol. 42.   (Urbana, Ill.)
1943.

569115

— PURSER (J. W. R.)
[Review of] The Use of rhyme in
Shakespeare's plays, by F. W. Ness.
IN The Modern Language Review, Vol.
38.   (Cambridge)   1943.

553690

Nethercot (A.H.) The Road to Tryermaine:
a study of the history, background
and purposes of Coleridge's "Christ-
abel". [With bibliographical notes
and Shakespearian references.]

(Chicago)   1939.

515677

Nethercot (A.H.) Sir William D'Avenant,
poet laureate and playwright-manager.
[With appendices and bibliographical
notes.] Port. Genealogical Table.

(Chicago)   1938.

496170

NEUMANN (JOSHUA H.)
Shakespearean criticism in the Tatler
and the Spectator. IN Publications
of the Modern Language Association of
America, Vol. 39.   (Menasha, Wis.)
1924.

428359

NEURATH, MARIE
They lived like this in Shakespeare's
England. Artist: Muriel Turner. 1968.

illus.   774869

[Neve (P.)] Cursory remarks on some
of the ancient English poets,
particularly Milton. [Including
Shakespeare.]

1789.

543791

NEVILLE (HARRY)
Crowner's quest [: an imaginary
inquest upon the death of Ophelia
in the form of a play]. IN New
Plays Quarterly, No. 12.
plan.   1950.

605301/12

NEVINSON (J. L.)
Shakespeare's dress in his portraits.
IN SHAKESPEARE QUARTERLY XVIII: 2.
pp. 101-106.
(New York)   1967.

605711

NEVO, RUTH
The Masque of greatness.
IN SHAKESPEARE STUDIES 3.   (Cincinnati,
Ohio)   1967.

771652

New and general biographical
dictionary, containing an historical
account of the lives and writings of
the most eminent persons in every
nation, particularly the British
and Irish. Vol.10 [including
Shakespear].

1762.

574981

New College Shakespeare Club, Oxford
see Societies and Clubs (Oxford. New
College Shakespeare Club).

New editors - Shakespeare: [a review
of] The Works of William Shakespeare,
edited by W. G. Clark, J. Glover and
W. A. Wright.   FROM [Dublin University
Magazine,] Vol. 63.   [Dublin] 1864.

558056

New facts regarding the life of
Shakspeare [, by J. P. Collier: a
review].   FROM The Mirror [of literature, amusement and instruction,
Vol. 26].   [1835.]

562631

New Orleans, U.S.A.

—— ROPPOLO (JOSEPH PATRICK)
American premieres of two Shakespearean
plays in New Orleans: The Two
gentlemen of Verona and Antony and
Cleopatra.   Reprinted from Tulane
University, Tulane Studies in English,
Vol. 7.   pp. [8].   (New Orleans, La.)
1957.

666580

—— ROPPOLO (JOSEPH PATRICK)

Hamlet in New Orleans. Reprinted from
Tulane University. Tulane Studies in
English. Vol.6. pp.[16] Chronological
Table. Bibliogs. (New Orleans, La.)
1956.

666581

New Place *see* **Stratford-upon-Avon**, New
Place

New Pocket Classics
LAMB (CHARLES and MARY [A.])
Tales from Shakespeare.   Edited [with
an introduction] by A. Ainger.
Revised by H. Y. Moffett.   Illustrated
by Maud and Miska Petersham. 1932.

399214

New Prize Library
LAMB (CHARLES and MARY [A.])
Tales from Shakespeare.
frontis.   [1949.]

598030

New Theatre *see* Leicester, New Theatre;
London, Theatres — New Theatre

NEW THEATRE MAGAZINE
Shakespeare Quatercentenary souvenir
issue [on] Bristol Shakespeare Festival.
Vol. V 2. (Bristol)   1964.

748949

New York

—— AMERICAN NATIONAL THEATER AND ACADEMY
Blevins Davis presents Hamlet at
Kronberg Castle, Elsinore, Denmark,
June 17-27, 1949.   pp. [24].   [New
York]
ports.   illus.   [1949.]
Privately printed.

607834

—— BEISWANGER (G.)
Dancers and makers of dance.
[Includes a criticism of the Ballet
Theatre's ballet Romeo and Juliet.]
IN Theatre Arts, Vol. 27. (New York)
illus.   1943.

548672

—— Beiswanger (G.) 'From eleven to two'
Signor Verdi's Falstaff in English
[at the Metropolitan Opera House,
New York]. Illus. In Theatre
Arts, Vol. 28.

(New York)   1944.

558366

—— CAMPBELL (O. J.)
Miss Webster and The Tempest [: a
criticism of Margaret Webster's pro-
duction of The Tempest at the Broadway
Theatre, New York]. FROM The American
Scholar, Vol. 14. (New York) 1945.

578272

—— Corbin (J.) Shakspere his own
stage-manager : a new method and
important discoveries in productions
of the New Theatre [New York].
Illus. From The Century Magazine,
Vol. 63.

(New York) 1911.

520178

—— GILDER (ROSAMOND)
Actors in their stride: Broadway in
review. [Includes a criticism of
Richard III at the Forrest Theatre,
New York.] IN Theatre Arts, Vol. 27.
(New York)
illus. 1943.

548672

—— GILDER (ROSAMOND)
Othello and Venus: Broadway in review.
[Includes a criticism of Margaret
Webster's production of Othello under
Theatre Guild auspices, starring
Paul Robeson.] IN Theatre Arts,
Vol. 27. (New York)
illus. 1943.

548672

—— Gilder (Rosamond) Shakespeare in New
York: 1947-1948. In Shakespeare
survey: an annual survey of
Shakespearian study & production.
[Vol.] 2.

(Cambridge) 1949.

598403

—— Houghton (N.) The Old Vic in New York
[including their Shakespearian
performances]. Illus. In Theatre
Arts, Vol.30.

(New York) 1946.

579721

—— Isaacs (H.R.) This insubstantial
pageant : The Tempest in the
making [i.e. Margaret Webster's
production in New York]. Illus.
In Theatre Arts, Vol. 29.

(New York) 1945.

567819

—— MANDERS (V. E. C.)
Shakespeare at St. Bernard's [School
for Boys in New York City].
IN SHAKESPEARE QUARTERLY II: 2.
pp. 123-126.
(New York) 1951.

605711

—— MASON (H.)
French theatre in New York: a list
of plays. [With introduction.
Including some of Shakespeare's
plays.] (New York)
bibliog. 1940.

520945

—— Maurice Evans presents in New York [at
the St. James Theatre] Shakespeare's
Hamlet in its entirety. Directed by
Margaret Webster. [Souvenir book.]
pp. 16. [New York]
ports. illus. [1938.]

599878

—— Meserole (Harrison T.)

Shakespeare in New York, 1823-24: the 'Mirror',
morals, and 'The Merry Wives of Windsor'. IN

SMITH, GORDON ROSS, ed.
Essays on Shakespeare [by various
authors]. (University Park, Penn.)
1965.

pp.228-238. 755528

—— NEW YORK CITY SHAKESPEARE TERCENTENARY
CELEBRATION COMMITTEE
Program of the community masque
"Caliban:by the yellow sands", by
P. MacKaye. Produced at the stadium
of the College of the City of New
York, May 23-27, 1916. pp. viii, 36.
[New York]
illus. plan. [1916.]

599877

—— O'DONAVAN (W. R.)
A Statue of Shakespeare [in the Central
Park, New York]. FROM [Lippincott's
Magazine,] Vol. 13. [Philadelphia]
1874.

553495

—— PIERPONT MORGAN LIBRARY, New York
English drama from the mid-sixteenth
to the later eighteenth century:
catalogue of an exhibition, October,
1945-March 1946. pp. 95. (New
York)
ports. facsimiles. [1946.]

650074

—— PLAYERS' CLUB, New York
The Players: Eleventh annual revival:
Troilus and Cressida, by W.Shakespeare
[at] B. S. Moss' Broadway Theatre,
New York, week of June 6th, 1932.
[Souvenir programme.] pp. [28.]
[New York]
ports. illus. facsimile. [1932.]

646353

—— The Players fifth annual classic
revival: King Henry IV, Part one,
at the Knickerbocker Theatre, New
York, May 31 to June 5, 1926.
[Souvenir programme.] pp. [32.]
[New York]
ports. illus. facsimiles. 1926.

599875

—[Reviews of the Shakespeare Season in New York by] M. K. Danziger, A. Griffin, M. C. Kuner and A. C. Sprague.   IN SHAKESPEARE QUARTERLY V:1954, pp. 311-316; VI:1955, pp. 423-427; VII:1956, pp. 393-398; VIII:1957, pp. 515-519; IX:1958, pp. 531-534; X:1959, pp. 569-572; XI:1960, pp. 467-468; XII:1961, pp. 472-473; XIII:1962, pp. 553-557; XIV:1963, pp. 441-443; XV:1964, pp. 419-422; XVI:1965, pp. 335-339; XVII: 1966, pp. 419-421.

605711

— STEINBERG (MOLLIE B.)
The History of the Fourteenth Street Theatre [including references to Shakespearean productions.   With an introduction by Eve Le Gallienne]. (New York)
ports.   facsimiles.   1931.

544831

— The Tempest [: the Broadway production directed by Margaret Webster.] Illus. From Life, Vol.18.

[Chicago]   1945.

578276

—[Theatre Guild, New York.] Paul Robeson as Othello, the Moor of Venice [: a souvenir book of the Margaret Webster production of Othello]. pp. [20.] Illus

[New York]   [1943.]

559677

— Theatre Guild, New York.] The Theatre Guild and Gilbert Miller present Helen Hayes and Maurice Evans in Shakespeare's "Twelfth Night". Directed by Margaret Webster. [Souvenir book.] pp.20. Ports. Illus.

[New York]   [1940.]

599879

— THEATRE GUILD, New York
The Theatre Guild presents Katharine Hepburn [in] As you like it, a comedy by William Shakespeare. Directed by M. Benthall.   [Souvenir book.] pp.[16] [New York]
ports.   illus.   [1950.]

612237

— THEATRE GUILD, NEW YORK
The Theatre Guild Inc. presents "The Taming of the Shrew" with Alfred Lunt and Lynn Fontanne.   Production directed by H. W. Gribble. [Souvenir book.] pp. [16.] [New York)
ports.   illus.   [1935.]

646354

— THEATRE INCORPORATED
Michael Redgrave [and] Flora Robson in The Tragedy of "Macbeth" [: a description of the Theatre Incorporated production and cast]. pp. [16.] [New York]
ports.   illus.   [1948.]

598973

— UNDERWOOD (MELA)
Joe and Uta [: notes on Jose Ferrer and Uta Ferrer, with special reference to their parts in Othello at the Broadway, New York.] FROM Collier's May 20, 1944.   (New York)
illus.   1944.

578275

— Vernon (G.) "As You Like It" [: a criticism of the performance at the Mansfield Theatre, New York]. From The Commonweal, Vol. 35.

(New York)   1941.

565599

— WILSON (R.)
"Macbeth" on film [: the Mercury Theatre's production].   IN Theatre Arts, Vol. 33.   (New York)
illus.   1949.

320431/33

— ZIEGFELD THEATRE, New York
[Souvenir booklet of Vivien Leigh and Laurence Olivier in the production of Bernard Shaw's Caesar and Cleopatra and Shakespeare's Antony and Cleopatra at the Ziegfeld Theatre.] pp. [16] [New York]
ports.   illus.   [1951.]

624735

New York Public Library

— BROWN (K.)
A Guide to the reference collections of New York Public Library. [Including the Shakespeare collection. With bibliographical notes.] (New York)
facsimiles.   1941.

534868

— GORDON, JOHN D.
The Bard and the book. Editions of Shakespeare in the seventeenth century: an exhibition [at the New York Public Library.] (New York)   1964.

747543

New York Shakespeare Festival

—   [NEWSPAPER CUTTINGS of New York Shakespeare Festival, 1957- .] Illus. [New York]   1957-

667412

— [Reviews of the Shakespeare Season in
New York by] M. K. Danziger, A. Griffin,
M. C. Kuner and A. C. Sprague. IN
SHAKESPEARE QUARTERLY V:1954, pp. 311-
316; VI:1955, pp.423-427; VII:1956,
pp. 393-398; VIII:1957, pp. 515-519;
IX:1958, pp. 531-534; X:1959, pp. 569-
572; XI:1960, pp. 467-468; XII:1961,
pp. 472-473; XIII:1962, pp. 553-557;
XIV:1963, pp. 441-443; XV:1964, pp.
419-422; XVI:1965, pp. 335-339; XVII:
1966, pp. 419-421; XVIII:1967, pp.
411-415 XIV:1968,pp. 385-386.   605711

New York Times: [10 supplements
commemorating the] Shakespeare
Tercentenary, 1616-1916.   (New York)
illus.   1916.

                    507557

New Zealand

——Making New Zealand: pictorial surveys
    of a century [1840-1940], Vol.2.
    [Including references to
    Shakespearean performances in New
    Zealand.]
            (Wellington, N.Z.)   1940.
    (New Zealand, Internal Affairs Department)

                    530008

— Shakespeare Memorial Theatre Company.
    Australia and New Zealand,1949-1950.
    Shakespeare Memorial Theatre presents
    The Tragedy of Macbeth [and] Much
    Ado about Nothing.[Souvenir booklet.]
    pp.[20.] Ports.Illus.

            (Evesham)   [1949.]

                    604346

NEWARK COUNTY TECHNICAL COLLEGE AND
SCHOOL OF ART
  Programmes of Shakespearian perform-
  ances.   (Newark)   1934-51.

                    488036

NEWBOLT ([Sir] HENRY [JOHN])
  A Note on Antony and Cleopatra.
  IN GOLLANCZ ([Sir] I.) ed., A Book of
  homage to Shakespeare.
    ports. illus. facsimiles. [1916.]

                    264175

NEWBOLT (Sir HENRY [JOHN])
  The Poet and his audience.   [With
  reference to Shakespeare's Measure
  for Measure and Croce.]   IN The
  English Review, Vol. 25.   1917.

                    271200

Newbolt, Henry John Sir *works relating to*

— AINSLIE (D.)
  Shakespeare['s Measure for Measure]
  and Croce: [a reply to The Poet and
  his audience, by Sir H. J. Newbolt.]
  FROM The English Review, 1918.
  pp. [5.]   [1918]

                    389195

NEWBURY GRAMMAR SCHOOL
  Programmes, etc., of Shakespearian
  performances.   [Newbury]
  illus.   [1922-]

                    432080

NEWCASTLE (W. CAVENDISH, [1st] Duke of)
  A Pleasante & merrye humor off a
  roge.   [Edited with a prefatory
  note by F. Needham, referring to
  likenesses in the play to The Winter's
  tale and Much ado about nothing.]
  pp. [46].   (Bungay)   1933.
  Welbeck Miscellany.

                    431337

Newcastle-upon-Tyne

——ARMSTRONG COLLEGE [UNIVERSITY OF DURHAM]
    Catalogue of an exhibition of early
    editions of the works of Shakespeare
    held in commemoration of the Tercen-
    tenary of The First Folio, 1623.
    With a preface by [E.] G. Craig.
    pp. 19.   [Newcastle-upon-Tyne]
                                1923.

                    414136

——PUBLIC LIBRARIES
    [List of Shakespearian productions in
    Newcastle.   Based upon the collection
    of Theatre Royal playbills 1812-64
    housed in the Newcastle Reference
    Library.]   IN Shakespeare Scrapbook
    Vol. 16.   ff. 6.   [Newcastle-upon-Tyne]
    typescript.   [1950.]

                    543533

——PUBLIC LIBRARIES
    William Shakespeare, select catalogue
    of books in Newcastle-upon-Tyne City
    Libraries.   pp. 36.   (Newcastle-
    upon-Tyne)   [1952].

                    624243

——THEATRE ROYAL, Grey Street
    Centenary week [souvenir], 1837-1937.
    pp. 16.   [Newcastle-upon-Tyne]
    facsimile.   1937.

                    462573

6-2

Newcomb (Wilburn W.) ed.
BARLEY (WILLIAM)
A New booke of tabliture, 1596. Lute
music of Shakespeare's time. Edited
and transcribed for keyboard with the
original tablature by W. W. Newcomb.
(University Park, Penn.)   1966.

757949

NEWDIGATE (B. H.)
Falstaff, Shallow and the Stratford
musters.   FROM London Mercury,
February, 1927.   1927.

449507

NEWDIGATE (BERNARD HENRY)
Michael Drayton and his circle.   [With
references to Shakespeare, and bibliographical references.]   (Oxford:
Shakespeare Head Press)
illus.   chronological tables.
facsimiles.   1941.

525587

NEWDIGATE (B. H.)
The Printers of the First Folio [:
a review of A Printer of Shakespeare,
by E. E. Willoughby.]   IN The
London Mercury, vol. 31.   1934-5.

438778

Newdigate-Newdegate ([Anne E.]Lady)
ed.,Gossip from a muniment-room.
passages in the lives of Anne and
Mary Fitton, 1574 to 1618. [With
references to Shakespeare.] [2nd
edn.] Ports. Genealogical Table.

1898.

466594

NEWMAN (FRANKLIN B.)
The Rejection of Falstaff and the
rigorous charity of the King.
IN Shakespeare Studies, 2. (Cincinnati,
Ohio)   1966.

761781

NEWMAN (JOEL) ed.
Music from Shakespeare's day [: Trio
in the Phrygian mode, by P. Philips;
Hexachord fantasy, by W. Daman;
Canzonet (Hold out, my heart), by
T. Morley, Fantasia, by T. Lupo] for
three recorders.   Transcribed by
J. Newman. (New York)   1964.
American Recorder Society Editions
No. 51.

745452

Newman, John Henry Cardinal *works relating to*

——Stockley (W.F.P.) Newman as Hamlet.
In The Month, Vol.147.

1926.

330905

NEWMAN NEAME LTD.
Stratford upon Avon [: pictorial
map.   With illustrations of scenes
from Shakespeare's plays, etc.]
1 sheet.   [1954.]

639498

Newport Lecture Association and Newport
Historical Society
WATSON (JOSEPH)
A Lecture on Shakespeare's enigmatical
work [i.e. Hamlet], embracing a new
theory.   Delivered before the Newport
Historical Society. (Newport, R.I.)
1878.

668406

NEWPORT PLAYGOERS' SOCIETY
Programmes, etc., of Shakespearian
performances, 1925-1945. (Newport,
Mon.)   [1925]-1945.

431404

Newspaper Cuttings

*In addition to the material listed below and in
the earlier catalogue under this heading, the
library currently collects newspaper cuttings
upon all aspects of the subject including
Shakespearian production and stage history,
book reviews, biography, etc. The newspaper
cuttings are classified and indexed*

——BENNETT (WILLIAM)
A Collection of playbills, portraits,
newspaper cuttings, and other material
relating to Covent Garden Theatre,
London.
2 vols.   1732-1922.

512634

——BENNETT (W.)
A Collection of playbills, portraits,
newspaper cuttings, and other material
relating to Drury Lane Theatre, and
other London theatres, etc.
2 vols.   1630-c.1880.

512636

——BENNETT (W.)
[Newspaper Cuttings.   Miscellaneous
newspaper cuttings including cuttings
relating to Shakespeare.   Collected
by W. Bennett.]

[1936-38.]

513752

——Broadcast productions of Shakespeare's
plays, reviews, etc.
illus.   1962-

Before 1962 this material is included in
the volumes of newspaper cuttings
relating generally to a particular play.

668168

—— Contemporaries of Shakespeare.
ports. illus. facsimiles. [1941]-

532645

—— COTTON (J.)
[Newspaper cuttings collected by J.
Cotton: literary and poetical. With
references to Shakespeare]. 2 vols.
ports. illus. [c.1890-1933].

467750

—— COTTON (J.)
[Newspaper cuttings collected by J.
Cotton: persons, places and events
in Bromsgrove and district. With
references to the Shakespeare Memorial
Theatre.] 3 vols.
ports. illus. 1870-1933.

467752

—— Gramophone and other recordings of
Shakespeare's works: reviews.
1962-

667633

—— Halliwell-Phillipps' "Outlines of the life
of Shakespeare." pp. [56.]
[1882-1888.]

497159

—— HERITAGE (GEORGE E.) ed.
Newspaper cuttings collected by
G. E. Heritage, 1864-c.1900.]
[c.1900.]

666677

—— MATTHEWS (B.)
[Newspaper cuttings etc. relating to
Shakespeare, 1894-1902, 1919-36.
Collected by B. Matthews.] 6 vols.
[Various]
[1894-1906.]

603247

—— New York Shakespeare Festival, 1957-
[New York]
illus. 1957-

667412

—— Newspaper cuttings relating to
Shakespeare. [1897-1926.]

538012

—— [Newspaper cuttings relating to the
formation of a new Shakespeare
centre in London sponsored by the
Globe-Mermaid Association of England
and America.] Illus.

1937-

494119

—— "Now am I in Arden", New Series [: topographical and historical notes relating
to Warwickshire and neighbouring counties
by] Mercian, [pseud. Including references to Shakespeare and Stratford-upon-
Avon. Newspaper cuttings from the
Birmingham News, Jan.-Dec. 1942].
pp. [80.] [Birmingham] [1942.]
For 1st Series, see files of the
Birmingham News, July 1940-July 1941,
catal. nos. 531189-90.

544461

—— PEARSON (H. S.)
[Newspaper and periodical cuttings
mainly relating to literary history
collected by H. S. Pearson. Containing cuttings about Shakespeare]
[c.1870-1920]

388846

—— Reviews, etc., of Shakespearian films.
illus. 1962-

Before 1962 this material is included in
the volumes of newspaper cuttings
relating generally to a particular play.

667821

—— Reviews of Shakespearian literature.
illus. 1962-

667631

Before 1962 this material is included in
the volumes of newspaper cuttings
relating generally to a particular play.

—— RHODES (R. C.) and others
Newspaper cuttings relating to Shakespeare,
Sheridan, etc. by R. C. Rhodes and others.
[1922-30.]

483543

—— [RODGERS (R. R.) ed.
A Collection of newspaper cuttings.
Including cuttings relating to
Shakespeare]. [1867-1904]

507548

—— Royal Shakespeare Theatre Company. 1962-

Before 1962 this material is included in
the volumes of newspaper cuttings
relating generally to a particular play.

667576

—— Scraps about theatricals [: a collection of newspaper cuttings, etc.
relating to Shakespeare and the
theatre.] [c.1835]

436163

—— SHAKESPEARE INSTITUTE
Newspaper cuttings: The Shakespeare
Institute, Stratford-upon-Avon.
1951-

634296

—— Shakespeare Memorial Theatre Company,
Stratford-upon-Avon, Foreign Tours.
1953-61. 642015
1962- included in Newspaper cuttings
relating to the Royal Shakespeare
Theatre Company.

667576

—— Shakespeare quatercentenary celebrations, 1964.
illus. 1962-1965.

668476

—— [Shakespeare's Birthplace and Museum.
Reports, cuttings, letters, etc.]

[1861-1910.]

496933

— Shakespeare's plays, and performances, etc. [1709-1912]. 2 vols.

769150

— Sir Henry Irving centenary, 1938. 1938.

481710

— Societies: Shakespeare and other societies. 1962-

668210

— The Stratford Shakespearean Festival of Canada. 1962-

Before 1962 this material is included in the volumes of newspaper cuttings relating generally to a particular play.

667634

— "This is my home": pen picture[s, i.e. articles on famous Warwickshire houses, including one on Anne Hathaway's cottage,] by Margaret McCartney. [Newspaper cuttings from the Birmingham News, 18th Oct.-27th Dec. 1941.] pp.[16.] [Birmingham] illus. [1941.]

544460

— WHITFIELD (J.   F.   )

[Theatrical scrapbooks, 1919-29, including newspaper cuttings and programmes of the Stratford-upon-Avon Shakespeare seasons, and of productions at Birmingham theatres. Collected by J.F. Whitfield.] Illus. 3 vols. [1919-29.]

668413-5

Newspapers

— THE MASK: a satirical review of the week in caricatures, edited and illustrated by Alfred Thompson. Nos. 1 to 14. 1879.

illus. 152836

— The SKETCH: an illustrated miscellany of music, the drama, society and the belles. Nos. 2 to 16 1879-80

illus. 60199

— STRATFORD-UPON-AVON HERALD and South Warwickshire Advertiser, 15th June, 1957. [An illustrated account of the visit of Queen Elizabeth and Prince Philip to Stratford, June 14th, 1957.] pp.8.

1957.

665542

— STRATFORD-UPON-AVON HERALD and South Warwickshire Advertiser, 24th April, 1964. The Shakespeare Quatercentenary Supplement, 1564-1964. 'Speak of me as I am'. (Stratford-upon-Avon) 1964.

illus. 668226

— THE SUNDAY TIMES COLOUR MAGAZINE, April 12, 1964 The Shakespeare mystery solved [: Mr. W.H.'s identity] by John Leslie Hotson. illus. 1964.

668228

— The Warwick and Warwickshire Advertiser and Leamington Gazette. Aug.6,1864, with supplement; July 27, Aug.3, 1872; Sept.12, 1908. 3 vols.

(Warwick) 1864-1908.

429879

— THE WEEKLY ORACLE: or universal library, No. 63. [1737.]

60561

NEWTON (ALFRED EDWARD)
Rare books, original drawings, autograph letters and manuscripts collected by the late A. E. Newton. For public sale at the Parke-Bernet Galleries, Inc., [April-Oct., 1941. Including Shakespeare items]. (New York) ports. illus. facsimiles. 3 vols. 1941.

537563

NEWTON (E. [R.])
Ballet music from Shakespeare's play The Tempest. Arranged for the pianoforte. pp. 16. [1924] Shakespeare Album.

397675

NEWTON (E. [R.])
Shakespeare's play A Midsummer night's dream. Incidental music to the fairy scene in a wood near Athens. Arranged for the pianoforte. pp. 17. [1925]

Shakespeare Album.

397676

NEWTON (E. [R.])
Shakespeare's play The Winter's tale. Ballet music. Arranged for the pianoforte. pp. 16. [1926]. Shakespeare Album.

397677

NEWTON (ERNEST RICHARD) ed.
The Vocal music to Shakespeare's plays. [From the collection by J. Caulfield, revised and supplemented.] 20 vols.

1922-25.

343592

23

[NEWTON (HENRY CHANCE)]
Some strange Shakespeariences: [a
report of a lecture by H. C. Newton,
delivered at the 107th session of the
Shakespeare Club.] FROM Stratford-
upon-Avon Herald, Oct. 24th 1930.
[Stratford-upon-Avon]   1930.

427397

NEWTON, JOHN MILLARD
Scrutiny's failure with Shakespeare.
IN The Cambridge quarterly, vol. 1,
no. 2.   (Cambridge)   1966.
pp. 144-177.

758239

NEWTON (R. G.)
Shakespearean settings for small
stages.   IN Drama, vol. 14.   1935.

463689

Ney, Marie *works relating to*

—— WATTS (B.)
Marie Ney and Shakespearian tradition.
IN The Amateur theatre and playwrights
journal, Vol. 1, No. 6.
port.   1934-35.

476088

NICHOLLS (FAITH)
An Actor's wife in Stratford.
Producer: P. Humphreys.   [Broadcast]
20th November, 1956.   ff. 9.
typescript.   1956.

665417

NICHOLS (BEVERLEY) ed.
A Book of ballads [, including "The
Friar of Orders Gray" composed from
fragments of ballads found in
Shakespeare's plays].   Selected and
with an introduction by B. Nichols.
Illustrated by H. M. Brock.   1934.

428935

NICHOLS (DOROTHY E.)
The Oregon Shakespeare Festival, 1967.
IN SHAKESPEARE QUARTERLY XVIII: 4.
pp. 421-423.   (New York)   1967.

605711

NICHOLS (DOROTHY)
Shakespeare on the West Coast, at
Ashland and San Diego.
IN SHAKESPEARE QUARTERLY XVI:4.
pp. 343-347.
(New York)   1965.

605711

NICHOLS (JAMES WILLIAM)
William Shakespeare on the stage: a study
of the figure of William Shakespeare in
British and American drama. A thesis
submitted to the University of Birmingham.
Bibliog. Typescript. (Birmingham)
1951.

649925

[Nichols (J.) ed.] A Select collection
of poems, with notes, biographical
and historical. [Including poems
on Shakespeare.] Ports   6 vols.

1780-82.

Wants Vols. 3 and 5.

504979

Nichols ([J.] B. [B.]) [ed.] Words
and days: a table-book of prose and
verse. With a preface by L.P.Smith
[and quotations from Shakespeare].
Frontis.

(Oxford)   1941.

528390

NICHOLS (W. B.)
The Mask of providence [: a novel of
the time of Charles I, containing
references to Shakespeare].   1936.

459362

NICHOLSON (A.)
Shakespeare's copy of Montaigne.
IN The Gentleman's Magazine, Vol. 283.
1897.

140342

Nicholson (B.) Dr. Mackay's thirteen
Celtic derivations [of words used
by Shakespeare.] In The Antiquarian
Magazine & Bibliographer, Vol.3.
1883.

.[1883.]

59317

NICHOLSON (BRINSLEY)
Hamlet's cursed hebenon. [With reply
"Hamlet's juice of cursed hebona" by
W. A. Harrison.]
IN Transactions of the New Shakespeare
Society, Series 1. Nos. 8-10. pp. 21-31,
295-321.   1880-6.
99113

NICHOLSON (BRINSLEY)
Kemp and the play of Hamlet – Yorick and
Tarlton – a short chapter in dramatic
history.
IN Transactions of the New Shakespeare
Society, Series 1. Nos. 8-10.
pp. 57-66.   1880-6.
99113

NICHOLSON (BRINSLEY)
On four passages in Henry V.
IN Transactions of the New Shakespeare
Society, Series 1. Nos. 8-10.
pp. 203-218.   1880-6.
99113

Nicholson (B.) On the army ranks of
Cassio and Iago. In The Antiquarian
Magazine & Bibliographer, Vol.1.
1882.
[1882.]

55895

NICHOLSON (BRINSLEY)
The Relation of the Quarto to the Folio
version of Henry V.
IN Transactions of the New Shakespeare
Society, Series 1. Nos. 8-10.
pp. 77-102.   1880-6.
99113

NICHOLSON (BRINSLEY)
Shakespeare and sea-glasses.
IN Transactions of the New Shakespeare
Society, Series 1. Nos. 8-10.
pp. 53-55.   1880-6.
99113

NICHOLSON ([J.] A.)
A Reply answered: The Hon. Ignatius
Donnelly's reply answered.   pp. 8.
(Stratford-on-Avon)   1889.

396674

Nicholson, John Aldwell *works relating to*

——Report of the testimonial and address
to the Rev. Dr. [J.] A. Nicholson, in
connection with the Shakespeare-Bacon
Controversy, presented on behalf of
the subscribers by the Rt. Hon.
Viscount Peel, at Leamington, Oct.16th,
1895: extracts from the press.
pp. 8.   1895.

396571

NICKS (GEORGE)
"That strain again": glee for three
voices; the words by Shakespeare
[in "Twelfth Night"].   pp. 3.
[?1800]

628455

NICKSON (HORACE)
[What is the Shakespeare mystery?]
An address delivered to the Birmingham
and the Stratford-on-Avon Rotary Clubs.
Reprinted from "Rotaria", October,
1930. pp. 7. (Birmingham) 1930.

558408

NICOLAI (C. L. R.) [pseud. i.e. Colin
Clair]
Shakespeare's England.   (Watford)
ports. illus. map.   [1957.]
The England of the Poets.

665690

NICOLAI [(CARL OTTO EHRENFRIED)]
[Overture] The Merry Wives of Windsor.
pp. 13.   [c.1900.]
Ashdown & Parry.   Overtures for the
Pianoforte, No. 67.

558613

NICOLAI [CARL OTTO EHRENFRIED]
Overture to Merry Wives of Windsor,
arranged from the full score for
the organ, by E. Evans.   pp. 18.
[c.1908.]

408797

NICOLAI [CARL OTTO EHRENFRIED]
The Merry Wives of Windsor.   [Over-
ture, transcribed by C. Zoeller.]
pp. 10.   [c.1910.]
Overture arranged from the full score
for the pianoforte by C. Zoeller,
No. 5.)

558612

NICOLL (ALLARDYCE)
The "Basic" use of microfilm [: at
the Shakespeare Institute].   IN
PMLA: Publications of the Modern
Language Association of America,
Vol. 68.   (Menasha, Wis.) 1953.

428321/68

NICOLL (ALLARDYCE)
Companions of Autolycus: [an article
on research in libraries, with references to Shakespeare.]   FROM Theatre
Arts Monthly, September, 1933.   pp.
711-20.
illus.   1933.

408896

NICOLL (ALLARDYCE)
Co-operation in Shakespearian scholarship.   [(42nd) Annual Shakespeare
Lecture of the British Academy, 1952)
pp. 18.   [1952.]

640821

NICOLL (ALLARDYCE)
The Development of the theatre: a
study of theatrical art from the
beginnings to the present day.   New
edn., revised. [With appendices
and bibliography.]
illus.   1937.   467984
_____ 3rd edn. revised and enlarged.
1948.   591192
_____ 4th edn. revised.
1958.   676764

NICOLL (A.)
The Doubtful plays [of Shakespeare.
Broadcast] 25th September, 1948.
ff. 4.
typescript.   1948.

596476

NICOLL (ALLARDYCE)
The English theatre.   [With reference
to Shakespeare, and a bibliography.]
illus.   1936.   456474
_____ Another edn. 1938. 520071

NICOLL (A.)
A History of early eighteenth century
drama, 1700-1750. [With references
to Shakespeare, a hand-list of plays,
and bibliographical notes.]   2nd edn.
(Cambridge)   1929.

566195

NICOLL (ALLARDYCE)
A History of early nineteenth century
drama, 1800-1850. [With a hand-list
of plays produced between 1800 and 1850
and references to Shakespeare.]
(Cambridge)
2 vols. 1930.
For Supplement to hand-list, by J. E.
Tobin, see in catal. no. 583399.

373490

NICOLL (ALLARDYCE)
A History of late nineteenth century
drama, 1850-1900. [With references
to Shakespeare, a hand-list of plays
produced between 1850 and 1900 and
bibliographical notes.] (Cambridge)
2 vols. 1946.

573723

NICOLL (A.)
A History of Restoration drama,
1660-1700 [: including a chapter
on "Adaptations of Shakespeare and
of other Elizabethan dramatists",
with a history of the playhouses,
1660-1700, and a hand-list of
Restoration plays.] 3rd edn. revised.
(Cambridge)
bibliog. 1940.

569878

NICOLL (ALLARDYCE)
A New Shakespeare [: Collins edition
of the complete works edited by
P. Alexander]. Broadcast 4th July,
1951. ff. 7.
typescript. 1951.

617919

NICOLL (ALLARDYCE)
'Passing over the stage'.
IN SHAKESPEARE SURVEY 12.
(Cambridge) 1959.

666150

NICOLL (A.)
Shakespeare [: a discussion of recent
Shakespearian publications].
IN The Year's work in English studies,
Vol. 26. (Oxford) 1947.

587254

NICOLL (ALLARDYCE)
Shakespeare. 1952.
Home Study Books.

625227

NICOLL, ALLARDYCE
Shakespeare and the court masque.
IN SHAKESPEARE JAHRBUCH. Bd. 94/1958.
pp. 51-62. (Heidelberg)

10531

NICOLL (ALLARDYCE)
Shakespeare's plays [: a lecture
given for the Istituto Internazionale
per la Ricerca Teatrale in Venice.]
[1964.]

740822

NICOLL (ALLARDYCE)

Stuart masques and the Renaissance
stage. 1937.

474954

NICOLL (ALLARDYCE)
Studies in the Elizabethan stage since
1900. IN SHAKESPEARE SURVEY 1.
(Cambridge) 1948.

590674

NICOLL, ALLARDYCE
What do we do with Shakespeare?
IN SHAKESPEARE JAHRBUCH. Bd. 96/1960.
pp. 35-46. (Heidelberg)

10531

NICOLL (ALLARDYCE) ed.

Shakespeare Survey: an annual survey
of Shakespearian study & production.
[Vol.] 1- 18. [With] indexes.
(Cambridge)
ports. illus. plans. dgms.
tables. facsimiles. bibliogs.
1948-
Shakespeare Survey 19- is edited by
Kenneth Muir.

590674

[NICOLL (ALLARDYCE) ed.]

Shakespeare survey list of books and
articles [No. 1] June 1946-58.
[Bibliographies taken from Shakespeare
survey: an annual survey edited by
A. Nicoll.]
typescript. 1946-58.

596641

Nicoll (Allardyce) ed.

SHARPHAM (EDWARD)
Cupid's whirligig (1607). Edited
from the First Quarto of 1607, with
an introduction & textual notes by
A. Nicoll. [Waltham St. Lawrence]
1926.
The Berkshire Series [Vol.] 1. Limited
edn. 500 copies.

332067

Nicoll (Allardyce) and Nicoll (Mrs.
Josephine [Calina]) eds.

HOLINSHED [R.]
Chronicle as used in Shakespeare's
plays. [Edited with an introduction
and a bibliography.] 1927.
Everyman's Library.

333612

NICOLL (Mrs. JOSEPHINE) [Calina]

Shakespeare in Poland. pp. 76.
bibliog. 1923.
Shakespeare Association. Shakespeare
Survey, Vol. 1.

305699

NICOLSON (Sir HAROLD [GEORGE])

Friday mornings, 1941-1944 [: articles
contributed to The Spectator.
Including an article: Shakespeare's
flowers]. 1944.

557060

NICOLSON (Sir HAROLD [GEORGE])
Marginal comment [: an article on
words used by Shakespeare]. IN
The Spectator, Vol. 176. 1946.

573327

NICOLSON (Sir HAROLD [GEORGE])

Some Shakespeare words.   IN Nicolson
(Sir H. [G.]) Comments, 1944-1948.
1948.

595785

Nicolson (Janet) Why we produce
Shakespeare in training colleges
and schools. In The Amateur Theatre
and Playwrights' Journal, Vol.4,No.75.
1937.

467093

NICOLSON (MARJORIE H.)

The Authorship of Henry the Eighth [:
an assertion that it was partly written
by J. Fletcher.   With bibliographical
notes].   FROM Publications of the
Modern Language Association of America,
Vol. 37.   (Menasha, Wis.)   1922.

554236

Niećko, Jacek
Main activities commemorating the fourth
centenary in Poland. IN

HELSZTYNSKI, STANISLAW, ed.
Poland's homage to Shakespeare.
Commemorating the fourth centenary of
his birth, 1564-1964. (Warsaw)
1965.

747846

NIELSEN (ELIZABETH)
"Macbeth": the nemesis of the post-
Shakespearian actor.
IN SHAKESPEARE QUARTERLY XVI: 2.
pp. 192-199.
(New York) 1965.

605711

NIELSON (FRANCIS)

A Study of Macbeth for the stage.
(New York)
plans.   1952.

629346

Nikitin (Nathalie V.) illus.

POSTGATE (ISA J.)
Woodnotes: poems [on Shakespeare,
and quotations from his plays.]
pp. [13.]   (New York)   [c.1840.]

479264

Nilsson, Christine *works relating to*

—— The "Hamlet" of [C. L.] A. Thomas [:
an opera], and the Ophelia of
Christine Nilsson.   FROM The Englishwoman's Domestic Magazine, Aug. 1,1869.
1869.

555515

NISBET (U.)
The Onlie begetter [: an essay
identifying Sir William Herbert
as the Mr. W.H. of Shakespeare's
Sonnets.]
port. bibliog.   1936.

451494

Nisbet, Ulric *works relating to*

—— EMPSON (W.)
The Onlie begetter, [a review].   IN
Life and Letters Today [Vol. 15].
[1936-7]

463697

NOBLE (HAROLD)
Hither, come hither: two-part song.
Words by Shakespeare [from "As you
like it"].   (Mortimer Series of
Part-Songs, No. 324)   pp. 4.   1952.

633326

Noble (H.)[ed.] Where the bee sucks.
Words by Shakespeare [from the
Tempest];music by [T.A.]Arne.
Arranged as a part song for T.T.B.B.
[with piano accompaniment] by H.
Noble. pp.6.

[1945.]

586796

NOBLE (IRIS)
William Shakespeare [: a novel].
(New York)
bibliog.   1961.

666948

NOBLE (PETER)
The Fabulous Orson Welles.
ports.   1956.

657159

NOBLE (R.)
Shakespeare's Biblical knowledge and
use of the Book of Common Prayer as
exemplified in the plays of the
First Folio.   1935.

437987

NOBLE (THOMAS TERTIUS)
Blow, blow, thou winter wind [: four
part song.   Words by] Shakespeare
[from As you like it.   Music by]
T. T. Noble.   pp. 8.   (York) 1924.
York Series, No. 923.

536615

NOCK (FRANCIS J.)
E. T. A. Hoffmann and Shakespeare.
IN Journal of English and Germanic
Philology, Vol. 53.   (Urbana, Ill.)
1954.

600780/53

NOLAN, EDWARD F.
Barron's simplified approach to
Shakespeare's "Othello".
(Woodbury, N.Y.)   1967.
Barron's educational series.

773400

NORDEN (JOHN)
Vicissitudo rerum: [an elegiacall
poeme.] 1600. With an introduction
by D. C. Collins. pp. [70.] 1931.
Shakespeare Association Facsimiles,
No. 4.

390120

NORGAARD (HOLGER)
[Review of] Shakespeare's use of
learning by V. K. Whitaker.   IN
English Studies, Vol. 36. (Amsterdam)
1955.

485643/36

NORMAN (ARTHUR M. Z.)
Daniel's The Tragedie of Cleopatra and
Antony and Cleopatra.
IN SHAKESPEARE QUARTERLY IX: 1.
pp. 11-18.
(New York) 1958.

605711

NORMAN (CHARLES)
The Muses' darling: the life of
Christopher Marlowe. [Containing
chapters: "Marlowe and Shakespeare"
and "Shakespeare and Harvey". With
a bibliography.]
illus. map. plan. facsimiles.
1947.

590727

Norman (C.) The Playmaker of Avon.
Illus.

(Philadelphia)   1949.

603779

NORMAN (CHARLES)
So worthy a friend: William Shakespeare.
Revised edn. (Collier Books) (New York)
1961.

667184

NORMAN (PHILIP)
The Accounts of the overseers of the
poor of Paris Garden, Southwark, 1608
to 1671. [Containing Shakespearian
references.]   IN Surrey Archaeological
Collections, Vol. 16. (Guildford)
1901.
Surrey Archaeological Society.

490519

NORMAND (W. G. NORMAND, [Lord])
Portia's judgement. FROM University
of Edinburgh Journal, Summer Number,
1939. (Edinburgh)   1939.

515200

Norris (H.) Costume & fashion, Vol.3 :
The Tudors, 1485-1603. Illustrated
by the author. [With references
to Shakespeare.] 1 in 2 vols.

1938.

492644

Norris (H.) No stunts with the
histories! : presenting Shakespeare
with accuracy. Illus. In The Amateur
Theatre and Playwrights' Journal,
Vol.4, No.75.

1937.

467093

North, Christopher, *pseud., see* **Wilson, John**

North (Sir Thomas) trans. see Plutarch.

NORTHAM (JOHN R.)
Dividing worlds.   Shakespeare's "The
Tempest" and Ibsen's "Rosmersholm".
(Oslo)   1965.
Kristiansand Museum pamphlet, No. 2.

755089

NORTHAMPTONSHIRE RECORD SOCIETY
"Northamptonshire in the reign of
Queen Elizabeth": catalogue of
exhibition of portraits and
manuscripts, March 28th - April 4th,
1936. pp. 16.   (Northampton)
port.   1936.

450564

Northcliffe Lectures in Literature
ALEXANDER (PETER)
Hamlet, father and son.   (Oxford)
1955.

645975

Northcliffe Lectures in Literature
MACKAIL (J. W.)
The Approach to Shakespeare.   (Oxford)
1930.   372498
_____ 2nd edn.   1933.   419850

NORTHCOTT (J.), CHURCH (W. E.) and
CATLING (T.) [eds.]
Annals of the Urban Club, and its
tributes to the immortal memory
of William Shakespeare. pp. 48.
ports. illus. 1902.

520909

Northumberland (Henry Percy, 1st Earl of)
see Henry the Fourth, Richard the
Second.

Northup (G.T.) An Introduction to
Spanish literature. [With references
to Shakespeare, and bibliographies.]

(Chicago)   1934.

436929

NORTON (ELLIOT)
The Cambridge Drama Festival.
IN SHAKESPEARE QUARTERLY X: 4.
pp. 597-602.
(New York) 1959.

605711

Norway

—— BJORNSON, BJORNSTJERNE MARTINIUS

A Defense [of his production of
"A Midsummer night's dream" at the
Christiania Theatre].   IN LEWINTER,
OSWALD, ed., Shakespeare in Europe
[by various authors].   1963.

667784

—— COLLIN (C.)
Shakespeare and the Norwegian drama.
IN GOLLANCZ ([Sir] I.) ed., A Book of
homage to Shakespeare.
ports. illus. facsimiles. [1916.]

264175

—— ECKHOFF, LORENTZ
Shakespeare in Norwegian translations.
IN SHAKESPEARE JAHRBUCH, Bd. 92/1956.
pp. 244-254.   (Heidelberg)

10531

Norwegian Studies in English
SMIDT (KRISTIAN)
Iniurious impostors and Richard III.
1963.

668033

NORWICH (CITY OF) SCHOOL
Programme of a performance of "Twelfth
Night" at the City of Norwich School,
Dec. 1937; with explanatory notes on
the music by M. N. Doe. ff. 4.
[Norwich]   1937.
Edition of "Twelfth Night" with MS.
notes referring to the music. 502842
MS. of music. 502843

506672

Norwich: Madder-Market Theatre

—— MONCK (W. NUGENT)
The Maddermarket Theatre and the
playing of Shakespeare.
IN SHAKESPEARE SURVEY 12.
(Cambridge)   1959.

666150

—— The Norwich Players, Maddermarket
Theatre, in extracts from "The Tempest".
Programme produced by W. Hughes.
[Broadcast] 15th June [1949].   (From
the Midland Theatres: a series of
theatre programmes introduced by
T. C. Kemp.)   ff. 4 [2] 22.
typescript.   [1949.]

605251

——[Programmes of Shakespeare performances.]
[1933]-

418307

—— RIGBY (C.)
Maddermarket Mondays: press articles
dealing with the famous Norwich
Players.   Foreword by B. Maine.
Published in commemoration of the
production of the whole of Shakespeare's
plays at the Maddermarket Theatre,
Norwich.   (Norwich)
port. illus.   1933.

416881

NORWOOD (GILBERT)
A Twisted masterpiece: [a discussion
on King Lear.]   IN The Contemporary
Review, Vol. 127.   1925.

320948

Noses

—— MARTIN (W. W)
Our noses.   Delivered at a meeting
of the Sette, held at Limmer's Hotel,
November 3rd, 1893.   [With references
to the mention of noses in
Shakespeare's plays.]
illus.   1893.
Sette of Odd Volumes.   Privately
Printed Opuscula, No. 32.
Edn. limited to 199 copies.

532141

NOSWORTHY (JAMES MANSFIELD)
All too short a date: internal evidence
in Shakespeare's sonnets.   IN Essays
in Criticism, Vol. 2.   (Oxford) 1952.

621866/2

NOSWORTHY (J. M.)
The Bleeding captain scene in Macbeth.
IN The Review of English Studies,
Vol. 22.   (Oxford)
bibliog.   [1946.]

579165

NOSWORTHY (JAMES MANSFIELD)
The Death of Ophelia. IN Shakespeare
Quarterly XV: 4. pp.345-348. (New York)
1964.

605711

NOSWORTHY (JAMES MANSFIELD)
"Hamlet" and the Player who could not
keep counsel. Reprinted FROM
Shakespeare Survey, No. 3, 1950.
(Cambridge)   1950.

668446

NOSWORTHY (JAMES MANSFIELD)
The Integrity of Shakespeare:
illustrated from "Cymbeline". Reprinted
FROM Shakespeare Survey, No. 8, 1955.
(Cambridge)   1955.

668448

Nosworthy (J.M.) King Lear - the
moral aspect. In English Studies,
Vol.21.

(Amsterdam)   1939.

510849

NOSWORTHY (JAMES MANSFIELD)
Macbeth at the Globe. Reprinted FROM
The Transactions of the Bibliographical
Society. "The Library", Sept.-Dec. 1947.
1948.

668449

NOSWORTHY (JAMES MANSFIELD)
The Marlowe Manuscript [: "Massacre in
Paris"]. Reprinted FROM The Transactions
of the Bibliographical Society. "The
Library", Sept.-Dec., 1945.
1945.

668443

NOSWORTHY (JAMES MANSFIELD)
Music and its function in the romances
of Shakespeare. Reprinted FROM
Shakespeare Survey, No. 11, 1958.
(Cambridge)   1958.

668447

NOSWORTHY (J. M.)
The Narrative sources of "The
Tempest".   IN The Review of English
Studies, Vol. 24.   (Oxford)
bibliog.   1948.

318239/24

NOSWORTHY (JAMES MANSFIELD)
A Reading of the play-scene in Hamlet.
[With bibliographical notes.]   IN
English Studies, Vol. 22.   (Amsterdam)
1940.

575606

Nosworthy (J.M.) [Review of] The
True Text of King Lear, by L.
Kirschbaum. In The Library, 5th
Series, Vol.1.

(Oxford)   1946.

586026

NOSWORTHY (JAMES MANSFIELD)
Shakespeare and "Sir Thomas More" [:
notes on the play]. Reprint FROM The
Review of English Studies, N.S. Vol.6,
No.21, 1955. (Oxford)   1955.

668445

NOSWORTHY, JAMES MANSFIELD
Shakespeare's occasional plays: their
origin and transmission.   1965.

747250

NOSWORTHY (JAMES MANSFIELD)
The Southouse Text of "Arden of
Feversham". Reprinted FROM The
Transactions of the Bibliographical
Society. "The Library", Sept. 1950.
1950.

668442

Nosworthy (J.M.) The Structural
experiment in Hamlet. [With bibliographical notes.] In The Review of
English Studies, Vol.22.

(Oxford)   [1946.]

579165

NOSWORTHY (JAMES MANSFIELD)
The Two angry families of Verona [:
Romeo and Juliet]. A reprint FROM
Shakespeare Quarterly, Vol.3, No.3,
July 1952. (New York)   1952.

668450

Notes drawn on the Avon bank for
general circulation.   [Shakespeare
Tercentenary Commemoration.]
FROM London Society, Vol. 5.
ports.   illus.   1864.

556283

Notes on chosen English texts

—— CARRINGTON, NORMAN THOMAS
Shakespeare: Antony and Cleopatra.
(Bath)   [1964.]

illus. Notes on chosen English
texts.   667962

——CARRINGTON (NORMAN THOMAS)
Shakespeare: Coriolanus. (Notes on
Chosen English Texts).
[1956.]

665241

—— CARRINGTON (NORMAN THOMAS)
Shakespeare: Cymbeline. (Notes on Chosen
English Texts). pp.79.   [1954.]

642525

——CARRINGTON (NORMAN THOMAS)
Shakespeare: Hamlet. (Notes on Chosen
English Texts) pp.88.   [1940.]

601682

—— CARRINGTON (NORMAN THOMAS)
Shakespeare: King Henry IV, Part I.
(Notes on Chosen English Texts)
pp.76. Dgm.   [1940.]

601687

—— CARRINGTON (NORMAN THOMAS)
Shakespeare: King Henry IV, Part I.
(Notes on Chosen English Texts) (Bath)
[1964]

742264

—— CARRINGTON, NORMAN THOMAS
Shakespeare: King Henry IV, part I.
Revised edition. (Bath) [1967]
illus. Notes on chosen English
texts.

772197

—— CARRINGTON (NORMAN THOMAS)
Shakespeare: King Henry IV. part 2.
(Notes on Chosen English Texts) pp.72.
[1954.]

645295

—— CARRINGTON (NORMAN THOMAS)
Shakespeare: King Lear. (Notes on
Chosen English Texts) (Bath)
[1962.]

667560

—— CARRINGTON (NORMAN THOMAS)
Shakespeare: King Richard II.
(Notes on Chosen English Texts)
pp.64. Dgm. [1940.]

601685

—— CARRINGTON (NORMAN THOMAS)
Shakespeare: Macbeth. (Notes on
Chosen English Texts) pp.56. Dgm.
[1939.]

504156

—— CARRINGTON (NORMAN THOMAS)
Shakespeare: Macbeth. (Notes on
Chosen English Texts) pp.72.
[1958.]

666254

—— CARRINGTON (NORMAN THOMAS)
Shakespeare: The Merchant of Venice.
(Notes on Chosen English Texts) pp.72.
Dgm. [1940.]

601684

—— CARRINGTON (NORMAN THOMAS)
Shakespeare: The Merchant of Venice.
(Notes on Chosen English Texts) pp.80.
[1958.]

666255

—— CARRINGTON, NORMAN THOMAS
Shakespeare: The Merchant of Venice.
Revised edition. (Bath)
illus. 1967.
Notes on chosen English texts.

767656

—— CARRINGTON (NORMAN THOMAS)
Shakespeare: Much ado about nothing.
(Notes on Chosen English Texts) pp.85.
Illus. [1961.]

666793

—— CARRINGTON, NORMAN T.
Shakespeare: Othello. (Bath) [1966.]

Notes on chosen English texts.
753353

—— CARRINGTON (NORMAN THOMAS)
Shakespeare: Romeo and Juliet.
1958.
Notes on Chosen English Texts.

666001

—— CARRINGTON (NORMAN THOMAS)
Shakespeare: Twelfth Night.
(Notes on Chosen English Texts)
pp.62. [1940.]

511819

—— CARRINGTON, NORMAN THOMAS
Shakespeare: Twelfth night. (Bath)
1965.

Notes on chosen English texts.
746636

—— CARRINGTON (NORMAN THOMAS)
Shakespeare: The Winter's Tale.
(Notes on Chosen English Texts)
pp.80. [1956.]

665240

—— EASTWOOD (W.)
Shakespeare: As you like it. pp. 56.
[1939.]

504155

—— HARDACRE, KENNETH
Shakespeare: King Richard III. (Bath)
[1964.]

illus. Notes on chosen English
texts. 668198

—— SMITH (T. W.)
Shakespeare: Julius Caesar. pp. 64.
[1940.]

511820

—— SMITH, T.W.
Shakespeare: Julius Caesar. (Revised
edition.) (Bath) [1965.]

illus. Notes on Chosen English
Texts. 744905

—— SMITH (T. W.)
Shakespeare: King Henry V. pp. 72.
dgm. [1940.]

601686

—— SMITH (T. W.)
Shakespeare: A Midsummer night's
dream. pp. 56.
dgm. [1940.]

601683

—— SMITH (T. W.)
Shakespeare: The Tempest. pp. 52.
dgm. [1940.]

601688

Notes on English Literature Series

—— COX, G.P.
The Winter's tale (Shakespeare).
(Oxford) 1967.

Notes on English literature.
767394

—— HARDY (Mrs. BARBARA GLADYS)

Twelfth Night. (Notes on English
Literature [Series])(Oxford: Blackwell)
1962.

667557

—— HARVEY (JOHN)
Macbeth. (Notes on English Literature)
pp.59. (Oxford) 1960.

666625

——MORRIS, HELEN
Antony and Cleopatra (W. Shakespeare).
(Oxford) 1968.
Notes on English literature.

773018

—— MORRIS, HELEN
King Lear. (Oxford) 1965.

Notes on English literature.
753070

Notes on Shakspeare's play "As you
like it". FROM [The Quarterly
Journal of Education,] Vol. 2.
[1869-70.]
Imperfect, all after Jan. 1870 wanting.

562353

Notes on Shakspeare's text: [reviews]
IN The Gentleman's Magazine, New Series,
Vol. 40. 1853.

18693

Nottingham Shakespeare Society.
[Programmes of plays, etc.]

1933-

418308

NOTTINGHAM UNIVERSITY
Shakespeare in art, a visual approach
to the plays: an exhibition of
paintings, drawings and other works
devoted to Shakespeariana subjects
from the seventeenth century to the
present day, and including designs
for stage-sets and illustrated editions
of the plays [held in the Nottingham
University Art Gallery, 13 Jan.-12 Feb.
1961. With introduction and notes by
W. M. Merchant.] pp. [58]. (Nottingham)
illus. facsimiles bibliog. 1961.

667004

NOTTINGHAM UNIVERSITY
[Shakespeare in Art Exhibition].
"Comment" No. 2 by T. G. Rosenthal.
Broadcast script. [Programme trans-
mitted] 12th January 1961. ff. 4.
1961.

667034

Novello &Company, Ltd. Shakespeare
music [:a list of] songs, duets,
trios, part-songs and incidental
music [published by] Novello
& Company. pp. 10.

[1940.]

594158

Novels and Short Stories
see also Fiction

—— APPLEBY (JOHN)
The Stuffed swan [: a novel relating
to Shakespeare]. 1956.

665437

—— BARKER (DUDLEY)
Grandfather's house [: a novel].
1951.

625559

——BARRIE ([Sir] J. M.)
My Lady Nicotine [: short stories
and sketches about smoking, including
a story relating to Shakespeare.]
5th edn. 1892.

524956

—— BENNETT (JOHN)
Master Skylark: a story of Shakspere's
time. Illustrations by R. B. Birch.
(New York) 1910. 642973
_____ Another edn. Illustrated by
H. C. Pitz. (Wants frontispiece)
1927. 437094

—— BLACK (W.)
Judith Shakespeare: a romance. New
and revised edn. 1893.

545572

——BLOOM, URSULA
How dark, my lady! a novel concerning
the private life of William Shakespeare.
1951.

621595

—— BOILEAU (ETHEL)
Ballade in G minor. [With references
to Shakespeare and Stratford-upon-
Avon.] [1938.]

504567

—— BOWERS, GWENDOLYN
At the Sign of the Globe [: a novel
about a boy in Shakespeare's London].
(New York) 1966.

760962

—— BOYCE (BURKE)
Cloak of folly [: a novel relating
to Edward de Vere, 17th Earl of
Oxford]. [1951.]

618901

—— BRAHMS (CARYL) [pseud. i.e. DORIS
CAROLINE ABRAHAMS] & SIMON (S. J.)
[pseud. i.e. SIMON JASHA SKIDELSKY]
No bed for Bacon [: a story of
Elizabethan times, relating to
Shakespeare].   1941.   528825
_____ Another edn.   (New York)
                1950.   608869

—— BROPHY (J.)
Gentleman of Stratford.   [With
author's postscript: Historical
origins, and a bibliography.]
                [1939.] 503254
_____ 3rd impression.
                1946.   571996

—— BUCKMASTER, HENRIETTA
All the living: a novel of one year
in the life of William Shakespeare.
                1963.

                         667484

—— BULLETT (GERALD)
The Alderman's son [: a novel relating to Shakespeare].   1954.

                         637516

—— BURGESS, ANTHONY, pseud.
Nothing like the sun: a story of
Shakespeare's love-life.   1964.

                         667815

—— Cabell ([J.] B.) Hamlet had an
Uncle : a comedy of honour.

                1940.

                         517244

—— CANTOR (A.)
Shakespeare at Sardi's [: a story].
IN Theatre Arts, Vol. 32-   (New
York)
illus.   1948-

                         320431/32

—— CHAMBRUN (Comtesse CLARA LONGWORTH DE)
Two loves I have: the romance of
William Shakespeare.   (Philadelphia)
ports.   1934.
Signed by the author.

                         626057

—— [Chovil (A.H.)] Arden vales: a novel
of Warwickshire, [with references
to Shakespeare,] by Peter Brook.

                1934.

                         422417

—— CHUTE (MARCHETTE GAYLORD)
The Wonderful winter [: a boy's
adventures in Shakespeare's London;
a novel].   Illustrated by Grace
Golden.
maps.   1962.

                         667765

—— CLAYTON (J.)
The Silver swan [: a novel with
Shakespeare as a character.]   [1939.]

                         497752

—— Cost (M.)[pseud of Peggy Morrison],
The Dark star [: a novel with
references to Shakespeare's plays].

                1939.

                         504566

—— COXHEAD (EILEEN ELIZABETH)
A Play toward [: a novel relating to
a school production of A Midsummer
Night's Dream].   1952.

                         624640

—— CRONYN (G. W.)
Mermaid Tavern: Kit Marlowe's
story.   [With references to
Shakespeare].   [1937]

                         478137

—— DALE (CELIA)
The Wooden O: a novel [about a Tudor
theatre].   1953.

                         633337

—— Dallow (M.) The Heir of Charlecote
[: a novel concerning David Lucy.
Including references to Shakespeare.] With illustrations by
C. Hutton.

                1938.

                         492413

—— DANIELL (D. S.)
The Time of the singing: a novel
[of Shakespeare's country.]   1941.

                         529726

—— DAVIES (ROBERTSON)
Tempest-tost:a novel. [With references to
Shakespeare's "The Tempest".]   1952.

                         625841

—— DISHER (MAURICE WILLSON)
Whitely wanton [: a novel relating
to Shakespeare].
illus.   1951.

                         618143

—— EGAN (P.)
The Life of an actor [: a novel,
with references to Shakespeare's
plays].   The poetical descriptions
by T. Greenwood.   [Etchings] by
T. Lane.   1892.

                         567378

—— ENGELL (ELSE)
The Birds of Shakespeare: a short
story [relating to Sir A. Geikie's
book of that title.]   IN Wilson
Bulletin, Vol. 11.   1937.

                         472343

—— Evans (J.R.) The Clue of the Shakespeare head. Frontis.

                [1933.]

                         451446

—— FISHER, EDWARD
The Best house in Stratford [: a novel].
                1965.

                         759086

— FISHER, EDWARD
    Love's labour's won. A novel about
    Shakespeare's lost years. (New York)
    1963.

        750237

— FISHER (EDWARD)

    Shakespeare & son: a novel.
                    1962.

        667428

— FOLEY (MARTHA)
    One with Shakespeare [: a short
    story]. FROM Story, vol. 18.
    pp. [6.] (New York)   1941.

        537397

— Frank (W.) The Bridegroom cometh :
    [a novel. With Shakespearian
    references.]

                1938.

        513804

— FURLONG (AGNES)
    Stratford adventure [: a novel].
    Illustrated by Rosemary Hay. 1951.

        618917

— GODDEN (RUMER)
    A Breath of air [: a novel based on
    The Tempest].   1950.

        610782

— Goudge (Elizabeth) The Dark lady :
    an episode in the life of William
    Shakespeare. From Britannia & Eve,
    December, 1938. pp. [8.] Illus.

                1938.

        494120

— GOUDGE (ELIZABETH)
    The Golden skylark and other stories.
    [Including The Dark lady: an episode
    in the life of William Shakespeare.]
                1941.

        528813

— GRAY, ELIZABETH JANET
    I will adventure [: a novel in which
    Shakespeare is a character]. 1964.

    illus.   742265

— GRIFFITHS (A.)
    Spirits under proof. [With
    references to Shakespeare.]
                1935.

        447311

— HALIDOM (M Y.)
    The Poet's curse: a tale [of an
    attempt by an American millionaire
    to get hold of Shakespeare's bones,
    and how the curse inscribed on the
    poet's tomb overtook the depredator].
                1911.
    Cover bears a copy of the inscription
    on Shakespeare's tomb.
        545173

— HATTON (CHARLES)
    Much ado about Mowbray [: a Shake-
    spearean mystery in Stratford today].
    1951.

        617855

— Heddle (Ethel F.) The Private life
    of William Shakespeare. [Illustrations
    by C. Caney.] From The Queen, April
    4th, 1934- May 16th, 1934. pp.[16.]

                1934.

        419845

— HILL (F. E.)
    To meet Will Shakespeare.   Illustrated
    by A. Burbank.   (New York)
    bibliog.   dgms.   1949.

        605032

— HILL (R. H.)
    Spring song in Warwick [: a story
    concerning Shakespeare's will].
    FROM Blackwoods Magazine, Vol. 253.
    [Edinburgh]   1943.

        541209

— HOLLAND (RUTH)

    One crown with a sun [: a novel on the
    life of Shakespeare].   1952.

        For French translation "La Vie
    passionnée de William Shakespeare",
    see Catal.No.665801.

        624637

— Innes (M.) Hamlet, revenge! : a story
    in four parts.

                1937.

        468360

— Jenkins (Elizabeth) The Phoenix' nest
    [: a novel of Shakespeare's time].

                1936.

        453013

— JEPSON (S.)
    Keep murder quiet [: a mystery story
    resembling the story of Hamlet].
                1940.

        519508

—   Jones ([Mrs.] E.B.) The Second Cecil:
    [a sequel to "In Burleigh's Days"; with
    Shakespeare as one of the characters.]

                [1917]

        393786

— JOWETT (MARGARET)
    A Cry of players [: a novel about
    a boy actor in the reign of
    Elizabeth I.]   Illustrated by
    A. Scott.   1961.

        667143

— KELSALL, FREDA M., and GIBSON, HARRY
                              NORMAN
    Double, double [: a novel on the
    identity of Shakespeare].   1965.

        747249

—KINGSMILL (HUGH) [pseud.]
   The Return of William Shakespeare [:
   a novel].   Revised edn.   IN
   Kingsmill (H.) [pseud.] The Dawn's
   delay.   1948.

                              592903

—KIPLING (R.)
   Proofs of Holy Writ [: a story
   with Shakespeare as one of the
   characters.]   Illustrated by
   A. R. M. Todd.   FROM The Strand
   Magazine, April, 1934.   pp. 10.
                              1934.

                              419969

—Lawrence (C.E.) Gloriana : a romance
   of the later days of Queen Elizabeth. [With Shakespeare as one of
   the characters.]

                              1939.

                              495936

—LEWIS (S.)
   Bethel Merriday [: a novel.   Including
   references to the tour of a Romeo and
   Juliet company].   1940.

                              542809

—Lidin (V.) Hamlet. **In** Soviet short
   stories.

                              [1942.]
   (Life and Literature in the Soviet Union, 2.)

                              534276

—Lofts (Norah) Here was a man: a romantic
   history of Sir Walter Raleigh, his
   voyages, his discoveries & his queen.
   [With Shakespearian references.]

                              .1936.

                              453147

—LONG (AMELIA R.)
   The Shakespeare murders.   (New York)
                   1939.   507777
   _____ Another edn.   (Dublin)
                   [1939]   565545

—   [Macdonell (A.G.)]   The Shakespeare
   murders, by Neil Gordon, [pseud.]

                              [1933.]
                              402168

—MARSH, NGAIO
   Death at the Dolphin [: a novel about
   a Shakespeare relic and the production
   of a play about Shakespeare].
                              1967.

                              763970

—Moore (J.[C.]) Overture beginners!
   [With references to 'Romeo and
   Juliet'.]

                              1936.

                              456687

—NOBLE (IRIS)
   William Shakespeare [: a novel].
   (New York)
   bibliog.   1961.

                              666948

—Norman (C.) The Playmaker of Avon.
   Illus.

   (Philadelphia)   1949.

                              603779

—NOYES (R. G.)
   Shakespeare in the eighteenth-century
   novel. [With bibliographical notes.]
   IN E.L.H.: a journal of English
   literary history, Vol. 11.   (Baltimore)
                              1944.

                              562838

—Oman (Carola) The Best of his family:
   [a novel about Shakespeare. With
   a bibliography]. Plan.

                              1933.

                              410741

—O'NEAL (COTHBURN MADISON)
   The Dark lady: a novel [relating to
   Shakespeare].   (New York)   1954.

                              644325

—OWEN (C.)
   The Phoenix and the dove: a novel
   [with Queen Elizabeth and Shakespeare
   as two of the principal characters].
                              1933.

                              402521

—Owens (P.) Picture of nobody: [a novel,
   with Shakespeare as one of the
   characters]. With a preface by
   L.A.G. Strong.

                              1936.

                              448124

—PARGETER (EDITH)
   This rough magic: a novel.   1953.

                              633058

—PORTER (T. H.)
   A Maid of the Malverns: a romance of
   Blackfriars Theatre.   [With refer-
   ences to Shakespeare.]   [1912]

                              392900

—POWEL (H. [W. H.])
   The Virgin Queene [: dealing with
   Elizabeth and Shakespeare.]   1928.

                              405583

—Robertson (T.W.) David Garrick: a
   love story.

                              1865.

                              522848

—SCOTT (Sir WALTER)
   Kenilworth, Vol. 1.   [With references
   to Shakespeare, pp. 339, 349-50, 354.]
                              1866.
   Waverley Novels, Vol. 22.

                              107724

— SETH-SMITH (E[LSIE] K.)
When Shakespeare lived in Southwark
[: the fictitious story of two
boys' adventures with the strolling
players].   Illustrated by J. Matthew.
1944.

554501

— SEVERN (EMMA)
Anne Hathaway, or, Shakspeare in
love.
3 vols.   1845.

446746

— SISSON (ROSEMARY ANNE)

Towards the "Globe": when Shakespeare
was a boy [; novel]. (Neusprachliche
Texte) (Lensing, Dortmund)
1959.

667519

— SISSON, ROSEMARY ANNE
The Young Shakespeare. Illustrated
by Denise Brown. [Famous Childhoods
Series.]   1959.

666308

— Speaight (R.) The Angel in the mist.
[With references to Shakespeare.]

1936.

450441

— Squire (J.C.) Professor
Gubbitts revolution. [a story on the
Bacon-Shakespeare controversy]. *In*
Squire (J.C.) Outside Eden: [short
stories].

1933.

403356

— STUART (FRANK)
Remember me [: a novel relating to
Shakespeare].   1951.

619042

— Trease (G.) Cue for treason [: a story
dealing partly with Shakespeare and
his time]. Frontis.

1940.

(Tales of Two Worlds, No.7.)

523002

— Tunstall (Beatrice) The Dark lady.

1939.

502760

— TURING, JOHN
My nephew Hamlet [: the journal of
Claudius, King of Denmark. A novel.]
Drawings by Jill McDonald.   1967.

illus.   764131

— TURNER (E. F.)
T leaves: a collection of pieces
for public reading. [Including
'Shakespeare on board', relating
to the ghost scene from Hamlet.]
3rd edn.   1885.

474962

— TYTLER (SARAH)
The American cousins: a story of
Shakespeare's country.   2nd and
cheap edn.   1899.
Digny's Popular Novel Series.

392895

— WHITE (ANNE TERRY)
Will Shakespeare and the Globe Theater.
Illustrated by C. W. Hodges.   1955.
World Landmark Books.

665060

—Williams (A.) Rue with a difference.
[Containing a description of a
performance of Hamlet.]

1939.

592761

— [WILLIAMS (R. F.)]
Shakspeare and his friends; or,
The Golden age of merry England
[: a novel] by the author of
"The Youth of Shakspeare".
(New York)   1847.

409504

— [Williams (R.F.)] The Youth of
Shakspeare, [a novel] by the
author of "Shakspeare and his
friends".
(New York)   1847.

417472

— Woodthorpe (R.C.) Rope for a convict
[: a novel relating to a Shakespeare Folio.]

1939.

506255

— Wynne (May) Hamlet: a romance from
Shakespeare's play. [Another copy.]

1930.

421195

—The Youth of Shakspeare [: a novel
by the author of "Shakespeare and
his friends" i.e. R. F. Williams.
A review].   FROM [The New Monthly
Magazine and Humorist, Vol. 55.]
[1839.]

560925

—ZEIGLER (WILBUR GLEASON)

It was Marlowe: a story of the secret
of three centuries. Illus. (Chicago)
1895.

668408

NOWOTTNY (WINIFRED M. T.)
Acts IV and V of Timon of Athens.
IN SHAKESPEARE QUARTERLY X: 4.
pp. 493-497.
(New York)   1959.

605711

NOWOTTNY (WINIFRED M. T.)
The Application of textual theory to
Hamlet's dying words.   IN The
Modern Language Review, Vol. 52.
                                        1957.

                                266816/52

NOWOTTNY (WINIFRED M. T.)
Formal elements in Shakespeare's
sonnets: Sonnets I-VI.   IN Essays
in Criticism, Vol. 2.   (Oxford)
                                        1952.

                                621866/2

NOWOTTNY (WINIFRED M. T.)
Justice and love in Othello.   IN The
University of Toronto Quarterly,
Vol. 21.   (Toronto)   1952.

                                596179/21

NOWOTTNY (WINIFRED M. T.)
Lear's questions.   IN SHAKESPEARE
SURVEY 10.   (Cambridge)   1957.

                                665485

NOWOTTNY, WINIFRED M.T.
   Shakespeare and "The Orator".
FROM Bulletin de la Faculté des
Lettres de Strasbourg, Mai-Juin 1965.
   (Strasbourg)   1965.

      pp.813-833.   765917

NOWOTTNY, WINIFRED M. T.
Shakespeare's tragedies.
IN SUTHERLAND, JAMES, and HURSTFIELD,
JOEL, eds., Shakespeare's world.
                                1964.

                                667808

NOWOTTNY (WINIFRED M. T.)
Some aspects of the style of "King
Lear".   IN SHAKESPEARE SURVEY 13.
(Cambridge)   1960.

                                666726

NOYES (ALFRED)
Christopher Marlowe.   IN GARVIN
(KATHARINE) ed., The Great Tudors.
                        .   1935.

                                431775

NOYES (ALFRED)
The Shadow of the master [: a poem].
IN GOLLANCZ ([Sir] I.) ed., A Book of
homage to Shakespeare.
   ports. illus. facsimiles.   [1916.]

                                264175

NOYES (A.)
Tales of the Mermaid Tavern [: poems].
(Edinburgh)   1924.

                                422875

Noyes (E.S.) On the dismissal of Lear's
   knights and Goneril's letter to
   Regan. From Philological Quarterly,
   vol.9.
              (Iowa)   1930.

                                442559

NOYES (ROBERT GALE)
   Ben Jonson on the English stage,
1660-1776.   [With references to
Shakespeare and an appendix "A
Chronology of the performances
of Ben Jonson's plays, 1660-1776."]
(Cambridge, [Mass.])   1935.
   Harvard Studies in English.

                                447454

NOYES (ROBERT GALE)
Shakespeare in the eighteenth-century
novel.   [With bibliographical notes.]
IN E.L.H.: a journal of English
literary history, Vol. 11. (Baltimore)
                                1944.

                                562838

NOYES (ROBERT GALE)
The Thespian mirror: Shakespeare in
the eighteenth-century novel.
(Brown University Studies, Vol. 15)
(Providence, R. I.)
ports. illus.   1953.

                                633632

NUGENT, ELIZABETH M.
   Shakespeare's Troilus and Cressida;
   Titus Andronicus; Timon of Athens;
   Pericles and Cymbeline. (New York)
                                1965.

        Monarch critiques of literature.
                                757008

NUGENT, F.M.
   Review notes and study guide to
Shakespeare's 'King Richard the third'.
(New York)   1964.

        Monarch critiques of literature.
                                756292

The "Nursery"

——EVANS (GWYNNE BLAKEMORE) ed.
   Introductions to the "Nursery", "The
   Comedy of Errors", "Midsummer night's
   dream", collations; edited by
   G. B. Evans.   (Charlottesville, Va.)
                                1964.
   Facsim. Shakespearean prompt-books of
   the seventeenth century, Vol. 3.
   Bibliographical Society of the Univer-
   sity of Virginia.

                                668305

NUTT (SARAH M.)
The Arctic voyages of William Barents
in probable relation to certain of
Shakespeare's plays.   [With bibliographical references.]   IN Studies
in Philology, Vol. 39.   (Chapel Hill,
N.C.) illus.   1942.

                                554520

NUTTALL, A.D.
   The Argument about Shakespeare's
   characters. FROM Critical Quarterly,
   Summer.   1965.

        pp.107-119.   753394

   _____ Another copy.   767185

NUTTALL, ANTHONY DAVID
   Two concepts of allegory: a study of
   Shakespeare's "The Tempest" and the
   logic of allegorical expression.
                                 1967.

                        761470

NUTTALL, A.D.
   William Shakespeare "The Winter's Tale".
                                 1966.

        Studies in English Literature,
   No.26.   755389

O. (W. H.) see Oakley (W. H.)

Oakeshott (B.N.) Hamlet, from a
   student's note-book. pp.[10]. From
   The Westminster Review, Vol.47,
   1897.

                        1897.

                        138545

OAKESHOTT (WALTER FRASER)
   Raleigh and "Love's labour's lost".
   IN Oakeshott (W. F.) The Queen and
   the poet [: Queen Elizabeth I and
   Sir Walter Raleigh].
   ports.   illus.   chronological
   table.   facsimiles.   1960.

                        694078

OAKESHOTT (WALTER [FRASER])
   Shakespeare and Plutarch.   IN
   GARRETT (JOHN) ed., Talking of
   Shakespeare [: a selection from the
   lectures delivered at the annual
   course for teachers at Stratford,
   1948-1953].   1954.

                        641471

Oakey (G.)[ed.,] Blow, blow, thou
   winter wind: words by Shakespeare
   [from As You Like It]; music by
   R.J.S.Stevens, arranged by
   G.Oakey. [Staff notation and tonic
   sol-fa.]   2 vols.

                   [c.1925.]

                        517031

Oakey (G.)[ed.,] Hark, hark! the lark
   at heaven's gate sings; arranged
   for two voices by G.Oakey. Words by
   Shakespeare [from Cymbeline];
   verse 2 by M.E.A.Yates. Music by
   F.Schubert. [Staff notation and
   tonic sol-fa.]   2 vols.

                   [1923.]

                        516972

Oakey (G.)[ed.,] O happy fair,
   arranged for S.S.C. by G.Oakey.
   Words from Shakespeare, [Midsummer
   Night's Dream]; music by W.Shield.
   [Staff notation and tonic sol-fa.]
   2 vols.

                   [1919.]

                        516999

Oakey (G.)[ed.,] Under the greenwood
   tree: words by Shakespeare [from
   As You Like It]. Melody by [T.A.]
   Arne, arranged by G.Oakey. [Staff
   notation and tonic sol-fa.]
   2 vols.

                   [1938.]

                        517012

Oakey (G.) ed., What shall he have
   that kill'd the deer: words by
   Shakespeare [from As You Like It];
   music by Sir H.[R.] Bishop,
   arranged by G.Oakey. [Staff notation
   and tonic sol-fa.]   2 vols.

                   [1926.]

                        517010

Oakey (G.)[ed.,] Where the bee sucks.
   Music by [T.A.] Arne and [W.]
   Jackson arranged by G.Oakey. [Words
   by Shakespeare from The Tempest.
   [Staff notation and tonic sol-fa.]
   2 vols.

                   [1926.]

                        516984

Oakey (G.)[ed.,] Ye spotted snakes:
   words by Shakespeare [from Midsummer
   Night's Dream]l music by R.J.S.
   Stevens, arranged by G.Oakey. [Staff
   notation and tonic sol-fa.]   2 vols.

                   [1926.]

                        517029

Oakley (E.S.) Shakespeare's religion.
   From "The Congregational Quarterly,
   Jan., 1935. pp.[3.]

                   [1935]

                        432016

O[AKLEY] (WILLIAM H.)
   Through the Shakespeare country: a
   tourlet of places around the Bard's
   district.   FROM Cycling, Vol. 103.
   illus.   1942.

                        534899

OATES, J.C.
   The ambiguity of Troilus and Cressida.
   IN Shakespeare Quarterly XVII: 2. pp.141-
   150. (New York)   1966.

                        605711

OBERLIN COLLEGE LIBRARY
   The Spanish drama collection in the
   Oberlin College Library: a descriptive
   catalogue, by P. P. Rogers.   Author
   list [and] Supplementary volume
   containing reference lists.   [Including
   entries of translations of some of
   Shakespeare's plays.]   (Oberlin,
   Ohio)
   2 vols.   1940-46.

                        526823

Oberon *see* **A Midsummer Night's Dream,**
General Works

OBERTELLO, ALFREDO
Shakespeare and Italy.   [1964.]

    typescript.   668338

OBEY (A.)
Lucrece.   Translated, by T. N.
Wilder, from "Le Viol de Lucrèce",
by A. Obey.   [A play based on
Shakespeare's poem, Lucrece.]
    1933.

    406189

[O'BRIEN (CECILIA)]
Shakespeare's young men.   FROM [The
Westminster Review,] New Series,
Vol. 50.   [1876.]

    554154

O'BRIEN, M.A.
A Critical commentary on Shakespeare's
'Henry V.'   1967.

    Macmillan critical commentaries.
    763619

Observations on Shakspeare's [plays].
FROM [The Repository of Modern
Literature,] Vol. 2.   [1823.]

    562352

O'CASEY (SEAN)
The Flying wasp: a laughing look-over
of what has been said about the things
of the theatre by the English dramatic
critics, [etc. With chapters "The
Public death of Shakespeare";
"Shakespeare lives in London lads",
and other Shakespearian references.]
    1937.

    463460

O'CASEY (SEAN)
Pictures in the hallway [: an autobiography, with a chapter "Shakespeare
taps at the window".]
  port.   1942.

    531372

O'Casey (S.) The Public death of
    Shakespeare. From Time and Tide,
    July 13th, 1935. pp.1036-1037.

    1935.

    438991

O'Casey (S.) Shakespeare lives in London
    lads: [a performance of Midsummer
    Night's Dream by the pupils of Sloane
    School]. In Time and Tide. Vol.17.

    1936.

    466069

O'Casey (S.) Shakespeare lives in
    London lads: [a performance of
    Midsummer Night's Dream, by pupils
    of Sloane School, Chelsea]. In
    School Drama, Vol.1, No.2.

    [1938.]

    522632

Occultism

— BUDD (F. E.)
    English literature and the occult.
    [With references to Shakespeare's
    plays.]   IN FRANKLYN (J.) ed.,
    A Survey of the occult [: an
    encyclopaedia.]
    bibliogs.   1935.
    Arthur Barker's Companion Series.

    491478

— HELINE (T.)
    The Occult in Shakespeare: The Merchant
    of Venice.   [With bibliographical ref-
    erences.] pp. 31.   (New York)
    1936.

    469128

— HELINE (T.)
    The Occult in Shakespeare: Romeo and
    Juliet.   [With bibliographical refer-
    ences.] pp. 36.   (New York)
    1936.

    469129

— POGSON (BERYL)
    In the East my pleasure lies: an
    esoteric interpretation of some
    plays of Shakespeare.   1950.

    613231

O'Connor (Evangeline M.) An Index to
    the works of Shakespere, giving
    references to notable passages
    [etc.]

    1887.

    453450

O'CONNOR (EVANGELINE M.)

Topical index to the Booklovers Edition
of Shakespeare, with explanations of
allusions and obscure and obsolete
words and phrases.   [1937]
    University Society, New York.
Booklovers Edition [-20].

    475465

O'CONNOR (F.)
The Road to Stratford [: the development of Shakespeare's character as
shown in his works]. FROM The
Irish Times, July 10th-13th and
15th-16th, 1946. [Dublin] 1946.

579645

O'Connor (Frank) The Road to
Stratford [: a critical study of
Shakespeare. With bibliographical
references.]

1948.

595326

O'CONNOR (FRANK)
Shakespeare's progress. (New York)
1961.

Collier Books.

667261

O'CONNOR (FRANK)
Towards an appreciation of literature.
[With references to Shakespeare.]
pp. 58. (Dublin) 1945.

568120

O'CONNOR (JOHN)
The Psychology of Shakespeare: [a
review of "Shakespeare's way: a
psychological study", by F. C. Kolbe.]
FROM Blackfriars, 1931. pp. [4.]
[Oxford] [1931]

390911

O'CONOR (N. J.)
Godes peace and the Queenes:
vicissitudes of a house [the
Manor House House at Weston-on-the-
Green, Oxfordshire] 1539-1615.
port. illus. maps. 1934.

428377

Odd Volumes (Sette of)
SIMON (A. L.)
Wine in Shakespeare's days and
Shakespeare's plays: [paper] read
at the 463rd meeting of the Sette of
Odd Volumes, 1931. pp. 35. 1931.
Edition limited to 199 copies.
This is No. 16 and bears the author's
autograph.

501289

Odd Volumes' (Sette of) Year-Boke,
No. 11 (1898-99). [Containing
account of Shakespeare Evening,
22nd November, 1898] [1899]
Edition limited to 199 copies; printed
for private circulation only. This
is No. 173.

470275

Oddoye (E. N. V.) trans.
LAMB (CHARLES and MARY ANN)
Lamb Adesai ni dze Shakespeare wodzi
le amli. [Ga text.] pp. 87.
1951.

665440

Ode to the genius of Shakespear.
[pp. 75-82.] [c.1760.]
Extracted from unknown work.

666347

Odell (G.C.D.) Shakespeare, from
Betterton to Irving. Ports. Illus.
(New York) 2 vols. 1920.

438152

ODELL (MARY T.)
The Old theatre, Worthing: the
Theatre Royal, 1807-1855. [With
references to Shakespearian productions.] (Aylesbury)
ports. illus. facsimiles.
1938.
Sign of the Dolphin.

487607

ODELL (MARY T.)
The Theatre Royal, 1807-1855: more
about the old theatre, Worthing,
its plays, players and playbills,
its proprietor and his playhouses.
Publishing under the Worthing Art
Development Scheme. [With references to Shakespearian productions.]
(Worthing)
ports. illus. facsimiles. 1945.
Sign of the Dolphin.

590855

ODELL (MARY T.)
The Theatre Royal, 1814-1819:
Mr. [T.] Trotter of Worthing and
the Brighton theatre. [With
references to Shakespeare productions.
Worthing pageant] published under the
Worthing Art Development Scheme.
(Worthing)
ports. illus. facsimiles. 1944.
Sign of the Dolphin.

558632

O'Donnell (Mary M.) The Genesis of a
fallacy in romantic Shakespearean
criticism: a dissertation submitted
to the Faculty of the Graduate
School of Arts and Sciences of the
Saint Louis University, in partial
fulfillment of the requirements for
the degree of doctor of philosophy.
[With a bibliography.]

(Saint Louis) 1940.

530253

O'DONNELL (NORBERT F.)
Shakespeare, Marston, and the university:
The sources of Thomas Goffe's "Orestes".
IN Studies in Philology, Vol. 50.
(Chapel Hill, N.C.) 1953.

554520/50

OESTEN (T.) [ed.]
The Mermaid's song from Weber's opera
Oberon, arranged for the pianoforte
by T. Oesten. pp. 5. [c.1900.]

558615

Of verbal criticism: an epistle to
Mr. Pope [: a poem, by D.Mallet.]

see: Mallet (D.)

OGBURN (CHARLTON)
The Renaissance man of England [:
the Earl of Oxford as William
Shakespeare]. pp. 37. (Atlanta,
Ga.)
port. 1949.

611989

OGBURN (Mrs. DOROTHY) and
        OGBURN (CHARLTON)

Shake-speare: the man behind the name
[; the case for Edward de Vere, 17th
Earl of Oxford, as the author of
Shakespeare's works]. Illus. (New York)
                                1962.

                        667432

OGBURN (Mrs. DOROTHY) and OGBURN
(CHARLTON)
This star of England "William Shakespeare", man of the Renaissance
[: a study of the Earl of Oxford
authorship theory]. (New York)
  ports. facsimiles. bibliog. 1952.

                        633249

OGBURN (VINCENT H.)
The Merry Wives quarto, a farce inter-
lude. [With bibliographical notes.]
IN Publications of the Modern
Language Association of America,
Vol. 57. (Menasha, Wis.) 1942.

                        544204

OGDEN (DUNBAR H.)
The 1962 season at Stratford, Connecticut.
  IN SHAKESPEARE QUARTERLY XIII: 4.
  pp. 537-540.
  (New York) 1962.

                        605711

OGDEN (DUNBAR H.)
The 1963 season at Stratford,
Connecticut.
IN SHAKESPEARE QUARTERLY XIV: 4.
pp. 437-439.
(New York) 1963.

                        605711

OGDEN (DUNBAR H.)
The 1964 season of the Ashland and San
Diego Shakespearian Festivals. IN
Shakespeare Quarterly XV: 4. pp.409-418.
(New York) 1964.

                        605711

OGDEN'S (W. B.) Ltd.
"Guinea Gold" cigarettes and "St.
Julian" tobacco. Scenes from
Shakespeare's plays: a series of
picture cards. pp. 11. [Liverpool]
                            [c.1900.]

                        489456

Ogg (D.) The Renaissance and Reformation.
[With a reference to Shakespeare and
the New Learning.] In Taylor (G.R.S.)
ed.,Great events in history.

                        1934.

                        420461

Ogilvie (V.) Three characters in Hamlet.
In Britain Today, No.138.Oct.,1947.

                        1947.

                        587767

OGILVY (J. D. A.)
The Forced gait of a shuffling nag.
(I Henry IV, III, i, 134). IN
Elizabethan studies and other essays
[, by various authors], in honor of
George F. Reynolds. [With biblio-
graphical notes.] (Boulder, Col.)
                                1945.
Colorado University Studies. Series
B. Studies in the Humanities. Vol.
2. No. 4.

                        569202

O'HAGAN (T.)
What Shakespeare is not. (Toronto)
  bibliog. 1936.

                        463636

Ohio State University, Contributions in
Languages and Literature
  KIRSCHBAUM (LEO)
  Shakespeare and the Stationers.
  (Columbus, Ohio)
  bibliog. 1955.

                        648104

Ohio State University, Contributions in
Languages and Literature
  MOORE (OLIN HARRIS)
  The Legend of Romeo and Juliet.
  (Columbus, Ohio)
  bibliog. 1950.

                        616127

Okerlund (G.) The Quarto version of
  Henry V as a stage adaptation. In
  Publications of the Modern Language
  Association of America, vol.49.

        (Menasha,Wis.) 1934.

                        432218

Old Age in Shakespeare

——COX (E. H.)
  Shakespeare and some conventions of old
  age. FROM Studies in Philology, Vol.
  39. (Chapel Hill, N.C.)
                                1942.

                        537258

—— MILES (L. W.)
  Shakespeare's old men. IN E.L.H.:
  a journal of English literary history,
  Vol. 7. (Baltimore) 1940.

                        529087

— SIMS (RUTH E.)
The Green old age of Falstaff. [With bibliographical notes.] FROM Bulletin of the History of Medicine, Vol. 13. (Baltimore)
1943.

569112

OLD COMEDIAN [pseud.]
The Life and death of David Garrick Esq., the celebrated English Roscius. Giving an account of his figure, face, voice and education, [etc.] Also [his] speech on retiring from the stage, in 1776, the procession and ceremony at his funeral, substance of his will; his prologues, epilogues, &c. [With] the life of Edward Alleyn [and] a curious anecdote of Alleyn, Shakespeare and Ben Jonson. pp. 64.
1779.

526662

Old English songs, edited by J. Coates. 2 vols. [1929.]
1(a) Lawn as white as driven snow (Autolycus' song in "Winter's Tale"). Words by Shakespeare. Music by W. Linley (1816).
(b) No more dams I'll make for fish (Caliban's song in "The Tempest") Words by Shakespeare; music by J. C. Smith (1756). pp. 5.
2. Come away, death!: song from "Twelfth Night". Words by Shakespeare; music by T. A. Arne. pp. 4.
594154

OLD VIC MAGAZINE: official organ of the Old Vic Theatre.
Vol. 1 (Oct. 1919-May 1920)-Vol. 11 (Sept. 1929-Dec. 1930) 11 vols.
1919-30.
Continued as The Old Vic and Sadler's Wells Magazine, catal. no. 397473.

326002

OLD VIC AND SADLER'S WELLS MAGAZINE: the official organ of both theatres.
Vol. 1 (1931)-Vol. 7 (1938-39).
7 vols. 1931-39.
Previously issued as The Old Vic Magazine, catal. no. 326002.
Ceased publication.
397473

Old Vic Theatre *see* London, Old Vic Theatre

Oldcastle, John Sir *works relating to*

— CLARK (ELEANOR G.)
Falstaff and Cobham. FROM A Christmas book, Dec. 1937.
pp. [12.] (New York) 1937.

598971

— FIEHLER (RUDOLPH)
How Oldcastle became Falstaff. IN Modern Language Quarterly, Vol. 16.
1955.

525289/16

— Oliver (L.M.) Sir John Oldcastle: legend or literature? [The Origin of Falstaff.] *In* The Library, 5th Series, Vol.1.
(Oxford) 1946.

586026

— SHAPTER (W.)
The Original of Falstaff: [Sir J. Oldcastle]. IN The Month, Vol. 93.
1899.

147490

— WAUGH (W. T.)
Sir John Oldcastle [: the original of Falstaff.] IN The English Historical Review, Vol. 20. 1905.

191450

Oldfield, Anne *works relating to*

— EGERTON (W.)
Faithful memoirs of the life, amours and performances, of Mrs. Anne Oldfield interspersed with several dramatical memoirs. [With an introduction by C. Cibber and references to Shakespeare.]
1731.

571427

OLDYS (WILLIAM)
Choice notes from his Adversaria [including a section on Shakespeare.] IN [YEOWELL (J.)] A Literary antiquary: memoir of William Oldys etc. (Reprinted from Notes and Queries.)
port. 1862.

389727

OLIPHANT (ERNEST HENRY CLARK)
Marlowe's hand in "Arden of Feversham": a problem for critics. IN The New Criterion, Vol. 4. 1926.

339555

OLIPHANT (ERNEST HENRY CLARK)
[A Review of] Shakespeare's Henry VI and Richard III, by P. Alexander. IN Modern Language Notes, vol. 45, December, 1930. (Baltimore) 1930.

439157

OLIPHANT (ERNEST HENRY CLARK)
The Shakespeare canon.   IN The
Quarterly Review, Vol. 259,
July, 1932.   1932.

405658

OLIPHANT (ERNEST HENRY CLARK)
Shakspere's plays: an examination.
IN The Modern Language Review, Vols.
3-4.   (Cambridge)
   2 vols.   1908-9.

266818

OLIPHANT (ERNEST HENRY CLARK)
"Sir Thomas More" [: a discussion
on Anthony Munday's authorship of
the play and whether Shakespeare
was concerned in the textual alter-
ation].   Reprinted from The Journal
of English and Germanic Philology,
Vol. 18.   (Urbana, Ill.)   [1919.]

554219

OLIVE (W. J.)
Sejanus and Hamlet.   IN WILLIAMS
(A. L.) ed., A Tribute to George
Coffin Taylor.   [Chapel Hill, N.C.]
                                   1952.

625745

OLIVE (W. J.)
"Twenty good nights" - The Knight of
the burning pestle, The Family of
love, and Romeo and Juliet.   IN
Studies in Philology, Vol. 47.
(Chapel Hill, N.C.)   1950.

554520/47

Oliver (B.) The Renaissance of the
   English public house.[With
   references to Shakespeare and
   bibliographical notes.] Illus.Plans.

1947.

585385

OLIVER (H.J.)
Coriolanus as tragic hero.
IN SHAKESPEARE QUARTERLY X: 1.
pp. 53-60.
(New York)   1959.

605711

Oliver (H.J.)[Review of]The Crown
   of life by G.W.Knight.In The
   Modern Language Review,Vol.42.

(Cambridge)   1947,

266816/42

OLIVER (HERBERT)
Shall I compare thee [: arranged
for] T.T.B.B.   Words by Shakespeare
[: Sonnet 18].   pp. 8.   1948.

601860

Oliver (L.M.) Sir John Oldcastle:
   legend or literature? [The origin
   of Falstaff.] In The Library,5th
   Series, Vol.1.

(Oxford)   1946.

586026

Olivia *see* Twelfth Night, General Works and
Criticism

[OLIVIER (Sir LAURENCE) and DENT
(ALAN [H.]) eds.]
Henry V: release script.   ff. 87.
(Two Cities Films Ltd.)
   typescript.   [1944.]

556035

[OLIVIER (Sir LAURENCE) and DENT (ALAN
[H.]) eds.]
Shakespeare's Henry V: revised treat-
ment for technicolor film.   ff. 64.
(Two Cities Films Ltd.)
   typescript.   [1944.]

548730

OLIVIER ([Sir] LAURENCE), REED (CAROL)
and FURSE (ROGER)
The Work of Roger Furse: the
relation of artist and director in
three interviews.   [With special
reference to "Hamlet".]   IN Film
To-day books [1.]
   ports.   illus.   [1948.]

589632

Olivier, Laurence Sir *works relating to*

—— ADLER (H.)
   Ralph Richardson and Laurence Olivier
   [: actors in Othello at the Old Vic].
   IN World Film News, Vol. 2.
   ports.   1938.

485420

—— Agee (J.) Films[: a review of
   Laurence Oliviers production of
   Henry V]. From The Nation, Vol.163.

(New York)   1946.

581633

—— Ashworth (J.) Olivier, Freud, and
   Hamlet. In Atlantic, Vol.183.

(Boston.Mass.)   1949

19347/183

—— BARKER (FELIX)
   The Oliviers [Laurence and Vivien]:
   a biography.
   ports.   illus.   1953.

633056

—— CAUSLEY (C.)
 Laurence Olivier's Richard III [: a
 poem].   IN Life and Letters, Vol. 54.
                        1947.

                        586006

—— Cinema [: a review of Laurence Olivier's
 production of Shakespeare's Henry V,
 as presented by Two Cities Films, Ltd.]
 FROM Time, Vol. 47.   [Chicago]
 illus.   map.   1946.

                        573947

—— Collector's prints, Shakespearean, 200-
 208: Henry V.   [Coloured prints from
 the film produced by Laurence Olivier
 and presented by Two Cities Films, Ltd.
 With an extract from the play on each
 print.]   [1945.]
 Brownlee Nineteen-forty-two.
                        569085

—— CROSS (BRENDA) ed.
 The Film Hamlet: a record of its
 production [by various authors].
 pp. 76.
  ports. illus. facsimiles. 1948.

                        591805

—— CROZIER (E.)
 Acting to-day: the work of Olivier
 and Richardson in Henry the Fourth.
 FROM Theatre Today, March 1946.
  ports.   illus.   1946.

                        568493

—— DARLINGTON, WILLIAM AUBREY
 Laurence Olivier [: a history of his
 acting career].
  illus.   1968.
 Great contemporaries.
                        776737

—— DENT (A.)
 Notes for a lecture on the film of
 "Hamlet".   ff. 7.
  typescript.   [1948.]

                        598972

—— DOONE (R.)
 Three Shakespearian productions [:
 Hamlet, with John Gielgud, Richard III,
 featuring Laurence Olivier, and King
 Lear, with Donald Wolfit].   IN The
 Penguin New Writing, 25. (Harmondsworth)
  illus.   1945.

                        564884

—— HALL (EVELYN)
 Laurence Olivier.   [With special
 reference to his Shakespearean
 performances.]   IN Britain Today,
 No. 139, Nov., 1947.
  illus.   1947.

                        587767

—— Hamlet, produced and directed by
 Sir Laurence Olivier for Two Cities
 Films: Records of the film, No. 16,
 published by the British Film
 Institute.   pp. [8.]   [1948.]

                        590201

—— Hamlet.   Produced and directed
 by Laurence Olivier.   A Two Cities
 film, 1948.   [Scenes from the film,
 with original set designs by
 R. Furse, adapted for use in miniature theatres.]   [1948.]

                        596187

—— HAY (LORNA)
 How Laurence Olivier plays King Lear:
 at the New Theatre, London.   IN
 Picture Post, Vol. 33.
  ports. illus.   1946.

                        494733/33

—— How Henry V was designed [: the design-
 ing of the costumes and setting in the
 Two Cities Films, Ltd. presentation of
 Laurence Olivier's film].   IN Picture
 Post, Vol. 26.
  illus.   1945.

                        565210

—— HUTTON (C. C.)
 The Making of Henry V [Laurence Olivier's
 production of Henry V, as presented by
 Two Cities Films, Ltd.]   pp. 72.
  ports. illus. map. plans. [1944.]

                        556042

—— [HUTTON (C. C.) ed.]
 The Story of Shakespeare's Henry V
 with illustrations from the [Two Cities
 Films, Ltd.] film presentation by
 Laurence Olivier [and drawings throughout by A. W. Dean].   pp. 32.
  ports.   illus.   [1946.]

                        572074

—— KOZELKA (PAUL)
 A Guide to the screen version of
 Shakespeare's Richard III. (Photoplay
 Studies).pp.16. Ports. Illus.[Maplewood,
 N.J.]   [1956.]

                        665547

—— LEJEUNE (CAROLINE A.)
 Three English films.   [Includes a
 review of Laurence Olivier's production
 of Henry V as presented by Two Cities
 Films, Ltd.]   IN Theatre Arts, Vol.
 29.   (New York)
  illus.   1945.

                        567819

—— LONDON FILM PRODUCTIONS, LTD.
 [London Films in association with
 Laurence Olivier.   Photographs
 and publicity material of the film
 Richard the Third.]   pp. 48. 1955.

                        665304

—— Olivier's Hamlet [: an article on the
 film, with critical letters].   pp. 4.
 FROM Time, Vol. 51.   [Chicago]
  ports. illus.   1948.

                        596203

—— POWELL (DILYS)
 "Hamlet" on the screen [: Sir Laurence
 Olivier's production].   IN Britain
 To-day, No. 147.   1948.

                        587767/147

POWELL (DILYS)
Laurence Olivier: a brief chronicle
[with an account of his Shakespearian
performances]. IN The Saturday Book,
6th year.
ports.   illus.   [1946.]

576899

[Richard the Third: release script
of the film presented by London Films
in association with Laurence Olivier.]
typescript.   [1955.]

665180

RIPLEY (A. C.)
Vaudeville pattern [: miscellaneous
essays in the cinema, theatre, etc.,
including two chapters on Laurence
Olivier's Henry V].
ports.   illus.   1942.

582752

STOKES (S.)
The Oliviers.   [With references to
Laurence Olivier's Shakespearean
performances].   IN Theatre Arts,
Vol. 29.   (New York)   1945.

567819

TWO CITIES FILMS, LTD.
G.C.F. presents Laurence Olivier's
Henry V by William Shakespeare
[: souvenir booklet].   pp. [16.]
[New York]
ports.   illus.   [1945.]

646355

TWO CITIES FILMS LTD.
Henry V.   [Production by Laurence
Olivier].   Release script [by Alan
[H.] Dent and Laurence Olivier].
ff. 87.
typescript.   [1944.]

556035

[TWO CITIES FILMS LTD.]
Laurence Olivier presents Hamlet
by William Shakespeare.   pp. [4.]
[1948.]

596213

[TWO CITIES FILMS, LTD.]
Laurence Olivier presents Hamlet by
Shakespeare [: photographs from the
film with a commentary in English,
French and Italian].   pp. [24].
[1949.]

600297

[TWO CITIES FILMS LTD.
Photographs of Laurence Olivier's
production of Hamlet.]   pp. [40.]
[1948.]

600249

[TWO CITIES FILMS LTD.
Photographs of Laurence Olivier's
production of Henry V.   ff. 12.]
[1944.]

555605

[TWO CITIES FILMS LTD.
Posters of Laurence Olivier's
production of Hamlet.]   [1948.]

600127

[TWO CITIES FILMS LTD.]
William Shakespeare's Henry V: revised
treatment for technicolor film.
[Production by Laurence Olivier.
Script] by Alan[H.]Dent & Laurence
Olivier.   ff. 64.
typescript.   [1944.]

548730

TYNAN, KENNETH PEACOCK, ed.
Othello: the National Theatre
production.   1966.

illus.   753063

WHITEHEAD, PETER, and BEAN, ROBIN
Olivier [and] Shakespeare: [being the
life of Sir Laurence Olivier, with still
photographs from his Shakespearian
films]. French translation by Marie-
Claude Apcher, and German translation
by V. Oleram.   1966.

753020

WILKINSON (F. W.)
Henry V [: a review of Laurence Olivier's
production as presented by Two Cities
Films, Ltd.]   IN Sight and Sound,
Vol. 13.   1944-5.

560963

ZIEGFELD THEATRE, New York
[Souvenir booklet of Vivien Leigh and
Laurence Olivier in the production of
Bernard Shaw's Caesar and Cleopatra
and Shakespeare's Antony and Cleopatra
at the Ziegfeld Theatre.]   pp. [16.]
[New York]
ports.   illus.   [1951.]

624735

O'LOUGHLIN (SEAN) and MUIR (KENNETH)
The Phoenix and the turtle.   FROM
The Dublin Magazine, Vol. 10, No. 2.
(N.S.)   (Dublin)   1935.

515689

O'LOUGHLIN (S.) [and] MUIR (K.)
The Voyage to Illyria: a new study
of Shakespeare.   1937.

469719

O'Loughlin, Sean *works relating to*

—— SPENCER (B. T.)
Three ways to Shakespeare [: a review
of The Voyage to Illyria: a new study
of Shakespeare, by K. Muir and
S. O'Loughlin, etc.] FROM Sewanee
Review, Vol. 47. (Sewanee) 1939.

530197

Olson (Alma L.) Scandinavia: the
background for neutrality. [With
a section entitled "Prince of
Denmark".]

(Philadelphia) 1940.

520074

OLSON (PAUL A.)
A Midsummer night's dream and the
meaning of court marriage. IN E.L.H.:
[: A Journal of English Literary
History] Vol. 24. (Baltimore, Md.)
1957.

430295/24

Olympic Theatre *see* **London**, Theatres —
Olympic Theatre

O'MALLEY, JUDITH MARIE
Justice in Shakespeare: three English
kings in the light of Thomistic thought.
(New York) 1964.

745723

OMAN (CAROLA MARY ANIMA)
The Best of his family [: a novel
about Shakespeare].
bibliog. plan. 1933.

410741

OMAN (CAROLA MARY ANIMA)
David Garrick [: a biography].
ports. illus. genealogical table.
bibliog. 1958.

681422

OMAN (J. [W.])
The Natural & the supernatural.
[With a chapter, "A Poet's awareness
and apprehension", as seen in
Shakespeare's plays and characters.]
(Cambridge) 1931.

383308

OMMANNEY (KATHARINE A.)
The Stage and the school. Pictures
by Ben Kutcher. [With chapters on
Shakespeare].
bibliogs. 1932.

469652

On "Hamlet". FROM The Institute
Magazine, Jan. 1912. [Birmingham]
1912.

536839

On Hamlet criticism. From [The London
University Magazine, June 1858.]

[1858.]

554158

On modern French poetry, with translations. [Containing references to
Ducis' adaptations of Shakespeare's
plays.] From [The London Magazine,]
Dec.1823.

1823.

561773

On Shakespear's monument at Stratford
upon Avon [: a poem.] IN [DODSLEY
(R.) ed.] A Collection of poems by
several hands. 5th edn. Vol. 2.
illus. 1758.

538519

On the character of Imogen. IN
[HONORIA, pseud., ed.] The Female
mentor; or, Select conversations,
Vol. 1. 1793. 556050
—————— Another copy. 49711

On the tragedy of Macbeth as represented
on the English stage. From Monthly
Prize Essays, Vol.1, No.2.

1846.

447568

O'NEAL (COTHBURN MADISON)
The Dark lady: a novel [relating to
Shakespeare]. (New York) 1954.

644325

O'Neill, Eugene Gladstone *works relating to*

—— HEYDRICK (B. A.) and MAY (A. A.) eds.
Macbeth, William Shakespeare [and]
The Emperor Jones, Eugene O'Neill.
(New York)
illus. 1933.
Noble's Comparative Classics.

414573

O'Neill (Moira)[pseud.] Macbeth as
the Celtic type. In Blackwood's
Edinburgh Magazine, Vol.150.

1891.

112932

ONG (W. J.)
Historical backgrounds of Elizabethan
and Jacobean punctuation theory.
[With references to Shakespeare.]
IN Publications of the Modern
Language Association of America,
Vol. 59. (Menasha, Wis.)
bibliog. 1944.

560393

ONG (WALTER J.)
Metaphor and the twinned vision: The
Phoenix and the turtle. IN The
Sewanee Review, Vol. 63. (Sewanee,
Tenn.) 1955.

641628/63

Onions (C.T.) Natural history:
animals. In Shakespeare's England,
vol.1. [With bibliographies.]
Illus. Facsimiles.

(Oxford) 1917.

435745

ONIONS (C. T.)
A Select glossary of musical terms,
with illustrative passages from
Shakespeare's works. IN Shakespeare's
England, vol. 2. (Oxford)
illus. facsimiles. bibliog. 1917.

435746

ONIONS (CHARLES TALBUT)
A Shakespeare glossary. 2nd edn.,
revised. (Oxford) 1925. 508432
_____ 2nd edn. revised. [New]
impression. 1929. 394557

Open Air Theatre, Regent's Park *see* London, Theatres — Regent's Park Open Air Theatre

Opera *see* Music

Opera Scores *see* Music Scores

Opera Texts *see* ENGLISH EDITIONS, [Play Title] Opera Texts

Ophelia *see* Hamlet, Characters — Ophelia

OPPELL (Baron von)
Beauty in Shakespeare and in Kant.
[With bibliographical notes.]
pp. 8. FROM The Hibbert Journal,
Vol. 40. 1942.

535148

ORAS (ANTS)
Lyrical instrumentation in Marlowe:
a step towards Shakespeare. IN
MATTHEWS (A. D.) and EMERY (C. M.)
eds., Studies in Shakespeare.
(University of Miami Publications in
English and American Literature,
Vol. 1, March 1953). (Coral Gables,
Fla.) 1953.

634188

Oratory and Rhetoric

ABERCROMBIE (DAVID)
How Garrick spoke Shakespeare.
[Broadcast] 9th March, 1951. ff. 8.
typescript. 1951.

620402

BURKE, KENNETH
Shakespearean persuasion [: the
rhetorical language of 'Antony and
Cleopatra']. FROM Antioch Review
Vol. XXIV: 1. (Yellow Springs, Ohio)
1964.

668301

CLARK (DONALD LEMEN)
Ancient rhetoric and English Renaissance
literature.
IN SHAKESPEARE QUARTERLY II: 3.
pp. 195-204.
(New York) 1951.

605711

CRANE (W. G.)
Wit and rhetoric in the Renaissance:
the formal basis of Elizabethan
prose style. (New York)
bibliog. 1937.
Columbia University. Studies in
English and Comparative Literature.

481097

JOSEPH (BERTRAM LEON)
Acting Shakespeare.
ports. glossary. 1960.

666541

—KENNEDY (M. B.)
   The Oration in Shakespeare. [With a
   bibliography and bibliographical notes.]
   (Chapel Hill, N.C.) 1942.

                         537591

— KNIGHT, GEORGE WILSON
   Shakespeare's rhetoric. Produced by
   G.M. MacBeth. B.B.C. radio script
   broadcast 17th December 1963.
                         1963.

        typescript.   667868

— LE PAGE (R. B.)
   The Dramatic delivery of Shakespeare's
   verse.   IN English Studies, Vol. 32.
   (Amsterdam)   1951.

                       485643/32

—MIRIAM JOSEPH, Sister
   Rhetoric in Shakespeare's time:
   literary theory of Renaissance
   Europe.   (New York)   1962.

                         667599

—MUIR, KENNETH
   Shakespeare and rhetoric.
   IN SHAKESPEARE JAHRBUCH.   Bd. 90/1954.
   pp. 49-68.   (Heidelberg)

                         10531

—PRIESTLEY (J.)
   A Course of lectures on oratory and
   criticism [with references to oratory
   and criticism in Shakespeare].
                    1777.   223509
   _____ Another edn.   (Dublin)
                    1781.   568834

— ROBERTS (D. R.)
   Shakespeare and the rhetoric of stylish
   ornamentation: an abstract of a dissertation presented to the Faculty of
   the Graduate School of Cornell University
   for the degree of Doctor of Philosophy.
   pp. [4.]   (Ithaca, N.Y.)   1936.

                         513778

— RYLANDS (GEORGE HUMPHREY WOLFESTAN)
   The Actor's speaking of Hamlet.
   [Broadcast] 12th Dec., 1951. ff.19.
     typescript.   1951.

                         624729

— Sansom (C.) On the speaking of
     Shakespeare. pp.12.

              1949.

(London Academy of Music and Dramatic Art)

                         608339

— WADE (J. E.)
   Medieval rhetoric in Shakespeare [:
   a dissertation submitted to the
   Faculty of] Saint Louis University
   [for the degree of Doctor of Philo-
   sophy].
     microfilm copy.   1942.
   University Microfilms.   Doctoral
   Dissertations Series.
     For an abstract of the dissertation
   see Microfilm Abstracts Vol. 5.No.2.
   Catal.no.569025.
                         575680

— WILLCOCK (GLADYS D.)
   Shakespeare and rhetoric.
   IN English Association, Essays and
   studies, Vol. 29, 1943.   Collected
   by Una [M.] Ellis-Fermor.   (Oxford)
                         1944.

           553238

ORCHARD (M.)

   Commentary and questionnaire on
   As you like it. pp. 32.   1927.
   Commentaries and Questionnaires
   in English Literature.
                  408527

ORCUTT (WILLIAM DANA)

   From my library walls: a kaleidoscope
   of memories.   [With references to
   Shakespeare.]
   port.   1946.

                  576555

Ord (H.) The Child and education in
   Shakespeare. In The Contemporary
   Review, Vol. 104.

                  1913.

                     247979

Ord (H.) London as shown by
   Shakespeare. Plan. In The Contemporary Review, Vol. 100.

             1911.

                     233746

Ordish (T.F.) The First folio Shakespeare
   1623. [From The Bookworm, Vol.1.]

                  [1888.]
                     482168

ORDISH (THOMAS FAIRMAN)
   Shakespeare in London, a fantasy [in
   verse].   (London Shakespeare Commemoration, 1913).   [With typescript
   original, signed by the author.]
   pp. [4], ff. [4].
   2 vols.   [1913.]

                     665063

Oregon Shakespeare Festival

——ASHLAND STUDIES IN SHAKESPEARE
Notes, comment, and reading-lists to
accompany classwork [in the Institute
of Renaissance Studies] established
by the English Department of Stanford
University in association with the
Oregon Shakespeare Festival.
Privately published and sponsored by
the Oregon Shakespeare Festival,
Southern Oregon College and Stanford
University of California. (Ashland, Ore.)
ports. illus. maps. plans. genealogical
tables. facsimiles. bibliog. 1954-

666259

——BAILEY (MARGERY)
The Shakespeare Festival of Oregon,
1949. IN Oregon Shakespeare Festival,
[Programmes, etc.] 8th season, 1948-
(Ashland, Ore.)
ports. illus. 1948-

626550

—— BAILEY (MARGERY)
Shakespeare in action. IN College
English, Vol. 15. (Chicago, Ill.)
1954.

598860/15

——BAILEY(MARGERY)

The Shakespeare stage in American theatre.
Reprint from Colorado Quarterly.Vol.pp.
[13] [.Boulder,Col.] 1953.

634768

—— DAVIDSON (LEVETTE J.)
Shakespeare in the Rockies.
IN SHAKESPEARE QUARTERLY IV: 1.
pp. 39-49.
(New York) 1953.

605711

—— HORN (ROBERT D.)
The Oregon Shakespeare Festival [:
reviews]. IN SHAKESPEARE QUARTERLY
VII, pp. 415-418, 1956; VIII, pp.
527-530, 1957; X, pp. 581-585, 1959;
XI, pp. 477-480, 1960; XII, pp. 415-
418, 1961; XIII, pp. 547-552, 1962.
(New York)

605711

—— INSTITUTE OF RENAISSANCE STUDIES
[Programmes] 1957- (Ashland, Ore.)
ports. illus. facsimile. 1957-

667287

—— JOHNSON (GLORIA E.)
Shakespeare at Ashland, Oregon - 1958.
IN SHAKESPEARE QUARTERLY IX.
pp. 543-547.
(New York) 1958.

605711

—— NICHOLS (DOROTHY E.)
The Oregon Shakespeare Festival, 1967.
IN SHAKESPEARE QUARTERLY XVIII: 4.
pp. 421-423. (New York) 1967.

605711

——NICHOLS (DOROTHY)
Shakespeare on the West Coast, at
Ashland and San Diego.
IN SHAKESPEARE QUARTERLY XVI: 4.
pp. 343-347.
(New York) 1965.

605711

——OGDEN (DUNBAR H.)
The 1964 season of the Ashland and San
Diego Shakespearian Festivals. IN
Shakespeare Quarterly XV: 4. pp.409-418.
(New York) 1964.

605711

——[Programmes, etc.] 8th season, 1948-
Ports. Illus. (Ashland, Ore.)

626550

—— PROSSER (ELEANOR)
Shakespeare at Ashland and San Diego.
IN SHAKESPEARE QUARTERLY XIV: 4.
pp. 445-454.
(New York) 1963.

605711

—— ROBINSON (HORACE W.)
Shakespeare, Ashland, Oregon.
IN SHAKESPEARE QUARTERLY VI:
pp. 447-451.
(New York) 1955.

605711

——SANDOE (JAMES)
The Oregon Shakespeare Festival.
IN SHAKESPEARE QUARTERLY I: 1.
pp. 5-11.
(New York) 1950.

605711

——SMITH (PETER D.)
The 1966 Festivals at Ashland, Oregon,
and San Diego, California.
IN SHAKESPEARE QUARTERLY XVII: 4.
pp. 407-417.
(New York) 1966.

605711

—— WADSWORTH (FRANK W.)
Shakespeare in action - a report.
IN College English, Vol. 16.
(Champaign, Ill.) 1955.

598860/16

Origin of Hamlet. IN All the year
round. New series, Vol. 22.
1879.

38535

O'Riordan (C.) Captain Falstaff and
other plays. Frontis.

1935.

445050

Orlando *see* **As You Like It**, General Works and Criticism

ORLEANS (Duc de)
D'une manière imparfaite (How imperfect is expression)
see: Music (Twelfth Night. Burlesques, parodies, additional songs, etc.)

Ornithology *see* **Natural History**

ORNSTEIN (ROBERT)
Character and reality in Shakespeare.
IN BLOOM (EDWARD A.) ed., Shakespeare 1564-1964: a collection of modern essays by various hands. (Providence. R.I.)   1964.
Brown University bicentennial publications.
                              744437

Ornstein (Robert)
The Ethic of the imagination: love and art in 'Antony and Cleopatra'. IN Stratford-upon-Avon Studies.
8: Later Shakespeare.   1966.

    illus. pp.31-46.   756101

ORNSTEIN (ROBERT)
The Great Lakes Shakespeare Festival.
IN SHAKESPEARE QUARTERLY XVIII: 1967, pp. 425-427; XIV: 1968, pp. 387-389.
(New York)
                              605711

Ornstein, Robert
Historical criticism and the interpretation of Shakespeare. IN

RABKIN, NORMAN, ed.
Approaches to Shakespeare [: 20th century critical essays]. (New York)
                              1964.

                   668298

ORNSTEIN (ROBERT)
The Human comedy: "Measure for measure", [by W. Shakespeare]. FROM The University of Kansas City Review, Vol. 24.   pp. [8.]   (Kansas City, Mo.)
                       1957.

                   666164

ORNSTEIN (ROBERT)
The Moral vision of Jacobean tragedy.
Bibliog. (Madison, Wis.)   1960.

                   698027

ORNSTEIN (ROBERT)
Seneca and the political drama of "Julius Caesar".   IN Journal of English and Germanic Philology, Vol. 57.   (Urbana, Ill.)   1958.

            600780/57

Ornstein (Robert)
Shakespeare's moral vision: Othello and Macbeth. IN

LEECH, CLIFFORD, ed.
Shakespeare: the tragedies.
A collection of critical essays.
(Chicago)   1965.

    Gemini books.   752332

ORNSTEIN (ROBERT) ed.
Discussions of Shakespeare's problem comedies [: All's well that ends well; Measure for measure; Troilus and Cressida. Selected from various authors]. (D. C. Heath and Co., Boston, Mass.)   1961.
Discussions of Literature.
                   667641

ORPINGTON BRANCH, British Empire Shakespeare Society
Programmes, etc.   (Orpington)
                   1941-57.

                   535366

ORR, PETER
The True histrionic: an appreciation of Sir John Gielgud on the occasion of his sixtieth birthday. Produced by John Powell. B.B.C. radio script broadcast 14th April 1964.   1964.

                   740867

ORRERY, R. BOYLE, 1st Earl of
The History of Henry the Fifth

For editions of this play see under English Editions: Henry the Fifth: Alterations &c.

Orsini (Napoleone) see Giordano-Orsini (Gian Napoleone)

Orsino *see* **Twelfth Night**, General Works and Criticism

ORTEGA Y GASSET, JOSÉ
Shylock.   IN LEWINTER, OSWALD, ed., Shakespeare in Europe [by various authors].   1963.

                   667784

Orthography *see* Name of Shakespeare

ORWELL (GEORGE)
Lear, Tolstoy and the fool [: a
discussion on Tolstoy's pamphlet
"Shakespeare and the drama"].   IN
Polemic, No. 7.   1947.
 For "Shakespeare and the drama" see
Catal. no. 204801.

586298

ORWELL (GEORGE)
Lear, Tolstoy and the fool.   IN
Orwell (G.) Shooting an elephant,
and other essays.   1950.

610432

Orwell (G.) Tolstoy and Shakespeare
[concerning Tolstoy's Essay on
Shakespeare. In The Listener, Vol.25.

1941.

526583

OSBORN (EDWARD BOLLAND) [ed.]
Shakespeare as sportsman [: quotations
from the plays].   IN Osborn (E. B.)
[ed.] Anthology of sporting verse.
1930.

438373

Osborn, Francis *works relating to*

—— WRIGHT (LOUIS BOOKER) ed.
     Advice to a son: precepts of Lord
     Burghley, Sir Walter Raleigh and
     and Francis Osborne.   (Ithaca, N.Y.)
      bibliogs.   1962.
     Folger Shakespeare Library.   Folger
     Documents of Tudor and Stuart
     Civilization.

667175

OSBORN (J. M.)
John Dryden: some biographical facts
and problems. [With references to
Shakespeare.] (New York)
 ports. facsimiles. genealogical
table. bibliog.   1940.

531316

OSBORNE (WILFRID J.)
Anne Hathaway's Cottage.   Published
by the Trustees and Guardians of
Shakespeare's Birthplace.   pp. 24.
(Stratford-upon-Avon)
 illus.   1947.

586597

[OSBORNE (W. J.)]
William Shakespeare [: some dates,
facts and inferences].   pp. 20.
 port. illus. genealogical table.
 facsimile.   [1948.]

597684

OSBORNE (WILLIAM ALEXANDER)
Some brief Shakespeare commentaries.
IN Osborne (W. A.) Essays and studies.
(Melbourne)   1946.

578948

OSBORNE (WILLIAM F.)
The Genius of Shakespeare, and
other essays.   (Boston)   1908.

415003

OSGERBY, J.R.
 William Shakespeare: Hamlet. 1965.

Guides to English literature.
744907

OSGOOD (C. G.)
The Voice of England: a history of
English literature. [With a
chapter on Shakespeare.]   (New
York)
 bibliog.   1935.

502978

OSLER ([Sir]WILLIAM)
Creators, transmuters, and transmitters
as illustrated by Shakespeare, Bacon,
and Burton [: reprint in "Osler in
Shakespeare, Bacon, and Burton", by
W. White].   FROM Bulletin of the
History of Medicine, Vol. 7.
(Baltimore)
 facsimile.   1939.

565596

Oslo Studies in English
ECKHOFF (LORENTZ)
Shakespeare: spokesman of the third
estate.   English translation by
R. I. Christophersen.   (Oslo)
1954.

647413

Osric *see* Hamlet, Characters — Osric

Ost (Franz) ed.
LAMB (CHARLES and MARY)
Six tales from Shakespere.   Mit
Anmerkungen zum schulgebrauch neu
herausgegeben von F. Ost. (Bielefeld)
 illus.   1923.
[English text with appendix and lexicon
in German]
 Velhagen & Klasings Sammlung franzö-
sischer und englischer schulausgaben.
English authors.   Bd. 28 B)

309089

OST (F.) ed.
Shakespeare and his time. [English texts.] Edited and annotated.
pp. 80. (Leipzig)
ports. illus. [c.1935]
English Treasure Series. Englische Lektüre und Kulturkunde in Einzelheften.
449471

Ost (Franz) ed.
Shakespeare in English literature.
pp. 77. [Leipzig] [1929.]
[English text.]
English Treasure Series: Englische Lektüre und Kulturkunde in Einzelheften.
362308

OSTROVSKY, ALEKSANDR NIKOLAEVICH
Easy money

For editions of this play see under English Editions: The Taming of the Shrew: Alterations &c.

OSTROWSKI, WITOLD
A Forgotten meaning of "The Tempest".
IN HELSZTYNSKI, STANISLAW, ed.,
Poland's homage to Shakespeare.
Commemorating the fourth centenary of his birth, 1564-1964. (Warsaw)
1965.

747846

O'SULLIVAN (MARY I.)
Hamlet and Dr. Timothy Bright. IN Publications of the Modern Language Association of America, Vol. 41.
(Menasha, Wis.) 1926.

428361

O'Sullivan (R.) Shakespeare and St. Thomas More. From The Catholic Times, July 5th, 1946.

1946.

579649

OSWALD (ARTHUR)
Stratford new and old. 2. Shakespeare's Stratford. FROM Country Life, April, 1932. pp. [4.]
illus. plan. 1932.

392856

Othello

General Works and Criticism
Bibliographies
Burlesques
Characters
— Iago
Cinematography
Illustrations
Literary Influence
Music; Opera
Novels; Plays; Poems
Sources and Background
Stage History and Production
— General Works
— 16th – 18th century
— 19th century
— 20th century
Study and Teaching; Tales
Textual History and Translation

Othello
— General Works and Criticism

__ ALEXANDER, NIGEL
Thomas Rymer and "Othello".
IN SHAKESPEARE SURVEY 21. (Cambridge)
pp. 67-77. 1968.

776762

__ ALLEN, NED B.
The Two parts of "Othello".
IN SHAKESPEARE SURVEY 21. (Cambridge)
pp. 1968.

776762

__ B* [pseud.]
Remarks on the tragedy of Othello.
FROM The New Universal Magazine,
Nov. 1751. 1751.

562350

__ BABCOCK (C. MERTON)
An Analogue for the name Othello.
IN Notes and Queries, Vol. 196.
1951.

5421/196

__ Bethell (S.L.) Shakespeare's imagery: the diabolic images in Othello. IN Shakespeare Survey [Vol.] 5. (Cambridge)
1952.

623798

-4

— [Bradley (A.C.)] Othello: a reading from A.C. Bradley's 'Shakespearean tragedy', by C. Hobbs. [Broadcast] 20th August, 1942. ff.2. Typescript.
1942.

536855

— BRADLEY (A. C.)
Shakespearean tragedy: lectures on Hamlet, Othello, King Lear, Macbeth. 2nd edn., (20th impr.)
1937.

For other editions of this work please check the main sequence under the author's name.

496470

— A Casebook on 'Othello', edited by L.F. Dean. [Text and criticism by various authors.] (New York: Thomas Y. Crowell)
1964.

Crowell Literary Casebooks.
748200

— CHEVERTON (F. J.)
A Study of "Jealousy" as suggested by a visit to Othello's Tower in the island of Cyprus. IN Rowley Regis Parish Church Magazine, July 1930.
1930.

384950

— DEAN (LEONARD F.)
A Casebook on "Othello" [: text and a selection of criticism]. (New York)
1964.
Crowell Literary Casebooks.
748200

— DORAN, MADELEINE
Good name in 'Othello' [: the importance of reputation in Renaissance society]. FROM Studies in English Literature 1500-1900. (Houston, Tex.) pp. 195-217.
1967.

777381

— Dramatic poems: Leonora, a tragedy [with remarks by the author including references to Othello [: and Etha and Aidalls, a dramatic poem.]
1801.

508290

— Draper (J.W.) Patterns of tempo and humor in "Othello". [With bibliographical notes.] Graph. In English Studies, Vol.28. (Amsterdam)
1947.

485643/28

— DRAPER (JOHN WILLIAM)
Shakespeare and Barbary. IN Studes anglaises, Grande-Bretagne, Etats-Unis, XIVᵉ Année, No. 4.
1961.

476080/14

— DUTT, SMARAJIT
Shakespeare's Othello: an oriental study. (Calcutta)
[1923].

311007

— ELLIOTT (GEORGE ROY)

Flaming minister: a study of "Othello" as tragedy of love and hate. (Durham, N.C.)
1953

635455

— Elliott (G.R.) Othello as a love-tragedy. From The American Review, Vol.8.
1937.

530193

— Empson (W.) The Best policy: [a study of the uses of the words "honest" and "honesty" in "Othello".] From Life and Letters To-day, Summer, 1936.
1936.

454861

— Empson (William) Honest in Othello. IN

EMPSON (WILLIAM)
The Structure of complex words. 1951.

617595

— EMPSON (W.) [and] GARRETT (G.)
Shakespeare survey: [Othello, Timon of Athens, and The Tempest. With an epilogue by R. Herring.]

[1937.]

472727

— EVERETT (BARBARA)

Reflections on the sentimentalist's "Othello". Reprinted from The Critical Quarterly, Summer, 1961. pp.[13]. (Hull)
1961.

667204

— FELDMAN (A. BRONSON)
Othello in reality. FROM The American Imago, Vol. 2, pp. 147-179. (Boston, [Mass.])
bibliog.
1954.

665619

— GARDNER, HELEN LOUISE
"Othello": a retrospect, 1900-67. IN SHAKESPEARE SURVEY 21. (Cambridge) pp. 1-11.
1968.

776762

— GILBERT (ALLAN H.   )

The Principles and practice of criticism. Othello, The Merry Wives, Hamlet. [Edited by Esther E. Jacoby.] Illus. (Detroit, Mich.)
1959.

666452

— GRANVILLE-BARKER (HARLEY)
Prefaces to Shakespeare. 2 vols.
1958.

665961-62

For other editions of this work check the main sequence under the author's name.

— HALLSTEAD, R. N.
Idolatrous love: a new approach to "Othello".
IN SHAKESPEARE QUARTERLY XIX: 2.
pp. 107-124. (New York)
1968.

605711

— HALSTEAD (WILLIAM L.)
Artifice and artistry in "Richard II"
and "Othello". IN Sweet smoke of
rhetoric: a collection of Renaissance
essays [by various authors]. (Coral
Gables, Fla.)   1964.

745483

— HAYES (ANN L.)
Othello. IN Carnegie Institute of
Technology, "Lovers meeting":
discussions of five plays by
Shakespeare. (Pittsburgh) 1964.

741508

— HEILMAN (ROBERT BECHTOLD)
Approach to "Othello". IN The
Sewanee Review, Vol. 64. (Sewanee,
Tenn.)   1956.

641628/64

— HEILMAN (ROBERT BECHTOLD)
Magic in the web: action & language
in Othello. (Lexington)
bibliog.   1956.

665290

— Heilman (R.B.) More fair than black:
light and dark in 'Othello". IN Essays in
Criticism, Vol.1. (Oxford)   1951.

621866

— HEILMAN (ROBERT BECHTOLD)

Wit and witchcraft: thematic form in
Othello. FROM Arizona Quarterly, Vol.12.
pp.16. (Tucson, Ariz.)   1956.

665392

— HIBBARD, GEORGE RICHARD
"Othello" and the pattern of
Shakespearian tragedy.
IN SHAKESPEARE SURVEY 21. (Cambridge)
pp. 39-46.   1968.

776762

— Jackson (Z.) Emendations in Shakspeare's
Othello. In The Gentleman's Magazine,
Vol. 102. Part 2.

1832.

18651

— Jenkins (Antoinette S.) The Jealous
husband in the plays of Chapman, Jonson,
Heywood, and Shakespeare, from 1597 to
1611. 1928. ([Abstract of] M.A. thesis,
University of North Carolina.) ll. 2.
Typescript.   [1945.]

569087

— JORDAN (HOOVER H.)
Dramatic illusion in "Othello".
IN SHAKESPEARE QUARTERLY I: 3.
pp. 146-152.
(New York) 1950.

605711

— JORGENSEN (PAUL A.   )

Honesty in Othello. IN Studies in
Philology, Vol.47. (Chapel Hill, N.C.)
1950.

554520/47

— KAULA (DAVID)
Othello possessed: notes on Shakespeare's
use of magic and witchcraft.
IN Shakespeare Studies, 2. (Cincinnati,
Ohio)   1966.

761781

— Kelcy (A.) Notes on Othello. From
Philological Quarterly, vol.12. (Iowa)
1933.

442563

— Kernan, Alvin B.
Othello: an introduction. IN

HARBAGE, ALFRED BENNETT, ed.
Shakespeare, the tragedies: a
collection of critical essays [by
various writers]. (Englewood Cliffs,
N.J.)   1964.

Twentieth century views. 742273

— KOTT (JAN)
Shakespeare our contemporary.
Translated by B. Taborski. Preface
by P. Brook. 1964.   741546
———— 2nd edn., revised.
1967.   766093
Includes "The Two paradoxes of
'Othello'" (in 2nd edn. only).

— LAW (R. A.)
"Almost damn'd in a fair wife."
IN University of Texas, Studies in
English, No. 15. (Austin, Texas)
1935.

442441

— Law (R.A.) Two Shakespearian pictures
of Puritans [as portrayed in passages in
Richard the Third and Othello.] In Texas,
University of. Studies in English, No.13
(Austin, Texas.)   1933.

434338

— Leatham (J.) The Exasperating tragedy
of 'Othello'. 2nd edn. pp.18. (Turriff)
[c.1920.]

(Shakespeare Studies, No.15)
566387

— Leavis (F.R.) Diabolic intellect and
the noble hero: a note on Othello.
In Scrutiny, Vol.6.

(Cambridge)   1937-38.

489751

— LEAVIS (FRANK RAYMOND)
Diabolic intellect and the noble hero.
IN The Common pursuit.   1952.

621408

— McGEE (ARTHUR)
Othello's motive for murder. IN
Shakespeare Quarterly XV: 1. pp.46-53.
(New York)   1964.

605711

—— McPEEK (JAMES ANDREW SCARBOROUGH)

The "Arts inhibited" and the meaning of "Othello". FROM Boston University. Studies in English, Vol.I. pp.[19.] (Boston, Mass.)
1955.

665671

—— MASON (PHILIP) [pseud. Philip Woodruff]
Prospero's magic: some thoughts on class and race [suggested by "Othello" and "The Tempest"].
1962.

710708

—— Matthews, G.N.
'Othello' and the dignity of man. IN

KETTLE, ARNOLD, ed.
Shakespeare in a changing world: essays [by various authors].
1964.

667797

—— MENDONÇA, BARBARA HELIODORA CARNEIRO de
"Othello": a tragedy built on a comic structure.
IN SHAKESPEARE SURVEY 21. (Cambridge)
pp. 31-38.
1968.

776762

—— MONEY (JOHN)

Othello's "It is the cause..." an analysis.
IN Shakespeare Survey [Vol.] 6. (Cambridge)
1953.

631770

—— MULLIK (B. R.)
Studies in dramatists, vol. 6:
Shakespeare's Othello. 2nd edn.
pp. 70. (Delhi)
bibliog.
1962.

667120

—— NOWOTTNY (WINIFRED M.   T.   )

Justice and love in Othello. IN The University of Toronto Quarterly, Vol.21.
(Toronto)
1952.

596179/21

—— ORNSTEIN (ROBERT)
Shakespeare's moral vision: Othello and Macbeth. IN LEECH, CLIFFORD, ed., Shakespeare: the tragedies.
A collection of critical essays.
(Chicago)
1965.
Gemini books.

752332

—— RIBNER (IRVING)
Othello and the pattern of Shakespearean tragedy. Reprinted from Tulane University, Tulane Studies in English. Vol. 5.
pp. [14]. (New Orleans, La.)
bibliogs.
1955.

666589

—— RICHMOND, HUGH
Love and justice: "Othello"'s Shakespearean context.
IN Pacific coast studies in Shakespeare.
Edited by W. F. McNeir and T. N. Greenfield. (Eugene: Ore.) 1966.

768009

—— ROSENBERG (MARVIN)
The Masks of Othello: the search for the identity of Othello, Iago, and Desdemona by three centuries of actors and critics. (Berkeley, Cal.)
frontis.
1961.

667256

—— (LAWRENCE J.)
Three readings in the Text of "Othello".
IN SHAKESPEARE QUARTERLY XIV: 2.
pp. 121-126.
(New York) 1963.

605711

—— ROSSETTI (RETO MARIO)
A Crux and no crux. [Othello's speech in IV.i.]
IN SHAKESPEARE QUARTERLY XIII: 3.
pp. 299-303.
(New York) 1962.

605711

—— RYMER (T.)
A Short view of tragedy. IN ADAMS (HENRY HITCH) and HATHAWAY (BAXTER) eds.
Dramatic essays of the neoclassic age. (New York) 1950.

611958

—— SEAMAN, JOHN E.
Othello's pearl.
IN SHAKESPEARE QUARTERLY XIX: 1.
pp. 81-85. (New York)
1968.

605711

—— SEDGEWICK (G. G.)
Of irony, especially in drama. [Including a chapter "Irony as dramatic preparation: Othello". With bibliographical notes.] (Toronto)
1935.   552715
Alexander Lectures in English at the University of Toronto, 1934.
———— [2nd edn.] Alexander Lectures.
1948.   599928

—— SHAW, JOHN
"What is the matter?" in Othello.
FROM Shakespeare Quarterly XVII: 2.
(New York) 1966.
pp. 157-161.

759521

—— SPROULE (ALBERT FREDERICK)
A Time Scheme for Othello.
IN SHAKESPEARE QUARTERLY VII.
pp. 217-226.
(New York) 1956.

605711

—— STOLL (E. E.)
Another Othello too modern [: refutation of G. G. Sedgewick.]
IN McMANAWAY (J. G.), DAWSON (G. E.) and WILLOUGHBY (E. E.) eds., Joseph Quincy Adams memorial studies.
(Washington)
bibliog.   1948.
G. G. Sedgewick's "Of irony", containing a chapter on Othello, is catal. no. 552715.

596748

—— STOLL (ELMER EDGAR)

Mainly controversy: Hamlet, Othello. IN Philological Quarterly, Vol.24. (Iowa)
1945.

592684/24

STOLL (ELMER EDGAR)
Slander in drama.
IN SHAKESPEARE QUARTERLY IV: 4.
pp. 433-450.
(New York) 1953.
605711

SUBBARAU, RENTALA VENKATA
Othello unveiled. (Madras) 1906.
196107

Swinburne (A.C.) "Othello": critical
comment. pp.[9.] In Harper's Monthly
Magazine, Vol.109, 1904. 1904.
185946

Tillotson (G.) Essays in [English
literary] criticism and research.
[Including an essay: 'Othello' and
'The Alchemist' at Oxford in 1610.]

(Cambridge) 1942.
531163

TRAVERSI (DEREK ANTONA)
Othello. IN LEECH, CLIFFORD, ed.
Shakespeare: the tragedies.
A collection of critical essays.
(Chicago) 1965.
Gemini books.
752332

WALPOLE (V.)
And Cassio high in oath' ('Othello',
II, iii, 227). IN The Modern
Language Review, Vol. 40.
(Cambridge) 1945.
571545

WATTS, ROBERT A.
The Comic scenes in "Othello".
IN SHAKESPEARE QUARTERLY XIX: 4.
pp. 349-354.
(New York) 1968.
605711

WEBB (HENRY J.   )

The Military background in 'Othello' IN
Philological Quarterly, Vol.30. (Iowa)
1951.

592684/30

WEST (ROBERT HUNTER)
The Christianness of "Othello". IN
Shakespeare Quarterly XV: 4. pp.333-343.
(New York) 1964.
605711

WILSON (EDWARD MERYON)

Othello, a tragedy of honour. [Broadcast]
May 12, 1952. ff.6. Typescript.
1952.
630864

WILSON (EDWARD MERYON)

Othello and the cardinal virtues.
[Broadcast] Sept. 21, 1952. pp.5.
Typescript. 1952.
630860

[Wilson (J.)] Dies Boreales Nos. 6 and 7.
Christopher under canvass: [conversations on
Othello.] In Blackwood's Magazine, Vol.67.
1850.

10167

WILSON (JOHN)
A Double-time-analysis of Macbeth and Othello.
IN Transactions of the New Shakespeare
Society, Series 1. No. 4.
pp. 351-387. and Series I   1875-8
Nos. 6-7. pp. 21-41.
40620 11987

Woodberry (G.E.) Makers of
literature: essays on Shelley [etc. With
a chapter Some actors' criticisms of
Othello, Iago and Shylock]. (New York)

1909.

404414

Othello
— Bibliographies

TANNENBAUM (S. A.)
Shakspere's Othello (a concise
bibliography). (New York)
frontis. 1943.
Elizabethan Bibliographies.
Edn. limited to 250 copies.
542195

Othello
— Burlesques
see also ENGLISH EDITIONS, Othello —
Alterations, etc.

[Dickens (C.)] O'Thello: Dickens's
earliest known manuscript. In The
Dickensian, Vol. 26.

1930.

375232

DOWLING (MAURICE G.)
Othello travestie: an operatic
burlesque burletta. pp. 33.
[Theatre Royal, Birmingham, prompt
book.] frontis. [?1834].
Duncombe's Edition.
Title-page shows minor variation from
57891.
455711

HUDSON (F.)
Othello the Second: a burletta in
two acts. IN HUDSON (F.) The Origin
of plum pudding [etc.]
illus. [1888].
516017

—— Iago [i.e. Sir R. Walpole] display'd.
The Contents: How Cassio [i.e. W.
Pulteney, Earl of Bath], accused Iago
of corruption; the various ways by
which Iago endeavour'd to destroy
Cassio; how Iago publish'd a libel
against Cassio; how he had it
whispered that Roderigo [i.e. John
Hervey, Baron Hervey] was the author
of it, [etc.] pp. 40. [c.1731.] 491339
————— Another edn. [c.1740.] 404423

—— KINGSMILL (H.) and MUGGERIDGE (M.)
Brave old world: a mirror for the
times. [Burlesque newspaper
articles including a parody of
Othello.] Illustrations by
S. Maiden. 1936.

457371

—— MOULTON (HOPE H.)
Othello: a burlesque in one act.
(Boston [Mass.]) 1927.

403885

—— NEILL (WILLIAM ALEXANDER) [pseud. A.
Cantab]
Othello: a tale of a Moor and an
Amour, by A. Cantab. pp. 12.
(Liverpool)

1856.

665103

Othello

— Characters

—— ARNOLD (AEROL)
The Function of Brabantio in "Othello".
IN SHAKESPEARE QUARTERLY VIII.
pp. 51-56.
(New York) 1957.

605711

—— ARTHOS (JOHN)
The Fall of Othello.
IN SHAKESPEARE QUARTERLY IX: 2.
pp. 93-104.
(New York) 1958.

605711

—— AUDEN (WYSTAN HUGH)
The Alienated city: reflections on
"Othello". pp. 14. FROM
"Encounter" [Vol. 17]. 1961.

666967

—— BAYLEY (JOHN)
The Characters of love: a study
in the literature of personality
[with special reference to the
works of Shakespeare]. 1960.

666701

—— Bonnard (G.) Are Othello and
Desdemona innocent or guilty?
In English Studies, Vol.30.

(Amsterdam) 1949.

485643/30

—— BUTCHER (PHILIP)
Othello's racial identity.
IN SHAKESPEARE QUARTERLY III: 3.
pp. 243-247.
(New York) 1952.

605711

—— COLES (Mrs. BLANCHE)
Shakespeare's four giants [i.e. Hamlet,
Macbeth, Othello and King Lear].
(Rindge, N.H.) 1957.

665631

—— DAVIES (HUGH SYKES)
"Very malice itself" [: talk on
Shakespeare's Othello]. Produced by
P. Stephenson. [Broadcast] 27th
November, 1953. ff. 9.
typescript. 1953.

643693

—— Draper (J.W.) Captain General
thello. In Anglia Zeitschrift
für Englische Philologie, Band 55.

1931.

397252

—— DRAPER (J. W.)
The Choleric Cassio. Reprinted
from the Bulletin of the History
of Medicine, Vol. 7. pp. [12].
bibliog. [1939.]

569108

—— Draper (J.W.) Desdemona: a compound
of two cultures. From Revue
de Littérature Comparée, [Tome]
50, 1933.

1933.

497548

—— DRAPER (J. W.)
Signior Brabantio, plaintiff. [With
bibliographical notes.] IN English
Studies, Vol. 22. (Amsterdam) 1940.

575606

—— DRAPER (J. W.)
"This poor trash of Venice" [: the
character of Roderigo]. pp. [8.]
FROM The Journal of English and
Germanic philology, Vol. 30,
No. 4, 1931. 1931.

444158

—— F. [pseud.]
Observations on Shakespeare's
character of Cassio. FROM [Literary
Panorama, Dec. 1808.] [1808.]

560927

—— FARJEON (H.)]
Shakespeare's characters, 16 -
Emilia [: scenes from Othello].
Arranged [with comments] by
H. Farjeon. [Broadcast] 24th-
29th September [1944]. ff. 21.
typescript. [1944.]

555599

——Flatter (R.) The Moor of Venice [:a study of "Othello"]. Port.

1950.

607172

—— GARDNER (HELEN LOUISE)
The Noble Moor. ([45th] Annual Shakespeare Lecture of the British Academy, 1955). pp. [18.] [1955.]

665364

—— GERARD (ALBERT)
"Egregiously an ass": the dark side of the Moor. A view of Othello's mind. IN SHAKESPEARE SURVEY 10. (Cambridge)   1957.

665485

—— GRUGEON, DAVID
'A' level English - 7: 'Othello'. Produced by P. Bacon. B.B.C. radio script broadcast 13th November 1967. typescript.   1967.

776828

—— HAPGOOD, ROBERT
The Trials of Othello. IN Pacific coast studies in Shakespeare. Edited by W. F. McNeir and T. N. Greenfield. (Eugene: Ore.)   1966.

768009

—— HUBLER (EDWARD)
The Damnation of Othello: some limitations on the Christian view of the play. IN SHAKESPEARE QUARTERLY IX: pp. 295-300. (New York) 1958.

605711

—— HUNTER, GEORGE KIRKPATRICK
Othello and colour prejudice. FROM Proceedings of the British Academy, vol. 53.   1967. pp. 139-163. illus. Annual Shakespeare Lecture, 1967.

775524

—— Jealousy: exemplified in the awful, tragical and bloody history of the lives and untimely deaths of Othello & Desdemona. pp. 24.   [c.1820.]

540103

—— JONES (ELDRED)
Othello's countrymen: the African in English Renaissance drama. illus.   1965.

742543

—— JORDAN (HOOVER H.)
Dramatic illusion in "Othello". IN SHAKESPEARE QUARTERLY I: 3. pp. 146-152. (New York) 1950.

605711

—— JORGENSEN (PAUL ALFRED)
"Perplex'd in the extreme": the role of thought in "Othello". IN Shakespeare 400: essays by American scholars on the anniversary of the poet's birth. Published in co-operation with the Shakespeare Association of America. illus.   1964.

667803

—— KIRSCHBAUM (L.)
The Modern Othello. IN ELH: a journal of English literary history, Vol. 11. (Baltimore) bibliog.   1944.

562838

——Kooistra (J.) On the character of Desdemona. In English studies, Vol.5.

(Amsterdam)   1923.

485647

—— LAWSON, ROBERT
The Epilepsy of Othello. REPRINTED FROM The Journal of Mental Science, April, 1880. (Lewes) pp. 11.

59878

—— PRIOR (MOODY ERASMUS)

Character in relation to action in Othello. Reprinted from Modern Philology, Vol.44, No.4. [Chicago] 1947.

667965

—— RANALD (MARGARET LOFTUS)
The Indiscretions of Desdemona. IN SHAKESPEARE QUARTERLY XIV: 2. pp. 127-139. (New York) 1963.

605711

—— RAPPOPORT (R.)
The Theme of personal integrity in "Othello", [from] "Theoria" No. 14. pp. 12. (Pietermaritzburg) 1960.

667030

—— Raymond (W.O.) Motivation and character portrayal in Othello. In University of Toronto Quarterly, Vol.17.

(Toronto)   1947.

596179

—— ROSS (LAWRENCE J.)
World and chrysolite in "Othello". IN Modern Language Notes, Vol. 76. 1961.

439157/76

—— SIEGEL (PAUL N.   )

The Damnation of Othello. Reprinted FROM PMLA, Publications of the Modern Language Association of America, Vol.68, No.5, Dec.1953. (New York) 1953.

668458

—— SNIDER (D. J.)
Shakespeare's tragedies. Othello [:
an analysis of the play. Part 2.]
FROM The Western [, Vol. 1]. [Saint
Louis] 1875.
Part 1 wanting.

563690

—— STEWART ([Mrs.] HELEN H.)
The Character of Desdemona. FROM
The Contemporary Review, 1911.
pp. [14.] [1911]

389206

—— STOLL (ELMER EDGAR)
Oedipus and Othello, Corneille, Rymer
and Voltaire. [English text. With
bibliographical notes.] Extrait de
la Revue Anglo-américaine, juin 1935.
pp. [16.] (Paris) [1935.]

569122

—— Stoll (E.E.) An Othello all-too modern.
[With bibliographical notes.] In
E.L.H.: a Journal of English
Literary History, Vol.13.

(Baltimore.Md.) 1946.

584757

—— STOLL (E. E.)
Shakespeare and other masters [: literary studies, including Othello the man;
Othello and Oedipus: Corneille,Rymer
and Voltaire; Iago. With references
to Othello in other studies, and bibliographical notes]. (Cambridge, Mass.)
1940.

532084

—— Strachey ([G.]L.) Othello [: an essay].
In Strachey ([G.]L.) Characters
and commentaries. [Edited with a
preface by J. Strachey.] Port.

1933.

41200C

—— TANNENBAUM (S. A.)
Cassio's hopes. FROM Philological
Quarterly, Vol. 18. (Iowa) 1939.

530194

—— TRAVERSI (DEREK A.)
Othello. FROM The Wind and the rain,
Vol. 6, No. 4. pp. 248-269. 1950.

639538

—— VILLIERS (JACOB I. DE)
The Tragedy of 'Othello'. FROM Theoria,
[Vol.] 7. pp.[8]. [Pietermaritzburg]
[1955.]

667026

—— Walters (J.C.) A Shakespearean
sisterhood: Imogen, Desdemona and
Hermione. In Manchester Literary
Club. Papers, Vol.32.

(Manchester) 1906.

518389

—— WALTON (J.
"Strength's abundance": a view of Othello.
IN Review of English Studies New Series,
Vol.11. (Oxford) 1960.

318239/N.S./11

Othello: Characters

— Iago

—— AUDEN (W. H.)
The Joker in the pack. IN Auden (W. H.)
comp., The Dyer's hand, and other essays.
1963.

713431

—— BABCOCK (WESTON)
Iago - an extraordinary honest man.
IN SHAKESPEARE QUARTERLY XVI: 4.
pp. 297-301.
(New York) 1965.

605711

—— BENEDICT [pseud.]
Shakspearian characters and their
representatives. No. 9. Iago.
IN Actors by daylight, No. 47,
Jan. 19, [1839]. [1839].

453717

—— BOWMAN (T. D.)
A Further study in the characterization and motivation of Iago. FROM
College English, Vol. 4. (Chicago)
1943.

563273

—— BROCK (J. H. E.)
Iago & some Shakespearean villains.
pp. 48. (Cambridge)
bibliog. 1937.

475488

—— CAMDEN (C.)
Iago on women. IN The Journal of
English and Germanic Philology, Vol.
48. (Urbana, Ill.)
1949.

600780/48

—— DRAPER (J. W.)
"Honest Iago". IN Publications of
the Modern Language Association of
America, Vol. 46. (Menasha, Wis.)
1931.

428366

—— Draper (J.W.) The Jealousy of Iago.
From Neophilologus, 25ste Jaargang,
Aflevering 1.

(Groningen) 1939.

510599

— GERARD, ALBERT
  Alack, poor Iago! Intellect and action
  in "Othello".
  IN SHAKESPEARE JAHRBUCH. Bd. 94/1958.
  pp. 218-232.   (Heidelberg)

                                10531

—GLAZ (A.   ANDRÉ)

  Iago or moral sadism. FROM The American
  Imago, Vol.19, No.4. (South Dennis,
  Mass.)   1962.

                          667479

—— HAWKES (TERRY)

  Iago's use of reason: reprinted from
  Studies in Philology, 58, 2, Pt. 1,
  April 1961. pp.[10]. [Chapel Hill,
  N.C.]   1961.

                          667043

— HEILMAN (ROBERT BECHTOLD)
  The Economics of Iago and others.
  IN PMLA: Publications of the Modern
  Language Association of America, Vol.
  68. (Menasha, Wis.)
                              1953.

                      428321/68

— HIRSCHFELD (JULIUS)
  What was Iago's crime in law? IN
  Journal of the Society of Comparative
  Legislation, New Series, Vol. 14.
                            1914.

                      283119/1914

—Jacox (F.) About Iago, and motiveless
  malignity. [With bibliographical
  notes.] From [The New Monthly
  Magazine,] Vol. 136.

                      [1866.]
                          558110

—KING (DONALD B.)
  Iago and St. Thomas [Aquinas].   FROM
  Blackfriars, Vol. 37.   pp. 473-9.
                          1957.

                          665940

—KNOWLES (Dom [M.] D.)
  Honest Iago. FROM [The Downside
  Review, Vol. 49, 1931].   pp. [11].
                          [1931.]

                          392123

— LERNER (LAURENCE DAVID)

  The Machiavel and the Moor [: characters
  of Iago and Othello in Shakespeare's
  'Othello']. (Essays in Criticism Vol.9,
  no.4, October 1959) ff.[22.] (Oxford)
                              1959.

                          666979

— McCloskey (J.C.) The Motivation of
  Iago. From College English, Vol.3.

       (Chicago)   1941.

                          537253

— [MAGINN (W.)]
  Shakspeare papers.   No. 8. Iago.
  FROM [Bentley's Miscellany,] Vol. 5.
                          [1839.]

                          562354

— MILLER (D. C.)
  Iago and the problem of time.
  IN English Studies, Vol. 22.
  (Amsterdam)
  bibliog.   1940.

                          575606

— MOORE (J. R.)
  The Character of Iago.   IN PROUTY
  (C. T.) ed., Studies in honor of
  A. H. R. Fairchild [, by various
  authors. With a bibliography and
  bibliographical notes]. (Columbia,
  Mo.)   port.   1946.
  University of Missouri Studies,
  Vol. 21, No. 1.

                          575822

—MUIR (KENNETH)
  The Jealousy of Iago.   IN English
  Miscellany, 2.   (Rome)
                          1951.

                      609696/2

—Nicholson (B.) On the army ranks of
  Cassio and Iago. In The Antiquarian
  Magazine & Bibliographer, Vol.1.
  1882.

                          [1882.]
                          55895

—RAND (FRANK PRENTICE)
  The Over garrulous Iago.
  IN SHAKESPEARE QUARTERLY I: 3.
  pp. 155-161.
  (New York) 1950.

                          605711

—[Richardson (D.L.)] Othello and Iago.
  From [Richardson (D.L.) Literary
  leaves, 2nd edn.] Vol.2.

                          [1840.]
                          579641

— ROSENBERG (MARVIN)
  In defense of Iago.
  IN SHAKESPEARE QUARTERLY VI.
  pp. 145-158.
  (New York) 1955.

                          605711

—SCRAGG, LEAH
  Iago – vice or devil?
  IN SHAKESPEARE SURVEY 21.   (Cambridge)
  pp. 53-65.   1968.

                          776762

— SHAFFER, ELINOR S.
  Iago's malignity motivated: Coleridge's
  unpublished "opus magnum".
  IN SHAKESPEARE QUARTERLY XIX: 3.
  pp. 195-203.   (New York)
                          1968.

                          605711

— SPIVACK (BERNARD)

  Shakespeare and the allegory of evil:
  the history of a metaphor in relation
  to his major villains. Bibliog. (New
  York)   1958.
                          665954

—— SPRAGUE (ARTHUR COLBY)
Edwin Booth's Iago: a study of a great
Shakespearian actor. IN The Theatre
Annual, 1947. (New York)
1947.

554521/1947

—— STEWART (JOHN INNES MACKINTOSH) [pseud.
Michael Innes]
Discoveries in Shakespeare, by M. Innes.
4: The Trial of Ancient Iago. Produced by Rayner Heppenstall. [Broadcast]
22nd June 1953. ff. 38.
typescript. [1953.]

634680

—— WARNKEN, HENRY L.
Iago as a projection of Othello.
IN PAOLUCCI, ANNE, ed., Shakespeare
encomium, 1564-1964 [by various
writers]. (New York) 1964.
City University of New York, City
College Papers.

747546

—— WEISINGER (HERBERT)
Iago's Iago. FROM The University of
Kansas City Review, Vol. 20. pp.
[8.] [Kansas City] [1953.]

665616

Othello
— Cinematography

—— BERNAD (MIGUEL A.)
Othello comes to town: Orson
Welles and Edmund Kean.
FROM Philippine Studies, Vol. 4.
pp. [12]. (Manila) 1956.

665654

—— KOZELKA (PAUL)
A Guide to the screen version of
Shakespeare's "Othello". Reprinted
from Audio-Visual Guide, October 1955.
pp. 16. (Maplewood, N.J.)
ports. illus. bibliog. 1955.
Photography Studies.

665549

—— LEJEUNE (C[AROLINE] A.)
Chestnuts in her lap, 1936-1946 [:
reviews and film articles. Including
"This wider cockpit: Henry the Fifth"
and "Potted Othello: A Story from
Othello"]. 1947.

583677

—— MACLIAMMOIR (MICHEAL)
Put money in thy purse: the diary of
the film Othello. With a preface by
O. Welles.
illus. 1952.

626652

—— UNITED ARTISTS CORPORATION LTD.
William Shakespeare's "Othello"
starring Orson Welles: script,
publicity material and photographs.
pp. 26.
typescript. 1954.

665294

Othello
— Illustrations
*The library's extensive collections of photo-
graphs and engravings are indexed but
mainly uncatalogued*

—— [De Saulles (W.H.)] Illustrations to
Macbeth,Hamlet,Othello,and As You
Like It: original pencil and pen-and-
ink drawings.] pp. [31.]

[c.1884.]

581627

Othello
— Literary Influence

—— Beckingham (C.F.) 'Othello' and 'Revenge
for Honour'. pp.[3.] In The Review
of English Studies, Vol.11. [1935]

[1935]

447384

—— CALDWELL (HELEN)
The Brazilian Othello of Machado
de Assis: a study of Dom Casmurro.
(Berkeley, Cal.) 1960.
Perspectives in Criticism.

697134

—— Q. (N.R.) Shakspeare fancies. No.2.
Desdemona and Felicia Dorothea
Hemans [: a comparison]. In The
Metropolitan Magazine, Vol. 23.

1838.

88823

—— VALENCY (M. J.)
The Tragedies of Herod & Mariamne
[: a study of the dramatized
versions of their story. With
references to Othello, a chronological
list and bibliographical notes].
(New York)
frontis. 1940.
Columbia University Studies in English
and Comparative Literature.

553106

— WATSON (SARA R.)
Shelley and Shakespeare [by D. L. Clark];
an addendum, A Comparison of Othello
and the Cenci.   IN Publications of
the Modern Language Association of
America, Vol. 55.   (Menasha, Wis.)
1940.
For Shelley and Shakespeare, by
D. L. Clark see catal. no. 515058.

525077

Othello
— Music; Opera
For music scores see under the heading
Music Scores, Othello

— BONAVIA (F.)
Verdi.   [With references to his opera
"Otello".]
ports. illus. facsimiles.   1947.

600803

— BRENNECKE (ERNEST)
"Nay, that's not next!"   The Significance
of Desdemona's "Willow Song".
IN SHAKESPEARE QUARTERLY IV: 1.
pp. 35-38.
(New York)   1953.

605711

— DEAN, WINTON
Verdi's "Otello": a Shakespearian
masterpiece.
IN SHAKESPEARE SURVEY 21.   (Cambridge)
pp.87-96.   1968.

776762

— Derwent [(G.H. Johnstone, 3rd Baron)]
Rossini and some forgotten nightin-
gales. [With a bibliography and
references to Othello]. Ports.
Illus.
1934.

420051

— EBERS (J.)
Seven years of the King's Theatre.
[With references to the operas "Otello"
and "Romeo e Giulietta".]
ports.   1828.

495693

— HUSSEY (D.)
Verdi [: a biography.   With references
to his operas "Otello" and "Falstaff".]
ports.   illus.   1940.
Master Musicians.   New Series.

514762

— KERMAN (JOSEPH)
Otello: traditional opera and the
image of Shakespeare.   IN Opera as
drama.
1957.

676796

— KERMAN (JOSEPH)
Verdi's Otello, or Shakespeare explained.
IN The Hudson Review, Vol. 6.   (New
York)
1953-54.

642968/6

— Klein, John W.
Verdi's 'Otello' and Rossini's. IN
Music & letters, Vol.45, No.2, April
1964: Shakespeare and music. 1964.

668211

— Reynolds (E.[E.]) Verdi's 'Otello'
and 'Falstaff'. From The Monthly
Musical Record. Jan.,1936.
1936.

446500

— ROSS, LAWRENCE J.
Shakespeare's "Dull clown" and
symbolic music. IN Shakespeare
Quarterly XVII: 2. pp.107-128. (New
York)   1966.

605711

— SLEZAK (L.)
Song of Motley: the reminiscences of
a hungry tenor.   [With references to
Verdi's opera Othello.]
ports.   illus.   .1938.

498638

— Toye (F.) Rossini: a study in tragi-
comedy, [containing references to
Rossini's opera 'Otello'.] Ports.
Facsimile.
1934.

419644

Othello
— Novels; Plays; Poems
see also ENGLISH EDITIONS, Othello —
Alterations, etc.

— BLACKLOCK (T.)
Prologue to Othello.   IN The Works
of the English poets, [edited] by
Dr. Samuel Johnson, Vol. 18.   1810.

3878

— BOYD (STEPHANIE)
The Two Othellos at the Old Vic: a
poem.   IN The Poetry Review, Vol. 47.
1956.

240749/47

— E. [pseud.]
English players in Paris [give a
performance of Othello]. From [The
New Monthly Magazine, Vol.5.]
[1822.]

561765

——Hauff (W.) Othello [translated] from the German [: a tale relating to a performance of Othello]. From [The Metropolitan Magazine, Vol. 26.]

[1839.]

558068

——The Long vacation: a satyr. Addressed to all disconsolate traders [containing references to Othello.] pp. 23.
1708. 488888
_____ Another edn. 1709. 435157

——LUDWIG (E.)
Othello: a novel. Translated from the German by F. von Hildebrand.
1949.

599111

——MEYNELL ([Mrs.] ALICE)
Reflexions: 2. In "Othello". IN Meynell ([Mrs.] A.) Poems, 1847-1923. Centenary edition. [Edited by Sir F. Meynell.] 1947.

589846

——Nathan (G.J.) The Avon flows [: a play combining part of the text of Romeo and Juliet, Othello and the Taming of the Shrew.]

(New York) 1937.

465371

—— Sansom (C.) Celestial meeting: a stage sketch for three women only [Viola, Desdemona, Lady Macbeth]. In Hampden (J.) [ed.] Plays without fees. pp.96. Dgms.

[1935].

439719

——SMART (CHRISTOPHER)
An Occasional prologue and epilogue to Othello, as it was acted at the Theatre-Royal in Drury-Lane, 7th March 1751. 2nd edn. pp. 8. [c.1750.]

633512

——[SMART (C.)]
The Prologue to Othello, as it was acted at the theatre in Drury-Lane and The Epilogue spoken by Desdemona. FROM The Midwife [; or The Old Woman's Magazine, Vol. 1]. 1751.

563203

—— Spink (W.) The Autocrat in the green-room: with a play [in four acts and in prose and verse, entitled: "Lesled, Lord of the Isles"] after "Othello".

1890.

522854

Othello
— Sources and Background

—— ALLEN (NED BLISS)
The Source of Othello. FROM Delaware Notes, 21st series, 1948. pp. 71-96. (Newark, Del.)

1948.

609565

——BALDENSPERGER (F.)
Was Othello an Ethiopian? IN Harvard studies and notes in philology and literature, Vol. 20. (Cambridge, Mass.)
1938.

478189

——CHARLTON (H. B.)
Shakespeare's Othello. IN Bulletin of the John Rylands Library, Manchester, Vol. 31. (Manchester) bibliogs. 1948.

182129/31

—— FONBLANQUE (ETHEL M. de)
The Italian sources of "Othello". IN The Fortnightly Review, Vol. 96.
1911.

234025

—— French (J.M.) Othello among the Anthropopaghi. In Publications of the Modern Language Association of America, vol.49. Map.

(Menasha,Wis.) 1934.

432218

—— JONES, EMRYS
"Othello", "Lepanto" and the Cyprus wars.
IN SHAKESPEARE SURVEY 21. (Cambridge) pp. 47-52. 1968.

776762

——Kahin (Helin A.) A Note on Othello, II, 1, 110-113 [Arden edn. With bibliographical notes]. In Modern Language Quarterly, Vol.1.

(Seattle) 1940.

525289

——KRAPPE (ALEXANDER HAGGERTY)
A Byzantine source of Shakespeare's "Othello". IN Modern Language Notes, Vol. 39. (Baltimore, Md.)
1924.

439157/39

——Stoll (E.E.) Source and motive in Macbeth and Othello. [With bibliographical notes.] In The Review of English Studies, Vol. 19.

(Oxford) 1943.

555539

___ SWINBURNE (ALGERNON CHARLES)
"Othello": critical comment.   FROM
Harper's Monthly Magazine, Oct. 1908.
   illus.   1908.

515796

___ WHITNEY (LOIS)
Did Shakespeare know Leo Africanus?
FROM Publications of the Modern
Language Association of America,
Vol. 37.   (Menasha, Wis.)
   bibliog.   1922.

554235

___ Wilson (H.S.) The Genesis of Othello.
In The Gentleman's Magazine,
Vol.266.

1889.

101717

Othello
— Stage History and Production, General Works
Newspaper reviews, playbills, theatre pro-grammes and theatrical illustrations — the library's extensive collection of this material is mainly uncatalogued but indexed
For texts of stage alterations and adaptations of the play see ENGLISH EDITIONS, Othello — Alterations, etc.

___ A Casebook on 'Othello', edited by
L.F. Dean. [Text and criticism by
various authors.] (New York: Thomas Y.
Crowell)   1964.

Crowell Literary Casebooks.
748200

___ Fernald (J.) The Play produced: an
introduction to the technique of
producing plays. Foreword by Flora
Robson. [Containing an excerpt from
Othello, with stage directions.]
Dgms.
[1933]
412544

___   Knight (J.) Signor Salvini and other
players of Othello. In Agate (J.[E.]) ed.,
The English dramatic critics.
[1932.]
399280

___ KOTT (JAN)
Shakespeare our contemporary.
Translated by B. Taborski.   Preface
by P. Brook.   1964.   741546
_____ 2nd edn., revised.
1967.   766093
Includes "The Two paradoxes of
'Othello'" (in 2nd edn. only).

___ PROGRAMMES OF SHAKESPEARIAN PERFORMANCES
Othello

This collection, which runs from the
latter half of the nineteenth century,
is continuously augmented by the addition of programmes of contemporary
productions.

499165

___ ROSENBERG (MARVIN)

The Masks of Othello: the search for
the identity of Othello, Iago, and
Desdemona by three centuries of actors
and critics. Frontis. (Berkeley, Cal.)
1961.

667256

___ SHATTUCK (C.)
Shakespeare's "Othello" and its actors.
FROM Players Magazine, Vol. 13.
(Peru, Nebraska)   1937.

563269

___ SPRAGUE (ARTHUR COLBY)
Shakespeare and the actors: the stage
business in his plays (1660-1905).
(Cambridge, Mass.)
   illus.   bibliog.   1945.
Othello, pp. 185-223.

563058

Othello
— 16th – 18th century

___ DRAPER (JOHN WILLIAM)
The Othello of Shakespeare's
audience.   (Paris)
   frontis.   table.   bibliog.
1952.

665281

___ HOSLEY (RICHARD)
The Staging of Desdemona's bed.
IN SHAKESPEARE QUARTERLY XIV: 1.
pp. 57-65.   (New York)   1963.

605711

___ ROSENBERG (MARVIN)
The "Refinement" of "Othello" in the
eighteenth century British theatre.
IN Studies in Philology, Vol. 51.
(Chapel Hill, N.C.)
1954.

554520/51

___ ROSS (LAWRENCE J.)
The Use of a "fit-up" booth in Othello.
IN SHAKESPEARE QUARTERLY XII: 4.
pp. 359-370.
(New York) 1961.

605711

—— A Satirical dialgoue between a sea
captain and his friend in town
address'd to the gentlemen who
deform'd the play of Othello,
M[arch] 7th, 1750; [with] a prologue
and epilogue. pp. [2.] [c.1750.]
  Epilogue only, Dialogue and Prologue
wanting.
                              633511

——SELTZER (DANIEL)
   Elizabethan acting in Othello.
   IN SHAKESPEARE QUARTERLY X: 2.
   pp. 201-210.
   (New York) 1959.
                              605711

——SMART (CHRISTOPHER)
   An Occasional prologue and epilogue to
   Othello, as it was acted at the Theatre
   -Royal in Drury-Lane, 7th March 1751.
   2nd edn.   pp. 8.
                          [c.1750.]

                              633512

—— [SMART (C.)]
   The Prologue to Othello, as it was acted
   at the theatre in Drury-Lane and The
   Epilogue spoken by Desdemona.   FROM
   The Midwife [; or, The Old woman's
   magazine, Vol. 1].   1751.

                              563203

——SPRAGUE (ARTHUR COLBY)
   Shakespearian players and performances.
   (Cambridge, Mass.)
     ports. illus.   1953.
   Edmund Kean as Othello, pp. 71-86.

                              635328

——STONE, GEORGE WINCHESTER
   Garrick and 'Othello.' IN Essays in
   English neoclassicism in memory of
   Charles B. Woods: Philological
   Quarterly, Vol.45, no.1, Jan. 1966.
   (Iowa City, Iowa)   1966.

       pp.304-320.   767563

——WHYTE (S.)
   Occasional address, spoken after
   Othello, Theatre-Royal, Crow Street,
   [Dublin] Aug. 3rd, 1789.   IN
   Whyte (S.) A Collection of poems on
   various subjects, including The Theatre,
   a didactic essay.   2nd edn.   (Dublin)
                             1792.

                              510480

Othello
— 19th century

——ALDEN (BARBARA)
   Differences in the conception of Othello's
   character as seen in the performances
   of three nineteenth century actors on
   the American stage, Edwin Forrest, Edwin
   Booth and Tommaso Salvini.   Filmed by
   the University of Chicago Library.
   (University of Chicago Doctoral Disser-
   tation.No. T 782)   (Chicago, Ill.)
   bibliog. typescript. microfilm, positive
   copy.   1 vol. in 1 reel, 35 mm.
                             1950.

                              665432

—— A Casebook on 'Othello', edited by
   L.F. Dean. [Text and criticism by
   various authors.] (New York: Thomas Y.
   Crowell)   1964.

     Crowell Literary Casebooks.
                              748200

——   Cook ([E.] D.) "Othello" in Paris.
   From The Theatre, Oct. 1, 1880.
                             1880.

                              516577

——CUMBERLAND (R.)
   News-paper critique of a tragedy of
   Shakespeare [: Othello].
   IN Cumberland (R.) The Observer,
   [edited] by A. Chalmers, [Vol. 2.]
                             1803.
   British Essayists.

                              459752

——   Dickens (C.) On Mr. Fechter's acting
   [of Iago]. From [The Atlantic Monthly,]
   Vol.24. [Boston, Mass.]   1869.

                              562638

——   The Drama. [E. Kean and C.M. Young in
   Othello at Drury Lane Theatre.] From [The
   London Magazine,] Jan. 1823.   1823.

                              561772

——   Hazlitt (W.) Essays. Selected and,
   edited [with introduction and notes]
   by F. Carr. [With a chapter, On Mr. Kean's
   Iago, and other Shakespearian references.]
                           [c.1896.]

   (Scott Library)

                              483486

——   Hazlitt (W.) On Mr. Kean's Iago. In
   Hazlitt (W.) The Round table [and]
   Characters of Shakespear's plays.

                             1936.

   (Everyman's Library, No.65)

                              473751

——   Head (June) Othello [: a performance
   at the Old Vic]. From Picture Post,
   August 8, 1942.   1942.

                              545621

IRVING ([Sir] HENRY)
Four favourite parts [: Hamlet; Richard III; Iago; King Lear].
IN The English Illustrated Magazine, 1892-3.
illus.   1893.

119734

MERCHANT, CHRISTINA
Delacroix's tragedy of Desdemona.
IN SHAKESPEARE SURVEY 21.   (Cambridge)
pp. 79-86.   1968.

776762

Morley (H.) On Fechter's Othello.
In Agate (J.[E.]) ed., The English dramatic critics.   [1932.]

399280

Morris (M.) Essays in theatrical criticism [including "Othello at the Lyceum"].   1882.

422874

Othello's costume. From Once a Week [, New Series, Vol.2].

1866.

554733

Parisian Critic, A. [pseud.]
Mr. Irving [as Hamlet] and Signor Salvini [as Othello]. From The Gentleman's Magazine, N[ew] S[eries], Vol. 14.   1875.

561328

SAINTSBURY (GEORGE EDWARD BATEMAN)
Mr. Irving's Iago.   IN Saintsbury (G. E. B.) A Second scrap book.
1923.

308680

S[eeley] ([Sir] J.R.) A Stage Iago.
In The Cornhill magazine, Vol.33.

1876.

38693

SPRAGUE (ARTHUR COLBY)
Edwin Booth's Iago: a study of a great Shakespearian actor.   IN The Theatre Annual, 1947.   (New York)   1947.

554521/1947

SPRAGUE (ARTHUR COLBY)
Shakespearian players and performances.
(Cambridge, Mass.)
ports.   illus.   1953.
Edwin Booth as Iago, pp. 121-135.

635328

WADSWORTH, FRANK W.
Hamlet and Iago: nineteenth-century breeches parts.   IN SHAKESPEARE QUARTERLY XVII: 2.   pp. 129-139.
(New York)   1966.

605711

White (R.G.) On the acting of Iago.   In The Atlantic Monthly.   Vol. 48.

(Boston)   1881.

39574

Othello

— 20th century

Adler (H.) Ralph Richardson and Laurence Olivier [: actors in Othello at the Old Vic.] Ports. In World Film News, Vol. 2.   1938.

485420

BOYD (STEPHANIE)
The Two Othellos at the Old Vic [: a poem].   IN The Poetry Review, Vol. 47.
1956.

240749/47

COLCHESTER REPERTORY COMPANY
Souvenir programmes to celebrate five hundred productions in Colchester, including the programme for the five hundredth play: Othello. pp. 40.
[Colchester.]
ports.   illus.   1950.

629840

CROSSE (G.)
Othello on the stage.   IN Macmillan's magazine, Vol. 87.   1902.

175820

Fisher (H.K.) The Theatre [: criticism of productions of] The Alchemist, Othello [and] King Richard II. In Life and Letters, Vol.54.
1947.

586006

GENNARO (G. de)
Anew McMaster as "Othello" [: portrait].
IN Gennaro (G. de) Pastels and paintings [: reproductions, with an] introduction by K. Van Haek.   pp. [12.]   (Dublin)
ports.   illus.   1945.
Signed by the author.

560995

Gilder (Rosamond) Othello and Venus:
Broadway in review. [Includes a criticism of Margaret Webster's production of Othello under Theatre Guild auspices, starring Paul Robeson.] Illus. In Theatre Arts, Vol.27. (New York)
1943.

548672

Kemp (T.C.) The Stratford Festival:
review of Othello. [Broadcast] 2nd August, 1948. ff. [3] Typescript.   1948.

596474

KEMP (THOMAS CHARLES)

Stratford 1954 [: "Othello" A radio talk]
produced by P. Humphreys. [Broadcast]
18th March, 1954. ff.6. Typescript.
1954.

643696

—— KITCHIN (LAURENCE)
"Othello" at Stratford-on-Avon.
Produced by G. MacBeth. [Broadcast]
18th October, 1961. 1961.

667767

—— Lovell (J.) Shakespeare's American
play [: an historical review of the
performances of Othello in America]. In
Theatre Arts, Vol. 28. (New York)
1944.

558366

——MacCarthy (Sir D.) Othello. IN

MacCARTHY (Sir DESMOND)
Theatre [: essays]. 1954.

642651

—— Othello [: an article]. In Play
pictorial, Vol.36. 1920.

571898

——Powell (P.) A Talk on Othello. In
Theatre Programme [: a radio review
of the stage:Shakespearean items.
Broadcast] 2nd April [1947].ff.[34.]
Typescript.

[1947.]

583268

—— Scheffauer (H.G.) The New vision
in the German arts: [essays. Including
The Chromatic Othello.] 1924.

443991

—— Smet (R. de) Othello in Paris and
Brussels. Translated by Sir B. [V.] Jackson.
Illus. In Shakespeare Survey: an annual
survey of Shakespearian study & production,
[Vol.] 3. (Cambridge) 1950.

606026

——STANISLAVSKY (KONSTANTIN) pseud.
Creating a role, translated by E. R.
Hapgood. 1963.

667656

——STANISLAVSKY (K. S.) pseud.
Director's plan for "Othello" Act III,
Scene IV. IN COLE (TOBY) and CHINOY
(HELEN KRICH) ed. Directing the play:
a source book of stagecraft, edited
with an illustrated history of directing
by T. Cole and Helen K. Chinoy.
ports. illus. dgms. facsimile. bibliog.
1954.

641766

——[STANISLAVSKY (KONSTANTIN)] pseud.
Stanislavsky produces Othello [at the
Moscow Art Theatre: the text of the
play, with instructions for production].
Translated from the Russian by Helen
Nowak.
frontis. plans. 1948.

592011

—— [Theatre Guild, New York.] Paul
Robeson as Othello, the Moor of Venice
[: a souvenir book of the Margaret
Webster production of Othello]. pp.[20]
Illus. [New York] [1943.]

559677

——TYNAN, KENNETH PEACOCK, ed.
Othello: the National Theatre
production. 1966.

illus. 753063

—— Underwood (Mela) Joe and Uta
[: notes on Jose Ferrer and Uta Ferrer,
with special reference to their parts
in Othello at the Broadway, New York].
Illus. From Collier's, May 20, 1944.
(New York) 1944.

578275

——WELLS, STANLEY
Shakespeare's text on the modern
stage [with special reference to
the National Theatre's "Othello".]
FROM Deutsche Shakespeare-
Gesellschaft West Jahrbuch 1967.
(Heidelberg)
pp. 175-193. 767901

— Study and Teaching; Tales

——ADAMSON (ELGIVA) and MOORE (KATHLEEN V.)
Notes on William Shakespeare's
"Othello". pp. 56. [Stratford,
Ontario] [1959.]

666392

——CARRINGTON, NORMAN T.
Shakespeare: Othello. (Bath) [1966.]

Notes on chosen English texts.
753353

——GRACE, WILLIAM JOSEPH
Review notes and study guide to
Shakespeare's 'Othello'. (New York)
1964.

Monarch critiques of literature.
757011

—Gray (P.) and Bradford (C.)
Shakespeare and modern drama: a
reading and writing handbook for
freshmen. [With essays, etc. on
Othello, and bibliographies.]

(Madison) 1939.

515775

——JORGENSEN, PAUL ALFRED
Othello: an outline-guide to the play.
(New York) 1964.

Barnes & Noble focus books.
743621

LAMB (CHARLES)
The Story of Othello. Preface and
C. Lamb's biography by G. M. Hunderfun.
English-Roumanian vocabulary by
H. Sascuteanu. pp. 24. [Bucharest]
[c.1930]
Library of English Rapid Readers, 1.

497777

LAMB (CHARLES) and LAMB (MARY ANN)
As you like it; and, Othello. pp.iii,
72. [Tokyo]
1949.
Easy Readings Series, 6.
627265

Mueller (W.R.) The Class of '50
reads "Othello". In College
English, Vol.10.

(Chicago) 1948-9.

598860/10

NOLAN, EDWARD F.
Barron's simplified approach to
Shakespeare's "Othello".
(Woodbury, N.Y.) 1967.
Barron's educational series.

773400

SHIPLEY, JOSEPH TWADELL, ed.
Othello: a scene-by-scene analysis with
critical commentary. (New York) 1963.

Study master series. 743617

Othello

— Textual History and Translation

CAMERON (K. W.)
"Othello", Quarto 1, reconsidered.
pp. [13]. FROM [Publications of
the Modern Language Association of
America, vol. 47.] [(Menasha, Wis.)]
[1932.]

438441

Cameron (K.W.) The Text of Othello:
an analysis. In Publications
of the Modern Language Association
of America, vol.49.

(Menasha,Wis.) 1934.
432218

Gallas (K.R.) [Review of] Othello in
French, by Margaret Gilman. In
English studies, Vol. 8.

(Amsterdam) 1926.
485650

HINMAN (C.)
The "Copy" for the second quarto of
Othello (1630). [With bibliographical notes.]
IN McMANAWAY (J. G.), DAWSON (G. E.)
and WILLOUGHBY (E. E.) eds., John
Quincy Adams memorial studies.
(Washington) 1948.

596748

LE BRETON (A.)
Le Théâtre romantique. [With a chapter
on Alfred de Vigny's translation of
Othello, and other references to
Shakespeare.] [c.1920.]

572306

MUIR, KENNETH
The Text of Othello. IN SHAKESPEARE
STUDIES, 1. (Cincinnati, Ohio)
1965.

750317

WALKER (ALICE) The 1622 Quarto and the
First Folio texts of Othello. IN Shakespeare
Survey. [Vol.] 5.
(Cambridge) 1952.

623798

Otsuka, Takanobu *works relating to*

ARAKI (KAZUO) and others, ed.
Studies in English grammar and
linguistics: a miscellany in
honour of Takanobu Otsuka. (Tokyo)
port. dgms. tables. bibliogs.
1958.

667095

OTWAY, THOMAS
The History and fall of Caius Marius

For editions of this play see under
English Editions: Romeo and Juliet:
Alterations &c.

Otway, Thomas *works relating to*

TAYLOR (ALINE MACKENZIE)
Next to Shakespeare: Otway's "Venice
Preserv'd" and "The Orphan" and their
history on the London stage.
(Durham, N.C.)
ports. illus. bibliogs. 1950.

615158

-5

Our sceptred isle : calendar 1942
[with] quotations from Shakespeare.
pp. [26.] Illus.

[Bognor Regis]   [1941.]

529561

Our Shakespeare Club <u>see</u> Birmingham,
Our Shakespeare Club

Our Traveler, pseud., <u>see</u> Travels in
France: a vignette of Talma

Outline Studies in Literature
edited by Maud E. Kingsley <u>see under</u>
Kingsley, Maud E.

Outlines to Shakespeare *see* Synopses

Over, Alan, and Bell, Mary, eds.
WHITER, WALTER
A Specimen of a commentary on Shakespeare,
being the text of the first (1794)
edition, revised by the author and never
previously published. Edited by A. Over.
Completed by Mary Bell.   1967.

764140

Overbury (Sir Thomas) the Elder, Works
relating to:- <u>see</u> MOORE (W. H.)
Baconian Studies.

OVERHOLSER (WINIFRED)
Shakespeare's psychiatry - and after.
IN SHAKESPEARE QUARTERLY X: 3.
pp. 335-352.
(New York) 1959.

605711

OVERMYER (GRACE)
America's first Hamlet [i.e. John
Howard Payne].   (New York)
port.   bibliog.   1957.

665530

OVID
Metamorphosis. The XV books of P.
Ovidius Naso entytuled metamorphosis,
translated out of Latin into English
meeter by A. Golding. (London: W.
Serez)   1567.

447653

Ovid *works relating to*

—— DORAN, MADELEINE
Some Renaissance 'Ovids'.   FROM
Literature and society, edited by
Bernice Slote.   (Lincoln, Neb.)
pp. 44-62.   1964.

777383

—— PALMATIER (M. A.)
A Suggested new source in Ovid's
Metamorphoses for Shakespeare's
Venus and Adonis.   Reprinted from
The Huntington Library Quarterly,
Vol. 24, No. 2, February 1961.
pp. 9.   [San Marino, Cal.]
bibliogs.   1961.

667081

—— SANDYS, GEORGE
Ovid's Metamorphosis Englished, mytho-
logiz'd, and represented in figures.
An Essay to the translation of Virgil's
AEnis.   1640.   [Facsimile of
commentary on Books I-IV, with an
introductory essay "Shakespeare's
other Ovid".
IN SHAKESPEARE STUDIES 3.   (Cincinnati,
Ohio)   1967.

771652

—— WRIGHT (F. A.)
Three Roman poets: Plautus, Catullus,
Ovid.   Their lives, times and works.
[With reference to Ovid's influence
on Shakespeare].
port.   illus.   facsimile.   1938.

479412

See also: MOORE (W. H.) Baconian studies.

OWEN (C.)
The Phoenix and the dove: a novel
[with Queen Elizabeth and Shakespeare
as two of the principal characters].
1933.

402521

OWEN (CHARLES A.   )

Comic awareness, style, and dramatic
technique in Much Ado About Nothing.
FROM Boston University Studies in
English, Vol.5, No.4. (Boston, Mass.)
1961.

667842

OWEN (EDWARD)
Ludovic Lloyd, a long-forgotten
Welshman: a contemporary and probable
acquaintance of William Shakespeare
and the possible exemplar of
Shakespeare's "Fluellen".   Reprinted
from the North Wales Guardian, Feb.-
April, 1931.   pp. 24.   (Wrexham)
1931.

396493

OWEN (JOANNES) the Epigrammatist. Works relating to: see Moore (W. H.) Baconian Studies.

OWEN, LEWIS J.
Richard II.
IN CARNEGIE INSTITUTE OF TECHNOLOGY, PITTSBURGH. Lectures on four of Shakespeare's history plays. (Pittsburgh, Pa.) 1953.

635454

OWEN (ORVILLE W.) [ed.]
The Tragical historie of Robert, Earl of Essex: [a play]. Deciphered from the works of F. Bacon. (Detroit) port. 1895.

451621

Owens (P.) Picture of nobody: [a novel, with Shakespeare as one of the characters.] With a preface by L.A.G. Strong.

1936.

448124

OWLETT, F.C.
Shakespeare and Charles Lamb [: address delivered at the Elian Club, London, March 17th, 1938]. 1938.

668474

OWLETT (F. C.)
The Spacious days and other essays [on English literature]. Published in conjunction with the Globe-Mermaid Association. [With references to Shakespeare.] 1937.

471612

OWST (G. R.)
Literature and pulpit in medieval England: a neglected chapter in the history of English letters & of the English people. [With references to Shakespeare.] (Cambridge) 1933.

402880

Oxberry's Dramatic biography, and histrionic anecdotes [with references to Shakespearean acting]. Vols. 1-5; New Series, Vol. 1. [Edited by Mrs. Oxberry.]
engraved t.ps. ports. 6 vols. 1825-27.
Subtitle of N.S., Vol. 1 reads "or, The Green-room spy" on printed t.p., and "and Green room spy" on engraved t.p. Vols. 3 and 5 imperfect.

557829

Oxford, Edward de Vere 17th Earl of *works relating to*

____ ALLEN (E.)
Curious "tributes" to Shakespeare [? or to Edward de Vere, 17th Earl of Oxford]. IN East Anglian Magazine, Vol. 4. (Ipswich) 1939.

510779

____ ALLEN (E.)
When Shakespeare died [: a suggestion that Shakespeare's plays were written by Edward de Vere, Earl of Oxford]. pp. 16. [1938.]

508269

____ ALLEN (E.)
Where are Shakespeare's portraits? IN East Anglian magazine, Vol. 4. (Ipswich) 1939.

510779

____ ALLEN (E.) and ALLEN (P.)
Lord Oxford & "Shakespeare": a reply to John Drinkwater. pp. 69. 1933.

407347

____ ALLEN (P.)
Anne Cecil, Elizabeth & Oxford: a study of relations between these three, with the Duke of Alençon added; based upon evidence drawn from (Chapman's?) A Lover's complaint [etc.]; and from various Shakesperean plays & poems. 1934.

417433

____ ALLEN (P)
The Life story of Edward de Vere as "William Shakespeare". frontis. 1932.

392091

____ ALLEN (P.)
Lord Oxford as Shakespeare. IN East Anglian Magazine, Vol. 2. (Ipswich) illus. 1937.

510777

____ ALLEN (P.)
The Plays of Shakespeare [i.e. Oxford] & Chapman in relation to French history. With an introduction by Marjorie Bowen. 1933.

407234

____ ALLEN (P.)
The Psychic in Shakespeare['s plays]. FROM Light [, Vol. 65]. [1945.]

563663

____ ALLEN (P.)
Shakespeare as a topical dramatist. FROM Poetry and the Play, 1929. pp. [18.] [1929]

389219

____ ALLEN (P.)
Talks with Elizabethans, revealing the mystery of "William Shakespeare" [: conversations with Elizabethan playwrights and poets, communicated through the automatic writing of Mrs. Hester Dowden. With references to Francis Bacon and the Earl of Oxford and bibliographical references.] ports. [1947.]

587016

— ALLEN (P.)
Topicalities in Shakespeare. IN
Downs (H .) ed., Theatre and stage,
Vol. 1.
ports. illus. dgms.   1934.
625661

— AMPHLETT (HILDA)
Who was Shakespeare? A new enquiry
[into the claim of the Earl of Oxford
to the authorship of Shakespeare's
plays.] With an introduction by
C. Humphreys.
ports. illus. facsimiles. bibliog.
1955.
648469

—BARRELL (C. W.)
Identifying "Shakespeare".   IN Scientific American.   Vol. 162.   (New York)
1940.
517843

— BARRELL (C. W.)
Verifying the secret history of
Shakespeare's sonnets [: a refutation of the theory that Shakespeare
can be identified in his sonnets as
a homo-sexual personality, and evidence
to show that the Earl of Oxford was
Shakespeare].   Illustrated by H. F.
Wood.   FROM Tomorrow, Vol. 5.   (New
York)
ports. illus. facsimiles.   1946.
574236

— BENEZET (LOUIS PAUL)
The Six loves of "Shake-speare" [: the
Earl of Oxford authorship theory]. Ports.
(New York)   1958.
665924

— BENHAM (W. G.)
Edward de Vere, Earl of Oxford,
'identified' as Shakespeare.
FROM The Essex Review, Vol. 29.
(Colchester)
illus.   pedigree.   1920.
395466

— BOWEN (GWYNNETH)
Shakespeare's farewell: paper read
under the title: 'The Date and authorship of The Tempest', at a meeting of
the Shakespeare Fellowship, February, 1
1951. pp. (ii), 20.   (Buxton)
[1951.]
Published by the author.
620076

— BOWEN (MARJORIE) [pseud.]
April 23rd doesn't impress me – why?
because I don't believe in
Shakespeare [: an attempt to prove
that Edward de Vere, 17th Earl of
Oxford, wrote Shakespeare].   pp. [4.]
FROM The Strand Magazine, April 1946.
1946.
579644

— BOYCE (BURKE)
Cloak of folly [: a novel relating
to Edward de Vere, 17th Earl of
Oxford].   [1951.]
618901

— CLARK (Mrs. EVA)
The Man who was Shakespeare [: the
life of Edward de Vere, 17th Earl
of Oxford.   With notes.]   (New
York)
ports. illus. facsimiles. bibliog.
1937.
478136

— Dawbarn (C.Y.C.)Oxford and the folio
plays: a supplement [to]
Baconiana,Oct.1938.pp.[80].Facsimiles.
1938.
(Bacon Society)
499944

—DOUGLAS (MONTAGU WILLIAM)
Lord Oxford and the Shakespeare Group:
a summary of evidence presented by
J. T. Looney, G. H. Rendall [and]
G. Slater.   3rd edn. [of The Earl of
Oxford as "Shakespeare"] contains
additional evidence and amendments.
(Oxford)
port.   bibliog.   1952.
627722

— DOUGLAS (M. W.)
Lord Oxford was "Shakespeare": a
summing up.   With an introduction
by G. H. Rendall [and bibliographies].
2nd edn. amended.
ports.   illus.   1934.
428118

— DWYER (J.J.)
Italian art in the poems and plays of
Shakespeare [: an argument in favour
of the true author of "Shakespeare"'s
work being Edward de Vere, 17th Earl
of Oxford] read at a meeting of the
[Shakespeare] Fellowship, January 26th,
1946. pp. 15.   (Colchester)
(Shakespeare Fellowship)   [1946.]
579794

— EGGAR (KATHARINE E.)
Shakespeare in his true colours.
pp. 8.   1951.
622316

— EGGAR (KATHERINE E.)
The Unlifted shadow: some misunderstood features in the life of
Edward de Vere, 17th Earl of Oxford,
1550-1604. pp. 8.   [Newport, Mon.]
[1954.]
644835

— FELDMAN (A. BRONSON)
Imaginary incest: a study of
Shakespeare's "Pericles".   FROM The
American Imago, Vol. 12, pp. 117-155.
(Boston [Mass.])
bibliog.   1955.
665620

— FELDMAN (A. BRONSON)
Othello in reality.   FROM The American
Imago, Vol. 2, pp. 147-179.   (Boston
[Mass.])
bibliog.   1954.
665619

FELDMAN (A. BRONSON)
Portals of discovery [: a study of
Shakespeare's "Comedy of errors"].
FROM The American Imago, Vol. 16,
pp. 77-107. (Boston, Mass.)
bibliog. [1959.]

666166

FORD, GERTRUDE C.
A rose by any name. Introduction by
Francis T. Carmody. (New York) 1964.

illus. 745724

Holland (H.H.) Shakespeare, Oxford and
Elizabethan times [: notes on
Shakespeare's plays.]

1933.

412431

KENT (W.)
The Real "Shake-speare" vindicated:
a reply to William Margrie's pamphlet.
pp. 7.
typescript. [1947.]
For W. Margrie's pamphlet, entitled "Shakespeare vindicated", see
catal. no. 580477.

580948

KENT (W.) and another
Edward de Vere, the seventeenth Earl
of Oxford, the real Shakespeare.
[1947.]
(The Shakespeare Fellowship)
582468

_____ 2nd edn. 1957. 665684

KITTLE (W.)
Edward de Vere, 17th Earl of Oxford,
and Shakespeare: external and contem-
porary evidence connecting the 17th
Earl of Oxford and the writer named
Shakespeare: with the background of
Elizabethan history needed for this
investigation; with the writer
Shakespeare's burial in Westminster
Abbey and the burial of Shakespeare
beneath the chancel of the church in
Stratford. (Baltimore)
ports. facsimiles. 1942. 542796

MARGRIE (W.)
Shakespeare vindicated: an exposure of
the Oxford and Bacon nonsense. The
essence of a speech delivered in a debate at Hope House, Westminster, on
December 5th, 1946, pp. [4].
[1946.]
For a reply to the above pamphlet
see 'The Real "Shake-Speare" vindicated'
by W. Kent (Catal. no. 580948)

580477

OGBURN (CHARLTON)
The Renaissance man of England [: the
Earl of Oxford as William Shakespeare].
pp. 37. (Atlanta, Ga.)
port. 1949.

611989

OGBURN (Mrs. DOROTHY) and
OGBURN (CHARLTON)
Shake-speare: the man behind the name
[; the case for Edward de Vere, 17th
Earl of Oxford, as the author of
Shakespeare's works]. Illus. (New York)
1962.

667432

OGBURN (Mrs. DOROTHY) and OGBURN
(CHARLTON)
This star of England "William Shakespeare", man of the Renaissance
[: a study of the Earl of Oxford
authorship theory]. (New York)
ports. facsimiles. bibliog. 1952.

633249

PHILLIPS (G.)
The Tragic story of "Shakespeare",
disclosed in the sonnets, and the life
of Edward de Vere, 17th Earl of Oxford.
1932.

392565

RANSON (F. L.)
Lavenham, Suffolk [containing references
to Shakespeare's connection with Lavenham and Edward de Vere, 17th Earl of
Oxford]. Foreword by M. W. Douglas.
pp. 79. [Ipswich]
illus. map. 1937.

557271

RANSON (F. L.)
Shakespeare was an East Anglian.
[With subsequent correspondence on
the same subject.] IN East Anglian
magazine, Vol. 2. (Ipswich)
ports. illus. 1937.

510777

RANSON (F. L.) ed.
Shakespearian page [: articles by
various authors chiefly relating to
the "Oxfordian" theory]. IN East
Anglian Magazine, Vol.2. (Ipswich)
1937.

510777

RAY (S.N.)
Shakespeare through X-ray: science
takes up the controversy [: an attempt
to prove that E. de Vere 17th Earl of
Oxford was Shakespeare]. IN The
Modern review, Vol. 69. (Calcutta)
ports. illus. 1941.

581255

RENDALL (G. H.)
Arthur Golding, translator - personal
and literary - Shakespeare and Edward
de Vere [: a review of An Elizabethan
Puritan, Arthur Golding, by L. T.
Golding]. FROM The Essex Review, Vol.
50. pp. 108-113. (Colchester)
1941.

541336

Rendall (G.H.) Personal clues in
Shakespeare poems and sonnets
[relating to Edward de Vere].

1934.

426741

—— Rendall (G.H.) Shakespeare : handwriting and spelling [as evidence
of the De Vere authorship of
Shakespearian plays and poems].
pp.55. Facsimiles.

1931.

415238

——RENDALL (G. H.)
Shakespeare in Essex and East Anglia
[: an essay dealing with the authorship
of the plays, with particular reference
to 2 Henry VI and Cymbeline. With
bibliographical references]. pp. 13.
[Colchester]   [1944.]

556041

—— Shakespeare Fellowship Quarterly [:
a periodical attempting to prove that
Edward de Vere, Earl of Oxford, wrote
the works of Shakespeare]. (New York)
9 vols.   1939-48.
Vols. 1-4 called News letter. All
published.

562696

——WARD (B. M.) and ALLEN (P.)
An enquiry into the relations between
Lord Oxford as "Shakespeare", Queen
Elizabeth and the Fair Youth of
Shakespeare's sonnets [with biblio-
graphical references].

[1936.]

530214

——WILSON (CORA P.)
The Shakespearean controversy: [the
seventeenth Earl of Oxford, Edward de
Vere, was the real Shakespeare.] ff.6.
typescript.   [c.1940.]

520264

Oxford

——Adams (W.[H.] D.) "Julius Caesar" at
Oxford. In The Theatre, Vol.13.

1889.

101204

——Boas (F.S.) Hamlet and Volpone at
Oxford. In The Fortnightly Review,
Vol.107. New series.

1920.

285541

——Boas (F.S.) "Hamlet" at Oxford:
new facts and suggestions. In
The Fortnightly Review. Vol.94.
New series.

1913.

247731

——BOAS (F. S.)
Oxford and Shakespeare.
IN GOLLANCZ ([Sir] I.) ed., A Book of
homage to Shakespeare.
ports. illus. facsimiles. [1916.]

264175

——Bodleian Library
HANSON (L. W.)
The Shakespeare Collection in the Bodleian
Library, Oxford. IN SHAKESPEARE SURVEY
14. (Cambridge)
facsimiles.   1951.

615854

——BODLEIAN LIBRARY
William Shakespeare 1564-1964.
A catalogue of the Quatercentenary
Exhibition in the Divinity School,
Oxford. (Oxford)   1964.

742974

——DRAGON SCHOOL
The Draconian. [Numbers containing
reports, etc., of the annual
Shakespearian productions]. [Oxford]
ports. illus.   1918-63.

458725

——HOLE (CHRISTINA)
English custom & usage. [With
references to Shakespeare's
birthday celebrations at Stratford-
upon-Avon and Oxford.]
illus. bibliog.   1941.

529397

——LEEDS (E. T.)
Appendix, including a monograph on
the Crosse Inn and the Tavern of
Oxford. IN ACHESON (A.) Shakespeare's
sonnet story, 1592-1598; with documentary evidence identifying Mistress
Davenant as the Dark Lady. New edn.
1933.

417420

—— Mr. W. Shakespeare, proctor [a
facetious attempt to prove that
Shakespeare was a proctor in the
University of Oxford]. IN The Shotover
papers; or, Echoes from Oxford.
[Vol. 1.] (Oxford)   1874-75.
All published.

558088

—— New College Shakespeare Club see
Societies and Clubs.

——   New Theatre. [Programmes of
performances, including Shakespearian
performances, 1900]- 1905.

[Oxford]   [1900]-1905.

464878

—— Oxford and Shakespeare-land : the
world's great travel shrine. 6th
edn. pp. 24. Illus. Maps.

1929.

(Great Western Railway)

499902

——Q. (D.)
Shakespeare, Oxford and an Oxford Inn.
IN Notes and Queries, Vol. 193.
(Oxford)   1948.

5421/193

——Rhodes (R.C.) Much ado about nothing
at Oxford, 1606. From The Shakespeare
Review, Vol.1.
1928.

467394

OXFORD COMPANION TO THE THEATRE, edited
by P. Hartnoll. 3rd ed.   1967.

illus.   763718

Oxford University Dramatic Society
see Societies and Clubs.

Oxford University Press. A List of
books on Shakespeare published by the
Oxford University Press; with those of
certain American and Australian universities and learned societies, and a
selection of books dealing with the
Shakespearian period. pp.11.

[Oxford]   [1937]

467391

OXFORD UNIVERSITY PRESS
Oxford music for Shakespeare year.
(New York)   1964.

750610

Oxley, B.T.

see GROSE, KENNETH H., and OXLEY, B.T.

OXYGEN NEWS
Shakespeare among Indians. Reprint of
a supplement issued to mark the
Quatercentenary of William Shakespeare.
(Calcutta)   [1964.]

illus.   744154

OYAMA (TOSHIKAZU)
The Folio copy of Richard III.   IN
Studies in English grammar and
linguistics: a miscellany in honour
of Takanobu Otsuka.   (Tokyo)
port. dgms. tables. bibliogs.
1958.

667095

OYAMA, TOSHIKAZU
Hamlet's dichotomy and the Elizabethan
demonology.   FROM The English review,
vol. V, nos. 1, 2, July 1967.
(Tokyo)   1967.

764572

OYAMA (TOSHIKAZU)
The Language of Feste, the Clown.
IN Studies in English grammar and
linguistics: a miscellany in honour
of Takanobu Otsuka.   (Tokyo)
port.   dgms.   tables.   bibliogs.
1958.

667095

OYAMA (TOSHIKAZU) Works edited by:-
see: Araki (Kazuo) and others.

"P"., [pseud.]
Passages in Shakspeare's Henry IV
elucidated.   FROM The Gentleman's
Magazine, July 1824.   pp. [4.]
1824.

402690

P. (E.K.M.)
A Country walk with the poets.
[With references to the flowers
mentioned in Shakespeare's plays.]
FROM The Victoria Magazine, Vol. 23.
1874.

563687

[P. (S.)]
A Particular account of the jubilee
held at Stratford-upon-Avon in
Warwickshire, on Wednesday the 6th
of September [1769], and the two
following days, to the immortal memory
of Shakespeare.   FROM [The Oxford
Magazine,] Vol. 3.   [Oxford]   [1769.]

558051

Pace, Richard *works relating to*

——   Wegg (J.) Richard Pace, a Tudor
diplomatist. [With a bibliography and
references to Pace in Shakespeare's Henry
the Eighth.]

1932.

401231

PACY (FRANK)
The Shakespeare Head Press at Stratford-
upon-Avon.   A paper read 5th May,
1916 at a meeting to commemorate the
Shakespeare tercentenary.   With a
note by E. I. Fripp on the proposed
publication (by the Shakespeare Head
Press) of the Chamberlains' accounts
of Stratford-upon-Avon.   Reprinted
from The Library Association Record,
July-Aug. 1916.   pp. 10.   (Aberdeen)
1916.

545619

PADELFORD (FREDERICK MORGAN)
Shakespeare;   The Forest of Arden
[: two poems].
IN GOLLANCZ ([Sir] I.) ed., A Book of
homage to Shakespeare.
ports.   illus.   facsimiles.   [1916.]

264175

PADEN (WILLIAM DOREMUS)
Tennyson in Egypt: a study of the
imagery in his earlier work. [With
references to Shakespeare's plays.]
(Lawrence, Kansas)
illus.   1942.
Kansas University Publications.
Humanistic Studies, No. 27.

539163

Padua University

——EVANS (GWYNNE BLAKEMORE) ed.
Introductions to [and] text of the
Padua "Macbeth", collations; edited
by G. B. Evans.   (Charlottesville,
Va.)   1960.
Facsim. Shakespearean prompt-books of
the seventeenth century, Vol. 4.
Bibliographical society of the
University of Virginia.

666707

——EVANS (GWYNNE BLAKEMORE) ed.
Introductions to [and] text of the
Padua "Measure for Measure" [and] "The
Winter's Tale", collations; edited
by G. B. Evans.   (Charlottesville, Va.)
                                1963.
Facsim. Shakespearean prompt-books of
the seventeenth century, Vol. 2.
Bibliographical Society of the University
of Virginia.

667611

PAFFORD (J. H. P.)
Music, and the songs in The Winter's Tale.
IN **SHAKESPEARE QUARTERLY** X: 2.
pp. 161-175.
(New York) 1959.

605711

PAGAN ([Miss] E. H. C.)
Astrology in Shakespeare, Parts 2-8.
FROM Modern Astrology, 1931-1934.
                                1931-4.
Wants Part 1.   Part 4 omitted in
numbering, owing to publisher's error.

430982

PAGAN (I. M.)
Sunset in Stratford [: a play about
William Shakespeare].   ff. 27.
([Stratford-upon-Avon])
typescript.   [1937]

477471

Page (E.R.) George Colman the elder:
essayist, dramatist, and theatrical
manager, 1732-1794. [With references
to Shakespeare, and a bibliography].

(New York)   1935.

(Columbia University Studies in English
and Comparative Literature,
No.120.)

447513

Page (F.) Shakespeare and Florio. In
Notes and Queries, Vol[s.] 184-5.
2 vols.
(Oxford)   1943.

544211

Page (H.E.) Rambles and walking tours
in Shakespeareland and the
Cotswolds. Illus. Maps.

1933.

406184

PAGE (JOSEPHINE)
The Winter's Tale, retold by Josephine
Page.   pp. vi, 70.   (Oxford)
illus.   1941.
Tales Retold for Easy Reading, Second
Series.

539921

Page (Nadine) Beatrice: "My Lady
Disdain". In Modern Language Notes,
vol.50.

(Baltimore)   1935.

446885

PAGE (NADINE)
The Public repudiation of Hero.
IN Publications of the Modern
Language Association of America,
Vol. 50.   (Menasha, Wis.)   1935.

448074

Pageantry in Shakespeare

——VENEZKY (ALICE S.)
Pageantry on the Shakespearean stage.
(New York)
illus.   bibliog.   1951.

619624

Pageants

——GILLIAM (L.) [ed.]
"English pageant" for St. George's Day
1941.   Arranged and produced by L.
Gilliam.   [With extracts from
Shakespeare.   Broadcast] 23rd April,
1941.   ff. 14.
typescript.   1941.

541845

—— HATCHER (O. L.)
A Book for Shakespeare plays and
pageants: Elizabethan and Shakespearean
detail for producers, stage managers,
actors, artists and students. [With
a bibliography.]
ports. illus. dgms.   [1916.]

455641

—— LANEHAM (R.)
Letter describing the magnificent
pageants presented before Queen
Elizabeth, at Kenilworth Castle in
1575. With an introductory preface,
glossarial and explanatory notes.
(Warwick and Leamington)
port.   1824.

566421

——[LANEHAM (R.)]
A Letter: wherein part of the entertainment untoo the Queenz Majesty at
Killingwoorth Castl, 1575 iz signified.
pp. 90. (Warwick)
                               1784.

414160

—— [RITSON (J.)]
The Stxcktxn [Stockton] Jubilee; or,
Shakespeare in all his glory: a
choice pageant for Christmas holidays,
1781 [containing passages from
Shakespeare applied to the principal
inhabitants of Stockton-on-Tees].
pp. [11].
manuscript.   1781.

533659

Pages *see* Children in Shakespeare

PAGET (E. N.)
Festival sonnets, Stratford-on-Avon
[by]E. N. P[aget].   pp. 54. [6.]
                              [c.1910]

638379

Paget (W.) illus.
JAMESON ([Mrs.] ANNA [B.])
Shakspeare's heroines: characteristics
of women, moral, poetical and historical.
                              [c.1890.]

376241

Paget (W.) illus.
LAMB (CHARLES and MARY [A.])
Tales from Shakespeare.   1901.

348881

Pain (Nesta) and Macqueen-Pope (W.[J.])
The Haymarket Theatre [: a history,
in the form of four plays. With
references to Shakespeare. Broadcast]
17th February, 2nd, 16th [and] 30th
March, 1944. pp. 13, ff. 14, 14, 15.
Typescript.   4 vols.

1944.

548003

PAINTER (WILLIAM)
The Goodly history of the true and
constant love between Romeus and
Julietta, abridged from "The Palace
of pleasure".   IN SHAKESPEARE (W.)
Romeo and Juliet. [Edited with an
introduction by H. Morley.]
                    1895.   530844
Cassell's National Library.
_____ Another edn. 1898. 527786
_____ Another edn. 1903. 550227

PAINTER (WILLIAM)
The Palace of pleasure: histories and
novels chosen and selected out of divers
authors; from the edition printed by
T. Marsh, 1575. Edited by J. Haslewood.
2 vols.   1813.

491699

PAINTER (W.)
The Palace of pleasure: Italian
and French novels done into English,
now again edited for the 4th time
by J. Jacobs.
3 vols.   1890.

108225

PAINTER (WILLIAM)
The Palace of pleasure. With an introduction by H. Miles and illustrations
by D. P. Bliss.   (Cresset Press)
4 vols.   1929.
Edn. limited to 500 copies on mould-
made paper and 30 copies on hand-made,
printed at the Oxford University Press.
The number of this copy is 379.

401118

[PAINTER (WILLIAM)]
The Story of Giletta [from The Palace
of pleasure].   IN SHAKESPEARE (W.)
All's well that ends well. [Edited
with an introduction by H. Morley.]
                               1889.
Cassell's National Library.
                               527798

Painter (William) [Paynter] trans.
BANDELLO (M.)
The Goodly history of the true and
constant love between Rhomeo and
Julietta.   Translated by W. Painter
from the French paraphrase by P.
Boaistuau of Bandello's version.
Reprinted from the edition issued by
the New Shakespeare Society in 1875
and edited by P. A. Daniel.   Frontispiece, etc. by F. T. Chamberlin.   pp.
lxxxii. (New Hampshire: Monadnock
Press)   1903.
Edn. limited to 115 copies on hand-
made paper and 10 on vellum.   418062

Painting *see* Art, Shakespeare in; Illustrations

Palembang

—KLAUS (A.)
Shakespeare in Palembang [: an account
of a presentation of the Merchant of
Venice in the Malay language]. FROM
The English Journal, Vol. 22. (Chicago)
1933.

533701

Pall Mall Shakespeare Gallery *see* **Boydell Shakespeare Gallery**

PALMATIER (M. A.)
A Suggested new source in Ovid's
Metamorphoses for Shakespeare's
Venus and Adonis. Reprinted from
The Huntington Library Quarterly,
Vol. 24, No. 2, February 1961.
pp. 9. [San Marino, Cal.]
bibliogs. 1961.

667081

PALMER (A. S.)
A New Shaksperian interpretation [of
Hamlet]. IN The Oxford and Cambridge
Review, No. 9, 1910. 1910.

228517

Palmer (C.) and Saintsbury (H.A.) eds.
We saw him act : a symposium on the
art of Sir Henry Irving; a series
of essays, articles and anecdotes,
personal reminiscences and dramatic
criticisms written by his contemporaries, collected and collated by H.A.
Saintsbury. Ports.

1939.

506641

Palmer (C.S.) A Possible approach to
the Shakespeare question. From The
Johns Hopkins Alumni Magazine, Vol.
25.

(Baltimore) 1937.

488671

PALMER, D.J.
Art and nature in "Twelfth Night".
FROM The Critical Quarterly, Autumn
1967. 1967.

pp.201-212. 766384

PALMER, DAVID JOHN
Stage spectators in Hamlet. FROM
English Studies, 47, Dec., 1966.
(Amsterdam) 1966.

758149

PALMER, DAVID JOHN, ed.
Shakespeare 'The Tempest': a
casebook. 1968.
Casebook series.

769357

PALMER (G. H.)
Intimations of immortality in the
sonnets of Shakespeare. pp. 57.
(Boston) 1912.
Ingersoll Lecture, 1912.

415004

PALMER (HAROLD E.)
Four stories from Shakespeare. Adapted
and rewritten with the thousand word
vocabulary. Illustrated by T. H.
Robinson. 1937.
Thousand-Word English Senior Series.

463628

PALMER (H. E.)
Four tales from Shakespeare. pp. 72.
[1944.]
[Evans International Series.] "Plain
English" Library.

555376

PALMER (J. [L.])
Ben Jonson [: a biography, with
references to Shakespeare.]
ports. illus. facsimile. 1934.

420415

PALMER (JOHN LESLIE)
Comic characters of Shakespeare [:
studies of Berowne, Touchstone, Shylock,
Bottom, Beatrice and Benedick. With
bibliographical notes]. 1946.

574450

PALMER (JOHN LESLIE)
Hamlet in modern dress. [A Review of
H. K. Ayliff's production of
Shakespeare's "Hamlet".] IN The
Fortnightly Review, Vol. 124. 1925.

325119

PALMER (JOHN LESLIE)
Political characters of Shakespeare
[: studies of Brutus, Richard II,
Richard III, Henry V and Coriolanus].
1945.

559355

PALMER (ROBERT)
A Pilgrimage to an English shrine:
[Stratford-on-Avon.] FROM The
Foresters' Miscellany, 1870. pp. [3.]
[Edinburgh] [1870]

389766

PALMER [(W.) ed.]
The New and complete English spouter;
or, An Universal key to theatrical
knowledge. A collection of prologues
and epilogues [including prologue and
epilogue to Richard the Third, and
prologue to Much ado about nothing.]
[1781.]

531636

PANDIT (K. G.)
Introduction to Shakespeare.
(Bombay) 1953.

641629

Parallelisms *see* Influence and Comparisons

——LAWRENCE (W. J.)
A Shakespearian pantomime.   IN The
Gentleman's Magazine. Vol. 284.
1898.

142601

PAOLUCCI, ANNE
Bradley and Hegel upon Shakespeare.
FROM Comparative Literature, XVI, 3.
1964.

pp.211-225.   747545

PAOLUCCI, ANNE
'Macbeth' and 'Oedipus Rex': a study
in paradox. FROM Shakespeare encomium,
1564-1964. (New York)   1964.

pp.44-70. City University of New
York, City College Papers, 1.
747547

PAOLUCCI (ANNE)
The Tragic hero in Julius Caesar.
IN   SHAKESPEARE QUARTERLY XI.
pp. 329-333.
(New York)   1960.

605711

PAOLUCCI, ANNE, ed.
Shakespeare encomium, 1564-1964 [by
various writers]. (New York) 1964.

City University of New York,
City College Papers, 1.   747546

Pape (Eric) illus.
SLAUGHTER (GERTRUDE)
Shakespeare and the heart of a child
[: a story for children].   (New York)
1922.

304949

Papé (Frank Cheyne) illus.
LAMB (CHARLES and MARY [A.])
Tales from Shakespeare.   1923.

310164

Papé (Frank Cheyne) illus.
LAMB (CHARLES and MARY [A.])
Tales from Shakspeare.   [1930]
["Chandos" Classics.]

383736

PAPP (JOSEPH)
Commentary.   IN Henry V.   Text
edited by C. J. Sisson.   (New York)
1962.
The Laurel Shakespeare.   F. Fergusson,
general editor.

667459

PAPP, JOSEPH
The Method and William Shakespeare.
IN Stratford Papers on Shakespeare
delivered at the 1963 Shakespeare
Seminar.   (Toronto)   1964.

668007

PARES (MARTIN)
A Pioneer; in memory of Delia Bacon,
February 2nd, 1811 to September 2nd, 1859.
(Francis Bacon Society) pp.60. Port.
Facsimiles. Bibliogs.   1958.

666036

PARES (MARTIN)
Will o' the wisp [: an examination of
the Bacon-Shakespeare controversy].
Re-printed from "Ariel", Spring 1958.
pp. 12.   [Winchester]
ports.   facsimiles.   [1958.]

665910

PARGETER (EDITH)
This rough magic: a novel. 1953.

633058

PARIATI, PIETRO
Cajo Marzio Coriolano

For editions of this play see under
English Editions: Coriolanus:
Opera Texts

PARIS (JEAN)
Shakespeare [: a biography]. Translated
by R. Seaver. (Evergreen Profile Book,
10) Ports. Illus. Chronological Tables.
Facsimiles. (New York)   1960.

666722

A PARISIAN CRITIC [pseud.]
Mr. Irving [as Hamlet] and Signor
Salvini [as Othello].   FROM The
Gentleman's Magazine, N[ew] S[eries],
Vol. 14.   1875.

561328

PARKER (A. A.)
Henry VIII in Shakespeare and Calderón.
[With bibliographical notes.]   IN
The Modern Language Review, Vol. 43.
(Cambridge)   1948.

266816/43

PARKER (ANTHONY)
William Shakespeare (1564-1616).   IN
Parker (A.) Great men of Warwickshire.
ports.   illus.   map.   1956.
Men of the Counties, 6.
653108

PARKER (CLIFTON)
Two songs from "As you like it":
It was a lover and his lass [and]
Under the greenwood tree.   [Words
by] Shakespeare.   pp. 5.   1958.
The Oxford Choral Songs.
666048

PARKER (ERIC) ed.
The Lonsdale anthology of sporting
prose & verse.   With an introduction.
[Containing quotations from Shakespeare.]
1932.

396568

PARKER (LOUIS NAPOLEON)
The Ode to Adelaide Ristori [with reference to her Shakespearian parts.]   IN
His Majesty's Theatre [London],
Adelaide Ristori memorial matinée
[programme], Nov. 30th, 1908.   pp. [4.]
port.   [1908.]

531801

PARKER (MARION DOMINICA HOPE)
The Slave of life: a study of
Shakespeare and the idea of justice.
bibliog.   1955.

647932

PARKER (R. B.)
Dramaturgy in Shakespeare and Brecht.
IN University of Toronto Quarterly,
April 1963.   pp. 18.   (Toronto)
                                        1963.

596179

Parker, R.   B.
Old books and Elizabethan printing. IN

STRATFORD PAPERS ON SHAKESPEARE
delivered at the 1961 Shakespeare
Seminar. (Toronto)   1962.

668005

PARKES (D.)
Epitaphs on the family of
Shakspeare.   FROM The Gentleman's
Magazine, July 1807.   pp. [2.]
frontis.   1807.

402683

PARKES (HENRY BAMFORD)
Nature's diverse laws: the double
vision of the Elizabethans.
FROM The Sewanee Review, Vol. 58.
(Sewanee, Tenn.)   1950.

620315

PARKS (EDD WINFIELD)
Simms's edition of the Shakespeare
apocrypha.   IN Studies in Shakespeare.
(University of Miami Publications in
English and American Literature,
Vol. 1, March 1953).   (Coral Gables,
Fla.)   1953.

634188

PARKS (G.B.)
The Development of The Two gentlemen
of Verona.   IN Huntington Library
Bulletin, No. 11.   (Cambridge, Mass.)
                                        1937.

477589

PARLIN (H T.)
A Study in Shirley's comedies of
London life. [With references to
Shakespeare.]   (Austin, Texas)
                                        1914.
University of Texas.   Studies in
English.

442433

Parodies *see* Burlesques

PARR (JOHNSTONE)
Shakespeare's artistic use of astrology;
The "Late eclipses" in King Lear; and
Edmund's birth under Ursa Major.   IN
Parr (J.) Tamburlaine's malady, and
other essays on astrology in Elizabethan
drama.   (University, Ala.)
bibliog.   1953.

638899

Parr, Nicholas *works relating to*

—M.   (C.   L.   )
A Note on Nicholas Parr's portrait of
Shakespeare, engraved c.1740, by C.L.M.
Illus. (Cleveland, [Ohio])   1907.

668399

Note: No. 12 of edition limited to 250
copies, privately printed.

PARROTT (T. M.)
The 'Academic tragedy' of 'Caesar
and Pompey'.   IN The Modern
Language Review, Vol. 5.   (Cambridge)
                                        1910.

266820

PARROTT (T. M.)
Errors and omissions in the Griggs
facsimile of the Second Quarto of
Hamlet.   IN Modern Language Notes,
Vol. 49.   (Baltimore)   1934.

428652

PARROTT (THOMAS MARC)
Further observations on Titus Andronicus.
IN SHAKESPEARE QUARTERLY I: 1.
pp. 22-29.
(New York)   1950.

605711

PARROTT (T. M.)
"God's" or "gods'" in King Lear, V.iii.17.
IN SHAKESPEARE QUARTERLY IV: 4.
pp. 427-432.
(New York)   1953.

605711

PARROTT (T.M.)
[Review of] William Shakspere's petty
school, by T.W. Baldwin.   FROM The
Journal of English and Germanic Philology, Vol. 43.

(Urbana, Ill.)   .1944.

578408

Parrott (T.M.) [Review of]
Shakespearian comedy and other
studies, by G.[S.] Gordon. From
The Journal of English and Germanic
Philology, Vol.44.

    (Urbana, Ill.)   1945.

             578406

Parrott (T.M.) [Review of]
Shakespearian comedy and other
studies, by G.[S.] Gordon. From
The Journal of English and Germanic
Philology, Vol.44.

    (Urbana, Ill.)   1945.

             578406

PARROTT (THOMAS MARC.)

[Review of] The Tempest. Edited by F.Kermode
(Arden Shakespeare) 5th edn. IN The Journal
of English and Germanic Philology, Vol.55.

      (Urbana. Ill.)   1956.

          600780/55

Parrott (T.M.) [A Review of] Art and
  artifice in Shakespeare, by E.E.Stoll.
In Modern language notes, Vol.50.

      (Baltimore)   1935.

          446885

PARROTT (T. M.)
[Review of] What happens in Hamlet,
by J. D Wilson; Hamlet, edited
by J. D. Wilson; and The Manuscript
of Shakespeare's Hamlet and the
problems of its transmission, by
J. D. Wilson. IN Modern language
notes, Vol. 52. (Baltimore) 1937.

         479896

Parrott (T.M.) Shakespearean comedy.

    (New York)   1949.

        603755

Parrott (T.M.) Shakespeare's revision
of "Titus Andronicus". In The
Modern Language Review, Vol. 14.

        1919.

        283257

PARROTT (THOMAS MARC)
The Taming of a shrew - a new study of
an old play. IN Elizabethan studies
and other essays[, by various authors],
in honor of George F. Reynolds. [With
bibliographical notes.] (Boulder,
Col.)   1945.

        569202

PARROTT (THOMAS MARC)
William Shakespeare: a handbook.
(Oxford)
ports.   illus.   1934.

        435938

PARRY (Sir CHARLES HUBERT HASTINGS)
England: John o' Gaunt's verse. The
words paraphrased from John o' Gaunt's
speech in Shakespeare's Richard II,
by Sir E. Howard. Set as a unison
song by C. H. H. Parry. pp. 4. 1919.
Year Book Press Series of Unison and
Part Songs, No. 156.

        520356

PARRY (Sir CHARLES HUBERT HASTINGS)
England. Words paraphrased from
Shakespeare by Sir E. Howard.
[Music] arranged by D. Wright for
soprano, alto, tenor and bass [with
piano accompaniment.] pp. 6.
         1960.
Year Book Press Music Series.

        667056

PARRY (JOHN)
A Guide to Shakespeare for Malayan
students. pp. 72.   1956.

        665366

Parry (R.St.J.) Henry Jackson,O.M.: a
memoir.[With a bibliography; extracts
from his correspondence, including
references to the Bacon- Shakespeare
controversy; a lecture: Was Shakspere
of Stratford the author of Shakespeare's
plays and poems?, delivered to the
Sheffield Branch of the British Empire
Shakespeare Society, 29 February,1912.
Port. Illus. (Cambridge)   1926.

        432383

PARSONS (G. H.) and other[s]
Warwickshire: an illustrated review
of the holiday, sporting, industrial
and commercial interests of the county.
With a foreword by Lord Leigh. Edited
by H. E. O'Connor. 2nd edn. [With
Shakespearian references.]
(Cheltenham: E. J. Burrow & Co. Ltd.)
map.   [1937].

        469726

PARSONS (HOWARD)
Emendations to three of Shakespeare's
plays: "The Merry Wives of Windsor",
"Love s Labour's Lost", "Comedy of
Errors". pp. 21.   [1953.]

        637816

PARSONS (H.)
Shakespearian emendations, Nos. [I]-IX.
[With relevant correspondence]. IN
The Poetry Review, Vols. 37-41.
        1946-50.
[No. 1.] The History of the First
Folio of "The Workes of William
Shakespeare". Nos. 2-9 [Emendations
to "As you like it".]

        246749/37

PARSONS, HOWARD
Shakespearian emendations and
discoveries.   1953.

        638911

PARSONS (J. D.)
Boycotted Shakespeare facts [containing
The Labeo-Shakespeare evidence,
Notes regarding Labeo, The Great
Taboo, Sir Sidney Lee and absolute
proof, Ben Jonson and Sir Sidney Lee].
pp. [65.]   1920.

392890

PARSONS (JOHN DENHAM)
R. Field and the first Shakespeare poem:
an essay on [E.] Arber's 40 years
neglected Transcript of the Stationers'
Company's Registers' Assignment Column
disclosure of a clerical error entry
of the copyright.   pp. 12.   (Chiswick)
1935.   436336
_____ Another copy.   With MS. letter
by author.   1935.   436337

[PARSONS (J. D.)]
A St. George's Day, 1932, authorship
claim, incorporated with which is a
criticism of Sir Edmund Chambers's
'William Shakespeare'.   pp. [34.]
[1933.]

408911

PARSONS (J. D.)
Sir Edward Clarke, P.C., K.C., on
Shakespeare's identity: a privately
issued challenge to the University
of Oxford, presenting Counsel's
Opinion upon the evidence submitted,
with some remarks on the replies of
the 21 Heads of Colleges.   pp. 24.
(Chiswick)   1931.

390059

[Parsons (P.)] Dialogues of the dead
with the living. [Including a
dialogue between Shakespeare and D.
Garrick.]

1779.

526001

PARSONS (PHILIP)
Shakespeare and the mask.
IN SHAKESPEARE SURVEY 16.
illus.   1963.

667523

A Particular account of the jubilee
held at Stratford-upon-Avon in
Warwickshire, on Wednesday the 6th of
September [1769], and the immortal
memory of Shakespeare [, by S.P.].
FROM [The Oxford Magazine,] Vol. 3.
[Oxford]
illus.   [1769.]

558051

PARTRIDGE (ASTLEY COOPER)
The Accidence of Ben Jonson's plays,
masques and entertainments. With
an appendix of comparable uses in
Shakespeare.   (Cambridge)
bibliog.   1953.

632347

PARTRIDGE, ASTLEY COOPER
Orthography in Shakespeare and
Elizabethan drama: a study of
colloquial contractions, elision,
prosody and punctuation.   1964.

667804

PARTRIDGE (A. C.)
The Problem of Henry VIII reopened:
some linguistic criteria for the two
styles apparent in the play.   With
a foreword by A. Nicoll.   pp. 35.
(Cambridge)   1949.

602352

PARTRIDGE (ASTLEY COOPER)
Shakespeare's orthography in "Venus
and Adonis" and some early Quartos.
IN SHAKESPEARE SURVEY 7.   (Cambridge)
1954.

639176

PARTRIDGE (ASTLEY COOPER)
Studies in the syntax of Ben Jonson's
plays [as a parallel to the syntax
of Shakespeare's plays].   (Cambridge)
chronological table. bibliog. 1953.

632786

PARTRIDGE (ERIC [H.])
Shakespeare's bawdy: a literary &
psychological essay and a comprehensive
glossary.   1947.

587277

Partridge (E.[H.]) Slang to-day and
yesterday. With a short historical
sketch, [references to Shakespeare]
and vocabularies of English, American
and Australian slang.

1933.

411402

PARTRIDGE (E. [H.])
Words, words, words! [With references to Shakespearean usage.]
1933.

410091

Partridge (E.[H.]) The World of words:
an introduction to language in general and to English and American in
particular. [With Shakespearian
references.] Dgms.

1938.

486846

Partridge, Eric H. *works relating to*

____MORTIMER (R.)
Old and blue [: review of]
Shakespeare's bawdy by E. [H.] Partridge.
IN The New Statesman and Nation, Vol.
34.   1947.

589227

____PEARSON (H.)
For adults only [: review of]
Shakespeare's bawdy by E. [H.] Partridge.
IN The Listener, Vol. 38.   1947.

589226

PASADENA PLAYHOUSE
Programmes of Midsummer Drama Festival
and miscellaneous material, 1935-41.
(Pasadena, Calif.)   1935-41.
  From 1942, incorporated in Pasadena
Playhouse News.   Programmes of
Shakespearian productions.
                              440898

Pasadena Playhouse news.   Vols. 14-
(Pasadena, Cal.)
  ports.   illus.   1935-
Wants Vols. 1-13, Vol. 14 Nos. 1-9.
Vol. 15 No. 2 not published.
                              472444

Pasadena Playhouse. A Record of
  William Shakespeare's plays at the
  Pasadena Community Playhouse.ff.[6].

       (Pasadena [Cal.]   [1937]

                              477473

PASCAL (ROY)
The Stage of the "Englische Komodianten"
- three problems.   [Containing references to Shakespeare's plays.]   FROM
The Modern Language Review, Vol. 35.
[With bibliographical notes.]   pp.
[10.]   (Cambridge)   1940.

                              527251

PASCAL (ROY) [ed.]
Shakespeare in Germany, 1740-1815
[: German criticisms and translations,
with an introduction in English].
(Cambridge)   1937.

                              469784

Pascal, Roy *works relating to*

___ KIES (P. P.)
  Review [of] Shakespeare in Germany,
  1740-1815, edited by R. Pascal.
  IN Modern Language Notes, Vol. 56.
  (Baltimore)   1941.

                              533477

___ POLAK (L.)
  [Review of] R. Pascal's Shakespeare in
  Germany, 1740-1815. 1937.   IN English
  Studies, Vol. 20.   (Amsterdam) 1938.

                              495114

___ R. (A.)
  [A Review of] Shakespeare in Germany,
  1740-1815, [edited] by R. Pascal.
  IN The Criterion, Vol. 17.   1937-38.

                              487675

PASINETTI (PIER MARIA)
Julius Caesar: the role of the tech-
nical adviser.   IN The Quarterly of
Film Radio and Television, Vol. 8.
(Berkeley, Cal.)   1953.

                              630462/8

Passages selected by distinguished
personages on the great literary trial
of "Vortigern and Rowena: a comi-
tragedy" "Whether it be - or be not
from the immortal pen of Shakespeare?"
[By Sir H. B. Dudley and Mary, Lady
Dudley.]   [1795.]   585432
  Vols. 2-3 wanting.
_____ Another edn.   4 vols.   Vol. 1,
5th edn., Vol. 3, 2nd edn.
           [1795-1807.]   113493

The Passionate Pilgrim

___ BARNFIELD (R.)
  Poems, 1594-1598.   Edited by E. Arber.
  [Contains two poems also attributed
  to Shakespeare and printed in The
  Passionate pilgrim: If musique and
  sweet poetrie agree;   As it fell upon
  a day.]   (Birmingham)   1883.
  English Scholar's Library.
                              53789

___ BARNFIELD (R.)]
  Poems: in diuers humors.   [Contains
  two poems also attributed to
  Shakespeare and printed in The Passionate
  Pilgrim: If musique and sweet poetrie
  agree;   As it fell upon a day.   IN
  SECCOMBE (T.) ed., An English garner.
  Vol. 8: Some longer Elizabethan poems.
                     1903.   270088
  _____ IN ARBER (E.) ed., An English
  garner.   Penshurst edition. [Vol. 10.]
  Some longer Elizabethan poems.
                     1939.   563357

___ Greg (W.W.) [Review of] Venus and
  Adonis, 1593; The Passionate pilgrim,
  1599; etc.: reproduced in facsimile
  from the earliest editions, with
  introductions by [Sir] S. Lee.   In
  The Library, New Series, Vol.7.

                              1906.

                              198827

PASTERNAK (BORIS)
Shakespeare [: a poem].   IN Pasternak
(B.) Selected poems.   Translated from
the Russian by J. M. Cohen.   [With]
drawings by Donia Nachshen.   pp. vi,
58.   1946.
  Russian Literature Library, [4.].

                              577203

Pasternak (B.) Some remarks by a
  translator of Shakespeare. From
  Soviet Literature, Sept. 1946.

         (Moscow)   1946.

                              581952

PASTERNAK (BORIS)

Translating Shakespeare.[Translated
by M.Harari.] FROM Twentieth Century,
Vol.164.pp.213-228.   1958.

                          665934

Pasternak, Boris *works relating to*

——FRANK (VICTOR S.   )

A Russian Hamlet: Boris Pasternak's
novel. IN The Dublin Review, Vol.232.
                                1958.

Pastoral Literature

——BAGCHI (JASODHARA)
The Pastoral on the Elizabethan stage
and Shakespeare.
IN Shakespeare commemoration volume,
edited by Taraknath Sen.   (Calcutta)
                               1966.

                          764382

——BATES, PAUL A.
Shakespeare's sonnets and pastoral poetry.
IN SHAKESPEARE JAHRBUCH.   Bd. 103/1967.
pp. 81-96.   (Weimar)

                          10531

——BRYANT (JERRY H.)
The Winter's Tale and the pastoral
tradition.
IN SHAKESPEARE QUARTERLY XIV: 4.
pp. 387-398.
(New York)   1963.

                          605711

——DRAPER (R. P.)
Shakespeare's pastoral comedy.
IN Etudes anglaises, 11ᵉ année.
                               1958.

                          476080/11

——EMPSON (W.)
Some versions of pastoral [: the
pastoral form in English literature.
With references to Shakespeare.]
                               1935.

                          444756

——LASCELLES (MARY MADGE)
Shakespeare's pastoral comedy.   IN
GARRETT (J.) More talking of
Shakespeare.   1959.

                          666126

——SMITH (H.)
Pastoral influence in the English
drama. [With references to "As
you like it".]   IN Publications
of the Modern Language Association
of America, Vol. 12.   (Baltimore)
                               1897.

                          428332

PATER (WALTER [HORATIO])
Love's labour's lost; Measure for
measure; Shakespeare's English kings.
IN Pater (W. [H.]) Appreciations,
with an essay on style.   1898.

                          540898

Paternity in Shakespeare

——QUILLER-COUCH (Sir A. [T.])
Paternity in Shakespeare.   pp.20.
                                [1932]
(British Academy Annual Shakespeare
Lecture. 1932.)
                          396735

——QUILLER-COUCH (Sir A. [T.])
Paternity in Shakespeare.   IN Quiller-
Couch (Sir A. [T.]) The Poet as citizen,
and other papers.   (Cambridge)
                               1934.

                          428734

        Paterson (J.) Kay's Edinburgh
portraits, Vol. 1. [Including "Mrs.
Siddons, at the Edinburgh Theatre."]
Ports.

                               1885.

                          403309

PATERSON (JOHN)
The Word in "Hamlet".
IN SHAKESPEARE QUARTERLY II: 1.
pp. 47-55.
(New York)   1951.

                          605711

PATERSON (MORTON)
The Stagecraft of the Revels Office
during the reign of Elizabeth.
IN PROUTY (CHARLES TYLER) ed.,
Studies in the Elizabethan theatre.
[Hamden, Conn.]
illus.   1961.

                          667053

Pathology *see* Medicine and Hygiene

[PATMORE (COVENTRY KERSEY DIGHTON)]
Macbeth [: an essay to prove that
Macbeth, before meeting the witches,
had already conceived and imparted
the idea of obtaining the crown of
Scotland illegitimately]. IN The
Germ, 1850.   1850.   580968
_____ A facsimile reprint.
                   1901.   157369

Paton, Allan Park *works relating to*

—— The Emphasis capitals of Shakspere
[: a review of] "The Tragedy of
Hamlet (Hamnet Edition) according
to the First Folio (spelling
modernized) with further remarks
on the emphasis capitals of Shakspere",
by A. P. Paton.   FROM The Theatre,
Feb. 1st, 1879.   1879.

                        530818

Paton (Sir J.N.) Compositions from
Shakespeare's Tempest: fifteen
engravings in outline.

                        1877.

                        421827

PATRICK (DAVID LYALL)
The Textual history of Richard III.
(Stanford, Cal.)   1936.
Stanford University.   University
Series.   Language and Literature,
Vol. 6, No. 1.
                        463300

PATRICK (FREDERICK JAMES)
The Birmingham Shakespeare Memorial Library.
IN SHAKESPEARE SURVEY 7.   (Cambridge)
                        1954.

                        639176

PATRICK (JOHN MAX)
The Problem of Ophelia.   IN Studies
in Shakespeare.   (Coral Gables, Fla.)
                        1953.
University of Miami Publications in
English and American Literature,
Vol. 1, March 1953.
                        634188

Patriotism

—— Bell (G.K.A.) ed.   Poems of patriotism.
Edited [with a preface.   Including
extracts from Shakespeare].

                        [1907.]

(The Golden Anthologies)

                        545333

—— EVANS (Dame EDITH)
The Patriotism of Shakespeare.   IN The
Queen's Book of the Red Cross.   In aid
of the Lord Mayor of London's fund for
the Red Cross and the Order of St. John
of Jerusalem.
port.   illus.   1939.

                        508871

—— GILBERT (ALLAN H.)
Patriotism and satire in Henry V.
IN Studies in Shakespeare.   (Coral
Gables, Fla.)   1953.
University of Miami Publications
in English and American Literature,
Vol. 1, March 1953.
                        634188

—— LINDABURY (R. V.)
A Study of patriotism in the
Elizabethan drama.   [With references
to Shakespeare.]
bibliog.   1931.
Princeton Studies in English.

                        390064

—— McKILLOP (A.D.)
The Poet as patriot: Shakespeare to
Wordsworth.   [With bibliographical
notes.]   IN The Rice Institute Pamphlet,
Vol. 29.   (Houston, Texas.)
                        1942.

                        563553

—— SINCLAIR (W. M.)]
The Patriotism of Shakespeare.   By
the Archdeacon of London.   FROM
Leisure Hour, 1902.   pp. [4.]
                        [1902]

                        389194

—— URWIN (E. C.)
For love of England: Christian citizenship lessons for boys and girls, based
on plays of W. Shakespeare;   concerning
Shakespeare and drink, Shakespeare and
gambling, Shakespeare and love of country.
                        1939.

                        504947

Patten (J.A.) Sir Walter Scott: a
character study. [With a chapter
"Shakespeare and Scott".] Port.

                        1932.

                        394493

Patten (N. van)

see: Van Patten (N.)

Patterne of painefull adventures:
containing the most excellent, pleasant
and variable Historie of the strange
accidents that befell unto Prince
Apollonius, the Lady Lucina, his wife
and Tharsia his daughter. [The original of Shakespeare's Pericles, Prince
of Tyre.] Gathered into English by
L. Twine. pp. 77. (New York) 1903.
Elston Press. [Shakespearean Reprints,
3. Edn. limited to 170 copies.

560448

PATTERSON ([Mrs.] H[ELEN] T.)
Shakespeare and the imagery of Victor
Hugo. IN Studies in Romance
Philology and French Literature
presented to John Orr by pupils,
colleagues and friends. (Manchester)
port. maps. bibliogs. 1953.

637179

Pattison (B.) Music and poetry of the
English renaissance.[Including
references to Shakespeare's songs.
With a bibliography, bibliographical
notes and musical examples.]

1948.

590557

PAUL (HENRY NEILL)
The Imperial theme in Macbeth. [With
bibliographical notes.] facsimile.
IN McMANAWAY (J. G.), DAWSON (G. E.)
and WILLOUGHBY (E. E.) eds., Joseph
Quincy Adams memorial studies.
(Washington) 1948.

596748

PAUL (H. N.)
Mr. Hughs' edition of Hamlet.
IN Modern Language Notes, November,
1934. pp. 438-443. (Baltimore)
1934.

428652

Paul (H.N.) Players' quartos and
duodecimos of Hamlet. In Modern
Language Notes, Vol.49.

(Baltimore) 1934.

428652

PAUL (HENRY NEILL)
The Royal play of Macbeth: when,
why, and how it was written by
Shakespeare. (New York)
ports. illus. facsimiles. 1950.

615509

PAUL (H. N.)
Shakespeare in Philadelphia.
IN Proceedings of the American
Philosophical Society, Vol. 76.
(Philadelphia) 1936.

463924

PAULL (HARRY MAJOR)
Critical notes on "As you like it".
FROM The Fortnightly Review, Vol. 85.
1906.

475798

PAUNCZ (ARPAD)
The Lear complex in world literature.
FROM The American Imago, Vol. 2,
pp. 51-83. (Boston [Mass.]) 1954.
bibliog.

665621

Pavier, Thomas *see* Textual History, The Quartos

PAXTON (WILLIAM)
The Temperance teaching of Shakespeare.
With a preface by Sir S. Chisholm.
pp. 20. (Edinburgh) 1908.

665324

Payne (B.I.) The Central figure:
Shakespeare [in the productions of
the Drama Department of the Carnegie
Institute of Technology]. In Theatre
Arts Monthly, Vol.23.

(New York) 1939.

510715

Payne (B.I.) The Ethical influence of
Shakespeare. Port. In The Amateur
Theatre and Playwrights' Journal,
Vol.4, No.75.

1937.

467093

PAYNE (BEN IDEN)
Talking of theatre, 2: Variations on
a theatre theme, No. 10. [Shakespeare
productions, with special reference to
W. Poel.] [Broadcast] 19th September,
1961. ff. 5.
typescript. 1961.

666977

Payne, John Howard *works relating to*

—— OVERMYER (GRACE)
America's first Hamlet [i.e. John
Howard Payne]. (New York)
port. bibliog. 1957.

665530

Peace

— Catalogue of the first four folio
editions of Shakespeare with Roger
Payne's bill for binding the First
Folio, from the library of H. B. H.
Beaufoy, sold by order of the
Beaufoy Trustees, July, 1912.
pp. 7.
   illus.   [1912.]

                              426551

PAYNE, WAVENEY R. N. afterwards
Mrs. W. R. N. FREDRICK
A Classification of Shakespearian
literature.   Projected thesis for
fellowship of the Library Association.
   typescript.   1966.

                         752253

PAYNE (WAVENEY R. N.)
The Shakespeare Memorial Library,
Birmingham.   IN Theatre Notebook,
Vol. 3.   1948-9.

                         584117/3

PAYNE (WAVENEY R. N.)
The Shakespeare Memorial Library,
Birmingham.   FROM The Library
Association Record, Vol. 60,
pp. 120-122.
   illus.   1958.

                         666268

PAYNE (WAVENEY R. N.)
The Shakespeare Memorial Library,
Birmingham Public Libraries [: Paper]
3 [of] Shakespeare in the Library: a
symposium.   IN Open Access, Vol. 10,
N.S., No. 2.   (Birmingham)   1962.

                         667074

PAYNE, WAVENEY R.N.
   The Shakespeare Memorial Library
   [Birmingham] IN The Library World,
   Feb. 1964.   1964.

        illus.   667968

PAYNE (WAVENEY R. N.)
The Special collection [: Shakespeare
Memorial Library, Birmingham].
Some present day problems.   FROM The
Library Association Record, Vol. 52,
pp. 231-232.   1950.

                         666267

— WAGGONER (G. R.)
An Elizabethan attitude toward peace
and war [: reflected in the plays of
Shakespeare and others].   IN
Philological Quarterly, Vol. 33.
(Iowa)   1954.

                         592684/33

PEACH (LAWRENCE DU GARDE)
"Merely players": a vague fantasy of
dreams and dollars [about Shakespeare,
written for broadcasting.]
   typescript.   1935.

                         434454

PEACH (L. du G.)
"Saint George's Day" [: a radio play
about St. George, Shakespeare, and
the sea.   Broadcast] 23rd April 1950.
ff. 17.
   typescript.   1950.

                         608872

PEACH (LAWRENCE DU GARDE)
The Swan of Avon: [a play written
for broadcasting.   With Shakespeare
as one of the characters.]   ff. 21.
   typescript.   [1934.]
Waterways of England, No. 6.
                         419569

Peach (L. du G.) The Swan of Avon
[: a play relating to Shakespeare.
Broadcast] 28th May, 1942. ff.15.
   Typescript.

                           1942.

                         534704

PEACH (L. du G.)
"Will Shakespeare", produced by
A. Macdonald.   [Broadcast in the]
Midland Regional (Children's Hour)
programme, 23rd April, [1938.]
ff. 27.
   typescript.   [1938.]

                         481192

PEACHAM (HENRY) Works relating to: see
Moore (W. H.) Baconian Studies.

PEARCE (JOSEPHINE A.)
Constituent elements in Shakespeare's
English history plays.   IN Studies
in Shakespeare.   (Coral Gables, Fla.)
                              1953.
   University of Miami Publications in
English and American Literature,
Vol. 1, March 1953.
                         634188

Pearce (Josephine A.) An Earlier
   Talbot epitaph. [Concerns the dating
   of Shakespeare's revision of Henry
   VI, Pt.1.] In Modern Language Notes,
   Vol.59.

        (Baltimore)   1944.

                         563869

PEARS, PETER

<u>see</u> BRITTEN, BENJAMIN <u>and</u> PEARS, PETER

PEARSON (EDMUND LESTER)
The Lost First Folio.   IN TARG (W.) ed.
Carrousel for bibliophiles. [With
bibliographical notes.]   (New York)
   illus.   facsimiles.   1947.

584407

PEARSON (HESKETH)
Beerbohm Tree: his life and laughter.
   ports.   illus.   chronological table.
                              1956.

657353

PEARSON (HESKETH)
Bernard Shaw: his life and personality.
[With references to Shakespeare and a
bibliographical note.]
   ports.   1942.

536261

Pearson (H.) The Fool of love: a life
   of William Hazlitt. [With a
   bibliography, and references to
   Shakespeare.] Port.

1934.

421185

PEARSON (H.)
'The Last actor managers'.
(1) H. B. Irving & Lewis Waller.
[Broadcast] 4th October, 1949.
ff. 8.
   typescript.   [1949.]

605259

PEARSON (HESKETH)
The Last actor-managers.   With
illustrations from the Raymond Mander
and Joe Mitchenson Theatre Collection.
pp. xii, 84.
   bibliog.   1950.

611578

PEARSON (HESKETH)
The Life of Oscar Wilde.   [With references to Shakespeare.]
   bibliog.   ports.   illus.   1946.

570763

PEARSON (HESKETH)
A Life of Shakespeare.   (Harmondsworth:
Penguin Books)
   port.   1942.   532572
   _____ Another edn.   1949.   601054

PEARSON (HESKETH)
Modern men and mummers [with references
to Shakespeare].   1921.

473413

Pearson (H.) Thinking it over:
   reminiscences.[With references
   to Shakespeare]. Port.

1938.

483084

PEARSON (HESKETH) and KINGSMILL (HUGH)
[pseud.]
This blessed plot [: the record of a
tour through England in the wake of
Shakespeare.]   Illustrated by M.
Weightman.   1942.

534309

Pearson, Hesketh *works relating to*

——FISHER (H. K.)
[Review of] A Life of Shakespeare [by]
H. Pearson.   IN Life and letters
to-day, Vol. 36.   1943.

544196

——WILLIAMS (C. [W. S.])
Biography "of course" [: a review of]
A Life of Shakespeare, [by] H. Pearson.
IN Time and Tide, Vol. 23.   1942.

544257

PEARSON (H. S.)
[Newspaper and periodical cuttings
mainly relating to literary history
collected by H. S. Pearson.   Containing
cuttings about Shakespeare]
                         [c.1870-1920]

388846

[Pearson (H.S.)] Shakespeare v. Bacon.
<u>From</u> The Central Literary Magazine,
Vol. 8.

(Birmingham)   1888.

559335

PEARSON ([Mrs.] LU E.)
Elizabethan love conventions.
[With a chapter on Shakespeare's
sonnets.]   (Berkeley, Cal.)
   bibliog.   1933.

407228

PEARSON ([Mrs.]LU EMILY)
Elizabethan widows.   [With references
to Shakespeare and bibliographical notes.]
IN Stanford Studies in Language and Lit-
erature, 1941.   Edited by H. Craig.
(Palo Alto,] Cal.)

1941.

537291

PEARSON (N. H.)
Antony and Cleopatra.   IN PROUTY
(CHARLES TYLER) ed., Shakespeare: of
an age and for all time: the Yale
Shakespeare Festival Lectures.   [New
Haven, Conn.]   1954.

640920

Peat (R.C.) Presenting Shakespeare[:
how and when to introduce the plays of
Shakespeare into the English school
syllabus]. Illus.

1947.

581860

PEATTIE (T. B.)
A Prince of humorists [: Sir John
Falstaff.] IN The Central Literary
Magazine, vol. 30. 1932.

407290

PEČÍRKA (JAROMÍR)
Shakespeare and the graphic arts. IN
CHARLES UNIVERSITY ON SHAKESPEARE:
essays edited by Z. Stříbrný. (Praha)
illus. 1966.

762631

Pedersen (L.) Elsinore: a guide and a
historical account, with special regard to its English memories, [and
references to Shakespeare.] Translated by Nina Sabra and P. Boisen.
pp. 56. Illus. Map.

(Helsingór) [1937.]

477618

Pediatrics *see* Medicine and Hygiene

PEDICORD (HARRY WILLIAM)
The Theatrical public in the time of
Garrick. (New York)
tables. bibliog. 1954.

646092

PEELE (GEORGE)
Merry conceited jests of George Peele,
gentleman, sometime student in Oxford,
wherein is showed the course of his
life, how he lived. Edited [with
notes] by C. Hindley. [The notes
contain references to Shakespeare's
plays.] pp. 48. 1871.

534344

Peele, George *works relating to*

——BRIDGEWATER (H.)
The Missing historical plays of
"Shakespeare" [: Edward I and Edward IV
attributed, respectively, to G. Peele
and T. Heywood.] Reprinted from
"Baconiana" [Vol. 17]. pp.16.
[1932.]
(Bacon Society, London)

549428

——HUBBARD (F. G.)
Repetition and parallelism in the
earlier Elizabethan drama. [With
notes on Kyd, Greene, Peele and Marlowe].
IN Publications of the Modern Language
Association of America, Vol. 20.
(Cambridge, Mass.)
1905.

428340

——TANNENBAUM (S. A.)
George Peele (a concise bibliography).
[With references to Shakespeare.]
(New York) pp, X, 36.
1940.
(Elizabethan Bibliographies, No. 15.)
Note: Edition limited to 300 copies.

525750

see also: MOORE (W. H.) Baconian studies.

Peers (E.A.) A History of the romantic
movement in Spain [with references
to Shakespeare.] 2 vols.

(Cambridge) 1940.

514600

Peerson, Martin *works relating to*

——ECCLES (MARK)
Martin Peerson and the Blackfriars.
IN SHAKESPEARE SURVEY 11. (Cambridge)
bibliog. 1958.

665816

PEERY (WILLIAM WALLACE)
The Hamlet of Stephen Dedalus. IN
The University of Texas Studies in
English, Vol. 31. (Austin, Tex.)
1952.

442432/31

PEERY (WILLIAM WALLACE)
Shakespeare and Nathan Field. [English
text.] FROM Neophilologus, 34ste
Jaargang. pp. [8.] (Groningen)
1950.

620108

PEERY (WILLIAM WALLACE)
Shakhisbeard at Finnegans Wake.
IN The University of Texas Studies
in English, Vol. 30. (Austin, Tex.)
1951.

442432/30

[PEGGE (SAMUEL)]
Anonymiana; or, Ten centuries of
observations on various authors and
subjects, [with references to Shakespeare].
Compiled by a late very learned and
reverend divine.   1809.   509689
_____ 2nd edn.   1818.   480936

Pellegrini, Giuliano
Symbols and significances. [: in
                    Elizabethan England].

IN Shakespeare Survey, 17. (Cambridge)
                                1964.

                    667822

Pe Maung Tin see Tin ([Pe] Maung)

PEMBERTON (CHARLES REECE) [pseud.
Pel Verjuice]
Four lectures on Shylock, Othello,
Richard II & Henry IV, King John;
delivered 1835.
  manuscript.   [1836].

                              57313

PEMBERTON (MADGE)
The Queen waits [: a play, with
reference to Shakespeare.]
IN MARRIOTT (J. W.) [ed.] The Best
one-act plays of 1940.   1941.

                            525593

PEMBERTON (T. E.)
Shakespeare Memorial Theatre,
Stratford-upon-Avon.   Concerning
the Shakespeare annual festival
(the first of the new century),
commencing on Monday, April 15th,
1901. (Stratford-upon-Avon)
  illus.   1901.
Another copy with different covers.

                            549759

Pembroke, Mary Herbert Countess of *works relating to*

——RENDALL (G. H.)
The Ben Jonson and the First Folio edition
of Shakespeare's plays.   [Containing
references to the Countess of
Pembroke.]   pp. 23.   (Colchester)
  port.   1939.

                            507045

Pembroke, William Herbert 3rd Earl of *works relating to*

——NISBET (U.)
The Onlie begetter [: an essay
identifying Sir William Herbert
as Mr. W.H. of Shakespeare's Sonnets.]
  port.   bibliog.   1936.

                            451494

——TAYLOR (DICK)
Clarendon and Ben Jonson as witnesses
for the Earl of Pembroke's character.
FROM Studies in English Renaissance
Drama.   pp. [23.]   [1960.]

                            666781

——TAYLOR (DICK)
The Earl of Pembroke and the youth of
Shakespeare's Sonnets: an essay in
rehabilitation.   Reprinted from
Studies in Philology, [Vol.] 56, 1.
pp. [29].   1959.

                            666782

——TAYLOR (DICK)
The Masque and the lance: the Earl
of Pembroke in Jacobean court
entertainments.   Reprinted from
Tulane University, Tulane Studies
in English.   Vol. 8.   pp. [33].
(New Orleans, La.)   1958.

                            666780

——TAYLOR (DICK)
The Third Earl of Pembroke as a patron
of poetry. Reprinted from Tulane
University. Tulane Studies in English.
Vol.5. pp.[27]. (New Orleans, La.)
                            1955.

                            666783

Pen and pencil sketches of the
picturesque.   No. 12.   Charlecote
Hall, Warwickshire.   FROM [Sixpenny
Magazine, Oct. 1862.]
  illus.   [1862.]

                            560923

PENDER (T.)
Fidele.   The words by W. Shakespeare
[from Cymbeline].   Set to music by
T. Pender.   pp. 6.   (Oxford)
                          [1943.]

                            546842

PENDER (T.)
Shall I compare thee.   The words
by W. Shakespeare [from the Sonnets].
Set to music by T. Pender.   pp. 5.
(Oxford)   [1943.]

                            546839

Pendered (Mary L.) John Martin, painter:
his life and times. [With references
to his Shakespearian illustrations].

1923.

450647

Pendlebury (B.J.) To Enid [with a
copy of Romeo and Juliet] and other
poems. pp.30.

1922.

428708

Pendley Shakespeare Festival

—— Programmes, etc. 1950-

666286

—— WILLIAMS (DORIAN)
Pendley and a pack of hounds
[: autobiography].
ports. illus. 1959.

687142

Penguin Shakespeare Library
LERNER, LAURENCE DAVID, ed.
Shakespeare's comedies: an anthology of
modern criticism. (Harmondsworth)
1967.

Penguin Shakespeare library.
763025

Penguin Shakespeare Library
SPENCER, TERENCE JOHN BEW ed.
Elizabethan love stories. With
introduction and glossary.
(Harmondsworth) 1968.
Penguin Shakespeare library.

768790

Penn, William *works relating to*

——WRIGHT (C.)
Shakespeare and Ben Jonson, William
Penn, Lord Macaulay and the
Athenaeum - or, its editor [: a
letter] to W. H. Dixon [relating
to the portrait of Shakespeare,
recently discovered at Stratford-
upon-Avon]. pp. 4. 1861.

558066

[PENNANT (THOMAS)]
Of London [including a paragraph on the
Globe Theatre.]
ports. illus. 1790.

389453

Pennant Key-Indexed Study Guides

LEEB, DAVID
Pennant key-indexed study guide to
Shakespeare's Julius Caesar.
(Philadelphia, Pa.) 1966.

Pennant key-indexed study guides.
761163

Pennsylvania University, Horace Howard
Furness Memorial Library see Furness
Memorial Library.

Pennsylvania University: Rosenbach
Fellowship in Bibliography
BOWERS (FREDSON THAYER)
On editing Shakespeare and the Eliza-
bethan dramatists. (Philadelphia,
Pa.) 1955.
Rosenbach Fellowship in Bibliography.

665021

[PENNY (Mrs. ANNE)]
Poems, with a dramatic entertainment,
by **** ****. [Including several
poems relating to Shakespeare.]
illus. [1771.]

550539

Penrhyn Players, Liverpool see
Liverpool

PENROSE (BOIES)
Tudor and early Stuart voyaging.
(Washington: Folger Shakespeare
Library)
illus. maps. 1962.
Folger Booklets on Tudor and Stuart
Civilization.

667843

Pensées choisies de William
Shakespeare. ff.96.
[1916]

[French Booklets, No.17.]

393764

Pepler (H.D.C.) Shakespeare as realist.
From G.K.'s Weekly, May 27,1937.
pp.[4.]
1937.

471792

Pepper (S.C.) The Basis of criticism
in the arts. [With a section
relating to Shakespeare's Sonnet 30.]

(Cambridge, Mass.) 1946.

576712

PEPUSCH, JOHANN CHRISTOPH
[Ah sweet Adonis.] A favourite
song sung by Mrs. Barbier in "Venus
and Adonis". [Words by C. Cibber.]
[?1715]

760958

PEPUSCH, JOHANN CHRISTOPH
[Beauty now alone shall move him]:
a favourite song, sung by Mr. Turner
in "Venus and Adonis." [Words by C.
Cibber.]   [?1715]

760951

PEPUSCH, JOHANN CHRISTOPH
[How pleasant is ranging ye fields.]
A favourit song sung by Margaritta de
l'Epine in "Venus and Adonis." [Words
by C. Cibber.]   [?1715]

760957

Pepys, Samuel *works relating to*

—— EMSLIE (MACDONALD)
Pepys' Shakespeare song.
IN SHAKESPEARE QUARTERLY VI.
pp. 159-170.
(New York)   1955.

605711

Percival (Maurice) illus.
WATKINS (R.)
Moonlight at the Globe: an essay in
Shakespeare production, based on
performance of A Midsummer night's
dream at Harrow School [produced on
the pattern of a supposed performance
at the Globe].   Drawings by M. Percival;
foreword by R. W. Moore.   [With bibliographical notes and musical examples.]
1946.

577562

Percival (Maurice) illus.
WATKINS (RONALD)
On producing Shakespeare.   With
drawings by M. Percival.
illus.   1950.

611567

PERCY (ESME)
Hamlet [: the actor's view] 4.
[Producer J. Davenport.   Broadcast
7th May, 1954.]   ff. 6.
typescript.   [1954].

643704

PERCY (JOHN)
Fairy glee ["In this house"] from
[Shakespeare's] Midsummer Night's
Dream.   pp. 4.   [c.1795.]

628456

Percy [J.] Glee for four voices (in
answer to Sigh no more ladies)
composed by [J.] Percy.   The words
from Shakespear.   pp. 5.

[c.1780].

520364

PERCY (JOHN)
I know a bank.   Words from
"A Midsummer's night's dream".
pp. [8.]   [c.1760.]
Select Songs, composed by J. Percy,
No. 17.

666044

[PERCY (Bishop THOMAS)]
Ballads that illustrate Shakespeare.
IN [Percy (T.) ed.,] Reliques of ancient
English poetry, Vol. 1.   2nd edn.
illus.   1767.   488504
——— 3rd edn.   1775.   488507

[PERCY (T.)]
The Percy letters.   General editors:
D. N. Smith and C. Brooks.   [With
references to the editions of
Shakespeare.]   [Baton Rouge, La.]
Vols. 1-6 only.   1944-61.

571997

"Perdita" (Mary Robinson) *works relating to*

—— Memoirs [containing references to
Shakespeare] of the late Mrs. Robinson
[pseud. "Perdita"] written by herself.
With some posthumous pieces.   [Edited
by her daughter, Mary E. Robinson].
ports.   4 vols.   1801.

556919

—— ROSE (K.)
Portrait the third: A Winter's tale,
Mrs. Robinson as "Perdita" by
Gainsborough, [Wallace Collection].
IN Rose (K.) Georgiana [: seven
dramatic portraits.]   pp. [viii,] 48.
1947.

591814

—— Steen (Marguerite) The Lost one: a
biography of Mary (Perdita) Robinson.
[With references to Shakespeare, and
a bibliography.] Ports.Illus.

1937.

466583

Pérez Galdós, Benito *works relating to*

—— SHOEMAKER (WILLIAM HUTCHINSON)
Galdós' "La de los tristes destinos"
and its Shakespearean connections.
IN Modern Language Notes, Vol. 71.
(Baltimore, Md.)
1956.

439157/71

Performance in aid of King George's
Pension Fund for Actors and
Actresses [at] His Majesty's
Theatre, Dec. 17, 1918 [: programme.
Including "Macbeth" and "Masks and
faces", by A. Brereton : an article
concerning two of the plays acted
at the performance.] pp. 12. Ports.

1918.

530615

Performances Stage *see* **Actors and Acting;**
Programmes; Stage History and Production

Pericles

——ANDERSON (MARGARET SPENCER WOOD)
The Mystery story of "Pericles".
IN Ashland Studies in Shakespeare,
1957. (Ashland, Ore.) 1957.

666259/1957

——APOLLONIUS [TYRIUS]
The Book of Apollonius [: a source
of Pericles]. Translated into
English verse [with introduction] by
R. L. Grismer and Elizabeth Atkins.
(Minneapolis)
bibliog. 1936.

470704

——ARTHOS (JOHN)
Pericles, Prince of Tyre: a study in
the dramatic use of romantic narrative.
IN SHAKESPEARE QUARTERLY IV: 3.
pp. 257-270.
(New York) 1953.

605711

——BAKER (H. T.)
The Relation of Shakspere's Pericles
to George Wilkins's novel, The
Painfull adventures of Pericles,
Prince of Tyre. IN Publications
of the Modern Language Association
of America, Vol. 23. (Baltimore)
1908.

428343

——BULLOUGH (GEOFFREY)
"Pericles" and the verse in Wilkins's
"Painfull adventures". IN
Hommage à Shakespeare: Bulletin de
la Faculté des Lettres de Strasbourg.
43ᵉ année, No. 8, mai-juin 1965.
illus. 766822

——CAMDEN (C.)
A Note on Pericles. IN Modern
Language Notes, Vol. 48. (Baltimore)
1933.

413924

——CRAIG (HARDIN)
Pericles and The Painfull adventures.
[With bibliographical notes.] IN
Studies in Philology, Vol. 45.
(Chapel Hill, N.C.) 1948.

554520/45

——EDWARDS (P.)
An Approach to the problem of "Pericles".
IN SHAKESPEARE SURVEY 5. (Cambridge)
1952.

623798

——FELDMAN (A. BRONSON)
Imaginary incest: a study of
Shakespeare's "Pericles". FROM The
American Imago, Vol. 12, pp. 117-155.
(Boston [Mass.])
bibliog. 1955.

665620

——FELPERIN (HOWARD)
Shakespeare's miracle play [Pericles].
IN SHAKESPEARE QUARTERLY XVIII: 4.
pp. 363-374.
(New York) 1967.

605711

——FISHER (H. K.)
Shakespeare - Greek and garden party
[: review of performances of Hamlet,
in modern Greek, and Pericles]. IN
Life and Letters To-day. Vol. 22.
1939.

510119

——FLEAY (FREDERICK GARD)
On the play of "Pericles".
IN Transactions of the New Shakespeare
Society, Series 1. No. 1. pp. 195-209.
1874.
4061

——GOOLDEN (P.)
Antiochus's riddle in Gower and
Shakespeare. IN Review of English
Studies, New Series, Vol. 6. (Oxford)
1957.

318239/N.S./6

——Gower (J.) The Story of the Prince
of Tyre, from J. Gower's Confessio
amantis. In Shakespeare (W.) Pericles.
[Edited with an introduction by
H. Morley.]
1889.

(Cassell's National Library.)

436517

——GRAY (H. D.)
Heywood's Pericles, revised by
Shakespeare. IN Publications of
the Modern Language Association of
America, Vol. 40. (Menasha, Wis.)
1925.

428360

——GREENFIELD, THELMA NELSON
A Re-examination of the "patient" Pericles.
IN SHAKESPEARE STUDIES 3. (Cincinnati,
Ohio) 1967.

771652

GREG (W. W.)
[Review of] Venus and Adonis, 1593;
Pericles, 1609; etc.: reproduced
in facsimile from the earliest editions,
with introductions by [Sir] S. Lee.
IN The Library, New Series, Vol. 7.
1906.

198827

HOENIGER (F. DAVID)
How significant are textual parallels?
A New author for Pericles?
IN SHAKESPEARE QUARTERLY XI: 1.
pp. 27-37.
(New York) 1960.

605711

HUTTON (W. H.)
"Pericles" at Stratford [: a criticism].
IN Literature, Vol. 6. 1900.

152699

James 1, Remonstrance for the Right
of Kings, etc. [With references
to "Pericles".]

(Cambridge) 1616.

124913

Kirschbaum (L.) A Census of bad
quartos. [With bibliographical
notes.] In The Review of English
Studies, Vol.14.

1938.

495115

LONG (JOHN HENDERSON)
Laying the ghosts in "Pericles".
IN SHAKESPEARE QUARTERLY VII:
pp. 39-42.
(New York) 1956.

605711

MUIR (K.)
Pericles, II.v. IN Notes and Queries,
Vol. 193. (Oxford) 1948.

5421/193

The Patterne of painefull adventures:
containing the most excellent, pleasant
and variable Historie of the strange
accidents that befell unto Prince
Apollonius, the Lady Lucina his wife
and Tharsia his daughter. [The original
of Shakespeare's Pericles, Prince of
Tyre.] Gathered into English by L.
Twine. pp. 77. (New York: Elston
Press) 1903.
[Shakespeare Reprints, 3.] Edn. limited
to 170 copies.

560448

Plutarch. Pericles. In Plutarch's Lives.
Translated from the original Greek,
with notes critical and historical
and a new life of Plutarch, by J.
and W. Langhorne. 5th edn.,corrected.
Vol.2.

1792.

581551

PROGRAMMES OF SHAKESPEARIAN PERFORMANCES
Pericles

This collection, which runs from the
latter half of the nineteenth century,
is continuously augmented by the
addition of programmes of contemporary
productions.

530759

SEILER (GRACE ELIZABETH)
Shakespeare's part in "Pericles".
(Ann Arbor, Mich.)
bibliog. typescript, 1951. micro-
film, positive copy. 1 reel, 35 mm.
[1952.]
University Microfilms. Doctoral
Dissertation Series.

647062

Spiker (S.) George Wilkins and the
authorship of Pericles. From
Studies in Philology, vol.30.

(Baltimore) 1933.

441596

TOMPKINS (JOYCE MARJORIE SANXTER)
Why Pericles? IN The Review of English
Studies, New Series, Vol. 3. (Oxford)
1952.

318239/N.S./3

TREWIN (JOHN COURTENAY)
The Night has been unruly [: the
theatre in England, 1769-1955].
Illustrated from the Raymond Mander
and Joe Mitchenson Theatre
Collection.
ports. illus. facsimiles. bibliog.
1957.
Pericles, Prince of Tyre, Stratford-
upon-Avon, 1900.

670241

WILKINS (GEORGE)
The Painfull adventures of Pericles,
Prince of Tyre [: a novel, printed
in 1608, and founded upon Shakespeare's
play]; edited by K. Muir. (Liverpool)
facsimile. 1953.
Liverpool Reprints, No. 8.

637758

Periodicals
see also **Newspapers**
*In addition to the items listed below, the stock
of the Birmingham Reference Library includes
over 2,000 sets of periodicals, many of them
are catalogued analytically here*

AMATEUR STAGE, Vol.XIX, No.4, April, 1964.
Shakespeare Quatercentenary. 1964.

illus. 744895

—— Amateur Theatre and Playwrights'
Journal, Vol.4, No.75, June, 1937
[Special Shakespeare number].
Ports. Illus.

467093.

—— Ashland Studies in Shakespeare: notes,
comment, and reading-lists to accompany
classwork [in the Institute of Renaissance Studies] established by the
English Department of Stanford University
in association with the Oregon
Shakespeare Festival.   Privately
published and sponsored by the Oregon
Shakespeare Festival, Southern Oregon
College and Stanford University of
California.   (Ashland, Ore.)
   ports. illus. maps. plans. genealogical
tables. facsimiles. bibliog.   1954-
666259

—— British theatre [edited by] P.Noble.
[With a biographical index and containing references to Shakespearean
productions, 1939-46]-   Ports.
Illus.

572015

—— CENTRAL LITERARY MAGAZINE
Special celebration number, William
Shakespeare 1564-1964. April 1964.

740859

—— [COMING EVENTS, February, 1964.]
Shakespeare. pp.22.

illus.   668223

—— THE DRACONIAN.   [Numbers containing
reports, etc., of the annual
Shakespearian productions.   [Oxford]
1918-63.

458725

—— The Drama; or, Theatrical Pocket
Magazine, Vols. 1-3 (May, 1821-
December, 1822.) [Containing
Shakespearian references.]
3 vols.
1821-2.

496188

—— ENGLISH: [Essays on Shakespeare]
Vol. 15: No. 86.   1964.

Pt. of 481151

—— ENGLISH STUDIES. XLV: II
Shakespeare Centenary number.
(Amsterdam)   1964.

485643/64

—— History today, February 1964 [:
Shakespeare issue].

illus.   667985

—— THE LISTENER and BB C Television Review,
Vol.LXXI, No.1830, April 23, 1964.
Shakespeare birthday number.

illus.   668225

—— THE LITERARY CRITERION
Special number on Shakespeare.
Vol.6, Winter, No.1. (Bombay) 1963.

756155

—— The Mask: a journal of the art of the
theatre.   Vols. 1-2; 4-15 (1909-1929).
(London and Florence)
   illus. plans. dgms. 14 vols. 1908-1929.
Not published 1916-17, 1919-22.
Ceased publication after 1929.   Vol. 3
wanting.   Vol. 8 (1918) issued as
monthly leaflet.   All but Nos. 2-3
wanting.

460751

—— THE MASK: a satirical review of the week
in caricatures, edited and illustrated
by Alfred Thompson. Nos. 1 to 14.
1879.

illus.   152836

—— The Monthly mirror, reflecting men
and manners.   With strictures on
their epitome, the stage [including
references to Shakespeare].   Vols. 1
and 3.
   2 vols.   ports.   illus.   [1795-7.]
All other volumes wanting.

520768

—— OLD VIC MAGAZINE: official organ of
the Old Vic Theatre.
   Vol. 1 (Oct. 1919-May 1920)-Vol. 11
(Sept. 1929-Dec. 1930)   11 vols.
1919-30.
   Continued as The Old Vic and Sadler's
Wells Magazine, catal. no. 397473.

326002

—— OLD VIC AND SADLER'S WELLS MAGAZINE:
the official organ of both theatres.
Vol. 1 (1931)-Vol. 7 (1938-39).
7 vols.   1931-39.
   Previously issued as The Old Vic
Magazine, catal. no. 326002.
Ceased publication.
397473

—— OXYGEN NEWS
Shakespeare among Indians. Reprint of
a supplement issued to mark the
Quatercentenary of William Shakespeare.
(Calcutta)   [1964.]

illus.   744154

—— Pasadena Playhouse News.   Vol. 14
(Nov.1935-June 1936) - Vol. 20 (July-
August, 1941).   (Pasadena, Cal.)
   ports.   illus.   1935-
Wants Vols. 1-13, Vol. 14, Nos. 1-9.
Vol. 15, No. 2 not published.
472444

—— PHILOLOGICAL QUARTERLY, Vol.45, No.1.
January. Essays in English neoclassicism
in memory of Charles B. Woods. (Iowa
City)   1966.

767563

—— Play pictorial: an illustrated
monthly journal.   Vols. 1, 3-[75].
[With programmes of, and articles
on Shakespearean performances.]
77 vols.   ports.   illus.
1902-[1939]

571864

—— Play Pictorial: the Stratford-upon-Avon
Festival, 1936. [Illustrated
souvenir.] pp.20.

1936.

450644

—— Play Pictorial, Vol.74, No.443.
    Diamond Jubilee Festival, Stratford-
    upon-Avon, 1939. pp. 20. Illus.

                            504804

—— PLAYS AND PLAYERS: Shakespeare
    birthday number, Vol. 2, No. 7.
    pp. 32.
      ports. illus. tables. 1955.

                            647239

—— PLAYS AND PLAYERS & THEATRE WORLD,
    Vols. 13— 1966—
                            766347

    see also Theatre World

——'POEL (WILLIAM)
    **Monthly letters written for the
    Shakespeare League Journal**, Nos. 1-52.
                            1915-19.

                    665890

        Includes autograph letter by W.Poel.

—— POEL (WILLIAM)
    Monthly letters [on Shakespeare's life
    and art, and the production of his
    plays, privately circulated among
    members of the London Shakespeare League
    and their friends, 1912-1924.   Selected
    and arranged [with foreword] by A. M. T.
      port.   1929.

                            362873

——A REVIEW OF ENGLISH LITERATURE
    Shakespeare number. Guest editor K.
    Muir. V: 2, April 1964   1964.

                        697306/64

—— ST. PANCRAS BOROUGH COUNCIL
    St. Pancras Journal. Vol.17, No.11.
                        1964.
    Shakespeare Quatercentenary Celebration
    Number.   740863

——SHAKESPEARE ASSOCIATION OF AMERICA
    Bulletin, Vol. 1 (1924) — Vol. 24
    (1949). [With annual bibliographies
    from 1927.] (New York)
      ports. illus. 24 vols. 1924-49.
    Wants Vol. 1, No. 3.   Continued as
    Shakespeare Quarterly, Catal. no. 605711.

                            400135

—— The Shakespeare Fellowship News-letter,
    1943, 1945-58.   (The Shakespeare
    Fellowship)
      15 vols.   1943-58.
    1944 wanting.   Continued by
    "Shakespearean authorship review".

                            666183

——Shakespeare Fellowship Quarterly [: a
    periodical attempting to prove that
    Edward de Vere, Earl of Oxford, wrote
    the works of Shakespeare].   Vols. 1-9.
    (New York)
      ports. illus. map. 9 vols.
                            1939-48.
    Vols. 1-4 called News letter.   All
    published.
                            562696

—— Shakespeare International Alliance,
    No. 2, April 1914.   1914.
    All others wanting.   Printed for
    private circulation only.

                            535364

——The Shakespeare Newsletter.   Vol. 1—
    (New York)
      ports. illus.   1951—

                            666182

——Shakespeare Quarterly, No. 1, Summer
    1948.   Issued under the auspices of
    the Austrian Shakespeare Society.
      ports. illus.   1948.
    All published.

                            610897

——The Shakespeare Quarterly Vol. 1—
    (Bethlehem, Pa.: Shakespeare
    Association of America)
      ports. illus.   1950—
    Previously issued as Shakespeare
    Association of America Bulletin, see
    catal. no. 400135.

                            605711

—— The Shakespeare Stage: the quarterly
    bulletin of the Shakespeare Stage
    Society, Nos. 1-7.   1953-54.

                            666647

——SHAKESPEARE STUDIES: an annual gathering
    of research, criticism, and reviews.
    Edited by J. Leeds Barroll. [Vol.] 1—
    (Cincinnati, Ohio)   1965—

                        750317

—— Shakespeare Survey: an annual survey
    of Shakespearian study & production.
    [Vol.] 1—   [With] indexes.
    (Cambridge)
      ports. illus. plans. dgms.
      tables. facsimiles. bibliogs.
                            1948—

                            590674

——Shakespeare Survey list of books and
    articles.   [Bibliographies taken
    from Shakespeare Survey, edited by
    A. Nicoll.]
      typescript.   1946-58.

                            596641

——Shakespearean Authorship Review, Nos.
    1— (The Shakespearian Authorship
    Society)   1959—
    Formerly "The Shakespeare Fellowship
    News-Letter".

                            666271

——SHOW: the magazine of the arts. A special
    report on the Bard today. Vol.IV, No.2:
    February 1964. (New York)   1964.

      illus.   740825

——Silver falcon. Published by the
    Shakespeare Society, Hunter
    College of the City of New York.
    pp.28.

                (New York)   1936.

                            598969

—The SKETCH: an illustrated miscellany of
music, the drama, society and the belles.
Nos. 2 to 76   1879-80

illus.   60199

—Stage, The; or, Theatrical Inquisitor,
Vol.1, 1828; Vol.2, Nos. 8-10,
1829. [Containing Shakespearian
articles.] Illus. 2 vols.
                               1828-29.

(i) Wants Vol.2, No.11 and any after.
(ii) No. 1 imperfect.

                                443576

—The Stage [with references to
Shakespearian performances].   Vol. 1
(1874)-
ports.   illus.
Wants Vol. 1, Nos. 1, 5, 7 (1874);
Vol. 2, all after No. 1 (1875); Vols.
3-44 (1876-1917); [Vol. 63] (1936).
Vols. [56], [58] imperfect.
                                59615

—"The Stage" year book.
Ports.Illus.

                   [1949]

                                597470

—Stratford-upon-Avon Herald and South
Warwickshire Advertiser, 15th June,
1957. [An illustrated account of
the visit of Queen Elizabeth and
Prince Philip to Stratford, June 14th,
1957.]   pp. 8.

                                665542

—Stratford-upon-Avon Scene, incorporating
Shakespeare Pictorial.   Vol. 1-3.
(Stratford-upon-Avon)
ports.   illus.   1946-50.
For Shakespeare Pictorial see catal.
no. 348579.
                                574721

—The Swan of Avon: a quarterly devoted
to new Shakespearian research,
Vol. 1, Nos. 1-3 (March-September
1948).   (Santa Barbara, Cal.:
Melander Shakespeare Society) 1948.
With additional corrected copy of
Vol. 1, No. 1.
All published.
                                618019

—Tallis's Dramatic Magazine and general
theatrical and musical review
[1850-1853].
ports. illus. 3 vols.   [1850-3].
1851 entitled Tallis's Drawing Room
Table Book.   From 1852-3 entitled
Tallis's Shakespere Gallery of
Engravings.
                                633014

—Theatre. Issued from the Bradford
Civic Playhouse. No.1- 11.   Illus.
Dgms.

       (Bradford)   1945-8.

                                562117

—Theatre notebook: a quarterly of
notes and research.   Vol. 1.
illus.   plans.   dgms.   1945-

                                584117

—Theatre Today, Nos. 1-[8].
ports. illus. plans. facsimiles.
                              1946-[9]
All published.   No. 8 entitled
Film and Theatre Today.
                                606680

—THEATRE WORLD, Vols. 41-61. Illus.
                              1945-65.

1. Vols. 1-40 wanting.
2. After Vol.61, No.491 incorporated
   in Plays and Players and called
   "Plays and Players & Theatre
   World".   Catal. no. 766347.

                                601552

—Theatrical Observer and Daily Bills
of the Play, No. 148, May 7, 1822-
No. 774, May 25, 1824.
3 vols.
Various numbers of 1822-24 and all
others wanting.
                                414174

—TIME [MAGAZINE]
Shakespeare, Midsummer Night's Box
Office.   [FROM "Time", July 4, 1960.]
pp. [12].   [Amsterdam]
ports.   illus.

                                667002

—WARWICKSHIRE & WORCESTERSHIRE MAGAZINE,
April, 1964. Shakespeare's anniversary
[: articles by various authors].
pp.35-43. (Leamington Spa)   1964.

                                728224

—The Warwickshire Journal: official
organ of the Warwickshire Rural
Community Council, Vol.1 (1938)-
[Containing Shakespearian articles].

    [Leamington Spa]   1938-51

                                481390

—THE WEEKLY ORACLE: or universal library,
No. 63.   [1737.]

                                60561

PERKIN (ROBERT L.)
Shakespeare in the Rockies: [reviews
of the Colorado Shakespeare Festival].
IN SHAKESPEARE QUARTERLY IX:1958, pp.
555-559; X:1959, pp. 587-591; XI:
1960, pp. 461-465; XII:1961, pp. 409-
413; XIII:1962, pp. 541-545; XIV:1963,
pp. 461-464; XV:1964, pp. 427-431;
XVII: 1966 pp. 423-426; XVIII: 1967,
pp. 417-420.   (New York)   605711

PERKINS, D.   C.
Model answers on Shakespeare's
'Henry IV, Part 1" [for General
Certificate of Education]. [Swansea]
                              [1966.]

                                759566

PERKINS, D. C.
Model answers on Shakespeare's
"Julius Caesar" [for General
Certificate of Education]. [Swansea]
1967.

767662

PERKINS, D.C.
Model answers on Shakespeare's
"Macbeth" [for General Certificate of
Education]. [Swansea]   1967.

763823

PERKINS, D.C.
Model answers on Shakespeare's
"Twelfth Night" [for General
Certificate of Education]. [Swansea]
1967.

763824

PERKINS (ELEANOR E.)
Prologue and epilogue.   IN RILEY
([Mrs.] ALICE C. D.) Shakespeare's
lovers in a garden: a flower masque.
Re-edited by the author.   pp. 32.
(Chicago: Drama League of America)
1927.   407981
_____ Music [by various composers.]
(Chicago)   [c.1927.]   407982

Perkinson (R.H.) [Review of] The True
text of King Lear, by L.Kirschbaum.
In Modern Language Quarterly,Vol.7.

(Seattle)   1946.

584762

PERKINSON (RICHARD HENRY)
Shakespeare's revision of the Lear story
and the structure of King Lear. [With
bibliographical notes.]   FROM Philological Quarterly, Vol. 22.   (Iowa City)
1943.

563274

PERRY (T. A.)
Emerson, the historical frame, and
Shakespeare.   IN Modern Language
Quarterly, Vol. 9.   (Seattle)
bibliog.   1948.

525289/9

PERRY (THOMAS A.)
Proteus, wry-transformed traveller.
IN SHAKESPEARE QUARTERLY V.
pp. 33-40.
(New York) 1954.

605711

Perry (W.) A Treatise on the identity
of Herne's Oak, shewing the maiden
tree to have been the real one.
pp.xii, 70. Illus.

1867.

-Presentation copy bound with a panel
of wood from the Oak on front cover.

474046

Persia

----AHMAD KHAN
Persian homage.   IN Gollancz ([Sir] I.)
ed., A Book of homage to Shakespeare.
ports.   illus.   facsimiles.
[1916]

264175

----DRAPER (JOHN WILLIAM)
Shakespeare and Abbas the Great.
IN Philological Quarterly, Vol. 30.
(Iowa)   1951.

592684/30

PERSICO (Count)
Romeo and Juliet.   [The Tomb of Juliet,
and Count Persico's story of Romeo
and Juliet.   IN The Portfolio of
entertaining and instructive varieties
in history, literature, science, &c.,
[New Series], No. 17, Nov. 14, 1829.
illus.   1929.

519904

Personality of Shakespeare *see* Shakespeare, William

Perspectives in Criticism
LANDRY, HILTON
Interpretations in Shakespeare's
sonnets.   1963.

667701

Perth

----BAXTER (P.)
The Drama in Perth: a history of
Perth's early plays, playhouses, play
bills, pageants, concerts, etc.
[With references to Shakespeare.]
(Perth)
illus.   1907.

575225

PERUGINI (MARK EDWARD)
The Omnibus box: social and theatrical
life in London and Paris, 1830-1850.
[Containing references to Shakespearean
performances of C. Kean.]
ports.   illus.   1933.

521174

PERUGINI (MARK EDWARD)
A Pageant of the dance & ballet
[: history from ancient times to
the present day. With references
to Shakespeare.]
  bibliog. ports. illus. chronological table.   1935.

               469985

[PETERSFIELD, Steep Shakespeare Players
Programmes, etc. of performances,
1926-1961. (Petersfield)

               464481

Petersham (Mrs. Maud and Miska)
LAMB (CHARLES and MARY [A.])
Tales from Shakespeare. Edited [with
an introduction] by A. Ainger. Revised
by H. Y. Maffett.   1932.
  New Pocket Classics.

               399214

PETERSON (DOUGLAS L.)
A Probable source for Shakespeare's
Sonnet CXXIX.
  IN SHAKESPEARE QUARTERLY V.
  pp. 381-384.
  (New York) 1954.

               605711

PETERSON, DOUGLAS L.
"Romeo and Juliet" and the art of moral
navigation.
IN Pacific coast studies in
Shakespeare. Edited by W. F. McNeir
and T. N. Greenfield. (Eugene: Ore.)
               1966.

               768009

PETERSON (DOUGLAS L.)
"Wisdom consumed in confidence": an
examination of Shakespeare's Julius
Caesar.
  IN SHAKESPEARE QUARTERLY XVI: 1.
  pp. 19-28.
  (New York) 1965.

               605711

Peterson (H.) The Lonely debate: dilemmas
from Hamlet to Hans Castorp.

     (New York)   1938.

               484763

    Petiška (Eduard). A Midsummer
night's dream: retold for children.
Photographs of puppets by J. Trnka.
[Translated by Jean Layton.] pp.35.
               1960.

               666875

PETTET (E. C.)
Coriolanus and the Midlands insurrec-
tion of 1607.   IN SHAKESPEARE
SURVEY 3. (Cambridge)   1950.

               606026

PETTET (E. C.)
Hot irons and fever: a note on some
of the imagery of "King John".   IN
Essays in Criticism, Vol. 4.   (Oxford)
    1954.

             621866/4

PETTET (E. C.)
The Imagery of "Romeo and Juliet".
IN English: the magazine of the English
Association, Vol. 8.   1950.

             481151/8

Pettet (E.C.) The Merchant of Venice
  and the problem of usury. In English
  Association, Essays and studies,
  Vol.31, 1945. Collected by V. de S.
  Pinto.

      (Oxford)   1946.

             571260

PETTET (E. C.)
[Review of] From Shakespeare to
Joyce, by E. E. Stoll.   IN English:
the magazine of the English
Association, Vol. 5.   (Oxford)
             1944-45.

             569018

PETTET (E. C.)
Shakespeare and the romance tradition.
With an introduction by H. S. Bennett.
  bibliogs.   1949.

             604783

PETTET (E. C.)
Shakespeare's conception of poetry.
IN English Association, Essays and
Studies, New Series, Vol. 3.   1950.

             610517

PETTET (E. C.)
Timon of Athens: the disruption of
feudal morality.   [With bibliographical
notes.]   IN The Review of English
Studies, Vol. 23.   (Oxford)   1947.

          318239/23

Pettigrew (Helen P.) Bassanio, the
  Elizabethan lover. [With bibliograph
  ical notes.] From Philological
  quarterly, Vol. 16.

     (Iowa)   1937.

             484073

PETTY (JOAN M.)
A Study of Winterset especially in the
light of Hamlet: Columbia University
[thesis] 1948.   IN GOLDING (NANCY L.)
A Survey of the proposed arrangements
of Shakespeare's Sonnets [etc.]
  bibliog.   microfilm, positive copy.
              [1948.]

             609350

PEYRE, HENRY MAURICE
Shakespeare and modern French
criticism. IN SCHUELLER, HERBERT M.,
ed., The Persistence of Shakespeare
idolatry. Essays in honour of
Robert W. Babcock. (Detroit) 1964.

             668300

PEYRE (HENRI [MAURICE])
Writers and their critics: a study
of misunderstanding [with references
to Shakespeare, and bibliographical
notes.] (Ithaca, N.Y.)   1944.
  Cornell University. Messenger Lectures
on the Evolution of Civilization, 1943.

             560639

Peyre (H.M.) ed., Essays in honor of
Albert [G.] Feuillerat [by various
writers. With a preface by C.Seymour,
bibliographical references and a
bibliography of the works of
A.G.Feuillerat, including his books
and articles on Shakespeare].

(New Haven [Conn.])   1943.

(Yale Romanic Studies, 22.)

560305

Pfister (G. A.) trans.
GATTI (G. M.)
The Two "Macbeths".   [A discussion
on Verdi's "Macbeth", and Bloch's
"Macbeth".   Translated from the Italian.]
IN The Sackbut, Vol. 3.   1923.

307946

Pforzheimer, Carl H. *works relating to*

— The Carl H. Pforzheimer Library,
English literature, 1475-1700 [: a
catalogue compiled by Emma V. Unger
and W. A. Jackson.   With a section
on Shakespeare].   (New York)
3 vols.   port.   illus.   facsimiles.
                              1940.
Privately printed.   No. 130 of an
edition limited to 150 copies.

539193

Phelps (C.H.) Shylock vs. Antonio: a
brief for plaintiff on appeal. In
The Atlantic monthly, vol.57.

(Boston,[Mass.])   1886.

84834

Phelps (H.P.) Hamlet from the actors'
standpoint: its representatives, and
a comparison of their performances.
[With a bibliography.] Ports.

(New York)   1890.

450749

Phelps (H.P.) Players of a century : a
record of the Albany stage, including
notices of prominent actors who have
appeared in America.   [With references
to Shakespeare.] 2nd edn.   Ports.

(Albany)   1880.

499293

Phelps, Samuel *works relating to*

—ALLEN (SHIRLEY)
A Successful people's theatre:
Samuel Phelps at Sadler's Wells
[and his presentation of
Shakespearean drama there].
IN Theatre Arts, Vol. 28.   (New York)
port.   illus.   1944.

558366

—Coleman (J.) [and] Coleman (E.)
Memoirs of Samuel Phelps. Port.

1886.

432386

—KENNEY (C. L.)
Mr. Phelps and the critics of his
correspondence with the Stratford
Committee.   [Shakespeare Tercentenary
Commemoration.]   pp. 8.   1864.

554142

—MORLEY (H.)
Phelps at Sadler's Wells [as Bottom
in Midsummer Night's Dream].   IN
WARD (A. C.) [ed.] Specimens of English
dramatic criticism, 17-20 centuries;
selected and introduced.   (Oxford) 1945.
The World's Classics.

563732

——[Portraits etc. of Samuel Phelps.]
ff.26.

[c.1830-c.1880]
437280

Phelps (W.L.) Notes on Shakespeare.
In Proceedings of the American
Philosophical Society, Vol.81.

1939.

518318

PHELPS (WILLIAM LYON)
A Plea for Charles the wrestler.
IN GOLLANCZ ([Sir] I.) ed., A Book of
homage to Shakespeare.
ports.   illus.   facsimiles.   [1916.]

264175

PHIALAS, PETER G.
Hamlet and the grave-maker. FROM
Journal of English and Germanic
Philology, Vol. 63, No.2.   1964.

pp.226-234.   756154

PHIALAS (PETER G.)
The Medieval in Richard II.
IN SHAKESPEARE QUARTERLY XII: 3.
pp. 305-310.
(New York)   1961.

605711

PHIALAS, PETER G.
'Richard II' and Shakespeare's tragic
mode. FROM Studies in Literature and
Language, Vol.V, No.3, Autumn 1963.
(Austin, Tex.)

756152

PHIALAS, PETER G.
Shakespeare's Henry V and the second
tetralogy. FROM Studies in Philology,
Vol.62: No. 2. (Chapel Hill, N.C.)
1965.

pp.155-175   756153

PHIALAS, PETER G.
Shakespeare's romantic comedies: the
development of their form and meaning.
(Chapel Hill, N.C.)   1966.

764560

Philadelphia, U.S.A.

——HANEY (J. L.)
Shakespeare and Philadelphia: an
address delivered before the City
Society of Philadelphia, November 28,
1934. pp. 41-73. (Philadelphia)
bibliog.   1936.
City History Society of Philadelphia,
Philadelphia History, Vol. 4, No. 3.

481972

——Jackson (J.) The Shakespeare tradition
in Philadelphia. In The
Pennsylvania Magazine, vol.40.

(Philadelphia)   1916.

410676

—— JAMES (R. D.)
Old Drury of Philadelphia: a history
of the Philadelphia stage, 1800-1835.
Including the Diary of W. B. Wood,
co-manager with W. Warren.
illus.   1932.

400591

—— PAUL (H. N.)
Shakespeare in Philadelphia.
IN Proceedings of the American
Philosophical Society, Vol. 76.
(Philadelphia)   1936.

463924

——POLLOCK (T. C.)
The Philadelphia theatre in the
eighteenth century, together with the
Day Book of the same period. [With
Shakespearian references.]
(Philadelphia)   1933.

440540

—— SAVAGE (HENRY L.)
The Shakspere Society of Philadelphia.
IN SHAKESPEARE QUARTERLY III: 4.
pp. 341-352.
(New York) 1952.

605711

—— WILSON (A.H.)
A History of the Philadelphia theatre,
1835 to 1855. [With Shakespearian
references]. (Philadelphia)   1935.

440184

Philadelphia City History Society Publications (Vol. 4, No. 3.)
HANEY (J. L.)
Shakespeare and Philadelphia: an
address delivered before the City
History Society of Philadelphia,
November 28, 1934.   [With a bibliography.] pp. 41-73.   (Philadelphia)
frontis.   1936.

481972

[PHILARETES, pseud.]
Work for chimny-sweepers; or, A
Warning for tobacconists. 1601.
With an introduction by S. H. Atkins.
1936.
Shakespeare Association Facsimiles,
No. 11.

452705

[PHILAZCHAIOTETOS]
Another Shaksperian pedigree, and
"Shakspere" the true mode of spelling
the name [by] $\Phi\iota\lambda\alpha\zeta\chi\alpha\iota o\tau\eta\tau os$.
FROM The Gentleman's Magazine, Jan.1817.
pp. [8.]   1817.

402687

PHILBRICK (NORMAN)
Act and scene division in the first
edition of Shakespeare [i.e. in
N. Rowe's edition of 1709. With
bibliographical references].   IN
The Theatre annual; a publication of
information and research in the arts
and history of the theatre, 1944.
(New York: Theatre Library Association)
illus.   facsimiles.   1945.

563989

PHILIPS, AMBROSE
Humfrey, Duke of Gloucester

For editions of this play see under
English Editions: Henry the Sixth,
Part II: Alterations &c.

Philips, Ambrose *works relating to*

——BRYAN (A. J.)
Ambrose Philips's Humfrey, Duke of
Gloucester: a study in eighteenth-
century adaptation.   IN CAFFEE (N. M.)
and KIRBY (T. A.) eds., Studies for
William A. Read.   (Louisiana)
port.   bibliog.   1940.

517139

PHILIPS, PETER, and others
Music from Shakespeare's day [: Trio
in the Phrygian mode, by P. Philips;
Hexachord fantasy, by W. Daman;
Canzonet (Hold out, my heart), by T.
Morley, Fantasia, by T. Lupo] for three
recorders. Transcribed by J. Newman.
(New York)   1964.

American Recorder Society Editions
No.51.   745452

Phillipps (James Orchard Halliwell-)
see Halliwell-Phillipps (J. O.)

PHILLIPPS (Sir T.)
A New notice of Shakespeare [in the
will of T. Whyttyngton of Shottre].
IN Archaeologia, Vol. 32.   1847.

27491

PHILLIPS (ADDISON LEROY)
Letting Shakespeare live again.
FROM Education, Vol. 58.   (Boston,
Mass.)   1938.

512382

PHILLIPS (E.)
William Shakespeare.   IN Phillips (E.)
Theatrum poetarum Anglicanorum.
Enlarged [edn.]   (Canterbury)
bibliog.   1800.

536162

PHILLIPS (GERALD WILLIAM) [pseud. JOHN
HUNTINGTON]
Lord Burghley in Shakespeare: Falstaff,
Sly and others.   1936.

456935

PHILLIPS (GERALD WILLIAM) [pseud.
John Huntingdon]
Shake spears sonnets, addressed to
members of the Shakespeare Fellow-
ship. pp. 23.   1954.
   Privately printed.

645438

PHILLIPS (GERALD WILLIAM)
Sunlight on Shakespeare's sonnets [:
with the text of the Sonnets].
                             1935.

432263

PHILLIPS (GERALD WILLIAM)
The Tragic story of "Shakespeare",
disclosed in the sonnets, and the life
of Edward de Vere, 17th Earl of Oxford.
                             1932.

393565

PHILLIPS (H. C. B.)
Literature: its relation to life.
[A lecture on Shakespeare's four
tragedies, Hamlet, Othello, Macbeth
and King Lear.] Bookshop practice:
talks on books and the bookshop.
No. 8.   FROM The Publishers' Circular,
December 12th, 1936. pp. [4.]
                             1936.

462918

PHILLIPS (HUBERT)
Shakespeare [: questions and answers].
                             [1947.]
News Chronicle "Quiz" [Series] No. 8.

583520

PHILLIPS (J. E.)
Adapted from a play by W. Shakespeare
[: Laurence Olivier's film production
of "Henry V", and the Old Vic radio
presentation of "Richard III" for
the Columbia Broadcasting System,
June 1946]. IN Hollywood Quarterly,
Vol. 2.   (Berkeley, Cal.)   1946-7.

592680/2

PHILLIPS (JAMES EMERSON)
Julius Caesar: Shakespeare as a screen
writer.   IN The Quarterly of Film
Radio and Television, Vol. 8.
(Berkeley, Cal.)   1953.

630462/8

PHILLIPS (JAMES EMERSON)
The State in Shakespeare's Greek and
Roman plays.   (New York)
 bibliog.   1940.
Columbia University Studies in English
and Comparative Literature No. 149.

522036

PHILLIPS, JAMES EMERSON
"The Tempest" and the Renaissance idea
of man.   IN McMANAWAY, JAMES GILMER,
ed., Shakespeare 400: essays by
American scholars on the anniversary
of the poet's birth.   Published in
co-operation with the Shakespeare
Association of America.
 illus.   1964.

667803

Phillips, James Emerson *works relating to*

——STIRLING (B.)
[Review of] The State in Shakespeare's
Greek and Roman plays, by J. E. Phillips.
IN Modern Language Quarterly, Vol. 2.
(Seattle)   1941.

533242

——TEETER (L.)
[Review of] The State in Shakespeare's
Greek and Roman plays, by J. E. Phillips.
IN Modern Language Notes, Vol. 58.
(Baltimore)   1943.

553688

Phillips (Leroy) and Crawford (Mary
M.) Shakespeare as we like him.
From The English Journal, December
1937.

(Chicago)   1937.

503861

Phillips (Mrs.), Marsh (F.) [and]
Vick (H.) Characters from the country: the Uley Village Players:
[a talk between] Mrs. Phillips [and
two members of her company,] F.
Marsh [and] H. Vick. [With references to Shakespearian productions.
Broadcast in] Midland programme, 2nd
August, 1938. ff. 6.

1938.

486181

PHILLIPS (M. F.)
It was a lover and his lass: four-
part song. Words [from As you
like it]. Music by M. F. Phillips.
[Supplement from]The Musical Times,
No. 1177. pp. 8. 1941.

524588

PHILLIPS (MONTAGUE FAWCETT)
Sigh no more, ladies: four-part song.
Words by Shakespeare [from "Much ado
about nothing]. pp. 8. 1948.
Novello's Part-song Book [No.] 1543.

599943

PHILLIPS (M. F.)
Under the greenwood tree: trio
for S.S.A. (unaccompanied). pp. 4.
1948.
Novello['s] Trios and Quartets for
Female and Boy's Voices.
597274

PHILLIPS, OWEN HOOD
The Law relating to Shakespeare,
1564-1964, [Parts] I, II. FROM The
Law Quarterly Review, April & July 1964.
1964.

740584

PHILLIPS (WILLIAM JOHN)
France on Byron: a dissertation
presented to the [University of
Pennsylvania] for the degree of Doctor
of Philosophy. [With references to
Shakespeare]. pp. 81. (Philadelphia:
University of Pennsylvania)
bibliog. 1941.

532151

PHILOLOGICAL QUARTERLY, Vol.45, No.1.
January. Essays in English neoclassicism
in memory of Charles B. Woods. (Iowa
City) 1966.

767563

Philosophy and Religion
see also Anthroposophy; Bible; Catholicism;
Death in Shakespeare; Dreams; Freemasonry;
Freewill and Determinism; Honour;
Humanism; Justice; Karma; Love, Courtship
and Marriage; Man and Nature; Morality;
Occultism; Patriotism; Platonism; Prayer
Book; Puritanism; Revenge; School of Night;
Science; Sin; Spiritualism; Stoicism; Sunday;
Supernatural; Theosophy; Truth

——Allen (D.C.) The Degeneration of man
and Renaissance pessimism. [With
references to Shakespeare.] From
Studies in Philology, Vol. 35.

[Chapel Hill, N.C.] 1938.

503671

——[Andrews (Constance E.)] The Transcenden-
talism of Shakespeare. From The
Church of the New Age Magazine,
June- Oct., 1933.

(Manchester) 1933.

438982

——Bacon (Delia [S.]) The Philosophy
of the plays of Shakspere unfolded.
With a preface by N. Hawthorne.

(Boston) 1857.

475380

——Banks (P.) Modern European drama and
religion [:with references to Shakespeare.] From The Aryan path, Vol.5.

(Bombay) 1934.

484130

___BATEN (A. M.)
The Philosophy of Shakespeare. [With
an introductory by De W. McMurray and
a bibliography]. (Kingsport,
Tennessee)
ports. 1937.

481130

___BATTENHOUSE (R. W.)
Measure for Measure and Christian
doctrine of the atonement. [With
bibliographical notes.] IN Publications of the Modern Language Association of America, Vol. 61. (Menasha,
Wis.) 1946.

581301

___BATTENHOUSE, ROY W.
Shakespearean tragedy: a Christian
approach. IN RABKIN, NORMAN, ed.,
Approaches to Shakespeare [: 20th
century critical essays]. (New
York) 1964.

668298

—— BAYNE (R.)
 Religion.   IN Shakespeare's England,
 Vol. 1.   (Oxford)
 bibliogs.   illus.   facsimiles.
  1917.

  435745

—— Bethell (S.L.) Poetry and belief.
 [With references to Shakespeare.]
 From Theology, July, 1939.

  1939.

  502655

—— BICKERSTETH (G. L.)
 The Philosophy of Shakespeare.
 FROM Aberdeen University Review, Vol.
 28.   (Aberdeen)   1941.

  535118

—— BROPHY (J.)
 Body and soul [: the relationship
 between them.   With references to
 Shakespeare's philosophy.]
 ports.   illus.   1948.

  591052

—— Broszinski (H.) Christian reality in
 "Macbeth".   From [Theology, Vol.
 50].   pp. [7.]

  [1947.]

  596214

—— Brucker (Louise H.M.) King Lear: an
 astro- philosophic interpretation.
 From Rosicrucian Magazine, February,
 1934.

  (Oceanside, Cal.   1934

  421108

—— BRYANT (J.   A.   )

 Hippolyta's view: some Christian aspects
 of Shakespeare's plays. Bibliog.
 [Lexington, Ky.]   1961.

  666829

—— Cadoux (A.T.) Shakespearean selves:
 an essay in ethics.

  1938.

  484522

—— CARR (JOHN) ed.
 What Shakespeare says: a Christian
 anthology.   pp. 60.   (Dublin)
 glossary.   1956.

  665319

—— CARTER (H.)
 The Spirit of Shakespeare: an hypothesis.
 IN The Quest, Vol. 11.   1920.

  408732

—— CHEVERTON (F. J.)
 Shakespeare's day [his religious message]:
 a sermon preached in Rowley Church,
 18th April, 1926 by the Rev. F.J.
 Cheverton;   [and] Stray thoughts on
 the sermon subject.   IN Rowley Regis
 Parish Church [Magazine] April 1926.
  1926.

  384946

—— CHOE, JAISOU
 Shakespeare's art as order of life.
 (New York)   1965.

  746859

—— COURSEN (HERBERT R.)
 In deepest consequence: "Macbeth".
 IN SHAKESPEARE QUARTERLY XVIII: 4.
 pp. 375-388.
 (New York)   1967.

  605711

—— CRAIG (HARDIN)
 A Cutpurse of the Empire: on
 Shakespeare cosmology.   IN WILLIAMS
 (A. L.) ed., A Tribute to George Coffin
 Taylor.   [Chapel Hill, N.C.]   1952.

  625745

—— Craig (H.) The Enchanted glass: the
 Elizabethan mind in literature.
 [With bibliographical notes, and
 references to Shakespeare].

  (New York)   1936.

  457122

—— CRAIG (H.)
 Shakespeare and the normal world.
 In The Rice Institute Pamphlet, Vol. 31.
  (Houston, Texas.)   1944.

  563555

—— CURRY (WALTER CLYDE)
 Shakespeare's philosophical patterns
 [as exhibited in "Macbeth" and "The
 Tempest".]   (Baton Rouge, La.)
  1937.   472128
 ——— 2nd edn.   bibliog.
  1959.   666437

—— Dennis (J.) Shakespeare's wise words
 [with quotations]. In The Leisure
 Hour, 1892.

  1892.

  115780

—— DOSSETOR, F.
 Religion in Shakespeare.
 IN PRITCHETT, VICTOR SAWDON, and
 others, Shakespeare: the comprehensive
 soul.   [Talks on the B.B.C.
 European English Service to celebrate
 the Shakespearian Quatercentenary.]
  1965.

  746585

—— DRAPER (JOHN WILLIAM)
 The Prince-philosopher and
 Shakespeare's Hamlet.   [With biblio-
 graphical references.]   FROM West
 Virginia University Studies III.
 Philological Papers, Vol. 2.
 (Morgantown, W. Va.)   1937.
 West Virginia University Bulletin.

  552428

—— Du Cann (C.G.L.) Other people's gods,
 III. The God of Shakespeare [: a
 suggestion that Shakespeare was a
 Freethinker]. From [The Freethinker,
 May 19th, 1946.]

  1946.

  579652

——EASTMAN (FRED) [pseud. Richard Morse]
Christ in the drama: the influence
of Christ on the drama of England
and America. The Shaffer Lectures
of Northwestern University, 1946.
(New York)
bibliog.   1947.

693407

——ECKHOFF (LORENTZ)
Shakespeare: spokesman of the third
estate. English translation by
R. I. Christophersen. (Oslo)
1954.
Oslo Studies in English No. 3.

647413

——EDWARDS, PHILIP W.
Shakespeare and the confines of art.
1968.

771308

——   Elliott (S.H.) Religion and
dramatic art, [containing a chapter
on Shakespeare.]

1927.

404178

——Ellis (O.C. de C.) Shakespeare as a
scientist, his philosophical background: a preliminary study of the
questionings explicit in his dialogue
and of the acceptances implicit in
his vocabulary. Reprinted from "The
Manchester Quarterly", July, 1933.
pp.3-43.
(Manchester)   1933.

536336

——Ferry (P.) The Deep implications of
Shakespeare's alleged Germanism. In
The Westminster review, Vol. 180.

1914.

248889

—— Fripp (E.I.) The Church of Shakespeare.
In The Modern churchman, Vol. 19.

(Oxford)   1929.

484171

—— FRYE (ROLAND MUSHAT)
Shakespeare and Christian doctrine.
1963.

667814

——GHURYE, (GOVIND SADASHIV)
Shakespeare on conscience and justice.
(Bombay)   1965.

763607

——Gill (F.C.) Homiletic values in
Shakespeare. From The London
Quarterly and Holborn Review,
October, 1937.
1937.

477470

——GRAVE (S. A.)
The Shakespearian pattern [: his view
of religion]. FROM [Theology, Vol.
50.]   [1947.]

587306

—— HANKINS (JOHN ERSKINE)
The Pains of the afterworld: fire,
wind and ice in Milton and
Shakespeare. IN P.M.L.A. Publications
of the Modern Language Association of
America, Vol. 71. (Menasha, Wis.)
1956.

428321/71

——HAPGOOD (ROBERT)
Shakespeare and the ritualists. IN
SHAKESPEARE SURVEY 15. (Cambridge)
1962.

667174

——HARRIS, BERNARD A.
Dissent and satire [: in Elizabethan
England]. IN SHAKESPEARE SURVEY 17.
(Cambridge)   1964.

667822

——HARRIS (F.)
The True Shakespeare: an essay in
realistic criticism, Parts 1-13.
[With quotations from the plays].
IN The Saturday Review, Vols. 85-86.
2 vols.   1898.

142978

——Harris (Mary Dormer) Shakespeare and
the religious drama. In Notes and
Queries, Vol.165.

1933.

416106

——HARRISON (CHARLES T.)
The Poet as witness [: the Christian
humanism of Dante and Shakespeare].
IN The Sewanee Review, Vol. 63.
(Sewanee, Tenn.)   1955.

641628/63

—— HARWOOD, ALFRED CECIL
Shakespeare's prophetic mind.
(Letchworth)   1964.

667829

——HAWKES, TERRY
Shakespeare and the reason: a study of
the tragedies and the problem plays.
1964.

668277

——HOLLIS (C.)
The Monstrous regiment [: the struggle
between Roman Catholicism and Protest-
antism, containing references to
Shakespeare's attitude towards
religion].   1929.

401683

——HOROWITZ, DAVID
Shakespeare: an existential view.
1965.
Studies in existentialism and
phenomenology.
768004

HUBLER (EDWARD)
    The Damnation of Othello: some limita-
    tions on the Christian view of the play.
    IN SHAKESPEARE QUARTERLY IX.
      pp. 295-300.
    (New York)   1958.
                         605711

HUTTAR, CHARLES A.
    The Christian basis of Shakespeare's
    Sonnet 146.
    IN SHAKESPEARE QUARTERLY XIX: 4.
      pp. 355-365.
    (New York)   1968.
                     605711

HUXLEY, ALDOUS LEONARD
    Shakespeare and religion.
    IN Aldous Huxley, 1894-1963: a
    memorial volume, edited by J. Huxley.
      illus.   1965.
                     746983

JAMES (D. G.)
    Scepticism and poetry: an essay on
    the poetic imagination. [With
    Shakespearian references.]   1937.
                     463037

JESSUP (BERTRAM)
    Philosophy in Shakespeare [: an Oregon
    Centennial Lecture delivered at the
    University of Oregon, April 8, 1959].
    pp.[ii],24. Bibliog. [Eugene]
                    1959.
                     666944

KAUFMANN (WALTER)
    Shakespeare: between Socrates and
    existentialism.   IN Kaufmann(W.)
    The Owl and the nightingale: from
    Shakespeare to existentialism [:
    review of European philosophy from
    1590 to date].
      bibliog.   1960.
                     692452

KENMARE (DALLAS) [pseud.]
    Shakespeare and Christianity.
    IN Kenmare (D.) [pseud.] The Face
    of truth: collected writings on
    poetry & religion. (Oxford:
    Shakespeare Head Press)   1939.
                     508981

             Kennedy (W.) Shakespeare's view
of human life. From Hibbert Journal,
Jan. 1933. ff. [14.]   1933.
                     402179

KNIGHT, GEORGE WILSON
    Shakespeare and religion: essays of
    forty years.   1967.
                     762034

KNIGHT, GEORGE WILSON
    Shakespeare and theology: a private
    protest. FROM Essays in Criticism, XV: 1.
    (Oxford)   1965.
      pp.95-104.   747548

KNIGHTS (LIONEL CHARLES)
    Some Shakespearean themes.
    bibliogs.   1959.
                     666303

KOENIGSBERGER (HANNELORE)
    The Untuned string: Shakespeare's
    concept of chaos. Microfilm,
    positive copy. (Ann Arbor, Mich.)
    Typescript, 1951. 1 reel, 35 mm.
                  [1952.]
    University Microfilms, Doctoral
    Dissertation Series.
                     647058

LAIRD (J.)
    Philosophical incursions into English
    literature. [With a chapter
    "Shakespeare on the wars of England"
    and bibliographical references.]
    (Cambridge)   1946.
                     576328

LAW (R. A.)
    Shakespeare in the Garden of Eden [and
    his interest in the two related theo-
    logical doctrines of the Fall of Man
    and Original Sin. With bibliographical
    notes]. IN University of Texas, Studies
    in English, [Vol. 21]. (Austin, Texas)
                    1941.
                     542174

LINGS, MARTIN
    Shakespeare in the light of sacred art.
                    1966.
                     751998

Lloyd (R.[B.]) The Rack of this
    tough world:christianity and King
    Lear.In The Quarterly Review,Vol.
    285.
                    1946.
                38702/285

MacCARTHY (SEÁN)
    Shakespeare the medievalist.
    FROM The Irish Ecclesiastical Record,
    Fifth Series Vol. 84. pp. [8].
    (Dublin)   1955.
                     665358

MASEFIELD (JOHN)
    Shakespeare and spiritual life. pp.
    32. (Oxford)   1924. 557231
    Romanes Lecture, 1924.
    200 copies printed; signed by the
    author.
          2nd impression.1924. 491857
          IN Masefield (J.) Recent prose.
    New and revised edn. 1932. 399415

MASSINGHAM (H. J.)
    The Tree of life. [With chapters on
    Shakespeare, dealing with his study
    of nature, philosophy and religion].
                    1943.
                     543975

MATTHEWS (HONOR M.   V.   )
    Character & symbol in Shakespeare's
    plays: a study of certain Christian and
    pre-Christian elements in their structure
    and imagery. (Cambridge)   1962.
                    667417

MENDL (ROBERT WILLIAM SIGISMUND)
Revelation in Shakespeare: a study of
the supernatural, religious and
spiritual elements in his art.   1964.

741028

MERCHANT, W. MOELWYN
Shakespeare's theology. IN A Review of
English Literature, October 1964.
1964.

697306

MOLDENHAWER (J. V.)
Shakespeare answers the query "What is
man?" FROM Anglican Theological
Review, Vol. 27.   (Evanston, Ill.)
1945.

593193

Morton (R.K.) The Faith of Shakespeare.
In Bibliotheca Sacra, vol.89.

(Pittsburgh,Pa.   1932.

405716

Morton (R.K.) Shakespeare : the man
and the message. From Education,
February 1934.

(Boston, Mass.)   1934.

503858

Moulton (R.G.) Shakespeare as a
dramatic thinker : a popular
illustration of fiction as the
experimental side of philosophy
[: a re-issue of "The Moral system
of Shakespeare."] New edn.

(New York)   1907.

491998

MUIR   KENNETH
"Timon of Athens" and the cash-nexus.
FROM The Modern quarterly miscellany,
No. 1.   [1947.]
pp. 57-76.

771893

Murry (J.M.) Heaven - and earth: [the
emergence of the modern world as
experienced by great minds; containing five chapters on Shakespeare and
other Shakespearian references.]

1938.

486666

Museus [pseud.] Shakespeare and the
life to come. In The Contemporary
review, Vol. 93.

1908.

208520

MYRICK (K. O.)
The Theme of damnation in Shakespearean
tragedy.   FROM Studies in Philology,
Vol. 38.   (Chapel Hill, N.C.) 1941.

529725

NAIK, M. K.
Humanitarianism in Shakespeare.
IN SHAKESPEARE QUARTERLY XIX: 2.
pp. 139-147.   (New York)
1968.

605711

NARASIMHAIAH (C. D.)
Ideas of self, sin, social impulse
and moral regeneration in
Shakespeare's plays.   IN The
Literary Criterion, Special number
on Shakespeare.   Vol. 6, Winter,
No. 1.   (Bombay)   1963.
pp. 94-110.

756155

NELSON (ROBERT JAMES)
Play within a play: the dramatist's
conception of his art; Shakespeare to
Anouilh. (Yale Romanic Studies: Second
Series, 5) (New Haven, [Conn.])
1958.

731490

Oakley (E.S.) Shakespeare's religion.
From The Congregational Quarterly,
Jan.,1935. pp.3.

[1935]

432016

OWST (G. R.)
Literature and pulpit in medieval
England: a neglected chapter in the
history of English letters & of the
English people.   [With references to
Shakespeare.]   (Cambridge) 1933.

402880

PARKER (MARION DOMINICA HOPE)
The Slave of life: a study of
Shakespeare and the idea of justice.
bibliog.   1955.

647932

PARSONS (PHILIP)
Shakespeare and the mask.
IN SHAKESPEARE SURVEY 16.
illus.   1963.

667523

Philosophy of William Shakespeare.
2nd edn.   1860.

474434

POPE (ELIZABETH MARIE)
Shakespeare on Hell.
IN SHAKESPEARE QUARTERLY I: 3.
pp. 162-164.
(New York) 1950.

605711

QUINN (MICHAEL)
Providence in Shakespeare's Yorkist
plays.
IN SHAKESPEARE QUARTERLY X: 1.
pp. 45-52.
(New York) 1959.

605711

RABKIN, NORMAN
Shakespeare and the common understanding.
(New York)   1967.

767392

RAMSEY (JAROLD W.)
Timon's imitation of Christ.
IN Shakespeare Studies, 2. (Cincinnati,
Ohio)   1966.

761781

The Religion of Shakespeare.   IN The
Modern Churchman, Vol. 6.
(Knaresborough)   1916–17.

565760

REYNOLDS (GEORGE FULLMER)

The Voice of Shakespeare. FROM
University of Colorado Studies,
Series in Language and Literature,
No.6.pp.[ii]12. (Boulder,Col.)
1957.

665716

ROBERTSON ([Rt. Hon.] J. M.)
A History of freethought, ancient
and modern, to the period of the
French Revolution.   [With references
to Shakespeare, a bibliography and a
biographical note of Robertson by
J. P. Gilmour].   4th edn., revised
and expanded.
ports.   2 vols.   1936.

455045

Rogers (L.W.) Shakespeare and theosophy.
In The Theosophist, Vol.58, Pt.1,

(Madras)   1937–

469480

Roscoe (J.E.)   Confessions of great
souls [: essays on religion in
literature, with references to
Shakespeare].

[c.1920.]

538352

Russell (A.J.) Their religion [i.e.
that of Abraham Lincoln, Robert
Burns, Shakespeare, etc.]

1934.

425197

RUSSELL (E. R.)
The Religion of Shakespeare.   FROM
The Theological Review, Vol. 13.
1876.

472755

SANDERS (C. R.)
Coleridge and the Broad Church movement:
studies in S.T. Coleridge, Dr. Arnold
of Rugby, J. C. Hare, Thomas Carlyle
and F. D. Maurice.   [With references
to Shakespeare, a bibliography and
bibliographical references.]   (Durham,
N.C.)   1942.
Duke University Publications.

542272

SANDERS, WILBUR
The Dramatist and the received idea.
Studies in the plays of Marlowe and
Shakespeare.   (Cambridge)   1968.

769240

Semper (I.J.) Hamlet without tears [:
the touchstone of Thomistic
philosophy applied to the problems
of Shakespeare's Hamlet. With
bibliographical notes].

(Dubuque, Iowa.)   1946.

580143

SIEGEL (PAUL N.)
Adversity and the miracle of love in
King Lear.
IN   SHAKESPEARE QUARTERLY VI:
pp. 325–336.
(New York)   1955.

605711

SIEGEL (PAUL N.)
Christianity and the religion of love in
Romeo and Juliet.
IN   SHAKESPEARE QUARTERLY XII: 4.
pp. 371–391.
(New York) 1961.

605711

SIEGEL, PAUL N.
Shakespeare in his time and ours.
(Notre Dame, Ind.)   1968.

776087

SIEGEL (PAUL N.)
Shakespearean tragedy and the Elizabethan
compromise.   (New York)
bibliog.   1957.

665533

SMITH (G.)
Shakespeare's religion and politics.
IN Macmillan's magazine, vol. 59,
Nov. 1888–April 1889.   1889.

100873

SMITH, MARION BODWELL
Dualities in Shakespeare [: the
humanist search for reconciliation of
opposites]. (Toronto)   1966.

757124

SOELLNER, ROLF
Shakespeare, Aristotle, Plato, and
the soul.
IN DEUTSCHE SHAKESPEARE-GESELLSCHAFT
WEST, JAHRBUCH 1968.   pp. 56–71.
(Heidelberg)
754129

SOUTHAM (B. C.)
Shakespeare's Christian sonnet?
Number 146.
IN SHAKESPEARE QUARTERLY XI: 1.
pp. 67–71.
(New York)   1960.

605711

SPALDING (KENNETH JAY)
The Philosophy of Shakespeare.
(Oxford)   1953.

632614

STEVENSON (ROBERT)
Shakespeare's religious frontier.
(The Hague)
bibliog.   1958.

665978

——[Stockley (W.F.P.)] Eat no fish
["King Lear" and Lent in Elizabethan
times]. In The Month, Vol.140.

1922.

307445

—— STRATHMAN (ERNEST ALBERT)
The Devil can cite Scripture.   IN
McMANAWAY (JAMES GILMER) ed.,
Shakespeare 400: essays by American
scholars on the anniversary of the
poet's birth.   Published in co-operation
with the Shakespeare Association of
America.
illus.   1964.

667803

—— SZENCZI (MIKLÓS)
The Nature of Shakespeare's realism.
IN SHAKESPEARE JAHRBUCH。   Bd. 102/
1966.   pp. 27-59.   (Weimar)

10531

——TARRANT (W. G.)
Shakespeare and religion.   pp. 24.
                             [c.1908.]
Unitarian Penny Library, 147.

407941

——TAYLOR (GEORGE COFFIN)
William Shakespeare, thinker.   FROM
University of North Carolina Extension
Bulletin, Vol. 26.   2nd Series:
Lectures in the Humanities, 1945-1946.
pp. 39-51.   (Chapel Hill, N.C.)
                                1946.

610453

——Taylor (H.) The Religious message of
Shakespeare. From The Congregaticna-
list. Vol.33.
                   [Durban]   1933.

420466

——THALER (ALWIN)

Shakespeare and our world。 Reprinted
from Tennessee Studies in Literature,
vol.2. pp.[16] (Knoxville, Tenn。)
                                1957.

666789

——THOMPSON (CRAIG R.)
The English Church in the sixteenth
century.   pp. 57.   (Washington, D.C.)
illus.   facsimiles.   bibliog.   1958.
Folger Shakespeare Library.   Folger
Booklets on Tudor and Stuart Civilization.

666180

——THOMPSON (CRAIG R.)
The English church in the sixteenth
century.   IN WRIGHT (LOUIS BOOKER)
and FREUND (Mrs. VIRGINIA) [LA MAR] eds.
Life and letters in Tudor and Stuart
England.   (Ithaca, N.Y.)
illus.   1962.
Folger Shakespeare Library: First
Folger Series, [Vol. 1].
                                667762

——TILLYARD (EUSTACE MANDEVILLE WETENHALL)
The Elizabethan world picture [:   an
exposition of the most ordinary beliefs
about the constitution of the world as
pictured in the Elizabethan age.   With
bibliographical notes and references
to Shakespeare's plays].   1943.

540616

——TRIBE, DAVID
Freethought and humanism in Shakespeare.
                            1964.

744461

——TRNKA (BOHUMIL)
Shakespeare's ethics and philosophy.   IN
CHARLES UNIVERSITY ON SHAKESPEARE:
essays edited by Z. Stríbrný.   (Praha)
illus.   1966.

762631

——ULANOV (BARRY)
Shakespeare and St. John of the Cross:
De Contemptu Mundi.   IN Sources and
resources: the literary traditions
of Christian humanism.   (Westminster,
Md.)
bibliog.   1960.

694579

——VYVYAN (JOHN)
Shakespeare and the rose of love:
a study of the early plays in
relation to the medieval philosophy
of love.   1960.

666532

—— WAIN (JOHN BARRINGTON)
The Mind of Shakespeare.
IN GARRETT (J.) More talking of
Shakespeare.   1959.

666126

——WARD (JOHN WILLIAM GEORGE)
The Sublimities of Shakespeare.
IN Ward (J. W. G.) Messages from
master minds [:   the spiritual
messages of eminent writers].
                            [1922.]

603468

——Webb (C.C.J.) Group theories of
religion and the individual. [With
references to Shakespeare and bibliographical notes.]

1916.

[Wilde Lectures in Natural and Comparative
Literature, 1914]

530692

——WERTSCHING (PAULINE)
Fate in Elizabethan drama: Columbia
University [thesis] 1948.   IN
GOLDING (NANCY L.) A Survey of the
proposed arrangements of Shakespeare's
Sonnets [etc.]
bibliog.   microfilm, positive copy.
                            [1948.]

609350

——WEST (REBECCA)
The Court and the castle: a study of
the interactions of political and
religious ideas in imaginative literature.   1958.

678977

——WILKES (G.)
Shakespeare from an American point of
view, including an inquiry as to his
religious faith and his knowledge of
law.   With the Baconian theory
considered.   [A review.]   IN The
Nonconformist, Vol. 38.   1877.

520508

——WILSON (ARTHUR HERMAN)
The Great theme in Shakespeare.   FROM
Susquehanna University Studies, Vol. 4.
pp. 62.   (Selinsgrove, Pa.) 1949.

608970

——Wilson (J.D.) Shakespeare and
humanity, from Les Langues Modernes
4te Annee, No.3. pp. [7.]

1947.

598382

PHIPSON (EMMA)
The Natural history similes in Henry VI.
IN Transactions of the New Shakespeare
Society, Series 1. Nos. 6-7.
pp. 354-384.   1877-9.

11987

The Phoenix and Turtle

—— ALVAREZ (ALFRED)
The Phoenix and the turtle [by]
William Shakespeare [: an essay].
IN WAIN (J. B.) Interpretations.
1955.

657285

——BATES (RONALD)
Shakespeare s "The Phoenix and Turtle".
IN SHAKESPEARE QUARTERLY VI.
pp. 19-30.
(New York) 1955.
605711

——   Bonnard (G.) Shakespeare's
contribution to R.Chester's "Love's
martyr" : The Phoenix and the turtle.
In English studies. Vol.19.
(Amsterdam)   1937.

485661

——   Dobree (B.) Talk [on The Phoenix and
the turtle]. In Shakespeare (W.) The
Phoenix and the turtle: a reading by
D.Leach [and a] talk by B.Dobrée.Produc(ed
by) B.Taylor. (Broadcast) 21st April,1948.
ff.10. Typescript   1948.

593002

—— ELLRODT (ROBERT) An Anatomy of 'The Phoenix
and the Turtle'. IN

Shakespeare Survey [Vol.] 15.
(Cambridge)   1962.

667174

——FURNIVALL (FREDERICK JAMES)
On Chester's "Love's Martyr": Essex is
not the turtle-dove of Shakspere's
"Phoenix and Turtle".
IN Transactions of the New Shakespeare
Society, Series 1. Nos. 6-7. 1877-9.
pp. 451-455.

11987

——   Guthrie (W.N.) Shakespeare's "The
Phoenix and the Turtle" : a liberal's
plea for symbolic orthodoxy. From
Anglican Theological Review,Vol.26.
(Evanston,Ill.)   1944.

578423

——KNIGHT (GEORGE WILSON)
The Mutual flame: on Shakespeare's
"Sonnets" and "The Phoenix and the
Turtle".
bibliog.   1955.

646278

——   Leishman (J.B.) [Review of] The
Phoenix and turtle, by W.Shakespeare
and others. 1937. In The Review of
English Studies, Vol.14.
1938.

495115

——MATCHETT, WILLIAM H.
The Phoenix and the turtle:
Shakespeare's poem and Chester's
"Loves martyr".   1965.

743752

——   Muir (K.) and O'Loughlin (S.) The
Phoenix and the turtle. From The Dublin
Magazine, Vol.10, No.2 (N.S.)
(Dublin.)   1935.

515689

——ONG (WALTER J.)
Metaphor and the twinned vision: The
Phoenix and the turtle.   IN The
Sewanee Review, Vol. 63.   (Sewanee,
Tenn.)   1955.

641628/63

——SELTZER (DANIEL)
"Their tragic scene": "The Phoenix and
turtle"and Shakespeare's love tragedies.
IN SHAKESPEARE QUARTERLY XII: 2.
pp. 91-101.
(New York) 1961.

605711

——   Thomson (W.) ed. The Sonnets of
William Shakespeare & Henry Wriothesley,
Third Earl of Southampton, with A Lover's
complaint and The Phoenix and Turtle.
Edited with an introduction.
(Oxford.)   1938.

480352

Phœnix Shakespeare Festival, Arizona

——BRYANT (JERRY H.)
The Phoenix Shakespeare Festival.
IN SHAKESPEARE QUARTERLY XII: 4.
pp. 447-451.
(New York) 1961.

605711

——BRYANT (JERRY H.) and YEATER (JAMES)
The Fourth Annual Phoenix Shakespeare
Festival.
IN SHAKESPEARE QUARTERLY XI.
pp. 473-476.
(New York) 1960.

605711

——CUTTS (ANSON B.)
The Phoenix Shakespeare Festival.
IN SHAKESPEARE QUARTERLY IX.
pp. 549-553.
(New York) 1958.

605711

——CUTTS (ANSON B.)
Third annual Phoenix Shakespeare
Festival.
IN SHAKESPEARE QUARTERLY X: 4.
pp. 593-596.
(New York) 1959.

605711

——PHOENIX LITTLE THEATRE, Arizona
Alfred Knight Shakespeare Section
Shakespeare festival [programme].
pp. 16. (Phoenix, Ariz.)
ports. illus. 1957.

665897

Phonetics *see* **Pronunciation**

Photographs *see* **Illustrations**

Physiognomy of Shakespeare *see* **Portraits of Shakespeare**

PIAVE, FRANCESCO MARIA
Macbeth [: opera libretto]

see under English Editions: Macbeth:
Opera Texts

Pichot, Amédée *works relating to*

——BISSON (L. A.)
Amédée Pichot: a romantic
Prometheus. [With references to
Shakespeare.] (Oxford)
ports. facsimiles. bibliog.
[1942.]

537587

Pickel (Margaret B.) Charles I as
patron of poetry and drama. [With
references to Shakespeare and a
bibliography].

1936.

456196

PICKERING & CHATTO, booksellers
A Catalogue of miscellaneous old
books, including a collection of
Shakespeareana. Part 6, S-W.
[Catalogue] No. 311. pp. [40.]
[1938.]

494019

Pickering & Chatto [Messrs.]
A Catalogue of old English plays
and poetry [with Shakespeare items].

[1918-1920]

282373

PICKERING & CHATTO, booksellers
English literature: a special selection
of prose, poetry and plays of the 17th,
18th and 19th centuries. Including a
collection of Shakespeareana and many
interesting and rare books on the
history of the British Stage.
[Catalogue] No. 278. pp. 68. [1932.]

400835

PICKERSGILL (EDWARD H.)
On the Quarto and the Folio of Richard III.
IN Transactions of the New Shakespeare
Society, Series 1. No. 3. pp. 77-124.
1875-6.

46·20

PICTON ([Sir] J. A.)
Falstaff and his followers: a
Shakespearean inquiry.   IN Manchester
Literary Club, Papers, Vol. 7.
(Manchester)   1881.

518370

Pictures *see* Illustrations

PIERCE (FREDERICK ERASTUS), MacCRACKEN
(HENRY N.) and DURHAM (WILLARD H.)
An Introduction to Shakespeare.   (New
York)
  port.   1913.   450748
  _____ Another edn.   1929.   466569

Pierce (Margery M.) Julius Caesar and
  the movies. From The English
  Journal, April 1937.

(Chicago)   1937.

503860

PIERPONT MORGAN LIBRARY, New York
English drama from the mid-sixteenth
to the later eighteenth century:
catalogue of an exhibition, October,
1945-March, 1946.   pp. 95.   (New
York)
  ports.   facsimiles.   [1946.]

650074

Pilcher (R.B.) Lecture on alchemists
  in art and literature. [Containing
  references to alchemy in Shakespeare.] pp.54. Ports. Illus.

1933.

(Institute of Chemistry of Great Britain
and Ireland).

414907

PILIKIAN, HOVHANNESS I.
The Copy for 'Mahumodo', 1964 [:
description of a play imitating
Shakespeare.] (Beirut)   1964.

illus.   745555

PILLAI (V. K. A.)
Shakespeare criticism, from the
beginnings to 1765: six lectures
delivered at the Presidency College
under the auspices of the University
of Madras.   1932.   401451
_____ [Review, by] F. T. Wood.
FROM Englische Studien, Bd. 69.
(Leipzig)   1934.   497792

——WOOD (F. T.)
[Review of] Shakespeare criticism, from
the beginnings to 1765: six lectures
delivered at the Presidency College
under the auspices of the University
of Madras, by V. K. A. Pillai.   FROM
Englische Studien, Bd. 69.   (Leipzig)
1934.

497792

Pillé (Henri) illus.
LAMB (CHARLES and MARY [A.])
Tales from Shakespeare.   Illustrated
with etchings by L. Monzies from
designs by H. Pillé.   [Gift edn.]
2 vols.   [1931]

389438

PINEAS, RAINER
Review notes and study guide to
Shakespeare's 'As you like it'. (New
York)   1964.

Monarch critiques of literature.
756285

PIÑEYRO (ENRIQUE)
The Romantics of Spain.   Translated
from the Spanish, with an introduction
and bibliography, by E. A. Peers.
[With references to Shakespeare.]
(Liverpool)   1934.
Studies in Hispanic Literature [Vol. 1].

433229

[Pinkerton (J.)] Remarks on the last
edition of Shakspere's Plays.   In
[Pinkerton (J.)] Letters of literature,
by R.Heron [pseud.].

1785.

78937

Pinter, Harold *works relating to*

——BROWN, JOHN RUSSELL
Mr. Pinter's Shakespeare.
IN Critical Quarterly, Vol. 5, No. 3.
1963.

692062

PINTO (VIVIAN DE SOLA)
Shakespeare and the dictators. [With bibliographical references.] IN DE LA MARE (WALTER [J.]) ed., Essays by divers hands: the Transactions of the Royal Society of literature of the United Kingdom, New Series, Vol. 21.
1944.

557508

PINVIN [WORCESTERSHIRE] DRAMATIC SOCIETY
Programmes, etc., of Shakespeare performances. (Pinvin) 1934-40.

452522

Piozzi ([Mrs.] H.L.) Anecdotes of Samuel Johnson, LL.D. during the last twenty years of his life. [Containing Shakespearian references.] New edn.

1822.

501058

Piozzi (Mrs.[Hester L.]) The Queeney letters: letters addressed to Hester Maria Thrale, by Dr. Johnson, Fanny Burney and Mrs. Thrale- Piozzi. Edited by the Marquis of Lansdowne. [Includes Shakespearian quotations by Mrs. Piozzi; and a bibliography.]

1934.
Curwen Press.)

419831

PIOZZI (Mrs. [HESTER L.]) and others Johnsoniana: anecdotes of Samuel Johnson, LL.D. With the diary of Dr. Campbell, and extracts from that of Madame d'Arblay. Newly collected and edited by Robina Napier. [Containing references to Shakespeare.]
port. 1892.

474421

Piper, Raymond, illus.
USHERWOOD, STEPHEN
Shakespeare play by play. illus. 1967.

764809

Pirated Editions *see* Textual History

PIRKHOFER (ANTON M.)
"A Pretty Pleasing Pricket" - on the use of alliteration in Shakespeare's Sonnets. IN SHAKESPEARE QUARTERLY XIV: 1.
pp. 3-14.
(New York) 1963.

605711

Pistol *see* Henry the Fourth, Characters; Henry the Fifth, Characters

PITCHER (SEYMOUR MAITLAND)
The Case for Shakespeare's authorship of "The Famous victories", with the complete text of the anonymous play. (New York)
port. facsimiles. bibliog.
1961.

666905

PITFIELD (THOMAS BARON)
Desdemona's song. Words by Shakespeare [from "Othello"]. pp. 4. 1957.

665756

PITT, D. BRYCE
Spot the lady

For editions of this play see under English Editions: Macbeth: Alterations &c.

Pizer (Lois D.) *see* Smith (John Harrington), Pizer (Lois D.) and Kaufman (Edward K.)

Place *see* Locality in Shakespeare

Plagiarism

——AUSTIN (WARREN B.)
A Supposed contemporary allusion to Shakespeare as a plagiarist. IN SHAKESPEARE QUARTERLY VI.
pp. 373-380.
(New York) 1955.

605711

——F. [pseud.]
Shakespeariana [: notes on the plagiarism of Shakespeare]. FROM The Mirror [of Literature, Amusement and Instruction, Vol. 19]. [1832.]

562355

——WHITE (H. O.)
Plagiarism and imitation during the English Renaissance: a study in critical distinctions. [With references to Shakespeare.]
(Cambridge, Mass.) 1935.
Harvard Studies in English.

431397

Plain Sheets, Toy Theatre *see* **Toy Theatre**

PLANCHÉ, JAMES ROBINSON
Oberon: a fairy opera: libretto

see under English Editions:
Midsummer Night's Dream: Opera Texts

Planché (J.R.) Recollections and
reflections : a professional autobiography. [With references to
Shakespeare.] New and revised edn.
Illus.

1901.

499275

Planché, James Robinson *works relating to*

—— GRANVILLE-BARKER (HARLEY)
Exit Planché - enter Gilbert. [With
references to Shakespeare.] IN
DRINKWATER (JOHN) ed., The Eighteen-
sixties: essays by Fellows of the
Royal Society of Literature.
illus. 1932.

393090

PLANTAGENET [pseud.]
Herne's Oak, Windsor Little Park.
FROM The Gentleman's Magazine,
[New Series] Vol. 13.
illus. 1840.

521907

Plants *see* **Flowers and Plants**

Platonism

—— SOELLNER, ROLF
Shakespeare, Aristotle, Plato, and
the soul.
IN DEUTSCHE SHAKESPEARE-GESELLSCHAFT
WEST, JAHRBUCH 1968. pp. 56-71.
(Heidelberg)
754129

—— VYVYAN (JOHN)
Shakespeare and platonic beauty.
1961.

666835

—— YATES (FRANCES A.)
Shakespeare and the Platonic tradition.
[With bibliographical references.]
FROM University of Edinburgh Journal,
Vol. 12. (Edinburgh) 1942.

542806

Platt ([J.]A.) 'Edward III' and
Shakespeare's Sonnets. *In* The
Modern language review, Vol. 6.

(Cambridge) 1911.

266821

PLATT (PETER)
English and French theories of tragedy
and comedy, based on the appreciation
of Shakespeare in France. Thesis
offered for the degree of Ph.D. in
the Faculty of Arts at the University
of Birmingham. [Birmingham]
bibliog. typescript. 1957.

665749

PLATT (PETER)
"Le Roi Lear en France". Disserta-
tion présentée à la Faculté des
Lettres de l'Université de Birmingham.
[Birmingham]
typescript. 1954.

644914

PLATTER (T.)
Travels in England, 1599. Rendered
into English from the German, with
introductory matter by [Mrs.] Clare
Williams.
facsimile. bibliog. 1937.

472112

Plautus, Titus Maccius *works relating to*

—— DRAPER (J. W.)
Falstaff and the Plautine parasite.
FROM The Classical Journal, April 1938.
(Menasha)
1938.

503857

—— GILL (E.)
A Comparison of the characters in the
Comedy of Errors with those in the
Menaechmi [of Plautus]. IN University
of Texas Studies in English, No. 5.
(Austin, Texas)

1925.

409501

Play pictorial: an illustrated monthly
journal. Vols. 1, 3-[75]. [With
programmes of, and articles on
Shakespearean performances.]
  ports. illus. 77 vols. 1902-[1939].

571864

Play Pictorial: the Stratford-upon-
Avon Festival, 1936. [Illustrated
souvenir.] pp. 20. 1936.

450644

Play Pictorial, Vol. 74, No. 443
Diamond Jubilee Festival, Stratford-
upon-Avon, 1939. pp. 20.
  illus. 1939.

504804

Playbills

*The Library's main collection of Shakespearian
playbills is being augmented from time to time
with new acquisitions. It is indexed*

___BENNETT (W.)
  A Collection of playbills, portraits,
  newspaper cuttings, and other material
  relating to Covent Garden Theatre,
  London.
  2 vols. 1732-1922.

512634

___BENNETT (W.)
  A Collection of playbills, portraits,
  newspaper cuttings, and other material
  relating to Drury Lane Theatre, and
  other London theatres, etc.
  2 vols. 1630-c.1880.

512636

___General volume [i.e. Playbills covering
  more than one play] 1847-1921. 438128
  All's well that ends well.
    1811-1852. 437128
  Henry VI. 1864. 437129
  Pericles. 1854. 437130
  Timon of Athens. 1816-1851. 437131
  For playbills of other Shakespearean
  plays, see pre-1932 catalogue.

___Leicester, New Theatre, Playbills
  [including Shakespeare's plays],
  seasons Sept. 11, 1837 - Jan. 1, 1838;
  Sept. 12 - Dec. 31, 1838. (Leicester)
  2 vols. 1837-8.

467386

___NEWCASTLE-UPON-TYNE PUBLIC LIBRARIES
  [List of Shakespearian productions in
  Newcastle. Based upon the collection
  of Theatre Royal playbills 1812-64
  housed in the Newcastle Reference
  Library.] IN Shakespeare Scrapbook
  Vol. 16. ff. 6. [Newcastle-upon-
  Tyne]
  typescript. [1950.]

543533

___Shakespeare Programmes and Play Bills
  with cuttings relating thereto.
  2 vols. 1901-1932.

170369

[THE PLAYERS CLUB, New York]
The Players fifth annual classic revival:
King Henry IV, Part one, at the Knickerbocker Theatre, New York, May 31 to
June 5, 1926. [Souvenir programme.]
pp. [32.] [New York]
  ports. illus. facsimiles. 1926.

599875

THE PLAYERS CLUB, New York
The Players eleventh annual revival:
Troilus and Cressida, by W. Shakespeare
[at] B. S. Moss' Broadway Theatre, New
York, week of June 6th, 1932.
[Souvenir programme.] pp. [28.]
[New York]
  ports. illus. facsimile. [1932.]

646353

Playfair (G.) Kean [: a biography.
  With references to Shakespearian
  performances, and a bibliography.]
  Ports. Illus. Genealogical Table.

1939.

498859

PLAYFAIR (GILES WILLIAM)
  My Father's son [: autobiography.
  With references to Shakespearean
  performances.]
  ports. illus. 1937.

469728

PLAYFAIR ([Sir] NIGEL)
  Richard Burbage. IN GARVIN (KATHARINE)
  ed., The Great Tudors. 1935.

431775

Playgoer's Society, Hull see Hull.

Playgoer's Theatre, Hull see Hull.

Playhouse Pocket-Companion; or,
Theatrical vade-mecum: containing
(1) a catalogue of all the dramatic
authors who have written for the
English stage, with a list of their
works, (2) a catalogue of anonymous
pieces, (3) an index of plays and
authors. To which is prefixed, a
critical history of the English stage.
1779.

488660

A Play-house to be lett; or, The
Stage-mutineers: a ballad opera,
by a Gentleman late of Trinity-College,
Cambridge.   As it is acted at the
Theatre-Royal in Covent Garden.
[Containing Shakespearian references.]
pp.40.   1733.

188792

Playing Cards

——BACON (JOHN H.) illus.
   "Shakespeare" playing cards [: set of
   53 cards with Shakespearian illustrations on the court cards].   (C. W.
   Faulkner)   [c.1900.]

615882

PLAYS AND PLAYERS & THEATRE WORLD,
Vols. 13- 1966-

766347

see also Theatre World

Plays and Players: Shakespeare birthday number, Vol. 2, No. 7.   pp. 32.
ports. illus. tables. 1955.

647239

Plays of Shakespeare *see* Attributed Plays; Comedies and the Comic; Early Plays; Greek and Roman Plays; History Plays; Later Plays; Tragedies *and under the titles of the separate plays*

Plays on Shakespeare
   Bibliographies
see also Burlesques; Imitations of Shakespeare
and under the titles of the separate plays

——ADAMS (O. F.)
   A Shakespearean fantasy [introducing
   characters from Shakespeare's plays].
   IN Adams (O. F.) A Motley jest:
   Shakespearean diversions.   [With a
   note by W. J. Rolfe.]   pp. [vii], 64.
   (Boston, [Mass.])   1909.

538105

——ALISON ([Miss] M. V.) and BAKER ([Miss]
E. M.)
   Entente shakespearienne: one-act play
   [in a mixture of English and French]
   produced at Solihull High School for
   Girls, March 1943.   ff. [13.]
   typescript.   1943.

548063

——ALLDRIDGE, JOHN
   Anne of Shottery [: a play]. 1964.

740342

——ALLEN (JOHN)
   Will Shakespeare, dramatist [: a
   play.   Broadcast for Schools]
   8th December, 1955.   ff. 14.
   typescript.

665243

——Allen (W.) David Garrick [: a play.
   With references to Shakespeare.
   Broadcast] from Birmingham, 19th
   June [1946]. ff.21.Typescript.

573103

——ALLGOOD (JILL) and HEMSLEY (H. [M.])
   "Hemsley's Hotel".   Episode 7 - "A
   Shakesperean episode" [in dramatic
   form].   Produced by Audrey Cameron.
   [Broadcast] 11th December, 1949.
   ff. [i] 12.
   typescript.

605260

——ARLETT (VERA ISABEL) and RUBINSTEIN
(HAROLD FREDERICK)
   Hamlet in Aldwych.   IN Arlett (V. I.)
   and Rubinstein (H. F.) Six London
   plays.   1950.   608442
   ———— IN New Plays Quarterly No. 3.
              [?1948.] 605301/3

——ASPIOTI (MARIE)
   So gracious is the time [: a play in
   one act with Shakespeare as one of the
   characters].   pp. 16.   [1949.]
   New Plays Quarterly [Supplement]

604279

——ATKINSON (H.)
   Shakespeare in Lypiatt [: a play].
   pp. [iv] 80.   1946.

568090

——AUDEN (W. H.)
   A Selection from "The Sea and the mirror":
   a commentary [in dramatic form] on
   Shakespeare's "The Tempest".   Produced
   by F. Hauser.   [Broadcast] 22nd July,
   1949.   ff. [ii] 5, 5A, 6-21.
   typescript.

605246

AYLMER (H.) and MAAS (BRIGID)
Tamburlaine, Parts I & II, by
Christopher Marlowe [: a dramatic
commentary on the first night production of the play, as an eye-witness
might have described it.   With
Shakespeare as one of the audience.]
Produced by D. Bower.   Broadcast
7th January, 1942.   ff. 12.
typescript.
Tudor First Nights, 1.

534908

BANESHIK (PERCY)
Elizabeth wears a wig: a comedy in
one act.   (French's Acting Edition,
No. 63)   pp. 40.   plan.   1947.

620769

Barber (E.) Crowner's quest. Adapted
by J.R.Gregson. Produced by
E.Wilkinson [in the British
Broadcasting Corporation's]
Northern Programme, August 5th, 1939.
Typescript.

503800

BARING ([Hon.] M.)
The Rehearsal [: a burlesque giving
an impression of what a rehearsal of
"Macbeth" must have been like when the
play was first produced].   IN Baring
([Hon.] M.) Diminutive dramas.
                    1911.   228752
    IN HAMPDEN (J.) ed., Nine modern
plays.   illus.   1935.   452763
  Teaching of English Series.
    Another edn.
  illus.   1947.   581860

BARLING (E[DITH] M.)
Back to G.B.S.; [or, A Midsummer
nightmare]: Shaw Tercentenary
Celebration, Malvern, A.D. 2156.
pp. 23.   [1931]

395652

BARRIE ([Sir] J. M.)
Shakespeare's legacy [: a play in
one act.]   pp. 27.   [1916.]
  Privately printed.   Edition
limited to 25 copies.
                            484136

BAXTER (ALICE H.) and PRIESTLEY (E.)
Shakespearian women [: musical
drama, utilizing songs of Shakespeare
and extracts from his plays.]
pp. 16.   [1949.]
  Macdonald Drama Library: Miniature
Musical Dramas, No. 2.
                            599925

BENNETT (CHARLES MOON) and JACKSON
(CHARLES VIVIAN)
Moving a playhouse: an event in
Shakespeare's life.   IN Masters and
masterpieces: classroom plays.
                            1958.

678077

BIRD (J. H.)
"The Shakespeare Jubilee of 1769";
or, Garrick's first Stratford Festival:
a dramatised chronicle produced by
W. I. Hughes.   [Broadcast] 27th April,
1949.   ff. [i] 39.

605254

[BLAIR-FISH (WALLACE WILFRED)]
Marchaunt-adventurers: an Elizabethan
comic romance, in five acts, by Blair.
[With Shakespeare as one of the
characters.]   ff. 8.
typescript.   [c.1913.]

534903

[BLAIR-FISH (WALLACE WILFRED)]
Shakespeare's country: a radio play
[about references to the Cotswolds
in Shakespeare's plays and with
Shakespeare as one of the characters]
by Blair [pseud.   Broadcast] 23rd
April, 1947.   ff. 25.
typescript.

583263

BOSTELMANN (LEWIS FREDERICK)
L'Envoi: the birth of the Folio [:
a play].   IN Bostelmann (L. F.)
Rutland: a chronologically arranged
outline of the life of Roger Manners,
6th Earl of Rutland, author of the
works issued in folio in 1623 under
the nom de plume "Shake-speare", [etc.]
(New York)   1911.

666340

BOSTELMANN (LEWIS FREDERICK)
Roger of Rutland: a drama in five acts.
2nd edn. amended and augmented.   IN
Bostelmann (L. F.) Rutland: a chronologically arranged outline of the life
of Roger Manners, 5th Earl of Rutland,
author of the works issued in folio in
1623 under the nom de plume "Shakespeare" [etc.].   (New York)
illus.   ports.   1911.

666340

Bourne (J.) Puck's good deed for the
day; or, Shakespeare is so modern.
In Bourne (J.) ed., 8 new one-act
plays of 1933.
                            1933.

415755

BOX (S.)
The Truth about Shakespeare.
IN MARRIOTT (J. W.) [ed.] The Best
one-act plays of 1939.   1940.

512038

BRAHMS (CARYL) [pseud. i.e. Doris
Caroline Abrahams] and SIMON (S. J.)
[pseud. i.e. Simon Jasha Skidelsky]
"Thank you, Mrs. Siddons": a play
devised for broadcasting.   [Broadcast]
18th February, 1944.   ff. 29.
typescript.

579578

Bridie (J.) Midsummer afternoon's
dream [: a play about a production
of Midsummer Night's Dream].   In
Bridie (J.) Tedious and brief.

1944.

558197

——[Bristol, St. Brendan's College. Queen Elizabeth comes to Bristol: a pageant. An adaptation of As You Like It. Bristol scenes by J.B. Thompson. Programmes, cuttings, etc.] Partly typescript. Illus.

[Bristol]   [1934]

433185

——   Britton (L.) Spacetime inn: [a play with Shakespeare as one of the characters].

1932.

398171

——BROWN (IVOR [J. C.])
William's other Anne [: a play about Shakespeare].   IN BOURNE (J.) ed. Twenty-five modern one-act plays.
1938.   476899
_____ [Broadcast script] 1st March, 1940. ff. [2], 18. 1940.   514551

——[Bull (J.) pseud.] The Jubilee; or, John Bull in his dotage : a grand national pantomime as it was to have been acted by His Majesty's subjects on the twenty-fifth of October, 1809 : [a parody of Garrick's Shakespeare Jubilee.] By the author of "Operations of the British Army of Spain" [i.e. John Bull,pseud. Words only.] pp. 40.

1809.

491340

——Burton (P.H.) "Her Majesty commands" [: a play, broadcast from] Cardiff, 22 Nov., 1938. ff. [1,] 29. Typescript.

491800

——Burton (P.H.) Master Shakespeare and Glendower: [a play broadcast from] Cardiff, 27 May, 1938. ff. [i], 22. Typescript.

487434

——CARLTON (GRACE)
The Wooing of Anne Hathaway: [a play.]
1938.   484302
_____ typescript. 1938.   491153

——[CARR (JOHN DICKSON)]
Appointment with fear, No. 8.   Fire burn and cauldron bubble [: a play relating to Shakespeare's Macbeth. Broadcast] 28th October, 1943.   pp. [II,] 20.
typescript.

550861

——Cheke (M.) This powerful rhyme: a comedy in three acts. [With reference to Shakespeare and his plays.] pp.[94]. Typescript.

[1934.]

425247

——CLEVERDON (D.)
"Shakespeare and his musicians", written and produced by D. Cleverdon: an enquiry into Shakespeare's use of music. [In dramatic form.] Broadcast 16th December 1948.   (Third Programme) ff. [i] 34. typescript.

599862

——[Colman (G.)] Man and wife; or, The Shakespeare Jubilee : a comedy. As it is performed at the Theatre Royal in Covent Garden. pp. vi, 60.

(Dublin)   1770.

531615

——COURNOS (J.)
Shylock's choice [a play].   IN HUEFFER (F. H. M.) and HUGHES (G.) [eds.] Imagist anthology, 1930.
1930.   401105
_____ IN The Fortnightly Review, Vol. 124.   1925. 325119

——COX (CONSTANCE) and WOLFIT (DONALD)
David Garrick: a comedy.   Adapted for broadcasting by Cynthia Pughe. [Broadcast] March 3rd, 1951. pp.55. typescript.

620405

——CRAIG (H. A. L.)
The School of night.   Production by D. Cleverdon. [Script of broadcast in B.B.C. Third Programme, October, 1960].   [British Broadcasting Corporation]
typescript.   1960.

667024

——CUNNINGHAM (W. McC.)
The Tragedy of Francis Bacon, Prince of England, by Sir Francis Bacon, assisted by Sir Myles Bodley and Sir Toby Matthews.   From the text and anagrammatic writing in the First Folio edition of the Shakespeare Hamlet.   (Los Angeles)
facsimiles.   frontis.   1940.

530591

——DANE (CLEMENCE) [pseud. i.e. Miss Winifred Ashton]
The Godson: a fantasy [about Shakespeare and the Davenant family]. illus.   1964.

742101

——   Dane (Clemence) [pseud.] Recapture: a Clemence Dane omnibus [including Will Shakespeare: a play].

1932.

399026

——DANE (CLEMENCE) [pseud. i.e. Miss Winifred Ashton]
The Unknown soldier [: a play with Shakespeare as a character].   IN Dane (C.) The Saviours: seven plays on one theme.   1942.

545488

—DANE (CLEMENCE) [psaud. of Miss Winifred Ashton]
Will Shakespeare: an invention.
[1921]
No. 4 of an edition, printed on hand-made paper, numbered and signed by the author, limited to 250 copies.

For other editions of this play check the main sequence under the author's name.

471776

—DANIELL (DAVID SCOTT)
The Great Garrick: a play. [Broadcast] 17th Feb. 1952. ff. 35.
typescript.

624730

—DANIELL (D. S.)
The Queen and Mr. Shakespeare: a play about William Shakespeare. [Broadcast] 18th June, 1940. ff. [1], 15.
typescript. 1940. 516332
_____ IN FULLER (M. H.) [ed.] Ten selected one-act plays.
1943. 546825

—Daniell (D.S.) Tygers hart [: a play about William Shakespeare.With Shakespeare as one of the characters.] (Children's Hour)[Broadcast]April 23rd, 1947. ff.34. Typescript.

583270

—DANIELL (DAVID SCOTT)
Tygers Hart [: a play about Shakespeare]. Produced by D. Boisseau. [Televised] 22nd April, 1954. ff. 26.
typescript.

643691

—DAVIE, IAN
A Play for Prospero: a Shakespearian extravaganza. 1966.

767654

—   Davis (Estelle H.) and Stasheff (E.)
Shakespearean nights: unified arrangements of interwoven scenes. Introduction by Lelitia Raubichek. Illus. (New York) 1935.

445069

—DRAMATIC AUTHORS' SOCIETY
Catalogue of dramatic pieces, the property of the members. [Including plays on Shakespeare.] pp. 40, [22.] 1860.

With MS. additions.

480226

—Dryhurst (E.) The Shakespeare murders: screen play. Director: E. M. Haynes. Shooting script.

1937.

(Fox British Pictures Ltd., Production 691)
Film entitled "The Claydon murder mystery"

479195

—FARROW (EMMA)
Perdita at home [: a play]. ff. 25. [Birmingham]
typescript. [1955]

665018

—FEIST (AUBREY)
Treasure in Arden: a light-hearted adventure [play] for Children's Hour. Produced by D. Davis. [Broadcast in six parts 14th January – 18th February 1955.]
typescript.

665041

—FELEY (RUTH A.)
Shakespeare on the razor's edge [: a play in one scene]. FROM Education, Vol. 53. (Boston, Mass.) 1933.

559546

—FELL (JAMES BLACK)
Bernard Shaw arrives: a fantasy in one act. pp. iv, 27. 1953.
French's Acting Edition No. 591.

630909

—GARNETT (LOUISE A.)
Will of Stratford: a midwinter night's dream in three acts, with a prologue and an epilogue. Revised [edn.] pp. 94. 1936.
Baker's [Royalty] Plays.

462357

—GEORGE (C.)
When Shakespeare's ladies meet: comedy for the fair sex in one act. pp. 23. (New York) 1942.
Dramatists Play Service, Inc.

544913

—GIBSON (WILLIAM)

A Cry of players: a preface in three acts [about William Shakespeare. Typescript] [1961.]

667023

—Gilbert (Sir W.S.) Rosencrantz and Guildenstern: a tragic episode in three tableaux, founded on an old Irish legend. In Boas (G.) ed.,Short modern plays.

1935.

[New Eversley Series.]

436624

—GITTINGS (R.)
Too much of water: a pre-Raphaelite tragi-comedy [relating to Ophelia and Millais' picture] written for broadcasting. Produced by S. Potter, 22nd July, 1943. ff. 15.
typescript.

542920

—GOODLOE ([ABBIE] C.)
To dream again: a comedy in one act [telling how Shakespeare came to write "The Tempest".] pp. [xii] 28. (New York)
plan. 1941.
Originally published under the title "Storm over Bermuda".

531790

——GOSFORTH (J. C.)
"The First night of Twelfth Night":
a dramatic reconstruction of a
Shakespearean première.   Based on
the book by L. Hotson.   Produced
by C. Shaw.   [Broadcast] 6th January,
1956.   ff. 24.
typescript.

665244

——GOW (R.)
"Enter Fanny Kemble": a play for
broadcasting.   ff. [1], 25.
typescript.   1940.

516587

——GOW (R.)
One man in his time: a fantastic
chronicle of the life and death of
Master William Shakespeare.   pp. 40.
typescript.   [1935.]

534909

——Gow (R.) The Stratford lad: three
scenes from the life of Shakespeare.
In Gow (R.) Plays for the classroom.

1933.

450738

——GRUNER (E. H.)
With golden quill: a cavalcade,
depicting Shakespeare's life and times.
With a Tudor cameo (as preamble) by
W. Jaggard [and a bibliography.]
(Stratford-on-Avon: Shakespeare Press)
ports.   illus.   1936.
Edn. limited to 500 copies.

459912

——HAIGH (VERONICA)
To dream again: a romantic play in
three acts [with Shakespeare as one
of the characters].
illus.   [1946.]
Guild Library.

588917

——HAMLEY ([Sir] E. B.)
Shakespeare's funeral.   IN Tales
from "Blackwood".   (Leipzig) 1880.
Collection of British Authors.
Tauchnitz Edition.

499877

——HAMMOND (H. J.)
Shakspeare: early life.   One-act
play.   ff. 21.   [Solihull]
typescript.   [1958.]

665979

——HARVEY, FRANK
The jesting swan [: a play].   1964.

740341

——Hay (H.H.) As Shakespeare was: a
drama.

1934.

427709

—— Hay (H.H.) The Great Elizabeth: a
play [with Shakespeare as one of the
characters].

(Boston)   1928.

395684

——Hayden (H.) The Immortal memory:
a new approach to the teaching
of Shakespeare [in dramatic form].
pp.[96]. Illus.

1936.

451445

——Hayes (G.M.) & Clarke (F.K.) Showing
up Shakespeare: [a play for
broadcasting.] ff. 18. Typescript.

[1934.]

419278

——HERRING (R.)
Harlequin Mercutio; or, Plague on your
houses: a ride through raids to resurrection [in verse].   FROM Life and
Letters to-day, Vols. 31 and 32.
1941-2.

534897

——HERRING (R.)
Harlequin Mercutio: or, A Plague on
both your houses: a ride through raids
to resurrection [: a verse pantomime
of present-day London, Mercutio and Hamlet
are taken to be two aspects, the spirit
and conscience, of the same person, Ego].
IN SCHIMANSKI (S.) and TREECE (H.) eds.,
Transformation [: an anthology].
1942.

543517

——Hinckley (Jane) The Lost key, and
First aid for Shakespeare: two
little plays. pp.16.

[1941.]

523909

——HONE (JOHN)
Hey, Will! Will!   A play in one act.
pp. 31.
plan.   1948.
French's Acting Edition, No. 5.

620768

——HYAMS (EDWARD)
"The Forger" [: a play relating to
Shakespeare].   Producer: H.B.Fortuin.
Broadcast 22nd August, 1955. ff. 35.
typescript.

665123

——JOHNSON (WILLIAM)
The Bishopton letter: an adventure play
[broadcast on the B.B.C. Midland Region,
children's programmes, 1962. Broadcast
script].

667772

——JOYCE (JAMES)
"The Second best bed": a usyless discussion on Hamlet or Hamnet.   A
Shakespearian dialogue by J. Joyce
arranged for broadcasting by J. K. Cross.
Production by N. Iliff.   Transmission:
1st January 1949: BBC Third Programme.
pp. [ii] 25.
typescript.

599861

—KITCHIN (LAURENCE)
Three on trial: an experiment in
biography. [Three plays: The Trial
of Lord Byron; The Trial of Dr.
Bowdler; and, The Trial of Machiavelli.]
With line drawings by A. Horner. 1959.

685314

—KOCH (F. H.) ed.
The Book of Shakespeare, the playmaker.
Written in collaboration by twenty
students of the University of North
Dakota for the Shakespeare Tercentenary
Commemoration. IN SANFORD (Mrs. ANNE P.)
ed., Plays for graduation days. (New
York)   1931.

453418

—Kurnitz (H.) "Fast and loose" [: a
screen play dealing with the stealing
of a valuable Shakespeare Manuscript.]
Film editor : E. Veron.

1939.

(Metro-Goldwyn-Mayer)

499945

—LAFORGUE (JULES)
Hamlet; or, The Consequences of
filial piety: a moral legend.
Translated and adapted for radio by
H. Reed. Produced by D. Cleverdon.
[Broadcast] 20th June [1954].
typescript.

665045

—LANDOR (W. S.)
Citation and examination of William
Shakespeare, Euseby Treen, Joseph
Carnaby and Silas Gough before Sir T.
Lucy touching deer-stealing, 1582.
1891.
For other editions of this work check
the main sequence under the author's
name.

390220

—LENNON (T.)
The Truth about Anne [: a play relating
to Anne Hathaway and Shakespeare].
(New York)   1942.
The Living Drama Series.

542238

—LITTLE (T.)
The Actor and the alderman's wife;
or, Kean and his little breeches, a
farce in three acts. pp. 29.
frontis.   [c.1824]

455702

—LYLE (MILLICENT)
Stratford tapestry: a one-act play.
pp. [ii.] 21.   1952.

626787

—LYNCH (EVANGELINE)
Shakespeare streamlined: a comedy in
one act [of which most of the dialogue
is made up of quotations from
Shakespeare's plays]. pp. 20 [vi].
(Evanston, Ill.)   1944.

558681

—LYTTON, DAVID
Mr. Melville's day in Stratford.
Produced by R.D. Smith. B.B.C. radio
script broadcast 25th February 1968.

typescript.   768972

—LYTTON (DAVID)
"Time come round": a supposition for
radio on the death of William
Shakespeare. Written and produced
by D. Lytton. [Broadcast] 27th April,
1956. ff. [i], 32.
typescript.

665271

—MacKAYE (PERCY)
The Mystery of Hamlet, King of Denmark;
or What we will: a tetralogy in
prologue to The Tragicall Historie
of Hamlet, Prince of Denmarke, by
W. Shakespeare. The Ghost of
Elsinore; The Fool in Eden Garden;
Odin against Christus; The Serpent
in the orchard.   (New York)
illus.   1950.

619928

—MADDERN (VICTOR) and BANKS (LYNNE REID)
Miss Pringle plays Portia: a comedy
in one act. pp. 27.   [1955.]
Deane's Series of Plays.

649434

—A Masque setting forth the true
honouring of our rare and precious
poet, William Shakespeare. pp. 45.
[1916.]
"Shakespeare Memorial National
Theatre, 1916", printed on cover.

494451

—MILLER (HELEN LOUISE)
The Shakespearean touch: a play for
American Education Week. FROM Plays,
the drama magazine for young people.
Vol. 14. pp. 12. (Boston, Mass.)
1954.

648776

—MORAN (MABEL M.)
The Shakespeare Garden Club:
comedy fantasy in one act.
pp. 17. (New York: Dramatists
Play Service, Inc.)   1938.

496022

—MORLEY (C. [D.])
Good theatre. IN CHURCH ([Mrs.]
VIRGINIA [W.]) ed., Curtain! A book
of modern plays. (New York) 1932.

453944

—MORRIS (T. B.)
Fair Youth and Dark Lady: a play
[relating to Shakespeare, Will Hughes
and the Dark Lady of the Sonnets].
pp. [32].   1938.
One-act Plays, No. 18.

534288

—MORRIS, T.B.
Stratford boy: a play.   1964.

667961

——MUIR (FRANK) and NORDEN (DENIS)
"Take it from here" [: script of
the radio programme, including a
burlesque on the life of Shakespeare.
Broadcast] 8th Jan., 1951. ff. 22.
  typescript.

622924

——MUSKERRY (W.)
Garrick; or, Only an actor.
A comedy: an original version of
the French and German pieces founded
on the same subject.   pp. 39.
                              [1886.]
French's Acting Plays.
                       418067

——Nathan (G.J.) The Avon flows [: a play
combining part of the text of Romeo
and Juliet, Othello and the Taming
of the Shrew].

(New York)   1937.

465371

——O'Riordan (C.) Captain Falstaff and
other plays. Frontis.

1935.

445050

——Pagan (I.M.) Sunset in Stratford
[: a play about William Shakespeare].
ff.27. Typescript.

([Stratford-upon-Avon])   [1937]

477471

——Peach (L. du Garde) "Merely
players": a vague fantasy of
dreams and dollars [about
Shakespeare, written for broadcasting.] Typescript.

1935.

434454

——PEACH (L. du G.)
"Saint George's Day" [: a radio play
about St. George, Shakespeare, and the
sea. Broadcast] 23rd April 1950.
ff. 17.
  typescript.

608872

——PEACH (L. du G.)
The Swan of Avon: [a play written for
broadcasting. With Shakespeare as one
of the characters.] ff. 21.
  typescript.   [1934.]   419569
Waterways of England, No. 6.
_____ [Broadcast script] 28th May,
1942. ff. 15.
  typescript.   534704

——Peach (L. du G.) "Will Shakespeare", produced by A. Macdonald. [Broadcast
in the] Midland Regional (Children's
hour) programme, 23rd April, [1938.]
ff. 27. Typescript.

481192

——Pemberton (Madge) The Queen waits
[: a play, with reference to Shakes-
peare]. In Marriott (J.W.) [ed.]
The Best one-act plays of 1940.

1941.

525593

——PILIKIAN, HOVHANNESS I.
The Copy for 'Mahumodo', 1964 [:
description of a play imitating
Shakespeare.] (Beirut)   1964.

illus.   745555

——PLOMLEY, ROY
Everybody's making money - except
Shakespeare: a comedy.   [1964.]

typescript.   740380

——Potter (S.) William Shakespeare:
dramatic reading. (Senior English.)
[Broadcast] 21 May, 1940.
ff. [1], 12. Typescript.

516588

——POWER (RHODA D.)
The Play's the thing [: a play about
acting and especially about
Shakespeare's Macbeth].   (Senior
English II, No. 9).   [Broadcast]
16th November, 1943.   ff. 12.
  typescript.   1944.

550859

——PRIMOST (SYDNEY)
The Pools of the gods: a play in
three acts.   With a foreword by
P. Tabori.   pp. 67.   1954.

646076

——REED (HENRY) of Birmingham
The Great desire I had (Shakespeare
and Italy) [: a play. Broadcast]
Oct. 26th, 1952.   ff. [ii], 44.
  typescript.

630861

——RILEY ([Mrs.] ALICE C. D.)
Shakespeare's lovers in a garden:
a flower masque.   Re-edited by the
author.   Prologue and epilogue by
Eleanor E. Perkins.   pp. 32.
(Chicago: Drama League of America)
                  1927.   407981
_____ Music [by various composers].
(Chicago)   [c.1927.] 407982

——ROBB (W. CUTHBERT)
The Shades of night; a comic opera
[in one act.   For schools and youth
clubs.   Libretto only].   pp. 16.
                              1952.

623706

——ROBERTS (C.)
The Second best bed.   IN BAYLISS
(A. E. M.) ed., Junior one-act plays
of to-day.   Third series.   1936.
Harrap's Junior Modern English Series.

457251

——ROGERS (R. E.)
The Boy Will.   IN COHEN (HELEN L.)
ed., One-act plays by modern authors,
edited [with introductions] by
Helen L. Cohen.
illus.   1921.

397663

——ROWLING (MARJORIE)
Bride for a bard [: a play.   Broad-
cast] 10th Sept. 1952.   ff. [ii] 19.
typescript.   1952.

630862

——RUBINSTEIN (H. F.)
After-glow: a play in one act.
[With Shakespeare as one of the
characters.] pp. 18.   1937.

472035

——Rubinstein (H.F.) Shakespeare's Globe:
play in one act. In The Amateur
Theatre and Playwrights' Journal,
Vol.4, No.75.

1937.

467093

——RUBINSTEIN, HAROLD FREDERICK
Unearthly gentleman. A Trilogy of one
act plays about Shakespeare.   1965.

746635

——Rubinstein (H.F.) and Bax (C.) Shakespeare: a play in five episodes. [With]
a preface by A.W. Pollard. pp.96.

[1934.]

[French's Acting Plays.]

415735

——Sansom (C.) Celestial meeting: a stage
sketch for three women only [Viola,
Desdemona, Lady Macbeth.] In
Hampden (J.) [ed.]Plays without
fees. pp.96. Dgms.

[1935].

439719

——SCHRAGER (VICTORIA)
How like a god: [a play in verse,
including Shakespearian characters]
by W. Shakespeare and Victoria
Schrager.   pp. 43.   (Northampton,
Mass.)   1939.

519134

——SCHULL (JOSEPH)
World of his own [: a play including reference to Shakespeare].
Produced by A. Campbell.   [Broadcast]
22nd June, 1953.   ff. 30.
typescript.

643689

——SEWELL (GEORGE)
The Tragedy of Sir Walter Raleigh.
As it is acted at the Theatre in
Lincolns-Inn-Fields. Third edition.
(London: John Pemberton)   1719.

The Epilogue refers to the
cutting and alteration of Shakespeare's
plays in the theatre.   436639

——SHAKESPEARE II [pseud.]
The Overman: the serio-comic history
of a twentieth century Hamlet.   [With
a preface signed William the Second,
pseud.] pp. 64.   1905.

547975

——Shaler (N.S.) Elizabeth of England:
a dramatic romance.   5 vols.

(Boston)   1903.

420074

—— Shaw ([G.]B.) "The Dark Lady of sonnets,"
produced by P. Creswell. [Broadcast
in the] National [programme], 22nd
April, 1938. ff. 4. Typescript.

481193

——SHAW (GEORGE BERNARD)
"The Dark lady of the sonnets".   Produced by D. Allen.   [Broadcast]
2nd October, 1955.   ff. [1], 18.
typescript.

665126

—— SHAW ([GEORGE] BERNARD)
Misalliance, The Dark lady of the
sonnets, [with a preface on
Shakespeare] and Fanny's first play.
1928.   504568
IN [Works, Standard Edn., Vol.
19.]   1932.   391891

——SHAW ([GEORGE] BERNARD)
Shakes versus Shav [: a puppet play].
IN Shaw ([G.] B.) [Works.   Standard
edn. Vol. 35.]   1950.

614733

——SHAW (GEORGE BERNARD)
Shakes versus Shav.   A puppet play.
(Stratford-upon-Avon)
illus.   [?1964.]

740198

——SHIRLEY, RAE
Jester of Stratford: a comedy in one
act.   1964.

740340

——Simpson (H.) and Houghton (C.) The
Unknown [: a play, with Shakespeare
as one of the characters]. ff.8.
Typescript.

[c.1935.]

534907

— Sitwell (Edith) "Romeo Coates" :
a portrait of failure. [A play
containing references to Romeo and
Juliet] adapted [for broadcasting]
and produced by S. Potter. Regional
programme, 23rd Feb., 1939. ff. 18.
Typescript.

498984

—SLADEN-SMITH (FRANCIS) [FRANK]

Sweet Master William: a play in one act.
(French's Acting Edition, No.731) pp.[2]
32.Plan.   1953.

636167

—SMITH (G.)
Tommy Jones's dream [: a play in
one act.] IN LOCK (A. B.) ed.,
Festival plays, Book two.   1951.

623436

—SMITH (R. P.)
Shakspeare in love.   IN Smith (R. P.)
The Sentinels & other plays.   Edited
[with a preface] by R. H. Ware and
H. W. Schoenberger. (Princeton, N.J.)
1941.

553951

—SOMERSET (CHARLES A.)
Shakespeare's birth day! or, The
Rival muses! A masque, in which
the question of tragedy or comedy,
which merits the palm? is decided.
[Theatre Royal, Birmingham, prompt
book] pp. [iv], 27.
manuscript.   [c.1840.]

666759

— Somerset (C.A.) Shakespeare's early
days: a drama in two acts. pp.16.
Illus.

[c.1883.]

(Dicks' Standard Plays, No.792.)

455700

—SQUIRE (Sir J. C.)
The Clown of Stratford: a comedy
in one act.   IN BOAS (G.) ed.,
Short modern plays.   1935.
[New Eversley Series]

436624

—The Stage-mutineers; or, A Play-house
to be lett: a ballad opera, by a
gentleman late of Trinity-College,
Cambridge.   As it is acted at the
Theatre-Royal in Covent Garden.
[Containing Shakespearian references.]
pp. 40.   1733.

188792

—   Stasheff (E.) and Davis (Estelle H.)
Shakespearean nights: unified arrangements
of interwoven scenes. Introduction by
Letitia Raubichek. Illus.
(New York)   1935.

445069

—STERNDALE-BENNETT (J.)
Shakespeare in Shoreditch: a play
in one act.   ff. 20. (Wateringbury)
typescript.   [1933.]

534906

— Stevens (Kate) Hiking with
Shakespeare. In Box (S.) ed.,
Monologues and duologues of to-day.

1935.

434937

—STEVENS (T. W.)
Highways Cross: [a play about
Shakespeare].   IN Stevens (T. W.)
The Nursery-maid of Heaven and other
plays.   1926.

395318

—STRONG (L. A. G.)
O rare Ben Jonson [: a radio play,
with Shakespeare as one of the
characters].   Produced by Mary H.
Allen.   [Broadcast]12th August,1945.
ff. 20.
typescript.

563287

—SUTTON (SHAUN)
Will loves Alice [: a play relating
to Shakespeare.   Broadcast] 19th Dec.,
1951.   pp. 31.
typescript.

622922

— Talbot (A.J.) Will Shakespeare's
bespoke supper: a Baconian night at
the Mermaid Tavern. In The One-act
theatre, the sixth book.

1935.

439266

—TANNENBAUM (S. A.)
The Knight and the crystal sphere:
a dramatic fantasy of Sir Walter
Ralegh and Queen Elizabeth.   [With
Shakespeare as one of the characters.]
pp. 70.   (New York)   1946.
Edn. limited to 250 copies.

587295

—Thompson (J.B.) Anne Hathaway sees
"Twelfth Night": written for
performance by the Bristol Drama
Club, in a Clifton garden, June,
1936. From St. Brendan's College
Magazine, Vol.3, No.1. Illus.

(Bristol)   1936.

455002

— Thomson (A.A.) The Second best bed;
or, The Truth about Shakespeare:
a comedy for broadcasting. ff.6.
Typescript.

[1934.]

422598

THORP (JOSEPHINE)
When fairies come [: a one act play,
with Shakespeare as one of the
characters]. IN SANFORD ([Mrs.]
A[NNE] P.) and SCHAUFFLER (R. H.) eds.,
Little plays for little people.
With an introduction by E. B. Sheldon.
(New York)   1939.

531538

TILLER (TERENCE)
The Conscience of the king: a study
of the fool in King Lear [in dramatic
form. Broadcast] May 7th, 1952.
pp. 42.
typescript.

624733

TREVELYAN (R. C.)
Thersites. FROM Life and Letters,
Vol. 11. pp. [9].   [1934]

428694

TUGMAN (CECIL C.)
The Workshop: a play. ff. [3] 12.
[Johannesburg]
typescript.   [1952.]

630854

TURNER (MARGARET)
My horn-book and my top: a play in
one act. pp. [vi], 30.   1951.
French's Acting Edition.

621421

TURNER (MARGARET)
There's rue for you: a play in one
act [on the childhood of Shakespeare].
pp. 24.   1950.
French's Acting Edition, No. 1290.

605566

WAITE (V.)
Will of Stratford. IN Waite (V.)
Three costume plays [: mainly for
schoolboy players]. With a foreword
by L. Banks.
dgms.   1944.

553770

WALKER (DEREK)
Most things do not happen: a theatrical
comedy. [B.B.C. Radio script of play
transmitted in the "Wednesday Matinee"
series, Home Service, 4th November 1959.
Typescript] pp. [ii], 32.

666445

WALKER (R. S.)
The Great Globe itself [: a play about
a rehearsal of The Tempest in 1611].
IN MARRIOTT (J. W.) [ed.,] One-act
plays of to-day. Sixth series.
frontis.   1934.
The Harrap Library.

424087

Wallis (C.) Thumb prints [: a play
for broadcasting.] ff.9. Typescript.

[1934.]

422599

Watts (N.B.) Morning glory [:a play,
including quotations from
Shakespeare. Broadcast] 16th
January [1950]. ff.32.Typescript.

609483

WEST (A. L.)
Shades of Shakespeare's women: entertainment in ten scenes. pp. 32.
1896.

395830

WILLIAMS (C. [W. S.])
A Myth of Shakespeare [: a play in
verse, containing representative scenes
and speeches from Shakespeare's plays.]
(Oxford)   1936.
The Oxford Bookshelf.

458510

WILLIAMS (C. [W. S.])
A Myth of Shakespeare. IN The
Appreciation of Shakespeare: a
collection of criticism, philosophic,
literary and esthetic, by writers and
scholar-critics of the eighteenth,
nineteenth, and twentieth centuries.
(Washington)   1949.

616565

WILLIAMS (C. [W. S.])
Shakespeare and Bacon: a scene from
an unpublished "Myth of Francis Bacon".
pp. [8]. FROM This Quarter, Dec. 1932.

401327

WILLIAMS (E. HARCOURT)
Little Tuk's dream [in which
Shakespeare appears]. IN Williams
(E. H.) Four fairy plays. pp. 30.
1920.

534289

WILLIAMS (EMLYN)
Spring, 1600: a comedy in three acts
[relating to Richard Burbage's company
acting Shakespeare's plays at the
Globe Theatre].   1946.

569754

WOOD (MARGARET LUCY ELIZABETH)
Instruments of darkness [: a prologue
to the murder of Duncan]. pp. [iv], 21.
plan.   1955.
French's Acting Edition, No. 340.

649352

Plays on Shakespeare
– Bibliographies

────NICHOLS (JAMES WILLIAM)
William Shakespeare on the stage: a
study of the figure of William
Shakespeare in British and American
drama. A thesis submitted to the
University of Birmingham. (Birmingham)
bibliog. typescript. 1951.
Illustrations wanting.

649925

Plimpton (G.A.) The Education of
Shakespeare. Illustrated from
schoolbooks in use in his time.

1933

407229

Pliny *works relating to*

────Baldwin (T.W.) A Note upon William
Shakespeare's use of Pliny.
[With bibliographical notes.] In
Craig (H.) ed.,Essays in dramatic
literature: the Parrott presentation
volume. Port.
(Princeton) 1935.

444399

PLOMER (H. R.)
The Printers of Shakespeare's plays
and poems. FROM The Library,
[New Series, Vol. 7.] 1906.

520173

PLOMLEY, ROY
Everybody's making money - except
Shakespeare: a comedy. [1964.]

typescript. 740380

Plots *see* Dramatic Art of Shakespeare; Sources of Shakespeare; Synopses

Plowman (M.) [J.M.] Murry's
"Shakespeare" [: a review]. From
The Adelphi, May, 1936. pp.105-111.

1936.

450638

Plowman (M.) Money and "The
Merchant." In The Adelphi, 1931.

[1931.]

396356

Plowman (M.) Notes on Macbeth. In
The Adelphi, Vol. 15.

1938-9.

509700

P[LOWMAN] (M.)
[Review of] Shakespeare, by M. Van
Doren. FROM The Adelphi, Vol. 17,
New Series. 1941.

527856

Plowman (M.) Some values in Hamlet.
In The Adelphi. Vol. 15.

1938-9.

509700

PLUMPTRE (E. H.)
Ecclesiastes; or the Preacher.
[With an appendix "Shakespeare and
Koheleth".] (Cambridge) 1888.
Cambridge Bible for Schools and
Colleges.

109059

PLUMSTEAD (MARY)
Sigh no more, ladies. Words by
Shakespeare. Music by Mary Plumstead.
pp. 4. 1955.

665338

PLUMSTEAD (MARY)
Take, O take those lips away. [Words
by] Shakespeare. Music by Mary
Plumstead. pp. 4. 1956.

665339

PLUTARCH
Lives of Octavius Caesar Augustus, Julius
Caesar, Marcus Brutus, Marcus Antonius,
Theseus, Alcibiades, Caius Martius
Coriolanus, from the 1579, 1595, 1603,
1612, edns. of Plutarch's Lives of the
noble Grecians and Romanes. Translated
out of Greek into French by J. Amyot
and out of French into English by Sir T.
North. With MS. notes by J.O. Halliwell-
Phillipps.] [1579-1612.]

496274

PLUTARCH
Lives, in 8 volumes.   Translated from
the Greek [with the life of Plutarch,
by J. Dryden.]   With notes historical
and critical from [A.] Dacier.
  ports.   illus.   7 vols.   1727.
Incomplete.   Vol. 8 wanting.
                              491781

PLUTARCH
Plutarch s Lives.   Translated from
the original Greek with notes
critical and historical and a new
life of Plutarch, by J. and W.
Langhorne.   5th edn., corrected.
[Including lives of Pericles,
Coriolanus, Lysander, Julius Caesar,
Demetrius, Antony and Brutus.]
  6 vols.   illus.   1792.

                          581550

PLUTARCH
Plutarch's Lives.   Translated from
the Greek with notes critical and
historical, and a new life of Plutarch,
by J. and W. Langhorne.   [Including
lives of Julius Caesar, Coriolanus,
Antony and Brutus.]
  8 vols.   1808.

                          513290

PLUTARCH
Lives of illustrious men, translated
from the Greek, with notes critical
and historical, and a life of Plutarch,
by J. and W. Langhorne.   New edn.
  ports.   2 vols.   1876.

                          487321

PLUTARCH
Lives of Alexander the Great and
Julius Caesar.   Translated by J. & W.
Langhorne.   [With an introduction
by H. Morley.]   1886.
  Cassell's National Library.
                          508015

PLUTARCH
Lives of Demetrius, Mark Antony, and
Themistocles, translated by J. Langhorne
and W. Langhorne.   [Edited, with
introduction, by H. Morley.]
                  1886.   414235
  Cassell's National Library.
  _____ Another edn.   1896.   414236

PLUTARCH
Shakespeare's Plutarch: a selection from
The Lives in [Sir T.] North's Plutarch
which illustrate Shakespeare's plays.
Edited, with a preface, notes, index of
names, and glossarial index, by W. W.
Skeat.   [Later edn.]   1904.

                          613447

PLUTARCH
Plutarch's Lives of Coriolanus, Caesar,
Brutus, and Antonius; in North's
translation.   Edited, with introduction
and notes, by R. H. Carr.   1906.

                          391793

PLUTARCH
Life of Julius Caesar in North's
translation.   Edited with introduction
and notes by R. H. Carr.   (Oxford)
                          1908.

                          545605

PLUTARCH
Julius Caesar from the histories of
Julius Caesar and Brutus in North's
Plutarch.   Put into Basic [English]
by A. P. Rossiter.
  table.   1933.
Psyche Miniatures, General Series,
No. 50.
                          403890

PLUTARCH
Shakespeare's Plutarch: the lives of
Julius Caesar, Brutus, Marcus Antonius
and Coriolanus in the translation of
Sir T. North.   Edited, with an intro-
duction, glossary and parallel passages
from Shakespeare's plays by T. J. B.
Spencer.   1964.
  Peregrine Books.
                          667944

Plutarch *works relating to*

—— The Coriolanus of Plutarch and
    Shakespeare.   From The Cornell
    Review, Vol. 4.

        (Ithaca [N.Y.])   1876.

                          558073

—— HEUER (HERMANN)
    From Plutarch to Shakespeare: a study
    of "Coriolanus".   IN SHAKESPEARE
    SURVEY 10.   (Cambridge)   1957.

                          665485

—— HONIGMANN (E. A. J.)
    Shakespeare's Plutarch.
    IN SHAKESPEARE QUARTERLY X: 1.
    pp. 25-33.
    (New York)   1959.
                          605711

—— LAW (R. A.)
    The Text of "Shakespeare's Plutarch"
    [: a study of the various editions
    of Sir Thomas North's translation of
    Plutarch's Parallel Lives, which showed
    it to be a source for several of
    Shakespeare's plays].   IN The Huntington
    Library Quarterly, Vol. 6.   (San
    Marino, Cal.)   1943.

                          549639

—— Shackford (Martha H.)

—— Plutarch in Renaissance England, with
    special reference to Shakespeare.
    [With a bibliography.] pp.54.
                          1929.

                          393979

—— Shakespeare's Plutarch: a selection
    from the lives in North's Plutarch
    which illustrate Shakespeare's plays.
    Edited by W. W. Skeat.   [A review.]
    IN The Nonconformist, Vol. 36.   1875.

                          520506

—— Trench (R.C.) Plutarch; his life,
his parallel lives and his morals:
five lectures. [With references to
Shakespeare.] 2nd edn.

1874.

68184

PLUTZIK (HYAM)
Horatio: a poem [that explores,
through a series of dramatic encounters,
the meaning of Hamlet's story].
(New York)   1961.

667596

PLYMOUTH SHAKSPERE LITERARY SOCIETY
Programmes, syllabuses, etc.]
(Plymouth)   1919-

453707

POCOCK (GUY [NOEL])
Brush up your reading.   Illustrated
by Anna Zinkeisen.   [With a chapter
on Shakespeare.]
bibliogs.   1942.

533027

POCOCK (GUY NOEL)
English men & women of ideas.   [Con-
taining chapters, "William Shakespeare
(1564-1616): the world's greatest
dramatist" and "Mrs. Siddons (1755-
1831): the supreme actress".] 1930.

427187

POEL (WILLIAM)
The Elizabethan Hamlet: [a review of
Shakespeare's Hamlet, by A. Clutton-
Brock.]   FROM The Hibbert Journal,
1922.   pp. [6.]   [1922]

389202

POEL (WILLIAM)
Monthly letters written for the
Shakespeare League Journal, Nos. 1-52.
1915-19.
Includes autograph letter by W. Poel.

665890

POEL (WILLIAM)
Monthly letters [on Shakespeare's
life and art, and the production
of his plays, privately circulated
among members of the London
Shakespeare League and their friends,
1912-1924.   Selected and arranged
[with foreword] by A. M. T.
port.   1929.

362873

POEL (W.)
The Playhouse of the sixteenth
century.   pp. 30.   [Edinburgh]
illus.   [c.1904.]

599944

Poel (W.) Shakespeare in the theatre.
Port.   1913.

431019

Poel (W.) Shakespeare's Jew and Marlowe's Christians.   In The Westminster
Review. Vol. 171.

1909,

POEL (WILLIAM)   218201.
William Poel's prompt-book of
Fratricide Punished [with text of
the play].   Edited, with an intro-
duction, by J. Isaacs.   pp. xx, 35.
facsimiles.   1956.
Society for Theatre Research.
Pamphlet Series No. 5.

658576

Poel, William *works relating to*

——CASSON (Sir LEWIS THOMAS)
The Influence of William Poel on the
modern theatre.   [Broadcast] 31st Dec.,
1951.   ff. 9.
typescript.   1951.

622923

—— DILLON (ARTHUR)
The Stage of the sixteenth century.
[Issued in connection with William
Poel's production of "Measure for
Measure" in 1893.]   pp. 19.
[London]   [?1893.]

665062

—— GLICK (CLARIS)
William Poel: his theories and influence.
IN Shakespeare Quarterly XV: 1.
pp.15-25. (New York)   1964.

605711

—— List of William Poel's productions,
1880-1932.   pp. [11.]
port.   [c.1933.]

622384

—— PAYNE (BEN IDEN)
Talking of theatre, 2: Variations
on a theatre theme, No. 10.
[Shakespeare productions, with special
reference to W. Poel.]   [Broadcast]
19th September, 1961.   ff. 5.
typescript.   1961.

666977

—— SPEAIGHT (ROBERT)
William Poel and the Elizabethan
revival.
ports.   illus.   chronological table,
bibliog.   1954.
Society for Theatre Research.   Annual
Publication [4] 1951-52.

641603

—— Sprague (A.C.) Shakespeare and William
Poel. In University of Toronto
Quarterly, Vol.17.

(Toronto)   1947.

596179

—— SPRAGUE (ARTHUR COLBY)
Shakespearian players and performances.
(Cambridge, Mass.)
ports. illus.   1953.
Enter William Poel, pp. 136-149.

635328

Poems of Shakespeare
see also under the titles of the individual plays

—— ALDEN (RAYMOND MACDONALD)
The 1710 and 1714 texts of Shakespeare's
poems.   IN Modern Language Notes,
Vol. 31.   (Baltimore, Md.) 1916.

439157/31

—— BALDWIN (THOMAS WHITFIELD)
On the literary genetics of Shakespere's
poems & sonnets.   (Urbana) 1950.

612745

—— DICKEY (FRANKLIN M.)
Not wisely but too well: Shakespeare's
love tragedies.   (San Marion, Cal.)
1957.
Huntington Library.

665754

—— ERSKINE (J.)
The Elizabethan lyric.
bibliog.   1931.
Columbia University Studies in
English and Comparative Literature.

404866

—— JANTZ (HAROLD S.)
Goethe and an Elizabethan poem [?
Shakespeare's].   IN Modern Language
Quarterly, Vol. 12.   (Seattle, Wash.)
1951.

525289/12

—— [Jortin (J.) ed.] Miscellaneous
observations upon authors, ancient
and modern [including Shakespeare.]
2 vols.
1731-2.

486890

—— LEVER (JULIUS WALTER)
Twentieth-century studies in
Shakespeare's Songs, Sonnets, and Poems;
3: The Poems.   IN SHAKESPEARE SURVEY
15.   (Cambridge)   1962.

667174

—— PRINCE, FRANK TEMPLETON
William Shakespeare: the poems.
1963.
Writers and their work.

667704

—— Rendall (G.H.) Personal clues in
Shakespeare poems & sonnets,
[relating to Edward de Vere].

1934.

426741

—— Ross (W.) The Story of Anne Whateley and
William Shaxpere, as revealed by "The
Sonnets to Mr. W.H." and other
Elizabethan poetry. [With a biblio-
graphy.]

(Glasgow)   1939.

510565

—— Saintsbury (G.[E.B.]) Shakespeare [:1.
Life and plays; 2. Poems. From
The Cambridge History of English
Literature, vol.5.] With an
appreciation [of the author] by
Helen J. Waddell.

(Cambridge)   1934.

(Cambridge Miscellany, 14.)

425998

—— Shakspeare's minor poems. From
[The Oxford and Cambridge Magazine,
Vol. 1].

1856.

554145

—— Williams (F.) Mr. Shakespeare of The
Globe. [With a bibliography.]
Ports. Illus. Map. Facsimiles.

(New York)   1941.

527721

—— Winsor (J.) Shakespeare's poems: a
bibliography of the earlier editions.
In Harvard College Library. Bulletins,
Vol.1, Nos. 9 and 10.

[Cambridge, Mass.]   1878-79.

14250

Poems on Shakespeare
see also Burlesques; Jubilees and
Commemorations *and under the titles of the
individual works*

——   [Aldington (Mrs. Hilda)] Good Frend
[: a poem]. In [Aldington (Mrs. Hilda)]
By Avon River [by] H.D. [pseud.]

(New York)   1949.

602772

—— Aldrich (T.B.) At Stratford-upon-
Avon [and] Ellen Terry in "The
Merchant of Venice". In Aldrich
(T.B.) Poems [and plays]. Revised
and complete Household Edition.
Illus.
(Boston, [Mass.])   1907.

544304

——ALDRICH (T. B.)
[Poem on Shakespeare.]   IN The
Shakespeare Tercentenary meeting
held at the Mansion House, May Day,
1916 [etc.]   pp. 18 [2.]   [1916.]
Printed at "The Sign of the Dolphin".

603467

——ARLOTT (J.)
Portrait of William Shakespeare (for
Clifford Bax) [: a sonnet].   IN
English: the magazine of the English
Association, Vol. 5.   (Oxford)
1944-45.

569018

——ARNOLD (MATTHEW)
Shakespeare [: a sonnet].   IN
Arnold (M.) Poetical works.   With
an introduction by Sir A. T. Quiller-
Couch.   (Oxford)
port.   1942.
For other editions of this poem please
check the main sequence under the
author's name.

569859

——AUNG (S. Z.)
From the Burmese Buddhists [: Burmese
poem with English translation].
IN GOLLANCZ ([Sir] I.) ed., A Book of
homage to Shakespeare.
ports. illus. facsimiles. [1916.]

264175

——BAILEY (R. E.)
Dark eyes and Will Shakespeare [: a
poem relating to the Dark Lady of
the Sonnets].   pp. 51.   (Milwaukee,
Wis.)
bibliog.   1944.

562120

——BAIN (R.)
Shakespeare and Dickens and me.
IN Bain (R.) Mice and men [: poems].
pp. 44.   (Glasgow)   1941.

529198

——BALMONT (K.)
Na otmeli vremen (On the shoal of time);
Vseobemlyushchi (The All-embracing).
Translated by N. Forbes.
IN GOLLANCZ ([Sir] I.) ed., A Book of
homage to Shakespeare.
ports. illus. facsimiles. [1916.]

264175

——BANCROFT (EDITH M.)
The Shakespeare Festival.   The
Prologue.   The Stratford Pilgrims
[: a parody of The Prologue to The
Canterbury Tales by G. Chaucer.]
IN The Journal of Education Vol. 71.
1939.

510161

——[BARHAM (R. H.)]
The Merchant of Venice: a legend of
Italy [in verse.]   IN [Barham (R. H.)]
The Ingoldsby Legends, with illustra-
tions by G. Cruikshank, J. Leech and
J. Tenniel.   1865.
For other editions of this poem please
check the main sequence under the author's
name.

37744

——BARNFIELD (R.)
Poems.   [With an introduction by
A. J. M. A. M. Summers.   Contains
a poem, Remembrance of some English
poets, with reference to Shakespeare].
(Fortune Press)
bibliog.   [1936].
No. 438 of an edn. of 500 copies.

453777

——BARR (J.)
American humorous verse.   Selected
and edited, with introduction and notes,
by J. Barr.   [Including "The Amateur
Orlando", a poem relating to
Shakespeare].   [1891.]
The Canterbury Poets.

459390

——BASSE (W.)
Elegy on Shakespeare.   IN DRINKWATER
(J.) [ed.] A Pageant of England's
life presented by her poets.
facsimile.   1934.

422901

——BASSE (W.)
On Mr. Wm. Shakespeare [: a poem].
IN ALDINGTON (R.) ed., Poetry of the
English-speaking world.   [With an
introduction by the editor.] 1947.

587865

——BAUM (PAULL FRANKLIN)
"Shakespeare" [: a study of Matthew
Arnold's sonnet].   IN Baum (P. F.)
Ten studies in the poetry of Matthew
Arnold.   (Durham, N.C.)   1958.

679765

——B[eerbohm] (M.) The Characters of Shakespeare [: verses].   In The Mask, Vol.
10.

(Florence)   1924.

482281

——Berenger ([R.]) Canto on the birth-day
of Shakspeare. In The World, [edited]
by A. Chalmers, [Vol.4.]

1802.

(British essayists, Vol.29.)

459739

——BERENGER (R.)
To Mr. Garrick, on his erecting a temple
and statue to Shakespear; [and] On the
birth-day of Shakespear; a cento, taken
from his works.   IN [DODSLEY (R.) ed.,]
A Collection of poems by several hands.
[5th edn.]   Vol. 6. 1758.   538523
——————— Another copy.   576735
——————— Another copy.   576741

——BINYON ([R.] L.)
England's poet [: a sonnet].
IN GOLLANCZ ([Sir] I.) ed., A Book of
homage to Shakespeare.
ports. illus. facsimiles. [1916.]

264175

——BIRCH (L.)
Dreams and realities: poems
[containing two poems on
Shakespeare - "In Shakespeare-Land",
and "To Shakespeare".] 1914.

481964

——BOAS (GUY)
The Repertory actor [: a poem relating
to Shakespeare's characters]. IN
Boas (G.) [ed.] An English book of
light verse. 1944.

548406

——BOND (R. W.)
1600 [: a poem on Shakespeare].
IN GOLLANCZ ([Sir] I.) ed., A Book of
homage to Shakespeare.
ports. illus. facsimiles. [1916.]

264175

——Bower (H.) Milton and Shakespeare : a
comparison. [A sonnet.] In
Bower (H.) The Painted book and
other poems.

(Bristol) 1897.

567624

——BOYAJIAN (ZABELLE C.)
Armenia's love to Shakespeare [: Armenian
poem with English translation.]
IN GOLLANCZ ([Sir] I.) ed., A Book of
homage to Shakespeare.
ports. illus. facsimiles. [1916.]

264175

——BRITTON (J. J.)
In memoriam, W. Shakspere,
April 23, 1616. IN [Newspaper
cuttings collected by J. Cotton:
literary and poetical. Vol. 2.]
ports. illus. [c.1890-1933]

467751

——BROWNING (ROBERT)
At the "Mermaid" [, with reference
to Shakespeare]. IN Browning (R.)
Poetical works. Vol. 14. 1919.

473873

——Browning (R.) The Names: a sonnet on
Shakespeare. In Cooke (G.W.) A Guide-
book to the poetic and dramatic
works of Robert Browning. [With a
bibliography.]

(Boston, [Mass.]) 1891.

529741

——BUNNER (H. C.)
My Shakspere [: a poem on an old copy
of Shakespeare]. IN LANG (A.) ed.,
Ballads of books. 1888.

94680

——BUTT (G.)
An Ode: Shakspere's chorus before
the battle of Agincourt - Henry V,
[and] An Epilogue to Shakspere's
Tragedy of King Lear. IN Butt (G.)
Poems, Vol. 1. 1793.

563232

——CAMPBELL (J.)
Scotland for ever, and other poems.
[With a sonnet on Shakespeare.]
pp. 80. (Birmingham) 1937.

471513

——CAMPBELL ([W.] W.)
Shakespeare [: a sonnet.]
IN GOLLANCZ ([Sir] I.) ed., A Book of
homage to Shakespeare.
ports. illus. facsimiles. [1916.]

264175

—— Chapman (R.) Shakespeare [: a poem].
In Bell (W.) ed., Poetry from Oxford
in wartime. pp. 94.

1945.

(Fortune Press)

559832

——CLERCQ (R. de)
Als deez' tijden groot [: Flemish poem
with English translation].
IN GOLLANCZ ([Sir] I) ed., A Book of
homage to Shakespeare.
ports. illus. facsimiles. [1916.]

264175

—— COLERIDGE (H.)
New poems, including a selection from
his published poetry [and two poems
on Shakespeare]. Edited [with a
preface] by E. L. Griggs. (Oxford)
port. 1942.

530450

——COLLINS (W. J. T.)
A Memory-haunted river [: a poem
on Shakespeare]. IN Collins (W.J.T.)
"Pilgrimage" and other poems.
pp. 69. (Newport [Mon.]) 1944.
No. 152 of edn. limited to 250
copies. signed by the author.

561252

——CONVERSE (FLORENCE)
Collected poems. [Including
Toast to Master Will]. 1937.

532416

——COOPER (J. G.)
The Tomb of Shakespear: a vision.
2nd edn. pp. 11. 1755. 474619
———— IN [Cooper (J. G.)] Poems on
several subjects, by the author of
the Life of Socrates.
frontis. 1764. 548210
———— IN [DODSLEY (R.) ed.] A Collection of poems by several hands. [5th
edn.] Vol. 5.
illus. 1758. 538522
——Another copy. 576734
——Another copy. 576740

——Cormack (Barbara) To Mary Arden
Shakespeare, mother of the sweetest
singer of all time. From
Chambers's Journal, April 1941.

524715

——COURTHOPE (W. J.)
The Tercentenary of Shakespeare's death
- 1916 [: a sonnet, with Italian
paraphrase].
IN GOLLANCZ ([Sir] I.) ed., A Book of
homage to Shakespeare.
ports. illus. facsimiles. [1916.]

264175

——Cruickshank (N.K.) While reading Shakespeare's sonnets [: a poem.] In
The Poetry Review, Vol.29.

1938.

492632

——CUMMINS ([Miss] P. D.)
The Defeated [: poems, including
some relating to Shakespeare.]
pp. viii, 64.   1947.

588931

——"D", [pseud.]
To Shakespeare: a sonnet. IN The
Journal of Education, New Series,
vol. 4.   1882.

408617

—— DAVENANT (Sir W.)
Three songs and an ode [in remembrance
of Master William Shakespeare].
Reprinted from Works, [1673].
pp. [8.]   1936.
No. 51 of an edn. of 75 copies
privately printed.
[Bache Matthews Christmas Booklet]

469919

——Davies (I.) Gold [: a poem on Shakes-
peare]. In Davies (I.) Tonypandy
and other poems.

1945.

562942

——Davies (M.) Shakespeare heroines [:
poems]. From [The New Monthly
Magazine,] Vol[s]. 5[-6. New
Series.]

[1874.]

558100

——DAVIES (W. H.)
Shakespeare works [: a poem].
IN GOLLANCZ ([Sir] I.) ed., A Book of
homage to Shakespeare.
ports. illus. facsimiles. [1916.]

264175

—— D[AVIS] (G.)
On the Second Centenary of the Death
of Shakespeare [: Broadside. 1816.]
IN [DAVIS (G.) A Collection of poems.]
broadsides and manuscript.
[1790-1819.]

413435

—— DAVIS (O. H.)
To William Shakespeare [: a sonnet].
IN The Central Literary Magazine,
Vol. 30. 1931-32.   1932.

407290

——De la Mare (W.[J.]) Collected poems.
[Containing poems on characters
from Shakespeare's plays.] With
decorations by B.Wolpe.

1942.

532029

——DE LA MARE (W. J.)
Ten characters from Shakespeare
[: poems]. IN The Monthly
Review, Vol. 7.   1902.

170751

——Dixon (W.M.) In Arcadia. [Includes
a poem "In remembrance of our
worthy Master Shakespere".]
pp.X, 84.

1933.

419828

——DIXON (W. M.)
In remembrance of our worthy Master
Shakespeare [: a quatorzain and a sonnet].
IN GOLLANCZ ([Sir] I.) ed., A Book of
homage to Shakespeare.
ports. illus. facsimiles. [1916.]

264175

——DOBSON ([H.] A.)
The Riddle, W.S., 1564-1616 [: a poem].
IN GOLLANCZ ([Sir] I.) ed., A Book of
homage to Shakespeare.
ports. illus. facsimiles. [1916.]

264175

——Douglas (Lord Alfred [B.]) Sonnets
[including one, To Shakespeare.]
pp. 77.

[1943.]

545230

——DOWDEN (E.)
Sent to an American Shakespeare
society [: a poem]. IN Dowden (E.)
Poems.
port.   1914.

250337

——DRAYTON (M.)
The Battaile of Agincourt. Elegies
upon sundry occasions [etc., including
"To my most dearely-loved friend
Henery Reynolds Esquire, of Poets
and Poesie", containing a reference
to Shakespeare. (Printed for
William Lee)
port.   1627.

560046

——DRINKWATER (J.)
For April 23rd, 1616-1916 [: a poem].
IN Drinkwater (J.) Olton pools [and
other poems]. Second impression.
pp. 42.   1916.

569404

——DRINKWATER (JOHN)
  For April 23rd, 1616-1916 [: a poem].
  IN GOLLANCZ ([Sir] I.) ed., A Book of
  homage to Shakespeare.
    ports. illus. facsimiles. [1916.]

                                264175

——DRINKWATER (J.)
  For April 23rd, 1616-1916; [and]
  Portia's housekeeping.
  IN Drinkwater (J.) Collected poems,
  1908-1922.
    2 vols. illus.   1923.
  No. 54 of edn. limited to 230 copies,
  signed by the author.

                                566422

—— DRINKWATER (J.)
  Shakespeare in Shoreditch [: a poem].
  IN FAITHFULL (LILIAN M.) The Evening
  crowns the day [: an autobiography].
    ports. illus.   1940.

                                516878

——The Druriad: or, Strictures on the
  principal performers of Drury-Lane
  Theatre: a satirical poem: with notes
  critical and explanatory. [With
  references to Shakespeare.] pp.28.

                  1798.

                                524911

——DUKES (A.)
  William Shakespeare to John Citizen
  [: a poem]. IN Shakespeare Memorial
  Theatre Fund, Theatre Royal, Drury
  Lane, Nov. 9th, 1926. Grand matinee
  in aid of the Fund. pp. 20.
    ports. illus.   1926.

                                436133

——Edwards (W.T.) Stratford-upon-Avon.
  In Wood (L.S.) and Burrows (H.L.)
  eds.,The Town in literature
  [: an anthology.] Frontis.

                  1925.

(The Teaching of English Series.)

                                437579

——ELTON (O.)
  Helena [: a sonnet].
  IN GOLLANCZ ([Sir] I.) ed., A Book of
  homage to Shakespeare.
    ports. illus. facsimiles. [1916.]

                                264175

——Emmons (Elise) The Lone eagle
  [: poems, including "Shakespeare's
  birthday","Anne Hathaway"].

      (Boston,[Mass.])   1928.

                                467846

——FALCONER (AGNES S.)
  Shakespeare's Beatrice [: a sonnet].
  FROM Chambers's Journal 1905.
  (Edinburgh)   1905.

                                390788

——[FENTON (E.)]
  An Epistle to Mr. Southerne, 1711
  [containing lines of verse on
  Shakespeare]. IN [Fenton (E.)]
  Poems on several occasions.
    frontis.   1717.

                                538120

——Field (P.) Souvenir: the 61st Division.
  [Containing a poem to Shakespeare.]
  pp.[8.] Ports. Illus.

      (Stratford-on-Avon)   1929.

                                420580

——Fridlander (D.) Of earth and the
    spirit: poems [including To
  Shakespeare.] pp. 95.

          (Oxford)   1938.

(Shakespeare Head Press.)

                                491323

—— FUNDUKLIAN (K. H.)
  To Shakespeare [: Armenian poem, with
  English translation].
  IN GOLLANCZ ([Sir] I.) ed., A Book of
  homage to Shakespeare.
    ports. illus. facsimiles. [1916.]

                                264175

——G.(H.J.L.) Medleys and songs without
    music [including Romeo and Juliet.]

                  1891.

                                498540

——[GARDEN (F.)]
  Miscellanies in prose and verse,
  including remarks on English plays,
  operas, farces and other publications,
  by Lord Gardenstone. [Including a
  poem on Shakespeare.]   (Edinburgh)
                              1792.

                                499065

——GARRICK, DAVID
  Songs relating to Shakspeare in
  "Harlequin's Invasion" written by
  David Garrick Esqr.   1805.
  MS single sheet.

                                772307

——GAYLEY (C. M.)
  Heart of the race [: a poem].
  IN GOLLANCZ ([Sir] I) ed., A Book of
  homage to Shakespeare.
    ports. illus. facsimiles. [1916.]

                                264175

——GOLLANCZ ([Sir] H.)
  [Hebrew ode with English paraphrase].
  IN GOLLANCZ ([Sir] I.) ed., A Book of
  homage to Shakespeare.
    ports. illus. facsimiles. [1916.]

                                264175

——GORELL (RONALD GORELL BARNES, 3rd Baron)
  W.S. to Stratford, Conn. IN Gorell
  (R. G. B.) All my yesterdays [and
  other poems].   1958.

                                680524

——GOSSE ([Sir] EDMUND)
With a copy of Shakespeare's sonnets.
IN Gosse ([Sir] E.) In russet & silver
[: poems]. 1894.

481473

—— GRAVES (A. P.)
The Fairies' homage [: a poem].
IN GOLLANCZ ([Sir] I.) ed., A Book of
homage to Shakespeare.
ports. illus. facsimiles. [1916.]

264175

——**Graves (A.P.) Shakespeare, April 23,
1864 [: a poem].** From [The Dublin
University Magazine, Vol. 62.]

[Dublin] 1864.

561335

——Gray (T.) Poems. [Including a poem
'William Shakespeare to Mrs. Anne'.]
Edited by A.L. Poole, [as revised
by L. Whibley, 1936].
1937.

(Hesperides Series.)

474419

—— Gray (T.) William Shakespeare to
Mrs. Anne. In Gray (T.) Poems.

(Oxford) [1939.]
(The World's Classics, 174.)

504786

——Gray [(T.)] and Collins [(W.)] Poems.
Edited by A.L. Poole. [Including
poems relating to Shakespeare.]
Ports. Facsimiles.

1937.

471548

——Green (R.L.) The Singing rose and other
poems [including poems on Shakespeare].

(Leicester) 1947.

585038

—— Green (T.) Poems. [Including Shakespeare:
an apostrophe. Printed at the]
Birmingham School of Printing.
pp.8.
(Birmingham) 1935.

446374

—— GRIERSON (H. J. C.)
Shakespeare and Scotland [: a poem].
IN GOLLANCZ ([Sir] I.) ed., A Book of
homage to Shakespeare.
ports. illus. facsimiles. [1916.]

264175

——HAFIZ IBRAHIM (M.)
To the memory of Shakespeare [: Arabic
poem, with a summary in English.]
IN GOLLANCZ ([Sir] I.) ed., A Book of
homage to Shakespeare.
ports. illus. facsimiles. [1916.]

264175

——Hall (S.) An Ape on Parnassus: poems
and imitations. [Including poems
in imitation of Shakespeare].
pp.80.

1936.

463879

——HARDY (T.)
To Shakespeare after 300 years [: a
poem]. IN GOLLANCZ ([Sir] I.) ed.,
A Book of homage to Shakespeare.
ports. illus. facsimiles. [1916.]

264175

—— HARDY (T.)
To Shakespeare [: facsimile of MS. of
poem.] IN Shakespeare Memorial
Theatre Fund, Theatre Royal, Drury
Lane, Nov. 9th, 1926. Grand matinée
in aid of the Fund. pp. [20].
ports. illus. 1926.

436133

——Hartnoll (Phyllis) The Maid's song
and other poems. [Including poems
on Shakespearian actors.] pp. 87.

1938.

491665

—— Hawley (W.D.) The Battle of
Edge-hill, and other poems. [With
references to Shakespeare.] Frontis.

1881.

397029

——HAYWARD (A.)
To [The lover of Shakespeare: a
poem]. IN [Fisher's] drawing-room
scrap-book, edited by Hon. Mrs.
Norton and C. Mackay, vol. 2.
illus. [1854]

454742

——HERRING (R.)
Harlequin Mercutio; or, Plague on
your houses: a ride through raids to
resurrection [in verse]. FROM Life
and Letters To-day, Vols. 31 and 32.
1941-2,

534897

——HERRING (R.)
Harlequin Mercutio; or, A Plague on
both your houses: a ride through raids
to resurrection [: a verse pantomime
of present-day London, Mercutio and
Hamlet are taken to be two aspects,
the spirit and conscience, of the same
person, Ego]. IN SCHIMANSKI (S.) and
TREECE (H.) eds., Transformation [: an
anthology].

1942.

543517

——HERSEE FAMILY
Poems by the family of Hersee.
[Containing poems relating to
Shakespeare.] All published in the
Warwick Advertiser. ([Warwick])
[c.1830-1840.]

463311

—— Holland (H.) Shakespeare dead,
1616 [: sonnet.] In Guiney
(Louise I.) [and Bliss (G.) eds.,]
Recusant poets, with a selection
from their work. [With bibliographical notes.]
1938

1. Saint Thomas More to Ben Jonson.

495299

—— [HUCKELL (J.)]
Avon: a poem.   pp. 78.   (Birmingham:
Printed for J. Baskerville)
1758.   5501
————   Another copy.   463129
On page 77 of this copy the signature
K2 is printed as 2K.   Contains
manuscript notes relating to the author.
————   Another edn.   pp. 59.
(Stratford-upon-Avon)
1811.   42690

—— Hunkin (Gladys) The Poets to
Shakespeare [: a sonnet]. In The
Poetry Review, Vol.33.

1942.

546123

—— HUNTER (EDWIN RAY)
A Man from Stratford entertains Ben
Jonson, in Stratford, August 7, 1623,
for Mistress Anne Shakespeare's funeral.
IN SHAKESPEARE QUARTERLY II: 2.
pp. 91-97.
(New York)   1951.
605711

—— IBBOT [B.]
A Fit of the spleen, in imitation of
Shakespeare [: a poem].   IN [DODSLEY
(R.) ed.] A Collection of poems by
several hands.   [5th edn.] Vol. 5.
illus.   1758.   538522
————   Another copy.   576734
————   Another copy.   576740

—— IGVAL (M.)
To Shakespeare: a tribute from the
East [: Urdu poem, with English
translation by] S. J. Singh.
IN GOLLANCZ ([Sir] I.) ed., A Book of
homage to Shakespeare.
ports.   illus.   facsimiles.   [1916.]

264175

—— IMAGE (S.)
Poems [edited by A. H. Mackmurdo.
Including poems on Shakespeare.]
port.   facsimile.   1932.

400764

——   IN SHAKESPEARE'S COUNTRY. pp.19.
Port. Illus.   1905.

667238

—— Jackson (Ada) Anne Shakespeare; and
Mary Shakespeare: poems. In Jackson
(Ada) The Widow, and other poems.

1933.

416088

—— Jaques (E.T.) The Bankside, Southwark.
[With references to Shakespeare.]
In The Pall Mall Magazine, vol.11.
1897. Illus.

1897.

357025

—— JERROLD (D. [W.])
Shakespeare's crab-tree.
IN Cambridge Garrick Club, Album.
Edited by a Member of the Club.
(Cambridge)   1836.

452001

—— JOHNSON (ALBERT EDWARD)
The Crown and the laurel [including
poems on Shakespeare.]   pp. 34.
(Oxford)   1953.

633361

—— Johnson (H.H.) The Voice of one,
[vol.2:] Love lyrics. [With poems
on Shakespearian characters.]
pp.39.
(Oxford)   1934.

(Shakespeare Head Press.)

420449

—— JOHNSON (R. U.)
Shakespeare [: a poem].
IN GOLLANCZ ([Sir] I.) ed., A Book of
homage to Shakespeare.
ports.   illus.   facsimiles.   [1916.]

264175

—— JOHNSON (S.)
The Drury-Lane Prologue; and the
Epilogue by David Garrick [spoken
at the opening of the Drury-Lane
Theatre], 1747.   Reproduced in
type-facsimile from the edition
printed by W. Webb.   pp. vi, 4,
xiii.   1924.
For other editions of this work check
the main sequence under the author's
name.

318787

—— JOHNSON (SAMUEL W.)
The Courtship of Anne Hathaway:
a dramatic poem.   With excerpts
from the plays and sonnets of
Shakespeare in modern English.
pp. 95.   (New York)   1952.

632782

—— KEATE (G.)
Prologue [and] Epilogue to the play
of King John, acted at Mr. Newcomb's
at Hackney, March 1769.
IN [PEARCH (G.) ed.] A Collection
of poems by several hands.   New edn.
Vol. 3.   1783.   99654
————   Another copy.   576745

—— Kemble (S.G.) Odes, lyrical ballads, and
poems on various occasions, [including
poems on Falstaff; The Shakespeare
Club, Coventry: a song; To Ophelia].

(Edinburgh)   1809.

521634

——Kemp (T.C.) Shakespeare [: a poem].
<u>In</u> The Central Literary Magazine,
Vol.32, July, 1936.

(Birmingham)   1936.

463922

——KENDALL (HARRIET)
Shakespeare [: a poem]. IN
Shakespeare Memorial Theatre Fund,
Theatre Royal, Drury Lane, Nov. 9th,
1926, Grand matinee in aid of the Fund.
pp. 20.
ports.   illus.   1926.

436133

——Koehring (Vera) Hamlet, on the time
clock [: a poem]. <u>In</u> Columbia
poetry, 1941. Edited with an
introduction by D.L.Clark.

(New York)   1941.

530399

——KOMAI (G.)
To Shakespeare: the greatest conqueror
of all.   [Japanese poem, with English
translation.]
IN GOLLANCZ ([Sir] I.) ed., A Book of
homage to Shakespeare.
ports. illus. facsimiles. [1916.]

264175

——La Barre (Julia) Stories of Shakespeare's popular comedies, told
in rhyme. pp.70. Port.

(Portland, Oregon)   1933.

415119

——Landor (W.S.) Complete works edited
[with preface and notes], vols.1-12,
by T.E. Webley, vols. 13-16, by
S. Wheeler. [Containing, "In
examination of Shakespeare" and
Shakespearean references.] Ports.
Illus.   16 vols.

1927-1936.

Limited edn. 525 sets.

339417

——Landor [W.S.] Poetry & prose [etc.,
including poems on Shakespeare].
With an introduction and notes by
E.K.Chambers. Port.

(Oxford)   1946.

569883

——LANGFORD (J. A.)
Poems of the fields and the town.
[With Ode to the memory of Shakespeare].
1859.

462979

——Lanyon (Carla L.) Shakespeare
answers the scholars. In The
Poetry Review.

1939.

510174

——LEIGH (C. LEIGH, [1st Baron])
Fifth epistle to a friend in town,
Warwickshire [including references
to Shakespeare] and other poems.
1835.

438403

——LEINO (E.)
Shakespeare - tunnelma [: Finnish poem
with English translation.]
IN GOLLANCZ ([Sir] I.) ed., A Book of
homage to Shakespeare.
ports. illus. facsimiles. [1916.]

264175

——LIU PO TUAN
Chinese homage [: Chinese poem, with
English paraphrase.]
IN GOLLANCZ ([Sir] I.) ed., A Book of
homage to Shakespeare.
ports. illus. facsimiles. [1916.]

264175

——Longfellow (H.W.) Sonnet on Mrs.
Kemble's readings from Shakspeare.
<u>In</u> Longfellow (H.W.) Voices of the
night, The Seaside and the fireside
and other poems. 2nd edn. Illus.

[1840.]

485392

——A Lyric ode on the fairies, aerial
beings and witches of Shakespeare.
pp. 18.   1776.
Imperfect.

599045

——M[acCURDY] (E. A. C.)
Wood-notes [: a poem relating to
Shakespeare]. IN M[acCurdy] (E. A. C.)
Parva seges [: poems].   pp. 39.
(Oxford)   1894.

587899

——MacLeish (A.) Verses for a centennial
[: a poem on Shakespeare]. <u>In</u>
MacLeish (A.) Streets in the moon
[: poems].

(Boston [Mass.]   1926.

530678

——Major (H.) Poems [including one on
Shakspere].

1865.

507657

——[MALLET (D.)]
An Epistle to Mr. Pope, occasioned
by Theobald's Shakespear and
Bentley's Milton [: a poem].
2nd edn.   pp. [ii], 14.   1733.

179160

——[MALLET (D.)]
Of verbal criticism: an epistle to
Mr. Pope occasioned by Theobald's
Shakespear, and Bentley's Milton [:
a poem.] pp. 14.   1733. 482783
The 2nd edn. was entitled An Epistle
to Pope, etc.
—————— IN Mallet (D.) Works, New edn.
Vol. 1.   1759. 157118

——MANCHESTER TERCENTENARY ASSOCIATION
Songs and recitations in commemoration
of the Shakespeare Tercentenary by
Shakespearean students and pupils in
Manchester schools.   3rd edn.,
enlarged.   pp. 31.   (Manchester)
1916.

591416

——MARTIN (J. S.)
A Winter's tale; and, Falstaff [: 2
poems].   IN Poetry of To-day, [New
Series, Vol. 18].   1945.

319077/N.S./18

——   Masefield (J.) Ode, recited by
Lady Keeble on the opening of the
Stratford Memorial Theatre by H.R.H.
the Prince of Wales, April 23, 1932.
[Printed at the Birmingham School
of Printing.] 4 ff.

1932.

397560

——[MAURICE (T.)]
Westminster Abbey, [including references
to Shakespeare] with other occasional
poems and a free translation of the
Oedipus Tyrannus of Sophocles [with a
preface by S. Johnson].
port.   illus.   1813.

546670

——MEYNELL ([Mrs.] ALICE)
Poems, [including The Two Shakespeare
Tercentenaries, of birth, 1864; of
death, 1916: To Shakespeare.]
Complete edn.
  port.   1923.   398093
  _____ Another edn. 1940. 520025
  _____ Another edn.   IN Meynell ([Mrs.
A.) Prose and poetry.   Centenary
volume.
  ports.   1947. 586379

——Michell (N.) A Vision of Shakespeare
[: a poem]. From [The New Monthly
Magazine, Vol.130].

[1864.]

581095

——MIDDLETON (THOMAS)
The Ghost of Lucrece [: a.continuation
of Shakespeare's poem.]   Reproduced
in facsimile from the unique copy in
the Folger Shakespeare Library, with
an introduction and an edited text by
J. C. Adams.   (New York)   1937.
Folger Shakespeare Library Publications.

479712

——MILNE (A. A.)
"The Harvest" [: a poem on Shakespeare.]
IN Shakespeare Memorial Theatre Fund,
Theatre Royal, Drury Lane, Nov. 9th,
1926.   Grand matinee in aid of the
Fund.   pp. [20].
  ports.   illus.   1926.

436133

——MILTON (JOHN)
On Shakespeare [: a poem].   IN
AUSLANDER (J.) and HILL (F. E.) [eds.]
The Winged horse anthology.   Educa-
tional edn.   (New York)   1929.
  John Milton's poem "On Shakespear, 1630"
was first printed in the prefatory
material to the Second Folio edition of
Shakespeare's plays, 1632.   539577

——MØLLER (N.)
Paa vej til Shakespeare.   (On the way
to Shakespeare.)   [: Danish poem with
English translation].
IN GOLLANCZ ([Sir] I.) ed., A Book of
homage to Shakespeare.
  ports.   illus.   facsimiles. [1916.]

264175

——Mutschmann (H.) Further studies
concerning the origin of Paradise
Lost. [With appendix: The Sources
of Milton's poem "On Shakespeare".]
pp.55.

(Tartu)   1934.

425388

——[NICHOLS (J.) ed.]
A Select collection of poems, with
notes, biographical and historical.
[Including poems on Shakespeare.]
6 vols.   ports.   1780–82.
Wants Vols. 3 and 5.

504979

——NOYES (A.)
The Shadow of the master [: a poem].
IN GOLLANCZ ([Sir] I.) ed., A Book of
homage to Shakespeare.
  ports.   illus.   facsimiles. [1916.]

264175

——Noyes (A.) Tales of the Mermaid
Tavern.

(Edinburgh)   1924.

422875

—— Ode to the genius of Shakespear.
[pp. 75–82.]   [c.1760.]
Extracted from unknown work.

666347

——On Shakespeare. In Fraser's Magazine,
Vol.21.

1840.

10621

——On Shakespear's monument at Stratford
upon Avon [: a poem.]   IN [DODSLEY
(R.) ed.] A Collection of poems by
several hands.   5th edn.   Vol. 2.
illus.   1758.

538519

——ORDISH (THOMAS FAIRMAN)
Shakespeare in London, a fantasy [in
verse].   (London Shakespeare
Commemoration, 1913).   [With typescript
original, signed by the author.]
pp. [4], ff. [4].
2 vols.   [1913.]

665063

——PADELFORD (F. M.)
Shakespeare [: a poem.]
IN GOLLANCZ ([Sir] I.) ed., A Book of
homage to Shakespeare.
ports. illus. facsimiles. [1916.]

264175

——PAGET (E. N.)
Festival sonnets, Stratford-on-Avon
[by]E. N. P[aget]. pp. 54. [6.]
[c.1910]

638379

——PARKER (L. N.)
Thd Ode to Adelaide Ristori [with
reference to her Shakespearian parts].
IN His Majesty's Theatre [London],
Adelaide Ristori memorial matinée
[programme], Nov. 30th, 1908. pp.[4.]
port. [1908.]

531801

——PASTERNAK (B.)
Shakespeare [: a poem].
IN Pasternak (B.) Selected poems.
Translated from the Russian by
J. M. Cohen. [With] drawings by
Donia Nachshen. pp. vi, 58. 1946.
Russian Literature Library.

577203

—— Pendlebury (B.J.) To Enid [with
a copy of Romeo and Juliet] and
other poems. pp.30.

1922.

428708

——[PENNY (Mrs. ANNE)]
Poems, with a dramatic entertainment,
by **** *****. [Including several
poems relating to Shakespeare.]
illus. [1771.]

550539

——Postgate (Isa J.) Woodnotes: poems
[on Shakespeare, and quotations from
his plays]. Illustrated by Nathalie
V. Nikitin. pp. [13.]

(New York) [c.1840.]

479264

——Quirk (C.J.) To Shakespeare's England
[: a sonnet]. In The Month, Vol.180.

1944.

562830

——RAMSEY (T. W.)
On re-reading Twelfth Night.
IN Ramsey (T. W.) Antares [: poems].
pp. 64. 1934.
Macmillan's Contemporary Poets.

432070

——REEVES ([Hon.] W. P.)
The Dream imperial [: a poem].
IN GOLLANCZ ([Sir] I.) ed., A Book of
homage to Shakespeare.
ports. illus. facsimiles. [1916.]

264175

——REID (A.)
Twelve variations on the theme of
Caliban. IN Reid (A.) Steps to a
viewpoint [: poems]. pp. 48.

1947.

585309

——[RENNELL] (J. R. RODD, [1st Baron])
The Tercentenary of Shakespeare's death
- 1916 [: a sonnet].
IN GOLLANCZ ([Sir] I.) ed., A Book of
homage to Shakespeare.
ports. illus. facsimiles. [1916.]

264175

——RENSHAW (C[ONSTANCE] A.)
Freeman of the hills [: poems,
including a poem "Shakespeare knew".]
(Oxford: Shakespeare Head Press)

1939.

499246

——Renshaw (C[onstance] A.) Shakespeare.
In Rendhaw (C[onstance] A.) Lest
we forget : [poems.] pp. xi, 83.

(Oxford) 1937.

(Shakespeare Head Press)

513982

——ROBERTS (C. G. D.)
To Shakespeare, 1916 [: a poem.]
IN GOLLANCZ ([Sir] I.) ed., A Book of
homage to Shakespeare.
ports. illus. facsimiles. [1916.]

264175

——ROBERTSON (J.)
Written on a blank leaf of
Shakespeare. IN [Robertson (J.)]
Poems by nobody. 1770.

483156

—— Robinson (E.A.) Collected poems,
[including 'Ben Jonson entertaihs a
Man from Stratford'.] New edn. Port.

1930.

398826

——ROSS ([Sir] R.)
Shakespeare, 1916 [: a sonnet].
IN GOLLANCZ ([Sir] I.) ed., A Book of
homage to Shakespeare.
ports. illus. facsimiles. [1916.]

264175

——Sampson (J.) In lighter moments: a
book of occasional verse and prose.
With illustrations by L. Wright [and
a foreword by Dora E. Yates. Containing "A Ryghte merrie and moralle
songe writ in praise of our excellente
poete Master Willm. Shakespeare.]

1934.

429645

——SANDYS ([Sir] J. E.)
Greek epigram on the tomb of Shakespeare
[with English translation.]
IN GOLLANCZ ([Sir] I.) ed., A Book of
homage to Shakespeare.
ports. illus. facsimiles. [1916.]

264175

—— SCHWARTZ (DELMORE)
  Coriolanus and his mother.   IN
  Schwartz (D.) Summer knowledge: new
  and selected poems, 1938-1958.   (New
  York)   1959.

                        689702

—— SCOTT (F. G.)
  Poems.   [Containing a sonnet
  "Shakespeare".]
  port.   1936.

                        458790

—— SCOTT (F. G.)
  "Shakespeare" [: a sonnet].
  IN GOLLANCZ ([Sir] I,) ed., A Book of
  homage to Shakespeare.
  ports. illus. facsimiles. [1916.]

                        264175

——[SEWARD (T.)]
  On Shakespear's monument at Stratford
  upon Avon.   IN [DODSLEY (R.) ed.,]
  A Collection of poems by several hands.
  3rd edn. Vol. 2.   1751.   576731
  ———— Another edn.   1755.   576737
  ———— Another edn.   1758.   538519

—— Sewell (J.W.) Rhymes en route
  [including a poem entitled
  "Quotations from Shakespeare
  (written during sickness)".]

                        [1911.]

                        532451

—— SEYMOUR (W. K.)
  Shakespeare [: a poem].
  IN Seymour (W. K.) Collected poems.
                                1946.

                        571002

——[SHENSTONE (W.)]
  Slender's ghost.   IN [DODSLEY (R.) ed.,]
  A Collection of poems by several hands.
  [5th edn.] Vol. 5.   1758.   538522
  ———— Another copy.   576734
  ———— Another copy.   576740
  ———— New edn., corrected. Vol. 5.
                       1782.   99650

—— Sidgwick (A.H.) Jones's wedding and
  other poems [including one on
  Shakespeare.] pp.96. Port.

                        1918.

                        405903

—— SIMMONS (B.)
  Minerva's owl and other poems.
  [Including several on Shakespeare.]
  pp. 64.   1933.

                        414224

——[SIMPSON (E. J.)]
  Time in the East, an entertainment [:
  experiences of an Intelligence Officer
  in the Middle East during the war
  1939-45], by E. John [pseud.   With
  "Five-line exercises in Shakespearian
  geography": limericks in several
  languages.]
  illus.   map.   1946.

                        569352

—— SKEMP (A. R.)
  Shakespeare [: a poem].
  IN GOLLANCZ ([Sir] I.) ed., A Book of
  homage to Shakespeare.
  ports. illus. facsimiles. [1916.]

                        264175

—— Sleigh (H.) Stratford-upon-Avon,
  April 23. In Sleigh (H.) The Great
  hope, and other poems.

     (Stratford-upon-Avon)   1921.

  (Shakespeare Head Press.)

—— SMITH (G. C. M.)
  Two sonnets: 1616, 1916.
  IN GOLLANCZ ([Sir] I,) ed., A Book of
  homage to Shakespeare.
  ports. illus. facsimiles. [1916.]

                        264175

—— SOMERS (A. C. C.)
  Shakspere's garden party [: a poem].
  IN The Manchester playgoer: the
  organ of the Manchester Playgoers'
  Club, Vol. 1.   (Manchester) 1910.

                        544467

—— Stanley (C.) Matthew Arnold [: a
  critical study. With references
  to his Sonnet on Shakespeare.]

     (Toronto)   1938.

                        495504

—— STEFÁNSSON (J.)
  An Eddic homage to William Shakespeare
  (culled from Eddic poems).   [With
  English translation.]
  IN GOLLANCZ ([Sir] I.) ed., A Book of
  homage to Shakespeare.
  ports. illus. facsimiles. [1916.]

                        264175

—— S[TEIN] (K. M.)
  Die schönste Lengevitch: [humorous
  verses, in German-American including
  a poem on Hamlet.]   1926.

                        396040

—— Stirling (W.F.) Orange groves: [poems.
  Including a poem on Shakespeare:
  "April 23rd".] pp.77.

                        1934.

                        421884

—— STOPES (Mrs. C. C.)
  The Making of Shakespeare [: a poem].
  IN GOLLANCZ ([Sir] I.) ed., A Book of
  homage to Shakespeare.
  ports. illus. facsimiles. [1916.]

                        264175

—— Strachey ([Jane Maria, Lady]) ed.,
  Poets on poets [: an anthology,
  with introduction and notes,
  including poems on Shakespeare by
  various poets].

                        1894.

                        432029

——SUCKLING (Sir J.)
A Supplement of an imperfect copy
of verses of Mr. William Shakespeare's,
by the author [i.e. Suckling.]
IN Suckling (Sir J.) Poems.   [With
notes on the text.]   1933.
No. 149 of an edition of 250 copies.

432710

——SWINBURNE (A. C.)
The Afterglow of Shakespeare.
IN Swinburne (A. C.) Selected poems,
with an introduction by [R.] L.
Binyon.   1939.
The World's Classics.

507798

——TAGORE ([Sir] R.)
Shakespeare [: an Indian poem, with
English translation.]
IN GOLLANCZ ([Sir] I.) ed., A Book of
homage to Shakespeare.
ports. illus. facsimiles. [1916.]

264175

——TASKER (REUBEN)
A "Presentation" of Shakespeare [No. 1:
verses on Shakespearian characters.
Anon.]   pp. [4.]   1954. 665515
_____ [No. 2: more verses on
Shakespearian characters]. pp. 12.
1956. 665516
_____ [No. 3: more verses on
Shakespearian characters]. pp. 16.
1958. 665965

——TAYLOR (J.)
Poems on various subjects.   Vol. 1.
[Containing a sonnet: "Shakspeare's
cliff".]   1827.

443705

—— Thom (R.W.) Coventry poems. [Containing
"Shakspeare Tercentenary poem".]
pp.86.

(Coventry)   [?1866]

432073

——Toole (H.) Birmingham Musical Festival,
1870. Second miscellaneous concert,
including a new cantata, Ode to
Shakespeare. Words by H. Toole.pp.15.

(Birmingham)   1870.

87760

—— TRENCH ([F.] H.)
Shakespeare [: a poem].
IN GOLLANCZ ([Sir] I) ed., A Book of
homage to Shakespeare.
ports. illus. facsimiles. [1916.]

264175

—— TRENCH (R. C.)
[Poem on Shakespeare.]   IN The
Shakespeare Tercentenary meeting held
at the Mansion House, May Day, 1916
[etc.]   pp. 18. [2.]   [1916.]
Printed at "The Sign of the Dolphin".

603467

——UNDERHILL (EVELYN)
William Shakespeare.   Died April 23,
1616 [: a poem].
IN GOLLANCZ ([Sir] I.) ed., A Book of
homage to Shakespeare.
ports. illus. facsimiles. [1916.]

264175

——VALLINS (G. H.)
At Stratford-on-Avon (Opening of
the Shakespeare Memorial Theatre,
April 23, 1932.)   IN Vallins (G. H.)
This dust, and other poems. pp. 64.
1935.
Macmillan's Contemporary Poets.

446623

——VANNUCCHIO [pseud.]
To Shakespeare: a sonnet.   IN The
Journal of Education, New Series,
vol. 4.   1882.

408617

——VERWEY (A.)
Grato m'è 'l sonno [: Dutch poem with
English paraphrase].   IN GOLLANCZ
([Sir] I.) ed., A Book of homage to
Shakespeare.
ports.   illus.   facsimiles.   [1916.]

264175

—— Ward (F.W.O.) Shakespeare [: a poem.]
From The Fireside Pictorial Annual,
1902.

1902.

501611

——Watson (Sir W.) Poems, 1878-1935,
[including a poem on Shakespeare,
and notes]. Port.

1936.

453391

—— WATTS-DUNTON (T.)
Christmas at the Mermaid.   IN The
Coming of love, and other poems,
pp. 81-147.   1898.

512706

——WHITE, ERIC WALTER, ed.
[Fifteen] poems for William Shakespeare
[commissioned from various poets to
celebrate the Quatercentenary].   With
an introduction.   (Stratford-upon-
Avon)   1964.

668308

——WHITEHEAD (W.)
To Mr. Garrick.   IN [DODSLEY (R.) ed.,]
A Collection of poems by several hands.
3rd edn. Vol. 2.   1751. 576731
_____ 4th edn. Vol. 4.
1755. 576737
_____ 5th edn. Vol. 2.
1758. 538519

——WILLETTS (A. J.)
Poems and sonnets, [including a sonnet
on Shakespeare.] pp. 94.
(Wolverhampton)   1896.

406875

WILLIAMS (J. O.)
Y Bardd a ganodd i'r byd.   [Welsh poem
with English paraphrase.]
IN GOLLANCZ ([Sir] I) ed., A Book of
homage to Shakespeare.
ports. illus. facsimiles. [1916.]

264175

WOOD (B. H.)
Shakespeare [: a poem].   IN The
Central Literary Magazine, Vol. 32,
July, 1935.   (Birmingham)
1936.   463922
_____ Another copy.   465871

YEYEN (W. A.)
Shakespeare [: Arabic poem, with a
summary in English.]
IN GOLLANCZ ([Sir] I.) ed., A Book of
homage to Shakespeare.
ports. illus. facsimiles. [1916.]

264175

ZANGWILL (I.)
The Two empires.
IN GOLLANCZ ([Sir] I.) ed., A Book of
homage to Shakespeare.
ports. illus. facsimiles. [1916.]

264175

Poetomachia *see* **Boy Actors**

Poetry of Shakespeare
see also **Grammar and Language; Imagery**
Versification

BARNES, T.R.
English verse: voice and movement from
Wyatt to Yeats.   1967.

With references to
Shakespeare.   764064

Beeching (H.C.) William Shakespeare :
player, playmaker and poet. A
reply to [Sir G.] G.Greenwood.
2nd edn. Facsimile signatures.

1909.

418668

Bethurum (Dorothy) The Immortal
word-smith : a study of Shakespeares
apparent poetic digressions. From
The Sewanee Review, Vol.36. pp.[14.]

(Sewanee, Tenn.)   1928.

447441

BONJOUR, ADRIEN
The Test of poetry.
IN SHAKESPEARE JAHRBUCH.   Bd. 100/1964.
pp. 149-158.   (Heidelberg)

10531

BRADBROOK (MURIEL CLARA)
Shakespeare and Elizabethan poetry:
a study of his earlier work in
relation to the poetry of the time.
port. illus.   1951.

619769

BROOKS (C.)
Shakespeare as a symbolist poet.
FROM The Yale Review, Vol. 34.
(New Haven, Conn.)   1945.

578270

CRAIG (H.)
Shakespeare's bad poetry [: portions
of] a paper read at the Shakespeare
Conference, Stratford-upon-Avon,
August 1947.   IN SHAKESPEARE SURVEY
1.   (Cambridge)
bibliog.   1948.

590674

CRUTTWELL (MAURICE JAMES PATRICK)
The Shakespearian moment and its place
in the poetry of the 17th century.
1954.

637658

DAICHES (DAVID)
The Living Shakespeare [No. 3]: His
poetry.   [Broadcast] 15th October 1958.
ff. 11.
typescript.   [1958.]

666023

David (R.[W.]) The Janus of poets :
an essay on the dramatic value of
Shakspeare's poetry both good and
bad.

(Cambridge)   1935.

(Harness Prize Essay, 1934)

438646

ELIOT (T. S.)
The Music of poetry: the third
W. P. Ker Memorial Lecture, delivered
in the University of Glasgow, 24th
February, 1942.   [Containing refer-
ences to the poetry of Shakespeare.]
pp. 28.   (Glasgow)   1942.
Glasgow University Publications, 57.

535800

ELIOT (T. S.)
The Sacred wood: essays on poetry
and criticism.   [Containing references to Shakespeare and an essay,
"Hamlet and his problems".]   4th edn.
1934.
Fountain Library.   427186

EMPSON (W.)
Seven types of ambiguity [: a study
of its effects in English verse.
With a criticism of Shakespearian
verse].   2nd edn. revised.   1947.

586456

FLEAY (FREDERICK GARD)
On metrical tests as applied to dramatic
poetry.   Part I. Shakspere.
IN Transactions of the New Shakespeare
Society, Series 1. No. 1. pp. 1-46.
1874.
4061

——GRANVILLE-BARKER (HARLEY)
On poetry in drama. [With references
to Shakespeare.] pp. 42. 1937.
Romanes Lecture, 1937.

467644

——GRAVES (ROBERT [RANKE])
The Common asphodel: collected essays
on poetry, 1922-1949. [With references
to Shakespeare, including the essay
"The Sources of The Tempest".]
frontis. 1949.

601433

——GRIERSON ([Sir] H. J. C.) and SMITH
(J. C.)
Shakespeare's predecessors;
Shakespeare; [and] Shakespeare's
contemporaries and successors in
drama. IN Grierson ([Sir] H. J. C.)
and Smith (J. C.) A Critical history
of English poetry. 1944.

553090

——HALLIDAY (FRANK ERNEST)
The Poetry of Shakespeare's plays.
facsimile. 1954.

639473

——Halliday, Frank Ernest
Reade him, therefore. IN

STRATFORD PAPERS ON SHAKESPEARE
delivered at the 1964 Shakespeare
Seminar. (Toronto) 1965.

745844

——HYETT ([Sir] F. A.)
Why is Shakespeare our greatest poet?
An address at the commemoration of
the Shakespeare Tercentenary at
Gloucester, May 3rd, 1916. pp. 20.
(Gloucester) 1916.

438429

——ISAACS (J.)
The Art of poetry. 3. Shakespeare's
poetic art. Produced by N. Iliff.
[Broadcast] 4th March, 1949.
ff. 14.
typescript. [1949.]

605258

——Joseph (B.) Verse in Elizabethan
drama ; talk [broadcast] 25th
April, 1950. ff.18. Typescript.

1950.

608871

——Knight (G.W.) The Burning oracle :
studies in the poetry of action.
[Including an essay entitled
The Shakespearian integrity.]

(Oxford) .1939.

502492

——NEMEROY (HOWARD)
The Marriage of Theseus and Hippolyta.
IN The Kenyon Review, Vol. 18.
(Gambier, Ohio) 1956.

594031/18

——PARKER (GEORGE)
William Shakespeare and the horse with
wings [; a lecture on the poetry of
Shakespeare delivered on Shakespeare
delivered on Shakespeare's birthday
at Stratford-on-Avon]. FROM Partisan
Review, July-August 1953. pp. [11].
[New York] 1953.

646235

——Pettet (E.C.) Shakespeare's conception
of poetry. In English Association.
Essays and studies, Vol.3.

1950.

610517

——POTTLE (F. A.)
The Idiom of poetry. [With notes and
references, including references to
Shakespeare.] (Ithaca, N.Y.) 1941.
Cornell University. Messenger Lectures
on the Evolution of Civilization, 1941.

536765

——Rashbrook (R.F.) Keats and others
[including Shakespeare : criticism
of their poetry]. From Notes and
Queries [Vol.192.]

.1947.

587305

——RICHMOND (W. K.)
Poetry and the people [: a survey of
English poetry from the earliest times
to the present. With references to
Shakespeare, including a chapter
entitled "Miracle, Mystery and
Shakespeare", and with bibliographical
notes]. 1947.

580803

——RYLANDS (G. [H. W.])
Shakespeare the poet. IN GRANVILLE-BARKER
(H.) and HARRISON (G. B.) eds., A
Companion to Shakespeare studies.
(Cambridge)
bibliogs. illus. tables. facsimiles.
                          1934. 418724
——— (New York) 1937. 479251
——— (Cambridge) 1945. 566174

——RYLANDS (GEORGE HUMPHREY WOLFESTAN)
Shakespeare's poetic energy. ([41st]
Annual Shakespeare Lecture of the
British Academy, 1951). pp. [21.]
[1951.]

634468

——SELLS (ARTHUR LYTTON)
Shakespeare. IN Sells (A. L.) The
Italian influence in English poetry
from Chaucer to Southwell.
ports. illus. bibliog. 1955.

647612

——SHERWOOD (MARGARET [P.])
The Formative faculty of poetry [:
with references to Shakespeare].
FROM The Aryan path, Vol. 7. (Bombay)
1936.

484132

SIPE, DOROTHY L.
Shakespeare's metrics. (New Haven, Conn.)   1968.
Yale studies in English, 167.

773050

Bitwell (Edith) A Poet's notebook [: notes on the necessity of poetry. Including notes on Shakespeare and two new poems by the author].

1943.

540875

SPENDER (S.)
Life and the poet.   [With references to Shakespeare.]   1942.
Searchlight Books.

531960

STAUFFER (D. A.)
The Nature of poetry.   [With references to Shakespeare.] (New York)
bibliog.   1946.

586113

Thaler (A.) Shakespeare on style, imagination and poetry. In PMLA, Publications of the Modern Language Association of America, Vol. 53.

1938.

499373

TILLYARD (EUSTACE MANDEVILLE WETENHALL)
Poetry, direct and oblique.   [With references to Shakespeare.]
1934.   418780
_____ Revised [edn.] 1945.   563733

VIVANTE (L.)
William Shakespeare 1564-1616. IN Vivante (L.) English poetry and its contribution to the knowledge of a creative principle.   1950.

608971

WAIN, JOHN BARRINGTON
Guides to Shakespeare.   FROM Encounter, March 1964, pp. 53-62.
1964.

668348

WILLCOCK (GLADYS DOIDGE)
Language and poetry in Shakespeare's early plays.   ([44th] Annual Shakespeare Lecture of the British Academy, 1954)   pp. 15.   [1954.]

665023

WILLIAMS (C.)
The English poetic mind.   [With a chapter "The Cycle of Shakespeare" and other Shakespearian references.]
1932.

392333

ZOCCA (LOUIS RALPH)
Elizabethan narrative poetry.   (New Brunswick, N.J.)
bibliog.   1950.

612741

Poets (The) and our wooden walls, [with references to Shakespeare.] In National Miscellany : a magazine of general literature. Vol. 4.

1855.

493348

POGSON (BERYL)
All's well that ends well: an esoteric interpretation. pp. 18.   1954.

665280

POGSON (BERYL)
In the East my pleasure lies: an esoteric interpretation of some plays of Shakespeare.   1950.

613231

POGSON (BERYL)
Romeo and Juliet: an esoteric inter- pretation. pp. 20.   [1954]

644241

POGSON, BERYL
Three plays by Shakespeare: an esoteric interpretation of Romeo and Juliet, All's well that ends well, The Winter's Tale.   1963.

667995

POGSON (BERYL)
The Winter's Tale: an esoteric interpretation. pp. 18. [c.1955.]

665844

POGUE, JIM C.
"The Two gentlemen of Verona" and Henry Wotton's "A Courtlie contro- uersie of Cupids cautels".   IN Four studies in Elizabethan drama, by Roma Ball, J. C. Pogue, J. L. Somer [and] E. J. Kettner. (Kansas State Teachers College, Emporia, Kan.) 1962. Emporia State Research Studies, Vol. 10, No. 4.   667737

POHL (FREDERICK JULIUS)
The Death-mask: a reprint from "Shakespeare Quarterly", Vol.12, No.2. (Shakespeare Association of America) pp.[12.] Illus. [New York]   1961.

667310

POINGDESTRE (E.)
A Summer day at Stratford-on-Avon. IN Temple Bar, Vol. 74.   1885.

82081

POINTER (JOHN)
Tell me where is fancy bred.   Four- part song.   Words [by] Shakespeare from "Merchant of Venice".   [Music] by J. Pointer.   IN The Musical Times, Vol. 58.   1917.

271406

POINTER (J.) [ed.]
Who is Sylvia?   Words by Shakespeare
[from Two Gentlemen of Verona], music
by [Sir] E. German, arranged for two
voices and pianoforte by J. Pointer.
School Music Review, Extra supplement,
Feb. 15, 1928.   pp. 8.   1928.

516958

POIRIER (M.)
Sidney's influences upon A Midsummer
night's dream.   [With bibliographical
notes.]   IN Studies in Philology,
Vol. 44.   (Chapel Hill, N.C.)   1947.

554520/44

POISSON, RODNEY
Coriolanus as Aristotle's magnanimous man.
IN Pacific coast studies in Shakespeare.
Edited by W. F. McNeir and T. N.
Greenfield.   (Eugene: Ore.)   1966.

768009

POKORNY (JAROSLAV)
Shakespeare in Czechoslovakia.   pp.66.
(Prague)
ports.   illus.   1955.

665081

POLAK (ALFRED LAURENCE)
More legal fictions: a series of cases
from Shakespeare.   Illustrated by
Diana Pullinger.   1946.

578252

POLAK (ALFRED LAURENCE)
"The Tempest" and "The Magic flute".
IN English, Vol. 9.   (Oxford)   1953.

481151/9

Polak (L.) [Review of] R. Pascal's
Shakespeare in Germany, 1740-1815.
1937.   In English Studies, Vol. 20.

(Amsterdam)   1938.

495114

Poland

HELSZTYŃSKI (STANISŁAW)
Polish translations of Shakespeare in
the past and today.
IN SHAKESPEARE JAHRBUCH.   Bd. 100/101.
1964/1965.   pp. 284-293.   (Weimar)

10531

HELSZTYNSKI, STANISŁAW, ed.
Poland's homage to Shakespeare.
Commemorating the fourth centenary of
his birth, 1564-1964. (Warsaw)
1965.

747846

KUNCEWICZOWA (MARIA)
Szekspir w Warszawie.   FROM Nowa
Polska Miesięcznik, Tom 2, 1943.
illus.
Published in London.

548062

PRAUSS (R.) and PRAUSS (Mrs. R.)
Bibliography of Polish Shakespeareana
up to Jan. 1st 1933.   Compiled on
behalf of the Birmingham Public Libraries
at the request of the British Embassy,
Warsaw.   pp. 88.
typescript.   [1934].

426524

POLANYI (KARL)
Hamlet.   IN The Yale Review, Vol. 43.
(New Haven, Conn.)   1954.

592685/43

POLIŠENSKÝ (JOSEF)
England and Bohemia in Shakespeare's day. IN
CHARLES UNIVERSITY ON SHAKESPEARE:
essays edited by Z. Stříbrný.   (Praha)
illus.   1966.

762631

Politics and Political Characters
see also Communism; Democracy; Dictatorship; Populace in Shakespeare; Royalty

BLOOM, ALLAN, and JAFFA, HARRY V.
Shakespeare's politics. (New York)
1964.

748156

DRAPER (J. W.)
Political themes in Shakespeare's later
plays.   [With bibliographical notes.]
FROM The Journal of English and Germanic
Philology, Vol. 35.   (Urbana, Ill.)
1936.

488673

ELLIS-FERMOR (UNA [M.])
The Frontiers of drama [: criticism of
the drama.   With chapters on Shakespeare's
political plays and Troilus and Cressida
and with bibliographical notes].
1945.

563985

FREEMAN, LESLIE
Shakespeare's kings and Machiavelli's
prince.   IN PAOLUCCI, ANNE, ed.,
Shakespeare encomium, 1564-1964 [by
various writers].   (New York)   1964.
City University of New York, City
College Papers.

747546

——GEYL (PIETER CATHARINUS ARIE)
Shakespeare as a historian.   IN
Geyl (P. C. A.) Encounters in history.
1963.

717642

——HIBBARD, GEORGE RICHARD
Politics in the romances. FROM Filološki
pregled, Vols. 1-2. (Beograd) 1964.

pp.103-116.   749527

——HUMPHREYS, ARTHUR RALEIGH
Shakespeare's political justice in
'Richard II' and 'Henry IV'.
IN Stratford Papers on Shakespeare
delivered at the 1964 Shakespeare
Seminar. (Toronto)   1965.

745844

——JAMESON, THOMAS H.
The Hidden Shakespeare: a study of the
poet's undercover activity in the
theatre. (New York)   1967.

767201

—— KEETON, GEORGE WILLIAM
Shakespeare's legal and political
background.   1967.

illus.   761262

——KNIGHTS (LIONEL CHARLES)
Poetry, politics and the English
tradition [: Shakespeare's handling
of political themes]. pp. 32.
1954.

640038

——KNIGHTS (L. C.)
Shakespeare and political wisdom: a
note on the personalism of "Julius
Caesar" and "Coriolanus". IN The
Sewanee Review, Vol. 61.   (Sewanee)
1953.

641628

——KNIGHTS (LIONEL CHARLES)
Shakespeare's politics.   With some
reflections on the nature of tradition.
pp. [18.]   [1957.] 665857
Annual Shakespeare Lecture of the
British Academy, 1957.
_____ IN Knights (L. C.) Further
explorations [: essays in criticism].
1965.   742545

——LEECH, CLIFFORD
Shakespeare, Cibber, and the Tudor
myth. FROM Shakespearean Essays, No.2.
(Knoxville, Tenn.) pp.79-95. 1964.

753396

——LEEMAN (F. W.)
A Socialist opens his Shakespeare.
FROM The Millgate, Vol. 39. 1944.

547453

——MacLURE (MILLAR)
Shakespeare and the lonely dragon.
IN University of Toronto Quarterly,
Vol. 24. (Toronto)   1954-55.
[The political hero in Shakespeare.]
596179/24

——MARRIOTT ([Sir] J. A. R.)
Shakespeare and politics. FROM Cornhill Magazine, Dec. 1927. pp. 678-690.
1927.

449505

——MORROW (D.)
Where Shakespeare stood: his part in
the crucial struggles of his day. With
an introduction by G. Hicks [and bibliographical notes.] pp. 89. (Milwaukee)
1935.

447816

——MOTT (L. F.)
A Political allusion in Shakespeare's
Richard III.   IN Fitz-Gerald (J. D.)
and Taylor (Pauline) eds., Todd memorial
volumes: philological studies, Vol. 2.
(New York)

1930.

398523

——MUIR (EDWIN)
The Politics of King Lear: the seventh
W. P. Ker Memorial Lecture delivered in
the University of Glasgow, 23rd April
1946.   pp. 24. (Glasgow)
1947. 586684
Glasgow University Publications, 72.
_____ IN Essays on literature and
society.   Enlarged and revised ed.
1965. 741672

——MUIR (KENNETH)
Shakespeare and politics.   IN
KETTLE (ARNOLD) ed., Shakespeare
in a changing world: essays [by
various authors].   1964.

667797

——PALMER (J. [L.])
Political characters of Shakespear
[: studies of Brutus, Richard II,
Richard III, Henry V and Coriolanus].
1945.

559355
reprint 568150

——PINTO (VIVIAN DE SOLA)
Shakespeare and the dictators.   [With
bibliographical references.]   IN
DE LA MARE (WALTER [J.]) ed., Essays
by divers hands: the Transactions of
the Royal Society of Literature of
the United Kingdom, New Series, Vol.21.
1944.

557508

——POWELL, JOHN ENOCH
Politics in Shakespeare.
IN PRITCHETT, VICTOR SAWDON, and
others, Shakespeare: the comprehensive soul. [Talks on the B.B.C.
European English Service to celebrate
the Shakespearian Quatercentenary.]
1965.

746585

——RABKIN (NORMAN)
Coriolanus: The Tragedy of Politics.
IN Shakespeare Quarterly XVII: 3.
(New York)   1966.

pp.95-212.   605711

—— REESE (MAX MEREDITH)
  Shakespeare and the welfare state.
  pp. 34.
   illus.   1953.

                              634860

—— RICHMOND, HUGH M.
  Shakespeare's political plays.
  (New York)   1967.

         Studies in language and
  literature.   765124

—— SIMPSON (RICHARD)
  The Political use of the stage in
  Shakspere's time.
  **IN Transactions of the New Shakespeare
  Society, Series 1.** No. 2.   pp. 371-395.
                     1874.
                              4061

—— SIMPSON (RICHARD)
  The Politics of Shakspere's historical plays.
  **IN Transactions of the New Shakespeare
  Society, Series 1.** No. 2.   pp. 396-441.
                     1874.
                              4061

—— SMITH (G.)
  Shakespeare's religion and politics.
  IN Macmillan's magazine, vol. 59, Nov.
  1888-April 1889.
                              1889.

                              100873

—— SPEAIGHT (R.)
  Shakespeare and politics: the Wedmore
  Memorial Lecture delivered before the
  Royal Society of Literature, May 21st,
  1946.   With a foreword by F. S. Boas.
  pp. 20.
                              [1946.]
  (Royal Society of Literature)
                              576035

—— SPEAIGHT (R.)
  Shakespeare and politics.   IN Bax (C.)
  ed. Essays by divers hands: the Transactions of the Royal Society of Literature
  of the United Kingdom, New Series, Vol.24.
                              1948.
  (Wedmore Memorial Lecture, 1946)
                              593464

—— Speaight, Robert
  Shakespeare and the political spectrum as
  illustrated by 'Richard II'. IN

  STRATFORD PAPERS ON SHAKESPEARE
    delivered at the 1964 Shakespeare
    Seminar. (Toronto)   1965.

                              745844

—— TALBERT (ERNEST WILLIAM)
  The Problem of order: Elizabethan
  political commonplaces and an example
  of Shakespeare's art [: Richard II.]
  (Chapel Hill, [N.C.])   1962.

                              668091

—— [VOIGT (F. A.)]
  The Political wisdom of the English poets
  [including Shakespeare] by the editor of
  "The Nineteenth Century and After".
  [With bibliographical notes.]   FROM The
  Nineteenth Century and After [Vol. 134].
                              1943.
  Note: Last page typescript.
                              547720

—— WEDGWOOD, CICELY VERONICA
  Shakespeare between two civil wars.
  IN Shakespeare celebrated: anniversary
  lectures delivered at the Folger Library
  [during 1964].   (Ithaca, N.Y.) 1965.

                              771817

—— WEST (REBECCA)
  The Court and the castle: a study of
  the interactions of political and
  religious ideas in imaginative
  literature.   1958.

                              678977

—— WOOD (F. T.)
  Shakespeare and the plebs.   IN The
  English Association, Essays and Studies,
  Vol. 18.   [Oxford]
                              1933.

                              404182

POLLARD (ALFRED WILLIAM)
  A Bibliographer's praise.
  IN GOLLANCZ ([Sir] I.) ed., A Book of
  homage to Shakespeare.
    ports. illus. **facsimiles.** [1916.]

                              264175

POLLARD (A. W.)
  The Bibliographical approach to
  Shakespeare: notes on new contri-
  butions.   IN The Library, 4th series,
  Vol. 14.   1934.

                              422285

POLLARD (A. W.)
  False dates in Shakespeare quartos.
  IN The Library.   3rd Series, Vol. 2.
                              1911.

                              235017

POLLARD (A. W.)
  The Foundations of Shakespeare's text.
  IN Aspects of Shakespeare: British
  Academy Lectures.   (Oxford) 1933.

                              401892

POLLARD (ALFRED WILLIAM)
  [Review of] William Shakespeare: a
  study of facts and problems, by [Sir]
  E. K. Chambers.   IN The Library,
  4th series, Vol. 9.   1931.

                              379873

POLLARD (A. W.)
  Review [of] The Text of Shakespeare's
  Hamlet, by B. A. P. van Dam.
  IN English studies, Vol. 6.
  (Amsterdam)   1924.

                              485648

Pollard (A.W.) [Review of] Hamlet:
  its textual history, by H.
  de Groot.   In English studies,
  Vol. 6.

           (Amsterdam)   1924.

                              485648

POLLARD (A. W.)
[Review of] The Works of Shakespeare.
Edited for the Syndics of the
Cambridge University Press by
Sir A. [T.] Quiller-Couch and J. D.
Wilson. [Vol. 1.] The Tempest.
IN The Library, 4th series, Vol. 2.
1922.

298823

POLLARD (ALFRED WILLIAM)
[Review of] William Shakespeare. The
Tragedie of Hamlet, Prince of Denmarke.
Edited by J. D. Wilson. IN The
Library, 4th series, Vol. 12. 1932.

393825

POLLARD (ALFRED WILLIAM)
Shakespeare's fight with the pirates
and the problems of the transmission
of his text: 2nd edn., revised with
an introduction. (Cambridge) 1937.
Shakespeare Problems [Series No. 1.]

472130

POLLARD (ALFRED WILLIAM)
Shakespeare's text. IN GRANVILLE-BARKER
(H.) and HARRISON (G. B.) eds., A
Companion to Shakespeare studies.
(Cambridge)
bibliogs.	illus.	tables.	facsimiles.
		1934.	418724
_____ (New York)		1937.	479251
_____ (Cambridge)		1945.	566174

POLLARD (ALFRED WILLIAM)
Verse tests and the date of "Sir Thomas
More". [A discussion on the "Shake-
spearean" passages in "The Book of
Sir Thomas More".] IN The Review of
English Studies, Vol. 1. 1925.

318239

Pollard, Alfred William *works relating to*

—— Dam (B.A.P. van) [Reply to A.W.
Pollard's, review of the author's]
The Text of Shakespeare's Hamlet.
In English studies, Vol, 7.

(Amsterdam) 1925.

485649

—— KOSTER (E. B.)
Review [of] Shakespeare's fight
with the pirates and the problems
of the transmission of his text,
by A. W. Pollard. 2nd edn. revised,
1920. IN English studies, Vol. 4.
(Amsterdam) 1922.

485646

—— McKERROW (R. B.)
[Review of] Shakespeare's hand in
the play of 'Sir Thomas More' papers
by A. W. Pollard [and others], with
the text of the Ill May Day Scenes,
edited by W. W. Greg. IN The
Library, 4th series, Vol. 4. 1924.

313752

—— [THOMAS (Sir HENRY) ed.]
A Select bibliography of the writings
of Alfred W. Pollard [including
Shakespeare items. With a brief
autobiography, "My first fifty years",
by A. W. Pollard. Edited with a
preface, and a chapter, "From fifty to
seventy-five", by Sir Henry Thomas].
pp. ix, 69. (Oxford)
port. 1938.
Edn. limited to 260 copies.

549399

Pollard (A.W.) & Bartlett (Henrietta
C.) A Census of Shakespeare's plays
in quarto, 1594-1709. Revised and
extended [and with an introduction]
by Henrietta C.Bartlett.

(New Haven, [Conn.]) 1939.

511666

Pollard (A.W.) and Huth (A.H.) On
the supposed false dates in certain
Shakespeare quartos. In The Library.
3rd series. Vol.1.

1910.

228048

POLLARD (ALFRED WILLIAM) and WILSON (JOHN
DOVER)
What follows if some of the good quarto
editions of Shakespeare's plays were
printed from his autograph manuscripts.
IN Transactions of the Bibliographical
Society, Vol. 15. 1920.

294089

POLLARD (ALFRED WILLIAM) and WILSON (JOHN
DOVER)
William Shakespeare. IN GARVIN
(KATHARINE) ed., The Great Tudors.
1935.

431775

POLLARD (ALFRED WILLIAM) and WILSON (JOHN
DOVER) eds.
Shakespeare problems. (Cambridge)
1920-56. see Shakespeare problems.

POLLARD (A. W.) [and others]
'Facsimile' reprints of old books,
by A. W. Pollard, G. R. Redgrave,
R. W. Chapman [and] W. W. Greg.
[With references to Shakespeare
reprints.] IN The Library, Vol. 6.
1926.

329554

POLLIN, BURTON R.
Hamlet, a successful suicide.
IN SHAKESPEARE STUDIES, 1.
(Cincinnati, Ohio) 1965.

750317

POLLOCK (J.)
Did Bacon sign Shakespeare?
[A Review of "Some acrostic signatures
of Francis Bacon", by W. S. Booth.]
IN The Cornhill Magazine. New
Series, vol. 27. 1909.

220424

POLLOCK (Lady JULIET)
The 'Hamlet' of the Seine.   IN The
Nineteenth Century, Vol. 20.   1886.

87957

POLLOCK (Lady [JULIET])
Macready as I knew him.   [With
references to Shakespeare.]
1884.   459998
_____ 2nd edn.   1885.   499292

POLLOCK (T. C.)
The Nature of literature, its
relation to science, language and
human experience. [With references
to Shakespeare's use of language.]
(Princeton)
bibliog.   1942.

548209

POLLOCK (T. C.)
The Philadelphia theatre in the
eighteenth century, together with
the Day Book of the same period
[with Shakespearian references.]
(Philadelphia)   1933.

440540

POLLOCK (W. H.)
Hamlets with differences.   IN The
Theatre, Vol. 30.   1897.

140753

Pollock (W.H.) Impressions of Henry
Irving, gathered in public and
private during a friendship of
many years. With a preface by H. B.
Irving [and Shakespeaeian references]

1908.

498878

POLLOCK (W. H.)
Macbeth on the stage.   IN The
Nineteenth Century and after,
Vol. 61.   1907.

201731

Pollock (W.H.) Plays and players. 3:
Should Shakespeare's plays be
acted? In The National Review,
Vol.19.

1892.

115355

Polonius *see* **Hamlet**, Characters — Polonius

POMERANZ, HERMAN
Medicine in the Shakespearean plays
and era.   FROM Medical Life, 41.
(New York)
pp. 479-532.   1934.

766274

Ponte, Lorenzo Da *works relating to*

—— EINSTEIN (A.)
Shakespeare and Da Ponte.
IN The Monthly Musical Record.
Vol. 56. 1936.   1936.

462309

POOL (PHOEBE) [ed.]
Poems of death.   With [a preface by
the editor and] original lithographs
by M. Ayrton.   [With extracts from
Shakespeare.]   1945.
New Excursions into English Poetry.

567469

POOL (R. M.) and WALSH (G.)
Antithetical views on twinning
found in the Bible and Shakespeare.
FROM Southern Medicine & Surgery.
Vol. 103.   (Charlotte, N.C.)
bibliog.   1941.

565605

POOL (R. M.) and WALSH (G.)
Laterality dominance in Shakespeare's
plays.   FROM Southern Medicine &
Surgery, Vol. 104.   (Charlotte, N.C.)
1942.

565606

POOL (R. M.) and WALSH (G.)
Shakespeare's knowledge of twins and
twinning.   FROM Southern Medicine &
Surgery, Vol. 102.   (Charlotte, N.C.)
bibliog.   1940.

565604

POOLE (E. F.)
Shakespeare and the secondary modern
school.   IN English in Schools, Vol.2.
1948.

618850/2

POOLE (JOHN F.) Ye Comedie of Errours
see ENGLISH EDITIONS, The Comedy of
Errors: Alterations &c.

Pope, Alexander *works relating to*

——BUTT (J.)
Pope's taste in Shakespeare: a paper
read before the Shakespeare Association,
March 22nd, 1935.   pp. 21.   1936.
The Shakespeare Association.

456087

DIXON, P.
Pope's Shakespeare. FROM Journal of
English and Germanic Philology, LXIII:
2, April, 1964.   1964.

    pp. 191-203.   668350

DOBELL (P. J. & A. E.)
A Catalogue of a remarkable collection
of publisher's agreements [etc.],
including the agreements made by
A. Pope, W. Warburton and I. Reed for
the publication of their respective
editions of Shakespeare.   No. 66.
1941.   pp. 12.   (Tunbridge Wells)
                                   1941.

                        528685

GRIFFITH (R. H.)
Alexander Pope: a bibliography.
[With references to his editions of
Shakespeare, etc., and a list of
bibliographical aids.]   (Austin)
2 vols.   1922-7.
University of Texas, Studies in English.

                        542224

MacDONALD (WILBERT LORNE)
Pope and his critics: a study in
eighteenth century personalities.
ports.   illus.   bibliog.   1951.

                        615972

[MALLET (D.)]
Of verbal criticism: an epistle to
Mr. Pope occasioned by Theobald's
Shakespear, and Bentley's Milton
[: a poem]. pp. 14.
                                   1733.
    The 2nd edn. was entitled An
Epistle to Mr. Pope, etc.

                        482783

[MALLET (D.)]
An Epistle to Mr. Pope, occasioned by
Theobald's Shakespear and Bentley's
Milton: [a poem]. 2nd. edn. pp.[ii], 14.
                                   1733.
    First edn. entitled Of Verbal
Criticism.
                        179160

MALLET (D.)
Of verbal criticism: [an epistle to
Mr. Pope, occasioned by Theobald's
Shakespear, and Bentley's Milton: a
poem.]   IN Mallet (D.) Works, New edn.
Vol. 1.
                                   1759.

                        157118

ROOT (R. K.)
The Poetical career of Alexander Pope.
[With notes, bibliographical references
and references to Shakespeare.]
(Princeton)
port.   1938.

                        500806

SHERBURN (G. [W.])
The Early career of Alexander Pope.
[With Shakespearian references.]
(Oxford)
port.   illus.   1934.

                        424469

TILLOTSON (G.)
On the poetry of Pope.   [With references to Shakespeare].   (Oxford)
                                   1938.

                        476469

POPE (ELIZABETH M.)
The Renaissance background of Measure
for Measure.   [With bibliographical
notes.]   IN SHAKESPEARE SURVEY 2.
(Cambridge)   1949.

                        598403

POPE (ELIZABETH MARIE)
Shakespeare on Hell.
IN SHAKESPEARE QUARTERLY I: 3.
pp. 162-164.
(New York)   1950.
                        605711

Pope (W. J. Macqueen-) see Macqueen-Pope
(W. J.)

POPE-HENNESSY ([Dame] UNA)
Three English women in America.
[With a chapter on Fanny Kemble
and references to Shakespeare.]
ports.   1929.

                        499259

POPOVIĆ (PAVLE)
Shakespeare in Serbia.
IN GOLLANCZ ([Sir] I.) ed., A Book of
homage to Shakespeare.
ports.   illus.   facsimiles. [1916.]

                        264175

POPOVIĆ (V.)
Shakespeare in post-war Yugoslavia.
IN SHAKESPEARE SURVEY 4.
(Cambridge)   1951.

                        615854

Populace in Shakespeare

Stirling (B.) The Populace in
Shakespeare. [With bibliographical notes.]

    (New York)   1949.

                        600905

STIRLING (B.)
Shakespeare's mob scenes: a reinterpretation [with particular reference
to Henry VI, Pt. 2, Julius Caesar and
Coriolanus.   With bibliographical
notes].   IN The Huntington Library
Quarterly, Vol. 8.   (San Marino, Cal.)
                                   1944-5.

                        562973

—— TUPPER (F.)
The Shaksperean mob.   IN Publications
of the Modern Language Association of
America, Vol. 27.   (Baltimore) 1912.

428347

Porcelain *see* Ceramics

POROHOVSHIKOV (PETER SERGE)
Shakespeare unmasked [: the claims of
Roger Manners, 5th Earl of Rutland, to
the authorship of Shakespeare. With
a preface by G. V. Vernadsky, and a
bibliography.]   (New York)
illus. facsimiles.   1940.

523046

PORT ELIZABETH PUBLIC LIBRARY
Shakespeare's quatercentenary, 1564-
1964: a list of the various editions
of Shakespeare's works in the library.
Revised edn. [Port Elizabeth.] 1967.

762623

PORTE (J. F.)
Elgar and his music: an appreciative
study.   [Containing a chapter
"Elgar and Shakespeare" and other
Shakespearian references.]
ports. illus. facsimile. 1933.

400648

Porter (E.G.) The Songs of Schubert.
[With reference to the Shakespeare
songs].

1937.

464064

PORTER (QUINCY)
Three Elizabethan songs [: God of
love; When I was fair and young;
Spring].   Published for the
Elizabethan Club, Yale University.
pp. [vi], 18.   [New Haven, Conn.]
1961.

667066

Porter ([Sir]R.K.) Travelling sketches
in Russia and Sweden, during
1805,1806,1807,1808. [With
references to Hamlet]. Illus.
2 vols.

1809.

450950

PORTER (T. H.)
A Maid of the Malverns: a romance of
Blackfriars Theatre.   [With references
to Shakespeare.]   [1912]

392900

Porteus (H.G.) Shakespeare reconsidered: [a review of] The Shakespearean Tempest, by G.W. Knight.
In The Bookman, Vol.83.

[1933].

405808

Portfolio of Shakespeariana,art,
literature, drama [: a collection
of illustrations].

[c.1905.]

594495

Porthcurno *see* Minack Theatre

Portia *see* Julius Cæsar, Characters; The Merchant of Venice, Characters

Porto (L. da) Giulietta and Romeo:
a story from the original Italian.
Illustrated with pictures painted
in Italy by the translator, Jessie
B. Evans. pp.49.

(Portland,Maine)   1934.

438976

Porto Rico University
LOVETT (R. M.)
[Shakespeare's permanence]: an address
delivered at the University of [Porto]
Rico on the occasion of the anniversary
of Shakespeare's birth.   pp. 15.
(Rio Piedras)   1940.

525046

Portraits and Monuments
*In addition to the material listed below and in
the earlier catalogue the library has a large
collection of Shakespearian portraits which is
indexed but not individually catalogued*

—— Atkinson (B.) William Shakespeare,
poet. With a photograph of a new
bust of Shakespeare by R. Aitken.
pp.13.
(Peekshill,N.Y.)   1934.

Edition limited to 130 copies.

442547

—— Autographic Mirror, The, [containing a photo-lithographic reproduction of the Droeshout portrait, with explanatory text,]

[1864]

57861

[Another copy.]

—— Beerbohm ([Sir] M.) The Poets' corner. [With a cartoon of Shakespeare.]

1904.

501838

—— BURBAGE (RICHARD)
A Facsimile of the remains of a portrait of William Shakespeare. 1851.

132018

——Chandos portrait. William Shakespeare, from the Chandos portrait in the possession of the Earl of Ellesmere. Engraved for the Shakespeare Society by S. Cousins.

.1849.

132010

—— Chesterton (G.K.) The Coloured lands [: essays, poems and short stories. With a caricature of Shakespeare.] Illus.

1938.

492252

——COOPER (R.)
Shakspeare [portrait] engraved by R. Cooper from the original in the collection of J. W. Croker. 1824.

132012

—— [The Droeshout Portrait of Shakespeare. Marshall's copy] from the edition of his Poems. 1640.

132015

—— Faed (J.) Shakspere in his study. Painted by John Faed, engraved in mezzotint by James Faed: [a prospectus.] pp.6.

1859.

420959

—— Folger Shakespeare Library Prints [1]: Portraits of Shakespeare. (Washington, D.C.)
12 plates. 1935.

475840

—— [Janssen Portrait of Shakespeare, Copy of.] 1 sheet. [c.1830.]

132009

—— [Repoussé metal portrait of] William Shakespeare.

[c.1900.]

418471

—— ROZENTHAL (L. GLÜCK)
The Immortal Shakespeare [: a portrait]. (Woolwich) [c.1900.]

623373

—— SMYTH (G. L.)
William Shakspeare. IN Smyth (G.L.) Biographical illustrations of St. Paul's Cathedral and Westminster Abbey.

1843.

68705

——TENNIEL (Sir JOHN)
Cartoons. Selected from the pages of "Punch", [1851-1901. Including a cartoon of Shakespeare.] [1901.]

517992

—— William Shakspeare, 1597, [portrait] from the original picture in the possession of Mr. Felton. 1796.

224068

Portraits and Monuments *works relating to*

—— Allen (E.) Where are Shakespeare's portraits? In East Anglian magazine, Vol.4.

(Ipswich) 1939.

510779

—— A[merican] L[ibrary] A[ssociation]
Portrait index: [an] index to portraits contained in printed books and periodicals. [Including a list of portraits of Shakespeare.]

(Washington) 1906.

(Library of Congress.)

199931

——Are you interested in "Shakespeare"? [Some Baconian theories about Shakespeare and the Shakespeare bust, addressed to the American forces stationed in this country.] pp. [5.]
[Birmingham]
illus. [1944.]
[Bacon Society]

549094

—— BAX (C.)
A Portrait of Shakespeare? [Formerly belonging to the Earl of Nithsdale.] FROM Country Life [, Vol. 97].
port. illus. 1945.

559338

——BRITTON (J.)
Essays on the merits and characteristics
of William Shakspere: also remarks on
his birth and burial-place, his monument,
portraits, and associations. IN
Britton (J.) Appendix to Britton's
autobiography.
illus.   1849.

28246

——BRITTON (J.)
Remarks on the monumental bust of
Shakespeare at Stratford-upon-Avon.
FROM The Gentleman's Magazine,
July 1816.   pp. [4.]   1816.

402685

—— Brophy (J.) The Human face. [With
references to Shakespeare.]
Ports. Illus.

1945.

564940

——Burgon (J.W.) The Portrait of a
Christian gentleman : a memoir of
Patrick Fraser Tytler, author of
the "History of Scotland". 2nd edn.
[With a reference to Shakespeare's
bust.]

1859.

491204

——Christie, Manson & Woods. Catalogue of
the collection of ancient and modern
pictures & drawings of the late
Baroness Burdett-Coutts [including
Shakespeare portraits] which will
be sold by auction May 4[-5], 1922.
pp. 72. Ports. Illus.

[1922.]

559103

—— COOK (C.)
Shakespeare [: description of a
portrait, engravings of which are
attributed to Robert Hancock].
IN Cook (C.) The Life and work of
Robert Hancock.
illus.   1948.

595794

——Cust ([Sir] L.[H.]) The Portraits of
Shakespeare. In Transactions of the
Bibliographical Society, Vol.9.

1908.

213085

—— DAWSON (G. E.)
The Arlaud-Duchange portrait of
Shakespeare.   Reprinted from The
Library, Dec., 1935. pp. 290-294.
(Bibliographical Society)
ports.   1935.

478518

—— DAWSON (G. E.)
A Note on the Arlaud-Duchange
portrait of Shakespeare.   IN The
Library, 4th Series, Vol. 18.
(Bibliographical Society)   1938.

487688

—— DRIVER, OLIVE WAGNER
The Shakespearean portraits and other
addenda. (A supplement to "The Bacon-
Shakespearean mystery). Revised edition.
(Northampton, Mass.)   1966.

illus.   762622

—— Effigies of the most famous English
writers from Chaucer to Johnson
[including Shakespeare], exhibited at
the Grolier Club, New York, December,
1891. [Catalogue].   pp. 78.   (New
York: Grolier Club)
illus.   1891.
Large paper edn. limited to 200 copies.

490489

—— ESDAILE ([Mrs.] KATHARINE A.)
English church monuments, 1510-1840.
With an introduction by S. Sitwell
[, references to Shakespeare and bibliographical references.]
illus.   1946.

579515

——Folkestone, Public Art Gallery.
Catalogue of an exhibition
entitled "Shakespeare as he
was and as artists have shown
him". From the private collection
of M.H. Spielmann. Oct. 1934.pp.15.

[Folkestone]   1934.

426130

—— GOWER ([Rt. Hon. Lord] RONALD [CHARLES
SUTHERLAND LEVESON])
The Shakespeare death-mask.   FROM
[The Antiquary, Vol. 2.]
illus.   [1880.]

553492

——GROLIER CLUB [OF] NEW YORK
Catalogue of an exhibition illustrative
of the text of Shakespeare's plays, as
published in edited editions; with a
collection of engraved portraits of
the poet.   (New York)   1916.
Edn. limited to 207 copies, on hand-
made paper.

511626

—— Hall (Lillian A.) Catalogue of dramatic
portraits in the Theatre Collection
of Harvard College Library. [Includ-
ing portraits of Shakespeare.]

(Cambridge, Mass.)   1930-34.

420683

——   Hind (Arthur Mayger) Martin Droeshout's
portraits: Shakespeare.IN Hind (A.M.) Engraving
in England in the sixteenth & seventeenth centuries:
a descriptive catalogue. Part 2. Facsimiles.
(Cambridge)   1955.

651163

—— HYDE (Mrs. MARY MORLEY CRAPO)
Shakespeare's head.
IN SHAKESPEARE QUARTERLY XVI: 1.
pp.139-143.
(New York) 1965.

605711

—— JARRATT (J. E.)
The Grafton portrait [of Shakespeare].
IN Bulletin of the John Rylands
Library, Manchester, Vol. 29.
(Manchester)   1945-46.

571535

—— JOHNSON (E. D.)
Will Shaksper's portrait [: an
analysis of the Droeshout portrait
on the second page of the First Folio].
pp. 8.   (Birmingham)
dgms.   facsimile. [1944.]   549914
———— Another copy.   558954

—— JONES (W.)
An Account of the Kenilworth Buffet,
with carved relievos illustrative of
Kenilworth Castle, in the Elizabethan
period, designed and manufactured by
Cookes and Sons, for the Grand
Exhibition, 1851.   [With references
to Shakespeare.]   pp. 22.
illus.   1851.

77896

—— Kingman (T.) An Authenticated
contemporary portrait of
Shakespeare. pp.87. Ports.
Illus.

(New York)   1932.

422094

—— M.   (C.   L.   )
A Note on Nicholas Parr's portrait of
Shakespeare, engraved c.1740, by C.L.M.
Illus. (Cleveland, [Ohio])   1907.
668399

No. 12 of edition limited to 250
copies, privately printed.

—— MERRIDEW (J.)
A Catalogue of engraved portraits of
nobility and others, connected with
the County of Warwick; [with]
biographical notices.   [Including
Shakespeare.] pp. viii, 83.
(Coventry)
port.   1848.   6510
Large paper copy.
———— [Extra illustrated with examples
from the collection of J. Macmillan.
Including Shakespeare.]   pp. [xx, 263,
34.] (Coventry)   1848.   301877

—— MINSTER (L.)
Look upon this picture.   IN The
Librarian, Vol. 26.   (Gravesend)
1937.

476071

—— MONROE (ROBERT D.)
Notes on a unique engraving and "lost"
portrait of Shakespeare.
IN SHAKESPEARE QUARTERLY XII: 3.
pp. 317-321
(New York)   1961.

605711

—— NATIONAL PORTRAIT GALLERY
O sweet Mr. Shakespeare, I'll have his
picture: the changing image of
Shakespeare's person, 1600-1800.
1964.

illus.   668095

—— NEVINSON (J. L.)
Shakespeare's dress in his portraits.
IN SHAKESPEARE QUARTERLY XVIII: 2.
pp. 101-106.
(New York)   1967.

605711

—— The Newly discovered portrait of
Shakespeare.   IN The London Review,
Vol. 2.   1861.

475.

—— D'DONAVAN (W. R.)
A Statue of Shakespeare [in the Central
Park, New York].   FROM [Lippincott's
Magazine,] Vol. 13.   [Philadelphia]
1874.

553495

—— POHL (FREDERICK JULIUS)

The Death-mask: a reprint from
"Shakespeare Quarterly", Vol.12, No.2.
(Shakespeare Association of America)
pp.[12.] Illus. [New York]   1961.

667310

—— PURCHAS (J. R. P.)
The Chandos portrait of Shakespeare.
IN The Antiquary, Vol. 41.
illus.   1905.

191811

—— RANSFORD (A.)
Grafton portrait of Shakespeare.
[With two notes by W. Jaggard.]
IN Notes and Queries, Vol. 166,
January-June, 1934.   1934.

422514

—— RAY (S. N.)
Shakespeare through X-ray; science
takes up the controversy [: an
attempt to prove that Edward de Vere,
17th Earl of Oxford was Shakespeare].
IN The Modern Review, Vol. 69.
(Calcutta)
ports.   illus.   1941.

581255

—— RENDALL (G. H.)
"Ashbourne" portrait of Shakespeare.
pp. 16.   (Colchester)
illus.   [1940.]

516325

—— SEWARD (T.)]
On Shakespear's monument at Stratford
upon Avon.   IN [DODSLEY (R.) ed.,]
A Collection of poems by several hands.
3rd edn., Vol. 2.   1751.   576731
————   4th edn.   1755.   576737
————   5th edn.   1758.   538519

—— Shakespeare portrait [with description].
In The Amateur Theatre and Playwrights'
Journal, Vol.4, No.75.

1937.

467093

—— Shakespeare portraits.   IN The Leisure
Hour, 1864.
illus.   1864.

83387

___ SMETHURST (W.)
The Ashbourne portrait of Shakespeare.
ff. [2,] 23.
port. illus. plan. typescript.
1943.
Only 9 copies made, of which this is
No. 2.

549760

____The So-called "Grafton portrait of
Shakespeare". In The Bulletin of
the John Rylands Library Manchester.
vol.17. 1933. Port.

(Manchester)   1933.

411706

___ SPIELMANN (M. H.)
The "Grafton" and "Sanders" portraits
of Shakespeare.   pp. [6.]   FROM The
Connoisseur, Feb. 1909.
ports.   1909.

521313

___ Spielmann (M.H.) The Janssen, or
Somerset, portrait of Shakespeare.
Ports. In The Connoisseur, Vol.24.

1909.

218524

____Spielmann (M.H.) The Janssen, or
Somerset, portrait of Shakespeare:
the more important copies, Part 2.
Illus. From The Connoisseur, Vol.32.

1912.

522118

___   Spielmann (M.H.) The Miniatures of
Shakespeare. Illus. In The Connoisseur
Vol. 45, 1916.

1916.

266905

___ SPIELMANN (M. H.)
[Shakespeare's portraiture: a reissue of]
The Title-page of the First Folio of
Shakespeare's plays: a comparative
study of the Droeshout portrait and the
Stratford monument.   Written for the
Shakespeare Association in celebration
of the First Folio Tercentenary, 1923.
[With bibliographical notes.]   pp. xi,56.
ports. illus. genealogical table.
facsimiles.   1931.
No. 22 of edn. limited to 50 copies.
Author's signature on ½ tp.   Date on tp.
1924, on cover 1931.   533661

___ SPIELMANN (M. H.)
"This figure that thou here seest put".
IN GOLLANCZ ([Sir] I) ed., A Book of
homage to Shakespeare.
ports. illus. facsimiles. [1916.]

264175

___ TIMBS (J.)
English eccentrics and eccentricites.
[With a reference to a Shakespeare
monument.]   New edn.
ports.   illus.   1877.

400637

____VERTUE (G.)
Note books [and autobiography.   Edited
with introduction and notes by a
committee appointed by the Walpole
Society.   With index to Vols. 1-5.
Contains references to Shakespeare].
(Oxford)
ports. facsimiles. illus. 1930-
The Walpole Society, Vols. 18, 20, 22,
24, 26, 29, 30.

376674

____WHELER (R. B.)
The Bust of Shakspeare at Stratford.
FROM The Gentleman's Magazine,
Jan. and March, 1815.   pp. [6.]
1815.

402685

____WIVELL (A.)
An Inquiry into the history, authenticity
and characteristics of the Shakspere
portraits.   pp. 46.
frontis.   facsimiles.   1848.

595514

___ WRIGHT (C.)
Shakespeare and Ben Jonson, William
Penn, Lord Macaulay and the Athenaeum -
or, its editor [: a letter] to
W. H. Dixon [relating to the portrait
of Shakespeare, recently discovered
at Stratford-upon-Avon].   pp. 4.
1861.

558066

Portraits of Greatness
ROSIGNOLI, MARIA PIA

The Life and times of Shakespeare.
Translator Mary Kanani.   (Feltham,
Mddx.)
illus.   1968.
Portraits of greatness.

777256

Portraits of Shakespearian Actors *see* Illustrations

PORTSMOUTH BRANCH, BRITISH EMPIRE
SHAKESPEARE SOCIETY
Programmes, etc.   [Portsmouth]
1934-8.

523297

PORTSMOUTH TEACHERS' DRAMATIC SOCIETY
[Programmes of Shakespeare performances.
(Portsmouth) 1925-1937].
illus.
Wants programme for 1924.   No perform-
ance 1931.

425732

— YOUNG ([Sir] G.)
Portugal and the Shakespeare tercentenary.
IN Gollancz ([Sir] I.) ed., A Book of
homage to Shakespeare.
ports. illus. facsimiles.   [1916].

264175

Posters *see* **Playbills**

Postgate (Isa J.) Woodnotes: poems
[on Shakespeare, and quotations from
his plays.] Illustrated by Nathalie
V. Nikitin. pp. [13.]

(New York)   [c.1840.]

479264

Posthumous parodies and other pieces
composed by celebrated poets but not
published in their works. [Including
parodies of passages from Shakespeare.
By H.Twiss].

1814.

516236

Pott (Mrs. [Constance M.]) The
Biliteral cipher [of Lord Bacon]:
hints for deciphering. pp.20.

[c.1903.]

558405

Pott (Mrs. [Constance M.]) Francis
Bacon and his secret society.

(Chicago)   1891.

500786

POTT (Mrs. [CONSTANCE M.]) ed.
The Promus of formularies and elegancies:
private notes, circ. 1594, hitherto
unpublished, by F. Bacon.   Illustrated
and elucidated by passages from
Shakespeare by Mrs. [Constance M.] Pott.
With preface by E. A. Abbott. 1883.

505532

___THEOBALD (R. M.)
Bacon's "Promus" and Shakespeare [: a
letter] to the editor of the "Nonconformist and Independent".   [A review
of The Promus of formularies and
elegancies, by F. Bacon.   Edited by
Mrs. Constance M. Pott, 1883.]   pp. 2.
[1883.]

555513

___WHITE (R. G.)
The Bacon-Shakespeare craze [: a
review of "The Promus of Bacon, illustrated by passages from Shakespeare",
by Mrs. Constance M. Pott, 1883].
IN The Atlantic Monthly, Vol. 51, 1883.
(Boston, Mass.)   1883.

60092

POTTER (RACHEL)
Macbeth: Handreichungen für den
Lehrer.   [English text.]   pp. 52.
(Dortmund)   1961.
Neusprachliche Unterricht in
Wissenschaft und Praxis, Bd. 4.

666852

Potter (S.) Coleridge and S.T.C.
[With references to Shakespeare
and with a bibliography.]

1935.

435813

POTTER (STEPHEN)
Henry IV - Part I; [and,] Henry IV -
Part II [: criticisms of the perform-
ances at the New Theatre, London].
IN The New Statesman and Nation, New
Series, Vol. 30.   1945.

568922

POTTER (STEPHEN)
How to appreciate Shakespeare [: a
demonstration.   Broadcast] 20th April,
1947.   ff. 23.
typescript.   1947.

583267

POTTER (STEPHEN)
Humour in three dimensions:
Shakespeare.   IN Potter (S.) Sense
of humour.
illus.   bibliog.   1954.

640447

POTTER (STEPHEN)
Notes on Shakespeare; and, The Lit
Shakespeare.   IN Potter (S.) The
Muse in chains: a study in education.
graph.   1937.

653584

Potter (S.) Shakespeare and Stratford.
In Theatre Today.

1946.

606680

Potter (S.) William Shakespeare:
dramatic reading. (Senior English.)
[Broadcast] 21 May, 1940. ff. [1],
12. Typescript.

1940.

516588

Potter (S.) and Keen (A.) Shakespeare discovery? : [a dramatized
story concerning Shakespeare's handwriting in a copy of Hall's
Chronicles, 1550]. Expert opinion
edited by N. Blakiston. Production
by S. Potter. [Broadcast] October
17th, 1940. ff. 21.

[1940.]

521688

Pottery *see* Ceramics

POTTLE (F. A.)
The Idiom of poetry. [With notes
and references, including references
to Shakespeare.] (Ithaca, N.Y.)
1941.
Cornell University. Messenger
Lectures on the Evolution of
Civilization.

536765

POTTS (ABBIE FINDLAY)
"Cynthia's Revels", "Poetaster", and
"Troilus and Cressida".
IN SHAKESPEARE QUARTERLY V.
pp. 297-302.
(New York) 1954.

605711

POTTS (ABBIE FINDLAY)
Hamlet and Gloriana's knights.
IN SHAKESPEARE QUARTERLY VI.
pp. 31-43.
(New York) 1955.

605711

POTTS (ABBIE FINDLAY)

Shakespeare and 'The Faerie Queene'.
(New York) 1958.

665996

Pound (E.[L.]) A B C of reading
[containing references to Shakespeare
and his work.]

1934.

419934

Pound (E.[L.]) Guide to kulchur. [With
reference to Shakespeare]. Illus.

1938.

486848

Powel (H.[W.H.]) The Virgin Queene:
[a novel, dealing with Elizabeth
and Shakespeare.]

(Boston,[Mass.] 1928.

405583

[Powell (Annie E.)] Coleridge's
Shakespearean criticism, edited
by T.M. Raysor: [a review signed
A.E. Dodds.] In Modern Language
Notes, 1932.

(Baltimore) 1932.

404117

POWELL (DILYS)
"Hamlet" on the screen [: Sir
Laurence Olivier's production].
IN Britain To-day, No. 147.
illus. 1948.

587767/147

POWELL (DILYS)
Laurence Olivier: a brief chronicle
[with an account of his Shakespearian
performances]. IN The Saturday Book,
6th year.
ports. illus. [1946.]

576899

Powell, Enoch

see Powell, John Enoch

Powell (Hugh) ed.
GRYPHIUS (ANDREAS)
Herr Peter Squentz [: a comedy based
on the Quince episode in Shakespeare's
"A Midsummer night's dream". German
text]. Edited, with introduction
and commentary [in English]. (Leicester:
[University College, Leicester])
illus. 1957.

675019

Powell (Hugh) ed.
SCHLEGEL (JOHANN ELIAS)
Vergleichung Shakespears und Andreas
Gryphs, [1741]. Faksimiledruck
herausgegeben mit Anhang und Nachwort
von H. Powell. (Leicester) 1964.

745370

POWELL (JOHN ENOCH)
Politics in Shakespeare. IN
PRITCHETT (VICTOR SAWDON) and others,
Shakespeare: the comprehensive soul.
[Talks on the B.B.C. European English
Service to celebrate the Shakespearian
Quatercentenary.] 1965.

746585

POWELL (PETER)
A Talk on Othello. IN Theatre
Programme [: a radio review of the
stage: Shakespearian items. Broad-
cast] 2nd April [1947.] ff. [34.]
typescript.
[1947.]

583268

POWER (RHODA [D.])
The Play's the thing [: a play about
acting and especially about
Shakespeare's Macbeth]. (Senior
English II, No. 9). [Broadcast]
16th November, 1943. ff. 12.
typescript. 1944.

550859

Power-Waters ([Mrs.] Alma) John
Barrymore : the authorized life.
[With references to his performances
in Shakespearean plays.] Foreword
by [J.] B. Atkinson. Port.

1942.

533679

Powers (Richard M.) illus.
LAMB (CHARLES and MARY ANN)
Tales from Shakespeare.   Illustrated
by R. M. Powers.   (New York)
illus.   1963.
Macmillan Classics,

747973

POWYS (J. C.)
The Pleasures of literature.
[Including a chapter entitled
Shakespeare, and with other references
to Shakespeare.]   1938.

491138

POWYS (L.)
Dorset essays [including one on
"Shakespeare's fairies".]   With
forty photographs by W. Goodden.
1935.

441390

POYNTER (FREDERICK NOEL LAWRENCE)
Gervase Markham. IN English Association.
Essays and Studies. New Series Vol. 15.
1962.

706391

POYNTER, FREDERICK NOEL LAWRENCE
Medicine and public health [: in
Elizabethan England.   FROM
SHAKESPEARE SURVEY 17.   (Cambridge)
1964.

740731

PRAGER, LEONARD
Shakespeare in Yiddish.
IN SHAKESPEARE QUARTERLY XIX: 2.
pp. 149-158.   (New York)
1968.

605711

PRAGUE THEATRE INSTITUTE
Theatre in Czechoslovakia: William
Shakespeare. [Articles by Z. Stribrny
and others. Ed. Ludmila Kopáčová.]
(Praha)   [1964.]

744460

PRAHL (A. J.)
Bemerkungen zu Gerhart Hauptmanns
Hamlet in Wittenberg.   [With biblio-
graphical notes.] FROM Monatshefte
für Deutschen Unterricht, Vol. 29.
(Madison, Wis.)   1937.

578414

Pratesi (Luigi) ed.
LAMB (CHARLES and MARY)
Tales from Shakespeare.   [English
text.]   Introduzione e note di
L. Pratesi.   (Livorno)
port.   1925.
[Biblioteca di Classici Stranieri]

330050

PRATT (FLETCHER)
Secret and urgent: the story of codes
and ciphers.   [With a chapter entitled
"Bacon or Shakespeare?"]
tables.   1939.

510108

PRATT (MARJORY B.)
Formal designs from ten Shakespeare
sonnets.   [With text of the sonnets,
from the Temple edition.]   pp. [46].
(New York)   1940.

522168

PRATT (SAMUEL M.)
Shakespeare and Humphrey Duke of
Gloucester: a study in myth.
IN SHAKESPEARE QUARTERLY XVI: 2.
pp. 201-216.
(New York)   1965.

605711

Pratt (T.) The Shakespeare Memorial
National Theatre. In Manchester
Literary Club. Papers, Vol.37.

(Manchester)   1911.

518393

PRAUSS (R. and Mrs. R.)
Bibliography of Polish Shakespeareana
up to Jan. 1st 1933.   Compiled on
behalf of the Birmingham Public
Libraries at the request of the
British Embassy, Warsaw.   pp. 88.
typescript.   [1934.]

426524

Prayer Book

— 'Noble (R.) Shakespeare's Biblical
knowledge and use of The Book of
Common Prayer as exemplified in
the plays of the first folio.

1935.

437987

Praz (M.) [Review of] Shakespeare and
the stoicism of Seneca, by T.S.
Eliot. In English studies, Vol. 10.

(Amsterdam)   1928.

485652

PRAZ (M.)
[Review of] The Problems of the
Shakespeare sonnets, by J. M.
Robertson.   IN English studies,
Vol. 10.   (Amsterdam)   1928.

485652

PRAZ (M.)
⌊Review of⌋ Les Sonnets elisabéthains,
par Janet G. Scott, and Aspects of
Elizabethan imagery, by Elizabeth
Holmes.   IN English studies,
Vol. 11.   (Amsterdam)   1929.

485653

PRAZ (M.)
⌊Review of⌋ The Real war of the
theatres, Shakespeare's fellows
in rivalry with the Admiral's men,
1594-1603, by R. B. Sharpe.
IN English studies, Vol. 19.
(Amsterdam)   1937.

485661

PRAZ (M.)
⌊Review of⌋ Shakespeare and "Sir
Thomas Moore", by S. A. Tannenbaum.
IN English studies, Vol. 12.
(Amsterdam)   1930.

485654

PRAZ (MARIO)
⌊Reviews of⌋ The Wheel of fire, The
Imperial theme, and The Shakespearian
tempest, by G. W. Knight.   IN
English studies, Vol. 15.   (Amsterdam)
1933.

485657

PRAZ (M.)
⌊Reviews of⌋ Shakespeare's imagery
and what it tells us, by Caroline
F. E. Spurgeon; Shakespeares
Bilder, von W. Clemen; ⌊and⌋ The
Jacobean drama, by U⌊na⌋ M. Ellis-
Fermor.   IN English studies,
Vol. 18.   (Amsterdam)   1936.

485660

PRAZ (M.)
The Romantic agony ⌊: a study of
the morbid tendencies of romantic
literature from 1800-1900, containing
references to Shakespeare and his
works.⌋   Translated from the Italian
by A. Davidson.
   frontis.   bibliog.   1933.

406496

PRAZ, MARIO
Shakespeare translations in Italy.
IN SHAKESPEARE JAHRBUCH, Bd. 92/1956,
pp. 220-231.   (Heidelberg)

10531

PRAZ (MARIO)
Shakespeare's Italy.   IN SHAKESPEARE
SURVEY 7.   (Cambridge)   1954.

639176

PRAZ (MARIO)
Studies in seventeenth-century imagery.
⌊With references to Shakespeare, and
bibliographical notes.⌋
   facsimiles.   1939.
Studies of the Warburg Institute,

497883

Predecessors of Shakespeare

―――ADAMS (J. Q.) [ed.]
Chief pre-Shakespearean dramas: a
selection of plays illustrating the
history of the English drama from
its origin down to Shakespeare.
   facsimile.   1924.

424814

―――BOAS (F. S.)
Shakspere and his predecessors.
                 1896.   505531
_____ New impression.1902.   498694
_____ 3rd imp.   (University Manuals)
                 1910.   466546
_____ 4th imp.   1918.   506814
_____ 5th imp.   1922.   418063
_____ 7th imp. with a new introductory
chapter.   1940.   521915

―――BOYD (J.)
Goethe's Knowledge of English literature.
⌊With bibliographical notes.   Including
chapters on Shakespeare, his predecessors
and contemporaries⌋.   (Oxford)
                 1932.
(Oxford Studies in Modern Languages and
Literature)

401515

―――CLEMEN (WOLFGANG H.)
English tragedy before Shakespeare:
the development of dramatic speech.
Translated ⌊from the German⌋ by
T. S. Dorsch.
   bibliog.   1961.

666756

―――DISRAELI (I.)
Amenities of literature: sketches and
characters of English literature [in-
cluding a chapter on The Predecessors
and contemporaries of Shakspere].
New edition, edited by the Earl of
Beaconsfield.

[1881.]

36382

―――EVERITT (E. B.) and ARMSTRONG (R. L.) eds.
Six early plays related to the
Shakespeare Canon.   (Copenhagen)
                 1965.
   Anglistica, Vol. XIV.

741510

―――LANIER (S.⌊C.⌋)
Shakspere and his forerunners: studies
in Elizabethan poetry and its development from early English.   ⌊With a
preface by H. W. Lanier.⌋
   ports.   illus.   facsimiles.   2 vols.
                 1903.

392888

―――LANIER (S. [C.])
Shakspere and his forerunners.   Edited
⌊with an introduction⌋ by K. Malone.
⌊With bibliographical notes.⌋   (⌊Works.⌋
Centennial edn. Vol. 3.)   (Baltimore)
   illus.   1945.

588454

——MANLY (J. M.) [ed.]
Specimens of the pre-Shakespearean
drama, with an introduction, notes
and a glossary. (Boston, [Mass.])
2 vols.   1925.
Athenaeum Press Series.

496468-9

——MURPHY (DOREEN)
Shakespeare's debt to his predecessors.
FROM The Irish Monthly, Vol. 62.
1934.

439142

——SYMONDS (J.A.)
Shakspere's predecessors in the English
drama. New edn.   1906.

472080

———— Another edn.   1913.   483089
———— 2nd edn.   1924.   401510

Prefaces *see* Introductions to Shakespeare's Plays

The Prefatory pages of the First
Folio, with a comment by Sir S.
Lee. 3rd edn. pp. [19].
(London Shakespeare League)
port.   1925.

424655

PRESCOTT (KATE H.)
Reminiscences of a Baconian. [New
York.]
illus. facsimiles. bibliog. 1949.

609757

Present remedies against the plague,
[1603,] etc. With an introduction
by W. P. Barrett.   1933.
Shakespeare Association Facsimiles,
No. 7.

403071

PRESSON, ROBERT K.
Boethius, King Lear and "Maystresse
Philosophie". FROM Journal of English
and Germanic Philology, Vol.64, No.3.
1965.

pp.406-424.   756149

PRESSON (ROBERT K.)
Shakespeare's "Troilus and Cressida"
& the legends of Troy. (Madison,
Wis.)   1953.

635838

PRESSON, ROBERT K.
Some traditional instances of setting
in Shakespeare's plays. FROM Modern
Language Review, January 1966, Vol.61,
No.I. (Cambridge)   1966.

pp.12-22.   756150

Prévost, A. F. L'Abbé *works relating to*

——CARPENTER (J. C.)
The Abbé Prévost and Shakespeare.
IN The Modern Language Review, Vol.
10.   (Cambridge)   1915.

266825

PRICE (CLAIR)
Stratford-upon-Avon.   IN JOHNSTONE
(K.) [and others] Introducing
Britain [: broadcast talks].
Revised 2nd edn.
illus.   1946.

573859

PRICE, GEORGE R.
Barron's simplified approach to
Shakespeare's Macbeth. (New York)
1966.

Barron's Educational series.
762646

PRICE (GEORGE R.)
Henry V and Germanicus.
IN SHAKESPEARE QUARTERLY XII: 1.
pp. 57-60.
(New York)   1961.

605711

PRICE, GEORGE R.
Reading Shakespeare's plays [: a
practical guide to the Elizabethan
background].   (Woodbury, N.Y.)
1962.
Barron's educational series.
769928

PRICE, GEORGE R.
A simplified approach to Shakespeare's
Hamlet. (New York: Barron's
Educational Series)   1964.

742492

PRICE (HEREWARD THIMBLEBY)
The Authorship of "Titus Andronicus".
FROM The Journal of English and
Germanic Philology, Vol. 42.   (Urbana,
Ill.)   1943.

563270

PRICE (HEREWARD THIMBLEBY)
Construction in Shakespeare.
(University of Michigan.   Contributions in Modern Philology, No.17)
pp. 42.   (Ann Arbor, Mich.) 1951.

617603

PRICE (HEREWARD THIMBLEBY)
The First Quarto of Titus Andronicus.
[With bibliographical notes.]   IN
English Institute Essays, 1947.
(New York)   1948.

530316/1947

PRICE (H. T.)
Function of imagery in Venus and
Adonis.   Reprinted from Papers of
the Michigan Academy of Science,
Arts and Letters, Vol. 31, 1945.
pp. [24].   [Ann Arbor, Mich.]
bibliog.   1947.

596024

PRICE (HEREWARD THIMBLEBY)
Mirror-scenes in Shakespeare.
IN McMANAWAY (J. G.), DAWSON (G. E.)
and WILLOUGHBY (E. E.) eds., Joseph
Quincy Adams memorial studies.
(Washington)   1948.

596748

PRICE (H. T.)
On some peculiarities in Shakespearean
texts.   IN Essays and studies by
members of the English department
of the University of Michigan.
(Ann Arbor [Mich.])   1932.
University of Michigan Publications.
Language and Literature.

404800

Price (H.T.) The Quarto and folio
texts of Henry V. From Philological
Quarterly, vol.12.

(Iowa)   1933.

442557

PRICE (HEREWARD THIMBLEBY)

[Review of] The Merchant of Venice. Edited
by J.R.Brown. (Arden Shakespeare) 7th edn.
IN The Journal of English and Germanic
Philology, Vol. 55.

(Urbana, Ill.)   1956.

600780/55

PRICE, HEREWARD THIMBLEBY
Shakespeare and his young contemporaries.
FROM Philological Quarterly, Vol.XLI,
No.1.   1962.

668388

PRICE (HEREWARD THIMBLEBY)
Shakespeare as a critic.   [With bibliographical notes.]   IN MAXWELL (B.) [and
others] eds., Renaissance studies in
honor of Hardin Craig.   (Iowa)
port.   1941.
Philological Quarterly, Vol. 20, No.
3; Iowa University [and Stanford
University.]

539442

PRICE (H. T.)
Shakespeare's imagery.   FROM
Michigan Alumnus Quarterly Review,
Vol. 50.   (Ann Arbor, Mich.)
                               1944.

581945

PRICE (H. T.)
Towards a scientific method of textual
criticism for the Elizabethan drama.
[With references to Shakespeare.]
Reprinted from The Journal of English
and Germanic philology, Vol. 36.
(Urbana, Ill.)   [1937.]

554218

PRICE, JOSEPH G.
From farce to romance.   All's well that
ends well 1756-1811.
IN SHAKESPEARE JAHRBUCH.   Bd 99/1963.
pp. 57-71.   (Heidelberg)

10531

PRICE (L. M.)
The Reception of English literature
in Germany [with chapters on
Shakespeare].   (Berkeley, Cal.)
bibliog.   1932.

414506

PRICE (NANCY)
Nettles and docks [: essays, with
references to Shakespeare].   Introduction by [W.] N. Birkett.
ports.   illus.   1940.

521800

Price (Norman M.) illus.
LAMB (CHARLES and MARY [A.])
Tales from Shakespeare.   With a front-
ispiece by N. M. Price and line drawings
by F. G. Moorsom.   [1933.]   406059
[Nelson's Famous Books.]
   Another edn. [1937.]   467563

Price (Norman M.) illus.
LAMB (CHARLES and MARY [A.])
Tales from Shakespeare.   [1939].

511665

PRICE (T. R.)
King Lear: a study of Shakspere's
dramatic method.   IN Publications
of the Modern Language Association
of America, Vol. 9.   (Baltimore)
                               1894.

428329

"Pride of Britain" Guides and Histories
TREWIN (JOHN COURTENAY)
The Pictorial story of Shakespeare &
Stratford-upon-Avon.   Foreword by
L. Fox.   (Pitkin Pictorials Ltd.)
pp. 24.
   ports. illus. map. facsimile. [1960.]

666649

PRIESTLEY (E.) and BAXTER (ALICE M.)
Shakespearian women [: a musical
drama, utilizing songs of Shakespeare
and extracts from his plays.]
pp. 16.   [1949.]
   Macdonald Drama Library: Miniature
Musical Dramas.

599925

PRIESTLEY (J. B.)
The English comic characters
[including those in Shakespeare's
plays.]   1937.
   Bodley Head Library.

493566

Priestley (J.B.) Falstaff and his
  circle. In MacLean (M.S.) and
  Holmes ([Mrs.]Elisabeth K.) eds.,
  Men and books.

                (New York)   1930.

                               413294

PRIESTLEY (JOHN BOYNTON)
  Shakespeare. IN Priestley (J. B.)
  The Art of the dramatist: a lecture,
  with appendices and discursive notes.
  [Hubert Henry Davies Fund Lecture,
  1956.]   1957.

                               670253

PRIESTLEY (J. B.)
  Theatre outlook [in England.
  With references to Shakespeare].
  pp. 76.
   ports. illus. maps. charts.
                               1947.

                               587192

PRIESTLEY (JOHN BOYNTON)
  What happened to Falstaff.
  Producer: J. Weltman. [Script
  of broadcast in Third Programme,
  September, 1960.]   (British
  Broadcasting Corporation) ff. 25.
   typescript.   1960.

                               667037

Priestley, John Boynton *works relating to*

——DE M. (S.)
    Falstaff and others: [a review of
    "The English comic characters", by
    J. B. Priestley.] FROM The Contemporary
    Review, Literary Supplement, 1925.
    pp. [3.]   [1925]

                               389227

——SPEAIGHT (ROBERT)

    Mr. Priestley, Falstaff and Establishment.
    FROM The Month, N.S. Vol.25, No.3.
                               1961.

                               667759

PRIESTLEY (JOSEPH)
  A Course of lectures on oratory and
  criticism [with references to oratory
  and criticism in Shakespeare].
                      1777.   223509
  _____   (Dublin)   1781.   568834

Priestley-Smith (H.) Come away, death:
  unaccompanied part-song for female
  voices. [Words by] Shakespeare
  [from Twelfth Night]. pp.4.

                               1914.

                               517043

Priestley-Smith (H.) O Mistress mine:
  part song for S.C.C. (unaccompanied).
  [Words by] Shakespeare [from
  Twelfth Night. Staff notation and
  tonic sol-fa.]   2 vols.

                1912.

                               517024

PRIESTMAN, BRIAN
  Music for Shakespeare - some practical
  problems. IN Music & letters,
  Vol. 45, No. 2, April 1964:
  Shakespeare and music.   1964.

                               668211

Primitivism

——HARRISON (T P.) Jr.
    Aspects of primitivism in Shakespeare
    and Spenser. IN University of Texas
    Studies in English, [No. 20].
    (Austin, Texas)
                               1940.

                               529715

PRIMOST (SYDNEY)
  The Pools of the Gods: a play in
  three acts. With a foreword by
  P. Tabori. pp. 67.   1954.

                               646076

PRINCE (FRANK TEMPLETON)

  The Sonnet from Wyatt to Shakespeare.
  IN Stratford-upon-Avon Studies,
  edited by J. R. Brown and B. Harris,
  Vol. 2. Elizabethan poetry. 1960.

                               666674

PRINCE, FRANK TEMPLETON

  William Shakespeare: the poems. 1963.

    Writers and their work, No. 165.
                               667704

Prince (P.A.) William Shakspeare.
  In Prince (P.A.) Parallel history:
  an outline of the history and
  biography of the world. 2nd edn.
  Vol.2.

                1843.

                               33335

Prince of Wales Theatre *see* London,
Theatres — Prince of Wales Theatre

Prince's Theatre *see* **London, Theatres —
Prince's Theatre**

PRING (BERYL)
Shakespeare and Russian films.
IN The Adelphi, vol. 4.   1932.

404903

PRINS (A. A.)
Review [of] The Humors & Shakespeare's
characters by J. W. Draper.
IN English Studies, Vol. 27.
(Amsterdam)   1946.

583562

Printing *see* **Textual History**

PRIOR (MOODY ERASMUS)

Character in relation to action in
Othello. Reprinted from Modern
Philology, Vol.44, No.4. [Chicago]
1947.

667965

PRIOR (MOODY ERASMUS)
Imagery as a test of authorship.
IN SHAKESPEARE QUARTERLY VI:
pp. 381-396.
(New York)   1955.

605711

PRIOR (M. E.)
The Language of tragedy [: an
exploration into the nature of
verse drama based on consideration
of English verse tragedy, including
reference to Shakespeare.] (New York)
bibliog.   1947.

590003

PRIOR (MOODY ERASMUS)
The Play scene in Hamlet.   [With
bibliographical notes.]   IN E.L.H.:
a journal of English literary
history, Vol. 9.   (Baltimore)   1942.

544179

PRIOR (MOODY ERASMUS)
The Thought of "Hamlet" and the modern
temper.   [With bibliographical notes.]
IN E.L.H.: a journal of English
literary history, Vol. 15.   (Baltimore)
1948.

430295/15

PRITCHARD (FRANCIS HENRY)
Studies in literature: an aid to
literary appreciation and composition.
[With references to Shakespeare and
bibliographies].   1919.

455527

PRITCHARD (FRANCIS HENRY)
Training in literary appreciation:
an introduction to criticism.   [With
references to Shakespeare.]
bibliog.   1922.

528130

PRITCHETT (VICTOR SAWDON) [ed.]
The Character of Macbeth [: scenes
from Macbeth.   Arranged with comments
by V. S. Pritchett].   (Forces Educational Broadcast.)   [Broadcast]
13th September, 1946.   ff. 9.
typescript.   1946.

579575

PRITCHETT, VICTOR SAWDON, and others
Shakespeare: the comprehensive
soul.   [Talks on the B.B.C.
European English Service to celebrate
the Shakespearian Quatercentenary.]
1965.

746585

[Procter (B.W.)] The Life of Edmund
Kean. Port.   2 vols.

1835.

522849

PROCTOR (G. L.)
An Introduction to English
literature [: studies of English
prose writers with excerpts from
their works.   With a section on
Shakespeare].   3rd edn.   (Stockholm)
ports.   facsimiles.   1944.

573970

PROCTOR (SIGMUND KLUSS)
Thomas De Quincey's theory of literature.
With references to Shakespeare.   (Ann
Arbor, Mich.)
bibliog.   1943.
Michigan University Publications,
Language and Literature, Vol. 19.

552714

A Production is born: Hamlet by
Bristol Old Vic Company at the Theatre
Royal, Bristol, January, 1948.   IN
LANDSTONE (C.) You and the theatre.
illus.   1948.
You Books.

597937

Production *see* **Stage History and Production**

Programmes
*In addition to the catalogued material listed
below, and in the earlier catalogue under this
heading, the library collects programmes of all
school, amateur and professional Shakespearian productions as they occur. The collections
are classified and indexed*

—— Abbots Langley & Bedmond Community
Players. Programmes, etc. of Shakespearean
performances, 1927–39.
(Abbots Langley)

440897

——AMERICAN SHAKESPEARE FESTIVAL THEATRE
AND ACADEMY, Stratford, Conn.
[Programmes, etc.]   [Stratford, Conn.]
ports.   illus.   [1955]–

665434

——AMERICAN SHAKESPEARE FOUNDATION
American Shakespeare celebration [for
the benefit of the Shakespeare
Memorial Fund] Metropolitan Opera
House, January 29, 1928 [: souvenir
programme]. pp. 72. [New York]
ports.   illus.   facsimile.

581625

——Antioch Shakespeare Festival
[Programmes, etc.]
[Yellow Springs, Ohio.]   1952–

645711

——BAALBECK INTERNATIONAL FESTIVAL,
1956

Open Air Theatre Company [Regent's
Park. English drama programme. With
details of the production of "Hamlet"
and "Twelfth Night", presented at the
1956 Baalbeck Festival].pp.[44,2]
Ports. Illus. [Beirut]

665896

——BAALBECK INTERNATIONAL FESTIVAL,
1957

The Old Vic Theatre Company.[English
drama programme. With details of "The
Merchant of Venice" and "Antony and
Cleopatra" presented at the 1957
Baalbeck Festival.]pp.[40] Ports.
Illus. [Beirut]

665903

——Bankside Players Society.

[Shakespearian performances. Programmes,
leaflets, etc. 1937   .]

464482

—— Barking Abbey School, Essex.
Programmes, etc. of Shakespearian
performances.   1934–

497014

——Belfast, ROYAL BELFAST ACADEMICAL
INSTITUTION
[Programmes of Shakespearian performances,]
1927–42.[Belfast]

449361

——BIRMINGHAM, THE CURTAIN PLAYERS
Programmes, etc., of Shakespeare &
other productions.   [Birmingham]
illus.   [1934–50.]

579647

—— [Birmingham. King Edward's School
Musical and Dramatic Society,
programmes, etc. of annual
performances of Shakespeare
plays.] 1922–

353682

——[Birmingham] ST. PHILIP'S GRAMMAR SCHOOL
Programmes of Shakespeare productions
1951–   (Birmingham)

666295

—— BIRMINGHAM AND MIDLAND INSTITUTE,
SHAKESPEARE AND DRAMATIC SOCIETY
[Programmes] 1923–

497940

—— Birmingham and Midland Institute,
Union of Teachers and Students.
Shakespeare and Dramatic Society.
Shakespeare Birthday Commemoration
[programmes], 1910–

[Birmingham]

245883

—— BIRMINGHAM UNIVERSITY LITERARY AND
DRAMATIC SOCIETY
Programme of King Henry IV, Part 1.
[With reviews of the production.]
(Birmingham)   1911.

768978

——BLACKBURN SHAKESPEARE SOCIETY
[Programmes, cuttings, etc., relating
to performances, 1935–7.
ports.   illus.

474538

—— Bolton School Dramatic Society.
[Programmes of Shakespeare performances,]
1934—   [Bolton]

425733

—— [Bournemouth] Leamor Players.
[Programmes of Shakespeare performances,
etc.]   1926–[?1935].

418310

——BOURNEMOUTH SCHOOL
  Programmes, etc., of Shakespearian
  performances.   (Bournemouth)
  illus.   [1932-]

                            440981

—— BOURNEMOUTH SHAKESPEARE PLAYERS
  [Programmes, etc.]   [Bournemouth]
  ports.   1947-55.

                            634275

——[Bournville Youths' Club.

  Programmes, etc., of Shakespeare
  performances.] Illus. [Birmingham]
                            [1932]-47.

                            455239

——   Bradford, Carlton Street Senior
  Evening Institute. [Programmes, etc. of
  Shakespearean performances.] [Bradford]
                            1911-30

                            419186

——   [Braintree Secondary Boys' School.
  Braintree Shakespeare Players. Reports,
  programmes, etc. of Shakespearean
  performances, 1944-51 .] Illus. [Braintree]

                            566860

——   [Brighton. Varndean School for boys.
  Shakespearian performances. Programmes,
  1934-   .] [Brighton]

                            479687

——   [Brighton College Preparatory School.
  Programmes and tickets of Shakespeare
  performances.]   1930-8.

                            417608

—— BRISTOL OLD VIC THEATRE
  W. Shakespeare's 'Hamlet', 'Measure for
  Measure' [and] 'Romeo & Juliet.'
  [: Souvenir of the American tour Spring
  1967.] (Bristol)

                            761648

——   [Bristol Shakespeare Society.
  Programmes of Shakespearian performances,
  1945-1949.] Illus. [Bristol]

                            566861

——   Bristol University Dramatic Society,
  [Programmes, etc., relating to
  Shakespearian performances 1937-1954.]
  [(Bristol)]

                            513887

—— British Empire Shakespeare Society
  see Societies (British Empire Shakespeare
  Society)

——   [Burton Shakespeare Society.
  Programmes, leaflets, cuttings, etc.,
  1937-   .]. (Burton-on-Trent)

                            464483

——   Buxton Theatre Festival,
  [including plays of Shakespeare.]
  Official souvenir, 1st (1937)- .
  Ports. Illus.

                            474048

—— CALIFORNIA SHAKESPEARE FESTIVAL.
  Programmes. Season 2-   . 1965-
  (Santa Clara, Cal.)

                            771363

——   [The Cambridge Arts Theatre.
  Marlowe Society & The A.D.C. Programmes,
  etc., of Shakespeare productions.] Illus.
  [Cambridge]   [1938-   .]

                            578432

——   [Cambridge]. Festival Theatre
  programmes. [With references to
  Shakespeare performances]. Illus.
  2 vols.   [1933-1938.]

                            418309

——   [Cardiff] Canton High School for
  Boys. Programmes, etc. of Shakespearian
  performances, 1927-35.   [Cardiff]

                            438036

——CATHOLIC UNIVERSITY OF AMERICA: SPEECH
  AND DRAMA DEPARTMENT
  The Story of Players Incorporated:
  "International Repertory Comapny"
  [1949-1954].   pp. 20.   [Washington]
  ports.   illus.   [1954.]

                            643996

——   [Chard School, Somerset,
  Programmes, etc. of Shakespearian
  performances, 1929-   .] [Chard]

                            495440

——   [Chelsea. Sloane School.
  Programmes, etc., of Shakespeare
  performances.]
                            [1934-   .]

                            452524

——   [Cheltenham, Dean Close School.
  Programmes, etc., of Shakespearian
  performances.] [Cheltenham]
                            [1934-   .]

                            440979

——   [Cheslyn Hay School. Shakespearian
  performances. Programmes, newspaper
  cuttings, etc.] Illus. [Brierley Hill]
  Illus. [Brierley Hill]
                            [1923-39]

                            460393

——CHILTERNS SCHOOL, Monks Risborough
  Programmes, etc., of Shakespearian
  performances.   (Monks Risborough)
                            1931-60.
  Wants programmes for 1932.

                            440980

——Chiswick Central School for Boys.
  Programmes [of performances of
  Shakespeare's plays.] 1928-

                            449337

——   Chiswick County School for Boys.
  Programmes, etc. of Shakespearian
  performances, 1933-   [Chiswick]

                            438037

— CLIFTON, ALL SAINTS' OLD BOYS' SOCIETY
Shakespearian performances: programmes,
etc. (Clifton) 1921-38.

463174

— CLIFTON ALL SAINTS' OLD BOYS' SOCIETY
"Summer Show": [programme of an
entertainment], All Saints' Hall,
July 14th & 15th [,1936]. [Shake-
spearian setting]. ff. 8. [Clifton]
cyclostyled. [1936]

463168

— COLORADO UNIVERSITY
Colorado Shakespeare Festival,
programmes [etc.] (Boulder, Col.)
1958-

666648

— Cornish Open-Air Shakespearean
Festivals. Programmes, etc. 1934-51.
[Truro]

424967

— Coventry Teachers' Shakespearian
Society. Shakespearian performances.
Programmes, cuttings, tickets, etc.
Illus. (Coventry) 1937-8.

473497

— [Cranbrook School, Programmes, etc.,
of Shakespearian plays, 1927-56.]
[(Cranbrook)]

431403

— Cranleigh School, [Surrey. Programmes,
tickets, etc., of Shakespearian
performances]. Illus. [Cranleigh]
1932-58.

410484

— [Croydon Histrionic Society.
Programmes of Shakespeare performances.]
[Croydon] [1930 - .]

424485

— Darlington Art Players. [Programmes,
etc. of Shakespearean performances.]
[Darlington.] 1928-37.

419074

— [Dartford Grammar School.
Shakespearian performances. Programmes,
photographs, tickets, etc., 1937-8]

479545

— [Denstone College. Programmes,
etc. relating to Shakespearean
performances.] 1933-

446874

— [Derby. Bemrose School. Programmes,
etc. of Shakespearian performances,
1934- .] [Derby]

494293

— DERBY SHAKESPEARE SOCIETY [formerly
British Empire Shakespeare Society,
Derby Branch]
Programmes, etc. (Derby) 1908-

217393

— [Dorset Shakespeare Players.
Performances: programmes, leaflets,
tickets, etc.] Illus. (Wareham)
1933-6.

488037

— DRURY LANE THEATRE
[Programme of performances of] Macbeth
[and] Winter's Tale, Oct.-Nov. 1878,
[under the managership of F. B.
Chatterton. With an address on Drury
Lane Theatre and the story of the
Winter's Tale by C. L. Kenney.]
pp. 32. 1878.

532018

— Drury Lane, Theatre Royal. Programme
[of] final performance [of] Sir J.
Forbes- Robertson's farewell season
in London. [Hamlet], June 6th,1913.
Ports.

471783

— Drury Lane, Theatre Royal,] Shakespeare tercentenary commemoration
performance, 2nd May, 1916.
[Programme.]

471777

— DRURY LANE, THEATRE ROYAL
Souvenir programme given by the
theatrical & musical professions as
a tribute to Miss Ellen Terry on the
occasion of her jubilee, Tuesday
afternoon, June 12th, 1906. pp. [27].

594119

— DUBLIN SHAKESPEARE SOCIETY
Programmes, etc. (Dublin) 1937-43.

488035

— [Dunfermline High School.
Programmes, etc., of Shakespearian
performances] Illus. [Dunfermline]
[1928-35]

440983

— [Durham County Drama Association,
Annual festivals: programmes.] [Durham]
1940-5.

535367

— Earle Grey Players see Toronto
Shakespeare Festival

— EASTBOURNE SHAKESPEARE SOCIETY
Programmes, etc. (Eastbourne)
[1952 -]

665443

— Edmonton County School
Shakespearean performances. Programmes,
cuttings, tickets, etc.
1931-3.

473499

— Ellesmere College (St. Oswald's
School). [Shakespearian] plays. Programmes.
[Shrewsbury] 1899 etc.

283951

— Embassy Theatre. [Programme of] Cymbeline, by W. Shakespeare and [G.]B. Shaw. [With a note by the collaborator, G.B.Shaw]. pp.[16].

1937.

477459

— Farnborough County Secondary School, Hants. Programmes of dramatic performances [including Shakespeare].

1930-4.

418311

— FIRST FOLIO THEATRE COMPANY [Programmes of Shakespearian performances, etc. pp. ii, 22.]

[1949-53.]

645710

— FOREST SHAKESPEARE PLAYERS Programmes.] (Newnham)

1949-55.

667778

— [Framlingham College. Programmes, photographs, etc. of Shakespearian performances, 1932-52.] (Framlingham)

454860

— Francis Holland Church of England School, London. Programmes, etc. of Shakespearian performances 1924-36.

438034

— Friern Barnet. Holly Park Senior School Shakespearian performances. Programmes, photographs, tickets, etc. 1935-37. Illus. (Friern Barnet)

472594

— Frome County Secondary School, [Programmes, etc., of Shakespeare plays 1923-37.] (Frome)

431406

— GARRICK THEATRE Souvenir of Shakespeare's play, The Merchant of Venice, as reproduced at the Garrick Theatre, London, [Oct., 1905. Text by A. Mackinnon, illustrations by C. A. Buchel.] pp. [8.] illus.

471784

— [Gillingham County School for Boys. Programmes, etc., of Shakespearian performances.] [Gillingham]

[1933-52.]

440978

— Goring Heath Endowed School, Oxon. Shakespearean Dramatic Performances. [Programmes, etc.] 1926-33. [Reading]

438038

— Gravesend County School, [Programmes, etc., of Shakespearian plays, 1926-35.] (Gravesend)

431402

— GREAT LAKES SHAKESPEARE FESTIVAL Programmes. 1966- (Cleveland, Ohio)

771362

— [Greenock Shakespeare Society. Programmes, tickets, etc.] Illus. [Greenock] 1938.

488034

— [Grimsby.] Wintringham Secondary School Dramatic Society. [Programmes of Shakespeare performances.] 1931- Illus. [Grimsby]

426697

— [Haileybury College. Shakespearian performances. Programmes, 1930-] ([Hertford])

484138

— Halstead. Gosfield School. Programmes etc. of Shakespearean performances, July 23rd 1937-54. (Halstead)

547085

— HARROGATE SHAKESPEAREAN FESTIVAL SOCIETY Posters, Programmes, etc. (Harrogate) 1942-7.

535368

— [Harrow School. Programmes, etc. of Shakespearian performances, 1941-] [Harrow]

566862

— HELLENIC DRAMATIC GROUP Shakespeare's week, Manolidou-Aroni-Horn present "Twelfth Night". [Souvenir programme. English and Greek text.] (Alexandria) 1945.

766817

— HIS MAJESTY'S THEATRE Adelaide Ristori memorial matinée [programme], Nov. 30th, 1908. [Including scenes from the Merchant of Venice, Hamlet, Taming of the Shrew and Macbeth, and an ode by L. N. Parker.] pp. [4.] port.

531801

— HIS MAJESTY'S THEATRE, [London] Coronation gala performance, by command of the King, June 27, 1911. [Including a scene from The Merry Wives of Windsor and Julius Caesar. Programme.] pp. [20]. 1911.

470977

— HOLLYWOOD SHAKESPEARE FESTIVAL [Programmes etc.] (West Hollywood, Calif.) 1958-

761652

— [Holt, Norfolk. Gresham's School. Programmes, etc. of Shakespearian performances, 1934-42 .] [Holt]

454865

— HONOURABLE SOCIETY OF THE MIDDLE TEMPLE [Programme of Shakespeare's Twelfth Night, acted by the Holywell Players in the Hall of the Middle Temple Society, June 28th, 29th and 30th, 1934. With a note "Shakespeare and the Middle Temple" by B. Williamson. With photographs.] pp. [6.] frontis. 1934.

421992

— Horsham, Sussex. Herons Ghyll School. Programmes, etc. of Shakespearean performances. 1930-51.

421988

— Huddersfield Co-operative Dramatic Society, [Programmes, etc., of Shakespeare performances, 1934-5 .] [(Huddersfield)]

431405

— [Huddersfield. Marion Rhodes Shakespearian Company performances. Programmes, tickets, etc., 1938.

([Huddersfield])

484094

— [Hull Boulevard School, (afterwards Kingston High School) Shakespearian performances. Programmes, cuttings, photographs, etc., 1933-7 .] [Hull]

479686

— Hull, Playgoers' Theatre. [Programmes, etc. of Shakespearian performances]. (Hull) 1929-34.

424484

— [Hurstpierpoint. St. John's College. Programmes of plays presented by the Shakspere Society.] [Hurstpierpoint.] [1905 -]

419852

— [Ilford County High School for Boys. Programmes, etc., of Shakespearian performances, 1936-   .] Illus.

497527

— IRVING (HENRY) & TERRY (ELLEN) Portraits, programmes etc., of Henry Irving and Ellen Terry. ff. 60. [c.1850-c.1910.]

437278

— Kemnay Secondary School, Aberdeenshire. Performances of Shakespearian plays [: programmes, photographs, etc.], 1924-

455261

— [Kenilworth, Knowle Hill School. Programmes, etc. of Shakespearean performances.]

[Kenilworth] 1933

418617

— Kettering Grammar School.

[Programmes and tickets of Shakespeare performances.] [Kettering] [1933 -7]

417607

— [Kilburn Grammar School. Programmes, etc. of Shakespearian performances, 1929-   .]

431751

— [Kilburn Polytechnic Dramatic Class. Programmes, etc., of Shakespeare performances.] [1930 -6]

452523

— Kingston High School (formerly Hull Boulevard Secondary School) see Hull above.

— [Kirkham Grammar School Literary and Dramatic Society. Programmes, etc. of Shakespeare performances, 1932-3 .] [Kirkham.]

416899

— Lancaster, St. Thomas's Girls' Central School. [Programmes of Shakespearian performances, illustrations of costumes, etc.] 1931-6. (Lancaster)

438195

— [Launceston College, Cornwall.

The College Players: programmes, etc. of Shakespeare performances, 1932-56.] [Launceston]

416901

— Leeds. Cockburn High School. [Programmes of Shakespeare performances,] 1915-34. [Leeds.]

416902

— Leicester, Little Theatre.

Programmes, etc. of Shakespearian performances, 1929-49. (Leicester)

438035

— Leicester, Robert Hall Players. Programmes of Shakespeare performances Feb., 1931- .] [Leicester]

416905

— Liverpool. PENRHYN PLAYERS DRAMATIC SOCIETY Programmes, etc. of performances of Shakespeare. [1919-35]

416907

—— LIVERPOOL SHAKESPEARE SOCIETY
Reports, programmes, etc. of
Shakespearian performances, 1949-

612236

—— [London Federation of Boys' Clubs.
Shakespearian performances. Programmes,
posters, etc., 1928-54 .]

479688

—— London Shakespeare Festival, 1910.
Diary [i.e.programme]. [Sir] H.B.
Tree begs to announce the sixth
year of the London Shakespeare
Festival, 28th March to 30th April,
1910. His Majesty's Theatre.pp.[16].

1910.
451683

—— LONDON SHAKESPEARE LEAGUE
Shakespeare Commemoration, 1905.
Romeo and Juliet, given by the
Elizabethan Stage Society, at the
Royalty Theatre, London, May 5, 1905:
[programme, etc.]

517666

—— LYCEUM THEATRE
Souvenir of King Henry the Eighth,
presented at the Lyceum Theatre,
5th Jan., 1892, by H. Irving.
Illustrated by [Sir] J. B. Partridge
[and others].   pp. [35].
ports. illus.   1892.   114644
—— Another copy.   471801

—— LYCEUM THEATRE
Souvenir of King Lear, presented at
the Lyceum Theatre, 10th Nov., 1892,
by H. Irving.   Illustrated by [Sir]
J. B. Partridge and H. Craven.
pp. [31].
ports.   illus.   1892.
Differs slightly from Catal. No. 145331.

471802

—— Maidstone Grammar School.

[Programmes, etc. of Shakespearian
performances]. Illus. [Maidstone]
[1932 -9.]

420928

—— [The Malvern Theatres. Malvern Festivals,
organised by the Birmingham Repertory
Theatre. Programmes and illustrated
souvenirs. Shaw Festival, 1929 (1st).
etc.]

359581

—— [March Grammar School. Shakespearian
performances. Programmes.] [March]
1929-59

488032

—— MARIN SHAKESPEARE FESTIVAL
Programmes, season 5-   1965-
(Ross, Cal.)

771365

—— [The MERMAID THEATRE.

Programmes, etc., of Shakespearian
productions, 1951-3.] Ports. Illus.

638756

—— [Merton. Raynes Park County School.
Programmes of Shakespearean performances,
1936-48 .]

528343

—— [MUSSELBURGH, Loretto School
Programmes of Shakespeare performances.]
(Musselburgh)   [1925-39.]

419851

—— [Muswell Hill Congregational

Church Social Circle, afterwards
Tetherdown Social Circle. Programmes,
etc. of Shakespearian performances,
1931-9 .]

500736

—— [Newark County Technical College
and School of Art. Shakespearian
performances. Programmes.] [Newark]
1934-51.

488036

—— [Newbury Grammar School. Programmes,
etc., of Shakespearian performances.]
Illus. [Newbury]   [1922-   ]

432080

—— Newcastle-on-Tyne. Theatre Royal,
Grey Street. Centenary week
[souvenir], 1837-1937. pp.16.
Facsimile.

[Newcastle-on-Tyne]   1937.

462573

—— Newport Playgoers' Society.
[Programmes, etc., of Shakespearian
performances, 1925-46] [(Newport, Mon.)]

431404

—— NORWICH (CITY OF) SCHOOL
Programme of a performance of "Twelfth
Night" at the City of Norwich School,
Dec. 1937; with explanatory notes on
the music by M. N. Doe.   ff. 4.
(Norwich)   1937.
Edition of "Twelfth Night" with MS.
notes referring to the music, Catal.
No. 502842.   MS. of the music,
Catal. No. 502843.

506672

—— Norwich. Maddermarket Theatre.
[Programmes of Shakespeare performances.]
[1933 -   ]

418307

—— NOTTINGHAM SHAKESPEARE SOCIETY
Programmes of plays, etc.   1907-

200755

—— Occasional Shakespearian performances
[: amateur and school productions].

This collection is continuously
augmented by the addition of
programmes of contemporary productions.

414580

— OLD VIC [and] SADLER'S WELLS
[Programmes of plays] Season 1916-63.
None issued 1939-40: no season.

518732

— OPEN AIR THEATRE, REGENT'S PARK, LONDON
Prospectus, programmes, etc. [1933 -]

408592

— Oxford
DRAGON SCHOOL
The Draconian. [Numbers containing
reports, etc., of the annual Shakespearian productions. [Oxford]
1918-63.

458725

— Oxford. New Theatre. [Programmes of
performances, including Shakespearian
performances, 1900]-1905.

[Oxford]

464878

— [Oxford University Dramatic Society.
Programmes, etc., of Shakespeare
performances.] Illus. [Oxford]
[1895-]

Wants 1901; 1903; 1905; 1908-9; 1911-20;
1922; 1925; 1928; 1931.

451509

— Pasadena Playhouse. Programmes of
Midsummer Drama Festival and miscellaneous
material, 1935-41. (Pasadena, Calif.)
1935-41.

From 1942, incorporated in Pasadena
Playhouse News. Programmes of Shakespearian
productions.

440898

— Pasadena Playhouse News. Vol. 14
(Nov. 1935-June 1936) - Vol. 20
(July-August, 1941). (Pasadena, Cal.)
ports. illus. 1935-
Wants Vols. 1-13, Vol. 14, Nos. 1-9.
Vol. 15, No. 2. not published.

472444

— PENDLEY SHAKESPEARE FESTIVAL
Programmes, etc. 1950-

666286

— PENRHYN PLAYERS DRAMATIC SOCIETY,
Liverpool
Programmes, etc. of performances of
Shakespeare, 1919-1935] [Liverpool]
ports. illus.
Society disbanded, 1935.

416907

— [Petersfield. Steep Shakespeare
Players. Programmes, etc. of performances,
1926-1961.] (Petersfield)

464481

— [Pinvin Dramatic Society.
Programmes, etc., of Shakespeare
performances.] [Pinvin.]
[1934-40]

452522

— [Plymouth Shakspere Literary Society.
Programmes, syllabuses. etc.] [Plymouth]
[1919 -]

453707

— Porthcurno, Minack Theatre. Antony
and Cleopatra. Programmes, illustrations and cuttings of the
performance at the Minack Theatre,
Porthcurno.]
[1937]

473457

— PORTHCURNO, MINACK THEATRE
[Programme and illustrations of
Miss Dorothea Valentine's production
of "The Tempest" at Porthcurno,
Cornwall, August, 1932.]

399402

— Portsmouth Teachers' Dramatic Society.
[Programmes of Shakespeare performances,
1925- 27 .] Illus. [Portsmouth]

(1) Wants programme for 1924.
(2) No performance 1931.

425732

— [Professional] performances of
Shakespeare's plays.
36 vols. c.1880-
This collection is continuously
augmented by the addition of programmes
of contemporary productions.

462500

— Richmond Shakespeare Society.
Programmes, cuttings, etc. [of
Shakespearian performances], 1934-

455238

— ROCHESTER CATHEDRAL CHOIR SCHOOL
Programmes, etc. of Shakespeare
performances, 1922-36. (Rochester)
[1922]-36.

416903

— Rugby. The Percival Guildhouse
Shakespearian performances. Programmes,
tickets, photographs, etc.
1936-55.

473498

— Shakespeare Festival matinee at the
New Theatre, (under the auspices
of the Shakespeare Association,)
April 29th, 1921. [Programme.]
pp.[8.]

471782

— Shakespeare Programmes and Play Bills
with cuttings relating thereto.
2 vols. 1901-1932.

170369

— SHEFFIELD CENTRAL SECONDARY SCHOOL
Programmes of Shakespearian performances. (Sheffield)
illus. 1918-38.

472593

SHEFFIELD EDUCATIONAL SETTLEMENT
Programmes, tickets, etc. of
Shakespearian performances.
[Sheffield]   1930-52.

425721

—— [Shipley. The Salt Girls' High School.
Shakespearian performances. Programmes, etc.]
Port. [Shipley]   1924-38.

488033

—— [Shrewsbury].   Celebration of the
500th anniversary of the Battle of
Shrewsbury, held at Shrewsbury,
19th to 25th July, 1903: official
programme [including programmes of
Shakespeare plays.]   pp. 21.
(Shrewsbury)
illus. plan.   1903.

458256

—— [Snaresbrook, Forest School.
Programmes, etc. of Shakespeare
performances, 1933-59.] [Snaresbrook]

416896

—— South Benfleet School. [Shakespearian
plays: programmes, tickets, photographs,
etc.] 1935-8.   (South Benfleet)

456665

—— SOUTHEND-ON-SEA SHAKESPEARE SOCIETY
Programmes, reports, etc. (Southend)
illus.   1921-

547087

—— SOUTHERN SHAKESPEARE REPERTORY THEATRE,
                    Coral Gables, Fla.
Souvenir programmes, 3rd season -
(Coral Gables, Fla.)   1963-

illus.   749762

Lacks 1st and 2nd season.

—— THE SOUTHSEA SHAKESPEARE ACTORS
[Programmes, etc.] [Southsea]
illus.   1950-

645707

—— [Southwark Shakespeare Festival.
Programmes, etc.] 1932-

420929

—— Southwell Grammar School.
Shakespearian performances. Programmes,
1923-38. (Southwell)

479949

—— STEWART HEADLAM SHAKESPEARE ASSOCIATION
Programmes, etc. of Shakespeare
performances, 1926-

416900

—— Stoke-on-Trent Shakespearian Society.
Programmes, photographs, etc. [of
Shakespearian performances]. Illus.
(Stoke-on-Trent)   1937-55

472596

—— Stourbridge. King Edward VI Grammar
School. [Programmes, etc. of
Shakespearean performances.]

[Stourbridge]   [1921 -]

417254

—— STOWE SCHOOL, Buckinghamshire
Programmes of Shakespeare productions,
1950-   [Stowe, Bucks.]

666296

—— [The Stratford Shakespearean Festival
of Canada.   Programmes, etc.]
[Stratford, Ont.]
ports.   illus.   [1953 -]

638761

—— [STRATFORD-UPON-AVON]
Opening of the Shakespeare Memorial
Theatre, Stratford-on-Avon.
Preliminary programme.   pp. 8.
(Stratford-on-Avon)   1879.
Differs from 113482.

558060

—— STRATFORD-UPON-AVON, ROYAL SHAKESPEARE
THEATRE
Programmes, Playbills, Posters.
                                 1882.
From 1963 souvenir programmes were
issued for each production.

176120

—— STRATFORD-UPON-AVON, ROYAL SHAKESPEARE
THEATRE
Programmes [Seasonal Summary]. 1919-

441948

—— [Stratford-upon-Avon.] Shakespeare
Festival Season, Stratford-upon-Avon,
1945 [: programme of activities for
members of the United States, Dominion
and Allied Continental Forces spending
a week in Stratford during the
Festival Season. Drawn up by the
British Council]. pp.24. Illus. Plan.

1945.

558597

—— Streatham, [London] Shakespeare
Players. Programmes, etc. of Shakespeare
performances, 1912-37

421989

—— [Taunton. Queen's College Dramatic
Society. Shakespearian performances.
Programmes, 1930-   ] [Taunton]

479685

—— THE TAVERNERS
[Shakespearian programmes, posters,
etc.]   [1947]-[1957]

645709

—— TAYLOR UNIVERSITY, Indiana.
Shakespeare festival. Programmes.
1952-   . (Upland, Ind.)

From 1959 onwards called Fine Arts
Festival.

771366

— TERRY (ELLEN) MEMORIAL PERFORMANCES
Programmes of Shakespeare and other
performances in aid of the Ellen Terry
Memorial Fund.
port.   1929-39.

429213

— THEATRE ROYAL, HAYMARKET
Performance of Hamlet, May 19, 1930,
in aid of King George's Pension Fund
for Actors and Actresses.   [Programme.]
pp. [26.]
ports.

471789

—   [Tonbridge School Dramatic Society.
Programmes, etc. of Shakespearian
performances, 1923-39.] Illus.
[Tonbridge.]

431743

— TORONTO SHAKESPEARE FESTIVAL
Programmes, etc.   [Toronto]
ports.   illus.   plans.   facsimiles.
[1950 -58.]

665433

— Truro Cathedral School.

Shakespearian Society. Programmes,
posters, tickets, etc. of performances.]
[Truro]   [1930-39.]

460001

— UTAH SHAKESPEAREAN FESTIVAL
[Programmes, etc.] (Cedar City, Utah)
1962-

illus.   668467

—   [Walsall, Queen Mary's Grammar School
Dramatic Society. Programmes of
Shakespeare performances. 1933-   ]
[Walsall]

416897

— WALTHAMSTOW SETTLEMENT, Shakespearean
Group
Programmes, etc., Feb. 20th 1943-57.
(Walthamstow)
547084

—   Wandsworth School Shakespearian
performances. Programmes, 1925-32, 1934-8.
(Wandsworth)

Wants 1933 programme.   472595

— WASHINGTON SHAKESPEARE SOCIETY
Programmes, 1926-54.   [Washington]
1929-30; 1938-39; 1939-40; 1940-41
wanting.
645713

—   [West Bromwich Grammar School.
Programmes, etc., of Shakespeare
performances.] [West Bromwich.]
[1930-47.]

451508

— WHITFIELD (J.   F.   )

[Theatrical scrapbooks, 1919-29,
including newspaper cuttings and
programmes of the Stratford-upon-Avon
Shakespeare seasons, and of productions
at Birmingham theatres. Collected by
J.F. Whitfield.] Illus.   3 vols.
[1919-29.]

668413-5

—   [Woodford College. Programmes, etc.,
of Shakespeare performances.]
[1931-7.]

45251y

—WORKSOP COLLEGE DRAMATIC SOCIETY
Programmes of Shakespeare performances,
Nov., 1931-45.   (Worksop)
416898

— YORK SETTLEMENT COMMUNITY PLAYERS
Programmes of Shakespearian performances.
(York)   [1934-]

479689

PROH PUDOR [pseud.]
On Shakespeare's sonnets.   FROM
Blackwood's Magazine, Aug. 1818.
(Edinburgh)   1818.

440104

Prolegomena to the works of Shakspeare.
(Sherwood and Co.)   pp. lxxx.
ports.   illus.   1825.

491858

[Prolegomena to] The Works of Shakspeare
from the text of Johnson, Steevens,
and Reed.   With a biographical memoir
by W. Harvey.   (Sherwood, Jones & Co.)
pp. lxxx.
ports.   illus.   [1825.]

60531

Prologues and Epilogues
see also under **Johnson, Samuel**

— BLACKLOCK (T.)
Prologue to Hamlet.   IN The Works of
the English poets, [edited] by
Dr. Samuel Johnson, Vol. 18.   1810.

3878

— BLACKLOCK (T.)
Prologue to Othello.   IN The Works of
the English poets, [edited] by Dr.
Samuel Johnson, Vol. 18.   1810.

3878

—— BUTT (G.)
An Epilogue to Shakspere's Tragedy of
King Lear. IN Butt (G.) Poems, Vol. 1.
1793.

563232

—— A Collection and selection of English
prologues and epilogues, commencing
with Shakespeare and concluding
with Garrick.
frontis. 4 vols. 1779.

401684

—— Epilogue to Shakespear's first part
of King Henry IV. IN [DODSLEY (R.)
ed.] A Collection of poems by several
hands. [5th edn.] Vol. 5.
illus. 1758.

538522

—— [HOADLY (J.)]
Epilogue to Shakespear's first part
of King Henry IV. IN [DODSLEY (R.)
ed.,] A Collection of poems by several
hands. [5th edn.] Vol. 5.
1758. 538522
_____ Another copy. 1758. 576734
_____ Another copy. 1758. 576740

—— KEATE (G.)
Prologue [and] Epilogue to the play of
King John, acted at Mr. Newcomb's at
Hackney, March 1769. IN [PEARCH (G.)
ed.,] A Collection of poems by several
hands, New edn. Vol. 3.
1783. 99654
_____ Another copy. 1783. 576745

—— MOLNÁR (F.)
Prologue to "King Lear". Adapted for
television and produced by E. Crozier.
ff. 26.
typescript. 1937.

475850

—— MOLNÁR (F.)
A Prologue to "King Lear". IN
TABORI (P.) ed., Hungarian anthology.
[With an introduction by J. Brophy
and woodcuts by G. P. Buday.] 1943.
Modern Reading Library, No. 5.

542692

—— MORE (HANNAH)
A Prologue to Hamlet. IN MORE (HANNAH)
Works in prose and verse. (Cork)
1789.

507445

—— MORE (HANNAH)
A Prologue to the Tragedy of King Lear.
IN More (H.) Works in prose and verse.
(Cork) 1789.

507445

—— [MORE (HANNAH)]
The Search after happiness: a pastoral
drama [in verse. With a prologue to
Hamlet, and a prologue to King Lear.]
6th edn. pp. 54. (Bristol) 1775.

490019

—— PALMER [(W.) ed.]
The New and complete English spouter;
or, An Universal key to theatrical
knowledge. A collection of prologues
[including prologue and epilogue to
Richard the Third, and prologue to
Much ado about nothing]. [1781.]

531636

—— SAVAGE (RICHARD) the poet
Prologue spoken at the revival of
Shakespeare's King Henry the Sixth,
at the Theatre-Royal in Drury-Lane.
IN Works [, collected and published
by T. Evans], Vol. 2. 1775.

537986

—— SMART (CHRISTOPHER)
An Occasional prologue and epilogue to
Othello, as it was acted at the
Theatre-Royal in Drury-Lane, 7th March
1751. 2nd edn. pp. 8. [c.1750.]

633512

—— [SMART (C.)]
The Prologue to Othello, as it was acted
at the theatre in Drury-Lane and The
Epilogue spoken by Desdemona. FROM
The Midwife [; or The Old Woman's
Magazine, Vol. 1]. 1751.

563203

—— WHYTE (S.)
Epilogue to Henry the Fourth, performed
at Castletown; [and] Occasional epilogue
to Henry the Fourth, performed at
Drumcree, Jan. 5, 1773. IN WHYTE (S.)
A Collection of poems on various subjects,
including The Theatre, a didactic essay.
2nd edn. revised by E. A. Whyte.
(Dublin) 1792.

510480

Prologues and Epilogues *works relating to*

—— BOWER (G. S.)
The Prologue and epilogue in English
literature (from Shakespeare to
Dryden). IN The New Monthly Magazine,
New [3rd] Series, Vol. 6. [1882.]

521086

—— Dryden (J.) Defence of the epilogue;
or, An Essay on the dramatick poetry
of the last age, [with references to
Shakespeare]. In Dryden (J.)
Dramatick works [edited by W. Congreve]
Vol. 3. Illus.

1763.

529693

— LEECH (CLIFFORD)
Shakespeare's prologues and epilogues.
IN ALLEN (D. C.) ed., Studies in honor
of T. W. Baldwin.   (Urbana, Ill.)
1958.

666314

— WILEY (AUTREY N.) ed.
Rare prologues and epilogues, 1642-
1700.   [With references to prologues
and epilogues to Shakespeare's plays.]
illus.   facsimiles.   bibliog.
1940.

520137

Prompt copies
see also **Birmingham**, Theatre Royal
Collection of Prompt copies; **Lena Ashwell
Players**

—— The Tragedy of Hamlet, prince of
Denmark, [edited by S. Barnet.
Signet Classic Shakespeare text.
(New York: New American Library)]
[1963]
Interleaved prompt copy with ms.
notes and stage directions by
R. D. Day.

768346

——   King Henry the Eighth: a tragedy.
Marked with the variations in the
manager's book at the Theatre-Royal
in Covent Garden. Frontis.   1786.

Interleaved with ms. notes and stage
directions by G.F. Cooke, with note and
signature on end-paper by E. Knight.

526709

—— The Merchant of Venice, [edited by K.
Myrick. Signet Classic Shakespeare text.
(New York: New American Library)]
[1965.]

761645

Interleaved prompt copy with ms.
notes and stage directions by R. Digby
Day.

——   William Charles Macready's
"King John": a facsimile prompt-book,
edited by C.H. Shattuck. Illus.
(Urbana, Ill.)   1962.

667486

Prompt copies *works relating to*

— BALD (ROBERT CECIL)
Shakespeare on the stage in Restoration
Dublin.   IN PMLA: Publications of
the Modern Language Association of
America, Vol. 56.   (Menasha, Wis.)
1941.

533611/56

— BYRNE (MURIEL ST. CLARE)
The Earliest 'Hamlet' prompt book
in an English library.   FROM Theatre
Notebook, Vol. 15, No. 1.   pp. [15].
facsimiles.   1960.

666983

— EVANS (GWYNNE BLAKEMORE) ed.
Shakespearean prompt-books of the
seventeenth century.   (Bibliographical
Society of the University of Virginia.
Charlottesville, Va.)   1960-
For setting out see under the author's
name.

— McMANAWAY (J. G.)
The Two earliest prompt books of
Hamlet.   pp. 34.   [New York]
1949.

604840

— SHATTUCK, CHARLES H.
The Shakespeare promptbooks: a
descriptive catalogue. (Urbana, Ill.)
1965.

753834

— SISSON (C. J.)
Shakespeare quartos as prompt-copies;
with some account of Cholmeley's
players and a new Shakespeare allusion.
[With bibliographical notes.]   IN
The Review of English Studies, Vol. 18.
(Oxford)   1942.

542539

The Prompter; or, Theatrical and
concert guide.   No. 1, June, 1834.
[With reference to Coriolanus]
1834.

453716

Pronunciation

— ELLIS (A. J.)
Syllabus of a lecture on the pronunciation of English in the sixteenth, fourteenth and thirteenth centuries, illustrated by passages from Shakspere, Chaucer and others, delivered, as they might have been at the time, [at the] Conversazione, Dec. 18, 1867, London Institution.   pp. 16.
table.   1867.

545617

— FIEDLER (H. G.)
A Contemporary of Shakespeare on phonetics and on the pronunciation of English and Latin, [i.e. "The Art of pronunciation" by R. Robinson, 1617]: a contribution to the history of phonetics and English sounds. [Presidential address, Modern Humanities Research Association, 1936.]   pp. 21. (Oxford)
bibliog.   facsimiles.   1936.

461805

— Jones (D.) Introductory remarks to the programme of Shakespeare in original pronunciation. [With passages from Shakespeare's plays. Broadcast] 28th December, 1949. ff.19. Typescript.

1949.

609485

— JONES (DANIEL) and EVANS (EILEEN M.)
Pronunciation of early 17th century English. [With extracts from Shakespeare's "As you like it", "Twelfth Night", "King Richard II" and "The Tempest".]   ([English through the centuries] No. 5-6: Shakespeare) (Linguaphone Institute).
gramophone record.   [c.1950.]

635187

— KÖKERITZ (HELGE)
Shakespeare's names: a pronouncing dictionary.   (New Haven [Conn.])
tables.   1959.
Yale Shakespeare Supplements.

666388

— KÖKERITZ (HELGE)
Shakespeare's pronunciation.   FROM Moderna Språk, Arg. 43.   pp. 19. (Malmö)   1949.

619423

— KÖKERITZ (HELGE)
Shakespeare's pronunciation. (New Haven, Conn.)
bibliog.   1953.

645615

— KUROKAWA (SHINICHI)
On Kökeritz' new theory on the development of M[iddle] E[nglish] "a" before [f, θ, s, r].   IN Studies in English grammar and linguistics: a miscellany in honour of Takanobu Otsuka.   (Tokyo) port. dgms. tables. bibliogs.
1958.

667095

— Phonetic transcription of a scene from "Romeo and Juliet". In American Speech. Reprints and monographs, No.1, p.64.

(New York)   1936.

465342

— QUIRK (RANDOLPH)
Shakespeare's pronunciation [: a talk]. Producer: P. H. Newby. [Broadcast 9th December 1954.]   ff. 10.
typescript.   1954.

665044

— Shaw (G.B.) The Art of talking for the talkies [with references to Shakespeare.]   Port.   In World Film News, Vol. 1.

1936.
485419

— Shewmake (E.F.) Shakespeare and Southern "You all". From American Speech, October 1938.

(New York)   1938.
506177

— "Take your choice": a scene from "Twelfth Night" in modern and in Elizabethan speech. Shakespearean pronounciation [sic] by F. G. Blandford. [Adapted for broadcasting].   ff. 14.
typescript.   1937.

475848

— UNGERER (GUSTAV)
Two items of Spanish pronunciation in Love's Labour's Lost.
IN SHAKESPEARE QUARTERLY XIV: 3. pp. 245-251.
(New York) 1963.

605711

— VIËTOR, WILHELM
A Shakespeare reader. In the old spelling and with a phonetic transcription. (New York)   1963.

749098

PROPER (IDA SEDGWICK)
Our elusive Willy: a slice of concealed Elizabethan history. [An attempt to prove that Shakespeare was the illegitimate son of Edward Seymour, Earl of Hertford.] (Manchester, Maine)
ports. illus.   1953.

637031

Property, Law of

— CLARKSON (P. S.) and WARREN (G. T.)
The Law of property in Shakespeare
and the Elizabethan drama. [With
a bibliography and bibliographical
notes.] (Baltimore) 1942.

541208

Prose in Shakespeare

— BORINSKI (LUDWIG)
Shakespeare's comic prose.
IN SHAKESPEARE SURVEY 8. (Cambridge)
1955.

647706

— BUELL (L. M.)
A Prose period in Shakespeare's career?
IN Modern Language Notes, Vol. 56.
(Baltimore)
tables. 1941.

533477

— BURRIS (QUINCY GUY)
"Soft! Here follows prose" - Twelfth
Night II.v.154.
IN SHAKESPEARE QUARTERLY II: 3.
pp. 233-239.
(New York) 1951.

605711

— CRANE (MILTON)
Shakespeare's prose. (Chicago, Ill.)
bibliog. 1951.

617443

— FISHER (A. Y.)
Note on Shakespeare's prose. FROM
Revue anglo-américaine, 1931.
pp. [8.] [Paris] [1931]

389218

— SUDDARD ([S. J.] MARY)
The Blending of prose, blank verse
and rhymed verse in "Romeo and Juliet".
FROM The Contemporary Review: Literary
Supplement, 1910. pp. [5.] [1910]

389209

— VICKERS, BRIAN
The artistry of Shakespeare's prose.
[Rev. version.] 1968.

767640

Proser (Matthew N.)
Hamlet and the name of action. IN

SMITH, GORDON ROSS, ed.
Essays on Shakespeare [by various
authors]. (University Park, Penn.)
1965.

pp.84-114. 755528

PROSER, MATTHEW N.
The heroic image in five Shakespearean
tragedies. (Princeton, N.J.) 1965.

748405

PROSSER (ELEANOR)
Colley Cibber at San Diego.
IN SHAKESPEARE QUARTERLY XIV: 3.
pp. 253-261.
(New York) 1963.

605711

PROSSER, ELEANOR
Hamlet and revenge [: the conflict
between obedience and conscience in
the light of Elizabethan attitudes].
1967.

766094

PROSSER (ELEANOR)
Shakespeare at Ashland and San Diego.
IN SHAKESPEARE QUARTERLY XIV: 4.
pp. 445-454.
(New York) 1963.

605711

PROSSER (ELEANOR)
Shakespeare in San Diego: the thirteenth
season.
IN SHAKESPEARE QUARTERLY XIII: 4.
pp. 529-535.
(New York) 1962.

605711

Proudfoot (Richard)
Shakespeare and the new dramatists of the
King's Men, 1606-1613. IN
Stratford-upon-Avon Studies.
8: Later Shakespeare. 1966.

illus. pp.235-261. 756101

Proust, Marcel *works relating to*

— Fowlie (W.) The Contemporary hero :
the world of Proust and Shakespeare.
In Fowlie (W.) The Spirit of France
: studies in modern French
literature.

1944.

553883

PROUTY (CHARLES TYLER)
The Contention and Shakespeare's
2 Henry VI: a comparative study.
(New Haven, Conn.)   1954.

641709

PROUTY (CHARLES TYLER)
An Early Elizabethan playhouse.
IN SHAKESPEARE SURVEY 6.   (Cambridge)
1953.

631770

PROUTY (C. T.)
George Gascoigne, Elizabethan courtier,
soldier, and poet.   [With references
to Shakespeare.]   (New York)
frontis.   bibliogs.   1942.

540708

PROUTY (CHARLES TYLER)
George Whetstone and the sources of
"Measure for measure". IN Shakespeare
Quarterly XV: 2. pp.131-145. (New York)
1964.

605711

PROUTY (CHARLES TYLER)
George Whetstone, Peter Beverly and
the sources of Much ado about nothing.
FROM Studies in Philology, Vol. 38.
(Chapel Hill, N.C.)   1941.

529724

PROUTY, CHARLES TYLER
Some observations on Shakespeare's sources.
IN SHAKESPEARE JAHRBUCH.   Bd. 96/1960.
pp. 64-77.   (Heidelberg)

10531

PROUTY (CHARLES TYLER)
The Sources of "Much Ado About
Nothing": a critical study.   With
the text of Peter Beverley's
"Ariodanto and Ieneura".   (New
Haven [Conn])   1950.

617510

PROUTY (CHARLES TYLER) ed.
Shakespeare: of an age and for all
time: the Yale Shakespeare Festival
Lectures.   [New Haven, Conn.] 1954.

640920

PROUTY (CHARLES TYLER) ed.
Studies in the Elizabethan theatre,
[by various authors.]   [Hamden,
Conn.]
illus.   plans.   bibliog.   1961.

667053

Prouty, Charles Tyler *works relating to*

—— EVANS (GWYNNE BLAKEMORE)
[Review of] The Contention and
Shakespeare's 2 Henry VI by C.T.Prouty.
IN Journal of English and Germanic
Philology, Vol. 53.   (Urbana, Ill.)
1954.

600780/53

Prouty (Mrs. Charles Tyler) and
Woglom (William Henry) trans.
FEUILLERAT (ALBERT GABRIEL)
The Composition of Shakespeare's
plays: authorship, chronology.
(New Haven, Conn.)   1953.

635608

Proverbs and Mottoes

—— Buckland (Anna J.) Shaksperian
mottoes, Nos. 3, 8-12. From
[Golden Hours, Vol.] 7.

[1874.]

579656

—— DARLINGTON (J.)
A Shakespearian vade-mecum: a
collection of colloquial expressions
and proverbial sayings, from the
works of Shakespeare.   [1891.]

409496

—— FALK (DORIS V.)
Proverbs and the Polonius destiny.
IN SHAKESPEARE QUARTERLY XVIII: 1.
pp. 23-36.
(New York)   1967.

605711

—— SMITH, CHARLES GEORGE, Professor of English
Shakespeare's proverb lore: his use of
the 'Sententiae' of Leonard Culman and
Publilius Syrus. (Cambridge, Mass.)
1963.

667800

—— TILLEY (MORRIS PALMER)
A Dictionary of the proverbs in
England in the sixteenth and seventeenth centuries: a collection of
the proverbs found in English
literature and the dictionaries of
the period.   (Ann Arbor, Mich.)
port.   bibliog.   1950.

617643

—TILLEY (M. P.)
  Elizabethan proverb lore in Lyly's
  Euphues and in Pettie's Petite Pallace,
  with parallels from Shakespeare.
  (Michigan University Pubns. Language
  and Literature, Vol. 2.)   (New York)
                                    1926.

                399822

— TILLEY (M. P.)
  Pun and proverb as aids to unexplained
  Shakespearean jests.   FROM Studies in
  Philology, Vol. 21.   (Chapel Hill,N.C.)
                                    1924.

                496552

—WHITING (B. J.)
  Proverbs in the earlier English drama,
  with illustrations from contemporary
  French plays, [and references to
  Shakespeare].   (Cambridge, Mass.)
                                    1938.
  (Harvard Studies in Comparative Liter-
  ature, Vol. 14)
                                491498

— WILSON (F. P.)
  English proverbs and dictionaries of
  proverbs.   [With quotations from
  Shakespeare.]   Reprinted from the
  Transactions of the Bibliographical
  Society: The Library [4th Series,
  Vol. 26.   With bibliographical notes].
  pp. [20.]
                                    1945.

                565126

— WILSON (FRANK PERCY)

  **The Proverbial wisdom of Shakespeare:
  presidential address of the Modern
  Humanities Research Association, 1961.
  pp.24. [Cambridge]**   1961.

                667086

Providence R.I.

— HASTINGS (WILLIAM THOMSON)
  Shakespeare in Providence.[(R.I.)]
  IN SHAKESPEARE QUARTERLY VIII.
  pp. 335-351.
  (New York)   1957.
                605711

Providence *see* Philosophy and Religion

PROWER (MAUDE)
  An Elizabethan playhouse: extract from
  a country gentleman's letter to his
  wife.   IN The Gentleman's Magazine,
  Vol. 295.   1903.

                179335

Pruvost (R.) Matteo Bandello and
  Elizabethan fiction.   [With a
  bibliography.]

            (Paris)   1937.

(Bibliothèque de la Revue de Littérature
            Comparée, Tome 113.)
                                495836|

Psychical Research *see* Spiritualism

Psychology

— ABENHEIMER (K. M.)
  Shakespeare's "Tempest": a psychological analysis.   IN The Psychoanalytic Review, Vol. 33.
  (New York)   1946.

                577280

— Adnès (A.) Shakespeare et la pathologie
    mentale. [With a bibliography.]

                        1935.

                437820

— ANDERSON, RUTH LEILA
  Elizabethan psychology and Shakespeare's
  plays. (New York)   1966.

        University of Iowa humanistic
  studies.   760093

— ARMSTRONG (E. A.)
  Shakespeare's imagination: a study
  of the psychology of association and
  inspiration.   [With bibliographical
  notes.]
  tables.   1946.

                569758

— BARTLETT (ALICE H.)
  **Shakespeare as a master psycho-analyst.
  FROM The Poetry Review, June 1933.**
                                    1933.

                405981

— BODKIN (MAUD)
  Archetypal patterns in poetry:
  psychological studies of imagination.
  [With references to Shakespeare.]
                                1934.

                428733

— BRADBY (M[ARY] K.)
  **Psycho-analysis and its place in life.
  [With a section on Hamlet].**
                                1919.

                277642

— BULLOUGH (GEOFFREY)
The Development of Shakespeare's
attitude to the mind.   IN Bullough (G.)
Mirror of minds, changing psychological
beliefs in English poetry [: revision
and enlargement of five Alexander
Lectures, delivered in Toronto
University, 1959].
bibliog.   1962.

707085

— Clark (C.) Shakespeare and psychology.
[With a bibliography.]

1936.

456686

— Clouston ([Sir]T.S.) The Hygiene of
mind. [With Shakespearian references].
Illus

1906.

455507

— CRUTTWELL (MAURICE JAMES PATRICK)
Physiology, and psychology in
Shakespeare's age.   IN Journal of
the History of Ideas, No. 12.
(Lancaster, Pa.)   1951.

519996/12

— DRAPER (JOHN WILLIAM)
The Humors & Shakespeare's characters.
[With a bibliography and bibliographical
notes.]   (Durham, N.C.)   1945.
Duke University Publications.

563425

— EDGAR (I. I.)
The Acquisition of Shakespeare's
medical and psychopathological knowledge.
[With bibliographical references.]
FROM The Canadian Medical Association
Journal, Vol. 33.   (Toronto)   1935.

506179

— EDGAR (I. I.)
Shakespeare's psychopathological
knowledge: a study in criticism
and interpretation.   [With bibliographical notes.]   FROM The Journal
of Abnormal and Social Psychology,
Vol. 30.   (Princeton)   1935.

506391

— FOREST (LOUISE C. T.)
A Caveat for critics against invoking
Elizabethan psychology.   [With refer-
ences to Shakespeare and bibliographical
notes.]   IN Publications of the
Modern Language Association of America,
Vol. 61.   (Menasha, Wis.)   1946.

581301

— HAMILTON (R.)
Shakespeare: the nemesis of pride.
FROM The Nineteenth Century and
after [Vol. 143].   pp. 335-340.
1948.

596209

— HOLLAND (NORMAN NORWOOD)
Freud on Shakespeare. (Publications in
the Humanities, No.47, Department of
Humanities, Massachusetts Institute of
Technology) (Cambridge, Mass.)
1961.

667527

— KANZER (MARK)
The Central theme in Shakespeare's
works.   IN The Psychoanalytic Review,
Vol. 38.   (New York)   1951.

289697/38

— LUCAS (FRANK LAURENCE)
Literature and psychology.   [With
references to King Lear, Othello and
Macbeth.]   1951.

613124

— McCURDY (HAROLD GRIER)
The Personality of Shakespeare: a
venture in psychological method.
(New Haven, Conn.)
graphs. tables. bibliog. 1953.

639770

— MACKENZIE (AGNES M.)
The Process of literature: an essay
towards some reconsiderations.
[A psychological study, with references
to Shakespeare and his plays.]
bibliog.   1929.

550205

— MUIR (KENNETH) [and] O'LOUGHLIN (SEAN)
The Voyage to Illyria: a new study
of Shakespeare.   1937.

469719

— PARTRIDGE (ERIC [H.])
Shakespeare's bawdy: a literary &
psychological essay and a comprehensive
glossary.   1947.

587277

— Shakespeare's Heart of Love: psycho-
physiology [of the Sonnets.   1st
article].   FROM The Journal of Man,
Vol. 1.   (Philadelphia)
port.   1872.

564841

— SHAND (A. F.)
The Foundations of character: a
study of the tendencies of the
emotions and sentiments [with
references to Shakespeare.] 1914.

286095

— SPENCER (T.)
Shakespeare and the nature of man [as
seen in his plays.   With bibliographical notes].   (Cambridge)   1943.
Lowell [Institute] Lectures, 1942.

544912

— VESSIE (P. R.)
Psychiatry catches up with Shakespeare.
FROM Medical Record, August 5, 1936.
(New York)   1936.

506180

— WEILGART (WOLFGANG J.)
Shakespeare psychognostic: character
evolution and transformation. (Tokyo)
bibliog.   1952.

649260

— YOUNG (H. M.)
The Sonnets of Shakespeare: a
psycho-sexual analysis.   (Columbia,
Miss.)   1937.

469785

Public Affairs, Shakespeare and *see* England in Shakespeare's Time

Public Health *see* Medicine and Hygiene

Publishing *see* Textual History

PUKNAT (ELIZABETH M.)
Romeo was a lady: Charlotte Cushman's
London triumph.   IN The Theatre
Annual, 1951.   1951.

554521/1950

PUMPHREY (MARY E.)
Shakespeare's birds.   FROM Friends'
Quarterly Examiner, Jan. and April,
1931.   pp. [24].   1931.

439152

Punctuation

—   Alden (R.M.) The Puncutation of
Shakespeare's printers. In Publications
of the Modern Language Association of
America, Vol.39.
(Menasha,Wis.)   1924.

428359

— ALEXANDER (P.)
Shakespeare's punctuation.   [With
bibliographical notes.]   pp. 24.
1945.
British Academy, [35th] Annual
Shakespeare Lecture.

564925

— CARTER (A. H.)
The Punctuation of Shakespeare's sonnets
of 1609.   [With bibliographical notes.]
IN McMANAWAY (J. G.), DAWSON (G. E.)
and WILLOUGHBY (E. E.) eds., John
Quincy Adams memorial studies.
(Washington)   1948.

596748

— The Emphasis capitals of Shakspere
[: a review of] The Tragedy of
Hamlet (Hamnet Edition) according to
the First Folio (spelling modernized)
with further remarks on the emphasis
capitals of Shakspere, by A. P. Paton.
FROM The Theatre, Feb. 1st, 1879.
1879.

530818

— GRAVES, ROBERT, and RIDING, LAURA
A Study in original punctuation
and spelling.   IN A Casebook on
Shakespeare's sonnets.   Edited
by G. Willen & V. B. Reed.   [Text
and critical essays.]   (New York:
Thomas Y. Crowell Co.]   1964.
Crowell Literary Casebooks.

668299

— McKENZIE (D. F.)
Shakespearian punctuation - a new
beginning.   IN The Review of English
Studies, New Series, Vol. 10.   1959.

318239/10

— 0393 Ong (W.J.) Historical backgrounds of
Elizabethan and Jacobean punctuation
theory. [With references to Shakespeare,
and bibliographical notes]. In
Publications of the Modern Language
Association of America,Vol.59.
(Menasha Wis.)   1944.

560393

— SHAW (GEORGE BERNARD)
Shakespear: a standard text.
IN Shaw [G. B.] on theatre.
1958.

693464

Puns

— BARNET (SYLVAN)
Coleridge on puns: a note to his
Shakespeare criticism.   IN Journal
of English and Germanic Philology,
Vol. 56.   1957.

600780/56

—   Kellett (E.E.) The story of the pun.
[With references to Shakespeare.] From
The Contemporary Review, Vol.146.pp.[9.]
[1934.]

428693

—KÖKERITZ (HELGE)
Punning names in Shakespeare.   IN
Modern Language Notes, Vol. 65.
(Baltimore, Md.)   1950.

439157/65

— MAHOOD (M. M.)
The Fatal Cleopatra; Shakespeare and
the pun.   IN Essays in Criticism,
Vol. 1.   (Oxford)   1951.

621866

—MAHOOD (MOLLY MAUREEN)
Shakespeare's wordplay.   1957.

665495

——   Nearing (H.) A Three-way pun in
Richard II. [With bibliographical notes.]
In Modern Language Notes, Vol.62.
(Baltimore,Md.)   1947.

439157/62

——   Siler (H.D.) A French pun in
"Love's Labour's Lost." In Modern
Language Notes, Vol.60.
(Baltimore)   1945.

571543

——   Tilley (M.P.) Pun and proverb as
aids to unexplained Shakespearean jests.
From Studies in Philology,Vol.21.
(Chapel Hill,N.C.)   1924

496552

Puppets *see* Marionettes and Puppets

PURCELL (HENRY)
Come unto these yellow sands.   Selected from "The Tempest". ff.[2.]
[?1750.]

639837

PURCELL (H.)
Come unto these yellow sands.
A Favorite Song in the Tempest.
pp. [4].   (Goulding & Co.)
[c.1799.]

465962

PURCELL [H.]
Come unto these yellow sands,
arranged by S. Nelson.   pp. [ii] 5.
[c.1840.]
Standard Songs.

600319

PURCELL (H.)
Come unto these yellow sands: song
and three part chorus.

IN Purcell (H.) Come, if you dare:
solo and chorus.   [c.1920.]
School Music Review.

594170

PURCELL (HENRY
Dance for Chinese man and woman.
(Chaconne, from "The Fairy Queen")
[an anonymous adaptation of
Shakespeare's "Midsummer Night's
Dream", 1692.   Air and variations.
Miniature score for piano and percus-
sion.]   IN MOORE (S. S.) The Road to
the orchestra.   (Edinburgh)
ports. illus. plans.   1939.

540811

PURCELL, HENRY
[Dear, dear, pretty, pretty pretty
youth.] A song in 'The Tempest' sung by
a girl and sett by Mr. H. Purcell.
[Words by Sir W. Davenant, J. Dryden
and T. Shadwell.]   [?1700]

760956

PURCELL (HENRY)
If love's a sweet passion, from The
Fairy Queen, an anonymous adaptation
of Shakespeare's "A Midsummer night's
dream".   IN Purcell (H.) Five songs
for soprano or tenor solo, chorus and
orchestra.   Published for the Purcell
Society.   pp. 24.
port.   [c.1930.]

550826

PURCELL (HENRY)
The Musick in the comedy of The
Tempest; in score.   pp. 39.
[c.1785]

632230

PURCELL (H.)
The Music in The Tempest.   pp. [iv]
50.   [B. Goodison]   [c.1790.]

602193

PURCELL (H.)
"Song of the birds" from the masque
in "Timon of Athens".   IN Purcell
(H.) Suite of five pieces for
pianoforte from the tragedy, masques
& sonatas of H. Purcell, arranged
by [Sir] H. J. Wood.   pp. 11.
1936.

-
536603

PURCELL (HENRY) and others
Sixteen standard songs of Shakespeare.
Music by Purcell, Arne, Bishop,
Schubert etc.   pp. 54.   [?1920.]

628133

Purcell, Henry *works relating to*

— Arundell (D.[D.]) Henry Purcell. [With references to his music to Shakespeare's plays.] Ports. Illus.

(Oxford)   1927.

[The World's Manuals]

344803

— Holland (A.K.) Henry Purcell, the English musical tradition. [With references to his music to Shakespeare's plays.] Port.

1932.

[Bell's Musical Publications)

400292

— MANDINIAN (E.)
Purcell's The Fairy Queen as presented by the Sadler's Wells Ballet and the Covent Garden Opera: a photographic record. With the preface to the original text [an anonymous adaptation of Shakespeare's A Midsummer Night's Dream], a preface by E. J. Dent and articles by C. Lambert and M. Ayrton. pp. 96.   1948.

590064

— MELLERS (WILFRID HOWARD)
Purcell and the Restoration theatre. IN Mellers (W. H.) Harmonious meeting: a study of the relationship between English music, poetry and theatre, c. 1500-1900.   1965.

742371

— Westrup (J.A.) Purcell. [With references to his music to Shakespeare's plays.] Ports. Illus. Facsimiles. Pedigree.

1937.

(Master Musicians, New Series)

463454

PURCHAS (J. R P.)
The Chandos portrait of Shakespeare. IN The Antiquary, Vol. 41.   1905.

191811

PURDIE, EDNA
Observations on some eighteenth-century German versions of the Witches' scenes in Macbeth.
IN SHAKESPEARE JAHRBUCH, Bd. 92/1956. pp. 96-109.   (Heidelberg)

10531

PURDOM (CHARLES BENJAMIN)
The Crosby Hall "Macbeth": notes on the production, a contribution to the Festival of Britain, at Crosby Hall, Chelsea, May 1951.   pp. 20.
1951.
Shakespeare Stage Society.

620879

PURDOM (CHARLES BENJAMIN)
Producing Shakespeare.
illus. dgms. bibliog. 1950.
Theatre and Stage Series.

611305

PURDOM (CHARLES BENJAMIN)
The Theatre at Stratford-upon-Avon. FROM Design for to-day, Nov. 1935. pp. [3.]
illus.   1935.

443819

Purgatory *see* **Catholicism**

Puritanism

— FLEAY (F. G.)
Shakespeare and Puritanism.   FROM Anglia, Bd. 7.   pp. [9.] [(Halle)] [1883.]

432002

— HALES (J. W.)
Shakespeare and puritanism.   pp. [14.] IN The Contemporary Review, Vol. 67, 1895.

1895.

129886

— HALLER (WILLIAM)
Elizabeth I and the Puritans.   (Ithaca, N.Y.)
illus.   1964.
Folger Booklets on Tudor and Stuart Civilization.

742217

— LAW (R. A.)
Two Shakespearian pictures of Puritans [as portrayed in passages in Richard the Third and Othello].   IN University of Texas Studies in English, No. 13. (Austin, Texas.)

1933.

434338

— MYERS (A. M.)
Representation and misrepresentation of the Puritan in Elizabethan drama: a thesis presented to the University of Pennsylvania for the degree of Doctor of Philosophy.
bibliog.   1931.

392216

PURSER (J. W. R.)
[Review of] Shakespeare and the
popular dramatic tradition, by
S. L. Bethell.   IN The Modern
Language Review, Vol. 40.
(Cambridge)   1945.

571545

PURSER (J. W. R.)
[Review of] The Use of rhyme in
Shakespeare's plays, by F. W. Ness.
IN The Moderr Language Review, Vol. 38.
(Cambridge)   1943.

553690

Pushkin, Aleksandr Sergyeevich *works relating to*

— GIBIAN (GEORGE)
Measure for Measure and Pushkin's
Angelo.   IN P.M.L.A.:   Publications
of the Modern Language Association
of America, Vol. 66.   (New York)
1951.

428321/66

— GIBIAN (GEORGE)
Pushkin's parody on "The Rape of Lucrece".
IN SHAKESPEARE QUARTERLY I: 4.
pp. 264-266.
(New York)   1950.

605711

— Gifford (H.) Shakespearean elements
in "Boris Godunov". [With
bibliographical notes.] In
The Slavonic and East European
Review, Vol.26.

1947-8.

309336/26

— LAVRIN (J.)
Pushkin and Shakespeare.
IN Lavrin (J.) Pushkin and Russian
literature.
port. maps. bibliogs. 1947.
English Universities Press.   Teach
Yourself History Library.

582261

— Pushkin: a collection of articles and
essays on the great Russian poet [by
various authors].   Title pages and
decorations by I. F. Rerberg.   Art
editor: M. P. Sokolnikov.
[Containing references to Shakespeare.
English text.]   (Moscow)
port. illus. facsimiles. 1939.
U.S.S.R. Society for Cultural Relations
with Foreign Countries.

535797

PUTNEY (RUFUS)
Venus agonistes.   Reprinted from
University of Colorado Studies.
Series in Language and Literature,
No. 4, July 1953.   pp. [15].
[Boulder, Colo.]   [1953.]

666115

Putney (R.) Venus and Adonis: amour
with humor. From Philological
Quarterly, Vol.20.

(Iowa)   1941.

539441

PUTNEY (RUFUS)
What "Praise to give?" Jonson vs.
Stoll [on Shakespeare's tragic
heroes.]   IN Philological Quarterly,
Vol. 23. No. 4.   (Iowa)   1944.

583399

PUTT (SAMUEL GORLEY)
[Review of] The Character of Hamlet
and other essays [by] J. E. Hankins.
IN Time and Tide, Vol. 23.   1942.

544257

PUTT (SAMUEL GORLEY)
A Shakespearean high Tory [: a review
of] Shakespeare and other masters,
[by] E. E. Stoll.   IN Time and Tide,
Vol. 23.   1942.

544257

Puzzles *see* Riddles and Puzzles

Pye, Henry James *works relating to*

— ALEXANDER (NIGEL)
Critical disagreement about Oedipus
and Hamlet.
IN SHAKESPEARE SURVEY 20.   (Cambridge)
1967.

766881

— DOUCE (F.)
Remarks on Mr. Pye's Comments on
Shakspeare [: a review]. FROM
[The] Gent[leman's] Mag[azine,
Vol. 77.   Part 2].   1807.

556073

PYLE (F.)
'Twelfth Night', 'King Lear' and
'Arcadia'.   IN The Modern Language
Review, Vol. 43.   (Cambridge)
bibliog.   1948.

266816/43

Pyles (T.) Rejected Q2 readings in the new Shakespeare Hamlet. [edited by J.D. Wilson: a review]. **In** ELH: a journal of English literary history, Vol.4.

1937.

483008

PYLES (THOMAS)
The Romantic side of Dr. Johnson [with references to Shakespeare and bibliographical notes]. IN E.L.H.: a journal of English literary history, Vol. 11. (Baltimore) 1944.

562838

Pyramus and Thisbe *see* A Midsummer Night's Dream, Sources and Background

Q. (D.)
[Review of] The Bacon-Shakespeare anatomy, by W. S. Melsome. [In 6 parts.] IN Notes and Queries, Vol. 190. 1946.

579129

Q. (D.)
Shakespeare, Oxford and Oxford Inn. IN Notes and Queries, Vol. 193. (Oxford) 1948.

5421/193

Q. (N. R.)
Shakspeare fancies. No. 1. Juliet and Lady Mary Wortley Montague [: a comparison]. IN The Metropolitan Magazine, Vol. 22. 1838.

88822

Q. (N. R.)
Shakspeare fancies. No. 2. Desdemona and Felicia Dorothea Hemans [: a comparison]. IN The Metropolitan Magazine, Vol. 23. 1838.

88823

Q. (N. R.)
Shakspeare fancies. No[s.] 3 [and] 4. Portia and Joanna Baillie [: a comparison]. IN The Metropolitan Magazine, Vol. 23. 1838.

88823

Q. (N. R.)
Shakspeare fancies. No[s.] 4-8. Cleopatra and Mme. de Stael [: a comparison]. IN The Metropolitan Magazine, Vols. 24-26. 3 vols. 1839.

88824

QUARLES (FRANCIS) Works relating to: see Moore (W. H.) Baconian Studies.

Quartos *see* Textual History, The Early Quartos

Quatercentenary 1964
General Works
Booklists
Commemorative Volumes
Exhibitions
Music
Periodicals

Quatercentenary 1964
-- General Works

— ARTS COUNCIL OF GREAT BRITAIN
Scottish Committee
List of events in Scotland to celebrate the Shakespeare Quatercentenary. (Edinburgh) 1964.

740736

— ASSOCIATED TELEVISION LTD., LONDON AREA
Man of the year. [Quatercentenary programme.] Script: Bill Oddie. Producer Peter Potter. ATV script transmitted 11th May 1964. typescript. 1964.

741625-8

— BATH DRAMA CLUB
The Marriage of true minds. A performance of extracts from Shakespeare's plays, with music. In celebration of the Quatercentenary. (Bath) typescript. 1964.

741623

— BECKERMAN (BERNARD)
The 1964 season at Stratford, Connecticut. IN Shakespeare Quarterly XV: 4. pp.397-401. (New York) 1964.

605711

— BIRMINGHAM PUBLIC LIBRARIES
Shakespeare Memorial Library [Visitors' book to the Shakespeare Quatercentenary exhibition held at the Art Gallery, Birmingham.] 1964.

740149

— Birmingham scraps and news cuttings. 1964.

764671

— DANZIGER (MARLIES K.)
Shakespeare in New York, 1964. IN Shakespeare Quarterly XV: 4. pp.419-422. (New York) 1964.

605711

— DAVIS, ARTHUR G.
Hamlet and the eternal problem of man.
(New York)   1964.

745118

Published by St. John's University
in celebration of the 400th Anniversary
Year of the birth of William
Shakespeare, 1564-1964.

—— EDWARDS, PAT
Shakespeare-poet of the world.
Produced by Pat Edwards. B.B.C. African
Service radio script broadcast 19th
April 1964.   1964.

typescript.   742218

—— EVANS, Mrs. BARBARA LLOYD
The Celebration, adapted from
Garrick's 'Jubilee'. Produced by
Edmund Marshall. B.B.C. radio script
broadcast 22nd April 1964.   1964.

668239

—— FOX, LEVI
Celebrating Shakespeare: a pictorial
record of the celebrations held at
Stratford-upon-Avon during 1964 to
mark the 400th anniversary of the
birth of William Shakespeare.
Prepared for the Shakespeare
Birthplace Trust.   (Stratford-upon-
Avon)
illus.   [1964.]

744155

—— FOX, LEVI
The Shakespeare anniversary book.
(Norwich)   1964.

illus. map.   667801

—— HELSZTYNSKI, STANISLAW, ed.
Poland's homage to Shakespeare.
Commemorating the fourth centenary of
his birth, 1564-1964. (Warsaw)
1965.

747846

—— HUTCHINSON, DAVID
Such sweet thunder (the universality
of Shakespeare). B.B.C. External
Services radio script broadcast 7th
April 1964.   1964.

typescript.   744457

—— ISAACS, JACOB
Shakespeare after 400 years.
FROM The Listener, November 10th.
1966.
pp. 685-687.

771374

—— LONDON
CORPORATION OF THE CITY OF LONDON
Festival of the city of London
souvenir programme 1964.   1964.

illus.   740729

—— MORRIS, PETER
Shakespeare on film: an index to
William Shakespeare's plays on film.
Prepared on the occasion of the 400th
anniversary of Shakespeare's birth.
(Ottawa)   1964.

746655

—— MORTON, ARTHUR LESLIE
Shakespeare's idea of history.
Issued for the fourth centenary of
Shakespeare's birth.
typescript.   1964.
Our History.   Pamphlet No. 33.

740829

—— NEWSPAPER CUTTINGS: Shakespeare
quatercentenary celebrations, 1964.
1962-1965.

illus.   668476

— NICOLL, ALLARDYCE
Shakespeare's plays [: a lecture given
for the Istituto Internazionale per la
Ricerca Teatrale in Venice.]   [1964.]

740822

— Niećko, Jacek
Main activities commemorating the fourth
centenary in Poland. IN

HELSZTYNSKI, STANISLAW, ed.
Poland's homage to Shakespeare.
Commemorating the fourth centenary of
his birth, 1564-1964. (Warsaw)
1965.

747846

— OGDEN (DUNBAR H.)
The 1964 season of the Ashland and San
Diego Shakespearian Festivals. IN
Shakespeare Quarterly XV: 4. pp.409-418.
(New York)   1964.

605711

— PERKIN (ROBERT L.)
Shakespeare in the Rockies: VII. IN
Shakespeare Quarterly XV: 4. pp.427-431.
(New York)   1964.

605711

— PRAGUE THEATRE INSTITUTE
Theatre in Czechoslovakia: William
Shakespeare. [Articles by Z. Stribrny
and others. Ed. Ludmila Kopáčová.]
(Praha)   [1964.]

744460

— PRITCHETT, VICTOR SAWDON, and others
Shakespeare: the comprehensive soul.
[Talks on the B.B.C. European English
Service to celebrate the Shakespearian
Quatercentenary.]   1965.

746585

—   Scrapbook relating to events
abroad.   1964.

752298

—   Scrapbook relating to events in
Great Britain.   1964.

752297

—— SHAKESPEARE ANNIVERSARY COMMITTEE
Shakespeare in North America.   (New
York)
illus.   1964.

740864

— SHEDD (ROBERT GORDON)
  The Great Lakes Shakespeare Festival,
  1964: "Henry VI" - and "Hamlet", too!
  IN Shakespeare Quarterly XV: 4.
  pp.423-426. (New York)   1964.

                    605711

— SIMPSON, DONALD HERBERT
  Shakespeare and the Commonwealth.
  [Published by] the Royal Commonwealth
  Society as its contribution to the
  four hundredth anniversary of the birth
  of William Shakespeare.   1964.

                    740585

— SPEAIGHT (ROBERT)
  Shakespeare in Britain. IN Shakespeare
  Quarterly XV: 4. pp.377-389. (New York)
                              1964.

        illus.   605711

— STRATFORD-UPON-AVON, Quatercentenary
  celebrations.   Scrapbook material.
                              1964.

                    753275

— SWINTON, MARJORY, comp.
  Shakespeare birthday book.   [1964.]

        illus. Windsor birthday books.
                              667978

— TAVISTOCK SHAKESPEARE SOCIETY
  Quatercentenary tribute to
  Shakespeare.   1964.

                    740855

— WAKELIN (ELLEN A.)
  [Scrolls presented to Sir Fordham
  Flower and L. Fox containing an account
  of the events in Stratford-upon-Avon
  at the Quatercentenary Birthday celebrations with a description of the
  Shakespeare Exhibition and the opening
  of the Stratford canal on July 11th
  1964.   With text and music of the
  Tercentenary Festal Song and the Tercentenary National Song to Shakespeare.]
  4 items in 1 reel, 35 mm.   [1964.]
  Microfilm, negative copy, made at
  Birmingham Reference Library, 1965.   744435

— WORLD THEATRE SEASON at the Aldwych
  Theatre, London, March 17 - June 13,
  1964. Presented by the governors of the
  Royal Shakespeare Company and Peter
  Daubeny in conjunction with the Sunday
  Telegraph. [Souvenir]   1964.

                    752257

— WRIGHT, LOUIS BOOKER
  The Britain that Shakespeare knew.
  FROM The National Geographic
  Magazine, May 1964, pp. 613-667.
  (Washington, D.C.)
        illus.   1964.

                    744138

Quatercentenary 1964

- Booklists

— DENT, ROBERT WILLIAM, and HABENICHT,
              RUDOLPH E., eds.
  Shakespeare: an annotated bibliography
  for 1964. FROM Shakespeare Quarterly,
  XVI: 3. (New York)   1965.

                    747853

— EAST SUFFOLK COUNTY LIBRARY
  William Shakespeare 1564-1616: a
  selection from the stock. (Ipswich)
                              1964.

                    740857

— HASTINGS
      PUBLIC LIBRARY
  A Shakespeare booklist published in
  commemoration of the Quatercentenary
  of the birth of William Shakespeare.
  (Hastings)   1964.

                    744462

— LEAMINGTON PUBLIC LIBRARY
  Shakespeare: a catalogue.
  (Leamington Spa)   1964.

                    740861

— PORT ELIZABETH PUBLIC LIBRARY
  Shakespeare's quatercentenary, 1564-
  1964: a list of the various editions
  of Shakespeare's works in the library.
  Revised edn. [Port Elizabeth.] 1967.

                    762623

— SCUNTHORPE PUBLIC LIBRARIES
  Shakespeare: a catalogue of books
  about the man, his times and his works.
  Shakespeare quatercentenary 1564-1964.
  (Scunthorpe)   [1964.]

                    667880

— UNDERWOOD, MARTIN
  William Shakespeare: a book list
  newly compiled and imprinted by
  St. Pancras Public Libraries to
  mark the 400th anniversary of his
  birth in 1564.   1964.

                    740827

Quatercentenary 1964

— Commemorative Volumes

— ANDHRA UNIVERSITY
  Shakespeare Quatercentenary
  celebrations.   24-27 February 1964.
  Souvenir.   (Waltair, India)   1965.

                    768977

— BLOOM, EDWARD A., ed.
Shakespeare 1564-1964: a collection
of modern essays by various hands.
(Providence, R.I.)   1964.
Brown University bicentennial
publications.

744437

— CHAPMAN, GERALD W., ed.
Essays on Shakespeare [by various
writers]. (Princeton, N.J.) 1965.

University of Denver. Shakespeare
Centennial Lectures.   749030

— CHARLES UNIVERSITY ON SHAKESPEARE: essays
[by various authors] edited by
Z. Stříbrný. (Praha)   1966.

illus.   762631

— CORDER, JIM W., ed.
Shakespeare 1964 [: a record of the
celebrations of the Shakespeare
Quatercentenary at Texas Christian
University]. (Fort Worth, Tex.)
                        1965.

illus.   745402

— DUTHIE (GEORGE IAN) ed.
Papers, mainly Shakespearian.   (Aberdeen)
                        1964.
Aberdeen University Studies, No. 147.

668205

— ENGLISH ASSOCIATION
Essays and Studies, 1964: Vol.17 of the
new series of Essays and Studies
collected by W.A. Armstrong.
Shakespeare Quatercentenary ed. 1964.

illus.   667820

— HOWARTH, ROBERT GUY, and others
Shakespeare at 400. A series of public
lectures given on the occasion of the
four-hundredth anniversary of William
Shakespeare's birth by members of the
Department of English, University of
Cape Town. (Cape Town)   1965.

typescript.   749535

— KETTLE (ARNOLD) ed.
Shakespeare in a changing world: essays
[by various authors].   1964.

667797

— McMANAWAY, JAMES GILMER, ed.
Shakespeare 400: essays by American
scholars on the anniversary of the
poet's birth.   Published in
co-operation with the Shakespeare
Association of America.
illus.   1964.

667803

— McNEIR, WALDO F. and GREENFIELD,
THELMA NELSON, eds.
Pacific coast studies in Shakespeare.
(Eugene: Ore.)   1966.

768009

— PAOLUCCI, ANNE, ed.
Shakespeare encomium, 1564-1964 [by
various writers]. (New York) 1964.

City University of New York, City
College Papers, 1.   747546

— SEN, TARAKNATH, ed.
Shakespeare commemoration volume.
Published by the Department of English,
Presidency College, Calcutta, under
the auspices of the Government of West
Bengal. (Calcutta)   1966.

764382

— SHAKESPEARE SEMINAR, 5-8 December 1964
[: lectures given at Sahitya Akademi,
New Delhi]. (New Delhi)   1964.

typescript.   744153

— SPENCER, TERENCE JOHN BEW, ed.
Shakespeare: a celebration, 1564-
1964.
illus.   maps.   1964.

667816

— STRASBOURG UNIVERSITY
La Faculté des Lettres
Hommage à Shakespeare: Bulletin de la
Faculté des Lettres de Strasbourg.
43e année, no.8, mai-juin 1965.

illus.   766822

— SUBRAHMANYAM, D. S., and others, eds.
Homage to Shakespeare, Quatercentenary
1964 [from] Sir C. Ramalinga Reddy
College.   (Eluru)
illus.   1964.

740823

— SUTHERLAND, JAMES, and HURSTFIELD, JOEL,
                               eds.
Shakespeare's world.   1964.

667808

— THALER, ALWIN, and SANDERS, NORMAN, eds.
Shakespearean essays.   1964.

Tennessee studies in literature,
special no: 2.   667977

— WRIGHT, LOUIS BOOKER, ed.
Shakespeare celebrated: anniversary
lectures delivered at the Folger
Library [during 1964].   (Ithaca, N.Y.)
                        1965.

771817

Quatercentenary 1964

Exhibitions

— ARTS COUNCIL OF GREAT BRITAIN
Shakespeare in art: paintings,
drawings and engravings devoted to
Shakespearean subjects [a catalogue].
illus.   1964.

740862

— ARTS COUNCIL OF GREAT BRITAIN
Scottish Committee
Shakespeare in Scottish art [: a
catalogue of the exhibition] at the
Arts Council Gallery, Edinburgh [to
celebrate Shakespeare's birth.
Compiled by B. Skinner].   (Edinburgh)
1964.

740735

— BIRMINGHAM PUBLIC LIBRARIES
Shakespeare Exhibition to celebrate
the quatercentenary of his birth and
the centenary of the Library.   In
the City Art Gallery 23rd April to
20th May.   Positive film of selected
exhibits.   (Birmingham)   [1964.]
1 reel 35 mm. contact prints.

772456

— BIRMINGHAM PUBLIC LIBRARIES
Shakespeare Memorial Library 1864-
1964.   [Catalogue of the] Shakespeare
Exhibition to celebrate the four
hundredth anniversary of his birth
and the centenary of the library.
In the City Art Gallery 23rd April
to 20th May.   (Birmingham)
illus.   1964.

756933

— BIRMINGHAM PUBLIC LIBRARIES
Shakespeare Memorial Library
[Visitors' book to the Shakespeare
Quatercentenary Exhibition held
at the Art Gallery, Birmingham.]
1964.

740149

— BIRMINGHAM PUBLIC LIBRARIES
Thirty frames of items from the
Shakespeare Exhibition mounted in
the Art Gallery, Birmingham.   1964.

766080

— BRITISH COUNCIL
Shakespeare exhibition: catalogue
of a display of recent writings on
Shakespeare, with examples of
modern texts, arranged by the
British Council.   [With supplements.]
1964.

740730

— BRITISH COUNCIL
Shakespeare Quatercentenary book
exhibitions.
typescript.   [1964.]

742420

— BRISTOL UNIVERSITY
Department of Drama
Shakespeare's England: [catalogue
of] an exhibition to mark the
anniversary of his birth.   (Bristol)
1964.

668233

— BRITISH MUSEUM, LONDON
William Shakespeare 1564-1616 and
Christopher Marlowe 1564-1593: an
exhibition of books, manuscripts and
other illustrative material held 23
April to 12 July 1964.   [1964.]

illus.   668011

— CHELTENHAM PUBLIC LIBRARY, ART GALLERY
& MUSEUM
"Everyman" and the theatre [: catalogue
of an exhibition presented] in
collaboration with the Cheltenham
Everyman Theatre Association.
[Cheltenham]   1964.

740732

— DAGENHAM PUBLIC LIBRARIES
Shakespeare Week 12-17 October 1964:
exhibitions, Shakespeare and his
contemporaries, Shakespeare - dressing
the part.   (Dagenham)   1964.

740856

— GORDON, JOHN D.
The Bard and the book. Editions of
Shakespeare in the seventeenth century:
an exhibition [at the New York Public
Library.] (New York)   1964.

747543

— GUILDHALL ART GALLERY, LONDON
Shakespeare and the theatre: an
exhibition of paintings, drawings
& stage designs arranged by the
Guildhall Art Gallery in collaboration with the Society for Theatre
Research.   [Catalogue.]   27th May
to 27th June, 1964.
illus.   1964.

740826

— HORNE (C. J.)
[Four hundred years of Shakespeare,
1564-1964.]   An Exhibition of the
main editions of William Shakespeare.
Arranged for the third Adelaide
Festival of Arts, March 7-21, 1964.
[Catalogue.]   (Adelaide)
illus.   1964.

740831

— HUGO, JEAN VICTOR, illus.
Shakespeare's Cotswolds: 13 scenes
of country life painted for the
[Stratford-upon-Avon] Shakespeare
exhibition, 1564-1964.   [1964.]

667983

— KENT RECORDS OFFICE, MAIDSTONE
[Shakespeare: his friends and literary
contemporaries. An exhibition to mark
the Shakespeare-Marlowe quatercentenary.
Press statement and caption cards.]
(Maidstone)   1964.

668236

—— MANCHESTER UNIVERSITY, WHITWORTH ART
GALLERY
   The Age of Shakespeare: catalogue
   [of an exhibition held to commemorate]
   the quater-centenary of Shakespeare's
   birth.   (Manchester)
   illus.   1964.

                          740728

—— MIDDLESEX COUNTY RECORD OFFICE
   Middlesex in Shakespeare's day:
   exhibition of records from the
   Middlesex County Record Office at the
   Middlesex Guildhall, Westminster.
                                      1964.

        illus.   740737

—— NATIONAL LIBRARY OF SCOTLAND, Edinburgh
and EDINBURGH UNIVERSITY LIBRARY
   Shakespeare: an exhibition of
   printed books to mark the Quatercentenary of his birth.   Drawn
   from the resources of the National
   Library of Scotland and the Library
   of the University of Edinburgh.
   (Edinburgh)   1964.

                          668235

—— NATIONAL PORTRAIT GALLERY
   O sweet Mr. Shakespeare, I'll have
   his picture: the changing image
   of Shakespeare's person, 1600-1800.
   illus.   1964.

                          668095

—— OXFORD UNIVERSITY, BODLEIAN LIBRARY
   William Shakespeare 1564-1964. A
   catalogue of the Quatercentenary
   Exhibition in the Divinity School,
   Oxford.   (Oxford)   1964.

                          742974

—— ST. ANDREWS UNIVERSITY
   Four hundredth anniversary of the
   birth of William Shakespeare: an
   exhibition [catalogue]. (St. Andrews)
                                      1964.

                          740858

—— ST. XAVIER HIGH SCHOOL, JAIPUR
   Shakespeare and the world: an
   exhibition at St. Xavier High School
   on 23rd April 1964. (Jaipur)   1964.

                          744152

—— Shakespeare's England exhibition,
   1564-1964.   1964.
   illus.

                          767941

—— STRATFORD-UPON-AVON, EDINBURGH, LONDON,
   The Shakespeare Exhibition [: Catalogue].
   illus.   [1964.]

                          667987

—— ULSTER MUSEUM, BELFAST
   Shakespeare in pictures [: catalogue
   of a Quatercentenary exhibition].
   (Belfast)   1964.

                          668234

—— WARWICK COUNTY MUSEUM
   In sweet musick is such art. An
   exhibition of English music 1580-1620
   arranged as the Warwickshire County
   Council's contribution to the 1964
   Shakespeare Festival. (Warwick)
                                      1964.

                          740734

—— WELLCOME HISTORICAL MEDICAL MUSEUM,
London
   Medicine and health in Shakespeare's
   England: an exhibition to commemorate
   the Quatercentenary of Shakespeare's
   birth.   [With an introduction by
   F. N. L. Poynter.]
   typescript.   1964.

                          740733

Quatercentenary 1964

- Music

—— CHAIKOVSKY, PETR ILICH, and others
   Romeo and Juliet: album for piano.
   Romeo und Julie: album für Klavier.
   [Music by various composers.] (Budapest)
                                      1964.

        illus.   746988

—— GARDNER, JOHN
   The Noble heart. Music by J. Gardner.
   Text arranged by J ^. Greenwood.
   Commissioned by and dedicated to the
   1964 Shakespeare Anniversary Council.
                                      1964.

                          751592

—— MELLERS, WILFRID HOWARD
   Rose of May. A threnody for Ophelia,
   for speaker, soprano, flute, clarinet
   and string quartet. The words by W.
   Shakespeare. Commissioned by the
   Cheltenham Festival 1964.   1965.

                          753249

—— PHILIPS, PETER, and others
   Music from Shakespeare's day [: Trio
   in the Phrygian mode, by P. Philips;
   Hexachord fantasy, by W. Daman;
   Canzonet (Hold out, my heart), by
   T. Morley; Fantasia, by T. Lupo] for
   J. Newman.   (New York)
                                      1964.
   American Recorder Society Editions No.51.

                          745452

Quatercentenary 1964

— Periodicals

— ABERDEEN TOWN COUNCIL
Shakespeare, Aberdeen 1964: a souvenir of the Shakespeare Quatercentenary celebrations 1964. (Aberdeen)
illus.

740838

— AMATEUR STAGE, Vol.XIX, No.4, April, 1964. Shakespeare Quatercentenary.

illus.   744895

— BIRMINGHAM POST
Shakespeare Quatercentenary commemorative supplement.   1964.

illus.   667881

— CENTRAL LITERARY MAGAZINE
Special celebration number, William Shakespeare 1564-1964. April 1964.

740859

— [COMING EVENTS, February, 1964.]
Shakespeare. pp.22.   1964.

illus.   668223

— ENGLISH: [Essays on Shakespeare]
Vol. 15: No. 86.   1964.

Pt. of 481151

— ENGLISH STUDIES. XLV: II
Shakespeare Centenary number. (Amsterdam)   1964.

485643/64

— FINDING OUT: the modern magazine for young people everywhere, Vol.8, No.7, [containing "Shakespeare's World"].
[1964.]

illus.   667986

— History today, February 1964 [: Shakespeare issue].   1964.

illus.   667985

— LIFE INTERNATIONAL
Shakespeare's world [and other articles] IN Life International, May 4, 1964. (New York)

pp.40-63. illus.   668227

— THE LISTENER and BBC Television Review, Vol.LXXI, No.1830, April 23, 1964. Shakespeare birthday number.

illus.   668225

— THE LITERARY CRITERION
Special number on Shakespeare. Vol.6, Winter, No.1. (Bombay) 1963.

756155

— NEW THEATRE MAGAZINE
Shakespeare Quatercentenary souvenir issue [on] Bristol Shakespeare Festival. Vol. V 2. (Bristol)   1964.

748949

— OXYGEN NEWS
Shakespeare among Indians. Reprint of a supplement issued to mark the Quatercentenary of William Shakespeare. (Calcutta)   [1964.]

illus.   744154

— A REVIEW OF ENGLISH LITERATURE
Shakespeare number. Guest editor K. Muir. V : 2, April 1964.

697306/64

— ST. PANCRAS BOROUGH COUNCIL
St. Pancras Journal.   Vol. 17, No. 11.   1964.

740863

— SHOW: the magazine of the arts. A special report on the Bard today. Vol.IV, No.2: February 1964. (New York)

illus.   740825

— STRATFORD-UPON-AVON HERALD and South Warwickshire Advertiser, 24th April, 1964. The Shakespeare Quatercentenary Supplement, 1564-1964. 'Speak of me as I am'. (Stratford-upon-Avon)   1964.

illus.   668226

— WARWICKSHIRE & WORCESTERSHIRE MAGAZINE, April, 1964. Shakespeare's anniversary [: articles by various authors]. pp.35-43. (Leamington Spa)   1964.

728224

— WORLD THEATRE, Vol.XIII. Nr.2
Shakespeare 1964 [: articles by various writers in English and French]. pp.73-147. (Bruxelles)   1964.

illus.   742319

QUAYLE (ANTHONY)
The Theatre from within. IN McBEAN (ANGUS) Shakespeare Memorial Theatre, 1948-1950: a photographic record.   With forewords by I. Brown and A. Quayle.   Photographs by A. McBean.   1951.

616917

"The Queen" Shakespeare Festival Supplement.   FROM "The Queen", May 7th, 1936.   pp. 21-44. ports.   illus.   1936.

451507

Queen Mary's Grammar School, Walsall see Walsall

Queen's Theatre *see* **London**, Theatres —
Queen's Theatre

QUENNELL, PETER
Shakespeare: the poet and his
background.
illus.   1963.

667625

Questors Theatre *see* **London**, Theatres —
Questors Theatre

[QUICK (HILDA M.)
Nine woodcuts of the chief characters
in "The Tempest" as dressed and played
in Miss Dorothea Valentine's production
at Porthcurno, Cornwall, August 1932]

399401

QUILLER-COUCH (Sir ARTHUR [THOMAS])
Cambridge lectures [on English literature, etc. Including lectures on
A Midsummer Night's Dream, Macbeth
and Antony and Cleopatra. With a
list of the author's works]. 1943.
Everyman's Library, No. 974.

540949

QUILLER-COUCH (Sir ARTHUR [THOMAS])
Paternity in Shakespeare. pp. 20.
                        [1932]
British Academy Annual Shakespeare
Lecture. 1932

396735

QUILLER-COUCH (Sir ARTHUR [THOMAS])
Paternity in Shakespeare. IN
Quiller-Couch (Sir A. [T.]) The Poet
as citizen, and other papers.
(Cambridge)   1934.

428734

QUILLER-COUCH (Sir ARTHUR THOMAS)
Shakespeare's "Julius Caesar".
Retold by [Sir] A. T. Quiller-Couch.
With introduction and notes by
E. Nagasawa. pp. iv, 64. (Tokyo)
                        [1951.]
Kenkyusha Pocket English Series.

627264

[QUILLER-COUCH (Sir ARTHUR THOMAS)
Shakespeare's workmanship.] Personal
choice [: a radio programme, in which]
J. [E.] Agate [reads] two passages
from "Shakespeare's workmanship", by
Sir A. [T.] Quiller-Couch. [Broadcast]
19th July, 1944. pp. 2.
typescript.   1944.

552383

QUILLER-COUCH (Sir ARTHUR [THOMAS])
Sir John Squire on Shakespeare [: a
review of his] Shakespeare as a
dramatist. IN London Mercury,
Vol. 32.   [1935]

444082

QUILLER-COUCH (Sir ARTHUR THOMAS)
Three prose tales [: King Henry the
Fourth; King Henry the Fifth;
Coriolanus.] IN [HOLMDAHL (FREDA)
ed.] A Further approach to Shakespeare.
With an introduction by H. E. Marshall.
illus.   1934.
Teaching of English Series.

429584

QUILLER-COUCH ([Sir] ARTHUR THOMAS)
The Warwickshire Avon. Illustrations
by A. Parsons.   1892.

460649

QUILLER-COUCH (Sir ARTHUR THOMAS)
The Workmanship of "Macbeth".
IN The Fortnightly Review, Vol. 102.
                          1914.

255614

QUILLER-COUCH (Sir ARTHUR [THOMAS])
The Workmanship of "The Merchant
of Venice". IN The Fortnightly
Review. Vol. 103, N.S.   1918.

272491

QUILLER-COUCH ([Sir] ARTHUR [THOMAS])
The Workmanship of "A Midsummer night's
dream". FROM The Fortnightly Review,
1915. pp. [11.]   [1915]

390790

Quiller-Couch, Arthur Thomas Sir *works
relating to*

—GREG (W. W.)
Review [of] The Works of Shakespeare,
edited for the Syndics of the
Cambridge University Press by Sir A.
[T.] Quiller-Couch and J. D. Wilson.
Vol. 1. The Tempest. Reprinted
from the Modern Language Review.
Vol. 17.   [1922.]

554224

— Memorabilia [including a review of
"Paternity in Shakespeare" by Sir
A. T. Quiller-Couch]. IN Notes
and Queries, Vol. 163, No. 14. 1932.

401809

— Murry (J.M.) "Shakespeare's workmanship", by Sir A.[T.] Quiller-Couch.
[a review.] *From* The Criterion,1931.
pp.[7.]

                          [1931.]

390914

——Pollard (A.W.) [Review of] The Works
of Shakespeare. Edited for the
Syndics of the Cambridge University
Press by Sir A.[T.] Quiller- Couch
and J.D. Wilson. [Vol.1.] The Tempest.
In The Library, 4th series, Vol.2.

1922.

298823

—— TANNENBAUM (S. A.)
How not to edit Shakspere: a review
[of "The 'New' Cambridge Shakespeare",
edited by Sir A. Quiller-Couch and
J. D. Wilson.] FROM Philological
Quarterly, vol. 10. (Iowa) 1931.

442561

QUILTER (R.)
Four Shakespeare songs. Third set:
Who is Silvia?; When daffodils
begin to peer; How should I your
true love know?; Sigh no more,
ladies. Low voice. pp. 16.
[1933.]

412185

QUILTER (ROGER)
Hark! hark! the lark: song. Words
by Shakespeare [from Cymbeline];
music by R. Quilter. pp. 5. 1946.

588778

QUILTER (ROGER)
It was a lover and his lass: two-part
song. Words by Shakespeare [from
"As you like it" and] music by
R. Quilter. pp. 8. 1935.
Boosey's Modern Festival Series.
No. 139.

560296

QUILTER (ROGER)
Suite from [Shakespeare's] "As you
like it", for pianoforte. pp. 12.
1920.

519019

Quin, James *works relating to*

—— The Life of Mr. James Quin, comedian.
With the history of the stage from
his commencing actor to his retreat
to Bath; anecdotes of persons of
distinction, literature and gallantry;
[and] a copy of his last will and
testament. [With references to
Shakespearian performances.
port. 1766.

483579

—— MACQUEEN-POPE (W. [J.])
The Rivals of old Drury. [James
Quin v. Charles Macklin and David
Garrick. With references to
Shakespeare.] FROM Millgate and
Playgoer, Vol. 40. (Manchester)
port. illus. 1945.

561327

——MANDER (RAYMOND) and MITCHENSON (JOE)
The China statuettes of Quin as
Falstaff. IN Theatre Notebook,
Vol. 12. 1958.

584117/12

—— SKINNER (O.)
Bath and James Quin. [With refer-
ences to Shakespeare.] Illustrations
from photographs in the Theatre
Collection, Harvard College Library.
FROM Scribner's Magazine. 1924.

521314

QUINCY (J. P.)
A Difficulty in Hamlet. IN The
Atlantic Monthly, vol. 49. 1882.

50019

QUINLAN (MAURICE J.)
Shakespeare and the Catholic burial
service.
IN SHAKESPEARE QUARTERLY V:
pp. 303-306.
(New York) 1954.

605711

QUINN (ARTHUR HOBSON)
A History of the American drama from
the Civil War to the present day.
[With a bibliography, a list of American
plays, 1860-1936, and references to
Shakespeare. Revised edn.]
ports. illus. 1937.

475161

QUINN (A. H.) and BLACK (M. W.)
F. E. Schelling. IN SCHELLING (F. E.)
[presentation of his bust to the
University of Pennsylvania.]
pp. viii, 30. (Philadelphia)
frontis. bibliog. 1935.

438954

QUINN, DAVID BEERS
Sailors and the sea [: in Elizabethan
England]. IN SHAKESPEARE SURVEY 17.
(Cambridge) 1964

667822

QUINN (MICHAEL)
Providence in Shakespeare's Yorkist
plays.
IN SHAKESPEARE QUARTERLY X: 1.
pp. 45-52.
(New York) 1959.

605711

QUINONES, RICARDO J.
Views of time in Shakespeare.
FROM Journal of the History of Ideas,
Vol. 26, No. 3, July-Sept. 1965.
    pp. 327-352.   1965.

                        767204

Quinton (A. R.) illus.
BRADLEY (A. G.)
The Avon and Shakespeare's country.
With illustrations in colour by
A. R. Quinton.   3rd edn.   (Abridged)
                                1927.

                        369286

Quippe Qui. [pseud.] Shakspeare's
"Julius Caesar" critically examined.
From The Shirburnian, Vol. 2. 2nd
Series.

        [Sherborne]   1865.

                    556070

Quirk (C.J.) To Shakespeare's
England [: a sonnet]. In The
Month, Vol. 180.

                    1944.

                    562830

QUIRK (RANDOLPH)
Shakespeare's pronunciation [: a talk].
Producer: P. H. Newby. [Broadcast
9th December 1954.]   ff. 10.
    typescript.   1954.

                    665044

Quiz Books

── DENT, ALAN HOLMES
    How well do you know your Shakespeare?
    Forty sets of questions and answers.
                        1964.

                        667819

──GROSS (FANNY)
    Shakespeare quiz book: 2000 questions
    and answers on all of Shakespeare's
    plays.   (New York)   1959.

                        666249

──GROSS (FANNY)
    The Shakespearean review book [: quiz
    book].   (New York)   1961.
    [Apollo Editions]

                        666831

── MACKENZIE, ALEXANDER
    Shakespeare quiz book.   Decorations
    by I. T. Morison.   1964.
    Collins quiz books.

                        667947

── PHILLIPS (H.)
    Shakespeare [: questions and answers].
                        1947.
    News Chronicle "Quiz" Series.

                        583520

Quotations
see also **Almanacs; Birthday Books**
For selections and anthologies see ENGLISH
EDITIONS, Selections and Anthologies

── AYSCOUGH (S.)
    An Index to the remarkable passages
    and words made use of by Shakspeare:
    [Vol. 3 of Shakspeare's Dramatic
    works.]   1790.

                    16262

── BARTLETT (J.)
    The Shakespeare phrase book.
    (Boston, [Mass.])   1881.

                    474429

── BARTON (R.) [ed.]
    Lend me your ears: an anthology of
    Shakespearean quotations...familiar,
    and not-so-familiar. [1943.] 544558
    _____ Revised and enlarged edn.
                    1946.   583691

── BATEN (A. M.)
    The Philosophy of Shakespeare.
    [With an introduction by De W.
    McMurray.]   (Kingsport, Tennessee)
    ports.   bibliog.   1937.

                        481130

── BATEN (A. M.) [ed.]
    Slang from Shakespeare, with literary
    expressions.   1931.

                        392826

──The Beauties of poetry display'd.
    Containing observations on the differ-
    ent species of poetry and the rules
    of English versification. Exemplified
    by a large collection of beautiful
    passages [including some from Shakes-
    peare], etc.   2 vols.

                        1757.

                    496925

── BLANÁR (I.)
    Shakespearian quotations: [Hungarian
    and English text.]
    illus.   [1928]
    Edn. limited to 3,000 copies.

                        392695

── Bonner (E.) Giving them fits in
    Guildford, with suits from
    Shakespeare [: quotations from
    the plays.]

        (Guildford)   1903.
                    494448

── BROWNING (DAVID CLAYTON) ed
    Everyman's dictionary of Shakespeare
    quotations.   1953.   635396
    Everyman's Reference Library.
    _____ Illustrations selected and
    edited by P. Hartnoll.
                    1964.   667999
    Everyman's Reference Library.

BYSSHE (E.)
The Art of English poetry, containing
Rules for making verses: A Collection
of the most natural, agreeable and
sublime thoughts that are to be found
in the best English poets [including
extracts from the plays and poems of
Shakespeare]; A Dictionary of rhymes.
1710.

520709

COSULICH (G.) [ed.]
Did Shakespeare say that? Timely
quotations [from Shakespeare]
suitable for the use of twentieth
century speakers and writers,
arranged alphabetically according
to subjects. (New York)   1944.

558211

DARLINGTON (J.)
A Shakespearian vade-mecum: a
collection of colloquial expressions
and proverbial sayings, from the
works of Shakespeare.   [1891]

409496

Dennis (J.) Shakespeare's wise words.
[With quotations]. In The Leisure
Hour, 1892.

1892

115780

Dictionary of quotations from the
British poets.   Part the first,
Shakspeare.   2nd edn.   1835.

391942

Eastcott (R.) Quotations from Shakespear, proving his knowledge of
music, and the high opinion he
entertained of it.   In Eastcott (R.)
Sketches of the origin, progress and
effects of music.

(Bath)   1793.

543684

Enfield (W.) Exercises in elocution,
selected from various authors.
Intended as a sequel to The Speaker.
New edn., [with] Counsels to young
men, in a letter from a father to
his son. [Containing selections from
Shakespeare's plays.] Illus.

1804.

496007

Fox (H.J.) The Student's topical
Shakespeare : thirty-seven plays
analyzed and topically arranged.
New edn., revised and enlarged.

(Boston)   1884.

498115

FOXTON (W.)
Shakespeare garden and wayside
flowers, with appropriate quotations
for every flower: a guide to
Shakespeare flora.   pp. 37.
frontis.   1934.

435628

Hancock (D.S.) Meteorology in Shakespeare: an attempt to prove the
poet's success as an observer of
meteorological phenomena, by
quotations from his works. ff.48.
Typescript.

[1934]

431750

Hartnoll (F.) Treasures from Shakespeare. pp.66.

(Scranton,Pa.)   1886.

419849

Hope (Constance) A Rose from Shakespeare's garden. In The Month, Vol.94,
July- Dec.1899.

1899.

150079

HOPE (CONSTANCE)
Shakespeare and the song of a lark.
IN The Month, Vol. 94.   1899.

150079

LEWIS (WILLIAM DODGE)
Shakespeare said it: topical
quotations from the works of
Shakespeare selected and annotated
by W. D. Lewis, with an introduction
by W. P. Tolley.   (Syracuse)
port.   1961.

667065

LOTHIAN, JOHN M.
Shakespeare's charactery. A book of
'characters' from Shakespeare [:
selected quotations]. (Oxford) 1966.

illus.   756373

LYNCH (EVANGELINE)
Shakespeare streamlined: a comedy
in one act [of which most of the
dialogue is made up of quotations from
Shakespeare's plays].   pp. 20 [vi].
(Evanston, Ill.)   1944.

558681

[Marks (J.I.) ed.] Quotations from
Shakspeare. Manuscript.

[c.1880.]

542625

MARSDEN, L. L. M.
Shakespearian quotations in everyday
use: a key to their source and
context.   [New ed.]   1964.

667946

Morgan (A.A.) The Mind of Shakspeare,
as exhibited in his works. With
illustrations by Sir J. Gilbert.

1876.

469838

— OSBORN (E. B.) [ed.]
Shakespeare as sportsman [: quotations
from the plays.] IN Osborn (E. B.)
[ed.] Anthology of sporting verse.
1930.

438373

— Pensées choisies de William
Shakespeare. pp.96.
[French Booklets, No.17.]
[1916]

393764

— Philosophy of William Shakespeare.
2nd edn. 1860.

474434

— [REES (T. J.) ed.]
Shakespeare on Swansea men and
matters: a selection of quotations
from Shakespeare's works. pp. 52.
(Swansea) [1914]

555585

— ROUTLEDGE (E.) [ed.]
Quotations from Shakespeare.
[c.1885.] 488088
"Quotation" Series.
1892. 396030

— SEN (N. B.)
Thoughts of Shakespeare: a treasury
of thoughts collected from the complete poetic and dramatic works and
classified under subjects. Foreword
by Sir Tej Bahandur Sapru. (Lahore)
frontis. [1952.]

636328

— SEN (N. B.) ed.
Wit and wisdom of Shakespeare
[: quotations from plays, poems
and sonnets]. (New Delhi: New
Book Society of India)
illus. 1961.

668094

— Shakspeare hand-book. 1860.

57883

— Shakespeare through the alphabet:
[quotations]. In The Amateur
Theatre and Playwrights' Journal,
Vol.4, No.75.

1937.

467093

— STEARNS (C. W.)
The Shakspeare treasury of wisdom
and knowledge. (New York)
illus. 1878.

584484

— STEVENSON (BURTON EGBERT) ed.
The Standard book of Shakespeare
quotations, compiled and arranged by
B. Stevenson. [1953.]

641659

— Stevenson (B.[E.]) ed., Stevenson's
book of Shakespeare quotations, being
also a concordance & a glossary of
the unique words & phrases in the
plays & poems.

1938.

481636

— Thesaurus dramaticus. Containing
celebrated passages, etc., in the
body of English plays, antient and
modern, digested under topics.
[Including passages from Shakespeare's
plays.]
frontis. 2 vols. 1724.

435158

— VENKATASIAH (M.) [ed.]
Longer moral quotations from
Shakespeare. 2nd edn. 1927.
Pocket Wisdom Series.

399213

— VENKATASIAH (M.) [ed.]
Short moral quotations from
Shakespeare. 2nd edn. 1927.
Pocket Wisdom Series.

399212

— Vest Pocket Shakespearean Manual of
quotations, characters, scenes and
plays. (Baltimore, Md.) 1955.

665845

— VIHERVAARA (LYYLI) [ed.]
Elämän kudelma: Shakespearen säkeitä
kuukauden joka päivälle poiminut
Lyyli Vihervaara. pp. 73. (Helsinki)
1928.
English and Finnish text.

430918

— Westacott (C.A.) The Compassionate
onlooker, William Shakespeare, 1564-
1616 [: quotations from Shakespeare's
works interspersed with notes by the
compiler, showing Shakespeare's
attitude to animals.] pp.8.

— [1941.]
(United Humanitarian League and the World
League against Vivisection and for the Protec-
tion of Animals.)

530215

R. (A.)
[A Review of] Shakespeare in Germany,
1740-1815,[edited] by R. Pascal.
IN The Criterion, Vol. 17. 1937-38.

487675

R. (E. M.)
Mr. Beerbohm Tree's Mark Antony. IN
The Westminster Review, Vol. 150.
1898.

144830

R. (J. G.)
The Shakespeare stage in Munich [: a
performance of King Lear]. IN
Literature, Vol. 7. 1900.

155394

R. (V.)
Violet eyes and Shakespeare. IN
Notes and Queries, Vol. 162. 1932.

401808

R. (W.)
Observations on the character of
Hamlet. FROM The Westminster
Magazine [, Vol. 12]. [1784.]

562346

R. (W.) [of] S- Hall, Suffolk
[Commentary on Shakespeare's plays:
manuscript notes]. 1780.
A Selection from these notes was
printed in "The Gentleman's Magazine",
Vol. 50. 1780.
On permanent deposit by Lord Cobham.

667993

R. (W. C.)
The Shakespeare Head Press - removal
to Oxford. IN The British Printer,
Vol. 42, No. 252. 1930.

401563

Rabelais, François *works relating to*

— Brown (H.) Rabelais in English literature.
[With appendix,* "Shakespeare and
Rabelais", and list of works and
editions cited.]

(Cambridge.Mass.) 1933.

419877

RABKIN (NORMAN)
Coriolanus: The Tragedy of Politics.
IN Shakespeare Quarterly XVII: 3.
(New York) 1966.

pp.95-212. 605711

RABKIN, NORMAN
Shakespeare and the common understanding.
(New York) 1967.

767392

RABKIN, NORMAN
Structure, convention, and meaning
in 'Julius Caesar'. FROM Journal
of English and Germanic Philology,
LXIII, 2. April 1964, pp. 240-254.
1964.

668326

Rabkin, Norman
Troilus and Cressida: the uses of the
double plot.

IN Shakespeare Studies, 1. (Cincinnati,
Ohio) 1965.

750317

RABKIN, NORMAN
"Venus and Adonis" and the myth of love.
IN Pacific coast studies in
Shakespeare. Edited by W. F. McNeir
and T. N. Greenfield. (Eugene: Ore.)
1966.

768009

RABKIN, NORMAN, ed.
Approaches to Shakespeare [: 20th
century critical essays]. (New York)
1964.

668298

RABKIN (NORMAN) ed.

see also Bluestone (Max) and Rabkin
(N.) eds.

RACE (SYDNEY)
J. P. Collier and his fabrications:
early poetical miscellanies and
Shakespeare papers. IN Notes and
Queries, Vol. 198. 1953.

5421/198

[RACHMANINOV (SERGYEI VASIL'EVICH) ed.]
Scherzo from A Midsummer night's dream
[by F.] Mendelssohn. [Arranged as a]
piano solo [by S. V.] Rachmaninoff.
pp. 17. (New York) 1933.

585681

Racial Prejudice
see also Jews

— CLARK (ELEANOR G.)
Racial antagonisms in Shakespeare.
FROM Opportunity: journal of negro
life, Vol. 14, No. 5. (New York)
illus. 1936.

524576

— JONES (ELDRED)
Othello's countrymen: the African
in English Renaissance drama.
illus. 1965.

742543

— MASON (PHILIP) [psued. PHILIP WOODRUFF]
Prospero's magic: some thoughts on
class and race [suggested by "Othello"
and "The Tempest"]. 1962.

710708

— WITHINGTON (R.)
Shakespeare and race prejudice. IN
Elizabethan studies and other essays
[, by various authors], in honor of
George F. Reynolds. [With biblio-
graphical notes.] (Boulder, Col.)
1945.
Colorado University Studies. Series
B. Studies in the Humanities. Vol.2.
No. 4.

569202

Racine, Jean *works relating to*

— CLARK (A. F. B.)
Jean Racine. [With references to
Shakespeare, and a bibliography].
(Cambridge, Mass.)   1939.
Harvard Studies in Comparative
Literature, Vol. 16.

510087

— HAZLITT (W.)
Sir Walter Scott, Racine, and
Shakespeare. IN Hazlitt (W.) The
Plain Speaker: opinions on books,
men and things.   1870.

11317

— SAVORY (D. L.)
Jean Racine: a public lecture given
in the Great Hall of the Queen's
University of Belfast on Wednesday,
6th December 1939 [on the occasion of
the] tercentenary of Racine. With a
preface by Sir R. [W.] Livingstone.
[Including references to Shakespeare.]
pp. 31. (Oxford)   1940.

514038

— STENDHAL, [pseud. i.e. Marie Henri
Beyle]
Racine and Shakespeare. Translated
by G. Daniels. Foreword by
A. Maurois. [New York]   1962.

667548

— STOLL (E. E.)
Phèdre [: an appreciation of the play
by Racine including comparisons with
Shakespeare. English text.] Extrait
de la Revue anglo-américaine, décembre
1934. pp. [16.] (Paris) [?1934.]

569086

— WILLIAMS (E. E.)
Tragedy of destiny: Oedipus Tyrannus,
Macbeth, Athalie. [With bibliograph-
ical notes.] pp. 35. (Cambridge,
Mass.)   1940.

527201

Rackham (A.) illus.
LAMB (C. and MARY [A.])
Great stories from Shakespeare.
(Daily Sketch Publications)
[c.1935.]

542597

Rackham (Arthur) illus.
LAMB (CHARLES & MARY [A.])
Tales from Shakespeare.
1899.   426116
Temple Classics for Young People.
_____ 4th edn. 1903.   513555
_____ Another edn. 1905.   532932
_____ Everyman's Library.
1908.   514212
_____ Edn. limited to 750 copies,
signed by the artist, of which this is
No. 263.   1909.   472999
_____ Everyman's Library.
1909.   563662
Imperfect, pp. iii-iv wanting.
_____ Everyman's Library.
1910.   550463
_____ Another copy with different covers.
1910.   555509
_____ Everyman's Library.
1930.   473752
_____ Another copy. Titlepage differs
from above.   1930.   550464
_____ Another edn. [1938.]   488212
_____ Literature of Yesterday and To-day.
1941.   524614

RADCLIFFE (Mrs. [ANNE])
On the supernatural in poetry. [With
references to Shakespeare.] FROM
[The New Monthly Magazine, Vol. 16.]
[1826.]

563682

RADFORD (Sir GEORGE HEYNES)
Falstaff. IN [BIRRELL (A.)] Obiter
dicta [: essays. 1st series].
4th edn.   1884.   454160
_____ IN BIRRELL (A.) Collected essays.
2nd edn. Vol. 1.   1902.   457255

RADFORD (Sir GEORGE [HEYNES])
Falstaff. IN Life & death of Sir
John Falstaff [: extracts from The
Merry Wives of Windsor, Henry IV, Parts
1 and 2, and Henry V.] (Birmingham)
frontis.   [1923.]
[The Bedside Series]

486578

RADOFF (M. L.)
Influence of French farce in Henry V
and The Merry Wives. IN Modern
Language Notes, Vol. 48. (Baltimore)
1933.

413924

RAE, T. I.
Scotland in the time of Shakespeare.
(Ithaca, N.Y.)   1965.

illus. Folger booklets on Tudor
and Stuart civilization. 749828

RAECK (K.)
Shakespeare in the German open-air theatre.
IN SHAKESPEARE SURVEY 3. (Cambridge)
1950.

606026

RAGG (LONSDALE)
Trees and gardens in Shakespeare's
plays. IN The Tree lover, Vol. 3.
1939-41.

574705

RAGLAN ([F. R. SOMERSET, 4th Baron])
The Hero: a study in tradition,
myth and drama. [With references
to Shakespeare, and a bibliography.]
1936.

456185

Railton (Herbert) and Hull (Edward) illus.
LEE ([Sir] S.)
Stratford-on-Avon, from the earliest
times to the death of Shakespeare.
New edn.
 map.   1904. 352668
    New edn. 1909. 364784

RAINFORTH (Miss)
Reading[s] of Shakspere's play[s],
with incidental songs, at Welbeck
Lodge, and the Music Hall, Leamington,
Nov. 25th, [?1857]; Dec. 9th, 1857;
Oct. 4th, 1858. [Programmes.] IN
[A Collection of concert programmes
of performances held chiefly in Midland
towns. pp. 60.]   [1857-88.]

       519021

RAITH (JOSEF)
Die Historie von den vier Kaufleuten
(Frederyke of Jennen) [with High
German, Middle-German, Dutch and
English versions of the legend].
Die Geschichte von der vertauschten
Wiege (The Mylner of Abyngton) [with
English version]. (Aus Schrifttum
und Sprache der Angelsachsen Bd.4)
(Leipzig)
 facsimiles.   1936.

       612563

RAJAN (BALACHANDRA)
Paradise Lost & the seventeenth century
reader [including comparisons with
Shakespeare].   1947.

       585307

Raleigh, Walter Sir *works relating to*

 — BRADBROOK (M[URIEL] C.)
  The School of Night: a study in the
  literary relationships of Sir Walter
  Ralegh. [Including a chapter
  "Shakespeare, the School, and Nashe",
  and other references to Shakespeare.
  With a bibliography.] (Cambridge)
          1936.

       458019

 — CLARK (ELEANOR G.)
  Ralegh and Marlowe: a study in Elizabethan fustian [i.e. the trick adopted
  by dramatists of using an historical
  or mythological episode as a cloak to
  avoid the censor. With bibliographical
  notes]. (New York)
  illus. facsimile. genealogical tables.
         1941.

       537084

 — LOFTS (NORAH)
  Here was a man: a romantic history of
  Sir Walter Raleigh, his voyages, his
  discoveries & his queen. [With
  Shakespearian references.]
        1936.

      433147

 — OAKESHOTT (WALTER FRASER)
  Raleigh and "Love's labour's lost".
  IN Oakeshott (W. F.) The Queen and
  the poet [: Queen Elizabeth I and
  Sir Walter Raleigh].
  ports. illus. chronological table.
  facsimiles.   1960.

      694078

 — STRATHMANN (E. A.)
  The Textual evidence for "The School
  of Night" [: a phrase from Love's
  labour's lost, Act 4, Scene 3;
  arguing whether this spelling is
  correct, and if so, whether it refers
  to Sir Walter Raleigh's circle, The
  School of Night.] IN Modern Language
  Notes, Vol. 56. (Baltimore) 1941.

      533477

 — THOMPSON (E. [J.])
  Sir Walter Ralegh: the last of
  the Elizabethans. [With references
  to Shakespeare.]
  ports. maps. bibliog. 1935.

      435812

 — WRIGHT (LOUIS BOOKER) ed.
  Advice to a son: precepts of
  Lord Burghley, Sir Walter Raleigh
  and Francis Osborne. (Ithaca, N.Y.)
  bibliogs.   1962.
  Folger Shakespeare Library. Folger
  Documents of Tudor and Stuart
  Civilization.

      667175

 — see also MOORE (W. H.) Baconian
  studies.

RALEIGH ([Sir] WALTER [ALEXANDER])
Johnson on Shakespeare. IN
Raleigh ([Sir] W. [A.]) Six essays
on Johnson. (Oxford) 1927.

      582451

RALEIGH ([Sir] WALTER [ALEXANDER])
Shakespeare. Reprinted.
      1913. 496450
English Men of Letters.
    Reprinted 1923. 391941
    Reprinted 1924. 551129

Raleigh (Sir Walter Alexander) ed.
JOHNSON [SAMUEL]
Johnson on Shakespeare: essays and
notes selected and set forth with an
introduction by [Sir] W. [A.] Raleigh.
(Oxford)   1925. 419956
    Another edn. 1931. 395359

Raleigh, Walter Alexander Sir *works relating to*

 — BUCHAN (J.)
  Shakespeare and Raleigh [: a review
  of "Shakespeare", by Sir W. A.
  Raleigh]. IN Buchan (J.) Comments
  and characters. 1940.

      519668

Ralli (A.) A History of Shakespearian
criticism.   2 vols.

1932.

391408

RALLI (A.)
Later critiques [: Carlyle and
Shakespeare, Shakespearian
criticism, Shakespeare's songs, and
other essays with Shakespearian
references.]   1933.

411682

Ralli, Augustus *works relating to*

—— Garrad (B.) [Review of] A History of
Shakespearian criticism by A.Ralli.
In The Modern Language Review
Vol.28. 1933.

1933.

415705

—— Spencer (H.) [Review of] A History of
Shakespearian criticism by A.Ralli.
In Modern Language Notes, December,
1934.

(Baltimore)   1934.

428652

—— Thomson (C[lara] L.) A History of
Shakespearian criticism, by A. Ralli:
[a review]. In The Criterion, Vol.12,
1932.

1932-33.

414720

Ramello, Giovanni *works relating to*

—— GRAY (H. D.)
[Review of] Hamlet 1603 [: Vol. I of
Studi sugli apocrifi shakespeariani]
by G. Ramello.   IN Modern Language
Notes, Vol. 46.   (Baltimore) 1931.

397731

RAMPTON (BETTINE)
The Story of Sadlers Wells.
Produced by L. Perowne. [Broadcast]
Nov. 17th, 1942.   ff. 11.
  typescript.   1942.

539869

RAMSEY (JAROLD W.)
Timon's imitation of Christ.
IN Shakespeare Studies, 2. (Cincinnati,
Ohio)   1966.

761781

RAMSEY (T. W.)
On re-reading Twelfth Night.
IN Ramsey (T. W.) Antares [: poems].
pp. 64.   1934.
Macmillan's Contemporary Poets.

432070

RAMSLAND, CLEMENT
The Taming of the Shrew

For editions of this play see under
English Editions: The Taming of
the Shrew: Alterations &c.

RANALD, MARGARET LOFTUS
The Betrothals of 'All's well that
ends well'.   IN The Huntington
Library Quarterly, Vol. 26.
(San Marino, Cal.)   1963.

494029

RANALD (MARGARET LOFTUS)
The Indiscretions of Desdemona.
IN SHAKESPEARE QUARTERLY XIV: 2.
pp. 127-139.   (New York) 1963.

605711

RANALD, MARGARET LOFTUS
Monarch notes and study guides:
Shakespeare's "The Taming of the shrew".
(New York)   1965.
Monarch critiques of literature.

757012

RANALD, MARGARET LOFTUS
Review notes and study guide to
Shakespeare. Selected comedies. (New
York)   1964.

Monarch critiques of literature.
756283

RANALD, MARGARET LOFTUS
Shakespeare's 'Coriolanus'. (New York)
1965.

Monarch critiques of literature.
756294

RANALD, MARGARET LOFTUS
Shakespeare's 'The Taming of the shrew'.
(New York)   1965.

Monarch critiques of literature.
757012

RANALD, MARGARET LOFTUS
Shakespeare's 'The Winter's tale'.
(New York)   1965.

Monarch critiques of literature.
756295

RAND (FRANK PRENTICE)
The Over garrulous Iago.
IN SHAKESPEARE QUARTERLY I: 3.
pp. 155-161.
(New York) 1950.

605711

Randolph, Thomas *works relating to*

— TANNENBAUM (S. A. and DOROTHY R.)
Thomas Randolph (a concise biblio-
graphy). [With references to
Shakespeare.] ff. 24. (New York)
typescript. 1947.
Elizabethan Bibliographies.

583239

Ranjee G. Shahani *see* Shahani (R. G.)

RANK ORGANIZATION, LTD.
[Romeo and Juliet, adapted for the
screen and directed by R. Castellani:
photographs, publicity material and
script.]
typescript. [1954.]
Signed by Laurence Harvey.

665120

Rank Organization Ltd. *works relating to*

— JORGENSEN (PAUL A.)
Castellani's "Romeo and Juliet":
intention and response. IN The
Quarterly of Film, Radio and Television,
Vol. 10. (Berkeley, Cal.) 1955.

630462/10

— LEWIN (WILLIAM) ed.
A Guide to the discussion of the
[J. Arthur Rank Organization] technicolor
screen version of Shakespeare's
Romeo and Juliet. Reprinted from Audio-
Visual Guide, Dec. 1954. (Maplewood,
N.J.) pp. 12.
ports. illus.
Photoplay Studies.

1955.

665548

RANKE, LEOPOLD von
[Shakespeare: from] History of
England, Volume IV, Chapter 6.
IN LEWINTER, OSWALD, ed., Shakespeare
in Europe [by various authors].
1963.

667784

RANNEY (OMAR)
Antioch Shakespeare Festival.
IN SHAKESPEARE QUARTERLY VI:
pp. 453-454.
(New York) 1955.

605711

RANSFORD (ALFRED)
Grafton portrait of Shakespeare.
[With two notes by W. Jaggard.] IN
Notes and Queries, Vol. 166, January-
June, 1934. 1934.

422514

RANSFORD (ALFRED)
John Hall, Shakespeare's son-in-law,
and Hall of Idlicote. IN Notes and
Queries, Vol. 161. 1931.
For a reply to this article see
BROOKS (E. ST. J.)

388854

Ransom (J.C.) On Shakespeare's
language. From The Sewanee Review,
Vol.55. pp.[18].

(Sewanee,Tenn.)
1947.

597421

RANSOM (JOHN CROWE)
Shakespeare at sonnets. FROM The
Southern Review, Winter, 1938.
[Baton Rouge, La.] 1938. 506182
_____ IN A Casebook on Shakespeare's
sonnets. Edited by G. Willen &
V. B. Reed. 1964. 668299
Crowell Literary Casebooks.

Ransom (J.C.) The World's body: [stud-
ies in poetic theory; containing a
chapter "Shakespeare at sonnets" and
other Shakespearian references.]

(New York) 1938.

486874

RANSOME (CYRIL)
Short studies of Shakespeare's plots.
1898. 424799
_____ Another edn. 1911. 527351
_____ Another edn. 1924. 533157

RANSOME (CYRIL)
Short studies of Shakespeare's plots:
Richard II. pp. iii, [38]. 1899.

665288

RANSON (F. L.)
Hamlet. IN East Anglian Magazine,
Vol. 4. (Ipswich) 1939.

510779

RANSON (F. L.)
Lavenham, Suffolk [containing references
to Shakespeare's connection with Lavenham
and Edward de Vere, 17th Earl of Oxford].
Foreword by M. W. Douglas. pp. 79. [Ipswich]
illus. map. 1937.

557271

RANSON (F. L.)
Shakespeare was an East Anglian.
[With subsequent correspondence
on the same subject.] IN East
Anglian magazine, Vol. 2. (Ipswich)
ports. illus. 1937.

510777

RANSON (F. L.) ed.
Shakespearian page [: articles by
various authors chiefly relating to
the "Oxfordian" theory]. IN East
Anglian Magazine, Vol. 2. (Ipswich)
1937.

510777

Rape of Lucrece *see* Lucrece

RAPHAEL (MARK)
Songs: Shall I compare thee to a
summer's day? (Shakespeare).
pp. [4.]   1961.

666894

RAPPOPORT (R.)
The Theme of personal integrity in
"Othello", [from] "Theoria" No. 14.
pp. 12.   (Pietermaritzburg) 1960.

667030

RASCOE (B.)
Shakespeare the mirror.   IN Rascoe
(B.) Titans of literature: from
Homer to the present.   1933.

409882

RASHBROOK (R. F.)
Keats and others [including Shakespeare:
criticism of their poetry].   FROM
Notes and Queries [Vol. 192.] 1947.

587305

RASHBROOK (R. F.)
The Winter's tale, V, i, 58-60.   IN
Notes and Queries, Vol. 192.   1947.

588005

RATCLIFF (S. C.) and JOHNSON (H. C.) eds.
Warwick County Records, vol. 1:
Quarter Sessions Order Book, Easter,
1625 to Trinity, 1637.   [Including
entries relating to John Hall, Thomas
Nash, and Stratford-upon-Avon.]
Edited [with introduction] by S. C.
Ratcliff and H. C. Johnson.   With a
foreword by Lord Hanworth.   (Warwick)
ports.   illus.   1935.
Warwickshire County Council, Records
Committee.

436276

Ratcliffe (Desmond) ed.
ARNE (T. A.)
Blow, blow, thou winter wind.   Words
[from As you like it] by Shakespeare;
arranged for S.A.T.B. (unaccompanied)
by D. Ratcliffe.   pp. 4.   1949.

604297

RATHBONE (G.)
How sweet the moonlight sleeps:
two-part song.   Words [from
Merchant of Venice].   Music by
G. Rathbone.   pp. 8.   1935.

524587

RATHBONE GEORGE)
Orpheus with his lute: two-part
song.   Words from Shakespeare's
"Henry VIII".   Music by G.
Rathbone.   pp. [7].   [1951]

666739

RATHBONE (G.)
Silvia: a four-part song.   pp. 4.
                               1931.
(The Musical Times)

594183

RATHBONE (G.)
Silvia: four-part song.   Words
by Shakespeare [from "Two Gentlemen
of Verona".]   The Musical Times,
No. 1067.   pp. 4.   1932.

516570

RATHKEY (W. A.)
"Vex not his ghost" [: a fantasy on
King Lear.]   IN English, Vol. 2.
(Oxford)   1939.

518293

Rationalism and Free-Thought *see* Philosophy and Religion

RATSEY (GAMALIEL)
The Life and death of Gamaliel Ratsey;
a famous thief, of England, executed at
Bedford the 26th of March last past,
1605 [with] "Ratsey's repentance, which
he wrote with his owne hand when hee was
in New-gate" [: a poem; and] "Ratseis
ghost; or, The Second part of his madde
prankes and robberies".   [With references
to Hamlet. 1605.   With an introduction
by S. H. Atkins.]   1935.
Shakespeare Association Facsimiles, 10.

435650

RATTRAY (R. F.)
Bernard Shaw: a chronicle and an
introduction.   [With Shakespearian
references.]   1934.

415233

RATTRAY (R. F.)
Shakespear as seen to-day.
IN The Quarterly Review, Vol. 287.
bibliog.   1949.

38702/287

RAUZZINI (VENANZIO)
The Dirge in Cymbaline [Cymbeline].
Harmonized by Mr. Rauzzini. Performed
at the Bath Concerts, with universal
applause. (Printed by Goulding & Co.)
                            [?1805.]

pp.168-169.   167103

Raven (A.A.) A Hamlet bibliography
and reference guide. 1877-1935.
(Chicago, Ill.)   1936.
                            456933

RAVEN-HART (HESTER E.) and CHISMAN
(ISABEL)
Manners and movements in costume
plays.   [With a glossary and
Shakespeare references.]   [1934].

443979

Rawley, William *works relating to*

—Theobald (B.G.) Dr.Rawley's epitaph
deciphered [**to discover allusions**
to the Bacon-Shakespeare question].
pp.20. Port. Facsimile.

(Bath)   [1940.]

(Bacon Society)

531019

RAY (B.) and RÅY (Sir P. C.)
The Shakespearean puzzle: endeavours
after its solution.   Parts 1-17.
FROM The Calcutta Review, Nov. 1939-
1941.   (Calcutta)
bibliog.   533633

RAY (JOSEPH E.)
A Book of inns.   No. 9: Around
Shakespeare's country.   pp. xii, 68.
illus.   1948.

598082

Raybould (A.) Our Catholic Shakespeare. _From_ The Catholic World,
vol.135.
(New York)   1932.

441602

Raymond (W.O.) Motivation and charac-
ter portrayed in Othello. _In_
University of Toronto Quarterly,
Vol.17.

(Toronto)   1947.

596179

Raynes Park County School, Merton see
Merton, Raynes Park County School.

RAYSOR (T. M.)
The Aesthetic significance of
Shakespeare's handling of time.
FROM Studies in philology, Vol. 32.
(Chapel Hill, N.C.)
bibliog.   1935.

484077

Raysor (T.M.) Intervals of time and
their effect upon dramatic values in
Shakespeare's tragedies. _From_ The
Journal of English and Germanic
Philology, Vol. 37.

1938.

503676

RAYSOR (T. M.)
Some marginalia on Shakespeare by
S. T. Coleridge.   IN Publications
of the Modern Language Association
of America. Vol. 42.   (Menasha,
Wis.)   1927.

428362

Raysor (Thomas Middleton) ed.
[COLERIDGE (SAMUEL TAYLOR)]
Coleridge's Shakespearean criticism.
[With an introduction.]
2 vols.   1930.   375324
_____ Another edn.   1960.   666711

Rea (J.D.) Hamlet and the ghost
again. _From_ The English Journal,
vol.18.

(Chicago)   1929.

442566

Rea (J.D.) Shylock and the Processus
Belial. _From_ Philological Quarterly,
Vol.8.

(Iowa)   1929.

539440

READ (CONYERS)
The Government of England under
Elizabeth.   IN Life and letters in
Tudor and Stuart England.
illus.   1962.
Folger Shakespeare Library.

667762

READ (CONYERS)
[Review of] Shakespeare's "histories":
mirrors of Elizabethan policy, by Lily
B. Campbell.   IN The American Historical
Review, Vol. 52.   (New York)   1947.

586017

Read (Conyers) ed.
LAMBARD (WILLIAM)
William Lambarde and local government:
his "Ephemeris" and twenty-nine charges
to juries and commissions; edited by
C. Read.   (Ithaca, N.Y.)
bibliogs.   1962.
Folger Shakespeare Library.   Folger
Documents of Tudor and Stuart Civiliza-
tion [1].

667176

READ (Sir HERBERT EDWARD)
Thieves of mercy [: an imaginary
conversation between Hamlet and the
pirate captain].   (Imaginary conversations, 8).   [Broadcast] April 20th,
1947.   ff. 16.
typescript.   1947.   583264
_____ IN HEPPENSTALL (R.) ed.,
Imaginary conversations: eight radio
scripts.   1948.   595750

READ (Sir HERBERT [EDWARD]) ed.
Surrealism, edited with an introduction
by H. Read; contributions by A. Breton,
H. S. Davies, P. Eluard, G. Hugnet.
[With Shakespearian references.]
illus.   1936.

458567

READE (C.)
Peg Woffington: a novel.
1853.   510548
_____ With an introduction by
[H.] A. Dobson and illustrations
by H. Thomson.   1899.   387983

READE (HUBERT)
How did Calderón know Shakespeare's
plays?   IN The Westminster Review,
Vol. 160.   1903.

179434

Reading Shakespeare

—— Bamborough (J.B.) Introducing
Shakespeare (1) : Shakespeare
today. [Broadcast] 17th November,
1949. ff. [1,] 8. Typescript.

1949.

605272

—— BAYLISS (Sir W.)
A Shakespeare reading and the readers'
Shakespeare. IN Good Words, 1898.

1898.

144615

—— DUNN (MARTHA B.)
My Shakespeare progress: [the reading
of Shakespeare]. IN The Atlantic
monthly, Vol. 98. (Boston, [Mass.])

1906.

198449

—— FITCH (G. H.)
Comfort found in good old books. [With
a chapter called, Shakespeare stands
next to the Bible. With a bibliography.]
(San Francisco)
port. illus. facsimiles. [1916.]

404405

—— FLEMING (J. R.)
The Highway of reading: a help to the
right choice of books. [With a chapter
entitled "Shakespeare's world".]

1936.

467943

—— [GRIERSON (W.)]
How to read Shakespeare. 1. King Lear:
2. The Tempest: 3. Macbeth. 4. The
Problem of Hamlet. By The Enquiring
Layman. FROM John O'London's Weekly,
Outline Supplement, 1931. pp. [6.]

1931.

390554

—— HARDMAN (D.)
The Pleasures of reading Shakespeare.
FROM Cambridge Public Library record
and book-list. Vol. 10. (Cambridge)

1938.

479346

—— POCOCK (G. [N.])
Brush up your reading. Illustrated
by Anna Zinkeisen. [With a chapter
on Shakespeare, and bibliographies.]

1942.

533027

—— RIDLEY (M. R.)
On reading Shakespeare. pp. 31.

1940.

(British Academy. [30th] Annual
Shakespeare Lecture)

522285

—— ROMILLY (G.)
"Tomorrow and tomorrow and tomorrow"
[: reading Shakespeare while a
prisoner of war in Germany. Broad-
cast] 21 st April, 1949. ff. 4.
typescript.

[1949.]

605243

—— SLADE (F. E.)
On reading Shakespeare. FROM The
Poetry Review [Vol. 31.]

1940.

521315

—— SMITH (L. P.)
On reading Shakespeare.
bibliog. 1933.
For other editions of this work check
the main sequence under the author's
name.

403807

Readings and Recitals of Shakespeare

—— MR. J.H. LEIGH'S reading of Richard III:
opinions of the London press.

[c.1900.]

667380

—— MR. J.H. LEIGH'S Shakespearean readings
[from 8 plays]: a few press opinions.

[c.1900.]

667381

—— RAINFORTH['S] (Miss)
Reading[s] of Shakspere's play[s],
with incidental songs, at Welbeck
Lodge, and the Music Hall, Leamington,
Nov. 25th, [?1857]: Dec. 9th, 1857;
Oct. 4th, 1858. [Programmes.] IN
[A collection of concert programmes of
performances held chiefly in Midland
towns. pp. 60.]

[1857-88.]

519021

—— [Shakespeare Festival, Stratford-upon-
Avon. Public lectures and recitals
arranged by the Shakespeare Memorial
Theatre, the University of Birmingham,
Shakespeare's Birthplace Trust, the
British Council, the Shakespeare
Institute, 1950-] [Stratford-on-Avon]

[1950]

645712

—— Shakespeare Recitals (The). In
Poetry Review, Vol.29.

1938.

492632

—— SHAW (IDA)
The Value of the Shakespeare recitals
[: part of The Vocal interpretation
of poetry, a report on the Teachers'
Conference held on Sept. 11th, 1943].
IN The Poetry Review, Vol. 34. 1943.

560954

Rebellion and loyalty; or, The Two
thrones [: essays, including one
on Shakespeare.]   [1885.]
[Library of National Information
and Popular Knowledge]
                            405779

REBILLON-LAMBLEY (KATHLEEN)
  Shakespeare's French.   IN WILLIAMS
  (MARY) and ROTHSCHILD (J. A. de) eds.,
  A Miscellany of studies in Romance
  languages & literatures presented to
  Léon E. Kastner.   (Cambridge) 1932.

                            391235

Recent literature of the Renaissance,
edited by H. Craig [and others]
see Craig (Hardin) and others, eds.

Recitals, Shakespearian *see* Readings and Recitals of Shakespeare

RECORD OFFICE (PUBLIC), LONDON
  Shakespeare in the Public Records.
                      .   1964.

          illus. Public Record Office
  handbooks, No.5. H.M. Stationery Office.
                            667809

Records *see* Stratford-upon-Avon

Red Bull Theatre *see* London, Theatres — Red Bull Theatre

REDDAWAY, THOMAS FIDDIAN
  London and the Court [: in Elizabethan
  England].   IN SHAKESPEARE SURVEY 17.
  (Cambridge)   1964.

                            667822

REDDING (C.)
  The Fac-simile Shakspeare [: on
  Booth's 1862-64 reprint of the
  Jaggard folio].   FROM [The New
  Monthly Magazine, Vol. 133.]
                            [1865.]

                            558106

REDFERN (JAMES)
  "Hamlet".   At the New [featuring
  Robert Helpmann: a criticism].   IN
  The Spectator, Vol. 172.   1944.

                            552304

REDFIELD, WILLIAM
  Letters from an actor [concerning the
  Gielgud-Burton production of Hamlet,
  1964].   1967.

                            764771

REDGRAVE (GILBERT R.)
  Photographic facsimiles [in] "Facsimile"
  reprints of old books, by A. W. Pollard
  [and others.   With references to
  Shakespeare reprints].   IN The Library,
  Vol. 6.   1926.

                            329554

REDGRAVE (Sir MICHAEL SCUDAMORE)
  The Actor's ways and means.
  (University of Bristol, Department
  of Drama, Rockefeller Foundation
  Lectures, 1952-3.)   pp. 90.
  ports. bibliog.   1953.

                            636851

REDGRAVE Sir MICHAEL SCUDAMORE
  Dame Edith Evans: a birthday tribute.
  Introducing extracts from "As you
  like it".   Produced by C. Lefeaux.
  B.B.C. radio script broadcast
  8th February 1968.
  typescript.   1968.

                            768973

REDGRAVE (Sir MICHAEL SCUDAMORE)
  Mask or face: reflections in an
  actor's mirror.
  ports.   1958.

                            678116

REDGRAVE (Sir MICHAEL SCUDAMORE)
  Shakespear and the actors.   IN
  GARRETT (JOHN) ed., Talking of
  Shakespeare [: a selection from the
  lectures delivered at the annual
  course for teachers at Stratford,
  1948-1953].   1954.

                            641471

REDGRAVE (Sir MICHAEL SCUDAMORE)
  Shakespeare and the Public Schools.
  IN CARLETON (P.) ed., The Amateur
  stage: a symposium.   1939.

                            508149

Redgrave, Michael Scudamore Sir *works relating to*

____FINDLATER (RICHARD)
  Michael Redgrave, actor.   With an
  introduction by H. Clurman.   [With
  a list of performances.]
  ports.   illus.   1956.

                            656327

____THEATRE INCORPORATED
  Michael Redgrave [and] Flora Robson
  in The Tragedy of "Macbeth" [: a
  description of the Theatre Incorporated production and cast].   pp. [16.]
  [New York]
  ports.   illus.   [1948.]

                            598973

REDGRAVE (Sir MICHAEL SCUDAMORE),
BIRCH (FRANK) and HOPE-WALLACE (PHILIP).
Dissecting a play: discuss[ion]
with illustrations from Macbeth [by]
members of the Aldwych Theatre cast.
[Broadcast] 6th February, 1948.
ff. 28.
   typescript.   1948.

                593004

[REDINGTON (J.) Publisher
A Collection of plain sheets of
Shakespearian characters.] (Hoxton)
10 sheets.   [?1887.]

                568502

REDLICH (HANS FERDINAND) ed.
Musik um Shakespeare: Music around
Shakespeare. Altenglische Virginal-
musik: Old English music for
virginals. Piano solo. pp. 44.
(Wien)
   facsimile.   1938.

                628450

REED (A. A.)
A Catalogue of books on Shakespeare
and his times. pp. 32.
               [1932]

                393885

REED, ALFRED
A Sea dirge: madrigal for mixed voices.
[Full fathom five] S.S.A.A.T.B.B., a
cappella. (New York)   1965.

     Frank choral library.
        764589

REED (CAROL), FURSE (ROGER) and OLIVIER
([Sir] LAURENCE)
The Work of Roger Furse: the relation
of artist and director described in
three interviews. [With special
reference to "Hamlet".] IN Film
To-day books [1].
   ports. illus.   [1948.]

                589632

REED (E.)
Bacon and Shake-speare parallelisms.
(Boston [Mass.])   1902.
   Photograph with signature of author
inserted.

                526717

REED (EDWIN)
Bacon vs. Shakspere: brief for
plaintiff.
   ports. illus. bibliog. facsimiles.
               1899.

                415113

REED (EDWIN)
Brief for plaintiff. Bacon vs.
Shakespeare. [3rd edn.] pp. 37.
(Chicago)   1890.   537990
Popular Topics, No. 1.
Bears author's signature.
      5th edn.   1892.   431082

REED (EDWIN) ed.
Noteworthy opinions, Pro and Con.
Bacon v. Shakspere. pp. 79.
(Boston [Mass.])
   port.   1905.

                313647

REED (H.)
Lectures on English history and tragic
poetry as illustrated by Shakspeare.
[Edited with an introduction and
notes by W. B. Reed.] (Philadelphia)
   bibliog.   1855.

                569831

REED (H.)
Lectures on the British poets.
[With references to Shakespeare.
Edited by W.B.R. i.e. W. B. Reed.]
New edn.   [1857]

                424820

REED (HENRY) of Birmingham
The Great desire I had (Shakespeare
and Italy) [: a play. Broadcast]
Oct. 26th, 1952. ff. [ii], 44.
   typescript.   1952.

                630861

REED (HENRY) of Birmingham
Hamlet once more. [Broadcast]
17th August, 1948. ff. 6.
   typescript.   1948.

                596479

Reed (Henry) of Birmingham, ed.
LAFORGUE (JULES)
Hamlet; or, The Consequences of filial
piety: a moral legend. Translated
and adapted for radio by H. Reed.
Produced by D. Cleverdon. [Broadcast]
20th June [1954].
   typescript.   [1954.]

                665045

Reed, Isaac *works relating to*

—— DOBELL (P. J. & A. E.)
   A Catalogue of a remarkable collection
   of publisher's agreements, [etc.]
   including the agreements made by
   A. Pope, W. Warburton and I. Reed
   for the publication of their respective
   editions of Shakespeare. No. 66,
   1941. pp. 12. (Tunbridge Wells)
                1941.

                528685

—— DOWDEN (E.)
   Some old Shakespearians. (From
   Reed's MS. note-books). IN Transactions of the Royal Society of
   Literature of the United Kingdom.
   2nd series, Vol. 25.
   ports.   1904.

                185685

—— [Review of] The Plays of William
   Shakspeare, [with] notes by S. Johnson
   and G. Steevens, 2nd edn. revised and
   augmented [by I. Reed, 1778]. IN
   The Monthly Review, Vol. 62. 1780.

                1462

—— [Review of] The Plays of William
Shakspeare, [with] notes by S. Johnson
and G. Steevens.   3rd edn. revised
and augmented by [I. Reed,] 1785.
IN The Monthly Review, Vol. 75.   1786.

1478

—— [Review of] The Plays of William
Shakspeare, in 15 volumes, with the
corrections and illustrations of various
commentators.   To which are added notes,
by S. Johnson and G. Steevens.   The
4th edn.   Revised and augmented; with
a glossarial index by the editor of
Dodsley's Collection of old plays [i.e.
I. Reed. 1793.]   IN The British
Critic, Vol. 1.   1793.

22191

REED (ROBERT RENTOUL)
Hamlet, the pseudo-procrastinator.
IN SHAKESPEARE QUARTERLY IX: 2.
pp. 177-186.
(New York)   1958.
605711

REED, ROBERT RENTOUL
The Occult on the Tudor and Stuart
stage.   1965.

743530

REED (ROBERT R.)
The Probable origin of Ariel.
IN SHAKESPEARE QUARTERLY XI: 1.
pp. 61-65.
(New York)   1960.
605711

Reed (W.H.) Elgar.   [With reference
to his Falstaff, and a bibliography.] Ports. Illus.

1939.

(Master Musicians. New Series)
496482

Rees (J.)[pseud.] Colley Cibber,
The Life of Edwin Forrest, with
reminiscences and personal
recollections. Port.

(Philadelphia)   1874.

Extra portrait of E. Forrest inserted.
522846

REES (JAMES) [pseud. Colley Cibber]
Shakespeare and the Bible, to which
is added prayers on the stage,
proper and improper.   (Philadelphia,
Pa.: Claxton, Remsen & Haffelfinger)
1876.

668402

REES (JOAN)
An Elizabethan eyewitness of "Antony
and Cleopatra".
IN SHAKESPEARE SURVEY 6.   (Cambridge)
1953.

631770

[REES (T. J.) ed.]
Shakespeare on Swansea men and matters:
a selection of quotations from
Shakespeare's works.   pp. 52.
(Swansea)   [1914.]

555585

REESE (GERTRUDE C.)
The Question of the succession in
Elizabethan drama.   [Including
the plays of Shakespeare.]
IN University of Texas, Studies in
English, [Vol. 22].   (Austin, Texas)
bibliog.   1942.

542175

REESE (MAX MEREDITH)
The Cease of majesty: a study of
Shakespeare's history plays.
bibliogs.   1961.

666842

REESE (MAX MEREDITH)
Shakespeare and the welfare state.
pp. 34.
illus.   1953.

634860

REESE (MAX MEREDITH)
Shakespeare; his world & his work.
illus. map. bibliog.   1953.

631880

REESE, MAX MEREDITH
William Shakespeare. Illustrated by D.
Chalmers.   1963.

illus. map.   667697

Reeve (F.A.) Shakespeare as a "best
seller" in France : [a review of three
new editions.] In The Publishers'
circular and booksellers' record,
Vol. 150.

1939.

503477

Reeve (W.N.) Lady Macbeth. [A paper]
Read March 10, 1851. In Leicester
Literary and Philosophical Society.
Report of Council [1854-55] and a
Selection of papers read before the
Society since its formation.

(Leicester)   1855.
465753

REEVES (Hon. WILLIAM PEMBER)
The Dream imperial [: a poem]
IN GOLLANCZ ([Sir] I.) ed., A Book of
homage to Shakespeare.
ports. illus. facsimiles. [1916.]

264175

Reformation

—— WARPEHA (MARY J.)
The Effect of the Reformation on
the English eighteenth century critics
of Shakespeare (1765-1807): a
dissertation submitted to the Faculty
of the Graduate School of Arts and
Sciences of the Catholic University
of America. pp. 92. (Washington)
bibliog.   1934.

428594

Regent's Park Open Air Theatre *see* London, Theatres — Regent's Park Open Air Theatre

Rehan, Ada *works relating to*

—— WALBROOK (H. M.)
The Shrew that Shakespeare drew:
[Ada Rehan as Katherina.] FROM The
Nineteenth Century, 1929. pp. [7.]
[1929]

389232

Reichart (W.A.) Hauptmann's German
"Hamlet". Reprinted from Papers of the
Michigan Academy of Science, Arts and
Letters, Vol.16, 1931. pp.477-487.
[Ann Arbor, Mich.]   1932.

452670

Reichart (W.A.) A Modern German Hamlet.
From The Journal of English and
Germanic philology, vol.31.

(Illinois)   1932.

444159

REID (A.)
Twelve variations on the theme of
Caliban.   IN Reid (A.) Steps to
a viewpoint [: poems].   pp. 48.
1947.

585309

REID (A. STODART)
The Historical Macbeth.   IN The
Manchester playgoer: the organ of
the Manchester Playgoers' Club,
Vol. 1. (Manchester)   1910.

544467

REID, B.L.
The Last act and the action of 'Hamlet'.
FROM the Yale Review Vol.54. (New Haven,
Conn.)   1964.

pp.59-80.   748960

REID, B.L.
'Macbeth' and the play of absolutes.
FROM: the Sewanee Review, Vol.73, No.1.
1965.

pp.19-46.   748962

REID (ERSKINE) and COMPTON (HERBERT)
The Dramatic peerage, 1892: personal
notes and professional sketches of the
actors and actresses of the London
stage.   Revised and corrected by the
profession.   [With references to
Shakespearian productions.] 1892.

485293

Reid (F.)Illustrators of the sixties
[containing references to
illustrators of Shakespeare's
works]. Illus.

(Chiswick Press)

1928.

405696

Reid (F.) Retrospective adventures
[: essays, including one entitled
Some reflections on 'A Midsummer
Night's Dream", and stories].

1941.

525746

[REID (Hon. WHITELAW)]
London Commemorations, winter of 1908-9.
Remarks at the Shakespeare anniversary,
Stratford-on-Avon, 345th birthday,
April 23rd, 1909, [etc.]   pp. 40.
1909.

511625

REIK (THEODOR)
From thirty years with Freud.   Translated from the German.   [Including
a chapter entitled The Way of all flesh,
relating to The Tempest and Hamlet,
and other Shakespeare references.]
1942.
International Psycho Analytical Library,
No. 32.

533357

Reincarnation

—— RUTTER (O.)
The Scales of Karma [: the law of
Karma and reincarnation. Containing
references to Shakespeare]. [1940.]

520030

Reinhardt, Max *works relating to*

CARTER (H.)
The Theatre of Max Reinhardt.   [With
references to productions of
Shakespeare's plays.]
ports. illus. plan.   1914.

539800

COCHRAN (C. B.)
Max Reinhardt and the English theatre,
[with references to Shakespeare.
Broadcast] 26th Nov., 1943.
typescript.   1943.

547089

Engel (F.) Max Reinhardt : das Werden
und Wirken eines Kunstler. [With
references to Shakespeare and Shakespearian illustrations by E. Stern.]
In Mosse Almanach, 1921.

(Berlin)   1920.

526140

WARNER BROTHERS
A Collection of photographs relating
to Max Reinhardt's production of
[the film] "A Midsummer night's
dream" as presented by Warner Brothers.
[1935]

452246

[Warner Brothers.] A Midsummer Night's
Dream: script [of the film produced
by M. Reinhardt.]

(Burbank, [Cal.])   1934.

452942

Warner Brothers. Press book and American
and English publicity material
relating to Max Reinhardt's production
of [the film] "A Midsummer Night's
Dream", as presented by Warner Brothers
[1935]

452245

REINIUS (J.)
On transferred appellations of
human beings, chiefly in English
and German: studies in historical
sematology. [Vol.] 1. [With
references to names in Shakespeare.]
(Göteborg)   1903.

524195

Relics of Shakespeare

FLEMING (JOHN F.)
A Book from Shakespeare's library
discovered by William Van Lennep.
IN Shakespeare 400: essays by
American scholars on the anniversary
of the poet's birth.   Published in
co-operation with the Shakespeare
Association of America.
illus.   1964.

667803

HAINES (CHARLES REGINALD)
What personal relics have we of
Shakespeare?   FROM The Antiquarian
Quarterly, [Vol. 2.].   pp. [12].
illus.   [1926.]

638759

JAGGARD (W.)
The Siddons Shakespeare relics.
IN Notes and Queries, Vol. 161.
1931.

388854

MATTHEWS (A.)
The Siddons Shakespeare relics.
IN Notes and Queries, Vol. 161.
1931.

388854

Roe (F.) and Roe (F.G.) Shakespeare's
chair? pp. [4.] Illus. From
The Connoisseur, July 1940.

1940.

515936

The Shakespeare brooch : [description
of a brooch supposed to have been
the personal property of Shakespeare.] pp. [2.]

[c.1880.]

512903

Shakspeare relic [: Shakespeare's
jug].   IN Tewkesbury Yearly
Register and Magazine.   Vol. 2.
(Tewkesbury)   1850.

572149

Shakspeare's gloves. In Once a Week,
[1st Series,] Vol.10.

1864.

39290

TAIT (HUGH)
Garrick, Shakespeare, and Wilkes.
pp.[13]. Reprinted from "The British
Museum Quarterly", Vol.24, No. 3-4.
[1959]

667275

URWICK (Sir H.)
Gloves: with special reference to
those of Shakespeare.   FROM The
Connoisseur, 1927.   pp. [7.]
illus.   [1927.]

389655

Religion *see* Philosophy and Religion

Remarks on the character of Richard
the Third as played by Cooke and
Kemble.   pp. 55.   1801.

462480

Remarks upon Cymbeline.   FROM [The
Oxford Magazine,] Vol. 7.   [Oxford]
[1771.]

554723

Renaissance

— Allen (D.C.) The Degeneration of man
  and Renaissance pessimism. [With
  references to Shakespeare.] From
  Studies in Philology, Vol. 35.

[Chapel Hill, N.C.]   1938.

503671

— BAUGH (A. C.) CHESTER (A. G.) and
  SHAABER (M. A.)
  Renaissance and Elizabethan literature
  [: part of the article "American
  bibliography for 1944" (English language
  and literature section).   Includes
  Shakespeare items].   IN Publications
  of the Modern Language Association of
  America, Vol. 59.   (Menasha, Wis.)
                      1944.   560393
  ———   IN Vol. 61.   1946.   581301

— Bush (D.) The Renaissance and English
  humanism. [With references to
  Shakespeare.]

1941.

[Alexander Lectures in English, University of
          Toronto, 1939.]

533493

— CRAIG (H.)
  Renaissance ideal: a lecture on
  Shakespeare.   FROM University of
  North Carolina Extension Bulletin,
  Vol. 24.   (Chapel Hill, N.C.)
  bibliog.   1944.

577764

— DRAPER (J. W.)
  Shakespeare's Coriolanus: a study
  in Renaissance psychology.   FROM
  West Virginia University Bulletin.
  Philological Studies. Vol. 3.
  (Morgantown, W. Va.)
  bibliog.   1939.

552429

— FOLGER SHAKESPEARE LIBRARY, Washington,
  D.C.
  Society and history in the Renaissance:
  report of a conference held at the
  Folger Library.   pp. [vi], 65.
  (Washington)   1960.

667006

— HAYDN (HIRAM COLLINS)
  The Counter-Renaissance.   (New York)
  bibliog.   1950.

616497

— Morrow (D.) Where Shakespeare stood:
  his part in the crucial struggles
  of his day. With an introduction
  by G. Hicks [and bibliographical
  notes.] pp.89.

(Milwankee)   1935.

447816

— Ogg (D.) The Renaissance and Reformation.
  [With a reference to Shakespeare
  and the New Learning.] In Taylor
  (G.R.S.) ed.,Great events in history.

1934.

420461

— POPE (ELIZABETH M.)
  The Renaissance background of
  Measure for Measure.   IN SHAKESPEARE
  SURVEY 2.   (Cambridge)
  bibliog.   1949.

598403

— SYMONDS (J. A.)
  The Drama of Elizabeth and James
  considered as the main product of
  the Renaissance in England.   [With
  references to Shakespeare.]   IN
  MARLOWE (C.) [Plays].   Edited by
  [H.] H. Ellis.
  port.   illus.   1902.
  The Mermaid Series.
  Large paper copy.

389466

— WATSON (CURTIS BROWN)

  Shakespeare and the Renaissance concept
  of honor. Bibliog. (Princeton, N.J.)
                            1960.

666749

— Young (S.) Shakspeare and the Venetians
  [: Shakespeare's work viewed in the
  light of some of the paintings of
  the Renaissance]. In Theatre Arts
  Monthly, Vol.14. Illus.

(New York)   1930.

379892

— see also CRAIG (HARDIN) and others
                        Works edited by:-

RENAN, JOSEPH ERNEST
Caliban: suite de La Tempête

For editions of this play see under
English Editions: The Tempest:
Alterations &c.

RENDALL (GERALD HENRY)
Arthur Golding, translator - personal
and literary - Shakespeare and Edward
de Vere [: a review of An Elizabethan
Puritan, Arthur Golding, by L. T.
Golding].   FROM The Essex Review,
Vol. 50.   pp. 108-113.   (Colchester)
                          1941.

541336

RENDALL (GERALD HENRY)
"Ashbourne" portrait of Shakespeare.
pp.16.   (Colchester)
   illus.   [1940.]

516325

RENDALL (G. H.)
Ben Jonson and the First Folio
edition of Shakespeare's plays.
[Containing references to the
Countess of Pembroke.]   pp. 23.
(Colchester)
   port.   1939.

507045

Rendall (G.H.) Personal clues in
   Shakespeare poems & sonnets [,
   relating to Edward de Vere].

1934.

426741

RENDALL (GERALD HENRY)
Shake-speare: handwriting and
spelling [as evidence of the De Vere
authorship of the Shakespearian
plays and poems].   pp. 55.
   facsimiles.   1931.

415238

RENDALL (GERALD HENRY)
Shakespeare in Essex and East Anglia
[: an essay dealing with the authorship of the plays, with particular
reference to 2 Henry VI and Cymbeline.
With bibliographical references].
pp. 13.   [Colchester]   [1944.]

556041

RENDALL (V.)
Wild flowers in literature [: an
anthology, containing quotations
from Shakespeare.]
   bibliog.   1934.

419646

RENDALL (VERNON) [ed.]
The Way of a man with a maid: an
anthology of courtship and wooing.
[Containing extracts from Shakespeare's
plays and sonnets].   1936.

459292

RENDLE (W.)
Old Southwark and its people.
[With references to Shakespeare.]
   illus. bibliog. plans. 1878.

507056

[RENNELL] (J. R. RODD, [1st Baron])
The Tercentenary of Shakespeare's
death - 1916 [: a sonnet].
IN GOLLANCZ ([Sir] I.) ed., A Book of
homage to Shakespeare.
   ports. illus. facsimiles. [1916.]

264175

RENO (RAYMOND H.)
Hamlet's quintessence of dust.
IN SHAKESPEARE QUARTERLY XII: 2.
   pp. 107-113.
(New York) 1961.

605711

RENSHAW (C[ONSTANCE] A.)
Freeman of the hills [: poems,
including a poem "Shakespeare knew".]
(Oxford: Shakespeare Head Press)
                                 1939.

499246

RENSHAW (C[ONSTANCE] A.)
Shakespeare.   IN Renshaw (C. A.)
Lest we forget [: poems].   pp. xi,
83.   (Oxford: Shakespeare Head
Press)   1937.

513982

RENTOUL (Sir GERVAIS)
Sometimes I think: random reflections
and recollections.   [With references
to Shakespeare.]
   port.   1940.

515422

RENTOUL (Sir G.)
This is my case: an autobiography.
[With references to Shakespearean
performances by the Oxford University
Dramatic Society.]
   ports. illus.   1944.

551873

RENWICK (WILLIAM LINDSAY)
[Review of] The Love-game comedy by
D. L. Stevenson.   IN The Review of
English Studies, Vol. 23.   (Oxford)
                                 1947.

318239/23

Repetition in Shakespeare's plays

— KREIDER (P. V.)
   Repetition in Shakespeare's plays.
   (Princeton: University of
   Cincinatti)
   bibliog.   1941.

529464

Report of the testimonial and address
to the Rev. Dr. [J.] A. Nicholson, in
connection with the Shakespeare-Bacon
Controversy, presented on behalf of
the subscribers by the Rt. Hon. Viscount
Peel, at Leamington, Oct. 16th, 1895:
extracts from the press.   pp. 8.
(Leamington)   1895.

396571

REPUBLIC PICTURES CORPORATION
[Orson Welles' Mercury production of
"Macbeth".   Script, publicity
material and photographs.] [1949.]

641789

Reputation of Shakespeare
see also **Allusions to Shakespeare; Influence and Comparisons; Jubilees and Commemorations** *and under the names of foreign countries*

—— Bardolatry abroad [: foreign interest in, and love of, Shakespeare]. IN The Times Literary Supplement, 1946.
1946.

580183

—— BROWN (I.[J.C.]) and FEARON (G.) Amazing monument: a short history of the Shakespeare industry. Ports. Illus.
1939.

497289

—— EVANS (G. B.) A Seventeenth-century reader of Shakespeare['s plays. With bibliographical notes]. IN The Review of English Studies, Vol. 21. (Oxford)
[1945.]

570955

—— HALLIDAY (FRANK ERNEST) The Cult of Shakespeare. Ports. Illus. Facsimiles. Bibliog.
1957.

665705

—— HARBAGE (ALFRED BENNETT) Shakespeare and the myth of perfection. IN McMANAWAY (JAMES GILMER) ed., Shakespeare 400: essays by American scholars on the anniversary of the poet's birth. Published in co-operation with the Shakespeare Association of America.
illus. 1964.

667803

—— LANCASTER (H. C.) The Alleged first foreign estimate of Shakespeare. [With bibliographical notes.] IN Modern Language Notes, Vol. 63. (Baltimore, Md.) 1948.

439157/63

—— MARDER, LOUIS His exits and his entrances: the story of Shakespeare's reputation. (Philadelphia, Pa.) 1963.

667597

—— MORGAN (PAUL) Our Will Shakespeare' and Lope de Vega: an unrecorded document. IN SHAKESPEARE SURVEY 16.
illus. 1963.

667523

—— The Shakespeare industry. IN Harper's Magazine, Vol. 179.
1939.

509706

—— SPENCER (TERENCE JOHN BEW) The Tyranny of Shakespeare. (Annual Shakespeare Lecture of the British Academy, 1959) pp. [19.]
bibliog. [1959.]

666610

Research *see* Study and Teaching

Return from Parnassus [Pt. 2]; or, The Scourge of Simony, [1606]. Anon. [Dramatic satire on contemporary poets including Shakespeare.] IN HAWKINS (T.) [ed.] The Origin of the English drama, Vol. 3. (Oxford) 1773. 2796
—— IN HAZLITT (W. C.) [ed.] A Select collection of old English plays. 4th edn. Vol. 9. 1874. 19290

The Return from Parnassus: [Pts. 1 & 2. Dramatic satire on contemporary poets including Shakespeare.] IN The Pilgrimage to Parnassus with the two parts of The Return from Parnassus. Edited by W. D. Macray. (Oxford)
1886.

98444

The Return from Parnassus, Part 1, 1597. [From the Rawlinson MS. D. 398. Dramatic satire on contemporary poets, including Shakespeare.] Edited by J. S. Farmer. 1912. Tudor Facsimile Texts, [Folio Series, Vol. 9.]

258901

The Return from Parnassus, 1606: [Pt. 2.] Anon. [Dramatic satire on contemporary poets, including Shakespeare.] Edited by J. S. Farmer. 1912. Tudor Facsimile Texts, [Vol. 91.]

258841

The Return from Parnassus [Pt. 2]; or, The Scourge of Simony 1606. [Dramatic satire on contemporary poets including Shakespeare.] IN SCHELLING (F. E.) ed., Typical Elizabethan plays. (New York)
frontis. 1926.

332001

RETZSCH ([FRIEDRICH AUGUST] MORITZ) Gallerie zu Shakespeare's dramatischen Werken. 1. Lieferung: Hamlet. Mit C. A. Böttiger's Andeutungen, herausgegeben von E. Fleischer. (Leipzig)
1828. 471794
This edn. has an English title-page and English descriptions to plates.

RETZSCH ([F. A.] M.) Gallerie zu Shakspeare's dramatischen Werken. 2te Lieferung: Macbeth. Mit C. A. Böttiger's Andeutungen. Herausgegeben von E. Fleischer. (Leipzig) 1833.

471795

RETZSCH ([F. A.] M.)
Gallerie zu Shakspeare's Dramatischen
Werken; Zweite Lieferung: Macbeth,
mit Andeutungen von C. A. Böttiger,
Deutsch, und in englischer Uebersetzung
von F. Shoberl.   2te Auflage.
Herausgegeben von E. Fleischer.
pp. [74].   (Leipzig)
illus.   1838.

435600

RETZSCH ([F. A.] M.)
Gallerie zu Shakspeare's dramatischen
Werken.   (Leipsig)
8 vols.   [?1840.]
1. Hamlet.   2. Macbeth.   3. Romeo
und Julia.   4. König Lear.   5. Der
Sturm.   6. Othello.   7. Die Lustigen
Weiber von Windsor.   8. König
Heinrich IV.
Similar to 43395 but with covers to
each part.

559487

RETZSCH ([F. A.] M.)
Gallery to Shakspeare's dramatic works.
In Outlines.   (Leipsic)
                    1847.   559486
German and English text.

RETZSCH ([F. A.] M.)
Gallery to Shakspeare's dramatic works.
In Outlines.   [With] explanations by
C. A. Boettiger, C. B. von Miltitz
[and] H. Ulrici.   (Leipsic)
2 vols.   1847.   164411-2

RETZSCH ([F. A.] M.)
Gallery to Shakspeare's Dramatic Works.
In Outlines.   2nd edn.   (Leipsic)
                    1860.   403289
_____ Explanations by C. A. Boettiger,
C. B. von Miltitz [and H. Ulrici.
[German and English text.]   2nd edn.
(Leipsic)   1860.   402832

RETZSCH (FRIEDRICH AUGUST
                    MORITZ)

The Merry Wives of Windsor [:
illustrations of scenes, with explanations
by H. Ulrici. Edited by E. Fleischer.
German and English Texts]. (Outlines
to Shakspeare. 7th Series.) pp.34.
13 plates.   1844.

311413

RETZSCH (FRIEDRICH AUGUST MORITZ)
Outlines to Shakespeare's dramatic
works, designed and engraved by
M. Retzsch.   4th edn., with a bio-
graphical sketch and explanations.
(Leipzig)   1878.

462960

Retzsch, Friedrich August Moritz *works relating to*

___ Retzsch's Outlines to Hamlet [: a
review].   IN The Foreign Quarterly
Review, Vol. 2.   1828.

29741

___ Retzsch's Outlines - Macbeth [: a
review].   IN The Foreign Quarterly
Review, Vol. 12.   1833.

29751

___ Retzsch's Outlines [to Macbeth, Hamlet
and Romeo and Juliet: a review].
IN The Foreign Quarterly Review,
Vol. 18.   1837.

29757

Revels Office

___ Boas (F.S.) Queen Elizabeth, the Revels
Office and Edmund Tilney. [With
references to Shakespeare]. pp.27.

(Oxford)   1938.

(Elizabeth Howland Lectures, 1937.)

481919

___ EDINBOROUGH (ARNOLD)
The Early Tudor Revels Office.
IN SHAKESPEARE QUARTERLY II: 1.
pp. 19-25.
(New York)   1951.

605711

___ FEUILLERAT (A.) ed.
Documents relating to the Revels at
Court in the time of King Edward VI
and Queen Mary.   (The Loseley MSS.)
With [preface], notes and indexes by
[the editor.]   (Materialien zur
Kunde des älteren englischen dramas,
Band 44)   1914.

400002

___ PATERSON (MORTON)
The Stagecraft of the Revels Office
during the reign of Elizabeth.
IN PROUTY (CHARLES TYLER) ed.,
Studies in the Elizabethan theatre,
[by various authors.]   [Hamden, Conn.]
illus. plans. bibliog. 1961.

667053

___ RECORD OFFICE (PUBLIC), LONDON
Shakespeare in the Public Records.
                    1964.

illus. Public Record Office
handbooks, No.5. H.M. Stationery Office.
                    667809

___ SISSON (C. J.) ed.
Thomas Lodge and other Elizabethans.
[Containing chapters on Sir George
Buck, Master of Revels.]
(Cambridge, [Mass.])
illus. plans. pedigrees. 1933.

408148

___ TANNENBAUM (S. A.)
Shakspere studies.   3. More about
the forged Revels Accounts
[attributed to Peter Cunningham.]
pp. 37.   (New York)   1932.

437497

Revenge

— ELLIOTT (GEORGE ROY)
   Scourge and minister: a study of
   "Hamlet" as tragedy of revengefulness
   and justice.   (Durham, N.C.)   1951.
   Duke University Publications.
                              617315

— PROSSER, ELEANOR
   Hamlet and revenge [: the conflict
   between obedience and conscience in
   the light of Elizabethan attitudes].
                              1967.

                              766094

— Simpson (P.) The Theme of revenge
   in Elizabethan tragedy. pp.38.

                              [1935]

(British Academy Annual Shakespeare Lecture,
                              1935.)

                              438945

A REVIEW OF ENGLISH LITERATURE
   Shakespeare number. Guest editor
   K. Muir. V : 2, April 1964.   1964.

                        697306/64

REW (Sir ROBERT HENRY)
   Farming in Shakespeare's time.   IN
   The Nineteenth Century and After,
   Vol. 99.   1926.

                              329555

REXA (DEZSO)
   Shakespeare in Hungary.   FROM Hungary
   Illustrated: a review of Hungary's
   past and present.   (Budapest)   1929.

                              602803

REYNOLDS (ERNEST RANDOLPH)
   Early Victorian drama (1830-1870).
   [With references to Shakespearean
   productions and with a bibliography.]
   (Cambridge)   1936.

                              458551

REYNOLDS (E. [R.])
   Verdi's "Otello" and "Falstaff".
   FROM The Monthly Musical Record,
   Jan., 1936.   1936.

                              446500

Reynolds (G.F.) Elizabethan stage
   conditions : talk [broadcast]
   18th July 1949. ff.8. Typescript.
   (Shakespeare and his world, 4).

                              1949.

                              605266

REYNOLDS (GEORGE FULLMER)
   Hamlet at the Globe.
   IN SHAKESPEARE SURVEY 9.   (Cambridge)
                              1956.

                              665210

REYNOLDS (GEORGE FULLMER)
   Mucedorus, most popular Elizabethan
   play?   IN Studies in the English
   Renaissance drama, edited by Josephine
   W. Bennett [and others].   1959.

                              684756

REYNOLDS (GEORGE FULLMER)
   [Review of] The Globe Playhouse: its
   design and equipment, by J. C. Adams.
   FROM The Journal of English and
   Germanic Philology, Vol. 42.   (Urbana,
   Ill.)   1943.

                              568673

REYNOLDS (GEORGE FULLMER)
   [Review of] Shakespeare's audience,
   by A. Harbage.   IN Modern Language
   Quarterly, Vol. 3.   (Seattle)   1942.

                              544203

REYNOLDS (GEORGE FULLMER)
   Some principles of Elizabethan staging:
   a dissertation [containing references
   to Shakespeare] submitted to the
   Faculty of the Graduate School of Arts
   and Literature in candidacy for the
   degree of Doctor of Philosophy
   (Department of English).   (Chicago:
   University of Chicago)   1905.
   This is W. J. Lawrence's copy, interleaved with manuscript notes.
                              500861

REYNOLDS (GEORGE FULLMER)
   The Staging of Elizabethan plays at
   the Red Bull Theater, 1605-1625.
   [Containing references to Shakespeare.
   With a bibliography.]   (New York)
                              1940.
   Modern Language Association of America.
   General Series, 9.
                              514989

REYNOLDS (G. F.)
   Troilus and Cressida on the Elizabethan
   stage.   IN McMANAWAY (J. G.),
   DAWSON (G. E.) and WILLOUGHBY (E. E.)
   eds., Joseph Quincy Adams memorial
   studies.   (Washington)
   bibliog.   1948.

                              596748

REYNOLDS, GEORGE FULLMER
   Two conventions of the open stage
   (as illustrated in King Lear?).
   FROM Philological Quarterly, vol. XLI,
   no. 1.   1962.

                              668390

REYNOLDS (GEORGE FULLMER)

   The Voice of Shakespeare. FROM
   University of Colorado Studies,
   Series in Language and Literature,
   No.6.pp.[ii]12. (Boulder,Col.)
                              1957.

                              665716

REYNOLDS (GEORGE FULMER)
   Was there a 'tarras' in Shakespeare's
   Globe?   IN SHAKESPEARE SURVEY 4.
   (Cambridge)   1951.

                              615854

REYNOLDS (GEORGE FULLMER)
What a theatre for Shakespeare should be.
IN SHAKESPEARE QUARTERLY I: 1.
pp. 12-17.
(New York)   1950.

    605711

REYNOLDS (GEORGE FULLMER)
William Percy and his plays, with a
summary of the customs of Elizabethan
staging.   [With references to the
production of Shakespeare's plays.]
Reprinted for private circulation from
Modern Philology, Vol. 12.   pp. [20.]
        1914.   498126
_____ Another copy.   Bears manuscript
notes by W. J. Lawrence.
        1914.   523726

REYNOLDS (GORDON)
Adventures in music: "A Midsummer
Night's Dream" [by F. Mendelssohn.
Broadcast] 20th February 1951.
ff. 11.
  typescript.   1951.

    616420

REYNOLDS (Sir JOSHUA)
Portraits: character sketches of Oliver
Goldsmith, Samuel Johnson, and David
Garrick, with other manuscripts of
Reynolds recently discovered among
the private papers of James Boswell.
Prepared for the press with intro-
ductions and notes by F. W. Hilles.
  ports. illus. facsimiles. bibliog. 1952.
Yale Editions of the Private Papers of
James Boswell.

    627913

REYNOLDS (LOU AGNES) and SAWYER (PAUL)
Folk medicine and the four fairies of
A Midsummer-Night's Dream.
IN SHAKESPEARE QUARTERLY X: 4.
pp. 513-521.
(New York)   1959.

    605711

Reynolds, William *works relating to*

—— WHITFIELD (CHRISTOPHER)
  The Kinship of Thomas Combe II,
  William Reynolds and William
  Shakespeare.   pp. 25.   (Newnham)
    genealogical tables.   1961.
  One of 100 copies printed by I. Bain
  at the Laverock Press.
        667104

Rhead (Louis) illus.
  LAMB (CHARLES and MARY)
  Tales from Shakespeare.   (New York)
          1918.   276032
  _____ Another edn.   [1926]   363006
  _____ Another edn.   [1938]   488210

Rhead (Louis) and Schoonover (Frank Earle)
illus.
  LAMB (CHARLES and MARY)
  Tales from Shakespeare.   [With a
  preface by L. Rhead.]   (New York)
        1918.

    394332

RHEDECYNIAN [pseud.]
Shakespeare, Handel and Gervinus.
FROM Notes and Queries, 1936.
        1936.

    462916

Rhetoric *see* Oratory and Rhetoric

Rhodes (Marion) Shakespearian Company,
Huddersfield <u>see</u> Huddersfield.

RHODES (R. C.)
Harlequin Sheridan: the man and the
legends.   [With Shakespearean
references.]
  illus.   bibliog.   1933.

    409056

Rhodes (R.C.) Much ado about nothing
  at Oxford,1606. <u>From</u> The Shakespeare
  Review, Vol.1.
        1928.

    467394

RHODES (R. C.) and others
Newspaper cuttings relating to Shakespeare,
Sheridan, etc. by R. C. Rhodes and others.
        [1922-30.]

    483543

Rhodes, Raymond Crompton *works relating to*

—— The First Folio [: a review of
  "Shakespeare's First Folio", by
  R. C. Rhodes.]   FROM The Contemporary
  Review, Literary Supplement, 1923.
  pp. [3.]   [1923]

    389223

Rhyme *see* Versification

RHYS (A.)
The Technical achievement of
Shakespeare's sonnets.   IN The
Poetry Review, Vol. 39.   1948-9.

246749/39

RHYS (E.)
"Julius Caesar": on the writing of
the play.   IN Her Majesty's Theatre.
Souvenir: Julius Caesar, 1898.
pp. [24.]
 illus.   1898.
The West-End Review.

583071

RHYS (ERNEST)
Shaw versus Shakespeare.   IN The New
Statesman and Nation, Vol. 3. (N.S.)
Jan.-June, 1932.   1932.

396297

Rhys ([Mrs.] Grace) Shakespeare and
Essex : the real Hamlet. In The
Nineteenth century and after, Vol.73.

1913.

243292

Ribbon *see* Shakespeare Riband

RIBNER (IRVING)
The English history play in the age of
Shakespeare. Bibliog. (Princeton,N.J.)
1957.

674365

RIBNER (IRVING)
The Gods are just: a reading of King
Lear. [From] The Tulane Drama Review.
Vol.2, No.3. pp.[21]. Bibliog. (New
Orleans, La.)   [1958]

666584

RIBNER, IRVING
 Julius Caesar: an outline guide to the
 play. (New York)   1964.

 Barnes & Noble focus books.
743622

RIBNER (IRVING)
Lear's madness in the nineteenth
century.   Reprinted from the
Shakespeare Association Bulletin,
Vol. 22, July 1947.   pp. [13.]
 bibliog.   [1947.]

666587

RIBNER (IRVING)
Macbeth: the pattern of idea and action.
Reprint from Shakespeare Quarterly,
Vol.10, Spring 1959. (Shakespeare
Association of America) pp.[14]
Facsimile. Bibliogs.   [c.1960.]

666585

RIBNER (IRVING)
 Marlowe and Shakespeare. IN
 Shakespeare Quarterly XV: 2. pp.41-53.
 (New York)   1964.

605711

RIBNER (IRVING)
Othello and the pattern of Shakespearean
tragedy. Reprinted from Tulane
University. Tulane Studies in English.
Vol.5. pp.[14]. Bibliogs. (New Orleans,
La.)   1955.

666589

RIBNER (IRVING)
Patterns in Shakespearian tragedy.
1960.

666641

Companion volume, entitled "Jacobean
tragedy" Catal. No. 705790.

RIBNER (IRVING)
Political issues in Julius Caesar.
Reprinted from The Journal of English
and Germanic philology. Vol.56, No.1.
pp.[13]. Bibliogs. (Urbana, Ill.)
1957.

666586

RIBNER (IRVING)
 The Political problem in Shakespeare's
 Lancastrian tetralogy.   IN Studies in
 Philology, Vol. 49.   (Chapel Hill,
 N.C.)   1952.

554520/49

RIBNER (IRVING)
 Shakespeare and legendary history:
 Lear and Cymbeline.   Reprint from
 Shakespeare Quarterly, Vol. 7,
 Winter 1956.   (Shakespeare Associa-
 tion of America)   pp. [6].
 bibliogs.   [?1957.]

666588

RIBNER (IRVING)
 Shakespeare criticism 1900-1964.
 IN BLOOM (EDWARD A.) ed., Shakespeare
 1564-1964: a collection of modern
 essays by various hands.   (Providence,
 R.I.)   1964.
 Brown University bicentennial
 publications.

744437

RIBNER (IRVING)
Shakespeare's history plays revisited. IN
Hommage a Shakespeare: Bulletin de
la Faculté des Lettres de Strasbourg.
43e année, No 8, mai-juin 1965.
 illus.   766822

RIBNER (IRVING)
Then I denie you starres: a reading
of Romeo and Juliet. IN Studies in
the English Renaissance drama, edited
by Josephine W. Bennett [and others].
1959.

684756

RIBNER (IRVING)
The Tragedy of "Coriolanus". IN
English Studies, Vol. 34. (Amsterdam)
1953.

485643/34

RIBTON-TURNER (CHARLES JAMES)
Shakespeare's land: a description of
central and southern Warwickshire.
(Leamington)
illus. maps. plans.
[c.1895.] 557115
_____ Another edn. 1932. 397264

RICE (CALE YOUNG)
A Pilgrim's scrip: poems for world
wanderers, [including one entitled
"At Stratford".] [1924.]

512919

Rice (S.[P.]) An Indian on Shakespeare
[: a review of "Shakespeare criticism"
by C. N. Menon.] From Asiatic
Review, Vol. 35.

1939.

494281

RICH (BARNABY)
Apolonius and Silla. [From Riche his
farewell to the military profession.
Possible source of incidents in Twelfth
Night.] IN SHAKESPEARE (W.) Twelfth-
Night. [Edited with an introduction
by H. Morley.] 1889. 436522
Cassell's National Library.
_____ Another edn. Imperfect, half
title-page wanting. 1897. 551384
_____ Another edn. 1901. 527796
_____ Another edn. 1906. 544398
_____ Another edn. 1908. 530847
_____ Another edn. 1909. 595238

RICH (BARNABY)
Rich's "Farewell to military profession"
1581 [: a collection of Elizabethan
short stories]. Edited by T.
Cranfill. (Austin, Tex.)
facsimiles. bibliog. 1959.
Facsimile reproduction of original
1581 edn.

688842

Rich, Barnaby *works relating to*

_____ BRUCE (DOROTHY H.)
The Merry wives and Two brethren
[i.e. Of two brethren and their
wives, by B. Riche.] IN Studies
in Philology, Vol. 39. (Chapel
Hill, N.C.)
bibliog. 1942.

554520

_____ CRANFILL (THOMAS MABRY) and BRUCE
(DOROTHY HART)
Barnaby Rich: a short biography.
(Austin, Tex.)
facsimiles. 1953.

638225

_____ JORGENSEN (PAUL ALFRED)
Barnaby Rich: soldierly suitor and
honest critic of women.
IN SHAKESPEARE QUARTERLY VII:
pp. 183-188.
(New York) 1956.

605711

_____ LIEVSAY (JOHN LEON)
A Word about Barnaby Rich. IN
Journal of English and Germanic
Philology, Vol. 55. (Urbana, Ill.)
1956.

600780/55

RICH (TOWNSEND)
Harington & Ariosto: a study in
Elizabethan verse translation, [i.e.
Sir John Harington's translation of
Ariosto's Orlando Furioso. With a
bibliography, bibliographical notes,
and references to Shakespeare.] (New
Haven, [Conn.])
facsimiles. 1940.
Yale Studies in English, Vol. 92.

521866

Richard the Second

General Works and Criticism

Sources and Background

Stage History and Production; Broadcasting

Study and Teaching; Tales

Textual History

Richard the Second

— General Works and Criticism

_____ ALTICK (R. D.)
Symphonic imagery in Richard II.
[With bibliographical notes.] IN
Publications of the Modern Language
Association of America, Vol. 62.
(Menasha, Wis.) 1947.

428321/62

_____ ATKINSON (A. D.)
Notes on "Richard II". IN Notes and
Queries, Vol. 194. 1949.

5421/194

——Barnett (T.D.) Notes on Shakespeare's
play of Richard II. pp. 67.

1890.

504582

—— BOGARD (TRAVIS)
Shakespeare's second Richard. IN PMLA:
Publications of the Modern Language
Association of America, Vol. 70.
(Menasha, Wis.)

1955.

428321/70

—— BONNARD, GEORGES ALFRED
The Actor in "Richard II".
IN SHAKESPEARE JAHRBUCH. Bd. 87/88/
1951/52. pp. 87-101. (Heidelberg)

10531

—— DEAN (LEONARD F.)
Richard II: the state and the image
of the theater. IN PMLA: Publications of the Modern Language Association of America, Vol. 67. (New York)
1952.

428321/67

—— DRAPER (JOHN WILLIAM)
The Character of Richard II. IN
Philological Quarterly, Vol. 21.
(Iowa)
1942.

592684/21

—— DRAPER (J. W.)
The Tempo of Richard II's speech.
IN Studia Neophilologica, Vol. 20,
1948. (Uppsala)
bibliog.
1948.

596342

—— FRENCH, A. L.
Who deposed Richard the Second?
FROM Essays in Criticism, Vol. 17,
No. 4, Oct. 1967. (Oxford) 1967.
pp. 411-433.

pt. of 621866

—— The Guardian. Vol. 1. [1713.
With Reflections on happiness and
misery, out of Richard II.] 1714.
Title page is dated 1714.

487143

—— The Guardian, Vol. 1, [1713. With
Shakespeare's Reflexions on happiness
and misery, out of his Richard II.]
frontis. 1756.

536048

—— HALL (H. T.)
Shaksperean fly-leaves. No. 5.
Richard the Second. pp. [30]
(Cambridge) 1866.

431977

—— HALSTEAD (WILLIAM L.)
Artifice and artistry in "Richard II"
and "Othello". IN Sweet smoke of
rhetoric: a collection of Renaissance
essays [by various authors]. (Coral
Gables, Fal.) 1964.

745483

—— HENINGER (S. K.)
The Sun-king analogy in Richard II.
IN SHAKESPEARE QUARTERLY XI.
pp. 319-327.
(New York) 1960.

605711

——HOCKEY (DOROTHY C.)
A World of rhetoric in Richard II.
In Shakespeare Quarterly XV: 3. pp.178-
191. (New York) 1964.

605711

—— KLIGER (S.)
The Sun imagery in Richard II.
IN Studies in Philology, Vol. 45.
(Chapel Hill, N.C.) 1948.

554520/45

—— KOTT (JAN)
Shakespeare our contemporary.
Translated by B. Taborski. Preface
by P. Brook. 1964. 741546
————— 2nd edn., revised.
1967. 766093
Includes "The Kings".

—— LEATHAM (J.)
"Richard II", the tragedy of kingship.
2nd edn. pp. 16. (Turriff)
[c.1920.]
Shakespeare Studies, No. 11.

566383

—— McAVOY (WILLIAM C.)
Form in "Richard II", II.i.40-66.
IN Journal of English and Germanic
Philology, Vol. 54. (Urbana, Ill.)
1955.

600780/54

—— McPEEK (JAMES ANDREW SCARBOROUGH)
Richard and his shadow world. FROM
The American Imago, Vol. 15. pp.
195-212. (Boston [Mass.]) 1958.

665935

—— MANZONI (Il Conte ALESSANDRO)
Letter to M. Chauvet on the unity of
time and place in tragedy. IN
LEWINTER (OSWALD) ed., Shakespeare
in Europe [by various authors].
1963.

667784

—— NEARING (H.)
A Three-way pun in Richard II.
IN Modern Language Notes, Vol. 62.
(Baltimore, Md.)
bibliog. 1947.

439157/62

—— OWEN, LEWIS J.
Richard II.
IN CARNEGIE INSTITUTE OF TECHNOLOGY,
PITTSBURGH. Lectures on four of
Shakespeare's history plays.
(Pittsburgh, Pa.) 1953.

635454

— Palmer (J.[L.]) Richard of Bordeaux.
   In Palmer (J.[L.]) Political
   characters of Shakespeare.

         1945.

             559355

— PHIALAS (PETER G.)
   The Medieval in Richard II.
   IN SHAKESPEARE QUARTERLY XII: 3.
   pp. 305–310.
   (New York) 1961.
             605711

— PHIALAS, PETER G.
   'Richard II' and Shakespeare's tragic
   mode. FROM Studies in Literature and
   Language, Vol. V, No. 3, Autumn 1963.
   (Austin, Tex.)

         756152

— Speaight, Robert
   Shakespeare and the political spectrum as
   illustrated by 'Richard II'. IN

   STRATFORD PAPERS ON SHAKESPEARE
   delivered at the 1964 Shakespeare
   Seminar. (Toronto) 1965.

         745844

— STEEL (A. [B.])
   Richard II. With a foreword by
   G. M. Trevelyan [and references to
   Shakespeare's play]. (Cambridge)
   bibliog. facsimile. 1941.

         528403

— STIRLING (BRENTS)
   Bolingbroke's "decision".
   IN SHAKESPEARE QUARTERLY II: 1.
   pp. 27–34.
   (New York) 1951.
             605711

— SUZMAN (ARTHUR)
   Imagery and symbolism in Richard II.
   IN SHAKESPEARE QUARTERLY VII.
   pp. 355–370.
   (New York) 1956.
             605711

— TALBERT (ERNEST WILLIAM)

   **The Problem of order: Elizabethan
   political commonplaces and an example
   of Shakespeare's art [; Richard II.]**
   (Chapel Hill, [N.C.]) 1962.

         668091

— THOMPSON (KARL F.)
   Richard II, martyr.
   IN SHAKESPEARE QUARTERLY VIII.
   pp. 159–166.
   (New York) 1957.
             605711

— TRAVERSI, DEREK ANTONA
   'Richard II'.   IN Stratford Papers
   on Shakespeare delivered at the 1964
   Shakespeare Seminar.   (Toronto)
            1965.

         745844

— TRAVERSI (DEREK ANTONA)
   Shakespeare from "Richard II" to
   "Henry V".   [1958.]

         665883

— URE (PETER)
   The Looking-glass of Richard II.
   IN Philological Quarterly, Vol. 34.
   (Iowa City) 1955.

         592684/34

— WALLIS (N. H.)
   The Ethics of criticism and other
   essays.   [Including some aspects
   of Shakespeare's Richard II and
   Henry V.] 1924.

         443990

— WILSON, JOHN DOVER
   The Political background of Shakespeare's
   "Richard II" and "Henry IV".
   IN SHAKESPEARE JAHRBUCH.   Bd 75/1939.
   pp. 36–51.   (Weimar)

         10531

Richard the Second

— Sources and Background

— ALBRIGHT (EVELYN M.)
   Shakespeare's Richard II and the Essex
   conspiracy.   IN Publications of the
   Modern Language Association of America,
   Vol. 42.   (Menasha, Wis.) 1927.

         428362

— ALBRIGHT (EVELYN M.)
   Shakespeare's Richard II, Hayward's
   History of Henry IV and the Essex
   conspiracy.   IN Publications of the
   Modern Language Association of America,
   Vol. 46.   (Menasha, Wis.) 1931.

         428366

— BLACK (M. W.)
   The Sources of Shakespeare's Richard II.
   [With bibliographical notes.]
   IN McMANAWAY (J. G.), DAWSON (G. E.)
   and WILLOUGHBY (E. E.) eds. Joseph
   Quincy Adams memorial studies.
   (Washington) 1948.

         596748

— BROOKS (HAROLD FLETCHER)
   **Shakespeare and "The Gouernour", Bk. II,
   ch. xiii.   Parallels with "Richard II"
   and the "More" addition.**
   IN SHAKESPEARE QUARTERLY XIV: 3.
   pp. 195–199.
   (New York) 1963.
             605711

— COOK, ARTHUR MALCOLM
   **The Lincolnshire background of
   Shakespeare's tragedy King Richard II.**
   (Lincoln) 1964.

    illus. map.   667828

—DANIEL (SAMUEL)
The Civil Wars. Edited with introduction and notes by L. [A.] Michel. (New
Haven, Conn.)
frontis. table. bibliog.   1958.

687162

—DODSON (SARAH)
Holinshed's Gloucester as a possible
source for Gaunt in Shakespeare's
"Richard II", II, i.   IN University
of Texas, Studies in English, No. 14.
(Austin, Texas)   1934.

442440

— Dodson (Sarah C.) The Northumberland of
Shakespeare and Holinshed. In
University of Texas, Studies in
English, 1939, [No.19].

(Austin, Texas)   1939.

511537

— Elson (J.J.) The Non-Shakespearian
Richard II and Shakespeare's Henry
IV, Part I. From Studies in
philology, Vol. 32.

(Chapel Hill, N.C.)   1935

484077

—HEFFNER (R.)
Shakespeare, Hayward and Essex.
IN Publications of the Modern Language
Association of America, Vol. 45.
(Menasha, Wis.)   1930.

428365

— HEFFNER (R.) and ALBRIGHT (EVELYN M.)
Comment and criticism: Shakespeare,
Hayward and Essex again. pp. [4.]
FROM [Publications of the Modern
Language Association of America, Vol.
47.] [Menasha, Wis.]
                                    [1932.]
Note: This is a continuation of the
discussion on an article by Evelyn M.
Albright (catal. no. 428366) by R.
Heffner (catal. no. 428365).

438445

— Holinshed's Chronicles: Richard II,
1398-1400, and Henry V. Edited by
R. S. Wallace and Alma Hansen.
                              1917.

391843

— HUMPHREYS, ARTHUR RALEIGH
Shakespeare's political justice in
'Richard II' and 'Henry IV'. IN
Stratford Papers on Shakespeare Seminar.
(Toronto)

1965.

745844

— LAW (ROBERT ADGER)
Deviations from Holinshed in "Richard II".
IN The University of Texas Studies in
English, Vol. 29.   (Austin, Tex.)
                              1950.

422432/29

— McLAREN (M.)
"By me...": a report upon the apparent
discovery of some working notes of
William Shakespeare in a sixteenth-
century book [i.e. Hall's Chronicles,
1550. Edited by R. W. Postgate.
With a comparison of passages from
Richard II with Hall and the notes.]
pp. [iv,] 68.
facsimiles.   1949.

600541

— SMITH (R. M.)
Froissart and the English chronicle
play. [With references to Richard II.]
(New York)   1915.
Columbia University. Studies in
English and Comparative Literature.

473400

—SPEAIGHT, ROBERT
Shakespeare and the political spectrum
as illustrated by 'Richard II'. IN
Stratford Papers on Shakespeare, deli-
vered at the 1964 Shakespeare Seminar.
(Toronto)

1965.

745844

— Woodstock [or, Richard II], a moral
history [: a play]. Edited, with
a preface [containing information
on the play as a source of Shakespeare's
Richard II, notes and a glossary] by
A. P. Rossiter.   1946.

574542

Richard the Second

— Stage History and Production; Broadcasting
*Newspaper reviews, playbills, theatre pro-
grammes and theatrical illustrations — the
library's extensive collection of this material
is mainly uncatalogued but indexed
For texts of stage alterations and adaptations of the play see* ENGLISH EDITIONS,
Richard the Second — Alterations, *etc.*

— ANTHONY (G.)
John Gielgud: camera studies [of
John Gielgud as Richard II, Shylock,
etc.] With an introduction by
M. Saint-Denis.   1938.

493613

— EDINBOROUGH (ARNOLD)
Canada's credible "Lear" and moving
"Richard". IN Shakespeare Quarterly XV:
4. pp.391-395. (New York)   1964.

605711

— Evans, Maurice, in King Richard II [: a
souvenir of the performance in New York.
With two articles: England's "skipping
king", by B. Atkinson, and Maurice Evans,
by B. Crowther]. pp. [16.] (New York)
illus. [1937.]

581626

— FARROW (EMMA)
Thrones and dominions: a recollection
of the history plays given at the
Shakespeare Memorial Theatre in the
Festival of Britain Season, 1951.
Richard II, Henery Iv, Part 1, Henry
IV, Part II, Henry V. (Birmingham)
typescript. [1951.]

630855

— FISHER (H. K.)
The Theatre [: criticism of productions
of] The Alchemist, Othello [and] King
Richard II. IN Life and Letters,
Vol. 54. 1947.

586006

— HILL (R. F.)
Dramatic Techniques and Interpretation
in 'Richard II'. IN

Stratford-on-Avon Studies,
edited by J.R. Brown and B. Harris,
Vol.3. Early Shakespeare.
1961.

668841

— HOWARD (LEON)
Shakespeare for the family. IN The
Quarterly of Film Radio and Television,
Vol. 8. (Berkeley, Cal.)
1954.

630462/8

— Isaacs (Edith J. R.) Broadway to a
national theatre : Broadway in
review [: including a review of
Richard II.] In Theatre Arts
Monthly, Vol. 21.

1937.

482353

— KEMP (THOMAS CHARLES)
The Stratford festival [: 1951].
Broadcast 11th April 1951. ff. 6.
typescript. 1951.

616351

— LAWRENCE (W. J.)
The Stage history of "King Richard
the Second". IN Gentleman's Magazine,
Vol. 283. 1897.

140342

— LEE (G. A.)
The Heraldry of Shakespeare's
"Richard II", at His Majesty's Theatre.
IN The Genealogical Magazine, Vol. 7.
illus. 1903.

182210

— McMANAWAY (JAMES GILMER)
"Richard II" at Covent Garden. IN
Shakespeare 400: essays by American
scholars on the anniversary of the
poet's birth. Published in co-
operation with the Shakespeare
Association of America.
illus. 1964.

667803

— MONTAGUE (C. E.)
F. R. Benson's Richard II. IN
WARD (A. C.) [ed.] Specimens of
English dramatic criticism, 17-20
centuries; selected and introduced.
(Oxford) 1945.
The World's Classics.

563732

— MONTAGUE (C. E.)
On Benson's Richard II. IN AGATE
(J. [E.]) ed., The English dramatic
critics. [1932.]

399280

— PROGRAMMES OF SHAKESPEARIAN PERFORMANCES
Richard the Second

This collection, which runs from the
latter half of the nineteenth century,
is continuously augmented by the addition of programmes of contemporary
productions.

499166

— Richard II [at] the Old Vic,
October 15th 1934. In Play pictorial,
Vol.65.

1934.

571927

— SPRAGUE (ARTHUR COLBY)
Shakespeare's histories: plays for
the stage.
illus. 1964.
Society for Theatre Research.
Richard II, pp. 29-49.

667707

— SYKES (E. F.)
"King Richard the Second": [the
production] at the Birmingham Repertory
Theatre, 1955. (Journal Notes, 7th
Series). ff. 30.
typescript. 1955.

665410

— THOMAS (MERLIN)
The Playing of Shakespeare at Avignon:
a report with excerpts from productions
of Henry IV and Richard II, played by
the Jean Vilar Company. Broadcast
18th November 1950. ff. 9.
typescript. 1950.

616418

—— TYTLER (ERNEST J.)
Richard the Second: filmstrip [of
the play produced at the Theatre
Royal, Brighton, by Tennent
Productions Ltd., Dec. 8, 1952];
and notes.
1 vol., 1 reel 35 mm.   [1952].

666693 & 666699

—— Usill (M.) and Boas (G.) "Richard II"
at Sloane School. In School Drama,
Vol.2, No.2.

[1939.]

523131

Richard the Second
— Study and Teaching; Tales

—— ADAMSON, ELGIVA, and MOORE, KATHLEEN V.
Notes on William Shakespeare's 'King
Richard II'. (Stratford, Ont.) 1965.

746654

—— Carrington (N.T.) Shakespeare:King
Richard II. pp.64. Dgm.

[1940.]

(Notes on Chosen English Texts)

601685

—— COLLEGE OF CAREERS, CAPE TOWN
STUDY-AID SERIES
Notes on Shakespeare's 'King Richard II'.
(Cape Town)   [1964.]

typescript.   740929

—— Dam (B.A.P. van) [Review of] The First
part of the reign of King Richard the
Second or Thomas of Woodstock, edited
by W[ilhelmina] P. Frijlinck. (Malone
Society Reprint, [Vol.59.] In English studies, Vol. 13.

(Amsterdam)   1931.

485655

—— HUMPHREYS, ARTHUR RALEIGH
Shakespeare: Richard II [: a study
guide].   1967.

Studies in English literature, 31.
758800

—— KEY FACTS LTD.
Richard II [: set of 25 cards for
revision for the General Certificate
of Education O level examination].
[1967.]

Key Facts, Shakespeare, 3.
763809

—— MORRIS, HELEN
King Richard II. (Oxford)   1966.

Notes on English literature.
762770

—— RANSOME (CYRIL)
Short studies of Shakespeare's plots:
Richard II.   pp. iii, [38]. 1899.

665288

—— SCANLAN, MARY H.
Review notes and study guide to
Shakespeare's 'Richard II'. (New York)
1964.

Monarch critiques of literature.
756293

—— SHIPLEY, JOSEPH TWADELL, ed.
Richard II: a scene-by-scene analysis
with critical commentary. (New York)
1964.

Study master series.   668335

—— WOOD (S.)
Richard II: questions and notes.
2nd edn.   pp. 46.   (Manchester)
[c.1900.]

545610

—— Woodstock [or, Richard II], a moral
history [: a play].   Edited, with
a preface [containing information
on the play as a source of
Shakespeare's Richard II, notes and
a glossary] by A. P. Rossiter. 1946.

574542

Richard the Second
— Textual History

—— HASKER (RICHARD E.)
The Copy for the First Folio Richard II.
IN Studies in Bibliography, Vol. 5.
(Charlottesville, Va.)
1952.

598680/5

—— [HOWARD (F.)
Drawings prepared for "The Spirit of
the plays of Shakespeare".   With the
plates and references descriptive of
the plates for the large paper edition
of Hamlet and Richard II.] [1827-33.]

436162

Kirschbaum (L.) A Census of bad
quartos. [With bibliographical
notes.] In The Review of
English Studies, Vol. 14.

1938.

495115

Richard the Third

General Works and Criticism
Cinematography
Plays; Poems; Fiction
Sources and Background
Stage History and Production
Study and Teaching; Tales
Textual History

Richard the Third

— General Works and Criticism

ARNOLD (AEROL)
The Recapitulation dream in Richard III
and Macbeth.
IN SHAKESPEARE QUARTERLY VI.
pp. 51-62.
(New York)   1955.

605711

BADAWI (M.   M.   )

The Paradox of Richard the Third.
Reprint from the Bulletin of the
Faculty of Arts, Alexandria University,
Vol.12, 1958. pp.[17.] (Alexandria)
[1958.]

667295

Bennett (J.O'D.) Much loved books: best
sellers of the ages. [Including,
Shakespeare's Hamlet and adventures
in the Furness Variorum; Shakespeare's
King Richard III. With a bibliography.]

1928.

412432

BERMAN (RONALD S.)
Anarchy and order in "Richard III" and
"King John".
IN SHAKESPEARE SURVEY 20.   (Cambridge)
1967.

766881

BOGARD (TRAVIS)
Shakespeare's second Richard. IN PMLA:
Publications of The Modern Language
Association of America, Vol. 70.
(Menasha, Wis.)

1955.

428321/70

BROOKE, NICHOLAS
Reflecting gems and dead bones:
tragedy versus history in "Richard
III".   FROM Critical Quarterly, 7.
1965.
pp. 123-134.

767184

CLEMEN, WOLFGANG H.
A commentary on Shakespeare's
"Richard III".   English version
by J. Bonheim.   1968.

768268

CUMBERLAND (R.)
A Delineation of Shakespear's charac-
ters of Macbeth and Richard [III].
A parallel between him and Aeschylus.
IN Cumberland (R.) The Observer,
[edited] by A. Chalmers, [Vol. 2.]
1803.
British essayists, Vol. 42.

459752

Davies (J.) The Shaksperian characters
of Richard the third, and Hamlet
contrasted: a paper read before
the Warrington Literary &
Philosophical Society, March 1882.
pp.20.

1882.

404418

DRAPER (J. W.)
Patterns of tempo in Richard III.
FROM Neuphilologische Mitteilungen,
50 Jahrgang, Nr. 1-2.   (Helsinki)
graph.   bibliog.   1949.

604847

HEILMAN, ROBERT BECHTOLD
Satiety and conscience: aspects
of 'Richard III'.   FROM Antioch
Review XXIV: 1.   (Yellow Springs,
Ohio)   1964.

668302

KANTOROWICS (ERNST HARTWIG)
Shakespeare: King Richard II.   IN The
King's two bodies: a study in mediaeval
political theology. (Princeton, N.J.)
illus. facsimiles. bibliog.   1957.

688618

KERNAN (ALVIN B.)
A Comparison of the imagery in "3
Henry VI" and "The True tragedie of
Richard Duke of York".   IN Studies
in Philology, Vol. 51.   (Chapel Hill,
N.C.)

1954.

554520/51

KOTT (JAN)
Shakespeare our contemporary.
Translated by B. Taborski.   Preface
by P. Brook.   1964.   741546
——— 2nd edn., revised.
1967.   766093
Includes "The Kings".

LAW (R. A.)
Richard the Third: a study in
Shakespeare's composition. [With
bibliographical notes.] IN Publications of the Modern Language Association of America, Vol. 60. (Menasha,
Wis.) 1945.

569026

Leatham (J.) The Life and death of
Richard Third. pp.19.

(Turriff) [c.1920.]

(Shakespeare Studies, No.17.)

566389

Legge (A.O.) An Estimate of the
character of Richard III. [With
references to Shakespeare.] In
Manchester Literary Club. Papers,
Vol.10.

(Manchester) 1884.

518371

LOWELL (J. R.)
Shakespeare's "Richard III". IN
Lowell (J. R.) Latest literary essays
and addresses. (Cambridge, Mass.)
port. 1891. 432337
No. 37 of 50 large paper copies printed
for Europe.
_____ IN The Atlantic Monthly, Vol. 68.
1891. 112935

LOWNE (E. G.)
An Essay on Shakspeare's historical
tragedy of Richard III [, Act 3,
Scene 7. A school essay]. ff.[11.]
manuscript. 1871.

536837

Palmer (J.[L.]) Richard of Gloucester.
In Palmer (J.[L.]) Political
characters of Shakespeare.

1945.

559355

Richard the Third, after the manner of
the ancients [: an account of
Shakespeare's play as it might have
been written by Euripides, Sophocles
or Aeschylus]. FROM [The London
Magazine,] June 1824.

1824.

561770

Roe (F.G.) Ghosts in art : the rise
of a tradition. [With illustrations
of ghost scenes from Shakespeare's
Richard III, Hamlet and Macbeth,
and bibliographical notes.] pp.[9.]
Illus. From The Connoisseur, Vol.
110.

1942.

541059

ROSSITER (ARTHUR PERCIVAL)
A Guide to Shakespeare-goers, 3:
'The Devil as avenging angel', or,
'The Meaning of Richard the Third.'
Produced by D. Bryson. [Broadcast]
7th July, 1953. ff. 17.
typescript. [1953.]

634504

SCHEFFAUER (H. G.)
The New vision in the German arts [:
essays. Including The Intensive
Shakespeare (Richard III).] 1924.

443991

Shanker (S.) Shakespeare pays
some compliments [in Richard
III]. In Modern Language
Notes, Vol.63.

(Baltimore, Md.) 1948

439157/63

SHOEMAKER (WILLIAM HUTCHINSON)
Galdós' "La de los tristes destinos"
and its Shakespearean connections.
IN Modern Language Notes, Vol. 71.
(Baltimore, Md.) 1956.

439157/71

SMITH (F. M.)
The Relation of Macbeth to Richard
the Third. [With bibliographical
notes.] IN Publications of the
Modern Language Association of America,
Vol. 60. (Menasha, Wis.) 1945.

569026

Spencer (H.) The Clock passage in
Richard III. In The Review of
English Studies, Vol.14.

1938.

495115

STALKER (A.)
Shakespeare, Marlowe and Nashe [:
critical examination of Richard III,
etc.] (Stirling) 1936.

462712

THOMAS (S.)
The Antic Hamlet and Richard III.
[With a bibliography.] (New York)
1943.

552067

WALKLEY (ARTHUR BINGHAM)
The Taming of tragedy (in "Richard III").
IN Frames of mind [: essays]. 1899.

544884

WILLIAMS (F. B.)
Clarence in the malmsey-butt. [With
special reference to Richard III.]
IN Modern Language Notes, Vol. 51.
(Baltimore) 1936.

463701

Richard the Third
— Cinematography

—— KOZELKA (PAUL)
A Guide to the screen version of
Shakespeare's Richard III.   pp. 16.
[Maplewood, N.J.]
  ports.   illus.   [1956.]
Photoplay Studies.

665547

—— LONDON FILM PRODUCTIONS, LTD.
[London Films in association with
Laurence Olivier.   Photographs
and publicity material of the film
Richard the Third.]   pp. 48. 1955.

665304

—— PHILLIPS (J. E.)
Adapted from a play by W. Shakespeare
[: Laurence Olivier's film production
of "Henry V" and the Old Vic radio
presentation of "Richard III" for the
Columbia Broadcasting System, June
1946].   IN Hollywood Quarterly Vol.2.
(Berkeley, Cal.)
                              1946-7.

592680/2

——   [Richard the Third: release script
of the film presented by London Films in
association with Laurence Olivier.]
Typescript.   [1955.]

665180

—— TYTLER (ERNEST J.   )

Richard the Third: filmstrip [from the
film made by London Film Productions
Ltd.].
     1. vol. 8vo., 1 reel 35 mm. [1950?].

666694 and 666700

Richard the Third
— Plays; Poems; Fiction
see also ENGLISH EDITIONS, Richard the
Third — Alterations, etc.

—— Binyon ([R.]L.) Brief candles [:a play
in blank verse concerning Richard
III.] With six engravings by
Helen Binyon [and references in the
introduction to Shakespeare's play
Richard III.] pp. 50.

1938.

(Golden Cockerel Press.)

489066

—— [BROOKE (C.)]
The Ghost of Richard the Third, 1614:
[a poem founded on Shakespeare's
play.] IN Miscellanies of the Fuller
Worthies' Library.   Edited, with
memorial-introductions and notes, by
A. B. Grosart.   Vol. 4.   1876.
  Printed for private circulation.
Edition limited to 156.

51102

—— Causley (C.) Laurence Olivier's Richard
III[: a poem]. In Life and Letters,
Vol. 54.

1947.

586006

—— [KNOX (E. G. V.)]
Malmsey wine [: a study of the Second
Murderer in Richard III, by] Evoe.
FROM Punch, Vol. 213.   [1947.]

587302

—— LESSING [(G. E.)]
Ausgewählte Prosa und Briefe.   Edited,
with notes, by H. S. White.   [Con-
taining "Gespenster auf der Bühne
(Shakespeare und Voltaire)" and
"Weisse's Richard III".]   (New York)
                              1888.
German Classics for American Students.

443693

—— PALMER [(W.) ed.]
The New and complete English spouter;
or, An Universal key to theatrical
knowledge.   A collection of prologues
and epilogues [including prologue and
epilogue to Richard the Third].
                              [1781.]

531636

—— SASSOON (S.)
First night: Richard III [: a
poem].   IN Sassoon (S.) Satirical
poems.   pp. 61.   1926.

536676

Richard the Third
— Sources and Background

—— Begg (Edleen) Shakespeare's debt to
Hall and Holinshed in Richard III.
[With bibliographical notes.]
From Studies in philology, Vol. 32.

(Chapel Hill, N.C.)   1935.

484077

—— CLEMEN (WOLFGANG)
Tradition and originality in
Shakespeare's "Richard III".
IN SHAKESPEARE QUARTERLY V.
pp. 247-257.
(New York)   1954.

605711

HALL [E.]
Passages illustrative of Shakspeare's
"Richard the Third" abridged from
the chronicles of [R.] Holinshed and
[E.] Hall. IN SHAKSPEARE [W.] King
Richard III. [Edited] with notes
[etc.] by J. Hunter. New edn. 1872.
[Longmans' Series of Hunter's Anno-
tated Shakespeare]

544997

LAW (R. A.)
Richard the Third, Act 1, Scene 4.
IN Publications of the Modern Language
Association of America, Vol. 27.
(Baltimore) 1912.

428347

LAW (R. A.)
Two Shakespearian pictures of Puritans
[as portrayed in passages in Richard
the Third and Othello]. IN University
of Texas Studies in English, No. 13.
(Austin, Texas.)
1933.

434338

LORDI (ROBERT J.   )
The Relationship of "Richardus Tertius"
to the main Richard III plays. FROM
Boston University Studies in English,
Vol.5, No.3. (Boston, Mass.)
1961.

667841

MacGibbon (D.) Elizabeth Woodville
(1437-1492) : her life and times.
[With references to Shakespeare's Henry VI, Pt 3 and Richard III; and a
bibliography.] Ports. Facsimiles.

1938.

488706

MOTT (L. F.)
A Political allusion in Shakespeare's
Richard III. IN FITZ-GERALD (J. D.)
and TAYLOR (PAULINE) eds., Todd
memorial volumes: philological
studies, Vol. 2. 1930.

398523

Thompson (C.J.S.) The Witchery of
Jane Shore, the Rose of London:
the romance of a Royal mistress.
[With references to Richard the
third]. Ports. Illus. Facsimiles.

1933.

417434

WILSON (JOHN DOVER)
Shakespeare's Richard III and The True
Tragedy of Richard the Third, 1594.
IN SHAKESPEARE QUARTERLY III: 4.
pp. 299-306.
(New York) 1952.

605711

Richard the Third
— Stage History and Production
*Newspaper reviews, playbills, theatre pro-
grammes and theatrical illustrations — the
library's extensive collection of this material
is mainly uncatalogued but indexed
For texts of stage alterations and adaptations of the play see* ENGLISH EDITIONS,
Richard the Third *— Alterations, etc.*

BARNES (T.)
Kean as Richard. IN HUDSON (D.)
Thomas Barnes of The Times. With
selections from his critical essays
never before reprinted, edited by
H. Child. [With a bibliography and
bibliographical notes.] (Cambridge)
port. illus. 1943.

545447

BARNES (T.)
Kean as Richard the Third.
IN WARD (A. C.) [ed.] Specimens of
English dramatic criticism, 17-20
centuries; selected and introduced.
(Oxford) 1945.
The World's Classics.

563732

CAUSLEY (C.)
Laurence Olivier's Richard III [: a
poem]. IN Life and Letters, Vol. 54.
1947.

586006

DAVIES (T.)
Garrick's first performance in
London [as Richard the Third].
IN WARD (A. C.) [ed.] Specimens of
English dramatic criticism, 17-20
centuries; selected and introduced.
(Oxford) 1945.
The World's Classics.

563732

DOONE (R.)
Three Shakespearian productions [:
Hamlet, with John Gielgud, Richard III,
with Laurence Olivier, and King Lear,
with Donald Wolfit]. IN The Penguin
New Writing, 25. (Harmondsworth)
illus. 1945.

564884

The Drama [: a criticism of a
performance of Richard III at
Covent Garden]. FROM [The London
Magazine,] April 1821. 1821.

563681

Duologues with the adjudicator.
The Blackburn Festival experiment
[extracts from the plays of
Shakespeare and other dramatists.]
IN The Amateur theatre and playwrights' journal, Vol. 4, No. 72.
1937-38.

482984

GILDER (ROSAMOND)
Actors in their stride: Broadway
in review. [Includes a criticism
of Richard III at the Forrest
Theatre, New York.] IN Theatre
Arts, Vol. 27. (New York)
illus. 1943.

548672

HAZLITT (WILLIAM)
On Edmund Kean's Richard. IN
AGATE (J. [E.]) ed., The English
dramatic critics. [1932.]

399280

Irving ([Sir]H.]B.]) Four favourite
parts [: Hamlet; Richard III; Iago;
King Lear]. Illus. In The English
Illustrated Magazine, 1892-3.

1893.

119734

KALSON, ALBERT E.
The Chronicles in Cibber's Richard
III. IN Studies in English
Literature, 1500-1900, Vol. 3,
No. 2: an offprint. 1963.

667776

KEMP (THOMAS CHARLES)
The Stratford festival [: the 1953
Shakespeare Memorial Theatre productions
of The Merchant of Venice and King
Richard III. Broadcast] 27th March,
1953. ff. 6.
typescript. 1953.

631924

"The London Chronicle" on Barry
as Richard III. In Agate (J.[E.]) ed.,
The English dramatic critics. [1932.]

399280

MacCARTHY (D.)
A Great repertory season [: a review
of the Old Vic Repertory Company's
productions at the New Theatre, London,
including Shakespeare's Richard III].
IN Picture Post, Vol. 25.
illus. 1944.

565209

MacCARTHY (D.)
Richard III and the Old Vic
Repertory [at the New Theatre,
London]. IN The New Statesman
and Nation, New Series, Vol. 28.
1944.

558344

Miller (T.) ed. The Old Vic Theatre
Company : a tour of Australia and
New Zealand [including a section
on "Richard III"]. Designed and
decorated by L.Sainthill. pp.60.
Ports. Illus. Facsimiles.

(Sydney) 1948.

(The British Council)

597842

MR. J.H. LEIGH'S reading of Richard III:
opinions of the London press.
[c.1900.]

667380

PALMER [(W.) ed.]
The New and complete English spouter;
or, An Universal key to theatrical
knowledge. A collection of prologues
and epilogues [including prologue and
epilogue to Richard the Third].
[1781.]

531636

Programmes of Shakespearian performances. Richard III, 1876- .]

499167

Remarks on the character of Richard
the Third as played by Cooke and
Kemble. pp. 55. 1801.

462480

"SENEX" [pseud.]
Observations on "Macbeth and
King Richard III: an essay in
answer to remarks on some of the
characters of Shakespeare", by
J. P. Kemble. FROM The Edinburgh
Monthly Magazine, August, 1817.
[Edinburgh] 1817.

440300

SPRAGUE (ARTHUR COLBY)
Shakespeare's histories: plays for
the stage.
illus. 1964.
Society for Theatre Research.
Richard III, pp. 121-141.

667707

Studies of old actors: 1. Garrick in
"Lord Hastings" 2. Mossop in "Cardinal
Wolsey" 3. Henderson in "Jacques".
From [The Dublin University Magazine]
Vol. 62.

[Dublin] 1863
579639

Walkley (A.B.) The Theatre in London.
Revival of King Richard III. In
Cosmopolis, Vol.6.

1897.

138551

Z. [pseud.]
On Garrick's delivery of a passage
in Shakspeare['s Richard III].
FROM [The New Monthly Magazine,
Vol. 4]. [1822.]

558072

Richard the Third
Study and Teaching; Tales

—— ADAMSON, ELGIVA, and MOORE, KATHLEEN V.
Notes on William Shakespeare's "Richard
III." [Stratford, Ontario]   1967.

766374

—— COLLEGE OF CAREERS, Cape Town
Study-Aid Series
Notes on Shakespeare's 'Richard III'.
Compiled by M. Arkin.   (Cape Town)
typescript.   [1964].

740926

—— HAEFFNER, PAUL
A Critical commentary on Shakespeare's
'Richard III'.   1966.

Macmillan critical commentaries.
753069

—— HARDACRE, KENNETH
Shakespeare: King Richard III. (Bath)
[1964.]

illus. Notes on chosen English
texts.   668198

——KEY FACTS LTD.
Richard III [: set of 25 cards for
revision for the General Certificate
of Education 0 level examination].
[1967.]

Key Facts, Shakespeare, 4.
763808

—— LORDI, ROBERT J., and ROBINSON, JAMES E.
Richard III: a scene-by-scene analysis
with critical commentary. (New York)
1966.

Study Master Series. 762658

—— NUGENT, F.M.
Review notes and study guide to
Shakespeare's 'King Richard the third'.
(New York)   1964.

Monarch critiques of literature.
756292

—— WHITE, J.W.R.
Shakespeare's Richard III: an
interpretation for students. (Adelaide)
1966.

761167

Richard the Third
— Textual History

—— BOWERS (FREDSON THAYER)
The Copy for the Folio Richard III.
IN SHAKESPEARE QUARTERLY X: 4.
pp. 541-544.
(New York)   1959.

605711

——CAIRNCROSS (ANDREW SCOTT)
The Quartos and the Folio text of
"Richard III".   IN The Review of
English Studies, New Series, Vol. 8.
(Oxford)   1957.

318239/8

—— CAMPBELL (O. J.)
[Review of] The Tragedy of King Richard
III, edited by H. Spencer. IN Modern
Language Notes, December, 1934.
(Baltimore)   1934.

428652

—— Dam (B.A.P. van) Shakespeare problems
nearing solution: Henry VI and
Richard III. From English Studies,
Vol.12, No.3.

(Amsterdam)   1930.

413985

——Greer (C.A.) The Relation of Richard III
to the True Tragedy of Richard
Duke of York and the third part
of Henry VI. From Studies in
Philology, vol.29.

(Baltimore)   1932.

441593

—— GREG (W. W.)
"Richard III" - Q5 (1612).   IN The
Library, 4th series, Vol. 17.   1937.

469402

—— GRIFFIN (W. J.)
An Omission in the Folio text of
Richard III.   IN The Review of English
studies, Vol. 13.   [1937.]

479772

—— Kirschbaum (L.) A Census of bad
quartos. [With bibliographical
notes.] In The Review of English
Studies, Vol. 14.

1938.

495115

—— MAAS (P.)
Two passages in Richard III.   [With
bibliographical notes.]   IN The
Review of English Studies, Vol. 18.
(Oxford)   1942.

542539

__ OYAMA (TOSHIKAZU)
The Folio copy of Richard III. IN
Studies in English grammar and
linguistics: a miscellany in honour
of Takanobu Otsuka. (Tokyo)
port. dgms. tables. bibliogs.
1958.

667095

___ PATRICK (D. L.)
The Textual history of Richard III.
(Stanford, Cal.)
1936.
Stanford University. University
Series. Language and Literature,
Vol. 6, No. 1.
463300

__ PICKERSGILL (EDWARD H.)
On the Quarto and the Folio of Richard III.
IN Transactions of the New Shakespeare
Society, Series 1. No. 3. pp. 77-124.
1875-6.

40620

__ SMIDT, KRISTIAN
Iniurious impostors and Richard III.
1963.
Norwegian studies in English.
668033

__ SPEDDING (JAMES)
On the corrected edition of Richard III.
IN Transactions of the New Shakespeare
Society, Series 1. No. 3. pp. 1-77.
1875-6.
40620

__ WALTON (J. K.)
The Copy for the folio text of
Richard III with a note on the copy
for the folio text of King Lear.
(Auckland)
tables. bibliogs. 1955.
Auckland University College,
Monograph Series, No. 1.
665102

__ WALTON (J. K.)
The Quarto copy for the Folio Richard III.
IN The Review of English Studies, New
Series, Vol. 10.
bibliog. tables. 1959.

318239/10

RICHARDS (A.)
Under the greenwood tree: canon in
the fourth below [: two-part song].
Words [from As you like it].
IN A Selection of songs, with words
by Shakespeare. [c.1925.]
Novello's School Songs.
520360

RICHARDS (GRANT)
Housman, 1897-1936 [: a biography].
With an introduction by Mrs. [Katharine
E.] Symons and appendices by G. B. A.
Fletcher and others. [Containing
references to Shakespeare's songs.]
(Oxford)
ports. illus. facsimiles. 1941.

529165

RICHARDS (IRVING T.)
The Meaning of Hamlet's soliloquy.
IN Publications of the Modern Language
Association of America, Vol. 48.
(Menasha, Wis.) 1933.

418268

RICHARDS (IVOR A.)
Coleridge on imagination [containing
Shakespearian references.]
port. 1934.

430016

Richards (I.A.) The Philosophy of
rhetoric. [With references to
Shakespeare.]

(New York) 1936.

(Mary Flexner Lectures on the Humanities,3.)

465250

RICHARDSON (A. D.)
The Early historical plays. IN
PROUTY (CHARLES TYLER) ed., Shakespeare:
of an age and for all time: the Yale
Shakespeare Festival Lectures. [New
Haven, Conn.] 1954.

640920

RICHARDSON (ALBERT EDWARD)
Shakespeare Memorial Theatre. FROM
The Builder, Vol. 142. pp. [6.] .
illus. 1932.

392673

Richardson (A.M.) It was a lover and
his lass [: words by] Shakespeare
[from As You Like It; music by]
A.M.Richardson. [Staff notation and
tonic sol-fa.] 2 vols.

1908-1930.

517003

Richardson (A.M.) O Mistress mine
[: words by Shakespeare [from
Twelfth Night. Music by] A.M.Richard-
son. [Staff notation and tonic
sol-fa.] 2 vols.

1908-[1926.]

517018

Richardson (A.M.) Under the greenwood
tree [: words by Shakespeare [from
As You Like It; music by] A.M.
Richardson. [Staff notation and
tonic sol-fa.] 2 vols.

1908-1923.

517001

RICHARDSON (B. J.)
Where the bee sucks. Harmonized
by B. J. Richardson. [Words by
Shakespeare from The Tempest.]
pp. 3. (J. Bland) [c.1790.]

599131

[RICHARDSON (D. L.)
Literary leaves: the chapters
extracted from Vol. 2 on Shakespeare's
Sonnets, Othello and Iago: on four
comic characters; and, Shylock.]
[1840.]

579641

RICHARDSON (L. J.)
Repetition and rhythm in Vergil
and Shakespeare. IN University
of California Chronicle, Vol. 32,
1930. (Berkeley, Cal.) [1930.]

400528

RICHARDSON (Sir RALPH DAVID)
Commentary. IN The First part of
King Henry the Fourth. Text edited
by C. J. Sisson. Commentary by
Sir R. Richardson. (New York)
1959.
The Laurel Shakespeare. F. Fergusson,
general editor.

667474

RICHARDSON (Sir RALPH DAVID)
Talk on the "Old Vic". IN Scenes
from the Taming of the Shrew.
(Theatre Programme: a radio review
of the stage.) [Broadcast] 2nd
September, 1947. ff. 3 10.
typescript. [1947.]

588385

RICHARDSON (WILLIAM)
Additional observations on
Shakespeare's dramatic character
of Hamlet in a letter to a friend.
IN LEECH, CLIFFORD, ed., Shakespeare:
the tragedies. A Collection of
critical essays. (Chicago) 1965.
Gemini books.

752332

RICHARDSON (WILLIAM)
Criticism on a scene in Shakspeare's
Richard III. IN The Mirror, [edited]
by A. Chalmers, [Vol. 2.] 1802
British essayists, Vol. 36.

459746

RICHARDSON (WILLIAM)
Essays on Shakespeare's dramatic
characters of Richard the Third, King
Lear, and Timon of Athens, an essay
on the faults of Shakespeare, and
additional observations on the character of Hamlet.
1784.

626051

[RICHARDSON (WILLIAM)]
A Philosophical analysis and illustration of some of Shakespeare's remarkable characters. (Edinburgh)
1774. 393425
_____ 3rd edn., corrected.
1784. 617252

Richardson, Ralph David, *Sir, works relating to*

— Adler (H.) Ralph Richardson and
Lawrence Olivier [:actors in Othello
at the Old Vic]. Ports. In World
Film News, Vol.2.

1938.

— Crozier (E.) Acting to-day : the work
of Olivier and Richardson in Henry
the Fourth. Ports. Illus. From
Theatre Today, March 1946.

1946.

568493

— HOBSON (HAROLD)
Ralph Richardson: an illustrated
study of Sir Ralph's work, with a
list of his appearances on stage and
screen. pp. 98. 1958.
Theatre World Monographs, No. 11.

677733

— Strachan (W.J.) "I have long dreamed"
[:a poem] on seeing Ralph Richardson
as Falstaff in Henry 1V. In Strachan
(W.J.) Moments of time : poems. pp.55.
Illus.

1947.

585234

Richardson, William *works relating to*

— Babcock (R.W.) William Richardson's
criticism of Shakespeare. From The
Journal of English and Germanic
philology, vol.28.

(Illinois) 1929.

444155

—) A Philosophical
analysis and illustration of some of
Shakespeare's remarkable characters.
[Review of. Reprinted from The
Monthly Review.] In The Monthly
Miscellany, Vol.2.

1774.

520767

Riche (Barnabe) see Rich (Barnaby)

Richepin, Jean *works relating to*

— SÉVRETTE (G.)
M. Jean Richepin's [lectures on]
Shakespeare. IN The Fortnightly
review, Vol. 102. 1914.

255614

RICHEY (A. M. S.)
Shakespeare: an appreciation.
FROM The Methodist Magazine, September,
1934. pp. [4.] 1934.

425722

RICHMOND, HUGH
Love and justice: "Othello"'s
Shakespearean context.
IN Pacific coast studies in Shakespeare.
Edited by W. F. McNeir and T. N.
Greenfield. (Eugene: Ore.) 1966.

768009

RICHMOND, HUGH M.
Shakespeare's political plays.
(New York) 1967.

Studies in language and
literature. 765124

RICHMOND (HUGH M.)
"To be or not to be" and the Hynne de
la Mort.
IN SHAKESPEARE QUARTERLY XIII: 3.
pp. 317-320.
(New York) 1962.

605711

Richmond (W.K.) Poetry and the people
[: a survey of English poetry from
the earliest times to the present.
With references to Shakespeare,
including a chapter entitled
"Miracle, Mystery and Shakespeare,"
and with bibliographical notes].

1947.

580803

Richmond Shakespeare Society. Programmes,
cuttings, etc. [of Shakespearian
performances], 1934-

455238

Richter (K.) [Review of] London for
Shakespeare lovers, by W. Kent.
From The English Literary and
Educational Review for Continental
Readers, Vol. 6, No. 1. pp. 40.
(Leipzig)

1935.

434833

Rickert (R. T.) see Foakes (Reginald A.)
and Rickert (R. T.)

Ricketts (Charles S.) illus.
SHAKESPEARE'S HEROINES: [souvenir
of the Sunday afternoon broadcasts.
Illustrated by C. S. Ricketts. With
foreword by Lilian Baylis, Sir F. R.
Benson and Edith Evans.] pp. [32.]
[British Broadcasting Company, Ltd.]
[1926.]

331149

RICKEY, MARY ELLEN
'Twixt the Dangerous Shores: Troilus
and Cressida again. IN Shakespeare
Quarterly XV: 1. 1964.

605711

Riddles and Puzzles

— AVALON HILL COMPANY
The Game of Shakespeare. [Contains
instructions for three game versions,
chesspieces, playing board, dice,
quotation cards and 52 page booklet
with synopses of all plays.]
(Baltimore, Md.) [1967.]

764235

— Shakespearian crossword [puzzles].
In The Amateur theatre and playwrights' journal, Vol. 2, Nos. 24,
28, 30, 34.

1935-36.

476089

— Shakespearian crossword [puzzles]. In
the Amateur theatre and playwrights'
Journal, Vol.4, No.75.

1937.

467093

RIDER (W.)
Views in Stratford-upon-Avon and its
vicinity. pp. [26]. (Warwick)
1828. 57315
———— [Large paper edn.]
1878. 399820

RIDLER (Mrs. ANNE) ed.
Shakespeare criticism 1919-35.
Selected with an introduction by
Anne Bradby [i.e. Mrs. A. Ridler].
(Oxford) 1936.
World's Classics.

458354

RIDLER, Mrs. ANNE, ed.
Shakespeare criticism, 1935-60,
selected with an introduction by A.
Ridler.   1963.

    World's classics.   667439

RIDLEY (MAURICE ROY)
Keats' craftsmanship: a study in
poetic development. [With
Shakespearian references.] (Oxford)
1933.

    414550

RIDLEY (MAURICE ROY)
The Living Shakespeare [No. 4]: Plot
and character in the plays. [Broad-
cast] 22nd October, 1958.   ff. 9.
typescript.   [1958.]

    666025

RIDLEY (M. R.)
On reading Shakespeare.   pp. 31.
1940.
(British Academy.   [30th] Annual
Shakespeare Lecture)

    522285

RIDLEY (MAURICE ROY)
Shakespeare's plays: a commentary.
frontis.   1937.

    472138

RIDLEY (MAURICE ROY)
William Shakespeare: a commentary.
1936.   452996
New Temple Shakespeare, [Vol. 40.]
_____ One of 25 copies for guests at
The Ivy, October 6, 1936.   Signed by
the author and publisher.
1936.   562375

Ridley, Maurice Roy *works relating to*

—— Murry (J.M.) Professors and poets [:
with a criticism of The New Temple
Shakespeare, edited by M.R.Ridley,
with special reference to his prefaces
to the Comedy of Errors and Hamlet.]
From The Aryan path, Vol.6.

    (Bombay)   1935.

    484131

—— SPENCER (B. T.)
Three ways to Shakespeare [: a review
of"Shakespeare's plays: a commentary",
by M. R. Ridley, etc.]   FROM Sewanee
Review, Vol. 47.   (Sewanee)   1939.

    530197

RIEMER, A   P
A reading of Shakespeare's 'Antony
and Cleopatra'. (Sydney)   1968.

    Sydney studies in Literature.
774921

Riga

—— Plays by William Shakespear staged
in Riga, Latvian Soviet Socialist
Republic in the post-war period.
typescript.   [1964.]

    740840

RIGBY (CHARLES)
Maddermarket Mondays: press articles
dealing with the famous Norwich Players.
Foreword by B. Maine.   Published in
commemoration of the production of the
whole of Shakespeare's plays at the
Maddermarket Theatre, Norwich. (Norwich)
port.   illus.   1933.

    416881

Right-handedness *see* Hand

RIGHTER (ANNE)
Shakespeare and the idea of the play.
1962.

    667378

Rignold, George *and* William Henry *works relating to*

——Lyric Theatre, [Shaftesbury Avenue,
London, Programme of] testimonial
benefit to W. [H.] Rignold, Dec. 5,
1902.   [With a reference to G. Rignold's
rendering of a fragment from Henry the
Fifth.] pp. [4.]
ports.   1902.

    471774

Riis (J.A.) Hamlet's castle. Illus.
In The Century Illustrated Monthly
Magazine. Vol.61.

(New York)   1900-01.

157026

Riley ([Mrs.]Alice C.D.) Shakespeare's
lovers in a garden: a flower masque.
Written for the Drama League of
America tercentenary celebration of
Shakespeare's birthday,1915. Re-
edited by the author. Prologue and
epilogue by Eleanor E. Perkins. pp.32
(Chicago)1.duo.1927.
Music [by various
composers
(Chicago)   [c.1927]

407981

407982

Rilke (R.M.) Requiem and other poems
[including "The Spirit Ariel"
(after reading Shakespeare's
Tempest)]. Translated from the
German with an introduction, by
J.B. Leishman. Port.

1935.

(Alcuin Press.)

437081

RILKE (R. M.)
The Spirit Ariel.   (After reading
Shakespeare's "Tempest".)
IN Rilke (R. M.) Later poems.
Translated by J. B. Leishman.
1938.

482573

RILLA (WALTER) [ed.]
Extracts from Schlegel's translation
of Shakespeare: a reading with introductory notes on the translation.
[Broadcast] 23rd April, 1947.   ff. 2.
typescript.   1947.
Introductory notes only

583271

RIMSKY-KORSAKOFF (NIKOLAI ANDREEVICH)
My musical life [: containing references to performances of Shakespearean
music].   Translated from the Russian
by J. A. Joffe and edited with an
introduction by C. V. Vechten.
ports.   1924.

314036

Rinder (F.) The Geographical distribution
of the First Folio Shakespeare.
From The Burlington Magazine, vol.2.

[1903.]

440806

RINGLER (WILLIAM A.)
Exit Kent.
IN SHAKESPEARE QUARTERLY XI.
pp. 311-317.
(New York)   1960.

605711

RINGLER (WILLIAM A.)
Hamlet's defense of the players.   IN
HOSLEY (RICHARD) ed., Essays on
Shakespeare and Elizabethan drama in
honour of Hardin Craig.
illus.   1963.

667532

Ripley (A.C.) Vaudeville pattern [:mis-
cellaneous essays on the cinema,
theatre, etc., including two chapters
on Laurence Olivier's Henry V]. Ports.
Illus.

1942.

582752

Ristori, Adelaide *works relating to*

── HIS MAJESTY'S THEATRE [LONDON]
Adelaide Ristori memorial matinée
[programme], Nov. 30th, 1908.
[Including scenes from The Merchant
of Venice, Hamlet, Taming of the
Shrew and Macbeth, and an ode by
L. N. Parker.]   pp. [4.]
port.   [1908.]

531801

── Lewes (G.H.) On Fechter and Ristori.
In Agate (J.[E.]) ed., The English
dramatic critics.

[1932.]

399280

Ritchie ([Lady]Anne [I.]T.) Chapters
from some memoirs. [Including
a chapter on Mrs. Kemble.]

1894.

433144

RITCHIE (JOHN) composer
Under the greenwood tree: song, with
pianoforte accompaniment by J.Ritchie.
Words by Shakespeare [from As you
like it].   pp. 3, [i].   [1951.]

616957

RITCHIE (ROBERT LINDSAY GRAEME) ed.
France: a companion to French studies.
[With Shakespearian references.]
map.   1937.
Methuen's Companions to Modern Studies.

462195

[Ritson (J.)] Cursory criticisms on
the edition of Shakspeare published
by Edmond Malone. In Monthly
extracts; or, Beauties of modern
authors, Vol.3.

1792.

520594

[Ritson (J.)] The Stxcktxn [Stockton]
Jubilee; or, Shakespeare in all his
glory: a choice pageant for Christmas
holidays, 1781 [containing passages
from Shakespeare applied to the
principal inhabitants of Stockton-on-
Tees]. pp. [11]. Manuscript.

1781.

533659

[RITSON (J.) ed.]
A Select collection of English songs.
[With preface, an essay on national
song, some songs of Shakespeare, and
music.]
3 vols.   1783.

460089

Ritson, Joseph *works relating to*

—— Literarius (T.) [pseud.] A Familiar
address to the curious in English
poetry: more particularly to the
readers of Shakspeare: criticisms of
J.Ritson's "Observations on the three
first volumes of the history of English
poetry", by T.Warton, and "Remarks
critical and illustrative on the text
and notes of the last edition of
Shakspeare", edited by G.Steevens,
1778.]   1784.

431752

—— Ritson on Shakspeare.   FROM
Blackwood's Magazine, Aug. 1819.
(Edinburgh)   1819.

440106

Ritual in Shakespeare

——HAPGOOD (ROBERT)
Shakespeare and the ritualists.
IN SHAKESPEARE SURVEY 15.
(Cambridge)   1962.

667174

RITZE (F. H.)
Shakespeare's men of melancholy -
his malcontents: Columbia University
[thesis].   1947.   IN GOLDING
(NANCY L.) A Survey of the proposed
arrangements of Shakespeare's Sonnets
[etc.]
microfilm, positive copy.   bibliog.
[1948.]

609350

RIVERS (JOHN)
Shakespeare à la française.   IN The
Library, New Series, Vol. 6.   1905.

191304

ROACH (J.)
Authentic memoirs of the green-room
(for 1801-1802) involving sketches
of the performers of the Theatres-
Royal, Drury Lane, Covent-Garden and
the Hay-Market.
2 vols.   [1801]-1802.
All other vols. wanting.

517672

Robarts (Edith) ed.
[LAMB (CHARLES and MARY A.)
Tales from Shakespeare, retold by
Edith Robarts.]
illus.   [1912.]
Stories for the Children.
Frontis, half title-page and title-page
wanting.

555508

ROBB (STEWART)
Shakespeare's alleged "schoolboy
howlers".   [A Few first and last
things; and Hidden names.] pp.[16].
[New York]
ports.   [1952.]

633534

ROBB (W. CUTHBERT)
The Shades of night; a comic opera
[in one act.   For schools and youth
clubs.   Libretto only].   pp. 16.
1952.

623706

The Robbers' cave; or, Four-horned
moon.   A drama in imitation of
Shakspeare, in five acts [in prose
and verse.   Anon.]   1843.

435592

ROBBINS (WILLIAM)
Hamlet as allegory.   IN The University
of Toronto Quarterly, Vol. 21.
(Toronto)   1952.

596179/21

Robert Hall Players, Leicester see
Leicester, Robert Hall Players.

Robert Spence Watson Memorial Lectures
JONES (Sir H.)
The Ethical idea in Shakespeare: the
Spence Watson lecture delivered to the
Newcastle-upon-Tyne Literary and
Philosophical Society, 1918.   IN
Jones (Sir H.) Essays on literature
and education, edited by H. J. W.
Hetherington.   [1924.]

315305

ROBERTON ([Sir] HUGH STEVENSON)
Dirge for Fidele for chorus (or
quartet) of men's voices (T.T.B.B.)
(Unaccompanied).   Poem from
Shakespeare's "Cymbeline".   pp. 4.
                                    1941.

                    528952

ROBERTON ([Sir] H. S.)
Dirge for Fidele for chorus (or
quartet) of mixed voices, S.C.T.B.
(Unaccompanied.)   Poem from
Shakespeare's "Cymbeline".   pp. 4.
                                    1941.

                    528951

ROBERTON (Sir HUGH STEVENSON)

Full fathom five, for four-part chorus
of men's voices.[Words by] Shakespeare
in "The Tempest" pp.6.
                            1941.

                    665800

ROBERTON ([Sir] HUGH STEVENSON)
Moon magic: [part-song] for chorus
of mixed voices S.C.T.B. (unaccompanied).
[Words] from The Merchant of Venice.
pp. 4.   1941.

                    525599

ROBERTS (CHARLES GEORGE DOUGLAS)
To Shakespeare, 1916 [: a poem
IN GOLLANCZ ([Sir] I.) ed. A Book of
homage to Shakespeare.
    ports. illus. facsimiles. [1916.]

                    264175

ROBERTS (CYRIL)
The Second best bed.   IN BAYLISS
(A. E. M.) ed., Junior one-act plays
of to-day.   Third series.   1936.
[Harrap's Junior Modern English
Series.]
                    457251

ROBERTS (Mrs. D. O.)
Shakespeare and Co. unlimited, by
Shakespeare & Co. [: spirit messages
received and] compiled by Mrs. D. O.
Roberts.   [1950.]

                    616141

ROBERTS (Mrs. DAISY OKE) and WOOLCOCK
(COLLIN E.)
Elizabethan episode, incorporating
Shakespeare and Co., Unlimited
[: spirit messages received and
compiled by Mrs. Daisy O. Roberts].
    port.   [1961.]

                    666936

ROBERTS (DONALD R.)
Shakespeare and the rhetoric of
stylistic ornamentation: an abstract
of a dissertation presented to the
Faculty of the Graduate School of
Cornell University for the degree
of Doctor of Philosophy.   pp. [4.]
(Ithaca, N.Y.)   1936.

                    513778

ROBERTS (EDWIN F.)
On Shakspere.   FROM [Hood's Magazine,]
Vol. 9.   1848.

                    558103

ROBERTS (ERIC)
'Amlet's tragedy or mine? [A story.
Broadcast] 23rd April, 1951. ff. 7.
typescript.   1951.

                    620399

Roberts (M.) The Spiritual plane in
Shakespeare [: a review of] Shakes-
peare's last plays by E.M.W.Tillyard.
In The London Mercury and Bookman,
Vol. 38.
                            1938.

                    495900

Roberts, Robert *works relating to*

—— BOWERS (FREDSON THAYER)
Robert Roberts: a printer of Shakespeare's
Fourth Folio.
    IN SHAKESPEARE QUARTERLY II: 3.
    pp. 241-246.
    (New York)   1951.
                    605711

ROBERTS (WILLIAM)
Shakespeare autographs.   FROM Chambers's
Journal, 1905.   pp. [4.]   (Edinburgh)
                            1905.

                    390788

Robertson (Beatrice Forbes-) see
Forbes-Robertson (Beatrice)

Robertson (F.) Planning a stage
fight : the duel in the Arts Theatre
[production of] "Hamlet". Illus.
In Picture Post, Vol.30.

                    1946.

                    581239

Robertson, Graham *works relating to*

—— Mr. Graham Robertson's new dressing
of "As you like it".   IN Cassell's
Magazine of Art, [vol. 20]. 1896-7.

                    137932

Robertson (J. Minto) Artistry of
"The Tempest". [From Great Thoughts,
July 1939.]

[1939.]

502652

ROBERTSON (J. MINTO)
"The Middle of humanity" as
Shakespeare saw it [: Shakespeare's
non-heroic characters]. FROM
Hibbert Journal, Jan. 1941. 1941.

524714

ROBERTSON (J. MINTO)
Understatement as an expression of
national and individual temperament
[containing references to Shakespeare].
FROM [London Quarterly & Holborn
Review. Vol. 171.] pp. 10-19.
[1946.]

596211

ROBERTSON (J. MINTO)
Wanted - a Shakespeare atlas and
gazetteer. IN English, Vol. 6.
1946.

481151/6

Robertson, J. Minto *works relating to*

—— PRAZ (M.)
[Review of] The Problems of the
Shakespeare sonnets, by J. M. Robertson.
IN English studies, Vol. 10.
(Amsterdam) 1928.

485652

ROBERTSON (JAMES)
Written on a blank leaf of Shakespeare
[: verses]. IN [Robertson (J.)]
Poems by Nobody. 1770.

483156

ROBERTSON (JOHN GEORGE)
The Knowledge of Shakespeare on the
continent at the beginning of the
eighteenth century. IN The Modern
Language Review, Vol. 1. (Cambridge)
1906.

266816

Robertson (J.G.) Lessing's dramatic
theory : an introduction to &
commentary on his Hamburgische
Dramaturgie. [Edited by Edna
Purdie. With a bibliographical
note and including references to
Shakespeare.] Illus.

(Cambridge) 1939.

497753

ROBERTSON (JOHN GEORGE)
The Life and work of Goethe, 1749-1832.
[With references to Shakespeare, and
bibliographical notes.]
ports. illus. 1932.

389376

ROBERTSON (JOHN MACKINNON)
Elizabethan literature. [Including
a chapter on Shakespeare.]
bibliog. 1932.
The Home University Library of Modern
Knowledge.

411891

ROBERTSON (J. M.)
A History of freethought, ancient and
modern, to the period of the French
Revolution. [With references to
Shakespeare, a bibliography and a bio-
graphical note of Robertson by J. P.
Gilmour.] 4th edn. revised and expanded.
ports. 1936.

455045

ROBERTSON (J. M.)
The Naturalistic theory of Hamlet.
IN The Criterion, Vol. 3. 1925.

328360

ROBERTSON (J. M.)
The Paradox of Shakespeare. IN Gollancz
([Sir] I. ed., A Book of homage to
Shakespeare.
ports. illus. facsimiles. [1916.]

264175

ROBERTSON (J. M.)
[Review of] William Shakespeare. A
Study of facts and problems, by [Sir]
E. K. Chambers. IN The Criterion,
Vol. 10.

1930-31.

388357

ROBERTSON (J. M.)
The Scansion of Shakespeare. IN The
Criterion, vol. 8.

[1929]

361188

ROBERTSON (J. M.)
The Shakespeare canon.

1922-
Part 4. Division 2.1: The Second part
of "Henry VI". 2: The Third part of
"Henry VI".

399360

ROBERTSON (J. M.)
Shakespearean idolatry. FROM The
Criterion, 1930. pp. [22.]
[1930.]

390921

Robertson, John Mackinnon Rt. Hon.
works relating to

— BOND (R. W.)
[A Review of] "Montaigne and
Shakespeare and other essays on
cognate questions", by J. M. Robertson.
IN The Modern Language Review, Vol. 5.
(Cambridge)   1910.

266820

— Hamlet once more [: a review of
"Hamlet once more", by J. M. Robertson.]
FROM The Contemporary Review, Literary
Supplement, 1923. pp. [3.] [1923.]

389225

— [A Review of] "The State of Shakespeare
study", by J.M. Robertson. In
The New Statesman and Nation,
Vol.1. (N.S.) Feb.- June, 1931.

1931.

396295

— Sykes (H.D.) [Review of] Shakespeare
and Chapman, by J. M. Robertson. In
The Modern Language Review. Vol. 13.

1918.

276260

Robertson (Sir Johnston Forbes-) see
Forbes-Robertson (Sir Johnston)

ROBERTSON (MARION)
Hamlet; and, Miracle in the Gorbals:
the stories of the ballets. With
decorations by Joyce Millen. pp.95.
1949.
The Ballet Pocket Series.

644595

ROBERTSON (THOMAS)
An Essay on the character of Hamlet,
in Shakespeare's tragedy of Hamlet.
Read [to the Royal Society of Edinburgh]
by [A.] Dalzel, July 21, 1788. IN
Transactions of the Royal Society of
Edinburgh, Vol. 2. (Edinburgh)
1790.

39022

ROBERTSON (T. W.)
David Garrick: a love story.
1865.   522848
———— Another edn. pp. 36.
French's Acting Edition.
[1881.]   455693

Robertson (W.G.) Time was: reminiscences. With a foreword by Sir J. Forbes-Robertson. Ports. Illus.

1931.

485744

Robeson, Paul LeRoy *works relating to*

— GILDER (ROSAMOND)
Othello and Venus: Broadway in
review. [Includes a criticism of
Margaret Webster's production of
Othello under Theatre Guild auspices,
starring Paul Robeson.] IN Theatre
Arts, Vol. 27. (New York)
illus.   1943.

548672

— [Theatre Guild, New York.] Paul
Robeson as Othello, the Moor of
Venice [: a souvenir book of the
Margaret Webster production of
Othello]. pp. [20.] Illus.

[New York]   [1943.]

559677

Robey, George Sir *works relating to*

— WILSON (ALBERT EDWARD)
Prime minister of mirth: the biography of Sir George Robey, C.B.E.
ports.   illus.   1956.
With Shakespearian references.
654604

ROBINS (EDWARD)
Echoes of the playhouse: reminiscences
of some past glories of the English
stage. [With chapters: "The English
Roscius (Thomas Betterton)", "An Irish
Shylock (Charles Macklin)", "A Very
good mimic (David Garrick)" and "The
Palmy days of Garrick". With bibliographical notes.] (New York)
ports.   illus.   1895.

545003

ROBINS (ELIZABETH)
Both sides of the curtain [: an
autobiography. With references
to Shakespeare].
port.   1940.

511246

ROBINS (ELIZABETH)
On seeing Madame Bernhardt's Hamlet.
IN The North American Review, Vol. 171.
(New York)   1900.

155377

ROBINSON (ANTHONY MEREDITH LEWIN)
The Grey copy of the Shakespeare First
Folio.   IN Quarterly Bulletin of the
South African Library, Vol. 5.   (Cape
Town)   1950.

601551/5

ROBINSON [CHARLES EDWARD RICKETTS]
Shakspere's "King John": its historical
character and dramatic features.   FROM
[The Workman's Magazine, 1873.]   [1873.]

553488

ROBINSON (E. A.)
Collected poems, [including 'Ben
Jonson entertains a man from
Stratford'.]   New edn.   (New York)
port.   1930.

398826

Robinson, Edwin Arlington *works relating to*

——LOWELL (AMY)
Edwin Arlington Robinson [: a
critical biographical essay with
references to Shakespeare.]
IN Lowell (A.) Tendencies in modern
American poetry.   (Oxford)
bibliog.   [1917.]

552574

ROBINSON (EILEEN)
The Shakespeare Memorial Library,
Stratford-upon-Avon: items of
interest to theatre research workers.
IN Theatre Notebook, Vol. 12.
                                    1958.

584117/12

ROBINSON (FREDERIC W.)
Commentary and questionnaire on King
Lear.   pp. 32.   1927.
Commentaries and Questionnaires in
English Literature, No. 79.
                                    408529

Robinson (H.C.) On books and their
writers [:excerpts from the author's
diaries and reminiscences, with
references to Shakespeare], edited
[with a preface] by Edith J. Morley.
Ports.   3 vols.

1938.

486402

ROBINSON (HERBERT SPENCER)
English Shakesperian criticism in the
eighteenth century.   (New York)
bibliog.   1932.

394328

ROBINSON (HORACE W.)
Shakespeare, Ashland, Oregon.
IN SHAKESPEARE QUARTERLY VI.
pp. 447-451.
(New York) 1955.

605711

ROBINSON, J. W.
Palpable hot ice: dramatic burlesque
in 'A Midsummer-night's dream'.
FROM Studies in Philology LXI.2.1.
(Chapel Hill, N.C.)   1964.

668309

ROBINSON, JAMES E.
Time and 'The Tempest'.   FROM Journal
of English and Germanic Philology
LXIII: 2, April 1964.   pp. 255-267.
                                    1964.

668349

ROBINSON (N. L.)
Shakespeare: an address delivered
at the Shakespeare Celebration
April 25th, 1932.   IN The Central
Literary Magazine.   Vol. 30. 1931-32.
                                    1932.

407289

Robinson (Richard G.) illus.
BURTON (HARRY McGUIRE)
Shakespeare and his plays.   With
illustrations by R. G. Robinson.
pp. [iv] 68.
port.   illus.   chart.   facsimiles.
bibliog.   1958.
Methuen's Outlines.

665794

Robinson, Robert *works relating to*

—— FIEDLER (H. G.)
A Contemporary of Shakespeare on
phonetics and on the pronunciation
of English and Latin [i.e. "The Art
of pronunciation" by R. Robinson,
1617]: a contribution to the history
of phonetics and English sounds.
[Presidential address, Modern Humanities
Research Association, 1936.]   pp. 21.
(Oxford)
facsimiles   bibliog.   1936.

461805

Robinson (William Heath) illus.
LAMB (CHARLES and MARY)
Tales from Shakespeare.   [1901.]

364017

Robson, Eleanor *works relating to*

___LIEBLER & CO.
Some excerpts from reviews having
reference to[Eleanor] Robson's
[performance as Juliet in Liebler &
Co's production of Shakespeare's
Romeo and Juliet, 1903]. pp. [24.]
(New York)
  ports.   illus.   [1903.]

646237

ROBSON (FLORA)
Commentary.   IN Macbeth.   Text edited
by C. J. Sisson.   (New York) 1962.
 The Laurel Shakespeare.   F. Fergusson,
general editor.

667472

Robson, Flora *works relating to*

___Theatre Incorporated. Michael
   Redgrave [and] Flora Robson in
   The Tragedy of "Macbeth" [:a
   description of the Theatre
   Incorporated production and
   cast]. pp. [16.] Ports. Illus.

[New York]   [1948.]

598973

Robson (W.W.) An Introduction to "The
Tempest" (the Davenant, Dryden,
Shadwell version). [Broadcast] 6th
[and] 8th January 1950. pp.6.
Typescript.

1950.

609487

ROBSON-SCOTT (WILLIAM DOUGLAS)
The Berlin stage, 1935-6.   IN
German life and letters Vol. 1.
(Oxford)   1936.

476079

ROCHDALE BRANCH, BRITISH EMPIRE SHAKESPEARE
SOCIETY
Leaflets, etc.   (Rochdale)   1925-45.

397915

ROCHESTER CATHEDRAL CHOIR SCHOOL
Programmes, etc. of Shakespeare performances, 1922-36.   (Rochester)
              [1922]-36.

ROCK AND CO
Views of Stratford-on-Avon and Warwick.
pp. [ii].
  12 plates.   [c.1855.]

573033

Rockefeller, John Davison *works relating to*

___HARRIS (J. C.)
Joel Chandler Harris, editor and essayist: miscellaneous literary, political,
and social writings.   Edited [with
introductions] by [Mrs.] Julia F. [C.]
Harris.   [Including, Shakespeare of
modern business: a study of the comparison made by O. L. Triggs between
Shakespeare and John D. Rockefeller.
With bibliographical notes.   (Chapel
Hill, N.C.)
  ports.   illus.   facsimiles. 1931.

536323

Rockelein (L.) see Moloney (J. C.) and
Rockelein (L.)

RODD (T.)
The Quarto editions of Shakespeare's
plays.   FROM The Gentleman's
Magazine, [New Series] Vol. 13.
              1840.

521907

RODDMAN, PHILIP
André Gide on Shakespeare.
IN PAOLUCCI, ANNE, ed., Shakespeare
encomium, 1564-1964 [by various
writers].   (New York)   1964.
 City University of New York, City
College Papers.

747546

Roddman (P.) Gide's Hamlet.pp.213-220.
From Partisan Review, Vol.2.

[New York]   1949.

604974

RODGER, IAN
An Anointed king [: 'Richard II'
rehearsed by the Royal Shakespeare
Theatre company]. Produced by Joe
Burroughs. B.B.C. radio script
broadcast 10th June 1964.   1964.

668246

Rodgers (J.) It was a lover and his
lass : part-song for S.A.T.B.
Words by Shakespeare [from As
You Like It]. Music by J.
Rodgers. pp.7.

[c.1925.]

594142

RODGERS (R.)
Falling in love with love [: song
from] a musical comedy, The Boys
from Syracuse, based on Shakespeare's
A Comedy of errors.   Lyrics by
L. Hart.   pp. 7.   1938.

514205

RODGERS (R.)
Oh, Diogenes! [: song from] a
musical comedy, The Boys from
Syracuse, based on Shakespeare's
A Comedy of errors.   Lyrics by
L. Hart. pp. 5.   1938.

514208

RODGERS (R.)
The Shortest day of the year [: song
from] a musical comedy, The Boys
from Syracuse, based on Shakespeare's
A Comedy of errors.   Lyrics by
L. Hart.   pp. 5.   1938.

514204

RODGERS (R.)
Sing for your supper [: song from]
a musical comedy, The Boys from
Syracuse, based on Shakespeare's
A Comedy of errors.   Lyrics by
L. Hart.   pp. 5.   1938.

514206

RODGERS (R.)
This can't be love [: song from]
a musical comedy, The Boys from
Syracuse, based on Shakespeare's
A Comedy of errors.   Lyrics by
L. Hart.   pp. 5.   1938.

514207

RODGERS (R.)
You have cast your shadow on the
sea [: song from] a musical comedy,
The Boys from Syracuse, based on
Shakespeare's A Comedy of errors.
Lyrics by L. Hart.   pp. 5.   1938.

514203

RODGERS (R. R.) ed.
A Collection of newspaper cuttings.
Including cuttings relating to
Shakespeare.   [1867-1904].

507548

Rodway (A.[J.]) Arms of Philip Massinger,
    emblazoned by A.[J.] Rodway.

[1912.]

73930

RODWAY (A. [J.])
Arms of Richard Burbage, emblazoned
by A. [J.] Rodway.   [1913.]

73930

RODWAY (PHYLLIS [I. I.] P.) and SLINGSBY
([Mrs.] LOIS [H.] R.)
Philip Rodway and a tale of two theatres,
by his daughters.   (Birmingham)
    ports.   illus.   pedigree.
            1934.   426686

ROE (FRANK GILBERT)
The Marlowe fiasco - Shakespeare is as
Shakespeare does.   [FROM "Queen's
Quarterly", Spring 1957.]   pp. [12]
[Kingston, Ontario]   1957.

666145

ROE (FRED and FREDERIC GORDON)
Shakespeare's chair?   pp. [4.]
FROM The Connoisseur, July 1940.
    illus.   1940.

515936

ROE (J. E.)
Sir Francis Bacon's own story.
(Rochester, N.Y.)
    port.   1918.

462482

ROERECKE (EDITH M.)
Baroque aspects of 'Antony and
Cleopatra'.   IN SMITH, GORDON ROSS,
ed., Essays on Shakespeare [by various
authors].   (University Park, Penn.)
pp. 182-195.   1965.

755528

ROESEN (BOBBYANN)
Love's labour's lost.
IN SHAKESPEARE QUARTERLY IV: 4.
pp. 411-426.
(New York)   1953.

605711

[ROFFE (A. T.)]
An Essay upon the ghost belief of
Shakespeare.   pp. 41.   [c.1860.]
    t.p. wanting.

526664

ROGERS (BRUCE)
The Format of the new Shakespeare [:
the Limited Editions Club edition].
IN Shakespeare: a review and a preview
[by various authors].   pp. [37.]
(New York: Limited Editions Club)
    illus.   [c.1939.]

564974

ROGERS (CARMEN)
Heavenly justice in the tragedies of
Shakespeare.   IN MATTHEWS (A. D.) and
EMERY (C. M.) eds., Studies in
Shakespeare.   (University of Miami
Publications in English and American
Literature, Vol. 1, March 1953).
(Coral Gables, Fla.)   1953.

634188

Rogers (J.D.) Voyages and exploration:
    geography: maps. In Shakespeare's
    England, vol.1. [With biblio-
    graphies.] Illus. Facsimiles.

(Oxford)   1917.

435745

ROGERS (L. W.)
Clairvoyance in Shakespeare.
IN The Theosophist, Vol. 58, Pt. 2.
(Madras)   1937.

469480

Rogers (L.W.) Ghosts in Shakespeare.
In The Theosophist, Vol.58, Pt.1.

(Madras)   1937.

469480

Rogers (L.W.) Shakespeare and theosophy.
In The Theosophist, Vol.58, Pt.1.

(Madras)   1937-

469480

Rogers (L.W.) Symbolical dreams in
Shakespeare. In The Theosophist,
Vol.58, Pt.2.

(Madras)   1937.

469480

Rogers, Paul *works relating to*

__ WILLIAMSON (AUDREY)
Paul Rogers [: a study of his work
for stage and screen].
port. illus. chronological table.
1956.
Theatre World Monographs No. 5.

654514

ROGERS (P. P.)
The Spanish drama collection in
the Oberlin College Library: a
descriptive catalogue. Author
list [and] Supplementary volume
containing reference lists.
[Including entries of translations
of some of Shakespeare's plays.]
(Oberlin, Ohio)
2 vols.   1940-46.

526823

ROGERS (R. E.)
The Boy Will. IN COHEN (HELEN L.)
ed., One-act plays by modern authors,
edited [with introductions] by
Helen L. Cohen.   (New York)
illus.   1921.

397663

Rogers (Walter S.) illus.
LAMB (CHARLES and MARY [A.])
Tales from Shakespeare.   (New York)
[c.1920.]

473389

ROGERS, WILLIAM HUDSON
Shakespeare and English history.
(Totowa, N.J.)   1966.

766606

Rogues and Vagabonds

__ FULLER (R.)
The Beggars' brotherhood [: a history
of beggars and knaves in England,
from the 16th to the 18th centuries.
With references to Shakespearian
characters].
ports. illus.   1936.

446969

__ McPEEK (J. A. S.)
Shakspere and the fraternity of
unthrifts: [a study of Copland's
"The Hye way to the spyttel hous"].
IN Harvard Studies and notes in
philology and literature, Vol. 14.
(Cambridge, Mass.)   1932.

398528

__ Whibley (C.) Rogues and vagabonds.
In Shakespeare's England, vol.2.
[With bibliographies.] Illus.
Facsimiles.

(Oxford)   1917.

435746

ROHDE (ELEANOUR S.)
Shakespeare's roses.   FROM Cornhill
Magazine, July, 1934.   pp. 28-32.
1934.

421735

Rohde (Eleanour S.) Shakespeare's wild
flowers: fairy lore, gardens, herbs,
gatherers of simples and bee lore.
Illus.

1935.

(Medici Society.)   443234

ROHDE (ELEANOR S.)
Shakespeare's wild flowers.
FROM The Cornhill Magazine, Vol.
151. pp. [11].   1935.

437095

Rohde (Eleanour S.) The Story of
the garden. [With references to flowers
mentioned by Shakespeare in his works.]
Illus.   (The Medici Society)

1932.

400147

Rohmkopfs Englische Reihe
MASEFIELD (JOHN)
William Shakespeare. Herausgegeben
von E. Wötzel. pp. 32. (Leipzig)
[c.1935.]

[English text.]
498654

RÖHRMAN (H.)
Marlowe and Shakespeare: a thematic
exposition of some of their plays.
(Arnhem)   1952.

628634

ROLFE (WILLIAM JAMES)
A Life of William Shakespeare.
ports.   illus.   1905.

394828

ROLFE (WILLIAM JAMES)
Shakespeare the boy; with sketches of
the home and school life, the games and
sports, the manners, customs and folk-
lore of the time.   (New York)
illus.   1896.

545571

Rolfe (W.J.) Shakespeare's allusions
to music. pp. [10.] From The
Looker-on, Vol. 2.

(New York)   1896.

494039

Rolfe (William James) ed.
CRAIK (G. L.)
The English of Shakespeare, illustrated in a philological commentary
on his Julius Caesar, [the commentary
preceded by a prolegomena and the
text of the play.]   Edited, from the
3rd revised London edn.   [6th
American edition.]   (Boston, [Mass.])
[1871.]

477169

Rolland, Romain
To my best friend - Shakespeare. IN

LEWINTER, OSWALD, ed.
Shakespeare in Europe [by various
authors].   1963.

667784

ROLLINS (HYDER EDWARD)
Thomas Deloney and Brian Melbancke:
notes on sources.   [With references
to Shakespeare.]   IN Harvard studies
and notes in philology and literature,
Vol. 19.   (Cambridge, Mass.) 1937.

464813

ROLLINS (HYDER EDWARD)
The Troilus-Cressida story from Chaucer
to Shakespeare.   IN Publications of
the Modern Language Association of
America, Vol. 32.   (Baltimore)   1917.

428352

Roman Plays *see* Greek and Roman Plays

Romano, Giulio *and* John Christopher *works relating to*

—— BAUGHAN (D.E.)
Shakespeare s probable confusion of the
two Romanos.   FROM The Journal of English
and Germanic Philology, Vol. 36.
(Urbana, Ill.)

1937.

488674

Romanticism

—— Barzun (J.[M.]) Romanticism and the
modern ego. [With references to
Shakespeare, bibliographical notes
and references.]

(Boston, [Mass.])   1944.

551143

—— BETHURUM (DOROTHY)
Shakespeare's comment on mediaeval
romance in Midsummer-night's dream
[and the influence of Chaucer's
Knight's Tale.]   IN Modern Language
Notes, Vol. 60.   (Baltimore)
bibliog.   1945.

571543

—— CHARLTON (H. B.)
Shakespeare's recoil from romanticism.
IN Bulletin of the John Rylands
Library, Vol. 15.   1931.

387635

—— Clement (N.H.) Romanticism in France.
[With a bibliography and references
to Shakespeare.]

(New York)   1939.

(Modern Language Association of America.
Revolving Fund Series, 9.)

496259

—— JAMES (D. G.)
The Romantic comedy [: a history of
English romanticism in terms of the
treatment of mythology by Blake,
Shelley, Keats, Coleridge and Newman.
With references to .Shakespeare and
bibliographical notes].   (Oxford)
1948.

593033

—— PETTET (E. C.)
Shakespeare and the romance
tradition.   With an introduction
by H. S. Bennett.
bibliogs.   1949.

604783

PRAZ (M.)
The Romantic agony: a study of the
morbid tendencies of romantic
literature from 1800-1900, containing
references to Shakespeare and his
works.] Translated from the Italian
by A. Davidson.
frontis. bibliog.   1933.

406496

Tynan (J.L.) The Influence of Greene on
Shakespeare's early romance. In PMLA,
Publications of the Modern Language
Association of America, vol.27.

(Baltimore)   1912.

428347

Wells (Stanley)
Shakespeare and romance. IN
Stratford-upon-Avon Studies.
8: Later Shakespeare.   1966.

illus. pp.49-101.   756101

WILLIAMS, JOHN ANTHONY
The Natural work of art: the
experience of romance in Shakespeare's
'Winter's Tale.' (Cambridge, Mass.)
1967.

LeBaron Russell Briggs Prize.
Honors essays in English, 1966.
763814

Romeo and Juliet

General Works and Criticism

Ballet

Characters

Cinematography

Illustrations

Music; Opera

Novels; Plays; Poems; Burlesques

Sources and Background

Stage History and Production

Study and Teaching; Tales

Textual History

Romeo and Juliet

— General Works and Criticism

ARCHER (W.)
The Local colour of "Romeo and Juliet".
FROM The Gentleman's Magazine,
November, 1884.   1884.

440302

Armstrong (E.) Italian studies. Edited
[with a preface] by Cecilia M. Ady.
[With an introduction "Edward
Armstrong, 1846- 1928", by W.H.Hutton;
bibliographical notes; and references
to Romeo and Juliet.] Port.

1934.

419175

Bamborough (J.B.) Introducing
Shakespeare (3) : "Romeo and
Juliet". [Broadcast] 1st
December, 1949. ff. [i,] 10.
Typescript.

1949.

605274

BONNARD (GEORGES A.)
Romeo and Juliet: a possible significance.   IN The Review of English
Studies, New Series, Vol. 2. (Oxford)
1951.

318239/2/2

BULGIN (RANDOLPH M.)
Dramatic imagery in Shakespeare: Romeo
and Juliet.   FROM Shenandoah, Vol. 21,
No. 2.   pp. [14].   (Lexington, Va.)
1960.

667234

CHANG, JOSEPH S. M. J.
The Language of paradox in "Romeo and
Juliet".   IN SHAKESPEARE STUDIES 3.
(Cincinnati, Ohio)   1967.

771652

Chapman (J.J.) The Young Shakespeare:
a study of Romeo. pp.[7.] In The
Atlantic Monthly, Vol.78, 1896.

(Boston)   1896.

136397

CHAPMAN (RAYMOND)
Double time in Romeo and Juliet.
IN Modern Language Review Vol. 44.
1949.

266816/44

CHARLTON (H. B.)
'Romeo and Juliet' as an experimental
tragedy.   pp. 45.
bibliog.   1939.
British Academy [29th] Annual
Shakespeare Lecture.

507457

DICKEY (FRANKLIN M.)
Not wisely but too well: Shakespeare's
love tragedies.   (San Marino, Cal.)
1957.
Huntington Library.

665754

DRAPER (JOHN WILLIAM)

Patterns of style in Romeo and Juliet.
FROM Studia Neophilologica, Vol. 21.
pp. 16.   (Uppsala)
[1949.]

608978

—DRAPER (JOHN WILLIAM)
Shakespeare's "star-crossed lovers".
IN Review of English Studies: a
quarterly journal of English literature and the English language, Vol.15.
1939.

513846

—DRIVER (TOM F.)
The Shakespearian clock: time and the
vision of reality in "Romeo and Juliet"
and "The Tempest". IN Shakespeare
Quarterly XV: 4. pp.363-370. (New York)
1964.

605711

—ERSKINE (J.)
Romeo and Juliet.   IN Erskine (J.)
The Delight of great books.   1928.

405093

—EVANS, ROBERT O.
The Osier cage: rhetorical devices in
Romeo & Juliet. (Lexington, Ky.)
1966.

764820

—GATTY (REGINALD ARTHUR ALLIX)
Romeo and Juliet [: a lecture].
manuscript.   [c.1925.]

637994

—GAW (ALLISON)
Actors' names in basic Shakespearean
texts, with special reference to
Romeo and Juliet and Much Ado.
FROM Publications of the Modern
Language Association of America,
Vol. 40.   (Menasha, Wis.)
bibliog.   1925.

554228

—GRANVILLE-BARKER (HARLEY)
Prefaces to Shakespeare.
2 vols.   1958.

665961-62

For other editions of this work check
the main sequence under the author's
name.

—HART (JOHN A.)
Romeo and Juliet.   IN Carnegie
Institute of Technology, Carnegie
Series in English, "Lovers' meeting":
discussions of five plays by
Shakespeare.   (Pittsburgh)   1964.

741508

—HELINE (T.)
The Occult in Shakespeare: Romeo
and Juliet.   pp. 36.   (New York)
bibliog.   1936.

469129

—KEIL (HARRY)
Scabies and the Queen Mab passage in
Romeo and Juliet.   FROM Journal of
the History of Ideas, Vol. 18.
pp. 394-410.   (Lancaster, Pa.) 1957.

665742

—LAMARTINE (ALPHONSE de)
Shakspeare.   IN Lamartine (A. de)
Biographies and portraits of some
celebrated people.
2 vols.   1866.

686407-8

—LAWLOR (JOHN)
"Romeo and Juliet".   IN Stratford-
upon-Avon Studies, edited by J. R.
Brown and B. Harris, Vol. 3.   Early
Shakespeare.   1961.

666841

—LEATHAM (J.)
"Romeo and Juliet", a true tragedy
of young love.   pp. 16.   (Turriff)
[c.1920.]
Shakespeare Studies, No. 16.

566388

—Le Gallienne (R.) The Burial of
Romeo and Juliet [:an essay]. In
Le Gallienne (R.) Prose fancies
(2nd series). 2nd edn.

[c.1902.]

413699

—LEVIN (HARRY TUCHMAN)
Form and formality in Romeo and Juliet.
IN SHAKESPEARE QUARTERLY XI: 1.
pp. 3-11.
(New York)   1960.

605711

—LINK (FREDERICK M.)
Romeo and Juliet: character and
tragedy.   FROM Boston University,
Studies in English, Vol. 1.   pp. [11.]
(Boston, Mass.)   1955.

665672

—[Maginn (W.)] Shakspeare papers,
No.3: Romeo. In Bentley's Miscellany,
Vol.2.

1837.

30952

—MALCOLMSON (D.)
Ten heroes [: a book on the making of
literature, giving ten patterns which
form the basis of all stories.   With
reference to Shakespeare's Romeo and
Juliet].   (New York)   1941.

536926

—MANNHEIM (LUCIE) [and others]
The Image of love [: a discussion
between Lucie Mannheim, M. Goring,
W. J. R. Turner, and J. Duncan; with
illustrations from Shakespeare's
"Romeo and Juliet", Schnitzler's
"Liebelei", Gogol's "Marriage", Ibsen's
"Doll's House" and Shaw's "Candida";
from the broadcast series The Living
image.   Broadcast] 25th January, 1943.
ff. 20.
typescript.   1943.

539874

OLIVE (W. J.)
"Twenty good nights" - The Knight of
the burning pestle, The Family of love,
and Romeo and Juliet.   IN Studies in
Philology, Vol. 47.   (Chapel Hill,
N.C.)   1950.

554520/47

PETERSON, DOUGLAS L.
"Romeo and Juliet" and the art of moral
navigation.
IN Pacific coast studies in
Shakespeare.   Edited by W. F. McNeir
and T. N. Greenfield.   (Eugene: Ore.)
1966.

768009

PETTET (E. C.)
The Imagery of "Romeo and Juliet".
IN English: the magazine of the
English Association, Vol. 8.
1950.

481151/8

POGSON (BERYL)
Romeo and Juliet: an esoteric interpretation.   pp. 20.
[1954]

644241

RIBNER (IRVING)
Then I denie you starres: a reading
of Romeo and Juliet.   IN Studies in
the English Renaissance drama, edited
by Josephine W. Bennett [and others].
1959.

684756

SATIN (JOSEPH)

Romeo and Juliet as Renaissance Vita
Nuova. FROM Discourse: A Review of the
Liberal Arts. Vol.3, No.2. pp.[19].
(Moorhead, Minn.)   1960.

667233

SIEGEL (PAUL N.   )

Christianity and the religion of love
in "Romeo and Juliet". A reprint FROM
Shakespeare Quarterly, Vol.12, No.4,
Autumn, 1961. (New York)   1961.

668455

SIMPSON (RICHARD)
On "evening mass" in Romeo and Juliet,
IV.i.38.
IN Transactions of the New Shakespeare
Society, Series 1. No. 3.   pp. 148-154.
1875-8.

40620

SMITH (GORDON ROSS)
The Balance of themes in 'Romeo and
Juliet'.   IN Smith (G. R.) ed.,
Essays on Shakespeare [by various
authors].   (University Park, Penn.)
pp. 15-66.   1965.

755528

SUDDARD ([S. J.] MARY)
The Blending of prose, blank verse
and rhymed verse in "Romeo and Juliet".
FROM The Contemporary Review: Literary
Supplement, 1910.   pp. [5.]   [1910]

389209

TANNENBAUM (SAMUEL AARON) and TANNENBAUM
(Mrs. DOROTHY ROSENZWEIG)
Shakspere's Romeo and Juliet: a concise
bibliography.   (New York)
1950.
Elizabethan Bibliographies, No. 41

608093

TANSELLE (G. THOMAS)
Time in "Romeo and Juliet". IN
Shakespeare Quarterly XV: 4. pp.349-361.
(New York)   1964.

605711

THOMPSON (D. W.)
"Full of his roperipe" and "roperipe
terms".   IN Modern Language Notes,
Vol. 53.   (Baltimore)   1938.
Romeo and Juliet,II, iv, 154.

493024

[Walker (J.C.)] Historical memoir on
Italian tragedy. [Contains (pp.50-62)
a parallel between L.Groto's tragedy of
Hadriana and Romeo and Juliet.]

1799.

59355

WICKHAM LEGG (J.)
Note upon the elf-locks in Romeo and Juliet
(I.iv.91 and 92).
IN Transactions of the New Shakespeare
Society, Series 1. No. 4.   pp. 191-193.
1875-6.

40620

Romeo and Juliet
— Ballet

AMBERG (G.)
Art in modern ballet [, including
illustrations of the ballets Hamlet
and Romeo and Juliet].   pp. 115.
210 plates.   [1947.]

581604

BEAUMONT (C. W.)
Supplement to Complete book of ballets.
[Including two ballet arrangements of
Romeo and Juliet.]
ports. illus.   1942.
For Complete book of ballets see
catal. no. 475178.

532109

BEISWANGER (G.)
Dancers and makers of dance.
[Includes a criticism of the Ballet
Theatre's ballet Romeo and Juliet.]
IN Theatre Arts, Vol. 27.   (New
York)
  illus.   1943.

                                548672

MORLEY (IRIS)
Romeo and Juliet in Moscow: a ballet.
IN Ballet, Vol. 4.
  illus.   1947.

                                591429

Morozov (M.[M.]) Ballet Romeo and
Juliet at the Bolshoi Theatre
[Moscow]. Illus. From Soviet
Literature, June, 1947.

        (Moscow)   1947.

                                599873

WYATT (E[UPHEMIA] V. R.)
Juliet on her toes [: Romeo and
Juliet as a ballet].   FROM The
Commonweal, Vol. 38.   (New York)
                                1943.

                                559502

Romeo and Juliet
– Characters

F. [pseud.]
False criticisms – Juliet and Portia.
FROM [The London University Magazine,
May 1842.]   [1842.]

                                558053

FARJEON (H.)
Shakespeare's characters – Capulet
[: scenes from Romeo and Juliet].
Arranged [with comments] by H. Farjeon.
[Broadcast 20 February, 1946.]   ff. 18.
  typescript.   [1945.]

                                569285

[FARJEON (H.)]
Shakespeare's characters – Mercutio
[: scenes from Romeo and Juliet].
Arranged [with comments] by
H. Farjeon.   [Recorded for broad-
casting] 2nd February [1944]. ff.15.
  typescript.   [1944.]

                                582325

GUIDO (ANGELINA)
The Humor of Juliet's nurse.
FROM Bulletin of the History of
Medicine, Vol. 17.   (Baltimore,
Md.)   1945.

                                583398

HERRING (R.)
Harlequin Mercutio; or, Plague on your
houses: a ride through raids to resurrection [: a verse-pantomime of present-
day London.   Mercutio and Hamlet are
taken to be two aspects, the spirit
and conscience, of the same person, Ego].
FROM Life and Letters To-day, Vols. 31
and 32.   1941-2.   534897
_____ IN SCHIMANSKI (S.) and TREECE (H.)
eds., Transformation [: an anthology].
                    1943.   543517

Holland (Norman Norwood)
Mercutio, mine own son the dentist. IN

SMITH, GORDON ROSS, ed.
Essays on Shakespeare [by various
authors]. (University Park, Penn.)
                                1965.

    pp.3-14.   755528

HOSLEY (RICHARD)
How many children had Lady Capulet?
IN SHAKESPEARE QUARTERLY XVIII: 1.
pp. 3-6.
(New York)   1967.

                                605711

McARTHUR (HERBERT)
Romeo's loquacious friend.
IN SHAKESPEARE QUARTERLY X: 1.
pp. 34-44.
(New York)   1959.

                                605711

MARTIN (HELENA FAUCIT [Lady])
On some of Shakespeare's female
characters: by one who has person-
ated them.   IV – Juliet.
IN Blackwood's Edinburgh Magazine,
Vol. 131.   1882.

                                50070

MEYNELL ([Mrs.] ALICE)
Harlequin Mercutio.   IN Meynell
([Mrs.] A.) Prose and poetry.
Centenary volume, edited by F. P[age
and others].
  ports.   1947.

                                586379

Q. (N. R.)
Shakspeare fancies.   No. 1. Juliet
and Lady Mary Wortley Montague [: a
comparison].   IN The Metropolitan
Magazine, Vol. 22.   1838.

                                88822

Thaler (A.) Mercutio and Spenser's
Phantastes. From Philological
Quarterly, Vol. 16.

    (Iowa City)   1937.

                                507528

Romeo and Juliet

— Cinematography

—Gielgud (V.) and Lejeune (C[aroline]
A.) Romeo and Juliet: a discussion
[of the film] between V. Gielgud
and C.A.Lejeune. Port. In World
Film News, Vol. 1.

1936.

485419

—GRANVILLE-BARKER (HARLEY)
Alas, poor Will!: comments on
Shakespeare's treatment on the screen
and through the microphone. FROM
The Listener, March 3rd, 1937.
illus. 1937.

464182

—HERBERT (M.)
William Shakespeare writes a pacifist
play: [a criticism of the film Romeo
and Juliet]. [FROM The Quiver, April,
1937].
illus. 1937.

471787

—HITCHCOCK (A.)
Much ado about nothing? 1: a reply
to [H.] Granville-Barker['s comments
on the screen representations of
Shakespeare.] FROM The Listener,
March 10th, 1937.
illus. 1937.

464183

—JORGENSEN (PAUL ALFRED)
Castellani's "Romeo and Juliet":
intention and response. IN The
Quarterly of Film, Radio and Television, Vol. 10. (Berkeley, Cal.)
1955.

630462/10

—[LEBRAN INC., MANILA]
Romeo at Julieta. Screen adaption,
Lebran, Inc., Manila. [Tagalog script
by Prudencio B. Mariano, with screen
directions in English by R. D. Brambles.]
(Manila)

[1951.]

638402

—LEWIN (WILLIAM) ed.
A Guide to the discussion of the
[J. Arthur Rank Organization]
technicolor screen version of
Shakespeare's Romeo and Juliet.
Reprinted from Audio-Visual Guide,
Dec. 1954. pp. 12. (Maplewood,N.J.)
ports. illus. 1955.
Photoplay Studies.

665548

—McCullie (H.) "Six-shooters" and
Shakespeare. [With references to
the film Romeo and Juliet.] Illus.
In World Film News, Vol. 2.

1937.

485420

—[METRO-GOLDWYN-MAYER
A Collection of photographs relating
to Irving G. Thalberg's production
of the film "Romeo and Juliet" as
presented by Metro-Goldwyn-Mayer.]
[1936]

468715

—[METRO-GOLDWYN-MAYER
English and American publicity
material relating to Irving G.
Thalberg's film production of
"Romeo and Juliet" as presented
by Metro-Goldwyn-Mayer.] [1936]

468716

—METRO-GOLDWYN-MAYER
[Publicity material relating to the
world première of the film Romeo and
Juliet, at Salzburg, 1936.]
illus. typescript. 1936.

465083

—PARAMOUNT PICTURES CORPORATION
Romeo and Juliet. A Paramount
Picture production by Franco Zeffirelli.
Release dialogue script.
typescript. 1968.
Script presented to the Shakespeare
Library and autographed by Leonard
Whiting.

777352

—RANK (JOSEPH ARTHUR) ORGANIZATION, LTD.
[Romeo and Juliet, adapted for the
screen and directed by R. Castellani:
photographs, publicity material and
script.]
typescript. [1954.]
Signed by Laurence Harvey.

665120

—Romeo and Juliet [: film supplement].
FROM Screen Pictorial, August, [1936].
pp. [11].
illus. [1936]

454858

—Romeo and Juliet: a motion picture
edition, produced for Metro-Goldwyn-
Mayer by I. G. Thalberg, directed by
G. Cukor [and] arranged for the screen
by T. Jennings.
illus. [1936] 457925
Arthur Barker Edition.
——— Random House Edition.

460419

—Romeo and Juliet. [Reviews of
the film.] IN World Film News,
Vol. 1.
illus. 1936.

485419

Romeo and Juliet

— Illustrations
The library's extensive collections of photographs and engravings are indexed but mainly uncatalogued

————— Retzsch's Outlines [to Macbeth, Hamlet and Romeo and Juliet: a review]. In The Foreign Quarterly Review, Vol.18.

1837.

29757

— Romeo and Juliet: [a] pictorial supplement [of a production at the New Theatre, London]. In The Amateur theatre and playwrights' journal, Vol. 2, No. 41. Illus.

1935-36.

476089

—Stock (F.R.) Pen and ink sketches [24 plates, many with quotations from "Hamlet", "Romeo and Juliet", etc.]

1859.

497975

Romeo and Juliet

— Music; Opera
For music scores see under the heading **Music Scores,** Romeo and Juliet

—Davidson (Gladys) Standard stories from the operas [including Romeo and Juliet.] Illustrated by L.R.Brightwell.   2 vols.

1939-40.

520271

— EBERS (J.)
Seven years of the King's Theatre. [With references to the operas "Otello" and "Romeo e Giulietta".] ports.   1828.

495693

—HAYWOOD (CHARLES)

William Boyce's "Solemn dirge" in Garrick's Romeo and Juliet production of 1750. A reprint from Shakespeare Quarterly, Vol.11, No.2. (Shakespeare Association of America, Inc., Bethlehem, Pa.)   1960.

667758

—Klein (H.) The Golden age of opera. [With references to Romeo and Juliet.] Ports.

1933.

406166

—LEISER (CLARA)
Jean de Reszke and the great days of opera. [With a foreword by A. Webber, [and references to "Romeo and Juliet"].
ports. illus. facsimiles. bibliog.

1933.

414221

— NEWMAN (E.)
Opera nights [: the stories of 29 operas, including chapters on Verdi's Falstaff and Gounod's Romeo and Juliet, with musical examples.]
ports.   illus.   1943.

545435

— Romeo e Giulietta [: a brief sketch of Gounod's opera]. In The Church Choirmaster and Organist, Vol. 1,1867.

1867.

527832

Romeo and Juliet

— Novels; Plays; Poems; Burlesques
see also **ENGLISH EDITIONS,** Romeo and Juliet — Alterations, etc.

—— G.(H.J.L.) Medleys and songs without music [including Romeo and Juliet.]

1891.

498540

—HALLIDAY (A.)
Romeo and Juliet travestie, or, The Cup of cold pison.   pp. 39.   (Lacy's Acting Edition, No. 633)   [1859] Theatre Royal, Birmingham, prompt book. Differs from 69798.

455741

—HERRING (R.)
Epitaph on Mercutio [: a poem]. IN Life and letters to-day, Vol. 36.
1943.

544196

— HERRING (R.)
Harlequin Mercutio: or, Plague on your houses: a ride through raids to resurrection [: a verse-pantomime of present-day London.   Mercutio and Hamlet are taken to be two aspects, the spirit and conscience, of the same person, Ego]. FROM Life and Letters To-day, Vols. 31 and 32.   1941-2.   534897
———— IN SCHIMANSKI (S.) and TREECE (H.) eds., Transformation [: an anthology]. 1943.   543517

KELLER (GOTTFRIED)
Romeo und Julia auf dem Dorfe.
Edited, with [introduction,] notes
and vocabulary by W. A. Adams.
(Boston[, Mass.]) 1900.
Heath's Modern Language Series.

577500

KELLER (GOTTFRIED)
A Village Romeo and Juliet [: a story].
Translated by P. B. Thomas [and]
B. Q. Morgan. (New York)
1955.
College Translations

665024

Kennedy (J.) Psyche & Eros; Romeo
& Juliet: two poems.

1935.

436526

LEWIS (S.)
Bethel Merriday [: a novel. Including
references to the tour of a Romeo and
Juliet company]. 1940.

542809

MACCOLL, EWAN
'Romeo and Juliet'. A radio ballad.
Produced by C. Parker. B.B.C. Script
broadcast 18th May, 25th May 1966.

typescript. 756954

MOORE (J. [C.])
Overture beginners! [A novel with
references to 'Romeo and Juliet'.]
1936.

456687

PENDLEBURY (B. J.)
To Enid [with a copy of Romeo and
Juliet] and other poems. pp. 30.
1922.

428708

Sitwell (Edith) "Romeo Coates" : a
portrait of failure. [A play containing references to Romeo and
Juliet] adapted [for broadcasting]
and produced by S. Potter. Regional
programme, 23rd Feb., 1939. ff. 18.
Typescript.

498984

STEVENS (H. C. G.)
High-speed Shakespeare: Hamlet,
Julius Caesar, Romeo and Juliet:
three tragedies in a tearing hurry.
pp. 60. 1934.

429426

Romeo and Juliet

— Sources and Background

ALLEN (M. S.)
Broke's Romeus and Juliet as a source
for the Valentine-Silvia plot in The
Two Gentlemen of Verona. IN
University of Texas, Studies in
English, [No. 18.] 1938. (Austin,
Texas)

498156

AXON (W. E. A.)
Romeo and Juliet before and in
Shakspere's time. IN Transactions
of the Royal Society of Literature
of the United Kingdom. 2nd series,
Vol. 26. 1905.

193553

[BANDELLO (M.)]
The Goodly history of the true and
constant love between Romeus and
Julietta. Abridged from Painter's
"Palace of Pleasure". IN SHAKESPEARE
(W.) Romeo and Juliet. [Edited
with an introduction by H. Morley.]
1903.
Cassell's National Library. New
Series.

550227

BANDELLO (M.)
The Goodly history of the true and constant love between Rhomeo and Julietta.
Translated by W. Painter from the French
paraphrase by P. Boaistuau of Bandello's
Version. Reprinted from the edition
issued by the New Shakespeare Society in
1875 and edited by P. A. Daniel. Frontispiece etc. by F. T. Chamberlin.
pp. lxxxii. (New Hampshire)
Monadnock Press 1903.
Edn. limited to 115 copies on hand-made
papers, and 10 on vellum.

418062

Bandello [M.] La Sfortunata morte di
dui infelicissimi amanti [the
source of Romeo and Juliet]. In
Bandello [M.] Le Novelle. 2a parte.

(Londra) 1740.

548835

Bandello (M.) The Story of Romeo and
Juliet: a source of Shakespeare's
play. Revised for modern readers by
Margherita Selvi. Translated by
Vera and H.B.Cotterill. [Italian
and English texts.] ff. 53.

[1940.]

[Harrap's] Bilingual Series.)

524347

—[Brooke (A.)] The Tragicall hystory
  of Romeus and Juliet: contayning in
  it a rare example of true
  constancie. [A poem by A.Brooke,
  based on a story by M.Bandello.]
  pp.77.

[c.1803.]

548840

—Bush (D.) Hero and Leander and Romeo
  and Juliet. pp.[4.] From Philological
  Quarterly, Vol.9, 1930.

(Iowa City,Iowa.)

452012

—CHARLTON (H. B.)
  France as chaperone of Romeo and
  Juliet. IN Studies in French
  language and mediaeval literature
  presented to Mildred K. Pope.
  (Manchester)
  port. illus. facsimiles. 1939.
  Publications of the University of
  Manchester.

511727

—Corte [(G. Dalla)] Account of Romeo
  and Juliet. [Taken from the History
  of Verona, 1594, and translated
  by J. Holmes].In The Antiquary,
  vol.3.

1881.

39584

—FREEMAN, ARTHUR
  Shakespeare and 'Solyman and Perseda'.
  IN The Modern Language Review, Vol.58.
  1963.

266816

—Juliet's tomb [: the story of the
  source of Shakespeare's Romeo and Juliet].
  FROM [Young Lady's Library, 1829.]
  [1829.]

559979

—LAW (R. A.)
  On Shakespeare's changes of his source
  material in "Romeo and Juliet". IN
  University of Texas, Studies in English,
  No. 9. (Austin, Texas)   1929.

442468

—LAW (R. A.)
  The Shoemakers' holiday, and Romeo and
  Juliet. FROM Studies in Philology,
  Vol. 21.   (Chapel Hill, N.C.) 1924.

496551

—MOORE (OLIN HARRIS)
  The Legend of Romeo and Juliet.
  (Ohio State University. Graduate
  School Monographs. Contributions
  in Languages and Literature, No. 13:
  Romance Languages Series 2). (Columbus,
  Ohio)
  bibliog.   1950.

616127

—Moore (O.H.) The Origins of the legend
  of Romeo and Juliet in Italy.
  From Speculum: a journal of mediaeval
  studies, vol.5.

(Cambridge,Mass.)   1930.

444460

—MOORE (O. H.)
  Shakespeare's deviations from "Romeus
  and Iuliet". IN Publications of the
  Modern Language Association of America,
  Vol. 52.   (Menasha, Wisc.) 1937.

485791

—NOSWORTHY (JAMES MANSFIELD)

  The Two angry families of Verona [:
  Romeo and Juliet]. A reprint FROM
  Shakespeare Quarterly, Vol.3, No.3,
  July 1952. (New York)

668450

—PAINTER (W.)
  The Goodly history of the true and
  constant love between Romeus and Julietta, abridged from "The Palace of
  pleasure". IN SHAKESPEARE (W.)
  Romeo and Juliet. [Edited with an
  introduction by H. Morley.]
                              1895.
  Cassell's National Library
                              530844

—PERSICO (Count)
  Romeo and Juliet. [The Tomb of
  Juliet, and Count Persico's story
  of Romeo and Juliet.   IN The
  Portfolio of entertaining and
  instructive varieties in history,
  literature, science, &c. [New
  Series], No. 17, Nov. 14,1829.
  illus.   1929.

519904

—PORTO (L. da)
  Giulietta and Romeo: a story from
  the original Italian. Illustrated
  with pictures painted in Italy by
  the translator, Jessie B. Evans.
  pp. 49. (Portland, Maine) 1934.

438976

—PRUVOST (R.)
  Matteo Bandello and Elizabethan
  fiction. [With references to
  Romeo and Juliet.] (Paris)
  bibliog.   1937.
  Bibliothèque de la Revue de Littérature
  Comparée.

495836

—SIEGEL (PAUL N.)
  Christianity and the religion of love in
  Romeo and Juliet.
  IN SHAKESPEARE QUARTERLY XII: 4.
  pp. 371-391.
  (New York) 1961.

605711

—STRUNK (WILLIAM)
  The Elizabethan showman's ape.
  IN Modern Language Notes, Vol. 32.
  (Baltimore, Md.)   1917.

439157/32

—TILLEY (MORRIS P.   )
A Parody of 'Euphues' in 'Romeo and
Juliet'. IN Modern Language Notes.
Vol.41.(Baltimore,Md.)   1926.

439157/41

—VILLAREJO (OSCAR M.)
Shakespeare's "Romeo and Juliet": its
Spanish source.
IN SHAKESPEARE SURVEY 20.   (Cambridge)
1967.

766881

—WALLEY (HAROLD REINOEHL)
Shakespeare's debt to Marlowe in
"Romeo and Juliet".   IN Philological
Quarterly, Vol. 21.   (Iowa)   1942.

592684/21

—Wheatley (H.B.) The Story of Romeo and
Juliet. In The Antiquary, Vols.5-6.
2 vols.

1882.

50011

—WILKINS (ERNEST HATCH)
The Tale of Julia and Pruneo.
IN Harvard Library Bulletin, Vol. 8.
(Cambridge, Mass.)

1954.

586792/8

Romeo and Juliet

— Stage History and Production
*Newspaper reviews, playbills, theatre pro-
grammes and theatrical illustrations — the
library's extensive collection of this material
is mainly uncatalogued but indexed
For texts of stage alterations and adaptations of the play see* ENGLISH EDITIONS,
Romeo and Juliet *— Alterations, etc.*

—ADAMS (J. C.)
Romeo and Juliet, as played on
Shakespeare's stage.   IN Theatre Arts
Monthly, Vol. 20.   (New York)
illus.   1936.

466068

—ADAMS (JOHN CRANFORD)
Shakespeare's use of the upper stage
in Romeo and Juliet, III.v.
IN SHAKESPEARE QUARTERLY VII;
pp. 145-152.
(New York)   1956.

605711

—AHO (JUHAIN)
Ensimainen suomalainen Shakespearen Ensi
- ilta suomessa.   [Finnish text, with
summary in English.]   IN Gollancs ([Sir]
I.) ed., A Book of homage to Shakespeare.
ports. illus. facsimiles.   [1916.]

264175

—Anderson (Madge) The Heroes of the
puppet stage. With illustrations by
the author, [a bibliography, and a
chapter, "The Japanese Romeo and
Juliet."]

1924.

544226

—Baker (H.B.) Some famous Juliets.
From The Gentleman's Magazine,
December, 1884.

1884.

440303

—Brown (J.M.) Three Macbeths and a
Romeo. [Illustrated by D. M.
Oenslager.] In Theatre Arts Monthly,
Vol. 9.

(New York)   1925.

328359

—BROWN (JOHN RUSSELL)
S. Franco Zeffirelli's "Romeo and Juliet".
IN SHAKESPEARE SURVEY 15.   (Cambridge)
1962.

667174

—CARR-DAVISON (GERTRUDE)
"Juliet".   IN The Theatre, Vol. 4.
(New Series)   1881.

59548

—Clapp (W.W.) The Drama in Boston. [With
facsimile of playbill for a
performance of Romeo and Juliet
Sept.28th 1796.] Ports. Illus.
Facsimiles. In Winsor (J.) ed.,
The Memorial history of Boston
including Suffolk County,Massa-
chusetts, 1630-1880, vol.4.

(Boston,Mass.)   1881.

59176

—DENT (ALAN HOLMES)
Stratford 1954 [: "Romeo and Juliet".
A radio talk] produced by P. Stephenson
for P. Humphreys.   [Broadcast]
30th April 1954.   ff. 8.
typescript.   1954.

643698

—Eich (L.M.) A Previous adaptation of
Romeo and Juliet. From The Quarterly
Journal of Speech, December 1937.

(Ann Arbor, Mich.)   1937.

503863

—   FINDLATER (RICHARD) and others
"Romeo and Juliet" at the Old Vic: a
discussion by R. Findlater, Elspeth
Huxley, A. Forge, D. Powell and H.A.L.
Graig. From The Critics, 1961. (B.B.C.
Script.) ff.13.   1961.

667036

—Fleming (W.H.) Dramatic notes. Romeo
and Juliet at Daly's Theatre. pp.
[2.] From The Looker-on, Vol. 2.

(New York)   1896.

496817

—Freedley (G.) An Early performance of
"Romeo and Juliet" in New York.
Facs. In Bulletin of the New York
Public Library, Vol. 40.

1936.

461612

—Hazlitt (W.) Prefatory remarks to
Oxberry's New English drama. [With
reference to Garrick's version of
Romeo and Juliet.] In Hazlitt
(W.) Complete works, edited by
P.P. Howe, vol. 9. Frontis.
(Centenary edn.)   1932.
  NOTE.- This edn. is limited
      to 1000 sets.

398714

—HOSLEY (RICHARD)
The Use of the upper stage in "Romeo
and Juliet".
IN SHAKESPEARE QUARTERLY V.
pp. 371-379.
(New York) 1954.

605711

—KERN (J. V.)
Playmates: a screen play. [Including
a performance of Romeo and Juliet in
swing style.]   Produced and directed
by D. Butler. (RKO Radio Pictures, Inc.)
  typescript.   [1941.]

550790

—LIEBLER & CO.
Some excerpts from reviews having
reference to [Eleanor] Robson's
[performance as Juliet in Liebler &
Co's production of Shakespeare's
Romeo and Juliet, 1903]. pp. [24.]
(New York)
  ports.   illus.   [1903.]

646237

—LONDON SHAKESPEARE LEAGUE
Shakespeare Commemoration, 1905.
Romeo and Juliet, given by the
Elizabethan Stage Society, at the
Royalty Theatre, London, May 5, 1905:
[programme, etc.]   1905.

517666

— Mary Anderson matinée, Theatre Royal
[Birmingham] Oct. 6th, 1917 [in aid
of the Catholic Hut Fund for soldiers
abroad.] Souvenir programme [of
balcony scene from Romeo and Juliet,
etc.] pp. 16.   [Birmingham]
  ports.   [1917.]

550283

—PROGRAMMES OF SHAKESPEARIAN PERFORMANCES
Romeo and Juliet

This collection, which runs from the
latter half of the nineteenth century,
is continuously augmented by the addition of programmes of contemporary
productions.

499168

—PUKNAT (ELIZABETH M.)
Romeo was a lady: Charlotte Cushman's
London triumph.   IN The Theatre Annual,
1951.

1951.

554521/1950

—Romeo and Juliet [at the New Theatre,
September 2nd, 1911]. In Play
Pictorial, Vol.18.

1911.

571880

—Romeo and Juliet at the New Theatre
[, London]. In Play pictorial,
Vol.67.

1935.

571929

—Romeo and Juliet : [a] pictorial
supplement [of a production at the
New Theatre, London.] In The Amateur theatre and playwrights' journal
Vol.2, No. 41. Illus.

1935-36.

476089

—Southern (R.) Stage-setting for amateurs
and professionals. [Including a
chapter on Romeo and Juliet.] Dgms.

1937.

474318

—STONE (GEORGE WINCHESTER)
"Romeo and Juliet": the source of
its modern stage career.   IN
McMANAWAY (JAMES GILMER) ed.,
Shakespeare 400: essays by American
scholars on the anniversary of the
poet's birth.   Published in co-operation
with the Shakespeare Association of
America.
  illus.   1964.

667803

—THEATRE ROYAL, BIRMINGHAM
Special [Mary Anderson] matinee,
Oct. 23rd, 1918; on behalf of the
Lady Mayoress's Prisoners of War Fund.
Souvenir programme [of the balcony
scene from Romeo and Juliet, etc.]
pp. 28.   [Birmingham]
  ports.   [1918.]   273584
  _____ Another copy.   273583

TIMBS (J.)
English eccentrics and eccentricities.
[With a passage on Romeo and Juliet
in America.]   New edn.
ports.   illus.   1877.

400637

—— Weiss (J.) Romeo and Juliet, Prague,
1946. Illus. In Theatre Today.

1946.

606680

—— Williams (H.) Henry Irving as Romeo.
Illus. Facsimiles In Theatre
Today.

1946.

606680

WILSON (F.)
Miss Alma Murray as Juliet.   pp. 16.
(Chiswick Press)   1887.

415112

WINTER (W.)
Romeo and Juliet; Shakspere on the
stage.   IN The Century Magazine,
Vol. 87.   (New York)
ports.   1914.

251086

Romeo and Juliet
— Study and Teaching; Tales

ADAMSON (ELGIVA) and MOORE
(KATHLEEN V.

Notes on William Shakespeare's "Romeo
and Juliet". pp.46. [Stratford,
Ontario]   [1960]

667087

BURTON (HARRY McGUIRE)

William Shakespeare: Romeo and Juliet.
(Guides to English Literature) pp.59.
[1962.]

667793

—— Capulet and Montague; or, the tragical
loves of Romeo and Juliet.   1823.

illus.   668480

CARRINGTON (NORMAN THOMAS)
Shakespeare: Romeo and Juliet.
1958.
Notes on Chosen English Texts.

666001

CLEMATIS PUBLICATIONS LIMITED
Clematis Theatre Guides.   Romeo and
Juliet by W. Shakespeare: a summary
and appreciation.   pp. 40.
[1952.]

631201

COLLEGE OF CAREERS
STUDY-AID SERIES
Notes on William Shakespeare's "Romeo
and Juliet."   1967.

764411

DUTCH (DANA E.)
Romeo and Juliet.   Adapted by
D. E. Dutch.   Illustrated by
H. C. Kiefer.   (Famous Authors
Illustrated.   [Treasury of Celebrated
Literature] No. 10)   pp. [32.]
(Bridgeport, Conn.)   1950.

616080

[GRIERSON (W.)]
The World's greatest love-tragedy
[Romeo and Juliet;] and Old stories
retold: Romeo and Juliet.   FROM
John O'London's Weekly, Outline
Supplement, 1931.   pp. 43.]
illus.   1931.

390556

HOSLEY, RICHARD
Romeo and Juliet: an outline guide to
the play. (New York)   1965.

Barnes & Noble focus books.
753074

JENKIN, LEONARD
Review notes and study guide to
Shakespeare's 'Romeo and Juliet'. (New
York)   1964.

Monarch critiques of literature.
757013

KEY FACTS LTD.
Romeo and Juliet [: set of 25 cards
for revision for the General
Certificate of Education O level
examination].   [1967.]

Key Facts, Shakespeare, 8.
763804

—— SHIPLEY, JOSEPH TWADELL, ed.
Romeo and Juliet: a scene-by-scene
analysis with critical commentary.
(New York)   1964.

Study master series. 743613

TERRY (JEAN F.)
Romeo and Juliet: a complete para-
phrase.   3rd edn.   pp. 64.
(Farnham, Surrey)   [1962.]
The Normal Shakespeare.

667255

—— Wheatley (H.B.) The Story of Romeo
and Juliet. In The Antiquary.
Vols. 5-6.

1882.

50011

— WINDROSS (RONALD)
Three Mediterranean plays: Shakespeare's
Romeo and Juliet: The Merchant of
Venice: [and,] Twelfth Night. Abridged
and simplified. Illustrated by
G. Irwin. (Tales from England. 2nd
Degree, No. 4) pp. 80. (Paris)
[1952.]

635256

Romeo and Juliet
— Textual History

— Allen (N.B.) Romeo and Juliet further
restored. In Modern Language Notes.
Vol. 54.

(Baltimore)   1939.

509539

— CANTRELL (PAUL L.) and WILLIAMS (GEORGE
WALTON)
The Printing of the Second Quarto of
"Romeo and Juliet". IN Studies in
Bibliography, Vol. 9. (Charlottesville,
Va.)   1957.

598680/9

— DAM (B. A. P. van)
Did Shakespeare revise Romeo and Juliet?
FROM Anglia [Neue Folge,] Bd. 39.
pp. 39-62. [Halle]   [1927]

455696

— DUTHIE (GEORGE IAN)
The Text of Shakespeare's "Romeo and
Juliet". IN Studies in Bibliography,
Vol. 4. (Charlottesville, Va.)
1951.

598680/4

—H[enley] (W.E.) The New "Romeo and
Juliet" [: review of Edition de
Luxe. With Introduction by E.Dowden
and illustrations by Sir F.B. Dicksee.
1884.] In The Magazine of Art, Vol.8.

1885.

78974

— HINMAN (CHARLTON)
The Proof-reading of the First Folio
text of "Romeo and Juliet".
IN Studies in Bibliography, Vol. 6.
(Charlottesville, Va.)   1953.

598680/6

— HOPPE (H. R.)
An Approximate printing date for
the First Quarto of Romeo and
Juliet. IN The Library, 4th Series,
Vol. 18. (Bibliographical Society)
1938.

487688

— HOPPE (H. R.)
The Bad Quarto of Romeo and Juliet:
a bibliographical and textual study.
[With bibliographical references.]
(Ithaca, N.Y.)
tables.   1948.
Cornell Studies in English, Vol. 36.

596308

— HOPPE (H R.)
Borrowings from "Romeo and Juliet"
in the 'bad' quarto of "The Merry
wives of Windsor". IN The Review
of English Studies, Vol. 20.
(Oxford)
bibliog.   [1944.]

562839

— HOPPE (H. R.)
The First Quarto of Romeo and Juliet:
a bibliographical and textual study.
IN Cornell University, Abstracts of
theses accepted in partial satisfaction
of the requirements for the Doctor's
degree, 1942. (Ithaca, N.Y.) 1943.

574488

— Hoppe (H.R.) The First quarto version
of Romeo and Juliet, II. vi and IV
v. 43ff. [With bibliographical
notes.] In The Review of English
Studies, Vol.14.

1938.

495115

— HOSLEY (RICHARD)
The Corrupting influence of the bad quarto
on the received text of Romeo and Juliet.
IN SHAKESPEARE QUARTERLY IV: 1.
pp. 11-33.
(New York) 1953.

605711

— HOSLEY (RICHARD)
Quarto copy for Q2 "Romeo and Juliet".
IN Studies in Bibliography, Vol. 9.
(Charlottesville, Va.)   1957.

598680/9

— Kirschbaum (L.) A Census of bad
quartos. [With bibliographical
notes.] In The Review of English
Studies, Vol.14.

1938.

495115

— SAMPLEY (A. M.)
Sixteenth century imitation of Romeo
and Juliet. IN University of Texas
Bulletin, Studies in English, No. 9.
(Texas)   1929.

442468

— SPALDING (THOMAS ALFRED)
On the First Quarto of Romeo and Juliet:
is there any evidence of a second hand in it?
**IN Transactions of the New Shakespeare
Society, Series 1.** No. 5. pp. 58-87.
1877-9.

40620

___ THOMAS (SIDNEY)
The Bibliographical links between the
first two Quartos of Romeo and Juliet.
IN The Review of English Studies,
Vol. 25.   1949.

318239/25

___ THOMAS (SIDNEY)
Henry Chettle and the First Quarto of
Romeo and Juliet.   IN The Review of
English Studies, New Series, Vol. 1.
(Oxford)   1950.

318239/2/1

___ WILSON (JOHN DOVER)
The New way with Shakespeare's texts,
2: Recent work on the text of Romeo
and Juliet.   IN SHAKESPEARE SURVEY 8.
(Cambridge)   1955.

647706

Romer (V.L.) Do Lamb's "Tales"
require re-writing? In The Bookman, Vol.
79. Port

[1930-31.]

384225

Romilly (G.)"Tomorrow and tomorrow and
tomorrow" [: reading Shakespeare
while a prisoner of war in Germany.
Broadcast] 21st August, 1949. ff.4.
Typescript.

[1949.]

605243

ROMNEY (GEORGE)

Shakespearian sketches commissioned for
Boydell's Shakespeare Gallery, from
manuscript notebooks in possession of
the Folger Shakespeare Library.
1 vol. in 1 reel. [c.1786.]
668411

Note: Microfilm negative copy, made at the
Folger Shakespeare Library, 1965.

ROOD, ARNOLD
Edward Gordon Craig, artist of the
theatre, 1872-1966: a memorial
exhibition in the Amsterdam Gallery.
(New York)   1967.

767189

Roosbroeck (Gustave Leopold van)
see Van Roosbroeck (G. L.)

ROOT, ROBERT KILBURN
Classical mythology in Shakespeare.
(New York)   1965.

Yale studies in English, XIX.
754007

Root (R.K.) The Poetical career of
Alexander Pope. [With notes, bibliographical references and references
to Shakespeare.] Port.

(Princeton)   1938.

500806

ROPPOLO (JOSEPH PATRICK)
American premieres of two
Shakespearean plays in New Orleans:
The Two gentlemen of Verona and
Antony and Cleopatra.   Reprinted
from Tulane University,   Tulane
Studies in English. Vol. 7.
pp. [8]. (New Orleans, La.)
bibliogs.   1957.

666580

ROPPOLO (JOSEPH PATRICK)

Hamlet in New Orleans. Reprinted from
Tulane University. Tulane Studies in
English. Vol.6. pp.[16] Chronological
Table. Bibliogs. (New Orleans, La.)
1956.

666581

ROSCELLI (WILLIAM JOHN)

Isabella, sin, and civil law [:
Isabella's attitude toward fornication
in Measure for Measure]. FROM The
University of Kansas City Review,
Vol.28, No.3. [Kansas City Mo.]
1962.

667838

Roscoe (J.E.) Confessions of great
souls [: essays on religion in
literature, with references to
Shakespeare.]

[c.1920.]

538352

ROSE (BARON THEODORE)
Medicine in the days and plays of
Shakespeare.   Reprinted from The
Birmingham Medical Review, Vol.17.
pp. 17.   [Birmingham]   [1952.]

632717

ROSE, BRIAN W.
The Tempest: a reconsideration of its
meaning. Bibliog. IN English Studies
in Africa Vol.I. (Johannesburg)
1958.

682610/1

Rose (Mrs.[Constance]) "Plain Mrs.
Rose [: reminiscences, with
Shakespearian references.] Ports.

(Cheltenham)   1936.

452685

ROSE (EDWARD)
The Division into acts of Hamlet.
IN Transactions of the New Shakespeare
Society, Series 1. No. 5.
pp. 1-8.   1877-9.

40620

ROSE (EDWARD)
The Inconsistency of the time in
Shakspere's plays.
IN Transactions of the New Shakespeare
Society, Series 1 Nos. 8-10. pp. 33-52.
                    1880-6.
                                99113

ROSE (EDWARD)
A Northern Hamlet [: Oehlenschlager's
"Amleth" compared with Shakespeare's
"Hamlet"]. FROM [Fraser's Magazine,]
New Series, Vol. 15.   1877.

                    560919

ROSE (EDWARD)
Sudden emotion: its effect upon different
characters, as shown by Shakspere.
IN Transactions of the New Shakespeare
Society, Series 1. Nos. 8-10. pp. 1-20.
                    1880-6.

                    99113

Rose (K.) Portrait the third: A Winter's
Tale,Mrs.Robinson as "Perdita",
by Gainsborough,[Wallace Collection].
In Rose (K.) Georgiana[:seven
dramatic portraits].pp.[viii,]48.

                    1947.

                    591814

ROSE (MARY)
Baconian myths: notes on two great
Englishmen and their defamers. [With
bibliographical notes.] pp. 39.
(Stratford-on-Avon)   [1913.]
Another copy with additional advertise-
ments.
                    573052

Rosen (William)
Antony and Cleopatra. IN

LEECH, CLIFFORD, ed.
Shakespeare: the tragedies.
A collection of critical essays.
(Chicago)   1965.

    Gemini books.   752332

ROSEN (WILLIAM)

Shakespeare and the craft of tragedy.
Bibliogs. (Cambridge, Mass.)
                        1960.

                    666556

Rosenbach (A.S.W.) A Book hunter's holiday: adventures with books and manu-
scirpts. [With references to Arden
of Feversham and other Shakespearian plays dealing with murder, and
those mentioning Christmas.] Ports.
Illus. Facsimiles.

        (Boston, [Mass.])   1936.

                    488945

ROSENBACH (ABRAHAM SIMON WOLF)
A Description of the four Folios of
Shakespeare, 1623, 1632, 1663-4, 1685
in the original bindings: [a] gift
to the Free Library of Philadelphia.
pp. 18.
facsimiles.   1945.

                    559567

Rosenbach (A.S.W.) The First
theatrical company in America.
[Including references to Shakes-
peare]. Reprinted from the
Proceedings of the American
Antiquarian Society for October,
1938. pp. 13. Facsimile.

    (Worcester, Mass.)   1939.

(American Antiquarian Society)

                    521905

Rosenbach, Abraham Simon Wolf *works relating to*

— HAYWARD (JOHN)
The Rosenbach-Bodmer Shakespeare
Collection.   IN The Book Collector,
Vol. 1.   1952.

                    649085/1

ROSENBACH COMPANY
William Shakespeare: a collection of
first and early editions of his works,
1594 to 1700 [: for sale by] the
Rosenbach Company. pp. v, 22
(Philadelphia)
illus. facsimiles.   1951.

                    633923

ROSENBERG (MARVIN)
In defense of Iago.
IN SHAKESPEARE QUARTERLY VI.
pp. 145-158.
(New York) 1955.
                    605711

ROSENBERG (MARVIN)

The Masks of Othello: the search for
the identity of Othello, Iago, and
Desdemona by three centuries of actors
and critics. Frontis. (Berkeley, Cal.)
                        1961.

                    667256

ROSENBERG (MARVIN)
The "Refinement" of "Othello" in the
eighteenth century British theatre.
IN Studies in Philology, Vol. 51.
(Chapel Hill, N.C.)   1954.

                    554520/51

ROSENBERG (MARVIN)
Reputation, oft lost without deserving...
IN SHAKESPEARE QUARTERLY IX.
pp. 499-506.
(New York) 1958.
                    605711

ROSENBERG (MARVIN)
Shakespeare on TV: an optimistic
survey. IN The Quarterly of Film
Radio and Television, Vol. 9.
(Berkeley, Cal.)   1954.

630462/9

ROSENFELD (SYBIL)
The Grieves Shakespearian scene designs.
IN SHAKESPEARE SURVEY 20.   (Cambridge)
1967.

766881

**Rosenfeld (Sybil) Strolling players
& drama in the provinces, 1660-
1765. [With references to Shakespeare.] Ports. Illus. Facsimiles.**

(Cambridge)   1939.

502621

ROSENHEIM (RICHARD)
The Mystic message of "The Tempest".
IN Rosenheim (R.) The Eternal drama:
a comprehensive treatise on the
syngenetic history of humanity,
dramatics, and theatre.   (New York)
illus. bibliog.   1952.

627222

ROSENTHAL (JEAN)
Commentary. IN The Tempest.   Text
edited by C. J. Sisson.   Commentary
by Jean Rosenthal.   (New York)
1961.
The Laurel Shakespeare.   F Fergusson,
General editor.

667464

ROSENTHAL (T.   G.   )

"Comment" No. 2 [: Shakespeare in Art
exhibition at Nottingham University.
B.B.C.] Broadcast script. [Programme
transmitted] 12th January 1961. ff.4.
1961.

667034

Roses *see* Flowers and Plants of Shakespeare

ROSIER (JAMES L.)
The Lex aeterna and King Lear.   IN
Journal of English and Germanic
Philology, Vol. 53.   (Urbana, Ill.)
1954.

600780/53

ROSIGNOLI, MARIA PIA
The Life and times of Shakespeare.
Translator Mary Kanani.   (Feltham,
Mddx.)
illus.   1968.
Portraits of greatness.

777256

ROSS (J. F.)
Hamlet: dramatist.   IN BRONSON
(B. H.) [and others] Five studies
in literature.   (Berkeley, Cal.)
1940.
California University, Publications
in English, Vol. 8, No. 1.

517365

ROSS (LAWRENCE J.   )

**The Meaning of strawberries in
Shakespeare. Offprint from "Studies in
the Renaissance" Vol.7. pp.16. Illus.**
[1961]

667083

ROSS, LAWRENCE J.
Shakespeare's "Dull clown" and
symbolic music. IN Shakespeare
Quarterly XVII: 2. pp.107-128. (New
York)   1966.

605711

ROSS (LAWRENCE J.)
Three readings in the text of "Othello".
IN SHAKESPEARE QUARTERLY XIV: 2.
pp. 121-126.   (New York) 1963.

605711

ROSS (LAWRENCE J.)
The Use of a "fit-up" booth in
Othello.   IN SHAKESPEARE QUARTERLY
XII: 4.   pp. 359-370.   (New York)
1961.

605711

ROSS (LAWRENCE J.)
World and chrysolite in "Othello"
[Act V Scene II line 179].   IN
Modern Language Notes, Vol. 76.
1961.

439157/76

ROSS (M. M.)
Milton's royalism: a study of the conflict of symbol and idea in the poems.
[With references to Shakespeare, a bibliography and bibliographical notes.]
(Ithaca, N. Y.)
1943.

(Cornell Studies in English, 34)

550881

ROSS (RAYMOND), WATT (H. A.) and
HOLZKNECHT (K. J.)
Outlines of Shakespeare's plays.
(New York)
bibliog.   illus.   maps.
1934.   427372
College Outline Series.
_____ Another edn. 1938.   488716

ROSS ([Sir] RONALD)
Shakespeare, 1916 [: a sonnet.]
IN GOLLANCZ ([Sir] I.) ed., A Book of
homage to Shakespeare.
ports. illus. facsimiles. [1916.]

264175

ROSS (T. A.)
A Note on The Merchant of Venice.
IN The British Journal of Medical
Psychology, Vol. 14.   (Cambridge)
1934.

433561

ROSS (W.)
The Story of Anne Whateley and William
Shaxpere, as revealed by "The Sonnets
to Mr. W.H." and other Elizabethan
poetry.   (Glasgow)
   bibliog.   1939.

510565

Rossetti, Dante Gabriel *works relating to*

— JONSON (G. C. A.)
   "The House of life" [: a comparison
   between Rossetti's and Shakespeare's
   sonnets.]   FROM The Poetry Review,
   1931.   pp. [17.]   [1931]

390920

ROSSETTI (RETO MARIO)
A Crux and no crux.   [Othello's speech in
IV.i.]
IN SHAKESPEARE QUARTERLY XIII: 3.
pp. 299-303.
(New York) 1962.

605711

[ROSSETTI (WILLIAM MICHAEL)]
Cordelia [: a poem.   With an etching
by F. M. Brown].   IN The Germ, 1850.
   1850.   580968
_____IN The Germ, 1850: a facsimile
reprint.   1901.   157369

Rossetti (W.M.) William Shakespeare.
   In Rossetti (W.M.) Lives of
   famous poets.

                          1878.

132582

Rossi, Ernesto *works relating to*

— BEATTY-KINGSTON (W.)
   Rossi on Hamlet.   FROM The Theatre,
   October, 1884.
                                1884.

498970

ROSSINI [GIOACCHINO ANTONIO]
Dramatic overtures to La Gazza ladra,
La Cenerentola, & Othello, arranged
as trios for two flutes & piano forte,
by H. Hill.   pp. 33.   [c.1850.]

558610

ROSSINI [(GIOACCHINO ANTONIO)]
Overture to Othello, arranged as a
duet, for...the piano forte, by
J. F. Burrowes.   pp. 19.   [c.1880.]

458154

Rossini, Gioacchino Antonio *works relating to*

—TOYE (F.)
   Rossini: a study in tragi-comedy,
   [containing references to Rossini's
   opera 'Otello'.]
   ports.   facsimile.   1934.

419644

ROSSITER (ARTHUR PERCIVAL)
Ambivalence: the dialectic of the
histories.   IN GARRETT (JOHN) ed.,
Talking of Shakespeare [: a selection
from the lectures delivered at the
annual course for teachers at Stratford,
1948-1953].   1954.

641471

ROSSITER (ARTHUR PERCIVAL)
Angel with horns; and other
Shakespeare lectures. Edited by G.
Storey. Bibliog.   1961.

666702

Rossiter (Arthur Percival)
Coriolanus. IN

LEECH, CLIFFORD, ed.
   Shakespeare: the tragedies.
   A collection of critical essays.
   (Chicago)   1965.

      Gemini books.   752332

ROSSITER (ARTHUR PERCIVAL)
A Guide for Shakespeare-goers, 1:
'The Gold standard' or, 'The Meaning
of The Merchant of Venice'.   Produced by D. Bryson.   [Broadcast]
23rd June, 1953.   ff. 16.
typescript.

634502

ROSSITER (ARTHUR PERCIVAL)
A Guide for Shakespeare-goers, 2:
'The Sex war in knockabout', or,
'The Meaning of The Taming of the
Shrew'.   Produced by D. Bryson.
[Broadcast] 30th June, 1953.   ff.18.
typescript.

634503

ROSSITER (ARTHUR PERCIVAL)
A Guide to Shakespeare-goers, 3:
'The Devil as avenging angel', or,
'The Meaning of Richard the Third'.
Produced by D. Bryson. [Broadcast]
7th July, 1953.   ff. 17.
   typescript.

634504

ROSSITER (ARTHUR PERCIVAL)
A Guide for Shakespeare-goers, 4:
'Pride of life'; or, The Meaning
of Antony & Cleopatra'.   Produced
by D. Bryson.   [Broadcast]
14th July, 1953.   ff. 17.
   typescript.

634505

ROSSITER (ARTHUR PERCIVAL)
A Guide for Shakespeare-goers, 5:
'Quarrel with the universe': or,
'The Meaning of King Lear'.   Produced
by P. Humphreys for D. Bryson.
[Broadcast] 21st July 1953.   ff. 17.
   typescript.

634506

ROSSITER (ARTHUR PERCIVAL)
Much ado about nothing.   IN MUIR
(KENNETH) ed., Shakespeare, the
comedies: a collection of critical
essays.   (Englewood Cliffs, N.J.)
                              1965.

748348

ROSSITER (A. P.)
Prognosis on a Shakespeare problem [:
the significance of the marginal notes,
supposedly by Shakespeare, in a copy
of Hall's "The Union of the two noble
and illustre families of Lancastre
and York".   With bibliographical
notes.]   pp. [14.]   FROM The Durham
University Journal, Vol. 33. No. 2.
(New Series Vol. 2, No. 2.)   (Durham)
                              1941.

526597

Rossiter (Arthur Percival) ed.
[PLUTARCH]
Julius Caesar, from the Histories of
Julius Caesar and Brutus in North's
Plutarch.   Put into Basic [English]
by A. P. Rossiter.
   table.   1933.
Psyche Miniatures, General Series,
No. 50.

403890

Rossolymos (D. M.) illus.
CLARKE (D. W.)
William Shakespeare [: his life and
works].   Drawings by D. M. Rossolymos.
pp. x, 86.
   glossary.   ports.   illus.   dgm.
   chronological table.   facsimile.
   bibliog.   1950.
Essential English Library.

607204

ROSTENBERG (LEONA)
Thomas Thorpe, publisher of "Shakespeares sonnets", from the Papers of the
Bibliographical Society of America, 1960.
pp.[22].

666962

ROTH, C.
The Background of Shylock.
Reprinted from The Review of
English Studies, Vol. IX, April
1933. pp. 9.

503661

ROTH (C.)
Magna Bibliotheca Anglo-Judaica:
a bibliographical guide to Anglo-
Jewish history.   [With a list of
works on Shakespeare and Jews.]
New edn., revised and enlarged.
(Jewish Historical Society) 1937.

483790

ROTHA, P. and MANVELL, A.R.
Shakespeare [films]. IN Rotha, P.
and Manvell, A.R. Movie parade,
1888–1949.   1950.

605986

ROTHE, H.
Shakespeare in German.
IN German Life and Letters, Vol.1,4.
(Oxford)   1937.

476079

ROTHSCHILD (JAMES ARMAND de)
Shakespeare and his day: a study of
the topical element in Shakespeare
and in the Elizabethan drama.   [With
bibliographical notes.]   1906.
Harness Prize Essay, 1901.
                             399712

ROTHWELL, JOHN
Swan's wake: a miscellany of books
about Shakespeare. Catalogue 16.
                             [1965.]

746118

ROTHWELL (W. F.)
Was there a typical Elizabethan
stage?   IN SHAKESPEARE SURVEY 12.
(Cambridge)
   bibliog.   1959.

666150

ROUDA (F. H.)
Coriolanus - a tragedy of youth.
IN SHAKESPEARE QUARTERLY XII: 2.
pp. 103-106.
(New York) 1961.
                             605711

Rouen, Siege of *see* France

ROUTH (HAROLD VICTOR)
Towards the twentieth century: essays
in the spiritual history of the
nineteenth.   [With references to
Shakespeare.]   (Cambridge) 1937.

473053

ROUTLEDGE (EDMUND)
Quotations from Shakespeare.
        [c.1885.]   488088
"Quotation" Series.
———— 3rd edn.   1892.   396030

Routledge's Sixpenny Series
LAMB [(CHARLES and MARY)]
Tales from Shakspeare. With 40
illustrations by Sir J. Gilbert.
pp. 64.   [1882].

               509233

Routledge's World Library
LAMB (CHARLES and MARY A.)
Tales from Shakespeare, designed for
the use of young people. [Edited]
with an introduction by H. R. Haweis.
           1886.

               544365

Rowbotham (J.F.) The Music of Shakes-
    peare. In Good Words, 1904.

               184416

Rowe, Harry *works relating to*

———— [Review of] Macbeth: a tragedy.
Written by W. Shakspeare. With notes
and emendations, by H. Rowe. 2nd
edn. [1799.] IN The Monthly Review,
Vol. 30.   1799.

               1514

ROWE (K. T.)
Elizabethan morality and the folio
revisions of Sidney's "Arcadia".
[With references to Shakespeare.]
FROM Modern Philology, Vol. 37.
(Chicago)   1939.

               530204

Rowe (N.) Jane Shore. Written in
imitation of Shakespear's style. In
Rowe (N.) Dramatick works, Vol.2.
Port. Illus.   1720.

               506885

ROWE (N.)
The Tragedy of Jane Shore: written
in imitation of Shakespear's style.
pp. 64.   [The Hague]   [c.1722.]

               531616

Rowe (N.) Tragedy of Jane Shore, in
imitation of Shakespear's style. pp.[80]
Frontis. (Bernard Lintot)   1736.

               474428

Rowe (N.) The Tragedy of Jane Shore,
written in imitation of Shakespear's style.
pp.82. (Henry Lintot)   1746.

               469642

Rowe (N.) The Tragedy of Jane Shore,
in imitation of Shakespear's style.
pp.[78](Henry Lintot)   1748.

               393765

Rowe (N.) The Tragedy of Jane Shore,
written in imitation of Shakespear's style.
New edn. pp.60. Frontis.

             [c.1750]

               441419

Rowe (N.) The Tragedy of Jane Shore,
written in imitation of Shakespear's
style. 9th edn. pp.72. Frontis. (T. Lowndes,
T. Caslon, and W. Nicoll)   1765.

               578074

Rowe (N.) Jane Shore: a tragedy in
imitation of Shakespeare's style. 1765.
In Rowe (N.) Works, vol.2.

             1766.

               411511

Rowe (N.) The Tragedy of Jane Shore,
written in imitation of Shakespeare's
style. 10th edn. pp.60. (Dublin)

             1767.

               508517

Rowe (N.) The Tragedy of Jane Shore.
Written in imitation of Shakespeare's style.
In The Theatre, Vol.2. (Edinburgh)

             1768.

               466135

Rowe (N.) Jane Shore: a tragedy, written
in imitation of Shakespeare's style. Marked
with the variations in the manager's book at
the Theatre-Royal in Drury-Lane. pp.63.
Frontis.   1776.

             517641

        [Another copy.] In The
New English Theatre, Vol.4.   1776.

             534335

ROWE (NICHOLAS)
The Tragedy of Jane Shore. Written
in imitation of Shakespeare's style.
As it is acted at the Theatre-Royal
in Drury-Lane and Covent-Garden.
pp. 16.   1777.

             624146

Rowe (N.) Jane Shore: a tragedy,
written in imitation of Shakespeare's
style. Marked with the variations in
the Manager's book, at the Theatre-
Royal in Drury-Lane, pp.60. Frontis.

             1783.

             490287

Rowe (N.) Jane Shore: a tragedy
[written in imitation of Shakespeare's style]
Adapted for theatrical representation, as
performed at the Theatres-Royal, Drury Lane
and Covent-Garden. pp.86. Frontis.
(John Bell)   1791.

             553178

ROWE (NICHOLAS)
Jeanne Shore; ou, Le Triomphe de la
fidélité, à la patrie et à la roiauté,
tragédie en cinq actes. Traduite
en vers françois,par L.D.C.V.G.D.N.
(Londres: Ph. Le Boussonnier & Co.)
1797.
640419

Rowe (N.) The Tragedy of Jane Shore.
[Written in imitation of Shakespeare's
style.] First acted at the Theatre Royal,
Drury Lane, 1713. [Theatre Royal,
Birmingham, prompt copy.] pp.107-164.
[Cambridge]   [1812]

Note: Extracted from Vol.1 of "English
drama purified, being a specimen of
select plays, etc." by J. Plumptre,
3 vols. 1812.
465066

Rowe (N.) Jane Shore; a tragedy
in five acts [in imitation of
Shakespeare's style]. As performed at
the Theatres Royal, Drury-Lane and
Covent-Garden. pp.42. Frontis.
(Edinburgh)   [c.1814]
(Oliver & Boyd)

483525

Rowe [N.] Jane Shore: a tragedy.
[Written in imitation of Shakespeare's
style.] Revised by J.P. Kemble. pp.55.
(John Miller)   1815.

394568

Rowe (N.) Jane Shore: a tragedy
in five acts. pp.47.   [c.1830]

(The British Dramatists. No.3)

456093

Rowe (N.) Jane Shore: a tragedy
in five acts [in imitation of Shakespeare].
From The London Stage, vol.1.
[c.1830]
455701

Rowe (N.) Jane Shore: a tragedy in
five acts, with remarks biographical
and critical, by D.-G. [i.e. George Daniel]
As performed at the Theatres Royal, London.
pp.49.   [?1830]

[Cumberland's British Theatre]

456092

Rowe (N.) Jane Shore [: a tragedy in
imitation of Shakespeare's style]. In The
Acting drama, containing sixty plays.
1839.

447828

Rowe (N.) Jane Shore: a tragedy, in
five acts [in imitation of Shakespeare's
style]. From [Dick's] British drama, No.1.
pp.[13].   1864.

522955

Rowe (N.) Jane Shore: a tragedy
in five acts. pp.51. [Theatre Royal,
Birmingham, prompt book.]
[c.1880]

(Lacy's Acting Edition. No. 584)

455843

Rowe (N.) Jane Shore [: a tragedy
in five acts, in imitation of
Shakespeare.] pp.[12] Illus.
[c.1883]

(Dicks' Standard Plays, No. 24)

455699

Rowe (N.) The Tragedy of Jane Shore.
Written in imitation of Shakespear's
style. In Hampden (J.) [ed.] Eighteenth
century plays.   [1928]

(Everyman's Library) 485768

Rowe (N.) The Tragedy of Jane Shore.
Written in imitation of Shakespear's style.
In Rowe (N.) Three plays: Tamerlane, The
Fair penitent, Jane Shore. Edited by J.R.
Sutherland, with introduction,
bibliography and notes.   1929.

Note: No. 61 of an edn. limited to 65 copies.
Signed by the editor.   480331

Rowe (N.) The Tragedy of Jane Shore.
[Written in imitation of Shakespeare's
style.] In Nettleton (G.H.) and
Case (A.E.) eds. British dramatists
from Dryden to Sheridan.

1939.
504288

ROWE (NICHOLAS)
Some account of the life of Mr. William
Shakespear (1709). With an introduction
by S. H. Monk. (Augustan Reprint
Society [Publication No. 17] Extra
Series No. 1). pp. 56. (Ann Arbor)
frontis.   1948.
A facsimile of original text.
Nicholas Rowe's "Life" of Shakespeare is
printed as an introduction to many
eighteenth-century editions of Shakespeare's
works. See English Editions: The
Complete Works.
622090

Rowe, Nicholas *works relating to*

── McKERROW (R. B.)
The Treatment of Shakespeare's text
by his earlier editors, 1709-1768.
pp. 35.   [1933.]
British Academy Annual Shakespeare
Lecture, 1933.
408968

── PHILBRICK (N.)
Act and scene division in the first
edition of Shakespeare [i. e. in N.
Rowe's edition of 1709. With bibliographical references]. IN The Theatre
Annual: a publication of information
and research in the arts and history of
the theatre, 1944. (New York)
illus. facsimiles.   1945.
(Theatre Library Association)
563989

—— Studies of old actors : 1. Garrick in
   "Lord Hastings". 2. Mossop in
   "Cardinal Wolsey". 3. Henderson in
   Jacques." From [The Dublin Univer-
   sity Magazine] Vol.62.

   [Dublin]   1863.

                579639

—— SUMMERS ([A.J.M.A.]M.)
   The First illustrated Shakespeare:
   [Rowe's edition of the Works, in six
   Volumes, adorn'd with cuts, 1709].
   FROM The Connoisseur, December, 1938.
   pp. [5.]
   illus.   1938.

                494121

—— WAGENKNECHT (E.)
   The First editor of Shakespeare: [N.
   Rowe]. IN The Colophon, Part 8.
   (New York)
   illus.   1931.

                396607

ROWELL (GEORGE RIGNAL)
   The Victorian Theatre: a survey.
   illus. bibliog.   1956.

                656283

ROWLEY (ALEC)
   It was a lover and his lass. Part-
   song for S.A.B. (unaccompanied).
   Words by [W.]Shakespeare [from
   "As you like it"]. pp. 8. 1951.

                620972

ROWLEY (ALEC)

When daisies pied. [From Love's Labour's
Lost. Arranged for soprano, alto, tenor
and bass.] (Enoch Choral Series, No.321)
(Edwin Ashdown Ltd.)   1962.

                667556

Rowley (Alec) ed.
ARNE (THOMAS [AUGUSTINE])
   Under the greenwood tree: arranged
   as a four-part song by A. Rowley.
   Words by Shakespeare [from "As you
   like it"].   pp. 8.   1943.

                542329

Rowley (A.) [ed.]
ARNE (THOMAS AUGUSTINE)
   When daisies pied. Words by
   Shakespeare [from Love's labour's
   lost].   Arranged as a four-part
   song by A. Rowley. pp. 4. 1943.
   Novello's Series of Short Choral
   Compositions. Musical Times.
                544419

Rowley (A.) [ed.]
COATES (ERIC)
   Tell me where is fancy bred: two-
   part song. Words [from Merchant
   of Venice]. Arranged by A. Rowley.
   pp. 8.   1933.
   Boosey's Modern Festival Series.
                524585

Rowley (A.) [ed.]
COATES (ERIC)
   Who is Sylvia?: two-part song.
   Words [from Two Gentlemen of Verona].
   Arranged by A. Rowley.   pp. 8.
                        1933.
   Boosey's Modern Festival Series.
                525600

Rowley (S.) When you see me, you
   know me: a chronicle - history
   [of King Henry VIII, and a probable
   source of Shakespeare's Henry VIII.]
   Edited, with an introduction and
   notes, by K. Elze.

   (Dessau)   1874.

                488647

ROWLEY (W.)
   All's lost by lust, and A Shoemaker,
   a gentleman. [Edited] with an
   introduction on Rowley's place in
   the drama [and notes] by C. W. Stork.
   [With references to Shakespeare.]
   (Philadelphia)   1910.
   University of Pennsylvania, Series
   in Philology and Literature.
                499285

ROWLING (MARJORIE)
   Bride for a bard [: a play. Broad-
   cast] 10th Sept. 1952. ff. [ii] 19.
   typescript.

                630862

ROWSE (ALFRED LESLIE)
   Elizabethan drama and society.
   IN GARRETT (JOHN) ed., Talking of
   Shakespeare [: a selection from the
   lectures delivered at the annual course
   for teachers at Stratford, 1948-1953].
                        1954.

                641471

ROWSE (A. L.)
   The English spirit: essays in
   history and literature. [With
   references to Shakespeare.]
   bibliog.   1944.

                553914

ROWSE (A. L.)
   [A Review of] "In Shakespeare's
   Warwickshire", by O. Baker. IN The
   Spectator, Vol. 159.   1937.

                476596

ROWSE (A. L.)
   [A Review of] "I, William Shakespeare,
   do appoint Thomas Russell, Esquire",
   by J. L. Hotson.   IN The Spectator,
   Vol. 159.   1937.

                476596

ROWSE, ALFRED LESLIE
   Shakespeare's Southampton, patron of
   Virginia.   1965.

   illus.   746572

ROWSE, ALFRED LESLIE
   William Shakespeare: a biography. 1963.

   illus.   667626

ROWSE (A. L.) and HARRISON (G. B.)
Queen Elizabeth and her subjects.
[With references to Shakespeare.]
ports.   1935.

431068

Roy (J.A.) Joseph Howe: a study in
achievement and frustration. [With
a bibliography, and reference to an
oration, by J. Howe, delivered during
the Tercentenary celebrations in
Halifax, Nova Scotia]. Ports. Illus.

(Toronto)   1935.

447665

Roy (P.T.) [Review of] Shakespeare-
Jahrbuch, Band 70. From The
English Literary and Educational
Review for Continental Readers,
vol. 6, No. 1. pp. 40.

(Leipzig)   1935.

434833

Royal College of Art, South Kensington

——LA DELL, EDWIN
Shakespeare lithographs 1964 [:
catalogue of a series published by
the Royal College of Art of work by
staff, students and invited guests.
With colour transparencies].   1964.

766241

Royal Court Theatre *see* London, Theatres — Royal Court Theatre

Royal General Theatrical Fund. Proceedings at the thirtieth Anniversary
Festival, July 1st, 1875. Henry Irving
in the chair. [Including references to
Shakespeare. From The Era.] pp. 48.

1875.

507847

Royal Institution, Hull

see: Hull, Playgoers' Theatre

Royal Italian Opera House Haymarket *see* London, Theatres — Royal Italian Opera House *Haymarket*

Royal Lyceum Theatre. Augustin Daly's
Company. [Programme of] 'As You
Like It' for Nov. 1891. pp.[4.]

1891.

421130

Royal Shakespeare Theatre *see* Stratford-upon-Avon, Royal Shakespeare Theatre

Royal Visits *see* Stratford-upon-Avon, Royal Visits

Royalty

—— Hofmannsthal, Hugo, Edler von
Shakespeare's kings and noblemen. IN

LEWINTER, OSWALD, ed.
Shakespeare in Europe [by various
authors].   1963.

667784

—— KIRSCH, JAMES
Shakespeare's royal self [: a
psychological study of 'Hamlet',
'King Lear' and 'Macbeth']. (New York)
1966.

760092

—— KNIGHT (GEORGE WILSON)
The Sovereign flower: on Shakespeare
as the poet of royalism, with related
essays and indexes to earlier volumes.
Indexes composed by Patricia M. Ball.
1958.

665908

——LA GUARDIA, ERIC
Ceremony and history: the problem of
symbol from "Richard II" to "Henry V".
IN Pacific coast studies in
Shakespeare. Edited by W. F. McNeir
and T. N. Greenfield. (Eugene: Ore.)
1966.

768009

—McNEAL (THOMAS H.)
Shakespeare's cruel queens.   IN The
Huntington Library Quarterly, Vol. 22.
bibliog.   1958.

494029/22

— SNYDER, KARL E.
Kings and kingship in four of
Shakespeare's history plays.
IN CORDER JIM W., ed., Shakespeare
1964 [: a record of the celebrations
of the Shakespeare Quatercentenary
at Texas Christian University].
(Fort Worth, Tex.)
illus.   1965.

745402

—WHITE (W.) and CHAPMAN (G.)
England's Royal characters in Shakespeare's
historical plays [: genealogical table].
1 sheet.   (Concord, N. H.)
1886.

454999

— WINNY, JAMES
The player king: a theme of
Shakespeare's histories.   1968.

770967

Royalty Theatre *see* London, Theatres — Royalty Theatre

Royde-Smith (Naomi [G.]) The
life of Mrs. Siddons: a psychological
investigation.   With references to
Shakespeare.]   Ports. Illus.

1933.

404014

[Roydon (M.)] A New sonet of Pyramus
and Thisbie[, claimed by A. Acheson
to have been parodied by Shakespeare
in A Midsummer Night's Dream. Here
attributed to Matthew Roydon.] In
Acheson (A.) Mistress Davenant, the
Dark Lady of Shakespeare's Sonnets.
2nd edn. Facsimile.

1913.

497276

ROYLE, E.
The Pattern of play in 'Twelfth Night'.
FROM Theoria, October, 1964. pp.1-12.
(Pietermaritzburg)   1964.

668359

ROYSTER (SALIBELLE)
An English teacher looks at England.
[With references to Stratford-on-Avon.]
FROM Education, Vol. 58.   (Boston,
Mass.)   1938.

512384

ROZENTHAL (L. GLÜCK)
The Immortal Shakespeare [: a por-
trait].   (Woolwich)   [c.1900.]

623373

RUBINSTEIN (HAROLD FREDERICK)
After-glow: a play in one act.
[With Shakespeare as one of the
characters.]   pp. 18.
1937.   472035
_____ IN ARMSTRONG (W.) ed., 8 new
one-act plays of 1937.   5th series.
1937.   472475

RUBINSTEIN (HAROLD FREDERICK)
Moneys from Shylock: [a play].
pp. 31.   [1940.]   515734
Nelson's Plays for Amateurs, No. 19.
_____ IN MARRIOTT (J. W.) [ed.] The
Best one-act plays of 1939.
1940.   512038

RUBINSTEIN, HAROLD FREDERICK
Prelude to a tragedy

For editions of this play see under
English Editions: Hamlet:
Alterations &c.

Rubinstein (H.F.) Shakespeare's Globe:
play in one act. In The Amateur
Theatre and Playwrights' Journal,
Vol.4, No.75.

1937.

467093

RUBINSTEIN, HAROLD FREDERICK
Unearthly gentleman. A Trilogy of one
act plays about Shakespeare.   1965.

746635

Rubinstein, Harold Frederick *works relating to*

—Wallis (N.H.) The Ethics of criticism
and other essays. [Including Two
modern plays on Shakespeare:
Shakespeare, by H.F.Rubinstein and
C.Bax;etc.]

1924.

443990

Rubinstein (H.F.) and Bax (C.) Shakespeare: a play in five episodes.
[With] a preface by A.W. Pollard.
pp.96.

[1934.]

[French's Acting Plays.]

415735

RUBOW (P. V.)
Shakespeare's sonnets.   [English
text.]   IN Orbis litterarum:
revue danois d'histoire littéraire.
Tome 4.   (Copenhague)
facsimiles. bibliog.   1946.

593482/4

RÜCKER (F. G.)
The Spirit of Caesar.   FROM The
Contemporary Review: Literary
Supplement, 1912.   pp. [3.]   [1912]

389205

Rueff (A.M.) The Life and activities
of Mr. Thomas Bowdler.   [From
Life and Letters To-day, Spring,
1938.]

1938.

488919

RUGBY, The Percival Guildhouse
Shakespearian performances
Programmes, tickets, photographs,
etc.   1936-55.

473498

RUGGLE (GEORGE) Works relating to:
see Moore (W. H.) Baconian Studies.

RUGGLES (ELEANOR) [Mrs. R. S. O'Leary]
Prince of players, Edwin Booth.
(New York)
ports. illus. facsimile. bibliog.
1953.

633250

Rugoff (M.A.) Donne's imagery : a
study in creative sources.   [With
bibliographical and Shakespearian
references.]

(New York)   1939.

507178

RULFS (DONALD J.)
The Romantic writers and Edmund Kean.
IN Modern Language Quarterly, Vol. 11.
1950.

525289/11

Rumania

——DUŢU (ALEXANDRU)
Recent Shakespeare performances in
Romania.
IN SHAKESPEARE SURVEY 20.   (Cambridge)
1967.

766881

——DUŢU, ALEXANDRU
Shakespeare in Rumania: a bibliographical essay.   With an introduction
by M. Gheorghiu.   (Bucharest) 1964.

742412

——GHEORGHIU, MIHNEA
Shakespeare in Rumania. FROM Rumanian
Review, 2: 1964. pp.71-80. (Bucharest)
1964.

742414

Rümelin, Gustav *works relating to*

——Shakespeare in Germany of to-day [: a
review of Shakespearestudien by G.
Rumelin].   From [The Broadway,
July 1872.]

553489

Rummel (Joseph) ed.
SULLIVAN ([Sir] ARTHUR [SEYMOUR])
Music to the masque in Shakespeare's
Merchant of Venice.   Arranged as
pianoforte duet by J. Rummel.   pp.
[iv], 68.   [c.1880]

472450

Runciman, John *works relating to*

——MERCHANT (W. M.)
John Runciman's 'Lear in the storm'.
IN Journal of the Warburg and
Courtauld Institutes, Vol. 17.
1954.

487462/17

RUSHTON (W. L.)
Shakespeare's euphuism.   1871.

573428

RUSK (R. L.) ed.
Letters to Emma Lazarus, in the
Columbia University Library.
[With references to Shakespeare.]
pp. 84.   (New York)   1939.

504572

RUSKIN (JOHN)
On "yon grey lines that fret the clouds",
in Julius Caesar, II.i.103-4.
IN Transactions of the New Shakespeare
Society, Series 1. Nos. 6-7.
pp. 409-412.   1877-9.

11987

RUSKIN (J.)
The Queenly power of women.   [With
references to Shakespeare's
characters].   IN International
University Society's Reading course:
text matter and biographical studies.
[Section 3.]   (Nottingham) [1936].

465268

Ruskin, John *works relating to*

——Dale (J.A.) Ruskin as critic of
Shakespeare. In Saint George, Vol.
10.

      (Birmingham)   1907.

          204838

—— Mr. Ruskin and Mr. Irving's Shylock.
FROM The Theatre, March 1, 1880.
          1880.

          516579

Russell (A.J.) Their religion [i.e.
that of Abraham Lincoln, Robert
Burns, Shakespeare, etc.]

          1934.

          425197

RUSSELL (BERTRAND ARTHUR WILLIAM, 3rd Earl)
Mr. Bowdler's nightmare: family bliss.
IN Nightmares of eminent persons and
other stories.   Illustrated by C. W.
Stewart.

          1954.

          649737

RUSSELL (BERTRAND ARTHUR WILLIAM, 3rd Earl)
The Psychoanalyst's Nightmare.   IN
Nightmares of eminent persons and other
stories.   Illustrated by C. W. Stewart.
          1954.

          649737

RUSSELL (D. A.)
Hamlet costumes from Garrick to Gielgud.
IN SHAKESPEARE SURVEY 9.   (Cambridge)
illus.   1956.

          665210

R[USSELL] (EDWARD RICHARD [RUSSELL,
1st Baron])
Ellen Terry as Portia.   FROM The
Theatre, Jan. 1880.   1880.

          516866

R[USSELL] (E. R. [RUSSELL, 1st Baron])
Henry Irving as Shylock.   FROM The
Theatre, Jan. 1880.   1880.

          515795

RUSSELL (E. R. [RUSSELL, 1st Baron])
The Merchant of Venice.   1: Shylock;
2:   The Minor characters.   pp. 53.
(Liverpool)   1888.

          421128

Russell (E.R. [Russell, 1st Baron])
Mr. Irving's interpretations of
Shakspeare. In The Fortnightly Review,
Vol.34. New Series. (Vol.40. Old
Series.)

          1883.

          62996

Russell (E.R. [Russell, 1st Baron])
The Religion of Shakespeare. From
The Theological Review. Vol.13.

          1876.

          472755

[RUSSELL (GEORGE WILLIAM)]
The Living torch, [by] A.E.   Edited
by M. Gibbon with an introductory
essay.   [Containing "Shakespeare
and the blind alley" and other
Shakespearian references].   1937.

          473582

RUSSELL (Rt. Hon. G. W. E.)
St. George and Shakespeare.
IN Russell (Rt. Hon. G. W. E.)
Sketches and snapshots.
frontis.   1910.

          434222

RUSSELL (J.)
Mendelssohn's "A Midsummer night's
dream" [: a description of the
music.   Broadcast] 19th August, 1946.
ff. 6.
typescript.   1946.

          579577

RUSSELL (JOHN)
Shakespeare's country.
illus.   map.   1942.
The Face of Britain [Series].

          532246

Russell (P.) Sir Henry Irving. pp.
63.

          [1895.]

(Men and Women of the Century, No. 1.)

          486852

Russell, Thomas *works relating to*

——HOTSON ([J.] L.)
I, William Shakespeare, do appoint
Thomas Russell, Esquire... [an account
of friends and associates of Shakespeare.
With bibliographical notes.]
ports.   illus.   maps.   facsimile.
genealogical tables. 1937.   474752
————— Another copy with inscription
signed by the author. 1937.   665445

RUSSELL (TRUSTEM WHEELER)
Voltaire, Dryden, & heroic tragedy.
[With references to Shakespeare,
bibliographical notes, and a bibliography.]   (New York)   1946.

          575212

RUSSELL (WILLIAM CLARK)
Representative actors: a collection of
criticisms, anecdotes, personal descriptions, etc. referring to many celebrated
British actors from the sixteenth to
the present century. With notes,
memoirs and a short account of English
acting. [With references to
Shakespearian actors.]
            [c.1870.] 483541
"Chandos" Classics.
_____ Another edn. [c.1872.] 427215

Russia
see also **Georgia; Hamlet, Russia; Latvia; Ukraine**

—Abraham (G.[E.H.]) Eight Soviet
    composers. [With references to
    Shakespearean music, bibliograph-
    ical notes and musical examples.]

            (Oxford)   1943.

                   545526

___ ANIKST (A.)
    Shakespeare in Russia.   FROM Soviet
    Literature, April-May 1946.
    (Moscow)   1946.

                   581951

___ BILAINKIN (G.)
    Maisky: ten years ambassador [i.e.
    Soviet ambassador to Britain. With
    references to his visits, in April
    1926 and 1936, to Stratford-on-Avon
    on the occasion of Shakespeare's
    birthday celebrations, and other refer-
    ences to Shakespeare.]
    ports.   illus.   1944.

                   548852

___ Boelza (I.[F.]) Handbook of Soviet
    musicians. Edited [with a foreword]
    by A.[D.] Bush. [With a biblio-
    graphy including references to
    Shakespearian music.] Ports.

                    1943.

[Life and Literature in the Soviet Union [4])

                   545155

___ BORISOVA, TAMARA
    Shakespeare on the Byelorussian
    stage.   [Moscow]
    typescript.   N.D.

                   741618

___ COATES (W. P.) and COATES (ZELDA K.)
    A History of Anglo-Soviet relations.
    [Containing an account of the presence
    of M. Maisky at Shakespeare's birthday
    celebrations at Stratford-on-Avon,
    April, 1926.]
    frontis.   1943.

                   548237

—CRAIG (EDWARD GORDON) [pseud.
                      Tom Fool]
    Craig in Moscow [: interview with D.
    Tutaev concerning Craig's production of
    Hamlet at the Moscow Art Theatre c.1909
    and his meeting with Stanislavsky.
    B.B.C.] Broadcast script. [Programme
    transmitted] 25 December 1960. ff.7.
                      1960.

                   667035

___ DANA (H. W. L.)
    Handbook on Soviet drama: lists
    of theatres, plays, operas, ballets,
    films, and books and articles about
    them.   [With references to
    Shakespeare.] (New York: American
    Russian Institute)   1938.

                   502494

—Dark (E.P.) The World against Russia?
    [With references to M.Maisky
    and the Shakespeare Birthday
    celebrations, 1926. With biblio-
    graphies and bibliographical
    notes.]

            (Sydney)   1948.

                   597921

—DRAPER (JOHN WILLIAM)
    Shakespeare and Muscovy.   IN The
    Slavonic and East European Review,
    Vol. 33.   1954-55.

                   309336/33

—DREYDEN (S.)
    "Midsummer night" in Siberia.
    IN Soviet War News, Vol. 10.
                      1943-4.

                   560942

—Ettinger (P.) Russian illustrations
    to Shakespeare : engravings by F.
    Konstantinov. <u>In</u> The Studio, Vol.
    118.

                      1939.

                   510178

___ GARRY (S.)
    Shakespeare through Russian eyes.
    [From articles by A. V. Lunacharsky
    and P. S. Kogan.]   pp. [4.]   FROM
    The Listener, Dec. 1934.
    illus.   1934.

                   428697

— Griffith (H.) ed., Playtime in
    Russia, by various authors. [With
    references to Shakespeare.] <u>Ports.</u>
    Illus.

                      1935.

                   434860

___ GYSEGHEM (A. van)
    Theatre in Soviet Russia. [With
    references to Shakespeare.]
    ports.   illus.   1943.

                   545305

—— HOUGHTON (N.)
    Moscow rehearsals: an account of
    methods of production in the Soviet
    theatre.   With an introduction by
    L. Simonson [and references to
    Shakespeare.]   (New York)
    illus.   1936.

                            457253

—— IVING (V.)
    Shakespeare ballet in Moscow: "The
    Merry Wives of Windsor", [music by
    V. Oransky, produced June 1942].
    IN Soviet war news, Vol. 5.   1942.

                            544254

—— Kotlyarevsky (N.) Shakespeare's
    influence on Russia, translated
    by Augusta C. Davidson. In Stephens
    (Winifred) ed. The Soul of Russia.
    [By various writers.] Illus.

                       1916.

                            438010

—— KOZINTSEV, GRIGORII MIKHAILOVICH
    Shakespeare: time and conscience.
    Translated from the Russian by Joyce
    Vining.   1967.

      illus.   767149

—— LAWRENCE (J.)
    Life in Russia.   [With references
    to Shakespearian performances.]
                    1947.

                          583615

—— LEHRMAN (EDGAR HAROLD)
    Soviet Shakespeare appreciation,
    1917-1952.   Typescript, 1954.
    Microfilm, positive copy.   (Ann
    Arbor, Mich.)   1 reel, 35 mm.
                    [1954.]
    University Microfilms.   Doctoral
    Dissertation Series.
                    647059

—— MACLEOD (J.)
    Actors across the Volga: a study of
    the 19th century Russian theatre and
    of Soviet theatres in war.   [With
    references to Shakespeare and a biblio-
    graphy.]
      ports.   illus.   1946.

                      566713

—— MACLEOD (J.)
    The New Soviet theatre [including
    a chapter "Shakespeare on the
    Soviet stage" and other Shakespearian
    references.]
      illus.   plan.   bibliogs.   1943.

                    538985

—— MARKOV (P. [A.])
    "Hamlet" at Moscow Art Theatre.
    IN Soviet War News, Vol. 10.
                  1943-4.

                    560942

—— Mikhailov (M.) The Study of
    Shakespeare in the Soviet Union,
    with a foreword by F.S.Boas. Illus.
    From The Anglo-Soviet Journal,
    Vol.6.

                  1945.

                    561323

—— MOISENCO (RENA)
    Twenty Soviet composers.   [With a
    reference to B. Assafiev's incidental
    music to Shakespeare's Macbeth and
    Merchant of Venice, and with biblio-
    graphical references.]   pp. 64.
                    [1942.]
    Workers' Music Association.   Keynote
    Series, Book I.

                    538872

—— MOROZOV (M. M.)
    Moscow discusses Shakespeare [at the
    annual Russian Shakespearian confer-
    ence, 1942].   IN Soviet war news,
    Vol. 4.   1942.

                    544253

—— MOROZOV (M. M.)
    Shakespeare on the Soviet stage.
    Translated by D. Magarshack, with an
    introduction by J. D. Wilson.   pp.72.
      ports.   illus.   1947.
    Soviet News.

                    582120

—— Othello in Moscow.   IN Picture
    Post, Vol. 26.
      illus.   1945.

                    565210

——   Pring (Beryl) Shakespeare and
    Russian films. In The Adelphi, Vol. 4.

                  1932.

                    404903

—— SEAR (H. G.)
    Russian music and Shakespeare.
    FROM The Musical Times, [Vol. 85].
                  1944.

                    550793

—— SIMMONS (E. J.)
    Catherine the Great and Shakespeare.
    pp. [17].   FROM [Publications of
    the Modern Language Association of
    America, Vol. 47.]   [(Menasha, Wis.)]
                    [1932]

                    438446

—— Simmons (E.J.) English literature and
    culture in Russia (1553-1840.)[With
    a chapter on The Early history of
    Shakspere in Russia; and biblio-
    graphies.]

      (Cambridge, Mass.)   1935.

  (Harvard Studies in Comparative Literature,12.)

                    437487

—— The Soviet Shakespeare [: article
    in shorthand].   IN Pitman's business
    education, Vol. 1, Oct. 1935-March 1936.
                  [1936]

                    454995

TRORY (E.)
Shakespeare in the U.S.S.R.
IN Trory (E.) Mainly about books.
(Brighton)
frontis.   tables.   1945.

564806

[Turgenev (I.S.)] The King Lear of the
Russian steppes. [Translated from
the Russian of I. Tourguenef by Mrs.
[Fanny] B. Palliser. From [London
Society,] Vol.22.

[1872.]

558071

VOITOLOVSKAYA (L.)
Khadji Mukan and William Shakespeare.
[Contains description of a performance
of "The Taming of the Shrew" in Soviet
Kazakhstan.]   IN Soviet War News,
Vol. 11.   1944.

560943

Rutgers University Studies in English
McGINN (D. J.)
Shakespeare's influence on the drama
of his age, studied in Hamlet.   (New
Brunswick, [N.J.])
bibliog.   1938.

486551

Rutherford (H.) illus.
EVANS (J. R.)
The Boyhood of Shakespeare.   [1947.]
Hutchinson's Books for Young People:
Historical Series.
599896

Rutland, Roger Manners 5th Earl of *works relating to*

BOSTELMANN (LEWIS FREDERICK)
Rutland: a chronologically arranged
outline of the life of Roger Manners,
5th Earl of Rutland, author of the
works issued in folio in 1623 under
the nom de plume "Shake-speare" [etc].
(New York)
ports. illus.   1911.
Signed by the author.
666340

POROHOVSHIKOV (P. S.)
Shakespeare unmasked [: the claims
of Roger Manners, 5th Earl of Rutland,
to the authorhsip of Shakespeare.
With a preface by G. V. Vernadsky, and
a bibliography.]   (New York)
facsimiles.   1940.

523046

SYKES (C. W.)
Alias William Shakespeare? [The
claims of Roger Manners, 5th Earl of
Rutland, to the authorship of
Shakespeare.]   With a preface by
A. Bryant [and bibliographical notes].
1947.

583729

SYKES (C. W.)
The Shakespeare mystery [: evidence
to show that Shakespeare's plays were
written by Roger Manners, 5th Earl of
Rutland].   pp. [6.] FROM The London
Mystery Magazine, Vol. 1.   [1949.]

604845

RUTLAND (WILLIAM RUTLAND)
Thomas Hardy.   [With references to
Shakespeare.]
ports. illus.   1938.
"Order of Merit" Series.
490733

RUTLEDGE (JEAN JACQUES)
La Quinzaine angloise à Paris; ou,
L'Art de s'y ruiner en peu de tems.
Ouvrage posthume du Docteur Stearne
[pseud. i.e. J. J. Rutledge]: tra-
duit de l'anglois par un Observateur
[or rather, an original work by
J. J. Rutledge].   (Londres) 1777.

606448

RUTTER (O.)
The Scales of Karma [: the law of
Karma and reincarnation.   Containing
references to Shakespeare].   [1940.]

520030

RUUTZ-REES (C[AROLINE])
Flower garlands of the poets, Milton,
Shakespeare, Spenser, Marot, Sannazaro.
Extrait [de] Mélanges offerts à
A. Lefranc par ses élèves et ses amis.
[English text.]   pp. 75-90.   1936.

497632

Ryder (S.), Anster (M.) and Baylis
(Lilian) The Shakespeare Festival:
correspondence. In The National
Review, vol.103.

1934.

430233

RYLANDS (GEORGE HUMPHREY WOLFESTAN)
The Actor's speaking of Hamlet.
[Broadcast] 12th Dec., 1951. ff.19.
typescript.   1951.

624729

RYLANDS (GEORGE HUMPHREY WOLFESTAN)
Festival Shakespeare in the West End.
IN SHAKESPEARE SURVEY 6.   (Cambridge)
1953.

631770

RYLANDS (GEORGE HUMPHREY WOLFESTAN)
Introduction.   IN The Comedies,
histories [and] tragedies.   Introduction[s] by T. Guthrie, J. G.
McManaway [and] G. Rylands.   Illustrations by E. Ardizzone, J. Farleigh
[and] Agnes M. Parker.   (New York)
3 vols.   1958-59.
Heritage Shakespeare.
666384-6.

RYLANDS (GEORGE HUMPHREY WOLFESTAN)
Introductory essay [entitled] On the
production of The Duchess of Malfi
[with references to Shakespeare].
IN WEBSTER (JOHN) The Duchess of
Malfi.   Illustrated by M. Ayrton.
1945.

561294

RYLANDS (G. [H. W.])
The Language of Shakespeare [: a
broadcast talk].   ff. 10.
  typescript.   1937.

465093

RYLANDS (GEORGE HUMPHREY WOLFESTAN)
The Poet and the player.
IN SHAKESPEARE SURVEY 7.   (Cambridge)
1954.

639176

RYLANDS (G. [H. W.])
[Review of H. G. Granville-Barker's
Prefaces to Shakespeare.   4th series.]
IN The New Statesman and Nation, New
Series, Vol. 31.   1946.

573326

RYLANDS (GEORGE HUMPHREY WOLFESTAN)
Review [of] Henry Irving [: a biography
by L. H. F. Irving.   Broadcast
2nd March, 1952].   ff. 12.
  typescript.

624732

RYLANDS (GEORGE HUMPHREY WOLFESTAN)
[Review of] Preface to Coriolanus
and other plays of Shakespeare by
H. Granville-Barker [broadcast
23rd April and] 3rd June, 1948.
ff. 9.
  typescript.

593006

RYLANDS (GEORGE HUMPHREY WOLFESTAN)
Shakespeare and his England.
[Broadcast] 21st April, 1947.
ff. 30.
  typescript.

583266

RYLANDS (GEORGE HUMPHREY WOLFESTAN)
Shakespeare and the stage.   (Forces
Educational Broadcast).   [Broadcast]
20th September, 1945.   ff. 12.
  typescript.

563609

RYLANDS (GEORGE HUMPHREY WOLFESTAN)
Shakespeare the poet.   IN
GRANVILLE-BARKER (H.) and HARRISON
(G. B.) eds., A Companion to Shakespeare
studies.   (Cambridge)
  bibliogs.   illus.   tables.   facsimiles.
                        1934.   418724
  ———(New York.)   1937.   479251
  ———(Cambridge)   1945.   566174

Rylands (G.[H.W.]) Shakespeare-
  yesterday and to-day [:the playing
  and presentation of Shakespeare].
  Talk [broadcast] 5th August, 1949.
  ff.6. Typescript. (Shakespeare and
  his world, 9)

605271

RYLANDS (GEORGE HUMPHREY WOLFESTAN)
Shakespeare's poetic energy.   ([41st]
Annual Shakespeare Lecture of the
British Academy, 1951).   pp. [21.]
                        [1951.]

634468

RYLANDS (G. [H. W.])
Shakespearian detection.   [Review
of] What happens in Hamlet, by
J. Dover Wilson [and] Shakespeare's
imagery by Caroline F. E. Spurgeon.
IN The New Statesman and Nation,
Vol. 10.   (New Series).   1935.

445577

RYLANDS (GEORGE HUMPHREY WOLFESTAN) [ed.]
The Ages of man: Shakespeare's image
of man and nature.   1939.

507797

RYLANDS (GEORGE HUMPHREY WOLFESTAN) ed.
Elizabethan tragedy: six representative
plays (excluding Shakespeare) selected
with an introduction by G. [H. W.]
Rylands.   1933.

412648

RYLANDS (GEORGE HUMPHREY WOLFESTAN)
      and BARTON (JOHN)

["As you like it" at Stratford-upon-
Avon: a discussion from the "Midland
Critics",broadcast April 19th,1957].ff5.
Typescript.

665513

RYLANDS (GEORGE HUMPHREY WOLFESTAN)
and BARTON (JOHN)
  "Cymbeline" [at Stratford: a
discussion.   Broadcast 15th July
1957].   ff. 7.
  typescript.

665665

RYLANDS (GEORGE HUMPHREY WOLFESTAN)
      and BARTON (JOHN)

"Julius Caesar" [at Stratford: a
discussion from the "Midland Critics".
Broadcast June 19th, 1957] ff 6.
Typescript

665543

RYLANDS (GEORGE HUMPHREY WOLFESTAN)
      and BARTON (JOHN)

["King John" at Stratford: a discussion.
Broadcast May 9th 1957]. ff 7.Typescript.

665521

RYLANDS (G. [H. W.]) and BENNETT (H. S.)
Stratford productions.   IN
SHAKESPEARE SURVEY 1.   (Cambridge)
                        1948.
Seasons 1946 and 1947.

590674

RYMER (THOMAS)
Reflections on the Julius Caesar.
IN LEECH, CLIFFORD, ed., Shakespeare:
the tragedies.   A collection of
critical essays.   (Chicago) 1965.
Gemini books.

752332

RYMER (THOMAS)
A Short view of tragedy.   IN
ADAMS (HENRY HITCH) and HATHAWAY
(BAXTER) ed., Dramatic essays of the
neoclassic age.   (New York)   1950.

611958

RYMER (THOMAS)
The Tragedies of the last age consider'd
and examin'd by the practice of the
ancients and by the common sense of all
ages;   in a letter to F. Shepheard.
Part 1.   2nd edn.   [With references
to Shakespeare].   1692.
For Part 2, "A Short view of tragedy,
etc." see catalogue number 1985.

466540

RYMER (THOMAS)
The Tragedies of the last age;   A
Short view of tragedy, with some
reflections on Shakespear.   IN The
Critical works of Thomas Rymer.
Edited with an introduction and
notes by C. A. Zimansky.   (New
Haven [Conn.])
bibliogs.   1956.

670354

Rymer, Thomas *works relating to*

____ALEXANDER, NIGEL
Thomas Rymer and "Othello".
IN SHAKESPEARE SURVEY 21.   (Cambridge)
pp. 67-77.   1968.

776762

____ DENNIS (J.)
The Impartial critick: or, some
observations upon a late book, entituled,
A Short view of tragedy, written by
Mr. Rymer (1693).   IN Dennis (J.)
Critical works, Vol. 1.   Edited [with
preface and notes] by E. N. Hooker.
(Baltimore)   1939.

503438

____STOLL (ELMER EDGAR)
Oedipus and Othello, Corneille, Rymer
and Voltaire.   [English text.   With
bibliographical notes.]   Extrait de
la Revue anglo-américaine, juin 1935.
pp. [16.]   (Paris)   [1935.]

569122

____WALCOTT (F. G.)
John Dryden's answer to Thomas Rymer's
"The Tragedies of the last age".
[With Shakespearian references and
bibliographical notes.]   FROM Philological Quarterly, Vol. 15.   (Iowa)
1935.

484068

S. [pseud.]
Shakspeare's Bertram.   FROM [The New
Monthly Magazine,] Vol. 4.   [1822.]

558107

S. (A. K.) <u>see</u> Smith (A. K.)

S. (C.)
An Ideal Hamlet: [Henry Irving as
Hamlet at the Lyceum Theatre,
October 31st, 1874].   FROM The
Theatre, December 1, 1880.   1880.

516327

S. (C. F.)
Shakespeare's "Henry VI".   IN The
Institute Magazine, Vol. 1.
(Birmingham)   1883.

45873

S. (E.) <u>see</u> Sandford (E.)

S. (E. B.)
A Polish source for Shakespeare [:   The
Counsellor, an English translation of
De optimo senatore, by L. Grimaldus
Goslicius, as a possible source for
the sayings and character of Polonius
in Hamlet].   IN More books: the
bulletin of the Boston Public Library,
6th Series, Vol. 15.   (Boston, [Mass.])
1940.

522784

Sabbath *see* Sunday

SABOL (ANDREW JOSEPH)
Two unpublished stage songs for the
'Aery of Children'.   IN Renaissance
News.   Vol. 13, 1960.   (New York)
illus.   bibliogs.   1960.

672073/1960

SACHS (EDWIN O.)
Modern opera houses and theatres.
Examples selected from playhouses
recently erected in Europe, with
descriptive text [etc.] Vols. 2-3
[with references to the Shakespeare
Memorial Theatre, Stratford-on-Avon].
illus.   plans.   dgms.   graphs.
tables.   2 vols.   1897-8.

560513

Sachs (W.) Psychoanalysis : its
meaning and practical applications.
[With a chapter on Hamlet.]

1934.

503202

SACKS (CLAIRE) and WHAN (EDGAR) eds.
Hamlet, enter critic.   (New York)
bibliog.   1960.

666637

Sadler's Wells Ballet Company and Sadler's Wells Theatre *see* **London**, Theatres — Sadler's Wells Theatre

[Sage (Abby)] The Hamlets of the stage. From [The Atlantic Monthly,] Vols. 23 and 24. [Boston, Mass.]
1869.

559341

SAGE (ABBY) and MACFARLAND (A. S.)
Stories from Shakespeare.
port. illus. [1882.] 401511
————— Another edn. [c.1895] 550468

SAHA (NARAYAN CHANDRA)
Tolstoy and Shakespeare.
IN Shakespeare commemoration volume, edited by Taraknath Sen. (Calcutta)
1966.

764382

SAHITYA AKADEMI
Shakespeare Seminar, 5-8 December 1964 [: lectures given at Sahitya Akademi, New Delhi]. (New Delhi)
typescript. 1964.

744153

Said (A. Samad) trans.
WYATT (HORACE GRAHAM)
Chĕrita-Chĕrita Shakespeare. Di-chĕritakan sa-mula oleh H. G. Wyatt. Di-tĕrjĕmahkan oleh A. Samad Said. (London. Kuala Lumpur: O.U.P.) 1958. Text in Malayan.

666153

Sailors and the Sea

————DOHERTY (W. O.)
Shakespeare's sea lore [: thesis.]
IN BANDEL (BETTY) The Debt of Shakespearian tragedy to early English comedy [etc.]
microfilm. bibliog. 1947.

597360

——— Ewen (C.[H.]L'E.) Shakespeare no seaman: the theme of an unpublished book. Reprinted from The Listener, 11th Aug., 1937. Revised and enlarged, October, 1938. pp.6. 1938.

493634

——— FALCONER, ALEXANDER FREDERICK
A glossary of Shakespeare's sea and naval terms including gunnery. 1965.

742927

——— FALCONER, ALEXANDER FREDERICK
Shakespeare and the sea. 1964.

illus. 667811

——— Grierson (H[elen]) Shakespeare and the sea. From Contemporary Review. 1910. pp.[10.]

389211

——— NICHOLSON (BRINSLEY)
Shakespeare and sea-glasses.
IN Transactions of the New Shakespeare Society, Series 1. Nos. 8-10.
pp. 53-55. 1880-6.

99113

——— QUINN, DAVID BEERS
Sailors and the sea [: in Elizabethan England]. IN SHAKESPEARE SURVEY 17. (Cambridge) 1964.

667822

——— Sharp (Mrs.[Elizabeth A.]) ed., Sea-music: an anthology of poems and passages descriptive of the sea.[With a prefatory note. Including poems by Shakespeare].
[The Canterbury Poets]
1887.

459394

——— SWALE (I.) ed.
The Voice of the sea [: an anthology of prose and poetry]. Edited [with a note. With extracts from Shakespeare].
illus. [1907.]
Wayfaring Books.

546919

——— Walker (N.W.G.) Was Shakespeare a seaman? From The P.L.A. Monthly,No.160.
1939.

512571

——— WATSON (H.F.)
The Sailor in English fiction and drama, 1550-1800. [With references to Shakespeare, a a bibliography.] 1931.

(Columbia University, Studies in English and Comparative Literature)

390618

——— Whymper (F.) The Sea: its stirring story of adventure, peril & heroism. Vol.4. [With references to Shakespeare's allusions to the sea and bibliographical notes.] Ports. Illus. Maps. [4 vols.]
[1877-1880.]

540700

ST. ANDREWS UNIVERSITY
Four hundredth anniversary of the birth of William Shakespeare: an exhibition [catalogue]. (St. Andrews)
1964.

740858

St. Brendan's College *see* Bristol

Saint-Denis, Michel *works relating to*

——Adler (H.) The Method of Michel
Saint Denis. [With references
to Shakespearian productions.]
<u>From</u> London Mercury, Vol. 39.

1938.

494283

St. James's Theatre *see* **London**, Theatres —
St. James's Theatre

St. James Theatre, New York <u>see</u>
New York

ST. JOHN ([Miss] CHRISTOPHER)
Ellen Terry: [a biography. With
Shakespeare refefences.] pp. 96.
ports. illus. 1907.
Stars of the Stage.

444816

St. John ([Miss] Christopher) Henry
Irving [: in memoriam. With
references to Shakespeare.] pp.
27. Port.

1905.

491429

St. John (Miss Christopher) ed.
TERRY (ELLEN)
Four lectures on Shakespeare.
port. 1932.

391411

ST. JOHN (JAMES AUGUSTUS)
Character of Lady Macbeth. FROM
[Tait's Edinburgh Magazine,] Vol. 15.
[Edinburgh] [1848.]

554730

St. Louis Pageant Drama Association
in celebration of the Shakespeare
Tercentenary. As you like it; as
produced by Margaret Anglin at
St. Louis, 1916. Preceded by a
community prologue enacted by citizens
of St. Louis. [St. Louis]
port. [1916.]

398925

St. Pancras

——St. Pancras Journal. Vol. 17, No. 11.
1964.

740863

——UNDERWOOD (MARTIN)
William Shakespeare: a book list
newly compiled and imprinted by
St. Pancras Public Libraries to
mark the 400th anniversary of his
birth in 1564. 1964.

740827

ST. PHILIP'S GRAMMAR SCHOOL, BIRMINGHAM
Programmes of Shakespeare productions,
1951- [Birmingham] 1951-

666295

ST. XAVIER HIGH SCHOOL, JAIPUR
Shakespeare and the world: an
exhibition at St. Xavier High School
on 23rd April 1964. (Jaipur) 1964.

744152

SAINTSBURY (GEORGE EDWARD BATEMAN)
A History of Elizabethan literature.
[With a bibliographical index and a
chapter on Shakespeare.]
1887. 536635
————— 2nd edn. 1898. 443968
————— 9th edn. 1913. 523512

SAINTSBURY (GEORGE EDWARD BATEMAN)
Mr. Irving's Iago. IN Saintsbury
(G. E. B.) A Second scrap book. 1923.

308680

SAINTSBURY (G. [E. B.])
Shakespeare. [From The Cambridge
History of English Literature, vol. 5.]
With an appreciation [of the author]
by Helen J. Waddell. (Cambridge)
1934.
Cambridge Miscellany.

425998

SAINTSBURY (G. [E. B.])
Shakespeare and the grand style.
IN JONES (PHYLLIS M.) [ed.] English
critical essays, twentieth century
[: an anthology], selected with an
introduction. 1933.
The World's Classics.

418096

SAINTSBURY (GEORGE EDWARD BATEMAN)
Shakespeare as touchstone.
IN GOLLANCZ ([Sir] I.) ed., A Book of
homage to Shakespeare.
ports. illus. facsimiles. [1916.]

264175

SAINTSBURY (GEORGE EDWARD BATEMAN)
The Two tragedies; a note [: the
tragic and the sentimental types of
tragedy, including references to
Shakespeare's tragedies]. IN
Blackwood's Magazine, Vol. 162.
(Edinburgh) 1897. 140338
————— IN Saintsbury (G. E. B.) The
Memorial volume: a new collection of
his essays and papers.
port. 1945. 563813

Saintsbury, George Edward Bateman *works relating to*

——K[NIGHTS] (L. C.)
  Shakespeare, by G. [E. B.] Saintsbury
  [: a review].   IN The Criterion,
  vol. 14, 1934–35.   [1934–35]

                              440552

SAINTSBURY (H. A.) and PALMER (C.) eds.
We saw him act: a symposium on the
art of Sir Henry Irving; a series
of essays, articles and anecdotes,
personal reminiscences and dramatic
criticisms written by his contemporaries, collected and collated by
H. A. Saintsbury.
  ports.   1939.

                              506641

Saker, E. *works relating to*

—— "A Midsummer-night's dream".
[Containing a discussion on this
comedy] as arranged for representation
by Edward Saker and produced by him
at the Alexandra Theatre, Liverpool,
Monday, March 29th, 1880, [and] at
Sadler's Wells Theatre, London, Monday,
June 28th, 1880.   IN The Theatre,
Vol. 2.   New Series.
  illus.   1880.

                              59546

SALE, ROGER
The Comic mode of "Measure for measure".
IN SHAKESPEARE QUARTERLY XIX: 1.
pp. 55–61.   (New York)
                          1968.

                              605711

Sale Catalogues *see* **Catalogues**

Salesmanship

——BURRUSS (W. B.)
  Shakespeare the salesman.   [With a
  preface entitled: 'About Bill Burruss',
  by J. C. Aspley.]   (Chicago)
                              1942.

                              548205

SALINGAR (L. G.)
The Design of Twelfth Night.
IN SHAKESPEARE QUARTERLY IX: 2.
pp. 117–139.
(New York)   1958.

                              605711

SALINGAR (L. G.)
Shakespeare in school.   IN The Use
of English, Vol. 1.
  bibliog.   1949.
Bureau of Current Affairs.

                              618851/1

SALINGER (HERMAN)
Shakespeare's tyranny over Grillparzer.
[With bibliographical notes.]   FROM
Monatshefte fur Deutschen Unterricht,
Vol. 31.   (Madison, Wis.)   1939.

                              578415

SALTER (F. M.)
The Play within the play of First
Henry IV.   IN Transactions of the
Royal Society of Canada, Section 2,
Series 3, Vol. 40.   (Ottawa) 1946.

                              584443

SALTER (F. M.)
Shakespeare's interpretation of
Hamlet.   FROM Transactions of the
Royal Society of Canada, 3rd. Series,
Vol. 42.   pp. 43.   [Toronto]
                              1948.

                              609970

SALTER (L.) ed.
The Willow song: unison song with
descant.   [Traditional air.]   pp. 4.
                              1940.

                              536586

"Saltire", pseud. <u>see</u> Wellstood (F. C.)

SALVINI (TOMMASO)
Leaves from the autobiography of
Tommaso Salvini.   [With references
to Shakespeare.]
  ports.   1893.

                              536675

SALVINI (TOMMASO)
On Shakespeare: King Lear.   FROM
The Theatre, December, 1883.   1883.

                              498965

Salvini, Tommaso *works relating to*

___ ALDEN (BARBARA)
Differences in the conception of Othello's
character as seen in the performances of
three nineteenth century actors on the
American stage, Edwin Forrest, Edwin
Booth and Tommaso Salvini.   Filmed by
the University of Chicago Library
(Chicago, Ill.)
bibliog. typescript. microfilm, positive
copy.   1 vol. in 1 reel, 35 mm.   1950.
University of Chicago Doctoral Dissertation No. T 782.
562429 665432

____HENLEY (W. E.)
Salvini.   IN The National Review,
Vol. 3.   1884.

70459

___ KNIGHT (J.)
Signor Salvini and other players of
Othello.   IN AGATE (J. [E.]) ed.,
The English dramatic critics.
[1932.]

399280

____A PARISIAN CRITIC [pseud.]
Mr. Irving [as Hamlet] and Signor
Salvini [as Othello].   FROM The
Gentleman's Magazine, N[ew] S[eries],
Vol. 14.   1875.

561328

SALZMAN (L. F.)
England in Tudor times: an account
of its social life and industries.
[With references to Shakespeare.]
illus.   1933.

426704

SAMARIN (ROMAN M.)
Our closeness to Shakespeare.
IN SHAKESPEARE SURVEY 16.
illus.   1963.

667523

SAMARIN (ROMAN M.   )

Shekspirovskaya Konferentsiya Stratforde
[1961]. FROM Vestnik Akademii Nauk SSSR,
1962; [and] Tenth International
Shakespeare Conference. FROM Soviet
Literature, 1962. pp.[4][4] (Moskva)
1962.

667312

SAMPLEY (A. M.)
Sixteenth century imitation of Romeo
and Juliet.   IN University of Texas
Bulletin, Studies in English, No. 9.
(Texas)   1929.

442468

SAMPSON (ANTONY)
The Printing of Shakespeare's plays.
IN Signature, New Series, No. 15.
facsimiles.   1952.

476085/2/15

Sampson (G.) Bach and Shakespeare[and]
Henry Irving, 1838-1905. In
Sampson (G.) Seven essays.

(Cambridge)   1947

582429

SAMPSON (GEORGE)
Literature in the class-room.
[With references to Shakespeare.]
IN English Association, Essays and
studies, vol. 20.   Collected by
G. Cookson.   (Oxford)
bibliog.   1935.

434627

Sampson (George) ed.
LAMB (CHARLES and MARY [A.])
Tales from Shakespeare.   Edited, with
an introduction and notes, by
G. Sampson.   Illustrated by J. A.
Walker.
port.   [1910.]

488211

SAMPSON (GODFREY)
A Spring song: unison song.
Words by Shakespeare [from "As you
like it"].   pp. 5.   1931.
Novello's School Songs.
594172

SAMPSON (GODFREY)
Under the greenwood tree: two-part
song.   Words by Shakespeare [from
As you like it]; music by
G. Sampson.   pp. 4.   1938.

519004

SAMPSON (JOHN)
In lighter moments: a book of occasional
verse and prose.   With illustrations
by L. Wright [and a foreword by Dora
E. Yates.   Containing "A Ryghte merrie
and moralle songe writ in praise of
our excellent poete Master Willm.
Shakespeare".]   1934.

429645

Samuel (R.) and Thomas (R.H.)
Expressionism in German life, literature and the theatre (1910-
1924) : studies. [With a bibliography, notes and references to
Shakespeare.] Illus.

(Cambridge)   1939.

495269

[SAMUELS (PHILIP FRANCIS)]
Five lectures on "Shakespeare" by
Samuels-Bacon [attempting to prove
that Bacon wrote "Shakespeare"].
pp. 47.   (Boston, Mass.)
1937.   479347
_____ New edn. with changes and
additions.   pp. 64.
port.   facsimile.   1943.   567357

San Diego Shakespeare Festival

——JOHNSON (CHARLES FREDERICK)
San Diego National Shakespeare Festival.
IN SHAKESPEARE QUARTERLY VIII.
pp. 531-534.
(New York) 1957.

605711

——NICHOLS (DOROTHY)
Shakespeare on the West Coast, at
Ashland and San Diego.
IN SHAKESPEARE QUARTERLY XVI: 4.
pp. 343-347.
(New York) 1965.

605711

——OGDEN (DUNBAR H.)
The 1964 season of the Ashland and San
Diego Shakespearian Festivals. IN
Shakespeare Quarterly XV: 4. pp.409-418.
(New York) 1964.

605711

——Programmes. Season 8- 1957-
(San Diego, Cal.)

771364

——PROSSER (ELEANOR)
Colley Cibber at San Diego.
IN SHAKESPEARE QUARTERLY XIV: 3.
pp. 253-261.
(New York) 1963.

605711

——PROSSER (ELEANOR)
Shakespeare at Ashland and San Diego.
IN SHAKESPEARE QUARTERLY XIV: 4.
pp. 445-454.
(New York) 1963.

605711

——PROSSER (ELEANOR)
Shakespeare in San Diego: the thirteenth
season.
IN SHAKESPEARE QUARTERLY XIII: 4.
pp. 529-535.
(New York) 1962.

605711

——SELLMAN (PRISCILLA M.)
The Old Globe's sixth season in San
Diego.
IN SHAKESPEARE QUARTERLY VII.
pp. 419-422.
(New York) 1956.

605711

——SMITH (PETER D.)
The 1966 Festivals at Ashland, Oregon,
and San Diego, California.
IN SHAKESPEARE QUARTERLY XVII: 4.
pp. 407-417.
(New York) 1966.

605711

——WHITAKER (VIRGIL KEEBLE)
Shakespeare in San Diego - the twelfth
season.
IN SHAKESPEARE QUARTERLY XII: 4.
pp. 403-408.
(New York) 1961.

605711

SANCTIS (FRANCESCO de)
History of Italian literature.
Translated by Joan Redfern. [With
references to Shakespeare.] (Oxford)
2 vols. [1932]

392213

Sandars Readership in Bibliography in
the University of Cambridge, Lectures
POLLARD (A. W.)
Shakespeare's fight with the pirates
and the problems of the transmission
of his text. 1917.

270483

Sanderlin (G.) The Repute of Shakespeare's sonnets in the early nineteenth century. In Modern Language
Notes. Vol. 54.

(Baltimore) 1939.

509539

SANDERS (CHARLES RICHARD)
Coleridge and the Broad Church movement:
studies in S. T. Coleridge, Dr. Arnold
of Rugby, J. C. Hare, Thomas Carlyle
and F. D. Maurice. [With references
to Shakespeare, a bibliography and
bibliographical references.] (Durham,
N.C.) 1942.
Duke University Publications.

542272

SANDERS (GERALD DeWITT)
A Shakespeare primer. (New York)
illus. dgms. facsimiles. bibliog.
1950.

612178

SANDERS (NORMAN)
The Comedy of Greene and Shakespeare.
IN Stratford-upon-Avon Studies,
edited by J. R. Brown and B. Harris,
Vol. 3. Early Shakespeare. 1961.

666841

SANDERS (NORMAN)
The Popularity of Shakespeare: an
examination of the Royal Shakespeare
Theatre's repertory. IN SHAKESPEARE
SURVEY 16.
illus. 1963.

667523

SANDERS, NORMAN
The Shift of power in 'Julius Caesar'.
FROM Review of English Literature, V:
2. pp.24-35. 1964.

744998

Sanders (Norman) ed. see Thaler (Alwin)
and Sanders (Norman) eds.

SANDERS, WILBUR
The Dramatist and the received idea.
Studies in the plays of Marlowe and
Shakespeare. (Cambridge) 1968.

769240

Sanders Portrait of Shakespeare *see* **Portraits and Monuments**

S[andford] (E.) Birmingham in
Shakespeare's time. pp. [8]. Illus.
Plan. From Some aspects of the life
and government of Birmingham through
its ten centuries: a supplement to
The Guildsman, October, 1938.

    (Birmingham)   1938.

        500745

SANDFORD (ERNEST)
The Wonder of our stage [: an address
delivered at the Central Literary
Association Shakespeare Celebration,
1935]. IN The Central Literary
Magazine, Vol. 32, July 1935. (Birmingham)
           1936.   463922
—— Another copy.   465871

SANDOE (JAMES)
King Henry the Sixth, Part 2: notes
during production. IN Theatre Annual,
Vol. 13. (New York)   1955.

        554521/13

SANDOE (JAMES)
The Oregon Shakespeare Festival.
IN SHAKESPEARE QUARTERLY I: 1.
pp. 5-11.
(New York)   1950.

       605711

SANDYS, GEORGE
Ovid's Metamorphosis Englished, mytho-
logiz'd, and represented in figures.
An Essay to the translation of Virgil's
AEneis. 1640. [Facsimile of
commentary on Books I-IV, with an
introductory essay "Shakespeare's
other Ovid".
IN SHAKESPEARE STUDIES 3.   (Cincinnati,
Ohio)   1967.

      771652

SANDYS (GEORGE) Works relating to: see
Moore (W. H.) Baconian Studies.

SANDYS (Sir JOHN EDWIN)
Education; and, Scholarship. IN
Shakespeare's England, Vol. 1.
(Oxford)
  bibliogs. illus. facsimiles.
           1917.

      435745

SANDYS ([Sir] JOHN EDWIN)
A Greek epigram on the tomb of
Shakespeare [with English translation].
IN GOLLANCZ ([Sir] I.) ed., A Book of
homage to Shakespeare.
  ports. illus. facsimiles. [1916.]

      264175

SANFORD, WENDY COPPEDGE
Theater as metaphor in 'Hamlet'.
(Cambridge, Mass.)   1967.
  LeBaron Russell Briggs prize, Honors
essays in English.
      778164

SANSOM (C.)
Celestial meeting: a stage sketch
for three women only [Viola,
Desdemona, Lady Macbeth]. IN
HAMPDEN (J.) [ed.] Plays without
fees. pp. 96.
  dgms.   [1935]

      439719

Sansom (C.) On the speaking of
Shakespeare. pp.12.   1949.

(London Academy of Music and Dramatic Art)

      608339

Santayana (G.) Hamlet. In Life and
Letters, Vol.1.

        1928.

      360846

Santayana (G.) Hamlet: an essay. In
Santayana (G.) Obiter scripta:
lectures, essays and reviews.

      1936.

      456684

SANTAYANA (GEORGE)
Sonnet.
IN GOLLANCZ ([Sir] I.) ed., A Book of
homage to Shakespeare.
  ports. illus. facsimiles. [1916.]

      264175

SANTAYANA (GEORGE)
Tragic philosophy. [With references
to Shakespeare and "Macbeth".] IN
Scrutiny, Vol. 4. (Cambridge)
          1935-6.
For note on this, entitled "Tragedy
and the 'medium'", by F. R. Leavis,
see catal. no. 564002.
      463798

Santayana, George *works relating to*

—— MAJOR (JOHN M.)
Santayana on Shakespeare.
IN SHAKESPEARE QUARTERLY X: 4.
pp. 469-479.
(New York)   1959.

      605711

Sanvic (Romain) pseud. [i.e. Robert de
Smet) see Smet (Robert de)

SAPTE (WILLIAM) ed.
"Stage-iana": 1,000 funny stories
of the playhouse, the play and the
players. [With references to
Shakespeare.] pp. [ii,] 96.
  frontis.   [1892.]

      563826

SARGEAUNT (G. M.)
The Classical spirit. [Containing
Troilus and Cressida; The Last phase;
and other Shakespearian references.]
[Bradford]   1936.

470852

SARGEAUNT (M[ARGARET] J.)
John Ford [: a critical study,
containing references to Shakespeare.]
(Oxford)
bibliog.   1935.

441150

SARGEAUNT (W. D.)
Macbeth: a new interpretation of
the text of Shakespeare's play.
1937.

462833

Sargent (G. F.) illus.
DALLY (F. F.)
The Apotheosis of Shakespeare and
other poems. (Maidstone) [1848.]

382910

SARGENT ([H.] M. [W.]) ed.
Shakespeare's carol [: Blow, blow,
thou winter wind.   Words from
As you like it.   Music by T. A.]
Arne, arr[anged by H.] M. [W.]
Sargent.   pp. 4.   (Oxford) [1937.]
Oxford Choral Songs.

522699

SARGENT (RALPH M.)
Sir Thomas Elyot and the integrity of
The Two Gentlemen of Verona.   IN
PMLA: Publications of the Modern
Language Association of America,
Vol. 65.   (New York)   1950.

428321/65

SARGENT (R. M.)
The Source of Titus Andronicus.
IN Studies in Philology, Vol. 46,
No. 2.   (Chapel Hill, N.C.) 1949.

554520/46

SARJEANT (J.)
Blow, blow, thou winter wind: song.
Words from As you like it.   pp. 8.
[c.1910.]
Differs from 347630.

520367

SARLOS (ROBERT K.)
Development and operation of the first
Blackfriars Theatre.   IN Studies in
the Elizabethan theatre, [by various
authors.]   [Hamden, Conn.]
illus. plans. bibliog.   1961.

667053

SARMENT (J.)
The Marriage of Hamlet: a play in
3 acts and prologue.   Translated
by Mrs. Dorothy Morland.
typescript.   [1935].

452528

SARSON (MAY)
Fear no more: unison song [from
Cymbeline].   pp. 4.   1933.
Novello's School Songs.

518986

SARSON (MAY)
A Merry note [When icicles hang by
the wall]: unison song [from'Love's
labour's lost'].   pp. 4.   1933.
Novello's School Songs.

594176

SASSOON (SIEGFRIED)
An Adjustment, by S. S.   [A dialogue
on cricket written in the style of
Shakespeare.]   With a foreword by
P. Gosse.   pp. [16.]   (Royston, Herts.:
Golden Head Press)
frontis.   1955.
No. 58 of edn. limited to 150 copies.
Initialled by the author.

646922

SASSOON (SIEGFRIED)
First night: Richard III [: a poem.]
IN Sassoon (S.) Satirical poems.
pp. 61.   1926.

536676

SATIN (JOSEPH)
Romeo and Juliet as Renaissance Vita
Nuova. FROM Discourse: A Review of the
Liberal Arts. Vol.3, No.2. pp.[19].
(Moorhead, Minn.)   1960.

667233

SATIN, JOSEPH
Shakespeare and his sources [for
thirteen of the plays]. (Boston)
1966.

764821

Satire

——CAMPBELL (O. J.)
Comicall satyre and Shakespeare's
"Troilus and Cressida".   (San Marino,
Cal.)
bibliog.   1938.
Huntington Library Publications.

495349

——CAMPBELL (O. J.)
Shakespeare's satire.   [With bibliographical notes.]   (Oxford) 1943.

553752

——CHAUDHURI (SUJATA)
Shakespeare and the Elizabethan satire
tradition.
IN Shakespeare commemoration volume,
edited by Taraknath Sen.   (Calcutta)
1966.

764382

——GILBERT (ALLAN H.)
Patriotism and satire in Henry V.
IN MATTHEWS (A. D.) and EMERY (C. M.)
eds., Studies in Shakespeare.   (Coral
Gables, Fla.)   1953.
University of Miami Publications in
English and American Literature,
Vol. 1, March 1953.

634188

_____HARRIS, BERNARD A.
Dissent and satire [: in Elizabethan
England]. IN SHAKESPEARE SURVEY 17.
(Cambridge) 1964.

667822

_____JOHNSON (E.) ed.
A Treasury of satire including the
world's greatest satirists, comic
and tragic, from antiquity to the
present time, selected and edited
with critical and historical backgrounds, an introduction on the nature
and value of satire [and containing a
section "Satiric overtones in
Shakespeare". (New York) 1945.

575899

_____UTLEY (F. L.)
The Crooked rib: an analytical index
to the argument about women in English
and Scots literature to the end of the
year 1568. [With an introductory
essay on satire and defense, bibliographical references and references
to Shakespeare.] (Columbus) 1944.
Ohio State University. Contributions
in Languages and Literature.
559112

_____WATKINS (W. B. C.)
Absent thee from felicity [: Swift's
satire compared with that of
Shakespeare]. FROM The Southern
Review, Autumn 1939. [Baton Rouge]
1939.

530198

_____WORCESTER (D.)
The Art of satire. [With references
to Shakespeare.] (Cambridge, Mass.)
bibliog. 1940.

526997

A Satirical dialogue between a sea
captain and his friend in town
address'd to the gentlemen who deform'd the play of Othello, M[arch]
7th, 1750; [with] a prologue and
epilogue. pp. [2.] [c.1750.]
Epilogue only, Dialogue and Prologue
wanting.
633511

SAUNDERS (J. W.)
Staging at the Globe, 1599-1613.
IN SHAKESPEARE QUARTERLY XI.
pp. 401-425.
(New York) 1960.
605711

SAUNDERS (J. W.)
Vaulting the rails [: the flexibility
of the Elizabethan stage].
IN SHAKESPEARE SURVEY 7. (Cambridge)
1954.

639176

SAUNDERS, J.W., ed.
Sheavyn, Phoebe
The Literary profession in the
Elizabethan age. 2nd edn., revised
throughout.
(Manchester) 1967.

764808

SAUNDERS (W.)
Debussy and Shakespeare. IN The
Musical Times, Vol. 71. 1930.

379876

SAVAGE (DEREK S.   )
Hamlet & the pirates: an exercise in
literary detection. 1950.

620065

SAVAGE (HENRY L.)
The Shakspere Society of Philadelphia.
IN SHAKESPEARE QUARTERLY III: 4.
pp. 341-352.
(New York) 1952.
605711

SAVAGE, JAMES E.
Notes on "A Midsummer night's dream".
FROM Studies in English, Vol.2, 1961.
(University, Miss.) 1961.

pp.65-78. 767190

SAVAGE, JAMES E.
"Troilus and Cressida" and Elizabethan
court factions. FROM Studies in English,
Vol.5. (University, Miss.) 1964.

pp.43-66. 767187

SAVAGE (RICHARD)
Prologue spoken at the revival of
Shakespeare's King Henry the Sixth, at
the Theatre-Royal in Drury-Lane.
IN Savage (R.) Works [, collected and
published by T. Evans], Vol. 2. 1775.

537986

Savage, Richard *works relating to*

_____JAGGARD (W.)
Richard Savage of Stratford-on-
Avon. Reprinted from The Library
Association Record. pp. [4.]
1924.
Printed for private circulation.

426448

SAVORY (Sir DOUGLAS LLOYD)
Jean Racine: a public lecture given in
the Great Hall of the Queen's University
of Belfast on Wednesday, 6th December
1939 [on the occasion of the] tercentenary of Racine. With a preface by
Sir R. [W.] Livingstone. (Including
references to Shakespeare]. pp. 31.
(Oxford) 1940.

514038

Savoy Theatre *see* **London**, Theatres — Savoy
Theatre

SAWYER (C. J.) Ltd.
"The Book beautiful": [catalogue
of] private press books, richly
decorated bindings, modern illuminated manuscripts, [etc. Including
Shakespeare items.] pp. 60. 1941.

535358

[SAXO GRAMMATICUS]
Extracts from the old translated "Historie
of Hamblet". IN SHAKSPEARE [W.]
Hamlet. [Edited] with notes [etc.] by
J. Hunter. New edn.
1874. 544998
[Longmans' Series of] Hunter's Annotated
Shakespeare.
———— Another edn. 1891. 527170

[SAXO GRAMMATICUS]
History of Hamlet. IN MORLEY (H.)
ed. Early prose romances. Edited
[with an introduction.] 1889.
Carisbrooke Library.

488224

[SAXO GRAMMATICUS]
Saxo's Amleth, translated by O. Elton,
Shakespeare's Hamlet, edited by
S. Humphries, and Milton's Areopagitica
[, with the preface by J. Thomson
reproduced from an edn. dated 1780.
With a note on Hamlet and Pascal by
J. de Marthold, an apologia by S.
Humphries, and a letter on the Bacon
theory by J. O. Halliwell-Phillipps].
ports. 1913.
Each work has its own tp., Hamlet and
Areopagitica being dated 1911. 10 copies
issued. Signature of O. Elton on front
endpaper. 569068

Saxo, *Grammaticus, works relating to*

————Sperber (H.) The Conundrums in
Saxo's Hamlet episode.
[With bibliographical notes.]
In PMLA, Vol.64.

(Menasha,Wis.) 1949.

428321/64

SAYERS (W. C. B.)
Library local collections. [With
a frontispiece, The Shakespeare in
the Birmingham Public Reference
Library.]
illus. bibliog. 1939.
Practical Library Handbooks.

496796

Scala Theatre *see* **London**, Theatres — Scala
Theatre

SCANLAN, MARY H.
Review notes and study guide to
Shakespeare's 'Richard II'. (New York)
1964.

Monarch critiques of literature.
756293

Scarfe, Norman
Shakespeare, Stratford-upon-Avon and
Warwickshire. IN

SPENCER, TERENCE JOHN BEW, ed.
Shakespeare: a celebration, 1564-1964.
1964.

illus. maps. 667816

Scenery

————BAGENAL (HOPE)
Shakespeare on a school stage.
IN Journal of the Royal Institute
of British Architects, 3rd Series,
Vol. 55.
illus. dgms. plan. 1948.

566031/3/55

———— Baughn (E.A.) The Background of
drama.[With references to stage scenery
in Shakespeare's plays.] In The Nine-
-teenth Century and after, Vol.61.
1907.

201731

———— Clark (B.H.) How to produce amateur
plays: a practical manual. [With
references to settings for Shakespeare's
plays.] Illus. Dgms. 1924.

565712

———— Craig (E.G.) Catalogue of an
exhibition of drawings and models
for 'Hamlet' and other plays.pp.24.
1912.

451684

———— Craig (E.G.) Catalogue of an
exhibition of drawings and models
for Hamlet, Macbeth, The Vikings and
other plays. [Held at the] City of
Manchester Art Gallery, November 1912.
pp.42. Illus.
(Manchester) 1912.

590358

———— Craig (E.G.) Exhibition of drawings
and models for Hamlet, Macbeth, The
Vikings and other plays. Arranged by The
United Arts Club, Dublin. [pp.21]. Illus.

1913.

450640

—— Craig (E.G.) An Exhibition of
drawings and models for Hamlet, Macbeth,
The Vikings and other plays. [Held in]
the City Art Gallery, Leeds.pp.[24].
Illus.   1913.

465734

—— Ffolkes (D.) Designing for
Shakespeare. Illus. In The Studio,
Vol.118.   1939.

510178

——HEVESI (A.)
Shakespeare as scenographer.
In The Mask, Vol. 2.
(Florence)   1909

460752

—— Hunt (T.B.) The Scenes as Shakespeare
saw them. In Craig (H.) ed., Essays in
dramatic literature: the Parrott
presentation volume. Port.
(Princeton)   1935.

444399

—— Hurry (L.) Settings & costumes for
Sadler's Wells ballets: Hamlet, 1942; Le
Lac des Cygnes and the Old Vic Hamlet,
1944. With an introduction by C.W.
Beaumont. Edited by Lillian Browse.pp.72.
Illus. Dgms.
(Ariel Books on the Arts)
1946.

574856

——INTERNATIONAL THEATRE INSTITUTE
Stage design throughout the world
since 1935. Texts and illustrations
collected by the National Centres of
the International Theatre Institute
chosen and presented by R.Hainaux.
[With] a sketch to serve as foreword
by J.Cocteau. Preface by K.Rae.
1956.

670902

——LEEPER (JANET)
Edward Gordon Craig: designs for
the theatre [including designs for
costumes and scenery for Shakespeare's
plays].   pp. 48.   (Harmondsworth)
40 plates.   1948.
King Penguin Books.

596804

——McDOWELL (J. H.)
Conventions of mediaeval art in
Shakespearian staging.   IN Journal
of English and Germanic Philology,
Vol. 47.   (Urbana, Ill.: University
of Illinois)
illus.   bibliog.   1948.

600780/47

——STAMM (RUDOLF)
Shakespeare's word-scenery; with
some remarks on stage-history and the
interpretation of his plays.
(Zürich)   1954.
Veröffentlichungen der Handels-
Hochschule St. Gallen, Reihe B,
Heft 10.

639793

—— Stopes (Mrs. Charlotte C.)
Elizabethan stage scenery. In The
Fortnightly Review, Vol.87.
1907.

201725

——WALKER (ROY)
In fair Verona [: the importance of
scenery in the production of Shakespeare's
plays.]   IN Twentieth Century, Vol. 156.
1954.

14975/156

Scenes from Shakespeare *see* ENGLISH EDITIONS, Selections and Anthologies

SCHAAR, CLAES
Conventional and unconventional in the
descriptions of scenery in Shakespeare's
Sonnets. FROM English Studies XLV: II.
pp.142-149. (Amsterdam)   1964.

745005

SCHAAR (CLAES)
An Elizabethan sonnet problem:
Shakespeare's sonnets, Daniel's Delia,
and their literary background. (Lund
Studies in English, 28) Bibliog. (Lund)
1960.

666636

SCHAAR (CLAES)
Elizabethan sonnet themes and the
dating of Shakespeare's 'sonnets'.
(Lund Studies in English, 32) (Lund)
1962.

667487

Schaefer, George *works relating to*

——George Schaefer's production of
"Macbeth" [: release script].
(Grand Prize Films Ltd.) [1961]

667309

SCHANZER (ERNEST)
Atavism and anticipation in
Shakespeare's style.   Reprinted
from Essays in Criticism Vol. 7.
ff. 242-256.   1957.

667097

SCHANZER (ERNEST)
The Central theme of A Midsummer night's
dream.   IN The University of Toronto
Quarterly, Vol. 20.   (Toronto)   1951.

596179/20

SCHANZER (ERNEST)
Daniel's revision of his "Cleopatra".
Reprint from The Review of English
Studies.   New Series.   Vol. 8,
No. 32.   pp. [7].   (Oxford) 1957.

667100

SCHANZER (ERNEST)
Heywood's "Ages" and Shakespeare.
Reprint from The Review of English
Studies Vol. 11.   pp. [14].   1960.

667098

SCHANZER (ERNEST)
The Marriage-contracts in "Measure
for measure".   IN SHAKESPEARE SURVEY
13.   (Cambridge)   1960.

666726

SCHANZER, ERNEST
A Midsummer-night's dream.
IN MUIR, KENNETH, ed., Shakespeare,
the comedies: a collection of
critical essays.   (Englewood Cliffs,
N.J.)   1965.

748348

SCHANZER (ERNEST)
The Moon and the fairies in "A
Midsummer Night's Dream". Reprint from
University of Toronto Quarterly. Vol.24,
No.3. pp.[13]. Bibliogs. (Toronto)
1955.

667096

SCHANZER (ERNEST)
The Problem of Julius Caesar.
IN SHAKESPEARE QUARTERLY VI.
pp. 297-308.
(New York)   1955.

605711

SCHANZER, ERNEST
The problem plays of Shakespeare: a
study of Julius Caesar; Measure for
Measure [and] Antony and Cleopatra.
1963.

667547

SCHANZER, ERNEST
The Structural pattern of 'The Winter's
tale'. From Review of English
Literature, V: 2. pp. 72-82. 1964.

744999

SCHANZER (ERNEST)
The Tragedy of Shakespeare's Brutus.
Reprinted from E L H, A Journal of
English Literary History, Vol. 22.
pp. 15.   1955.

667099

SCHAPPES, MORRIS U.
Shylock and anti-semitism.   FROM
Jewish Currents.   (New York)   1962.
pp. 3-12.

769986

SCHARTAU (H. W.)
Ariel's song ("Where the bee sucks"):
two-part song [from The Tempest].
IN A Selection of songs, with words
by Shakespeare.   [c.1925.]
Novello's School Songs.

520360

SCHECHTER (ABRAHAM)

King Lear : warning or prophecy?pp.28.
(Brooklyn,N.Y.)   1956.

665403

SCHEFFAUER (HERMAN GEORGE)
The New vision in the German arts:
[essays.   Including The Intensive
Shakespeare (Richard III), and The
Chromatic Othello.]   1924.

443991

SCHEIT, KARL
Leichte Stücke aus Shakespeares Zeit:
aus Lautentabulaturen übertragen und
für Gitarre bearbeitet. [Text in four
languages.] (Wien)   1965.

Musik für Gitarre.   746989

SCHELLING (FELIX EMANUEL)
The Common folk of Shakespeare.
IN GOLLANCZ ([Sir] I.) ed., A Book of
homage to Shakespeare.
ports. illus. facsimiles. [1916.]

264175

SCHELLING (FELIX EMANUEL)
The Dial-statue of the Shakespeare
garden [at the Horace Howard Furness
Memorial].   FROM The University of
Pennsylvania Library Chronicle,
Vol. 6.   [Philadelphia]
illus.   1938.

552432

SCHELLING (FELIX EMANUEL)
The Return to Shakespearean orthodoxy.
IN Proceedings of the American
Philosophical Society, Vol. 70.
(Philadelphia)   1931.

390363

SCHELLING (FELIX EMANUEL)
Shakespeare and biography: an address
delivered at a meeting of the Friends
of the Library held May 15, 1934.
[With bibliographical references.]
FROM The University of Pennsylvania
Library Chronicle, Vol. 2. (Philadelphia)
1934.

552433

Schelling (F.E.) Shakespeare and
Shallow, by [J.] L. Hotson:
[a review.] In Modern Language
Notes, 1932.

(Baltimore)   1932.

404117

SCHELLING (F. E.)
Shakespeare biography and other papers,
chiefly Elizabethan [and Shakespearian].
(Philadelphia)   1937.

466772

SCHELLING (FELIX EMANUEL)
Shakespeare books in the library of
the Furness Memorial.   FROM The
University of Pennsylvania Library
Chronicle, Vol. 3.   (Philadelphia)
bibliog.   1935.

552430

Schelling, Felix Emanuel *works relating to*

__QUINN (A. H.) and BLACK (M. W.)
F. E. Schelling.   IN SCHELLING (F. E.)
⌊presentation of his bust to the
University of Pennsylvania.   With a
bibliography.⌋   pp. viii, 30.
(Philadelphia)
frontis.   1935.

438954

Schering, Arnold *works relating to*

__BLOM (E.)
Beethoven's pianoforte sonatas
discussed [: with references to
A. Schering's theory that certain
Beethoven compositions are based on
Shakespeare's plays.⌋
illus. bibliog.   1938.

486835

[Scherling (E.von)] The History of
King Lear in an early 15th
century manuscript : [the Brut,
middle-English text, with an introduction.] From Rotulus, Vol. 4,
Winter 1937.

(Leyden)   1937.
498871

Schiller, Johann Christoph Friedrich von *works relating to*

__BERGMANN (A.)
Programm der hoheren Burgerschule zu
Fulda für das Schuljahr 1876/77. Voran
geht eine Abhandlung des Rectors: Remarks on some German tragedies written
after the model of Shakespeare's Macbeth;
with particular regard to that of Schiller.
pp. 28. (Fulda)
1877.

405602

__BOAS (FREDERICK SAMUEL)
Joan of Arc in Shakespeare, Schiller,
and Shaw.
IN SHAKESPEARE QUARTERLY II: 1.
pp. 35-45.
(New York) 1951.
605711

__EWEN (F.)
The Prestige of Schiller in England,
1788-1859. [With Shakespearian references and a bibliography.] (New York)
1932.
Columbia University Studies in English
and Comparative Literature)
403388

__MEAKIN (ANNETTE M. B.)
Goethe and Schiller, 1785-1805: the
story of a friendship. [With references to Shakespeare.]   3 vols.
ports.   1932.

393700

__WITTE (WILLIAM)
Time in 'Wallenstein' and 'Macbeth'.
IN Aberdeen University Review
Vol. 34, ⌊No.⌋ 3.   pp. 8.
(Aberdeen)   1952.

633542

Schipper (J.) A History of English
versification. [With references
to the blank verse of Shakespeare.]

(Oxford)   1910.
327526

Schlauch (Margaret) The Pound of flesh
story in the north. From The Journal
of English and Germanic philology,
vol.30.

(Illinois)   1931.
444157

SCHLAUCH, MARGARET
The Social background of Shakespeare's
malapropisms.   IN HELSZTYNSKI,
STANISLAW, ed., Poland's homage to
Shakespeare.   Commemorating the
fourth centenary of his birth, 1564-
1964.   (Warsaw)   1965.

747846

SCHLEGEL (AUGUST WILHELM von)
A Course of lectures on dramatic art and
literature.   Translated from the German
by J. Black.   ⌊With criticisms of
Shakespeare's comedies, tragedies and
histories.⌋
2 vols.   1815.   2889
_____ Another edn.   Revised by A. J. W.
Morrison. port.   1846.   57198
_____ Another edn.   1879.   8232
_____ Bohn's Standard Library.
1889.   527346
_____ Another edn.   1909.   455642

SCHLEGEL (AUGUST WILHELM von)
Lectures on German literature from
Gottsched to Goethe, given at the
University of Bonn and taken down by
G. Toynbee in 1833.   With Toynbee's
"Continuation to Heine" [& references
to Shakespeare⌋.   With introduction,
notes and a portrait, edited by H. G.
Fiedler.   pp. 96.   (Oxford)
tables.   bibliog.   1944.

552830

Schlegel, August Wilhelm von *works relating to*

——ATKINSON (MARGARET EDITH)
August Wilhelm Schlegel as a translator
of Shakespeare: a comparison of three
plays with the original. pp.ix,67.
Bibliog. (Oxford)   1958.

666138

——LAZENBY (MARION C.)
The Influence of Wieland and Eschenburg
on Schlegel's Shakespeare translation:
a dissertation submitted to the Board
of University Studies of The Johns
Hopkins University in conformity with
the requirements for the degree of
Doctor of Philosophy, 1941.   pp. 37.
(Baltimore) bibliogs.   1942.

560977

——ORSINI, GIAN NAPOLEONE GIORDANO
Coleridge and Schlegel reconsidered.
FROM Comparative Literature, Vol.16,
No.2.   1964.

pp.97-118.   748966

——RILLA (W.) [ed.]
Extracts from Schlegel's translation of
Shakespeare: a reading with introduc-
tory notes in the translation.
[Broadcast] 23rd April, 1947.   ff. 2.
typescript.   1947.
Introductory notes only.

583271

——Struble (G.G.) Schlegel's translation
of Twelfth Night. From The Quarterly
Journal of the University of North
Dakota. Vol.19, No.2.

(Grand Forks,N.D.)   1929.

442293

——TOYNBEE (G.)
Continuation to Heine [of] A. W. [von]
Schlegel's Lectures on German literature
from Gottsched to Goethe given at the
University of Bonn and taken down by
G. Toynbee in 1833.   [With references
to Schlegel and Shakespeare.]   Edited
by H. G. Fiedler.   pp. 96.   (Oxford)
tables.   bibliog.   1944.

552830

SCHLEGEL (CARL WILHELM FRIEDRICH von)
Literary notebooks, 1797-1801.   [With
references to Shakespeare.   German
text.]   Edited, with introduction and
commentary [in English] by H. Eichner.
facsimile.   1957.

675711

SCHLEGEL, JOHANN ELIAS
Vergleichung Shakespears und Andreas
Gryphs, [1741]. Faksimiledruck
herausgegeben mit Anhang und Nachwort
von H. Powell. (Leicester)   1964.

745370

Schlesinger, E. G.
see Barber, H. W. and others

SCHMIDT (ALBERT F.)
The Yeoman in Tudor and Stuart
England.   pp. ii, 49.
(Washington, D.C.)
illus. plan. dgm. facsimiles. 1961.
Folger Shakespeare Library.   Folger
Booklets on Tudor and Stuart
Civilization.

667129

Schmidt, Alexander *works relating to*

——F. (A. I.)
Some recent helps in the study of
Shakespeare [: a review of] 2. Dr.[A.]
Schmidt's Shakespeare-lexicon, Vol. 1.
1874, etc.   FROM The Penn Monthly,
Vol. 5.   (Philadelphia)   1874.

555525

SCHMIDT-IHMS, M.
Shakespeare in the German-speaking
world with special reference to 'Hamlet'.
FROM Theoria, October 1964. pp.21-34.
(Pietermaritzburg)

668361

SCHMIDT-IHMS (M.   )
Shakespeare's influence on German drama.
FROM Theoria, [Vol.] 3. pp.[14].
[Pietermaritzburg]   1955.

667025

SCHNITTKIND (HENRY T.) and (DANA ARNOLD)]
William Shakespeare, 1564-1616.
IN Living biographies of famous men,
by H. Thomas and D. L. Thomas [pseuds.]
(New York)
ports.   chronological table.   1946.

581343

SCHOENBAUM, SAMUEL
As you like it: an outline-guide to
the play. (New York)   1965.

Barnes and Noble focus books.
753358

SCHOENBAUM, SAMUEL
Internal evidence and Elizabethan
dramatic authorship: an essay in
literary history and method.   1966.

752033

SCHOFF (FRANCIS G.)
Aspects of Shakespearean criticism,
1914-1950 [: a commentary centered
on British and American criticism of
Hamlet].   (Ann Arbor, Mich.)
bibliog.   typescript, 1952.   microfilm, positive copy.   1 reel, 35 mm.
[1953.]
University Microfilms.   Doctoral
Dissertation Series.

647061

SCHOFF (FRANCIS G.)
Claudio, Bertram, and a note on inter-
pretation.
 IN SHAKESPEARE QUARTERLY X: 1.
 pp. 11-23.
 (New York)   1959.
                             605711

SCHOFF (FRANCIS G.)
Horatio: a Shakespearian confidant.
IN SHAKESPEARE QUARTERLY VII.
 pp. 53-57.
 (New York)   1956.
                             605711

SCHOFF (FRANCIS G.)
King Lear: moral example or tragic
protagonist?
 IN SHAKESPEARE QUARTERLY XIII: 2.
 pp. 157-172.
 (New York) 1962.
                             605711

Scholarship *see* Criticism, Shakespearian; Study and Teaching

Scholderer (V.) The Development of
 Shakespeare's fools. In The Library,
 New Series, Vol.10.
                       1909.
                             222151

Scholes (P.A.) Elgar's 'Falstaff'
 reconsidered. From The Musical Times,
 Aug. 1st and Sept. 1st, 1929.
                       1929.
                             516572

SCHOLES (P. A.)
 The Puritans and music in England
 and New England: a contribution
 to the cultural history of two
 nations.   [With references to
 Shakespeare.]
 illus. bibliog.   1934.
                             426700

Scholes (P.A.) Shakespeare as musician.
 In The Teacher's World, April 5,
 1916. pp.48. Illus.
                       1916.
                             432005

SCHOLES (ROBERT E.)
 Dr. Johnson and the bibliographical
 criticism of Shakespeare.
 IN SHAKESPEARE QUARTERLY XI.
 pp.163-171.
 (New York)   1960.
                             605711

Schöninghs Englische Schulausgaben
LAMB (CHARLES & MARY)
 Tales from Shakespeare [: English
 text.]   Herausgegeben von F. Behrens.
 pp. 79.   (Paderborn)   [1930.]
                             369246

School Drama: a magazine for
schools, boys' and girls' clubs,
Vols. 1-3 (1938-40.)
3 vols. illus.
From Vol. 2, No. 2 incorporating
the "Mime Review".   All published.
                             522632

School of Night

— Bradbrook (Muriel C.) The School of
  Night: a study in the literary
  relationships of Sir Walter Raleigh.
  [Including a chapter "Shakespeare,
  the School and Nashe" and other
  references to Shakespeare.With a
  bibliography.]
        (Cambridge)   1936.
                             458019

— CRAIG (H. A. L.)
  The School of night.   Production
  by D. Cleverdon. [Script of
  broadcast in B.B.C. Third Programme,
  October, 1960].   [British Broadcasting
  Corporation]
  typescript.   1960.
                             667024

— SCHRICKX (W.)
  Shakespeare and the School of Night:
  an estimate and further interpretations.   FROM Neophilologus, 34 ste
  Jaargang.   pp. [10].   (Groningen)
                           1950.
                             608851

— STRATHMANN (E. A.)
  The Textual evidence for "The School
  of Night" [: Love's labour's lost,
  Act 4, Scene 3].   IN Modern Language
  Notes, Vol. 56.   (Baltimore)
  bibliog.   1941.
                             533477

School Productions *see* Programmes; Societies and Clubs; Stage History and Production; Study and Teaching *and under the names of schools and places where the schools are situated*

Schools *see* Education and Knowledge; Study and Teaching

SCHRADE (L.)
 Beethoven in France: the growth
 of an idea.   [With references to
 Shakespeare's influence in France.]
 (New Haven, [Conn.])
 bibliog.   1942.
 Louis Stern Memorial Fund.
                             557321

SCHRAGER (VICTORIA)
How like a god [: a play in verse,
including Shakespearian characters]
by W. Shakespeare and Victoria Schrager.
pp. 43.   (Northampton, Mass.) 1939.

519134

SCHREIBER (C. F.)
Deutschland ist Hamlet.   IN
Publications of the Modern Language
Association of America, Vol. 28.
(Baltimore)   1913.

428348

SCHREIBER (FLORA RHETA)
Television's "Hamlet".   IN The Quarterly
of Film Radio and Television, Vol. 8.
(Berkeley, Cal.)   1953.

630462/8

Schreiber (Morris) ed.
LAMB (CHARLES and MARY A.)
Favorite tales from Shakespeare.
Edited for modern readers by M. Schreiber.
Illustrated by D. Lynch.   (New York)
1956.

665531

SCHRICKX (W.)
Shakespeare and the School of Night:
an estimate and further interpretations.   FROM Neophilologus, 34 ste
Jaargang.   pp. [10].   (Groningen)
1950.

608851

SCHRICKX (W.)
Shakespeare's early contemporaries:
the background of the Harvey-Nashe
polemic and "Love's labour's lost".
(Antwerpen)
bibliog.   1956.

665395

SCHRICKX (W.)
Solar symbolism and related imagery
in Shakespeare.   FROM Revue Belge de
Philologie et d'Histoire, Tome 29.
pp. 17.   (Bruxelles)   1951.

634250

SCHUBERT, FRANZ.   For music scores
by Schubert see under the heading
MUSIC SCORES: CYMBELINE and THE TWO
GENTLEMEN OF VERONA.

Schubert, Franz *works relating to*

——CAPELL (R.)
Schubert and Shakespeare.   IN
Shakespeare Quarterly, No. 1, Summer
1948.   Issued under the auspices of
the Austrian Shakespeare Society.
ports.   illus.   1948.
All published.

610897

Schücking (L.L.) The Baroque character
of the Elizabethan tragic hero.
pp.29.
1938.

(British Academy. [28th] Annual Shakespeare
Lecture)

487921

SCHÜCKING (LEVIN LUDWIG)
Character and action: King Lear.
IN LEECH, CLIFFORD, ed., Shakespeare:
the tragedies.   A collection of
critical essays.   (Chicago) 1965.
Gemini books.

752332

Schucking (L.L.) The Churchyard-scene
in Shakespeare's 'Hamlet', v.i. an
afterthought? pp.[10]. In The
Review of English studies, vol.11.
[1935].

[1935].

447384

SCHÜCKING (LEVIN LUDWIG)
Hamlet, III.1.148 f.   FROM Review
of English studies, Vol. 4. 1928.

497594

Schucking (L.L.) The Meaning of Hamlet.
[With a bibliography.] Translated
from the German by G.[S.] Rawson.

(Oxford)   1937.

469658

Schücking (L.L.)[Review of] Shakespeare's influence on the drama of
his age, studied in Hamlet [by]
D.J.McGinn. In Beiblatt zur Anglia
[Bd.] 53.

(Halle)   1942.

576459

SCHÜCKING (LEVIN L.)
The Sociology of literary taste.
[With references to Shakespeare.]
Translated from the German by E. W.
Dickes.
bibliog.   1944.
International Library of Sociology
and Social Reconstruction.

550198

see also Ebisch (Walther) and Schücking
(L. L.)

Schücking, Levin L. *works relating to*

— ALEXANDER (PETER)
[Review of] The Meaning of Hamlet by
L. L. Schücking. 1937.   IN The Review
of English Studies, Vol. 14.   1938.

495115

—Dam (B.A.P. van) [Review of] Zum
Problem der Ueberlieferung des Ham-
let-Textes, von L.L.Schucking.   In
English studies, Vol. 14.

(Amsterdam)   1932.

485656

—Knights (L. C.)
A Review of The Meaning of Hamlet, by
L. L. Schücking.   IN The Criterion,
Vol. 17.   1937–38.

487675

— KOSZUL (A. [H.])
[Review of] L. L. Schücking's Der Sinn
des Hamlet, 1935 [, and of its English
translation] The Meaning of Hamlet,
by G. Rawson, 1937.   IN English
Studies, Vol. 20.   (Amsterdam)   1938.

495114

—MacCARTHY (D.)
Shakespearean criticism: [review of]
Character problems in Shakespeare's
plays, by L. L. Schücking.   IN
MacCarthy (D.) Drama.   1940.

522304

— SPENCER (B. T.)
Three ways to Shakespeare [: a
review of The Meaning of Hamlet, by
L. L. Schucking, translated by
G. Warson, etc.]   FROM Sewanee Review,
Vol. 47.   (Sewanee)   1939.

530197

SCHUELLER, HERBERT M., ed.
The Persistence of Shakespeare idolatry.
Essays in honour of Robert W. Babcock.
(Detroit)   1964.

668300

SCHULL (JOSEPH)
World of his own [: a play including reference to Shakespeare].
Produced by A. Campbell.   [Broadcast]
22nd June, 1953.   ff. 30.
typescript.   1953.

643689

SCHULTZE (H. M.)
A Day in Elizabethan London, [from]
J. Finnemore's Social life in England.
[With references to Shakespeare, notes
in German and "Wörterbuch".]   pp. 24,
16.   (Kiel)   1926.
Französische und englische Schullektüre.
Ergänzungsheft, 5.

425704

Schultz (J.H.) A Glossary of Shakes-
peare's hawking language.   In
University of Texas, Studies in
English, [No.18.] 1938.

(Austin, Texas.)   1938.

498156

SCHULZ (HERBERT C.)
A Shakespeare haunt in Bucks.?
IN SHAKESPEARE QUARTERLY V.
pp. 177–178.
(New York)   1954.

605711

SCHUMANN (ROBERT [ALEXANDER])
A Midsummer Night's Dream: a letter
[referring to Mendelssohn's music].
IN Schumann (R. [A.]) On music and
musicians.   1947.

587117

SCHURÉ (EDOUARD)
Shakespeare and the laic theatre.
IN Schuré (E.) The Genesis of tragedy.
Authorized translation by F. Rothwell.
1936.

587218

Schutt (J.H.) Prof. Moulton and Shakespeare's Merchant of Venice.   In
English studies, Vol. 6.

(Amsterdam)   1924.

485648

Schutt (J.H.) Review [of] Shakespeare-
Worterbuch von L. Kellner.   In
English studies, Vol. 5.

(Amsterdam)   1923.

485647

SCHUTTE (WILLIAM M.)
Henry IV, Part 2.   IN Lectures on four
of Shakespeare's history plays.
pp. [v], 69.   (Pittsburgh: Carnegie
Institute of Technology)   1953.

635454

SCHUTTE (WILLIAM METCALF)
Joyce and Shakespeare: a study in
the meaning of "Ulysses".   (New Haven,
Conn.)   1957.
Yale Studies in English, 134.

665579

SCHWARTZ (DELMORE)
Coriolanus and his mother.   IN
Schwartz (D.) Summer knowledge: new
and selected poems, 1938–1958.   (New
York)   1959.

689702

SCHWARTZ (ELIAS)
The Idea of the person and Shakespearian
tragedy.

IN SHAKESPEARE QUARTERLY XVI: 1.
pp. 39–47.
(New York)   1965.

605711

SCHWARZ (ALFRED)
Otto Ludwig's Shakespearean criticism.
IN LEVIN (H. [T.]) ed., Perspectives
of criticism.   (Cambridge [Mass.])
frontis.   1950.
Harvard Studies in Comparative Literature, 20.

610100

Science

BRONOWSKI, JACOB
Shakespeare's view of nature.
IN PRITCHETT, VICTOR SAWDON, and
others, Shakespeare: the comprehensive soul.   [Talks on the B.B.C.
European English Serivce to celebrate
the Shakespearian Quatercentenary.]
                                  1965.

746585

CRAIG (HARDIN)
Shakespeare and the here and now.
IN P.M.L.A.: Publications of the
Modern Language Association of America,
Vol. 67.   (New York)   1952.

428321/67

Science, Shakespeare and
Hall, Marie Boas
Scientific thought. [: in Elizabethan
England].

IN Shakespeare Survey, 17. (Cambridge)
1964.

667822

Scofield, Paul *works relating to*

TREWIN (JOHN COURTENAY)
Paul Scofield: an illustrated study
of his work, with a list of his
appearances on stage and screen.
ports.   illus.   1956.
Theatre World Monograph No. 6.

656877

Scotland
see also Quatercentenary 1964

Cargill (A.) Shakespeare in Scotland.
In Chambers's Journal, 6th Series,Vol.7.
1904.

184934

Did Shakespeare visit Scotland? [An
article on a chapter in William
Shak speare: a biography, by C. Knight.]
From Chambers' Edinburgh Journal, 1844.
pp.[4].   1844.

390780

FERGUSSON (Sir JAMES)
Shakespeare's Scotland.   pp. 21.
(Edinburgh)   1957.
Andrew Lang Lecture, 1956.

665479

Grierson (H.J.C.) Shakespeare and
Scotland [: a poem]. In Gollancz ([Sir]I.)
ed., A Book of homage to Shakespeare.
Ports. Illus. Facsimiles.

[1916.]

264175

Harries (F.J.) Shakespeare and the
Scots.
(Edinburgh)   [1932.]

393157

Mossner (E.C.) Hume and the Scottish
Shakespeare. [A discussion on "Douglas" by
J. Home, with reference to Shakespeare.] In
The Huntington Library Quarterly Vol.3.
1940.

518263

RAE, T. I.
Scotland in the time of Shakespeare.
(Ithaca, N.Y.)   1965.

illus. Folger booklets on Tudor
and Stuart civilization.   749828

Twice-told tales,42: Was Shakespeare
ever in Scotland? (From Chambers's
Edinburgh Journal for July 18, 1835). In
Chambers's Journal, 8th series,Vol.4.
1935.

444111

SCOTT (CLEMENT [WILLIAM])
America by the Avon [: an account of
the dedication to Stratford of the
Fountain and Clock Tower presented by
G. W. Childs; performed by Sir H. B.
Irving].   IN Scott (C. [W.]) Blossom-
land and fallen leaves.   3rd edn.
port.   [1892.]

590633

SCOTT (CLEMENT WILLIAM)
Henry Irving's Hamlet.   IN AGATE
(J. [E.]) ed., The English dramatic
critics.   [1932.]

399280

S[COTT] (CLEMENT [WILLIAM])
Miss Ellen Terry's first appearance.
FROM The Theatre, New Series, Vol. 10.
1887.

530837

SCOTT (CLEMENT WILLIAM)
Some notable "Hamlets" of the present
time (Sarah Bernhardt, [Sir] H. [B.]
Irving, W. Barrett, [Sir H.] B. Tree
and [Sir J.] Forbes Robertson). New
and cheaper edn. with a new chapter on
H. B. Irving by W. L. Courtney.
Illustrated by W. G. Mein.
  ports.   1905.

                    540625

Scott, Clement *works relating to*

___ HAPGOOD, ROBERT
    His heart upon his sleeve: Clement Scott
    as a reviewer of Shakespearian productions.
    IN DEUTSCHE SHAKESPEARE-GESELLSCHAFT
    WEST, JAHRBUCH 1967.   pp. 70-82.
    (Heidelberg)
                    754129

___ WALBROOK (H. M.)
    The Drama in Clement Scott's day.
    FROM "The Fortnightly Review", April
    1934.   pp. 472-480.   1934.

                    427396

SCOTT (FREDERICK GEORGE)
Poems.   [Containing a sonnet
"Shakespeare".]
  port.   1936.

                    458790

SCOTT (FREDERICK GEORGE)
"Shakespeare" [: a sonnet].
IN GOLLANCZ ([Sir] I.) ed., A Book of
homage to Shakespeare.
  ports. illus. facsimiles. [1916.]

                    264175

SCOTT (HARDIMAN)
Shakespeare Library at Birmingham.
FROM Radio Newsreel [broadcast]
23rd April 1952.   ff. [9.]
  typescript.   1952.

                    624731

Scott, Janet G. *works relating to*

___ Praz (M.) [Review of] Les Sonnets
    Elisabéthains, les sources et
    l'apport personnel, par Janet G.
    Scott. In English studies, Vol.11.

       (Amsterdam)   1929.

                    485653

Scott (Kenneth William) *see* Cordasco
  (Francesco) and Scott (K.W.)

[SCOTT (MARGARETTA)
Shakespeare's use of music; and
Foss (H. J.) Vaughan Williams' music
to Dickens' "Christmas Carol",
Music Magazine (16).   [Broadcast]
December 24th, 1944.   ff. 15.
  typescript.   1944.

                    556038

Scott (Mrs.) Marian) Chautauqua
  caravan [:experiences of a member of
  a Chautauqua entertainment group.
  With references to Shakespearian
  performances]. Ports.Illus.

       (New York)   1939.

                    585833

Scott (Marion M.) Beethoven: [a
  biography. With references to
  Shakespeare and a bibliography.]
  Ports. Illus. Facsimiles.

                    1934.

(Master Musicians. New Series.)

                    420559

SCOTT (MARY A.)
The Book of the courtyer [by Castiglione]:
a possible source of Benedick and
Beatrice.   IN Publications of the
Modern Language Association of America.
Vol. 16.   1901.

                    428336

SCOTT (MARY A.)
Elizabethan translations from the
Italian: the titles of such works,
now first collected and arranged,
with annotations.   [With references
to Shakespeare.]   IN Publications of
the Modern Language Association of
America, Vols. 10, 11, 13 and 14.
(Baltimore)
  4 vols.   1895-99.

                    428330

Scott (Sir W.) Essay on the drama,
  [with references to Shakespeare].
  Reprint of edn. 1818. In Gibbon (E.)
  The Crusades., [etc. Edited by
  A. Murray.]
                    1870.

                    446617

Scott, Walter Sir *works relating to*

___ BIGGINS, D.
    "Measure for Measure" and "The Heart
    of Mid-Lothian". IN Études Anglaises,
    Grande-Bretagne, États-Unis, XIVe Année,
    No. 3.   1960.

                    476080/14

___ BUCHAN (J.)
    Sir Walter Scott: [his life and work.
    With references to Shakespeare, and a
    bibliography.]
    port.   1932.

                    390597

—— CRICHTON-BROWNE ([Sir] J.)
"Hamlet" and "Lammermoor".   FROM The
Contemporary Review, 1910.
[1910.]

389221

—— GORDON (R. K.)
Shakespeare and some scenes in the
Waverley novels.   FROM Queen's Quarterly,
Vol. 45.   (Kingston, Ontario)
1938.

530202

—— HAZLITT (W.)
Sir Walter Scott, Racine, and Shakespeare.
IN The Plain Speaker: opinions on
books, men and things.
1870.

11317

—— Patten (J.A.) Sir Walter Scott: a
character study. [With a chapter
"Shakespeare and Scott".] Port.

1932.

394493

——— SECCOMBE (T.) [and others]
Scott centenary articles: essays by
T. Seccombe, W. P. Ker, G. Gordon,
W. H. Hutton, A. McDowall and R. S. Rait.
[With references comparing Scott with
Shakespeare.]
1932.

397158

—— Smith (J.C.) Scott and Shakespeare.
In English Association, Essays and
studies, Vol. 24, 1938. Collected
by [R.] L. Binyon.

(Oxford)   1939.

499319

SCOTT (WALTER SIDNEY)
The Georgian theatre [: with
biographical sketches of some of
its leading figures, and references
to Shakespeare].
ports.   illus.   1946.

578657

Scott (William Douglas Robson) see
Robson-Scott (William Douglas)

SCOTT (WILLIAM HERBERT)
Edward German: an intimate biography,
[with reference to his Shakespearean
music and a list of his compositions.]
ports.   illus.   1932.

397767

SCOTT (WILLIAM INGLIS DUNN)

Shakespeare's melancholics [: eight
Shakespearian characters examined in
the light of modern psychological
knowledge.] Foreword by H. Yellowlees.
1962.

667396

Scott, William O.
Proteus in Spenser and Shakespeare:
the lover's identity.

IN Shakespeare Studies, 1. (Cincinnati,
Ohio)   1965.

750317

SCOTT (WILLIAM O.)
Seasons and Flowers in "The Winter's
Tale".
IN SHAKESPEARE QUARTERLY XIV: 4.
pp. 411-417.
(New York)   1963.

605711

SCOTT-GILES (CHARLES WILFRID)
Shakespeare's heraldry.   Illustrated
by the author.
glossary.   genealogical tables.
facsimiles.   1950.

605192

SCOTT-JAMES (ROLFE ARNOLD)
The Making of literature: some principles
of criticism examined in the light of
ancient and modern theory.   [With
references to Shakespeare.]   1946.
bibliog.

580334

SCOTT-JAMES (ROLFE ARNOLD)
Modernism and romance [:   in literature.
With references to Shakespearean
criticism.]
1908.

454785

SCOTT-JAMES (ROLFE ARNOLD)
The "New way" of playing Shakespeare.
IN The Contemporary Review, Vol. 105.
1914.

251087

Scott- Maxwell (Florida) From London
town to Stratford-on-Avon. From
Scottish Motor Transport Magazine,
July, 1934. pp.[6.] Illus.

(Edinburgh)   1934.

422167

SCOUFOS (ALICE LYLE)
The "Martyrdom" of Falstaff.
IN Shakespeare Studies, 2. (Cincinnati,
Ohio)   1966.

761781

SCOUTEN (ARTHUR H.)
The Increase in popularity of Shakespeare's
plays in the eighteenth century: a
caveat for interpretors of stage history.
IN SHAKESPEARE QUARTERLY VII.
pp. 189-202.
(New York)   1956.

605711

SCOUTEN (A. H.)
Shakespeare's plays in the theatrical
repertory when Garrick came to
London.   IN University of Texas,
Studies in English [No. 24] 1944.
(Austin [Texas])
bibliog.   1945.

563674

Scouten, Arthur H., ed., see
Lennep, William Van, and others, eds.

SCOUTEN (ARTHUR H.) and HUGHES (LEO)
A Calendar of performances of
1 Henry IV and 2 Henry IV during the
first half of the eighteenth century.
FROM The Journal of English and
Germanic Philology, Vol. 43.   (Urbana,
Ill.)
bibliog.   1944.

578407

SCRAGG, LEAH
Iago - vice or devil?
IN SHAKESPEARE SURVEY 21.   (Cambridge)
pp. 53-65.   1968.

776762

Scrap-book Collections

___ American Scrap Book.   1950-

460402

___ Green (T.) Shakespeareana: newscuttings,
illustrations, portraits relating
to Shakespeare and his works,
collected from various sources.
2 vols.
                       1923-27.

449072

___ HERITAGE (GEORGE E.)
[Letters, autographs etc. mainly of
Shakespearian interest, collected
by G. Heritage of Birmingham.
[Birmingham]
port.   illus.   facsimiles.   1880.

666771

___ HERITAGE (GEORGE E.   )
[Portraits, mainly of Sir Henry Irving,
collected by G.E. Heritage, c.1870-1905.]
                       [c.1905.]

666678

___ HERITAGE (GEORGE E.)
Shakespearian and other portraits
collected by G. E. Heritage, c.1790-
c.1910.]   [c.1910.]

666676

___ HILL (J.)
Note books relating to William
Shakespeare.   (Note books, Vols. 42-
43)   manuscript.   2 vols.
                       c.1887-c.1905.

661048

___ KNIGHT (GEORGE WILSON)
Dramatic papers: material relating
to the Shakespearian and other
productions of G. Wilson Knight,
at Hart House Theatre, Toronto, and
in England.]
illus.   1926-

634261

___ Scraps about theatricals[: a collection
of newspaper cuttings, etc.,
relating to Shakespeare and the
theatre].

[c.1835]

436163

___ SHAKESPEARE QUATERCENTENARY 1964
Birmingham scraps and news cuttings.
                       1964.

764671

___ SHAKESPEARE QUATERCENTENARY 1964
Scrapbook relating to events in
Great Britain.   1964.

752297

___ SHAKESPEARE QUATERCENTENARY 1964
Scrapbook relating to events abroad.
                       1964.

752298

___ Topographical prints, etc.,
including prints relating to
Shakespeare.   [c.1800-1880.]

564701

___ TURNER (JAMES)
Shakespeare illustrated: drawings,
engravings and prints after the first
artists, including the Boydell Gallery
and other curious collections.   Culled
from many sources by a member of the
Birmingham Shakespeare Reading Club.
(Birmingham)
37 vols.   1898.

665136-72

Screens (Furniture)

___ SMITH (H. C.)
Byron's pictorial screen: its theatri-
cal side, with recollections of the
Regency stage [including Shakespearean
actors and actresses].   IN Country Life,
Vol. 98.
                          1945.

570906

SCRIMGEOUR, GARY J.
The Messenger as a dramatic device in
Shakespeare.
IN SHAKESPEARE QUARTERLY XIX: 1.
pp. 41-54.   (New York)
                     1968.

605711

Scudamore Family *works relating to*

___ FEIL (J. P.)
.   Dramatic references from the Scudamore
     papers.   IN SHAKESPEARE SURVEY 11.
     (Cambridge)
         ports.   illus.   bibliog. 1958.

665816

SCUNTHORPE PUBLIC LIBRARIES
     Shakespeare: a catalogue of books
     about the man, his times and his works.
     Shakespeare quatercentenary 1564-1964.
     (Scunthorpe)   [1964.]

667880

Sea *see* Sailors and the Sea

SEAGER (HERBERT WEST)
     Natural history in Shakespeare's time.
                                    1896.
     Large paper edition.
                                    471781

SEALE (DOUGLAS)
     Commentary.   IN King John.   Text
     edited by C. J. Sisson.   (New York)
     illus.   1963.
     Laurel Shakespeare.
                                    667608

SEAMAN, JOHN E.
     The blind curtain and Hamlet's guilt.
     FROM Western Humanities Review, Vol.19,
     No.4, Autumn 1965. (Salt Lake City, Utah)
                                    1965.

         pp.345-353.   766827

SEAMAN, JOHN E.
Othello's pearl.
IN SHAKESPEARE QUARTERLY XIX: 1.
pp. 81-85.   (New York)
                     1968.

605711

SEAR, H.G.
     Castelnuovo-Tedesco and the
     Shakespearian theatre. IN Musical
     Times, Vol.79.
                              1938.

495901

Sear (H.G.) Korngold and [his
     music to Shakespeare's] Much Ado.
     From The Sackbut, Vol. 12.

                     1932.

520177

SEAR (H. G.)
     Russian music and Shakespeare.   FROM
     The Musical Times, [Vol. 85]. 1944.

550793

SEARS (WILLIAM P.)
     The Ancient borough of Southwark: a
     center of literary and historic
     interest.   [With references to
     Shakespeare.]   FROM Education, Vol.
     58.   (Boston, Mass.)   1938.

512385

SEARS (WILLIAM P.)
     A London shrine for Shakespeare.
     FROM The English Journal, December
     1937.   (Chicago)   1937.

503862

SEATON (ETHEL)
     Antony and Cleopatra and the Book
     of Revelation.   IN The Review
     of English Studies, Vol. 22.
     (Oxford)   [1946.]

579165

SEATON (ETHEL)
     Comus and Shakespeare.   IN English
     Association, Essays and studies, Vol.
     31, 1945.   Collected by V. de S.
     Pinto.   (Oxford)

                              1946.

571260

SEATON (ETHEL)
     Literary relations of England and
     Scandinavia in the seventeenth century.
     [With references to Shakespeare.]
     (Oxford)
      bibliog.   ports.   illus.   1935.
     Oxford Studies in Modern Languages and
     Literature.

441821

SEATON (ETHEL)
     Richard Galis and the Witches of
     Windsor.   IN The Library, Fourth
     Series, Vol. 18.   pp. 268-78.
                                   1938.
     Transactions of the Bibliographical
     Society, Second Series

487688

SEATON (ETHEL) [and] LEA (KATHLEEN [M.])
     "I saw young Harry" [: Sir Richard
     Vernon's description of Henry, Prince
     of Wales and his companions in arms
     (I Henry IV, iv, i, 97)].   IN The
     Review of English Studies, Vol. 21.
     (Oxford)   [1945.]

570955

SEBESTYÉN (KAROLY)
     The Cult of Shakespeare in Hungary.
     IN The Hungarian Quarterly. Vol. 3.
                                   1937.

482328

SEC (FONG F.)
Stories from Shakespeare.   pp. [xv],
74. (Shanghai)   1929.

438364

SECCHI (NICCOLÒ)
Self-interest [: a play].
Translated by W. Reymes.   Edited
by Helen A. Kaufman.   (Seattle)
bibliog.   1953.

670494

Secchi, Nicolo *works relating to*

__KAUFMAN (HELEN ANDREWS)
Nicolò Secchi as a source of "Twelfth
Night".
IN SHAKESPEARE QUARTERLY V:
pp. 271-280.
(New York) 1954.

605711

SECCOMBE (T.)
William Shakespeare (1564-1616).
IN The Bookman, Vol. 25.
illus.   1903.

181448

SECCOMBE (T.) and ALLEN (J. W.)
The Age of Shakespeare (1579-1631).
With an introduction by [J. W.] Hales.
2 vols.   1919-20. 436478
Handbooks of English Literature.
_____ Another edn.1925-8.   416097

SECCOMBE (T.) [and others]
Scott centenary articles: essays by
T. Seccombe, W. P. Ker, G. Gordon,
W. H. Hutton, A. McDowall and R. S.
Rait. [With references comparing
Scott with Shakespeare.]   1932.

397158

Second Maiden's Tragedy

__Lacy (J.) Old English drama: The
Second maiden's tragedy. From [The
London Magazine,] Aug. 1824.

1824.

554150

SECORD (ARTHUR WELLESLEY)
I.M. of the First Folio Shakespeare
and other Mabbe problems.   IN Journal
of English and Germanic Philology,
Vol. 47. (Urbana, Ill.: University
of Illinois)   1948.

600780/47

SEDGEWICK (GARNETT GLADWIN)
Of irony, especially in drama.
[Including a chapter "Irony as
dramatic preparation: Othello".]
(Alexander Lectures in English at
the University of Toronto, 1934)
(Toronto)   1935.   552715
_____ 2nd edn.   1948.   599928

Sedgewick, Garnett Gladwin *works relating to*

__STOLL (ELMER EDGAR)
Another Othello too modern [: refutation of G. G. Sedgewick. With bibliographical notes.]   IN McMANAWAY (J. G.),
DAWSON (G. E.) and WILLOUGHBY (E. E.)
eds., John Quincy Adams memorial
studies. (Washington)   1948.
G. G. Sedgewick's "Of irony", containing
a chapter on Othello, is catal. no.
552715.

596748

SEDGFIELD (W. R.)
Photograph of Shakespeare's birthplace,
Stratford-upon-Avon. (Henry T. Cooke
& Son, Fine Art Repository, Warwick)
[c.1860]

391936

Sedgwick (W.E.) Herman Melville : the
tragedy of mind. [With references
to Shakespeare. Edited, with a
foreword, by Mrs. Sarah C. Sedgwick.]

(Cambridge, Mass.)   1945.

565576

SEDLEY, Sir CHARLES
Beauty the conquerour, or, The Death
of Marc Antony.

For editions of this play see under
English Editions: Antony and
Cleopatra: Alterations &c.

S[eeley] ([Sir] J.R.) Shakspere's
"Macbeth" and another. In The
Cornhill magazine, Vol.32.

1875.

38692

S[eeley] ([Sir] J.R.) A Stage Iago.
In The Cornhill magazine, Vol.33.

1876.

38693

SEIDEN (MELVIN)
Malvolio reconsidered.   FROM The
University of Kansas City review,
Vol. XXVII, No. 2.   1961.

667735

SEIDLIN (O.)
Georg Brandes, 1842-1927. [With references to his work,"William Shakespeare: a critical study."] IN Journal of the History of Ideas, Vol. 3. (Lancaster, Pa.)
bibliog.   1942.

546115

SEILER (GRACE ELIZABETH)
Shakespeare's part in "Pericles". (Ann Arbor, Mich.)
bibliog. typescript, 1951. micro-film, positive copy. 1 reel, 35 mm.
[1952.]
University Microfilms.   Doctoral Dissertation Series.

647062

SELBY, CHARLES
King Richard ye third; or, Ye Battel of Bosworth Field.

For editions of this play see under English Editions: Richard the Third: Alterations &c.

SELDEN (J.) Works relating to: see Moore (W. H.) Baconian Studies.

SELENUS (GUSTAVUS) pseud. [i.e. Augustus II, Duke of Brunswick-Luneberg] Works relating to:- see Moore (W. H.) Baconian Studies.

[SELKIRK (J. B.) pseud.] i.e. James Brown of Selkirk
Bible truths with Shakspearian parallels.
2nd edn.   1864.   392706
_____ 4th edn.   [1879] 541997

SELLMAN (PRISCILLA M.)
The Old Globe's sixth season in San Diego.
IN SHAKESPEARE QUARTERLY VII.
pp. 419-422.
(New York) 1956.

605711

SELLS (ARTHUR LYTTON)
The Italian influence in English poetry from Chaucer to Southwell.
ports. illus. bibliog. 1955.
With a chapter on Shakespeare.

647612

SELTZER (DANIEL)
Elizabethan acting in Othello.
IN SHAKESPEARE QUARTERLY X: 2.
pp. 201-210.
(New York) 1959.

605711

Seltzer (Daniel)

The Staging of the last plays. IN Stratford-upon-Avon Studies.
8: Later Shakespeare.   1966.

illus. pp.127-165.   756101

SELTZER (DANIEL)
"Their tragic scene": The Phoenix and turtle and Shakespeare's love tragedies.
IN SHAKESPEARE QUARTERLY XII: 2.
pp. 91-101.
(New York) 1961.

605711

Selvi (Margherita) ed.
BANDELLO (M.)
The Story of Romeo and Juliet (a source of Shakespeare's play), revised for modern readers, translated by Vera and H. B. Cotterill. [In Italian and English.] pp. 53. [1921.] 295637
Harrap's Bilingual Series.
_____ Another edn.   [1940.] 524347

S[EMAR] (J.)
Getting on with it.   ["Hamlet" in America.]   IN The Mask, Vol. 15 (1929).
(Florence)   1929.

369443

SEMPER (ISIDORE JOSEPH)
The Ghost in Hamlet.   FROM The Catholic World, Vol. 162.   (New York)   1946.

575827

SEMPER (ISIDORE JOSEPH)
The Ghost in Hamlet:_ pagan or Christian?
IN The Month, Vol. 195.   1953.

404303/195

Semper (I.J.) Hamlet without tears [: the touchstone of Thomistic philosophy applied to the problems of Shakespeare's Hamlet. With bibliographical notes].
(Dubuque, Iowa)   1946.

580143

Semper (I.J.) In the steps of Dante and other papers [including Shakespeare and St.Thomas More, and Shakespeare and war].

(Dubuque)   1941.

545882

SEMPER (ISIDORE JOSEPH)
The Jacobean theater through the eyes of Catholic clerics.
IN SHAKESPEARE QUARTERLY III: 1.
pp. 45-51.
(New York)   1952.

605711

SEMPER (ISIDORE JOSEPH)
Shakespeare and St. Thomas More.
FROM The Catholic Educational Review, Vol. 39. pp. [7.] (Washington, D.C.)
1941.

537392

SEN (N. B.) ed.
Thoughts of Shakespeare: a treasury of thoughts collected from the com-plete poetic and dramatic works and classified under subjects.   Foreword by Sir Tej Bahandur Sapru.   (Lahore)
frontis.   [1952.]

636328

SEN (N. B.) ed.
Wit and wisdom of Shakespeare
[: quotations from plays, poems
and sonnets]. (New Delhi: New
Book Society of India)
illus.   1961.

668094

SEN (SAILENDRA KUMAR)
Capell and Malone, and modern critical
bibliography. Introduction by A. Nicoll.
(Calcutta)   1960.

667618

SEN (SAILENDRA KUMAR)
A Neglected critic of Shakespeare:
Walter Whiter.
IN SHAKESPEARE QUARTERLY XIII: 2.
pp. 173-185.
(New York) 1962.

605711

SEN (SAILENDRA KUMAR)
"The Noblest Roman of them all":
Malone and Shakespearian scholarship.
IN Shakespeare commemoration volume,
edited by Taraknath Sen.   (Calcutta)
1966.

764382

SEN (SAILENDRA KUMAR)
What happens in Coriolanus.
IN SHAKESPEARE QUARTERLY IX.
pp. 331-345.
(New York) 1958.

605711

SEN (TARAKNATH)
Hamlet's treatment of Ophelia in the
nunnery scene.   IN The Modern
Language Review, Vol. 35.   (Cambridge)
bibliog.   1940.

527506

SEN (TARAKNATH)
Shakespeare's short lines.
IN Shakespeare commemoration volume,
edited by Taraknath Sen.   (Calcutta)
1966.

764382

SEN, TARAKNATH, ed.
Shakespeare commemoration volume.
Published by the Department of English,
Presidency College, Calcutta, under
the auspices of the Government of West
Bengal. (Calcutta)   1966.

764382

SEN GUPTA (SUBODH CHANDRA)
The Art of Bernard Shaw.   [With
references to Shakespeare.]
(Oxford)   1936.

453808

SEN GUPTA (SUBODH CHANDRA)
Shakespeare the man.   IN Shakespeare
commemoration volume, edited by
Taraknath Sen.   (Calcutta) 1966.

764382

SEN GUPTA (SUBODH CHANDRA)
Shakespearean comedy.   (Calcutta)
1950.

611217

SEN GUPTA, SUBODH CHANDRA
Shakespeare's historical plays.
1964.

668307

SEN GUPTA (SUBODH CHANDRA)
The Whirligig of time: the problem
of duration in Shakespeare's plays.
1961.

667103

Sen Gupta, Subodh Chandra *works relating to*

RIBNER (IRVING)
Shakespeare's history plays revisited. IN
Hommage a Shakespeare: Bulletin de
la Faculté des Lettres de Strasbourg.
43ᵉ année, No. 8, mai-juin 1965.
illus.   766822

SENCOURT (R.) [pseud. i.e. Robert Edmonde
Gordon George]
The Consecration of genius: an essay
to elucidate the distinctive significance and quality of Christian art by
analysis and comparison of certain
masterpieces.   [With references to
Shakespeare.]
illus.   bibliog.   1947.

577751

Seneca *works relating to*

CRAIG (H.)
Shakespeare and the history play [: der-
ivations from Seneca.   With bibliograph-
ical notes].   IN McManaway (J. G.),
Dawson (G. E.) and Willoughby (E. E.) eds.
John Quincy Adams memorial studies.
(Washington)
1948.

596748

ELIOT (THOMAS STEARNS)
Shakespeare and the stoicism of Seneca.
IN Eliot (T. S.) Selected essays,
1917-1932.   1932.

397201

EVANS (GARETH LLOYD)
Shakespeare, Seneca and the kingdom of
violence.   IN DOREY (THOMAS ALAN) and
DUDLEY (DONALD REYNOLDS) eds., Roman
drama.
illus.   1965.
Studies in Latin literature and its
influence.

746340

EWBANK (INGA-STINA)
The Fiend-like queen: a note on
"Macbeth" and Seneca's "Medea".
IN SHAKESPEARE SURVEY 19 [Macbeth].
(Cambridge) pp. 82-94.   1966.

755342

__ HUNTER (GEORGE KIRKPATRICK)
Seneca and the Elizabethans: a case-
study in "influence".
IN SHAKESPEARE SURVEY 20. (Cambridge)
1967.

766881

__ MENDELL (C.W.)
Our Seneca [: Senecan influence on English
drama, particularly pre-Elizabethan and
Shakespearian plays. With verse translations
of the Oedipus of Sophocles and the Oedipus
of Seneca]. (New Haven)   1941.

537613

__ JOHNSON (F. R.)
Shakespearian imagery and Senecan
imitation. bibliogs.
IN McMANAWAY (J. G.), DAWSON (G. E.)
and WILLOUGHBY (E. E.) eds., Joseph
Quincy Adams memorial studies.
(Washington)   1948.

596748

__ ORNSTEIN (ROBERT)
Seneca and the political drama of
"Julius Caesar". IN Journal of
English and Germanic Philology, Vol.
57. (Urbana, Ill.)   1958.

600780/57

"SENEX", [pseud.]
Observations on "Macbeth and King Richard
III: an essay in answer to remarks on
some of the characters of Shakespeare",
by J. P. Kemble. FROM The Edinburgh
Monthly Magazine, August, 1817.
[Edinburgh]   1817.

440300

SENG (PETER J.)
Songs, time and the rejection of
Falstaff. IN SHAKESPEARE SURVEY 15.
(Cambridge)   1962.

667174

SENG, PETER J.
The Vocal songs in the plays of
Shakespeare: a critical history.
(Cambridge, Mass.)   1967.

763845

SENIOR (W.)
The Old Wakefield theatre. [With
references to Shakespeare.]
(Wakefield)
frontis.   1894.

536679

SENNETT (MABELL)
As you like it: a new point of
view. pp. 31.   1930.
Psychological Aid Society
Publications: Illustrative Exercise
Series.

402647

SENNETT (MABELL)
His erring pilgrimage: a new interpretation of "As you like it". (Bacon
Society)
bibliog. facsimile.   [1949.]

598902

SENTER (JOHN H.)
Was Shakespeare a lawyer? An address
delivered before the annual meeting
[of the Vermont Bar Association]
Oct. 27, 1903. pp. 60. (Montpelier,
Vt.)   1903.

666341

Serbia

__ POPOVIC (P.)
Shakespeare in Serbia.
IN GOLLANCZ ([Sir] I.) ed., A Book of
homage to Shakespeare.
ports. illus. facsimiles. [1916.]

264175

Sermons

__ BEECHING [H. C.]
The Shakespeare sermon. Reprinted
from the Stratford-upon-Avon Herald,
April 28, 1911. pp. 9. [1911]

389769

__ BUNN (ALFRED)
The Reprover admonished: a sermon
[in defence of the English theatre,
including references to Shakespeare],
by A Churchman [i.e. A. Bunn].
(Birmingham: J. Drake)   1824.

668369

__ CHEVERTON (F. J.)
Shakespeare's day, [his religious
message]: a sermon preached in
Rowley Church, 18th April, 1926 by
the Rev. F. J. Cheverton; [and]
Stray thoughts on the sermon subject.
IN Rowley Regis Parish Church
[Magazine] April 1926.   1926.

384946

__ HART (ALFRED)
Shakespeare and the homilies [: a new
Shakespearean source-book] and other
pieces of research into the Elizabethan
drama. (Melbourne)   1934.

429387

__ Trench (R.C.) Every good gift from
above : a sermon preached in the
parish church of Stratford-upon-Avon
on Sunday, April 24, 1864 at the
celebration of the tercentenary of
Shakespeare's birth. 2nd edn.
pp. 20.

1864.

511208

SERONSY (CECIL C.)
"Supposes" as the unifying theme in "The
Taming of the Shrew".
IN SHAKESPEARE QUARTERLY XIV: 1.
pp. 15-30.
(New York) 1963.

605711

Seronsy (Cecil C.) <u>see</u> Michel
(Laurence A.) and Seronsy (C. C.)

SERRAILLIER, IAN
Stories from Shakespeare: the enchanted
island. Illustrated by P. Farmer.
1964.

667996

Servants

___ STUART (DOROTHY M.)
The English Abigail [: a study of the
English maidservant drawn from history
and literature. With references to
Shakespeare].
ports. illus. 1946.

573508

SERVISS (GARRETT PUTMAN)
The New Shakespeare-Bacon controversy
[: a review of Mrs. Gallup's "Bi-
literal Cypher"]. IN The Cosmopolitan,
Vol. 32. 1902.

172513

SETH-SMITH (E[LSIE] K.)
When Shakespeare lived in Southwark
[: the fictitious story of two boys'
adventures with the strolling
players]. Illustrated by J. Matthew.
1944.

554501

SETON (MATTHEW)
Recent Shakesperian revivals at the
Lyceum, Drury Lane and the Queen's.
FROM [The New Monthly Magazine, New
Series, Vol. 11.] [1877.]

560924

Settings *see* Scenery

SETTLE, ELKANAH
The Siege of Troy

For editions of this play see under
English Editions: Troilus and
Cressida: Alterations &c.

SETTLE (RONALD)

O Mistress Mine. Words by Shakespeare.
Vocal score. pp.5. [1961.]

667058

Seven Ages of Man *see* As You Like It, Seven Ages of Man

Seventeenth century studies, presented
to Sir H.[J.C.] Grierson. [With
references to Shakespeare, and a
bibliography.] Port. Illus.

(Oxford) 1938.

476132

Severn (Emma) Anne Hathaway, or,
Shakspeare in love [: fiction].
3 vols.
1845.

446746

Severs ([W.]K.) Imagery and drama.[With
references to Shakespeare and
bibliographical notes.]From Durham
University Journal, Vol.41.pp.[10]

(Durham) 1948.

596747

SÉVRETTE (GASTON)
M. Jean Richepin's [lectures on]
Shakespeare. IN The Fortnightly
Review, Vol. 102. 1914.

255614

[SEWARD (THOMAS)]
On Shakespear's monument at Stratford
upon Avon. IN [DODSLEY (R.) ed.,]
A Collection of poems by several hands.
3rd edn. Vol. 2. 1751. 576731
_____ 4th edn. 1755. 576737
_____ 5th edn. 1758. 538519

SEWELL (ARTHUR)
Character and society in Shakespeare.
(Oxford) 1951.

620174

Sewell (A.) Notes on the integrity of
Troilus and Cressida. [With biblio-
graphical notes.] In The Review of
English Studies, Vol. 19.

(Oxford) 1943.

555539

SEWELL (A.)
The Physiology of beauty [: an
examination of the functions of
literary criticism from a physio-
logical standpoint. With references
to Shakespeare]. With an introduction by L. [T.] Hogben. 1931.

406087

Sewell (A.) Place and time in
Shakespeare's plays. In Studies in
Philology,Vol.42.

(Chapel Hill, N.C.) 1945.

569039

SEWELL (ARTHUR)
Sense and Shakespeare [: review of]
The Real Shakespeare [by] W. Bliss.
IN The New Statesman and Nation,
Vol. 34.   1947.

589227

SEWELL (ELIZABETH)
Bacon and Shakespeare: postlogical
thinking.   IN Sewell (E.) The Orphic
voice, poetry and natural history
[: their inter-relation as symbolised
by Orphic myth in the works of major
Western writers].   1961.

696957

SEWELL (GEORGE)
The Tragedy of Sir Walter Raleigh.
As it is acted at the Theatre in
Lincolns-Inn-Fields. Third edition.
(London: John Pemberton)   1719.

The Epilogue refers to the
cutting and alteration of Shakespeare's
plays in the theatre.   436639

SEWELL, J. W.
Hamlet: a travesty in one act.

For editions of this play see under
English Editions: Hamlet:
Alterations &c.

Sex

___ADAMS (JOHN F.)
All's well that ends well: the paradox
of procreation.

IN SHAKESPEARE QUARTERLY XII: 3.
pp. 261-270.
(New York) 1961.
605711

___BARRELL (C. W.)
Verifying the secret history of
Shakespeare's sonnets [: a refutation
of the theory that Shakespeare can be
identified in his sonnets as a homo-
sexual personality, and evidence to
show that the Earl of Oxford was
Shakespeare].   Illustrated by H. F.
Wood.   FROM Tomorrow, Vol. 5. (New York)
ports.   illus.   facsimiles. 1946.

574236

___BAX (C.)
Sex and art.   [With references to
Shakespeare.] FROM The English Review,
Sept. 1934.   pp. 336-343.
1934.

427413

___CALDERWOOD, JAMES L.
Styles of knowing in All's Well. FROM
Modern Language Quarterly, 25: 3.
(Seattle)   1964.

pp.272-294.   747856

___KOTT (JAN)
Shakespeare our contemporary.
Translated by B. Taborski.   Preface
by P. Brook.   1964.   741546
_____ 2nd edn., revised.
1967.   766093
Includes "Titania and the ass's
head".

___PARTRIDGE (ERIC [H.])
Shakespeare's bawdy: a literary &
psychological essay and a comprehensive
glossary.   1947.

587277

___ SIMPSON (LUCIE)
The Sex bias of Measure for Measure.
IN The Fortnightly Review, Vol. 121.
1924.

312919

___WEST (ROBERT HUNTER)
Sex and pessimism in King Lear.
IN SHAKESPEARE QUARTERLY XI: 1.
pp. 55-60.
(New York) 1960.

605711

SEYLER (ATHENE)
"The Supporting rôle" [in acting].
Broadcast 16th October, 1955. ff.7.
typescript.   1955.

665125

Seymour, E. H. *works relating to*

___Remarks, critical, conjectural and
explanatory upon the plays of Shakspeare [etc.], by E. H. Seymour [: a
review. With bibliographical notes.]
From[The Monthly] Rev[iew, Vol. 51].

1806.

558070

Seymour (H.) Ben Jonson's"Poet-ape"
shewn to be Thomas Dekker, not
Shakespeare as commonly supposed.
Reprinted from Baconiana", January
1937. pp. [8.]

1937.

(The Bacon Society).

497670

Seymour (H.) John Barclay's Argenis and
cypher key. Reprinted from Baconiana, Feb. 1931. pp. 15.

1931.

(The Bacon Society.)

497671

Seymour (Mary) Shakespeare stories
simply told: tragedies and
histories. Illus.

1893.

516785

SEYMOUR (ROBERT)
New readings of old authors:
Shakespeare.   Designed and drawn on
stone. [Collected edn.]   [1841.]
  Imperfect, 6 parts only out of 25.
(Coriolanus; As you like it;
Midsummer night's dream; Troilus and
Cressida; King Richard II; King Henry
IV, pt. 1.)

508110

SEYMOUR (WILLIAM KEAN)
Shakespeare [: a poem].   IN
Seymour (W. K.) Collected poems.

1946.

571002

SHAABER (M. A.)
"The First rape of faire Hellen" by
John Trussell.
IN SHAKESPEARE QUARTERLY VIII:
pp. 407-448.
(New York)   1957.

605711

SHAABER (M. A.)
The Folio text of 2 Henry IV.
IN SHAKESPEARE QUARTERLY VI:
pp. 135-144.
(New York)   1955.

605711

SHAABER (MATTHIAS ADAM)
The Furness Variorum Shakespeare.
IN Proceedings of the American
Philosophical Society, Vol. 75.
(Philadelphia)   1935.

450515

SHAABER (MATTHIAS ADAM)
"A living drollery" (The Tempest, 111,iii,
21). Baltimore)
    bibliog.   1945.
                              371543

SHAABER (MATTHIAS ADAM)
Problems in the editing of Shakespeare:
text.   IN English Institute Essays,
1947.   (New York)
    bibliog.   1948.

530316/1947

SHAABER (MATTHIAS ADAM)
[Review of] The Editorial problem in
Shakespeare: a survey of the founda-
tions of the text, by W. W. Greg.
IN Modern Language Notes, Vol. 59.
(Baltimore)   1944.

563869

SHAABER (M. A.)
[Review of] A Shakespeare handbook
by R. M. Alden.   IN Modern Language
Notes, February, 1934.   (Baltimore)
                                 1934.

428652

SHAABER (M. A.)
[Review of] Shakespearian comedy
and other studies, by G. [S.] Gordon.
IN Modern Language Notes, Vol. 60.
(Baltimore)   1945.

571543

Shaaber (M.A.) A Textual dilemma
in I Henry IV. In Modern Language
Notes, Vol.54.

(Baltimore)   1939.

509539

SHAABER (MATTHIAS ADAM)
The Unity of Henry IV.   bibliog.
IN McMANAWAY (J. G.), DAWSON (G. E.)
and WILLOUGHBY (E. E.) eds., Joseph
Quincy Adams memorial studies.
(Washington)   1948.

596748

Shaaber (M. A.) joint author see
Black (M. W.) and Shaaber (M. A.)

Shackford (C.C.) Hamlet's "antic
  disposition". From The Cornell
  Review, Vol. 4.

(Ithaca [N.Y.])   1876.

560059

SHACKFORD (MARTHA HALE)
Plutarch in Renaissance England, with
special reference to Shakespeare.
pp. 54.   [Wellesley, Mass.]
bibliog.   1929.

393979

SHACKFORD (MARTHA HALE)
Shakespeare, Sophocles: dramatic modes.
pp. 37.   (Natick, Mass.)   1957.

666100

SHADWELL, THOMAS
The History of Timon of Athens, the
man-hater.

For editions of this play see under
English Editions: Timon of Athens:
Alterations &c.

SHADWELL, THOMAS
The Tempest; or, The Enchanted island

For editions of this play see under
English Editions: The Tempest:
Alterations &c.: Dryden, Davenant
and Shadwell's version

Shadwell, Thomas *works relating to*

——Hooker (Helene M.) Dryden's and
    Shadwell's Tempest. [With biblio-
    graphical notes.] In The Huntington
    Library Quarterly, Vol.6.

(San Marino, Cal.)   1943.

549639

___IACUZZI (A.)
The Naive theme in The Tempest as a
link between Thomas Shadwell and
Ramón de la Cruz.   IN Modern Language
Notes, Vol. 52.   (Baltimore) 1937.

479896

___MILTON (W. M.)
Tempest in a teapot [: discussing
whether T. Shadwell wrote an opera,
The Tempest.]   IN E.L.H., Vol. 14.
(Baltimore, Md.)
bibliog.   1947.

430295/14

— Squire (W.B.) The Music of Shadwell's
"Tempest" [composed by P.Humphrey].
pp. [14.] From The Musical
quarterly, Vol.7.

(New York)   1921.

523728

SHAFFER, ELINOR S.
Iago's malignity motivated: Coleridge's
unpublished "opus magnum".
IN SHAKESPEARE QUARTERLY XIX: 3.
pp. 195-203.   (New York)
1968.

605711

SHAH (C. R.)
Shakespearean plays in Indian languages.
[Parts] 1-2.   FROM The Aryan Path,
Vol. 26.   pp. [6, 4.]   (Bombay)
2 vols.   1955.

665272-3

SHAHANI (RANJEE G.)
Kalidasa and Shakespeare.   FROM The
Aryan path, Vol. 7.   (Bombay)
1936.   484132
_____ FROM The Poetry Review, May-
June, 1942.   1942.   534898

Shahani (R.G.)   The Sentimental
autobiography of Shakespeare.
From [The Asiatic Review, New
Series,] Vol. 36.

1940.

521316

Shahani (R.G.) Shakespeare in Indian
literary criticism. In Indian
Art and Letters, Vol.7.

1933.

417843

SHAHANI (R. G.)
Shakespeare through Eastern eyes.
With an introduction by J. M. Murry,
and an appreciation by E. Legouis.
[1932.]

397671

SHAHANI (R. G.)
The Shakespearian vision.   FROM
Poetry Review, August, 1935. 1935.

438990

Shahani, Ranjee G. *works relating to*

—   Burdett (O.[H.]) Shakespeare through
Eastern eyes, by R.G. Shahani: [a review.]
In The London Mercury, Vol. 26.

[1932.]

402135

—— K[nights] (L.C.) Shakespeare through
Eastern eyes, by R.G. Shahani:
[a review.] In The Criterion, Vol.12,
1933.

1932-33.

414720

— WESTBROOK (Mrs.)
Shakespeare through Eastern eyes, by
R. G. Shahani: [a review.]   IN The
Asiatic Review, Vol. 29.   1933.

415141

Shakespeare, Anne *see* Family of Shakespeare

Shakespeare, John *see* Family of Shakespeare

Shakespeare, Mary *see* Family of Shakespeare

SHAKESPEARE II [pseud.]
The Overman: the serio-comic history
of a twentieth century Hamlet.
[With a preface signed William the
Second,pseud.]   pp. 64.   1905.

547975

Shakespeare, William

see also Allusions to Shakespeare; Birthday Celebrations; Criticism, Shakespearian; Influence and Comparisons; Life of Shakespeare; Philosophy and Religion; Portraits and Monuments; Relics of Shakespeare; Reputation of Shakespeare; Stratford-upon-Avon

___ ADAMS (W. H. D.)
Sword and pen; or, English worthies in the reign of Elizabeth.   3rd edn. [With a chapter on Shakespeare, select passages on Shakespeare in verse and prose from various authors and bibliographical notes.]
illus.   1875.

441044

___ ADDICOTE (W.)
The Myth [: Shakespeare].   IN The Mask, Vol. 15 (1929).   (Florence)
1929.

369443

___ ANSPACHER (L. K.)
Shakespeare as poet and lover and the enigma of the sonnets.   pp. [vi,] 55. (New York)   1944.

556395

___ ARCHER (T.)
What is known about Shakespeare. FROM The Graphic [, Vol. 37].
port.   illus.   1888.
Imperfect, p. 486 wanting.

564291

___ ATKINSON (B.)
William Shakespeare, poet.   With a photograph of a new bust of Shakespeare by R. Aitken.   pp. 13. (Peekshill, N.Y.)   1934.
Edition limited to 130 copies.

442547

___ BAGEHOT (WALTER)
Shakespeare - the man.   IN Bagehot (W.) Literary studies.   Edited, with a prefatory memoir by R. H. Hutton. New edn. Vol. 1.
port.   1895.   474726
_____ IN Booklovers Edition [of] Shakespeare [Vol. 11.]   (University Society, New York)   [1937].   475456

___ BARRELL (C. W.)
Identifying "Shakespeare".
IN Scientific American, Vol. 162. (New York)   1940.

517843

___ [Barton (R.)] Farrago; containing essays, moral, philosophical, political and historical, on Shakespeare, [etc.] Vol.1.

(Tewkesbury)   1792.

523175

___ Baten (A.M.) Do you believe in yourself? [Containing a chapter on Shakespeare and other Shakespearian references.]

(Grand Rapids)   1935.

440777

___ BAX (C.)
Shakespeare and Smith [: thoughts on Shakespeare arising from seeing a performance of A Midsummer night's dream].   IN Bax (C.) Evenings in Albany.
frontis.   1945.

561874

___ BEECHING (H. C.)
The Benefit of the doubt.
IN GOLLANCZ ([Sir] I.) ed., A Book of homage to Shakespeare.
ports.   illus.   facsimiles.   [1916.]

264175

___ [Beeching (H.C.)] Provincial letters and other papers [including a section on Shakespeare] by the author of Pages from a Private Diary.

1906.

433728

___ BENSON ([Sir] F. R.)
Shakespeare's message.   IN The Shakespeare International Alliance, No. 2, April 1914.   1914. Printed for private circulation only.

535364

___ BERRYMAN (JOHN)
Shakespeare at thirty.   IN The Hudson Review, Vol. 6.   (New York)
1953-54.

642968/6

___ BLISS (W.)
The Real Shakespeare: a counterblast to commentators.   1947.

583383

___ Bliss (W.) Shakespeare a murderer! From "The Month", July, 1933. pp.[10.]
1933.

408588

___ BOAS (F. S.)
Shakspere and his predecessors.   New impression.   1902. For other editions of this work check the main sequence under the author's name.

498694

___ Bradley (A.C.) Oxford lectures on poetry. 2nd edn. [Including Shakespeare the man. With bibliographical notes.]

1917

533634

—— BRITTON (J.)
Essays on the merits and characteristics
of William Shakspere: also remarks on
his birth and burial-place, his monument,
portraits, and associations.   IN
Britton (J.) Appendix to Britton's
autobiography.
illus.   1849.

28246

—— BROWN, IVOR JOHN CARNEGIE
The Man Shakespeare. Produced by H.
Burton. B.B.C. script transmitted for
T.V. 18th April 1965.   1965.

typescript.   744467

—— Brown(I.[J.C.]) Mr.William
Shakespeare: the man behind the
monument.From Harper's Bazaar,
April, 1945.

1945.

579643

—— BRYCE ([J. BRYCE, 1st] Viscount)
Some stray thoughts.
IN GOLLANCZ ([Sir] I.) ed., A Book of
homage to Shakespeare.
ports. illus. facsimiles. [1916.]

264175

—— BULLOUGH, GEOFFREY
Shakespeare the Elizabethan. FROM
Proceedings of the British Academy,
Vol.L.   1964.

pp.121-141. British Academy,
Annual Shakespeare Lecture.   748305

—— BURRUSS (W. B.)
Shakespeare the salesman.   [With
a preface entitled: "About Bill
Burruss", by J. C. Aspley.]
(Chicago)   1942.

548205

—— BURTON (HARRY McGUIRE)
Shakespeare and his plays.   With
illustrations by R. G. Robinson.
pp. [iv] 68.
port. illus. chart.   facsimiles.
bibliog.   1958.
Methuen's Outlines.

665794

—— C. [pseud.]
Shakspere and his age: reflections
on modern play.   FROM [Stray Leaves
Quarterly, Jan. 1874].   [Liverpool]
[1874]

554727

—— CAINE ([Sir] T. [H.] H.)
Two aspects of Shakspere's art.
IN The Contemporary Review, Vol. 43.
1883.

60100

—— CARLYLE (T.)
On Shakespeare.   FROM The Hero as poet.
pp. 29.
1904.

De La Mare [Booklets]

For other editions of this work check
the main sequence under the author's
name.

564104

—— Carr (P.) Days with the French
Romantics in the Paris of 1830
[, including a chapter entitled
"Discovery of Shakespeare"]. Ports.
Illus.

1932.

572683

—— Carter (H.) The Spirit of Shakespeare:
an hypothesis. In The Quest, vol.11.

1920.

408732

—— [Central Literary Magazine. Index of
articles relating to Shakespeare
and poetry, contained in the Central
Literary Magazine, Vols. 1-31,
1873-1934]. ff.6. Typescript.

[Birmingham]   [c.1935]

471779

—— CHAMBERS ([Sir] E.K.)
Shakespearean gleanings [: essays on
Shakespeare and his works.   With bibli-
ographical notes].   Frontis.
(Oxford)   1944.

555503

—— Chapman (W.H.) Shakespeare: the
personal phase. Ports. Illus.

[Los Angeles]   [1920]

437258

—— CHATEAUBRIAND (Le Vicomte F. A. R. de)
Recollections of Italy, England and
America, with essays on various
subjects in morals and literature
Vol. 1.   [1815.]
Includes a chapter on Shakespeare.

579640

—— CHUBB (E. W.)
Stories of authors, British and
American.   [With a chapter "About
Shakspere".]
ports.   1911.

524720

—— CLARK (CUMBERLAND)
Shakespeare's world.   (Southampton)
bibliog.   1940.

617014

—— CLARKE ([Mrs.] MARY [V.] COWDEN)
Shakespeare's self [as revealed in
his writings.]   pp. 13. [Birmingham]
[1943.] 539326
Privately printed.
———— Another copy.   546035

—— Cohen (Helen L.) William Shakespeare
[: an appreciation]. Port.
From Scholastic, April 15, 1940.

[New York]   1940.

525315

COLLIER (D. W.)
The Immortal memory of William
Shakespeare [: an address delivered
at the Shakespeare Celebration, 1936].
IN The Central Literary Magazine,
Vol. 32, July, 1936.   (Birmingham)
                              1936.   463922
_____ Another copy. 1936.   465871

Cowie (D.) The British contribution:
some ideas and inventions that have
helped humanity. [With a chapter on
Shakespeare and] foreword by
L. [C.M.] S.Amery. Illus.

1941.

524267

CRAIG (HARDIN)
Man successful. IN Shakespeare
Quarterly XV: 2. pp.11-15. (New York)
                              1964.

605711

Craig (H.) Renaissance ideal: a
lecture on Shakespeare. [With a
bibliography.] From University of
North Carolina Extension Bulletin,
Vol.24.

(Chapel Hill, N.C.)   1944.

577764

CRAIG (H.)
Shakespeare and the normal world.
In The Rice Institute Pamphlet, Vol. 31.
(Houston, Texas.)   1944.

563555

Craig (H.) Shakespeare as an
Elizabethan : talk [broadcast]
10th July 1949. ff.10. Typescript.
(Shakespeare and his world, 1).

605263

DALGLEISH (W. S.)
Great authors, from Chaucer to Pope,
[including] Shakespeare.
ports.   1909.
[Royal English Class-Books.]
                              445107

D'Amato (G.A.) A Man named Shakspere.
In D'Amato (G.A.)Portraits of
ideas. Illustrated by A.Duccini.

(Boston,Mass.)   1947.

592425

Dent (A.) Introducing Shakespeare.
(Forces Educational Broadcast).
[Broadcast] 22nd October, 1945.
ff.9. Typescript.

567026

DENT (R. K.)
Shakespeare and his England.   IN
Dent (R. K.) Lecture notes and other
manuscripts, Vol. II.
manuscript.   [c.1890-1920]

389903

DIXON (W. M.)
Shakespere, the Englishman: portion
of an address delivered to the
Library Association, 5th May, 1916.
FROM The Hibbert Journal, Vol. 14.
                              1916.

474790

DOBBS (L. [G.])
Shakespeare revealed.   Edited, with
an introductory memoir, by Hugh
Kingsmill [pseud.]
port.   bibliog.   [1949.]

604031

DOWDEN (E.)
Introduction to Shakespeare.   Reprinted.
port.   illus.   1897.

For other editions of this work check
the main sequence under the author's name.

413743

DOWDEN (E.)
Shakspere: a critical study of his
mind and art.   20th edn.   [c.1930.]
For other editions of this work
check the main sequence under the
author's name.
                              409497

EMERSON (ANNE)
What price Shakespeare? [A monologue.]
Broadcast 19th March, 1951. ff. 5.
typescript.   1951.

616352

EMERSON (R. W.)
Shakespeare; or, the poet.   IN Emerson
(R. W.) English traits, Representative
men, & other essays.   [With an intro-
duction by E. Rhys, and a bibliography.]
                              1932.
(Everyman's Library)

For other editions of this work check
the main sequence under the author's name.
                              473749

EVANS, Sir BENJAMIN IFOR
Shakespeare's world.   IN SUTHERLAND,
JAMES, and HURSTFIELD, JOEL, eds.,
Shakespeare's world.   1964.

667808

FAY (M.)
We need a Shakespeare now!   FROM
The Millgate, Vol. 35.   [Manchester]
                              1940.

522656

FINNEMORE (J.)
Famous Englishmen, Vol. 1, Alfred to
Elizabeth.   [With a chapter, William
Shakespeare.]   2nd edn.
ports.   illus.   1931.

428110

—Fonseka (J.P.de) Breakspeare and
Shakespeare. From The Month,
May 1933. pp.[6.]

1933.

406219

—FOX, LEVI
The Shakespeare anniversary book.
(Norwich)   1964.

illus. map.   667801

—Furness (H.H.) [Jr.,] On Shakespeare,
"or, What you will": oration delivered before the Harvard Chapter of
Phi Beta Kappa, June 25, 1908. Reprinted from the Harvard Graduates'
Magazine, Sept. 1908. pp. 25.

[Cambridge, Mass.]   1908.

488383

—Fyfe (H.H.) A New light on Shakespeare. From Queen's Quarterly,
vol.40.

(Kingston,Ont.)   1933.

441605

— GALLOWAY (DAVID)
Shakespeare: seven radio talks on
CBC University of the air.
(Canadian Broadcasting Corporation)
(Toronto)
bibliog.   1961.

666934

— GALSWORTHY (JOHN)
The Great tree [: an essay on
Shakespeare]. IN Galsworthy (J.)
Forsytes, Pendyces and others.
1935.

436156

— GANNON (D.)
Musings on Shakespeare. pp. 91.
[Buenos Aires]
frontis.   [1922]

585177

—GARRETT (JOHN) ed.
Talking of Shakespeare [: a selection
from the lectures delivered at the
annual course for teachers at
Stratford. 1948-1953.   1954.

6414¯1

— GASQUET (Cardinal F. A.)
Shakespeare.
IN GOLLANCZ ([Sir] I.) ed., A Book of
homage to Shakespeare.
ports. illus. facsimiles. [1916.]

264175

— GIBBS ([Sir] P.)
Short sketches of great writers.
2. The Spirit of Shakspere. IN
Gibbs ([Sir] P.) Knowledge is power:
a guide to personal culture. 1906.

589328

— GILFILLAN (G.)
Shakspere - a lecture. IN A Third
Gallery of Portraits, pp. 501-536.
(Edinburgh)   1854.   84518
——— FROM Gilfillan (G.) Galleries
of literary portraits. [Edinburgh]
[1856]. 431270
——— (Everyman's Library)
1927. 473750

—GILLIES (A.)
Herder's essay on Shakespeare: "Das
Herz der Untersuchung". IN The
Modern Langauge Review, Vol. 32.
(Cambridge)   1937.

477224

— GOETHE ([J. W. von)]
Criticisms, reflections and maxims;
translated, with an introduction,
by W. B. Ronnfeldt. [Containing
Goethe on Shakespeare: Shakespeare
and no end; The First edition of
"Hamlet"; On "Hamlet"; Stray
thoughts on Shakespeare; English
drama in Paris.]   [1897]
The Scott Library.

473909

—GOETHE (JOHANN WOLFGANG von)
Shakespeare: zum Shäkespears Tag;
Shakespeare und kein ende!; Ludwig
Tiecks Dramaturgische Blätter. IN
Goethe the critic: a selection from
his writings on the arts. With
introduction and notes by G. F. Senior,
revised and completed by C. V. Bock.
(Manchester)
chronological table. bibliog. 1960.
German Texts.

699370

— GRANVILLE-BARKER (H.)
The Perennial Shakespeare. pp. 28.
1937.
Broadcast National Lectures.
476606

—HAMMERTON ([Sir] J. A.)
Other things than war, musings and
memories [: miscellaneous essays on
books, personalities, etc., including
Will Shakespeare live?]
ports. illus. dgm.   [1943.]

546296

—HARDING (D. P.)
Shakespeare the Elizabethan. IN
PROUTY (CHARLES TYLER) ed., Shakespeare:
of an age and for all time: the Yale
Shakespeare Festival Lectures. [New
Haven, Conn.]   1954.

640920

—HARDMAN (DAVID)
What about Shakespeare?
bibliog.   1938.   492175
Discussion Books.
——— Another edn.   1947. 667520

—   Harper (C.G.) Shakespeare the
countryman. In The Cyclists' Touring
Club Gazette, Vol. 51 (N.S.) 1932.

401791

___ HARRIS (F.)
The Man Shakespeare and his tragic
life-story.   (New York)
                    1909   464563
Author's signature on front end-paper.
    _____ 2nd and revised edn.
                  1911.   388841
    _____ Another edn. 1935.   447803

___ HARRIS (F.)
The True Shakespeare: an essay in
realistic criticism. Parts 1-13
[discovering Shakespeare's personal
character in his dramatic characters].
IN The Saturday Review, Vols. 85-86.
2 vols.   1898.

               142978

___ HARRIS (J. C.)
Joel Chandler Harris, editor and
essayist: miscellaneous literary,
political and social writings.
Edited [with introductions] by [Mrs.]
Julia [F.] C. Harris.   [Including
an essay on Tolstoy's criticism of
Shakespeare.] (Chapel Hill, N.C.)
ports. illus. facsimiles. bibliog.
              1931.

               536323

___ HAZLITT (WILLIAM)
On posthumous fame - whether
Shakspeare was influenced by a love
of it?   IN Hazlitt (W.) The Round
table [and] Characters of Shakespear's
plays.   1936.
Everyman's Library, No. 65.

               473751

___ Healy (T.F.) Shakespeare was an
    Irishman. In The American Mercury,
Vol.51.

       (New York)   1940.

               525051

___ Hearn (L.) Complete lectures on art,
    literature and philosophy. [Containing
    a lecture, Shakespeare; and references
    to Shakespeare's plays]. Edited by
    R. Tanabé, T. Ochiai and I. Nishizaki.

       (Tokyo)   1932.

               412511

___ HENLEY (W. E.)
Shakespeare [: an essay].   IN Views
and reviews; essays in appreciation.
              1892.

               170110

___ Henty (W.) Shakespeare's "der adventure".
    In The Antiquary, vol.4.

              1881.

              39585

___ Hodgson (Sir A.) Shakespearean
    jottings collated in a lecture
    delivered in the Stoneleigh
    Institute, Stoneleigh, Warwickshire.
    pp.32. Illus.
              1902.

(Privately printed. Chiswick Press.)

              419183

___ Hotson ([J.] L.) "Not of an age":
Shakespeare. From Sewanee Review,
vol.49. pp. [18].

    (Sewanee, Tenn.)   1941.

              537396

___ HOWARTH (HERBERT)
Shakespeare's gentleness.   IN
SHAKESPEARE SURVEY 14.   (Cambridge)
              1961.

              666755

___ Howe (J.) Shakspeare. In Howe (J.)
    Poems and essays.

       (Montreal)   1874.

              483637

___ Hunt (L.) Leigh Hunt as poet and
    essayist: the choicest passages
    from his works. [Including an essay
    on Shakespeare.] Selected and edited
    with a biographical introduction [and
    a bibliography], by [W.] C. [M.].
    Kent. Port.

              1889.

(Cavendish Library)

              485876

___ HUNT (L.)
Shakespeare's birthday.   IN MAKOWER
(S. V.) and BLACKWELL (B. H.) [eds.]
A Book of English essays (1600-1900).
(Oxford)   1935.
The World's Classics.

              540665

___ Hunt (L.) Table-talk, [with] Imaginary
    conversations of Pope and Swift
    [and one entitled "Associations
    with Shakspeare".]

              1870.
              485878

___ HUTTON (L.)
William Shakespeare, 1564-1616 [:
an essay].   IN Literary landmarks
of London.   1885.

              77022

___ HYETT ([Sir] F. A.)
Why is Shakespeare our greatest poet?
An address at the commemoration of
the Shakespeare Tercentenary at
Gloucester, May 3rd, 1916.   pp. 20.
(Gloucester)   1916.

              438429

___ IRVING (Sir HENRY)
Biographical introduction and an essay
on Shakespeare and Bacon.   IN The
Complete works of William Shakespeare.
ports. illus. 6 vols. [c.1905.]
Bijou Shakespeare.

              543951

___ [JACKSON (W.)]
Letter 14: On Shakspeare.
IN [Jackson (W.)] Thirty letters
on various subjects.   Vol. 1.
              1783.

              546667

——James (S.B.) The Tragedy of
Shakespeare. In The Month,
vol.154.

1929.

369446

——JESSUP, FRANK
On behalf of Shakespeare.
IN Stratford Papers on Shakespeare
delivered at the 1962 Shakespeare
Seminar.   (Toronto)   1963.

668006

——JOHNSON (PAMELA H.)
Book talk - the personality of
Shakespeare.   [Broadcast] 12th March,
1945.   ff. 3.
typescript.

558619

——JOHNSON [SAMUEL]
Character of Shakspeare.   IN
Johnson [S.] The Beauties of Johnson,
consisting of selections from his
works by A. Howard.
port.   [c.1834.]

518887

——JOHNSON (SAMUEL)
Johnson on Shakespeare: essays and
notes selected and set forth with
an introduction by [Sir] W. [A.]
Raleigh.   (Oxford)   1925.   419956
[Oxford Miscellany]
——— Another edn.   1931.   395359

——JOHNSTON (Sir H. [H.]) ed.
A Book of great authors [: Homer,
Shakespeare, etc.]
illus.   [1932]
Collins' Boys' Library of Famous Men.

416259

——JUSSERAND (J. J.)
What to expect of Shakespeare.
IN Jusserand (J. J.) The School for
ambassadors, and other essays.
(New York)
frontis.   1925.

485228

——KEMENOV (V.)
Shakespeare: on the occasion of
the 330th anniversary of his death.
FROM Voks Bulletin, No. 5-6.
(Moscow: U.S.S.R. Society for
Cultural Relations with Foreign
Countries)   1946.

581624

——KENNEDY (AUBREY LEO)
The Two greatest Englishmen:
Shakespeare and Churchill?   IN The
Quarterly Review, Vol. 296.   1958.

38702/296

——KING (T.)
Shakespeare, the master-builder.
FROM The Aryan Path, Vol. 18.
(Bombay)   1947.

587357

——KINGSMILL (HUGH) [pseud.]
Frank Harris [containing a chapter
"The Saturday Review and Shakespeare"].
port.   1932.

392945

——KITTREDGE (G. L.)
Shakspere: an address delivered
April 23, 1916, in Sanders Theatre,
Harvard College.   With preface and
notes by R. Ishikawa.   pp. [88.]
[1929]
Kenkyusha Pocket English Series.

397850

——Knickerbocker (W.S.) Shakespeare. In
Knickerbocker (W.S.) ed. Twentieth
century English [: essays on the
understanding and use of the English
language, by various authors].

(New York)   1946.

575898

——KNIGHT (GEORGE WILSON)
Shakespeare's world.   IN Knight (G. W.)
Hiroshima [and] On prophecy and the
sun-bomb [: essays and literary
studies].   1946.

577189

——LAMBORN (E. A. G.) and HARRISON (G. B.)
Shakespeare, the man and his stage.
ports.   illus.   facsimiles.
1924.   436484
[The World's Manuals.]
——— Another edn.   1928.   425284

——LANGDON-DAVIES (JOHN)
Young Shakespeare: a collection of
contemporary documents compiled and
edited by J. Langdon-Davies.
(Jonathan Cape)
illus.   [1964.]
Jackdaw, No. 9.

667833

——LE BRETON (A.)
Le Théâtre romantique.   [With a
chapter on Alfred de Vigny's translation
of Othello, and other references to
Shakespeare.]   [c.1920.]

572306

——LEE ([Sir] SIDNEY)
Great Englishmen of the sixteenth
century [including "Shakespeare's
career" and "Foreign influences on
Shakespeare".]   2nd edn.
ports.   bibliogs.   1907.   411890
——— 2nd edn.   (Harrap Library, 30)
1925.   396028

——[Leisure Hour. Articles relating to
Shakespeare and Johnson. From
Leisure Hour, 1864.] Ports.
Illus. pp.24.

[1864.]

405982

——Lewis ([P.]W.) Was Shakespeare a
John Bull?   In Lewis ([P.]W.)
The Mysterious Mr. Bull.

1938.

495350

—Lindsay (J.) A Short history of
culture. [With chapters : "William
Shakespeare", and "Shakespearian
tragedy."] Illus.

1939.

500639

—Lovett (R.M.) [Shakespeare's
permanence]: an address delivered at
the University of [Porto] Rico on
the occasion of the anniversary of
Shakespeare's birth. pp. 15.

(Rio Piedras)   1940.
([Porto] Rico University Bulletin, Series XI,
No.1.)

525046

—LUCE (M.)
The Character of Shakespeare.
IN GOLLANCZ ([Sir] I.) ed., A Book of
homage to Shakespeare.
ports. illus. facsimiles. [1916.]

264175

—Lyde (H.W.) The Immortal memory
of William Shakespeare: an
address delivered at the
Shakespeare Celebrations 23rd
April, 1931. In The Central
Literary Magazine. Vol.30.
1931-32.

1932.

407289

—McCURDY (HAROLD GRIER)
The Personality of Shakespeare: a
venture in psychological method.
(New Haven, Conn.)
graphs. tables. bibliog. 1953.

639770

—MacDONALD (G.)
A Dish of orts, chiefly papers on
the imagination and on Shakspere.
Enlarged edn.
port.   1893.   436476
_____ Illustrated by C. Cuneo &
G. H. Evison.   1908.   399704

—Mace (C.A.) Historical years
[: a miscellany. With a chapter,
William Shakespeare.] Port.

[1925.]

415001

—Mair (A.W.) Praise of Shakespeare
[: Greek] dialogue [with English
translation]. In Gollancz ([Sir]I.)
ed.,A Book of homage to Shakespeare.
Ports. Illus. Facsimiles.

[1916.]

264175

—Man (W.L.) and White (T.A.S.) Lecture
on Shakespeare. [With, The Tercentenary celebration of Shakespeare
at Stratford, 1864, by T.A.S.White.]
pp.42. Ports. Illus.

(Maidstone)   1887.

419185 ____

—MASEFIELD (JOHN)
Shakespeare and spiritual life.
2nd impression. pp. 32. (Oxford)
1924.   491857
Romanes Lectures, 1924.
_____ Another copy.   200 copies
printed; signed by the author.
1924.   557231
_____ IN Masefield (J.) Recent prose.
New and revised edn. 1932.   399415

—Mathew (F.) An Image of Shakespeare
[as revealed in his works.]

(New York)   1923.

444967

—Matthews ([J.]B.) Shakespeare as an
actor. In North American Review,
Vol.195.

(New York)   1912.

236981

—MATTHISON (A. L.)
Nothing about Shakespeare.   IN
Matthison (A. L.) Nothing about
paint [: essays].   (Birmingham)
1944.   547270
_____ Another copy.   546854

—MEIGHEN (Rt. Hon. A.)
"The Greatest Englishman of history"
[i.e. Shakespeare:] an address.
With a foreword by Sir R. [A.] Falconer.
pp. 39. (Toronto)
port.   1936.

472827

—METCALF (JOHN CALVIN)
Know your Shakespeare.   (Boston
[Mass.])
illus. facsimiles. bibliog.
1949.

604460

—MILNE (A. A.)
More lost diaries, with acknowledge-
ments to M. Baring: the lost diary
of Shakespeare.   IN The Saturday
Book, 6th year.   [1946.]

576899

—MITCHELL (D. G.)
English lands, letters and kings.
[With chapters on Shakespeare.]
2 vols.   1890.

436903

—MOHRBUTTER (A.)
Queen Elizabeth and her influence
on English politics and culture.
[With a chapter "Great writers:
William Shakespeare", and notes
in German.]   pp. 52, 19.   (Kiel)
ports. illus. map.   1927.
Franzosische und englische Schullekture,
Erganzungsheft, 37.

425705

—Morley (G.) Shakespeare the welldoer.
In The Quest, vol.9.

1918.

408730

—— Morton (R.K.) Shakespeare : the man and the message. From Education, February 1934.

(Boston, Mass.)   1934.

503858

—— MOULTON (R. G.)
Shakespeare as the central point in world literature.   IN GOLLANCZ ([Sir] I.) ed., A Book of homage to Shakespeare.
ports. illus. facsimiles. [1916.]

264175

—— MOWAT (R. B.)
Makers of British history.   Book 1: 1066-1603.   [Containing a chapter on Shakespeare.]
ports.   illus.   [1926]

427185

—— MUIR (KENNETH) and O'LOUGHLIN (S.)
The Voyage to Illyria: a new study of Shakespeare.   1937.

469719

—— MULLIK (B.   R.   )

Studies in Dramatists, vol. 3: Shakespeare - general. 3rd edn. revised and enlarged. Bibliog. (Delhi)
1959.

667114

—— O'CONNOR (F.)
The Road to Stratford [: the development of Shakespeare's character as shown in his works.]   FROM The Irish Times, July 10th-13th and 15th-16th, 1946. [Dublin]   1946.

579645

—— O'CONNOR (F.)
The Road to Stratford [: a critical study of Shakespeare. With bibliographical references.]   1948.

595326

—— O'HAGAN (T.)
What Shakespeare is not.   (Toronto)
bibliog.   1936.

463636

—— On Shakespeare. [Study and poem].
In Fraser's Magazine, vol.21.

1840.

10621

—— Osborne (W.A.) Some brief Shakespeare commentaries. In Osborne (W.A.) Essays and studies.

(Melbourne)   1946.

578948

—— OSLER ([Sir] W.)
Creators, transmuters, and transmitters as illustrated by Shakespeare, Bacon, and Burton [: reprint in Osler on Shakespeare, Bacon, and Burton, by W. White].   FROM Bulletin of the History of Medicine, Vol. 7.
(Baltimore)
facsimile.   1939.

565596

—— OST (F.) ed.
Shakespeare and his time.   [English texts.]   Edited and annotated.
pp. 80.   (Leipzig)
port.   illus.   [c.1935]
English Treasure Series.   Englische Lekture und Kulturkunde in Einzelheften.

449471

—— PEARSON (H.) and KINGSMILL (H.) [pseud.]
This blessed plot [: the record of a tour through England in the wake of Shakespeare.]   Illustrated by M. Weightman.   1942.

534309

—— [PEGGE (S.)]
Anonymiana; or, Ten centuries of observations on various authors and subjects [including Shakespeare]. Compiled by a late very learned and reverend divine.   2nd edn.   1818.

480936

—— Pepler (H.D.C.) Shakespeare as realist. From G.K.'s Weekly, May 27, 1937. pp.[4.]

1937.

471792

—— Phelps (W.L.) Notes on Shakespeare.
In Proceedings of the American Philosophical Society, Vol.81.

1939.

518318

—— POCOCK (G. N.)
English men & women of ideas. [Containing a chapter, William Shakespeare (1564-1616): the world's greatest dramatist].   1930.

427187

—— Pollard (A.W.) and Wilson (J.D.)
William Shakespeare. In Garvin (Katharine) ed.,The Great Tudors.

1935.

431775

—— Pound (E.[L.]) Guide to kulchur. [With references to Shakespeare.] Illus.

1938.

486848

PRICE (H. T.)
Shakespeare as a critic. [With
bibliographical notes.] IN
MAXWELL (B.) [and others] eds.,
Renaissance studies in honor of
Hardin Craig. (Iowa)
port. 1941.
Philological Quarterly, Vol. 20, No.3;
Iowa University [and Stanford University.]

539442

Prince (P.A.) William Shakspeare.
In Prince (P.A.) Parallel history:
an outline of the history and
biography of the world. 2nd edn.
Vol.2.

1843.

33335

RAILSTON (MARGARET)
William Shakespeare: an appreciation.
IN BELLOC (HILAIRE) The Aftermath;
or, Gleanings from a busy life...
1920.
[The Reader's Library]

388786

Rascoe (B.) Shakespeare the mirror.
In Rascoe (B.) Titans of literature:
from Homer to the present.

1933.

409882

RATTRAY (R. F.)
Shakespear as seen to-day. IN The
Quarterly Review, Vol. 287.
bibliog. 1949.

38702/287

RAY (B.) and RAY (Sir P. C.)
The Shakespearean puzzle: endeavours
after its solution. Parts 1-17.
FROM The Calcutta Review, Nov. 1939-
1941. (Calcutta)
bibliog. 533633

REESE (MAX MEREDITH)
Shakespeare: his world & his work.
illus. map. bibliog. 1953.

631880

REYNOLDS (Sir JOSHUA)
Portraits: character sketches of Oliver
Goldsmith, Samuel Johnson, and David
Garrick, with other manuscripts of
Reynolds recently discovered among the
private papers of James Boswell.
Prepared for the press with introduc-
tions and notes by F. W. Hilles.
ports. illus. facsimiles. bibliog.
1952.
Yale Editions of the Private Papers of
James Boswell.
With a chapter on Shakespeare. 627913

Richey (A.M.S.) Shakespeare: an
appreciation. From The Methodist
Magazine, September, 1934. pp.[4.]

425722

Roberts (E.F.) On Shakspere. From
[Hood's Magazine,] Vol. 9.

1848.

558103

Robinson (N.L.) Shakespeare: an
address delivered at the Shakespeare
Celebration, April 25th, 1932. In
The Central Literary Magazine.
Vol.30. 1931-32.

407289

[RUSSELL (G. W.)]
The Living torch, [by] A.E. Edited
by M. Gibbon with an introductory
essay. [Containing "Shakespeare and
the blind alley" and other Shakespearian
references]. 1937.

473582

Rylands (G.H.W.) Shakespeare and his
England.[Broadcast] 21st April,
1947. ff.30. Typescript.

583266

SAINTSBURY (G. [E. B.])
A History of Elizabethan literature.
[With a bibliographical index and a
chapter on Shakespeare.]
1887.
For other editions of this work check
the main sequence under the author's
name.

539185

SENGUPTA (SUBODH CHANDRA)
Shakespeare the man.
IN Shakespeare commemoration volume,
edited by Taraknath Sen. (Calcutta)
1966.

764382

Shahani (R.G.) The Sentimental
autobiography of Shakespeare.
From [The Asiatic Review, New
Series,] Vol. 36.

[1940].

521316

Shakespeare not a man of parts.
IN All the Year Round, Vol. 11.
1864.

38504

Shakespeare the bookman: a legal
document which shows that he was
the possessor of a library, and
challenges the theory that he was
illiterate. From The Sphere, April
21st, 1934. pp.[4.]

419847

Shakespeare's mind. In The Times
Literary Supplement, 1946.

1946.

580183

— SHERLOCK (M.)
Letters from an English traveller
[including one on Shakespeare].
Translated from the French original
printed at Geneva. With notes.
pp. xiv, 74.   1780.

536094

— Sherman (S.P.) On contemporary
literature. [With a chapter,
Shakespeare, our contemporary, and
other references to Shakespeare.]

(New York)   1917.

530369

— Sisson (C.J.) The Mythical sorrows
of Shakespeare. pp.28.

[1934.]

(British Academy Annual Shakespeare
Lecture, 1934.)

422579

— SISSON (CHARLES JASPER)
Shakespeare.   (British Book News.
Bibliographical Series of Supplements.
Writers and their Work, No. 58)
pp. 50.
port.   bibliog.   1955.

645584

— Sisson, Charles Jasper
Shakespeare the writer. IN

STRATFORD PAPERS ON SHAKESPEARE
delivered at the 1960 Shakespeare
Seminar. (Toronto)   1961.

667140

— Slade (F.E.) On reading Shakespeare.
In The Poetry review, Vol.31.

1940.

524163

— SMITH (HALLETT D.)
In search of the real Shakespeare.
IN The Yale Review, Vol. 40.   1951.

592685/40

— SMYTH (G. L.)
William Shakspeare.   IN Smyth (G. L.)
Biographical illustrations of St. Paul's
Cathedral and Westminster Abbey.
                  1843.   68705
        ———— IN Smyth (G. L.) The Worthies
of England.   1850.   546938

— STEPHEN ([Sir] L.)
Self-revelation of Shakespeare.
IN Booklovers Edition [of] Shakespeare
[Vol. 11].   [1937]
University Society, New York.

475456

— Stephen ([Sir]L.) Shakespeare as a
man. In The National Review, Vol.37.

1901.

158872

— STEPHENS (J.)
Essayes and characters, 1615. IN
HALLIWELL (J. O.) Books of characters.
                              1857.
Contains a character of "A Base
mercenary poet", believed to be
modelled on Shakespeare.
Edn. limited to 25 copies.

59738

— SUMNER (MARY B.)
Essay on William Shakspere.   pp. xvi,
64.
manuscript.   ports.   illus.
facsimiles.   1907.

592300

—[Swanwick (Anna)] William Shakespeare,
1564-1616. From Swanwick (Anna)
Poets, the interpreters of their
age.

[1892]

431269

— SYMON ([Sir] J. H.)
Shakespeare quotation: a lecture
delivered before the Adelaide
University Shakespeare Society at
Adelaide.   pp. 63.   1901.
Printed for private circulation.

395747

— TITTERTON (W. R.)
An Afternoon tea philosophy [: essays,
with a chapter "The Extinction of
Shakespeare"].   pp. 96.   1909.

424824

— TUCKER (W. J.)
College Shakespeare [: an account of
his life and work.]
bibliog.   port.   1932.

392299

— URBAN (SYLVANUS) [pseud.]
Table talk: The Study of Shakespeare;
Judge Madden on Shakespeare; What we
know concerning Shakespeare; The
Shakespeare of Stratford and the
Shakespeare of "Hamlet".   IN The
Gentleman's Magazine, Vol. 286.
                              1899.

147488

—[Vredenburg (E.W.)] Memoir of Shakespeare. In The Shakespeare Birthday
Book. With 4 illustrations in colour
by J.H. Bacon & others. pp.67.

[1921].

438184

— WAREING (ALFRED [J.])
Enter Shakespeare.   IN ISAAC (WINIFRED
F. E. C.) Alfred Wareing: a biography.
With forewords by J. Bridie, I. Brown,
Rt. Hon. W. Elliot and Sir J. R.
Richmond.
ports. illus. facsimiles.   [1950.]

614427

WEBER[-EBENHOF] (ALFRED [von])
Farewell to European history. 1947.
International Library of Sociology
and Social Reconstruction.
Includes a chapter "The Loosening
of dogma and the break-through into
the depths: Shakespeare".
585106

WHIBLEY (CHARLES)

Shakespeare: the poet of England. FROM
Blackwood's Magazine, No. 1207. pp.[14.]
1916.

667278

WHIPPLE (E. P.)
Shakespeare, the man and the dramatist.
IN The Atalntic Monthly, vol. 19.
1867.

19365

WHITE (W.)
Osler on Shakespeare, Bacon, and
Burton. With a reprint of his
"Creators, transmuters, and trans-
mitters as illustrated by Shakespeare,
Bacon, and Burton." [With biblio-
graphical notes.] FROM Bulletin of
the History of Medicine, Vol. 7.
(Baltimore)
facsimile. 1939.

565596

WILKES (J.)
William Shakespeare. IN Wilkes (J.)
Encyclopaedia Londinensis, Vol. 23.
[Edited by G. Jones.] 1828.
Portrait wanting.
537155

William Shakspeare. FROM Every Month,
Vol. 1. (Liverpool)
port. 1864.

555516

William Shakespeare. FROM Great
Thoughts, [Vol. 9.]
port. illus. [1888.]

550795

WILLIAMS (C. [W. S.])
William Shakespeare. IN Williams
(C. [W. S.]) Stories of great names.
With notes by R. D. Binfield. (Oxford)
map. 1937.

479406

Wilson (H.S.) Guesses at Shakespeare.
pp.[5.] In The Gentleman's Magazine,
Vol.281. 1896.

1896.

136240

WILSON [J.]
A Few words on Shakespeare. IN
Wilson [J.] Essays, critical and
imaginative, Vol. 3: Works, Vol. 7.
1857.

34601

WILSON (J. D.)
The Elizabethan Shakespeare: Annual
Shakespeare Lecture, 1929. IN
Proceedings of the British Academy,
[Vol. 15] 1929. [1932] 401892
_____ IN Aspects of Shakespeare:
British Academy lectures.
1933. 390430

WILSON (J. D.)
The Essential Shakespeare: a biographical adventure. [With bibliographical
notes.] (Cambridge)
port. 1932. 391410
_____ Another edn. 1946. 574449

[WILSON (JOHN DOVER)
The Essential Shakespeare.] Personal
choice [: a radio programme in which]
D. Bower [reads] a passage from "The
Essential Shakespeare", by J. D. Wilson.
[Broadcast] 21st February, 1944.
pp. 4.
typescript.

547998

WORDSWORTH (WILLIAM)
[Two] letters [relating to
Shakespeare]. IN BROUGHTON (L. N.)
ed., Some letters of the Wordsworth
family, now first published. With
a few unpublished letters of Coleridge
and Southey and others. (Ithaca, N.Y.)
frontis. 1942.
Cornell Studies in English, 32.

542115

YEATMAN (J. P.)
The Gentle Shakspere: a vindication.
3rd edn. (augmented). (Shakespeare
Society of New York)
ports. facsimile. 1904. 405091
_____ 4th edn. (augmented). (Derby)
ports. facsimile. 1906. 467158

YOUNG (GEORGE MALCOLM)
Shakespeare and the termers. Annual
Shakespeare Lecture, 1947. IN
Proceedings of the British Academy,
1947. [1951.]

620388

ZANONI [pseud.]
Ibsen and the drama [with a chapter
"Shakspere vindicated".] [1895.]

495585

The Shakespeare Almanack for 1870.
1870.
Second copy, interleaved
467485

Shakespeare and Co. Unlimited, by
Shakespeare & Co. [: spirit messages
received and] compiled by Mrs. D. O.
Roberts. [1950.]

616141

Shakespeare and Co. Unlimited
Elizabethan episode, incorporating
Shakespeare and Co., Unlimited [:
spirit messages received and compiled
by Mrs. Daisy O. Roberts].
port. [1961.]

666936

Shakespeare and mental pathology [:
a review of "Shakespeare et la pathologie mentale" by A. Adnès].   IN
The British Medical Journal, Jan.-
June, 1935.   1935.

437530

Shakespeare and Terpsichore.   FROM
All the Year Round [, Vol. 19].
1868.

554164

Shakespeare, and the new discovery
[by J. P. Collier of a 1632 folio
with MS. corrections].   FROM Fraser's
Magazine, Vol. 47.   1853.

558097

SHAKESPEARE ANNIVERSARY COMMITTEE
Shakespeare in North America. (New
York)
illus.   1964.

740864

[SHAKESPEARE ASSOCIATION
Notices of meetings, accounts, etc.
Nov., 1932-9.]
416906

Shakespeare Association of America.
Bulletin.   Vol. 1 (1924) - Vol. 24
(1949).   [With annual bibliographies
from 1927.]   (New York)   24 vols.
ports.   illus.   1924-49.
Note: 1.   Wants Vol. 1. No. 3.
       2.   Continued as Shakespeare
            Quarterly, catal. no. 605711

400135

Shakespeare Association of Japan.
Catalogue of the exhibition of
Shakespeariana under the patronage
of the Shakespeare Association of
Japan and the British Ambassador,
held at Maruzen Co.,Ltd. Tokyo,
May 1933. pp.82.

[Tokyo]   1933.

407934

Shakespeare-Bacon Controversy *see* Bacon-Shakespeare Controversy

Shakespeare Birthday Book *see* Birthday Books

Shakespeare Birthplace etc. Trust
see Stratford-upon-Avon (Birthplace,
etc.)

Shakspere Club, Stratford-upon-Avon
see Societies and Clubs.

Shakespeare Club, Wilson, N.C. *see*
Societies and Clubs.

Shakespeare Conference (Stratford-
upon-Avon) *see* Stratford-upon-Avon
(Conferences).

Shakespeare Deeds *see* Life of Shakespeare, Documents

Shakespeare discovery; is it the
poet's own handwriting? [: the
discovery of annotations probably
made by Shakespeare in a copy of
E. Hall's Union of the families
of Lancaster and York, 1550].
IN The Listener, Vol. 24.
illus.   map.   1940.

522770

Shakespeare done into French.   [By
J. R. Ware.   A Criticism of Le Juif
de Venise, translated by F. Dugué.]
IN The Atlantic Monthly, Vol. 6.
(Boston, Mass.)   1860.

19352

Shakespeare Exhibition *see* Exhibitions

Shakespeare Fellowship
PHILLIPS (GERALD WILLIAM) [pseud.
John Huntingdon]
Shake spears sonnets, addressed to
members of the Shakespeare Fellow-
ship.   pp. 23.   1954.
Privately printed.

645438

The Shakespeare Fellowship Newsletter,
1943, 1945-58.   15 vols.
1944 wanting.   Continued as
"Shakespearean Authorship Review".

666183

Shakespeare Fellowship Quarterly [: a
periodical attempting to prove that
Edward de Vere, Earl of Oxford, wrote
the works of Shakespeare].   Vol. 1
(Dec. 1939 - Nov. 1940) - Vol. 9,
No. 2 (1948).   (New York)
ports.   illus.   map.   9 vols.
1939-48.
Vols. 1-4 called News letter.   All
published.

562696

Shakespeare Festival *see* Festivals

Shakespeare Gallery *see* Boydell
Gallery; Illustrations

Shakspeare hand-book [:quotations].

1860.

57883

Shakespeare - his biographers and
critics. From Dublin University
Magazine, Vol.61.

[Dublin]   1863.

554156

"Shakespeare in Art" Exhibition
see Nottingham

Shakespeare in Israel: A Bibliography
for the years ca. 1950-1965. IN
Shakespeare Quarterly XVII: 3. pp.291-
306. (New York)   1966.

605711

Shakespeare in Washington [: an
article on the Folger Shakespeare
Library]. IN Theatre Arts, Vol. 27.
(New York)   1943.

                    548672

Shakespeare Head Press Publications

——Ariel, the Stratford-upon-Avon
Messenger, No. 1, May 5th, 1926.
[Issued during the General Strike.]
ff. 1. (Printed by the Shakespeare
Head Press)   1926.

                    392851

—— Bransom (J.S.H.) The Tragedy of
King Lear.
          (Oxford)   1934.

                    417733

——England's Helicon, reprinted from the
edition of 1600, with additional poems
from the edition of 1614 [: a collection
of Elizabethan poetry.   With introduction and notes by H. Macdonald].
facsimile.   1925.   556957
The Haslewood Books.
———— No. 19 of 50 special copies.
              1925.   573557

——FRIPP (E. I.)
Note on the proposed publication (by
the Shakespeare Head Press) of the
Chamberlains' accounts of Stratford-
upon-Avon.   IN PACY (F.) The
Shakespeare Head Press at Stratford-
upon-Avon.   A paper read, 5th May,
1916 at a meeting to commemorate the
Shakespeare tercentenary.   Reprinted
from The Library Association Record,
July-Aug. 1916. – pp. 10. (Aberdeen)
                              1916.

                    545619

——JONSON (B.)
Poems, [including 'To the reader'
and 'To the memory of my beloved
the author, Mr. William Shakespeare,
and what he hath left us'.]   Edited
by B. H. Newdigate, [with a preface
and notes.] (Oxford)
port.   facsimiles.   1936.

                    451673

— Law (E.) Shakespeare's garden,
Stratford-upon-Avon. pp.34.
Illus.

          (Stratford-upon-Avon)   1924.

                    411878

—— List of books printed and published
by A. H. Bullen in the house of
Julius Shaw, the friend of Shakespeare
and the first witness to the poet's
will.   pp. 16. (Stratford-upon-
Avon)
illus.   1915.

                    545618

——The Phoenix and turtle, by W. Shakespeare,
J. Marston, G. Chapman, B. Jonson and
others: [facsimile reproduction of
"Poeticall essaies, 1601"] edited, [with
introduction and notes] by B. H.
Newdigate.   pp. xxiv, 31.   (Oxford)
frontis.   1937.

                    467868

——RENSHAW (C[ONSTANCE] A.)
Freeman of the hills [: poems,
including a poem "Shakespeare knew".]
(Oxford)   1939.

                    499246

——SHAKESPEARE
Works.   (Stratford-on-Avon)
ports.   10 vols. 1904-1907. 517534
No. 40 of 1,000 copies printed on hand-
made paper.
———— No. 722 of 1,000 copies printed
on hand-made paper.   498104

——SHAKESPEARE
Works.   [With glossary.]   (Oxford)
port.   1934.   426228
———— Another edn. 1944.   550173

——SHAKESPEARE
The Players' Shakespeare.   (Ernest Benn,
Ltd.)   7 vols.   1923-7.   305149
The Merchant of Venice; Love's labour's
lost; A Midsommer night's dream;
Cymbeline; Julius Caesar; Macbeth;
King Lear.   Printed litteratim from the
First Folio of 1623, and illustrated by
artists interested in the modern stage.
With introduction by H. Granville-Barker.
Printed at the Shakespeare Head Press.
———— Edition limited to 106 signed
copies.   Lacks "King Lear".

                    488544

——Shakespeare's Songs.   [Edited by
A. H. Bullen.]   pp. [viii], 33.
                    1907.   205814
Edn. limited to 510 copies: No. 35.
———— Another copy, No. 478. 399479
———— Another edn.   1912.   559905
———— Another edn.   pp. 40.   No. 393
of an edn. limited to 400 copies.
                    1920.   419584

——Shakespeare's Sonnets.   (Stratford-
upon-Avon)   1912.
Edn. limited to 510 copies, of which
this is No. 494.

                    547445

—— Shakespeare's sonnets.   [Edited with
a prefatory note by G. W. Phillips.]
(Oxford)   1934.   420135
———— Another copy.   421941

——SHAKESPEARE
The Sonnets of William Shakespeare [:
the text prepared for the Stratford
Town Edition, by H. A. Bullen].
(Oxford)   1945.

                    559695

——SYKES (H. D.)
Sidelights on Shakespeare.   (Stratford-
upon-Avon)   1919.

                    279416

Shakespeare Head Press *works relating to*

— PACY (F.)
The Shakespeare Head Press at Stratford-
upon-Avon.   A paper read, 5th May,
1916 at a meeting to commemorate the
Shakespeare tercentenary.   With a note
by E. I. Fripp on the proposed publication (by the Shakespeare Head Press) of
the Chamberlains' accounts of Stratford-
upon-Avon.   Reprinted from the Library
Association Record, July-Aug. 1916.
pp. 10.   (Aberdeen)   1916.

545619

— [Prospectus of] The Works of William
Shakespeare, gathered into one
volume. pp.[4.]

(Oxford)   1934.

421991

Shakespeare Institute
see also **Stratford-upon-Avon**, Summer School

—   Birmingham University. The
Shakespeare Institute, Stratford-upon-
Avon. pp.8. [Birmingham].
[1954.]

646236

— Director's report, 1951-1957- [and]
News letter [No. 2] 1956-57-1962.
(Stratford-upon-Avon: Shakespeare
Institute)   1951-1962.
All issued.
667503

— DUBNO (MARIA)
The Birmingham University Shakespeare
Institute Library, Stratford-upon-Avon
[: Paper] 2 [of] Shakespeare in the
Library: a symposium. IN Open Access,
Vol.10, N.S., No.2. (Birmingham)
1962.

667074

— Newspaper cuttings: The Shakespeare
Institute, Stratford-upon-Avon.
1951-

634296

— NICOLL (ALLARDYCE)
The "Basic" use of microfilm [: at the
Shakespeare Institute]. IN PMLA:
Publications of the Modern Language
Association of America, Vol.68. (Menasha,
Wis.)   1953.

428321/68

— [SHAKESPEARE FESTIVAL, STRATFORD-UPON-AVON
Programme of public lectures and
recitals, &c., including the Annual
Summer School, arranged each year by
the Royal Shakespeare Theatre, the
University of Birmingham, the
Shakespeare Birthplace Trust, and the
British Council, at Stratford-upon-
Avon.]   (Birmingham and Stratford-
upon-Avon)   1947-

645712

—   The SHAKESPEARE INSTITUTE AT
STRATFORD-UPON-AVON: a centre for
postgraduate study of sixteenth- and
seventeenth-century life and literature.
pp.16. Illus. (Birmingham)
1962.

667280

— see also Stratford-upon-Avon Studies

The Shakespeare International Alliance,
No. 2, April 1914.   1914.
All others wanting.   Printed for
private circulation only.
535364

Shakespeare-Jahrbuch see under
German Shakespeariana: Societies
Deutsche Shakespeare-Gesellschaft.

Shakespeare-land: the world's great
travel shrine. [2nd edn.] pp. 22.
(Great Western Railway Company)
port.   illus.   maps.   1913.

549761

The Shakespeare Library *edited by* Sir I. Gollancz

— LODGE (THOMAS)
Lodge's 'Rosalynde', [1590]: the
original of Shakespeare's "As you
like it".   Edited, [with introduction and notes, etc.] by W. W.
Greg.   [2nd edn.]   1931.

388882

— The Shakspere allusion-book: a collection of allusions to Shakspere from
1591 to 1700, originally compiled by
C. M. Ingleby, L[ucy] T. Smith and
F. J. Furnivall, with the assistance
of the New Shakspere Society.   Re-
edited, revised, and re-arranged, with
an introduction by J. Munro (1909), and
now re-issued with a preface by Sir E.
[K.] Chambers.
2 vols.   1932.
392943

— SIDGWICK (F.)
The Sources and analogues of A Midsummer-night's dream.
facsimile.   1908.
Large paper copy.
480726

——The Troublesome reign of King John: the original of Shakespeare's "Life and death of King John". Edited [with introduction, appendixes and notes] by F. J. Furnivall and J. Munro. (Chatto & Windus)
  facsimile. 1913. 240792
  ———— Another copy. With Oxford University Press label pasted over imprint. 1913. 542629

Shakespeare Library, Birmingham <u>see</u> Birmingham

Shakespeare Lodge of Freemasonry
Stratford-upon-Avon

—— MASONRY: hymns, odes, songs Written and compiled for the Masonic jubelee [sic], at Shakespear Lodge, Stratford on Avon, 4th June, 1793. pp. 22. (Birmingham) [1793.]
  Photostat copy made Nov. 1951 from the original at Shakespeare's Birthplace.
  621222

Shakespeare-mad [: Shakespeare's three-hundredth birthday in London and Stratford.] <u>In</u> All the Year Round. Vol.11.
  1864.
  38504

Shakespeare Made Easier

—— STOPFORTH (LOURENS MARTHINUS DANIEL)
  Henry the Fourth, Part 1: retold in modern English prose. (Cape Town: Nasionale Boekhandel Bpk.)
  [1962.]
  Shakespeare Made Easier.
  667584

—— STOPFORTH (LOURENS MARTHINUS DANIEL)
  Henry the Fifth retold in modern English prose. (Cape Town)
  illus. [1963.]
  Shakespeare Made Easier.
  668209

—— STOPFORTH (LOURENS MARTHINUS DANIEL)
  Macbeth: retold in modern English prose. (Nasionale Boekhandel, Cape Town) [1962.]
  Shakespeare Made Easier
  667583

—— STOPFORTH, L.M.D.
  The Tempest, retold in modern English prose by L.M.D. Stopforth. [c.1963.]

  illus. Shakespeare made easier.
  668208

Shakespeare Memorial National Theatre *see* National Theatre Project

Shakespeare Memorial Theatre, Stratford-upon-Avon *see* Stratford-upon-Avon (Royal Shakespeare Theatre)

Shakespeare music. In three acts. <u>In</u> All the Year Round, Vol.9.
  1863.
  38502

The SHAKESPEARE NEWSLETTER

Vol.1- Ports. Illus. (New York)
  1951-
  666182

[Shakspeare portfolio: illustrations to Shakspeare, by R. Smirke and others.]
95 plates. [1821-34]
Imperfect, 3 plates missing.
  426536

Shakespeare Press Publications

—— CHAMBRUN (C[LARA] LONGWORTH de)
  My Shakespeare, rise!: recollections of John Lacy, one of His Majesty's players. With preface by A. Maurois. Illustrated by R. Genicot. (Stratford-on-Avon: Shakespeare Press) 1935.
  442986

—— Gesta Romanorum: the old English versions, edited from manuscripts in the British Museum and University Library Cambridge; with an introduction and notes [including bibliographical notes] by Sir F. Mac___n. [Including "Theodosius th'emperoure": the tale of King Lear; and "Selestinus a wyse emperoure" and "Ancelmus the emperour", the last two containing incidents used by Shakespeare in The Merchant of Venice.] (Roxburghe Club)
  engraved tp. 1838.
  552609

—— GRUNER (E. H.)
  With golden quill: a cavalcade, depicting Shakespeare's life and times. With a Tudor cameo (as preamble) by W. Jaggard. (Stratford-on-Avon)
  ports. illus. bibliog. 1936.
  Edn. limited to 500 copies.
  459912

—— JAGGARD (W.)
Shakespeare and the Tudor Jaggards.
[Privately reprinted from the
"Stratford-upon-Avon Herald"].
pp. 12.   (Stratford-on-Avon)
illus.   [1934.]
Issue limited to 500 copies.

419567

—— JAGGARD (W.)
Shakespeare once a printer and
bookman: lecture at Stationers'
Hall, London, 20th Oct., 1933.
pp. 34.   (Stratford-on-Avon)
port.   illus.   [1934.]
Printing Trade Lectures.   Twelfth
Series.
Edn. limited to 450 copies.

419570

Shakespeare Problems *edited by* A. W. Pollard and John Dover Wilson

—— [1] POLLARD (A. W.)
Shakespeare's fight with the pirates
and the problems of the transmission
of his text.   (Cambridge)
                    1920-   287221
_____ 2nd edn. revised with an introduction.   1937.   472130

—— 2. POLLARD (A. W.), GREG (W. W.),
THOMPSON (E. M.), WILSON (J. D.) &
CHAMBERS (R. W.)
Shakespeare's hand in the play of Sir
Thomas More; with the text of the
Ill May Day Scenes, edited by W. W.
Greg.   (Cambridge)
bibliog.   1923.

308052

—— 3. ALEXANDER (PETER)
Shakespeare's Henry VI and Richard III.
With an introduction by A. W. Pollard.
(Cambridge)
bibliog.   1929.

359794

—— 4. WILSON (JOHN DOVER)
The Manuscript of Shakespeare's Hamlet
and the problems of its transmission:
an essay in critical bibliography.
(Cambridge)
2 vols.   1934.

421320

—— 5. YATES (FRANCES AMELIA)
A Study of Love's labour's lost.
(Cambridge)
bibliog.   1936.

450742

—— 6. DUTHIE (GEORGE IAN)
The "Bad" Quarto of Hamlet: a critical
study.   [With a foreword by W. W.
Greg.]   (Cambridge)
bibliog.   1941.

522178

—— 7. WALKER (ALICE)
Textual problems of the First Folio:
Richard III, King Lear, Troilus &
Cressida, 2 Henry IV, Hamlet, Othello.
(Cambridge)
bibliog.   1953.

633690

——8. SISSON (CHARLES JASPER)
New readings in Shakespeare.
(Cambridge)
2 vols.   facsimiles.   1956.

665182-3

Shakespeare Quarterly, No. 1, Summer
1948.   Issued under the auspices of
the Austrian Shakespeare Society.
ports.   illus.   1948.
All published.

610897

The Shakespeare Quarterly Vol. 1-
(Bethlehem, Pa.:   Shakespeare
Association of America)
ports.   illus.   1950-
Previously issued as Shakespeare
Association of America Bulletin, see
catal. no. 400135.

605711

Shakespeare Quatercentenary 1964 <u>see</u>
Quatercentenary 1964

Shakespeare rare print collection.
Edited by S. Eaton.   Connoisseur edn.
                    1900.   176137
Published for private circulation.
_____ No. 470 of edn. published for
private circulation. 1900.   548051

Shakespeare Riband

—— GROVES (SYLVIA)
Coventry ribbons and ribbon pictures.
[With references to the Shakespeare
riband.]   IN Country Life, Vol. 103.
illus.   1948.

170680/103

SHAKESPEARE SEMINAR, 5-8 December 1964
[: lectures given at Sahitya Akademi,
New Delhi]. (New Delhi)   1964.

typescript.   744153

SHAKESPEARE SOCIETY OF JAPAN
Shakespeare studies, Vol.1, 1962-
                    (Tokyo)

667505

THE SHAKESPEARE SOCIETY OF WASHINGTON
Programmes, 1926-54.   [Washington]
1929-30; 1938-39; 1939-40; 1940-41
wanting.

645713

Shakespeare Stage Society

—— PURDOM (CHARLES BENJAMIN)
The Crosby Hall "Macbeth": notes on
the production, a contribution to
the Festival of Britain, at Crosby
Hall, Chelsea, May 1951.   pp. 20.
1951.
Shakespeare Stage Society.

620879

—— The SHAKESPEARE STAGE: the
quarterly bulletin of the Shakespeare
Stage Society, Nos. 1-7.
1953-54.

666647

SHAKESPEARE STUDIES: an annual gathering
of research, criticism, and reviews.
Edited by J. Leeds Barroll. [Vol.] 1-
(Cincinnati, Ohio)   1965-

750317

Shakespeare Survey: an annual survey
of Shakespearian study & production.
[Vol.] 1-   [With]indexes.
(Cambridge)
ports.   illus.   plans.   dgms.
tables.   facsimiles.   bibliogs.
1948-

590674

Shakespeare Survey list of books and
articles [Nos. 1-35].   [Bibliographies
taken from Shakespeare Survey: an
annual survey edited by A. Nicoll.]
typescript.   1946-58.

596641

Shakespeare talks with uncritical
people [concerning Shakespeare's
plays.]   IN The Monthly packet of
evening readings for members of the
English Church.   New series, Vols.
25-28.
4 vols.   1878-9.

530287

Shakespeare v. Perkins: the concluding
argument.   [A reply to The Battle of
the commentators, by F. Bowen, in
North American Review, Vol. 78.]
FROM [Putnam's Monthly Magazine,]
Vol. 3.   [New York]   1854.
For "Battle of the commentators" by
F. Bowen, see catal. no. 41808.

562636

Shakespeare's Birthplace, etc. Trust *see*
Stratford-upon-Avon, Birthplace

Shakespeare's Brooch *see* **Relics of**
Shakespeare

Shakespeare's Cliff *see* **Kent**

Shakespeare's Company *see* **Stage History and**
Production, Elizabethan and Jacobean Period

Shakespeare's Country *see* **Warwickshire and**
Shakespeare's Country

Shakespeare's England: an account of
the life & manners of his age.   [By
various writers.   (Oxford)
bibliogs.   illus.   facsimiles.
2 vols.   1917.

435745

SHAKESPEARE'S ENGLAND. By the Editors of
Horizon Magazine in consultation with
L.B. Wright.   1964.

illus. Cassell Caravel books.
743838

"Shakespeare's England" Exhibition 1912 *see*
London, Earl's Court

Shakespeare's England exhibition,
1564-1964.   1964.
illus.

767941

Shakespeare's great vision: where are
his words from?   FROM My Magazine,
1931.   pp. [8.]
illus.   [1931]

390792

Shakespeare's heart of love: psycho-
physiology [of the Sonnets.   1st
article].   FROM the Journal of Man,
Vol. 1.   (Philadelphia)
port.   1872.

564841

Shakspere's house.   FROM The
Gentleman's Magazine, Sept. 1847.
pp. [2.]   1847.

402701

Shakespeare's mind. In The Times
Literary Supplement, 1946.
1946.

580183

Shakspere's real life story.
pp. [4.]   (Bacon Society)   [1938.]

506944

Shakespeare's Spirit, pseud. see
Shatford (Sarah T.)

SHAKESPEARE'S TOMB, STRATFORD-ON-AVON [and] STRATFORD JUBILEE. FROM The Mirror of Literature, Amusement and Instruction, April 28th, 1827. Illus. pp.[32.]   1827.

667042

Shakespeare's young men.   IN The Westminster Review, N.S. Vol. 50.
1876.

19440

Shakespearean Authorship Review, Nos. 1-   (The Shakespearian Authorship Society)   1959-
Formerly The Shakespeare Fellowship News-Letter.

666271

Shakespearean Authorship Society formerly The Shakespeare Fellowsnip.

see: Shakespeare Fellowship.

Shakesperian melodies.   No. 1: The Passionate shepherd; No. 2: Green sleeves.   IN The Literary garland, New series, Vol. 3.   (Montreal)
1845.

480852

Shakspearean notes [on Hamlet, Antony and Cleopatra, Troilus and Cressida, and Macbeth].   No[s. 1 and] 2. FROM [Dublin University Magazine, Vol. 63.]   [Dublin] pp. 12. 1864.

559982

Shakespearean prompt-books of the seventeenth century see EVANS (G. BLAKEMORE) ed.

SHAKESPEAREAN RESEARCH OPPORTUNITIES: the report of the Modern Language Association of America conference. Edited by W. R. Elton.   No. 1- (Riverside, Cal.)   1965-

762628

Shaksperean Show-book.   [Programmes of a fancy fair, for the benefit of the Chelsea Hospital for Women; with original literary contributions, illustrations and music.   Edited by J. S. Wood.]   (Manchester)
[1884.] 69016
_____ [Another copy, imperfect.] (Manchester)   [1884.] 616770

SHALER (NATHANIEL SOUTHGATE)
Elizabeth of England: a dramatic romance.   (Boston)
5 vols.   1903.

420074

Shallow, Robert

— DRAPER (J. W.)
Robert Shallow, Esq., J.P.   FROM Neuphilologische Mitteilungen [Bd.] 38. [Helsinki]   1937.

497629

—[FARJEON (H.)]
Shakespeare's characters - Shallow and Silence [: scenes from Henry IV, Part 2].   Arranged [with comments] by H. Farjeon.   [Broadcast Sept. 4th, 1945.]   ff. 18.
typescript.   1945.

563610

— Newdigate (B.H.) Falstaff, Shallow and the Stratford musters. From London Mercury, February, 1927.

1927.

449507

SHAND (A. F.)
The Foundations of character: a study of the tendencies of the emotions and sentiments [with references to Shakespeare.]   1914.

286095

SHAND (J.)
"Macbeth" at the Prince's Theatre [London].   IN The Adelphi, Vol. 4.
1926-27.

368487

SHANKER (S.)
Shakespeare pays some compliments [in Richard III].   IN Modern Language Notes, Vol. 63.   (Baltimore, Md.)   1948.

439157/63

Shapin (Betty) An Experiment in memorial reconstruction [to show that the variance between the first Quarto and authentic texts of "Hamlet" may be attributed to the faulty memory of a hypothetical reporter making a deduced memorial reconstruction]. In The Modern Language Review, Vol.39.

(Cambridge)   1944.

563897

SHAPIRO (ISAAC ABY)
The Bankside theatres: early engravings. IN SHAKESPEARE SURVEY 1.   (Cambridge) bibliog.   illus.   plans.   facsimiles.
1948.

590674

Shapiro (I.A.)An Original drawing of the Globe Theatre.[With bibliographical notes.] Illus. In Shakespeare survey: an annual survey of Shakespearian study & production, [Vol.] 2.

(Cambridge)   1949.

598403

SHAPIRO (ISAAC ABY)
[Review of] A Companion to Shakespeare studies, edited by H. Granville-Barker and G. B. Harrison.   IN Adult Education, Vol. 7.   1934-5.

472305

SHAPIRO, ISAAC ABY
  Robert Fludd's stage-illustration
  [: the problem of identifying an
  illustration of the stage of Blackfriars
  Theatre]. FROM Shakespeare Studies 2.
  [Cincinnati, Ohio]   [1966.]

      pp.192-209.   761646

    SHAPIRO (ISAAC ABY)
  Shakespeare and Mundy. IN Shakespeare
  Survey, [Vol.] 14. (Cambridge)
                              1961.

                          666755

  SHAPIRO (ISAAC ABY)
    The Significance of a date.   facsimiles.
  IN SHAKESPEARE SURVEY 8.   (Cambridge)
    1955.

                          647706

  SHAPIRO, STEPHEN A.
    The Varying shore of the world:
  ambivalence in "Antony and Cleopatra".
  FROM Modern Language Quarterly,
  vol. 27, no. 1, March.   (Irvine,
  Cal.)   1966.
    pp. 18-32.
                          767191

  SHAPTER (W.)
    The Original of Falstaff: [Sir J.
  Oldcastle].   IN The Month, Vol. 93.
                              1899.

                          147490

  SHARMAN (CECIL)
    I know a bank: two-part song [from
  A Midsummer night's dream].   FROM
  The School Music Review, No. 451.
  pp. [4.]   1929.   518988
  _____ Another copy.   Differs from
  above.   1929.   594177

  SHARMAN (CECIL)
    Tell me where is fancy bred: two-
  part song [from The Merchant of
  Venice].   pp. 4.   1929.

                          519001

  SHARMAN (CECIL)
    When daisies pied: two-part song
  [from Love's labour's lost].   pp. 4.
                              1930.

                          519006

  SHARMAN (CECIL)
    When icicles hang by the wall: two-
  part song.
  [from Love's labour's lost].   pp. 8.
                              1931.
  Winthrop Rogers Edition of Choral Music
  for Festivals.
                          560291

  SHARP (Mrs. [ELIZABETH AMELIA]) ed.
    Sea-music: an anthology of poems and
  passages descriptive of the sea.
  [With a prefatory note.   Including
  poems by Shakespeare].   1887.
    [The Canterbury Poets]
                          459394

  SHARP (ROBERT FARQUHARSON)
    Travesties of Shakespeare's plays.
  IN Transactions of the Bibliographical
  Society, 2nd Series, Vol. 1 (: The
  Library, 4th series, Vol. 1.) 1920.

                          285638

SHARP (T.)
  An Epitome of the county of Warwick,
  containing a brief account of the
  towns, villages, and parishes.
  [With a chapter, Stratford-on-Avon].
                    1835.   61141
  _____ Another copy. 1835.   410630

SHARP (WILLIAM) [pseud. Fiona Macleod]
  "Timon of Athens".   pp. [7.]   IN
  Harper's Monthly Magazine, Vol. 116,
  1907-8.
    illus.   1908.

                          208781

SHARPE (ELLA FREEMAN)
  Collected papers on psycho-analysis.
  Edited by Marjorie Brierley. [Contains]
  "The Impatience of Hamlet"; "From
  King Lear to The Tempest"; [and] "An
  Unfinished paper on Hamlet".
  bibliog.   1950.

                          605922

SHARPE (ELLA [FREEMAN])
  The Impatience of Hamlet.   IN The
  International Journal of Psycho-analysis,
  Vol. 10.   1929.

                          361576

SHARPE (ELLA FREEMAN)
  An Unfinished paper on "Hamlet: Prince
  of Denmark".   Edited, with an intro-
  duction, by Marjorie Brierley.   IN
  The International Journal of Psycho-
  Analysis, Vol. 29.   (Institute of
  Psycho-Analysis)   1948.

                          306178/29

SHARPE (ROBERT BOIES)
  Irony in the drama: an essay on
  impersonation, shock, and catharsis.
  (Chapel Hill, N.C.)   1959.

                          685352

SHARPE (ROBERT BOIES
  The Real war of the theatres:
  Shakespeare's fellows in rivalry with
  the Admiral's men, 1594-1603.
  Repertories, devices, and types.
  (Boston)   1935.
    The Modern Language Association of
  America.   Monograph Series, 5.

                          443036

Sharpe, Robert Boies *works relating to*

——BALD (R. C.)
    [Review of] The Real war of the theatres:
  Shakespeare's fellows in rivalry with
  the Admiral's men, 1594-1603, by
  R. B. Sharpe.   FROM Englische Studien,
  Bd. 72.   (Leipzig)   1937.

                          497805

—— PRAZ (M.)
    [Review of] The Real war of the
  theatres, Shakespeare's fellows in
  rivalry with the Admiral's men, 1594-
  1603, by R. B. Sharpe.   IN English
  Studies, Vol. 19.   (Amsterdam) 1937.

                          485661

SHARPE (WILLIAM)
Hamlet.   FROM Modern Thought [, Vol.1].
                              [1879.]

                              554719

[SHATFORD (SARAH TAYLOR)]
Jesus' teachings, by Shakespeare's
Spirit, [pseud].   (New York) 1922.

                              434101

[SHATFORD (SARAH TAYLOR)]
My proof of immortality, with my
demiséd act.   By Shakespeare's Spirit
[pseud.] (New York)   1924.

                              430035

[SHATFORD (SARAH TAYLOR)]
This book for Him I name for Jesus'
sake, by Shakespeare's Spirit [pseud.]
[New York]   [1920]

                              434100

SHATTUCK, CHARLES H.
   The Shakespeare promptbooks: a
   descriptive catalogue. (Urbana, Ill.)
                              1965.

                              753834

SHATTUCK (CHARLES HARLEN)
Shakespeare's "Othello" and its actors.
FROM Players Magazine, Vol. 13.
(Peru, Nebraska)   1937.

                              563269

Shaw (Byam) illus.
LAMB (CHARLES and MARY [A.])
Tales from Shakspeare.   Illustrations
[from drawings made for the Chiswick
Shakespeare].   2nd impression. 1907.

                              457223

SHAW (G.)
Sigh no more, ladies: two-part song
for equal voices [from Much ado
about nothing].   (York)   1937.
York Series.

                              519000

Shaw (G.) Six Shakespeare songs for
   chorus and piano: [What shall he have
   that kill'd the deer, (As You Like
   It); When icicles hang by the wall,
   (Love's Labour's Lost); Over hill,
   over dale, [and] Ye spotted snakes,
   (Midsummer Night's Dream); Hey,
   Robin, jolly Robin, [and] When that
   I was and a little tiny boy,
   (Twelfth Night). pp. 38.

                              [1912.]

                              520352

SHAW (G.)
Tell me, where is fancy bred?: a
two part song [from The Merchant
of Venice].   pp. 4.   1937.
York Series

                              519002

SHAW (GEOFFREY,
When icicles hang by the wall. [Words
from Shakespeare's] Love's labour's
lost.   pp. 8.   1912.
Joseph Williams, Modern Festival Series
of Part Songs.   (St. Cecilia Series)

                              631058

Shaw (Geoffrey) ed.
ARNE [THOMAS AUGUSTINE]
Come away, death.   Words from
Shakespeare's "Twelfth Night".
Arranged for S.A.T.B. by G. Shaw.
pp. 4.   1909.
Novello's Part-song Book, Second
Series, No. 1169.

                              594179

Shaw (Geoffrey) ed.
ARNE [THOMAS AUGUSTINE]
Where the bee sucks.   Words from
Shakespeare's "The Tempest".   Arranged
as a part-song (S.A.T.B.) unaccompanied,
by G. Shaw.   pp. 4.   1909.
Novello's Part-song Book, Second
Series, No. 1112.

                              594178

Shaw (G.B.)   The Art of talking for
   the talkies [with references to
   Shakespeare.] Port. In World
   Film News, Vol. 1.

                              1936.

                              485419

[SHAW (GEORGE BERNARD)]
Barry Sullivan, Shakespear and Shaw,
by G.B.S.   FROM [Strand Magazine]
Vol. 94.
illus.   1947.

                              586889

SHAW, GEORGE BERNARD
Cymbeline refinished

For editions of this play see under
English Editions: Cymbeline:
Alterations &c.

SHAW (GEORGE [BERNARD])
"The Dark Lady of the sonnets",
produced by P. Creswell.   [Broadcast
in the] National [Programme],22nd April,
1938.   ff. 14.
typescript.

                              481193

SHAW (GEORGE BERNARD)
"The Dark lady of the sonnets".   Produced by D. Allen.   [Broadcast]
2nd October, 1955.   ff. [1], 18.
typescript.

                              665126

SHAW (GEORGE BERNARD)
The Dying tongue of great Elizabeth
[: a review of Beerbohm Tree's
production of "Much ado about nothing",
1905].   IN Shaw [G. B.] on theatre.
                              1958.

                              693464

Shaw (G.B.) Forbes Robertson's Hamlet.
In Ward (A.C.)[ed.] Specimens of
English dramatic criticism:
selected and introduced.

   (Oxford)   1945.

(The World's Classics)

                              563732

SHAW (GEORGE BERNARD)

John Barrymore's Hamlet. IN Shaw [G.B.]
on theatre.   1958.

693464

SHAW ([GEORGE] BERNARD)

London music in 1888-89: [criticisms
contributed to the "Star" newspaper.
With Shakespearian references.
(Works, Standard Edn., Vol. 32.)]
port.   1937.

470414

SHAW ([GEORGE]BERNARD)

Misalliance, The Dark lady of the
sonnets, [with a preface on Shakespeare],
and Fanny's first play.
                1928.   504568
_____ IN Works, Standard Edn., Vol.19.
                1932.   391891

Shaw (G.B.) Note. In Embassy Theatre.
[Programme of Cymbeline, by W.
Shakespeare and [G.]B. Shaw.
pp.[16].
                                     1937.

477459

SHAW (GEORGE BERNARD)

On cutting Shakespear. IN Shaw [G.B.]
on theatre.   1958.

693464

SHAW ([GEORGE] BERNARD)

Our theatres in the nineties [: criti-
cisms contributed to the Saturday
Review including criticisms of some of
Shakespeare's plays. (Works Standard
Edn. Vols. 12, 13, 16.)]
3 vols.   1932.

388864

SHAW ([GEORGE] BERNARD)

Pen portraits and reviews.   [With
references to Shakespeare: Works,
Standard Edn., Vol. 21.]   1932.

391893

SHAW (GEORGE BERNARD)

Plays & players: essays on the theatre.
Selected with an introduction by
A. C. Ward.   1952.
   World's Classics.

628613

Shaw ([G.]B.) Prefaces [to plays, etc.
With references to Shakespeare.]

1934.

421515

SHAW (GEORGE BERNARD)

Shakes versus Shav.   A Puppet play.
(Stratford-upon-Avon)
   illus.   [?1964.] 740198
_____ IN Shaw (G. B.) [Works.
Standard edn. Vol. 35.] 1950. 614733

SHAW (GEORGE BERNARD)

Shakespear: a standard text.
IN Shaw [G. B.] on theatre.   1958.

693464

SHAW (GEORGE BERNARD)

Shakespear and the Stratford-upon-
Avon Theatre: a plea for reconstruction.   IN Shaw [G. B.] on
theatre.   1958.

693464

SHAW (GEORGE BERNARD)

Shaw on Shakespeare: an anthology of
Bernard Shaw's writings on the plays
and production of Shakespeare. Edited
and with an introduction by E. Wilson.
                               1962.

666943

SHAW (GEORGE BERNARD)

Sullivan, Shakespear and Shaw.   IN
The Atlantic Monthly, Vol. 180.
(Boston, Mass.)   1947.   19347/180
_____ IN Shaw [G. B.] on theatre.
                1958.   693464

Shaw, George Bernard *works relating to*

—ARMSTRONG (WILLIAM A.)
   Bernard Shaw and Forbes-Robertson's
   Hamlet. IN Shakespeare Quarterly XV: 1.
   pp.27-31. (New York)   1964.

605711

— BARLING (E[DITH] M.)
   Back to G.B.S.; [or, A Midsummer
   nightmare]: Shaw Tercentenary Celebration, Malvern, A.D. 2156.   pp. 23.
                               [1931]

395652

— BOAS (FREDERICK SAMUEL)
   Joan of Arc in Shakespeare, Schiller,
   and Shaw.
   IN SHAKESPEARE QUARTERLY II: 1.
   pp. 35-45.
   (New York) 1951.

605711

— CHESTERTON (GILBERT KEITH)
   Shakespeare and Shaw.   IN Chesterton
   (G. K.) Sidelights on new London and
   Newer York, and other essays. 1932.

392229

— COLBOURNE (M.)
   The Real Bernard Shaw.   [With
   Shakespearian references.]
      ports.   illus.   1939.

507611

—COLLINS (P. A. W.)
   Shaw on Shakespeare.
   IN SHAKESPEARE QUARTERLY VIII.
   pp. 1-13.
   (New York)   1957.

605711

— Duffin (H.C.) The Quintessence of Bernard
   Shaw. Revised and enlarged edn. [With
   references to Shakespeare.]

1939.

501318

— Harris (F.) Shaw on Shakespeare : an open letter. <u>In</u> The Academy, Vol. 80.

1911.

231465

— HENDERSON (A.)
Bernard Shaw, playboy and prophet. Authorized [biography. With references to Shakespeare.]
ports. illus. 1932.

399241

— KRABBE (HENNING)
Bernard Shaw on Shakespeare and English Shakespearian acting. (Aarhus Universitet Acta Jutlandica. Humanistisk Serie 41. Aarsskrift 27. Supplementum B.) pp. 66. (København)
bibliog. 1955.

665061

— MacCARTHY (Sir DESMOND)
Shaw [: essays on his development as a dramatist.] 1951.
Includes "Dark lady of the sonnets: Mr. Shaw on Shakespeare".

613875

— PEARSON (H.)
Bernard Shaw: his life and personality. [With references to Shakespeare.]
bibliog. ports. 1942.

536261

— RATTRAY (R. F.)
Bernard Shaw: a chronicle and an introduction. [With Shakespearian references.] 1934.

415233

— RHYS (E.)
Shaw versus Shakespeare. IN The New Statesman and Nation, Vol. 3. (N.S. Jan.-June, 1932. 1932.

396297

— Sen Gupta (S.C.) The Art of Bernard Shaw. [With references to Shakespeare].

(Oxford) 1936.

453808

— SHAW ([GEORGE] BERNARD)
Shakes versus Shav [: a puppet play]. IN Works. Standard edn. Vol. 35. 1950.

614733

— SILVERMAN (ALBERT H.)
Bernard Shaw's Shakespeare criticism. IN PMLA: Publications of the Modern Language Association of America, Vol. 72. (Menasha, Wis.) 1957.

428321/72

— SMITH (J. PERCY)
Superman versus man: Bernard Shaw on Shakespeare. IN The Yale Review. New Series, Vol. 42. (New Haven, Conn.)
1952. 592685/N.S.42
_____ IN Stratford Papers on Shakespeare. (Toronto) 1963. 668006

— STAMM (RUDOLF)
George Bernard Shaw and Shakespeare's "Cymbeline". IN D.C. Allen, ed. "Studies in honor of T.W. Baldwin." (Urbana, Ill.) 1958.

666314

— WEST (E. J.)
G.B.S., music and Shakespearean blank verse. IN Elizabethan studies and other essays [, by various authors], in honor of George F. Reynolds. (Boulder, Col.)
bibliog. 1945.
Colorado University Studies. Series B. Studies in the Humanities. Vol. 2. No. 4.

569202

— WEST (E. J.)
G.B.S. on Shakespearean production. IN Studies in Philology, Vol. 45. (Chapel Hill, N.C.)
bibliog. 1948.

554520/45

— WEST (EDWARD J.)
Shaw, Shakespeare and Cymbeline. IN The Theatre Annual, 1950. (New York)
1950.

554521/1950

— ZBIERSKI (HENRYK)
Shakespeare criticism and the influence of George Bernard Shaw in the light of his "Dark Lady of the Sonnets". IN Poland's homage to Shakespeare. Commemorating the fourth centenary of his birth, 1564-1964. (Warsaw) 1965.

747846

SHAW (IDA)
The Value of the Shakespeare recitals [: part of The Vocal interpretation of poetry, a report on the Teachers' conference held on Sept. 11th, 1943]. IN The Poetry Review, Vol. 34. 1943.

560954

SHAW, JOHN
Cleopatra and Seleucus. FROM A Review of English Literature, Vol.7, no.4, Oct. 1966. 1966.

pp.79-86. 762625

SHAW, JOHN
Fortune and nature in "As you like it." FROM Shakespeare Quarterly, Vol.6, no.1, Winter 1955. (New York) 1955.

pp.45-50. 759523

SHAW, JOHN
King Lear: the final lines. FROM Essays in Criticism, Vol.16, no.3, July 1966. (Oxford) 1966.

pp.261-267. 759522

SHAW (JOHN)
The Staging of parody and parallels in
"I Henry IV".
IN SHAKESPEARE SURVEY 20.   (Cambridge)
1967.

766881

SHAW, JOHN
"What is the matter?" in Othello.
FROM Shakespeare Quarterly XVII: 2.
(New York)   1966.

pp.157-161.   759521

Shaw, Julius *works relating to*

—— The Shakespeare Head Press, Stratford-
upon-Avon. List of books printed and
published by A.H.Bullen in the house
of Julius Shaw, the friend of
Shakespeare and the first witness to
the poet's will. pp. 16. Illus.

(Stratford-upon-Avon)   1915.

545618

Shaw (M.[F.]) I know a bank: two-part
s.s. Words by W.Shakespeare [from
Midsummer Night's Dream]. pp.4.

1923.

(Cramer's Library of Unison and Part-Songs by
Modern Composers, No.7.)

560295

Shaw (M.[F.]) Over hill, over dale:
two-part s.s. Words by W.Shake-
speare [from Midsummer Night's
Dream]. pp.4.

1923.

(Cramer's Library of Unison and Part Songs by
Modern Composers, No.8.)

560294

Shaw (M.[F.]) This England. First
performed at the Royal Silver
Jubilee celebrations in Liverpool
Cathedral, May 5th and 12th, 1935.
Words by Shakespeare [from Richard
the Second]. Set to music for choir
and organ (or orchestra). pp.18.

(Oxford)   [1935.]

568497

Shaw (M.[F.]) You spotted snakes:
two-part song. Words by W.Shake-
speare [from Midsummer Night's
Dream]. pp.4.

1927.

(Cramer's Library of Unison and Part-Songs by
Modern Composers, No.36.)

560293

SHEARER (NORMA)
Juliet.   IN SHAKESPEARE (W.) Romeo and
Juliet: a motion picture edition.
Produced for Metro-Goldwyn-Mayer.
illus.   [1936]   457925.
Arthur Barker Edition.
—————— Random House Edition.

460419

SHEARMAN ([Sir] MONTAGUE)
History of football in England (from
"Athletics and football".   4th edn.)
[With references to Shakespeare.]
IN GARNETT (R.) [and others] eds.,
The International library of famous
literature, Vol. 13.
ports.   illus.   [c.1900.]

403693

SHEAVYN, PHOEBE
The Literary profession in the
Elizabethan age. 2nd edn., revised
throughout, by J.W. Saunders.
(Manchester)   1967.

764808

SHEDD (ROBERT G.)
The Great Lakes Shakespeare Festival in
Lakewood, Ohio: reaching new audiences.
IN SHAKESPEARE QUARTERLY XIII: 4.
pp. 559-563.
(New York) 1962.

605711

SHEDD (ROBERT G.)
The Great Lakes Shakespeare Festival:
consolidation and expansion.
IN SHAKESPEARE QUARTERLY XIV: 4.
pp. 455-459.
(New York)   1963.

605711

SHEDD (ROBERT GORDON)
The Great Lakes Shakespeare Festival,
1964: "Henry VI" - and "Hamlet", too!
IN Shakespeare Quarterly XV: 4.
pp.423-426. (New York)   1964.

605711

SHEDD (ROBERT GORDON)
The "Measure for Measure" of
Shakespeare's 1604 audience. (Ann
Arbor, Mich.)
bibliog.   typescript, 1953. micro-
film, positive copy.   1 reel, 35 mm.
1953.
University Microfilms.   Doctoral
Dissertation Series.

647063

SHEDD (ROBERT G.)
Shakespeare at Antioch, 1957: past
record and present achievement.
IN SHAKESPEARE QUARTERLY VIII:
pp. 521-525.
(New York)   1957.

605711

Sheep Shearing *see* Natural History

Sheffield

—— KEETON (G. W.) ed.
All right on the night: the book of
the Sheffield Central Secondary School
Boys' Shakespeare Society.   (Sheffield)
ports.   illus.   1929.

417053

—— Shakespeare in Sheffield [: a criticism of the Sheffield Shakespeare
Club]. pp. 24. (Stamford) 1822.

621024

—— SHEFFIELD CENTRAL SECONDARY SCHOOL
Programmes of Shakespearian performances. (Sheffield)
illus. 1918-1938.

472593

—— Sheffield Educational Settlement.
Programmes, tickets, etc. of
Shakespearian performances.

[Sheffield] 1930-52

425721

SHELDON (ESTHER K.)
Sheridan's "Coriolanus": an 18th-century
compromise.
IN SHAKESPEARE QUARTERLY XIV: 2.
pp. 153-161.
(New York) 1963.

605711

Shelley, Percy Bysshe *works relating to*

—— Blunden (E.) Shelley: a life story
[containing references to Shakespeare].
Port.

1946.

569129

—— CLARK (D. L.)
Shelley and Shakespeare [: Shelley's
knowledge of Shakespeare and his
indebtedness to him.] IN Publications
of the Modern Language Association
of America, Vol. 54. (Menasha, Wis.)
bibliog. 1939.

515058

—— JONES (F. L.)
Shelley and Shakespeare [by D. L. Clark]:
a supplement. IN Publications of the
Modern Language Association of America,
Vol. 59. (Menasha, Wis.) 1944.
For Shelley and Shakespeare, by
D. L. Clark, see catal. no. 515058.

560393

—— Langston (B.) Shelley's use of
Shakespeare. [With biblio-
graphical notes.] In The
Huntington Library Quarterly,
Vol.12.

(San Marino,Cal.)
1948-9.

494029/12

—— WATSON (SARA R.)
Shelley and Shakespeare [by D. L. Clark]
an addendum, A Comparison of Othello
and The Cenci. IN Publications of
the Modern Language Association of
America, Vol. 55. (Menasha, Wis.)
1940.
For Shelley and Shakespeare, by D. L.
Clark, see catal. no. 515058.

525077

Shelly (P.V.D.) The Living Chaucer.
[With bibliographical references,
and references to Shakespeare.]

(Philadelphia) 1940.

525010

[SHENSTONE (WILLIAM)]
Slender's ghost. IN [DODSLEY (R.) ed.,]
A Collection of poems by several
hands. [5th edn.] Vol. 5.
1758. 538522
_____ New ed., corrected.
1782. 99650

SHEPHERD (F. N.)
Shakspeare's birthplace: an artist's
pilgrimage to Stratford-upon-Avon.
pp. 16.
illus. 1864.

409500

Sheppard, Jack *works relating to*

—— BLEACKLEY (H.)
Jack Sheppard. [With a dialogue be-
tween Julius Caesar and Jack Sheppard.]
(Edinburgh)
ports. illus. 1933.
Notable British Trials

405062

SHEPPARD (Sir JOHN TRESIDDER)
Shakespeare's small Latin. IN The
Rice Institute Pamphlet, Vol. 44.
(Honston, Tex.) 1957.

288765/44

SHERBO (ARTHUR)
Dr. Johnson on Macbeth: 1745 and 1765.
IN The Review of English Studies.
New Series, Vol. 2. (Oxford) 1951.

318239/2/2

SHERBO (ARTHUR)
Dr. Johnson's "Dictionary" and
Warburton's "Shakespeare". IN
Philological Quarterly, Vol. 33.
(Iowa) 1954.

592684/33

SHERBO (ARTHUR)
The Proof-sheets of Dr. [S.] Johnson's
preface to Shakespeare. IN Bulletin of
the John Rylands Library, Vol.35, pp.206-
210. (Manchester)
1952.

182129/35

SHERBO (ARTHUR)
Samuel Johnson, editor of Shakespeare.
With an essay on "The Adventurer".
(Urbana, Ill.)
tables. bibliog.   1956.
Illinois Studies in Language and
Literature, Vol. 42.

665393

SHERBO (ARTHUR)
Warburton and the 1745 Shakespeare.
IN The Journal of English and Germanic
Philology, Vol. 51. (Urbana, Ill.)
1952.

600780/51

Sherbo, Arthur ed.
JOHNSON, SAMUEL
Johnson on Shakespeare.   Edited by
A. Sherbo with an introduction by
B. H. Bronson.   (New Haven, Conn.)
1968.
Yale edition of the works of Samuel
Johnson, Vols. VII, VIII.

774916-7

Sherbo (Arthur) ed.
JOHNSON (SAMUEL)
Notes to Shakespeare.   (Los Angeles:
William Andrews Clark Memorial Library)
3 vols.   1956-58.
Augustan Reprint Society Publications,
Nos. 59-60, 65-66, 71-73.

666070

Sherburn (G.[W.]) The Early career
of Alexander Pope. [With Shakespearian references.] Port. Illus.

(Oxford)   1934.

424469

[SHERIDAN (RICHARD BRINSLEY)]
Verses to the memory of Garrick.
Spoken as a monody at the Theatre Royal
in Drury-Lane.   [With references to
Shakespeare.]   pp. 15.
frontis.   1779.   540725
_____ 2nd edn.   1779.   480078

Sheridan, Richard Brinsley *works relating to*

RHODES (R. C.)
Harlequin Sheridan: the man and the
legends. [With Shakespearean
references.]
illus.   bibliog.   1933.

409056

SHELDON (ESTHER K.)
Sheridan's "Coriolanus": an 18th-
century compromise.   IN SHAKESPEARE
QUARTERLY XIV: 2.   pp. 153-161.
(New York)   1963.

605711

SHERLEY, LORRAINE
"King Lear": the stage, not the
closet.   IN CORDER, JIM W., ed.,
Shakespeare 1964 [: a record of the
celebrations of the Shakespeare
Quatercentenary at Texas Christian
University].   (Fort Worth, Tex.)
illus.   1965.

745402

SHERLOCK (MARTIN)
Letters from an English traveller
[including one on Shakespeare].
Translated from the French original
printed at Geneva.   With notes.
pp. xiv, 74.   1780.

536094

Sherman (L.A.) Shakespeare's first
principles of art. pp.[13]. In
Publications of the Modern Language
Association of America, Vol.10,1895.

(Baltimore)   1895.

428330

SHERMAN (S. P.)
On contemporary literature.   [With
a chapter, "Shakespeare, our contemporary", and other references to
Shakespeare.]   (New York) 1917.

530369

Sherwood (Margaret [P.]) The Formative
faculty of poetry [:with references to
Shakespeare.] *From* The Aryan path,
Vol. 7.

(Bombay)   1936.

484132

Sherzer (Jane) American editions of
Shakespeare, 1753-1866. In Publications
of the Modern Language Association
of America, Vol.22.

(Baltimore)   1907.

428342

Shewmake (E.F.) Shakespeare and Southern "You all". *From* American Speech,
October 1938.

(New York)   1938.

506177

SHEWRING (WALTER)
Come away, come away, Death: [a song].
Words from Twelfth Night. pp. 4.
(York)   1937.

472839

SHIELD (WILLIAM)
Honour, riches, marriage-blessing:
two-part song.   Words by Shakespeare
[from] "The Tempest".   Arranged by
R. Dunstan.   IN STEVENS (R. J. [S.])
The Cloud-capp'd towers: part song
for S.S.A.A.   [c.1920.]
  School Music Review No. 252.

                                    594167

SHIELD (WILLIAM)
The Load-stars [: a glee for three
voices] from Shakespeare['s Midsummer
Night's Dream].   pp. 5.   [c.1815.]

                                    600309

SHIELD (WILLIAM)
A New edition of Shakespear's "Poor
Barbara" [from "Othello": a glee].
pp. 6.   [?1795]
  Composer's signature on p. 6.

                                    628457

SHIELD (W.)
O happy fair; or, The Loadstars,
composed by W. Shield. [Words
from Midsummer night's dream.]
pp. [3.]   [c.1880.]
  Novello's Standard Glee Book.

                                    538796

SHIELD [W.]
Shakespeare's Duel and Lodestars,
set to music by Mr. Shield.   pp. 5.
                        [c.1796.]
  Signed by the composer.

                                    602192

Shillman (B.) The Play of Macbeth:
  its importance as tragedy: a
  lecture delivered to the British
  Empire Shakespeare Society, Dublin
  Branch. With a foreword by W.F.
  Trench. pp.28. Port.

                (Dublin)   [1926.]

                                    408187

SHIPLEY, JOSEPH TWADELL, ed.
  As you like it: a scene-by-scene
  analysis with critical commentary.
  (New York)   1964.

        Study master series.   668336

SHIPLEY, JOSEPH TWADELL, ed.
  Hamlet: a scene-by-scene analysis with
  critical commentary. (New York) 1963.

        Study master series.   743611

SHIPLEY, JOSEPH TWADELL, ed.
  Julius Caesar: a scene-by-scene analysis
  with critical commentary. (New York)
  1963.

        Study master series.   743612

SHIPLEY, JOSEPH TWADELL, ed.
  King Lear: a scene-by-scene analysis
  with critical commentary. (New York)
  1965.

        Study master series.   743610

SHIPLEY, JOSEPH TWADELL, ed.
  Macbeth: a scene-by-scene analysis with
  critical commentary. (New York) 1964.

        Study master series.   743614

SHIPLEY, JOSEPH TWADELL
  The Merchant of Venice: a scene-by-
  scene analysis with critical commentary.
  (New York)   1964.

        Study master series.   743615

SHIPLEY, JOSEPH TWADELL, ed.
  A Midsummer Night's Dream: a scene-by-
  scene analysis with critical commentary.
  (New York)   1964.

        Study master series.   743616

SHIPLEY, JOSEPH TWADELL, ed.
  Othello: a scene-by-scene analysis with
  critical commentary. (New York) 1963.

        Study master series.   743617

SHIPLEY, JOSEPH TWADELL, ed.
  Richard II: a scene-by-scene analysis
  with critical commentary. (New York)
                                    1964.

        Study master series.   668335

SHIPLEY, JOSEPH TWADELL, ed.
  Romeo and Juliet: a scene-by-scene
  analysis with critical commentary.
  (New York)   1964.

        Study master series. 743613

SHIPLEY, JOSEPH TWADELL, ed.
  Shakespeare's Sonnets: analytical notes
  and critical commentary. (New York)
                                    1963.

        Study master series. 743618

SHIPLEY, THE SALT GIRLS' HIGH SCHOOL
Programmes, etc., of Shakespearian
performances.   [Shipley]
  port.   1924-38.

                                    488033

Shipping *see* Sailors and the Sea

SHIRLEY, FRANCES ANN
  Shakespeare's use of off-stage sounds.
  (Lincoln, Neb.)   1963.

                                    667763

Shirley, James *works relating to*

— NASON (A. H.)
  James Shirley, dramatist: a biographical and critical study. [With
  references to Shakespeare.]   (New
  York)
  ports.   facsimiles.   bibliog.
                                    1915.
  Author's autograph on end paper.

                                    499297

— PARLIN (H. T.)
A Study in Shirley's comedies of London life [with references to Shakespeare]. (Austin, Texas) 1914. University of Texas, Studies in English, No. 2.

442433

— TANNENBAUM (S.A.) & TANNENBAUM (DOROThY R.)
James Shirley (a concise bibliography). ff. 42. (New York) typescript. 1946. Elizabethan Bibliographies, No. 34.

571626

SHIRLEY (J. W.)
Falstaff, an Elizabethan glutton. FROM Philological quarterly, Vol. 17. pp. 271-287. (Iowa) 1938.

493045

SHIRLEY, RAE
Jester of Stratford: a comedy in one act. 1964.

740340

SHIRLEY (WILLIAM)
Edward the Black Prince; or, The Battle of Poictiers: an historical tragedy after the manner of Shakespeare, as acted at the Theatre-Royal, Drury-Lane. pp. xvi, 72. 1750. 392237
_____ Another edn. (Dublin) 1750. 445736
_____ Regulated from the prompt-book by Mr. Hopkins, 1777. IN Bell's British Theatre, Vol. 16. 1778. 58016
_____ Another edn. 1779. 490017
_____ IN Sharpe's British Theatre, Vol. 3. 1804. 164735
_____ IN The British Theatre, Vol.14. 1808. 29708
_____ Hodgson's Juvenile Drama. [?1822] 171965
_____ IN The London Stage, Vol. 4. [c.1830] 69992
_____ IN British drama illustrated, Vol. 3. 1865. 58681
_____ Dicks' Standard Plays, No.116. [c.1883] 455698

SHOEMAKER (F.)
Extensions and exemplification of a modern aesthetic approach to world literature: Hamlet as example. IN Shoemaker (F.) Aesthetic experience and the humanities. [Edited by L. Grey.] (New York) bibliogs. 1943.

560536

SHOEMAKER (NEILLE)
The Aesthetic criticism of "Hamlet" from 1692 to 1699. IN SHAKESPEARE QUARTERLY XVI: 1. pp. 99-103. (New York) 1965.

605711

SHOEMAKER (WILLIAM HUTCHINSON)
Galdós' "La de los tristes destinos" and its Shakespearean connections. IN Modern Language Notes, Vol. 71. (Baltimore, Md.) 1956.

439157/71

Shoreditch *see* London

Shoreditch Shakespeare Festival

Faithfull (Lilian M.) The Evening crowns the day [: an autobiography. With references to Shakespeare and the Shoreditch Shakespeare Festival, July 6th, 1933.]
1940.

516878

SHORT (ERNEST HENRY)
Theatrical cavalcade [: a review of the British stage during the last fifty years. With references to Shakespeare.]
illus. 1942.

537042

A Short account of Stratford-on-Avon. (Pumphrey Bros.) [c.1880]

42699

Shorthand *see* Textual History, The Quartos

Shorthand, Works in

— LAMB (C. & MARY [A.])
Tales from Shakespeare: Hamlet. Illustrations by Astrid F. Gescheidt. Gregg shorthand plates by Winifred K. Richmond. pp. 46. (New York) [1931]

446936

— The Soviet Shakespeare [: article in shorthand]. IN Pitman's business education, Vol. 1, Oct. 1935-March 1936. [1936]

454995

Shottery *see* Warwickshire and Shakespeare's Country

SHOW: the magazine of the arts. A special report on the Bard today. Vol.IV, No.2: February 1964. (New York) 1964.

illus. 740825

SHOWELL (CHARLES)
Shakespeare's Avon from source to Severn. Illustrated with pen & ink drawings by the author. (Birmingham)
map. 1901. 156575
Large paper edn.: No. 61 signed by the author.
_____ Another copy. 169670

Showmen see Actors and Acting

SHROEDER (JOHN W.)
The Great Folio of 1623: Shakespeare's plays in the printing house. (Ann Arbor, Mich.) 1956.

665387

SHROEDER (JOHN W.)
'The Taming of a shrew' and 'The Taming of the shrew': a case re-opened. IN Journal of English and Germanic Philology, Vol. 57. (Urbana, Ill.) 1958.

600780/57

Shropshire

——KEEN (ALAN)
"In the quick forge and working-house of thought..." Lancashire and Shropshire and the young Shakespeare. Reprinted from the Bulletin of the John Rylands Library, Vol. 33. pp. [16]. (Manchester) 1951.

618919

SHUCHTER, J. D.
Prince Hal and Francis: the imitation of an action.
IN SHAKESPEARE STUDIES 3. (Cincinnati, Ohio) 1967.

771652

SHUKER, ARTHUR D.
The Dictator, according to Shakespeare's "The Merchant of Venice".

For editions of this play see under English Editions: The Merchant of Venice: Alterations &c.

SHULMAN, ROBERT
Shakespeare and the drama of Melville's fiction.
IN Pacific coast studies in Shakespeare. Edited by W. F. McNeir and T. N. Greenfield. (Eugene: Ore.) 1966.

768009

SHURTER (ROBERT L.)
Shakespearean performances in pre-revolutionary America. FROM The South Atlantic Quarterly, January 1937. (Durham, N.C.) 1937.

503864

SHUTTLEWORTH (BERTRAM)
Irving's Macbeth. IN Theatre Notebook, Vol. 5. 1950-51.

584117/5

Shylock *see* The Merchant of Venice, Characters — Shylock

SIBELIUS (JEAN JULIUS CHRISTIAN)
Vorspiel, erste und zweite Suiten für kleines Orchester aus der Musik zu Shakespeares "Der Sturm", Op. 109 Nr. 1-3. (København) 3 vols. [1954.]

641741-43

Siberia *see* Russia

SIBLEY (GERTRUDE M.)
The Lost plays and masques, 1500-1642 [including those having Shakespearian subjects]. (Ithaca, N.Y.) 1933. Cornell Studies in English.

407209

SICHEL (EDITH)
Michel de Montaigne [: a biographical study. With references to Shakespeare.]
ports. illus. facsimiles. bibliog. 1911.

432265

SICHEL (WALTER)
Types and characters: a kaleidoscope, [including a study of Shylock.]
port. [1925.]

487916

Sickness *see* Medicine and Hygiene

[Siddons (J.H.)] The Autobiography of an
actor. from The Theatre, June, 1883, etc

1883.

498969

SIDDONS (SARAH)
Directions and alterations.   IN Othello,
the Moor of Venice, a tragedy.   Printed
exactly agreeable to the representation,
by H. Garland.   pp. 86.
[c.1765.]   666730
Tp. wanting.   Mrs. Siddons' working
copy, with directions and alterations
in her hand.   Letters written by Fanny
Kemble and R. J. Lane inserted;   notes
by Mrs. C. Fitzhugh on endpapers.

666730

Siddons, Sarah *works relating to*

——An Artist's love story, told in the
letters of Sir T. Lawrence, Mrs. Siddons
and her daughters.   Edited by O. G.
Knapp.
   ports.   facsimiles.   1904.

503947

——BAILEY (PRISCILLA)
Sarah Siddons: a great actress.
pp. 48.
   ports.   illus.   facsimile.   1953.
"Women of Renown" Series.

634123

——BEAUFOY (GWENDOLYN)
Leaves from a beech tree.   [Containing
letters from Mrs. Siddons to her son
George Siddons].   (Oxford)
   ports.   illus.   1930.

456377

——BOADEN (J.)
Memoirs of Mrs. Siddons, interspersed
with anecdotes of authors and actors.
2nd edn.
   port.   2 vols.   1831.   515808
_____ No. 64 of an edition limited to
150 copies.   1 vol.   1893.   521715
_____ Another edn.   1896.   427216

——BRAHMS (CARYL) and SIMON (S. J.) [pseuds.]
"Thank you, Mrs. Siddons": a play
devised for broadcasting.   [Broadcast]
18th February, 1944.   ff. 29.
   typescript.

579578

——FFRENCH (YVONNE)
Mrs. Siddons: tragic actress.
   bibliog.   ports.   illus.   genealogical table.   1936.

458676

——HAZLITT (W.)
On the art of Mrs. Siddons.
IN AGATE (J. [E.]) ed., The English
dramatic critics.   [1932.]

399280

——HUNT (L.)
Mrs. Siddons.   IN WARD (A. C.) [ed.]
Specimens of English dramatic
criticism, 17-20 centuries;   selected
and introduced.   (Oxford) 1945.
The World's Classics.

563732

——JAGGARD (W.)
The Siddons Shakespeare relics.   IN
Notes and Queries, Vol. 161.   1931.

388854

——Kemble (Frances A.) On the stage. From
The Cornhill Magazine. Vol.8.

1863.

524713

——Lawrence (Sir T.) An Artist's love
story, told in the letters of Sir
T. Lawrence, Mrs. Siddons and her
daughters. Edited by O. G. Knapp.
Ports. Facsimiles.

1904.

503947

——   Matthews (A.) The Siddons Shakespeare
relics.   In Notes and Queries, Vol.161.

1931.

388854

——   Maurois (A.) Mape: the world of
illusion: [studies of Goethe, Balzac,
Mrs. Siddons.] Translated by E. Sutton.
1926.

397321

——Maurois (A.   Portrait d'une
actrice (Mrs. Siddons): an extract
from Méipe. Edited [with an
introduction]. With a special
preface [for this edition] by the
author. pp. 78.

(Cambridge)   1927.

512861

——   Paterson (J.) Kay's Edinburgh
portraits, Vol. 1. [Including "Mrs.
Siddons, at the Edinburgh Theatre."]
Ports.

1885.

403309

——Pedigree of the Kemble Family and the
related Family of Ward of Herefordshire,
London and elsewhere, compiled at the
Hereford Public Library, [including
Sarah Siddons].   ff. 6.
   manuscript.   1934.
Photostat reproduction made at the
Birmingham Reference Library, 1935.

453825

——POCOCK (G. N.)
  English men & women of ideas.
  [Containing a chapter "Mrs. Siddons
  (1755-1831): the supreme actress".]
                          1930.

                    427187

——   Royde-Smith (Naomi [G.] The Private
  life of Mrs. Siddons: a psychological
  investigation. [With references to
  Shakespeare.] Ports. Illus.

                    1933.

                  404014

——SPRAGUE (ARTHUR COLBY)
  Shakespearian players and performances.
  (Cambridge, Mass.)
   ports. illus.   1953.
  Mrs. Siddons as Lady Macbeth, pp. 57-70.

                    635328

——TAYLOR (J.)
  Mrs. Siddons's strange dress for
  Rosalind. IN AGATE (J. [E.]) ed.,
  The English dramatic critics.
                          [1932.]

                    399280

——YOUNG (J. C.)
  Others - and Mrs. Siddons. IN
  WARD (A. C.) [ed.] Specimens of English
  dramatic criticism, 17-20 centuries;
  selected and introduced.   (Oxford)
                          1945.

  The World's Classics.

                    563732

SIDERIS, JOANNIS
  Shakespeare in Greece.   FROM Theatre
  Research.   1964.
   pp. 85-99.   illus.

                    773830

Sidgwick (A.H.) Jones's wedding and
  other poems [including one on
  Shakespeare.] pp.96. Port.

                    1918.

                  405903

SIDGWICK (F.)
  The Sources and analogues of 'A
  Midsummer-night's dream'.
   facsimile.   1908.
  The Shakespeare Library.
  Large paper copy.

                    480726

SIDNELL (MICHAEL J.)
  A Moniment without a tombe: the
  Stratford Shakespearian Festival
  Theatre, Ontario.   IN English Associa-
  tion, Essays and Studies, 1964: Vol.
  17 of the new series of Essays and
  Studies collected by W. A. Armstrong.
  Shakespeare Quatercentenary ed.
   illus.   1964.

                    667820

Sidney, Philip Sir *works relating to*

——Bill (A.H.) Astrophel; or, The Life
  and death of the renowned Sir
  Philip Sidney. [With a bibliography and references to Shakes-
  peare] Ports. Illus.

                    1938.

                  477095

——DANBY, JOHN FRANCIS
  Elizabethan and Jacobean poets.
  Studies in Sidney, Shakespeare,
  Beaumont & Fletcher.   1964.

                    744906

  Note: Previously published under title
  'Poets on Fortune's hill', 1952.

——McKeithan (D.M.) "King Lear" and
  Sidney's "Arcadia". In University
  of Texas. Studies in English,
  No.14.

       (Austin,Texas.)   1934.

                  442440

—— Moore (W.H.) Baconian Studies
   [:cypher analyses of various
   works]. Manuscript.   83 vols.

                    1936-1940.
  Vol.69. Sidney'[s Works]. Facsimiles.

                  462661

——MYRICK (K. O.)
  Sir Philip Sidney as a literary crafts-
  man. [With references to Shakespeare.]
  (Cambridge, Mass.)
   bibliog.   1935.
  Harvard Studies in English, 14.

                    438837

—— Poirier (M) Sidney's influence
   upon A Midsummer Night's Dream.
   [With bibliographical notes.]
   In Studies in Philology,Vol.44.

       (Chapel Hill.N.C.)
                          1947.

                  554520/44

——PYLE (F.)
  "Twelfth Night", "King Lear" and
  "Arcadia".   IN The Modern Language
  Review, Vol. 43.   (Cambridge)
   bibliog.   1948.

                    266816/43

—— Rowe (K.T.) Elizabethan morality and
   the folio revisions of Sydney's
   Arcadia. [With references to
   Shakespeare.] From Modern
   Philology, Vol.37.

       (Chicago)   1939.

                  530204

—Tannenbaum (S.A.) Sir Philip Sidney
  [a concise bibliography). [With
  references to Shakespeare.]
  pp.x,69. (Elizabethan Bibliographies, No.23)

(New York)   1941.

Note : Edn. Limited to 300 copies.

535255

—Thaler (A.) Shakespeare and Sir
  Philip Sidney : the influence
  of "The Defense of Poesy". [With
  bibliographical notes.]

(Cambridge,Mass.)   1947.

601357

—Warren (C.H.) Sir Philip Sidney : a
  study in conflict. [containing
  references to Shakespeare.]
  Ports. Illus.

[1936.]

457050

SIEGEL (PAUL N.   )
  Adversity and the miracle of love in
  "King Lear". A reprint FROM Shakespeare
  Quarterly, Vol.6, No.3, Summer, 1955.
  (New York)   1955.

668454

SIEGEL (PAUL N.   )

Christianity and the religion of love
in "Romeo and Juliet". A reprint FROM
Shakespeare Quarterly, Vol.12, No.4,
Autumn, 1961. (New York)   1961.

668455

SIEGEL (PAUL N.   )

The Damnation of Othello. Reprinted
FROM PMLA, Publications of the Modern
Language Association of America, Vol.68,
No.5, Dec.1953. (New York)
                              1953.

668458

SIEGEL (PAUL N.   )

Leontes, a jealous tyrant. Reprint
FROM The Review of English Studies.
N.S. Vol.1, No.4, Oct.1950.
                              1950.

668456

SIEGEL (PAUL N.)
  Measure for Measure: the significance
  of the title.
  IN SHAKESPEARE QUARTERLY IV: 3.
  pp. 317-320.
  (New York) 1953.

605711

SIEGEL (PAUL N.)
A Midsummer Night's Dream and the
wedding guests.
IN SHAKESPEARE QUARTERLY IV: 2.
pp. 139-144.
(New York)   1953.

605711

SIEGEL, PAUL N.
  Shakespeare and the neo-chivalric cult
  of honor. FROM The Centennial Review,
  Vol.8, No.1. (East Lansing, Mich.)
                              1964.

pp.39-70.   749832

SIEGEL, PAUL N.
  Shakespeare in his time and ours.
  (Notre Dame, Ind.)   1968.

776087

SIEGEL (PAUL N.)
  Shakespearean tragedy and the Elizabethan compromise.   (New York)
  bibliog.   1957.

665533

SIEGEL (PAUL N.)
  Shylock and the Puritan usurers.
  IN MATTHEWS (A. D.) and EMERY (C. M.)
  eds., Studies in Shakespeare.
  (Coral Gables, Fla.)   1953.
  University of Miami Publications in
  English and American Literature,
  Vol. 1, March 1953.
                              634188

SIEGEL (PAUL N.   )

Willy Loman and King Lear. Reprinted
FROM College English, March 1956.
(Chicago)   1956.

668453

SIENKIEWICS (HENRYK)
  Dlaczego moglem czytac Szekspira.
  (Why I was able to read Shakespeare).
  [Polish text, with English translation
  by L. A. Tadema.]
  IN GOLLANCZ ([Sir] I.) ed., A Book of
  homage to Shakespeare.
  ports. illus. facsimiles. [1916.]

264175

SIEVEKING (A. F.)
  Coursing, fowling and angling;
  fencing and duelling; horsemanship;
  dancing, [and] games.   IN
  Shakespeare's England, vol. 2.
  (Oxford)
  illus. facsimiles. bibliog.
                              1917.

435746

Signature *see* Autographs of Shakespeare

Silence, William *see* Henry the Fourth, Characters

Siler (H.D.) A French pun in "Love's Labour's Lost". In Modern Language Notes, Vol.60.

(Baltimore)   1945.

571543

SILVER, FREDERICK
Sonnet 18. Words by W. Shakespeare, music by F. Silver, arrangement for mixed chorus unaccompanied (S.A.T.B.)
1963.

Williamson choral series.
667684

Silver (G.) Paradoxes of defence, 1599. With an introduction by J.D. Wilson.

(Shakespeare Association Facsimiles, No.6.)

1933.

403070

Silver falcon [: a periodical] published by the Shakespeare Society, Hunter College of the City of New York. pp. 28. (New York) 1936.

598969

SILVERMAN (ALBERT H.   )

Bernard Shaw's Shakespeare criticism. IN PMLA: Publications of the Modern Language Association of America, Vol.72. (Menasha,Wis.)

1957.

428321/72

Similes *see* Imagery

Simison (Barbara D.) A Source for the first Quarto of Henry V. In Modern Language notes, Vol. 46.

(Baltimore)

1931.

397731

SIMISON (BARBARA D.)
Stage directions: a test for the playhouse origin of the First Quarto Henry V. FROM Philological Quarterly, Vol. 11. (Iowa)
bibliog.   1932.

484065

ŠIMKO (JÁN)
Shakespeare in Slovakia.   IN
SHAKESPEARE SURVEY 4.   (Cambridge)
1951.

615854

ŠIMKO (JÁN)
Some recent Shakespearean productions in Czechoslovakia.
IN SHAKESPEARE JAHRBUCH.   Bd. 100/101.
1964/1965.   pp. 294-304.   (Weimar)

10531

Simmons (B.) Minerva's owl and other poems. [Including several on Shakespeare.] pp.64.

1933.

414224

Simmons (E.J.) Catherine the Great and Shakespeare. pp.[17]. From [Publications of the Modern Language Association of America, vol.47.]

[(Menasha,Wis.)]   [1932]

438446

Simmons (E.J.) English literature and culture in Russia (1553-1840.) [With a chapter on the Early history of Shakspere in Russia; and biblio-graphies.]

(Cambridge, Mass.)   1935.

(Harvard Studies in Comparative Literature, 12.)

437487

Simms, William Gilmore *works relating to*

——PARKS (EDD WINFIELD)
Simms's edition of the Shakespeare apocrypha. IN MATTHEWS (A. D.) and EMERY (C. M.) eds., Studies in Shakespeare. (Coral Gables, Fla.)
1953.
University of Miami Publications in English and American Literature, Vol.1, March 1953.

634188

——VANDIVER (EDWARD P.)
Simms's Border romances and Shakespeare. IN SHAKESPEARE QUARTERLY V.
pp. 129-139.
(New York) 1954.

605711

SIMON (ANDRÉ LOUIS)
Wine in Shakespeare's days and
Shakespeare's plays: [paper] read at
the 463rd meeting of the Sette of Odd
Volumes, 1931.   pp. 35.   1931.
(Sette of Odd Volumes, Privately
Printed Opuscula, No. 93.
Edition limited to 199 copies.   This
is No. 16 and bears the author's auto-
graph.

501289

Simon (H.W.) The Reading of
   Shakespeare in American
   schools and colleges: an
   historical survey. [With
   bibliographies.]

(New York)   1932.

407352

SIMON (H. W.)
Shakespeare - teller of stories.
IN SHAKESPEARE (W.) Five great
tragedies: Romeo and Juliet, Julius
Caesar, Hamlet, King Lear, Macbeth.
Cambridge text as edited by W. A.
Wright, with introductions by
J. Masefield [and Stories of the plays,
by J. W. McSpadden.   Edited by H. W.
Simon.]   (New York) 1939.
Pocket Books.

504059

Simon (H.W.) Why Shakespeare. From
   The English Journal, vol.23.

(Chicago)   1934.

442569

SIMON (S. J.) [pseud. i.e. SIMON JASHA
SKIDELSKY] & BRAHMS (CARYL) [pseud. i.e.
DORIS CAROLINE ABRAHAMS]
No bed for Bacon [: a story of Eliza-
bethan times, relating to Shakespeare].
                         1941. 528825
_____ [Another copy]   (New York)
                         1950. 608869

SIMON (S. J.) [pseud. i.e. Simon Jasha
Skidelsky] and BRAHMS (CARYL) [pseud.
i.e. Doris Caroline Abrahams]
"Thank you, Mrs. Siddons": a play
devised for broadcasting.   [Broadcast]
18th February, 1944.   ff. 29.
typescript.   1944.

579578

SIMONINI (R. C.)
Language lesson dialogues in Shakespeare.
IN SHAKESPEARE QUARTERLY II: 4.
pp. 319-329.
(New York)   1951.

605711

SIMONSON (LEE)
The Art of scenic design: a pictorial
analysis of stage setting and its
relation to theatrical production.
(New York)   1950.
Includes "More ways than one: six
interpretations of Hamlet".

614523

SIMONSON (L.)
The Stage is set [: a history of
stage-setting and scenery.   With
references to Shakespeare and a
chapter on The Scenic revival in
Shakespeare's England.]   (New York)
illus. plans. dgms. bibliog.   1937.

550764

Simonson (L.) ed ,Theatre art. With an
   introduction[and illustrations of
   scenery for some of Shakespeare's
   plays.]
                     (New York)   1934.

(Museum of Modern Art.)

420487

SIMONSON (L.) and KOMISARJEVSKY (F. F.)
Settings & costumes of the modern
stage, [including some Shakespeare
settings].   Edited by C. J. Holme.
illus.   1933.
"Studio" Winter Number, 1933.

411962

SIMPSON (CLAUDE MITCHELL) [ed.]
Elizabethan & Shakespearean musicke
for the recorder.   Selected and
arranged [with an introduction] for
ensembles of two, three, four and
more players.   With historical notes
by R. Lamson.   pp. xiii, 31.
(Boston, Mass.)   1941.

549897

SIMPSON, DONALD HERBERT
   Shakespeare and the Commonwealth.
   [Published by] the Royal Commonwealth
   Society as its contribution to the
   four hundredth anniversary of the birth
   of William Shakespeare.   1964.

740585

[SIMPSON (EVAN JOHN)] [pseud. Evan John]
Time in the East, an entertainment
[: experiences of an Intelligence
officer in the Middle East during the
war, 1939-45], by E. John [pseud.
With Five-line exercises in Shakespearian geography: limericks in
several languages.]
illus.   map.   1946.

569352

SIMPSON (F.)
New Place: the only representation
of Shakespeare's house from an
unpublished manuscript.   IN
SHAKESPEARE SURVEY 5.   (Cambridge)
facsimiles.   1952.

623798

Simpson (H.) and Braun (Mrs. Charles)
   A Century of famous actresses, 1750-
   1850. [With an appendix of characters
   and plays, and references to Shakespeare.] Ports.

[1913.]

421583

SIMPSON (H.) and HOUGHTON (C.)
The Unknown [: a play, with
Shakespeare as one of the characters].
ff. 8.
  typescript.   [c.1935.]

534907

SIMPSON (J. G.)
Commentary & questionnaire on The
Tempest.   [Reprint].   pp. 32.
                                1933.
Commentaries and Questionnaires in
English Literature.

547451

SIMPSON (JOHN PALGRAVA)
A New Hamlet: [Edwin Booth as Hamlet]
at the Princess's Theatre, Nov. 6th,
1880.   FROM The Theatre, December 1,
1880.
  illus.

516326

SIMPSON (LUCIE)
The Secondary heroes of Shakespeare,
and other essays.   [1950.]

614783

Simpson (Lucie) The Sex bias of
  Measure for Measure. In The
  Fortnightly Review, Vol.121.

1924.

312919

Simpson (Lucie) Shakespeare's
  "Cleopatra." In The Fortnightly
  Review, Vol.129.

1928.

347485

SIMPSON (P.)
Actors and acting; and, The Masque.
IN Shakespeare's England, vol. 2.
(Oxford)
  bibliogs.   illus.   facsimiles.
                                1917.

435746

SIMPSON (P.)
The Art of Ben Jonson.   [With references
to Shakespeare.]   IN English Association,
Essays and studies, Vol. 30, 1944.
Collected by C. H. Wilkinson.   (Oxford)
                                1945.

559548

Simpson (P.) The "Headless bear" in
  Shakespeare and Burton. From
  Queen's Quarterly, vol.39.

(New York)   1932.

441604

SIMPSON (P.)
The Play of 'Sir Thomas More' and
Shakespeare's hand in it.   IN The
Library.   3rd Series.   Vol. 8.
                                1917.

272685

SIMPSON (PERCY)
Proof-reading in the sixteenth, seven-
teenth and eighteenth centuries.
[With Shakespearian references.]
  illus.   facsimiles.   1935.
[Oxford Books on Bibliography]

434325

SIMPSON (PERCY)
[Review of] Shakespeare and Jonson:
their reputations in the seventeenth
century compared, by G. E. Bentley.
IN The Review of English Studies,
Vol. 21.   (Oxford)   [1945.]

570955

SIMPSON (PERCY)

Studies in Elizabethan drama. (Oxford)
                                1955.

679264

Simpson (P.) The Theme of revenge
  in Elizabethan tragedy. pp.38.

[1935].

(British Academy Annual Shakespeare lecture,
                                1935.)

438945

SIMPSON (PERCY) and GRAY (HENRY DAVID)
Shakespeare or Heminge?   A rejoinder
and a surrejoinder.   By H. D. Gray
and P. Simpson.   IN The Modern
Language Review Vol. 45.   1950.

266816/45

SIMPSON (RICHARD)
On "evening mass" in Romeo and Juliet,
IV.i.38.
IN Transactions of the New Shakespeare
Society, Series 1. No. 3.   pp. 148-154.
                                1875-8.

40620

SIMPSON (RICHARD)
On some plays attributed to Shakspere.
IN Transactions of the New Shakespeare
Society, Series 1.   No. 3.   pp. 155-180.
                                1875-6.

40620

SIMPSON (RICHARD)
The Political use of the stage in
Shakspere's time.
IN Transactions of the New Shakespeare
Society, Series 1. No. 2.   pp. 371-395.
                                1874.
                                      4061

SIMPSON (RICHARD)
The Politics of Shakspere's historical plays.
IN Transactions of the New Shakespeare
Society, Series 1. No. 2.   pp. 396-441.
                                1874.

4061

SIMPSON (RICHARD)
The School of Shakspere. Vol. 1.
Prefatory notice. Appendix: The
stories of the plays of "Captain Stucley"
and "Nobody and Somebody", Biography of
Sir Thomas Stucley. The Famous History
of the Life and Death of Captain Thomas
Stukeley. Nobody and Somebody.
Vol. 2. Histrio-Mastix. The Prodigal
Son. Jack Drums Entertainement. A
Warning for Faire Women. Faire Em.
An Account of Robert Greene, and his
attacks on Shakspere and the Players.
Index and Glossary. 2 vols. 1878. 516383
(New York)

SIMPSON (ROBERT RITCHIE)
Shakespeare and medicine.
(Edinburgh)
  chart. facsimiles.   1959.

                666120

SIMPSON (SAMUEL RALEIGH)

Shakespeare in Edinburgh [:conversations
upon certain events in the life of
Shakespeare]. pp.90. (Edinburgh)
                          [1960.]

        666557

SIMS (RUTH E.)
The Green old age of Falstaff. FROM
Bulletin of the History of Medicine,
Vol. 13. (Baltimore)
  bibliog.   1943.

                569112

Simson (Lena, Lady)

  see: Ashwell (Lena)

Sin

——LAW (R. A.)
    Shakespeare in the Garden of Eden [and
    his interest in the two related
    theological doctrines of the Fall of
    Man and Original Sin.] IN University
    of Texas, Studies in English, [Vol.21].
    (Austin, Texas)
      bibliog.   1941.

                    542174

[SINCLAIR (W. M.)]
The Patriotism of Shakespeare.
By the Archdeacon of London.
FROM Leisure Hour, 1902.   pp. [4.]
                          [1902]

                389194

Singer, Samuel Weller *works relating to*

——The Corrector of Shakspeare.   Collier
    and Singer [: reviews of various
    books on the Collier controversy].
    FROM [The Edinburgh Review,] Vol. 103.
    [Edinburgh]   1856.

                    563685

——Notes on Shakspeare's text: [reviews
    of] The Text of Shakspeare vindicated
    from the interpolations and corruptions
    advocated by John Payne Collier, Esq.,
    in his "Notes and emendations", by
    S. W. Singer, etc.   IN The Gentleman's
    Magazine, New Series, Vol. 40.   1853.

                18693

Singh (Sardar Jogundra) trans.
IGVAL (M.)
To Shakespeare: a tribute from the East
[: Urdu poem, with English translation
by] S. J. Singh.
IN GOLLANCZ ([Sir] I.) ed., A Book of
homage to Shakespeare.
  ports. illus. facsimiles. [1916.]

                264175

SINGLETON (ESTHER)
The Shakespeare garden. Illustrated
from photographs and old woodcuts.
[With an introduction by Eva T. Clark.]
  bibliog.   [1931.] 398227
_____ New edn.   (New York)
                    1931.   391269

[SINGLETON (H.) illus.]
The Shakspeare gallery, containing a
select series of scenes and characters,
accompanied by criticisms and remarks:
on fifty [forty] plates [designed by
H. Singleton].   1792.   63822
_____ Another copy.   7383
  pp. 127-260 and all plates wanting.
_____ Large paper copy.   Title page,
pp. 79-260 and plates to these pages
wanting.   544675

Sinistrality *see* Hand

Sinnett (A.P.) New light on Shakespeare.
  In The National Review, Vol.37.

                1901.

                    158872

Sinsheimer (H.) Shylock: the history
  of a character; or, The Myth of
  the Jew. [With a foreword by J.M.
  Murry and a bibliography.] Ports.
  Illus.

            1947.

                580875

SIPE, DOROTHY L.
Shakespeare's metrics.   (New Haven,
Conn.)   1968.
  Yale studies in English, 167.

773050

Sir C. Ramalinga Reddy College, Eluru
SUBRAHAMANYAM, D.S., and others, eds.
Homage to Shakespeare, Quatercentenary
1964 [from] Sir C. Ramalinga Reddy
College.   (Eluru)
  illus.   1964.

740823

Sir Thomas More: a play

—— Addy (S.O.) Robert Wilson and
  'Sir Thomas More' : Wilson's
  first play. In Notes and
  Queries, Vol.154, 1928.

(High Wycombe)   [1928.]

348919

——   Bald (R.C.) The Booke of Sir Thomas
  Moore and its problems; [and] The
  Shakespearian additions in the Booke of
  Sir Thomas More. [With bibliographical
  notes.] Facsimiles. In Shakespeare survey:
  an annual survey of Shakespearian study
  & production, [Vol.] 2. (Cambridge)
                              1949.

598403

—— BRITISH MUSEUM, LONDON
  Facsimiles of the Shakespeare deed and
  a leaf of the Sir Thomas More play in
  the British Museum.   1964.

668012

—— CHAMBER (R. W.)
  Man's unconquerable mind: studies of
  English writers, from Bede to A. E.
  Housman and W. P. Ker.   [Including
  Shakespeare.]
  port. illus.   1939.

496608

——CHAMBERS (R. W.)
  Some sequences of thought in
  Shakespeare and in the 147 lines of
  'Sir Thomas More'.   Reprinted from
  The Modern language review, Vol. 26.
  pp. [30]. (Cambridge)   1931.

475799

——COLLINS (D. C.)
  On the date of "Sir Thomas More" [:
  the possibility of three pages being
  in Shakespeare's hand.]   IN The
  Review of English Studies, Vol. 10.
                              1934.

428644

—— Golding (S.R.) Further notes on
  Robert Wilson and 'Sir Thomas
  More'. In Notes and Queries,
  Vol.154-5, 1928.

(High Wycombe) 2 vols.   [1928]

348919

—— HARRISON (G. B.)
  The Date of "Sir Thomas More".   [A
  discussion on the "Shakespearean"
  passages in "The Book of Sir Thomas
  More".]   IN The Review of English
  Studies, Vol. 1.   1925.

318239

——HUBER (R. A.)
  On looking over Shakespeare's "Secretarie".
  IN Stratford papers on Shakespeare,
  delivered at the 1960 Shakespeare
  Seminar sponsored by the Universities
  of Canada in co-operation with the
  Stratford Festival Theatre.   (Toronto)
  facsimiles.   1961.

667140

——LAW (R. A.)
  Is Heywood's hand in "Sir Thomas More"?
  IN Studies in English, No. 11:
  University of Texas Bulletin.
  (Austin, Texas)   1931.

442438

——   MacNALTY (Sir ARTHUR SALUSBURY)
  Shakespeare and Sir Thomas More.   IN
  English Association. Essays and Studies,
  1959. New Series,Vol.12.
                              1959.

684452

——NOSWORTHY (JAMES MANSFIELD)
  Shakespeare and "Sir Thomas More" [:
  notes on the play]. Reprint FROM The
  Review of English Studies, N.S. Vol.6,
  No.21, 1955. (Oxford)   1955.

668445

——OLIPHANT (E. H. C.)
  "Sir Thomas More" [: a discussion
  on Anthony Munday's authorship of
  the play, and whether Shakespeare
  was concerned in the textual altera-
  tion].   Reprinted from The Journal
  of English and Germanic philology,
  Vol. 18.   (Urbana, Ill.)   [1919.]

554219

——POLLARD (A. W.)
  Verse tests and the date of "Sir Thomas
  More".   [A discussion on the "Shake-
  spearean" passages in "The Book of
  Sir Thomas More".]   IN The Review of
  English Studies, Vol. 1.   1925.

318239

—— SEMPER (I. J.)
  In the steps of Dante and other papers
  [including Shakespeare and St. Thomas
  More].   (Dubuque)   1941.

545882

——   Shapiro (I.A.)
  The Significance of a date. Facsimiles.
  IN Shakespeare Survey, [Vol.] 8
  (Cambridge)   1955.

647706

——SIMPSON (P.)
  The Play of 'Sir Thomas More' and
  Shakespeare's hand in it.   IN The
  Library.   3rd Series, Vol. 8.
                              1917.

272685

——Speeches from Sir Thomas More. In
Flower (D.) and Munby (A.N.L.)
eds. English poetical autographs :
a collection of [46] facsimiles of
autographs poems from Sir Thomas
Wyat to Rupert Brooke. pp. 25.

1938.

491927

——Spurgeon (Caroline F.E.) Imagery in the
Sir Thomas More fragment. In The
Review of English Studies. Vol.6.

[1930.]

377862

——TANNENBAUM (S. A.)
Anthony Mundy, including the play of
"Sir Thomas Moore" (a concise biblio-
graphy). pp. viii, 36. (New York)
1942.
Elizabethan Bibliographies.
Edition limited to 250 copies

539395

——Tannenbaum (S.A.) Dr. Greg and the
"Goodal" notation in "Sir Thomas
Moore". In Comment and criticism.
Reprinted from P.M.L.A. (Publica-
tions of the Modern Language
Association of America,) Vol.44.
pp.[14.]

[Menasha, Wis.] 1929.

413468

——TANNENBAUM (S. A.)
More about "The Booke of Sir Thomas
Moore". Reprinted from P.M.L.A.
(Publications of the Modern Language
Association of America,) Vol. 43.
pp. [12.] [Menasha, Wis.]
facsimile. 1928.

413469

——Tannenbaum (S.A.) Robert Wilson
and 'Sir Thomas More'. In
Notes and Queries, Vol.154, 1928.

(High Wycombe) [1928.]

348919

——TANNENBAUM (S. A.)
Shakspere studies. 2. An object
lesson in Shaksperian research [:
the Collier forgery in the manuscript
of Sir Thomas More. A reply to
W. W. Greg.] pp. 23. (New York)
facsimile. 1931.
Limited edn.: 250 copies. Signed
by the author.

413467

——Tannenbaum (S.A.) Shakspere's
unquestioned autographs and "the
addition" to "Sir Thomas Moore."
Reprinted from "Studies in Philology,
[Vol.] 22. pp. 133-160. Facsimiles.

(Baltimore) 1925.

488382

——WENTERSDORFF, KARL P.
The Date of the additions in the "Booke
of Sir Thomas More".
IN DEUTSCHE SHAKESPEARE-GESELLSCHAFT
WEST, JAHRBUCH 1965. pp. 305-325.
(Heidelberg)

754129

——WILSON (JOHN DOVER)
The New way with Shakespeare's texts:
an introduction for lay readers, 3:
In sight of Shakespeare's manuscripts.
IN SHAKESPEARE SURVEY 9. (Cambridge)
1956.

665210

SISSON (CHARLES JASPER)
A Colony of Jews in Shakespeare's
London. IN English Association,
Essays and studies, Vol. 23. Collected
by S. C. Roberts. (Oxford)
bibliog. 1938.

484755

Sisson, Charles Jasper
King John, a history play for Elizabethans
IN

STRATFORD PAPERS ON SHAKESPEARE
delivered at the 1960 Shakespeare
Seminar. (Toronto) 1961.

667140

SISSON (CHARLES JASPER)
The Laws of Elizabethan copyright: the
Stationers' view. [Reprinted from the
Transactions of the Bibliographical
Society, The Library, March, 1960.]
pp.20. 1960.

667159

SISSON (CHARLES JASPER)
The Living Shakespeare [No. 9]: The
Roman plays. [Broadcast] 26th
November 1958. pp. 13.
typescript. [1958.]

666031

Sisson (C.J.) Lost plays of Shakespeare's age. [With summary of
original sources.] Plan. Facsimiles.

(Cambridge) 1936.

450440

SISSON (CHARLES JASPER)
The Magic of Prospero. Bibliog. IN
Shakespeare Survey,[Vol.]11.
(Cambridge) 1958.

665816

SISSON (CHARLES JASPER)
The Mythical sorrows of Shakespeare.
pp. 28. [1934.] 422579
British Academy Annual Shakespeare
Lecture, 1934.
——— IN Studies in Shakespeare:
British Academy lectures, selected
and introduced by P. Alexander.
1964. 667830
Oxford Paperbacks, No. 81.

SISSON (CHARLES JASPER)

New readings in Shakespeare. (Shakespeare
Problems, 8) Facsimiles. (Cambridge)
2 vols.   1956.

665182-3

SISSON (CHARLES JASPER)
The Red Bull Company and the importunate
widow.   IN SHAKESPEARE SURVEY 7.
(Cambridge)
facsimiles.   1954.

639176

Sisson (C.J.) [Review of]Shakespeare
and Jonson: their reputations in the
seventeenth century compared,by G.F.
Bentley.In The Modern Language
Review, Vol.41.

(Cambridge)   1946.

584763

Sisson (C.J.) [Review of] H.B.
Charlton's "Shakespearian Comedy.
1938".   In The Modern Language
Review, Vol. 33.

1938.

492625

Sisson (C.J.) [Review of] Shakespearian
comedy and other studies, by G.[S.]
Gordon. In The Modern Language
Review. Vol.39.

(Cambridge)   1944.

563897

Sisson (C.J.) [Review of] Shakespeare-
Jahrbuch. Vol.69. [1933]. In
Modern Language Review, July, 1934.

1934.

428653

SISSON (CHARLES JASPER)
Shakespeare.   pp. 50.
port.   bibliog.   1955.
British Book News.   Bibliographical
Series of Supplements.   Writers and
their Work.

645584

SISSON (CHARLES JASPER)
Shakespeare quartos as prompt-copies;
with some account of Cholmeley's
players and a new Shakespeare allusion.
IN The Review of English Studies,
Vol. 18.   (Oxford)
bibliog.   1942.

542539

Sisson, Charles Jasper
Shakespeare the writer. IN

STRATFORD PAPERS ON SHAKESPEARE
delivered at the 1960 Shakespeare
Seminar. (Toronto)   1961.

667140

SISSON (CHARLES JASPER)

Shakespeare's friends: Hathaways and
Burmans at Shottery. Bibliog. IN
Shakespeare Survey [Vol.] 12.
(Cambridge)   1959.

666150

SISSON (CHARLES JASPER)

Shakespeare's Helena and Dr. William
Harvey. With a case-history from
Harvey's practice. IN Essays and
Studies, Vol.13, N.S., 1960.

1960.

691985

SISSON, CHARLES JASPER
Shakespeare's London.   IN SPENCER,
TERENCE JOHN BEW, ed., Shakespeare:
a celebration, 1564-1964.
illus.   maps.   1964.

667816

SISSON (CHARLES JASPER)
Shakespeare's tragic justice.
(Ontario)   [1961.]

667250

SISSON (C. J.)
Studies in the life and environment
of Shakespeare since 1900 [: reviews].
IN SHAKESPEARE SURVEY 3.   (Cambridge)
1950.

606026

SISSON (CHARLES JASPER)
The Theatres and companies.   IN
GRANVILLE-BARKER (H.) and HARRISON
(G. B.) eds., A Companion to Shakespeare
studies.   (Cambridge)
bibliogs.   illus.   tables.
facsimiles.   1934.   418724
_____ (New York)   1937.   479251
_____ (Cambridge) 1945.   566174

SISSON (CHARLES JASPER)
Tudor intelligence tests: Malvolio
and real life.   IN HOSLEY (RICHARD) ed.,
Essays on Shakespeare and Elizabethan
drama in honour of Hardin Craig.
illus.   1963.

667532

Sisson, Charles Jasper *works relating to*

——STEPHENSON (ANTHONY A.)
New Readings for old, the text of
Shakespeare [: review of New Readings
in Shakespeare by C. J. Sisson] IN
The Month, New Series, Vol. 15. 1956.

404303/2/15

Sisson (E.O.) [Review of] W.C.
Curry's "Shakespeare's philosophical patterns. 1937". In
The Modern Language Review, Vol.
33.

1938.

492625

SISSON (ROSEMARY ANNE)
The Globe Theatre: a story of
Shakespeare's London. [B.B.C. Radio
script of programme transmitted in
Home Service (Schools), 19th November
1959.] pp. 11.
　　typescript.　　　　　　　　[1959.]
Stories from British History.
　　　　　　　　　　　　666446

SISSON (ROSEMARY ANNE)

Towards the "Globe": when Shakespeare
was a boy [; novel]. (Neusprachliche
Texte) (Lensing, Dortmund)
　　　　　　　　　　1959.

　　　　　　　667519

SISSON (ROSEMARY ANNE)
The Young Shakespeare.　　Illustrated
by Denise Brown.　　　　1959.
　[Famous Childhoods Series]
　　　　　　　　　666308

SITWELL (Dame EDITH)

King Lear [from Notebook on William
Shakespeare]. In The Atlantic, Vol.185,
No.5. (Concord. N.H.)　　　1950.

　　　　　19347/185

SITWELL (Dame EDITH)

Macbeth [from Notebook on William
Shakespeare]. In The Atlantic, Vol.185,
No.4. (Concord, N.H.)　　　1950.

　　　　　19347/185

SITWELL (Dame EDITH)

A Note on "Measure for Measure". In
The Nineteenth Century and After,
Vol. 140.　　　　　　　　1946.

　　　　　578009

SITWELL (Dame EDITH)

A Notebook on William Shakespeare.
[With bibliographical notes.]
　　　　　　　　　1948.

　　　　　594672

SITWELL (Dame EDITH)

Of the clowns and fools of Shakespeare.
[With bibliographical notes.] From
[Life and Letters Today, Vol.57]. pp.[8].
　　　　　　　　　　　　[1948]

　　　　　596219

SITWELL (Dame EDITH)

A Poet's notebook [: notes on the
necessity of poetry. Including notes on
Shakespeare and two new poems by the
author].　　　　　　　1943.

　　　　　540875

SITWELL (Dame EDITH)
"Romeo Coates": a portrait of failure.
[A play containing references to
Romeo and Juliet] adapted [for broad-
casting] and produced by S. Potter.
Regional programme, 23rd Feb., 1939.
ff. 18.
　　typescript.

　　　　　498984

SITWELL (SACHEVERELL)
Dance of the quick and the dead: an
entertainment of the imagination.
[With Shakespearian references.]
　illus.　　　　　　　　1936.

　　　　　458272

SITWELL (SACHEVERELL)
Sacred and profane love [: a banquet
of the five senses. With references
to Shakespeare].
　illus.　　　　　　　　1940.

　　　　　520730

SITWELL (SACHEVERELL)
Splendours and miseries [: a miscellany,
dealing with events of the past four
years. With references to H. Fuseli's
illustrations of Shakespeare].
　illus.　　　　　　　　1943.

　　　　　546694

SIVARAMAN (K. M.), RANGANATHAN (S. R.)
and SUNDARAM (C.)
Reference service and bibliography.
[Including references to Shakespeare.]
(Madras)
2 vols.　　　　　　　　1940-1.
Madras Library Association.　Publica-
tion Series.

　　　　　539617

Six stories from Shakespeare.
Retold by J. Buchan, H. [S.] Walpole,
Clemence Dane, F. B. Young, W. [L. S.]
Churchill, Viscount Snowden.
Illustrations by F. Matania.　　1934.

　　　　　428744

Sixteen standard songs of Shakespeare.
Music by Purcell, Arne, Bishop,
Schubert etc.　pp. 54.　[?1920.]

　　　　　628133

SJÖGREN (GUNNAR)
A Contribution to the geography of "Hamlet".
IN SHAKESPEARE JAHRBUCH.　Bd. 100/101.
1964/1965.　PP. 266-273.　(Weimar)

　　　　　10531

SJÖGREN (GUNNAR)
Hamlet and the Coronation of Christian IV.
IN SHAKESPEARE QUARTERLY XVI: 2.
pp. 155-160.
(New York)　1965.

　　　　　605711

SJÖGREN, GUNNAR
The Setting of Measure for Measure.
FROM Revue de Littérature Comparée,
XXXV. pp[35-39]　　　　1961.

　　　　　667855

SKARD (S.)
The Use of color in literature: a
survey of research.　[With references
to Shakespeare.]　IN Proceedings of
the American Philosophical Society,
Vol. 90.　(Philadelphia, [Pa.])
　bibliogs.　　　　　　　1946.

　　　　　578022

SKEAT (WALTER WILLIAM)
[Review of] A Shakespearian Grammar,
by E. A. Abbott, 3rd edn., 1870.
IN The Academy, Vol. 1.   [1870]

50601

SKEAT (WALTER WILLIAM)
Shakespeare's Plutarch: a selection
from the Lives in [Sir T.] North's
Plutarch which illustrate Shakespeare's
plays. Edited, with a preface, notes,
index of names, and glossarial index,
1904.

613447

SKEFFINGTON (FLORENCE [V.])
William Shakespeare: biography
and selections from his writings.
pp. 32.   (Taylorville, Ill.)
port. illus. bibliog. [c.1920]
Studies of Great American and English
Authors.

396971

SKEMP (ARTHUR ROWLAND)
Shakespeare [: a poem].
IN GOLLANCZ ([Sir] I.) ed., A Book of
homage to Shakespeare.
ports. illus. facsimiles. [1916.]

264175

The SKETCH: an illustrated miscellany of
music, the drama, society and the belles.
Nos. 2 to 76   1879-80

illus.   60199

The Sketch: a journal of art and
actuality.   Vols. 1-58.   Feb.,1893-
July, 1907.
57 vols.   ports.   illus.
[1893-1907.]
Wants Vol. 25.
480254

SKINNER (BASIL) ed.
Shakespeare in Scottish art [: a
catalogue of the exhibition] at the
Arts Council Gallery, Edinburgh [to
celebrate Shakespeare's birth.]
(Edinburgh)   1964.

740735

SKINNER (O.)
Bath and James Quin. [With refer-
ences to Shakespeare.] Illustra-
tions from photographs in the Theatre
Collection, Harvard College Library.
FROM Scribner's Magazine.   1924.

521314

**Skinner (O.) Mad folk of the theatre:
ten studies in temperament. [Containing
"Will-of-Avon's-Night" and other
Shakespearian references.] Ports.
Illus. (Indianapolis)   1928.**

442504

Skottowe, A. *works relating to*

— Review of "The Life of Shakspeare",
by A. Skottowe.   FROM The Gentleman's
Magazine, Aug. 1824.   pp. [2.]
1824.

402691

SKULSKY, HAROLD
King Lear and the meaning of chaos.
IN Shakespeare Quarterly XVII: 1.
pp.3-17. (New York)   1966.

605711

SLACK (ROBERT C.)
Measure for Measure.   IN Shakespeare:
lectures on five plays, by A. F.
Sochatoff [and others].   pp. xii, 83.
(Pittsburgh)   1958.

666185

SLACK (ROBERT C.)
The Realms of gold and the dark comedies.
IN "Starre of Poets".   Discussions of
Shakespeare. (Pittsburgh, Pa.:
Carnegie Institute of Technology)
1966.

766812

Slade (F.E.) On reading Shakespeare.
From The Poetry Review [Vol.31.]

1940.

521315

Slade (W.A.) The Folger Shakespeare
Library.   From The Library Journal, July,
1932. pp.[7.] Illus.

(New York)   [1932]

396013

SLADEN-SMITH (FRANCIS) [FRANK]
Sweet Master William: a play in one
act.   pp. [2], 32.
plan.   1953.
French's Acting Edition, No. 731.

636167

Slang

— ALEXANDER (ROSE)
Slang and popular phrases used by
Shakespeare, etc.   pp. 64.   [Los
Angeles, Cal.]   [1936]

461090

— BATEN (A. M.) [ed.]
Slang from Shakespeare, with literary
expressions.   [Dallas, Texas] 1931.

392826

— PARTRIDGE (E. [H.])
Shakespeare's bawdy: a literary &
psychological essay and a comprehensive
glossary.   1947.

587277

— **Partridge (E.[H.]),Slang to-day and
yesterday. With a short historical
sketch, [references to Shakespeare]
and vocabularies of English,
American and Australian slang.**

1933.

411402

— Partridge (E.[H.]) Words, words,
   words! [with references to
   Shakespearean usage.]

                           1933.

                    410091

Sledd, James ed. see Harrison, Thomas
Perrin and others eds.

Sleep

——,CAMDEN (C.)
   Shakespeare on sleep and dreams.
   IN Rice Instutute Pamphlet, Vol. 23.
   (Houston, Texas)   [1936]

                    464030

——,STEWART (CAROL) [ed.]
   Poems of sleep and dream.   [Including
   extracts from Shakespeare].   With
   original lithographs by C. Colquhoun.
                              1947.
   New Excursions into English Poetry.

                    589908

SLEIGH (H.)
   Stratford-upon-Avon, April 23.
   IN Sleigh (H.) The Great hope, and
   other poems.   (Stratford-upon-Avon:
   Shakespeare Head Press)   1921.

                    478200

Slender *see* The Merry Wives of Windsor, General Works and Criticism

SLINN (L. A.)
   Guide to Warwickshire.   [With references to Shakespeare].   Illustrated
   by W. Green.   (Worcester)
   map.   [1949.]

                    597038

SLOAN (J.)
   The Moneylender of Venice.   In
   Shylock, a different play struggles
   to be born.   pp. [6].   FROM
   Commentary, Vol. 5.   [New York]
                              1948.

                    597810

.oane School, Chelsea see Chelsea

Slovakia

——SIMKO (J.)
   Shakespeare in Slovakia.
   IN SHAKESPEARE SURVEY 4.   (Cambridge)
                              1951.

                    615854

Sly, Christopher *see* The Taming of the Shrew, General Works and Criticism

SMALL (MIRIAM R.)
   Charlotte Ramsay Lennox, an eighteenth
   century lady of letters.   [With a
   chapter, Miscellaneous works of
   Mrs. Lennox; Shakespear illustrated,
   etc. and other Shakespearian references.]   (New Haven, [Conn.])
   port.   illus.   1935.
   Yale Studies in English.

                    447408

SMALL (S. A.)
   The Ending of "The Two Gentlemen of
   Verona".   IN Publications of the
   Modern Language Association of America,
   Vol. 48.   (Menasha, Wis.)   1933.

                    418268

       Small (S.A.) 'The Jew': [a
   probable source of Shakespeare's Merchant
   of Venice.]   In The Modern Language
   Review, Vol. 26.

                    (Cambridge)   1931.

                           390362

SMALL (S. A.)
   [Review of] Shakespeare and the tragic
   theme, by A. H. R. Fairchild.   IN
   Modern Language Notes, Vol. 61.
   (Baltimore, Md.)   1946.

                    579125

   Small (S.A.) The Shaksperian keynote
   in comedy. From Birmingham- Southern
   College Bulletin, June, 1928.

          (Birmingham, Alabama)   1928.

                           446219

SMALL (W. FARQUHARSON)
   "Return journey to the Old Vic".
   [Broadcast] 30th October, 1949.
   pp. [ii] 26.
   typescript.   [1949.]

                    605244

SMART (CHRISTOPHER)
   An Occasional prologue and epilogue to
   Othello, as it was acted at the
   Theatre-Royal in Drury-Lane, 7th March
   1751.   2nd edn.   pp. 8.   [c.1750.]

                    633512

[SMART (C.)]
The Prologue to Othello, as it was
acted at the theatre in Drury Lane
and The Epilogue spoken by Desdemona.
FROM The Midwife [; or, The Old
Woman's Magazine, Vol. 1].   1751.

563203

SMART, JOHN SEMPLE
Shakespeare, truth and tradition.
With a memoir by W. M. Dixon and
preface by P. Alexander.   (Oxford)
1966.

773599

SMEATON (OLIPHANT)
The Life and works of William
Shakespeare.   1937.
Everyman's Library.

572119

[SMEDLEY (W. T.)]
Avon Valley Argus [and] Limpley Stoke
Dispatch. [Journal of the Limpley
Stoke Hydro No. 1, July-Sept., 1934
issued by W. T. Smedley and including
references to Shakespeare].   1934.

433183

Smedley (W.T.) The Mystery of Francis
Bacon. Port. Illus.

(San Francisco)   [1920]

475381

SMET (ROBERT de) [pseud. Romain Sanvic]
Othello in Paris and Brussels. Translated by Sir B. [V.] Jackson.
illus.
IN SHAKESPEARE SURVEY 3.   (Cambridge)
1950.

606026

SMETHURST (WILLIAM)
The Ashbourne portrait of Shakespeare.
ff. [2,] 23.
port.   illus.   plan.   typescript.
1943.
Only 9 copies made, of which this is
No. 2.

549760

SMIDT, KRISTIAN
Injurious impostors and Richard III.
1963.

Norwegian studies in English,
No.12.   668033

SMIDT, KRISTIAN
The Quarto and the Folio Lear. FROM
English Studies XLV: II. pp.149-162.
(Amsterdam)   1964.

745006

SMIRKE (ROBERT)
Illustrations to Shakspeare.   IN
[Shakspeare portfolio.]
95 plates.   [1821-34]
Imperfect, 3 plates missing.

426536

SMIRKE (R.)
The Seven ages of man.   Described
by Shakespeare, depicted by R. Smirke.
ports.   1864.

480375

SMIRNOV (ALEKSANDR ALEKSANDROVICH)
Shakespeare: a Marxist interpretation.
Translated from the Russian by Sonia
Volochova, Sidonie Kronman, A. Goldstein,
A. Morais, Zena Rautbort and the
Editorial Committee: Angel Flores,
Charles Birchall, E. P. Greene, Paul S.
Leitner, Lola H. Sachs.   3rd edn.
revised.   pp. 93.   (New York) 1936.

457904

SMIRNOV, ALEKSANDR ALEKSANDROVICH
Shakespeare: a Marxist interpretation.
IN RABKIN, NORMAN, ed., Approaches to
Shakespeare [: 20th century critical
essays].   (New York)   1964.

668298

Smirnov, Aleksandr Aleksandrovich *works relating to*

— West (A.) Shakespeare: a revaluation.
[A Review of Shakespeare: A Maxist
interpretation, by A. A. Smirnov.]
In Left review, Vol. 2.

1935[-37]

456238

S[mith] (A.K.) Herne, the hunter: a
legend of Windsor Forest. pp.48.
Frontis.

[c.1830]

431981

Smith, Adam *works relating to*

—— Lothian, John Maule
Adam Smith as a critic of Shakespeare. IN

DUTHIE, GEORGE IAN, ed.
Papers, mainly Shakespearian. 1964.

Aberdeen University studies,
No. 147.   668205

SMITH, ALBERT JAMES
Shakespeare stories.   1963.

World of English series.
667682

SMITH (ALBERT RICHARD) and REACH (ANGUS
BETHUNE)
The Man in the moon, Vol. 2.   [With
imaginary conversation between
Shakespeare and The Man in the moon.
illus.   1847.
Imperfect.   Vol. 1 wants pp. 1-185.
Vol. 2 wants title page.

446494

SMITH (ALEXANDER BRENT)
Fear no more: three part song.
[Music by] A. B. Smith. [Words by]
Shakespeare [from Cymbeline.] pp. 7.
1926.
Elkin & Co's Choral Series, 1518.

488615

Smith (C.A.) Shakespeare's present
indicative s-endings. With plural
subjects: a study in the grammar
of the First Folio. In Publications
of the Modern Language Association
of America, Vol.11.

(Baltimore) 1896.

428331

SMITH, CHARLES GEORGE
Shakespeare's proverb lore: his use of
the 'Sententiae' of Leonard Culman and
Publilius Syrus. (Cambridge, Mass.)
1963.

667800

SMITH (CHARLES J.)
The Effect of Shakespeare's influence
on Wordsworth's "The Borderers".
IN Studies in Philology, Vol. 50.
(Chapel Hill, N.C.) 1953.

554520/50

SMITH (CYRIL KEGAN)

"Getting ready at Stratford"[:
Shakespeare Memorial Theatre.Broadcast]
6th March 1958.ff.6. Typescript.
1958.

665770

SMITH (DANE FARNSWORTH)
Plays about the theatre in England
from The Rehearsal in 1671 to the
Licensing Act in 1737, or, The Self-
conscious stage and its burlesque
and satirical reflections in the
age of criticism. [With appendices].
(Oxford)
illus. bibliog. 1936.

468347

SMITH (DAVID NICHOL)
Authors and patrons. IN Shakespeare's
England, Vol. 2. (Oxford)
illus. facsimiles. bibliogs.
1917.

435746

SMITH, DAVID NICHOL
Eighteenth century essays on
Shakespeare [by various authors]. 2nd
ed. (Oxford) 1963.

667615

SMITH (DAVID NICHOL) [ed.]
Shakespeare criticism: a selection
with an introduction. (Oxford)
1926. 419635
World's Classics.
_____ Another edn. 1930. 473891

SMITH (FRED MANNING)
The Relation of Macbeth to Richard the
Third. IN Publications of the Modern
Language Association of America, Vol.
60. (Menasha, Wis.)
bibliog. 1945.

569026

SMITH (G.)
Shakespeare's religion and politics.
IN Macmillan's magazine, vol. 59,
Nov. 1888-April 1889. 1889

100873

SMITH (G.)
Tommy Jones's dream [: a play in one
act.] IN LOCK (A. B.) ed., Festival
plays, Book two. 1951.

623436

SMITH (G. G.)
Shakespeare on the screen. FROM
The Emory University Quarterly,
Vol. 3. pp. [8]. [Atlanta, Ga.]
1947.

596844

SMITH (GEORGE CHARLES MOORE)
Two sonnets: 1616; 1916.
IN GOLLANCZ ([Sir] I.) ed., A Book of
homage to Shakespeare.
ports. illus. facsimiles. [1916.]

264175

SMITH (GORDON ROSS)
The Balance of themes in "Romeo and
Juliet". IN Essays on Shakespeare
[by various authors]. (University
Park, Penn.) pp. 15-66. 1965.

755528

SMITH (GORDON ROSS)
Brutus, virtue, and will.
IN SHAKESPEARE QUARTERLY X: 3.
pp. 367-379.
(New York) 1959.

605711

SMITH, GORDON ROSS
A classified Shakespeare bibliography,
1936-1958. 1963.

6c,j51

SMITH, GORDON ROSS
Isabella and Elbow in varying contexts
of interpretation. FROM Journal of
General Education, vol. 17, no. 1,
April 1965. (University Park, Pa.)
1965.

pp. 63-78.

766496

SMITH, GORDON ROSS, ed.
Essays on Shakespeare [by various
authors]. (University Park, Penn.)
1965.

755528

SMITH (H.)
Pastoral influence in the English
drama. [With references to "As
you like it".] IN Publications of
the Modern Language Association of
America, Vol. 12. (Baltimore) 1897.

428332

[SMITH (H.)]
Punch's Apotheosis, by T[heodore] H[ook].
IN Smith (J.) and Smith (H.) Rejected
Addresses.   New edn. Illustrations by
G. Cruikshank.
1869.

7686

[SMITH (H.)]
Punch's Apotheosis, by T[heodore] H[ook].
IN [Smith (J.) and Smith (H.)] Rejected
addresses.   [Edited] by A. Boyle.
ports.   illus.   1929.

356643

SMITH (HALLETT DARIUS)
In search of the real Shakespeare.
IN The Yale Review, Vol. 40. 1951.

592685/40

SMITH (HALLETT D.)
Leontes' Affectio.
IN SHAKESPEARE QUARTERLY XIV: 2.
pp. 163-166.
(New York) 1963.
605711

SMITH (HALLET D.)
"No cloudy stuffe to puzzell intellect":
a testimonial misapplied to Shakespeare.
IN SHAKESPEARE QUARTERLY I: 1.
pp. 18-21.
(New York) 1950.
605711

SMITH (HAROLD CLIFFORD)
Byron's pictorial screen: its theatrical
side, with recollections of the Regency
stage [including Shakespearean actors
and actresses].   IN Country Life,
Vol. 98.
illus.   1945.

570906

SMITH (HARRY BACHE)
First nights and first editions [: an
autobiography.   With a foreword by
W. L. Phelps.   Containing references
to Shakespeare].   (Boston, [Mass.])
ports.   illus.   facsimiles.
1931.

537731

SMITH (IRWIN)
"Gates" on Shakespeare's stage.
IN SHAKESPEARE QUARTERLY VII:
pp. 159-176.
(New York) 1956.
605711

SMITH (IRWIN)
Notes on the construction of the Globe
model.
IN SHAKESPEARE QUARTERLY II: 1.
pp. 13-18.
(New York) 1951.
605711

SMITH, IRWIN
Shakespeare's Blackfriars playhouse:
its history and design.   1966.

748775

SMITH (IRWIN)
Shakespeare's Globe playhouse: a
modern reconstruction in text and
scale drawings, based upon the reconstruction of the Globe by J. C. Adams,
with an introduction by J. G. McManaway.
(New York)
illus.   plans.   1956.

665477

SMITH (IRWIN)
Theatre into Globe.
IN SHAKESPEARE QUARTERLY III: 2.
pp. 113-120.
(New York) 1952.
605711

SMITH (IRWIN)
Their exits and reentrances [actors in
Shakespeare's plays].
IN SHAKESPEARE QUARTERLY XVIII: 1.
pp. 7-16.
(New York) 1967.
605711

SMITH (J. PERCY)
Superman versus man: Bernard Shaw on
Shakespeare.   IN The Yale Review,
New Series, Vol. 42.   (New Haven,
Conn.)   1952.   592685/N.S.42
_____ IN Stratford Papers on
Shakespeare delivered at the 1962
Shakespeare Seminar.   (Toronto)
1963.   668006

SMITH (JAMES) [1777-1849)]
Macbeth travestie, by M[omus] M[edlar].
IN [Smith (J.) and Smith (H.)]
Rejected addresses, or The New theatrum
poetarum.   1812.   519723
_____ 13th edn.   1813.   519724
_____ 18th edn., carefully revised,
with an original preface and notes.
port.   illus.   1833.   523513
_____ 21st edn., carefully revised,
with an original preface and notes.
port.   illus.   1847.   523699
_____ [Edited] with an introduction
and notes by A. D. Godley.
frontis.   1904.   501348
_____ Another edn.   [1907] 497448
_____ [Edited] by A. Boyle.
ports.   illus.   1929.   356643

SMITH (JAMES)
Much ado about nothing: notes from
a book in preparation.   IN Scrutiny,
Vol. 13.   (Cambridge)   1945-6.

573398

SMITH (JAMES CRUICKSHANK)
Scott and Shakespeare.   IN English
Association, Essays and studies,
Vol. 24, 1938.   Collected by
[R.] L. Binyon.   (Oxford) 1939.

499319

SMITH (JAMES CRUICKSHANK) and GRIERSON
([Sir] HERBERT JOHN CLIFFORD)
Shakespeare's predecessors;
Shakespeare; [and] Shakespeare's
contemporaries and successors in drama.
IN GRIERSON ([Sir] H. J. C.) & SMITH
(J. C.) A Critical history of English
poetry.   1944.

553090

SMITH (JOHN CHRISTOPHER)
No more dams I'll make for fish
(Caliban's song in "The Tempest").
Words by Shakespeare; music by
J. C. Smith (1756). Edited by
J. Coates. IN Old English songs (1).
pp. 5. [1929.]

594154

SMITH (JOHN CHRISTOPHER)
No more dams I'll make for fish.
[Words by Shakespeare, with] abbre-
viated form of the [music] by
J. C. Smith. IN The Tempest.
Arranged and condensed for little
theater production by T. P. Robinson.
(New York) 1942.
The Players' Shakespeare.

542834

SMITH (JOHN CHRISTOPHER)
Up and down. [Words by Shakespeare]
from "A Midsummer night's dream".
Arranged by R. Dunstan. IN ARNE [T.A.]
While you here do snoring lie.
[1921.]
School Music Review, No. 255.

594166

SMITH (JOHN CHRISTOPHER)
You spotted snakes: unison song
from "The Fairies". Arr. R. Graves.
Words from 'A Midsummer-night's
dream'. pp. 4. [1956.]

665355

SMITH, JOHN HARRINGTON
The Comedy of errors: a scene by
scene analysis with critical
commentary. (New York) 1966.
Study master series.

768543

SMITH (JOHN HARRINGTON), PIZER (LOIS D.),
and KAUFMAN (EDWARD K.)
Hamlet, Antonio's Revenge and the Ur-
Hamlet.
IN SHAKESPEARE QUARTERLY IX.
pp. 493-498.
(New York) 1958.

605711

SMITH (JOHN HAZEL)
The Cancel in the Quarto of "2 Henry IV"
revisited. IN Shakespeare Quarterly
XV: 3. pp.173-178. (New York) 1964.

605711

SMITH (JOHN HAZEL)
Shylock: "devil incarnation" or
"poor man ... wronged"? IN The
Journal of English and Germanic
Philology, Vol. 60. (Urbana, Ill.)
1961.

6000780/60

Smith (John Moyr) illus.
LAMB (CHARLES and MARY)
Tales from Shakespeare. Shakespeare
for children. New edn. 1885.

394333

SMITH, JONATHAN
The Language of Leontes.
IN SHAKESPEARE QUARTERLY XIX: 4.
pp. 317-327.
(New York) 1968.

605711

SMITH (LAURENCE DWIGHT)
The Baconian biliteral cipher [and
references to the Bacon-Shakespeare
controversy]. IN Smith (L. D.)
Cryptography: the science of secret
writing.
bibliog. dgms. tables. 1944.

553061

SMITH (LEWIS WORTHINGTON)
Chronology and verse in Shakespeare.
FROM The English Journal, Vol. 21.
(Chicago) 1932.

442571

SMITH (LOGAN PEARSALL)
On reading Shakespeare. FROM Life
and Letters, Sept., 1932. pp. [80.]
bibliog. [1932]

396012

SMITH (LOGAN PEARSALL)
On reading Shakespeare.
bibliog. 1933. 403807
_____ Another edn. Revised and
corrected. (Crown Constables)
1934. 425617

Smith, Logan Pearsall *works relating to*

— AGATE (J. [E.])
On reading Shakespeare [: a review of
L. P. Smith's book]. IN Agate (J. [E.])
Thursdays and Fridays [: articles
contributed to the Daily Express and
John O'London's Weekly]. 1941.

530462

— KINGSMILL (H.) [pseud.]
Shakespeare criticism [: a review
of "On reading Shakespeare", by
L. P. Smith.] IN The English Review,
Vol. 56, 1933. 1933.

408264

— KNICKERBOCKER (W. S.)
Mr. Stoll's Shakspere [: reviews
of 'Art and artifice in Shakespeare'
by E. E. Stoll and 'On reading
Shakespeare' by L. P. Smith].
FROM Sewanee Review, Vol. 42.
pp. [20]. (Sewanee, Tenn.) 1934.

447442

— K[nights] (L.C.) On reading Shakespeare
by L.P. Smith: [a review.] In The
Criterion, Vol.12, 1933.

1932-33.

414720

— LASS (A. H.)
On reading Shakespeare [: a review of
"On reading Shakespeare" by L. P.
Smith.] FROM The English Journal,
October, 1934. (Chicago, Ill.)
1934.

492292

SMITH (L[UCY] TOULMIN), FURNIVALL (F. J.) and INGLEBY (C. M.)
The Shakspere allusion-book: a collection of allusions to Shakspere from 1591 to 1700, originally compiled by C. M. Ingleby, L[ucy] T. Smith and F. J. Furnivall, with the assistance of the New Shakspere Society. Re-edited, revised, and re-arranged, with an introduction by J. Munro (1909), and now re-issued with a preface by Sir E. [K.] Chambers.
2 vols.   1932.
The Shakespeare Library.
                                 392943

SMITH, MARION BODWELL
Dualities in Shakespeare [: the humanist search for reconciliation of opposites]. (Toronto)   1966.
                                 757124

Smith (Paul Gerard), Spigelgass (L.) and Grayson (C.) The Boys from Syracuse see English Editions (Comedy of Errors: Alterations, etc.)

SMITH (PETER D.)
The 1966 Festivals at Ashland, Oregon, and San Diego, California.
IN SHAKESPEARE QUARTERLY XVII: 4.
pp. 407-417.
(New York) 1966.
                                 605711

SMITH (PETER D.)
"Sharp wit and noble scenes": a review of the 1961 season of the Stratford, Ontario, Festival.
IN SHAKESPEARE QUARTERLY XIII: 1.
pp. 71-77.
(New York) 1962.
                                 605711

SMITH (PETER D.)
"Toil and trouble": a review of the 1962 season of the Stratford, Ontario, Festival.
IN SHAKESPEARE QUARTERLY XIII: 4.
pp. 521-527.
(New York) 1962.
                                 605711

SMITH (PETER [D.])
"A Trifling foolish banquet". IN Stratford Papers on Shakespeare delivered at the 1963 Shakespeare Seminar. (Toronto)   1964.
                                 668007

SMITH (RICHARD PENN)
The Sentinels & other plays. Edited [with a preface] by R. H. Wake and H. W. Schoenberger. (Princeton, N.J.)
                                 1941.
Includes "Shakespeare in love".
                                 553951

SMITH (ROBERT METCALF)
Fly-specks and folios, [including the Shakespeare First Folio]. IN The Colophon, Vol. 1. N.S. No. 1.
  facsimiles.   1935.
                                 438235

SMITH (ROBERT METCALF)
Froissart and the English chronicle play. [With references to Shakespeare.] (New York)
  bibliog.   1915.
Columbia University, Studies in English and Comparative Literature.
                                 473400

SMITH (ROBERT METCALF)
A Good word for Oswald. IN WILLIAMS (A. L.) A Tribute to George Coffin Taylor. [Chapel Hill, N.C.] 1952.
                                 625745

SMITH (ROBERT METCALF)
Hamlet said "pajock". FROM The Journal of English and Germanic Philology, Vol. 44. (Urbana, Ill.)
  bibliog.   1945.
                                 578405

SMITH (ROBERT METCALF)
Interpretations of Measure for Measure.
IN SHAKESPEARE QUARTERLY I: 4.
pp. 208-218. (New York) 1950.
                                 605711

SMITH (ROBERT METCALF)
King Lear and the Merlin tradition.
IN Modern Language Quarterly, Vol. 7. (Seattle)
  bibliog.   1946.
                                 584762

SMITH (ROBERT METCALF)
Macbeth's cyme once more. IN Modern Language Notes, Vol. 60. (Baltimore)
  bibliog.   1945.
                                 571543

SMITH (ROBERT METCALF)
The Pursuit of a First Folio.
IN The Colophon. New series, Vol. 3. No. 1. (New York)   1938.
                                 478439

SMITH (ROBERT METCALF)
Why a First Folio Shakespeare remained in England. IN Review of English Studies: a quarterly journal of English literature and the English language, Vol. 15.   1939.
                                 513846

SMITH, SHEILA MARY
'This great solemnity': a study of the presentation of death in 'Antony and Cleopatra'. FROM English Studies, 45: 2.
pp.113-176. (Amsterdam)   1964.
                                 750612

SMITH (T. W.)
Shakespeare: Julius Caesar.   pp. 64.
               [1940.]   511820
Notes on Chosen English Texts.
_____ Revised edition.   (Bath)
  illus.   [1965.]   744905

SMITH (T. W.)
Shakespeare: King Henry V.   pp. 72.
  dgm.   [1940.]
Notes on Chosen English Texts.
                                 601686

SMITH (T. W.)
Shakespeare: A Midsummer night's
dream.   pp. 56.
  dgm.   [1940.]
Notes on Chosen English Texts.

        601683

SMITH (T. W.)
Shakespeare: The Tempest.   pp. 52.
  dgm.   [1940.]
Notes on Chosen English Texts.

        601688

SMITH (TOULMIN)
On the Bond-story in The Merchant of
Venice, and a version of it in the
Cursor Mundi.
IN Transactions of the New Shakespeare
Society, Series 1. No. 3.   pp. 181–189.
                    1875–6.

        40620

SMITH (W. F.)
Much ado about nothing: a complete
paraphrase.   3rd edn.   pp. 66.
                [c.1905.]
Normal Tutorial Series.

        545615

SMITH (WARREN DALE)
The Duplicate revelation of Portia's death.
IN SHAKESPEARE QUARTERLY IV: 2.
pp. 153–161.
(New York)   1953.

        605711

SMITH (WARREN D.)
The Elizabethan rejection of judicial
astrology and Shakespeare's practice.
IN SHAKESPEARE QUARTERLY IX: 2.
pp. 159–176.
(New York)   1958.

        605711

SMITH (WARREN DALE)
The Elizabethan stage and Shakespeare's
entrance announcements.
IN SHAKESPEARE QUARTERLY IV: 4.
pp. 405–410.
(New York)   1953.
        605711

SMITH (WARREN DALE)
Evidence of scaffolding on Shakespeare's
stage.   IN The Review of English
Studies, New Series, Vol. 2.   (Oxford)
                  1951.

        318239/2/2

SMITH (WARREN DALE)
The Henry V choruses in the First Folio.
IN Journal of English and Germanic
Philology, Vol. 53.   (Urbana, Ill.)
                  1954.

        600780/53

SMITH (WARREN DALE)
More light on "Measure for Measure".
IN Modern Language Quarterly, Vol. 23,
No. 4.   1962.

        525289/1962

SMITH (WARREN DALE)
New light on stage directions in
Shakespeare.   IN Studies in Philology,
Vol. 47.   (Chapel Hill, N.C.)
                  1950.

        554520/47

SMITH (WARREN DALE)
Shakespeare's Shylock. IN Shakespeare
Quarterly XV: 3. pp.193–199. (New York)
                  1964.

        605711

SMITH (WARREN DALE)
Shakespeare's stagecraft as denoted
by the dialogue in the original
printings of his texts.   (Ann Arbor,
Mich.)
  typescript, 1947. microfilm,
positive copy.   1 reel, 35 mm.
                  [1950.]

        612610

SMITH (WARREN DALE)
Stage business in Shakespeare's dialogue.
IN SHAKESPEARE QUARTERLY IV: 3.
pp. 311–316.
(New York)   1953.

        605711

SMITH (WARREN [DALE])
The Third type of aside in Shakespeare.
IN Modern Language Notes, Vol. 64.
(Baltimore)
  bibliog.   1949.

        439157/64

SMITH (WARREN HUNTING)
Architecture in English fiction.
[With references to Shakespeare.]
(New Haven, [Conn.])
  illus.   1934.
Yale Studies in English, 83.

        429738

SMITH (WILLIAM)
Evesham and neighbourhood.   Revised,
extended and partially re-written
by K. G. Smith.   With an introduction
by E. A. B. Barnard.   Illustrated by
E. H. New and B. C. Boulter.   [Con-
taining references to Shakespeare and
Stratford-upon-Avon].   5th edn.
(Evesham)
  illus.   maps.   1930.
Homeland Handbooks, No. 25.

        460695

Smith, William Henry *works relating to*

———The Art of cavilling: [an answer to
W. H. Smith on the Bacon-Shakespeare
question].   FROM Blackwood's Magazine,
Nov. 1856.   (Edinburgh)   1856.

        440113

Smithson (E.W.) Ben Jonson's pious
fraud [: with appendix Jonson's
Ode in the First Folio, 1623.] In
The Nineteenth century and after,
Vol. 74.

                1913.

        247982

Smollett, Tobias George *works relating to*

——HEILMAN (R. B.)
Falstaff and Smollett's Micklewhimmen.
[With bibliographical notes.] IN The
Review of English Studies, Vol. 22.
(Oxford)

[1946.]

579165

——KAHRL (G. M.)
The Influence of Shakespeare on Smollett.
[With bibliographical notes.]
IN CRAIG (H.) ed., Essays in dramatic
literature: the Parrott presentation
volume. (Princeton)
port.   1935.

444399

SMYTH (GEORGE LEWIS)
William Shakspeare.   IN Smyth (G. L.)
Biographical illustrations of St. Paul's
Cathedral and Westminster Abbey.
                1843.   68705
————— IN Smyth (G. L.) The Worthies
of England.   1850.   546938

Smyth (J.) David Garrick. pp. 80.

[1887.]

486282

**Smyth (Mary W.) Dante and Shakespeare.
In The Nineteenth century and after,
Vol. 64.**

1908.

213154

Smythe (A.J.) The Life of William
Terriss, actor. With an introduction
by C.[W.] Scott [and containing
references to Shakespearian
performances.] Ports. Illus.

1898.

420109

SMYTHE (PERCY ELLESMERE)
A Complete paraphrase of Hamlet, Prince
of Denmark. (Sydney)   [1959.]

666318

SMYTHE (PERCY ELLESMERE)
Critical notes, appreciation and
exercises on Shakespeare's Macbeth.
pp. 91. (Sydney)   [1939]

509833

SMYTHE (PERCY ELLESMERE)
Julius Caesar: critical notes,
appreciation and exercises. pp. 84.
(Sydney)   [1941.]

532133

SMYTHE (PERCY ELLESMERE)
The Merchant of Venice: a complete
paraphrase. pp. 76. (Sydney)
[1959.]

666319

SMYTHE (PERCY ELLESMERE)
A Midsummer night's dream: critical
notes, appreciation and exercises [on
the play by Shakespeare]. pp. 87-
116. (Sydney)   [1941.]

532132

SMYTHE (PERCY ELLESMERE)
The Tempest: critical notes,
appreciation and exercises. pp. 50.
(Sydney)   [1941.]

532131

SMYTHIES, WILLIAM GORDON
Charles John Kean [: a poem].
IN Golden Leisures.
pp. 32.   c.1868.

69859

SNARESBROOK, FOREST SCHOOL
Programmes, etc., of Shakespeare
performances.   (Snaresbrook)

1933-59.

416896

SNIDER (DENTON JACQUES)
Antony and Cleopatra [: an analysis
of the play].   FROM The Journal of
Speculative Philosophy, Vol. 10.
(St. Louis)   1876.

556085

SNIDER (DENTON JACQUES)
Historical drama - Coriolanus.
FROM The Western [, Nov. and Dec.
1875]. [Saint Louis, Missouri]
[1875.]

554157

SNIDER (DENTON JACQUES)
A Midsummer night's dream [: an
analysis of the play]. FROM The
Journal of Speculative Philosophy,
Vol. 8.   (St. Louis)   1874.

556082

SNIDER (DENTON JACQUES)
Shakespeare's comedy "As you like it"
[: an analysis of the play].   Re-
printed from The Journal of Speculative
Philosophy, Vol. 7.   FROM The
Western[, Jan. 1876]. [Saint Louis]
[1876.]
Imperfect, all after Jan. 1876 wanting.

562632

SNIDER (DENTON JACQUES)
Shakspeare's "Cymbeline" [: an
analysis of the play]. FROM The
Journal of Speculative Philosophy,
Vol. 9. [St. Louis]   1875.

556084

SNIDER (DENTON JACQUES)
Shakespeare's "Tempest" [: an
analysis of the play].   FROM
The Journal of Speculative Philosophy,
Vol. 8. (St. Louis)   1874.

556083

SNIDER (D. J.)
Shakespeare's tragedies. King Lear
[: an analysis of the play, Part 1.]
FROM The Western [, Vol. 1]. [Saint
Louis]   1875.

563689

SNIDER (D. J.)
Shakespeare's tragedies. Othello
[: an analysis of the play, Part 2].
FROM The Western [, Vol. 1].
[Saint Louis]   1875.

563690

SNIDER (DENTON JACQUES)
The Tragedy of Julius Caesar [: an
analysis of the play]. FROM The
Western, Vol. 2. [Saint Louis]
[1876.]

558058

SNIDER (DENTON JACQUES)
The Two Gentlemen of Verona [: an
analysis of the play]. FROM The
Journal of Speculative Philosophy,
Vol. 10. (St. Louis)   1876.

556086

SNOWDEN ([P. SNOWDEN,] Viscount)
The Merchant of Venice. Illustrated
by F. Matania. FROM The Strand
Magazine, Dec., 1933.   1933.
Shakespeare's Plays as Short Stories.

419770

Snowden ([P.] Snowden, Viscount) The
Merchant of Venice. In Six stories
from Shakespeare. Illustrations by
F. Matania.

1934.

428744

SNUGGS (HENRY L.)
Shakespeare and five acts: studies in
a dramatic convention. (New York)
tables. bibliog.   1960.

666574

SNYDER (KARL E.)
Kings and kingship in four of
Shakespeare's history plays. IN
Shakespeare 1964 [: a record of the
celebrations of the Shakespeare
Quatercentenary at Texas Christian
University]. (Fort Worth, Tex.)
illus.   1965.

745402

SNYDER (SUSAN)
King Lear and the Prodigal Son.
IN SHAKESPEARE QUARTERLY XVII: 4.
pp. 361-369.
(New York) 1966.
605711

SOCHATOFF, A. FRED
Much ado about nothing. IN
Shakespeare: lectures on five plays,
by A. F. Sochatoff [and others].
(Pittsburgh, Pa.)   1958.
Carnegie series in English.
666185

SOCHATOFF (A. FRED)
The Tragedies.
IN "Starre of Poets". Discussions of
Shakespeare. (Pittsburgh, Pa.:
Carnegie Institute of Technology)
1966.

766812

SOCHATOFF, A. FRED
Twelfth Night. IN "Lovers meeting":
discussions of five plays by
Shakespeare. (Pittsburgh, Pa.)
1964.
Carnegie series in English.
741508

Societies and Clubs

——ABBOTS LANGLEY & BEDMOND COMMUNITY PLAYERS
Programmes, etc. of Shakespearean
performances. (Abbots Langley)
1927-9.

440897

——ADELAIDE UNIVERSITY SHAKESPEARE SOCIETY
Symon ([Sir] J. H.)
Shakespeare quotation: a lecture
delivered before the Adelaide University
Shakespeare Society at Adelaide.
pp. 63.   1901.
Printed for private circulation.

395747

—— AUSTRALIAN ENGLISH ASSOCIATION
Howarth (R. G.)
Shakespeare's Tempest. A public
lecture delivered for the Australian
English Association on Oct. 1, 1936.
pp. 55. (Sydney)   1936.

472072

—— Bacon Society see Bacon-Shakespeare
controversy.

BACON SOCIETY OF AMERICA
Constitution: adopted May 15th, 1922.
pp. [8.] (New York)   1922.

403988

—— BELFAST, ROYAL BELFAST ACADEMICAL
INSTITUTION
Programmes of Shakespearian performances.
(Belfast)   1927-42.

449361

—— [Bermondsey and Oxford Boys' Club.]
Shakespeare in a boys' club: [the
performance of Macbeth by the
Bermondsey and Oxford Boys' Club],
by J.R.P.Moon. In School Drama,
Vol.1, No.3.

[1938.]

522632

——BIRMINGHAM, HANDSWORTH PRIVATE DRAMATIC
ASSOCIATION
Record of performances, 1861-1914,
including Much ado about nothing and
Twelfth Night.
manuscript.   1861-1914.

514092

——BIRMINGHAM, KING EDWARD'S SCHOOL
Musical and Dramatic Society. Programmes etc. of annual performances
of Shakespeare's plays, 1922-

353682

——BIRMINGHAM. OUR SHAKESPEARE CLUB
Waterhouse (Rachel)
Shakespeare and the Birmingham Liberals
["Our Shakespeare Club"]. IN The
Central Literary magazine XXXIX:
7th April 1964.   pp. 17-24.

740859

——BIRMINGHAM AND MIDLAND INSTITUTE,
SHAKESPEARE AND DRAMATIC SOCIETY
[Programmes] 1923-

497940

——BIRMINGHAM AND MIDLAND INSTITUTE, UNION
OF TEACHERS AND STUDENTS, SHAKESPEARE
AND DRAMATIC SOCIETY
Shakespeare Birthday Commemoration.
[Programmes], 1910-12; 1916-17;
1919-23; 1928-50.   [1910-50]
 1913-1915; 1918 wanting. 1924-1927
not issued.

245883

——BLACKBURN SHAKESPEARE SOCIETY
[Programmes, cuttings, etc., relating
to performances, 1935-7.
ports.   illus.   1935-7.

474538

——BOLTON SCHOOL DRAMATIC SOCIETY
Programmes of Shakespearian performances,
1934-
425733

——BOLTON SHAKESPEARE SOCIETY
Proceedings.   10th annual meeting,
May, 1926.   With resumé of ten years'
work and list of members for the year
1925-26.   pp. [10].   [Bolton]
1926.

477461

——BOURNEMOUTH, LEAMOR PLAYERS
Programmes of Shakespeare performances,
etc.   1926-[1935]

418310

——BOURNEMOUTH SHAKESPEARE PLAYERS
Programmes, etc.   (Bournemouth)
ports.   1947-55.

634275

——BOURNVILLE YOUTHS' CLUB
Programmes, etc., of Shakespeare
performances.   (Birmingham)
illus.   1932-47.

455239

——BRISTOL SHAKESPEARE SOCIETY
Programmes, etc. of Shakespearian
performances, 1945-1949.   (Bristol)
illus.   1945-1949.

566861

British Empire
Shakespeare Society Branches

——AUCKLAND (NEW ZEALAND) BRANCH
Programmes, etc.   [Auckland, N.Z.]
[1933]-5.

418028

—— BATH AVON BRANCH
Programmes, leaflets, etc.
1926-1932.
Branch ceased to exist in 1933.

397911

—— Brentwood Branch.   Minute Book, 1911-
1935.   (Brentwood)
Note: Mainly manuscript.

622538

——BRIDGWATER BRANCH
Programmes, etc.   1931-4.

397913

——BUCKLEY (DORIS)
The "B[ritish] E[mpire] S[hakespeare]
S[ociety]".   IN The Amateur Theatre
and Playwrights' Journal, Vol. 4,
No. 75.   1937.

467093

——DUBLIN BRANCH
Shillman (B.)
The Play of Macbeth: its importance
as tragedy: a lecture delivered to
the British Empire Shakespeare Society,
Dublin Branch.   With a foreword by
W. F. Trench.   pp. 28.   (Dublin)
port.   [1926.]

408187

——DUNEDIN (NEW ZEALAND) BRANCH
Programmes, etc.   1916-
Dunedin Shakespeare Club was affiliated
with the British Empire Shakespeare
Society in 1923.

397914

——DURBAN BRANCH
Annual reports, 4th (1931)-3.
[Durban]

488038

——EPSOM BRANCH
Programmes, etc.   1931-32.

416596

——GLASGOW BRANCH
Report and financial statement,
[1913]-44.
Wants 1918-19, 1923-24, 1925-26.

419662

—— [Notes on meetings of the British
Empire Shakespeare Society].   IN
The Poetry Review, Vols. 4-5.
1914.

253079

——ORPINGTON BRANCH
Programmes, etc.   (Orpington)
1941-57.

535366

—— PORTSMOUTH BRANCH
Programmes, etc.   (Portsmouth)
[1934]-38.

523297

—— ROCHDALE BRANCH
Leaflets, etc.   1925-45.

397915

—— SHEFFIELD BRANCH
Parry (R. St. J.)
Henry Jackson, O.M.: a memoir [with
extracts from his correspondence,
including references to the Bacon-
Shakespeare controversy; a lecture:
Was Shakspere of Stratford the author
of Shakespeare's plays and poems?]
delivered to the Sheffield Branch of
the British Empire Shakespeare Society,
29 February, 1912.   (Cambridge)
port. illus. bibliog. 1926.

432383

—— TUNBRIDGE WELLS BRANCH
Programmes, etc.   1937-45.

547086

—— UPPER NORWOOD BRANCH
Programmes, etc. relating to
Shakespearian performances.   1934-39.

497015

—— BURTON SHAKESPEARE SOCIETY
Programmes, leaflets, cuttings, etc.,
1937-   (Burton-on-Trent)
464483

——CHELTENHAM
The Cheltonian. [Edited by members
of Cheltenham College. With a
reference to the College Shakespeare
Society.] April 1905.   pp. [28.]
[1905]

390856

——CLIFTON, ALL SAINTS OLD BOYS' SOCIETY
Programmes, etc., of Shakespearian
performances. [Clifton] 1921-38.

463174

——CLIFTON SHAKSPERE SOCIETY
Handlist of books in the library of
the Clifton Shakspere Society.
ff. 29.   [Clifton]
typescript.   [1936.]

471797

—— CORNISH OPEN-AIR SHAKESPEAREAN FESTIVAL
Programmes, etc.   [Truro] 1934-51.

424967

——COVENTRY TEACHERS' SHAKESPEARIAN SOCIETY
Shakespearian performances.
Programmes, cuttings, tickets, etc.
(Coventry)
illus.   1937-[8]

473497

——DARLINGTON ART PLAYERS
Programmes, etc. of Shakespearean
performances.   [Darlington]
1928-37.

419074

——DERBY SHAKESPEARE SOCIETY [formerly
British Empire Shakespeare Society,
Derby Branch]
Programmes, etc. (Derby) 1908-

217393

——DUBLIN SHAKESPEARE SOCIETY
Programmes, etc.   (Dublin)
1937-1943.

488035

—— Dunedin [New Zealand] Shakespeare
Club see under British Empire
Shakespeare Society, above.

—— DURHAM COUNTY DRAMA ASSOCIATION
Programmes of annual festivals.
(Durham)   1940-5.

535367

—— EASTBOURNE SHAKESPEARE SOCIETY
Programmes, etc.   (Eastbourne)
[1952]-

665443

—— ELIZABETHAN STAGE SOCIETY
[Poel (W.)]
The Playhouse of the sixteenth century.
pp. 30.   [Edinburgh]
illus.   [c.1904.]

599944

——ELIZABETHAN STAGE SOCIETY
Shakespeare Commemoration, 1905.
Programme; Romeo and Juliet, given
by the Elizabethan Stage Society at
the request of the London Shakespeare
League, at the Royalty Theatre, London,
May 5, 1905: [programme. With rules,
etc. of the London Shakespeare League.]
1905.

517666

——GLOBE-MERMAID ASSOCIATION OF ENGLAND AND
AMERICA
Leaflets, etc., 1935-37.
464484

—— Globe-Mermaid Association of
England and America. Newspaper
cuttings relating to the formation of a new Shakespeare centre
in London sponsored by the Globe-
Mermaid Association.] Illus.

1937-45

494119

—— GREENOCK SHAKESPEARE SOCIETY
Programmes, tickets, etc.
(Greenock)
illus.   1938.

488034

—— GRIMSBY, WINTRINGHAM SECONDARY SCHOOL
DRAMATIC SOCIETY
Programmes of Shakespeare performances.
(Grimsby)
illus.   1931-

426697

HARROGATE SHAKESPEAREAN FESTIVAL SOCIETY
Posters, programmes, etc.   (Harrogate)
1942-7.

535368

HULL PLAYGOERS' SOCIETY
[Programmes, etc. of Shakespearian
performances.]   (Hull)   1929-34

424484

HUNTER COLLEGE SHAKESPEARE SOCIETY,
NEW YORK
Silver falcon [: a periodical].
Published by the Shakespeare Society,
Hunter College of the City of New York.
pp. 28.   (New York)   1936.

598969

HURSTPIERPOINT, ST. JOHN'S COLLEGE
Programmes of plays presented by the
Shakspere Society.   (Hurstpierpoint)
[1905]-

419852

KEMNAY SECONDARY SCHOOL, ABERDEENSHIRE
Performances of Shakespearian plays
[: programmes, photographs, etc.],
1924-

455261

KIRKHAM GRAMMAR SCHOOL LITERARY AND
DRAMATIC SOCIETY
Programmes, etc. of Shakespeare
performances.   [Kirkham]   [1932]-3.

416899

LADIES' GUILD OF FRANCIS ST. ALBAN
Stewart (Mrs. [Helen] H.)
Light on the "Hamlet": historical
associations and prototypes.   pp. 51.
[1912.]

559069

LEIGHTON HOUSE SOCIETY
Speaight (R.)
Shakespeare's search for a hero [: a
lecture delivered to the Leighton
House Society on Nov. 6th, 1936].
FROM Blackfriars, May-June, 1937.
1937.

472754

LIVERPOOL SHAKESPEARE SOCIETY
Reports, programmes, etc. of
Shakespearian performances, 1949-
1949-

612236

London Shakespeare League

Booth (J. [B.])
A Century of theatrical history, 1816-
1916: the "Old Vic" [Royal Victoria
Hall, Lambeth.]   pp. 72.
port.   illus.   1917.   269128
_____ Another copy.   422907

[HEADLAM (S. D.)]
The Three objects of the London
Shakespeare League.   pp. 8.   1920.

285411

LITTLEWOOD (S. R.)
The London Shakespeare Commemoration
League: its purposes and its story.
pp. 16.   1928.

424656

Ordish (Thomas Fairman)
Shakespeare in London, a fantasy [in
verse].   (London Shakespeare
Commemoration, 1913).   [With typescript original, signed by the author.]
pp. [4], ff. [4].
2 vols.   [1913.]

665063

POEL (WILLIAM)
Monthly letters written for the
Shakespeare League Journal, Nos. 1-52.
1915-19.
Includes autograph letter by W. Poel.

665890

Poel (William)
Monthly letters [on Shakespeare's life
and art, and the production of his
plays, privately circulated among
members of the London Shakespeare
League and their friends, 1912-1924.
Selected and arranged [with foreword]
by A. M. T.
port.   1929.

362873

The Prefatory pages of the First
Folio, with a comment by Sir S. Lee.
3rd edn.   pp. [19].
port.   1925.

424655

Shakespeare Commemoration, 1905.
Programme; Romeo and Juliet, given
by the Elizabethan Stage Society at
the request of the London Shakespeare
League, at the Royalty Theatre, London
May 5, 1905 [: programme.   With
rules, etc. of the London Shakespeare
League.]   1905.

517666

MANCHESTER, SHAKESPEARE TERCENTENARY
ASSOCIATION
Songs and recitations in commemoration
of the Shakespeare Tercentenary by
Shakespearean students and pupils in
Manchester schools.   3rd edn.,
enlarged.   pp. 31.   (Manchester)
1916.

591416

MULBERRY CLUB
Timbs (J.)
English eccentrics and eccentricities.
[With a passage on the Mulberries, a
Shakespearian Club.]   New edn.
ports.   illus.   1877.

400637

— NATIONAL JUNIOR SHAKESPEARE CLUB
Nesbit (E[dith])
Twenty beautiful stories from
Shakespeare. Official text for members
of the National Junior Shakespeare
Club. Illustrated by M. Bihn.
Edited and arranged, [with a preface],
by E. T. Roe. (Chicago) 1926.

422519

— New Shakspere Society
[HALLIWELL-PHILLIPPS (J. O.)]
Which shall it be? New lamps or old?
Shaxper of Shakespeare?: questions
submitted to members of the New
Shakspere Society. pp. 16. (Brighton)
[Proof copy] 1879.
Unique copy, with cancelled preface,
and corrections by the author.
494717

— NEW SHAKSPERE SOCIETY
Swinburne (A. C.)
Report of the first anniversary
meeting of the newest Shakespeare
society [i.e. New Shakspere Society],
April, 1876. FROM The Examiner,
April 1, 1876. 1876.

555523

— NEW SHAKSPERE SOCIETY, Series VI
[Shakespeare's England]
No. 5, Appendix: Southwark in the
time of Shakspere: the Bankside,
theatres, stews &c., [by W. Rendle].
pp. 32. plans. 1878.
Autographed by the author.
The other New Shakespeare Society and
Shakespeare Society publications are
listed in the earlier catalogue 1879-
1931.
508207

— NEW YORK SHAKESPEARE SOCIETY
Yeatman (J. P.)
The Gentle Shakspere: a vindication.
3rd edn. (augmented). (Shakespeare
Society of New York)
ports. facsimile. 1904.

405091

— Newspaper cuttings: Shakespeare
and other societies. 1962-

668210

— NOTTINGHAM SHAKESPEARE SOCIETY
Programmes of plays, etc. 1907-

200755

— OLDMINSTER SHAKESPEARE CLUB
A Very modest club. FROM Chambers's
Journal, [1862.] pp. [3.] [1862.]

390783

— OXFORD, NEW COLLEGE SHAKESPEARE CLUB
Bowman (H. [E.])
Middle-East window [: memories,
including a reference to the New
College Shakespeare Club, Oxford].
With an introduction by Sir R. Storrs.
ports. illus. map. 1942.

533148

Oxford University Dramatic Society

— COGHILL (N.)
The Taming of the Shrew by the O[xford]
U[niversity] D[ramatic] S[ociety].
IN Picture Post, Vol. 28.
illus. 1945.

572595

— MACKINNON (A.)
The Oxford amateurs: history of
theatricals at the university.
[Including references to Shakespearian
productions by the O.U.D.S.] 1910.

226892

— Programmes, etc. of Shakespeare
performances. (Oxford) [1895-]
Wants 1901; 1903; 1905; 1908-9;
1911-20; 1922; 1925; 1928; 1931.

451509

— Rentoul (Sir G.) This is my case : an
autobiography. [With references to
Shakespearean performances by the
Oxford University Dramatic Society.]
Ports. Illus.

1944.

551873

— PASADENA PLAYHOUSE
Programmes of Shakespeare performances,
etc. (Pasadena, Calif.) 1935-41.

440898

— PENRHYN PLAYERS DRAMATIC SOCIETY
Programmes, etc. of performances of
Shakespeare. (Kirkdale)
ports. illus. 1919-35.

416907

— PETERSFIELD, STEEP SHAKESPEARE PLAYERS
Programmes, etc. of performances,
1926-1961. (Petersfield)
464481

— Philadelphia SAVAGE (HENRY L.)
The Shakspere Society of Philadelphia.
IN SHAKESPEARE QUARTERLY III: 4.
pp. 341-352.
(New York) 1952.
605711

— PHILADELPHIA SHAKESPEARE SOCIETY
Furness (H. H.)
The Homage of the Shakspere Society
of Philadelphia. IN GOLLANCZ ([Sir] I.)
ed., A Book of homage to Shakespeare.
ports. illus. facsimiles. [1916.]

264175

— PLYMOUTH SHAKSPERE LITERARY SOCIETY
Programmes, syllabuses, etc.
(Plymouth) [1919]-

453707

——PORTSMOUTH TEACHERS' DRAMATIC SOCIETY
Programmes of Shakespeare performances, 1925-37.   (Portsmouth)
illus.   [1925-37.]
Wants programme for 1924.   No
performance 1931.

425732

——RICHMOND SHAKESPEARE SOCIETY
Programmes, cuttings, etc., of
Shakespearian performances.   1934-

455238

Shakespeare Association

——Barrett (W.P.) Chart of plays, 1584-
1623. Published under the auspices
of the Shakespeare Association.
pp.39.

(Cambridge)   1934.

421734

——BUTT (J.)
Pope's taste in Shakespeare: a
paper read before the Shakespeare
Association, March 22nd, 1935.
pp. 21.   1936.

456087

——ELLIS-FERMOR (UNA [M.])
Some recent research in Shakespeare's
imagery: a paper read before the
Shakespeare Association, March 19th,
1937. pp. 39.   1937.

472302

——In commemoration of the First Folio
Tercentenary: a re-setting of the
preliminary matter of the First Folio,
with a catalogue of Shakespeariana
exhibited in the Hall of the Worshipful
Company of Stationers.   Introduction
by Sir I. Gollancz.   pp. 56.
facsimiles.   1923.
Half t.p. missing.

428768

——ISAACS (J.)
Production and stage-management at
the Blackfriars Theatre.   pp. 28.
1933.   414993
_____ Another copy.   415677

——Notices of meetings, accounts, etc.
1932-39.

416906

——Shakespeare Association Facsimiles:
rare texts illustrating life and thought
in Shakespeare's England.   General
editor: G. B. Harrison.   1931-
(No. 1) GIFFORD (G.)
A Dialogue concerning witches and
witchcraftes, 1593. With an introduction by Beatrice [M. I.] White.
bibliog.   1931.   390117
(No. 2)   GUILPIN (E.)
Skialetheia; [or, A Shadow of truth
in certaine epigrams and satyres,]
1598.   pp. [84.]   Anon.
1931.   390118

(No. 3)   M[ARKHAM (G.)]
A Health to the gentlemanly profession
of serving-men, 1598.   By I.M.   With
an introduction by A. V. Judges.
pp. [94].   1931.   390119
(No. 4)   NORDEN (J.)
Vicissitudo rerum: [an elegiacall poeme.]
1600.   With an introduction by D. C.
Collins.   pp. [70.] 1931.   390120
(No. 5)   COCKAINE (Sir T.)
A Short treatise on hunting, 1591.
With an introduction by W. R. Halliday.
1932.   403069
(No. 6)   SILVER (G.)
Paradoxes of defence, 1599.   With an
introduction by J. D. Wilson.
1933.   403070
(No. 7)   Present remedies against the
plague, etc.   With an introduction by
W. P. Barrett.   1933.   403071
(No. 8)   BUCKMINSTER (T.)
An Almanack and prognostication for
the year 1598.   With an introduction
by E. F. Bosanquet.   pp. [62].
1935.   437589
(No. 9)   Battle of Nieuport, 1600:
two news pamphlets and a ballad.
With an introduction on news in Eliza-
bethan England, by D. C. Collins.
pp. [50].   facsimile.   1935.   437590
(No. 10)   The Life and death of
Gamaliel Ratsey, a famous thief of
England, executed at Bedford, 26th March,
1605; [Ratseys repentance: a poem by
G. Ratsey, 1605, and Ratseis ghost,
1605.]   1935.   435650
(No. 11)   Work for chimny-sweepers;
or, A Warning for tobacconists.   1660.
With an introduction by S. H. Atkins.
1936.   452705
(No. 12)   DAY (J.)
The Ile of guls.   1606.   With an
introduction by G. B. Harrison.
1936.   452706
(No. 13)   [DALLINGTON (Sir R.)]
The View of Fraunce.   1604.   With
an introduction by W. P. Barrett.
1936.   452707
(No. 14)   MORLEY (T.)
A Plaine and easie introduction to
practicall musicke, [1597].   With an
introduction by E. H. Fellowes.
1937.   467403
(No. 15)   [DU LAURENS (A.)]
A Discourse of the preservation of
the sight: of melancholike diseases;
of rheumes, and of old age, by A.
Laurentius, [and] translated by R.
Surphlet, 1599.   With an introduction
by S. V. Larkey.   (Oxford)
1938.   483395
——Shakespeare Festival matinee at the
New Theatre, (under the auspices of
the Shakespeare Association), April
29th, 1921.   [Programme.]   pp. [8.]
1921.

471782

——Shakespeare Quarto Facsimiles see
English Editions [: the Separate
Plays].

——WHITE (BEATRICE [M. I.])
An Index to the Elizabethan stage;
and William Shakespeare: a study
of facts and problems, by Sir E. [K.]
Chambers.   (Oxford) 1934.   420692
_____ Another copy.   Different
imprint.   430175

——WILLCOCK (GLADYS D.)
Shakespeare as a critic of language.
pp. 30.   1934.

425740

— WILSON (F. P.)
The English jestbooks of the sixteenth
and early seventeenth centuries [: a
paper read before the Shakespeare
Association, Nov. 26, 1937]. Reprinted
from the Huntington Library Quarterly,
Vol. 2, No. 2. pp. [38.] [San
Marino, Cal.]
bibliog. 1939.

550832

Shakespeare Association of America

— Bulletin. Vol. 1 (1924) – Vol. 24
(1949). [With annual bibliographies
from 1927.] (New York)
ports. illus. 24 vols. 1924–49.
Wants Vol. 1 No. 3. Continued as
Shakespeare Quarterly, catal. no. 605711.

400135

— HYDE (Mrs. MARY MORLEY CRAPO)
The Shakespeare Association of America.
IN Shakespeare 400: essays by
American scholars on the anniversary
of the poet's birth. Published in
co-operation with the Shakespeare
Association of America.
illus. 1964.

667803

— The Shakespeare Quarterly, Vol. 1–
(Bethlehem, Pa.)
ports. illus. 1950–
Previously issued as Shakespeare
Association of America Bulletin,
see catal. no. 400135.

605711

— SHAKESPEARE ASSOCIATION OF JAPAN
Catalogue of the exhibition of
Shakespeariana under the patronage
of the Shakespeare Association of
Japan and the British Ambassador,
held at Maruzen Co. Ltd. Tokyo,
May 1933. pp. 82. [Tokyo] 1933.

407934

— Shakespeare Club of Alloa. FROM
Blackwood's Magazine, May, 1817.
(Edinburgh) 1817.

440102

— The Shakespeare Fellowship Newsletter,
1943, 1945–58. (The Shakespeare
Fellowship)
15 vols. 1943–58.
1944 wanting. Continued by
'Shakespearean authorship review'.

666183

— Shakespeare Fellowship Quarterly [: a
periodical attempting to prove that
Edward de Vere, Earl of Oxford, wrote
the works of Shakespeare]. Vol. 1
(Dec. 1939 – Nov. 1940) – Vol. 9, No.
2 (1948). (New York)
ports. illus. map. 9 vols. 1939–48.
Vols. 1–4 called News letter. All
published.

562696

— SHAKESPEARE LADIES CLUB (London 1736–)
Avery (Emmett Langdon)
The Shakespeare Ladies Club.
IN SHAKESPEARE QUARTERLY VII.
pp. 153–158. (New York) 1956.

605711

Shakespeare Society, London

— COLLIER (J. P.)
Notes and emendations to the text
of Shakespeare's plays, from early
manuscript corrections in a copy
of the Folio, 1632.
facsimile. 1852.

420950

— Plays edited by the Shakespeare
Society. FROM The Gentleman's
Magazine, March 1845. pp. [28.]
1845.

402699

— [Portrait of] William Shakespeare,
from the Chandos portrait in the
possession of the Earl of Ellesmere.
Engraved by S. Cousins. 1849.

132010

— SHAKESPEARE SOCIETY OF JAPAN
Shakespeare studies, Vol.1, 1962–
(Tokyo)
1962–

667505

— THE SHAKESPEARE SOCIETY OF WASHINGTON
Programmes, 1926–54. [Washington]
1929–30; 1938–39; 1939–40; 1940–41
wanting.

645713

— The Shakespeare Stage: the quarterly
bulletin of the Shakespeare Stage
Society, Nos. 1–7. 1953–54.

666647

— Shakespearean Authorship Review, Nos. 1–
(The Shakespearean Authorship Society)
1959–
Formerly "The Shakespeare Fellowship
News-Letter".

666271

—SHEFFIELD CENTRAL SECONDARY SCHOOL BOYS'
SHAKESPEARE SOCIETY
Keeton (G. W.) ed.
All right on the night: the book of
the Sheffield Central Secondary School
Boys' Shakespeare Society. (Sheffield)
ports. illus.   1929.

417053

—SHEFFIELD EDUCATIONAL SETTLEMENT
Programmes, tickets, etc. of
Shakespearian performances.
[Sheffield]   1930-

425721

—SHEFFIELD SHAKESPEARE CLUB
Shakespeare in Sheffield [: a
criticism of the Sheffield Shakespeare
Club]. pp. 24. (Stamford) 1822.

621024

—SOUTHEND-ON-SEA SHAKESPEARE SOCIETY
[Programmes, reports, etc.]
[Southend]
illus.   1921-

547087

— THE SOUTHSEA SHAKESPEARE ACTORS
[Programmes, etc.] [Southsea]
illus.   1950-

645707

—STEWART HEADLAM SHAKESPEARE ASSOCIATION
Programmes. etc. of Shakespeare
performances, 1926-

416900

—STOKE-ON-TRENT SHAKESPEARIAN SOCIETY
Programmes, photographs, etc. of
Shakespearian performances. (Stoke-
on-Trent)
illus.   1937-55.

472596

—STRATFORD-UPON-AVON, ROYAL SHAKSPEAREAN
CLUB
Account of the second commemoration of
Shakspeare, celebrated at Stratford-
upon-Avon on Friday 23rd of April, 1830
... Dedicated to the members of the
Royal Shakspearean Club. (Leamington)
[1830.]

64331

—STRATFORD-UPON-AVON SHAKESPEARE CLUB
Papers, etc., 1901, 1903-4.
Reprinted from the Stratford-upon-
Avon Herald. pp. 20. (Stratford-
upon-Avon)   1901-04.

593467

—Stratford-on-Avon Shakspere Club.
Rules. pp. [6.] [Stratford-
on-Avon]   1874.

570141

—SUNDAY SHAKESPEARE SOCIETY
[Annual reports, etc.] 1874, 1918-
1957.   1874-1957.
Nos. from 1874 to 1917 missing.

449338

— THE TAVERNERS
[Shakespearian programmes, posters,
etc.]   [1947]-[1957]

645709

—TAVISTOCK SHAKESPEARE SOCIETY
Quatercentenary tribute to Shakespeare.
1964.

740855

— TORONTO SHAKESPEARE SOCIETY
[Dramatic Papers: material relating to
the Shakespearian and other productions
of G. Wilson Knight, at Hart House
Theatre, Toronto, and in England.]
illus.   1926-

634261

—ULEY PLAYERS
Castle (G.), Awdry (Diana) and Vick (H.)
Characters from the country [: experiences of Diana Awdry and H. Vick with
the Uley Players with special references to Shakespearian productions.
Broadcast] 9th May, 1938 (Midland).
ff. 7.
typescript.   1938.

482433

—ULEY PLAYERS
Phillips (Mrs.), Marsh (F.) [and] Vick (H.)
Characters from the country: the Uley
Village Players: [a talk between]
Mrs. Phillips [and two members of her
company,] F. Marsh [and] H. Vick.
[With references to Shakespearian pro-
ductions.   Broadcast in] Midland
programme, 2nd August, 1938.   ff. 6.
1938.

486181

— The Unnamed Society's 21st birthday
1915-1936 [souvenir.   With an account
of the society by N. Cardus, and list
of productions including The Tempest.]
pp. 20.   [Manchester]
illus.   [1936].

459001

—URBAN CLUB
Church (W. E.), Northcott (J.) and
Catling (T.) [eds.]
Annals of the Urban Club, and its
tributes to the immortal memory of
William Shakespeare. pp. 48.
ports. illus.   1902.

520909

—VIC-WELLS ASSOCIATION
[Newsletter]. Nos. 1-83. (March,
1946)   1946-53.

638014

—WALSALL, QUEEN MARY'S GRAMMAR SCHOOL
DRAMATIC SOCIETY
Programmes of Shakespeare performances,
1933-. (Walsall)   [1933]-

416897

—WARRINGTON LITERARY & PHILOSOPHICAL
SOCIETY
Davies (J.)
The Shaksperian characters of
Richard the Third and Hamlet contrasted:
a paper read before the Warrington
Literary & Philosophical Society,
March 1882. pp. 20.   1882.

404418

—WHEELING SHAKESPEARE CLUB (VIRGINIA)
Proceedings of the Wheeling
Shakespeare Club, on the anniversary
of Shakespeare's birth, April 23d,
1877.   pp. 8.   [Wheeling, Va.]
1877.

558061

—WILSON (N.C.) SHAKESPEARE CLUB
Daniels (J.)
Tar heel editor.   [Containing ref-
erences to the Shakespeare Club,
Wilson, N.C.]   (Chapel Hill, N.C.)
ports. illus. maps.   1939.

569949

— WINCHESTER COLLEGE SHAKSPERE SOCIETY
Noctes Shaksperianae. A series of
papers by late and present members,
edited by C.H. Hawkins. Re-issue for
the Quingentenary. (Winchester) 1893.

668479

SOCIETY FOR TEACHERS OF ENGLISH
Hudson (Arthur Kenneth)
Shakespeare and the classroom, compiled
for The Society for Teachers of English.
With a foreword by B. Miles.
  bibliog.   1954.   638927
_____ 2nd edn.
  bibliog. discography.
                1960.   666837

SOCIETY FOR THEATRE RESEARCH
Poel (William)
William Poel's prompt-book of Fratricide
Punished [with text of the play].
Edited, with an introduction, by
J. Isaacs.   pp. xx, 35.
  facsimiles.   1956.

658576

SOCIETY FOR THEATRE RESEARCH
Sprague (Arthur Colby)
The Stage business in Shakespeare's
plays: a postscript.   pp. 35.
  port.   1954.

639849

Soellner, Rolf
Baroque passion in Shakespeare and his
contemporaries.

IN Shakespeare Studies, 1. (Cincinnati,
Ohio)   1965.

750317

SOELLNER, ROLF
Shakespeare, Aristotle, Plato, and
the soul,
IN DEUTSCHE SHAKESPEARE-GESELLSCHAFT
WEST, JAHRBUCH 1968.   pp. 56-71.
(Heidelberg)
                        754129

Soldiers
see also **Armour**

— BOAS (F. S.)
The Soldier in Elizabethan and later
English drama: the Giff Edmonds
Memorial Lecture [1940.   With references to Shakespeare's soldiers.]
IN CHAPMAN (R. W.) ed., Essay by
divers hands: the Transactions of
the Royal Society of Literature of
the United Kingdom, New Series, Vol. 19.
                            1942.

538168

— BROOKS (C.)
Shakespeare and the soldier [: scenes
from Henry V, with introduction and
comments by C. Brooks].   (Forces
Educational Broadcast) [Broadcast]
20th December, 1946.   ff. 9.
  typescript.   1946.

582328

— COOPER ([Rt. Hon. Sir A.] D.)
Sergeant Shakespeare [: evidence of
Shakespeare's supposed connection
with the army].   1950.

602964

—JORGENSEN (PAUL A.)
Shakespeare's military world.
                          1956.

665390

—WAVELL (ARCHIBALD JOHN ARTHUR WAVELL,
2nd Earl)
Shakespeare and soldiering.   IN
Essays by Divers Hands, New Series,
Vol. 27.   1955.

647127

Soliloquies

—CLEMEN, WOLFGANG H.
Shakespeare's soliloquies.   1964.

Modern Humanities Research
Association, Presidential address,
1964.   667878

—MUIR, KENNETH
Shakespeare's soliloquies. FROM
Ocidente, LXVII, August, 1964. (Lisboa)
pp.45-59.   1964.

668041

— Peterson (H.) The Lonely debate:
_dilemmas from Hamlet to Hans Castorp.

(New York)   1938.

484763

SOLOVIEV (V. [S.])
Plato. Translated from the Russian
by R. Gill. [Containing a comparison
of the characters of Socrates and
Hamlet]. pp. 83.
port. 1935.

445799

Some Remarks on The Tragedy of Hamlet,
Prince of Denmark. Written by
Mr. William Shakespeare (1736).
Anonymous [attributed to Thomas Hanmer].
With an introduction by C. D. Thorpe.
pp. [ii] 8, viii, 63, [2]. (Ann Arbor)
1947.
Augustan Reprint Society, Series Three:
Essays on the Stage, No. 3. A facsimile
of original text.

622089

SOMER (JOHN L.)
Ralph Crane and "an olde play called
Winter's Tale". IN Four Studies
in Elizabethan Drama, by Roma Ball,
J. C. Pogue, J. L. Somer [and]
E. J. Kettner. (Kansas State
Teachers College, Emporia, Kan.)
1962.
Emporia State Research Studies,
Vol. 10, No. 4.

667737

SOMEREN-GODFERY (M. van)
Fear no more the heat o'the sun:
from Cymbeline. pp. 7. 1928.

515427

SOMERS (ALEX C. C.)
Shakspere's garden party [: a poem].
IN The Manchester playgoer: the
organ of the Manchester Playgoers'
Club, Vol. 1. (Manchester) 1910.

544467

SOMERSET, CHARLES A.
The Death of Shylock.

For editions of this play see under
English Editions: The Merchant of
Venice: Alterations &c.

SOMERSET (CHARLES A.)
Shakespeare's birth day! or, The
Rival muses! A masque, in which
the question of tragedy or comedy,
which merits the palm? is decided.
[Theatre Royal, Birmingham, prompt
book] pp. [iv], 27.
manuscript. [c.1840.]

666759

SOMERSET (CHARLES A.)
Shakspeare's early days: a historical
play in two acts, with remarks bio-
graphical and critical, by D.-G. [i.e.
George Daniel]. As performed at the
Theatres Royal, London. [Theatre
Royal, Birmingham, prompt book.]
[?1831].
[Cumberland's British Theatre].
Interleaved; MS. notes and alterations
throughout.

455844

SOMERSET (C. A.)
Shakespeare's early days [: a drama
in two acts]. pp. 16.
illus. [c.1883].
Dicks' Standard Plays.

455700

SOMERVELL (Sir A.)
Blow, blow thou winter wind: two
part song [from "As you like it"].
1925.
Boosey's Modern Festival Series.

528953

SOMERVELL ([Sir]A.)
Two songs of Autolycus: 1. Will you
buy any tape? 2. Lawn as white as
driven snow. Music by [Sir] A.
Somervell; words [from Winter's Tale].
pp. 6. 1931.
Singing Class Music - Edward Arnold's
Series.

536605

SOMERVELL (Sir A.)
Under the greenwood tree: two part
song [from "As you like it"].
pp. 4. 1925.
Boosey's Modern Festival Series.

528955

SOMMER (HEINRICH OSKAR)
Critical introduction [containing
references to Shakespeare's "Troilus
and Cressida", bibliographical foot-
notes], index and glossary. IN
[LE FÈVRE (R.)] The Recuyell of the
historyes of Troye. Written in French
by R. Lefèvre; translated and printed
by W. Caxton (about 1474).
tables. facsimiles. 2 vols. 1894.
No. 1 of edn. limited to 12 copies,
signed by the publisher D. Nutt.

573703

Songs of Shakespeare

——ATKINS (R.)
Shakespeare in song, presented with
gramophone records. [Broadcast]
June 28th [1942]. ff. 3.
typescript.
[1942.]

534703

——Bennett ([Mrs]Irene) Shakespeare and
his use of the ballad. In The
Welsh secondary schools review,
Vol.34, No.1.
[Port Talbot] 1948.

594541

——CLEVERDON (D.)
Music in Shakespeare [: a programme
illustrating Shakespeare's dramatic
use of music and songs, with a
commentary by D. Cleverdon. Broadcast]
January 27th [1947]. ff. 51.
typescript.
[1947.]

582329

——CLINTON-BADDELEY (V. C.)
Words for music. [With references to
songs of Shakespeare.] (Cambridge)
1941.

523117

—DAY (C. L.) and MURRIE ([Mrs.] ELEANORE B.)
English song-books, 1651-1702: a
bibliography, with a first-line index
of songs. [Including Shakespearian
songs.]
  facsimiles.   1940.
(Bibliographical Society. [Miscellan-
eous Publications.])

              521492

— GATTY (REGINALD ARTHUR ALLIX)
Shakespeare in character and song:
As you like it; The Tempest; and,
Twelfth Night.   ff. 35.
  manuscript.   [c.1925.]

              637992

—HABER (T. B.)
What fools these mortals be: Housman's
poetry and the lyrics of Shakespeare.
IN Modern Language Quarterly, Vol. 6.
(Seattle)
  bibliog.   1945.

              571544

—HOWE (BEA)
Through the year: script [containing
seasonal poems, interspersed with
Shakespearean songs. Broadcast
28th January, 1944].   ff. 6.
  typescript.   1944.
Note: Only the titles of the
Shakespearean songs appear in the text.

              555601

—ING (CATHERINE)
The Lyrics of Spenser, Shakespeare
and Donne. IN Ing (C.) Elizabethan
lyrics: a study in the development
of English metres and their relation
to poetic effect.
  bibliog.   1951.

              620170

—KEMPSON (ETHEL M.)
Shakespeare's songs.   FROM The Institute
Magazine, Vol. 15. [Birmingham]
                   1910.

              537163

— Langford (A.) Music for Shakespeare,
No.1 : The Songs in the plays.
[Broadcast] April 15th, 1950.
ff. 9. Typescript.

             1950.

              609059

—Nichols (B.) ed.,A Book of ballads
[, including "The Friar of Orders
Gray" composed from fragments of
ballads found in Shakespeare's
plays]. Selected and with an
introduction by B. Nichols.
Illustrated by H.M. Brock.

             1934.

             428935

— PATTISON (B.)
Music and poetry of the English renaissance. [Including references to
Shakespeare's songs. With a bibliography, bibliographical notes and musical
examples.]
                  1948.

           590557

— RALLI (A.)
Later critiques: [Carlyle and Shakespeare, Shakespearian criticism,
Shakespeare's songs, and other essays
with Shakespearian references.]
               1933.

           411682

— RICHARDS (G.)
Housman, 1897-1936 [: a biography].
With an introduction by Mrs. [Katharine
E.] Symons and appendices by G. B. A.
Fletcher and others. [Containing
references to Shakespeare's songs.]
(Oxford)
  ports. illus. facsimiles.   1941.

          529165

— SENG, PETER J.
The Vocal songs in the plays of
Shakespeare: a critical history.
(Cambridge, Mass.)   1967.

          763845

— VOGEL (RUTH R.)
An Evaluation of the love songs in
Shakespeare's dramatic works:
Columbia University [thesis] 1948.
IN GOLDING (NANCY L.) A Survey of
the proposed arrangements of
Shakespeare's Sonnets [etc.]
  bibliog.   microfilm, positive copy.
           [1948.]

          609350

— WYSONG, J. N.
The Influence of Shakespeare's songs
on the poetry of A. E. Housman.
IN SHAKESPEARE QUARTERLY XIX: 4.
pp. 333-339.
(New York)   1968.
           605711

SONNECK (OSCAR GEORGE THEODORE)
A Bibliography of early secular
American music (18th century) [:
containing references to Shakespearian
music]. Revised and enlarged by
W. T. Upton. (Washington) 1945.
Library of Congress, Music Division.

          569666

SONNECK (O. G. T.)
Early opera in America [with references
to The Tempest, Macbeth and Romeo and
Juliet.] (New York)
  ports. illus. tables. facsimile.
             1915.

          499284

Sonnets

General Works
Authorship
Identity of the principal figures
Individual Sonnets
Order and Dating
Textual History

Sonnets

— General Works

—AKRIGG, GEORGE PHILIP VERNON
The Shakespeare of the sonnets.
FROM Queen's Quarterly, Spring.
(Kingston, Ont.)   1965.
pp. 78-90.

766382

—ANSPACHER (L. K.)
Shakespeare as poet and lover and the
enigma of the sonnets.   pp. [vi,] 55.
(New York)   1944.

556395

—BALDI, SERGIO
Shakespeare's sonnets as literature.
IN Shakespeare celebrated: anniversary
lectures delivered at the Folger Library
[during 1964].   (Ithaca, N.Y.)   1965.

771817

—BALDWIN (THOMAS WHITFIELD)
On the literary genetics of Shakespere's
poems & sonnets   (Urbana)   1950.

612745

—BANERJEE (SRIKUMAR)
The Sonnets of Shakespeare.
IN Shakespeare commemoration volume,
edited by Taraknath Sen.   (Calcutta)
1966.

764382

—BATES, PAUL A.
Shakespeare's sonnets and pastoral poetry.
IN SHAKESPEARE JAHRBUCH.   Bd. 103/1967.
pp. 81-96.   (Weimar)

10531

—BERRY (FRANCIS)
"Thou" and "you" in Shakespeare's
sonnets.   IN Essays in Criticism,
Vol. 8.   (Oxford)   1958.

621866/8

—BRADDY, HALDEEN
Shakespeare's sonnet plan and the
effect of folk belief. FROM Midwest
Folklore, 1962, Vol.12, no.4. (El Paso,
Tex.)   1962.

pp.235-240.   763278

—BRAY ([Sir] D. [de S.])
Difficult passages in the sonnets
re-examined.   IN Notes and Queries,
Vol. 190-1.   1946.

579129

—BROADBENT, JOHN BARCLAY
Shakespeare's sonnets.   IN Broadbent
(J. B.) Poetic love.   1964.

727140

—BYVANCK (W. G. C.)
Reading Shakespeare's sonnets.
IN GOLLANCZ ([Sir] I.) ed., A Book of
homage to Shakespeare.
ports.   illus.   facsimiles.   [1916.]

264175

—A Casebook on Shakespeare's sonnets.
Edited by G. Willen & V.B. Reed. [Text
and critical essays.] (New York: Thomas
Y. Crowell Co.]   1964.

Crowell Literary Casebooks.
668299

—CHAPMAN (J. A.)
Marching song [: an essay on
Shakespeare's Sonnets].   IN English
Association, Essays and studies,
Vol. 28, 1942.   Collected by
R. W. Chapman.   (Oxford)   1943.

541298

—CRAIG (E. G.)
On the 154 Sonnets of Shakespeare.
IN The Mask, Vol. 9.   (Florence)
1923.

460758

—OE MONTMORENCY (J. E. G.)
The Mystery of Shakespeare's sonnets.
IN The Contemporary Review, Vol. 101.
1912.

236965

—[ELLIS (C.)]
Shakspeare and the Bible: fifty
sonnets with their scriptural harmonies.
Interpreted by C. E[llis].
port.   facsimile.   1896.   135407
_____ Another copy without advertise-
ments.   1896.   574389

—ELLIS (C.)
Shakspeare and the Bible: Shakspeare;
A Reading from The Merchant of Venice;
Shakspeariana;   Sonnets.   With their
scriptural harmonies interpreted.
port.   1897.
This copy has (i) Cover title "The
Christ in Shakspeare"   (ii) Bethnal
Green Free Library slip pasted to title-
page   (iii) Author's autograph on
dedication leaf.

418061

—ELMEN (PAUL)
Shakespeare's gentle hours.   [Time in
the Sonnets.]
IN SHAKESPEARE QUARTERLY IV: 3.
pp. 301-309.
(New York)   1953.

605711

—GOSSE ([Sir] E.)
With a copy of Shakespeare's sonnets.
IN Gosse ([Sir] E.) In russet & silver
[: poems]. 1894.

481473

—GRUNDY (JOAN)
Shakespeare's sonnets and the Eliza-
bethan sonneteers. IN SHAKESPEARE
SURVEY 15. (Cambridge) 1962.

667174

—HAYES (ANN L.)
The Sonnets.
IN "Starre of Poets". Discussions of
Shakespeare. (Pittsburgh, Pa.:
Carnegie Institute of Technology)
1966.

766812

—HERBERT (THOMAS WALTER)

Sound and sense in two Shakespeare
sonnets. Reprinted from Tennessee
Studies in Literature, Vol.3. pp.[10]
Bibliog. (Knoxville, Tenn.)
1958.

666788

—HERRNSTEIN, BARBARA, ed.
Discussions of Shakespeare's sonnets
[by various writers]. (Boston)
1964.

Discussions of literature.
748157

—HUBLER (EDWARD)
The Sense of Shakespeare's Sonnets.
(Princeton, N.J.) 1952.
Princeton Studies in English, No. 33.

626396

—HUNTER (G. K.)
The Dramatic technique of Shakespeare's
sonnets. IN Essays in Criticism,
Vol. 3. (Oxford) 1953.

621866/3

—INGE (W. R.)
Did Shakespeare unlock his heart?
IN Inge (W. R.) A Pacifist in trouble
[: essays.] 1939.

508356

—JOHN (L. C.)
The Elizabethan sonnet sequences:
studies in conventional conceits.
[With references to the sonnets of
Shakespeare, and notes.] (New York)
bibliog. 1938.
Columbia University, Studies in English
and Comparative Literature.

528609

—JONSON (G. C. A.)
"The House of Life": [a comparison
between Rossetti's and Shakespeare's
sonnets.] FROM The Poetry Review,
1931. pp. [17.] [1931]

390920

—JONSON (G. C. A.)
Shakespeare's sonnets. FROM The
Poetry Review, 1931. pp. [19.]
[1931]

390913

—KERMODE (FRANK)
Shakespeare's sonnets [: a talk].
Producer: P. H. Newby, reader:
A. Jacobs. [Broadcast January 4th,
1955.] ff. 19.
typescript. 1955.

665042

—KNIGHT (GEORGE WILSON)
The Mutual flame: on Shakespeare's
"Sonnets" and "The Phoenix and the
Turtle".
bibliog. 1955.

646278

—KNIGHT, GEORGE WILSON
Shakespeare's sonnets. Produced
by George MacBeth. B.B.C. radio
script broadcast 23rd April 1964.
1964.

668243

—KNIGHT (GEORGE WILSON)
Time and eternity. IN HERRNSTEIN
(BARBARA) ed., Discussions of
Shakespeare's sonnets [by various writers].
(Boston) 1964.
Discussions of literature.

748157

—KNIGHTS (L. C.)
Shakespeare's sonnets. IN Scrutiny,
Vol. 3. (Cambridge) 1934.

448195

—Knights (L.C.) Shakespeare's Sonnets.
[With bibliographical notes.]
In Knights (L.C.) Explorations :
essays in criticism, mainly on
the literature of the seventeenth
century.
1946.

572014

—KOTT (JAN)
Shakespeare our contemporary.
Translated by B. Taborski. Preface
by P. Brook. 1964. 741546
_____ 2nd edn., revised.
1967. 766093
Includes "Shakespeare's bitter
Arcadia" (in 2nd edn. only).

—KRIEGER, MURRAY
A Window to criticism: Shakespeare's
'Sonnets' and modern poetics.
(Princeton, N.J.) 1964.

748258

—LANDRY, HILTON
Interpretations in Shakespeare's sonnets.
1963.

Perspectives in criticism, No.14.
667701

—LEISHMAN (JAMES BLAIR)

Themes and variations in Shakespeare's
sonnets. 1961.

666734

——LEISHMAN (JAMES BLAIR)
Variations on a theme in
Shakespeare's sonnets.   IN [DAVIS
(H.) and GARDNER (HELEN L.) eds.]
Elizabethan and Jacobean studies.
(Oxford)   1959.

687986

—— LEVER (JULIUS WALTER)
The Elizabethan love sonnet.   1956.

653678

—— Lowell (J.R.)[Letter to James T.Fields
concerning the text of his proposed
edition of Shakespeare's Sonnets]
In Letters. Vol.1.

1894.

121420

—— MACKENZIE (BARBARA A.)
Shakespeare's Sonnets: their relation
to his life.   pp. x, 82.   (Cape Town)
bibliog.   1946.

575544

——MASSON (DAVID I.)
Free phonetic patterns in Shakespeare's
sonnets.   FROM Neophilologus, 38.
Jaargang.   (Groningen)   1954.

647042

——MORRIS (T. B.)
Fair Youth and Dark Lady: a play
[relating to Shakespeare, Will Hughes
and the Dark Lady of the Sonnets].
pp. [32].   1938.
One-act Plays, No. 18.

534288

—— MURRY (JOHN MIDDLETON)
Shakespeare and love; Shakespeare's
dedication; The Creation of Falstaff;
Coriolanus; The Mortal moon; IN
Murry (J. M.) John Clare and other
studies.   1950.

611291

——NEARING (HOMER)
Shakespeare as a nondramatic poet:
Sonnet XXIX.
IN SHAKESPEARE QUARTERLY XIII: 1.
pp. 15-20.
(New York) 1962.

605711

——NEJGEBAUER (A.)
Twentieth-century studies in
Shakespeare's Songs, Sonnets and
Poems.   2: The Sonnets.   IN
SHAKESPEARE SURVEY 15.   (Cambridge)
1962.

667174

——NOWOTTNY (WINIFRED M. T.)
Formal elements in Shakespeare's
sonnets: Sonnets I-VI.   IN Essays
in Criticism, Vol. 2.   (Oxford)
1952.

621866/2

——PALMER (G. H.)
Intimations of immortality in the
sonnets of Shakspere.   pp. 57.
(Boston)   1912.
Ingersoll Lecture, 1912.

415004

——Pearson ([Mrs.] Lu E.)Elizabethan
love, conventions. [With a
chapter on Shakespeare's sonnets,
and a bibliography.]

1933.

407228

—— PIRKHOFER (ANTON M.)
"A Pretty Pleasing Pricket" - on the use
of alliteration in Shakespeare's Sonnets.
IN SHAKESPEARE QUARTERLY XIV: 1.
pp. 3-14.
(New York)   1963.

605711

——Platt ([J.]A.) 'Edward III' and
Shakespeare's Sonnets.   In The
Modern language review, Vol. 6.

(Cambridge)   1911.

266821

—— PRINCE (FRANK TEMPLETON)

The Sonnet from Wyatt to Shakespeare.
IN Stratford-upon-Avon Studies, edited
by J.R. Brown and B. Harris, Vol.2.
Elizabethan poetry.   1960.

666674

——PROH PUDOR [pseud.]
On Shakspeare's sonnets.   FROM
Blackwood's Magazine, Aug. 1818.
(Edinburgh)

440104

——Ransom (J.C.) Shakespeare at sonnets.
From The Southern Review, Winter,
1938.

[Baton Rouge]

506182

———— IN RANSOM (J. C.) The World's
body [: studies in poetic theory].
(New York)   1938.

486874

——RHYS (A.)
The Technical achievement of
Shakespeare's sonnets.   IN The Poetry
Review, Vol. 39.   1948-9.

246749/39

——[RICHARDSON (D. L.)]
Shakespeare's Sonnets.   [With biblio-
graphical notes.]   FROM [Richardson
(D. L.) Literary leaves. 2nd edn.]
Vol. 2.   [1840.]

579641

—— RUBOW (P. V.)
Shakespeare's sonnets. [English
text.] IN Orbis litterarum: revue
Danois d'histoire littéraire.
Tome 4. (Copenhague)
bibliog. facsimiles. 1946.

593482/4

—— SANDERLIN (G.)
The Repute of Shakespeare's sonnets
in the early nineteenth century.
IN Modern Language Notes. Vol. 54.
(Baltimore) 1939.

509539

—— SCHAAR, CLAES
Conventional and unconventional in the
descriptions of scenery in Shakespeare's
Sonnets. FROM English Studies XLV: II.
pp.142-149. (Amsterdam) 1964.

745005

—— SHIPLEY, JOSEPH TWADELL, ed.
Shakespeare's Sonnets: analytical notes
and critical commentary. (New York)
1963.

Study master series. 743618

—— SMITH (HALLET D.)
"No cloudy stuffe to puzzell intellect":
a testimonial misapplied to Shakespeare.
IN SHAKESPEARE QUARTERLY I: 1.
pp. 18-21.
(New York) 1950.

605711

—— Tannenbaum (S.A.) Shakspere's
Sonnets (a concise bibliography.)

(New York) 1940.

(Elizabethan Bibliographies, No. 10.)
Edn. limited to 300 copies.

513225

—— UNGARETTI, GIUSEPPE
Notes on Shakespeare's art of poetry.
IN LEWINTER, OSWALD, ed., Shakespeare
in Europe [by various authors]
1963.

667784

—— VISWANATHAM, K.
The Sonnets of Shakespeare. FROM
"Triveni", January 1965.
(Machilipatnam, India) 1965.
pp. 16-26.

768975

—— WILSON, JOHN DOVER
An introduction to the sonnets of
Shakespeare, for the use of historians
and others. 1963.

667945

—— WINNY, JAMES
The master-mistress: a study of
Shakespeare's sonnets. 1968.

775734

—— WINTERS (YVOR)
Poetic style in Shakespeare's sonnets.
IN HERRNSTEIN (BARBARA) ed., Discussions
of Shakespeare's sonnets [by various
writers]. (Boston) 1964.
Discussions of literature.

748157

Sonnets

— Authorship

—— ALLEN (P.) and WARD (B. M.)
An Enquiry into the relations between
Lord Oxford as "Shakespeare", Queen
Elizabeth and the Fair Youth of
Shakespeare's sonnets. pp. 15.
bibliog. [1936.]

530214

—— BARRELL (C. W.)
Verifying the secret history of
Shakespeare's sonnets. Illustrated,
by H. F. Wood. FROM Tomorrow, Vol.5.
(New York)
ports. illus. facsimiles. 1946.

574236

—— Chapman (J.A.) The Riddle of the
sonnets. From The Poetry Review,
Vol. 29.

1938.

494278

—— DAVIES (R. [R. H.])
Notes upon some of Shakespeare's
sonnets pp. 46, [ii].
(Kensington)
port. 1927.
[Cayme Press Pamphlet, No. 6.]
Differs from 337784.

559342

—— Denning (W.H.) Dressing old words
new (authorship controversy): a
tentative exposition, in part,
of external matter affecting the
construction of Shakespeare's
sonnets, and other things. pp.10.

[c.1930.]

(Bacon Society, London.)

422160

—— DODD (A.)
Francis Bacon's diary: Shake-speare's
Sonnets. Who wrote them? When were
they written? Why were they written?
Were they a diary from youth to old
age? Proof that the Sonnets were
written after Shaksper's death.
pp. 22. (Bacon Society)
facsimiles. 1947.

583254

—DODD (A.)
The Marriage of Elizabeth Tudor: an inquiry into her alleged marriage with the Earl of Leicester and the alleged births of her two sons, Francis Bacon and the Earl of Essex: an historical research based on one of the themes in "Shakespeare's Sonnets".
ports. illus. facsimiles. bibliog. 1940.
522465

—DODD (A.)
When was "Shake-speares sonnets" first published?: a lecture delivered to the Bacon Society, London. pp. 24. 1937.
471285

—EAGLE, RODERICK L.
The secrets of the Shakespeare sonnets. With facsimile reproduction of the 1609 edition of the sonnets and "A Lover's complaint". 1965.
744898

— Feely (J.M.) The Cypher in the sonnets : the dedication key. pp. 68. Facsimiles.
(Rochester, N.Y.) 1940.
523045

—JAMES (G.)
Francis Bacon in the Sonnets. pp. 38. (Birmingham) 1900. Bacon-Shakespeare Pamphlets.
552893

—NAAE (T. T.)
The Key to Shakespeare by the anatomy of the figure on the title-page of the Folio of 1623 of Shakespeare Plays, being an exposition of this First Folio, with notes to The Tempest, Love's Labor's Lost, and Sonnets. [Dealing with the Bacon-Shakespeare question]. New enlarged edn. (Boston) ports. illus. facsimiles. 1935.
442863

—PHILLIPS (GERALD WILLIAM) [pseud. John Huntingdon]
Shake spears sonnets, addressed to members of the Shakespeare Fellow-ship. pp. 23. 1954. Privately printed.
645438

—PHILLIPS (G. W.)
Sunlight on Shakespeare's sonnets [: with the text of the sonnets]. 1935.
432263

—PHILLIPS (G. W.)
The Tragic story of "Shakespeare", disclosed in the sonnets, and the life of Edward de Vere, 17th Earl of Oxford. 1932.
393565

—RENDALL (G. H.)
Personal clues in Shakespeare: Poems & sonnets [, relating to Edward de Vere]. 1934.
426741

—SPAIN (MARGARET M.)
Who wrote Shakespeare's sonnets? pp. 32. (Dublin) 1946.
596764

—THOMSON (W.) ed.
The Sonnets of William Shakespeare & Henry Wriothesley, Third Earl of Southampton, with A Lover's complaint and The Phoenix & turtle. Edited with an introduction. (Oxford) 1938.
480352

— Titherley (A.W.) Shakespeare's sonnets as from the pen of William Stanley, sixth Earl of Derby. pp. 61.
(Liverpool) 1939.
502981

— VENTON, W. B.
Analyses of Shake-speares sonnets using the cipher code [to prove that Edward VI was the author]. 1968.
772619

Sonnets

— Identity of the principal figures

— B[oaden] (J.) To what person the sonnets of Shakespeare were actually addressed. [With bibliographical notes.] From [The] Gent[leman's] Mag[azine, Vol. 102. Part 2].
1832.
556077

— COOK, I. R. W.
William Hervey and Shakespeare's Sonnets. IN SHAKESPEARE SURVEY 21. (Cambridge) pp. 97-106. 1968.
776762

— De Montmorency (J.E.G.) The "Other poet" of Shakespeare's sonnets [: Edmund Spenser]. In The Contemporary Review, Vol.101.
1912.
236965

— DOUGLAS (Lord A. [B.])
The True history of Shakespeare's Sonnets. [Containing the text of the sonnets.]
port. 1933.
403354

— GITTINGS (ROBERT WILLIAM VICTOR)

Shakespeare's rival: a study in three
parts [with special reference to Gervase
Markham]. Ports. Illus. Bibliog.
1960.

666664

— GRAY (H. D.)
Shakespeare's rival poet.   IN
Journal of English and Germanic
Philology, Vol. 47.   (Urbana, Ill.:
University of Illinois)
bibliog.   1948.

600780/47

— HIGHET (GILBERT)
People, places and books [: essays].
(New York)
bibliogs.   1953.
Includes "The Autobiography of
Shakespeare" [: criticism of the
Sonnets].

647495

— HILLARD (KATE)
On the study of Shakespeare's sonnets.
FROM Lippincott's Magazine, Vol. 15.
(Philadelphia)   1875.

555527

— HOTSON, JOHN LESLIE
Mr. W.H. [: the friend to whom
Shakespeare wrote his Sonnets]. 1964.

illus.   667798

— HOTSON, JOHN LESLIE
The Shakespeare mystery solved [:
Mr. W.H.'s identity]. FROM The Sunday
Times Colour Magazine, April 12, 1964.

illus.   668228

— KEEN (FRANCES)
Phoenix: an inquiry into the poems of
Robert Chester's "Love's martyr" (1601),
and the "Phoenix' nest" (1593), in
relation to Shakespeare's "Sonnets" and
"A Lover's complaint"; arising from
recent discoveries which point to the
identity of the youth of the sonnets
[etc.]   broadsheet.   1957.
No. 79 of edn. limited to 250 copies,
published by the author.

665748

— LEIGH (G. A.)
The Rival poet in Shakespeare's
sonnets.   pp. [15].   IN The
Westminster Review, Vol. 147, 1897.

138545

— MACDONALD (K. C.)
Blessed Robert Southwell, S.J.,
and William Shakespeare.   [With
references to "Mr. W.H." in
connection with the Sonnets.]
IN The Month, vol. 158.   1931.

389959

— MASSEY (G.)
The Secret drama of Shakespeare's
sonnets.   1888.
Edition limited to 100 copies for
subscribers only.

506259

— MASSEY (G.)
The Vilification of Shakspeare and
Bacon: a chapter from "The Secret
drama of Shakspeare's sonnets".
pp. 36.   1888.

540603

— MUGGERIDGE (MALCOLM)
The Earnest atheist: a study of Samuel
Butler.   [With a critical account of
"Shakespeare's Sonnets reconsidered",
by S. Butler]
port.   1936.

456605

— NISBET (U.)
The Onlie begetter [: an essay
identifying Sir William Herbert as
the Mr. W.H. of Shakespeare's Sonnets.]
port. bibliog.   1936.

451494

— (Richardson (D.L.)) Shakespeare's
Sonnets. [With bibliographical
notes.] From [Richardson (D.L.)
Literary leaves. 2nd edn.] Vol. 2.

[1840.]

579641

— Shakespeare's heart of love: psycho-
physiology [of the Sonnets.   1st
article].   FROM The Journal of Man,
Vol. 1.   (Philadelphia)   1872.

564841

— Shakespeare's secret: a new & correct
interpretation of Shakespeare's
sonnets, with a word-for-word interpretation of each sonnet & a running
commentary, and a re-arrangement of
the "Dark Lady" sonnets, by R. M.
Holzapfel.   (Dublin: Melander
Shakespeare Society)
port. illus. facsimile.   1961.

666741

— STALKER (A.)
Shakespeare and the rival poet.
IN Notes and Queries, Vol. 163.
1932.

401809

— STALKER (A.)
The Sonnets of Shakespeare: imaginary
conversations between Coleridge and
Lamb.   [With a MS. notes by the author.]
pp. 36.   (Stirling)   1933.

416882

— STEVENSON, DAVID
The Meditations of William Shakespeare.
An Introduction to the Shakespeare
anagrams [in the Sonnets]. (New York)
1965.

illus.   746860

— Stopes (Mrs. Charlotte C.) The
Friends in Shakespeare's sonnets.
In Transactions of the Royal Society
of Literature of the United Kingdom.
Second Series, Vol. 27.

1907.

201930

—TAYLOR (DICK)
The Earl of Pembroke and the youth of
Shakespeare's Sonnets: an essay in
rehabilitation. Reprinted from
Studies in Philology, [Vol.] 56, 1.
pp. [29]   1959.

666782

—Thomas ([P.]E.) Women, nature and
poetry. [Containing references to
the sonnets of Shakespeare.] In
Thomas ([P.]E.) Feminine influence
on the poets.

1910.

236222

— Walters (J.C.) Shakespeare's note
book: a new suggestion on the
sonnets: [report of a paper read by
J.C.Walters]. In Manchester
Literary Club. Papers, Vol.30.

(Manchester)   1904.

518388

— WILDE (OSCAR)
The Portrait of Mr. W.H. [Willie
Hughes.] pp. 78. (Portland,
Maine)   1901.
Edition limited to 425 copies.

562744

— WILDE (OSCAR)
The Portrait of Mr. W.H. [Willie
Hughes.] The greatly enlarged version
prepared by the author after the
appearance of the story in 1889 but
not published. Edited with an
introduction by V. Holland.
facsimile.   1958.

665972

— YOUNG (H. M.)
The Sonnets of Shakespeare: a psycho-
sexual analysis. (Columbia, Miss.)
1937.

469785

Sonnets

— Individual Sonnets

— BANKS (T. H.)
Shakespeare's sonnet No. 8 [: a
criticism]. IN Modern Language
Notes, Vol. 63. (Baltimore, Md.)
1948.

439157/63

— CLARKSON (P. S.) [and] WARREN (C. T.)
Pleading and practice in Shakespeare's
Sonnet XLVI. IN Modern Language
Notes, Vol. 62. (Baltimore, Md.)
bibliog.   1947.

439157/62

—DAVIS (JACK M.) and GRANT (J. E.)
A Critical dialogue on Shakespeare's
Sonnet 71. FROM "Texas Studies in
Literature and Language". Vol. 1,
No. 2. pp. [19.] (Austin, Tex.)
1959.

666995

— HUTTAR, CHARLES A.
The Christian basis of Shakespeare's
Sonnet 146.
IN SHAKESPEARE QUARTERLY XIX: 4.
pp. 355-365.
(New York) 1968.

605711

—HUTTON (J.)
Analogues of Shakespeare's sonnets,
153-54: contributions to the
history of a theme. FROM Modern
Philology, Vol. 38. (Chicago) 1941.

537254

— LANDRY, HILTON
The Marriage of true minds: truth and
error in Sonnet 116.
IN SHAKESPEARE STUDIES 3. (Cincinnati,
Ohio)   1967.

771652

— LEVIN (RICHARD)
Sonnet CXXIX as a "dramatic" poem.
IN SHAKESPEARE QUARTERLY XVI: 2.
pp. 175-181.
(New York) 1965.

605711

— MATTINGLY (G.)
The Date of Shakespeare's Sonnet CVII.
IN Publications of the Modern
Language Association of America,
Vol. 48. (Menasha, Wis.) 1933.

418268

— MURRY (J. M.)
Notes on Shakespeare: Sonnet 107.
FROM The New Adelphi, 1929. pp. [4.]
[1929]

389198

— Pepper (S.C.) The Basis of criticism
in the arts. [With a section
relating to Shakespeare's Sonnet 30.]

(Cambridge, Mass.)   1946.

576712

— PETERSON (DOUGLAS L.)
A Probable source for Shakespeare's
Sonnet CXXIX.
IN SHAKESPEARE QUARTERLY V.
pp. 381-384.
(New York) 1954.

605711

— SOUTHAM (B. C.)
Shakespeare's Christian sonnet?
Number 146.
IN SHAKESPEARE QUARTERLY XI: 1.
pp. 67-71.
(New York) 1960.

605711

—   Stalker (A.) Shakespeare's
sonnet" 126. In Notes and Queries,
Vol. 162.

1932.

401808

——STONE (WALTER B.)
Shakespeare and the sad augurs.
IN The Journal of English and Germanic
Philology, Vol. 52.   (Urbana, Ill.)
1953.

600780/52

——THONON, ROBERT
"Still" or "skill": a note on
Shakespeare's Sonnet CVI.
IN SHAKESPEARE JAHRBUCH.   Bd. 97/1961.
pp. 203-207.   (Heidelberg)

10531

Sonnets

— Order and Dating

——BATESON (F. [N.] W.)
Elementary, my dear Hotson!: a caveat
for literary detectives. IN
HERRNSTEIN, BARBARA, ed.
Discussions of Shakespeare's sonnets
[by various writers]. (Boston)
1964.

Discussions of literature.
748157

——Bray ([Sir] D. [de S.]) Shakespeare's
sonnet-sequence [:introduction, follow-
ed by the sonnets.]

1938.

489057

——FORT (J. A.)
The Order and chronology of
Shakespeare's sonnets.   IN The Review
of English studies, Vol. 9.   [1933.]

414489

——FORT (J. A.)
The Time-scheme of the first series
of Shakespeare's Sonnets.   FROM
The Nineteenth Century, 1926.
pp. [8.]   [1926]

389229

——GOLDING (NANCY L.)
A Survey of the proposed arrangements
of Shakespeare's Sonnets: Columbia
University [thesis] 1948.
 bibliog. [etc.]   microfilm, positive
copy.   5 vols. in 1 reel 35 mm.
[1948.]

609350

——GRAY (H. D.)
The Arrangement and the date of
Shakespeare's sonnets.   IN Publications of the Modern Language Association of America, Vol. 30.   (Baltimore)
1915.

428350

——HARBAGE (ALFRED BENNETT)
Dating Shakespeare's sonnets.
IN SHAKESPEARE QUARTERLY I: 2.
pp. 57-63.
(New York)   1950.

605711

——HOTSON (JOHN LESLIE)
More light on Shakespeare's Sonnets.
IN SHAKESPEARE QUARTERLY II: 2.
pp. 111-118.
(New York)   1951.

605711

——HOTSON ([J.] L.)
Shakespeare's sonnets dated, and other
essays [on Shakespeare].
 port.   illus.   facsimiles.   1949.

602546

——HOTSON ([J.] L.)
When Shakespeare wrote the Sonnets.
IN The Atlantic Monthly, Vol. 184.
(Boston, Mass.)   1949.

19347/184

——NOSWORTHY (J. M.)
All too short a date: internal
evidence in Shakespeare's sonnets.
IN Essays in Criticism, Vol. 2.
(Oxford)   1952.

621866/2

—— SCHAAR (CLAES)

An Elizabethan sonnet problem:
Shakespeare's sonnets, Daniel's Delia,
and their literary background. (Lund
Studies in English, 28) Bibliog. (Lund)
1960.

666636

——SCHAAR (CLAES)
Elizabethan sonnet themes and the
dating of Shakespeare's 'Sonnets'.
(Lund)   1962.
Lund Studies in English.

667487

——Shahani (R.G.) The Sentimental
autobiography of Shakespeare.
[Relates to Shakespeare's sonnet-
sequence, by Sir D. de S. Bray]
From [The Asiatic Review, New
Series,] Vol. 36.

[1940.]

521316

—— STIRLING (BRENTS)
More Shakespeare sonnet groups.
IN HOSLEY (RICHARD) ed., Essays on
Shakespeare and Elizabethan drama
in honour of Hardin Craig.
 illus.   1963.

667532

—STIRLING, BRENTS
The Shakespeare sonnet order:
poems and groups. (Berkeley, Cal.)
1968.

774506

—STIRLING (BRENTS)
Sonnets 127-154.   IN BLOOM (EDWARD A.)
ed., Shakespeare 1564-1964: a collection of modern essays by various
hands.   (Providence, R.I.) 1964.
Brown University bicentennial
publications.

744437

—WARD (B. R.)
Shakespeare's Sonnets.   FROM [Poetry
and the Play, 1929-30].   pp. [12.]
[1929]

389214

Sonnets

— Textual History

—BENNETT, JOSEPHINE WATERS
Benson's alleged piracy of "Shake-
speare's Sonnets" and of some of
Jonson's works.   IN Studies in
Bibliography, Vol. 21.
(Charlottesville, Va.)   1968.
pp. 235-248.

598680

—CARTER (A. H.)
The Punctuation of Shakespeare's
sonnets of 1609.   IN McMANAWAY (J. G.),
DAWSON (G. E.) and WILLOUGHBY (E. E.)
eds., Joseph Quincy Adams memorial
studies.   (Washington)   1948.

596748

—HUBLER (EDWARD)
Shakespeare's sonnets and the
commentators. IN Hubler (E.) and others.
The Riddle of Shakespeare's sonnets.
1962.

667289

—LANDRY, HILTON
Malone as editor of Shakespeare's sonnets.
IN Bulletin of the New York Public
Library, Vol.67, No.7. (New York) 1963.

136894/67

— ROSTENBERG (LEONA)
Thomas Thorpe, publisher of
"Shake-speares sonnets", from the
Papers of the Bibliographical Society
of America, 1960.   pp. [22].   1960.

666962

Sonnets on Shakespeare *see* Poems on
Shakespeare

Sophocles *works relating to*

— ALEXANDER (NIGEL)
Critical disagreement about Oedipus
and Hamlet.
IN SHAKESPEARE SURVEY 20.   (Cambridge)
1967.

766881

— Bowra (C.M.) Sophoclean tragedy.
[With references to Shakespeare,
and bibliographical notes.]

(Oxford)   1944.

549175

— Earp (F.R.) The Style of Sophocles.
[With a chapter, Change of style
in Shakespeare.]

(Cambridge)   1944.

548213

—Richard the Third, after the manner
of the ancients [: an account of
Shakespeare's play as it might have
been written by Euripides, Sophocles
or Aeschylus].   FROM [The London
Magazine,] June 1824.

561770

—STOLL (ELMER EDGAR)
Oedipus and Othello, Corneille, Rymer
and Voltaire.   [English text.]
Extrait de la Revue anglo-américaine,
juin 1935.   pp. [16.]   (Paris)
bibliog.   [1935.]

569122

— STOLL (ELMER EDGAR)
Reconciliation in tragedy: Shakespeare
and Sophocles.   FROM The University
of Toronto Quarterly, Vol. 4.   (Toronto)
1934.

440599

—WILLIAMS (E. E.)
Tragedy of destiny: Oedipus Tyrannus,
Macbeth, Athalie.   pp. 35.
(Cambridge, Mass.)
bibliog.   1940.

527201

SORELL (WALTER)
Shakespeare and the dance.
IN SHAKESPEARE QUARTERLY VIII:
pp. 367-384.
(New York) 1957.

605711

SORENSEN (F.)
"The Masque of the Muscovites" in
Love's labour's lost.   IN Modern
Language Notes, vol. 50.
(Baltimore)   1935.

446885

Sotheby and Company, Catalogues *see* Catalogues

Sotheran, Henry, Ltd. Catalogues *see* Catalogues

SOTHERN (E. H.)
My remembrances: the melancholy
tale of "me". [With references
to Shakespeare.]
ports.   illus.   facsimiles.
                               1917.

481761

Sound in Shakespeare's Plays

— SHIRLEY, FRANCES ANN
Shakespeare's use of off-stage sounds.
(Lincoln, Neb.)   1963.

667763

— SPRAGUE (A. C.)
Off-stage sounds, [including references
to Shakespeare. With bibliographical
notes.]   FROM University of Toronto
Quarterly, Vol. 15.   (Toronto)
                               1945.

578420

— WOOD (W. W.)
A Comparison between Shakespeare and
his contemporaries in their use of
music and sound effects.   IN Northwestern University, Summaries of
doctoral dissertations.   June–Sept.
1944, Vol. 12.   (Chicago) 1945.

586199

Sources of Shakespeare

see also Bandello, M.; Castiglione, Count B.;
Hall, E.; Holinshed, R.; Ovid; Painter, W.;
Plautus; Plutarch

see also ENGLISH EDITIONS, The Comedy
of Errors; Henry the Fifth; King John; King
Lear; Measure for Measure; Richard the Third;
The Taming of the Shrew — Alterations, etc.

— APPIAN, of Alexandria [Appianus]
Shakespeare's Appian: a selection
from the Tudor translation of
Appian's "Civil Wars".   Edited by
E. Schanzer.   (Liverpool)
  facsimiles.   1956.
English Reprint Series, No. 13.

665309

— BULLOUGH (GEOFFREY) ed.
Narrative and dramatic sources of
Shakespeare.
  bibliog.   1957–

665704

— Gesta Romanorum: the old English versions,
edited from manuscripts in the British
Museum and University Library, Cambridge;
with an introduction and notes [including
bibliographical notes] by Sir F. Madden.
[Including Theodosius th'emperoure, the
tale of King Lear; and Selestinus a wyse
emperoure and Ancelmus the emperour, both
containing incidents used by Shakespeare
in The Merchant of Venice.]   (Shakespeare
Press)
  engraved tp.   1838.
Shakespeare Press   552609

— [GLANVILLE (B. de)]
Batman uppon Bartholome, his booke
De proprietatibus rerum [with the
translation of the same by J. Trevisa];
newly corrected, enlarged and amended.
                               1582.

335387

— GRIFFIN, ALICE, ed.
The sources of ten Shakespearean plays.
(New York)   1966.

754717

— KOLBING (E.) ed.
The Romance of Sir Beues of Hamtoun.
Edited from six manuscripts and the
old printed copy, with introduction,
notes and glossary.
  3 vols.   1885–1894.
Early English Text Society.   Extra
Series 46, 48, 65.
  Regarded as a source book of Hamlet
by R. Zenker.   See catal. no. 466558.

124881

—LA PRIMAUDAYE (P. de)
The French Academie, wherin is discoursed
the institution of maners. [Containing
a possible source of "The Seven ages of
man" in "As you like it".] Newly translated into English by T. B[owes]. 2nd
edn. (Londini: Impensis G. Bishop)
1589.

469179

—SPENCER, TERENCE JOHN BEW ed.
Elizabethan love stories. With
introduction and glossary.
(Harmondsworth) 1968.
Pengiun Shakespeare library.

768790

Sources of Shakespeare *works relating to* see also Classical Literature and Shakespeare *and under titles of Shakespeare's separate works*

— AKRIGG (GEORGE PHILIP VERNON)
Shakespeare's living sources - an
exercise in literary detection. FROM
Queen's Quarterly, Kingston, Ontario,
Vol.65. pp.239-250. [Kingston, Ontario]
[1958.]

666457

—— ALDEN (R. M.)
A Shakespeare handbook. Revised
and enlarged by O. J. Campbell.
[With an introductory note by
F. E. Schelling.]
port. bibliog. 1932.

402816

—— ATTWATER (A. L.)
Shakespeare's sources. IN GRANVILLE-
BARKER (H.) and HARRISON (G. B.) eds.,
A Companion to Shakespeare studies.
(Cambridge)
bibliogs. illus. tables. facsimiles.
1934. 418724
_____ (New York) 1937. 479251
_____ (Cambridge) 1945. 566174

—— BALDENSPERGER (F.)
Le Siège de Rouen, 1591-1592, et son
importance pour l'information de
Shakespeare. IN Comparative
literature studies [: Cahiers de
littérature comparée], Vol. 3.
(Cardiff)
bibliog. 1941.

548007

——BALDWIN (THOMAS WHITFIELD)
On the literary genetics of Shakespere's
poems & sonnets. (Urbana) 1950.

612745

——BARROLL (J. LEEDS)
Shakespeare and Roman history.
IN The Modern Language Review,
Vol. 53. 1958.

266816/53

—BOND (R. W.)
Studia otiosa: some attempts in
criticism. [With chapters on
Shakespeare's sources.] 1938.

483739

—BORINSKI (LUDWIG)
The Origin of the euphuistic novel and
its significance for Shakespeare. IN
D.C. Allen, ed. "Studies in honor of
T.W. Baldwin" (Urbana, Ill.)
1958.

666314

—BROOKE ([C. F.] T.)
Willobie's Avisa. [With references
to Shakespeare.] IN PEYRE (H. M.)
ed., Essays in honor of Albert [G.]
Feuillerat [by various writers].
(New Haven [Conn.]) 1943.
Yale Romanic Studies, 22.

560305

——BULLOUGH, GEOFFREY
The Lost "Troilus and Cressida".
IN English Association, Essays and
Studies, Shakespeare Quatercentenary
ed.
illus. 1964.

667820

—COWL (RICHARD PAPE)
Shakespeare's Italian sources. [By
R.P. Cowl.] ff.12. [1949.]

641610

—CRAIG (HARDIN)
Motivation in Shakespeare's choice
of materials. IN SHAKESPEARE SURVEY 4.
(Cambridge) 1951.

615854

—CRAIG (H.)
Shakespeare and Wilson's "Arte of
Rhetorique": an inquiry into the
criteria for determining sources.
FROM Studies in Philology, Vol. 28.
(Baltimore)
1931.

441592

— F. [pseud.]
Shaksperiana [: notes on the plagiarism
of Shakespeare]. IN The Mirror of
Literature, Amusement and Instruction,
Vol. 19. 1832. 471959
_____ Another copy. 562355

——FARMER (R.)
An Essay on the learning of Shakespeare:
addressed to Joseph Cradock, Esq.
pp. 50. (Cambridge) 1767.
For other editions of this work check
the main sequence under the author's
name.

536326

—Goldschmidt (E.P.) & Co., Ltd. Catalogue 50 : Sources of English literature before 1640; books offered
for sale. [Containing sources of
Shakespeare and other Shakespeariana.]
Illus.

[1938.]

494025

— GUTTMAN (SELMA)
The Foreign sources of Shakespeare's
works: an annotated bibliography of
the commentary written on this subject
between 1904 and 1940 with lists of
certain translations available to
Shakespeare. (New York)
bibliog. 1947.

588412

— HARMON (ALICE)
How great was Shakespeare's debt to
Montaigne? IN Publications of the
Modern Language Association of
America, Vol. 57. (Menasha, Wis.)
bibliog. 1942.

544204

— HARRISON (THOMAS PERRIN)
Shakespeare and Marlowe's "Dido,
Queen of Carthage". IN Texas
University, Studies in English,
Vol. 35. (Austin, Tex.) 1956.

442432/35

— HARRISON (T. P.)
Shakespeare and Montemayor's "Diana".
IN University of Texas, Studies in
English, No. 6. (Austin, Texas)
1926.

442435

— HART (A.)
Shakespeare and the homilies [: a
new Shakespearean source-book] and
other pieces of research into the
Elizabethan drama. (Melbourne)
1934.

429387

— HONIGMANN (E. A. J.)
Shakespeare's "lost source-plays".
IN The Modern Language Review,
Vol. 49. (Cambridge) 1954.

266816/49

— HUME (M. [A. S.])
Some Spanish influences in Elizabethan
literature. [With reference to
Shakespeare.] IN Transactions of the
Royal Society of Literature. Second
Series. Vol. 29.
1909.

222619

— HUMPHREYS, ARTHUR RALEIGH
Shakespeare and the Tudor perception of
history.
IN Shakespeare celebrated: anniversary
lectures delivered at the Folger Library
[during 1964]. (Ithaca, N.Y.) 1965.

771817

— HUMPHREYS, K. W.
Shakespeare's library: an address to
the Birmingham Central Literary
Association.
typescript. 1968.

775442

— HUNTINGTON LIBRARY AND ART GALLERY
Tudor drama: an exhibition selected
from source materials in the
Huntington Library. [Including
Shakespeare sources and items. Hand
list.] pp. 25. (San Marino, Cal.)
facsimiles. 1934.

560854

— Isaacs (J) Shakespeare and his sources:
talk [Broadcast] 16 July 1949.
ff. 14. Typescript. (Shakespeare
and his world, 3)

1949.

605265

— JUSSERAND (J. J.)
The English novel in the time of
Shakespeare. Translated from the
French by Elizabeth Lee. Revised
and enlarged by the author.
illus. 1890. 468118
No. 65 of 65 copies of this edition
printed on Japanese paper, bearing the
publisher's (T. F. Unwin's) autograph.
_____ Another edn. 1908. 455816

— KEEN (A.)
Hall and Shakespeare [: the relation
between E. Hall's "Union of the noble
houses of Lancaster and York" and
Shakespeare's historical plays. FROM
The Times Literary Supplement, April
26th 1947.]

[1947.]

586801

— KUHL (E. P.)
Shakespeare and Hayward [: a discussion
on the relations between Shakespeare's
Richard II and Henry IV and Hayward's
works on the same subject.] FROM
Studies in Philology, Vol. 25.
[Chapel Hill, N.C.]
bibliog. 1928.

554223

— LAW (R. A.)
Some books that Shakespeare read.
FROM The Library Chronicle of the
University of Texas, Vol. 1.
[Austin, Tex.] 1944.

567009

— LENNOX (Mrs. [CHARLOTTE])
Dedication of "Shakspeare illustrated"
to the Earl of Orrery. IN
JOHNSON [S.] The Beauties of Johnson,
consisting of selections from his
works by A. Howard.
port. [c.1834.]

518887

— LOTHIAN (J. M.)
Shakespeare's knowledge of Aretino's
plays. IN The Modern Language
Review, Vol. 25. (Cambridge)
1930.

379829

——McDOWELL (MINNIE M.)
Shakespeare's likeness to Castiglione,
an indication of probable indebtedness:
a thesis submitted for the degree of
Master of Arts. ff. 117. (Washington)
bibliog. typescript. 1935.
Copy made at the Birmingham Reference
Library from the original typescript
in Washington University.

472781

——Manchester, John Rylands Library.
Catalogue of an exhibition of the
works of Shakespeare, his sources,
and the writings of his principal
contemporaries. With an introductory
sketch, and sixteen facsimiles. Tercentenary of the death of Shakespeare,
1616. April 23, 1916.

(Manchester)   1916.

494549

——MUIR (KENNETH)
Shakespeare's sources, I: Comedies
and Tragedies.   1957.

665480

——MUIR, KENNETH
Source problems in the histories.
IN SHAKESPEARE JAHRBUCH. Bd. 96/1960.
pp. 47-63.   (Heidelberg)

10531

——PROUTY, CHARLES TYLER
Some observations on Shakespeare's sources.
IN SHAKESPEARE JAHRBUCH. Bd. 96/1960.
pp. 64-77.   (Heidelberg)

10531

——RIBNER (IRVING)
Shakespeare and legendary history:
Lear and Cymbeline.   Reprint from
Shakespeare Quarterly, Vol. 7,
Winter 1956.   (Shakespeare Associa-
tion of America)   pp. [6]
bibliogs.   [?1957.]

666588

——RICH (T.)
Harington & Ariosto: a study in
Elizabethan verse translation, [i.e.
Sir John Harington's translation of
Ariosto's Orlando Furioso. [With
references to Shakespeare.] (New
Haven, [Conn.])
bibliogs.   facsimiles.   1940.
Yale Studies in English, Vol. 92.

521866

——SATIN, JOSEPH
Shakespeare and his sources [for
thirteen of the plays]. (Boston)
1966.

764821

——SCOTT (MARY A.)
Elizabethan translations from the
Italian: the titles of such works,
now first collected and arranged,
with annotations. [With references
to Shakespeare.] IN Publications
of the Modern Language Association of
America, Vols. 10, 11, 13 and 14.
(Baltimore)
4 vols.   1895-99.

428330

——Bisson (C.J.) ed.,Thomas Lodge and
other Elizabethans. Illus. Plans.
Pedigrees.

(Cambridge,[Mass.]   1933.

408148

——SPENCER (TERENCE JOHN BEW)
Shakespeare and the Elizabethan Romans.
IN SHAKESPEARE SURVEY, 10.   (Cambridge)
1957.

665485

——SPIVACK (BERNARD)

Shakespeare and the allegory of evil:
the history of a metaphor in relation
to his major villains. Bibliog. (New
York)   1958.

665954

——STARNES (D. T.)
Shakespeare and Apuleius [: Shakespeare's
knowledge and use of Apuleius' Golden
Ass.]   IN Publications of the Modern
Language Association of America, Vol.60.
(Menasha, Wis.)   1945.
bibliog.

569026

——STOLL (E. E.)
Source and motive in Macbeth and
Othello.   IN The Review of English
Studies, Vol. 19.   (Oxford)
bibliog.   1943.

555539

——TESLAR (JOSEPH ANDREW)
Shakespeare's worthy counsellor [:
influence on Shakespeare's texts of
the treatise "De optimo senatore" by
Laurentius Grimalius Goslicki and the
influence of John Zamoyski on Goslicki].
(Rzym)
port.   illus.   facsimiles.   bibliog.
1960.

666938

——Thaler (A.) Shakspere, Daniel and
Everyman. [With bibliographical
notes.] From Philological quarterly,
Vol. 15.

(Iowa)   1935.

484068

——Tynan (J.L.) The Influence of Greene on
Shakespeare's early romance. In PMLA,
Publications of the Modern Language
Association of America, vol.27.

(Baltimore)   1912.

428347

——WADMAN (H.)
Who wrote in the margin? [: a description of the find of a copy of E. Hall's
"Union of the noble houses of Lancaster
and York", 1550, with marginal notes
attributed to Shakespeare.] FROM
Picture Post, Apr. 26, 1941.
illus.   facsimiles.   1941.

524716

WHITAKER (V. K.)
Shakespeare's use of his sources.
IN MAXWELL (B.) [and others] eds.,
Renaissance studies in honor of
Hardin Craig. (Iowa)
port. bibliog. 1941.
Philological Quarterly, Vol. 20,
No. 3; Iowa University [and Stanford
University].

539442

WHITAKER (VIRGIL KEEBLE)
Shakespeare's use of learning: an
inquiry into the growth of his mind
& art. (San Marino, Cal.) 1953.
bibliog.
Huntington Library.

637660

WILSON (F. P.)
Shakespeare's reading. IN SHAKESPEARE
SURVEY 3. (Cambridge) 1950.

606026

WRIGHT (T.)
On some early Latin stories imitated
at a later period by Chaucer and
Shakespeare. Communicated to the
Society of Antiquaries by T. Wright.
[Reprinted] from The Archaeologia,
Vol. 32. pp. 8. 1848.

554141

ZEEVELD (W. G.)
The Influence of Hall on Shakespeare's
English historical plays. IN A
Journal of English literary history.
Vol. 3. (Baltimore)
1936.

469240

SOUSTER (GERALD)
To Shakespeare (after seeing "Much ado
about nothing") [: a poem]. IN
Poetry of To-day, New Series, Vol. 11.
1939.

518304

A South African's homage [: Sechuana
text with English translation.]
IN GOLLANCZ ([Sir] I.) ed., A Book of
homage to Shakespeare.
ports. illus. facsimiles. [1916.]

264175

SOUTH BENFLEET SCHOOL
Shakespearian plays: programmes,
tickets, photographs, etc.
(South Benfleet) 1935-8.

456665

SOUTHALL (RAYMOND)
Measure for measure and the Protestant
ethic. IN Essays in Criticism,
Vol. 11. 1961. 1961.

621866/1961

SOUTHALL, RAYMOND
'Troilus and Cressida' and the spirit
of capitalism. IN KETTLE, ARNOLD,
ed., Shakespeare in a changing
world: essays [by various authors].
1964.

667797

SOUTHAM (B. C.)
Shakespeare's Christian sonnet?
Number 146.
IN SHAKESPEARE QUARTERLY XI: 1.
pp. 67-71.
(New York) 1960.

605711

Southampton, Henry Wriothesley 3rd Earl of
works relating to

AKRIGG, GEORGE PHILIP VERNON
Shakespeare and the Earl of
Southampton.
illus. 1968.

771926

BUCKLAND, EMILY A.
The Rainsford family, with sidelights
on Shakespeare, Southampton, Hall and Hart.
Ports. Illus. Genealogical Tables.
(Worcester) [1932.]

405462

GRAY, H.D.
Shakespeare, Southampton and Avisa.
IN Stanford Studies in Language and
Literature, 1941. Edited by H. Craig.
([Palo Alto,] Cal.) 1941.

537291

GRAY, H.D.
Shakespeare's rival poet.
[With bibliographical notes]. IN
Journal of English and Germanic
Philology, Vol.47. (Urbana, Ill.)
1941.

(University of Illinois)

600780/47

LEE, Sir S.
Shakespeare and the Earl of Southampton.
FROM Cornhill Magazine, 1898. pp.[14.]
[1898.]

390916

ROWSE, ALFRED LESLIE
Shakespeare's Southampton, patron of
Virginia. 1965.

illus. 746572

Sharpe (R.B.)
The Real war of the theatres: Shakespeare's
fellows in rivalry with the Admiral's men,
1594-1603. Repertories, devices and types.
[With bibliographical footnotes.] (Boston)
1935.

(The Modern Language Association of America.
Monograph Series, 5.)

443036

——THOMSON, W., ed.
The Sonnets of William Shakespeare &
Henry Wriothesley, Third Earl of
Southampton, with A Lover's Complaint
and The Phoenix & Turtle. Edited with an
introduction. (Oxford)   1933.

480352

SOUTHEND-ON-SEA SHAKESPEARE SOCIETY
Programmes, reports, etc. [Southend]
illus.   1921-

547087

SOUTHERN (RICHARD)
The Mystery of the Elizabethan stage.
Producer Leonie Cohn. [Script of
broadcast, March, 1960]   (British
Broadcasting Corporation)   ff. 10.
typescript.   1960.

666910

SOUTHERN (RICHARD)
On reconstructing a practicable
Elizabethan public playhouse.
IN SHAKESPEARE SURVEY 12. (Cambridge)
illus.   plan.   dgms.   1959.

666150

Southern Oregon College

Ashland Studies in Shakespeare: notes,
comment, and reading-lists to accompany
classwork [in the Institute of
Renaissance Studies] established by
the English Department of Stanford
University in association with the
Oregon Shakespeare Festival. Privately
published and sponsored by the Oregon
Shakespeare Festival, Southern Oregon
College and Stanford University of
California.   (Ashland, Ore.)
ports. illus. maps. plans. genealogical
tables. facsimiles. bibliog.   1954-
666259

SOUTHERN SHAKESPEARE REPERTORY THEATRE,
                     Coral Gables, Fla.
Souvenir programmes, 3rd season -
(Coral Gables, Fla.)   1963-

illus.   749762

Note: Lacks 1st and 2nd season.

SOUTHGATE (HENRY)
The Way to woo and win a wife: choice
extracts [including quotations from
Shakespeare,] with some original
matter.
illus.   1876.

486983

THE SOUTHSEA SHAKESPEARE ACTORS
[Programmes, etc.]   [Southsea]
illus.   1950-

645707

Southwark *see* London

SOUTHWARK PUBLIC LIBRARIES AND CUMING
MUSEUM
Shakespeare Tercentenary, Second
Folio, 1632-1932: a catalogue of
Shakespeare editions, playbills,
broadsides, exhibited in the Central
Libraries.   Inaugurated by Sir Frank
R. Benson, April 1932.   pp.48. [1932]

393886

SOUTHWARK SHAKESPEARE FESTIVAL
Programmes, etc.   1932-

420929

Southwell, Robert *works relating to*

—— DEVLIN (CHRISTOPHER)
The Life of Robert Southwell, poet and
martyr. Genealogical Tables. Bibliog.
                               1956.

654447

—— MACDONALD (K. C.)
Blessed Robert Southwell, S.J., and
William Shakespeare.   [With refer-
ences to "Mr. W.H." in connection
with the sonnets.]   IN The Month,
Vol. 158.   1931.

389959

SOUTHWELL GRAMMAR SCHOOL
Shakespearian performances.   Programmes.
(Southwell)   1923-38.

479949

SOUTHWORTH (J. G.)
The Poetry of Thomas Hardy.   [With
references to Shakespeare.]   (New
York)   1947.

589789

Souvenirs, Theatrical *see under* [Play Title]
Stage History and Production

Soviet Russia *see* **Russia**

SOWERBUTTS (J. A.)
Sigh no more, ladies: four-part song
(S.A.T.B.) Words [from Much ado
about nothing]. pp. 7. 1920.
Novello's Part-song Book, Second
Series.

594136

SPAIN (MARGARET M.)
Who wrote Shakespeare's sonnets? pp.32.
(Dublin)

1946.

596764

Spain

——CRAWFORD (J. P. W.)
Spanish drama before Lope de Vega.
Revised edn. [with Shakespearian
references.] (Philadelphia) 1937.

472074

——FRASER (J. A.)
Spain and the West Country. [With
references to Spanish influence on
Shakespeare, and editions of his
works in Spain.]
bibliog. ports. illus. facsimiles.
1935.

440349

——HUME (MARTIN [ANDREW SHARP])
Some Spanish influences in Elizabethan
literature. [With reference to
Shakespeare.] IN Transactions of the
Royal Society of Literature. Second
Series. Vol. 29. 1909.

222619

—— MERRY DEL VAL (ALFONSO, [Marquis de])
Shakespeare, from a Spaniard.
IN GOLLANCZ ([Sir] I.) ed., A Book of
homage to Shakespeare.
ports. illus. facsimiles. [1916.]

264175

——NORTHUP (G.T.)
An Introduction to Spanish literature.
[With references to Shakespeare and
bibliographies.] (Chicago)
1934.

436929

——THOMAS (Sir H.)
Shakespeare in Spain. pp. 24.
bibliog. [1949.]
British Academy. [39th] Annual
Shakespeare Lecture.

604892

SPALDING (KENNETH JAY)
The Philosophy of Shakespeare.
(Oxford) 1953.

632614

SPALDING (THOMAS ALFRED)
On the First Quarto of Romeo and Juliet:
is there any evidence of a second hand in it?
**IN Transactions of the New Shakespeare
Society, Series 1.** No. 5. pp. 58-87.
1877-9.

40620

SPALDING (THOMAS ALFRED)
On the witchcraft in Macbeth.
IN Transactions of the New Shakespeare
Society, Series 1. No. 5. pp. 27-40.
1877-9.

40620

SPARGO (JOHN WEBSTER)
An Interpretation of Falstaff.
Reprinted from Washington University
Studies, Vol. 9, Humanistic Series,
No. 2. pp. 119-133. [Washington]
1922.

479850

SPARGO (JOHN WEBSTER)
The Knocking at the gate in Macbeth:
an essay in interpretation. bibliog.
IN McMANAWAY (J. G.), DAWSON (G. E.)
and WILLOUGHBY (E. E.) eds., Joseph
Quincy Adams memorial studies.
(Washington) 1948.

596748

SPEAIGHT (G.)
Juvenile drama: the history of the
English toy theatre. [With lists
of publishers and plays published
for the juvenile drama, and references
to Shakespeare.]
illus. bibliog. 1946.

578246

Speaight (J.) Some Shakespeare fairy
characters for string quartet,
(Hawkes Concert Edition.)
2 vols.

1916.

403995

Speaight (R.) Acting : its idea
and tradition. [With references
to Shakespeare and a bibliography.]
pp. 95.

1939.

502113

Speaight (R.) The Angel in the mist:
[a novel. With references to
Shakespeare.]

1936.

450441

SPEAIGHT (ROBERT)

The Christian theatre. (Faith and Fact
Books, 118) Bibliog. 1960.

693060

SPEAIGHT (ROBERT)
Interpretations of Shakespeare [: a
review of "The Crown of Life" by
G. W. Knight.] FROM Time and Tide,
Vol. 28.   1947.

587304

SPEAIGHT, ROBERT
Marlowe: the forerunner. FROM A Review
of English Literature, Vol.7, no.4,
Oct.1966.   1966.

pp.25-41.   762624

SPEAIGHT (ROBERT)

Mr. Priestley, Falstaff and Establishment.
FROM The Month, N.S. Vol.25, No.3.
1961.

667759

SPEAIGHT (ROBERT)
Nature and grace in Macbeth.   (Giff
Edmonds Memorial Lecture, 1952.)
IN Essays by Divers Hands, New Series,
Vol. 27.   1955.

647127

SPEAIGHT (ROBERT)
Nature in Shakespearian tragedy.
1955.

648479

SPEAIGHT (ROBERT)
The 1960 Season at Stratford-upon-Avon.
IN SHAKESPEARE QUARTERLY XI:
pp. 445-453.
(New York) 1960.

605711

SPEAIGHT (ROBERT)
The Old Vic and Stratford-upon-Avon,
1960-61.
IN SHAKESPEARE QUARTERLY XII: 4.
pp. 425-441.
(New York) 1961.

605711

SPEAIGHT (ROBERT)
A Programme on the development of
the Shakespeare Memorial Theatre,
Stratford-upon-Avon.   Introduced by
R. Speaight.   Produced by D. Cleverdon.
[Script of Broadcast, April, 1960]
(British Broadcasting Corporation)
ff. 15.
  typescript.   1959.

666906

SPEAIGHT (ROBERT)
Shakespeare and politics: the Wedmore
Memorial Lecture delivered before the
Royal Society of Literature, May 21st,
1946.   With a foreword by F. S. Boas.
pp. 20.   [1946.] 576035
Royal Society of Literature.
_____ IN Bax (C.) ed., Essays by divers
hands: the Transactions of the Royal
Society of Literature of the United
Kingdom, New Series, Vol. 24.
1948. 593464

SPEAIGHT, ROBERT
Shakespeare and the political
spectrum as illustrated by 'Richard II'.
IN Stratford Papers on Shakespeare
delivered at the 1964 Shakespeare
Seminar.   (Toronto)   1965.

745844

SPEAIGHT (ROBERT)
Shakespeare in Britain [: reviews of
productions].   IN SHAKESPEARE
QUARTERLY XIV:1963, pp. 419-432;
XV:1964, pp. 377-389; XVI:1965,
pp. 313-323; XVII:1966, pp. 389-398;
XVIII:1967, pp.389-397; XIX:1968,
pp. 367-375.   (New York)

605711

SPEAIGHT (ROBERT)
Shakespeare's search for a hero [: a
lecture delivered to the Leighton
House Society on Nov. 6th, 1936.]
FROM Blackfriars, May-June, 1937.

472754

SPEAIGHT (ROBERT)
William Poel and the Elizabethan
revival.   (Society for Theatre
Research.   Annual Publication [4]
1951-52.)
  ports.   illus.   chronological
  table.   bibliog.   1954.

641603

Special library resources, edited
by Rose L. Vormelker, Vol. 1.
[Includes the Horace Howard Furness
Memorial Library of Shakespeareana,
University of Pennsylvania.]
(New York)   1941.
  Special Libraries Association,
[United States]

529758

[Specimen pictures from Collins' Stage
Shakespeare.]   [?1903-05.]
  Apparently a traveller's sample volume.

551119

SPECKING (INEZ)
A Shakespeare for children.   (New
York)   1954.

665070

SPEDDING (FRANK)
The Morning chase: two-part [song.
Words by] W. Shakespeare [from "Titus
Andronicus"].   pp. 8.   1959.
The Oxford Choral Songs.

666471

SPEDDING (JAMES)
On the corrected edition of Richard III.
IN Transactions of the New Shakespeare
Society, Series 1. No. 3.   pp. 1-77.
1875-6.
40620

SPEDDING (JAMES)
On the division of the acts in Lear, Much
ado, and Twelfth Night.
IN Transactions of the New Shakespeare
Society, Series 1.   No. 5.   pp. 11-26.
1877-9.

40620

SPEDDING (JAMES)
On the several shares of Shakspere and
Fletcher in the play of "Henry VIII".
IN Transactions of the New Shakespeare
Society, Series 1.No. 1.   pp. 1-24. of
Appendix.   1874.

4061

S[PEDDING] (JAMES)
The Proper division of "King Lear"
into acts.   FROM The Gentleman's
Magazine, May 1850.   pp. [4.]
1850.

402703

S[PEDDING] (JAMES)
The Proper division of "Much ado about
nothing" into acts.   FROM The
Gentleman's Magazine, June 1850.
pp. [4.]

402704

SPEDDING (JAMES)
Reviews and discussions: literary,
political and historical, not relating
to Bacon.   1879.

125328

S[PEDDING] (JAMES)
Who wrote Shakspere's "Henry VIII".
FROM The Gentleman's Magazine, Aug.
1850, Oct. 1850.   pp. [12.] 1850.

402705

Speech *see* Grammar and Language; Oratory and Rhetoric

Speed (Lancelot) illus.
LAMB (CHARLES and MARY [A.])
Tales from Shakespeare [with an intro-
duction and notes].
[c.1915.] 552918
[Illustrated Scarlet Library]
_____ Another edn. [1939.]   511664

SPEED (LANCELOT) illus.
Lamb (Charles and Mary A.)
Tales from Shakespeare [Illustrated
Scarlet Library] [c.1915]   552918
--- Another edition [1934]   426015
--- Another edition [1939]   511614

Spelling *see* Grammar and Language

SPENCE (JAMES LEWIS THOMAS CHALMERS)
British fairy origins [including
references to Shakespeare.]
bibliogs.   1946.

575668

SPENCER (BENJAMIN T.)
Antony and Cleopatra and the paradoxical
metaphor.
IN SHAKESPEARE QUARTERLY IX.
pp. 373-378.
(New York)   1958.

605711

SPENCER (B. T.)
King Lear: a prophetic tragedy.
FROM College English, Vol. 5.
(Chicago)   1944.

578274

SPENCER (BENJAMIN TOWNLEY)
The Man who was Shakespeare [: a review
of] "The Man who was Shakespeare", by
[Mrs.] Eva T. Clark; "Shakespeare, man
and artist", by E. I. Fripp; "In
Shakespeare's Warwickshire and the
unknown years", by O. Baker; "I, William
Shakespeare, do appoint Thomas Russell,
Esquire", by L. Hotson; [and]
"Shakespeare rediscovered", by [Comtesse]
Clara L. de Chambrun. pp. [12.]   FROM
Sewanee Review, Vol. 47.   (Sewanee,
Tenn.)   1939.

533675

SPENCER (BENJAMIN TOWNLEY)
Philip Massinger.   IN Seventeenth
century studies [: first series].
Edited by R. Shafer.   (Princeton)
bibliog.   1933.

481322

SPENCER (BENJAMIN TOWNLEY)
The Stasis of Henry IV, Part II.
IN Tennessee Studies in Literature,
Vol. 6.   (Knoxville)   1961.

692773/6

SPENCER (BENJAMIN TOWNLEY)
Three ways to Shakespeare [: a review
of The Voyage to Illyria: a new study
of Shakespeare, by K. Muir and S.
O'Loughlin; The Meaning of Hamlet,
by L. L. Schucking, translated by
G. Rawson; Shakespeare's plays: a
commentary, by M. R. Ridley].   FROM
Sewanee Review, Vol. 47.   (Sewanee)
1939.

530197

Spencer (B.T.) 2 Henry IV and the
theme of time. From University of
Toronto Quarterly, Vol.13.

(Toronto)   1944.

578419

SPENCER, CHRISTOPHER
A word for Tate's 'King Lear'. FROM
Studies in English Literature 1500-1900,
Vol.3, No.2. (Houston, Tex.) 1963.

pp.241-251.   753400

Spencer (Christopher) ed.
DAVENANT (Sir WILLIAM)
Macbeth, from the Yale manuscript:
an edition, with a discussion of the
relation of Davenant's text to
Shakespeare's.   (New Haven, [Conn.])
facsimiles.   bibliogs.   1961.
Yale Studies in English, 146.

666874

SPENCER (CHRISTOPHER) ed.
Five Restoration adaptations of
Shakespeare, edited with an introduction.
(Urbana: University of Illinois Press)
1965.

751887

SPENCER (HAZELTON)
The Art and life of William Shakespeare.
(New York)
ports. illus. map. facsimiles. bibliog.
1940.

513809

Spencer (H.) The Clock passage in
Richard III. In The Review of
English Studies, Vol. 14.

1938.

495115

SPENCER (HAZELTON)
D'Avenant's Macbeth and Shakespeare's.
IN Publications of the Modern Language
Association of America, Vol. 40.
(Menasha, Wis.)   1925.

428360

SPENCER (HAZELTON)
Hamlet under the Restoration.
FROM Publications of the Modern
Language Association of America,
Vol. 38.   (Menasha, Wis.)
bibliog.   1923.

554229

SPENCER (HAZELTON)
How Shakespeare staged his plays:
some notes on the dubiety of non-
textual evidence.   FROM The Johns
Hopkins Alumni Magazine.   Vol. 20,
No. 3.   (Baltimore)   1932.

440786

SPENCER (HAZELTON)
Improving Shakespeare: some bibliographical notes on the Restoration
adaptations.   IN Publications of
the Modern Language Association of
America, Vol. 41.   (Menasha, Wis.)
1926.

428361

SPENCER (HAZELTON)
A Nice derangement: the irregular
verse-lining in 'A Midsummer night's
dream', Act V. Sc. 1. ll. 1-84.
IN The Modern Language Review, Vol.
25.   (Cambridge)   1930.

379829

S[pencer] (H.) [Review of] "Shakespeare's Titus Andronicus : The
First Quarto, 1594. [Edited]
by J.Q. Adams. 1936." In Modern
Language Notes, Vol.53.

(Baltimore)   1938.

493024

Spencer (H.) [Review of] M.W.
Black and M.A.Shaaber's "Shakespeare's
seventeenth-century editors : 1632-
1685. 1937". In Modern Language
Notes. Vol. 53.

(Baltimore)   1938.

493024

Spencer (H.) [Review of J.] L.
Hotson's "I, William Shakespeare,
do appoint Thomas Russell, Esquire.
1938". In Modern Language Notes,
Vol.53.

(Baltimore)   1938.

493024

SPENCER (HAZELTON)
[Review of] Shakespeare's problem
comedies, by W. W. Lawrence.
IN Modern Language Notes, 1932.
(Baltimore)

404117

Spencer (H.) [Review of] A History
of Shakespearian criticism by
A. Ralli. In Modern Language
Notes, December, 1934.

(Baltimore)   .

428652

SPENCER (H.)
[Review of] Poets and playwrights:
Shakespeare, Jonson, Spenser, Milton,
by E. E. Stoll.   IN Modern Language
Notes, Vol. 46.   (Baltimore) 1931.

397731

SPENCER (HAZELTON)
Seventeenth-century cuts in Hamlet's
soliloquies.   IN The Review of English
Studies, Vol. 9.   [1933.]

414489

SPENCER (HAZELTON) ed.
Elizabethan plays, written by
Shakespeare's friends, colleagues,
rivals, and successors; to wit:
Christopher Marlowe, John Lyly, Robert
Greene, Thomas Kyd, Ben Jonson, George
Chapman, Thomas Dekker, John Marston,
Thomas Heywood, Francis Beaumont,
John Fletcher, John Webster, Thomas
Middleton, William Rowley, Philip
Massinger, John Ford and James Shirley.
Edited, with new texts based on the
original folios, quartos, and octavos.
port.   1934.
420590

Spencer, Hazelton *works relating to*

CAMPBELL (O. J.)
[Review of] The Tragedy of King
Richard III edited by H. Spencer.
IN Modern Language Notes, December,
1934.   (Baltimore)   1934.

428652

————KAHIN (HELEN A.)
[Review of] The Art and life of
William Shakespeare, by H. Spencer;
A Note on Othello, II, i, 110-113
[Arden edn. With bibliographical
notes]. IN Modern Language Quarterly,
Vol. 1. (Seattle) 1940.

525289

————KRANENDONK (A. G. van)
[Review of] The Art and life of
William Shakespeare, by H. Spencer.
IN English Studies, Vol. 22.
(Amsterdam) 1940.

575606

————PARROTT (T. M.)
[Review of] Elizabethan plays, written
by Shakespeare's friends, etc. edited
by H. Spencer. IN Modern Language
Notes, January, 1934. (Baltimore)
1934.

428652

SPENCER (MARGUERITA)

Two Shakespeare songs for two-part
singing: I know a bank [and] Where the
bee sucks. Arranged by Marguerita
Spencer. (Gordon V. Thompson Limited,
Toronto) 1961.

667426

SPENCER, TERENCE JOHN BEW
The Course of Shakespeare criticism.
IN SUTHERLAND, JAMES, and HURSTFIELD,
JOEL, eds., Shakespeare's world.
1964.

667808

SPENCER, TERENCE JOHN BEW
The Decline of Hamlet. IN Stratford-
upon-Avon Studies. 5: Hamlet.
1963.

667698

SPENCER (TERENCE JOHN BEW)
The Great rival: Shakespeare and the
classical dramatists. IN BLOOM
(EDWARD A.) ed., Shakespeare 1564-1964:
a collection of modern essays by various
hands. (Providence, R.I.) 1964.
Brown University bicentennial publications.

744437

SPENCER (TERENCE JOHN BEW)
"Greeks" and "Merrygreeks": a background to "Timon of Athens" and "Troilus
and Cressida". IN HOSLEY (RICHARD) ed.,
Essays on Shakespeare and Elizabethan
drama in honour of Hardin Craig.
illus. 1963.

667532

SPENCER, TERENCE JOHN BEW
The Roman plays; 'Titus Andronicus',
'Julius Caesar', 'Antony and Cleopatra',
'Coriolanus'. 1963.

British Book News. Bibliographical
Series of Supplements. Writers and their
Work, no.157. 667502

SPENCER (TERENCE JOHN BEW)
Shakespeare and the Elizabethan Romans.
IN SHAKESPEARE SURVEY 10. (Cambridge)
1957.

665485

SPENCER, TERENCE JOHN BEW
Shakespeare and the noble woman.
IN DEUTSCHE SHAKESPEARE-GESELLSCHAFT
WEST, JAHRBUCH 1966. pp. 49-62.
(Heidelberg)

754129

SPENCER (TERENCE JOHN BEW)
Shakespeare as seen by his contemporaries. IN Shakespeare: a celebration,
1564-1964.
illus. maps. 1964.

667816

SPENCER (TERENCE JOHN BEW)
Shakespeare learns the value of
money: the dramatist at work on
Timon of Athens. IN SHAKESPEARE
SURVEY 6. (Cambridge) 1953.

631770

SPENCER (TERENCE JOHN BEW)

**Shakespeare v. The Rest: the old
controversy.** IN Shakespeare Survey
[Vol.] 14. (Cambridge) 1961.

666755

SPENCER (TERENCE JOHN BEW)
The Tyranny of Shakespeare. pp. [19.]
bibliog. [1959.] 666610
(Annual Shakespeare Lecture of the
British Academy, 1959)
————— IN Studies in Shakespeare:
British Academy lectures, selected
and introduced by P. Alexander.
1964. 667830

SPENCER, TERENCE JOHN BEW ed.
Elizabethan love stories. With
introduction and glossary.
(Harmondsworth) 1968.
Penguin Shakespeare library.

768790

SPENCER, TERENCE JOHN BEW, ed.
Shakespeare: a celebration, 1564-1964.
illus. maps. 1964.

667816

SPENCER (TERENCE JOHN BEW) ed.
Shakespeare's Plutarch: the lives of
Julius Caesar, Brutus, Marcus Antonius
and Coriolanus in the translation of
Sir T. North. Edited, with an
introduction, glossary and parallel
passages from Shakespeare's plays.
1964.
Peregrine Books.

667944

SPENCER (THEODORE)

**Death and Elizabethan tragedy: a
study of convention and opinion in
the Elizabethan drama.** (Cambridge,
Mass.) 1936.

453812

SPENCER (THEODORE)

Editions of Shakespeare. From The New
Republic, January 10, 1944. (New York)
1944.

559547

SPENCER (THEODORE)

Hamlet and the nature of reality.
In E L H: a Journal of English Literary
History, Vol. 5. 1938.

499385

SPENCER (THEODORE)

The Isolation of the Shakespearian hero:
the Furness Lecture at Wellesley College
for 1944. From The Sewanee Review, Vol.52.
(Sewanee, Tenn.) 1944.

578421

SPENCER (THEODORE)

Shakespeare and Milton. In
Modern Language Notes, Vol.53.
(Baltimore) 1938.

493024

SPENCER (THEODORE)
Shakespeare and the nature of man.
(Cambridge)
bibliog. 1943. 544912
Lowell [Institute] Lectures, 1942.
_____ 2nd edn. (New York)
1949. 611935

SPENCER (THEODORE)

The Two Noble Kinsmen. From Modern
Philology, Vol. 36. (Chicago)
1939.

530567

Spencer, Theodore *works relating to*

—ALEXANDER (P.)
[Review of] Shakespeare and the
nature of man, by T. Spencer. IN
The Modern Language Review, Vol. 39.
(Cambridge) 1944.

563897

—COX (E. H.)
[Review of] Shakespeare and the nature
of man, by T. Spencer. IN Modern
Language Quarterly, Vol. 5. (Seattle)
1944.

563896

—— KNIGHTS (LIONEL CHARLES)
Shakespeare and the Elizabethan climate
[: review of] Shakespeare and the
nature of man, by T. Spencer. IN
Scrutiny, Vol. 12. (Cambridge)
1943-4.

564002

----KNOX (R. S.)
[Review of] Shakespeare and the nature
of man, by T. Spencer. FROM University
of Toronto Quarterly, Vol. 13.
(Toronto) 1944.

578418

—— Shakespeare's world [: review of]
Shakespeare and the nature of man,
by T. Spencer. IN The Times
Literary Supplement, Jan. 29, 1944.

558345

——WILSON (J. S.)
Shakespeare in the interpretation of
the time [: review of] Shakespeare's
satire, by O. J. Campbell; [and]
Shakespeare and the nature of man,
by T. Spencer. FROM The Virginia
Quarterly Review, Vol. 19.
(Charlottesville, Va.) 1943.

565603

SPENDER (STEPHEN)
The Alike and the other. IN Hubler (E.)
and others. The Riddle of Shakespeare's
sonnets. 1962.

667289

Spender (S.) Life and the poet.
[With references to Shakespeare.]

1942.

(Searchlight Books, No. 18)

531960

SPENS (JANET)
Spenser's Faerie Queene, an interpretation [with Shakespearian references.]
1934.

428270

Spenser, Edmund *works relating to*

——ATKINSON (DOROTHY F.)
Edmund Spenser: a bibliographical
supplement [to F. I. Carpenter's
"A Reference guide to Edmund Spenser".
With Shakespearian references.]
(Baltimore) 1937.

471903

——BENNETT (JOSEPHINE W.)
The Evolution of "The Faerie Queene".
[With bibliographical notes and references to Shakespeare.] (Chicago)
tables. 1942.

544478

—— DE MONTMORENCY (J. E. G.)
The "Other poet" of Shakespeare's
sonnets [: Edmund Spenser]. IN
The Contemporary Review, Vol. 101.
1912.

236965

——HARRISON (THOMAS PERRIN)
Aspects of primitivism in Shakespeare
and Spenser. IN University of Texas,
Studies in English, [No. 20].
(Austin, Texas) 1940.

529715

——HARRISON (T. P.)
Flower lore in Spenser and Shakespeare:
two notes. [With bibliographical
notes.] IN Modern Language Quarterly,
Vol. 7, (Seattle) 1946.

584762

——KRANENDONK (A. G. van)
Spenserian echoes in A Midsummer-night's
dream. FROM English studies, Vol. 14.
(Amsterdam) 1932.

441442

——MAYHALL (JANE)
Shakespeare and Spenser: a commentary
on differences. IN Modern Language
Quarterly, Vol. 10. (Seattle, Wash.)
1949.

525289/10

——MILLICAN (C. B.)
Spenser and the Table Round: a study
in the contemporaneous background
for Spenser's use of the Arthurian
legend [containing Shakespearian
references].
illus. 1932.
Harvard Studies in Comparative
Literature.

398063

——POTTS (ABBIE FINDLAY)
Hamlet and Gloriana's knights.
IN SHAKESPEARE QUARTERLY VI:
pp. 31-43.
(New York) 1955.

605711

—— POTTS (ABBIE FINDLAY)

Shakespeare and 'The Faerie Queene'.
(New York) 1958.

665996

——PROPER (IDA SEDGWICK)
Our elusive Willy: a slice of concealed
Elizabethan history. [An attempt to
prove that Shakespeare was the illegitimate son of Edward Seymour, Earl of
Hertford.] (Manchester, Maine)
ports. illus. 1953.

637031

——THALER (A.)
Mercutio and Spenser's Phantasies.
FROM Philological Quarterly, Vol. 16.
(Iowa City) 1937.

507528

——THALER (A.)
Spenser and "Much ado about nothing".
IN Studies in Philology, Vol. 37.
(Chapel Hill, N.C.) 1940.

522312

—— WATKINS (WALTER BARKER CRITZ)
Shakespeare & Spenser. (Princeton,
N.J.)
bibliog. 1950.

611909

——WILLIAMS, FRANKLIN B., Jr.
Spenser, Shakespeare, and Zachary Jones.
IN SHAKESPEARE QUARTERLY XIX: 3.
pp. 205-212. (New York)
1968.

605711

—— see also MOORE (W. H.) Baconian studies.

SPERBER (H.)
The Conundrums in Saxo's Hamlet
episode. IN PMLA, Vol. 64.
(Menasha, Wis.)
bibliog. 1949.

428321/64

SPEVACK, MARVIN
A Complete and systematic concordance
to the works of Shakespeare.
(Hildesheim) 1968-

767574

SPEVACK, MARVIN
Hero and villain in Shakespeare: [an
essay] on dualism and tragedy. FROM
Tennessee Studies in Literature,
Vol.XII,1967. (Knoxville, Tenn.)
1967.

pp.1-11. 766079

SPIEGLER (C. G.)
"Julius Caesar" - a liberal education:
a modern approach to the teaching of
a classic. FROM High points in the
work of the High Schools of the City
of New York, May 1936. [New York]
1936.

506185

SPIELMANN (MARION HARRY)
The "Grafton" and "Sanders" portraits
of Shakespeare. pp. [6.] FROM
The Connoisseur, Feb. 1909. 1909.
ports.

521313

SPIELMANN (M. H.)
The Janssen, or Somerset, portrait
of Shakespeare. IN The Connoisseur,
Vol. 24.
ports. 1909.

218524

SPIELMANN (M. H.)
The Janssen, or Somerset, portrait
of Shakespeare: the more important
copies, part 2. FROM The
Connoisseur, Vol. 32.
illus. 1912.

522118

SPIELMANN (M. H.)
The Miniatures of Shakespeare.
IN The Connoisseur, Vol. 45, 1916.
illus.

266905

SPIELMANN (M. H.)
A Shakespearean revival: Macbeth.
IN The Magazine of Art, [Vol. 12],
1889.   1889.

103127

SPIELMANN (MARION HARRY)
[Shakespeare's portraiture: a reissue
of] The Title-page of the First Folio
of Shakespeare's plays: a comparative
study of the Droeshout portrait and
the Stratford monument. Written for
the Shakespeare Association in celebration of the First Folio Tercentenary
1923.   pp. xi, 56.
  bibliog. ports. illus. genealogical
table. facsimiles.   1931.
  No. 22 of edn. limited to 50 copies.
Author's signature on half tp.   Date
on tp. 1924, on cover 1931.
                              533661

SPIELMANN (MARION HARRY)
"This figure, that thou here seest put".
IN GOLLANCZ ([Sir] I.) ed., A Book
of homage to Shakespeare.
   ports. illus. facsimiles. [1916.]

264175

Spigelgass (Leonard), Grayson (C.)
and Smith (P. G.) The Boys from
Syracuse see English Editions (Comedy
of Errors: Alterations,etc.)

Spiker (S.) George Wilkins and the
   authorship of Pericles. From
   Studies in Philology, vol.30.

          (Baltimore)   1933.

441596

**Spink (W.) The Autocrat in the
greenroom [containing references to
Shakespeare]; with a play [in four
acts in prose and verse, entitled:
"Lesled: Lord of the Isles"] after
Othello.**

                          1890.

522854

SPINK, WILLIAM
Lesled, Lord of the Isles.

For editions of this play see under
English Editions: Othello:
Alterations &c.

Spiritualism

— ALLEN (P.)
   **Talks with Elizabethans, revealing the
   mystery of "William Shakespeare"
   [: conversations with Elizabethan playwrights and poets, communicated through
   automatic writing of Mrs. Hester Dowden.
   With references to Francis Bacon and
   the Earl of Oxford and bibliographical
   references.]**
      ports.
                                [1947.]

587016

——ARCHER (F.)
   "Genius is mediumistic" says Robert
   Lynd --- Shakespeare was possibly
   the spirit influence behind Keats's
   poetry. FROM Psychic News [August
   2nd 1947].   [1947.]
    Incomplete.

586803

——DODD (A.)
   The Immortal master [: "Shake-
   speare", i.e. Francis Bacon].
   A [psychic] study.
     ports.   facsimiles.   [1943.]

543149

——[DODD (A.)]
   "Shake-speare" speaks again to his
   countrymen [: a spirit message
   purporting to have come from Francis
   Bacon].   pp. 3.   [1942.]

549423

——DOUGLAS (M. W.)
   The Shakespeare mystery - a discarnate
   solution.   IN Light, Vol. 68.
                                1948.

267861/68

—— EWEN (C.[H.] L'E)
   Shakespeare, automatist or nothing.
   [With bibliographical notes.] pp.[ii]8.
   (Paignton)
                                1946.

574459

——ROBERTS (Mrs. DAISY OKE)
   Shakespeare and Co. unlimited, by
   Shakespeare & Co. [: spirit messages
   received and] compiled by Mrs. D. O.
   Roberts.   [1950.]

616141

—— ROBERTS (Mrs. DAISY OKE) and WOOLCOCK
                    (COLLIN E.   )
   Elizabethan episode, incorporating
   Shakespeare and Co., Unlimited [: spirit
   messages received and compiled by Mrs.
   Daisy O. Roberts]. Port.   [1961.]

666936

——[SHATFORD (SARAH T.)]
   Jesus' teachings, by Shakespeare's
   Spirit [pseud.]. (New York) 1922.

434101

——[SHATFORD (SARAH T.)]
   My proof of immortality, with my
   demiséd act.   By Shakespeare's Spirit
   [pseud.] (New York)   1924.

430035

——[SHATFORD (SARAH T.)]
   This book for Him I name for Jesus'
   sake, by Shakespeare's Spirit [pseud.].
   [New York]   [1920]

434100

——WASHBURN (O. R.)
   Who are these? Writings from psychic
   sources [including a communication
   from Shakespeare's spirit].
   (Philadelphia)   1941.

533043

SPIVACK (BERNARD)
Falstaff and the Psychomachia.
IN SHAKESPEARE QUARTERLY VIII.
pp. 449-459.
(New York) 1957.
605711

SPIVACK (BERNARD)
Shakespeare and the allegory of evil:
the history of a metaphor in relation
to his major villains. (New York)
bibliog. 1958.
665954

SPIVEY (GAYNELL CALLAWAY)
Swinburne's use of Elizabethan drama.
[With references to Shakespeare.]
IN Studies in Philology, Vol. 41.
(Chapel Hill, N.C.)
bibliog. 1944.
563556

Splendour Books
GOULDEN (SHIRLEY)
Tales from Shakespeare. Illustrated
by Nardini.
illus. 1964.
Splendour Books.
668324

SPOFFORD (HARRIET ELIZABETH PRESCOTT)
Woods of Warwick [: a poem]. FROM
Atalanta, Vol. 1. 1887.
515798

Sport
see also Angling; Archery; Bowls; Cricket;
Cycling; Duelling; Falconry; Fencing;
Football; Gambling; Hawking; Hunting;
Swimming

——DAWSON (GILES EDWIN)
London's Bull-baiting and bear-baiting
arena in 1562. IN Shakespeare Quarterly
XV: 1. pp.97-101. (New York) 1964.
605711

——[DUNKIN (R.)]
Sport in Shakespeare. IN [Dunkin (R.)]
The Snaffle papers [on sport], by
"Snaffle". With drawings by H. Dixon.
1898.
483855

——G[em] (T.H.) Shakespeare as a
sportsman. From Baily's Magazine of
Sports and Pastimes, Vol.22.
1872.
559985

——Henn (T.R.) Field sports in Shakespeare. In [Darton (F.J.H.) ed.,]
Essays of the year, 1933-1934.
1934.
425666

——Madden (Rt. Hon. D.H.) The Diary
of Master William Silence: a
study of Shakespeare & of Elizabethan sport. New edn.
1907.
425346

——OSBORN (E. B.) [ed.]
Shakespeare as sportsman [: quotations
from the plays.] IN Osborn (E. B.)
[ed.] Anthology of sporting verse.
1930.
438373

——PARKER (E.) ed.
The Lonsdale anthology of sporting
prose & verse. With an introduction.
[Containing quotations from
Shakespeare.] 1932.
396568

—— Shakespeare's England, vol. 2.
[With chapters on Sports in
Shakespeare's time.] (Oxford)
illus. facsimiles. bibliogs.
1917.
435746

——Sieveking (A.F.) Games. In Shakespeare's
England, vol.2. [With bibliographies.] Illus. Facsimiles.
(Oxford) 1917.
435746

——STONE (LILLY C.)
English sports and recreations.
pp. ii, 50. (Washington, D.C.)
illus. facsimiles. bibliog.
1960. 666785
Folger Shakespeare Library. Folger
Booklets on Tudor and Stuart Civilisation.
_____ IN Life and letters in Tudor and
Stuart England. (Ithaca, N.Y.)
illus. 1962. 667762
Folger Shakespeare Library.

SPRAGUE, ARTHUR COLBY
The Doubling of parts in Shakespeare's
plays. 1966.
752780

SPRAGUE (ARTHUR COLBY)
Edmund Kean as Othello. IN A
Casebook on 'Othello', edited by
L. F. Dean. (New York) 1964.
Crowell Literary Casebooks.
748200

SPRAGUE (ARTHUR COLBY)
Edwin Booth's Iago: a study of a great
Shakespearian actor. IN The Theatre
Annual, 1947. (New York)
554521/1947

SPRAGUE (ARTHUR COLBY)
Falstaff Hackett.   IN Theatre Notebook,
Vol. 9.   1955.

584117/9

SPRAGUE (ARTHUR COLBY)
Gadshill revisited.[Falstaff and his critics.]
IN SHAKESPEARE QUARTERLY IV: 2.
pp. 125-137.
(New York)   1953.

605711

SPRAGUE, ARTHUR COLBY
The Moments of seriousness in Shakespearian
comedy.
IN DEUTSCHE SHAKESPEARE-GESELLSCHAFT
WEST, JAHRBUCH 1965.   pp. 240-247.
(Heidelberg)

754129

SPRAGUE (ARTHUR COLBY)
Off-stage sounds, [including references
to Shakespeare.]   FROM University of
Toronto Quarterly, Vol. 15.   (Toronto)
bibliog.   1945.

578420

SPRAGUE (ARTHUR COLBY)
Shakespeare and melodrama.
IN Essays and Studies, 1965.

742617

SPRAGUE (ARTHUR COLBY)
Shakespeare and the actors: the stage
business in his plays (1660-1905).
(Cambridge, Mass.)
illus.   bibliog.   1945.

563058

SPRAGUE (ARTHUR COLBY)
Shakespeare and the audience: a study
in the technique of exposition.
(Cambridge, Mass.)   1935.

445223

Sprague (A.C.) Shakespeare and
William Poel. In University of
Toronto Quarterly, Vol.17.

(Toronto)   1947.

596179

SPRAGUE (ARTHUR COLBY)
Shakespeare on the New York stage [:
reviews].   IN SHAKESPEARE QUARTERLY
V:1954, pp. 311-316; VI:1955, pp.
423-427; VII:1956, pp. 393-398.
(New York)

605711

SPRAGUE, ARTHUR COLBY
Shakespeare's histories: plays for
the stage.   1964.

illus. Society for Theatre
Research.   667707

SPRAGUE, ARTHUR COLBY
Shakespeare's unnecessary characters.
FROM Shakespeare Survey, 20.
pp. 75-82.   1967.

769994

SPRAGUE (ARTHUR COLBY)
Shakespearian players and performances.
Ports. Illus. (Cambridge, Mass.)
                              1953.

635328

SPRAGUE (ARTHUR COLBY)
The Stage business in Shakespeare's plays:
a postscript. (Society for Theatre
Research. Pamphlet Series No. 3) pp.35.
Port.   1954.

639849

Sprague, Arthur Colby *works relating to*

— BALDWIN (THOMAS WHITFIELD)
[Review of] Shakespeare and the
audience, by A. C. Sprague.   IN
Modern Language Notes, Vol. 52.
(Baltimore)   1937.

479896

— BENNETT (HENRY STANLEY)
"Business" in Shakespeare [: review
of] Shakespeare and the actors, by
A. C. Sprague.   IN The New Statesman
and Nation, New Series, Vol. 29.
                              1945.

563861

— BOAS (F. S.)
[Review of] Shakespeare and the actors,
by A. C. Sprague.   IN The Modern
Language Review, Vol. 41.   (Cambridge)
                              1946.

584763

— FISHER (H. K.)
[Review of] Shakespeare and the actors:
the stage business in his plays from
1660-1905, by A. C. Sprague; [and]
A Macbeth production, by J. Masefield.
IN Life and Letters, Vol. 46.   1945.

567808

— GRANVILLE-BARKER (H.)
[Review of] Shakespeare and the actors:
the stage business in his plays (1660-
1905), by A. C. Sprague.   IN Modern
Language Notes, Vol. 60.   (Baltimore)
                              1945.

571543

— HARRISON (G. B.)
[Review of] Shakespeare and the audience
by A. C. Sprague.   IN The Modern
Language Review, Vol. 32.   1937.

477224

— JENKIN (BERNARD)
[Review of] Shakespeare and the actors:
the stage business [in his plays (1660-
1905), by A. C. Sprague.]   IN The
Review of English Studies, Vol. 21.
(Oxford)   [1945.]

570955

SPRIGGS (CHARLES O.)
Hamlet on the eighteenth century stage.
FROM The Quarterly Journal of Speech,
Vol. 22. (Ann Arbor, Mich.)
bibliog. 1936.

488668

SPRING ([H.] P.)
The Healing power of the word:
Shakespeare and Goethe. IN Spring
([H.] P.) The Spirit of literature.
(Winter Park, Fla.) 1945.
Human Science Series.

579395

Spring, according to Shakspeare.
FROM The Day of Rest [, May 1865].
[1865.]

559989

SPROULE (ALBERT FREDERICK)
A Time Scheme for Othello.
IN SHAKESPEARE QUARTERLY VII.
pp. 217-226.
(New York) 1956.

605711

SPRUNT (MARGARET)
Did Lady Macbeth really faint?
Reprinted from The Liverpool
University College Magazine. pp. 12.
(Liverpool) 1887.

493947

SPURGEON (CAROLINE F. E.)
Imagery in the Sir Thomas More
fragment. IN The Review of English
Studies. Vol. 6. [1930.]

377862

SPURGEON (CAROLINE FRANCES ELEANOR)
Shakespeare's imagery and what it
tells us. (Cambridge)
illus. charts. 1935. 439768
_____ Another copy 617013

SPURGEON (CAROLINE FRANCES ELEANOR)
Shakespeare's iterative imagery.
IN Aspects of Shakespeare: British
Academy lectures. (Oxford)
1933. 401892
_____ IN Proceedings of the British
Academy, 1931. [1933.] 407052
_____ IN Studies in Shakespeare:
British Academy lectures, selected
and introduced by P. Alexander.
1964. 667830
Oxford Paperbacks, 81.

SPURGEON (CAROLINE F. E.)
The Use of imagery by Shakespeare
and Bacon. IN The Review of
English studies, vol. 9. [1933.]

414489

Spurgeon, Caroline F. E. *works relating to*

—— BOSANQUET (THEODORA)
Shakespeare's imagery and what it tells
us. [A review of the book by
Caroline F. E. Spurgeon.] IN English:
the magazine of the English Association,
Vol. 1. (Oxford) 1936.

481151

—— KNIGHTS (L. C.)
"Work for scholars". [Review of]
"Shakespeare's imagery and what it
tells us" by Caroline F. E. Spurgeon.
IN The Spectator, Vol. 155. 1935.

445578

—— PRAZ (M.)
[Reviews of] Shakespeare's imagery
and what it tells us, by Caroline
F. E. Spurgeon; Shakespeares Bilder,
von W. Clemen; [and] The Jacobean
drama, by U[na] M. Ellis-Fermor.
IN English Studies, Vol. 18.
(Amsterdam) 1936.

485660

—— RYLANDS (G. [H. W.])
Shakespearian detection. [Review of]
"Shakespeare's imagery", by Caroline
F. E. Spurgeon. IN The New Statesman
and Nation, Vol. 10. (New Series)
1935.

445577

SPURGEON (CHARLES HADDON)
The Treasury of David: containing
an original exposition of the Book of
Psalms; a collection of illustrative
extracts from literature; homiletical
hints; and lists of writers upon
each psalm. [Including quotations
from Shakespeare.]
6 vols. ports. illus. [1915.]

419866

SQUIRE (Sir J. C.)
The Clown of Stratford: a comedy
in one act. IN BOAS (G.) ed.,
Short modern plays. 1935.
[New Eversley Series]

436624

SQUIRE (Sir JOHN COLLINGS)
If it had been discovered in 1930 that
Bacon really did write Shakespeare.
FROM The London Mercury, 1931.
pp. [13.]

390791

SQUIRE (Sir JOHN COLLINGS)
Life at the Mermaid [and other essays,
including If one were descended from
Shakespeare, and, The Descendants of
Shakespeare.] [1927] 390219
Collins' Kings' Way Classics.
_____ Another edn. [1930] 546573

SQUIRE ([Sir] JOHN COLLINGS)
Literary affairs in London.
[Shakespeare Tercentenary Commemoration.]
FROM The Dial[, Vol. 61].   [Chicago]
1916.

559990

SQUIRE (Sir JOHN COLLINGS)
Professor Gubbitt's revolution [: a
story on the Bacon-Shakespeare contro-
versy].   IN Squire (Sir J. C.) Outside
Eden [: short stories].   1933.

403356

[SQUIRE (J. C.)]
Shakespeare and the Second Chamber.
[On the authorship of Shakespeare's
works.]   FROM [Squire (J. C.)]
Essays at large.   By Solomon Eagle.
pp. [8.]   [1922]

394975

SQUIRE (Sir J. [C.])
Shakespeare as a dramatist.   1935.

440464

SQUIRE (J. C.)
The Shakespeare Memorial Theatre.
FROM The Architectural Review,
June 1932: Shakespeare Memorial
Theatre Number.
   illus.   plans.   1932.

393576

SQUIRE (Sir J. [C.])
Water-music; or, A Fortnight of Bliss
[: further reminiscences.   Random
thoughts of the author, while canoeing
on the Cherwell, the Avon and the
Thames, with W. Bliss.   With references to Stratford].   1939.

501210

SQUIRE (W. B.)
Music.   IN Shakespeare's England,
vol. 2.   (Oxford)
   illus.   facsimiles.   bibliog.
1917.

435746

SQUIRE (W. B.)
The Music of Shadwell's "Tempest"
[composed by P. Humphrey.]   pp. [14.]
FROM The Musical quarterly, vol. 7.
(New York)   1921.

523728

SQUIRE (W. B.)
Shakespearian operas.   IN GOLLANCZ
([Sir] I.) ed., A Book of homage to
Shakespeare.
   ports.   illus.   facsimiles.   [1916.]

264175

SRINIVASA IYENGAR (KADAGANALLUR
                    RAMASWAMI)

Crime and punishment in Shakespeare.
pp.66. Reprinted from the Journal of
the Annamalai University, Vol.22.
(Annamalainagar)   1960.

667202

SRINIVASA IYENGAR (K. R.)
Imogen.   pp. [15.]   FROM The Visva-
Bharati Quarterly, Nov. 1946–Jan. 1947.
[Santiniketan]   1946.

667133

SRINIVASA IYENGAR (KADAGANALLUR
                    RAMASWAMI)

Introduction to Mannan Lear.
[Typescript.]   [?1959.]

668367

SRINIVASA IYENGAR (KADAGANALLUR RAMASWAMI)
   Shakespeare: his world and his art.
1964.

741021

Squire, John Collings, *Sir, works relating to*

——Quiller- Couch (Sir A.[T.]) Sir John
    Squire on Shakespeare: [a review
    of his] Shakespeare as a dramatist.
    In London Mercury, Vol.32.

[1935].

444082

—— RYLANDS (G. [H. W.])
    [Review of] Shakespeare as a dramatist,
    by Sir John [C.] Squire.   IN The
    Spectator, vol. 155.   1935.

445578

Staël, Mme de *works relating to*

——Q. (N. R.)
    Shakspeare fancies.   No[s.] 4-8.
    Cleopatra and Mme. de Stael [: a com-
    parison].   IN The Metropolitan Magazine,
    Vols. 24-26.

1839.

88824

STAFFORD (JOHN)
Henry Norman Hudson and the Whig use
of Shakespeare.   IN PMLA: Publications
of the Modern Language Association of
America, Vol. 66.   (New York) 1951.

428321/66

The Stage; or, Theatrical Inquisitor,
Vol. 1, 1828; Vol. 2, Nos. 8-10,
1829. [Containing Shakespearian
articles]
illus.   1828-29.
Vol. I No. 1 imperfect.

443576

The Stage; [with references to
Shakespearian performances.]
Vol. 1 (1874)-
  ports.   illus.
Wants Vol. 1, Nos. 1, 5, 7 (1874);
Vol. 2, all after No. 1 (1875);
Vols. 3-44 (1876-1917); [Vol. 63]
(1936).   Vols. [56], [58] imperfect.

59615

"The Stage-Cat" pseud. <u>see</u> Fagan
(Mrs. Elizabeth)

Stage History and Production
  Bibliography
  General Works
  Elizabethan and Jacobean Period
  Restoration and 18th century
  19th century
  20th century
see also Actors, Portraits of; Actors and
Acting; Boy Actors; Festivals; Masques;
Marionettes and Puppets; Programmes;
Scenery; Societies; Study and Teaching
and under titles of the separate plays

*see also under the names of towns and
cities where theatres are situated*

*Newspaper reviews, playbills, theatre pro-
grammes and theatrical illustration — the
library's extensive collection of this material
is mostly uncatalogued but indexed*

Stage History and Production

  Bibliography

[FIELD (J.)]
Bibliotheca histrionica; a catalogue of
the theatrical and miscellaneous library
of J. Field, contain[ing] specimens of
the early drama.   [Including
Shakespearian items.   To] be sold by
auction, by Mr. S. Sotheby, 22d January,
1827, and five following days.   [Prices
obtained added in MS.]   [1827.]

540083

Fletcher (I.K.) [bookseller,]
Actors and acting : works relating
to the theatre. Catalogue 17
[with supplement. Including
Shakespearian actors and actresses].
pp. 48, 12.

1940.

520840

Fletcher (I.K.) [bookseller.] Histories of theatres : books, manuscripts
and prints, theatrical architecture
and stage design. Catalogue 18.
[With Shakespearian items.] pp. 24.

1940.

520841

Fletcher (I.K.) [Bookseller.] History
of drama : books and manuscripts,
Shakespeare, theatrical periodicals
and anti-theatrical works. Catalogue
20. pp. 32.

(Newport, Mon.)   1940.

520955

Fletcher (J.K.) Ltd. Theatre: a
collection of plays, playbills,
prints, portraits, and books on
marionettes, dancing, conjuring,
the circus, opera and many other
aspects of the theatre. Catalogue
No.36. [Including Shakespeare
items.] pp.72.

(Newport)   1933.

405830

Fletcher (J.K.) Ltd.,Theatre, including
books, manuscripts, playbills, prints
& drawings relating to actors, plays
& theatres, ballet, circus, conjuring
& marionettes. Catalogue 54, Spring,
1936. [Including Shakespearian items.]
Frontis.

1936.

449120

—[HINTON (P. F.)]
R. Crompton Rhodes collection.
(Dramatic library of the Theatre
Royal, Birmingham.) [Now in the
Birmingham Reference Library,
Catalogue of] Plays in manuscript.
ff. 26.
  typescript.   [1937].

479810

—Low (David) Ltd., Books on the
theatre: pamphlets and plays,
history of the theatre, including
lives of actors and actresses,
theatre construction and design,
commedia del'arte. [Including
Shakespeare items.] Catalogue 32.
pp. 54.

[1940.]

518014

Stage History and Production

General Works

—Acton-Bond [A.] The Amateur and
Shakespeare. In The Poetry Review,
[Vol.4.]

1914.

253079

—AGATE (J. [E.]) ed.
The English dramatic critics: an antho-
logy, 1660-1932. [With references to
Shakespeare and the drama.] [1932.]

399280

—ANDREWS (C. B.)
The Theatre, the cinema and ourselves.
[With references to Shakespeare.]
pp. 52.
  ports.   illus.   1947.

588433

—Arthur (Sir G.[C.A.]) From Phelps to
Gielgud: reminiscences of the
stage through sixty-five years.
[Containing references to Shakes-
peare]. With an introduction by
J. Gielgud. Ports.

1936.

448594

—ATKINS (R.)
Acting in Shakespeare's plays.   IN
DOWNS (H.) ed., Theatre and stage,
Vol. 1.
  ports.   illus.   dgms.   1934.

425661

—Atkins (R.) Shakespeare and the
theatre. In Drama, Vol.12,,1933-34.

424896

—Bamford (T.W.) Practical make-up
for the stage. With a foreword by
E.Thesiger. Ports. Illus. Tables.

1940.

(Theatre and Stage Series)

518555

—Baynham (W.) The Glasgow stage. [With
references to Shakespearian productions.] Frontis.

(Glasgow)   1892.

No. 206 of edn. limited to 400 copies.

556918

—BERRY, FRANCIS
The Shakespeare inset: word and picture.
1965.

743789

—BOYD (A. K.)
The Technique of play production.
[Containing Shakespeare references.]
1934.

443980

—Brandon- Thomas (J.) Practical stage-
craft for amateurs. Edited by D.C.
Keir. With a preface by Marie
Tempest. [Containing references to
Shakespeare]. Illus.

1936.

452456

—   Brereton (A.) Shakespearean scenes
and characters: with descriptive notes
on the plays, and the principal
Shakespearean players from Betterton to
Irving. Port. Illus.   1886.

526715

—BRITISH COUNCIL
Shakespeare in the British theatre [:
a British Council exhibition on tour
1956-57]. pp. 20.
  discography.   [1956.]

665565

—BROOK (D.)
The Romance of the English theatre.
[With references to Shakespeare.]
  ports.   illus.   1946.

572379

—Brook (P.) Style in Shakespeare production. Illus. In Orpheus : a symposium of the arts, Vol.1.

1948.

588410

—Brown (I.[J.C.]) The British and
their bard. In Theatre Arts Monthly,
Vol.20.

(New York)   1936.

466068

—Brown (I.[J.C.]) Producing Shakespeare. From The Fortnightly Review, June 1933.

406761

— BROWN (J. M.)
Shakespeare the designer's touchstone. IN ISAACS ([Mrs.] EDITH J. R.) Theatre: essays on the arts of the theatre.
illus.   1927.

403880

— BROWN, JOHN RUSSELL
The Study and practice of Shakespeare production.   IN SHAKESPEARE SURVEY 18.   (Cambridge)   1965.

749826

— BROWN (JOHN RUSSELL)
Theater research and the criticism of Shakespeare and his contemporaries.
IN SHAKESPEARE QUARTERLY XIII: 4. pp. 451-461.
(New York) 1962.

605711

— BROWNE (E. MARTIN)
The Essentials of Shakespeare.   IN The Amateur theatre and playwrights' journal, Vol. 4, No. 75.
illus.   1937-38.

482984

— BRUŠÁK (K.)
The New conception of dramatic space. Translated from the Czech by Dora Round.   [With references to Shakespeare.]   IN Daylight: European arts and letters, yesterday, today, tomorrow, Vol. 1.
illus.   plan.   1941.

531506

— Byrne (M[uriel] St.C.) Photographs of theatrical productions [of Shakespeare's plays. In 3 parts.] In Theatre Notebook, Vols.1-2.

1947-48.

584117

—CHILD (H.)
Shakespeare in the theatre from the Restoration to the present time.
IN GRANVILLE-BARKER (H.) and HARRISON (G. B.) eds., A Companion to Shakespeare studies.   (Cambridge) bibliogs. illus. tables. facsimiles.
                    1934.   418724
_____ (New York) 1937.   479251
_____ (Cambridge) 1945.   566174

—CHILD (H.)
Shakespeare: the theatre from then until now [: a broadcast talk].
ff. 9.
typescript.   1937.

465084

—Clark (B.H.) How to produce amateur plays: a practical manual. [With references to settings for Shakespeare's plays.] Illus. Dgms.

1924.

565712

— COOKMAN, A. V.
Shakespeare's contemporaries on the modern English stage.
IN SHAKESPEARE JAHRBUCH.   Bd. 94/1958. pp. 29-41.   (Heidelberg)

10531

— COUNCIL FOR THE ENCOURAGEMENT OF MUSIC AND THE ARTS]
A History of Shakespearean production [: an exhibition of pictures, play-bills, books, etc.] arranged by the Arts Council of Great Britain and the Society for Cultural Relations with the U.S.S.R.   Exhibited by the National Book League.   Jan. 15- Feb. 28, 1948. [Catalogue, poster etc.] pp. 36. Illustrated t.p.   1948.

588769

— CRAIG (EDWARD GORDON)
The Art of the theatre, together with an introduction.   Preface by R. G. Robertson.   pp. 55.   (Edinburgh)
illus.   1905.   499291
No. 107 of an edn. of 150 copies.
_____ [2nd edn.]
illus.   1924.   443885

— Craig (E.G.):] Biographical note [with references to his Shakespeare productions]. In The Mask, Vol.6, No.1.
            (Florence)   1913.

416075

—CRAIG (E.G.)
The Theatre advancing [: essays. Including two essays, "Shakespeare's collaborators", "The True Hamlet", and with other references to Shakespeare.] Illus.   1921.

413534

— DARLINGTON (W.A.)
Through the fourth wall [: essays on the theatre. With references to Shakespeare.]
                                    1922.

443806

— DAVIES, ROBERTSON
Changing fashions in Shakespearean production.   IN Stratford Papers on Shakespeare delivered at the 1962 Shakespeare Seminar.   (Toronto)
                                    1963.

668006

— DILLON (A.)
The Staging of Shakespeare.   IN The Westminster Review, Vol. 154.
                                    1900.

155210

—   Doran (J.) Love for, and the lovers of, Shakspere. <u>From</u> The Gentleman's Magazine, February 1856. pp. [8.]

402714

— DORAN (J.)
"Their Majesties' Servants". Annals of the English stage, from Thomas Betterton to Edmund Kean. Actors - authors - audiences.
   ports. 2 vols.   1864.   487918
   _____ (New York)   1865.   499699
   _____ Edited and revised by R. W. Lowe.
   ports. illus. 3 vols. 1888. 504121
Edn. limited to 300 copies: No. 13.
   _____ People's edn.
   ports. illus.   1897. 402657

— DOUGLASS (A.)
Footlight reflections: the musings of one who has spent sixty years in the theatrical profession. [With references to Shakespeare]
   ports.   1934

470204

— DOWNS (H.) ed.
Theatre and stage: a modern guide to amateur dramatic, operatic and theatrical work. [Including articles, and references to Shakespeare.]
   2 vols. ports. illus. dgms.
               1934.

425661

— ENGEL [J. J.]
Practical illustrations of rhetorical gesture and action, adapted to the English drama. From a work on the same subject by [J. J.] Engle, by H. Siddons. [With references to Shakespeare and] with engravings, expressive of the various passions, and representing the modern costume of the London theatres. 1807.

539955

— The Era [: the official organ of entertainment], Vols. 29-103, (Jan., 1867-Sept. 21st, 1939.)
   illus.   73 vols. 1867-1939.
Wants all from 21st Oct. 1914 to 26th Dec. 1917 and from Jan.1933 to Aug. 1935. Ceased publication Sept. 21st, 1939.

100557

— Ffolkes (D.) Designing for Shakespeare. Illus. <u>In</u> The Studio, Vol. 118.

1939.

510178

— FITZGERALD (P.)
Shakespearean representations, their laws and limits. IN The Gentleman's Magazine, Vol. 294.   1903.

176630

— FORBES-WINSLOW (D.)
Daly's: the biography of a theatre. [Containing references to Shakespearian performances.]
   ports.   illus.   1944.

553734

— FOSS (G. R.)
What the author [Shakespeare] meant [: studies of Shakespearian productions.]
   illus.   1932.

400302

— FREEDLEY (G.) and REEVES (J. A.)
A History of the theatre. [With references to Shakespeare.] (New York)
   ports. illus. facsimile.   1941.

577566

— FROST (H. W.)
The Stage as it was. [Part] 1. [With references to Shakespeare's plays.] FROM [The Galaxy,] Oct. 1873. [New York]

557130

— G. (G.M.) The Stage censor: an historical sketch, 1544-1907. [With references to Shakespeare.] Ports. Facsimile.
                   1908.

544214

— Gabain (M[arjorie]) "Unser Shakespeare": Professor Jessher on the art of the producer. <u>In</u> New English Weekly, Vol.4.

1933-34.

419220

— A GALLERYITE [pseud.]
Gallery unreserved: a collection of experiences, opinions and stories connected with the gallery and galleryites. With a foreword by W. S. Maugham, and contributions by many famous authors and actors. [With references to Shakespeare.]
   ports.   illus.   1931.

469998

— GORELIK (M.)
New theatres for old [: an account of the rise and fall of stage and screen techniques. With references to Shakespeare's plays.]
   ports. illus. glossary. bibliog.
                 1947.
International Theatre and Cinema.

589664

— GREET (Sir P. B.)
I Believe in Shakespeare. IN The Amateur theatre and playwrights' journal, Vol. 1, No. 5.
   port.   1934-35.

476088

— Guthrie (T.) The Producer should
    experiment with Shakespeare. Illus.
    <u>In</u> The Amateur Theatre and Playwrights
    Journal, Vol.4, No.75.

                    1937.

                        467093

—— GUTHRIE (TYRONE)
    Shakespeare produced on the modern
    stage [: a broadcast talk]. ff. 8.
    typescript.   1937.

                465085

—— GUTHRIE ([Sir] TYRONE)
    Theatre prospect. [With references
    to Shakespeare.] pp. 87.
    illus.   1932.
    Adelphi Quartos [3].

                402311

—— HALLIDAY (FRANK ERNEST)
    Four centuries of Shakespearean
    production. IN History today, February
    1964 [: Shakespeare issue].
    illus.   1964.

                667985

—— HARBAGE, ALFRED BENNETT
    The Role of the Shakespearean producer.
    IN SHAKESPEARE JAHRBUCH. Bd. 91/1955.
    pp. 161-173.   (Heidelberg)

            10531

— Hatcher (O.L.) A Book for Shakespeare
    plays and pageants: Elizabethan
    and Shakespearean detail for
    producers, stage managers, actors,
    artists and students. [With a
    bibliography.] Ports. Illus. Dgms.

                [1916]

                455641

— Haweis (H.R.) Shakspere and the
    stage. <u>In</u> Haweis (H.R.) Arrows
    in the air [: essays].

                1878.

                434221

— Heaton (Elizabeth) Remarks on the
    production of Shakespeare. <u>In</u>
    London Mercury, Vol.33.

               1936.

               452192

— HOWARTH (HERBERT)
    Metre and emphasis: a conservative
    note. IN SMITH, GORDON ROSS, ed.
    Essays on Shakespeare [by various
    authors] (University Park, Penn.)
    pp. 211-226.   1965.

                755528

— Humpherson (F.) Shakespeare for
    amateurs [: a manual for producers].
    Illus. Dgms.

                [1935]

                447813

— ISAACS ([Mrs.] EDITH J. R.) ed.
    Theatre: essays on the arts of the
    theatre. [With references to
    Shakespeare.]
    illus.   1927.

                403880

—— JACKSON (Sir BARRY VINCENT)
    Producing the comedies. IN
    SHAKESPEARE SURVEY 8. (Cambridge)
                    1955.

                647706

—— Jacobs (R.) Covent garden, its romance
    and history. [With Shakespearian
    references.]
                   1913.

                420529

—— Kelly (Mary) Village theatre. [With
    references to Shakespeare]

                   1939.

    ["Little Theatre" Series]

                510564

—— KERNODLE (GEORGE RILEY)
    The Open stage: Elizabethan or
    existentialist? IN SHAKESPEARE SURVEY
    12. (Cambridge)   1959.

                666150

—— KNIGHT (GEORGE WILSON)
    Principles of Shakespearian production,
    with especial reference to the
    tragedies.   1936.   450763
    ————— [With an appendix: Drama and
    the university.] (Harmondsworth)
                1949.   602532
    Pelican Books.

—— KNIGHT, GEORGE WILSON
    Shakespearian production, with especial
    reference to the Tragedies. 1964.

    illus.   668001

—— KOMISARJEVSKY (THEODORE)
    The Theatre and a changing civilisa-
    tion. [With references to
    Shakespeare.]   1935.
    Twentieth Century Library.

                429283

—— KOPECKÝ (JAN)
    Shakespeare's forgotten theatre: a
    contribution to the problems of the
    theatre today. IN
    CHARLES UNIVERSITY ON SHAKESPEARE:
    essays edited by Z. Stříbrný. (Praha)
    illus.   1966.

                762631

—— LANGHAM, MICHAEL
    An Approach to staging Shakespeare's
    works. IN Stratford Papers on
    Shakespeare delivered at the 1961
    Shakespeare Seminar. (Toronto)
                   1962.

                668005

——LAWRENCE (W. J.)
Old theatre days and ways. [With references to Shakespeare.]
ports. illus. 1935.

443093

—— LEAVER (P.), HARRIS (V.) [and] MACQUEEN-POPE (W. [J.])
The Stones of Drury Lane: the romance and drama of London's famous playhouse, [with references to Shakespeare], in eight [broadcast] episodes. Transmission 18th May – 13th July, 1942. typescript. 8 vols.

536846

——Leaves from the portfolio of a manager. No. 6. A Few more words on Shakspeare; [and] On criticism in general, more particularly on theatrical criticism. From [The Dublin University Magazine,] Vol.37. [Dublin] 1851.

564838

—— LEECH (CLIFFORD)
The "Capability" of Shakespeare. IN SHAKESPEARE QUARTERLY XI. pp. 123–136.
(New York) 1960.

605711

—— Liszt (R.G.) The Last word in make-up (:make-up encyclopedia. [With a foreword by W. D. Russell, and with instructions for make-up for Shakespearian characters.] Illus.

1939.

503084

—— MacOwan (M.) Producing Shakespeare. [Broadcast] 5th August, 1948. ff.8. Typescript.

596475

——Macqueen-Pope (W.J.) Theatre Royal, Drury Lane [: a history, from 1663 to the present day. With a foreword by I. Novello and references to Shakespearian performances]. Ports. Illus. Facsimiles.

1945.

569914

—— MARSHALL (NORMAN)
The Producer and the play. 2nd edn. revised and enlarged.
illus. 1962.

708207

—— MERCHANT, WILLIAM MOELWYN
Shakespeare in production: tradition or betrayal? FROM Antioch Review, XXIV.1. (Yellow Springs, Ohio) 1964.

668303

—— MERCHANT, WILLIAM MOELWYN
Visual elements in Shakespeare studies. IN SHAKESPEARE JAHRBUCH, Bd. 92/1956. pp. 280–290. (Heidelberg)

10531

—— MITCHELL (L.)
Shakespeare's lighting effects. FROM Speech Monographs, Vol. 15. pp. 72–84. [Ann Arbor, Mich.] 1948.
Speech Association of America.

605191

——Nathaniel (Sir)[pseud.] Shakspeare and the stage: a vexed question. [With bibliographical notes.] From [The New Monthly Magazine, Vol.130].

[1864.]

579655

——Newspaper cuttings on Shakespeare's plays, and performances, etc. 2 vols. [1709–1912]

769150

——NEWTON (R. G.)
Shakespearean setting for small stages. IN Drama, Vol. 14. 1935.

463689

—— NICOLL (ALLARDYCE)
The Development of the theatre: a study of theatrical art from the beginnings to the present day. New edn., revised. [With appendices and bibliography.]
illus. 1937. 467984
———— 3rd edn. revised and enlarged. 1948. 591192
———— 4th edn. revised. 1958. 676764

—— NICOLL (ALLARDYCE)
The English theatre. [With references to Shakespeare, and a bibliography.]
illus. 1936. 456474
———— Another edn. 1938. 520071

—— ODELL (G. C. D.)
Shakespeare, from Betterton to Irving. (New York) 2 vols.
ports. illus. 1920.

438152

——Oxberry's Dramatic biography, and histrionic anecdotes [with references to Shakespearean acting] Vols. 1–5; New Series, Vol. 1. [Edited by Mrs. Oxberry.]
engraved t.ps. ports. 6 vols. 1825–27.
Subtitle of N.S., Vol. 1 reads "or, The Green-room spy" on printed t.p., and "and Green room spy" on engraved t.p. Vols. 3 and 5 imperfect.

557829

—— OXFORD COMPANION TO THE THEATRE, edited by P. Hartnoll. 3rd ed. 1967.

illus. 763718

— Playhouse pocket-companion; or,
Theatrical vade-mecum: containing (1)
a catalogue of all the dramatic authors
who have written for the English stage,
with a list of their works, (2) a
catalogue of anonymous pieces, (3) an
index of plays and authors. To which
is prefixed, a critical history of the
English stage. 1779.

488660

— POEL (W.)
Shakespeare in the theatre.
port. 1913.

431019

— Pollock (W.H.) Plays and players.3:
Should Shakespeare's plays be
acted? In The National Review,
Vol.19.
1892.

115355

— REYNOLDS (GEORGE FULLMER)
What a theatre for Shakespeare should be.
IN SHAKESPEARE QUARTERLY I: 1.
pp. 12-17.
(New York) 1950.

605711

— RYLANDS (G. [H. W.])
Shakespeare and the stage. (Forces
Educational Broadcast). [Broadcast]
20th September, 1945. ff. 12.
typescript.

563609

— RYLANDS (G. [H. W.])
Shakespeare - yesterday and to-day
[: the playing and presentation of
Shakespeare]. Talk [braodcast]
5th August 1949. ff. 6.
typescript.
Shakespeare and his world, 9.

605271

— SANDFORD (E.)
The Wonder of our stage [: an address
delivered at the Central Literary
Association Shakespeare Celebration,
1935]. IN The Central Literary
Magazine, Vol. 32, July, 1935.
(Birmingham) 1936. 463922
_____ Another copy. 465871

— Scott-James (R.A.) The "New way" of
playing Shakespeare. In The
Contemporary Review, Vol. 105.

1914.

251087

— Scraps about theatricals [: a collection of newspaper cuttings, etc.,
relating to Shakespeare and the
theatre.] [c.1835].

436163

— The SHAKESPEARE STAGE: the
quarterly bulletin of the Shakespeare
Stage Society, Nos. 1-7.
1953-54.

666647

— SHAW (GEORGE BERNARD)
On cutting Shakespear. IN Shaw [G. B.]
on theatre. 1958.

693464

— SIMONSON (L.)
The Stage is set [: a history of
stage-setting and scenery. With
references to Shakespeare and a
chapter on The Scenic revival in
Shakespeare's England.] (New York)
illus. plans. dgms. bibliog.
1937.

550764

— SIMONSON (L.) ed.
Theatre art. With an introduction,
[and illustrations of scenery for
some of Shakespeare's plays.]
(New York: Museum of Modern Art)
1934.

420487

— SIMPSON (DONALD HERBERT)
Shakespeare and the Commonwealth.
[Published by] the Royal Commonwealth
Society as its contribution to the
four hundredth anniversary of the
birth of William Shakespeare. 1964.

740585

— Sketch, The: a journal of art and actuality.
Vols.1-49. Feb. 1893 - Apr. 1905. Ports.
Illus. 35. fol. [1893-1905]

Note: Wants Vols. 12, 16-25, 35, 36, and 48.

480254

— SOCIETY FOR THEATRE RESEARCH
The Theatre of the British Isles,
excluding London: a bibliography,
compiled by A. Loewenberg. pp. ix, 75.
1950.

605472

— SPRAGUE (ARTHUR COLBY)
The Doubling of parts in Shakesepare's
plays. 1966.

752780

— SPRAGUE (ARTHUR COLBY)
Shakespeare and the actors: the
stage business in his plays (1660-
1905). (Cambridge, Mass.)
illus. bibliog. 1945.

563058

— SPRAGUE (ARTHUR COLBY)
Shakespeare's histories: plays for
the stage.
illus. 1964.
Society for Theatre Research.

667707

— SPRAGUE (ARTHUR COLBY)
Shakespearian players and performances.
(Cambridge, Mass.)
ports. illus. 1953.

635328

—SPRAGUE (ARTHUR COLBY)
The Stage business in Shakespeare's
plays: a postscript. pp. 35.
port.   1954.
Society for Theatre Research.
Pamphlet Series No. 3.

639849

— The Stage" year book, 1949-
ports. illus.-

597470

—STAMM (RUDOLF)
Shakespeare's word-scenery; with
some remarks on stage-history and the
interpretation of his plays.
(Zürich)   1954.
Veröffentlichungen der Handels-
Hochschule St. Gallen, Reihe B,
Heft 10.

639793

— The Theatre annual: a publication
of information and research in the
arts and history of the theatre, 1942-
(New York)
illus. facsimiles.   1943-
Theatre Library Association.

554521

— Theatre notebook: a quarterly of
notes and research.   Vol. 1.
illus. plans. dgms.   1945-

584117

— Theatre Programme [: a radio review
of the stage: Shakespearian items
including an introductory sketch "The
Plain man's guide to Shakespeare", by
P. Watts; a discussion "How the plain
man can appreciate Shakespeare", by
I. J. C. Brown and W. Bridges-Adams;
and a talk on Othello, by P. Powell.
[Broadcast] 2nd April [1947].
ff. [34.]
typescript.

583268

— Theatre Programme, Second Series,
No. 1 [: a radio review of the stage
by Shakespearian actors. With references to Shakespeare's plays. Broad-
cast] 9th October [1946]. pp. [38].
typescript.

579576

—Theatre World, Vol. 41-
ports. illus.   1945-
Vols. 1-40 wanting.

601552

— "TIME"
Shakespeare, Midsummer night's box office.
[From "Time", July 4, 1960.] pp. [12]
[Amsterdam]
ports. illus.   1960.

667002

— TOLMAN (A. H.)
The Views about Hamlet and other essays
[including Shakespeare's stage and
modern adaptations.]   (Boston, [Mass.])
bibliog.   1904.   544884
_____ Another edn.   1906.   450751

—TOMLINS (F. G.)
Remarks on the present state of the
English drama.   [Containing references
to Shakespeare.] pp. 15.   1851.

443577

—WALKER (ROY)
In fair Verona [: the importance of
scenery in the production of
Shakespeare's plays.]   IN Twentieth
Century, Vol. 156.   1954.

14975/156

—WARD (A. C.)
Dramatic critics and Shakespeare.
[Reprinted] from "Specimens of
English dramatic criticism, 17-20
centuries".   FROM The Periodical,
Vol. 26.   (Oxford)   1945.

579653

—Ward (A.C.)[ed.] Specimens of English
dramatic criticism, 17-20 centuries;
selected and introduced. [With
articles on Shakespearian actors
and productions, and a bibliographical note.]

(Oxford)   1945.

[World's Classics]

563732

—WATKINS (RONALD)
On producing Shakespeare.   With
drawings by M. Percival.
illus.   1950.

611567

—Webster (Margaret) On directing
Shakespeare. In Gassner (J.[W.])
Producing the play. [With a biblio-
graphy.] Illus. Dgms.

(New York)   1941.

536928

—WEBSTER (MARGARET)
Producing Mr. Shakespeare.   IN Theatre
Arts, Vol. 26.   (New York)
1942.   546127
_____ IN Theatre Arts Anthology: a
record and a prophecy.   Edited by
Rosamond Gilder, H. R. Isaacs, R. M.
MacGregor [and] E. Reed.   (New York)
1950.   614298

—WEBSTER (MARGARET)

Shakespeare without tears. With an
introduction by J.M. Brown. (New York)
1942.

536056

— WEST (E. J.)
G.B.S. on Shakespearean production.
IN Studies in Philology, Vol. 45.
(Chapel Hill, N.C.)
bibliog.   1948.

554520/45

WILSON (A. E.)
Theatre guyed: the Baedeker of
Thespia. With Tittivations by
Tom Titt and an Overture by Sydney
Horler. [Including a chapter
"Brighter Shakespeare", and other
references to Shakespeare]. 1935.

434180

— WISE, ARTHUR
Weapons in the theatre [: the problems
of mounting stage fights].
illus. 1968.

777351

Stage History and Production

— Elizabethan and Jacobean Period
see also Actors and Acting, Elizabethan
and Jacobean Period; **Audiences; Boy
Actors; Dramatic Art of Shakespeare;
London,** Theatres — Blackfriars Theatre,
Curtain Theatre, Globe Theatre, Swan
Theatre, The Theatre; **Revels Office**

Adams (J.C.) Shakespeare's stage:
new facts and figures. In Theatre
Arts Monthly. Vol.20.

1936.

466068

— ADAMS (J. Q.)
Elizabethan playhouse manuscripts and
their significance for the text of
Shakespeare. FROM The Johns Hopkins
Alumni Magazine. Vol. 21.
(Baltimore) 1932.

440787

— Adams (J.Q.) Shakespearean playhouses :
a history of English theatres from
the beginnings to the Restoration.
[With a bibliography.] Ports. Illus.
Maps. Plans.

[1920.]

500863

— ARCHER (W.)
A Sixteenth century playhouse.
IN The Universal Review, [Vol. 1,]
May-Aug. 1888.
illus.

97617

— Archer (W.) and Lawrence (W.J.) The
Playhouse. In Shakespeare's England,
vol.2. [With bibliographies.] Illus.
Facsimiles.

(Oxford) 1917.

435746

— ARMSTRONG (WILLIAM A.)
Actors and theatres [: in Elizabethan
England]. IN SHAKESPEARE SURVEY, 17.
(Cambridge) 1964.

667822

— ARMSTRONG (WILLIAM A.)
The Audience of the Elizabethan private
theatres: reprint from Review of
English Studies, New Series, Vol.10,
No.39, August 1959. pp.[16]. (Oxford)

667045

— ARMSTRONG (WILLIAM A.)
The Elizabethan private theatres:
facts and problems. pp. 18.
1958.
The Society for Theatre Research
Pamphlet Series No. 6.

682084

— BALD (ROBERT CECIL)
The Entrance to the Elizabethan theater.
IN SHAKESPEARE QUARTERLY III: 1.
pp. 17-20.
(New York) 1952.

605711

— BECKERMAN (BERNARD)
Shakespeare at the Globe, 1599-1609.
(New York) 1962.

667186

— BENNETT (HENRY STANLEY)
Shakespeare's audience. pp. 16.
bibliog. 1944. 553066
British Academy, [34th] Annual
Shakespeare Lecture.
＿＿＿ IN Studies in Shakespeare:
British Academy Lectures, selected and
introduced by P. Alexander.
1964. 667830
Oxford Paperbacks 81.

— BENNETT (H. S.)
Shakespeare's stage and audience.
FROM Neophilologus, 33ste Jaargang.
(Groningen) 1949.

604848

— BENTLEY (G. E.)
The Jacobean and Caroline stage:
dramatic companies and players.
[Including an alphabetical list of
players of the time giving biographical
summaries, and references to performances of Shakespeare's plays.] (Oxford)
bibliog. tables. 2 vols. 1941.

523172

— BENTLEY (GERALD EADES)
Shakespeare and his theatre. 1964.

668034

— BERRY, HERBERT
Dr. Fludd's engravings and their
beholders.
IN SHAKESPEARE STUDIES 3. (Cincinnati,
Ohio) 1967.

771652

— BETHELL (S. L.)
Shakespeare & the popular dramatic
tradition. [With an introduction
by T. S. Eliot.]
bibliog. frontis. 1944.

550623

— BOAS (F. S.)
Queen Elizabeth, the Revels Office and
Edmund Tilney. [With references to
Shakespeare] pp. 27. (Oxford)
1938.
(Elizabeth Howland Lectures, 1937.)

481919

— BRADBROOK (M[URIEL] C.)
Elizabethan stage conditions: a study
of their place in the interpretation
of Shakespeare's plays. (Harness
Prize Essay, 1931) 1932.

390338

— BRADBROOK (MURIEL CLARA)

The Rise of the common player: a study
of actor and society in Shakespeare's
England. 1962.

illus. 667324

— BRADLEY (A. C.)
Oxford lectures on poetry. 2nd edn.
[Including Shakespeare's theatre and
audience.]
bibliog. 1914. 552475
_____ Another edn. 1917. 533634

— BRERETON (J.Le G.)
De Witt at the Swan. IN Gollancz
([Sir] I.) ed., A Book of homage to
Shakespeare. Ports. Illus. Facsimiles.
[1916.]
264175

— BROWN (ARTHUR)
The Play within a play: an Elizabethan
dramatic device. Reprinted from
"Essays and Studies". pp. [13.]
1960.

666970

— BROWN (ARTHUR)
Studies in Elizabethan and Jacobean
drama since 1900. IN SHAKESPEARE
SURVEY 14. (Cambridge) 1961.

666755

— BROWN, IVOR JOHN CARNEGIE
How Shakespeare spent the day. 1963.

667544

— BROWN (IVOR JOHN CARNEGIE)
Shakespeare in his time. (Edinburgh)
ports. illus. maps. facsimiles.
1960.

666531

— BUCKLEY (E. R.)
The Elizabethan playwright in his
workshop. IN The Gentleman's
Magazine, Vol. 294. 1903.

176630

— C. [pseud.]
Shakespere and his age: reflections
on modern play. FROM [Stray Leaves
Quarterly, Jan. 1874]. [Liverpool]

554727

— Cardiff Public Libraries. The
Elizabethan theatre : a lecture by
S.L.Bethell. Reading list [With
references to Shakespeare] pp. 3.

(Cardiff) 1939.

497461

— CARRINGTON, NORMAN THOMAS, ed.
The theatre in Shakespeare's day:
filmstrip [and notes].
1 vol., 1 reel 35 mm. [1963.]
Brodie educational filmstrip.
667549-50

— CHAMBERS ([Sir] E. K.)
William Shakespeare: an epilogue
[concerning his observations on the
stage and his stage imagery.] IN
The Review of English Studies, Vol.
16. (Oxford)
bibliog. 1940.

525063

— CHUTE (MARCHETTE GAYLORD)
Shakespeare and his stage.
illus. 1953.
Pathfinder Library.

636327

— COLSON (P.)
Dulwich Gallery and the Shakespearian
stage. FROM "Apollo", March, 1935.
pp. 3.
illus.

432006

— Cutts (John P.)
New findings with regard to the 1624
protection list. [Identity of King's Men
theatre musicians]
IN SHAKESPEARE SURVEY: 19
[Macbeth]
(Cambridge) 1966.

pp.101-110. 755342

— DILLON (ARTHUR)
The Stage of the sixteenth century.
[Issued in connection with William
Poel's production of "Measure for
Measure" in 1893.] pp. 19.
[London] [?1893.]

665062

— Feasey (Lynette)[ed.] On the playbill
in old London [:plays of pre-
Elizabethan and Elizabethan times,
with a history of the playhouses.
Including a play entitled Katharine
of Aragon; from the Life of Henry
the Eighth by W.Shakespeare and John
Fletcher.]Ports.Illus.

1948.

591995

—FISHER (H. W.)
A First performance in Shakespeare's
time.   IN AtJantic Monthly, Vol. 81.
1898.

142809

—FISHER, SIDNEY T.
The Theatre, the Curtain, & the Globe
[: views of Elizabethan playhouses
examined in a letter to R. Pennington].
(Montreal)   1964.

illus.   747539

—FOAKES (REGINALD ANTHONY)
The Profession of playwright.   IN
Stratford-upon-Avon Studies, edited
by J. R. Brown and B. Harris, Vol. 3.
Early Shakespeare.   1961.

666841

—FOAKES (REGINALD ANTHONY) and RICKERT
(R. T.)
An Elizabethan stage drawing?
IN SHAKESPEARE SURVEY 13.
(Cambridge)
illus.   1960.

666726

—Folger Shakespeare Library Prints [3]:
The Shakespearian theatre.
(Washington, D.C.)
12 plates.   1935.

475842

—FORMAN ([SIMON])
Book of plays 1611.
IN Transactions of the New Shakespeare
Society, Series 1. No. 4.
pp. 413-420.   1875-6.

40620

—GARDINER (H. C.)
Mysteries' end: an investigation of
the last days of the medieval religious
stage.   [With reference to
Shakespeare.]   (New Haven, [Conn.])
bibliogs.   1946.
Yale Studies in English, Vol. 103.
Published on the Kingsley Trust
Association Publication Fund.

584870

— Going to the play with Shakespeare.
FROM All the Year Round [, Vol. 6.].
1862.

559987

— GREEN (J. R.)
Three phases in English history
[with a section "The Theatre and
people in Shakespeare's time"].
IN GARNETT (R.) [and others] ed.
The International library of famous
literature, vol. 6.
ports.   illus.   [c.1900.]

403686

—HARBAGE (ALFRED BENNETT)
Cavalier drama: an historical and
critical supplement to the study
of the Elizabethan and Restoration
stage.   (New York)
bibliog.   1936.
Modern Language Association of America.

465835

—HARBAGE (ALFRED BENNETT)
Shakespeare and the rival traditions.
(New York)
bibliogs.   1952.

630614

—HARBAGE (ALFRED BENNETT)
Theatre for Shakespeare.   (Alexander
Lectures [in English] 1954-55.)
(Toronto)   1955.

665178

—Harrison (G.B.)   Elizabethan plays
and players. Map.

1940.

513577

—HARRISON (G.B.)
Shakespeare at work, 1592-1603.   Ports.
Illus.
1933.
412172

—HARRISON (G. B.)
Shakespeare in his theatre [: a
broadcast] talk.   ff. 7.
typescript.   1937.

460675

—HARRISON (G.B.)
Shakespeare under Elizabeth.   Ports.
Illus.
1933.
407353

—HART (A.)
Plays abridgment: Part 1: The Length
of Elizabethan and Jacobean plays;
Part 2: The Time allotted for the
representation of Elizabethan and
Jacobean plays; Part 3: Acting
versions of Elizabethan and Jacobean
plays.   IN Hart (A.) Shakespeare and
the homilies, and other pieces of
research into the Elizabethan drama.
(Melbourne)   1934.

429387

—HENSLOWE (PHILIP) [HINCHLOW]

Diary. [Concerned mainly with financial
transactions in connection with theatres
managed by Henslowe, 1590-1604.] Edited
with supplementary material, introduction
and notes by R.A. Foakes and R.T.
Rickert. Dgm. Glossary. Facsimiles.
Bibliog. (Cambridge)   1961.

666746

— HEVESI (A.)
Shakespeare as scenographer.
IN The Mask, Vol. 2.
(Florence)   1909.

460752

— HILLEBRAND (H. N.)
The Child actors: a chapter in
Elizabethan stage history.
([Urbana], Ill.)
bibliog.   1926.
University of Illinois. Studies in
language and literature, Vol. 11.
Nos. 1 [and] 2.

423798

— HODGES (C. W.)
An Elizabethan playhouse, 1599-1613;
a conjectural reconstruction [: a
drawing in cross section].
1 sheet.   [1948.]
For a full account of the playhouse
see "Shakespeare and the players", by
C. W. Hodges. catal. no. 595096.

595883

— HODGES (CYRIL WALTER)
The Lantern of taste.   IN
SHAKESPEARE SURVEY 12.   (Cambridge)
illus.   1959.

666150

— HODGES (C. W.)
Shakespeare and the players.   With
a foreword by A. Nicoll.
illus.   plans.   1948.

595096

— HODGES, CYRIL WALTER
Shakespeare's theatre.   1964.

illus.   667785

— HODGES (CYRIL WALTER)
Unworthy scaffolds: a theory for
the reconstruction of Elizabethan
playhouses.   IN SHAKESPEARE SURVEY
3.   (Cambridge)
illus.   1950.

606026

— HOSLEY (RICHARD)
The Gallery over the stage in the public
playgouse of Shakespeare's time.
IN SHAKESPEARE QUARTERLY VIII.
pp. 15-31.
(New York)   1957.

605711

— HOSLEY (RICHARD)
The Origins of the Shakespearian playhouse.   IN McMANAWAY (JAMES GILMER)
ed., Shakespeare 400: essays by
American scholars on the anniversary of
the poet's birth.   Published in co-
operation with the Shakespeare Association of America.
illus.   1964.

667803

— HOSLEY (RICHARD)
Shakespeare's use of a gallery over
the stage.   IN SHAKESPEARE SURVEY
10.   (Cambridge)   1957.

665485

— HOTSON ([J.] L.)
The Projected amphitheatre.   IN
SHAKESPEARE SURVEY 2.   (Cambridge)
bibliog.   1949.

598403

— HOTSON (JOHN LESLIE)
Shakespeare's arena.   IN The Atlantic,
Vol. 193.   (Boston, Mass.)   1954.

19347/193

— HOTSON (JOHN LESLIE)
Shakespeare's wooden O [: Shakespeare's
stage in its true perspective].
illus.   plans.   dgms.   1959.

666317

— ISAACS (J.)
Production and stage-management at
the Blackfriars Theatre.   pp. 28.
(Shakespeare Association)
                          1933.   414993
_____ Another copy.   415677

— JEWKES (WILFRED THOMAS)
Act division in Elizabethan and
Jacobean plays.   1583-1616.
(Hamden, Conn.)
bibliog.   1958.

666288

— K. (A.J.) [Players in Shakespeare's
time;] license of the Duke of York's
Company of Players, 1611; illustra-
tions of [phrases used by]
Shakespeare [in his plays; and the
orthography of Shakespeare]. From
The Gentleman's Magazine, [New
Series] Vol.13.

1840.

521907

— KIRSCHBAUM (L.)
Shakespeare's stage blood and its critical significance.   [With bibliographical notes.]   IN PMLA, Vol. 64.
(Menasha, Wis.)

1949.

428321/64

— LAMBORN (E. A. G.) and HARRISON (G. B.)
Shakespeare, the man and his stage.
ports. illus. facsimiles.
                          1924.   436484
[The World's Manuals.]
_____ Another edn.   1928.   425284

— LAWRENCE (W. J.)
Act-intervals in early Shakespearean
performances.   FROM Review of English
Studies, Vol. 4.   1928.

496553

— LAWRENCE (W. J.)
A Forgotten playhouse custom of
Shakespeare's day.
IN GOLLANCZ ([Sir] I.) ed., A Book
of homage to Shakespeare.
ports. illus. facsimiles. [1916.]

264175

— LAWRENCE (W. J.)
Shakespeare's supers.   IN The New
Statesman and Nation.   Vol. 1.
(N.S.) Feb.-June, 1931.

396295

—Lawrence (W.J.) Speeding up Shakespeare. In The Criterion, vol.14.

[1934-35].

440552

—Lawrence (W.J.) Speeding up Shakespeare: studies of the bygone theatre and drama. Ports. Illus.

1937.

477622

— LAWRENCE (W. J.)
Those nut-cracking Elizabethans: studies of the early theatre and drama. illus. facsimile. 1935.

436141

— LINDABURY (R. V.)
A Study of patriotism in the Elizabethan drama. [With references to Shakespeare.]
bibliog. 1931.
Princeton Studies in English, No. 5.

390064

— LONG (JOHN H.)
Music for the replica staging of Shakespeare. IN MATTHEWS (A. D.) and EMERY (C. M.) eds., Studies in Shakespeare. (Coral Gables, Fla.) 1953.
University of Miami Publications in English and American Literature, Vol. 1, March 1953.

634188

— LONG (JOHN HENDERSON)
Shakespeare's use of music: a study of the music and its performance in the original production of seven comedies. Facsimiles. Bibliog.(Gainesville,Fla.) 1955.
665100

— MACKINTOSH (F. H.)
An Evening with Shakspere, A.D. 1611. (The New play, [articles] I [and] II.) FROM The Bellman, Vol. 10. (Minneapolis)
illus. 1911.

564496

— McMANAWAY (JAMES G.)
A New Shakespeare document [: a warrant from the Lord Chamberlain for the payment to the financial agent of the King's Men for their performance of twenty-one plays before King Charles I and Queen Henrietta Maria in 1630-31.] IN SHAKESPEARE QUARTERLY II: 2.
pp. 110-122. (New York) 1951.

605711

— MacOWAN (MICHAEL)
The Living Shakespeare [No. 2]: His theatre. [Broadcast] 8th October, 1958. ff. 8.
typescript. 1958.

666020

— MANTZIUS (KARL)
A History of theatrical art in ancient and modern times. Translation by Louise von Cossel. Vol. 3: The Shakespearian period in England. [Another copy] Ports. Illus. 1904.

667211

— MATTHEWS (BACHE [ed.]
Elizabethan and Stuart playhouses, players and play production, etc.: contemporary references.
illus. plans. dgms. manuscript, typescript and cuttings. [c.1920.]

603513

— [MATTHEWS (BACHE) ed.]
Poor scoundrels: some notes on Shakespeare's fellows. [Extracts from 16th and 17th century books relating to players and playhouses of the period.] ff. [8.] 1933. No. 97 of an edn. of 100 copies privately printed. [Bache Matthews Christmas Booklets, 1933.]

433450

— MATTHEWS ([JAMES] BRANDER)
How Shakspere learnt his trade. IN The North American Review, Vol. 177. 1903.

180487

— MATTHEWS ([JAMES] BRANDER)
Shakespeare as an actor. IN North American Review, Vol. 195. (New York) 1912.

236981

— MILLS (J.)
Shakespeare and the Elizabethan stage. IN The Henrician, Vol. 11. (Evesham) 1938.

513851

— MOORE (J.R.)
The Songs of the public theaters in the time of Shakespeare. From The Journal of English and Germanic philology, vol. 28.
(Illinois) 1929.
444156

— MORETON, W.H.C.
Shakespeare came to Shoreditch.
1964.
illus. 667825

— MYERSCOUGH-WALKER (R.)
Stage and film décor. [With references to Shakespeare and the Elizabethan theatre.] With a foreword by C. B. Cochrane.
illus. dgms. 1940.

522306

— NAGLER (ALOIS MARIA)
Shakespeare's stage. Translated by R. Manheim. (Yale Shakespeare Supplements) Facsimile. Bibliog. (New Haven)
1958.

666158

— NAGLER (ALOIS MARIA)
Sixteenth-century continental stages. IN SHAKESPEARE QUARTERLY V: pp. 359-370.
(New York) 1954.

605711

—NICOLL (ALLARDYCE)
"Passing over the stage".   IN
SHAKESPEARE SURVEY 12.   (Cambridge)
1959.

666150

—NICOLL (ALLARDYCE)
Studies in the Elizabethan stage since
1900.   IN SHAKESPEARE SURVEY 1.
(Cambridge)   1948.

590674

—PASCAL (R.)
The Stage of the "Englische Komödianter"
- three problems.   [Containing references to Shakespeare's plays.]
FROM The Modern Language Review,
Vol. 35.   pp. [10.]   (Cambridge)
bibliog.   1940.

527251

—PICKEL (MARGARET B.)
Charles I as patron of poetry and
drama.   [With references to
Shakespeare.]
bibliog.   1936.

456196

—[POEL (W.)]
The Playhouse of the sixteenth century.
pp. 30.   [Edinburgh]
illus.   [c.1904.]

599944

—POEL (W.)
Shakespeare in the theatre.
port.   1913.

431019

—PROUTY (CHARLES TYLER)
An early Elizabethan playhouse.
IN SHAKESPEARE SURVEY 6.   (Cambridge)
1953.

631770

—PROUTY (CHARLES TYLER) ed.
Studies in the Elizabethan theatre,
[by various authors.]   [Hamden,
Conn.]
illus.   plans.   bibliog.   1961.

667053

—PROWER (M.)
An Elizabethan playhouse: extract
from a country gentleman's letter to
his wife.   IN The Gentleman's
Magazine, Vol. 295.   1903.

179335

—REESE (MAX MEREDITH)
Shakespeare: his world & his work.
illus.   map.   bibliog.   1953.

631880

—Reynolds (G.F.) Elizabethan stage
conditions : talk [broadcast]
18th July 1949. ff.8. Typescript.
(Shakespeare and his world,4).

1949.

605266

—REYNOLDS (G. F.)
Some principles of Elizabethan staging:
a dissertation [containing references
to Shakespeare] submitted to the Faculty
of the Graduate School of Arts and
Literature in candidacy for the degree
of Doctor of Philosophy (Department of
English).   (Chicago: University of
Chicago)   1905.
   This is W. J. Lawrence's copy, interleaved with manuscript notes.

500861

—REYNOLDS (G.F.)
The staging of Elizabethan plays at
the Red Bull Theater, 1605-1625.
[Containing references to Shakespeare.
With a bibliography.]
               [New York]   1940.
[Modern Language Association of America.
General Series, 9.]   514989

—REYNOLDS, GEORGE FULLMER
Two conventions of the open stage (as
illustrated in King Lear?).   FROM
Philological Quarterly, vol.XLI, no.1.
1962.

668390

—REYNOLDS (G. F.)
William Percy and his plays, with a
summary of the customs of Elizabethan
staging.   [With references to the
production of Shakespeare's plays.]
Reprinted for private circulation from
Modern Philology, Vol. 12.   pp. [20.]
(Chicago)   1914.   498126
_____ Another copy with manuscript
notes by W. J. Lawrence.   523726

—ROTHSCHILD (J. A. de)
Shakespeare and his day: a study of
the topical element in Shakespeare
and in the Elizabethan drama.
(Harness Prize Essay, 1901)
bibliog.   1906.

399712

—ROTHWELL (W. F.)
Was there a typical Elizabethan stage?
IN SHAKESPEARE SURVEY 12.
(Cambridge)
bibliog.   1959.

666150

—SAUNDERS (J. W.)
Vaulting the rails [:   the flexibility
of the Elizabethan stage].
IN SHAKESPEARE SURVEY 7.   (Cambridge)
1954.

639176

—Seltzer (Daniel)
The Staging of the last plays. IN
Stratford-upon-Avon Studies.
8: Later Shakespeare.   1966.

   illus. pp.127-165.   756101

—SEMPER (ISIDORE JOSEPH)
The Jacobean theater through the eyes
of Catholic clerics.
IN   SHAKESPEARE QUARTERLY III: 1.
pp. 45-51.
(New York)   1952.

605711

—Shakespeare's theatre and plays.
(Pictorial Education Quarterly,
June 1954)
ports.   illus.   map.   1954.

641380

—SHAPIRO (I. A.)
The Bankside theatres: early engravings.
IN SHAKESPEARE SURVEY 1.   (Cambridge)
bibliog.   illus.   plans.   facsimiles.
1948.

590674

—SHAPIRO, ISAAC ABY
Robert Fludd's stage-illustration
[: the problem of identifying an
illustration of the stage of Blackfriars
Theatre]. FROM Shakespeare Studies 2.
[Cincinnati, Ohio]   [1966.]

pp.192-209.   761646

—SHARPE (R. B.)
The Real war of the theatres:
Shakespeare's fellows in rivalry
with the Admiral's men, 1594-1603.
Repertories, devices, and types.
(Boston)
bibliog.   1935.
The Modern Language Association of
America.   Monographs Series, 5.

443036

—SHIRLEY, FRANCES ANN
Shakespeare's use of off-stage sounds.
(Lincoln, Neb.)   1963.

667763

—SIMPSON (P.)
Actors and acting: the masque.
IN Shakespeare's England, vol. 2.
(Oxford)
illus.   facsimiles.   bibliog.
1917.

435746

—SISSON (C. J.)
The Theatres and companies.   IN
GRANVILLE-BARKER (H.) and HARRISON
(G. B.) eds., A Companion to
Shakespeare studies.   (Cambridge)
illus.   tables.   facsimiles.
                 1934.   418724
_____ (New York)   1937.   479251
_____ (Cambridge) 1945.   566174

—   Smith (G.C.M.) Plays performed in
Cambridge Colleges before 1585.   In
Fasciculus Ioanni Willis Clark dicatus.
1909.

398908

—SMITH (IRWIN)
"Gates" on Shakespeare's stage.
IN SHAKESPEARE QUARTERLY VII:
pp. 159-176.
(New York)   1956.

605711

—SMITH (IRWIN)
Their exits and reentrances [actors in
Shakespeare's plays].
IN SHAKESPEARE QUARTERLY XVIII: 1.
pp. 7-16.
(New York)   1967.

605711

—SMITH (WARREN DALE)
The Elizabethan stage and Shakespeare's
entrance announcements.
IN SHAKESPEARE QUARTERLY IV: 4.
pp. 405-410.
(New York)   1953.

605711

—SMITH (WARREN DALE)
Evidence of scaffolding on
Shakespeare's stage.   IN The Review
of English Studies.   New Series,
Vol. 2.   (Oxford)   1951.

318239/2/2

—SMITH (WARREN DALE)
New light on stage directions in
Shakespeare.   IN Studies in Philology,
Vol. 47.   (Chapel Hill, N.C.) 1950.

554520/47

—SMITH (WARREN DALE)
Shakespeare's stagecraft as denoted
by the dialogue in the original
printings of his texts.   (Ann Arbor,
Mich.)
typescript, 1947.   microfilm,
positive copy.   1 reel, 35 mm.
[1950.]

612610

—SMITH (WARREN DALE)
Stage business in Shakespeare's dialogue.
IN SHAKESPEARE QUARTERLY IV:
pp. 311-316.
(New York) 1953.

605711

—SORELL (WALTER)
Shakespeare and the dance.
IN SHAKESPEARE QUARTERLY VIII:
pp. 367-384.
(New York)   1957.

605711

—SOUTHERN (RICHARD)
The Mystery of the Elizabethan stage.
Producer Leonie Cohn.   [Script of
broadcast, March, 1960].   (British
Broadcasting Corporation)   ff. 10.
typescript.   1960.

666910

—SOUTHERN (RICHARD)
On reconstructing a practicable
Elizabethan public playhouse.
IN SHAKESPEARE SURVEY 12.
(Cambridge)
illus.   plan.   dgms.   1959.

666150

—Spencer (H.) How Shakespeare staged
his plays: some notes on the
dubiety of non- textual evidence.
From The Johns Hopkins Alumni
Magazine. Vol.20, No.3.

(Baltimore)   1932.

440786

—Sprague (A.C.) Off-stage sounds,
[including references to Shakespeare.
With bibliographical notes.] From
University of Toronto Quarterly,
Vol.15.

(Toronto)   1945.

578420

—STAMM (RUDOLF)
Elizabethan stage-practice and the
transmutation of source material
by the dramatists.   IN SHAKESPEARE
SURVEY 12.   (Cambridge)   1959.

666150

STEVENS (T. P.)
Elizabethan playhouses in Southwark.
FROM Southwark Diocesan Gazette,
vol. 23.   pp. [2]
illus.   1942.

540155

STOPES (Mrs. Charlotte C.)
Burbage's "Theatre".   IN The Fortnightly Review. Vol. 92.

1909.
220427

Stopes (Mrs. Charlotte C.) Elizabethan
stage scenery. In The Fortnightly
Review, Vol. 87.

1907.

201725

STRATFORD-UPON-AVON STUDIES. 9:
Elizabethan Theatre.   1966.

illus.   756653

STYAN (J. L.)
The Actor at the foot of Shakespeare's
platform.   IN SHAKESPEARE SURVEY 12.
(Cambridge)   1959.

666150

STYAN, JOHN LOUIS
Shakespeare's stagecraft. (Cambridge)
1967.

766182

SYMONDS (J. A.)
The Drama of Elizabeth and James
considered as the main product of the
Renaissance in England. [With refer-
ences to Shakespeare.]   IN MARLOWE (C.)
[Plays].   Edited by H. [H.] Ellis.
port.   illus.   1902.
The Mermaid Series.
Large paper copy.

389466

Thaler (A.) Shakespeare and democracy
[: revaluations, critical and
historical; "Country" plays and
strolling players; Poets, plays and
actors. With bibliographical
references.]

(Knoxville, Tenn.)   1941.

531788

Thaler (A.) The Travelling players
in Shakspere's England. [With
bibliographical notes.]Reprinted
for private circulation from Modern
philology, Vol.17. pp. [26.]

[Chicago]   1920.

523732

Thorndike (A.H.) Shakespeare's
theater, [i.e. the stage in
Shakespeare's time. With bibliographical notes.] Illus. Map. Plans.

(New York)   1925.

522855

TYTLER (ERNEST J.   )

Elizabethan theatre: filmstrip and
notes. 1.vol.   ,1 reel 35 m.m. 1960.

666560-1

VENEZKY (ALICE S.)
Pageantry on the Shakespearean stage.
(New York)
illus.   bibliog.   1951.

619624

WALLACE (C.W.)
The First London Theatre: materials
for a history.   [1576-1602.]
([Lincoln, Neb.]) 1.   .1913
([Nebraska] University Studies, Vol. 13,
nos. 1-3.)

499282

WHEATLEY (HENRY BENJAMIN)
The London stage in Elizabeth's reign.
(Royal Institution of Great Britain)
pp. 7.   1890.

665455

WICKHAM, GLYNNE WILLIAM GLADSTONE
The Cockpit reconstructed.   FROM New
Theatre Magazine.   Vol. 7, no. 2,
Spring.   (Bristol)   1967.

771372

WIKLAND (ERIK)
Elizabethan players in Sweden, 1591-92:
facts and problems.   Translated by
P. Hort.   Translations from the Latin
by C. E. Holm.   (Stockholm)
ports. illus. map. genealogical tables.
facsimiles. bibliog.   1962.

667260

WILSON (FRANK PERCY)
The Elizabethan theatre.   FROM Neophilologus, 39. Jaargang. (Groningen)
1955.

665002

Wilson (J.D.) "They sleepe all the
act." From Review of English
Studies, Vol.4.

1928.

497598

WRIGHT (G. R.)
The English stage in the year 1638.
[With facsimile list of 24 plays
presented at Court,1638.]   IN The
Journal of the British Archaeological
Association, vol. 16.   1860.

118739

WRIGHT (LOUIS BOOKER)
Shakespeare's theatre and the dramatic
tradition.   pp. 36.   (Washington, D.C.)
ports. illus. maps. facsimiles. bibliog.
1958.   666181
Folger Shakespeare Library.   Folger
Booklets of Tudor and Stuart Civilization.
_____ IN Life and letters in Tudor and
Stuart England.   (Ithaca, N.Y.)
illus.   1962.   667762
Folger Shakespeare Library.

YATES (FRANCES A.)
English actors in Paris during the
lifetime of Shakespeare.   IN The
Review of English Studies, Vol. 1.
1925.

318239

— YATES, FRANCES AMELIA
The Stage in Robert Fludd's memory system.
IN SHAKESPEARE STUDIES 3.   (Cincinnati, Ohio)   1967.

771652

— ZBIERSKI (HENRYK)
Shakespeare and the "War of the theatres": a reinterpretation.
(Poznańskie Towarzystwo Przyjaciół Nauk.   Wydział Filologiczno-Filozoficzny.   Prace Komisji Filologicznej.   Tom 16, Zeszyt 5)
(Poznań)
illus.   map.   bibliog.   1957.

665635

Stage History and Production
Restoration and 18th century
see also **Actors and Acting**, Restoration and 18th century

— ALLARD (L.)
La Censure théâtrale sous la Restauration.   IN Harvard Studies and notes in philology and literature, vol. 14.   1932.

398528

— ALLEMAN (G. S.)
Matrimonial law and the materials of Restoration comedy;   an essential portion of a dissertation in English, presented to the Graduate School in partial fulfillment of the requirements for the degree of Doctor of Philosophy [in the] University of Pennsylvania.   [With references to Shakespeare.]   (Philadelphia)
tables. bibliog   1942.

540880

— ALLEN (R. J.)
Life in eighteenth century England [: brief text and plates.   With references to performances of Shakespeare at Drury Lane].   (Boston, [Mass.])
                                        1941.
Illustrative Set No. 4, Museum Extension Publications, Museum of Fine Art. Boston.

531544

— An Answer to the memoirs of Mrs. Billington, with the life and adventures of Richard Daly, Esq., and an account of the present state of the Irish theatre. Written by a gentleman, well acquainted with several curious anecdotes of all parties. pp. 71.

1792.

507040

— ANTHONY (ROSE)
The Jeremy Collier stage controversy, 1698-1726: a dissertation for the degree of Doctor of Philosophy.
(Milwaukee, Wisc.)
port.   bibliogs.   1937.

475522

— ASHLEY (L. R. N.)
Colley Cibber: a bibliography.
FROM Restoration and 18th Century Theatre Research.   Vol. 6, No. 1.
(Chicago, Ill.)   pp. 14-27. 1967.

761650

— AVERY (E. L.)
[Colley] Cibber, "King John", and the students of the law.   IN Modern Language Notes, Vol. 53.   (Baltimore)
                                        1938.

493024

— Avery (E.L.) I Henry IV and 2 Henry IV [: performances] during the first half of the eighteenth century. [With bibliographical notes.] From The Journal of English and Germanic Philology, Vol.44.

(Urbana, Ill.)   1945.

578402

— BAGSTER-COLLINS (J. F.)
George Colman, the younger, 1762-1836. [With references to Shakespeare.]
(New York)
port.   bibliogs.   1946.

580081

— BARKER (R. H.)
Mr. Cibber of Drury Lane.   (New York)
bibliog.   1939.
Columbia University Studies in English and Comparative Literature.

510733

— BAX (C.)
Pretty witty Nell: an account of Nell Gwyn and her environment.   [With references to Shakespeare.]
bibliog.   ports.   illus.   map.
                                        1932.

469984

— BEDFORD (A.)
The Evil and danger of stage-plays; shewing their natural tendency to destroy religion, and introduce a general corruption of manners [containing references to Shakespeare's plays].
(Bristol)   1706.

568216

— BEDFORD (ARTHUR)
A Serious remonstrance in behalf of the Christian religion, against the horrid blasphemies and impieties which are still used in the English play-houses.   1719.

621146

— BENTLEY (G. E.)
The Jacobean and Caroline stage: dramatic companies and players. [Including an alphabetical list of players of the time giving biographical summaries, and references to performances of Shakespeare's plays.] (Oxford)
tables. bibliogs. 2 vols.   1941.

523172

—BETTERTON (T.)
The History of the English stage from
the Restauration to the present time.
Including the lives, characters and
amours of the most eminent actors and
actresses. With instructions for
public speaking, by T. Betterton [or
more probably William Oldys]. With
Memoirs of Mrs. Anne Oldfield [and
references to Shakespeare. Edited by
E. Curll].
  ports. 1741.

576640

— Byrne (M.[uriel] St. C.) A History of
Shakespearean production in England, Part I:
1700-1800: scenes and characters in the
eighteenth century. [Filmstrips and
explanatory notes.] Made in collaboration
with the Arts Council of Great Britain.
[With bibliographies.] Dgm. Facsimile.
Typescript. 2 vols. 35 mm. 1948.

603733-4

— CAMPBELL (LILY B.)
The Rise of a theory of stage presentation in England during the eighteenth
century. [With references to
Shakespeare.] FROM [Publications of
the Modern Language Association of
America, Vol. 32]. pp. 163-200.
(New York)
  bibliog. [1917.]

554232

— [CHETWOOD (W. R.)]
The British theatre, containing the
lives of the English dramatic poets
[including Shakespeare] with an
account of all their plays [etc.]
(Dublin) 1750.

592245

— CIBBER (COLLEY)
An Apology for the life of Colley Cibber;
with an historical view of the stage
during his own time. Written by
himself.
  port. 1740.
For other editions of this work check
the main sequence under the author's
name.

504560

— [CIBBER (T.)]
An Apology for the life of Mr. The[ophilus]
Cibber, comedian: a proper sequel to
the Apology for the life of Mr. Colley
Cibber, comedian, with an historical
view of the stage; [doubtfully ascribed
to H. Fielding]. Supposed to be
written by himself. In the style and
manner of the poet laureat. 1740. 493428
  __ Another edn. (Dublin) 1741.

560447

— COLLIER (J.)
A Farther vindication of the Short
view of the profaneness and immorality
of the English stage. In which the
objections of a late book [by Edward
Filmer] entitled: A Defence of
plays, are consider'd. pp. 46.
1708.

605280

— COLLIER (J.)
A Short view of the immorality and
profaneness of the English stage,
together with the sense of antiquity
upon this argument. 1698. 466547
  _____ 2nd edn. 1698. 466548
  _____ 4th edn. 1699. 491991

— COLMAN (G.) [the elder]
Prose on several occasions; accompanied with some pieces in verse.
[With references to Shakespeare.]
frontis. 3 vols. 1787.

473264

— A Companion to the theatre; or, a key
to the play; containing the stories
of the most celebrated dramatick
pieces; the plan, character and
design of each performance is exhibited and explain'd; with remarks on
each representation. 2nd edn.
1740.

57158

— A Companion to the theatre: or, A
View of our most celebrated dramatic
pieces [, including plays of
Shakespeare]: in which the plan,
characters, and incidents of each are
particularly explained. Interspersed
with remarks historical, critical and
moral. (Dublin) 1751.

579753

— A Companion to the theatre; or, A View
of our most celebrated dramatic pieces,
in which the plan, characters and
incidents of each are particulary
explained; interspersed with remarks,
historical, critical and moral; [with]
a brief account of the lives and
writings of the English dramatic poets,
with a list of their plays, 1538-1750,
[and] the lives of the principal actors
as well as poets. (Dublin) 1756.

551195

— CONGREVE (W.)
Amendments of Mr. Collier's false
and imperfect citations, etc. from
the Old bachelor, Double dealer,
Love for love, Mourning bride.
IN Congreve (W.) Dramatic works,
Vol. 2. 1773.

568221

— COTTON (W.)
The Story of the drama in Exeter,
during its best period, 1787 to 1823.
With reminiscences of Edmund Kean.
[Including accounts of performances
of Shakespeare's plays.] pp. [iv,]66.
  port. 1887.

535317

— Covent Garden Journal [: an account of
the destruction of the old theatre
by fire 1808, of the rise of the new
theatre, and of the subsequent
occurrences that took place therein.
With an appendix and references to
Shakespeare. Edited by J.J.Stockdale].
Illus. 2 vols.
1810.

538118

— [CROKER (Rt. Hon. J. W.)]
Familiar epistles to Frederick J[one]s,
Esq. on the present state of the Irish
stage [in connection with his management of the Theatre Royal, Dublin, by
T.D.C. With references to Shakespeare
and Shakespeare characters]. 2nd edn.,
with considerable additions. (Dublin)
1804.

519657

— CUNNINGHAM (P.)
The Story of Nell Gwyn and the sayings
of Charles II. With the author's latest
corrections. Edited with introduction,
additional notes and a life of the author
by H. B. Wheatley. [With references to
Shakespeare]
 port. [1892]. 511122
Hutchinson's Library of Standard Lives.
———— New edn., with an introduction
[and notes] by J. Drinkwater.
 ports. illus. 1927. 511083
Privately printed for the Navarre Society.

— DAVIES (T.)
Dramatic miscellanies: critical observations on several plays of Shakspeare,
with a review of his principal characters and those of various eminent
writers as represented by Mr. Garrick
and other celebrated comedians; with
anecdotes of dramatic poets, actors, etc.
 port. 3 vols. 1783-4. 467493
———— Another edn. (Dublin)
 1784. 522856

— DENNIS (J.)
Critical works. Edited [with preface,
introduction and notes] by E. N. Hooker.
[Contains "An Essay on the genius and
writings of Shakespear"; "The Impartial
critick" (1693); "The Person of
quality's answer to Mr. Collier's letter,
being a disswasive from the play-house";
(1704); and other references to
Shakespeare.] (Baltimore)
 2 vols. 1939-43.

503438

— DENNIS (J.)
The Person of quality's answer to
Mr. Collier's letter, being a
disswasive from the play-house (1704).
IN Dennis (J.) Critical works.
Edited [with a preface and notes] by
E. N. Hooker. (Baltimore) 1939.

503438

— [DERRICK (S.)]
A General view of the stage, by
Mr. Wilkes. [With references to
Shakespeare]. 1759.

93998

— [Dibdin (T.J.)] Reminiscences of
 Thomas Dibdin, of the Theatres
 Royal, Covent-Garden, Drury-Lane,
 Haymarket, &c. Port. 2 vols.

1827.

495702

— [DRAKE (J.)]
The Antient and modern stages
survey'd; or, Mr. Collier's View
of the immorality and profaneness
of the English stage set in a true
light. [With references to
Shakespeare.] 1699.

551003

— The Druriad: or, Strictures on the
 principal performers of Drury-Lane
 Theatre: a satirical poem: with
 notes critical and explanatory.
 [With references to Shakespeare.]
 pp. 28.

1798.

524911

— EVANS (GWYNNE BLAKEMORE) ed.
Shakespearean prompt-books of the
seventeenth century. (Bibliographical
Society of the University of Virginia.
Charlottesville, Va.) 1960-
 For setting out see under the author's
name.

— [GARRICK (D.)]
An Essay on acting in which will be
consider'd the mimical behaviour of a
certain fashionable faulty actor [and]
a short criticism of his acting Macbeth.
[By D. Garrick: a criticism of himself.]
pp. 27. 1744.

57899

— [GILDON (C.)]
A Comparison between the two stages
[i.e. Drury Lane and Lincoln's Inn
Fields]: a late Restoration book
of the theatre. [With references
to Shakespeare] Edited with an
introduction and notes by S. B. Wells.
(Princeton)
 facsimile. bibliog. 1942.
Princeton Studies in English.

563408

— GRAY (C. H.)
Theatrical criticism in London to 1795.
[With references to Shakespeare and a
bibliographical note.] 1931.
 Columbia University Studies in English
and Comparative Literature.

390261

— HARBAGE (A.)
Sir William Davenant, poet venturer,
1606-1668. [With a chapter:
"Adaptations of Shakespeare" and
other references to Shakespeare.]
(Philadelphia)
 port. bibliog. 1935.

436086

— HOGAN (CHARLES BEECHER)
Shakespeare in the theatre, 1701-1800:
a record of performances in London.
(Oxford)
 2 vols. 1952-57.

625548

— How do you do? Nos. 1-8 (30th July-
 5th November, 1796). [A general
 periodical, with special sections on
 the stage including references to
 Shakespearian productions.]

1796.

524910

— KELLY (J. A.)
German visitors to English theaters
in the eighteenth century.   [With
Shakespearian references and a bibliographical appendix.]   (Princeton, N.J.)
1936.

466543

— The Laureat, or, The Right side of
Colley Cibber;   containing explanations, amendments and observations
on a book intituled "An Apology for
the life of Colley Cibber".   [With]
The History of the life, manners and
writings of Aesopus.   1740.

614553

— LEECH (CLIFFORD)
Shakespeare, Cibber, and the Tudor
myth.   FROM Shakespearean Essays,
No. 2.   (Knoxville, Tenn.)
pp. 79-95.   1964.

753396

— LICHTENBERG (G. C.)
Lichtenberg's visits to England, as
described in his letters and diaries.
Translated and annotated by Margaret
L. Mare and W. H. Quarrell.   [With
a biographical introduction by
Margaret L. Mare, and including refer-
ences to Shakespeare's plays.]   (Oxford)
port.   bibliog.   1938.
Oxford Studies in Modern Languages and
Literature.

484591

— The Life of John Philip Kemble, a
proprietor, and stage manager of
Covent Garden Theatre, interspersed
with family and theatrical anecdotes.
pp. [iv], 52.   [1809].
Frontispiece by Isaac Cruikshank.

621022

— THE LONDON STAGE, 1660-1800: a calendar
of plays, entertainments & afterpieces.
Compiled from the playbills, newspapers
and theatrical diaries of the period.
(Carbondale, Ill.)
illus.   bibliogs.   1960-
Part 1. 1660-1700, ed. by W. Van Lennep.
2. 1700-1729, ed. by E. L. Avery.
3. 1729-1747, ed. by A. H. Scouten.
4. 1747-1776, ed. by G. W. Stone.

696196

— LYNCH (JAMES J.)
The Shakespearean heritage of the mid-
century stage [and] The Shakespearean
revival.   IN Lynch (J. J.) Box, pit
and gallery: stage and society in
Johnson's London.   (Berkeley, Cal.)
illus.   map.   facsimilés.   1953.

638320

— LYNCH (KATHLEEN M.)
The Social mode of Restoration comedy.
[With references to Shakespeare.]
(New York)
bibliog.   1926.
Michigan University.   Language and
Literature.

422446

— MacMILLAN (D.) ed.
Drury Lane Calendar, 1747-1776;
compiled from the playbills and edited
with an introduction.   [Containing
Shakespearian references]   (Oxford)
1938.
Published in co-operation with the
Huntington Library.

482401

— MACQUEEN-POPE (W. [J.])
The Rivals of old Drury.   [J. Quin
v. C. Macklin and D. Garrick.   With
references to Shakespeare.]   FROM
Millgate and Playgoer, Vol. 40.
(Manchester)
port.   illus.   1945.

561327

— MATTHEWS (BACHE [ed.]
Extracts from the diaries of Samuel
Pepys and his contemporaries relating
to plays, playhouses and players.
[With references to Shakespeare.]
typescript.   [c.1920.]

603508

— The Monthly mirror, reflecting men and
manners.   With strictures on their
epitome, the stage [including references to Shakespeare].   Vols. 1 and 3.
ports.   illus.   2 vols.   [1795-7.]
All other volumes wanting.

520768

— MORGAN ([J.] A.)
William Shakespeare's literary
executor: the first Shakespearean
revival.   IN Magazine of American
History, Vol. 16.   (New York)   1886.

88042

— Nethercot (A.H.) Sir William D'Avenant,
poet laureate and playwright-manager.
[With appendices and bibliographical
notes.]   Port.   Genealogical Table.

(Chicago)   1938.

496170

— PAGE (E. R.)
George Colman the elder: essayist,
dramatist, and theatrical manager,
1732-1794.   [With references to
Shakespeare.]   (New York)
bibliog.   1935.
Columbia University.   Studies in
English and Comparative Literature,
No. 120.

447513

— Rosenfeld (Sybil) Strolling players
& drama in the provinces, 1660-
1765.   [With references to
Shakespeare.]   Ports.   Illus.
Facsimiles.

(Cambridge)   1939.

502621

— Scott (W.S.) The Georgian theatre [:
with biographical sketches of some
of its leading figures, and
references to Shakespeare].   Ports.
Illus.

1946.

578657

—SCOUTEN (ARTHUR H.)
The Increase in popularity of Shakespeare's
plays in the eighteenth century: a
caveat for interpretors of stage history.
IN SHAKESPEARE QUARTERLY VII.
pp. 189-202.
(New York) 1956.
605711

—SCOUTEN (A. H.)
Shakespeare's plays in the theatrical
repertory when Garrick came to London.
IN University of Texas, Studies in
English [No. 24] 1944. (Austin [Texas],
bibliog. 1945.
563674

—Scouten (A.H.) and Hughes (L.) A
Calendar of performances of
1 Henry IV and 2 Henry IV during
the first half of the eighteenth
century. [With bibliographical
notes.] From The Journal of English
and Germanic Philology, Vol.43.
(Urbana, Ill.) 1944.
578407

—SEWELL (GEORGE)
The Tragedy of Sir Walter Raleigh.
As it is acted at the Theatre in
Lincolns-Inn-Fields. Third edition.
(London: John Pemberton) 1719.

The Epilogue refers to the
cutting and alteration of Shakespeare's
plays in the theatre. 436639

—Shakespeare's Plays, as they are now
performed at the Theatre Royal in
London [: a review of Bell's edition
of Shakespeare's plays.] In The
Monthly Review; or, literary journal,
Dec.1773-July 1774, Vol.50.
482038

—Shurter (R.L.) Shakespearean perform-
ances in pre-revolutionary America.
From The South Atlantic Quarterly,
January 1937.
(Durham, N.C.)
503864

— SMITH (D.F.)
Plays about the theatre in England from
The Rehearsal in 1671 to the Licensing
Act in 1737, or, The Self-conscious
stage and its burlesque and satirical
reflections in the age of criticism.
[With bibliographical notes and
appendices]. Illus. (Oxford)
1936.
468347

— The Stage-mutineers; or, A Play-house
to be lett: a ballad opera, by a
Gentleman late of Trinity-College,
Cambridge. As it is acted at the
Theatre-Royal in Covent-Garden.
[Containing Shakespearian references.]
pp. 40. 1733.
188792

—Summers ([A.J.M.A.]M.) The Playhouse
of Pepys. [With references to
Shakespeare.] Ports. Illus.
Facsimiles.
1935.
436146

—SUMMERS ([A. J. M. A.] M.)
The Restoration theatre [: an account
of the technique of the playwrights
and the practical staging of plays.
With references to Shakespeare].
illus. facsimiles. 1934.
417668

—SUTHERLAND (J. R.)
Shakespeare's imitators in the
eighteenth century. IN The Modern
Language Review, Vol. 28, 1933.
415705

—Thespian dictionary; or, Dramatic
biography of the eighteenth century,
containing sketches of the principal
managers, dramatists [etc.] of the
United Kingdom, and forming a concise
history of the English stage.
port. 1802.
485290

— Thorp (W.) ed.,Songs from the
Restoration theater. Edited [with
introduction and notes.] Ports.
(Princeton) 1934.
431797

— Wewitzer (R.) A Brief dramatic chronology of actors, &c. on the London
stage, from the introduction of
theatrical entertainments into England
to the present time. New edn. [with]
miscellaneous appendix.
1817.
501291

—WEWITZER (R.)
A Theatrical pocket book; or, Brief
dramatic chronology from the earliest
periods of history. With a list of
British dramatists and of actors,
etc. on the London stage. 1814.
479703

—Whincop (T.) Scanderbeg; or, Love and
liberty. To which are added, A
List of all the dramatic authors
[including Shakespeare], with some
account of their lives; and of all
dramatic pieces published in English,
to the year 1747. Illus.
1747.
484913

—Wilcox (J.) The Relation of Molière
to Restoration comedy. [With
references to Shakespeare and a
bibliography.]
(New York) 1938.
491575

— **Wilkes [T.]** A General view of the stage.

1759.

497696

—WOEHL (A. L.)
Some plays in the repertories of the patent houses [i.e. the playhouses established by Thomas Killigrew and William Davenant. With references to plays of Shakespeare.] IN Studies in speech and drama [by various authors]: in honor of Alexander M. Drummond. (Ithaca, N.Y.)
bibliog. 1944.

561280

— WOOD (F. T.)
Theatrical performances at Bath in the eighteenth century. [With references to Shakespearian performances.] IN Notes and Queries, Vol. 192-3.
1947-8.

588005

— [Woodward (J.)] Some thoughts concerning the stage in a letter to a lady. pp.13.

1704.

605281

Stage History and Production

— 19th century
see also **Actors and Acting**, 19th century

— A Beckett (A.W.) Green-room recollections. [With references to Shakespeare.]
(Bristol) [1896]

(Arrowsmith Series Vol.25.)

473286

— ALLEN (SHIRLEY)
A Successful people's theatre: Samuel Phelps at Sadler's Wells [and his presentation of Shakespearean drama there]. IN Theatre Arts, Vol. 28. (New York)
port. illus. 1944.

558366

— ARCHER (W.)
The Theatrical 'world' for 1893. [Containing Shakespearian references.]
[1894]

433540

— ARCHER (W.)
The Theatrical "World", 1893-1897. [With references to Shakespearian plays.]
5 vols. [1894]-1898.
Vol. for 1893 had added portraits.
Vol. for 1896 has letter written by author inserted.

503948

— ARCHER (W.)
The Theatrical 'world' of 1897. With an introduction by S. Grundy and a synopsis of playbills of the year, by H. G. Hibbert, [containing Shakespearian references]. 1898.

416052

— BEVINGTON (MERLE M.)
The Saturday review, 1855-1868: representative educated opinion in Victorian England. [With references to Shakespearian productions.] (New York)
bibliogs. 1941.
Columbia University. Studies in English and Comparative Literature.

538464

— BOAS (F. S.)
From Richardson to Pinero: some innovators and idealists. [With references to Kean in Shakespearian parts]. 1936.

457592

—BOBSON (G.)
Shakspeare and the drama: a letter to T. Smith, scene-painter and tragedian at the Amphitheatre. FROM Blackwood's Magazine, May 1846. (Edinburgh)

440111

—Broadbent (R.J.) Stage whispers. [With references to Shakespeare.]

1901.

511085

— [BUCKE (C.)]
The Italians; or, The Fatal accusation: a tragedy. With a preface, containing the correspondence of the author with the committee of Drury Lane Theatre, P. Moore, Esq., and Mr. Kean. By the author of "The Philosophy of nature" 6th edn. 1819.
Preface signed C. B.

518507

— BUNN (A.)
The Stage: both before and behind the curtain. [With references to Shakespeare's plays.]
3 vols. 1840.

460013

— C. [pseud.] Shakespere and his age: reflections on modern play. *From* [Stray Leaves Quarterly, Jan.1874].

[Liverpool]

554727

— CARLISLE (CAROL JONES)
The Nineteenth-century actors versus the closet critics of Shakespeare. IN Studies in Philology, Vol. 51. (Chapel Hill, N.C.) 1954.

554520/51

—COOK ([E.] D.)
A Book of the play: studies and
illustrations of histrionic story,
life and character. [With references
to Shakespeare.] 3rd and revised edn.
1881.

460703

—COOK ([E.] D.)
Nights at the play: a view of the
English stage. [Containing criticisms
of Shakespeare performances.]
1883. 443987
_____ Another edn.
2 vols. 1883. 443573

—CRAIG (EDWARD GORDON)
Index to the story of my days: some
memoirs, 1872-1907.
ports. illus. 1957.

673655

—CROSSE (G.)
Fifty years of Shakespearean playgoing. 1940.

522290

—CROSSE (GORDON)
Shakespearean performances which I
have seen, from January, 1890 to
July, 1953.
manuscript. 21 vols. 1890-1953.

641917-37

—CROSSE (GORDON)
Shakespearean playgoing, 1890-1952.
Ports. Illus.
1953.

635983

— Dickins (R.) Forty years of Shakespeare on the English stage, August
1867 to August 1907 : a student's
memories.

[c.1910.]

517665

— DISHER (M. WILSON)
Greatest show on earth, as performed
for over a century at Astley's (afterwards Sanger's) Royal Amphitheatre of
Arts, Westminster Bridge Road.
ports. 1937.
Includes "Shakespeare on horseback"
[: William Cooke's equestrian versions
of "Richard III", "Macbeth" &c.]

498856

— DRAKE (F. C.)
Shakspere in modern settings.
IN The Cosmopolitan, Vol. 35.
1903.

180954

— The Drama; or, Theatrical Pocket
Magazine, Vols. 1-3 (May, 1821-
December, 1822.) [Containing
Shakespearian references.]
3 vols.

1821-2.

496188

— DU BOIS (A. E.)
The Beginnings of tragic comedy in
the drama of the nineteenth century:
a summary of a dissertation submitted
to the Johns Hopkins University, 1932.
pp. [39]. (Baltimore) 1934.

477157

— FELHEIM (MARVIN)
The Theater of Augustin Daly: the
late nineteenth century American
stage. (Cambridge [Mass.])
ports. illus. 1956.

656407

— FULLER (E.) ed.
The Dramatic year (1887-88): brief
criticisms of important theatrical
events [including Shakespearian
drama] in the United States. With
a sketch of the season in London,
by W. Archer. 1888.

563825

— GLICK (CLARIS)
William Poel: his theories and
influence. IN Shakespeare Quarterly XV: 1.
pp.15-25. (New York) 1964.

605711

— Going to the play with Shakespeare.
FROM All the year round [, Vol. 6.]
1862.

559987

— GOODWIN (T.)
Sketches and impressions, musical,
theatrical, and social (1799-1885);
including a sketch of the Philharmonic
Society of New York. [With chapters
relating to Shakespeare. Edited,
with a preface,] from the after-dinner
talk of T. Goodwin, by R. O. Mason.
(New York) 1887.

544466

— HACKETT (J. H.)
Notes and comments upon certain plays
and actors of Shakespeare, with
criticisms and correspondence.
3rd edn. (New York)
port. 1864.

458144

— HAPGOOD, ROBERT
His heart upon his sleeve: Clement Scott
as a reviewer of Shakespearian productions.
IN DEUTSCHE SHAKESPEARE-GESELLSCHAFT
WEST, JAHRBUCH 1967. pp. 70-82.
(Heidelberg)

754129

— HAZLITT (W.)
Dramatic criticism. IN Hazlitt (W.)
Complete works, edited by P. P. Howe,
Vol. 18.
frontis. 1933.
Centenary edition.
This edition limited to 1,000 sets.

412886

— HAZLITT (W.)
Dramatic essays. Selected and
edited, with notes and an introduction, by W. Archer and R. W. Lowe.
frontis. 1895.

443801

— HAZLITT (WILLIAM)
Essays.   Selected and edited [with
introduction and notes] by F. Carr.
[With references to Shakespeare].
                                    [c.1896.]
Scott Library.
                                        483486

— HAZLITT (WILLIAM)
A View of the English stage;   or, A
Series of dramatic criticisms.
                            1818.   507033
_____ Another edn.   1821.   524273

— Hollingshead (J.) Gaiety chronicles.
[With references to Shakespeare.]
Ports. illus.

                            1898.
                                    499276

— HORMANN (H.)
Ludwig Tieck, theatrical reformer [:
his theories on staging, with references
to various Shakespearian productions
and bibliographical notes].   FROM The
Quarterly Journal of Speech, Vol. 31.
(Detroit)   1945.

                                    576840

— HUNT (L.)
Dramatic criticism, 1808-1831.
Edited by L. H. Houtchens and [Mrs.]
Carolyn W. Houtchens.   1950.

                                    609880

— Hunt (L.) Dramatic essays. [With
references to Shakespeare.]Selected
and edited with notes and an
introduction by W. Archer and R.W.
Lowe. Frontis.
                            1894.
                                    473279

— [ISAACS (Mrs. EDITH J. R.) and GILDER
(ROSAMOND)]
Augustin Daly: the end of the
resident company.   [With references
to Daly's Shakespearean productions.]
IN Theatre Arts, Vol. 27.   (New York)
illus.   1943.

                                    548672

— Lamb (C.) The Art of the stage, as
set out in Lamb's dramatic essays.
With a commentary by P.[H.] Fitz-
gerald. [Including references to
Shakespeare and the drama.] Port.

                            1885.
                                    416076

— Lee ([Sir]S.) Shakespeare and the
modern stage, with other essays.

                            1907.
                                    434418

— MacQueen-Pope (W.[J.]) Carriages at
eleven: the story of the Edwardian
theatre [1897-1914.With references to
performances of Shakespeare's plays.]
Ports.Illus.

                    1947.

                            585827

— Manvers (D.) A Series of theatrical
observations, admonitions and
criticisms; received by J.P.Warde:
[mainly relating to his own
performances. With references to
Shakespearian productions].
Vol.1. Manuscript.

                    [1815-1819.]
                                    515584

— Max, pseud.

At the Lyceum [: a criticism of F.R.
Benson's Shakespearian performances].
In The Saturday Review. Vol.89. 1900.

                                    153040

— MORLEY (H.)
The Journal of a London playgoer from
1851 to 1866.   (Books and Papers,
1851-1866, [Vol.] 2.)   [With references to Shakespearian performances.]
                            1891.

                                    470203

— MORRIS (M.)
Essays in theatrical criticism.
[With references to Shakespeare.]
                            1882.

                                    422874

— Morris (M.) On some recent theatrical
criticims. From Macmillan's
Magazine, Vol.48. pp. [8.]

                            1883.
                                    599868

— MURAOKA (AKIRA)
Shakespeare in Stageland, 1816-1856.
IN ARAKI (KAZUO) and others, eds.,
Studies in English grammar and linguis-
tics: a miscellany in honour of
Takanobu Otsuka.   (Tokyo)
port. dgms. tables. bibliogs. 1958.

                                    667095

— Odell (Mary T.) The Old theatre,
Worthing: the Theatre Royal, 1807-
1855.   [With references to Shakespearian productions.] Ports.
Illus. Facsimiles.

                    (Aylesbury)   1938.

(Sign of the Dolphin)

                                    487607

— ODELL (MARY T.)
The Theatre Royal, 1807-1855: more
about the old theatre, Worthing, its
plays, players and playbills, its
proprietor and his playhouses.
Published under the Worthing Art
Development Scheme.   [With references
to Shakespearian productions.]
(Worthing: Sign of the Dolphin)
ports. illus. facsimiles.   1945.

                                    590955

—ODELL (MARY T.)
The Theatre Royal, 1814-1819:
Mr. [T.] Trotter of Worthing and
the Brighton theatre.   Published
under the Worthing Art Development
Scheme.   [With references to
Shakespeare productions.]   (Worthing:
Sign of the Dolphin)
illus.   1944.

558632

—PASCOE (C. E.) and others, eds.
Dramatic notes: a chronicle of the
London stage, 1879-1893 [1st-14th
issues].   [Edited] by C. E. Pascoe,
W. H. Rideing, A. Brereton and
C. Howard.   [With references to
Shakespearean drama.]
illus.   10 vols.   1883-93.
All published.

545668

—PERVGINI (M. E.)
The Omnibus box: social and
theatrical life in London and Paris,
1830-1850.   [Containing references
to Shakespearean performances of
Kean.]
ports.   illus.   1933.

521174

—Planché (J.R.) Recollections and
reflections : a professional autobiography. [With references to
Shakespeare.] New and revised edn.
illus.

1901.

499275

—Programmes of professional performances
of Shakespeare's plays.
36 vols.   c.1880-
This collection is continuously
augmented by the addition of programmes
of contemporary productions.

462500

—The Prompter; or, Theatrical and
concert guide.   No. 1, June, 1834.
1834.

453716

—REYNOLDS (E. [R.])
Early Victorian drama (1830-1870).
[With references to Shakespearean
productions.]   (Cambridge)
bibliog.   1936.

458551

— ROSENFELD (SYBIL)
The Grieves Shakespearian scene designs.
IN SHAKESPEARE SURVEY 20.   (Cambridge)
1967.

766881

—ROWELL (GEORGE RIGNAL)
The Victorian theatre: a survey.
illus.   bibliog.   1956.

656283

—Royal General Theatrical Fund.
Proceedings at the thirtieth
Anniversary Festival, July 1st, 1875.
Henry Irving in the chair. [Including
references to Shakespeare. From
The Era.] pp. 48.

1875.

507847

—Senior (W.) The Old Wakefield theatre.
[with references to Shakespeare.]
Frontis.

(Wakefield)   1894.

536679

— SETON (M.)
Recent Shakesperian revivals at the
Lyceum, Drury Lane and the Queen's.
FROM [The New Monthly Magazine, New
Series, Vol. 11.]   [1877.]

560924

— SHAW ([GEORGE] BERNARD)
Our theatres in the nineties [:
criticism contributed to the Saturday
Review including criticisms of some
of Shakespeare's plays.]
3 vols.   1932.
Works, Standard Edn.,Vols. 12, 13, 16.

388864

— SHAW ([GEORGE] BERNARD)
Pen portraits and reviews.   1932.
Works, Standard Edn., Vol. 21.

391893

— SHAW (GEORGE BERNARD)
Plays & players: essays on the theatre.
Selected with an introduction by
A. C. Ward.   1952.
World's Classics.

628613

— SHAW (GEORGE BERNARD)
Shaw on Shakespeare: an anthology
of Bernard Shaw's writings on the
plays and production of Shakespeare.
Edited and with an introduction by
E. Wilson.   1962.

666943

— SPER (F.)
The Periodical press of London,
theatrical and literary (excluding the
daily newspaper) 1800-1830.   With a
foreword by A. Nicoll.   pp. 58.
(Boston, [Mass.])   1937.

472835

— SPRAGUE (ARTHUR COLBY)
Shakespeare and melodrama.   IN
Essays and Studies, 1965.   1965.

742617

— SPRAGUE (ARTHUR COLBY)
Shakespearian players and performances.
(Cambridge, Mass.)
ports. illus.   1953.
Enter William Poel, pp. 136-149.

635328

—The Stage; [with references to
Shakespearian performances]
Vol. 1 (1874)-
ports. illus.
Wants Vol. 1, Nos. 1, 5, 7 (1874);
Vol. 2, all after No. 1 (1875);
Vols. 3-44 (1876-1917); [Vol. 63]
(1936). Vols. [56], [58] imperfect.

59651

— [STURGIS (J. R.)]
The Shakspeare revival in London.
[Containing references to Sir H.
Irving and Ellen Terry.] FROM
[International Review, Vol. 6.]
[New York] [1879.]

554169

— TELBIN (W.)
Art in the theatre: scenery. IN
The Magazine of Art, [vol. 12], 1889.

103127

—Theatre Royal, Drury Lane. Proceedings
of the Sub-Committee during the
season 1834-5 : a selection from the
minutes of the Sub-Committee, with
documents, correspondence, etc.

1835.

502036

—Theatrical Inquisitor (The) and
Monthly Mirror, Vols. 5, 8. 9, 11,
12. [With references to Shakespearian performances.] Illus.
5 vols.
1814-1818.

Vols. 1-4, 6-7, 10, 13 to 16 and N.S.
Vol. 1. wanting.

485740

—Theatrical John Bull. Nos. 1-21
(May 29 - Oct. 16, 1824). (Birmingham)
1825.

460428

—Theatrical Observer and Daily Bills
of the Play, No. 148, May 7, 1822.
pp. [2.]

414174

—The Theatrical register, and general
amusement guide, No.4, Oct.22, 1838.
[Including Shakespearian performances]
pp.23-32.

1838.

453719

— THORNELL (J. H.) ed.
The Bill of the play: an illustrated
record of the chief dramas, plays,
operas bouffe etc. produced during
the year 1881 [including plays by
Shakespeare.] With illustrations
by H. Ludlow. [1882.]

501364

— TOLLES (W.)
Tom Taylor and the Victorian drama.
[With references to Shakespeare.]
(New York)
bibliog. 1940.
Columbia University. Studies in
English and Comparative Literature.

520946

— WAGNER (L.)
The Stage, with the curtain raised.
[With references to Shakespeare.
New, revised and enlarged edn.]
pp. 32. [1880]

511087

— WAITZKIN (L.)
The Witch of Wych Street: a study
of the theatrical reforms of Madame
Vestris. [With Shakespearian
references.] pp. 67. (Cambridge,
Mass.)
illus. bibliog. 1933.
Harvard Honors Theses in English.

423999

— WALBROOK (H.M.)
The Drama in Clement Scott's day.
From "The Fortnightly Review", April
1934. pp.472-480.

427396

— WALKLEY (A. B.)
Playhouse impressions: [articles
reprinted chiefly from the Speaker,
National Observer and the Star.
Including articles on Shakespeare's
plays.] 1892.

460100

— WHYTE (F.)
The Victorian stage, [with
Shakespearian references.] IN
The Pall Mall Magazine, Vol. 12.
illus. 1897.

357026

Stage History and Production

— 20th century
see also **Actors and Acting,** 20th century

— ADLER (H.)
The Method of Michel Saint Denis.
[With references to Shakespearian
productions.] FROM London Mercury,
Vol. 39. 1938.

494283

——ADVANCE PLAYERS ASSOCIATION LTD.
Eight years of actor-management, 1937-45:
a record of the productions [including
Shakespeare productions] of Advance
Players Association Ltd., founded for
the presentation of classical plays,
and plays of an educational nature.
Under the direction of Donald Wolfit.
pp. 16.
   ports.   [1945.]

           565121

—— AGATE (JAMES EVERSHED)
Agate's folly: a pleasaunce [:
personal recollection and miscellaneous
essays on the theatre and other topics.
With references to Shakespearian per-
formances].   1925.

           580370

——AGATE (J. [E.])
The Amazing theatre [: dramatic criticisms of Shakespearian and other plays,
1937-39.]   1939.

           507616

——Agate (J.[E.]) At half- past eight:
essays of the theatre, 1921-1922.
Reprinted from the Saturday
Review.
          1923.

           420104

——AGATE (J. [E.])
Brief chronicles: a survey of the plays
of Shakespeare and the Elizabethans in
actual performance.   1943.

           543094

——AGATE (J. E.)
Buzz, buzz! Essays of the theatre.
[With references to Shakespeare.]
               [1918]

           469988

——Agate (J.[E.]) The Contemporary
theatre, 1944 and 1945 [: a week-by-
week survey of the London
commercial theatre. With references
to Shakespearean productions].

          1946.

           578652

——AGATE (J. [E.])
Ego: the autobiography of James Agate
[with references to Shakespearian
actors and performances.]
   ports.   illus.   1935.

           434148

——AGATE (J. [E.])
Ego 2: more of the autobiography
of J. Agate, [a diary from 7th August
1934 to 24th June, 1936.]
   ports.   illus.   plan.   1936.

           458022

——AGATE (J. [E.])
Ego 3: still more of the autobiography
[: a diary from August 9th 1936, to
July 19th 1938.]
   ports.   illus.   1938.

           489926

——AGATE (J. [E.])
Ego 4: yet more of the autobiography
of James Agate [: a diary from
July 21st, 1938 to June 17th, 1940].
   ports.   illus.   1940.

           518338

——AGATE (J. [E.])
Ego 5: again more of the autobiography
of James Agate [: a diary from
July 28, 1940 to August 3, 1942].
                1942.

           537804

——AGATE (J. [E.])
Ego 6: once more the autobiography
of James Agate [: a diary from
August 3, 1942 to December 16, 1943.]
   ports.   illus.   facsimile.   1944.

           550335

——[Agate (J.E.)] Ego 7 : even more of
the autobiography of James [E.]
Agate [: a diary from January 1 to
December 31, 1944. With references
to Shakespeare]. Ports. Facsimiles.

          1945.

           564236

——AGATE (J. [E.])
Ego 8: continuing the autobiography
of James Agate [: a diary from
January 1st to December 31st, 1945.
With references to Shakespeare].
   ports.   illus.   1946.

           580478

——AGATE (J. [E.])
Ego 9: concluding the autobiography
of James [E.] Agate [: a diary from
Jan. 1st 1946 to June 2nd 1947.
With references to Shakespeare.]
   ports.   illus.   1948.

           594059

——AGATE (J. [E.])
Fantasies and impromptus [: miscel-
laneous essays, containing
Shakespearian references].   1923.

           416072

——Agate (J.[E.]) First nights: [dramatic
criticisms, Oct. 1930- April 1934.
Reprinted from The Sunday Times]

          1934.

           425220

——Agate (J.[E.]) Here's richness: an
anthology [from his works, containing
references to Shakespearian
performances and actors]. With a
foreword by O.Sitwell.

          1942.

           535417

——AGATE (J. [E.])
Immoment toys: a survey of light
entertainment on the London stage,
1920-1943.   1945.

           560085

—AGATE (J. [E.])
    More first nights [: dramatic criti-
    cisms, April, 1934 - Feb., 1937.
    Reprinted from The Sunday Times.
    With references to Shakespeare.]
                    1937.

              473984

—Agate (J.[E.]) My 100 years of
    playgoing. From John O'London's
    Weekly. Dec. 7th, 1935. pp.viii.
    Ports.

                    1935.

              446498

—Agate (J.[E.]) My theatre talks.

                  1933.

              401747

—AGATE (J. [E.])
    Red letter nights: a survey of the
    post Elizabethan drama in actual
    performance on the London stage,
    1921-1943.   1944.

              550347

—AGATE (J. E.)
    A Short view of the English stage,
    1900-1926.   1926.
    The To-day Library.

              423989

—[AGATE (J. E.)]
    A Shorter Ego: the [abridged]
    autobiography of James Agate
    [containing references to
    Shakespearian performances and
    actors].
    ports.   3 vols.   1945-1949.

              568085

—AGATE (J. [E.])
    Their hour upon the stage.
    [Containing criticisms of
    Shakespearian performances.]
    (Cambridge)   1930.
    No. 19 of an edn. limited to 56
    copies signed by the author.

              416071

—AGATE (J. [E.])
    These were actors: extracts from a
    newspaper cutting book, 1811-1833.
    Selected and annotated. [With many
    references to Shakespearian actors,
    actresses and performances.] [1943.]

              546209

—Agate (J.[E.]) Those were the nights
    [:an anthology of dramatic criticism
    1880-1906.With references to
    Shakespearian performances]
    Ports.Illus.

              [1947.]

              587179

—AGATE (J. [E.])
    Thurdsays and Fridays [: articles
    contributed to the Daily Express
    and John O'London's Weekly, including
    On reading Shakespeare: a review of
    L. P. Smith's book; The Majesty of
    Lear; As I like it; A Fine Coriolanus;
    Shakespeare in lounge suits; Mr.
    Gielgud as Lear].   [1941.]

              530462

—ALLEN (A. B.)
    Drama through the centuries and play
    production to-day. [Containing
    references to Shakespeare].
    illus.   dgms.   [1936]

              459417

—Archer (C.) William Archer: life, work,
    and friendships. [With a biblio-
    graphic appendix, and references to
    Shakespeare.] Ports. Illus.

              1931.

              522373

—ARCHER (W.)
    The Criticism of acting. [Including
    references to Shakespeare.] FROM
    The New Review, Vol. 12. [1895.]

              515794

—ARMSTRONG (WILLIAM A.   )

    The Art of Shakespearean production in
    the twentieth century. IN English
    Association. Essays and Studies. New
    Series, Vol.15.   1962.

              706391

—Atkins (R.) Shakespeare on his stage.
    In The Amateur theatre and playwrights'
    journal, Vol. 4, No. 71. Port.
    Illus.

             1937-38.

              482984

—The Australian Elizabethan Theatre
    Trust: the first year. pp. 35.
    ports.   illus.   [1956.]

              665398

—Baxter ([A.]B.) First nights and
    noises off [:dramatic criticism,
    1943-46. With references to
    Shakespearian productions.]Ports.

              [1949.]

              599113

—BAXTER (Sir ARTHUR BEVERLEY)
    First nights and footlights [: a
    collection of dramatic criticisms].
    ports.   illus.   1955.

              650931

—— Baxter (P.) The Drama in Perth: a
history of Perth's early plays,
playhouses, play bills, pageants,
concerts, etc. [With references
to Shakespeare.] Illus.

(Perth)   1907.

575225

—— BEERBOHM (MAX)
Around theatres [: dramatic criticisms,
including Shakespearean performances,
from the "Saturday Review".] (New
York)
2 vols.   1930.

449853

—— BENTLEY (ERIC RUSSELL)
Doing Shakespeare wrong.   IN
Perspectives, No. 3.
1953.   643398/3
_____ IN Bentley (E. R.) In search
of theater.   1954.   647405

—— BISHOP (G. W.)
Barry Jackson and the London theatre.
With a foreword by C. B. Cochran [and
references to Shakespeare].   Illustrations from the designs of Paul Shelving.
port.   1933.   402720
_____ No. 136 of the first edn.,
limited to 200 copies, signed by the
author and artist.   1933.   433802

—— BOAS (GUY)
Shakespeare and the young actor: a
guide to production.   [Including
accounts of Shakespeare performances
at Sloane School, Chelsea.]
ports.   illus.   1955.

646761

—— BOAS (G.)
Shakespeare in modern dress.   FROM
Blackwood's Magazine, February, 1939.

502659

—— Bottomley (G.) Voice and stage.
[Including references to Shakespeare.]
From The Dublin Magazine, October,
1941.

(Dublin)

530200

—— BRAHMS (CARYL) [pseud. i.e. DORIS CAROLINE
ABRAHAMS]
The Rest of the evening's my own [:
a criticism of the English theatre,
1953-1963].   1964.
Includes a chapter on Shakespeare.

724399

—— BROOK (PETER)
Style in Shakespeare production.
IN The Penguin New Writing, Vol. 36.
(Harmondsworth)   1949.

586205/36

—— BROWN (FLORENCE WARNER)
Shakespeare and Gielgud, co-authors of men.
IN SHAKESPEARE QUARTERLY XII: 2.
pp. 133-138.
(New York)   1961.

605711

—— Brown (I.[J.C.]) Producing Shakespeare.
In The Fortnightly Review, N.S.
Vol.133.

1933.

409013

—— Brown (I.[J.C.]) Shakespeare- new ways
for old: a critical commentary on
post-war methods of Shakespearian
production. In The Amateur Theatre
and Playwrights' Journal, Vol.4, No.75.

1937.

467093

—— BROWN (J. M.)
Seeing things [: essays on the theatre,
personalities and life, reprinted from
articles contributed weekly to "The
Saturday Review of Literature".   With
references to Shakespearian productions].
1946.

580620

—— BROWN (J. M.)
Two on the aisle: ten years of the
American theatre in performance
[including Shakespeare on the
contemporary stage.]   (New York)
1938.

529720

—— BROWN, JOHN RUSSELL
English criticism of Shakespeare
performances today.
IN DEUTSCHE SHAKESPEARE-GESELLSCHAFT
WEST, JAHRBUCH 1967.   pp. 163-174.
(Heidelberg)

754129

—— BROWN (JOHN RUSSELL)
Three adaptations.   IN SHAKESPEARE
SURVEY 13.   (Cambridge)
ports.   illus.   1960.

666726

—— BROWN, JOHN RUSSELL
Three kinds of Shakespeare: 1964
productions at London, Stratford-
upon-Avon and Edinburgh.   IN
SHAKESPEARE SURVEY 18.   (Cambridge)
1965.

749826

—— BROWNE (ELLIOTT MARTIN)
English Hamlets of the twentieth century.
IN SHAKESPEARE SURVEY 9.   (Cambridge)
1956.

665210

—— BYRNE (M[URIEL] ST. C.)
Fifty years of Shakespearian production, 1898-1948.   IN SHAKESPEARE
SURVEY 2.   (Cambridge)
illus.   1949.

598403

—— BYRNE (MURIEL ST. C.)
Modern Shakespearean production:
talk [broadcast] 29th July 1949.
ff. 11.
typescript.
Shakespeare and his world.

605270

—CARLETON (P.) ed.
The Amateur stage: a symposium by Flora
Robson, S. Box, M.[S.] Redgrave, L. du G.
Peach, G. Makin, P. Carleton. [With
references to Shakespeare.]   1939.

508149

— CARTER (H.)
The Theatre of Max Reinhardt.   [With
references to productions of
Shakespeare's plays.]
ports. illus. plan.   1914.

539800

—CASSON (Sir LEWIS THOMAS)
The Influence of William Poel on the
modern theatre. [Broadcast] 31st
Dec., 1951.   ff. 9.
typescript.

622923

—CATHOLIC UNIVERSITY OF AMERICA: SPEECH
AND DRAMA DEPARTMENT: PLAYERS INCORPORATED
The Story of Players Incorporated:
"International Repertory Company"
[1949-1954].   pp. 20.   [Washington]
[1954.]

643996

—CHADWICK (S.)
"Theatre Royal": the romance of the
Huddersfield stage, with a record of
the Wareing International Repertory
seasons [and] a foreword by E. Woodhead.
[Containing references to Shakespeare
and the Huddersfield Shakespeare
Festival.] pp. vi, 40. (Huddersfield)
ports. illus.   1941.

526135

— Charques (R.D.) ed., Footnotes to
the theatre [: articles by various
authors. With references to Shakespeare.] Ports. Illus.

1938.

492878

— Chisholm (C.) Repertory: an outline
of the modern theatre movement;
production, plays, management.
[With references to Shakespeare
and a bibliography.] Illus.

1934

426702

—CLURMAN (H.)
The Fervent years: the story of the
Group Theatre and the thirties.
[With references to Shakespeare's
plays.]
ports.   illus.   1946.
[International Theatre and Cinema]

577742

— COGHILL, NEVILL
University contributions to Shakespeare
production in England.
IN SHAKESPEARE JAHRBUCH.   Bd. 93/1957.
pp. 175-185.   (Heidelberg)

10531

—COLE (WENDELL)
Elizabethan stages and open-air
performances in America a half century
ago. IN The Quarterly Journal of Speech,
February 1961. pp.[10.]

667771

—   Corbin (J.) Shakspere his own
stage-manager: a new method and important
discoveries in productions of the New
Theatre [New York]. Illus. From The
Century Magazine, Vol.83. (New York)
1911.

520178

520178

—Courtney (W.L.) Rosemary's letter-
book: the record of a year [partly
reprinted from the Daily Telegraph
and the Glasgow Herald, and including
references to Shakespeare and the
plays]. Frontis.

1909.

435767

—CRAIG (E. G.)
Catalogue of an exhibition of drawings
and models for "Hamlet" and other
plays.   pp. 24.   1912.

451684

—CRAIG (E. G.)
Catalogue of an exhibition of drawings
and models for Hamlet, Macbeth, The
Vikings and other plays.   [Held at
the] City of Manchester Art Gallery,
November 1912.   pp. 42.   (Manchester)
illus.   1912.

590358

—CRAIG (E. G.)
Exhibition of drawings and models for
Hamlet, Macbeth, The Vikings and
other plays.   Arranged by The United
Arts Club, Dublin.   [pp. 21].
illus.   1913.

450640

—CRAIG (E. G.)
An Exhibition of drawings and models
for Hamlet, Macbeth, The Vikings
and other plays.   [Held in] the
City Art Gallery, Leeds.   pp. [24].
illus.   1913.

465734

— Craig (E.G.) A Production: thirty-two
collotype plates of designs projected
or realised for The Pretenders of
Henrik Ibsen, and produced at the
Royal Theatre, Copenhagen, 1926.
[With an introduction containing
references to Shakespeare.]

(Oxford)   1930.

513156

— CROFT (R. M.)
The Theatre: the return of William
Shakespeare['s plays to London theatres].
IN The New English Review, Vol. 13.
1946.

577268

— CROSSE (G.)
  Fifty years of Shakespearean playgoing.

        1940.

        522290

— CROSSE (GORDON)
  Shakespearean performances which I have
  seen, from January, 1890 to July, 1953.
  [by Gordon Crosse] Manuscript. 21 vols.

        1890-1953.

        641917-37

— CROSSE (GORDON)
  Shakespearean playgoing, 1890-1952.
  Ports. Illus.

        1953.

        635983

— DAVID (RICHARD)
  Actors and scholars: a view of
  Shakespeare in the modern theatre.
  IN SHAKESPEARE SURVEY 12.
  (Cambridge)   1959.

        666150

— DAVID (RICHARD)
  Drams of eale: a review of recent
  Shakespearian productions. IN
  SHAKESPEARE SURVEY 10. (Cambridge)
        1957.

        665485

— DAVID (RICHARD)

  Plays pleasant and plays unpleasant : a
  review of Shakespeare productions during
  the winter of 1953-4.Illus.IN Shakespeare
  Survey, [Vol.],8 (Cambridge)
        1955

        647706

— DE BANKE (CECILE)

  Shakespearian stage production then & now.
  With a foreword by H.Miller.Ports.Illus.
  Plans.Dgms.Tables.Bibliogs.
        1954.

        639042

— DENT (A.)
  Preludes & studies [: biographical
  studies, dramatic criticisms, including
  criticisms of Shakespearian performances, and journeys]. With a prefatory
  letter from Sir M. Beerbohm.
  ports. illus.   1942.

        532557

— Dent (E.J.) A Theatre for everybody:
  the story of the Old Vic and
  Sadler's Wells. Illustrated by Kay
  Ambrose. [With references to
  Shakespeare and a bibliography.]
  Ports. Illus.

        1946.

        578232

— Desmond (S.) London nights of long
  ago. [With references to Shakespearian
  performances.] Ports. Illus.

        1927.

        519055

— DOONE (R.)
  Three Shakespearian productions [:
  Hamlet, with John Gielgud, Richard III,
  with Laurence Olivier, and King Lear,
  with Donald Wolfit]. IN The Penguin
  New Writing, 25. (Harmondsworth)
  illus.   1945.

        564884

— DOWNER (ALAN S.)
  A Comparison of two stagings: Stratford-
  upon-Avon and London.
  IN SHAKESPEARE QUARTERLY VI:
  pp. 429-433.
  (New York) 1955.

        605711

— DOWNER (ALAN S.)
  For Jesus' sake forbear: Shakespeare vs.
  the modern theater.
  IN SHAKESPEARE QUARTERLY XIII: 2.
  pp. 219-230.
  (New York) 1962.

        605711

— DOWNER, ALAN S.
  Shakespeare in the contemporary American
  theatre.
  IN SHAKESPEARE JAHRBUCH. Bd. 93/1957.
  pp. 154-174.   (Heidelberg)

        10531

— DUȚU (ALEXANDRU)
  Recent Shakespeare performances in
  Romania.
  IN SHAKESPEARE SURVEY 20. (Cambridge)
        1967.

        766881

— EVANS (GARETH LLOYD)
  Shakespeare, the twentieth century
  and "behaviourism".
  IN SHAKESPEARE SURVEY 20. (Cambridge)
        1967.

        766881

— FARJEON (H.)
  The Shakespearean scene: dramatic
  criticisms.   [1949.]

        599137

— FULLER (ROSALINDE)
  A Shakespeare tour in wartime.
  IN Theatre arts, Vol. 24. (New
  York)   1940.

        525084

— GARNETT (E.)
  "Troilus and Cressida" and the critics.
  IN The Contemporary Review, Vol.103.
        1913.

        243280

    William Poel's production

—— GASSNER (J. W.)
Interpreting Shakespeare.   IN
Gassner (J. [W.]) Producing the
play.   (New York)
   illus.   dgms.   bibliog.   1941.

536928

—— GIELGUD (J.)
Granville-Barker's Shakespeare.
IN Theatre Arts, Vol. 31.   (New
York)   1947.

320431/31

——GLICK (CLARIS)
William Poel: his theories and
influence. IN Shakespeare Quarterly XV: 1.
pp.15-25. (New York)   1964.

605711

——Grein (J.T.) Premières of the year
[1900. With references to
Shakespearian performances].

1901.

541907

—— GUTHRIE (Sir TYRONE)
In various directions: a view of
theatre.
   illus.   1965.
Includes "Hidden motives in five
Shakespearean plays" and "Shakespeare
on stage".

749576

——GUTHRIE (Sir TYRONE)
The Living Shakespeare [No. 2]:
The plays in production.   [Broadcast]
8th October, 1958.   ff. 9.
   typescript.

666021

—— GUTHRIE, Sir TYRONE
Shakespeare in my life.   Produced
by Joseph Hone.   B.B.C. radio
script broadcast 23rd April 1964.

668244

——HARBAGE (ALFRED BENNETT)
Theatre for Shakespeare.   (Alexander
Lectures [in English] 1954-55.)
(Toronto)   1955.

665178

——HEGGIE (BARBARA)
Profiles [: a study of Margaret Webster
as a Shakespearian producer].   FROM
The New Yorker, May 20, 1944.   (New
York)
   port.

578278

——HOPE-WALLACE (P.)
Shakespeare season: Donald Wolfit [at
the] Scala [London].   IN Time and
Tide, Vol. 25.   1944.

562807

—— Houghton (N.) The Old Vic in New York
[including their Shakespearian
performances]. Illus. In Theatre
Arts, Vol. 30.

(New York)   1946.

579721

—— HUBLER (EDWARD)
The Princeton theatrical season
1963-1964. IN Shakespeare Quarterly
XV: 4. pp.403-407. (New York)   1964.

605711

—— HUNT (HUGH)
Contemporary Shakespeare production.
IN The Director in the theatre [:
essays].   1954.

644064

—— HUNT (HUGH)

Old Vic prefaces: Shakespeare and the
producer. Ports. Illus.   1954.

638360

—— HURRY (L.)
Settings & costumes for Sadler's Wells
ballets: Hamlet, 1942; Le Lac des
Cygnes and the Old Vic Hamlet, 1944.
With an introduction by C. W. Beaumont.
Edited by Lillian Browse.   pp. 72.
   illus.   dgms.   1946.
Ariel Books on the Arts.

574856

—— International news [: reports from
correspondents].   IN SHAKESPEARE
SURVEY 1-   (Cambridge)   1948-
From [vol.] 4, 1951 called
"International notes".

590674

—— IRVING (H. B.)
[Summary of lecture] The Theatre of
to-day.   IN The Poetry Review,
[Vol. 4.]   1914.

253079

—— KEMP (THOMAS CHARLES)
Acting Shakespeare: modern tendencies
in playing and production, with special
reference to some recent productions.
IN SHAKESPEARE SURVEY 7.   (Cambridge)
                             1954.

639176

—— KEMP (T. C.)
Birmingham Repertory Theatre: the
playhouse and the man [i.e. Sir Barry
Jackson.   A record of performances,
1924-43].   With a foreword by Sir
Barry Jackson [and references to
Shakespeare].   (Birmingham)
   port.   illus.   1943.

544087

—— KITCHIN (LAURENCE)
Drama in the sixties: form and inter-
pretation.
   illus.   1966.
Includes chapters "On stage" and
"Shakespeare".

750383

—KNIGHT (GEORGE WILSON)
Dramatic papers: material relating
to the Shakespearian and other
productions of G. Wilson Knight,
at Hart House Theatre, Toronto, and
in England.
ports. illus. plans.   1926–

632461

— KOMISARJEVSKY (T.)
Myself and the theatre.   [With
references to Shakespearian produc-
tions].
ports.   illus.   1929.

454084

— KOMISARJEVSKY (T.)
The Theatre and a changing civilisation.
[With references to Shakespeare.]
                              1935.
Twentieth Century Library.

429283

— KOMISARJEVSKY (T.) and SIMONSON (L.)
Settings & costumes of the modern
stage [including some Shakespeare
settings].   Edited by C. J. Holme.
illus.   1933.
Studio Winter Number, 1933.
                          411962

— LINTON (C. D.)
Some recent trends in Shakespearean
staging.   IN E.L.H.: a journal of
English literary history, Vol. 7.
(Baltimore)
bibliog.   1940.

529087

— A Living theatre: the Gordon Craig
School [for the art of the theatre,
at] the Arena Goldoni; The Mask [:
a journal of the art of the theatre,
published at the Arena Goldoni].
pp. 74. (Florence)
illus.   1913.

416075

— MacCARTHY (D.)
The Court Theatre 1904–1907: a
commentary on criticism.   With
an appendix containing reprinted
programmes of the "Vedrenne-Barker
performances".   [With references
to Shakespeare]   1907.

473280

— MacCarthy (D.) Drama [: literary
essays on many of the plays
produced on the London stage since
1913, including plays of Shakespeare].

1940.

522304

— McDOWELL (J. H.)
Shakespeare and modern design.
IN Journal of English and Germanic
Philology, Vol. 46.   (Urbana, Ill.:
University of Illinois)
bibliog.   1947.

600780/46

— Macgeorge (N.) The Arts in Australia
[: an anthology of articles and essays.
With references to Shakespearian
productions]. Ports. Illus.
        (Melbourne)   1948.

597932

—MacLIAMMÓIR (M.)
Three Shakespearian productions: a
conversation.   IN SHAKESPEARE SURVEY 1.
(Cambridge)
illus.   1948.

590674

— McMANAWAY, JAMES GILMER
Shakespearian productions in America
in 1955–56.
IN SHAKESPEARE JAHRBUCH.   Bd. 93/1957.
pp. 145–153.   (Heidelberg)

10531

— McMULLAN (F.)
Producing Shakespeare.   IN PROUTY
(CHARLES TYLER) ed., Shakespeare: of
an age and for all time: the Yale
Shakespeare Festival Lectures.   [New
Haven, Conn.]   1954.

640920

— MACQUEEN-POPE (W. [J.])
Carriages at eleven: the story of
the Edwardian theatre [1897–1914.
With references to performances of
Shakespeare's plays.]
ports.   illus.   1947.

585827

— MANDER (R.) and MITCHENSON (J.)
Merely players [: some broadcast
memories of Shakespearean productions
and the actors that played in them,
of the past 50 years;   recalled by
gramophone records].   Presented by
F. [H.] Grisewood.   ff. 4.
typescript.   1941.

527618

—Marshall (N.) The Other theatre [: a
record of the non-commercial theatre,
1925–1946. With a chapter on the
Shakespeare Memorial Theatre and
references to other Shakespearian
productions]. Illus.

1947.

582293

—The Mask: a journal of the art of the
theatre.   Vols. 1–2; 4–15 (1909–1929).
(London and Florence)
illus. plans. dgms.   14 vols.
                          1908–1929.
Not published 1916–17, 1919–22.
Ceased publication after 1929.
Vol. 3 wanting.   Vol. 8 (1918) issued
as monthly leaflet.   All but Nos. 2–3
wanting.

460751

— MILES (BERNARD) [pseud. John Bancroft]
Rehearsing Shakespeare [: Macbeth].
Broadcast 28th November, 1950.
ff. 12.
typescript.

616419

—— MR. J.H. LEIGH'S Shakespearean readings
   [from 8 plays]: a few press opinions.
                                    [c.1900.]

                                    667381

—— MITCHELL (L.)
   The Effect of modern stage conventions
   on Shakespeare.   IN Theatre Arts,
   Vol. 26.   (New York)   1942.

                                    546127

—— Mottram (R.H.) The Maddermarket
   Theatre. [With] prologue by
   N. Monck [and] epilogue by
   J. Sprott. pp.20. Frontis.

        (Norwich)   [1928.]

                                    418614

—— Nathan (G.J.) The Critic and the
   drama. [With references to
   Shakespeare.]

                            [1922.]

                                    443954

—— NATHAN (G. J.)
   Materia critica [: a critic's notes
   on dramatic criticism and the theatre
   in general.   With references to
   Shakespeare].   (New York)   1924.

                                    544438

—— O'CASEY (S.)
   The Flying wasp: a laughing look-over
   of what has been said about the things
   of the theatre by the English dramatic
   critics, [etc.   With a chapter "The
   Public death of Shakespeare", and
   other Shakespearian references.]
                                    1937.

                                    463460

—— PAPP (JOSEPH)
   The Method and William Shakespeare.
   IN STRATFORD PAPERS ON SHAKESPEARE
   delivered at the 1963 Shakespeare
   Seminar. (Toronto)   1964.

                                    668007

—— Payne (B.I.) The Central figure:
   Shakespeare [in the productions of
   the Drama Department of the Carnegie
   Institute of Technology]. In Theatre
   Arts Monthly, Vol.23.

        (New York)   1939.

                                    510715

—— PAYNE (BEN IDEN)
   Talking of theatre, 2: Variations
   on a theatre theme, No. 10.
   [Shakespeare productions, with special
   reference to W. Poel.]   [Broadcast]
   19th September, 1961.   ff. 5.
   typescript.

                                    666977

—— Play pictorial: an illustrated monthly journal.
   Vols. 1, 3-[75]. [With programmes of, and
   articles on Shakespearean performances.]
   Ports. Illus.   1902-[1939.]
   77 vols.

                                    571864

—— PLAYS AND PLAYERS & THEATRE WORLD,
   Vols. 13-   1966-

   see also Theatre World   766347

—— Priestley (J.B.) Theatre outlook
   [in England. With references to
   Shakespeare]. pp.76. Ports. Illus.
   Maps. Charts.

        1947.

                                    587192

—— 'Programmes of professional performances
   of Shakespeare's plays.
   36 vols.   c.1880-
   This collection is continuously
   augmented by the addition of programmes
   of contemporary productions.

                                    462500

—— PURDOM (CHARLES BENJAMIN)
   Harley Granville Barker: man of the
   theatre, dramatist and scholar.
   [With a list of his writings]
   ports. illus. facsimile.   1955.

                                    651120

—— PURDOM (CHARLES BENJAMIN)
   Producing Shakespeare.
   illus. dgms. bibliog. 1950.
   Theatre and Stage Series.

                                    611305

—— RIGBY (C.)
   Maddermarket Mondays: press articles
   dealing with the famous Norwich Players.
   Foreword by B. Maine.   Published in
   commemoration of the production of
   the whole of Shakespeare's plays at
   the Maddermarket Theatre, Norwich.
   (Norwich)
   port.   illus.   1933.

                                    416881

—— RYLANDS (GEORGE HUMPHREY WOLFESTAN)
   Festival Shakespeare in the West
   End.   IN SHAKESPEARE SURVEY 6.
   (Cambridge)   1953.

                                    631770

—— Scott ([Mrs.] Marian) Chautauqua
   caravan [:experiences of a member of
   a Chautauqua entertainment group.
   With references to Shakespearian
   performances]. Ports. Illus.

        (New York)   1939.

                                    585833

—— [Scrap Book of] Shakespeare programmes
   and play bills with cuttings relating
   thereto.
   2 vols.   1901-1932.

                                    170369

—— Shakespeare on foreign stages [: 5
   illustrations].   IN Theatre arts
   monthly, vol. 16.   1932.

                                    402620

— Shakespeare productions in the United Kingdom, 1950–65. A List compiled from its records by the Shakespeare Memorial Library, Birmingham.   IN SHAKESPEARE SURVEY 5–19. (Cambridge)   1952–1966.

623798

— SHAW (GEORGE BERNARD)
Shaw on Shakespeare: an anthology of Bernard Shaw's writings on the plays and production of Shakespeare. Edited and with an introduction by E. Wilson.   1962.

666943

— SHORT (E. [H.])
Theatrical cavalcade [: a review of the British stage during the last fifty years.   With references to Shakespeare.]
illus.   1942.

537042

— ŠIMKO (JÁN)
Some recent Shakespearean productions in Czechoslovakia.
IN SHAKESPEARE JAHRBUCH.   Bd. 100/101. 1964/1965.   pp. 294–304.   (Weimar)

10531

— SPEAIGHT (ROBERT)
Shakespeare in Britain.
IN SHAKESPEARE QUARTERLY XIV: 1963, pp. 419–432; XVI: 1965, pp. 313–323. (New York)

605711

— SPEAIGHT (ROBERT)
William Poel and the Elizabethan revival.   (Society for Theatre Research.   Annual Publication [4] 1951–52.)
ports.   illus.   chronological table.   bibliog.   1954.

641603

— SPRAGUE (ARTHUR COLBY)
Shakespearian players and performances. (Cambridge, Mass.)
ports.   illus.   1953.
Shakespearian playgoing, pp. 150–176.

635328

— Study and stage [: a criticism of H. Granville-Barker's presentation of Shakespeare].   IN The Times Literary Supplement, 1946.   1946.

580183

— Theatre 1954–5–   [: annual review of dramatic productions and publications, with reference to Shakespeare;   edited by] Ivor Brown.
illus.   1955–

650967

— THEATRE TODAY No.4
Re-thinking Shakespeare. Produced by G. Hughes. I T V television script broadcast 5th April 1965.

typescript.   744156

— THEATRE WORLD, Vols. 41–61. Illus. 1945–65.

1. Vols. 1–40 wanting.
2. After Vol.61, No.491 incorporated in Plays and Players and called "Plays and Players & Theatre World".   Catal. no. 766347.

601552

— TREWIN (J. C.)
The Post-war theatre: a survey. [With references to Shakespearian performances.]   IN ELWIN (M.) ed., Pleasure ground: a miscellany of English writing.
illus.   1947.

582769

— TREWIN, JOHN COURTENAY
Shakespeare on the English stage, 1900–1964: a survey of productions, illustrated from the Raymond Mander and Joe Mitchenson Theatre Collection. 1964.

illus.   667799

— TREWIN (JOHN COURTENAY)
We'll hear a play [: a note-book of the theatre].   With an introduction by Sir B. Jackson.   1949.
Includes references to Shakespeare.

611287

— Vickers (J.), The Old Vic in photographs. With an introduction by J.Burrell [and references to Shakespearian productions.] pp.[vi],90.

1947.

588346

— WALBROOK (H. M.)
A Playgoer's wanderings [: reminiscences of the theatre.   With references to Shakespeare.]
ports.   illus.   1926.

443959

— WALKER (ROY)
Unto Caesar: a review of recent productions.   IN SHAKESPEARE SURVEY 11. (Cambridge)
ports.   illus.   bibliog.   1958.

665816

— WALKER (ROY)
The Whirligig of time: a review of recent productions.   IN SHAKESPEARE SURVEY 12.   (Cambridge)
ports.   illus.   bibliog.   1959.

666150

— WEBSTER (MARGARET)
Shakespeare today.   [With an] introduction by M. R. Ridley.   1957.

665453

— WEIMANN (ROBERT)
Shakespeare on the modern stage: past significance and present meaning.
IN SHAKESPEARE SURVEY 20.   (Cambridge) 1967.

766881

——WELLS, STANLEY
   Shakespeare's text on the modern stage.
   IN DEUTSCHE SHAKESPEARE-GESELLSCHAFT
   WEST, JAHRBUCH 1967. pp. 175-193.
   (Heidelberg)

                 754129

——WEST, ALICK
   The Importance of Shakespeare in the
   contemporary English theatre.
   IN SHAKESPEARE JAHRBUCH. Bd. 103/1967.
   pp. 97-135.   (Weimar)

           10531

——Williams (H.) Four years at the
   Old Vic, 1929-1933. [With references
   to Shakespeare's plays.] Ports.
   Illus.

            1935.

              443094

——Williams (H.) Old Vic saga. Ports.Illus.
   Facsimiles.

          1949.

              602439

——Williams (H.) Producing Shakespeare's
   plays. In Downs (H.) ed.,Theatre
   and stage, Vol.1. Ports. Illus. Dgms.

           1934.

            425661

——Williams (H.) ed.. Vic-Wells: the work
   of Lilian Baylis. [A collection of
   appreciations by those who knew her
   best. With references to Shakespeare.]
   Photographs by A. McBean.

          1938.

           481118

——WILLIAMSON (AUDREY)
   Old Vic drama: a twelve years' study
   of plays and players. With a foreword by Dame Sybil Thorndike [and
   references to Shakespeare].
   ports. illus. bibliog. 1948.

          594695

——WILLIAMSON (AUDREY)

   Old Vic drama, 2, 1947-1957. Ports.
   Illus.   1957.

          665668

——WILLIAMSON (AUDREY)

   Theatre of two decades [: 1930-1950].
   ports. illus.   1951.
   Includes chapters "Homes of Shakespeare"
   and "Shakespeare and the Elizabethans"
   [: productions, 1930-50].

          618557

——Wilson (A.E.) Post-war theatre [:plays
   produced in London since June
   20,1945,including plays of
   Shakespeare].

        [1949.]

          603205

——WISE, ARTHUR
   Weapons in the theatre [: the problems
   of mounting stage fights].
   illus.   1968.

          777351

——WOOD (ROGER) and CLARKE (MARY)

   **Shakespeare at the Old Vic: the Old
   Vic Five-Year First Folio Plan, 1953-4—
   1957-8. Ports. Illus. 5 vols.**
             1954-8.

   1956-7 and 1957-8 by Mary Clarke.

        644305

—— WORLD THEATRE, Vol.XIII. Nr.2
   Shakespeare 1964 [: articles by various
   writers in English and French]. pp.73-
   147. (Bruxelles)   1964.

   illus.   742319

—— WORSLEY (THOMAS CUTHBERT)
   The Fugitive art: dramatic commentaries 1947-1951.
   illus.   1952.

       628091

—— WORSLEY (THOMAS CUTHBERT)
   Stratford and Shakespearian production.
   IN LUMLEY (FREDERICK) ed., Theatre in
   review. [By] E. [W.] Blom [and
   others]. (Edinburgh)
   ports. illus.   1956.

       657684

——YOUNG (S.)
   Immortal shadows: a book of dramatic
   criticism [including performances of
   some Shakespeare plays]. 1948.

       598301

Stagecraft of Shakespeare *see* Dramatic Art of Shakespeare; Stage History and Production, Elizabethan and Jacobean Period

STALKER (ARCHIBALD)
   Is Shakespeare's will a forgery?
   FROM Quarterly Review, April 1940.

       515964

STALKER (ARCHIBALD)
   Shakespeare and the rival poet.
   IN Notes and Queries, Vol. 163.
          1932.

       401809

Stalker (A.) Shakespeare and Tom
   Nashe [: imaginary conversations
   between Coleridge and Lamb.]

   (Stirling)   1935.

       435912

STALKER (ARCHIBALD)
Shakespeare, Marlowe and Nashe [:
critical examinations of Richard III,
Henry V, etc.]   (Stirling)   1936.

462712

STALKER (ARCHIBALD)
Shakespeare's "sonnet" 126.   IN
Notes and Queries, Vol. 162.

1932.

401808

STALKER (ARCHIBALD)
The Sonnets of Shakespeare: imaginary
conversations between Coleridge and
Lamb.   [With a MS. note by the author.]
pp. 36.   (Stirling)   1933.

416882

STAMM (RUDOLF)
Elizabethan stage-practice and the
transmutation of source material by
the dramatists.   IN SHAKESPEARE
SURVEY 12.   (Cambridge)   1959.

666150

STAMM (RUDOLF)

**George Bernard Shaw and Shakespeare's
"Cymbeline". IN D.C. Allen, ed.
"Studies in honor of T.W. Baldwin."
(Urbana, Ill.)**   **1958.**

666314

STAMM (RUDOLF)
The Glass of Pandar's praise: the
word-scenery, mirror passages, and
reported scenes in Shakespeare's
"Troilus and Cressida".   IN English
Association, Essays and Studies,
Shakespeare Quatercentenary ed.
  illus.   1964.

667820

STAMM (RUDOLF)
Hamlet in Richard Flatter's translation.
IN English Studies, Vol. 36.
(Amsterdam)   1955.

485643/36

STAMM (RUDOLF)
Modern 'theatrical' translations of
Shakespeare.   IN SHAKESPEARE SURVEY
16.
  illus.   1963.

667523

STAMM (RUDOLF)
Shakespeare's word-scenery; with
some remarks on stage-history and the
interpretation of his plays.
(Zürich)   1954.
  Veröffentlichungen der Handels-
Hochschule St. Gallen, Reihe B,
Heft 10.

639793

STAMM (RUDOLF)
Sir William Davenant and Shakespeare's
imagery.   IN English Studies, Vol. 24.
(Amsterdam)
  bibliog.   1942.

575608

STAMPFER (J.   )

The Catharsis of "King Lear". IN
Shakespeare Survey. [Vol.] 13.
(Cambridge)   1960.

666726

Standen, Anthony Sir *works relating to*

——ASHE (GEOFFREY)
Shakespeare and a Catholic exile.
IN The Month, New Series Vol. 5.
1951.

404302/2/5

——ASHE (GEOFFREY)
Shakespeare's first manuscript?
IN The Month, New Series Vol. 6.
1951.

404302/2/6

STANDFAST (W. G.)
The Beauties of Shakspere: fifty-two
engravings.   [1875.]

666346

STANESBY (SAMUEL) illus.
Lewis (E. G.)
Shakespearean creations.   Illuminated
by S. Stanesby.   [?1866.]

368396

STANFORD (Sir CHARLES VILLIERS)

The Rain it raineth every day [: When
that I was and a little tiny boy, from
Twelfth Night]. (Boosey & Co.)
[N.D.]

667877

STANFORD (WILLIAM BEDELL)
Ghosts and apparitions in Homer,
Aeschylus and Shakespeare.   FROM
Hermathena: papers on literature,
science and philosophy, by members
of Trinity College, Dublin, No. 56.
(Dublin)
  bibliog.   1940.

538659

STANFORD (W. B.)
Greek metaphor: studies in theory
and practice.   [With references
to Shakespeare's use of metaphor.]
(Oxford)   1936.

539700

STANFORD UNIVERSITY
Ashland Studies in Shakespeare: notes,
comment, and reading-lists to accompany
classwork [in the Institute of
Renaissance Studies] established by
the English Department of Stanford
University in association with the
Oregon Shakespeare Festival.
(Ashland, Ore.)
  illus. bibliog.   1954-

                     666259

Stanford University
GRAY (H. D.)
The Original version of "Love's
labour's lost", with a conjecture as
to "Love's labour's won". pp. 55.
([Palo Alto] Cal.)   1918.

                     288847

STANISLAVSKY (KONSTANTIN) pseud.
An Actor prepares [: learning to act
for the Moscow Art Theatre, with references to Shakespeare. Translated, with
a foreword, by Elizabeth R. Hapgood].
  port.   1936.

                     464580

STANISLAVSKY (KONSTANTIN) pseud.
Creating a role. Translated by E. R.
Hapgood.
                1963.

                     667656

STANISLAVSKY (KONSTANTIN) pseud.
Director's plan for "Othello", Act III,
Scene IV.   IN COLE (TOBY) and CHINOY
(HELEN KRICH) ed. Directing the play:
a source book of stagecraft, edited with
an illustrated history of directing by
T. Cole and Helen K. Chinoy.
  ports. illus. dgms. facsimiles. bibliog.
                   1954.

                     641766

[STANISLAVSKY (KONSTANTIN)] pseud.
Stanislavsky produces Othello [at the
Moscow Art Theatre: the text of the
play, with instructions for production].
Translated from the Russian by Helen
Nowak.
  frontis. plans.   1948.

                     592011

Stanislavsky, Konstantin *works relating to*

——CRAIG (EDWARD GORDON) [pseud. Tom Fool]
  Craig in Moscow [: interview with D.
  Tutaev concerning Craig's production
  of Hamlet at the Moscow Art Theatre
  C. 1909 and his meeting with Stanislavsky,
  B.B.C.] Broadcast script. [Programme
  transmitted] 25 December 1960. ff.7.

                     667035

STANLEY (A. J.) publisher
The "Reliable" guide to Stratford-
on-Avon. pp. 24.   (Stratford-
on-Avon)
  illus. plan.   [c.1915.]

                     665287

**Stanley (C.) Matthew Arnold [: a
critical study. With references
to Shakespeare.]**

    (Toronto)   1938.

                     495504

Stanley, Thomas Sir *works relating to*

——MALONE (E.)
  Autograph letter, dated 28 April, 1791,
  addressed to the incumbent of Tong
  Church, Salop, together with a copy of
  a letter in reply and a copy of an
  inscription, concerning the epitaph on
  the tomb of Sir Thomas Stanley in Tong
  Church, said to have been written by
  Shakespeare. IN A Collection of
  seventy-six original letters mainly
  addressed to the members of the
  Pakington Family.
  manuscript.   [1539]-1829.

                     500985

——WHITE (W.)
  All round the Wrekin. [With a reference to a rhyming epitaph on the tomb
  of Sir Thomas Stanley in Tong church,
  said to have been written by
  Shakespeare.]   1860.   27886
  ——— 2nd edn.   1860.   462078

STARKE (A. H.)
Sidney Lanier: a biographical and
critical study. [With notes and
references to Shakespeare.]
(Chapel Hill, N.C.)
  ports. illus. facsimiles. bibliog.
                   1933.

                     410765

STARKIE (W. J. M.)
Wit and humour in Shakespeare.
IN GOLLANCZ ([Sir] I.) ed., A Book
of homage to Shakespeare.
  ports. illus. facsimiles. [1916.]

                     264175

STARNES (DeWITT TALMAGE)
Bilingual dictionaries of Shakespeare's
day. IN Publications of the Modern
Language Association of America, Vol.
52. (Menasha, Wis.)   1937.

                     485791

STARNES (DeWITT TALMAGE)
More about Dryden as an adapter of
Shakespeare. IN University of Texas,
Studies in English, No. 8. (Austin,
Texas)   1928.

                     442436

Starnes (D.T.) More about the Prince
Hal legend. [With bibliographical
notes.] From Philological quarterly,
Vol. 15.

(Iowa)   1936.

484070

STARNES (DeWITT TALMAGE)
[Review of] Shakespeare and the tragic
theme, by A. H. R. Fairchild.   IN
Modern Language Quarterly, Vol. 6.
(Seattle)   1945.

571544

STARNES (DeWITT TALMAGE)
Shakespeare and Apuleius [:
Shakespeare's knowledge and use of
Apuleius' Golden Ass.] IN Publications
of the Modern Language Association of
America, Vol. 60.   (Menasha, Wis.)
bibliog.   1945.

569026

Starnes, Dewitt Talmage *works relating to*

——HARRISON, THOMAS PERRIN and others, eds.
Studies in honor of DeWitt T. Starnes,
edited by T. P. Harrison, A. A. Hill,
E. C. Mossner, J. Sledd.   (Austin,
Tex.)   1967.

772917

STARNES (DeWITT TALMAGE) and TALBERT
(ERNEST WILLIAM)
Classical myth and legend in Renaissance
dictionaries: a study of Renaissance
dictionaries in their relation to the
classical learning of contemporary
English writers.   (Chapel Hill, N.C.)
illus.   facsimiles.   1955.
Includes a chapter "Shakespeare and
the dictionaries".

656476

STARR (N. C.)
The Dynamics of literature [including
criticism of Shakespeare's works and
bibliographical notes].   (New York)
1945.

575539

STASHEFF (E.) and DAVIS (ESTELLE H.)
Shakespearean nights: unified arrangements of interwoven scenes.   Introduction by Letitia Raubicheck.
(New York)
illus.   1935.

445069

Statham (H.H.) The Morality of Shakespeare. In The Nineteenth century
and after, Vol. 63.

1908.

208524

Stationers' Company, London

——DICKEY (FRANKLIN)
The Old man at work: forgeries in the
Stationers' Registers.
IN SHAKESPEARE QUARTERLY XI: 1.
pp. 39-47.
(New York)   1960.

605711

——In commemoration of the First Folio
Tercentenary: a re-setting of the
preliminary matter of the First Folio,
with a catalogue of Shakespeariana
exhibited in the Hall of the Worshipful
Company of Stationers.   Introduction
by Sir I. Gollancz.   pp. 56.
(Shakespeare Association)
facsimiles.   1923.
Half t.p. missing.

428768

——KIRSCHBAUM (LEO)
Shakespeare and the Stationers.
(Ohio State University.   Graduate
School Monographs.   Contributions
in Languages and Literature, No.15:
English Series 5.)   (Columbus,
Ohio)
bibliog.   1955.

648104

STATON, WALTER F.
Ovidian elements in 'A Midsummer Night's
Dream". IN The Huntington Library
Quarterly, Vol.26. (San Marino, Cal.)
1963.

494029

Statues *see* Portraits and Monuments

Stauffer (D.A.) The Art of biography
in eighteenth century England. [With
bibliographical references, a]
bibliographical supplement [and
references to Shakespeare's influence
on biography].   2 vols.

(Princeton)   1941.

531285

STAUFFER (D. A.)
The Nature of poetry.   [With references to Shakespeare.]   (New York)
bibliog.   1946.

586113

STAUFFER (D. A.)
Shakespeare's world of images: the
development of his moral ideas.
(New York)   1949.

605572

STAUNTON (H.)
Shakespeare.   IN The Imperial
dictionary of universal biography:
a series of original memoirs of
distinguished men by various writers,
conducted by J. Eadie [and others,
and edited by] J. F. Waller.   Vol. 3.
ports.   illus.   [1865.]

505393

[STEAD (W. T.)]
First impressions of the Theatre.
1 - My first play: "The Tempest",
at His Majesty's.   IN The Review
of Reviews, Vol. 30.   1904.

186085

STEAD (W. T.)
First impressions of the theatre.
[Reviews on 'The Taming of the
shrew', 'King Lear', and 'Hamlet',
and an article: 'Shakespeare at
Stratford'.]   IN The Review of
Reviews, Vol. 31.   1905.

189564

STEADMAN (JOHN M.)
Falstaff as Actaeon: a dramatic emblem.
IN SHAKESPEARE QUARTERLY XIV: 3.
pp. 231-244.
(New York) 1963.

605711

STEARNS (C. W.)
The Shakspeare treasury of widsom
and knowledge.   (New York)
illus.   1878.

584484

Stearns (M.W.) Hamlet and Freud.
In College English, Vol.10.

(Chicago)   1948-9.

598860/10

Steeds (P.) Two lesser known plays
[: summary of a lecture on 'Measure
for Measure' and 'Troilus and
Cressida']. In The Poetry Review,
[Vol.4.]

1914.

253079

STEEL (ANTHONY BEDFORD)
Richard II.   With a foreword by
G. M. Trevelyan [and references to
Shakespeare's play.]   (Cambridge)
facsimile.   1941.

528403

STEEL, CHRISTOPHER
A Shakespeare symphony: symphony no.3
for baritone solo, S A T B and orchestra,
Opus 25.   1966.

763624

STEELE (R. R.), SIMPSON (P.) and
ONIONS (C. T.)
The Sciences: Alchemy.   IN
Shakespeare's England, vol. 1.
(Oxford)
illus.   bibliogs.   facsimiles.
1917.

435745

Steen (Marguerite) Ellen Terry. [With
Shakespearian references]. In
The Post Victorians.

1933.

412642

Steen (Marguerite) The Lost one: a
biography of Mary (Perdita) Robinson.
[With references to Shakespeare,
and a bibliography.] Ports.Illus.

1937.

466583

Steevens, George *works relating to*

— BOADEN (J.)
A Letter to G. Ste[e]vens, Esq.
containing a critical examination
of the papers of Shakspeare,
published by Mr. S. Ireland [: a
review].   IN The Monthly Mirror,
Vol. 1.   1796.

520768

— M. [pseud.]

Sketch of the life, and brief observations
on the Shakespeare of the late G. Steevens,
Esq. &c. Frontis. From The European
Magazine, Vol.61.   [1812.]

564837

—[Review of] The Plays of William
Shakspeare, [with] notes by
S. Johnson and G. Steevens.   2nd
edn. revised and augmented [by
I. Reed, 1778].   IN The Monthly
Review, Vol. 62.   1780.

1462

—[Review of] The Plays of William
Shakspeare, [with] notes by
S. Johnson and G. Steevens.   3rd
edn. revised and augmented by
[I. Reed,] 1785.   IN The Monthly
Review, Vol. 75.   1786.

1478

—[Review of] The Plays of William
Shakspeare, in 15 volumes, with the
corrections and illustrations of
various commentators.   To which are
added notes, by S. Johnson and
G. Steevens.   The 4th edn.   Revised
and augmented; with a glossarial index
by the editor of Dodsley's Collection
of old plays [i.e. I. Reed].   IN The
British Critic, Vol. 1.   1793.

22191

STEEVES (G. W.)
Medical allusions in the writings
of Francis Bacon.   Reprinted from
the Proceedings of the Royal Society
of Medicine, 1913.   Vol. 6.   pp. 21.
1913.

558421

Stefan (Paul) <u>see</u> Werfel (Franz V.)
and Stefan (Paul)

STEFÁNSSON (JÓN)
An Eddic homage to William Shakespeare
(culled from Eddic poems).   [With
English translation.]

IN GOLLANCZ ([Sir] I.) ed., A Book
of homage to Shakespeare.
ports.   illus.   facsimiles.   [1916.]

264175

STEFÁNSSON (JÓN)
Shakespeare at Elsinore.   IN The
Contemporary Review, Vol. 69.
1896.

134265

STEHLÍKOVÁ (EVA)
Thersites, a deformed and scurrilous
Grecian.   IN
CHARLES UNIVERSITY ON SHAKESPEARE:
essays edited by Z. Stříbrný.   (Praha)
illus.   1966.

762631

STEIN (ARNOLD)
Macbeth and word-magic.   FROM The
Sewanee Review, Vol. 59.   pp. [14].
[Sewanee, Tenn.]   1951.

636334

Stein (Elizabeth) Caxton's Recuyell
and Shakespeare's Troilus. <u>In</u>
Modern Language Notes, vol.45,1930.

(Baltimore)

439157

STEIN (ELIZABETH P.)
David Garrick, dramatist.   [With
Shakespearian references.]   (New York)
ports.   illus.   bibliog.   1938.
The Modern Language Association of
America, Revolving Fund Series.

483092

Stein (Jess M.) Horace Walpole and
Shakespeare. <u>From</u> Studies in Philology, vol.31.

(Baltimore)   1934.

441600

S[TEIN] (KURT M.)
Die Schönste Lengevitch: [humorous
verses including a poem on Hamlet.]
With an introduction by R. [T.]
Atwater.   (Chicago)   1926.

396040

STEINBERG (MOLLIE B.)
The History of the Fourteenth Street
Theatre [including references to
Shakespearean productions.   With an
introduction by Eva Le Gallienne].
(New York)
ports.   facsimiles.   1931.

544831

STEMPEL (DANIEL)
The Transmigration of the crocodile.
IN SHAKESPEARE QUARTERLY VII,
pp. 59-72.
(New York)   1956.

605711

STENDHAL, pseud. [i.e.
Marie Henri Beyle]

Racine and Shakespeare. Translated by
G. Daniels. Foreword by A. Maurois.
[New York]   1962.

667548

Stendhal, *pseud.* Marie Henri Beyle *works relating to*

—— Green (F.C.) Stendhal [: a study of
his life and works, with references
to Shakespeare.]

(Cambridge)   1939.

497745

ŠTĚPÁNEK (VLADIMÍR)
The Importance of Shakespeare for the
formation of modern Czech literature. IN
CHARLES UNIVERSITY ON SHAKESPEARE:
essays edited by Z. Stříbrný.   (Praha)
illus.   1966.

762631

STEPHEN (Sir LESLIE)
Men, books and mountains: essays.
Collected, and with an introduction,
by S. O. A. Ullmann.
bibliog.   1956.
Includes a chapter "Did Shakespeare
write Bacon?"

657613

STEPHEN ([Sir] LESLIE)
Self-revelation of Shakespeare.   IN
Booklovers Edition [of] Shakespeare
[Vol. 11].   [1937].
University Society, New York.

475456

STEPHEN ([Sir] LESLIE)
Shakespeare as a man.   IN The National
Review, Vol. 37.   1901.

158872

[Stephens (G.)] Introductory remarks
and an analysis of the characters.
In Shakespeare (W.) "The Tempest":
an outline sketch of the play.
pp.33.
(Stockholm)   1836.

417288

STEPHENS (J.)
Essayes and characters, 1615.
IN HALLIWELL (J. O.) Books of characters.   1857.
Contains a character of "A Base
mercenary poet", believed to be
modelled on Shakespeare.   Edn. limited
to 25 copies.

59738

STEPHENSON (ANTHONY A.)

New Readings for old., the text of Shakespeare
[:review of New Readings in Shakespeare by
C.J.Sisson] IN The Month, New Series, Vol.15.

1956.

404303/2/15.

STEPHENSON (ANTHONY A.)
The Significance of "Cymbeline".
IN Scrutiny, Vol. 10.   (Cambridge)
bibliog.   1942.

538076

STEPPAT ([Mrs.] MARGARET [A. A.])
Shakespeare in the classroom:
preparatory study and exercises in
dramatic work which lead up to the
reading of the plays.   pp. 86.
1933.

411351

Sterling (T. S.) and Holme (J. W.) eds.
LAMB (CHARLES and MARY [A.])
Tales from Shakespeare.   Abridged
and simplified by T. S. Sterling and
J. W. Holme.   (Allahabad)   1924.
The Victory Series for Indian Students,
No. 5.

465620

STERN (EDWARD SAMUEL) and WHILES (WILLIAM
HERBERT)
Three Ganser states and Hamlet [: an
examination of the case of Hamlet from
a psychiatric viewpoint, giving reasons
for believing that he suffered from a
particular state of mind called the
Ganser state, named after Dr. Ganser].
FROM The Journal of Mental Science,
Vol. 88.   1942.
For a reply to this article, by T. M.
Davie, see catal. no. 552445.

550831

STERN (P. Van D.)
... And William Shakespeare.   IN
Ten years and William Shakespeare:
a survey of the publishing activities
of The Limited Editions Club from
Oct. 1929 to Oct. 1940 [by various
authors].   pp. 82.   ([New York]:
Limited Editions Club)
port.   illus.   1940.

528141

STERNBECK (A.)
A Gateway to Shakespeare: stories
from Shakespeare.   [English text
with German notes.]   (Leipzig)
port.   illus.   1930.
Französische und englische Schulbibliothek, Reihe A, Bd. 198.

450313

Sternbeck (Alfred) ed.
[LAMB (CHARLES and LAMB (MARY ANN)]
Stories from Shakespeare's plays
(Hamlet, Macbeth).   Herausgegeben
[mit Anmerkungen] von A. Sternbeck.
pp. 30.   (Bielefeld)   1926.
Velhagen & Klasings Franșösische und
Englische Lesebogen Nr. 36.

332412

STERNDALE-BENNETT (JOHN)
Shakespeare in Shoreditch: a play in
one act.   ff. 20.   (Wateringbury)
typescript.   [1933.]

534906

STERNE (L.)
Letters.   [With references to
Shakespeare and David Garrick.]
Edited [with preface and introduction]
by L. P. Curtis.   (Oxford)
ports.   illus.   facsimile.   maps.
1935.

433218

STERNE, RICHARD L.
John Gielgud directs Richard Burton
in "Hamlet".   A journal of rehearsals
[with the prompt-script].   (New
York)
illus.   1967.   767568
--- 2nd edn.   1968.   776088

STERNFELD (FREDERICK W.)
The Dramatic and allegorical function
of music in Shakespeare's tragedies.
IN Annales Musicologiques, Tome 3.
1955.

637889/3

STERNFELD (FREDERICK WILLIAM)
Lasso's music for Shakespeare's "Samingo".
IN SHAKESPEARE QUARTERLY IX: 2.
pp. 105-116.
(New York)   1958.

605711

STERNFELD, FREDERICK WILLIAM
Music and ballads [: in Elizabethan
England].   IN SHAKESPEARE SURVEY 17.
(Cambridge)   1964.

667822

STERNFELD, FREDERICK WILLIAM
Music in Shakespearean tragedy.   1963.

illus. Studies in the history
of music.   667660

STERNFELD, FREDERICK WILLIAM
Ophelia's version of the Walsingham
song.   IN Music & letters, Vol. 45,
No. 2, April 1964: Shakespeare and
music.

668211

STERNFELD (FREDERICK W.   )

Shakespeare's use of popular song.
Bibliog. IN [Davis (H.) and Gardner
(Helen L.) eds.,] Elizabethan and
Jacobean studies. (Oxford)
                                    1959.

                          687986

STERNFELD (FREDERICK W.)
Twentieth-century studies in
Shakespeare's songs, sonnets, and
poems.   1: Songs and music.   IN
SHAKESPEARE SURVEY 15.   (Cambridge)
                                    1962.

                          667174

STEVENS (DENIS)
The Five songs in Shakespeare['s]
"As you like it", adapted and arranged
from sources contemporary with the
play.   pp. 8.
   illus.   [1956.]
Hinrichsen Edition No. 1564.

                          665584

STEVENS (G. A.)
Distress upon distress; or, Tragedy
in true taste: a heroi-comi-parodi-
tragedi-farcical burlesque in two
acts.   With annotations [etc.] by
Sir Henry Humm [i.e. G. A. Stevens]
and notes by Paulus Purgantius
Pedasculus [i.e. G. A. Stevens.   A
satire on Sir T. Hanmer's and W.
Warburton's editions of Shakespeare.]
                                    1752.

                          481297

STEVENS (HAROLD CHARLES GILBARD)
Hamlet in modern-rush.   IN Stevens
(H. C. G.) Sir Herbert is deeply
touched, [etc.: three one-act plays.
With a foreword by G. Graves].   pp. 40.
                                    1931.

                          387514

STEVENS (HAROLD CHARLES GILBARD)
High-speed Shakespeare: Hamlet,
Julius Caesar, Romeo and Juliet:
three tragedies in a tearing hurry.
pp. 60.   1934.
   "Hamlet" is a reprint of "Hamlet in
modern-rush".

                          429426

STEVENS, JOHN,
   Music and illusion in Shakespeare.
Produced by R. Layton. B.B.C. radio
script broadcast 22nd November 1964.

     typescript.   744465

STEVENS, JOHN
Shakespeare and the music of the
Elizabethan stage: an introductory
essay.   IN HARTNOLL, PHYLLIS, ed.,
Shakespeare in music: essays by
J. Stevens, C. Cudworth, W. Dean,
R. Fiske.   With a catalogue of
musical works.   1964.

                          668315

Stevens   (Kate) Hiking with
Shakespeare.   In Box (S.) ed.,
Monologues and duologues of
to-day.

                          1935.

                          434937

STEVENS (RICHARD JOHN SAMUEL)
The Cloud cap't towers: glee for six
voices, composed by R. J. S. Stevens.
pp. [4.]   [c.1880.]

                          538780

STEVENS (RICHARD JOHN SAMUEL)
The Cloud-capp'd towers: part song
for S.S.A.A. (unaccompanied).
Arranged by R. Dunstan.   pp. [7.]
                                    [c.1920.]
School Music Review.

                          594167

STEVENS (RICHARD JOHN SAMUEL)
The Cloud-capt towers.
            [from "The Tempest"]
Adapted for men's voices.   IN
DAVY [J.] The Bay of Biscay.   [Words
by] A. Cherry.   (Curwen)   [c.1925.]

                          594181

STEVENS (RICHARD JOHN SAMUEL)
O mistress mine: glee for five voices,
composed by R. J. S. Stevens.   pp. 5.
                                    [?1785]

                          594120

STEVENS (RICHARD JOHN SAMUEL)
Sigh no more, ladies: glee for 5
voices, composed by R. J. S. Stevens.
pp. [4.]   (J. Bland)   [c.1790.]

                          599130

STEVENS (RICHARD JOHN SAMUEL)
Sigh no more ladies: a duett by
J. R. S. Stevens.   ff. [2.]
                                    [c.1795.]

                          600306

STEVENS (RICHARD JOHN SAMUEL)
Sigh no more ladies, composed by
R. J. S. Stevens: glee [for five
voices].   pp. 19-23.   [c.1800.]

                          568591

STEVENS (RICHARD JOHN SAMUEL)
Sigh no more ladies: glee for five
voices.
                           pp. 193-
196.   [1822.]
   Composer's signature on p. 193.

                          628454

STEVENS (RICHARD JOHN SAMUEL)
Sigh no more, ladies.   IN STANFORD
([Sir] C. V.) ed., The National song
book.   1906.

                          520195

STEVENS (R. J. [S.])
Sigh no more, ladies; arranged for
male voices (T.T.B.B.) by T. F. Dunhill.
pp. 5.   1930.

                          414144

STEVENS (RICHARD JOHN SAMUEL)
Ye spotted snakes: glee for four
voices. Music [by] R. J. S. Stevens
[etc.]. pp. 25. [c.1800.]

552144

STEVENS (RICHARD JOHN SAMUEL)
Ye spotted snakes. pp. [4.]
[c.1880.]
Novello's Standard Glee Book.

538795

Stevens, Richard John Samuel *works relating to*

—— CUDWORTH, CHARLES
Two Georgian classics: Arne and
Stevens. IN Music & letters, Vol. 45,
No. 2, April 1964: Shakespeare and
music. 1964.

668211

STEVENS (T. P.)
Elizabethan playhouses in Southwark.
FROM Southwark Diocesan Gazette,
vol. 23. pp. [2.]
illus. 1942.

540155

STEVENS (T. P.)
Shakespeare and Southwark. pp. 12.
(Putney)
illus. [1945.]

567507

STEVENS (THOMAS WOOD)
Highways Cross: [a play about
Shakespeare]. IN Stevens (T. W.)
The Nursery-maid of Heaven and other
plays. (New York) 1926.

395318

STEVENSON (ALLAN H.)
The Case of the decapitated cast or "The
Night-walker" at Smock Alley.
IN SHAKESPEARE QUARTERLY VI:
pp. 275-296.
(New York) 1955.

605711

STEVENSON (ALLAN H.)
Shakespearian dated watermarks. IN
Studies in Bibliography Vol. 4.
(Charlottesville, Va.) 1951.

598680/4

STEVENSON (BURTON EGBERT) ed.
The Standard book of Shakespeare
quotations, compiled and arranged
by B. Stevenson. [1953.]

641659

STEVENSON (BURTON [EGBERT]) ed.
Stevenson's book of Shakespeare
quotations, being also a concordance
& a glossary of the unique words &
phrases in the plays & poems.
1938.

481636

STEVENSON, DAVID LLOYD
The Achievement of Shakespeare's
Measure for Measure. (Ithaca, N.Y.)
1966.

763846

STEVENSON (D. L.)
The Love-game comedy [: love and courtship
in literature, from the Middle Ages to
Elizabethan times. With bibliographical
notes and a bibliography]. (New York)
1946.
(Columbia University Studies in English
and Comparative Literature, No. 164.)

575213

STEVENSON, DAVID [L.]
The Meditations of William Shakespeare.
An Introduction to the Shakespeare
anagrams [in the Sonnets]. (New York)
1965.

illus. 746860

STEVENSON (DAVID L.   )

The Role of James I in Shakespeare's
'Measure for Measure'. IN E.L.H. Vol.26,
No.2. (Baltimore, Md.) 1959.

430295/26

Stevenson, David L. *works relating to*

—— RENWICK (W. L.)
[Review of] Stevenson (D. L.) The Love-
game comedy. IN The Review of English
Studies, Vol. 23. (Oxford)
1947.

318239/23

STEVENSON (Sir JOHN ANDREW)
And will he not come again. [Words
by W. Shakespeare from "Hamlet".]
A glee for three voices, with an
accompaniment for the pianoforte or
harp. pp. 4. [c.1825.]

639840

STEVENSON (Sir JOHN ANDREW)
The Fairy glee, with chorusses and
accompaniments for two performers
on the piano forte.   The words
from Shakespear [or rather, anonymous].
pp. [ii] 22.   (Dublin)   [1800]
   Probably sung at a performance of
"A Midsummer Night's Dream".

628451

STEVENSON (Sir J. A.)
Tell me where is fancy bred?
Duetto ... arranged for two treble
voices by [Sir] H. R. Bishop.   Sung
in Shakespeare's Comedy of Errors.
pp. 7.   [c.1880.]

458155

STEVENSON (Sir JOHN ANDREW)
That strain again [: song].   The
words by Shakespeare [from Twelfth
Night].   pp. 12-13.   [Dublin]
                           [c.1800]

646819

STEVENSON (ROBERT)
Shakespeare's cardinals and bishops.
FROM The Crozer Quarterly, Vol. 27.
pp. 23.   (Chester, Pa.)   1950.

620111

STEVENSON (ROBERT)
Shakespeare's interest in Harsnet's
"Declaration".   IN P.M.L.A.:
Publications of the Modern Language
Association of America, Vol. 67.
(New York)   1952.

428321/67

STEVENSON (ROBERT)
Shakespeare's religious frontier.
(The Hague)
bibliog.   1958.

665978

STEVENSON (T. J.)
Shylock.   FROM The English Journal,
vol. 17.   pp. [10.]   (Chicago)
                               1928.

537393

STEVENSON-REECE (GEORGE)
I knew Ellen Terry.   [Woman's hour,
broadcast] 25th October, 1948.   ff. 4.
typescript.

596478

STEWART (BAIN TATE)
The Misunderstood dreams in the plays
of Shakespeare and his contemporaries.
IN Essays in honor of Walter Clyde
Curry [by various authors].
(Nashville, Tenn.)
port.   bibliog.   1955.
Vanderbilt Studies in the Humanities.

671926

STEWART (CAROL)
Poems of sleep and dream.
[Including extracts from Shakespeare.]
Chosen by Carol Stewart with original
lithographs by R. Colquhoun.   1947.
New Excursions into English Poetry.

589908

STEWART ([Mrs.] HELEN HINTON)
The Character of Desdemona.   FROM
The Contemporary Review, 1911.
pp. [14.]

389206

STEWART (Mrs. [HELEN HINTON])
Light on the early "Hamlet": historical
associations and prototypes.   pp. 51.
(Ladies' Guild of Francis St. Alban)
                               [1912.]

559069

STEWART (HUMPHREY JOHN)
Scenes from Shakespeare's "The Tempest":
suite for organ.   No. 1. "The Shipwreck".
pp. 8.   No. 2. "The Enchanted isle".
pp. 6.   No. 3. "Ferdinand and Miranda".
pp. 6.   No. 4. "Caliban".   pp. 6.
No. 5. "Ariel".   pp. 12.   No. 6. "The
Masque of Ceres" wanting. (Philadelphia)
5 vols.   [1929.]

575719

STEWART (JOHN INNES MACKINTOSH) [pseud.
Michael Innes]
   The Blinding of Gloster [in the
third act of King Lear.]   IN The
Review of English Studies, vol. 21.
(Oxford)
bibliog.   [1945.]

570955

Stewart (John Innes Mackintosh) [pseud.
            Michael Innes]

Character and motive in Shakespeare: some
recent appraisals examined. [With
bibliographical notes.]
                               1949.

597958

STEWART (JOHN INNES MACKINTOSH) [pseud.
Michael Innes]
   "The Danish tragedy":   a programme
embodying conjectural scenes from
Thomas Kyd's lost play, circa 1585,
the immediate source of Shakespeare's
"Hamlet".   [Broadcast] 5th March 1958.
ff. 41.
typescript.

665786

STEWART (JOHN INNES MACKINTOSH) [pseud.
MICHAEL INNES]
Discoveries in Shakespeare, by M.
Innes.   1: A Visitor to Dorset
Garden [during a rehearsal of Macbeth].
Produced by Rayner Heppenstall.
[Broadcast] 2nd April, 1953.   ff.21.
typescript.

634678

STEWART (JOHN INNES MACKINTOSH) [pseud.
MICHAEL INNES]
Discoveries in Shakespeare, by M.
Innes.   3: A Smack of Hamlet.
Produced by Rayner Heppenstall.
[Broadcast] 21st May, 1953.   ff. 19.
typescript.

634679

STEWART (JOHN INNES MACKINTOSH) [pseud.
MICHAEL INNES]
Discoveries in Shakespeare, by M.
Innes.   4: The Trial of Ancient
Iago.   Produced by Rayner Heppenstall.
[Broadcast] 22nd June, 1953. ff. 38.
 typescript.

634680

STEWART (JOHN INNES MACKINTOSH) [pseud.
Michael Innes]
 "A Discovery of the Bermudas": an
inquiry into the sources of "The
Tempest".   Produced by R. Heppenstall.
[Broadcast] 29th September, 1959.
ff. 37.
 typescript.

666285

Stewart (John Innes Mackintosh) [pseud.
                    Michael Innes]

Hamlet, revenge! : a story in four parts,
by Michael Innes
                    1937.

468360

Stewart (John Innes Mackintosh) [pseud.
                    Michael Innes]

The Hawk and the handsaw [: Shakespearean
criticism in dramatic form, introducing
characters from"Hamlet"]. Written by M.
Innes   ]Produced by R. Heppenstall.
[Broadcast on the] Third Programme: 21st
November 1948. ff.[i] 47. Typescript.

599860

Stewart (John Innes Mackintosh) [pseud.
                    Michael Innes]
'Julius Caesar' and 'Macbeth' : two notes
on Shakespearean technique. [With bibliographical notes.] In The Modern Language
Review, Vol.40.
            (Cambridge.)   1945.

571545

Stewart (John Innes Mackintosh) [pseud.
                    Michael Innes]
"The Mysterious affair at Elsinore" :written
and recorded by M. Innes   Producer:
D. Cleverdon. [Broadcast] 26th June, 1949.
ff. [ii] 13. Typescript.

605247

STEWART (JOHN INNES MACKINTOSH) [pseud.
MICHAEL INNES]
 The Road to Dunsinane [: a critical
speculation on Macbeth in dramatic
form].   Broadcast 1st November, 1950.
ff. 19, 23-58.
 typescript.

616417

STEWART (JOHN INNES MACKINTOSH) [pseud.
Michael Innes]
 Shakespeare's characters: talk
[broadcast] 23rd July 1949.   ff. 10.
 typescript.
 Shakespeare and his world.
                    605268

STEWART (JOHN INNES MACKINTOSH) [pseud.
Michael Innes]
 Shakespeare's men and their morals.
IN GARRETT (J.) More talking of
Shakespeare.   1959.

666126

STEWART (JOHN INNES MACKINTOSH) [pseud.
Michael Innes]
 "Steep tragic contrast": Macbeth.
IN LEECH, CLIFFORD, ed., Shakespeare:
the tragedies.   A collection of
critical essays.   (Chicago) 1965.
 Gemini books.

752332

STEWART (P.)
An Eighteenth-century adaptation of
Shakespeare [i.e. The Universal
passion, by J. Miller: an adaptation
of Much ado about nothing].   IN
University of Texas, Studies in
English, No. 12.   (Austin, Texas)
                    1932.

442439

STEWART, STANLEY
Romeo and necessity.
IN Pacific coast studies in
Shakespeare.   Edited by W. F. McNeir
and T. N. Greenfield.   (Eugene: Ore.)
                    1966.

768009

STEWART HEADLAM, SHAKESPEARE ASSOCIATION
Programmes, etc. of Shakespeare performances, 1926-

416900

Stidolph (Ada B.) The Children's
 Shakespeare [: The Merchant of Venice,
 A Midsummer Night's Dream and As You
 Like it, in story form]. With
 preface by C.W.Barnett-Clarke. 2nd
 edn. Ports.

[c.1905.]

527186

STILL (COLIN)
An Interpretation of Shakespeare's
"Tempest".   IN Still (C.) The Timeless
theme: a critical theory formulated
and applied.   1936.

456789

STILLMAN (CLARA G.)
Samuel Butler, a mid-Victorian
modern.   [With references to
Shakespeare.]
ports. illus. bibliog. 1932.

399122

STINSON (JAMES)
Reconstructions of Elizabethan public
playhouses.   IN Studies in the
Elizabethan theatre, [by various
authors.]   [Hamden, Conn.]
illus. plans. bibliog.   1961.

667053

STIRK (S. D.)
A Note on Gerhart Hauptmann's "Hamlet
in Wittenburg".   IN The Modern
Language Review, Vol. 32.
(Cambridge)   1937.

477224

STIRLING (BRENTS)
Anti-democracy in Shakespeare: a
re-survey.   IN Modern Language
Quarterly, Vol. 2.   (Seattle)
  bibliog.   1941.

                          533242

STIRLING (BRENTS)
Bolingbroke's "decision".
IN SHAKESPEARE QUARTERLY II: 1.
pp. 27-34.
(New York) 1951.
                          605711

STIRLING (BRENTS)
Brutus and the death of Portia.
IN SHAKESPEARE QUARTERLY X: 2.
pp. 211-217.
(New York) 1959.
                          605711

STIRLING (BRENTS)
Cleopatra's scene with Seleucus:
Plutarch, Daniel, and Shakespeare.
IN Shakespeare 400: essays by American
scholars on the anniversary of the
poet's birth.   Published in co-
operation with the Shakespeare Association of America.
  illus.   1964.

                          667803

STIRLING (BRENTS)
Julius Caesar in revision.

  IN SHAKESPEARE QUARTERLY XIII: 2.
pp. 187-205.
(New York) 1962.
                          605711

STIRLING (BRENTS)
More Shakespeare sonnet groups.
IN Essays on Shakespeare and Eliza-
bethan drama in honour of Hardin
Craig.
  illus.   1963.

                          667532

STIRLING (BRENTS)
The Populace in Shakespeare.   (New
York)
  bibliog.   1949.

                          600905

STIRLING (B.)
[Review of] The State in Shakespeare's
Greek and Roman plays, by J. E.
Phillips.   IN Modern Language
Quarterly, Vol. 2.   (Seattle) 1941.

                          533242

STIRLING (BRENTS)
[Review of] Shakespeare and democracy,
by A. Thaler.   IN Modern Language
Quarterly, Vol. 3.   (Seattle) 1942.

                          544203

STIRLING, BRENTS
The Shakespeare sonnet order:
poems and groups. (Berkeley, Cal.)
                          1968.

                          774506

STIRLING (BRENTS)
Shakespeare's mob scenes: a reinterpretation [with particular reference
to Henry VI, Pt. 2, Julius Caesar
and Coriolanus.]   IN The Huntington
Library Quarterly, Vol. 8.   (San
Marino, Cal.)
  bibliog.   1944-5.

                          562973

STIRLING, BRENTS
Sonnets 127-154.   IN BLOOM, EDWARD A.,
ed., Shakespeare 1564-1964: a
collection of modern essays by
various hands.   (Providence, R.I.)
                          1964.
Brown University bicentennial
publications.
                          744437

STIRLING (BRENTS)
Theme and character in Hamlet.
IN Modern Language Quarterly, Vol. 13.
(Seattle, Wash.)   1952.

                          525289/13

STIRLING (BRENTS)
Unity in Shakespearian tragedy: the
interplay of theme and character.
(New York)   1956.

                          665317

STIRLING (BRENTS)
The Unity of Macbeth.
IN SHAKESPEARE QUARTERLY IV: 4.
pp. 385-394.
(New York) 1953.
                          605711

STIRLING (W. F.)
Orange groves [: poems.   Including
a poem on Shakespeare: "April 23rd".]
pp. 77.   1934.

                          421884

STOCHHOLM, JOHANNE M.
Garrick's folly: the Shakespeare
Jubilee of 1769 at Stratford and Drury
Lane.   1964.

  illus.   667802

Stock (F.R.) Pen and ink sketches [:
24 plates, many with quotations from
"Hamlet", "Romeo and Juliet", etc.]

                          1859.

                    497975

[STOCKDALE (J. J.) ed.]
Covent Garden Journal [: an account
of the destruction of the old theatre
by fire in 1808, of the rise of the
new theatre, and of the subsequent
occurrences that took place therein.
With an appendix and references to
Shakespeare].
  2 vols.   illus.   1810.

                    538118

STOCKELBACH (Mrs. LAVONIA)
The Birds of Shakespeare.   pp. 52.
[Verona, N.J.]
  illus.   1940. 525216
Privately printed.   Signed by author.
_____ Another edn.   (London)
pp. 94, 30 plates. [1954] 642669

Stockholm *see* Sweden

STOCKLEY (W. F. P.)
The Bacon-Shakespeare matter.   IN
The Westminster Review, Vol. 180.
1913.

248889

[STOCKLEY (W. F. P.)]
Eat no fish ["King Lear" and Lent
in Elizabethan times].   IN The
Month, Vol. 140.   1922.

307445

STOCKLEY (W. F. P.)
Newman as Hamlet.   IN The Month,
Vol. 147.   1926.

330905

STOCKLEY (W. F. P.)
Reading Julius Caesar.   pp. 91.
(Dublin)   [1914]

478682

STOCKS (H. C. L.)
You spotted snakes - Die wiber fraith:
unison song.   The English words [from
A Midsummer night's dream] by
Shakespeare; Y Cyfiethiad Cymraeg
gan T. G. Jones.   [Music by] H. C. L.
Stocks.   pp. 4.   (Llangollen)
1939.

542324

[Stockton] Stxcktxn Jubilee (The); or,
Shakespeare in all his glory: a
choice pageant for Christmas
holidays, 1781 [containing passages
from Shakespeare applied to the
inhabitants of Stockton-on-Tees. By
J.Ritson.] pp. [11]. Manuscript.

1781.

533659

STOCKWELL (LA TOURETTE)
Dublin theatres and theatre customs
(1637-1820).   (Kingsport, Tenn.)
ports.   illus.   bibliog.   1938.
No. 153 of an edition limited to
500 copies.

498814

Stoddart (Jane T.) Antonio in "The Merchant of Venice:" a character study.
In The Bookman, Vol.29.

905-6.

193733

Stoffel, C. *works relating to*

— The Prosody of Shakespeare [: a
review of "William Shakespeare,
prosody and text", by B. A. P. van
Dam and C. Stoffel].   IN The
Saturday Review, Vol. 90, 1900.
1901.

155380

Stoicism

— BOYCE (B.)
The Stoic "consolatio" and Shakespeare.
IN PMLA, Vol. 64.   (Menasha, Wis.)
bibliog.   1949.

428321/64

STOKE-ON-TRENT SHAKESPEARIAN SOCIETY
Programmes, photographs, etc. [of
Shakespearian performances.   (Stoke-
on-Trent)
illus.   1937-55.

472596

Stoker (B.) The Art of Ellen Terry.
Illus. In The Playgoer, Vol.1.

1902.

159497

STOKER (BRAM)
Manuscript letter.   IN Romeo and Juliet,
a tragedy in five acts, as arranged for
the stage by H. Irving and presented at
the Lyceum Theatre, March 8th, 1882.
pp. 79.   (Bickers & Son)   1882.

511204

Stoker (B.) Personal reminiscences
of Henry Irving.   Revised edn.
Ports.

1907.

487372

STOKER (M. E.) and STOKER (J. T.)
Shakespeare's "Twelfth night"; filmstrip and notes.   pp. 28.   2 vols.
bibliog.   1954.

646079-80

STOKES (LESLIE)
Macready's farewell: the actor's
retirement from the stage in 1851,
compiled from his diaries and other
contemporary sources.   [Broadcast]
April 22nd, 1951.   pp. 16.
typescript.

620398

STOKES (ROY)
Bacon and "Shakespeare". [With
subsequent correspondence on the
same subject] IN East Anglian
Magazine, Vol. 2. (Ipswich)
ports. facsimiles. 1937.

510777

STOKES (S.)
The Oliviers [with references to
Laurence Olivier's Shakespearean
performances]. IN Theatre Arts,
Vol. 29. (New York)
illus. 1945.

567819

STOKES (W.)
All Shakespeare's Tales: Tales
from Shakespeare by C. and Mary
Lamb, and Tales from Shakespeare
by W. Stokes. Illustrated by
Maria L. Kirk. (New York) 1911.

407351

STOLL (ELMER EDGAR)
Another Othello too modern [: refutation
of G. G. Sedgewick. With bibliographical
notes.]
IN McMANAWAY (J. G.), DAWSON (G. E.)
and WILLOUGHBY (E. E.) eds., Joseph
Quincy Adams memorial studies.
(Washington) 1948.

596748

Stoll (E.E.) Art and artifice in Shakespeare: a study in dramatic contrast
and illusion.

(Cambridge) 1933.

410663

STOLL (ELMER EDGAR)
Art and artifice in the Iliad; or,
The Poetical treatment of character
in Homer and Shakespeare. FROM
The Johns Hopkins Alumni Magazine,
Vol. 24. (Baltimore) 1935.

488670

STOLL (ELMER EDGAR)
The Dramatic texture in Shakespeare.
FROM "The Criterion", July, 1935.
pp. [22].

437097

STOLL (ELMER EDGAR)
From Shakespeare to Joyce: authors
and critics; literature and life.
(New York)
bibliog. 1944.

552070

STOLL (E. E.)
Hamlet and The Spanish Tragedy, Quartos
I and II: a protest. FROM Modern
Philology, Vol. 35. (Chicago, Ill.)
bibliog. 1935.

488666

STOLL (ELMER EDGAR)
Hamlet and The Spanish Tragedy again.
FROM Modern Philology, Vol. 37.
(Chicago) 1939.

530203

STOLL (E. E.)
Hamlet, the man. pp. 29. 1935.
English Association Pamphlet.

436031

STOLL (ELMER EDGAR)
Heroes and villains: [characters of]
Shakespeare, Middleton, Byron, Dickens.
IN The Review of English Studies,
Vol. 18. (Oxford)
bibliog. 1942.

542539

STOLL (E. E.)
Jacques, and the antiquaries.
IN Modern Language Notes, Vol. 54.
(Baltimore) 1939.

509539

STOLL (ELMER EDGAR)
Kent and Gloster [: their characters
as revealed in "King Lear"]. FROM
Life and letters, Dec. 1933-Feb. 1934.
pp. [15.]

416889

STOLL (ELMER EDGAR)
Mainly controversy: Hamlet, Othello.
IN Philological Quarterly, Vol. 24.
(Iowa) 1945.

592684/24

STOLL (ELMER EDGAR)
Molière and Shakespeare. FROM
The Romanic Review, Vol. 35. (New
York)
bibliog. 1944.

578269

STOLL (ELMER EDGAR)
"Multi-consciousness" in the theatre.
IN Philological Quarterly, Vol. 29.
(Iowa) 1950.

592684/29

STOLL (ELMER EDGAR)
Not fat or thirty. [Hamlet]
IN SHAKESPEARE QUARTERLY II: 4.
pp. 295-301.
(New York) 1951.

605711

Stoll (E.E.) The Objectivity of the
ghosts in Shakspere. In Publications
of the Modern Language Association
of America, Vol.22.

(Baltimore) 1907.

428342

STOLL (ELMER EDGAR)
Oedipus and Othello, Corneille, Rymer
and Voltaire. [English text.]
Extrait de la Revue anglo-américaine,
juin 1935. pp. [16.] (Paris)
bibliog. [1935.]

569122

Stoll (E.E.) An Othello all-too modern.
[With bibliographical notes.] In
E.L.H. : a Journal of English
literary History, Vol.13.

(Balitmore, Md.) 1946.

584757

STOLL (ELMER EDGAR)
Othello: tragedy of effect. IN A
Casebook on 'Othello', edited by
L. F. Dean. [Text and criticism
by various authors.] (New York:
Thomas Y. Crowell) 1964.
Crowell Literary Casebooks.

748200

STOLL (E. E.)
Phèdre [: an appreciation of the play
by Racine including comparisons with
Shakespeare. English text].
Extrait de la Revue anglo-américaine,
décembre 1934. pp. [16.] (Paris)
[?1934].

569086

STOLL (ELMER EDGAR)
Recent Elizabethan criticism. [With
references to Shakespeare.] IN
E.L.H.: A Journal of English literary
history, Vol. 6. (Baltimore) 1939.

513732

STOLL (ELMER EDGAR)
Reconciliation in tragedy: Shakespeare
and Sophocles. FROM The University
of Toronto Quarterly, Vol. 4.
(Toronto) 1934.

440599

STOLL (ELMER EDGAR)
Shakespeare and other masters [:
literary studies.] (Cambridge, Mass.)
bibliog. 1940.

532084

Stoll (E.E.) Shakespeare forbears.
[Shakespeare's treatment of love.]
In Modern Language Notes. Vol.54.

(Baltimore) 1939.

509539

Stoll (E.E.) Shakespeare studies:
historical and comparative in method.
[2nd edn. With bibliographical
notes.]

(New York) 1942.

539383

Stoll (E.E.) Shakespeare's Jew. From
University of Toronto Quarterly,
January 1939.

(Toronto)

502375

STOLL (ELMER EDGAR)
Shakespeare's young lovers. (Oxford)
1937.
Alexander Lectures [in English], 1935.

477167

STOLL (ELMER EDGAR)
Slander in drama.
IN SHAKESPEARE QUARTERLY IV: 4.
pp. 433-450.
(New York) 1953.

605711

STOLL (ELMER EDGAR)
Source and motive in Macbeth and Othello.
IN The Review of English Studies,
Vol. 19. (Oxford)
bibliog. 1943.

555539

STOLL (E. E.)
Symbolism in Shakespeare. IN The
Modern Language Review, Vol. 42.
(Cambridge)
bibliog. 1947.

266816/42

STOLL (E. E.)
"The Tempest" [: a critical essay.]
pp. [28]. FROM [Publications of
the Modern Language Association of
America, vol. 47.] [(Menasha, Wis.)]
[1932.]

438440

STOLL (ELMER EDGAR)
The Tragic fallacy, so-called [, in
modern drama]. Reprinted from the
University of Toronto Quarterly,
Vol. 5. [With references to
Shakespeare.] pp. [25.] (Toronto)
bibliog. 1936.

568679

Stoll, Elmer Edgar *works relating to*

—— BENNETT (HENRY STANLEY)
[Review of] Shakespeare and other
masters, by E. E. Stoll. IN The
Review of English Studies, Vol. 18.
(Oxford) 1942.

542539

—— DAVIS (B. E. C.)
[Review of] Shakespeare and other
masters, by E. E. Stoll. IN The
Modern Language Review, Vol. 38.
(Cambridge) 1943.

553690

—— DOBRÉE (BONAMY)
Art and artifice in Shakespeare [: a
review of "Art and artifice in
Shakespeare", by E. E. Stoll]. IN
The Criterion, Vol. 13, 1933-34.

424895

—— KNICKERBOCKER (W. S.)
Mr. Stoll's Shakspere [: reviews of
'Art and artifice in Shakespeare'
by E. E. Stoll, etc.] FROM Sewanee
Review, Vol. 42. pp. [20].
(Sewanee, Tenn.) 1934.

447442

—— LAW (ROBERT ADGER)
[Review of] Shakespeare and other masters,
by E. E. Stoll. IN Modern Language
Quarterly, Vol. 2. (Seattle) 1941.

533242

— MAXWELL (BALDWIN)
[Review of] Shakespeare and other
masters, by E. E. Stoll.   IN Modern
Language Notes, Vol. 58.   (Baltimore)
1943.

553688

— The Myth hunt, psycho-analysis in
criticism [: review of] From
Shakespeare to Joyce, by E. E. Stoll.
IN The Times Literary Supplement,
Mar. 18, 1944.
port.

558345

— PARROTT (T. M.)
[A Review of] Art and artifice in
Shakespeare, by E. E. Stoll.   IN
Modern language notes, Vol. 50.
(Baltimore)
1935.

446885

— PETTET (E. C.)
[Review of] From Shakespeare to Joyce,
by E. E. Stoll.   IN English: the
magazine of the English Association,
Vol. 5.   (Oxford)
1944-45.

569018

— PUTNEY (R.)
What "praise to give?"   Jonson vs.
Stoll [on Shakespeare's tragic heroes].
IN Philological Quarterly, Vol. 23,
No. 4.   (Iowa)
1944.

583399

— PUTT (SAMUEL GORLEY)
A Shakespearean high Tory [: a review
of] Shakespeare and other masters,
[by] E. E. Stoll.   IN Time and Tide,
Vol. 23.
1942.

544257

— RYLANDS (G. [H. W.])
[Review of] Stoll (E. E.) Shakespeare's
young lovers.   IN The New Statesman
and Nation, N. S., Vol. 15.
1938.

485147

— SPENCER (BENJAMIN TOWNLEY)
This Elizabethan Shakespeare [: reviews
of "Shakespeare", by M. Van Doren;
"The Hamlet of Shakespeare's audience",
by J. W. Draper; "Shakespeare in
America", by Esther C. Dunn; [and]
"Shakespeare and other masters", by
E. E. Stoll.   FROM Sewanee Review,
Vol. 49.   (Sewanee)
1941.

537257

— SPENCER (H.)
[Review of] Poets and Playwrights:
Shakespeare, Jonson, Spenser, Milton,
by E. E. Stoll.   IN Modern Language
Notes, Vol. 46.   (Baltimore)
1931.

397731

— STONIER (G. W.)
Back to Shakespeare [: review of]
From Shakespeare to Joyce, by E. E.
Stoll.   IN The New Statesman and
Nation, New Series, Vol. 27.   1944.

554748

— SUTHERLAND (J. R.)
[Review of] From Shakespeare to Joyce:
by E. E. Stoll.   IN The Review of
English Studies, Vol. 21.   (Oxford)
[1945.]

570955

— YAO SHEN
Some chapters on Shakespearean criticism:
Coleridge, Hazlitt and Stoll.   A disser-
tation submitted for the degree of
Doctor of Education in English,
University of Michigan.   (Ann Arbor,
Mich.)
bibliogs.   microfilm. 1 reel 35 mm.
1944.
University Microfilms.   Doctoral
Dissertations Series.

603942

STONE (GEORGE WINCHESTER)
David Garrick's significance in the
history of Shakespearean criticism:
a study of the impact of the actor
upon the change of critical focus
during the eighteenth century.
IN P.M.L.A.: Publications of the
Modern Language Association of America,
Vol. 65.   (New York)
1950.

428321/65

STONE (GEORGE WINCHESTER)
Garrick, and an unknown operatic
version [by Captain Edward Thompson]
of "Love's labour's lost".   IN The
Review of English Studies, Vol. 15.
1939.

513846

STONE, GEORGE WINCHESTER
Garrick and 'Othello.' IN Essays in
English neoclassicism in memory of
Charles B. Woods: Philological
Quarterly, Vol.45, no.1, Jan. 1966.
(Iowa City, Iowa)

pp.304-320.   767563

STONE (G. W.)
Garrick's handling of Macbeth.
pp. 20.   FROM Studies in Philology,
Vol. 38.   (Chapel Hill, N.C.)
bibliog.
1941.

533678

STONE (G. W.)
Garrick's long lost alteration of
Hamlet.   IN Publications of the
Modern Language Association of
America, vol. 49.   (Menasha, Wis.)
1934.

432218

STONE (GEORGE WINCHESTER)
Garrick's presentation of Antony and
Cleopatra.   IN The Review of English
Studies, Vol. 13.   [1937.]

479772

STONE (GEORGE WINCHESTER)
Garrick's production of King Lear: a
study in the temper of the eighteenth
century mind.   IN Studies in Philology,
Vol. 45.   (Chapel Hill, N.C.)
bibliog.   1948.

554520/45

STONE (GEORGE WINCHESTER)
The God of his idolatry: Garrick's
theory of acting and dramatic composition
with especial reference to Shakespeare.
[With bibliographical notes.]

IN McMANAWAY (J. G.), DAWSON (G. E.)
and WILLOUGHBY (E. E.) eds., Joseph
Quincy Adams memorial studies.
(Washington)   1948.

596748

STONE (GEORGE WINCHESTER)
"A Midsummer night's dream" in the hands
of Garrick and Colman.   IN Publications
of the Modern Language Association of
America, Vol. 54.   (Menasha, Wis.)
bibliog.   1939.

515058

STONE (GEORGE WINCHESTER)
"Romeo and Juliet": the source of its
modern stage career.   IN McMANAWAY
(JAMES GILMER) ed., Shakespeare 400:
essays by American scholars on the
anniversary of the poet's birth.
Published in co-operation with the
Shakespeare Association of America.
illus.   1964.

667803

STONE (GEORGE WINCHESTER)
Shakespeare in the periodicals, 1700-
1740.   A study of the growth of a
knowledge of the dramatist in the
eighteenth century.   IN SHAKESPEARE
QUARTERLY II: 1951, pp. 221-231;
III: 1952, pp. 313-328.   (New York)

605711

STONE (GEORGE WINCHESTER)
Shakespeare's "Tempest" at Drury Lane
during Garrick's management.
IN SHAKESPEARE QUARTERLY VII.
pp. 1-7.
(New York) 1956.

605711

Stone (George Winchester) ed. see
Lennep (Willem van) and others, eds.

[STONE (Sir JOHN BENJAMIN)]
Sir Benjamin Stone's pictures: records
of national life and history reproduced
from [his] photographs.   Vol. 1:
Festivals, ceremonies and customs.
[With notes on, and a photograph of,
the Shakespeare Birthday Festival at
Stratford-on-Avon.]   [1905]

389427

STONE (LILLY C.)
English sports and recreations.
pp. ii, 50.   (Washington, D.C.
illus. facsimiles. bibliog.
1960.   666785
Folger Shakespeare Library.   Folger
Booklets on Tudor and Stuart Civilization.
_____ IN Life and letters in Tudor and
Stuart England.   (Ithaca, N.Y.)
illus.   1962.   667762
Folger Shakespeare Library.

STONE (NORMAN)
Blow, blow, thou winter wind.   Part-
song for T.T.B.B.   pp. 8.   1938.
Elkin New Choral Series, 1983.

479845

STONE (NORMAN)
Fear no more the heat o' the sun.
pp. 8.   1949.
Cramer's Choral Library, No. 57.

666655

[STONE (NORMAN) ed.]
Where the bee sucks.   Air by T. [A.]
Arne.   Arranged for mixed voices
(S.C.T.B.) [by] N. Stone.   pp. 6.
(Oxford)   1947.
Oxford Choral Songs, No. 1660.

588733

STONE (WALTER B.)
Shakespeare and the sad augurs.
IN The Journal of English and Germanic
Philology, Vol. 52.   (Urbana, Ill.)
1953.

600780/52

STONIER (GEORGE WALTER)
Back to Shakespeare [: review of]
From Shakespeare to Joyce, by
E. E. Stoll.   IN The New Statesman
and Nation, New Series, Vol. 27.
1944.

554748

STONIER (GEORGE WALTER)
Gog Magog, and other critical essays.
[With an essay "Footnote to Verdi's
Falstaff".]   1933.

411258

STONIER (GEORGE WALTER)
Ophelia [: an imaginary conversation
between Ophelia, Hamlet and other
characters in the play].   [Broadcast]
April 24th, 1947.   pp. 33.
typescript.   1947.   583265
Imaginary Conversations, 9.
_____ IN HEPPENSTALL (R.) ed.,
Imaginary conversations: eight radio
scripts.   1948.   595750

Stopes (Mrs. Charlotte C.)   **Burbage's
"Theatre".**   **In The Fortnightly Review,
Vol. 92.**

1909.

220427

STOPES (Mrs. CHARLOTTE C.)
Elizabethan stage scenery.   IN The
Fortnightly Review, Vol. 87.   1907.

201725

**Stopes (Mrs. Charlotte C.) The Friends
in Shakespeare's sonnets.   In
Transactions of the Royal Society of
Literature of the United Kingdom.
Second Series, Vol. 27.**

1907.

201930

STOPES (Mrs. CHARLOTTE CARMICHAEL)
The Making of Shakespeare [: a poem].
IN GOLLANCZ ([Sir] I.) ed., A Book
of homage to Shakespeare.
ports. illus. facsimiles. [1916.]

264175

STOPES (Mrs. CHARLOTTE C.)
The Scottish and English Macbeth.
IN Transactions of the Royal Society
of Literature, 2nd series, Vol. 18.
1897.

138775

Stopes, Charlotte C. *works relating to*

— G. [pseud.]
Shakespeare's family: a record of the
ancestors and descendants of William
Shakespeare, with some account of the
Ardens, by Mrs. C. G. Stopes: [a review].
IN The Antiquary, Vol. 37.
1901.

159938

— Shakespeare's family [: a review].
IN The Genealogical Magazine, Vol. 5.
illus. 1901.

170191

— Shakespeare's family [: a review].
IN Berks, Bucks & Oxon archaeological
journal, Vol. 7. (Reading) [1901-2.]

577765

Stopford (R.W.) and Jeffreys (M.V.C.)
Play production, for amateurs and
schools. [With Shakespearian references, and a bibliography.] Illus.

1933.

473240

STOPFORTH (LOURENS MARTHINUS DANIEL)
Henry the Fourth, Part 1: retold
in modern English prose. (Cape
Town: Nasionale Boekhandel Bpk.)
[1962.]
Shakespeare Made Easier
667584

STOPFORTH, LOURENS MARTHINUS DANIEL
Henry the Fifth retold in modern
English prose. (Cape Town)
illus. [1963.]
Shakespeare Made Easier.
668209

STOPFORTH (LOURENS MARTHINUS
DANIEL)

Macbeth: retold in modern English
prose. (Shakespeare Made Easier)
(Nasionale Boekhandel, Cape Town)
[1962.]

667583

STOPFORTH, LOURENS MARTHINUS DANIEL
The Tempest, retold in modern English
prose.
illus. [c.1963.]
Shakespeare Made Easier.
668208

STOPPARD, TOM
Rosencrantz and Guildenstern are dead.
[A play based on Shakespeare's 'Hamlet'.]
1967.

759531

STOREY (GRAHAM)
The Success of "Much ado about nothing".
IN GARRETT (J.) More talking of
Shakespeare. 1959.

666126

Stories and Sketches
LAMB (CHARLES and MARY ANN)
Seven tales from Shakespeare.
Annotated and slightly adapted by
P. A. Ter Weer. 3rd edn. (Zwolle)
1950.

615444

Stories for the Children
[LAMB (CHARLES and MARY A.)
Tales from Shakespeare, retold by
Edith Robarts.]
illus. [1912.]
Frontis, half title-page and title-
page wanting.

555508

Stories from Shakespeare. pp. 95.
illus. 1934.
The Children's Shakespeare.
438385

Stories Old and New
LAMB (CHARLES and MARY A.)
Tales from Shakspeare.
illus. [1918.]

665189

Storr (E.B.) Shakespeare's Brutus:
a character study. pp.[9.] From
London Quarterly and Holborn Review,
July, 1935.

438989

STOTHARD (THOMAS)
Shakspeare's Seven ages of man illustrated. Drawn by T. Stothard;
engraved by W. Bromley. pp. [iv],
ii, 14, 7 plates. (W. Bromley)
1799.

Covers to four parts, published by
H. D. Symonds, possibly belonging to
another edn.

458809

STOURBRIDGE, King Edward VI Grammar
School
Programmes, etc. of Shakespearean
performances. 1921-

417254

STOVALL (FLOYD)
Whitman, Shakespeare, and democracy.
IN The Journal of English and Germanic
Philology, Vol. 51. (Urbana, Ill.)
1952.

600780/51

STOVALL (FLOYD)
Whitman's knowledge of Shakespeare.
IN Studies in Philology, Vol. 49.
(Chapel Hill, N.C.)   1952.

554520/49

STOWE (Mrs. [HARRIET ELIZABETH BEECHER])
Visit to Shakespeare's house and tomb.
[Extracted from the author's "Sunny
memories in foreign lands"]   IN The
Leisure Hour, 1864.
illus.   1864.

83387

Stowe, James *works relating to*

—— HODGSON (Mrs. W.)
A Shakespearian forgery [: one of the
Shakespearian frauds by William Henry
Ireland, purporting to be a print of
an etching of the Globe Theatre by
James Stowe].   IN Apollo, Vol. 37.
(Mundesley-on-Sea)
facsimiles.   1943.

542421

STOWE SCHOOL, BUCKINGHAMSHIRE
Programmes of Shakespeare productions,
1950-   [Stowe, Bucks.]

666296

STOWELL (HELEN ELIZABETH)

Reading Shakespeare's plays. Port. Illus.
(Welwyn, Herts)   1962.

667200

STRACHAN (WALTER JOHN)
"I have long dreamed" [: a poem] on
seeing Ralph Richardson as Falstaff
in Henry IV.   IN Strachan (W. J.)
Moments of time: poems.   pp. 55.
illus.   1947.

585234

STRACHEY ([Sir EDWARD)
Shakespeare in Love's labour's lost.
IN The Atlantic Monthly, Vol. 71.
(Boston, [Mass.])   1893.

119144

Strachey (G.L.) Shakespeare's final
period. In The Independent Review,
Vol.3.
1904.

184000

STRACHEY, [G.] L.
Spectatorial Essays, with a Preface
by James Strachey.   1964.

728003

Contributions to "The Spectator"
including several on Shakespearian
subjects.

Strachey, Giles Lytton *works relating to*

—— SANDERS (CHARLES RICHARD)
Lytton Strachey as a critic of Eliza-
bethan drama.   IN Philological
Quarterly, Vol. 30.   (Iowa) 1931.

592684/30

STRACHEY ([JANE MARIA, Lady]) ed.
Poets on poets [: an anthology,
with introduction and notes,
including poems on Shakespeare,
by various poets].   1894.

432029

STRACHEY (MARJORIE)
King Lear at the Théâtre Antoine
[: the French translation by P. Loti
and E. Vedel.]   IN The Independent
review, Vol. 8.   1906.

193889

STRACHEY, WILLIAM
A True reportory of the wracke, and
redemption of Sir Thomas Gates Knight;
upon, and from the Ilands of the
Bermudas ... July 15. 1610.   IN
Purchas his Pilgrimes ... The Fourth
Part ... 1625.
pp. 1734-53.

110817

Stratford as connected with Shakespeare,
and the Bard's rural haunts.
(Stratford-upon-Avon)   1851.

759520

Stratford, Connecticut

—— AMERICAN SHAKESPEARE FESTIVAL THEATRE
AND ACADEMY
Programmes, etc.   (Stratford, Conn.)
ports.   illus.   1955-

665434

—— AMERICAN SHAKESPEARE FESTIVAL THEATRE
AND ACADEMY
Study guide [to] 'Julius Caesar',
'Twelfth Night', 'Falstaff (Henry IV,
Part II)   (Stratford, Conn.)
illus.   1966.

758152

—— BECKERMAN (BERNARD)
The Season at Stratford, Connecticut.
IN SHAKESPEARE QUARTERLY XV: 1964,
pp. 397-401; XVI: 1965, pp. 329-333;
XVII: 1966, pp. 403-6; XVIII: 1967,
pp. 405-408.

605711

—— BECKERMAN, BERNARD
Stratford (Connecticut) revisited 1968.
IN SHAKESPEARE QUARTERLY XIX: 4.
pp. 377-380.
(New York) 1968.
605711

—— GRIFFIN (ALICE)
The American Shakespeare Festival.
IN SHAKESPEARE QUARTERLY VI:
pp. 441-446.
(New York) 1955.
605711

—— HOSLEY (RICHARD)
The Second season at Stratford,
Connecticut.
IN SHAKESPEARE QUARTERLY VII:
pp. 399-402.
(New York) 1956.
605711

—— HOUSEMAN (JOHN) and LANDAU (JACK)
The American Shakespeare Festival:
the birth of a theatre. pp. 96.
(New York)
ports. illus. 1959.
666462

—— McGLINCHEE (CLAIRE)
Stratford, Connecticut, Shakespeare
Festival [: reviewed] IN SHAKESPEARE
QUARTERLY VIII:1957, pp. 507-510;
IX:1958, pp. 539-542; X:1959, pp.
573-576; XI:1960, pp. 469-472; XII:
1961, pp. 419-423. (New York)
605711

—— Newspaper cuttings [relating to
the] American Shakespeare Festival
Theatre and Academy, Stratford,
Connecticut. 1962-
667632

—— OGDEN (DUNBAR H.)
The Season at Stratford, Connecticut.
IN SHAKESPEARE QUARTERLY XIII: 1962,
pp. 537-540; XIV: 1963, pp. 437-439.
(New York)
605711

Stratford, Ontario

—— DAVIES (ROBERTSON) and others
Thrice the brinded cat hath mew'd: a
record of the Stratford Shakespearean
Festival in Canada, 1955 [by] R. Davies,
T. Guthrie, [L.] B. Neel [and] Tanya
Moiseiwitsch. (Toronto)
ports. illus. 1955.
665216

—— EDINBOROUGH (ARNOLD)
Canada's achievement [: 1962
Shakespeare Festival at Stratford,
Ont.] IN SHAKESPEARE SURVEY 16.
illus. 1963.
667523

—— EDINBOROUGH (ARNOLD)
Reviews of the Stratford Shakespearean
Festival of Canada. IN SHAKESPEARE
QUARTERLY V:1954 pp. 47-50; VI:1955
pp. 435-440; VII:1956 pp. 403-406;
VIII:1957 pp. 511-514; IX:1958 pp.
535-538; X:1959 pp. 577-580; XI:1960
pp. 455-459; XIV:1963 pp. 433-436;
XV:1964 pp. 391-395; XVI:1965 pp.
325-327; XVII:1966 pp. 398-402; XVIII:
1967, pp. 399-403; XIX:1968,pp.381-384.
(New York) 605711

—— FISHER (SIDNEY)
An Exhibit of Shakespeare books from
the collection of S. Fisher. Exhibited
at the Stratford Shakespearean
Festival, 1956, Stratford, Ontario.
(Montreal) 2 vols. 1956-7.
668430-1

—— FISHER, SIDNEY
An Exhibit of Shakespeare books: a
loan exhibition from the collection of
Mr. S. Fisher of Montreal ... at the
Stratford Shakespearean Festival,
Stratford, Ontario. (Montreal)
1964.
illus. 746651

—— GANONG (JOAN)
Backstage at Stratford [Ontario]; with
twelve pages of photographs of the
ninth season. (Toronto) 1962.
667325

—— GUTHRIE (Sir TYRONE)
Shakespeare at Stratford, Ontario. IN
Shakespeare Survey, [Vol.] 8. (Cambridge)
1955.
647706

—— GUTHRIE (Sir TYRONE)
Shakespeare in Canada. Producer:
Elisabeth Rowley. Broadcast 4th
November, 1955. ff.8. Typescript.
665122

—— GUTHRIE (Sir TYRONE)
Shakespeare's other Stratford [: account
of the Shakespeare Festival in Stratford,
Ontario during the summer of 1953.
Broadcast 30th December 1953]. ff.5.
Typescript.
643695

—— GUTHRIE (Sir TYRONE), DAVIES (ROBERTSON)
and MACDONALD (GRANT)
Renown at Stratford: a record of
the Shakespeare Festival in Canada,
1953. [Illustrations by G.
Macdonald.] (Toronto) 1953.
637120

—— GUTHRIE (Sir TYRONE), DAVIES (ROBERTSON)
and MACDONALD (GRANT)
Twice have the trumpets sounded: a
record of the Stratford Shakespearean
Festival in Canada, 1954. [Illus-
trations by G. Macdonald.] (Toronto)
1954.
649573

—HALL (PETER REGINALD FREDERICK) and
LANGHAM (MICHAEL)
  Talking of theatre: two Stratfords
  [Stratford-upon-Avon and Stratford,
  Ontario.]   [B.B.C. script,
  24th November 1959.]   pp. 11.
  typescript.

666447

—In retrospect [: a talk on the
  productions of the 1962 season].
  IN Stratford Papers on Shakespeare
  delivered at the 1962 Shakespeare
  Seminar. (Toronto)   1963.

668006

—   Newspaper cuttings. The Stratford
  Shakespearean Festival of Canada.
                                1962-

667634

— SIDNELL (MICHAEL J.)
  A Moniment without a tombe: the
  Stratford Shakespearian Festival
  Theatre, Ontario.   IN English
  Association, Essays and Studies.
  Shakespeare Quatercentenary ed.
   illus.   1964.

667820

— SMITH (PETER D.)
  "Sharp wit and noble scenes": a review
  of the 1961 season of the Stratford,
  Ontario, Festival.
   IN SHAKESPEARE QUARTERLY XIII: 1.
  pp. 71-77.
  (New York) 1962.

605711

— SMITH (PETER D.)
  "Toil and trouble": a review of the 1962
  season of the Stratford, Ontario, Festival.
   IN SHAKESPEARE QUARTERLY XIII: 4.
  pp. 521-527.
  (New York) 1962.

605711

—   STRATFORD PAPERS ON SHAKESPEARE
  delivered at the 1960-   Shakespeare
  Seminars sponsored by the Universities
  of Canada in co-operation with the
  Stratford Festival Theatre. [Edited by
  B.A.W. Jackson.] (Toronto)
                                1961-

667140

— THE STRATFORD SHAKESPEAREAN FESTIVAL OF
  CANADA
   Programmes, etc.   (Stratford, Ont.)
    ports.   illus.   [1953]-

638761

—The STRATFORD SHAKESPEAREAN
         FESTIVAL OF CANADA

  The Stratford Festival, 1953-1957: a
  record in pictures and text. With a
  foreword by the Rt.Hon.V.Massey and
  an introduction by H.Whittaker.
  pp.xxii, 61 Plates. (Toronto)
                                1958.

665967

—The STRATFORD SHAKESPEAREAN
         FESTIVAL OF CANADA

  A [Tenth] 10th season souvenir collection
  of costume designs from the Stratford
  Festival, Stratford, Ontario, Canada,
  1962. ff.23.   [1962.]

667323

— SUMMERSON (JOHN NEWENHAM) ed.
  [The Critics.]   Edinburgh International
  Festival edition [including a criticism
  of the Canadian Stratford Company in
  Shakespeare's Henry the Fifth].
  Chairman: J. [N.] Summerson.
  Producer: J. Weltman.   [Broadcast]
  9th September, 1956.   ff. [25.]
   typescript.

665431

STRATFORD PAPERS ON SHAKESPEARE

delivered at the 1960-   Shakespeare
Seminars sponsored by the Universities
of Canada in co-operation with the
Stratford Festival Theatre. [Edited by
B.A.W. Jackson.] (Toronto)
                              1961-

667140

Stratford-upon-Avon

General Works
Birthday Celebrations
Birthplace, etc.
Church of the Holy Trinity
Conferences
— Falcon Hotel
Grammar School
Guides
Libraries
Maps
New Place
Royal Shakespeare Theatre
— Festival
Royal Visits
Shakespeare Hotel
Shakespeare Memorial Library
Summer School
Views

Stratford-upon-Avon

– General Works

— ALDRICH (T. B.)
At Stratford-upon-Avon [: a poem].
IN Aldrich (T. B.) Poems [and plays].
Revised and complete Household Edition.
(Boston, [Mass.])
illus.   1907.

544304

— ANDERSON (D.)
Shakespeare at home.   FROM The Theatre,
June 1, 1880.

516578

— Ariel, the Stratford-upon-Avon Messenger.
No. 1, May 5th, 1926.   [Issued during
the General Strike.]   ff. 1.
(Shakespeare Head Press)   1926

392851

— Bickley (W.B.) The Gilde of the Holy
Cross [Stratford-on-Avon]: its
constitution and ordinances.1 sheet.

(Birmingham)   [c.1890].

474710

— BIRMINGHAM WEEKLY POST
Background to Shakespeare, Stratford-
on-Avon supplement, June 13, 1952.
pp. 8.   (Birmingham)
ports.   illus.

624739

— BLOOM, URSULA
Rosemary for Stratford-on-Avon.
1966.

illus.   748629

— Britton (J.) Essays on the merits and
characteristics of William Shakspere;
also remarks on his birth and burial-
place, his monument, portraits, and
associations. Illus. In Britton (J.)
Appendix to Britton's auto-biography.

1849.

28246

— Brooke (C.F.T.) Shakespeare remembers
his youth in Stratford. In Essays
and studies in honor of Carleton
Brown. Published in cooperation
with the Modern Language Association
of America. Port. Illus.

(New York)   1940.

531874

— BROOKE (CHARLES FREDERICK TUCKER)
Shakespeare's moiety of the Stratford
tithes.   IN Modern Language Notes.
Vol. 40.   (Baltimore, Md.)
1926.

439157/40

— BROWN (I. [J. C.]) and FEARON (G.)
Amazing monument: a short history of
the Shakespeare industry.
ports.   illus.   1939.

497289

— Bullock (G.) Marie Corelli: the life
and death of a best-seller. [With
references to Shakespeare and
Stratford-upon-Avon.] Ports. Illus.

1940.

510660

— BURRITT (E.)
Stratford-upon-Avon and Shakespeare;
his fame, past and prospective.
IN Burritt (E.) Walks in the Black
Country and its green border-land.
frontis.   1868.   343492
_____ [2nd edn.]   frontis.
1869.   302572
_____ [2nd edn.   Another copy.]
1869.   516429
_____ [2nd edn.]   1872.   42438

— CAMPBELL (T.)
Diary of a visit to England in 1775.
Newly edited from the M.S., [with
the life of T. Campbell and notes]
by J. L. Clifford.   With an introduction by S. C. Roberts [and references to Stratford-upon-Avon].
(Cambridge)
port.   facsimile.   1947.

582643

— Carr (R.) And malt does more than
Shakespeare can -   [:a consideration of entertainment in Stratford-
on-Avon.] Illus.   In World Film News
Vol. 2.

1937.

485420

— CARUS-WILSON, E. M.
The First half-century of the
Borough of Stratford-upon-Avon.
FROM Economic History Review,
Vol. 18, 2nd series. 1965.
pp. 46-63.

768965

— Charques (R.D.) ed., Footnotes to
the theatre [: articles by various
authors. With references to
Shakespeare.] Ports. Illus.

1938.

492878

— CHRISTON (CAROLINE)
We mustn't upset the staff [: experiences of a Stratford-on-Avon hotel
proprietor].   1951.

617075

— COOK (ROBERT BEILBY)
A Pilgrimage to Stratford-on-Avon.
Reprinted from the Yorkshire Weekly
Post.   pp. 12.   (York)   1892.

633183

—— COOPER (W.)
Henley-in-Arden: an ancient market
town and its surroundings. [With
references to Shakespeare and
Stratford-upon-Avon.] (Birmingham)
port. illus. maps. bibliog.
1946.

568864

—— D.U.K.Films, Ltd. The Upstart crow
[:script of a film dealing mainly
with Shakespearian associations of
Stratford]. ff.28. Typescript.

[1948.]

598970

—— DEFOE (DANIEL)
A Tour through England & Wales.
With an introduction by G. D. H.
Cole. [With a description of
Shakespeare's grave at Stratford-on-
Avon.]
2 vols. bibliog. [1928]
Everyman's Library.

399006

—— Dowden (E.) Shakespeare. In Homes
and haunts of famous authors.
Illus.

1906.

415649

—— Extenta manerii de veteri Stratford.
(Extenta burgi de Stratford [1252]).
pp. 8. [Middle Hill] [1840]
[Privately printed: Middle Hill Press]

431327

—— A Fine day at Stratford-upon-Avon"
[and] "Another day at Stratford" [with
letters from Richard Greene and
Joseph Greene] "'Touching' Shakespeare's
monument at Stratford-upon-Avon".
IN Fraser's Magazine, Vol. 30. 1844.

10630

—— FOX (LEVI)

Shakespeare's town and country. pp.[48].
Illus. Map. [Norwich] [1959.]

666229

—— FOX (LEVI)
Some new sidelights on Stratford-
upon-Avon's medieval Guild buildings.
Reprinted from the Transactions of
the Birmingham Archaeological Society,
Vol. 70. (Oxford) illus. 1954.
Signed by the author

642021

—— FOX (L.)
Stratford-upon-Avon. With drawings
by H. Wright, a foreword by F. Flower
[and a bibliography.] pp. [vi,] 40.
(Bristol)
maps. [1949.]
[The Garland of England, 3]

599154

—— FOX, LEVI
Stratford-upon-Avon: an appreciation.
illus. 1963.
Jarrold tableau series.

667982

—— FOX (LEVI)
Stratford-upon-Avon and the
Shakespeare country. pp. [32.]
(Norwich)
illus. [1955]
The Window Book Series.

646804

—— FRIPP (E. I.)
Note on the proposed publication (by
the Shakespeare Head Press) of the
Chamberlains' accounts of Stratford-
upon-Avon. IN PACY (F.) The
Shakespeare Head Press at Stratford-
upon-Avon. Reprinted from The Library
Association Record, July-Aug. 1916.
pp. 10. (Aberdeen) 1916.

545619

—— Gower ([Rt. Hon.] Lord R.[C.] Suther-
land-[Leveson-]) Records and reminiscences, selected from "My reminiscences" and "Old Diaries". [With
references to Shakespeare monuments
at Stratford-upon-Avon.] Ports.
Illus.

1903.

494415

—— HALL (E. V.)
Testamentary Papers. [1931-7]
1. Wills from Shakespeare's town
and time. pp. 36.
2. _____ 2nd series. pp. 46.
illus.
3. Marlowe's death at Deptford Strand:
wills of jurors at the inquest, with
some other wills. pp. 37.

380309

—— HARNESS (WILLIAM)
Stratford-upon-Avon a hundred years
ago: extracts from the travel diary
of the Reverend William Harness.
IN SHAKESPEARE SURVEY 14. (Cambridge)
1961.

666755

—— Hathaway Farm. Rules and regulations
of the Hathaway Farm Club. pp.32.
Illus.

(Birmingham) [1935]

447609

—— HAWTHORNE (NATHANIEL)
The English notebooks. [With refer-
ences to Shakespeare and Stratford-
upon-Avon.] Based upon the original
manuscripts in the Pierpont Morgan
Library and edited by R. Stewart.
(New York) 1941.
Modern Language Association of America,
General Series, 13.

536106

—— HAWTHORNE (NATHANIEL)
Recollections of a gifted woman [:
Delia S. Bacon.] IN Hawthorne (N.)
Our old home, Vol. 1. 1863.

61344

—Howells (W.D.) Experiences of a true
Baconian in Shakespeare's town. In
North American Review, Vol.195.

(New York)   1912.

236981

—HUNT (PETER) and HEARST (STEPHEN)
Stratford-upon-Avon.   "About Britain"
No. 12).   [Television programme]
23rd April, 1954.   Produced by
S. McCormack.   ff. 26.
typescript.

643692

—HYDE (D.)
An rud tharla do Ghaedheal ag Stratford
ar an abhainn: How it fared with a
Gael at Stratford-on-Avon.   [Gaelic
text with English translation.]
IN GOLLANCZ ([Sir] I.) ed., A Book of
homage to Shakespeare.
ports. illus. facsimiles. [1916.]

264175

—[IRVING (W.)]
The Sketch book of Geoffrey Crayon,
Gent. [With a chapter on Stratford-
on-Avon.] 5th edn.   2 vols.
1821.

For later editions of this work check
the main sequence under the author's
name.

513969

—Irving (W.) and Fairholt (F.W.) Shakes-
peare's home; visited and described.
With a letter from Stratford by J.F.
Sabin and the complete prose works of
Shakespeare. With etchings by J.F.
and W. W. Sabin.

(New York)   1877.

57062

—JAGGARD (GEOFFREY)
The Battle of Stratford-upon-Avon.
Broadcast October 23rd, 1960.
ff. 5.   [Birmingham]
typescript.

666993

—JAGGARD, GEOFFREY
Companion to Stratford: Shakespeare's
town as he knew it. [With] Street
ballads by A. Jaggard [and] new
illustrations.   1964.

map.   667835

—JAGGARD (GERALD)
Stratford mosaic: the Shakespeare
Club and a medley of memories.
ports.   illus.   1960.

666512

—Jaggard (W.) Richard Savage of
Stratford-on-Avon. Reprinted
from "The Library Association
Record". pp.[4.]

1924.

Printed for private circulation.

426448

—JONES (F. W.)
Stratford-upon-Avon town planning
scheme.   IN Midland Joint Town
Planning Advisory Council.   Regional
Planning Exhibition and Conference.
Report of proceedings, Town Hall,
Birmingham, 20th-24th June, 1927.

402885

—LAFFAN (BERTHA)
The Poet's cradle.   IN The Theatre,
Vol. 12.
illus.   1888.

99108

—LEE ([Sir] S.)
"As you like it" and Stratford-on-
Avon.   FROM The Gentleman's
Magazine, October, 1885.

440305

—LEE ([Sir] S.)
Stratford-on-Avon.   From earliest
times to the death of Shakespeare.
With illustrations by E. Hull.
pp. 77.   1885.
Large paper copy.

394203

New edn.   1902.   509093

—LYLE (MILLICENT)
Stratford tapestry: a one-act play.
pp. [ii.] 21.   1952.

626787

—LYTTON (DAVID)
On living in Stratford-on-Avon in
August.   [Broadcast] 20th August
1957.   ff. 8.
typescript.

665696

—MADDEN (EVA)
Along the road to Stratford.   FROM
The Landmark, 1928.   pp. [5.]
illus.

389200

—MAIS (STUART PETRE BRODIE)
Arden and Avon.   Illustrations by
R. A. Maynard.
map.   1951.

615394

—MARTIN (L.) and MARTIN ([Mrs.] SYLVIA)
Shakespeare-on-Avon [: the growth of
the fame of Stratford-on-Avon, with
special reference to the Flower family].
IN Forum, Vol. 109.   (Philadelphia,
Pa.)   1948.

146116/109

—MASONRY: hymns, odes, songs
Written and compiled for the Masonic
jubelee [sic], at Shakespear Lodge,
Stratford on Avon, 4th June, 1793.
pp. 22.   (Birmingham)   [1793.]
Photostat copy made Nov. 1951 from
the original at Shakespeare's Birthplace.

621222

—— MILLER (H.)
Visit to Stratford-on-Avon. [Extracted from the author's "First impressions of England and its people", 1847] IN The Leisure Hour, 1864.
illus.

83387

—— MORITZ (CHARLES P.)
Travels in England in 1782 [: a reprint of "Travels, chiefly on foot, through several parts of England in 1782, described in Letters to a Friend", translated from the German by a lady, and published in 1795]. With an introduction by H. Morley.
1886.   507035
Cassell's National Library.
_____ With an introduction by P. E. Matheson.
illus.   1924.   316943

—— MOULT (T.)
Shakespeare's Stratford.   IN The British Annual of Literature, Vol. 4.
illus.   1947.

590588

—— MOWAT (R. B.)
Americans in England.   [With references to Stratford-upon-Avon]
ports.

447336

—— Newdigate (B.H.) Falstaff, Shallow and the Stratford musters. From London Mercury, February, 1927.

449507

——Newspaper cuttings relating to Stratford-upon-Avon.

1918-

301496

—— NICHOLLS (FAITH)
An Actor's wife in Stratford.
Producer:P. Humphreys.   [Broadcast]
20th November, 1956.   ff. 9.
typescript.

665417

—— OSWALD (A.)
Stratford new and old, 2: Shakespeare's Stratford.   FROM Country Life, April, 1932.   pp. [5.]
illus.

392856

—— PALMER (R.)
A Pilgrimage to an English shrine [: Stratford-on-Avon.]   FROM The Foresters' Miscellany, 1870.   pp. [3.]

389766

—— POINGDESTRE (E.)
A Summer day at Stratford-on-Avon.
IN Temple Bar, Vol. 74.   1885.

82081

—— Potter (S.) Shakespeare and Stratford.
In Theatre Today.

1946.

606680

—— PRICE (CLAIR)
Stratford-upon-Avon.   IN JOHNSTONE (K.) [and others] Introducing Britain [: broadcast talks].
Revised 2nd edn.
illus.   1946.

573859

—— Ratcliff (S.C.) and Johnson (H.C.) eds.,Warwick County Records, vol.1: Quarter Sessions Order Book, Easter 1625 to Trinity, 1637 [including entries relating to Stratford-upon-Avon]. Edited [with introduction] by S.C. Ratcliff and H.C. Johnson. With a foreword by Lord Hanworth.
Ports. Illus.
(Warwick)   1935.

(Warwickshire County Council, Records
Committee.)

436276

—— RICE (C. Y.)
A Pilgrim's scrip: poems for world wanderers [including one entitled "At Stratford"].   [1924.]

512919

—— Rose (Mrs.[Constance]) "Plain Mrs. Rose" [: reminiscences, with references to Shakespeare and Stratford-upon-Avon.] Ports.

(Cheltenham)   1936.

452685

—— ROYSTER (SALIBELLE)
An English teacher looks at England. [With references to Stratford-on-Avon.]   FROM Education, Vol. 58.
(Boston, Mass.)   1938.

512384

—— SCARFE (NORMAN)
Shakespeare, Stratford-upon-Avon and Warwickshire.   IN Shakespeare: a celebration, 1564-1964.
illus.   maps.   1964.

667816

—— SCOTT (C. [W.])
America by the Avon [: an account of the dedication to Stratford of the Fountain and Clock Tower presented by G. W. Childs; performed by Sir H. B. Irving].   IN Scott (C. [W.]) Blossomland and fallen leaves.   3rd edn.
port.   [1892.]

590633

—— SCOTT-MAXWELL (FLORIDA)
From London town to Stratford-on-Avon.   FROM Scottish Motor Transport Magazine, July,1934.   pp. [6.]
(Edinburgh)
illus.

422167

— [SEWARD (T.)]
On Shakespear's monument at Stratford
upon Avon.   IN [DODSLEY (R.) ed.,]
A Collection of poems by several hands.
3rd edn., Vol. 2.   1751.   576731
_____ 4th edn.   1755.   576737
_____ 5th edn.   1758.   538519

— SHEPHERD (F. N.)
Shakspeare's birthplace: an artist's
pilgrimage to Stratford-upon-Avon.
pp. 16.
   illus.   1864.

                              409500

— SQUIRE (Sir J. [C.])
Water-music: or, A Fortnight of Bliss
[further reminiscences. Random thoughts
of the author while canoeing on the
Cherwell, the Avon, and the Thames, with
W. Bliss. With references to Stratford.]
                              1939.

                              501210

— Stratford as connected with
Shakespeare; and the Bard's rural
haunts.   (Stratford-upon-Avon)
                              1851.

                              759520

— STRATFORD-ON-AVON HYDRO, LIMITED
Prospectus. [Advance copy.   With
references to Shakespeare.]
pp. [15.]
   illus.   [1911.]

                              397685

— Stratford-upon-Avon Scene, incorporating Shakespeare Pictorial.
Vols. 1-3.   (Stratford-upon-Avon)
ports. illus.   1946-50.
For Shakespeare Pictorial see catal.
no. 348579.

                              574721

— Styles (P.) The Borough of Stratford-
upon-Avon and the parish of
Alveston. [Reprinted from The
Victoria history of the county of
Warwick, Vol.3.] Architectural
descriptions by J.W.Bloe. [With
bibliographical notes.] pp. 72.
Illus. Maps. Plans.

                              1946.

                         574868

— TIMBS (J.)
English eccentrics and eccentricities.
[With a reference to a Shakespeare
monument.]   New edn.
ports.   illus.   1877.

                              400637

— TOMLINSON (W.)
A Walk to Shottery from Stratford-
on-Avon.   IN Manchester Literary
Club, Papers, Vol. 12.   (Manchester)
                              1886.

                              518373

— TORRINGTON (J. BYNG, 5th Viscount)
The Torrington diaries; containing
the tours through England and Wales,
of the Hon. J. Byng (5th Viscount
Torrington) between 1781 and 1794.
[With references to Shakespeare and
Stratford-upon-Avon.]   Edited by
C. B. Andrews.
   ports. illus. genealogical table.

                              1934-

                              424032

— TREWIN (J. C.)
The Story of Stratford upon Avon.
Photography by E. Daniels.   pp. 80.
   facsimile.   bibliog.   1950.

                              607314

— TYTLER (SARAH)
The American cousins: a story of
Shakespeare's country.   2nd and
cheap edn.   1899.
Digby's Popular Novel Series.

                              392895

— The Very heart of England: Shakespeare's
home on the Avon. pp.[14.] Illus.
From My Magazine, November, 1933.

                              414574

— WARD (A. C.)
A Literary journey through wartime
Britain [: an account of the bombing
of literary landmarks during the War.
With references to Shakespeare and
Stratford-on-Avon].   Illustrated
by F. T. Chapman.   (Oxford)
   maps.   1943.

                              557332

— WARD (H. S.)
Stratford-on-Avon and the Vale of
the Red Horse.   IN The Bookman,
Vol. 25.
   illus.   1903.

                              181448

— Ward (H.S.) and Ward ([Mrs.] C.W.)
Shakespeare's town and times. 3rd
edn. enlarged. Illus. Maps.

                              [1908]

                              452945

— WELLSTOOD (FREDERICK CHRISTIAN) [pseud.
"Saltire"]
An inventory of the civic insignia and
other antiquities belonging to the
Mayor and Corporation of Stratford-
upon-Avon; with historical notes.
pp. 30.   (Stratford-upon-Avon)
   port. illus. facsimiles.   1940.

                              642293

— [WELLSTOOD (F. C.)]
Stratford-upon-Avon races in the
eighteenth century.   By "Saltire".
Reprinted from the Stratford-upon-
Avon Herald, May, 1921.   pp. 32.
[Stratford-upon-Avon]

                              296928

—— WHELER (R. B.)
History and antiquities of Stratford-
upon-Avon: a description of the
Collegiate Church, the life of
Shakspeare [with an] account of the
Jubilee celebrated at Stratford, in
honour of [Shakespeare, 1769].
(Stratford-upon-Avon)
illus.   [1906.]

520159

—— WILLIAMS (GWYN)
Welshmen in Shakespeare's Stratford.
IN The Honourable Society of Cymmro-
dorion, Transactions, 1954.

1955.

255163/1954

—— Willis (N.P.) Loiterings of travel:
[poems, letters and reminiscences.]
Vol.1. [Containing references to
Stratford-on-Avon.]

1840.

436185

—— WINTER (WILLIAM)
Shakespeare's England.   (Boston, Mass.)
                1890. 450765
_____ Author's edn.   (Edinburgh)
                1891. 496258
_____ Author's edn.   (Edinburgh)
                1894. 565610
_____ New edn.   1902. 420262
_____ (New York)
ports.   illus.   1910. 627562

—— WISE (J. R. [de C.])
Shakspere: his birthplace and its
neighbourhood.   Illustrated by
W. J. Linton.   1861.

513644

—— WOODCOCK ([Mrs.] GWEN)
Historic haunts of England.   [With
a chapter on Stratford-on-Avon and
references to Shakespeare].
illus.   map.   1938.

481633

Stratford-upon-Avon

— Anne Hathaway's Cottage *see* Birthplace, etc. *below*

Stratford-upon-Avon

— Birthday Celebrations
see also **Jubilees and Commemorations; Quatercentenary 1964; Tercentenary 1864**

—— BILAINKIN (G.)
Maisky: ten years ambassador [i.e.
Soviet ambassador to Britain.   With
references to his visits, in April
1926 and 1936, to Stratford-upon-Avon
on the occasion of Shakespeare's
birthday celebrations, and other references to Shakespeare].
ports.   illus.   1944.

548852

—— COATES (W. P.) and COATES (ZELDA K.)
A History of Anglo-Soviet relations.
[Containing an account of the
presence of M. Maisky at Shakespeare's
birthday celebrations at Stratford-
on-Avon, April, 1926.]
frontis.   1943.

548237

—— DARK (E. P.)
The World against Russia?   [With
references to M. Maisky and the
Shakespeare Birthday celebrations,
1926.]   (Sydney)
bibliogs.   1948.

597921

—— HOLE (CHRISTINA)
English custom & usage.   [With
references to Shakespeare's
birthday celebrations at Stratford-
upon-Avon and Oxford.]
illus.   bibliog.   1941.

529397

—— ICHIKAWA([Mrs.] HARNKO)
Japanese lady in Europe.   Edited
and with an introduction by W. Plomer.
[With a chapter on the Shakespeare
Festival, Stratford-on-Avon]. 1937.

462840

—— MORLEY (G.)
Round Shakespeare's table.   An
account of the birthday celebrations
held at Stratford-on-Avon in honour
of the poet.   pp. [viii,] 68.
(Birmingham)
port.   [1908.]
Differs from 207289.

546574

—— MORLEY (G.)
A Shakespearean commemoration of
sixty years ago [i.e. 1829].
FROM The Sun.   October, 1889 to
September, 1890.   (Paisley) 1890.

570694

—— Newspaper Cuttings relating to Shakespeare's
Birthday Celebrations at Stratford-upon-
Avon.

1901-

171100

—— [REID (W.)]
London Commemorations, winter of
1908-9.   Remarks at the Shakespeare
anniversary, Stratford-on-Avon,
345th birthday, April 23rd, 1909,
[etc.]   pp. 40.   1909.

511625

—— Review of A Descriptive account of
the late Gala Festival at Stratford
upon Avon, in commemoration of the
Natal Day of Shakespeare.   FROM The
Gentleman's Magazine, July 1828.
pp. [4.]

402694

—— SLEIGH (H.)
Stratford-upon-Avon, April 23.
IN Sleigh (H.) The Great hope,
and other poems.   (Stratford-upon-
Avon: Shakespeare Head Press)
1921.

478200

—— [STONE (Sir J. B.)]
Sir Benjamin Stone's pictures: records
of national life and history repro-
duced from [his] photographs.   Vol. 1:
Festivals, ceremonies, and customs.
[With notes on, and a photograph of
the Shakespeare Birthday Festival at
Stratford-on-Avon].   [1905.]

389427

—— Stratford-upon-Avon: Shakespeare
Birthday Celebrations.   Programmes,
menus, etc.   [Stratford-upon-Avon]
1955-

667154

—— WAKELIN (ELLEN A.)
[Scrolls presented to Sir Fordham
Flower and L. Fox containing an account
of the events in Stratford-upon-Avon
at the Quatercentenary Birthday celebrations with a description of the
Shakespeare Exhibition and the opening
of the Stratford canal on July 11th
1964.   With text and music of the
Tercentenary Festal Song and the Tercentenary National Song to Shakespeare.]
4 items in 1 reel. 35 mm.   [1964.]
Microfilm, negative copy, made at
Birmingham Reference Library, 1965. 744435

Stratford-upon-Avon

— Birthplace, etc.
see also New Place, *below*

—— Anne Hathaway's Cottage: [how to make
a model from a folding plan.]
[c.1830.]
(Clarke's Little Modeller No. 11.)

457728

—— B. (J. H.)
Shakespeare land: a visit to Hathaway
Farm Shottery [made by members and
friends of the Birmingham Rotary Club].
Reprinted from the Evesham Journal and
Four Shires Advertiser, Sept. 1929.
FROM The Review, Vol. 1.   (Birmingham)
1930.

501610

—— The Birth place of Shakspeare.
IN The London Journal, Vol. 1.
1845.

414301

—— BOAS (F. S.)
The Shakespeare Conference at
Stratford-on-Avon [1947]: centenary
of the purchase of the birthplace.
FROM Queen's Quarterly, Vol. 54.
pp. [8].   (Kingston, Ont.)   1947.

596578

—— [BROWN (I. J. C.)]
The Shakespeares; and, The Birthplace,
[by G. Fearon].   pp. 61.   ([Stratford-
upon-Avon])
port. illus. genealogical table.
[1939.]

502917

—— BURMAN (J.)
Old Warwickshire families and houses.
[With a chapter: Anne Hathaway's
cottage.]   (Birmingham)
illus.   pedigrees.   1934.
_____ Another copy

425232-3

—— CARNEGIE (A.)
Copy of conveyance from Andrew
Carnegie of Skibo Castle, co.
Sutherland, esq., to the Trustees
and Guardians of Shakespeare's
Birthplace, of land adjoining the
Birthplace in Stratford upon Avon
[co. War.], together with two messuages
and premises built thereon.   With
incidental papers annexed.
11 July, 1903.
plan.   manuscript.

493919

—— Centenary commemoration of the purchase
of Shakespeare's birthplace, 1847-1947:
souvenir programme of a garden party
held in the garden of Shakespeare's
birthplace, 20th August 1947.
pp. [10.]   [Stratford-on-Avon]
illus.

586072

—— Centenary of the purchase of
Shakespeare's birthplace, 1847-1947:
guide to a select commemorative
exhibition displayed at Shakespeare's
birthplace.   pp. [8.]   [Stratford-
on-Avon]
illus.   [1947.]

586071

—— [CLIFTON (H.)]
History of the Hathaway families, 1200-
1600.   Manuscript.   3 vols.

[c.1925.]

516283

— CLOPTON FAMILY
A Collection of charters, deeds and
other documents relating to the
Clopton Family and estates in Clopton,
Stratford-upon-Avon and elsewhere.
manuscript. 2 vols. 1934.
Photostat reproductions made at the
Birmingham Reference Library from the
originals in the possession of the
Trustees of Shakespeare's Birthplace,
Stratford-upon-Avon.

451723

— [Fearon (G.)] The Birthplace; and,
The Shakespeares, [by I.J.C.Brown.)
pp. 61. Illus.

([Stratford-upon-Avon]) [1939.]

502917

— FLOWER (F.)
Buying Shakespeare's house [: a broadcast talk on the centenary of the
purchase of Shakespeare's birthplace
at Stratford-on-Avon. Broadcast]
16th September, 1947. ff. 6.
typescript. 1947.

587050

— FOX, LEVI
Anne Hathaway's cottage: a **pictorial**
guide. (Norwich) [1963.]

illus. 667679

— FOX, LEVI
Celebrating Shakespeare: a pictorial
record of the celebrations held at
Stratford-upon-Avon during 1964 to
mark the 400th anniversary of the
birth of William Shakespeare.
Prepared for the Shakespeare Birthplace Trust. (Stratford-upon-Avon)
illus. [1964.]

744155

— FOX (L.)
The Heritage of Shakespeare's birthplace. IN SHAKESPEARE SURVEY 1.
(Cambridge)
illus. bibliog. 1948.

590674

— FOX (LEVI)
The Shakespeare collections of
Shakespeare's birthplace and the Royal
Shakespeare Theatre, Stratford-upon-Avon:
[Paper] 1 [of] Shakespeare in the
Library: a symposium. IN Open Access,
Vol.10, N.S., No.2. (Birmingham)
1962.

667074

— FOX (LEVI)
Shakespeare's birthplace: a history
and description. pp. [20].
(Norwich)
illus. [1954.] 642340
A Cotman-Photo Book.
———— A Wensum Colour Book.
[1964.] 667954

— FOX (LEVI)
Shakespeare's Birthplace Library,
Stratford-upon-Avon. Reprinted
from Archives, Vol. 5. pp. [10].
[1961.]
Local Archives of Great Britain, 20.

667308

— FOX (LEVI)
The Shakespearian gardens [: the
gardens administered by the
Shakespeare Birthplace Trust].
pp. [28.] (Norwich)
illus. [1954.]

645424

— FOX, LEVI
The Shakespearian properties,
described by L. Fox. (Norwich)
pp. [16].
illus. map. [1964.]
Wensum series colour books.

667954

— [FURNIVALL (F. J.)]
Modern Shakespearean criticism, as
exhibited in a letter [on the birth-
place] which was published in the
Stratford-on-Avon Herald of Friday,
9th November, 1888. (Brighton)
1888.
Edition of 10 copies only.

496256

— HABGOOD (E. C.) and EAGLE (R. L.)
The Stratford birthplace. Reprinted
from "Baconiana". pp. [13].
1940. 513779
———— 2nd edn. pp. 12.
illus. 1947. 583256

— [HAWTHORNE (N.)]
Shakespeare's birthplace [: an
extract from Recollections of a
gifted woman i.e. Delia S. Bacon].
FROM The Ladies' Treasury, May 1,
1864.
illus.

561763

— HILL (J.)
Shakespeare's birthplace and
adjoining properties. Reprinted
from The Stratford-upon-Avon
Herald. pp. 41. [Stratford-
upon-Avon] 1885.

431332

— HOWITT (W.)
Shakespeare. IN Howitt (W.) Homes
and haunts of the most eminent British
poets.
illus. [?1872]

85170

— [HOWITT (W.)]
The Shakespeare fix [: an article on
the birthplace and family of
Shakespeare]. IN Howitt's Journal,
Vol. 2. 1847.

408552

—— Inventory of documents concerning
the Archer family of Umberslade Hall,
in Tamworth co. War., belonging to
the Rt. Hon. the Earl of Plymouth,
XII-XIX Cent.]   [c.1920.]
  The documents included in the
inventory were deposited at
Shakespeare's Birthplace Library,
Stratford-upon-Avon, 1946.

660596

——   Jewitt (L.) The Museums of England,
with special reference to objects of art
and antiquity: The Shakspere Museum;
Stratford-on-Avon. In The Art Journal,
New Series, Vol.10.

1871.

13102

—— KNIGHT (C.)
Birth-place of Shakspere. [Extract]
from "Shakspere: a biography", by
C. Knight.   FROM The Penny Magazine,
Vol. 11. [New Series.]
  illus.   1842.

557123

—— Landor (W.S.) Shakespeare's house. In
Landor (W.S.) The Last fruit off
an old tree [: imaginary conversations and other works in prose and
verse].

1853.

577129

—— LANE, SAM and ROSINA
A Pictorial guide to replicas of
William Shakespeare's birthplace, and
his wife Anne Hathaway's thatched
cottage, together with Chaucer Lane:
part of the old English village in
Victoria, B.C., Canada. (Victoria,
B.C.)
  illus.   [1960.]

765924

—— LAW (E.)
Shakespeare's garden, Stratford-
upon-Avon. pp. 34.   (Stratford-
upon-Avon: Shakespeare Head Press)
  illus.   1924.

411878

—— McCARTNEY (MARGARET)
"This is my home": pen picture[s,
i.e. articles on famous Warwickshire
houses, including one of Anne
Hathaway's cottage. Newspaper
cuttings from the Birmingham News,
18th Oct. - 27th Dec. 1941].
pp. [16.] [Birmingham]
  illus.

544460

—— Mansinha (M.) At the birth-place of
Shakespeare. Illus. In The Modern
Review, Vol.64.

(Calcutta)   1938.

493025

—— OSBORNE (W.J.)
Anne Hathaway's Cottage.   Published
by the Trustees and Guardians of Shakespeare's Birthplace. pp. 24. Illus.

(Stratford-upon-Avon)   1947.

586597

—— The Royal visit to Stratford-upon-
Avon, April 20th, 1950: a pictorial
record.   Birmingham Post and Mail
photographs. pp. [24.]
(Birmingham)
  ports. illus.   1950.

608548

—— [SEDGFIELD (W. R.)
Photograph of Shakespeare's birthplace,
Stratford-upon-Avon.   (Henry T.
Cooke & Son, Fine Art Repository,
Warwick)]   [c.1860.]

391936

—— Shakespeare and Cervantes [: correspondence between the Royal Academy of
Spain (La Real Academia Española) and
the trustees of Shakespeare's birthplace on the occasion of the recent
national celebration at Madrid of the
tercentenary of the publication of the
first part of Cervantes's "Don Quixote".
Reprinted] from The Times, 9th June,
1905. pp. [3].

531020

—— Shakespeare Birthplace, &c., Trust
Act, 1961.   9 & 10 Eliz. 2 Ch. 38.
pp. 14.   1961.

667290

—— [SHAKESPEARE BIRTHPLACE, ETC., TRUST]
Annual meeting of the Trustees, 1898-
1951.   Reprinted from the Stratford-
upon-Avon Herald. [Stratford]
1898-1951.
Wants 1903-4.

441970

—— [SHAKESPEARE FESTIVAL, STRATFORD-UPON-AVON.
Programme of public lectures and recitals,
&c., including the Annual Summer School,
arranged each year by the Royal Shakes-
peare Theatre, the University of
Birmingham, the Shakespeare Birthplace
Trust, and the British Council, at
Stratford-upon-Avon.] (Birmingham and
Stratford-upon-Avon)   1947-

645712

—— The Shakespeare property at Stratford.
IN The Leisure Hour, 1864.
  illus.

83387

—— Shakespeare's birth-place [: an
extract from Recollections of a
gifted woman i.e. Delia S. Bacon,
by N. Hawthorne].   FROM The Ladies'
Treasury, May 1, 1864.
  illus.

561763

— [Shakespeare's Birthplace and Museum. Reports, cuttings, letters, etc.]

[1861-1910.]

496933

— SHAKESPEARE'S BIRTHPLACE LIBRARY
English books published between 1500 and 1640 with S.T.C. references.
ff. 20. [Stratford-upon-Avon]
1955.
For Pollard and Redgrave's Short title catalogue, see catal. no. 333393.

665253

— SHAKESPEARE'S BIRTHPLACE TRUST

Descriptions, and regulations for the admission of visitors to the buildings of the Trust]. pp. [4]. [Stratford-upon-Avon]
illus. map. [1947.]

580949

— SHAKESPEARE'S BIRTHPLACE TRUST
Hall's Croft, Old Town: souvenir programme of the official opening, 4th April, 1951. pp. [12], [4], [4]. [Stratford-on-Avon]
illus. map.

616082

— Shakspere's house. FROM The Gentleman's Magazine, Sept. 1847. pp. [2.]

402701

— STOWE (Mrs. [HARRIET E. B.])
Visit to Shakespeare's house and tomb. [Extracted from the author's "Sunny memories in foreign lands"]. IN The Leisure Hour, 1864.
illus.

83387

— [WELLSTOOD (FREDERICK CHRISTIAN)]
A Calendar of deeds relating to Coventry deposited in the Record Room at Shakespeare's Birthplace, Stratford-upon-Avon, by Major Charles H. Gregory-Hood.
typescript. [1943.]

549543

— WELLSTOOD (F. C.)
Catalogue of the books, manuscripts, works of art, antiquities and relics exhibited in Shakespeare's birthplace. [With a preface by Sir A. D. Flower.]
New edn. with a supplementary list of recent additions. (Stratford-upon-Avon)
ports. illus. plans. facsimiles. 1937.

490699

— WELLSTOOD (FREDERICK CHRISTIAN)
Catalogue of the books, manuscripts, works of art, antiquities and relics exhibited in Shakespeare's birthplace.
New edition, with a supplementary list of recent additions. (Stratford-upon-Avon)
ports. illus. plans. facsimiles.
1944.

666390

— WELLSTOOD (FREDERICK CHRISTIAN)

An Inventory of the civic insignia and other antiquities belonging to the Mayor and Corporation of Stratford-upon-Avon; with historical notes.
pp. 30. (Stratford-upon-Avon)
port. illus. facsimiles. 1940.

642293

— WELLSTOOD (F. C.)
List of manorial documents preserved in the Record room of the Shakespeare Birthplace Trust, Stratford-upon-Avon. Reprinted from the Genealogists' Magazine, September, 1942. pp. 258-263.

537162

— The Yankee author at Shakespeare's birthplace. (From the popular entertainment "The World and his wife"). IN Routledge's Comic reciter, edited and selected by J. E. Carpenter.
[1867.]

521649

Stratford-upon-Avon

— Church of the Holy Trinity
see also **Grave of Shakespeare**

— Arbuthnot (G.) A Guide to the Collegiate Church of Stratford-on-Avon. 3rd edn. pp.20. Illus.

[Stratford-on-Avon] 1901.

479549

— BEESLEY (G. J.)
My Shakespeare autograph book. [In aid of Shakespeare's Church Fund.]
FROM Strand Magazine, 1903. pp. [9.]

390787

— The Collegiate Church of the Holy Trinity, Stratford-on-Avon. 4th edn.
pp. 28. (Gloucester)
illus. plan. [1946.]

585760

— FISHER (T.)
A Series of antient allegorical, historical and legendary paintings which were discovered, in the summer of 1804, on the walls of the Chapel of the Holy Trinity, at Stratford upon Avon, in Warwickshire. Also views and sections, illustrative of the architecture of the Chapel. [Pts. 1-4. With Appendix No. 1.] pp. 4. 1807.
No more published.

525089

— KNOWLES (E. H.)
An Architectural account of the collegiate church of the Holy Trinity.
IN NEIL (S.) The Home of Shakespeare.
pp. 80.   (Warwick)
                          [?1871]   394908
_____ 2nd edn.   [1878]   508515
_____ 11th edn.   With forty-eight
engravings.   [c.1898] 467567

— NEALE (J. P.) and LE KEUX (J. [H.])
Views of the ancient church of the
Holy Trinity, Stratford upon Avon.
With an historical and architectural
description.   pp. 16.
                      1825.   467246
_____ [Large paper edn.]
                      1825.   608382

— STOWE (Mrs. [HARRIET E. B.])
Visit to Shakespeare's house and
tomb.   [Extracted from the author's
"Sunny memories in foreign lands"]
IN The Leisure Hour, 1864.
  illus.

                      83387

Stratford-upon-Avon

Conferences

— BENNETT (H. S.)
The Shakespearean conference [at
Stratford, 1948.   Broadcast]
2nd September, 1948.   ff. 2.
  typescript.

                      605255

— BOAS (F. S.)
The Shakespeare Conference at
Stratford-on-Avon [1947]:   centenary
of the purchase of the birthplace.
FROM Queen's Quarterly, Vol. 54.
pp. [8].   (Kingston, Ont.)

                      596578

— [Programmes and cuttings relating to
the Shakespeare Conference at Stratford-
on-Avon, organised by G. B. Harrison,
and J. Garrett.]
  ports.   illus.   3 vols.   [1937-39]
Newspaper cuttings relating to Shakespeare
Conferences, 1946- is included in Newspaper Cuttings, Stratford-upon-Avon,
1947-, Catal. no. 587955.   Programmes in
666573.
                      474540

— SAMARIN (ROMAN M.   )
Shekspirovskaya Konferentsiya Stratforde
[1961]. FROM Vestnik Akademii Nauk SSSR,
1962; [and] Tenth International
Shakespeare Conference. FROM Soviet
Literature, 1962. pp.[4][4] (Moskva)

                      667312

— SHAKESPEARE CONFERENCES, Stratford-upon-
Avon [Programmes, reports, etc.] 1st—
[Stratford-upon-Avon.]   1946-

- 1. Material relating to the Conferences
  included in Newspaper Cuttings,
  Stratford-upon-Avon, Catal.No.587955.
- 2. From 7th (1955) called International
  Shakespeare Conference.

                      666573

Stratford-upon-Avon

Exhibition 1964 *see* **Quatercentenary 1964,**
Exhibitions

Stratford-upon-Avon

— Falcon Hotel

— BARNARD (WALKER) & SON, auctioneers
The "Falcon Hotel" and adjoining property, Stratford on Avon.   To be sold
at the Grand Hotel, Birmingham, 29th
April, 1920.   pp. [8.]   (Stratford-
on-Avon)
  illus.   plan.

                      624737

Stratford-upon-Avon

Festival *for Shakespeare birthday celebrations see* Birthday Celebrations, *above*
*For Royal Shakespeare Theatre Festival
season see* Royal Shakespeare Theatre
Festival, *below*

Stratford-upon-Avon

— Grammar School

— The Grammar School of King Edward the
Sixth (Shakespeare's school) in
Stratford-upon-Avon.   pp. 19.
  illus.   plan.   1919.
Printed at the Sign of the Dolphin in
Venezia type, a facsimile of that
used by Nicolas Jenson in Venice in
1470.
                      428692

—— WATKINS (LESLIE)
The Story of Shakespeare's school,
1853-1953. pp. xii, 60. (Stratford-
upon-Avon)
ports. illus.   1953.

637013

Stratford-upon-Avon

— Guides *see also* Warwickshire and
Shakespeare's Country

—— ADAMS (E.) publisher
Hand book for visitors to Stratford-
upon-Avon. pp. 47. (Stratford-
upon-Avon)
illus.   1857.

453751

—— BRITISH COUNCIL
Stratford-upon-Avon. IN [British
Council, Guides to places in the
United Kingdom, compiled for the
United States Armed Forces.]
illus.   [1944-5.]

562395

—— FOX (LEVI)
The Borough town of Stratford-upon-
Avon. (Corporation of Stratford-
upon-Avon)
ports. illus. plans. facsimiles.
                        1953.

633407

— FOX, LEVI
Stratford-upon-Avon: a concise
pictorial guide.   [c.1964.]

illus. A Cotman-photo book.
                      667980

—— FOX, LEVI
Stratford-upon-Avon deutsche Farbenausgabe
Übertragen von A.N. Court. (Norwich)
                        [1963]

illus. map.   667677

— FOX, LEVI
Stratford-upon-Avon en coleurs: nouveau
guide illustré, traduction en français
par A.N. Court. (Norwich)   [1963]

illus. map.   667678

— Fox's Penny guide to Stratford-on-Avon,
with plan of the town, showing chief
places of interest. New & revised
edn.   pp. 23. (Stratford-on-Avon)
genealogical table.   [c.1900.]

478517

—— HEUWOOD (JOHN) Ltd.
Illustrated guide to Stratford-on-
Avon.   pp. 32.   (Manchester)
map.   [c.1920]

478516

—— PUMPHREY BROS.
A Short account of Stratford-on-Avon.
                        [c.1880]

42699

—— ROCK BROTHERS & PAYNE, publishers
Stratford-upon-Avon, the home of
William Shakspeare, pictorially
illustrated. [With descriptive
text.] pp. 16.   1864.

460330

—— STANLEY & BOLTON, publishers
The "Reliable" guide to Stratford-
on-Avon, with a plan of the town.
Containing descriptions of places
of historic interest, and the relics
of Shakespeare. pp. 24. (Stratford-
on-Avon)
illus.   [c.1910.] 418066
_____ Another edn. [c.1915.] 665287

— Stratford-upon-Avon: official guide.
pp. 64.   (Cheltenham)
illus.   map.   plan.   [c.1935.]

550471

— Stratford-upon-Avon: official guide.
(Stratford-upon-Avon)
ports. illus. maps.   [1950]-

607015

—— The Stratford-upon-Avon visitor's handbook, 1952- . Including the official
accommodation register of hotels [etc.].
(Stratford-upon-Avon)
illus. map.   [1952]-
Note: From 1955 Accommodation Register
only issued.

623134

—— WARD (H. S. and [Mrs.] CATHARINE W.)
The Shakespearean guide to Stratford-
on-Avon. With chapters on Warwick,
Kenilworth and "the Shakespeare
country" generally. Illustrated
by W. T. Whitehead. 2nd edn.
port.   [c.1900]

467566

— Ward & Lock's Illustrated guide to,
and popular history of Stratford-
upon-Avon, the home of Shakespeare;
with excursions in the neighbourhood.
illus. maps.   [1881]

467564

Stratford-upon-Avon

— Hall's Croft *see* Birthplace, etc.

Stratford-upon-Avon

— Jubilee *see* Jubilees and Commemorations

STRATFORD-UPON-AVON STUDIES, 3
Early Shakespeare.
illus. chronological tables.
bibliogs. 1961.

666841

STRATFORD-UPON-AVON STUDIES, 4
Contemporary theatre. 1962.

710729

STRATFORD-UPON-AVON STUDIES, 5
Hamlet. 1963.

667698

STRATFORD-UPON-AVON STUDIES, 6
Restoration theatre. 1965.

740808

STRATFORD-UPON-AVON STUDIES, 7
American poetry. 1965.

747636

STRATFORD-UPON-AVON STUDIES, 8
Later Shakespeare.
illus. 1966.

756101

STRATFORD-UPON-AVON STUDIES, 9
Elizabethan theatre.
illus. 1966.

756653

The Stratford-upon-Avon visitor's
handbook, 1952- . Including the
official accommodation register of
hotels [etc.] [Stratford-upon-
Avon] [1952]-
illus. map.
From 1955 Accommodation Register
only issued.

623134

STRATHMANN(ERNEST ALBERT)
The Devil can cite Scripture. IN
Shakespeare 400: essays by American
scholars on the anniversary of the
poet's birth. Published in co-
operation with the Shakespeare
Association of America.
illus. 1964.

667803

STRATHMANN (ERNEST ALBERT)
[Review of] The Passionate Pilgrim,
by William Shakespeare. The third
edn., 1612, reproduced in facsimile
from the copy in the Folger
Shakespeare Library. IN Modern
Language Quarterly, Vol. 2.
(Seattle) 1941.

533242

STRATHMANN (ERNEST ALBERT)
The Textual evidence for "The School
of night" [: a phrase from Love's
labour's lost, Act 4, Scene 3;
arguing whether this spelling is
correct, and if so, whether it refers
to Sir Walter Raleigh's circle, The
School of Night.] IN Modern Language
Notes, Vol. 56. (Baltimore)
bibliog. 1941.

533477

Stratton (Helen) illus.
LAMB ([CHARLES and MARY A.])
A Midsummer night's dream. With songs
set to music [arranged] by T. M. Hardy.
pp. [iv], 72. 1915.
Lamb Shakespeare for the Young.

436485

STRAUSS (T.)
Maurice Evans [Shakespearean actor
and producer, and his career].
IN Theatre Arts, Vol. 26. (New
York)
illus. 1942.

546127

STRAVINSKY (IGOR FEDOROVITCH)
Three songs from William Shakespeare,
1953, for mezzo-soprano, flute,
clarinet and viola. Vocal score.
pp. 12. 1954.

641744

Strawberries

—— ROSS (LAWRENCE J.)
The Meaning of strawberries in
Shakespeare. Offprint from "Studies
in the Renaissance" Vol. 7. pp. 16.
illus. [1961]

667083

Streatfeild (R.A.) Verdi and "King
Lear". In The Musical Times, Vol.
46.

1905.

192174

STREATHAM SHAKESPEARE PLAYERS
Programmes, etc. of Shakespeare
performances, 1912-1937.

421989

STŘIBRNÝ (ZDENĚK)
"Henry V" and history. IN Shakespeare
in a changing world: essays [by
various authors]. 1964.

667797

STŘÍBRNÝ, ZDENĚK
Shakespeare in Czechoslovakia.
IN Shakespeare celebrated: anniversary
lectures delivered at the Folger Library
[during 1964]. (Ithaca, N.Y.) 1965.

771817

STŘÍBRNÝ (ZDENĚK)
Shakespeare today.   IN
CHARLES UNIVERSITY ON SHAKESPEARE:
essays edited by Z. Stříbrný.   (Praha)
illus.   1966.

762631

STŘÍBRNÝ, ZDENĚK, ed.
Charles University on Shakespeare:
essays [by various authors].
(Praha)
illus.   1966.

762631

STRINDBERG, JOHAN AUGUST
Letters to the Intimate Theatre [on
acting, directing and the use of
scenery, with special reference to
Shakespeare]. Translated and
introduced by W. Johnson.   1967.

illus.   760268

Strindberg, Johan August *works relating to*

—ANDERSSON (HANS)
Strindberg's "Master Olaf" and
Shakespeare.   pp. 63.   (Uppsala)
                     1952.
Essays and Studies on English Language
and Literature, 11.

637182

—BULMAN (JOAN)
Strindberg and Shakespeare:
Shakespeare's influence on
Strindberg's historical drama.
bibliog.   1933.

402520

STROEDEL (WOLFGANG)
90th anniversary celebration of the
Deutsche Shakespeare-Gesellschaft.
IN SHAKESPEARE QUARTERLY V:
pp. 317-322.
(New York)   1954.

605711

Stronach (G.) A Critic criticised . Mr.
Sidney Lee and the Baconians [:a
letter to the editor.]   In The Pall
Mall Magazine, Vol. 32.

1904.

405657

STRONACH (GEORGE)
Mr. Sidney Lee and the Baconians:
a critic criticised.   [A revised
version of a letter originally
published in the Pall Mall Magazine,
Vol. 32.]   pp. 24.   [1904.]

549420

STRONG (L. A. G.)
Common sense about poetry.   [With
references to Shakespeare.]
bibliog.   1931.

521376

STRONG (L. A. G.)
O rare Ben Jonson [: a radio play,
with Shakespeare as one of the
characters].   Produced by Mary H.
Allen.   [Broadcast] 12th August,
1945.   ff. 20.
typescript.

563287

STRONG (LEONARD ALFRED GEORGE)
Shakespeare and the psychologists.
IN Talking of Shakespeare [: a
selection from the lectures delivered
at the annual course for teachers at
Stratford. 1948-1953.]   1954.

641471

STRONG (LEONARD ALFRED GEORGE) and
REDLICH (MONICA)
Life in English literature: an
introduction for beginners.
Part 1.   Chaucer to Ben Jonson.
[Containing four chapters on
Shakespeare.]   1932.

397618

Strong (Pablo M.) trans.
LAMB (CHARLES)
Tales from Shakespeare (Macbeth-
Hamlet).   Trad[ucción] de P. M. Strong.
[Spanish and English text.]   pp. 79.
(Madrid)   1936.
Nuevos Textos Bilingües.

459906

STROUD (T. A.)
Hamlet and The Seagull.
IN SHAKESPEARE QUARTERLY IX.
pp. 367-372.
(New York)   1958.

605711

STROUP (THOMAS BRADLEY)
Cordelia and the Fool.
IN SHAKESPEARE QUARTERLY XII: 2.
pp. 127-132.
(New York)   1961.

605711

Stroup (T.B.) Launce and Launcelot.
From The Journal of English and
Germanic philology, vol.30.

(Illinois)   1931.

444158

STROUP (THOMAS BRADLEY)
The Structure of "Antony and
Cleopatra".   IN Shakespeare 400:
essays by American scholars on the
anniversary of the poet's birth.
Published in co-operation with the
Shakespeare Association of America.
illus.   1964.

667803

STROUT, ALAN LANG
John Wilson (Christopher North) as a
Shakespeare critic.   A study of
Shakespeare in the English Romantic
Movement.
IN SHAKESPEARE JAHRBUCH.   Bd. 72/1936.
pp. 93-123.   (Weimar)

10531

Strout (A.L.) A Note on Shakespearean
    criticism. [With bibliographical
    notes.] From Philological quarterly,
    Vol. 11.

            (Iowa)   1932.

                484065

Struble (G.G.) Schlegel's translation
    of Twelfth Night. From The Quarterly
    Journal of the University of North
    Dakota. Vol.19. No.2.

    (Grand Forks,N.D.)   1929.

                442293

STRUNK (WILLIAM)
    The Elizabethan showman's ape.   IN
    Modern Language Notes, Vol. 32.
    (Baltimore, Md.)   1917.

                439157/32

STRUNK (WILLIAM)
    Foreword to Romeo and Juliet.
    IN SHAKESPEARE (W.) Romeo and Juliet:
    a motion picture edition.   Produced
    for Metro-Goldwyn-Mayer.
    illus.   [1936]   457925
    Arthur Barker Edition.
    _____ Random House Edition.
                [1936]   460419

STUART (BETTY KANTOR)
    Truth and tragedy in King Lear.
    IN SHAKESPEARE QUARTERLY XVIII: 2.
    pp. 167-180.
    (New York)   1967.
                605711

STUART (DOROTHY MARGARET)
    The English Abigail [: a study of
    the English maidservant drawn from
    history and literature.   With refer-
    ences to Shakespeare].
    ports. illus.   1946.

                573508

STUART (FRANK)
    Remember me [: a novel relating to
    Shakespeare].   1951.

                619042

Studies in English Literature

—— BECK, RICHARD J.
    Shakespeare: Henry IV.   1965.

        Studies in English Literature No.24.
                744903

—— BROOKE, NICHOLAS
    Shakespeare: King Lear.   1963.

        Studies in English literature,
    No.15.   667688

—— BROWN, JOHN RUSSELL
    Shakespeare: the Tragedy of Macbeth.
                1963.

        Studies in English literature,
    No. 14.   667689

—— FENDER, STEPHEN
    Shakespeare: A Midsummer night's
    dream.   1968.
    Studies in English literature.

                772579

—— HUMPHREYS, ARTHUR RALEIGH
    Shakespeare: Richard II [: a study
    guide].   1967.

        Studies in English literature, 31.
                758800

—— JAMIESON, MICHAEL
    Shakespeare: As you like it. 1965.

        Studies in English Literature
    No.25.   744406

—— MOODY, A.D.
        Shakespeare: 'The Merchant of Venice'.
                1964.

                668323

—— MUIR, KENNETH
    Shakespeare: Hamlet.   1963.

        Studies in English literature,
    No.13.   667796

—— MULRYNE, J.R.
    Shakespeare: Much ado about nothing.
                1965.

        Studies in English Literature
    No.16.   744405

—— NUTTALL, A.D.
    William Shakespeare "The Winter's Tale".
                1966.

        Studies in English Literature,
    No.26.   755389

Studies in English Literature Mouton & Co.

—— TOOLE, WILLIAM B.
    Shakespeare's problem plays: studies
    in form and meaning.   (The Hague)
                1966.
    Studies in English literature Vol. XIX.

                773660

—— WYNKOOP (WILLIAM M.)
    Three children of the universe:
    Emerson's view of Shakespeare, Bacon,
    and Milton.   (Mouton: The Hague)
    illus.   1966.
    Studies in English Literature.

                763098

Studies in Existentialism and Phenomenology

—HOROWITZ, DAVID
   Shakespeare: an existential view.
                              1965.
   Studies in existentialism and
   phenomenology.
                              768004

Studies in Language and Literature

—McFARLAND, THOMAS
   Tragic meanings in Shakespeare.
   (New York)   1966.

         Studies in language and literature.
                              754716

—RICHMOND, HUGH M.
   Shakespeare's political plays.
   (New York)   1967.

         Studies in language and
   literature.   765124

Studies of old actors: 1. Garrick
in "Lord Hastings" 2. Mossop in
"Cardinal Wolsey" 3. Henderson in
"Jacques".   FROM [The Dublin
University Magazine] Vol. 62.
[Dublin]   1863.

                           579639

Studies of Shakspeare in the plays of
King John, Cymbeline, Macbeth [etc.]
with observations on the criticism
and the acting of those plays, by
G. Fletcher [: a review].   FROM
[The Dublin University Magazine,]
Vol. 31. [Dublin]   1848.

                           556076

Studies of undeveloped characters in
Shakspeare, from sketches and
suggestions in his plays.   No[s.] 1
and 4.   FROM [The Monthly Chronicle,
Jan. and April 1839.]
Nos. 2-3 and all after No. 4 wanting.

                           562635

Study-Aid Series see College of Careers,
Study-Aid Series

Study and stage [: a criticism of
   H.G.Granville-Barker's presentation
   of Shakespeare]. In The Times
   Literary Supplement, 1946.

                           580183

A Study in Shakespeare: Timon of
Athens.   FROM [The Oxford and
Cambridge Magazine,] Vol. 1.   1856.

                           554146

Study and Teaching
see also Criticism *works relating to*; Education
and Knowledge; Filmstrips

—ALEXANDER (A. G.)
   English stones [: how Shakespeare is
   taught, a criticism].   FROM Peabody
   Journal of Education, Vol. 17.
   (Nashville, Tenn.)   1939.

                           527917

—ATTINGHAM PARK, Shrewsbury

   Programmes of Shakespeare courses.
   [Shrewsbury, etc.]   1954-

                           667173

—BARNES (T. R.)
   Producing Shakespeare in school.
   IN The Use of English, Vol. 3.
                              1952.

                           618851/3

—BARTON, ARTHUR
   Enter Will Shakespeare! [: personal
   experience of methods of teaching
   Shakespeare]   B.B.C. radio script
   broadcast 25th September 1964.

                           668248

—BARTON (G.)
   Shakespeare - and all that at Bedford
   school. Illus. From Athene: the official
   organ of the Society for Education in Art,
   Vol.1. (Bedford)   1941.

                           554728

—BATE, JOHN
   How to find out about Shakespeare.
   (Oxford)   1968.

      Commonwealth and international library
      Libraries and technical information
      division.   774957

—Bennett (R.) Classroom dramatics.
   [With references to Shakespeare's
   plays.]

                              1938.

                           489964

—BOAS (GUY)
   Shakespeare and the young actor: a
   guide to production.   [Including
   accounts of Shakespeare performances
   at Sloane School, Chelsea.]
   ports.   illus.   1955.   646761
   ───── 2nd edn.   1961.   667197

—— BOAS, GUY
A Teacher's story [: autobiography].
illus. 1963.
Includes a chapter on Shakespeare.

715037

—— BOAS (G.) and HAYDEN (H.) eds.
School drama: its practice and
theory, [by various authors.]
Edited for the School Drama
Committee of the British Drama League,
With a preface by G. Whitworth.
[With references to Shakespeare.]
illus. dgms. bibliog. 1938.

491670

—— BOWER (D.)
"Shakespeare and the cinema" and
"Shakespeare, poetry, acting and
schools"[by] J. Garrett. [Broadcast]
9th March, 1945. ff. 6.
typescript. 1945.
The Arts, No. 5.
For reprint entitled "Shakespeare on
the screen and in the school", see
catal. no. 561343.

558618

—— BREWER (J. S.)
English studies or essays in English
history and literature. [Containing
essays: "On Shakspeare" and "On the
study of Shakspeare".] Edited with
a prefatory memoir by H. Wace.
1881.

421032

—— BRIDGE (G. F.)
Shakspere in schools. FROM The
Journal of Education, Aug., 1936.

454859

—— Butler (H.M.) Shakespeare plays in
schools. pp.57.
([Singapore]) [1921.]

472873

—— CARLETON (P.) ed.
The Amateur stage: a symposium by Flora
Robson, S. Box, M.[S.] Redgrave, L. du
G. Peach, G. Makin, P. Carleton. [With
references to Shakespeare.] 1939.

508149

—— Carroll (S.W.) The Teaching of
Shakespeare in schools. In
Conference of Educational Associa-
tions, 24th annual report, 1936.

449139

—— Cook (H.C.) Acting Shakespeare in
the classroom. In The Play way.
Illus. Plans.

1931.

426883

—— Cooper (L.) Methods and aims in the
study of literature: a series of
extracts and illustrations. [With
references to Shakespeare and bibliographical notes.]

(Ithaca, N.Y.)

(Cornell Studies in English, 31.)

525573

—— Corson (H.) An Introduction to the
study of Shakespeare.

1907.

404403

—— CRAIG (HARDIN)
Proof and probability in the study
of Shakespeare and his contemporaries.
FROM The McNeese Review, Vol. 7.
pp. 19. [Lake Charles]
typescript. 1955.

665663

—— CRAIG (H.)
Trend of Shakespeare scholarship.
IN SHAKESPEARE SURVEY 2.
(Cambridge) 1949.

598403

—— Crawford (H.J.) How to read Shakespeare. In The Teacher's World,
April 5, 1916. pp.48. Illus.

1916.

432005

—— CRAWFORD (MARY M.) and PHILLIPS (L.)
Shakespeare as we like him.
FROM The English Journal, December
1937. (Chicago)

503861

—— CRUMP (G.)
Shakespeare in the schools: [a broadcast talk]. ff. 11.
typescript. 1937.

465088

—— DILTZ (B. C.)
Poetic pilgrimage: an essay in
education [and the study of poetry.
With references to Shakespeare].
(Toronto)
bibliogs. 1942.

544612

—— DONALD (LOUISE)
Shakespeare in the schoolroom. FROM
Aberdeen University Review, Vol. 32.
pp. [4]. [Aberdeen] 1948.

607649

—— ELLIS-FERMOR (UNA [M.])
The Study of Shakespeare: an
inaugural lecture delivered at
Bedford College, University of
London on October 28th 1947.
pp. 16. 1948.

593027

—— Fifty Oxford and Cambridge Local
Examination papers on Shakespeare,
junior and senior.
pp. 96.   1876-92.
Relfe Brothers' Ten Years' Examination
Series.

124818

——FOLGER SHAKESPEARE LIBRARY, Washington,D.C.
Tudor and Stuart history: a report of
the Folger Library Conference on needs
and opportunities; held in celebration
of the fourth centenary of the accession
of Queen Elizabeth I.   pp. 41.
(Washington)   1959.

666450

——FOWLER (J. H.)
The Art of teaching English: lectures
and papers.   [With a chapter on the
study of Shakespeare.]
bibliog.   1932.

388869

——FOWLER (W. W.)
Essays in brief for war-time.   [With
a chapter "A Shakespearean problem".]
(Oxford)   1916.

422534

—— GARRETT (J.)
Shakespeare on the screen and in the
school [: a broadcast talk].   II -
A Hold upon happiness.   FROM The
Listener, Vol. 33.   (Wembley)
illus.   1945.
For broadcast script, see catal. no.
558618.

563665

—— GARRETT (J.)
Shakespeare, poetry, acting and
schools; and Shakespeare and the
cinema [by] D. Bower.   [Broadcast]
9th March, 1945.   ff. 6.
typescript.   1945.
The Arts, No. 5.
For reprint entitled "Shakespeare on
the screen and in the school", see
catal.no. 563665.

558618

—— GIBSON (CHRISTINE M.)
On teaching Shakespeare.   FROM The
English Journal, Vol. 31.   (Chicago)
1942.

565602

—— GORDON (P.)
Shakespeare - with music [: plans
and materials for the use of music
in the teaching of Shakespeare in
high schools, with particular reference to Twelfth night].   FROM The
English Journal, Vol. 31.   (Chicago)
1942.

565601

—— HALLER (WILLIAM)
"What needs my Shakespeare?"
IN SHAKESPEARE QUARTERLY III: 1.
pp. 3-16.
(New York)   1952.

605711

—— HALLIDAY (FRANK ERNEST)
The Enjoyment of Shakespeare.
illus.   1952.

629718

—— THE HARROVIAN: LXXVII: 24.
[Tributes to Ronald Watkins.]   1964.

668237

——Hayden (H.) The Immortal memory:
a new approach to the teaching
of Shakespeare [in dramatic
form.] pp.[96]. Illus.

1936.

451445

——HEADLAM (S. D.)
A Few notes for teachers and others
as to how to get the most educational
value out of the acted Shakespeare
play.   pp. [2.]   (London
Shakespeare League)   [1923.]

424654

——Hill (R.) Streamline Shakespeare [:
an essay on the teaching and production of Shakespeare in schools.]
From The English Journal, June 1938.

503669

—— HILL (W. K.)
How to set a literature paper, illus-
trated from As you like it.   IN The
Educational Review, Vol. 18.   (Old
Series.)   1900.

157146

—— How to read and enjoy Shakespeare.
pp. 60.   (Odham's Press, Ltd.)
illus.   [1933.]

413903

——HOWARTH (ROBERT GUY)

Shakespeare by air: broadcasts to
schools.pp.64. (Sydney)

1957.

665865

—— HUDSON (ARTHUR KENNETH)
Shakespeare and the classroom, compiled
for The Society for Teachers of English.
With a foreword by B. Miles.
bibliog.   1954.   638927
_____ 2nd edn. bibliog. discography.
1960.   666837

—— HUGHES (D.)
The Public schools and the future
[with a chapter "Shakespeare and
School Certificate"].   (Cambridge)
1942.
Current Problems.

530797

——ILLSLEY (W. A.)
A Shakespeare manual for schools.
pp. 96.   (Cambridge)
illus.   glossary.   bibliog.   1957.

665679

— ISAACS (J.)
Shakespearian scholarship.   IN
GRANVILLE-BARKER (H.) and HARRISON
(G. B.) eds., A Companion to
Shakespeare studies.   (Cambridge)
bibliogs. illus. tables. facsimiles.
                                1934.   418724
_____ (New York)   1937.   479251
_____ (Cambridge)   1945.   566174

— Kranendonk (A.G.van) New methods for the
study of literature. [With references to Shakespeare.] In English
studies, Vol. 17.

(Amsterdam)   1935.

485659

— LANG (Mrs. A.) [ed.]
The Approach to Shakespeare [: selections from the plays, stories from the
plays, and sources]; with an introduction.   6th edn.
port. illus.   1927.   544399
The Teaching of English Series.
For "A Further approach to Shakespeare"
see under Holmdahl (Freda).
_____ 7th edn.   1928.   544400
_____ Another edn. 1929.   563643
_____ Another edn. 1932.   501588

— LEAVIS (F. R.)
The Approach to Shakespeare.
IN Leavis (F. R.) Education & the
university: a sketch for an
'English school'.
bibliog.   1943.

544927

— Liddell (M.H.) Botching Shakespeare.
In Atlantic Monthly, Vol.82.

(Boston,Mass.)   1898.

144045

— LUSHINGTON (V.)
On the study of Shakspere.   FROM
The Working Men's College Magazine,
Vol. 2.   1860.

558055

— LYTLE (C.F.)
When Shakespeare holds the stage:
learning through acting. [With
bibliographical notes.] From The
English Journal, Vol.32. (Chicago)
                                 1943.

578424

— McCAUL (R. L.)
A Worksheet for a Shakespearean
drama.   FROM Education, Vol. 58.
(Boston, Mass.)   1938.

512383

— MACDONELL (AMICE)
The Production of school plays.
[With references to Shakespeare's
plays.]
frontis. bibliog.   1934.

428986

— McGREGOR (J. S. I.) ed.
Notes on Shakespeare's plays [: notes
for schools], No. 1.   (Cape Town)
                                [1949]
A Midsummer night's dream; Henry IV
Part I; Macbeth; The Merchant of
Venice; King Lear; Twelfth Night.

613220

—   Maguire (G.P.) Macbeth in a
Hungarian school. In The Hungarian
Quarterly, Vol.4.
(Budapest)   1938.

496057

— Malm (Marguerite) Interpreting
Shakespeare to youth. From The
English Journal, April 1937.

(Chicago)

503859

— MERRILL(J.) and FLEMING (MARTHA)
Play-making and plays: the dramatic
impulse and its educative use in the
elementary and secondary school. [With
an introduction by C.A. Scott, a
bibliography and references to Shakespeare.
Illus.   1930.

403624

— MIKHAILOV (M.)
The Study of Shakespeare in the
Soviet Union, with a foreword by
F. S. Boas.   FROM The Anglo-Soviet
Journal, Vol. 6.
illus.   1945.

561323

— Mueller (W.R.) The Class of
'50 reads "Othello". In
College English, Vol.10.

(Chicago)   1948-9.

598860-10

— Muir (K.) Shakespeare in the school
library.   In The School library
review, Vol. 2.

(Sharnbrook)   1939.

522774

— MUIR (KENNETH)
Shakespeare texts for school libraries.
IN The School Library Review, Vol. 3.
No. 4.   (Sharnbrook)   1944.

560962

— MURPHY (G. H.)
Shakespeare and the ordinary man.
FROM The Dalhousie Review, Vol. 15.
(Halifax, N.S.)   1935.

514306

— Murphy (G.H.) Shakespeare and the
ordinary man. With a foreword by
Sir J. Chisholm. pp. 41.

(Toronto)   1939.

502333

—— NICOLL (ALLARDYCE)
Companions of Autolycus [: an article
on research in libraries, with references to Shakespeare.] FROM Theatre
Arts Monthly, September, 1933. pp.
711-20.
illus.

408896

—— NICOLL (ALLARDYCE)
Co-operation in Shakespearian scholarship. [(42nd] Annual Shakespeare
Lecture of the British Academy, 1952)
pp. 18.

640821

—— Nicolson (Janet) Why we produce
Shakespeare in training colleges
and schools. In The Amateur Theatre
and Playwrights' Journal, Vol.4,
No.75.

1937.

467093

—— OMMANNEY (KATHARINE A.)
The Stage and the school. Pictures
by Ben Kutcher. [With chapters on
Shakespeare.]
bibliogs. 1932.

469652

—— Peat (R.C.) Presenting Shakespeare [:
how and when to introduce the plays
of Shakespeare into the English
school syllabus]. Illus.

1947.

581860

—— PHILLIPS (A. L.)
Letting Shakespeare live again.
FROM Education, Vol. 58.
(Boston, Mass.) 1938.

512382

—— POOLE (E. F.)
Shakespeare and the secondary modern
school. IN English in Schools,
Vol. 2. 1948.

618850/2

—— POTTER (S.)
How to appreciate Shakespeare [: a
demonstration. Broadcast] 20th
April, 1947. ff. 23.
typescript.

583267

—— POTTER (STEPHEN)
Notes on Shakespeare. IN Potter (S.)
The Muse in chains: a study in
education.
graph. 1937.

653584

—— SALINGAR (L. G.)
Shakespeare in school. IN The Use
of English, Vol. 1. (Bureau of
Current Affairs)
bibliog. 1949.

618851/1

—— SAMPSON (G.)
Literature in the classroom.
[With references to Shakespeare]
IN English Association, Essays and
Studies, vol. 20. Collected by
G. Cookson. (Oxford)
bibliog. 1935.

434627

—— SANDERS (GERALD DeWITT)
A Shakespeare primer. (New York)
illus. dgms. facsimiles. bibliog.
1950.

612178

—— Shakespeare Survey: an annual
survey of Shakespearian study &
production. [Vol.] 1- [With]
indexes. (Cambridge)
ports. illus. plans. dgms.
tables. facsimiles. bibliogs.
1948-

590674

—— SHAKESPEAREAN RESEARCH OPPORTUNITIES:
the report of the Modern Language
Association of America conference.
Edited by W. R. Elton. No. 1-
(Riverside, Cal.) 1965-

762628

—— SIMON (H. W.)
The Reading of Shakespeare in American
schools and colleges: an historical
survey. [With bibliographies.]
(New York)

1932.

407352

—— Simon (H.W.) Why Shakespeare. From
The English Journal, vol.23.

(Chicago) 1934.

442569

—— STEPPAT ([Mrs.] MARGARET [A. A.])
Shakespeare in the classroom:
preparatory study and exercises in
dramatic work which lead up to the
reading of the plays. pp. 86.
1933.

411351

—— STOWELL (HELEN ELIZABETH)

Reading Shakespeare's plays. Port. Illus.
(Welwyn, Herts) 1962.

667200

—— TAGGERT (LOUISE) and HAEFNER (G. E.)
Two methods of teaching Macbeth.
FROM The English Journal, vol. 23.
(Chicago) 1934.

442570

—— TOWNSEND (C. L.)
Shakespeare and the wide, wide
world. FROM The English Journal,
vol. 19. (Chicago) 1930.

442567

—— VAN CLEVE (C. F.)
The Teaching of Shakespearean plays
in American secondary schools.
pp. 9.   (Nashville, Tenn.) 1937.
George Peabody College for Teachers.

567010

—— WALTER (JOHN HENRY)
Shakespeare in schools.   IN SHAKESPEARE
SURVEY 10.   (Cambridge)   1957.

665485

—— WEISINGER (HERBERT)
The Study of Shakespearian tragedy
since Bradley: a reprint from
Shakespeare Quarterly, Vol. 6.
pp. [10].   [New York]   [1955]

665615

—— WESTHAM HOUSE ADULT RESIDENTIAL
COLLEGE Barford

**Programmes of courses on Shakespeare for
adult students.** [Barford, etc.]
1954-

667172

—— WILSON (A. H.)
English essays and essentials [for
students of courses at Susquehanna
University.   Including a section
on Shakespeare.] pp. 63.
(Selinsgrove, Pa.)
bibliog.   1941.

552436

—— Wilson (J.D.) The Study of Shakespeare. From University of
Edinburgh Journal, Summer Number,
1936.

(Edinburgh)

515199

—— WOOD (S.)
The New teaching of Shakespeare in
schools.   With illustrations from
the plays of "Julius Caesar" and
"A Midsummer night's dream". pp. 57.
bibliog.   1947.

590045

—— WORTH (MARTIN)
Producing Macbeth [: introductory
scripts to a production of Macbeth
for schools].   Televised January-
March, 1958.   (Associated
Rediffusion Ltd.)
typescript.

665945

—— WORTH (MARTIN)

**Twelfth Night, a Shakespearean series
[: nine introductory scripts to a
production of Twelfth Night for schools].
Televised January-March, 1959.
Typescript. (Associated-Rediffusion Ltd.).**

666169

—— WRIGHT (LOUIS BOOKER)
An Obligation to Shakespeare and
the public.   IN SHAKESPEARE SURVEY
16.
illus.   1963.

667523

—— WRIGHT, PETER
Success in Shakespeare [: a guide
to 'O' and 'A' level examinations].
(Stockport)   [1968]

773078

Study and Teaching: Manuals
see also Barnes and Noble Focus Books;
Barrons Educational Series; College of
Careers, Cape Town, Study Aid Series;
Dinglewood Shakespeare Manuals; Guides to
English Literature Series; Monarch Critiques
of Literature; Notes on Chosen English Texts;
Outline Studies in Literature; Studies in
English Literature; Study Master Series;
Wadsworth Guides to Literary Study *and
also under titles of the individual plays and
poems*

—— AMERICAN SHAKESPEARE FESTIVAL THEATRE AND
ACADEMY, Stratford, Conn.
Study guide [to] 'Julius Caesar',
'Twelfth Night', 'Falstaff (Henry IV,
Part II)'. (Stratford, Conn.) 1966.

illus.   758152

—— BECKER (KATE H.)
English outlines for the busy teacher.
(Belmont, N.C.)
No. 1.   As you like it.   pp. 24.
                  1931.   446917
No. 4.   Henry the Fifth.   pp. 41.
                  1931.   446916
No. 8.   Julius Caesar.   pp. 48.
                  1933.   446915
No. 10. Macbeth.   pp. 53.
                  1935.   446914
No. 14. The Merchant of Venice. pp.40.
                  1939.   507778
No. 18. Hamlet.   pp. 39.
                  1944.   557779

—— BERKELEY (DAVID S.)
A Guide to Shakespearean tragedy.
(Stillwater, Okla.)
typescript. bibliogs.   1960.

666834

—— BOAS (F. S.)
An Introduction to the reading of
Shakespeare.
ports.   illus.   facsimiles.
bibliog.   1930.
The World's Manuals.

488357

—BRANSOM (LAURA)
Living Shakespeare [: the stories of
the plays].
  illus.   [1949 –53]
For "Teachers' companion to Living
Shakespeare", see Catal. no. 636356.

           604746

—BRANSOM (LAURA)
Living Shakespeare: teachers' companion [: scenes suitable for acting
by children]. Illustrated by Molly
Wilson.   1953
 For 'Living Shakespeare' [: the
stories of the plays] see Catal. no.
604746.

           636356

—BUTLER (P.)
Analytical questions on Shakespearean
plays. (New Orleans)   1936.

           455272

—COLIJN (I.)
An Introduction to Shakespeare for
secondary schools. [With notes
in Dutch.] pp. 52. (Zutphen)
 ports. illus. facsimile. bibliog.
         1958.

           666410

—HENGESBACH (J.) [ed.]
Readings on Shakespeare: illustrative
of the poet's art, plots and characters. Ein lesebuch für höhere
Schulen, insebondere Gymnasien und
zum Studium. [English text, with
preface and notes in German.] (Berlin)
 bibliog.   1901.

           452582

—[HOLMDAHL (FREDA)]
A Further approach to Shakespeare [:
selections from the plays, stories
from the plays] including three prose
tales by Sir A. T. Quiller-Couch.
With an introduction by H. E.
Marshall.
 illus.   1934.
"Teaching of English" Series.
For the Approach to Shakespeare see
under Lang (Mrs. Andrew).

           429584

—ILLSLEY (W.   A.

A Shakespeare manual for schools.pp.96.
Illus. Glossary. Bibliog. (Cambridge).
         1957.

          665679

—MacCRACKEN (H. N.), PIERCE (F. E.) and
DURHAM (W. H.)
An Introduction to Shakespeare.
 port.   1913. 450748
  _____ (New York) 1929. 466569

—McGREGOR (J. S. I.) ed.
Notes on Shakespeare's plays [: notes
for schools], No. 1. (Cape Town)
         [1949]
 A Midsummer night's dream; Henry IV
Part I; Macbeth; The Merchant of Venice;
King Lear; Twelfth Night.

          613220

—PARRY (JOHN)
A Guide to Shakespeare for Malayan
students. pp. 72.   1956.

         665366

—Reading a Shakespeare play: outlines
and suggestions. (New Hudson
Shakespeare) Nos. 1-3. [1931]
  1. Macbeth; As you like it;
A Midsummer night's dream. pp. 27.
  2. Hamlet; Julius Caesar; Twelfth
Night. Edited by G. P. W. Earle.
pp. 31.
  3. King Lear; Henry the Fourth:
Part 1; The Tempest. By G. P. W.
Earle. pp. 46.

         393730

—REDGRAVE (Sir MICHAEL SCUDAMORE)
Shakespeare and the public schools.
IN CARLETON (P.) ed., The Amateur
stage: a symposium.   1939.

         508149

—SANDERS (GERALD DeWITT)
A Shakespeare primer. Illus. Dgms.
Facsimiles. Bibliog. (New York)

         1950.

        612178

Study Master Series

— HENDERSON, ARCHIBALD
Much ado about nothing. A scene-by-
scene analysis with critical commentary.
(New York)   1966.

   Study master series. 756595

— KIMBROUGH, ROBERT
Troilus and Cressida: a scene-by-scene
analysis with critical commentary.
(New York)   1966.

   Study master series. 762645

—LORDI, ROBERT J., and ROBINSON, JAMES E.
Richard III: a scene-by-scene analysis
with critical commentary. (New York)
        1966.

   Study Master Series. 762658

— NAUMAN, JANET
Henry IV Part One. A scene-by-
scene analysis with critical
commentary. (New York) 1964.
Study master series.

        746819

— SHIPLEY, JOSEPH TWADELL, ed.
**As you like it: a scene-by-scene
analysis with critical commentary.**
(New York)   1964.

   Study master series. 668336

— SHIPLEY, JOSEPH TWADELL, ed.
Hamlet: a scene-by-scene analysis with critical commentary. (New York) 1963.

Study master series.   743611

— SHIPLEY, JOSEPH TWADELL, ed.
Julius Caesar: a scene-by-scene analysis with critical commentary. (New York) 1963.

Study master series.   743612

— SHIPLEY, JOSEPH TWADELL, ed.
King Lear: a scene-by-scene analysis with critical commentary. (New York) 1965.

Study master series.   743610

— SHIPLEY, JOSEPH TWADELL, ed.
Macbeth: a scene-by-scene analysis with critical commentary. (New York) 1964.

Study master series.   743614

— SHIPLEY, JOSEPH TWADELL, ed.
The Merchant of Venice: a scene-by-scene analysis with critical commentary. (New York) 1964.

Study master series.   743615

— SHIPLEY, JOSEPH TWADELL, ed.
A Midsummer Night's Dream: a scene-by-scene analysis with critical commentary. (New York) 1964.

Study master series.   743616

— SHIPLEY, JOSEPH TWADELL, ed.
Othello: a scene-by-scene analysis with critical commentary. (New York) 1963.

Study master series.   743617

— SHIPLEY, JOSEPH TWADELL, ed.
Richard II: a scene-by-scene analysis with critical commentary. (New York) 1964.

Study master series.   668335

— SHIPLEY, JOSEPH TWADELL, ed.
Romeo and Juliet: a scene-by-scene analysis with critical commentary. (New York) 1964.

Study master series.   743613

— SHIPLEY, JOSEPH TWADELL, ed.
Shakespeare's Sonnets: analytical notes and critical commentary. (New York) 1963.

Study master series.   743618

— SMITH, JOHN HARRINGTON
The Comedy of errors: a scene by scene analysis with critical commentary.   (New York)   1966.
Study master series.
768543

STULL (JOSEPH S.)
Cleopatra's magnanimity: the dismissal of the Messenger.
IN SHAKESPEARE QUARTERLY VII,
pp. 73-78.
(New York) 1956.

605711

STUNZ (ARTHUR N.)
The Date of Macbeth.   IN E.L.H.: a journal of English literary history, Vol. 9.   (Baltimore)
bibliog.   1942.

544179

STURGIS, JULIAN RUSSELL
Much ado about nothing: opera libretto

see under English Editions:
Much Ado About Nothing: Opera texts

[STURGIS (JULIAN RUSSELL)]
The Shakspeare revival in London.
[Containing references to Sir H. Irving and Ellen Terry.] FROM
[International Review, Vol. 6.]
[New York]   [1879.]

554169

Sturt (Mary) Francis Bacon: a biography [with Shakespearian references and a bibliography]. Ports. Illus. Facsimile.   1932.

397730

STYAN (J. L.)
The Actor at the foot of Shakespeare's platform.   IN SHAKESPEARE SURVEY 12.
(Cambridge)   1959.

666150

STYAN (JOHN LOUIS)

The Elements of drama [: an analysis of its verbal, visual and aural elements]. Bibliog.   1960.

692824

STYAN, JOHN LOUIS
Shakespeare's stagecraft. (Cambridge) 1967.

766182

Style
see also Baroque

— BENNETT (PAUL E.)
The Statistical measurement of a stylistic trait in Julius Caesar and As you like it.
IN SHAKESPEARE QUARTERLY VIII.
pp. 33-50.
(New York) 1957.

605711

Style

— Bett (H.) Some secrets of style.
[With references to Shakespeare.]
1932.

398437

—— BRADBROOK (MURIEL CLARA)
Fifty years of the criticism of
Shakespeare's style: a retrospect.
IN SHAKESPEARE SURVEY 7.   (Cambridge)
1954.

639176

— DOWNS (E. V.)
English literature: the rudiments
of its art and craft. [With references to Shakespeare.]
 bibliogs.   1920.   527216
The New Teaching Series.
_____ 2nd and revised edn.
1926.   574422

— EARP (F. R.)
The Style of Sophocles. [With a
chapter "Change of style in
Shakespeare".] (Cambridge) 1944.

548213

— Elton (O.) Essays and addresses
[including a lecture in 'Style in
Shakespeare].   1939.

506134

— FOAKES, REGINALD ANTHONY
Contrasts and connections: some notes
on style in Shakespeare's comedies and
tragedies.
IN SHAKESPEARE JAHRBUCH. Bd. 90/1954.
pp. 69-81.   (Heidelberg)

10531

— HAPGOOD (ROBERT)
Shakespeare's thematic modes of speech:
"Richard II" to "Henry V".
IN SHAKESPEARE SURVEY 20. (Cambridge)
1967.

766881

— HILL (R. E.)
Shakespeare's early tragic mode.
IN SHAKESPEARE QUARTERLY IX.
pp. 455-469.
(New York)   1958.

605711

— Lawrence (C.E.) The Gentle art of
authorship [with references to
Shakespeare.]   1924.

517920

— Mathews (W.) Literary style, and
other essays. [With references to
Shakespeare.]
(Toronto)   1881.

519832

— MILNER (IAN)
Shakespeare's climactic style. IN
CHARLES UNIVERSITY ON SHAKESPEARE:
essays edited by Z. Stříbrný. (Praha)
illus.   1966.

762631

— NOSWORTHY (J. M.)
The Integrity of Shakespeare: illustrated from Cymbeline.
IN SHAKESPEARE SURVEY 8.   (Cambridge)
1955.

647706

— PIRKHOFER (ANTON M.)
"A Pretty Pleasing Pricket" - on the use
of alliteration in Shakespeare's Sonnets.
IN SHAKESPEARE QUARTERLY XIV: 1.
pp. 3-14.
(New York)   1963.

605711

— Saintsbury (G.[E.B.]) Shakespeare
and the grand style. In Jones (Phyllis M.)
[ed.] English critical essays, twentieth
century [: an anthology], selected with
an introduction.
(The World's Classics)
1933.

418096

— SCHANZER (ERNEST)
Atavism and anticipation in
Shakespeare's style.   Reprinted
from Essays in Criticism Vol. 7.
ff. 242-256.   1957.

667097

— SEN (TARAKNATH)
Shakespeare's short lines.
IN Shakespeare commemoration volume,
edited by Taraknath Sen.   (Calcutta)
1966.

764382

— Thaler (A.) Shakespeare and Sir
Philip Sidney: the influence of "The
Defense of Poesy". [With bibliographical
notes.]
(Cambridge.Mass.)   1947.

601357

— Thaler (A.) Shakespeare on style,
imagination and poetry. In PMLA,
Publications of the Modern Language
Association of America,Vol.53.
1936.

499373

— Weston (H.) Form in literature: a
theory of technique and construction. With
a preface by J. Drinkwater [and
references to Shakespeare]. Dgms.
1934.

427713

Styles (P.) The Borough of Stratford-
upon-Avon and the parish of
Alveston. [Reprinted from The
Victoria history of the county of
Warwick, Vol.3.] Architectural
descriptions by J.W.Bloe. [With
bibliographical notes.] pp.72. Illus.
Maps. Plans.

1946.

574868

STYLES, PHILIP
The Commonwealth [: in Elizabethan
England].   IN SHAKESPEARE SURVEY 17.
(Cambridge)   1964.

667822

Styles, Philip *works relating to*

——Shakespeare's county [: a review of
The Victoria history of the county
of Warwick, Vol.3. Barlichway
Hundred. Edited by P.Styles]. In
The Times Literary Supplement, 1946.

580183

SUBRAHMANYAM, D. S., and others, eds.
Homage to Shakespeare Quatercentenary
1964 [from] Sir C. Ramalinga Reddy
College   (Eluru)
illus.   1964.

740823

SUBBARAU, RENTALA VENKATA
Othello unveiled.   (Madras) 1906.

196107

SUCKLING (Sir JOHN)
A Supplement of an imperfect copy of
verses of Mr. William Shakespeare's
by the author [: Excerpt from Lucrece,
with addition by Suckling.]   IN
Suckling (Sir J.) Works in prose and
verse.   Edited by A. H. Thompson.
                    1910.   400780
_____ IN Suckling (Sir J.) Poems.
                    1933.   432710
No. 149 of an edition of 250 copies.

Suddard ([S.J.]Mary) Ben Jonson and
Shakespeare.   From The Contemporary
Review [Vol. 99.]

[1911.]

318538

SUDDARD ([S. J.] MARY)
The Blending of prose, blank verse
and rhymed verse in "Romeo and Juliet".
FROM The Contemporary Review: Literary
Supplement, 1910.   pp. [5.]   [1910]

389209

Sūdraka *works relating to*

——FADDEGON (B.)
Mrcchakatikā [by Sūdraka] and King
Lear.   IN India antiqua: oriental
studies presented to J. P. Vogel on
the fiftieth anniversary of his
doctorate.   (Leyden: Kern Institute)
dgms.   1947.

589687

[Suffield (J.)] Bacon v. Shakespeare.
From The Central Literary Magazine,
Vol. 8.

(Birmingham)   1888.

559336

Suicide *see* Death in Shakespeare

Sullivan (Sir Arthur Seymour) see
Music Scores (Henry the Eighth;
The Merchant of Venice; Much ado
about nothing; Twelfth Night)

Sullivan, Barry *works relating to*

——LAWRENCE (W. J.)
Barry Sullivan: a biographical
sketch [containing references to
Shakespearian productions.]
ports.   1893.
Author's extra-illustrated copy.
Contains author's signature.
                          500865

—— SHAW (GEORGE BERNARD)
Sullivan, Shakespear and Shaw.   IN
The Atlantic Monthly, Vol. 180.
(Boston, Mass.)   1947. 19347/180
_____ FROM [Strand Magazine] Vol. 94.
illus.   1947. 586889
_____ IN Shaw [G. B.] on theatre.
                    1958.   693464

SULLIVAN ([Sir] E.)
The Defamers of Shakespeare [: a
criticism of "The Shakespeare problem
re-stated", by Sir G. G. Greenwood].
IN The Nineteenth Century.   Vol. 65.
1909.

216975

SULLIVAN ([Sir] EDWARD)
Francis Bacon as a poet.   IN The
Nineteenth Century and After, Vol. 66.
1909.

220446

SULLIVAN ([Sir] E.)
An Italian book of etiquette in
Shakespeare's day [: The Civile
Conversation of S. Guazzo.]
IN The Nineteenth century and after,
Vol. 73.   1913.

243292

Sullivan ([Sir] E.) A Libel on Ben
   Jonson. In The Nineteenth century
   and after, Vol. 74.

1913.

247982

SULLIVAN ([Sir] E.)
Shakespeare and the waterways of
North Italy.   IN The Nineteenth
century and after, Vol. 64.
   bibliog.   1908.

213154

Sullivan ([Sir] E.) What Shakespeare
   saw in nature. In The Nineteenth
   century and after, Vol. 73.

1913.

243292

Sullivan, Edward Sir *works relating to*

— GREENWOOD ([Sir] G. G.)
   The Vindicators of Shakespeare: a
   reply to Sir Edward Sullivan.
   IN The Nineteenth Century and After.
   Vol. 65.   1909.

216975

SULLIVAN (F.)
Cyme, a purgative drug [: a discussion
on the text of two lines of Macbeth].
IN Modern Language Notes, Vol. 56.
(Baltimore)   1941.

533477

Sumarokov, Aleksandr *works relating to*

— LANG (D. M.)
   Sumarokov's 'Hamlet': a misjudged
   Russian tragedy of the eighteenth
   century.   IN The Modern Language
   Review, Vol. 43.   (Cambridge)
   bibliog.   1948.

266816/43

Summer

— MUSEUS [pseud.]
   Shakespeare's summer.   FROM The
   Contemporary Review, Literary Supple-
   ment, 1910.   pp. [4.]

389208

SUMMERS ([ALPHONSUS JOSEPH MARY AUGUSTUS]
MONTAGUE)
A Bibliography of the Restoration
drama.   (Fortune Press)   [1935].
   Edn. limited to 250 copies.

436088

SUMMERS ([ALPHONSUS JOSEPH MARY
AUGUSTUS] MONTAGUE)
The First illustrated Shakespeare:
[Rowe's edition of the Works, in
six volumes, adorn'd with cuts,
1709].   FROM The Connoisseur,
December, 1938.   pp. [5.]
   illus.

494121

SUMMERS ([ALPHONSUS JOSEPH MARY
AUGUSTUS] MONTAGUE)
The Gothic quest: a history of
the Gothic novel.   [With
Shakespearian references.]
   ports.   illus.   [1938.]
Fortune Press.

492225

SUMMERS ([ALPHONSUS JOSEPH MARY
AUGUSTUS] MONTAGUE)
The Playhouse of Pepys.   [With
references to Shakespeare.]
   ports.   illus.   facsimiles.
1935.

436146

SUMMERS ([ALPHONSUS JOSEPH MARY
AUGUSTUS] MONTAGUE)
The Restoration theatre [: an
account of the technique of the
playwrights and the practical
staging of plays. With references
to Shakespeare].
  illus. facsimiles.   1934.

417668

SUMMERSON (JOHN NEWENHAM) ed.
[The Critics.] Edinburgh International
Festival edition [including a criticism
of the Canadian Stratford Company in
Shakespeare's Henry the Fi...].
Chairman: J. [N.] Summerson.
Producer: J. Weltman. [Broadcast]
9th September, 1956. ff. [25.]
  typescript.

665431

SUMNER (MARY B.)
Essay on William Shakspere.   pp. xvi,
64. manuscript. ports.   illus.
facsimiles.   1907.

592300

SUMNER'S TY-PHOO TEA LTD.
Characters from Shakespeare: [a series
of 25 picture cards.]   pp. [20.]
[Birmingham]   [1937.]

480109

[Sun Life Assurance Society.] The Seven
  ages [: advertisement booklet based
  on Shakespeare's Seven Ages of Man.
  Illustrated by reproductions from
  Boydell's Illustrations to Shakes-
  peare]. pp.[16.]

[1927.]

419853

Sund (Marcus W.) ed.
LAMB (CHARLES and MARY [A.])
Tales from Shakespeare.   Annotated
by L. S. Kwei.   (Shanghai)   [1929]
English Classics Series.

438360

SUNDARAM (C.), SIVARAMAN (K. M.) and
RANGANATHAN (S. R.)
Reference service and bibliography.
[Including references to Shakespeare.]
(Madras)
2 vols.   1940-1.
Madras Library Association.
Publication Series, 9, 10.

539617

Sunday

——————   Hessey (J.A.) Sunday: its origin,
  history and present obligation. [Con-
  taining references to Shakespeare's use
  of the words "Sunday" and "Sabbath".]
  (Bampton Lectures, 1860)   1889.

398666

SUNDAY SHAKESPEARE SOCIETY
[Annual reports, etc.] 1874, 1918-
1957.
  Nos. from 1874 to 1918 missing.

449338

Sundials *see* Time in Shakespeare

Supernatural
see also Fairies; Folklore; Ghosts; Magic;
Spiritualism; Witches and Witchcraft

—— ALLEN (P.)
The Psychic in Shakespeare['s plays].
FROM Light[, Vol. 65]   [1945.]

563663

—— BUSHNELL (N. S.)
Natural supernaturalism in "The
Tempest".   pp. [15].   FROM
Publications of the Modern Language
Association of America, vol. 47.
[(Menasha, Wis.)   [1932]

438442

——COURVILLE, XAVIER de
Shakespeare and the marvellous.
IN Revue d'histoire du théâtre,
quinzième année, [no.] 1, jan.-mar.,
1963.

621867

——CRAWFORD (ALEXANDER W.)
The Apparitions in "Macbeth".   IN
Modern Language Notes, Vol. 39.
(Baltimore, Md.)   1924.

439157/39

—— De M[ontmorency] (J.E.G.) The
Supernatural in literature. [With
references to Shakespeare.] In The
Contemporary Review, Vol.101.

1912.

236965

—— Doran (Madeleine) On Elizabethan
"credulity". With some questions
concerning the use of the marvelous
in literature [and references to
the supernatural in Shakespeare's
plays]. In Journal of the history of
ideas, Vol.1.

(New York)   1940.

519996

— DORAN (MADELEINE)
That undiscovered country: a problem
concerning the use of the supernatural
in Hamlet and Macbeth.   IN Renaissance
studies in honor of Hardin Craig.
(Iowa)
   port.   bibliog.   1941.
Philological Quarterly, Vol. 20, No. 3.
Iowa University [and Stanford University]

539442

— Hardy (T.J.) Books on the shelf
   [: essays. With references to
   Shakespeare.]

1934.

421879

— Hodgson (S.H.) The Supernatural in
   English poetry: Shakspere; Milton;
   Wordsworth; Tennyson. In Hodgson
   (S.H.) Outcast essays and verse
   translations.

1881.

175842

— Oman (J.[W.]) The Natural & the supernatural. [With a chapter, "A Poet's
   awareness and apprehension", as seen
   in Shakespeare's plays and characters]

(Cambridge)   1931.

383308

— OYAMA, TOSHIKAZU
   Hamlet's dichotomy and the Elizabethan
   demonology.   FROM The English review,
   vol. V, nos. 1, 2, July 1967.
   (Tokyo)

764572

— RADCLIFFE (Mrs. [ANNE])
   On the supernatural in poetry.
   [With references to Shakespeare.]
   FROM [The New Monthly Magazine,
   Vol. 16.]   [1826.]

563682

— REED, ROBERT RENTOUL
   The occult on the Tudor and Stuart
   stage.   1965.

743530

— Rogers (L.W.) Clairvoyance in Shakespeare.
   In The Theosophist, Vol.58, Pt.2.

(Madras)   1937.

469480

— Rogers (L.W.) Symbolical dreams in
   Shakespeare.   In The Theosophist,
   Vol.58, Pt.2.

(Madras)   1937.

469480

— ROSE (BRIAN W.)
   The Tempest: a reconsideration of
   its meaning.   IN English Studies
   in Africa, Vol. I.   (Johannesburg)
                              1958.

682610/1

— Shakspeare and the supernatural.
   FROM Chambers' Journal [, Vol. 31].
                              [1874.]

554731

— The Shakespearean angels and devils:
   1. The angels; 2. Fairies and witches.
   In The Contemporary Review, Vols.
   105 [and] 106.   2 vols.

1914.

251087

— The Supernatural element in Shakespeare. In The Westminster Review,
   Vol.52.

1877.

19442

— THORNTON (G. H.)
   English composition [using the subject
   "Shakespeare's treatment of the
   supernatural" as an example for essay
   writing].   Edited by [Sir] J. Adams.
                              [1906.]
   The Self Educator [Vol. 1].

528701

— TONGE (MILDRED)
   Black magic and miracles in Macbeth.
   FROM The Journal of English and
   Germanic philology, vol. 31.
   (Illinois)   1932.

444160

— WEST (R.H.) The Invisible world: a study of
   pneumatology in Elizabethan drama. [With
   reference to Shakespeare, a bibliography
   and notes.] (Athens, Georgia)
                              1939.

529590

Superstitions *see* **Folklore**

Surgery *see* **Medicine and Hygiene**

Surrealism *see* **Art in Shakespeare**

Stratford-upon-Avon

– Libraries
see also Birthplace, etc. *above;* Shakespeare
Memorial Library, *below*

—— CALTHROP (D. C.)
  Andrew Carnegie [, the Stratford-upon-
  Avon Free Library] and Mr. William
  Shakespeare. IN The New Liberal
  Review, Vol. 5.   1903.

                        176911

Stratford-upon-Avon

– Maps

—— Geographers' street plan of Stratford
  upon Avon. Produced under the
  direction of Phyllis Pearsall.
  Scale 6" to one mile.   [1964.]

                        667984

—— NEWMAN NEAME LTD.
  Stratford upon Avon [: pictorial map.
  With illustrations of scenes from
  Shakespeare's plays, etc]. 1 sheet.
                          [1954.]

                        639498

—— [Pictorial map of] Stratford-upon-
  Avon. [With illustrations of
  scenes from Shakespeare's plays.]
  Published for the Travel Association
  of Great Britain and N. Ireland
  (Tourist Division of the British
  Tourist and Holidays Board)
  sheet.   [1948.]

                        590831

Stratford-upon-Avon

– New Place

—— FOX, LEVI
  New Place: Shakespeare's home.
  illus.   [c.1964.]
  A Cotman-photo book.

                        667981

—— HALLIWELL[-PHILLIPS] (J. O.)
  An Historical account of the New
  Place, Stratford-upon-Avon, the last
  residence of Shakespeare.
  illus.   1864.
  Contains a list of subscribers to the
  New Place fund, which is not included
  in catal. no. 22279.

                        507068

—— MORRISON (J. H.)
  The Underhills of Warwickshire: an
  essay in family history. [With
  references to Shakespeare and New
  Place.]
  illus. maps. facsimiles. genealogical
  charts. Privately printed. 1932.

                        396911

—— National Shakespearian Fund established
  by J. O. Halliwell in 1861 [for the
  purchase of New Place Gardens, Anne
  Hathaway's Cottage, etc. at Stratford-
  on-Avon]. Vellum sheets headed
  'Shakespearian Census' intended for
  the recording of subscriptions.
                    [1861.]

                        472927

—— SIMPSON (F.)
  New Place: the only representation of
  Shakespeare's house from an unpublished
  manuscript. IN Shakespeare Survey
  [Vol.] 5. (Cambridge)
  facsimiles.   1952.

                        623798

—— Watts (P.R.) Shakespeare's "double"
  purchase of New Place. From The
  Australian Law Journal, Vol. 20.

          (Sydney)   1947.

                        599946

Stratford-upon-Avon

– Quatercentenary 1964

Stratford-upon-Avon

– Royal Shakespeare Theatre *formerly
  Shakespeare Memorial Theatre*

——   American Shakespeare Foundation.
  American Shakespeare celebration [for
  the benefit of the Shakespeare Memorial
  Fund] Metropolitan Opera House, January
  29, 1928 [: souvenir programme]. pp.72.
  Ports. Illus. Facsimile. [New York]

                        581625

——   Architectural Review, June 1932:
  Shakespeare Memorial Theatre Number.
  Illus. Plans.

                        393576

— ["Architecture Illustrated".
Portfolio of architectural illustrations.
Theatres and cinemas I, containing
illustrations of designs submitted for
the Shakespeare Memorial Theatre].
[c.1930-33]

407444

— [Articles on the new Shakespeare
Memorial Theatre] From The Architect
& Building News, April 1932. pp.[66].
Illus. Plans.

392855

— Baldwin (Rt. Hon. S.)

Shakespeare: a speech delivered at the
opening of the Shakespeare Memorial Theatre
at Stratford-on-Avon, April 23, 1932.
In Baldwin (Rt.Hon. S.) This torch of
freedom.   1935.

443270

— BIRMINGHAM WEEKLY POST

Background to Shakespeare [: the]
Stratford-on-Avon supplement, June 13, 1952.
pp.8. Ports. Illus. (Birmingham)

624739

— BRIDGES-ADAMS (W.)
The Shakespeare country, with a history of
the Festival Theatre and its company. pp.48.
Port. Illus. Map. Plan.   1932.

391905

— Bridges-Adams (W.) The Theatre:
Stratford's diamond jubilee [: a
broadcast talk]. ff.9. Typescript.
1939.

499919

— Charteris (S.) The Home of lovely
players: a memory of Stratford-upon-Avon,
where, on April 23, 1932, the Shakespeare
Memorial Theatre was opened by the Prince
of Wales. [Printed at the] Birmingham
School of Printing. pp.24. (Birmingham)
1935.

435577

— Chesterton (A.K.) Brave enterprise:
a history of the Shakespeare Memorial
Theatre, Stratford-upon-Avon. pp.62.
Ports. Illus.   1934.

421321

— Craig (E.G.) A Book about the
Shakespeare Memorial Theatre[: "The
Shakespeare Memorial Theatre", by
Muriel C. Day and J.C. Trewin]
reviewed.
1931.

409342

— Ellis ([Mrs.] Ruth) The Shakespeare
Memorial Theatre. [With a bibliography.]
Ports. Illus.   1948.

593363

— EVANS (GARETH LLOYD)
Shakespeare, the twentieth century
and "behaviourism".
IN SHAKESPEARE SURVEY 20.   (Cambridge)
1967.

766881

— FEARON (G.)
What can we learn at Stratford?
IN The Amateur Theatre and Playwrights' Journal, Vol. 4, No. 75.
1937.

467093

— FRY (E. M.)
Shakespeare's Stratford - and ours.
IN The Architectural Review, June 1932:
Shakespeare Memorial Theatre Number.
illus.   plans.

393576

— Herring (E.M.) The Stratford theatre:
under the builder's scaffold. Illus. In
Theatre arts monthly, Vol. 16.
1932.

402620

— Hussey (C.) The New Shakespeare
Memorial Theatre. Illus. Plan. In
The Listener, Vol. 7.   1932.

394419

— Hussey (C.) Shakespeare Memorial
Theatre: Stratford new & old, 1.
pp.[4]. Illus. Plan. From Country Life,
April, 1932.

392856

— ISAAC (WINIFRED F. E. C.)
Alfred Wareing: a biography.
With forewords by J. Bridie, I.
Brown, Rt. Hon. W. Elliot and
Sir J. R. Richmond.
ports. illus. facsimiles. [1950.]

614427

— JELLICOE (G. A.)
The Development of the theatre plan.
IN The Architectural Review, June 1932:
Shakespeare Memorial Theatre Number.
illus.   plans.

393576

— Jellicoe (G.A.) The Shakespeare
Memorial Theatre, Stratford-upon-Avon.
With a foreword by W. Bridges-Adams and
illustrations from photographs by F.R.
Yerbury. Maps. Plans. Alcuin Press.
1933.

403886

— Kemp (T.C.) Birmingham Repertory
Theatre: the playhouse and the man [i.e.
Sir B.V. Jackson. A record of performances,
1924-43]. With a foreword by Sir Barry V.
Jackson [and references to Shakespeare and
the Shakespeare Memorial Theatre]. Port.
Illus. (Birmingham)   1943.

544087

— LYTTON (DAVID)

"A Marvellous convenient place" [: a
programme to mark the twenty-fifth
anniversary of the building of the
Shakespeare Memorial Theatre,
Stratford-upon-Avon. Broadcast]
25th April 1957. ff.49. Typescript.

665563

—   Marston ([J.] W.) Address on the
inauguration of the Shakespeare Memorial
Theatre at Stratford-upon-Avon, April
23rd, 1879. pp.8.

479548

—   Masefield (J.) Ode recited by Lady
Keeble on the opening of the Stratford
Memorial Theatre by H.R.H. the Prince of
Wales, April,23, 1932. [Printed at the
Birmingham School of Printing.] 4ff.
                                      1932.

397560

— MATTHISON (A.   L.

Stratford. Illus. IN Matthison (A.L.)
Elephants on the Stratford Road, and
other essays and sketches. Ports. Illus.
(Birmingham)   1953.

647184

— MONTAGUE (C. E.)
   Playgoing at Stratford-on-Avon.
   IN Dramatic values.   3rd edn., revised.
   pp. 187-196.   1931.
   Phoenix Library, [Vol. 76.]

473893

—   The New Shakespeare Memorial Theatre,
Stratford-on-Avon. Illus. In The
Illustrated London News, Vol.180.
                                      1932.

399155

—   The New Shakespeare Memorial Theatre;
The Shakespeare Theatre as an instrument;
The Construction of the Shakespeare Memorial
Theatre. In The Architect & Building News,
vol. 130.   1932.

397501

—   [Newspaper cuttings collected by
J. Cotton: persons, places and events in
Bromsgrove and district. With references
to the Shakespeare Memorial Theatre.]
Ports. Illus.   1870-1933.
3 vols.

467752

—   Opening ceremonial by H.R.H. the
Prince of Wales, April 1932. [Souvenir]
pp.26. Port. Illus.

393894

—   Opening of the Shakespeare Memorial
Theatre, Stratford-on-Avon. Preliminary
programme. pp.8. (Stratford-on-Avon)
                                      1879.

Differs from 113482.

558060

—   Purdom (C.B.) The Theatre at
Stratford-upon-Avon. From Design for
to-day, Nov. 1935. pp.[3.] Illus.

443819

—   Richardson (A.E.) Shakespeare Memorial
Theatre. pp.6. Illus. From The Builder,
Vol. 142.   1932.

392673

—   Sachs (E.O.) Modern opera houses
and theatres. Examples selected from
playhouses recently erected in Europe,
with descriptive text [etc.] Vols. 2-3
[with references to the Shakespeare
Memorial Theatre, Stratford-on-Avon].
Illus. Plans. Dgms. Graphs. Tables.
2 vols.   1897-8.

560513

—   The Shakspere memorial [: the opening
of the Shakespeare Memorial Theatre at
Stratford-on-Avon]. From The Theatre,
May 1, 1879.

530820

—   The Shakespeare Memorial Theatre.
From Journal of the Institution of
Municipal and County Engineers, Vol.58.
Illus.   1931.

390214

—   Shakespeare Memorial Theatre. Illus.
In Heating and Ventilating Engineer, vol.5.
                                      1932.

395388

—Shakespeare Memorial Theatre.

Ceremony of laying the foundation
stone by Lord Ampthill, Stratford-
upon-Avon, 2nd July 1929. pp.[14.]
Frontis.

624880

—   Shakespeare Memorial Theatre Fund.
Theatre Royal, Drury Lane. Nov. 9th., 1926.
Grand matinee in aid of the Fund. [Programme,
with foreword by W.L. Courtney, poems by
T. Hardy, A.A. Milne, A. Dukes, Harriet
Kendall, and an article, "Spring in Arden",
by H.C. Bailey.] pp.[20.] Ports. Illus.

436133

—   Shakespeare Memorial Theatre
Number of the Architectural Review, June 1932
Illus. Plans.

393576

—   Shakespeare Memorial Theatre.
Royal opening, April 23rd, 1932[.:
supplement to "Evesham Journal and
Four Shires Advertiser"] pp.4. Ports.
Illus.

393954

— SHAW (GEORGE BERNARD)

Shakespear and the Stratford-upon-Avon
Theatre: a plea for reconstruction. IN
Shaw [G.B.] on theatre.   1958.

693464

—   Stratford Memorial Theatre.
In The Poetry Review, vol. 23.
1932.

409337

—   Stratford-upon-Avon Herald.
Special souvenir Supplement for
the opening of the new Shakespeare
Memorial Theatre. April 23rd, 1932.
pp.56. Ports. Illus.

392672

—   Towndrow (F.E.) Brickwork of the
Shakespeare Memorial Theatre. From
"The Brick Builder", June, 1932. pp.[3.]

419972

—   Trewin (J.C.) and Day (M[uriel] C.)
The Shakespeare Memorial Theatre. With
forewords by Sir F.[R.] Benson and W.
Bridges-Adams. Ports. Illus. Plan.
Facsimiles.   1932.

391217

—   Vallins (G.H.) At Stratford-on-Avon.
Opening of the Shakespeare Memorial
Theatre, April 23, 1932.) In Vallins (G.H.)
This dust, and other poems. pp.64.
1935.

(Macmillan's Contemporary Poets)

446623

—   Wenban (R.) [Coloured drawing of the
opening performance at the Shakespeare
Memorial Theatre, Stratford, April, 1932.
With a note on] Shakespeare's "Prince of
Wales". In The National Graphic, vol.1
(New Series)

397496

— WILENSKI (R. H.)
Eric Kennington and the sculptures at
Stratford.   IN The Architectural Review,
June, 1932:   Shakespeare Memorial Theatre
Number.
illus.   plans.

393576

— WILLIAMSON (AUDREY)
Theatre of two decades [: 1930-1950].
ports.   illus.   1951.
Includes a chapter "Homes of Shakespeare".

618557

— YORKE (F. R. S.)
Inside the theatre, and Notes on the
Shakespeare Memorial Theatre.   IN The
Architectural Review, June 1932:
Shakespeare Memorial Theatre Number.
illus.   plans.

393576

Stratford-upon-Avon: Royal Shakespeare Theatre:

— Festival:General Works

—   Bancroft (Edith M.) The Shakespeare
Festival. The Prologue. The Stratford
Pilgrims [: a parody of The Prologue
to The Canterbury Tales by G. Chaucer].
In The Journal of Education. Vol.71.
1939.

510161

—   Bridges-Adams (W.) The Shakespeare
country, with a history of the Festival
Theatre and its company. pp.48. Port.
Illus. Map. Plan.   1932.

391905

— BRIDGEWATER, LESLIE
The Stratford series of Shakespeare
songs. Vol.1-   1964-

740242

—   Brown (I. [J.C.])
The British and their bard. In
Theatre Arts Monthly, Vol.20. (New York)
1936.

466068

—   Buckley (R.R.) F.R. Benson and the
Stratford-on-Avon Festival. In The World's
Work, Vol.17.   1910-11.

231462

—   [Buckley (R.R.) ed.,] A Handbook
to Stratford-upon-Avon Festival, with
articles by [Sir] F.R. Benson,
A. Hutchinson, R.R. Buckley, C.J. Sharp.
[Edited with a preface.] (Shakespeare
Memorial Council.)   1913.

399807

—   Charques (R.D.) ed., Footnotes to
the theatre [: articles by various authors.
With references to Shakespeare]. Ports.
Illus.   1938.

492878

— Crucial years [: an account of new
productions and policies at the
Royal Shakespeare Theatre, Stratford-
upon-Avon, 1962].   1963.

667521

—   Darlington (W.A.) I do what I like [:
autobiography. With references to Shakespearian productions and the Shakespeare
Memorial Theatre]. Ports.   1947.

585381

— ENGLISH COUNTIES PERIODICALS LIMITED

Shakespeare festival souvenirs.
[Booklets]. Ports. Illus. [Leamington Spa].
1960—67

666809

— Forster (Elizabeth) Some Stratford yesterdays [: reminiscences of Stratford Festivals. Broadcast] 22nd April, 1947. ff.8. Typescript.

581998

— **Guthrie (T.) Where is the brontosaurus now? [: an article on the Shakespeare Memorial Theatre and the Old Vic.** From The London Mercury, June, 1938.]

488923

— HALL, PETER REGINALD FREDERICK
People today: Peter Hall talking to Ian Rodger. Produced by Joe Burroughs. B.B.C. radio script broadcast 12th July 1964.

668242

— HALL (PETER REGINALD FREDERICK) and LANGHAM (MICHAEL)

Talking of theatre: two Stratfords [Stratford-upon-Avon and Stratford, Ontario.] [B.B.C. Radio script of programme transmitted in Network Three, 24th November 1959. Typescript.] pp.11.

666447

— Hope-Wallace (P.)

Stratford at the crossroads. In The Penguin new writing, 32.
1947.

587237

— KEMP (THOMAS CHARLES) and TREWIN (JOHN COURTENAY)

The Stratford Festival: a history of the Shakespeare Memorial Theatre. Ports. Illus. (Birmingham)   1953.

630388

— Marshall (N.) The Shakespeare Memorial Theatre. Illus. In Marshall (N.) The Other theatre [: a record of the non-commercial theatre, 1925-1946].
1947.

582293

— Milliken (R.T.R.) The Masque of the rose, 1912. Produced at the Memorial Theatre, Stratford-on-Avon, by H. Herbert, and enacted by Stratford Townsfolk, in costumes, [etc.] suggested and designed by R.T.R. Milliken, Kathleen Baker, and the actors in the masque. pp.18. ([Stratford-on-Avon])
[1912]

479720

— Mr.Harold V.Neilson's Shakespeare Memorial Theatre.1919-1933 [a selection of press opinions].pp.23. [Loughborough]
[c.1935.]

649960

— Newspaper cuttings relating to foreign **tours** by the Shakespeare Memorial **Theatre Company,** Stratford-upon-Avon.
1953-1961.
642015
1962 - included in Newspaper cuttings relating to the Royal Shakespeare Theatre Company.

667576

— **Newspaper cuttings relating to the Royal Shakespeare Theatre Company.**
1962-

Before 1962 newspaper reviews of Stratford Festival productions are included in the collection of newspaper cuttings relating to each play.

667576

— **Programme of public lectures and recitals, &c., including the Annual Summer School, arranged each year by the Royal Shakespeare Theatre, the University of Birmingham, the Shakespeare Birthplace Trust, and the British Council, at Stratford-upon-Avon.]** (Birmingham and Stratford-upon-Avon)   1947-

645712

— Programmes, Playbills, Posters.
1882-
From 1963 souvenir programmes were issued for each production.

176120

— Programmes [Seasonal Summary].   1919-

441948

— Royal Shakespeare Theatre Company, 1960-1963, edited by J. Goodwin. illus.   1964.

667787

— SANDERS (NORMAN)
The Popularity of Shakespeare: an examination of the Royal Shakespeare Theatre's repertory.   IN SHAKESPEARE SURVEY 16.
illus.   1963.

667523

— Shakespeare Memorial Theatre, 1948-1950: a photographic record.   With forewords by I. Brown and A. Quayle.   Photographs by A. McBean.
1951.

616917

— Shakespeare Memorial Theatre, 1951-53: a photographic record [by A. McBean]. With a critical analysis by I. [J. C.] Brown.
1953.

637577

— Shakespeare Memorial Theatre, 1954-56: a photographic record [by A. McBean]. With a critical analysis by I. [J. C.] Brown.
1956.

665371

— Shakespeare Memorial Theatre, 1957-1959: a photographic record [by A. McBean].   With an introduction by I. [J. C.] Brown.
1959.

666315

—   Shore (S.) Rough island story:
newsreel (and unreal) of the depression,
1931-1935. Pictures by J.T. Gilroy. [With
references to the Shakespeare Memorial
Theatre.]   1935.

445800

— Souvenir booklets.   Festivals,
1949-1962.
   illus.
Ceased publication.

604347

— Souvenir booklets of foreign tours.
   (Stratford-upon-Avon)
   illus.   1949.

604346

— SPEAIGHT (ROBERT)
A Programme on the development of
The Shakespeare Memorial Theatre,
Stratford-upon-Avon.   Introduced
by R. Speaight.   Produced by D.
Cleverdon.   [Script of Broadcast,
April, 1960].   (British Broadcasting
Corporation)   ff. 15.
   typescript.   1959.

666906

— WORSLEY (THOMAS CUTHBERT)
Stratford and Shakespearian productions.
IN LUMLEY (FREDERICK) ed., Theatre in
review.   [By] E. [W.] Blom [and
others].   (Edinburgh)
   ports.   illus.   1956.

657684

Stratford-upon-Avon: Royal Shakespeare Theatre:

— Festival 1900

— TREWIN (JOHN COURTENAY)
The Night has been unruly [: the
theatre in England, 1769-1955].
Illustrated from the Raymond Mander
and Joe Mitchenson Theatre Collection.
   ports. illus. facsimiles. bibliog.
                                    1957.
pp. 194-212: Pericles, Prince of Tyre,
Stratford-upon-Avon, 1900.

670241

— Festival 1901

— PEMBERTON (T. E.)
   Shakespeare Memorial Theatre,
   Stratford-upon-Avon.   Concerning
   the Shakespeare annual festival
   (the first of the new century),
   commencing on Monday, April 15th,
   1901.   (Stratford-upon-Avon)
      illus.   1901.
   Differs from 157520.

549759

— Festival 1902

—   The Shakespeare festival at
Stratford-on-Avon, by H.S. Ward. Illus.
In The Playgoer. Vol. 2.
                                    1902.

171877

— Festival 1905 –

—   Impressions of the Theatre;VIII: (16)
Shakespeare at Stratford. Illus. In
The Review of Reviews, Vol.31.
                                    1905.

189564

—   Interviews on topics of the month, XIV:
The Shakespeare Festival: Mr. F.R. Benson.
Ports. In The Review of Reviews, Vol.31.
                                    1905.

189564

— Stead (W.T.) First impressions of the
   theatre. [Include reviews on 'The
   Taming of the Shrew,' 'King Lear'
   and 'Hamlet' and an article:
   Shakespeare at Stratford.] In The
   Review of Reviews, Vol.31.

1905.

189564

—   Theatre book, 1905 [-1909. MS.
notebook giving details of receipts and
expenses at the Stratford-on-Avon Memorial
Theatre during the winter seasons Oct. 1905
to Sept. 1909]. pp.62.   [1905-1909.]

539400

— Festival 1907

— Shakespeare Festival [1907]: plays and players at Stratford-on-Avon. Ports. Illus. From The Windsor Magazine, 1907.

599881

— Festival 1908

— The Shakespeare Festival: plays and players at Stratford-on-Avon. From Windsor Magazine, 1908. pp.[22.] Illus.

389193

— Festival 1909

—Grindon (Mrs. [Rosa E.])

The Story and the poetry of Shakespeare's play of Cymbeline: lecture delivered in the Picture Gallery, Memorial Theatre, Stratford-on-Avon, April 20, 1909. pp.26. (Manchester)

431988

— Festival 1919 –

— Legge (R.H.) The Shakespeare Festival at Stratford-upon-Avon. [The Work of W.] Bridges-Adams and [Sir T.] Beecham. From The Musician, Vol. 1. 1919.

520181

— WHITFIELD (J.   F.   )

Theatrical scrapbooks, 1919-29, including newspaper cuttings and programmes of the Stratford-upon-Avon Shakespeare seasons, and of productions at Birmingham theatres. Collected by J.F. Whitfield.] Illus.   3 vols.
[1919-29.]

668413-5

— Festival 1922 –

— Cardozo (J.L.) A Holiday at Stratford-on-Avon: [Shakespeare birthday festival. With remarks on the Shakespeare performances.] In English studies, Vol.4. (Amsterdam) 1922.

485646

— Festival 1927 –

— Mackarness (R.S.P.) Shakespeare's Birthday Festival: the Stratford Theatre, and other things. From The Landmark, 1927. pp.[4.] Illus.

389199

— Festival 1934

— Shakespeare Festival, The: correspondence by M. Auster, Lilian Baylis and S. Ryder. In The National Review, vol. 103.   1934.

430233

— Festival 1935 –

— Shakespeare Festivals, 1935, 1936, 1938, 1939.   IN Play pictorial, Vols. 66, 68, 72, 74.   3 vols.
1935-[1939.]

571928

Festival 1936

—   Play Pictorial: The Stratford-upon-
Avon Festival, 1936. [Illustrated souvenir]
pp.20.

450644

—   "The Queen" Shakespeare Festival Supplement. From "The Queen", May 7th, 1936.
pp.21-44. Ports. Illus.

451507

—   Stratford-upon-Avon Festival, 1936:
[scenes from] eight festival plays. In
The Amateur theatre and playwrights'
Journal, Vol.3, No.53. Illus.
1936-37.

476090

— Festival 1937

—   Fearon (G.) The Stratford-upon-Avon
festivals. From Theatre World, June, 1937.
pp.[16.] Ports. Illus.

471791

—   Fraser (M.F.K.) First night
impressions at Stratford: [Shakespeare
Birthday Festival, 1937. A talk broadcast
from Midland Regional] ff.4. Typescript.
1937.

472376

—   Stratford-upon-Avon Festival, 1937
[: scenes from 8 plays]. In The Amateur
theatre and playwrights' Journal, Vol.4,
No.75. Illus.   1937-38.

482984

— Festival 1938

—   Kemp (T.C.) First night impressions
of the Stratford Festival [: a broadcast
talk]. ff.6. Typescript. ([Birmingham])
[1938.]

481281

— Festival 1939

—   Brown (I. [J.C.]) First night
impressions of the Stratford Festival
[: a broadcast talk]. ff.7. Typescript.
([Birmingham])   1939.

499918

—   Play Pictorial, Vol.74, No.443.
Diamond Jubilee Festival, Stratford-upon-
Avon, 1939. pp.20. Illus.

499919

—   Stratford-upon-Avon Diamond Jubilee
Festival, 1939. In Play pictorial,
Vol. 74.

571936

— Festival 1941

—   Charteris (S.) The Shakespeare Festival.
pp.[3.] Illus. From The English-Speaking
World, Vol. 23,   1941.

535362

—   Shakespeare Festival, Stratford-upon-
Avon, 1941: Theatre World souvenir. pp.12.
Ports. Illus.   [1941.]

541606

— Festival 1946 –

— BENNETT (H. S.) and RYLANDS (G. [H. W.])
Stratford productions.   IN SHAKESPEARE
SURVEY 1.   (Cambridge)   1948.

590674

—   Hope-Wallace (P.) The Stratford
festival [: a criticism of the 1946
productions]. In Time and Tide, Vol.27.
1946.

585995

—   Shakespeare Festival, 1946.
Programme from the Shakespeare
Memorial Theatre. Produced by E. Livesey.
[Broadcast] 18th April, 1946. ff.15.
Typescript.

570710

— Shakespeare Festival Season, Stratford-upon-Avon, 1946. [Programme.] pp.27. Illus. Plan. [Birmingham]

569621

— Festival 1947

— Collier (J.W.) Sir Barry Jackson at Stratford - the second year. In Dobson's theatre year-book, 1948-9. 1948.

595952

— Dent (A.) The Stratford Festival [1947. Broadcast] 13th May 1947. ff.4. Typescript.

582326

— Kemp (T.C.) The Stratford Festival [1947. Broadcast] 15th April, 1947. ff.7. Typescript.

581999

— Festival 1948 —

— Brown (I. [J.C.]) The Stratford season [1948: a review of the opening play "King John"]. In Britain To-day, No. 146. 1948.

587767/146

— Kemp (T.C.) The Stratford Festival: review of Hamlet and The Taming of the Shrew. [Broadcast] 12th May, 1948. ff.7. Typescript.

591374

— Kemp (T.C.) The Stratford Festival: review of King John and The Merchant of Venice. [Broadcast] 22nd April, 1948. ff.6. Typescript.

591373

— Kemp (T.C.) The Stratford Festival: review of Othello. [Broadcast] 2nd August, 1948. ff.[3.] Typescript.

596474

— Kemp (T.C.) The Stratford Festival: review of The Winter's Tale. [Broadcast 10th June, 1948. ff.3. Typescript.

596465

— Kemp (T.C.) The Stratford Festival: review of Troilus and Cressida. [Broadcast] 9th July, 1948. ff.3. Typescript.

593009

— Shakespeare Memorial Theatre, 1948-1950: a photographic record. With forewords by I. Brown and A. Quayle. Photographs by A. McBean. 1951.

616917

— Festival 1949 —

— Byrne (Muriel St. C.) A Stratford production: Henry VIII. Illus. In Shakespeare Survey: an annual survey of Shakespearian study & production, [Vol.] 3. (Cambridge) 1950.

606026

— DENT (ALAN HOLMES), HOBSON (HAROLD) and BROWN (IVOR JOHN CARNEGIE)

[Critics' Forum: review of Anthony Quayle's production of Macbeth and John Gielgud's production of Much Ado About Nothing at Stratford-on-Avon. Broadcast 20th April 1949] ff.20. Typescript.

609295

— [Dent (A.H.), Hobson (H.) and Kemp (T.C.)] Critics review [: of Tyrone Guthrie's production of Henry VIII at Stratford. Broadcast] 18th July, 1949. ff.5. Typescript.

605252

— Kemp (T.C.) 'The Stratford Festival'. Review of 'Macbeth', 'Much Ado about Nothing', 'A Midsummer Night's Dream', 'Cymbeline', 'Othello' and 'King Henry VIII'. [Broadcast] 3rd May [and] 20th July 1949. ff.7,7. Typescript. 2 vols.

605253

— Worsley (T.C.) The Stratford Festival, 1949. Illus. In Penguin New Writing. Edited by J. Lehmann. (Harmondsworth) 1949.

(Penguin Books)

586205/38

– Festival 1950

GRIFFIN (Mrs. ALICE)
The 1950 season at Stratford-upon-Avon –
a memorable achievement in stage history.
IN SHAKESPEARE QUARTERLY II: 1.
pp. 73-78.
(New York)   1951.

605711

KEMP (THOMAS CHARLES)

The Stratford Festival [performance of
King Lear]. Broadcast 19th July, 1950.
ff.3. Typescript.

614640

. Kemp (T.C.) The Stratford Festival
[: a review of] "Julius Caesar" and "Much
Ado About Nothing". [Broadcast] 14th June,
1950. ff.5. Typescript.

609488

. Kemp (T.C.) The Stratford Festival
[: a review of "Measure for Measure" and
"King Henry the Eighth." Broadcast]
5th April, 1950. ff.6. Typescript.

609484

Stratford-upon-Avon

– Festival 1951 –

FARROW (EMMA)
Thrones and dominions: a recollection of
the history plays given at the Shakespeare
Memorial Theatre in the Festival of
Britain Season 1951. Richard II, Henry IV,
Part I, Henry IV, Part II, Henry V.
Typescript. (Birmingham)   [1951]

630855

HUME (GEORGE)

Stratford 1951 [: festival]. Broadcast
19th February, 1951. ff.6. Typescript.

616350

KEMP (THOMAS CHARLES)
The Stratford festival [:1951]. Broadcast
11th April, 1951 ff.6.Typescript.

616351

KEMP (THOMAS CHARLES)

The Stratford Festival [: 1951
production of Henry V. Broadcast]
August 10th, 1951. ff.v. Typescript.

620379

KEMP (THOMAS CHARLES)

The Stratford Festival [: 1951 productions
of Henry IV Part 2 and The Tempest].
Broadcast 28th June, 1951. ff.5. Typescript.

617918

Shakespeare Memorial Theatre, 1951-53:
a photographic record [by A. McBean].
With a critical analysis by I. [J. C.]
Brown.   1953.

637577

WILSON (JOHN DOVER) and
    WORSLEY (THOMAS CUTHBERT)

Shakespeare's histories at Stratford, 1951.
Photographs by A. McBean. Illus.

1952.

624931

Stratford-upon-Avon

– Festival 1952

KEMP (THOMAS CHARLES)
Stratford festival [: the 1952 Shakespeare
Memorial Theatre productions of As You
Like It and Macbeth. Broadcast] 7th July,
1952. ff.6.Typescript.

627709.

KEMP (THOMAS CHARLES)
Stratford,1952 [: the Shakespeare Memorial
Theatre productions of Coriolanus and The
Tempest. Broadcast] 9th April, 1952.ff.5.
Typescript.

624728

LEECH (CLIFFORD)
Stratford 1952.
IN SHAKESPEARE QUARTERLY III: 4.
pp. 353-357.
(New York)   1952.

605711

– Festival 1953

KEMP (THOMAS CHARLES)

The Stratford Festival [: 1953
production of 'Antony and Cleopatra' at
the Shakespeare Memorial Theatre.]
Produced by P. Humphreys. [Broadcast]
30th April, 1953. ff.6. Typescript.

634516

— KEMP (THOMAS CHARLES)

The Stratford festival [: 1953
production of 'King Lear' at the Shakespeare
Memorial Theatre] Produced by P. Humphreys.
[Broadcast] 16th July, 1953. ff.7.
Typescript.

634524

— KEMP (THOMAS CHARLES)

The Stratford Festival [: 1953 production
of 'The Taming of the Shrew' at the
Shakespeare Memorial Theatre]. Produced
by P. Humphreys. [Broadcast] 11th June, 1953
ff.6. Typescript.

634523

— KEMP (THOMAS CHARLES)

The Stratford festival [: the 1953
Shakespeare Memorial Theatre
productions of The Merchant of
Venice and King Richard III. Broadcast.]
27th March, 1953. ff.6. Typescript.

631924

— LEECH (CLIFFORD)
Stratford 1953.
IN SHAKESPEARE QUARTERLY IV: 4.
pp. 461-466.
(New York) 1953.

605711

— KEMP (THOMAS CHARLES)

Stratford 1954: "A Midsummer night's
dream". [A radio talk] produced by
P. Humphreys. [Broadcast] 29th March,
1954. ff.6. Typescript.

643697

— KEMP (THOMAS CHARLES)

Stratford 1954 [: "Othello" A radio talk]
produced by P. Humphreys. [Broadcast]
18th March, 1954. ff.6. Typescript.

643696

— ROYAL SHAKESPEARE THEATRE
Shakespeare Memorial Theatre, 1954-56:
a photographic record [by A. McBean].
With a critical analysis by I.[J.C.]
Brown.   1956.

665371

— SYKES (E.   F.   )
Segregation of the role of Diomedes.
Supplementary note to comments on
Byam Shaw's production at Stratford-
upon-Avon [of] "Troilus and Cressida".
(Journal notes. 6th Series). ff.16.
Typescript.   1954.

665406

— Festival 1954 –

— DAVID (RICHARD)
Stratford 1954.
IN SHAKESPEARE QUARTERLY V.
pp. 385-394.
(New York)   1954.

605711

— DENT, ALAN HOLMES
Stratford 1954 [:"Romeo and Juliet".
A radio talk] produced by P. Stephenson
for P. Humphreys. [Broadcast] 30th April,
1954. ff.8. Typescript.

643698.

— DENT (ALAN HOLMES)

Stratford 1954 [: "The Taming of the
Shrew". A radio talk] produced by P.
Harvey for P. Humphreys. [Broadcast]
9th June, 1954. ff.9. Typescript.

643699

— DENT (ALAN HOLMES)

Troilus and Cressida at Stratford-on-
Avon. [Radio talk] produced by
P. Humphreys. [Broadcast] 15th July,
1954. ff.5. Typescript.

643700

— Festival 1955

— COX (TRENCHARD) and others
Twelfth Night.   [Shakespeare Memorial
Theatre, Stratford, 1955.]   Extract
from "Midland Critics".   [Critics:
T. Cox, Evelyn Gibbs, H. Folkes and
J. C. Moore.   Chairman: J. English.
Broadcast] 21st April, 1955.   ff. 7.
typescript.

665046

— DAVID (RICHARD)

The Tragic curve: a review of two
productions of Macbeth: at the Old Vic,
winter 1954-5, and at the Shakespeare
Memorial Theatre, Stratford-upon-Avon,
summer 1955. Illus. IN Shakespeare Survey,
[Vol.] 9. (Cambridge)   1956.

665210

— MOORE (JOHN CECIL) and others
Macbeth: Stratford-upon-Avon:
Shakespeare Memorial Theatre [1955].
Extract from "The Midland Critics"
broadcast 15th June, 1955. Critics:
J. [C.] Moore, R. Henriques, Evelyn
Gibbs, H. Folkes, chairman: J.English
ff.4, 4a-6. Typescript.   1955.

649312

— SYKES (E. F.)
All's Well That Ends Well": [the]
Stratford-on-Avon Shakespeare Memorial
Theatre [production], Festival Season
1955. (Journal Notes. 7th Series). ff.29.
Typescript.   1955.

665407

— SYKES (E. F.)
"Macbeth": [the] Stratford-upon-Avon
Memorial Theatre [production], Festival
Season 1955. (Journal Notes. 7th Series)
Chart. Typescript.   1955.

665411

— SYKES (E. F.)

The Merry Wives of Windsor": [the]
Stratford-upon-Avon Shakespeare
Festival Season [production] 1955.
(Journal Notes. 7th Series) ff.[19.]
Typescript.   1955.

665412

— SYKES (E. F.)

"Much Ado About Nothing": [the]
Stratford-upon-Avon Memorial
Theatre [production] Festival
Season 1955. (Journal Notes. 7th Series).
ff.5. Typescript.

665413

— SYKES (E. F.)

"Titus Andronicus": [the production]
at the Memorial Theatre, Stratford-
upon-Avon, 1955 Festival Season.
(Journal Notes. 7th Series). ff.[33.]
Typescript.   1955.

665414

— SYKES (E. F.)

"Twelfth Night": [the] Stratford-upon-
Avon Shakespeare Memorial Theatre
[production] Festival Season 1955.
(Journal Notes. 7th Series). ff.25.
                                    1955.

665416

— TREWIN (JOHN COURTENAY)
The Night has been unruly [: the
theatre in England, 1769-1955].
Illustrated from the Raymond Mander
and Joe Mitchenson Theatre Collection.
ports. illus. facsimiles. bibliog.
                                    1957.
pp. 259-77: Titus Andronicus
Stratford-upon-Avon, 1955.

670241

— Festival 1956

— BROWN (JOHN RUSSELL)
Shakespeare festivals in Britain, 1956.
IN SHAKESPEARE QUARTERLY VII.
pp. 407-410.
(New York) 1956.

605711

— ENGLISH (JOHN) ed.
"Hamlet": extract from "The Midland
Critics". [Broadcast] 22nd May, 1956.
Chairman: J. English. pp. 9.
typescript.

665311

— ENGLISH (JOHN) ed.
Measure for measure [: the Stratford
Memorial Theatre 1956 production.
Extract from] "The Midland Critics".
Chairman: J. English. [Broadcast]
14th October, 1956. ff. [8.]
typescript.

665512

— Festival 1957

— BYRNE (MURIEL ST. CLARE)
The Shakespeare Season at the Old Vic,
1956-57 and Stratford-upon-Avon, 1957.
IN SHAKESPEARE QUARTERLY VIII.
pp. 461-492.
(New York) 1957.

605711

— RYLANDS (GEORGE HUMPHREY WOLFESTAN)
and BARTON (JOHN)

["As you like it" at Stratford-upon-
Avon: a discussion from the "Midland
Critics", broadcast April 19th, 1957].
Typescript.

665513

— RYLANDS (GEORGE HUMPHREY WOLFESTAN)
and BARTON (JOHN)

"Cymbeline" [at Stratford: a discussion.
Broadcast 15th July 1957]. ff.7.
Typescript.

665665

— RYLANDS (GEORGE HUMPHREY WOLFESTAN)
and BARTON (JOHN)

"Julius Caesar" [at Stratford: a
discussion from the "Midland Critics".
Broadcast June 19th, 1957] ff.6.
Typescript.   1957.

665543

— RYLANDS (GEORGE HUMPHREY WOLFESTAN)
and BARTON (JOHN)

["King John" at Stratford: a discussion.
Broadcast May 9th 1957]. ff.7. Typescript.

665524

— Shakespeare Memorial Theatre, 1957-
1959: a photographic record [by
A. McBean]. With an introduction
by I. [J. C.] Brown.   1959.

666315

—— TREWIN (JOHN COURTENAY) and
          BARTON (JOHN)

"The Tempest" [at Stratford: a discussion
Broadcast, 15th August 1957.] ff.7.
Typescript.

                    665666

— Festival 1958

—— BYRNE (MURIEL ST. CLARE)
    The Shakespeare season at the Old Vic,
    1957-58 and Stratford-upon-Avon, 1958.
    IN SHAKESPEARE QUARTERLY IX.
    pp. 507-530.
    (New York) 1958.
                605711

—— SMITH (CYRIL KEGAN)

"Getting ready at Stratford" [:
*S*hakespeare Memorial Theatre.
Broadcast] 6th March 1958. ff.6.
Typescript.

                665770

— Festival 1959

—— BRAHMS (CARYL)[pseud. i.e. DORIS CAROLINE
ABRAHAMS]
    The Rest of the evening's my own [:
    a criticism of the English theatre,
    1953-1963.   1964.
      Includes a chapter on Shakespeare.

              724399

—— BYRNE (MURIEL ST. CLARE)
    King Lear at Stratford-on-Avon, 1959.
    IN SHAKESPEARE QUARTERLY XI.
    pp. 189-206.
    (New York) 1960.
             605711

—— BYRNE (MURIEL ST. CLARE)
    The Shakespeare Season at the Old Vic,
    1958-59 and Stratford-upon-Avon, 1959.
    IN SHAKESPEARE QUARTERLY X: 4.
    pp. 545-567.
    (New York) 1959.
             605711

— Festival 1960 –

—— BAYLEY (P.   C.   )

Shakespeare, old drama and new theatre.
IN Critical Quarterly, Vol.2. (Hull)
                1960.

              692062/2

—— Royal Shakespeare theatre company
1960-1963, edited by J. Goodwin.
(New York)
    illus.   1964.   773834
    ————— Another edn.   (London)
                1964.   667787

—— SPEAIGHT (ROBERT)
    The 1960 Season at Stratford-upon-Avon.
    IN SHAKESPEARE QUARTERLY XI.
    pp. 445-453.
    (New York) 1960.
             605711

—— SPEAIGHT (ROBERT)
    The Old Vic and Stratford-upon-Avon,
    1960-61.
    IN SHAKESPEARE QUARTERLY XII: 4.
    pp. 425-441.
    (New York)   1961.

             605711

— Festival 1961 –

—— KITCHIN (LAURENCE)
    "Othello" at Stratford-on-Avon.
    Produced by G. MacBeth.   [Broadcast]
    18th October, 1961.

             667767

—— TREWIN (JOHN COURTENAY)
    The Old Vic and Stratford-upon-Avon
    1961-1962.
    IN SHAKESPEARE QUARTERLY XIII: 4.
    pp. 505-519.
    (New York) 1962.
             605711

— Festival 1962 –

—— Brown (J.R.) Acting Shakespeare today: a
review of performances at the Royal Shakespeare
Theatre, 1962.

IN Shakespeare Survey [Vol.] 16. 1963.

      illus.   667523

—— Crucial years [: an account of new
productions and policies at the
Royal Shakespeare Theatre, Stratford-
upon-Avon, 1962]. 1963.

667521

˜ Festival 1963

—— SPEAIGHT (ROBERT)
Shakespeare in Britain.
IN SHAKESPEARE QUARTERLY XIV.
pp. 419-432.
(New York) 1963.

605711

— Festival 1964
see also **Quatercentenary 1964**

—— RODGER, IAN
An Anointed king [: 'Richard II'
rehearsed by the Royal Shakespeare
Theatre company]. Produced by
Joe Burroughs. B.B.C. radio script
broadcast 10th June 1964.

668246

—— SPEAIGHT (ROBERT)
Shakespeare in Britain.
IN SHAKESPEARE QUARTERLY XV.
pp. 377-389.
(New York) 1964.

605711

— Festival 1965

—— Brown (John Russell)
The Royal Shakespeare Company 1965.
IN SHAKESPEARE SURVEY: 19
[Macbeth]
(Cambridge) 1966.

pp.111-118. 755342

—— SPEAIGHT (ROBERT)
Shakespeare in Britain.
IN SHAKESPEARE QUARTERLY XVI.
pp. 313-323.
(New York) 1965.

605711

— Festival 1966

—— SPEAIGHT (ROBERT)
Shakespeare in Britain.
IN SHAKESPEARE QUARTERLY XVII: 4.
pp. 389-398.
(New York) 1966.

605711

˜ Festival 1967

—— SPEAIGHT (ROBERT)
Shakespeare in Britain.
IN SHAKESPEARE QUARTERLY XVIII: 4.
pp. 389-397. (New York) 1967.

605711

Festival 1968

—— SPEAIGHT (ROBERT)
Shakespeare in Britain.
IN SHAKESPEARE QUARTERLY XIX.
pp. 367-375.
(New York) 1968.

605711

Stratford-upon-Avon
— Royal Visits

—— Royal visit to Stratford-upon-Avon,
April 20th 1950: a pictorial record.
Birmingham Post and Mail photographs.
pp.[24.] Ports. Illus. (Birmingham)
1950.

608548

—— Stratford-upon-Avon Herald and South
Warwickshire Advertiser, 15th June,
1957. [An illustrated account of
the visit of Queen Elizabeth and
Prince Philip to Stratford, June 14th,
1957.] pp. 8. 1957.

665542

Stratford-upon-Avon

— Shakespeare Hotel

KNIGHT, FRANK & RUTLEY, auctioneers
[A Sale catalogue of] the Shakespeare
Hotel, Stratford-on-Avon, Warwickshire.
Offered for sale by Messrs. Knight,
Frank & Rutley in conjunction with
Messrs. Walker Barnard & Son.   pp. [12.]
illus.   1919.

624738

Stratford-upon-Avon

— Shakespeare Institute *see under*
Shakespeare Institute

Stratford-upon-Avon

— Shakespeare Memorial Library

FOX (LEVI)

The Shakespeare collections of
Shakespeare's birthplace and the Royal
Shakespeare Theatre, Stratford-upon-Avon:
[Paper] 1 [of] Shakespeare in the
Library: a symposium. IN Open Access,
Vol.10, N.S., No.2. (Birmingham)
1962.

667074

Items of interest to theatre research
workers.   ff. 4.   (Stratford-upon-
Avon)   1957.

665891

ROBINSON (EILEEN)
The Shakespeare Memorial Library,
Stratford-upon-Avon: items of interest
to theatre research workers.   IN
Theatre Notebook, Vol. 12.   1958.

584117/12

Stratford-upon-Avon

— Shakespeare Memorial Theatre
see Royal Shakespeare Theatre *above*

Stratford-upon-Avon

— Summer School

[Programme of public lectures and recitals,
&c., including the Annual Summer School,
arranged each year by the Royal Shakes-
peare Theatre, the University of
Birmingham, the Shakespeare Birthplace
Trust, and the British Council, at
Stratford-upon-Avon.] (Birmingham and
Stratford-upon-Avon)   1947-

645712

Stratford-upon-Avon

— Views

BATES (MARJORIE C.)
Stratford-on-Avon and Broadway village:
16 views in colour, after the original
drawings by Marjorie C. Bates.   [With
descriptions.]   pp. [40.]   1932.

391915

[BLAIR (A.)]
Graphic illustrations of Warwickshire
[including Stratford-on-Avon.]
1829.   2391
_____ Another copy. 1829.   5474
_____ [Large paper edn., with illus-
trations on india paper.]
1829.   5473
_____ Another edn.   Edited] by
J. Jaffray.   1862.   64408
_____ Another copy   1862.   5475

COLYER (S. W.)
Shakespeare's country: a book of
[33] photographs: with a foreword
by Lord Willoughby de Broke.   1947.
Fair Britain Series.

583360

COSSINS (J. A.)
[A Collection of photographs of
England and Wales.   Vol. 2:
Warwickshire, etc., including
Stratford-upon-Avon.]
[c.1890.]
Not published.

454849

CUNLIFFE (J. W.)
England in picture, song and story:
[containing a chapter "The Shakespeare
country".]   With notes on the illustrations by Margaret B. Pickel.
(New York)
ports.   1936.

460140

Exhibition of water-colour drawings
by Mme. [Georgina M.] de L'Aubinière
[: catalogue], comprising "A Day
in Shakespeare's Land," [etc].

1891.

(The Modern Gallery.)

520536

Folger Shakespeare Library Prints
[4]: Stratford-on-Avon. 20 plates.

(Washington, D.C.)   [1935]

475843

FOX (L.)
Shakespeare's town, Stratford-upon-Avon:
a pictorial record.   pp. 40.
(Coventry)
port.   1949.

600424

NEIL (S.)
The Home of Shakespeare, illustrated
in thirty-three engravings by F. W.
Fairholt. [With An Architectural
account of the collegiate church of
the Holy Trinity by E. H. Knowles]
pp. 80.   (Warwick)
                    [?1871]   394908
_____ 2nd edn.   [1878]   508515
_____ 11th edn.   [c.1898] 467567

RIDER (W.)
Views in Stratford-upon-Avon and its
vicinity, illustrative of the
biography of Shakspeare, with
descriptive remarks.   [Large paper
edn.]   pp. [26.]   1878.

399820

[SEDGFIELD (W. R.)
Photograph of Shakespeare's birthplace,
Stratford-upon-Avon.   (Henry T. Cooke
& Son, Fine Art Repository, Warwick)
                              [c.1860]

391936

Souvenir of Stratford upon Avon:
[album of nine photographs].

[c.1880.]

515565

SWINYARD (LAURENCE)
Shakespeare's Stratford-on-Avon.
Sketches by E. E. Briscoe.   pp. [20]
                              [1951.]

617923

TREWIN (JOHN COURTENAY)
The Pictorial story of William
Shakespeare and Stratford upon Avon.
Foreword by L. Fox.   pp. 24.
ports.   illus.   [1954.]

640453

TREWIN (JOHN COURTENAY)
The Pictorial story of Shakespeare
& Stratford-upon-Avon.   Foreword
by L. Fox.   pp. 24.
ports.   illus.   map.   facsimile.
                              [1960.]
Pitkin Pictorials Ltd., "Pride of
Britain" Guides and Histories.

666649

[Views of Stratford-on-Avon and
Warwick]   pp. [ii].   [Rock and
Co.]
12 plates.   [c.1855.]

573033

STRATFORD-UPON-AVON HERALD
Special souvenir Supplement for
the opening of the new Shakespeare
Memorial Theatre.   April 23rd,
1932.   pp. 56.   [Stratford-upon-
Avon]
ports.   illus.

392672

Stratford-upon-Avon Herald and South
Warwickshire Advertiser, 15th June,
1957.   [An illustrated account of
the visit of Queen Elizabeth and
Prince Philip to Stratford, June 14th,
1957.]   pp. 8.

665542

Stratford-upon-Avon Herald and
South Warwickshire Advertiser,
24th April, 1964.   The Shakespeare
Quatercentenary Supplement, 1564-
1964.   'Speak of me as I am'.
(Stratford-upon-Avon)
illus.

668226

Stratford-upon-Avon: official guide.
pp. 64.   (Cheltenham)
illus.   map.   plan.   [c.1935.]

550471

Stratford-upon-Avon: official guide.
[Stratford-upon-Avon]
ports.   illus.   maps.   [1950]-

607015

Stratford-upon-Avon, Quatercentenary
celebrations _see_ Quatercentenary 1964.

Stratford-upon-Avon Scene, incorporating
Shakespeare Pictorial.   Vol. 1-3.
(Stratford-upon-Avon)
ports.   illus.   1946-50.
For Shakespeare Pictorial see catal.
no. 348579.

574721

STRATFORD-UPON-AVON STUDIES, 1
Jacobean theatre.
bibliogs.   1960.

666673

STRATFORD-UPON-AVON STUDIES, 2
Elizabethan poetry.
illus.   bibliogs.   1960.

666674

Surrey, Henry Howard, Earl of *works relating to*

—— FLEMING (JOHN F.)
A Book from Shakespeare's library
discovered by William Van Lennep.
IN Shakespeare 400: essays by
American scholars on the anniversary
of the poet's birth.   Published in
co-operation with the Shakespeare
Association of America.
illus.   1964.

667803

Sussex

—— SURTEES (S. [F.])
Shakespeare's provincialisms: words
in use in Sussex.   pp. 8.   (Dinsdale-
on-Tees)   1889.

388845

—— Wright (J.) Shakespeare and Sussex.
From Sussex County Magazine [Sept.
1946].

[Eastbourne]

579650

SUTHERLAND (JAMES RUNCIEMAN)
How the characters talk.   IN
Shakespeare's world.   1964.

667808

SUTHERLAND (JAMES RUNCIEMAN)
The Language of the last plays.
IN GARRETT (J.) More talking of
Shakespeare.   1959.

666126

SUTHERLAND (JAMES RUNCIEMAN)
The Moving pattern of Shakespeare's
thought.   IN DUTHIE (GEORGE IAN) ed.,
Papers, mainly Shakespearian. 1964.
Aberdeen University studies, No. 147.

668205

SUTHERLAND (JAMES RUNCIEMAN)
[Review of] Shakespeare's imagination
by E. A. Armstrong.   IN The Review of
English Studies, Vol. 23.   (Oxford)
1947.

318239/23

SUTHERLAND (JAMES RUNCIEMAN)
[Review of] From Shakespeare to Joyce:
authors and critics; literature and
life, by E. E. Stoll.   IN The Review
of English Studies, Vol. 21.   (Oxford)
[1945.]

570955

SUTHERLAND (JAMES RUNCIEMAN)
Shakespeare's imitators in the
eighteenth century.   IN The Modern
Language Review. Vol. 28. 1933.

415705

SUTHERLAND (JAMES RUNCIEMAN) and
HURSTFIELD (JOEL) eds.
Shakespeare's world.   1964.

667808

SUTHERLAND (RAYMOND CARTER)
The Grants of arms to Shakespeare's
father.
IN   SHAKESPEARE QUARTERLY XIV: 4.
pp. 379-385.
(New York)   1963.

605711

SUTHERLAND (W. O. S.)
Polonius, Hamlet and Lear in Aaron
Hill's "Prompter".   IN Studies in
Philology, Vol. 49.   (Chapel Hill,
N.C.)   1952.

554520/49

Sutherland-Leveson-Gower (Rt. Hon.
Lord Ronald Charles) see Gower
(Rt. Hon. Lord R. C. Sutherland-
Leveson)

SUTTON (Sir B. E.)
Shakespeare on the art of war.
IN Journal of the Royal United
Service Institution, Vol. 89.
1944.

564001

Sutton ([E.]G.) 'We band of
brothers': a memorial tribute
to F.R.Benson [broadcast] April
26th 1950. ff. [1,] 46. Typescript.

608873

SUTTON (SHAUN)
Will loves Alice [: a play relating
to Shakespeare.   Broadcast] 19th Dec.,
1951.   pp. 31.
typescript.

622922

SUTTON COLDFIELD, BISHOP VESEY'S GRAMMAR
SCHOOL
Prospectus, [1940.   With "A Note on
Shakespeare: his connection with
Sutton Coldfield and the Grammar
School".]   pp. 26.   [Sutton Coldfield]
illus.   [1940]

521873

SUZMAN (ARTHUR)
Imagery and symbolism in Richard II.
IN SHAKESPEARE QUARTERLY VII:
pp. 355-370.
(New York) 1956.

605711

SWALE (INGRAM) ed.
The Voice of the sea [: an anthology
of prose and poetry]. Edited [with
a note. With extracts from
Shakespeare].
illus. [1907.]
Wayfaring Books.

546919

SWAN HILL NATIONAL THEATRE
Swan Hill Shakespeare Festival
programmes [etc.] (Swan Hill,
Victoria) 1949-

666302

The Swan of Avon: a quarterly devoted
to new Shakespearian research,
Vol. 1, Nos. 1-3 (March-September
1948). (Santa Barbara, Cal.:
Melander Shakespeare Society) 1948.
With additional corrected copy of
Vol. 1, No. 1.
All published.

618019

Swan Theatre *see* London, Swan Theatre

SWANDER, HOMER D.
Cymbeline and the "blameless hero"
FROM E L H, Vol.31, No.3. (Baltimore,
Maryland) 1964.

pp.259-270. 747850

SWANDER, HOMER D.
"Cymbeline": religious idea and dramatic
design.
IN Pacific coast studies in Shakespeare.
Edited by W. F. McNeir and T. N.
Greenfield. (Eugene: Ore.) 1966.

768009

SWANDER (HOMER D.)
The Design of "Cymbeline". (Ann
Arbor, Mich.)
bibliog. typescript, 1953. micro-
film, positive copy. 1 reel, 35 mm.
1953.
University Microfilms. Doctoral
Dissertation Series.

647064

SWANDER, HOMER D.
Twelfth Night: critics, players, and a
script. FROM Educational Theatre Journal.
(Columbia) 1964.

pp.114-121. 747851

SWANDER (HOMER D.   )

The Use of Shakespeare: a cautionary
essay. FROM Spectrum, Vol.4, No.1,
Winter, 1960. (Santa Barbara, Cal.)

668439

[SWANSEA LITTLE THEATRE
Songs for tenor voice and pianoforte,
composed for the production of
Twelfth Night at the Swansea Little
Theatre in December, 1938, by Thomas
Warner]. ff. [4].
manuscript. 1938.

512988

SWANSTON (HAMISH F. G.)
The Baroque element in "Troilus and
Cressida". FROM "The Durham
University Journal", New Series
Vol. 19. pp. 14-23. (Durham)
1957.

665776

SWANTON (ERNEST W.)
Country notes and a nature calendar.
[With a chapter on Shakespeare's
flowers] (Haslemere)
1938. 481893
2nd edn.
illus. 1951. 621078

[SWANWICK (ANNA)]
William Shakespeare, 1564-1616.
FROM Swanwick (A.) Poets, the
interpreters of their age. [1892]

431269

SWART (J.)
I know not "seems": a study of Hamlet.
IN A Review of English literature.
Vol. 2. 1961.
bibliogs.

697306/1961

Sweden

— KING (J. C.)
Twelfth Night at Stockholm.
IN Theatre Today.
illus. [1947.]

606680

— MOLIN, NILS
Shakespeare translated into Swedish.
IN SHAKESPEARE JAHRBUCH, Bd. 92/1956.
pp. 232-243. (Heidelberg)

10531

— WIKLAND (ERIK)
Elizabethan players in Sweden,
1591-92: facts and problems.
Translated by P. Hort.   Translations
from the Latin by C. E. Holm.
(Stockholm)
ports. illus. map. genealogical
tables. facsimiles. bibliog.
                              1962.

                    667260

SWEET (GEORGE ELLIOTT)
Shake-speare: the mystery [of the
authorship].   (Stanford, Cal.)
tables. bibliog. 1956.   665726
_____ Another edn.   (London)
                  1963.   667657

Swift, Jonathan *works relating to*

— WATKINS (W. B. C.)
Absent thee from felicity [: Swift's
satire compared with that of
Shakespeare].   FROM The Southern
Review, Autumn 1939.   [Baton Rouge]

                    530198

Swimming

— HEDGES (S. G.)
Swimming complete; illustrated by
S. Lewis.   [With quotations from
Shakespeare.]
                    [1939.]

                    499999

SWINBURNE (ALGERNON CHARLES)
The Age of Shakespeare.
                  1908.   469787
No. 2 of a large-paper edition limited
to 110 copies.
_____ 2nd impression.
                  1909.   395714

SWINBURNE (ALGERNON CHARLES)
Dramatic poets, 2: William Shakespeare;
The Afterglow of Shakespeare.   IN
Swinburne (A. C.) Selected poems, with
an introduction by [R.] L. Binyon.
                              1939.
The World's Classics.

                    507798

SWINBURNE (ALGERNON CHARLES)
General introduction.   IN SHAKESPEARE
(W.) Complete works, Vol. 1.
(Oxford)   1933.
The World's Classics.

                    530180

SWINBURNE (ALGERNON CHARLES)
Note on the historical play of
King Edward III.   FROM The
Gentleman's Magazine, Vol. 245.
                              1879.

                    556081

SWINBURNE (ALGERNON CHARLES)
"Othello": critical comment.   pp.
[9.]   IN Harper's Monthly Magazine,
Vol. 109, 1904.   185946
_____ FROM Harper's Monthly Magazine,
Oct. 1908.
illus.   515796

SWINBURNE (ALGERNON CHARLES)
Report of the first anniversary
meeting of the newest Shakespeare
society [i.e. New Shakspere Society],
April 1, 1876.   FROM The Examiner,
April 1, 1876.

                    555523

SWINBURNE (ALGERNON CHARLES)
A Study of Shakespeare.   2nd edn.
                  1880.   399707
_____ 3rd edn. revised.
                  1895.   394928
_____ 5th impression.
                  1909.   428133
_____ Another edn.   [With a preface
by Sir E. Gosse.]   (Golden Pine edn.)
                  1918.   407940
_____ New impression.
                  1920.   482877

SWINBURNE (A. C.)
William Shakespeare [: a sonnet].
IN WHITING (B. J.) [and others] eds.,
The College survey of English
literature, Vol. 2.   (New York)
ports. illus. maps. facsimiles.
bibliogs.   1944.

                    556884

Swinburne, Algernon Charles *works relating to*

— Brocklehurst (J.H.) Swinburne's "The Age of Shakespeare": a review. <u>In</u> Manchester Literary Club. Papers, Vol.35.

(Manchester)   1909.

518392

— SPIVEY (GAYNELL C.) Swinburne's use of Elizabethan drama. [With references to Shakespeare.] IN Studies in Philology, Vol. 41. (Chapel Hill, N.C.) bibliog.   1944.

563556

Swinnerton (F.[A.]) The Georgian literary scene: a panorama [including references to Shakespeare. With a bibliography.]

1935.

432939

SWINSON (ARTHUR) The First night of "Vortigern" [: a programme in dramatic form on the production in 1796 of the play "Vortigern" by W. H. Ireland, which he claimed was by William Shakespeare.] Television broadcast 25th June, 1958. ff. 52. typescript.

665904

SWINTON, MARJORY, comp. Shakespeare birthday book.   [1964.]

illus. Windsor birthday books. 667978

SWINYARD (LAURENCE) Shakespeare's Stratford-on-Avon. Sketches by E. E. Briscoe.   pp.[20]. [1951.]

617923

Switzerland

— ENGEL (CLAIRE E.) Shakespeare in Switzerland in the XVIIIth century.   IN Comparative Literature Studies: Cahiers de littérature comparée, Vols. 17-18. (Cardiff)   1945.

579159

Swordsmanship *see* **Fencing**

S[YDENHAM] (H. R.) Kuwia na kuwiwa [: an account of an African performance of Shakespeare's Merchant of Venice]. FROM "Central Africa", August 1934.

427412

SYDENHAM OF COMBE ([GEORGE SYDENHAM CLARKE, 1st Baron]) The First Baconian [i.e. J. Wilmot]. Reprinted from Baconiana.   Feb. 1933. pp. 8.   [Bacon Society, London] 1933.   422158
_____ Another edn.   pp. 5. port.   illus.   [1944.]   549421

Sydney Studies in Literature RIEMER, A. P. A Reading of Shakespeare's 'Antony and Cleopatra'.   (Sydney)   1968.

774921

SYKES (C. W.) Alias William Shakespeare?   [The claims of Roger Manners, 5th Earl of Rutland, to the authorship of Shakespeare.]   With a preface by A. Bryant. bibliog.   1947.

583729

Sykes (C.W.) The Shakespeare mystery [:evidence to show that Shakespeare's plays were written by Roger Manners, 5th Earl of Rutland]. pp. [6 .] From The London Mystery Magazine, Vol.1.

[1949.]

604845

Sykes, C. W. *works relating to*

— HOUSE (HUMPHREY)
  Reviews of Alias William Shakespeare,
  by C. W. Sykes and The Real
  Shakespeare, by W. Bliss.   IN
  CALDER-MARSHALL (A.) ed., Books and
  authors [: reviews.   Broadcast]
  16th July, 1947.   pp. 18.
    typescript.

587749

SYKES (ERNEST F.)
  "All's well that ends well", Stratford-
  upon-Avon Shakespeare Memorial Theatre
  [production], Festival season 1955.
  ff. 29.
    typescript.   1955.
  Journal Notes.   7th Series.

665407

SYKES (ERNEST F.)
  "The Comedy of Errors":   Midland
  Theatre Company [production] at
  Coventry Technical College, Nov. 14th
  1955.   ff. 7.
    typescript.   1956.
  Journal Notes.   7th Series.

665408

SYKES (ERNEST F.)
  "Hamlet":   [the] Peter Brook-Scofield
  production, prior to Moscow, at
  Birmingham Alexandra Theatre.
    typescript.   [1955.]
  Journal [Notes. 7th Series].

665409

SYKES (ERNEST F.)
  John English's production of "Much ado
  about nothing" [at the] Arena Theatre,
  Birmingham, 1954.   ff. 32.
    typescript.   [1954.]

665405

SYKES (ERNEST F.)
  "King Richard the Second":   [the
  production] at the Birmingham Repertory
  Theatre, 1955.   ff. 30.
    typescript.   1955.
  Journal Notes.   7th Series.

665410

SYKES (ERNEST F.)
  "Macbeth":   Stratford-upon-Avon
  Memorial Theatre [production],
  Festival Season 1955.
    chart.   typescript.   1955.
  Journal Notes.   7th Series.

665411

SYKES (ERNEST F.)
  "The Merry Wives of Windsor":
  Stratford-upon-Avon Shakespeare Festival
  Season [production] 1955.   ff. [19.]
    typescript.   1955.
  Journal Notes.   7th Series.

665412

SYKES (ERNEST F.)
  "Much ado about nothing":   Stratford-
  upon-Avon Memorial Theatre [production]
  Festival Season 1955.   ff. 5.
    typescript.   1955.
  Journal Notes.   7th Series.

665413

SYKES (ERNEST F.)
  Segregation of the role of Diomedes.
  Supplementary note to comments on
  Byam Shaw's production at Stratford-
  upon-Avon [of] "Troilus and Cressida".
  ff. 16.
    typescript.   1954.
  Journal Notes.   6th Series.

665406

SYKES (ERNEST F.)
  "Titus Andronicus":   [the production]
  at the Memorial Theatre, Stratford-
  upon-Avon, 1955 Festival Season.
  ff. [33.]
    typescript.   1955.
  Journal Notes.   7th Series.

665414

SYKES (ERNEST F.)
  "Troilus and Cressida":   Sir W. Walton's
  opera;   libretto by C. Hassall.   Some
  jottings regarding the Covent Garden
  Opera Company's performance at the
  Coventry Theatre, April 1955.   ff. 15.
    typescript.   [1955.]

665415

SYKES (ERNEST F.)
  "Twelfth Night":   Stratford-upon-Avon
  Shakespeare Memorial Theatre
  [production] Festival Season 1955.
  ff. 25.   1955.
    Journal Notes.   7th Series.

665416

Sykes (H.D.)   The Authorship of "A
  Yorkshire tragedy".   From The Journal
  of English and Germanic Philology,
  Vol.16.

                 (Urbana, Ill.)   1917.

510468

SYKES (H. D.)
  The Authorship of "The Two noble
  kinsmen".   IN The Modern Language
  Review, Vol. 11.   (Cambridge)
                                     1916.

266431

SYKES (H. D.)
[Review of] Shakespeare's Henry VI
and Richard III, by P. Alexander.
IN Review of English Studies,
Vol. 6.   1930.

377862

SYKES (H. D.)
[Review of] The Origin and development
of 1 Henry VI, in relation to
Shakespeare, Marlowe, Peele and
Greene, by A. Gaw.   FROM Review of
English Studies, Vol. 4.   1928.

497596

Sykes (H.D.) [Review of] Shakespeare
and Chapman, by J. M. Robertson.
In The Modern Language Review. Vol.
13.

1918.

276260

Sykes, Henry Dugdale *works relating to*

— Frijlinck (W.P.) [Review of] Sidelights
on Elizabethan drama, by H.D.Sykes.
In English studies, Vol. 8.

(Amsterdam)   1926.

485650

Sylvain, Aleksandr *works relating to*

— NOWOTTNY, WINIFRED M.T.
Shakespeare and "The Orator".
FROM Bulletin de la Faculté des
Lettres de Strasbourg, Mai-Juin 1965.
(Strasbourg)

pp.813-833.   765917

Symbolism *see* Imagery

SYMON (Sir J. [H.])
Shakespeare at home.   (Adelaide)
1905.

422630

SYMON ([Sir] J. H.)
Shakespeare quotation: a lecture
delivered before the Adelaide University
Shakespeare Society, at Adelaide.
pp. 63.   (Stirling [Australia])
(Printed for private circulation)
1901.

395747

SYMONDS (JOHN ADDINGTON)
The Drama of Elizabeth and James
considered as the main product of
the Renaissance in England.   [With
references to Shakespeare.]   IN
MARLOWE (CHRISTOPHER) [Plays] Edited
by [H.] H. Ellis.
port.   illus.   [1902]
The Mermaid Series.
Large paper copy.

389466

SYMONDS (JOHN ADDINGTON)
Shakspere's predecessors in the English
drama.   New edn.   1906.   472088
_____ New edn.   1913.   483089
_____ 2nd edn.   1924.   401510

Symons (T.) Come away death [: a song.
Words from Twelfth Night by]
Shakespeare: [music by] T.Symons.
pp.8.

[1934.]

536606

Synopses
see also under the titles of the individual plays

— Cartmell (V.H.) ed. Plot outlines of
100 famous plays [including six plays
of Shakespeare.]

(Philadelphia)   1945.

587356

— HARBAGE, ALFRED
William Shakespeare: a reader's
guide.   (New York)   1963.

667623

— HOLZKNECHT (KARL JULIUS)
Outlines of Tudor and Stuart plays,
1497-1642.   (New York)
illus.   table.   bibliog.   1952.
College Outline Series.

666111

— KELLER (HELEN R.)
The Reader's digest of books.   New
and enlarged edn.   [With outlines
of Shakespeare's plays.]   [1937]

468376

— McSPADDEN (JOSEPH WALKER)

Shakespeare's plays in digest form:
outlines of all the plays of
Shakespeare. With an article on
Shakespeare's stage, by Sue G. Walcutt.
Illus. Map. (Thomas Y. Crowell Co.,
[New York])   1961.

667419

— MAGILL (LEWIS MALCOLM) and AULT (NELSON A.)
Synopses of Shakespeare's complete
plays.   (Ames, Iowa)
  port.   1952.
Littlefield College Outlines.

630285

— RANSOME (C.)
Short studies of Shakespeare's plots.
                    1898.   424799
_____ Another edn. 1911. 527351
_____ Another edn. 1924. 533157

— STOWELL (HELEN ELIZABETH)

Reading Shakespeare's plays. Port. Illus.
(Welwyn, Herts)   1962.

667200

— USHERWOOD, STEPHEN
Shakespeare play by play. Illustrated
by R. Piper.   1967.

  illus.   764809

— WATT (H. A.), HOLZKNECHT (K. J.) and
  ROSS (R.)
Outlines of Shakespeare's plays.
  (New York)
  illus. maps. bibliogs. 1934. 427372
College Outline Series.
_____ Another edn. 1938. 488716
_____ Another edn. 1941. 530370

— WILLIAMS (G. C.) and FOULKES (W. R.)
Shakespearean synopses.   1928.

396606

SYPHER (WYLIE)
Hamlet: the existential madness.
FROM The Nation [Vol. 162].   (New
York)   1946.

581634

SYPHER (WYLIE)
Shakespeare as casuist: Measure for
Measure.   FROM The Sewanee Review,
Vol. 58.   (Sewanee, Tenn.)   1950.

619298

SZENCZI (MIKLÓS)
The Nature of Shakespeare's realism.
IN SHAKESPEARE JAHRBUCH.   Bd. 102/
1966.   pp. 27-59.   (Weimar)

10531

SZYFMAN (ARNOLD)
"King Lear" on the stage: a producer's
reflections.   IN SHAKESPEARE SURVEY
13.   (Cambridge)   1960.

666726

T. (S.)
Compendium of county history:
Warwickshire.   [With references to
Shakespeare.]   FROM The Gentleman's
Magazine, Jan. 1825.

401837

Taborski (Boleslaw) trans.
  KOTT (JAN)
Shakespeare our contemporary.   Translated
by B. Taborski.   Preface by P. Brook.
                               1964.

741546

Taggert (Louise) and Haefner (G.E.)
  Two methods of teaching Macbeth.
  From The English Journal, vol.23.

        (Chicago)   1934.

442570

TAGORE ([Sir] R.)
Shakespeare [: an Indian poem,
with English translation].
IN GOLLANCZ ([Sir] I.) ed.,
A Book of homage to Shakespeare.
  ports. illus. facsimiles.

                               [1916.]

264175

TAINE (HIPPOLYTE)
[Shakespeare's characters: excerpts
from] A History of English Literature,
Book II.   IN LEWINTER (OSWALD) ed.,
Shakespeare in Europe [by various
authors].   1963.

667784

TAIT (HUGH)

Garrick, Shakespeare, and Wilkes.
pp.[13]. Reprinted from "The British
Museum Quarterly", Vol.24. No. 3-4.
                               [1959]

667275

TALBERT, ERNEST WILLIAM
Elizabethan drama and Shakespeare's
early plays: an essay in historical
criticism.   1963.

667960

TALBERT (ERNEST WILLIAM)

The Problem of order: Elizabethan
political commonplaces and an example
of Shakespeare's art [; Richard II.]
(Chapel Hill, [N.C.])   1962.

668091

Talbot (A.J.) Was Hamlet a minor? In
  Drama, [N.S.] Vol.17, 1938-39.

510799

TALBOT (A. J.)
Will Shakespeare's bespoke supper:
a Baconian night at the Mermaid
Tavern.   IN The One-act theatre,
the sixth book.   1935.

439266

Talbot (F.) Trades and crafts of
  Shakespeare. From [Belgravia,
  March 1875.]

554160

TALBOT (W.)
  Shakespeare: a select bibliography
  of books issued during the past
  six years.   FROM The Publishers'
  Circular and Booksellers' Record.
  pp. [4.]   1932.

394977

Talbot Epitaph see Henry the Sixth

Tales from Shakespeare

see also Lamb, Charles and Mary A. *and under
the titles of the separate plays*

—— BAZAGONOV, MIKHAIL SERAFIMOVICH, pseud.
  Shakespeare in the red. Tales from
  Shakespeare by a Soviet Lamb. 1964.

741515

—— BRANSOM (LAURA)
  Living Shakespeare [: the stories of
  the plays]. 5 vols.
  illus.   [1949 -53]
  For "Teachers' companion to Living
  Shakespeare", see Catal. no. 636356.

604746

—— BRANSOM (LAURA)
  Living Shakespeare: teachers' companion [: scenes suitable for acting
  by children].   Illustrated by Molly
  Wilson.   1953
  For 'Living Shakespeare' [: the
  stories of the plays] see Catal. no.
  604746.

636356

—— BUCKMAN, IRENE
  Twenty tales from Shakespeare. With
  a foreword by Dame Peggy Ashcroft.
                          1963.

  illus.   667675

—— BURNS (J. J.)
  The Story of English kings according
  to Shakespeare.   (New York)
  ports.   illus.   1900.

572120

—— CARTER (R.)
  Shakespeare's stories of the English
  kings.   With illustrations by
  Gertrude D. Hammond.   1928.
  "Told Through the Ages".

392830

—— CARTER (T.)
  Stories from Shakespeare.   Illustra-
  tions by Gertrude D. Hammond.
                     1914.   528729
  _____ Another edn.   ("Told Through
  the Ages")   1931.   392831
  _____ Another edn. 1934.   552919

—— Cheever (J.) Homage to Shakespeare.
  From Story, November, 1937.

  (New York)

503865

—— CHUTE (MARCHETTE GAYLORD)
  Stories from Shakespeare. (Mentor Book)
  (New York)   1959.

666242

—— DEUTSCH (BABETTE)
  The Reader's Shakespeare [: stories
  of the most popular plays].   With
  decorations by W, Chappell [and
  musical examples].   (New York)
  bibliog.   1946.

581692

—— DODD (E. F.)
  Six tales from Shakespeare.   (Madras)
  frontis.   1953.
  Macmillan's Stories to Remember in
  Simple English.

640466

—— DODD (E. F.)
  Three Shakespeare comedies [: As you
  like it; A Midsummer night's dream;
  and, Much ado about nothing, retold].
  pp. 56.   (Madras)   1953.

644192

—— DODD (E.   F.   )
  Three Shakespeare histories: England
  under the Plantagenet Kings, Richard II,
  Henry IV, and Henry V as depicted in
  Shakespeare's historical plays.
  (Macmillan's Stories to Remember)
  Illus. (Macmillan and Co. Ltd., Madras)
                          1962.

667416

—— DODD (E. F.)
  Three Shakespeare tragedies [: Romeo
  and Juliet; Hamlet; and Othello,
  retold].   (Madras)
  ports.   illus.   1956.
  Macmillan's Stories to Remember:
  Senior Series.

665491

—— GILBERT (M.)
  The Short story Shakespeare.   [Each
  volume containing the story in prose
  with dialogue from the play.]
  (Bournemouth)
  illus.   5 vols.   [1947-8]
  For setting out, see under Gilbert (M.)

587528

—— GOULDEN, SHIRLEY
  Tales from Shakespeare.   Illustrated
  by Nardini.
  illus.   1964.
  Splendour Books.

668324

— GREEN, ROGER LANCELYN
Tales from Shakespeare.   Illustrated
by Richard Beer.   Foreword by
Christopher Fry.
2 vols.   1964-5.

                  740347

— HARRISON (G. B.)
New tales from Shakespeare.   Illus-
trated by C. W. Hodges.
            1938.   487748
_____ "Teaching of English" Series.
            1939.   510478

— HARRISON (G. B.)
More new tales from Shakespeare.
Illustrated by C. W. Hodges.
            1939.   498254
_____ "Teaching of English" Series.
            1940.   510479

— [HOLMDAHL (FREDA)]
A Further approach to Shakespeare [:
selections from the plays, stories
from the plays] including three prose
tales by Sir A. T. Quiller-Couch.
With an introduction by H. E. Marshall.
illus.   1934.
"Teaching of English" Series.
For "The Approach to Shakespeare" see
under: Lang (Mrs. Andrew)

                  429584

— HUDSON (R.)
Tales from Shakespeare.
illus.   [1933.]
[School and Adventure Library]

                  412174

— LA BARRE (JULIA)
Stories of Shakespeare's popular
comedies, told in rhyme.   pp. 70.
(Portland, Oregon)
port.   1933.

                  415119

— Macauley (Miss [Elizabeth W.]) Tales
of the drama: founded on the
tragedies of Shakspeare, etc.
Ports. Illus.

      (Exeter)   1833.

                  431998

— MACFARLAND (A. S.) and SAGE (A.)
Stories from Shakespeare.
port.   illus.   [1882]   401511
_____ Another edn.
            [c.1895.]   550468

— MacLEOD (MARY)
The Shakespeare story-book.   With
introduction by [Sir] S. Lee.   4th
edn.   1911.   388842
      (Darton's Romance Readers)
3 vols.   [1911.]   530993
_____ 6th edn.   1 vol.
            1922.   405778
_____ 12th edn.   1944.   559960

— McSPADDEN (J. W.)
Stories of the plays.   IN SHAKESPEARE
(W.) Five great tragedies: Romeo and
Juliet, Julius Caesar, Hamlet, King
Lear, Macbeth.   Cambridge text as
edited by W. A. Wright, with introductions by J. Masefield.   [Edited with
a chapter, Shakespeare - teller of
stories, by H. W. Simon.]   (New York)
                  1939.

Pocket Books, 3.

                  504059

— MARTIN (CONSTANCE M.)
Stories from Shakespeare.   Illustrated
by Mary Gordon.   pp. 48.   [1935]
"Riverside" Readers.

                  475742

— MAUD (CONSTANCE and MARY)
Shakespeare's stories in modern
English.   With bilingual notes
by W. V. Doherty and B. Shen.
Edited by N. B. Pitman.   (Shanghai)
                 [1932]

                  438363

— Miller (Daphne) Stories from
Shakespeare. pp.[24.] Illus.

      (Oxford)   1934.

(Little Giant Books.)

                  421213

— MURRAY (GEOFFREY)

Let's discover Shakespeare [:eight of
Shakespeare's plays retold for
children]. Illus. Bibliog.
                  1957.

                  665641

— MURRAY (GEOFFREY)

Let's discover more Shakespeare [:
eight of Shakespeare's plays retold for
children]. Port.   1960.

                  666667

— Nesbit (E[dith]) The Children's
Shakespeare.   Illustrated by R.
Klep.

      (New York)   1938.

                  496765

— NESBIT (E[DITH])
Twenty beautiful stories from
Shakespeare.   Official text for
members of the National Junior
Shakespeare Club.   Illustrated
by M. Bihn.   Edited and arranged,
[with a preface,] by E. T. Roe.
(Chicago)   1926.

                  422519

— NESBIT (EDITH) and CHESSON (HUGH)
The Merchant of Venice and other stories.
Illustrated by F. Brundage and M. Bowley.
pp.64. Illus.   [c.1920.]

                  667236

— Old stories retold. 1. King Lear;
2. The Tempest; 3. Macbeth; [4]
Hamlet, by [W. Grierson.] FROM
John O' London's Weekly (Outline
Supplement) 1931. pp. [7.]
illus.
King Lear is imperfect.

390553

— PAGE (JOSEPHINE)
The Winter's Tale, by William
Shakespeare. Retold by Josephine
Page. pp. vi, 70. (Oxford)
illus. 1941.

539921

— PALMER (H. E.)
Four stories from Shakespeare.
Adapted and rewritten with the thousand
word vocabulary. Illustrated by
T. H. Robinson. 1937.
Thousand-Word English Senior Series.

463628

— PALMER (H. E.)
Four tales from Shakespeare.
pp. 72. [1944.]
[Evans International Series.]
"Plain English" Library.

555376

— QUILLER-COUCH ([Sir] A. T.)
Historical tales from Shakespeare.
New illustrated edn.
1905. 467082
Another edn. [1910] 391318

— SEC (FONG F.)
Stories from Shakespeare. pp. [iv],
74. (Shanghai) 1929.

438364

— SERRAILLIER, IAN
Stories from Shakespeare: the enchanted
island. Illustrated by P. Farmer.
1964.

667996

— Seymour (Mary) Shakespeare stories
simply told: tragedies and
histories. Illus.

1893.

516785

— Shakespeare stories for boys and girls.
Illustrated by J. H. Bacon, H. Copping
and others. [1933.]
The Modern Library for Boys and Girls.

407216

— Shakespeare tales for boys and girls,
Illustrated by J. H. Bacon. [1932.]
[Golden Treasury Library]
Includes "When Shakespeare was a
boy", by F. J. Furnivall.

399215

— Shakespeare's plays as short stories.
[1] King Lear, by H. [S.] Walpole:
(2) Julius Caesar, by the Rt. Hon. W.
[L. S.] Churchill; (3) The Merchant
of Venice, by [P. Snowden] Viscount
Snowden; (4) Coriolanus, by J. Buchan;
(5) Hamlet, by F. B. Young; (6) The
Taming of the Shrew, by Clemence Dane.
Illustrated by F. Matania. FROM The
Strand Magazine, Oct., 1933–March, 1934.

419970

— SIMON (H. W.)
Shakespeare – teller of stories.
IN SHAKESPEARE (W.) Five great
tragedies: Romeo and Juliet,
Julius Caesar, Hamlet, King Lear,
Macbeth. Cambridge text as edited
by W. A. Wright, with introductions
by J. Masefield [and Stories of the
plays, by J. W. McSpadden. Edited
by H. W. Simon.] (New York) 1939.
Pocket Book, 3.

504059

— Six stories from Shakespeare. Retold by
J. Buchan, H.[S.] Walpole, Clemence
Dane, F.B. Young, W.[L.S.]Churchill,
Viscount Snowden. Illustrations by
F. Matania.

1934.

428744

— SMITH, ALBERT JAMES
Shakespeare stories. 1963.

World of English series.

667682

— SPECKING (INEZ)
A Shakespeare for children. (New
York) 1954.

665070

— STERNBECK (A.)
A Gateway to Shakespeare: stories
from Shakespeare. Zusammengestellt
und erklärt. Worterbuch [&c.]
(Leipzig)
port. illus. 1930.
Französische und englische Schulbibliothek.
English text, with notes &c. in German.

450313

— STIDOLPH (ADA B.)
The Children's Shakespeare [: The
Merchant of Venice, A Midsummer
night's dream and As you like it,
in story form]. With preface by
C. W. Barnett-Clarke. 2nd edn.
ports. [c.1905.]

527186

— Stories from Shakespeare. pp. 95.
illus. 1934.
The Children's Shakespeare.

438385

— Stories from Shakespeare for young
students. [6th edn.] [Tokyo]
[1931]

397844

——The Stories of Shakespeare's plays.
(Oxford)
   illus.   2 vols.   1939.
Tales Retold for Easy Reading, Second
Series.

521397

—— WHITE (ANNA T.)
   Three children and Shakespeare [:
   the stories of A Midsummer night's
   dream, The Merchant of Venice,
   Julius Caesar and The Taming of
   the shrew, told mainly in Shakespeare's
   own words.]   With drawings by
   Beatrice Tobias.   (New York) 1938.

492184

—— WINDROSS (RONALD)
   Two comedies: Much ado about nothing;
   The Winter's tale.   The stories of
   these abridged and simplified.
   Illustrated by M. Abauzit.   (Paris:
   Marcel Didier)   1962.
      Tales from England, 3rd degree, No. 31.

668153

—— WINDROSS (RONALD)

   Two tragedies: Othello [and] Hamlet;
   abridged and simplified. Illustrated
   by H. Breton. (Tales from England)
   (Didier, Paris)   1961.

667330

—— WYATT (H. G.)
   Stories from Shakespeare.   (Oxford)
      illus.   1934.
   Stories Retold.

421720

—— WYATT (H. G.)
   More stories from Shakespeare.
   (Oxford)
      illus.   1933.
   Stories Retold.

418059

—— WYATT (HORACE GRAHAM)
   Chĕrita-Chĕrita Shakespeare.
   Di-chĕritakan sa-mula oleh H. G. Wyatt.
   Di-tĕrjĕmahkan oleh A. Samad Said.
   (London.   Kuala Lumpur; O.U.P.)
                         1958.
   Text in Malayan.

666153

—— ZACHRISSON (R. E.)
   Shakespeare stories.   Compiled and
   annotated for the use of Swedish
   schools, with a Shakespeare biblio-
   graphy.   [English and Swedish text.]
   Fjarde upplagan.   (Stockholm)
                   1926.   417273
   ——— Ordlista.   (Stockholm)
                   1928.   417285
   [Moderna Engelska Forfattare.]

TALFOURD, FRANCIS
Macbeth travestie

For editions of this play see under
English Editions: Macbeth:
Alterations &c.

TALFOURD, FRANCIS
Shylock, or, The Merchant of Venice
preserved

For editions of this play see under
English Editions: The Merchant of
Venice: Alterations &c.

TALFOURD (Sir THOMAS NOON)
Memoirs of Charles Lamb.   Edited
and annotated by P. Fitzgerald.
[With Shakespearian references.]
   ports.   1892.

485278

Tallis's dramatic magazine and general
theatrical and musical review [1850-
1853].
   ports.   illus.   3 vols.
1851 entitled Tallis's drawing room
table book.   From 1852-3 entitled
Tallis's Shakespeare gallery of
engravings.

633014

Talma, François **Joseph** *works relating to*

—— EGGLI (E.)
   Talma à Londres en 1817.   IN WILLIAMS
   (MARY) and ROTHSCHILD (J. A. de) eds.,
   A Miscellany of studies in Romance lang-
   uages & literatures presented to Léon
   E. Kastner.   (Cambrdige)
                         1932.

391235

—— Travels in France: a vignette of Talma.
   [An account of Talma and his performance
   of Hamlet, taken from Our Traveler's
   "Travels in France"]   IN Theatre Arts,
   Vol. 28.   (New York)
      port.   1944.

558366

The Taming of a shrew

For editions of this play see under
English Editions: The Taming of
the Shrew: Alterations &c.

Taming of the Shrew
General Works and Criticism

Burlesques; Plays

Stage History and Production

Study and Teaching; Tales

Taming of the Shrew
— General Works and Criticism

— BRADBROOK, MURIEL CLARA
Dramatic rôle as social image: a study
of The Taming of the Shrew.
IN SHAKESPEARE JAHRBUCH. Bd. 94/1958.
pp.132-150.   (Heidelberg)

10531

— BRUNVAND (JAN HAROLD)
The Folktale origin of The Taming of
the Shrew.
IN SHAKESPEARE QUARTERLY XVII: 4.
pp. 345-359.
(New York) 1966.

605711

— CHARLTON (H. B.)
The Taming of the Shrew [: a study].
Reprinted from "The Bulletin of the
John Rylands Library", Vol. 16, No. 2,
July 1932. pp. 25.   (Manchester)
1932.

401475

— CRAIG (H.)
The Shrew and A Shrew: possible settle-
ment of an old debate [over the relation
between The Taming of the Shrew and The
Taming of a Shrew].   IN Elizabethan
studies and other essays [by various
authors], in honor of George F. Reynolds.
[With bibliographical notes.] (Boulder,
Col.)   1945.
(Colorado University Studies. Series B.
Studies in the Humanities, Vol. 2. No.4.)
569202

— DAM (B. A. P. van)
The Taming of a shrew.   Offprint
from English Studies, [Vol.] 10.
pp. 97-106.   (Amsterdam)   [1928.]

554220

— DEELEY (R. M.)
A Genealogical history of Montfort-sur-
Risle and Deeley of Halesowen.
[Including a reference to Christopher
Sly]
ports. illus. maps. pedigrees.
1941.

531802

— Draper (J.W.) "Kate the Curst". From
The Journal of Nervous and Mental
Disease, Vol. 89, No. 6.

(Richmond, Va.)   1939.

527855

— DUTHIE (G. I.)
The Taming of a Shrew and The Taming
of the Shrew.   IN The Review of
English Studies, Vol. 19.   (Oxford)
bibliog.   1943.

555539

— FLEAY (FREDERICK GARD)
On the authorship of The Taming of the Shrew.
**IN Transactions of the New Shakespeare
Society, Series 1.** No. 1.   pp. 85-129.
1874.

4061

— FULLER-MAITLAND (J. A.)
Bianca's music-lesson.
IN GOLLANCZ ([Sir] I.) ed., A Book
of homage to Shakespeare.
ports. illus. facsimiles. [1916.]

264175

— GATTY (REGINALD ARTHUR ALLIX)
The Taming of the Shrew [: a lecture].
manuscript.   1928.

637993

— GATTY (REGINALD ARTHUR ALLIX)
The Taming of the shrew, from William
Shakespeare.   ff. 19.
typescript.   [?1930.]

624888

— GRAY (H. D.)
The Taming of a Shrew [: a theory
that "A Shrew" is a bad quarto based
upon "The Shrew" before it underwent
revision. With bibliographical notes].
IN MAXWELL (B.) [and others] eds.,
Renaissance studies in honor of Hardin
Craig.   (Iowa)
port.   8vo.1941.
Philological Quarterly, Vol. 20, No.3;
Iowa University [and Stanford University])
539442

— HIBBARD, GEORGE RICHARD
The Taming of the shrew: a social comedy.
FROM Shakespearean Essays, special
number: 2. (Knoxville, Tennessee)
1964.

pp.15-28.   749528

— HOUK (R. A.)
"Doctor Faustus" and "A Shrew".   IN
Publications of the Modern Language
Association of America, Vol. 62.
(Menasha, Wis.)
bibliog.
1947.

428321/62

— HOUK (R. A.)
The Evolution of The Taming of the
Shrew.   IN Publications of the Modern
Language Association of America,
Vol. 57.   (Menasha, Wis.)
bibliog.
1942.

544204

— HOUK (R. A.)
Shakespeare's Shrew and Greene's
Orlando. IN Publications of the
Modern Language Association of America,
Vol. 62.   (Menasha, Wis.)
bibliog.   1947.

428321/62

— HOUK (R. A.)
Strata in The Taming of the Shrew.
IN Studies in Philology, Vol. 39.
(Chapel Hill, N.C.)
bibliog.   1942.

554520

— JORGENSEN (PAUL ALFRED)
The Taming of the Shrew: entertainment
for television.   IN The Quarterly of
Film, Radio and Television, Vol. 10.
(Berkeley, Cal.)
                            1956.

630462/10

— KUHL (E. P.)
The Authorship of The Taming of the
Shrew.   FROM Publications of the
Modern Language Association of America,
Vol. 40.   (Menasha, Wis.)
bibliog.   1925.

554227

— KUHL (E. [P.])
Shakspere's "Lead apes in Hell" and
the ballad of "The Maid and the palmer".
FROM Studies in Philology, Vol. 22,
No. 4.   (Chapel Hill, N.C.)   1925.

436043

— KUHL (ERNEST PETER)
Shakspere's purpose in dropping Sly.
IN Modern Language Notes, Vol. 36.
(Baltimore, Md.)   1921.

439157/36

— LEATHAM (J.)
The Taming of the Shrew.   2nd edn.
pp. 20.   (Turriff)   [c.1920.]
Shakespeare Studies, No. 14.

566386

— MILLER (H. C.)
A Shakespearean music lesson [in
The Taming of the Shrew].   IN
Notes and Queries, Vol. 165.
                            1933.

416106

— PARROTT (T. M.)
The Taming of a shrew   a new study of
an old play.   IN Elizabethan studies
and other essays [, by various authors],
in honor of George F. Reynolds. [With
bibliographical notes.] (Boulder, Col.)
                            1945.
Colorado University Studies.   Series B.
Studies in the Humanities. Vol. 2.No.4.

569202

— PHILLIPS (G. W.)
Lord Burghley in Shakespeare: Falstaff,
Sly and others.   1936.

456935

— ROSSITER (ARTHUR PERCIVAL)
A Guide for Shakespeare-goers,2: 'The
Sex war in knockabout', or, 'The Meaning
of the Taming of the Shrew'. Produced
by D. Bryson. [Broadcast] 30th June,
1953. ff. 18.
typescript.

634503

— SERONSY (CECIL C.)
"Supposes" as the unifying theme
in "The Taming of the Shrew".
IN SHAKESPEARE QUARTERLY XIV: 1.
pp. 15-30.   (New York)   1963.

605711

— SHROEDER (JOHN W.)
'The Taming of a shrew' and 'The
Taming of the shrew': a case
re-opened.   IN Journal of English
and Germanic Philology, Vol. 57.
(Urbana, Ill.)   1958.

600780/57

— TAYLOR (G. C.)
Two notes on Shakespeare [2: The
Strange case of Du Bartas in The
Taming of a Shrew. bibliog.]
IN Renaissance studies in honor of
Hardin Craig.   (Iowa)
port.   1941.

539442

— THOMAS (S.)
A Note on "The Taming of the shrew".
IN Modern Language Notes, Vol. 64.
(Baltimore)
bibliog.   1949.

439157/64

— TILLYARD (EUSTACE MANDEVILLE WETENHALL)
The Fairy-tale element in The Taming
of the Shrew.   IN BLOOM (EDWARD A.)
ed., Shakespeare 1564-1964: a
collection of modern essays by various
hands.   (Providence, R.I.)   1964.
Brown University bicentennial
publications.

744437

— Tolman (A.H.) Shakespeare's part in
the "Taming of the Shrew". In
Publications of the Modern Language
Association of America, Vol.5.

(Baltimore)   1890.

428325

— TOLMAN (A. H.)
The Views about Hamlet and other essays
[including Shakespeare and The Taming
of the Shrew.]   (Boston [Mass.])
illus. bibliog.   1904.   544888
_____ Another edn.   1906.   450751

— WALDO (TOMMY RUTH) and HERBERT (THOMAS
WALTER)
Musical terms in The Taming of the
shrew: evidence of single authorship.
IN SHAKESPEARE QUARTERLY X: 2.
pp. 185-199.
(New York) 1959.

605711

— WENTERSDORF (KARL P.)
The Authenticity of The Taming of the
Shrew.
IN SHAKESPEARE QUARTERLY V:
pp. 11-32.
(New York) 1954.

605711

Taming of the Shrew

— Burlesques; Plays
   see also ENGLISH EDITIONS, The Taming
   of the Shrew — Alterations, etc.

BANGS (J. K.)
   Katharine: a travesty [in four acts].
   [New York]   1888.
   Bears author's signature.

                              547689

A BRIDAL ODE on the marriage
Catherine and Petruchio. ff.19.
                              1779.

                              667060

   Positive photostat copy made from
   the original in Glasgow University
   Library, by Birmingham Reference
   Library, 1961.

Taming of the Shrew

— Stage History and Production
   Newspaper reviews, playbills, theatre pro-
   grammes and theatrical illustrations — the
   library's extensive collection of this material
   is mainly uncatalogued but indexed
   For texts of stage alterations and adaptat-
   ions of the play see ENGLISH EDITIONS,
   The Taming of the Shrew — Alterations, etc.

ADELPHI THEATRE
   The Taming of the Shrew: portfolio
   of players [and programme. With a
   note by O. Stuart.]   pp. [12.]
   ff. [9.]   [1904.]

                              420918

COGHILL (N.)
   The Taming of the shrew, by the
   O[xford] U[niversity] D[ramatic]
   S[ociety].   IN Picture Post,
   Vol. 28.
   illus.   1945.

                              572595

DENT (ALAN HOLMES)
   Stratford 1954 [: "The Taming of the
   Shrew".   A radio talk] produced by P.
   Harvey for P. Humphreys. [Broadcast]
   9th June, 1954. ff. 9.
   typescript.

                              643699

JAYNE, SEARS
   The Dreaming of The Shrew. IN
   Shakespeare Quarterly XVII: 1. pp.41-56.
   (New York)   1966.

                              605711

Kemp (T.C.) The Stratford Festival
   :review of Hamlet and The Taming
   of the Shrew.[Broadcast] 12th
   May,1948.ff.7. Typescript.

                              591374

KEMP (THOMAS CHARLES)
   The Stratford Festival [: 1953 production of 'The Taming of the Shrew'
   at the Shakespeare Memorial Theatre].
   Produced by P. Humphreys. [Broadcast]
   11th June 1953.   ff. 6.
   typescript.

                              634523

MARSHALL (F. A.)
   On Shakespeare's "Taming of the Shrew",
   as played at the Gaiety Theatre by
   Mr. Augustus Daly's Company.   IN The
   Theatre, Vol. 12.   1888.

                              99108

PROGRAMMES OF SHAKESPEARIAN PERFORMANCES
   The Taming of the Shrew

   This collection, which runs from
   the latter half of the nineteenth
   century, is continuously augmented
   by the addition of programmes of
   contemporary productions.

                              499169

Stead (W.T.) First impressions of the
   theatre. [Include reviews on 'The
   Taming of the Shrew', 'King Lear'
   and 'Hamlet' and an article:
   Shakespeare at Stratford] In
   The Review of Reviews, Vol.31.

                              1905.

                              189564

Taming of the Shrew [at the Adelphi
   Theatre, November 29th, 1904]. In
   Play pictorial, Vol.5.

                              1905.

                              571867

"The Taming of the Shrew": Goetz's
   masterpiece.   FROM The Theatre,
   Feb. 1880.

                              530824

THEATRE GUILD, NEW YORK
   The Theatre Guild Inc. presents "The
   Taming of the Shrew" with Alfred Lunt,
   and Lynn Fontanne.   Production directed
   by H. W. Gribble.   [Souvenir book] pp.
   [16.]   [New York]
   ports.   illus.   [1935.]

                              646354

VOITOLOVSKAYA (L.)
   Khadji Mukan and William Shakespeare.
   [Contains description of a perform-
   ance of The Taming of the Shrew in
   Soviet Kazakhstan.]   IN Soviet
   War News, Vol. 11.   1944.

                              560943

— WALBROOK (H. M.)
    The Shrew that Shakespeare drew: [Ada
    Rehan as Katharina.]   FROM The
    Nineteenth Century, 1929.   pp. [7.]

                            389232

— Zinkeisen (Doris) Designing for the stage.
    [With settings for "The Taming of the
    Shrew".] pp. 78. Illus.

                    [1938.]

    ("How to do it" series, No. 18.) (The Studio)

                    487004

Taming of the Shrew

— Study and Teaching; Tales

— DANE (CLEMENCE) [pseud.]
    The Taming of the Shrew.   IN Six
    stories from Shakespeare.   Illustra-
    tions by F. Matania.
                    1934.   428744
    _____   FROM The Strand Magazine,
    March, 1934.   [1934.] 419970
    Shakespeare's Plays as Short Stories, 6.

— DAVIS (S.)
    Shakespeare's Taming of the Shrew,
    retold by S. Davis and illustrated
    by Alice B. Woodward.   pp. 84.
                    1932.
    Shakespeare Retold [for Little People].

                    452673

— RANALD, MARGARET LOFTIS
    Monarch notes and study guides:
    Shakespeare's "The Taming of the shrew".
    (New York)   1965.
    Monarch critiques of literature.

                    757012

TANGER (GUSTAV)
    The First and Second Quartos and the First
    Folio of Hamlet: their relation to each
    other.
    IN Transactions of the New Shakespeare
    Society, Series 1.   Nos. 8-10.
    pp. 109-200.   1880-6.
                            99113

Tannenbaum (S.A.) The Assassination of
    Christopher Marlowe : a new view.
    [With references to Shakespeare.]
    pp. 75.

            (New York)   1928.

(Privately printed.)
Note: Edition limited to 100 copies.

                    499298

TANNENBAUM (SAMUEL AARON)
    Cassio's hopes.   FROM Philological
    Quarterly, Vol. 18.   (Iowa) 1939.

                    530194

        Tannenbaum (S.A.) A Crux in
    Much Ado and its solution. In Modern
    Language Notes, Vol. 46.

            (Baltimore)   1931.

                    397731

TANNENBAUM (SAMUEL AARON)
    Dr. Greg and the "Goodal" notation in
    "Sir Thomas Moore".   IN Comment and
    criticism.   Reprinted from P.M.L.A.
    (Publications of the Modern Language
    Association of America,) Vol. 44.
    pp. [14.]   [Menasha, Wis.] 1929.

                    413468

TANNENBAUM (SAMUEL AARON)
    Elizabethan bibliographies.   (New York)
    Samuel Daniel.   pp. x, 37.
                    1942.   537463
    Michael Drayton.   pp. viii, [ii], 54.
                    1941.   527192
    John Ford.   pp. viii, [ii], 26.
                    1941.   527115
    George Gascoigne.   pp. x, 22.
                    1942.   537464
    Thomas Heywood.   pp. 43.
                    1939.   503813
    Thomas Kyd.   pp. ix, 34.
                    1941.   525229
    Thomas Lodge.   pp. [x], 30.
                    1940.   513226
    John Lyly. pp. xi, 38.
                    1940.   516633
    John Marston.   pp. viii, 34.
                    1940.   518618
    Philip Massinger.   pp. viii, 40.
                    1938.   491492
    Thomas Middleton.   pp. viii, 35.
                    1940.   518619
    Michel Eyquem de Montaigne.
                    1942.   533356
    Anthony Mundy.   pp. viii, 36.
                    1942.   539395
    Thomas Nashe.   pp. viii, [ii,] 31.
                    1941.   527144
    George Peele.   pp. x, 36.
                    1940.   525750
    Sir Philip Sidney.   pp. x, 69.
                    1941.   535255
    John Webster.   pp. x, 38.
                    1941.   525230

    Shakspere's King Lear.
                    1940.   523926
    Shakspere's Macbeth. 1939.   509096
    Shakspere's The Merchant of Venice.
                    1941.   524621
    Shakspere's Othello. 1943.   542195
    Shakspere's Sonnets. 1940.   513225

TANNENBAUM (S. A.)
    How not to edit Shakspere: a review
    [of "The 'New' Cambridge Shakespeare",
    edited by Sir A. Quiller-Couch and
    J. D. Wilson].   FROM Philological
    Quarterly, vol. 10.   (Iowa) 1931.

                    442561

TANNENBAUM (SAMUEL AARON)
The Knight and the crystal sphere: a
dramatic fantasy of Sir Walter Ralegh
and Queen Elizabeth. [With
Shakespeare as one of the characters.]
pp. 70. (New York)   1946.
Edn. limited to 250 copies.

587295

TANNENBAUM (SAMUEL AARON)
More about "The Booke of Sir Thomas
Moore". Reprinted from P.M.L.A.
(Publications of the Modern Language
Association of America,) Vol. 43.
pp. [12.] [Menasha, Wis.]
facsimile.   1928.

413469

Tannenbaum (S.A.) Robert Wilson
and 'Sir Thomas More'. In
Notes and Queries, Vol.154,
1928.

(High Wycombe)

348919

TANNENBAUM (SAMUEL AARON)
Shakspere studies.   (New York)
1.   Slips of the tongue. Reprinted,
with corrections and additions, from
the Shakespeare Association Bulletin,
Vol. 5.   pp. 14.   Limited edn.: 50
copies.   Signed by the author.
               1930.   413466
2.   An Object lesson in Shakesperian
research: [the Collier forgery in the
manuscript of "Sir Thomas More".   A
reply to W. W. Greg.]   pp. 23.
facsimile.   Limited edn.: 250 copies.
Signed by the author.
               1931.   413467
3.   More about the forged Revels
Accounts [attributed to Peter Cunningham.]
pp. 37.   1932.   437497
4.   The New Cambridge Shakspere and
The Two Gentlemen of Verona.   Reprinted,
with additions and corrections, from
the Shakespeare Association Bulletin.
pp. 68.   Limited edn.: 200 copies.
               1939.   515136

TANNENBAUM (S. A.)
Shakspere's unquestioned autographs
and "the addition" to "Sir Thomas
Moore".   Reprinted from Studies in
Philology, [Vol.] 22.   pp. 133-160.
(Baltimore)
facsimiles.   1925.

488382

TANNENBAUM (S. A.)
Shaksperian scraps and other Elizabethan
fragments. [With a foreword by
J. Q. Adams, and notes.]   (New York)
facsimiles.   1933.

411561

Tannenbaum (S.A.) Shall a King smite
a King? From Philological quarterly,
Vol. 15.

(Iowa)   1936.

484069

TANNENBAUM (S. A.)
Some emendations of Shakspere's text;
and A Neglected Shakspere document.
Reprinted from The Shakespeare
Association Bulletin, Vol. 6, No. 3.
pp. [8.]   1931.

413465

Tannenbaum (S.A.) Textual errors in
the Furness Variorum. In Modern
Language Notes, vol.45, 1930.

(Baltimore)

439157

Tannenbaum (S.A.) That monster custom
(an emendation of Hamlet.) From
Philological quarterly, Vol. 15.

(Iowa)   1936.

484070

Tannenbaum, Samuel Aaron *works relating to*

—— Craig (H.) The Handwriting of the
Renaissance: the development and
characteristics of the script of
Shakespeare's time, by S.A.
Tannenbaum: [a review.] In Modern
Language Notes, 1932.

(Baltimore)

404117

——FORSYTHE (R. S.)
[Review of] Shakspere and "Sir Thomas
Moore", by S. A. Tannenbaum.   IN Modern
Language Notes, Vol. 46.   (Baltimore)
               1931.

397731

——McKERROW (R. B.)
[Review of] Shakspere Forgeries in the
Revels Accounts, by S. A. Tannenbaum.
IN Modern Language Notes, Vol. 46.
(Baltimore)
               1931.

397731

—— Praz (M.) [Review of] Shakespeare and
"Sir Thomas Moore", by S. A. Tannenbaum.   In English studies, Vol. 12.

(Amsterdam)   1930.

485654

TANNENBAUM (SAMUEL AARON and DOROTHY
ROSENZWEIG)
Annual bibliography of Shakespeariana,
1927-1948.   FROM Shakespeare
Association [of America] Bulletin,
Vols. 3-24.   (New York)
22 vols.   1928-1949.
From 1949 continued as "Shakespeare:
an annotated bibliography", see
catal. no. 623676.

399585

TANNENBAUM (SAMUEL AARON and DOROTHY
ROSENZWEIG)
Elizabethan bibliographies.   (New York)
Roger Ascham.   ff. 27.   typescript.
               1946.   575563
Beaumont & Fletcher.   [With a]
Supplement.   3 vols.
            1938-46.   491491
Nicholas Breton.   ff. i, 34.
typescript.   1947.   587877
George Chapman.   [With a] Supplement.
3 vols.   1938-46.   491493
Thomas Dekker.   [With a] Supplement.
3 vols.   1939-45.   503814
Robert Greene.   [With a] Supplement.
3 vols.   1939-45.   503815
George Herbert.   ff. 52.   typescript.
            1946.   574351
John Heywood.   ff. [iii,] 31.
typescript.   1946.   578075
Ben Jonson.   [With a] Supplement.
3 vols.   1938-[47].   488230
Marie Stuart in her relations to the
arts.   1946.   568107
Christopher Marlowe.   [With a
Supplement.]   3 vols.
         1937-47.   469603
Thomas Randolph.   ff. 24.   typescript.
           1947.   583239
James Shirley.   ff. 42.   typescript.
          1946.   571626
Cyril Tourneur.   ff. 14.   typescript.
          1946.   572412

Shakspere's Romeo and Juliet.
typescript.   1950.   608093
Shakspere's Troilus & Cressida.
pp. x, 44.   illus.   1943.   546539

TANNER (VIRGINIA)
Broadcasting Shakespeare.   FROM The
English Journal, October 1934.
(Chicago, Ill.)

                488667

TANSELLE (G. THOMAS)
Time in "Romeo and Juliet". IN
Shakespeare Quarterly XV: 4. pp.349-361.
(New York)   1964.

             605711

TANSELLE (G. THOMAS) and DUNBAR
(FLORENCE W.)
Legal language in Coriolanus.
IN SHAKESPEARE QUARTERLY XIII: 2.
pp. 231-238.
(New York) 1962.
             605711

TANTON (ERNEST C.)
The Mirror to human nature.   11. The
Life of King Henry V.   FROM The
Methodist Magazine, Nov. 1935.
pp. [2.]

             444408

TAPP (F.) [ed.]
Orpheus with his lute.   Words from
"Henry VIII".   Arrangement for
mixed voices by F. Tapp; music by
R. V. Williams.   pp. [ii] 6.
             1937.

             601861

Taranath (Rajeev)
Coriolanus, 'The Waste Land' and the
Coriolan poems. IN

THE LITERARY CRITERION
Special number on Shakespeare. Vol.6,
Winter, No.1. (Bombay)   1963.

   pp.111-120.   756155

[TARLTON (R.)]
Tarlton's Jests, 1638.   Facsimile
reproduction: superintended by
E. W. Ashbee.   [?1876]
Edn. limited to 100 copies, printed
for private circulation: No. 3.

              2565

Tarlton, Richard *works relating to*

— BRYANT (JOSEPH ALLEN)
Shakespeare's Falstaff and the mantle
of Dick Tarlton.   IN Studies in
Philology, Vol. 51.   (Chapel Hill,
N.C.)   1954.

         554520/51

Tarrant (W.G.) Shakespeare and
religion. pp.24.
           [c.1908.]

(Unitarian Penny Library,147.)

          407941

TASKER (REUBEN)
A "Presentation" of Shakespeare [No. 1:
Verses on Shakespearian characters.
Anon.]   pp. [4.]   1954. 665515
_____ [No. 2: More verses on
Shakespearian characters].   pp. 12.
       1956.   665516

Tasso, Torquato *works relating to*

— Leigh (G.A.) The Rival poet in
Shakespeare's sonnets [i.e. Tasso].
pp.[15]. In The Westminster Review,
vol.147, 1897.

            138545

TATE, NAHUM
History of King Lear.

For editions of this play see under
English Editions: King Lear:
Alterations &c.

Tate, Nahum *works relating to*

—— BLACK, JAMES
An Augustan stage-history: Nahum Tate's
"King Lear." FROM Restoration and 18th
Century Theatre Research, Vol.6, no.1.
(Chicago, Ill.)   1967.

pp.36-54   761649

—— SPENCER, CHRISTOPHER
A word for Tate's 'King Lear'. FROM
Studies in English Literature 1500-1900,
Vol.3, No.2. (Houston, Tex.) 1963.

pp.241-251.   753400

—— WILLIAMS, T. D. DUNCAN
Mr. Nahum Tate's "King Lear".
FROM Studia neophilologica, vol. 38,
no. 2, 1966.   (Uppsala)   1967.
pp. 290-300.

767900

TATE (Sir ROBERT WILLIAM) [ed.]
Carmina Dublinensia [: translations
by the editor into Greek and Latin
verse with original texts including
extracts from Shakespeare.   2nd edn.]
(Dublin)   1946.
[Dublin University Press Series]

572002

TATLOCK (JOHN STRONG PERRY)
The Siege of Troy in Elizabethan
literature especially in Shakespeare
and Heywood.   IN Publications of
the Modern Language Association of
America, Vol. 30.   (Baltimore)
1915.

428350

TATLOCK (J. S. P.)
The Welsh 'Troilus and Cressida'
[MS. Peniarth 106, National Library
of Wales] and its relation to the
Elizabethan drama.   IN The Modern
Language Review, Vol. 10.
(Cambridge)   1915.

266825

[Taunton.   Queen's College Dramatic
Society.   Shakespearian performances.
Programmes, 1930-   ].

[Taunton]

479685

TAUPIN (RENÉ)
The Myth of Hamlet in France in
Mallarmé's generation.   IN Modern
Language Quarterly, Vol. 14.
(Seattle, Wis.)   1953.

525289/14

THE TAVERNERS
[Shakespearian programmes, posters,
etc.]   [1947]-[1957]

645709

TAVISTOCK SHAKESPEARE SOCIETY
Quatercentenary tribute to Shakespeare.
1964.

740855

Tayler, Edward William *works relating to*

—— FRYE (DEAN)
The Weeded garden and the fecund woods:
review article.   IN Shakespeare
Studies, 2.   (Cincinnati, Ohio)
1966.

761781

TAYLOR, ALINE MACKENZIE
Dryden's 'Enchanted isle' and
Shadwell's 'Dominion'.   FROM Studies
in philology, Extra series, no. 4.
(Chapel Hill, N.C.)   1967.
pp. 39-53.

776820

TAYLOR (ALINE MACKENZIE)
Next to Shakespeare: Otway's "Venice
Preserv'd" and "The Orphan" and their
history on the London stage.
(Durham, N.C.)
ports. illus. bibliogs. 1950.

615158

TAYLOR (DICK)
Clarendon and Ben Jonson as witnesses
for the Earl of Pembroke's character.
FROM Studies in English Renaissance
Drama.   pp. [23.]   [1960.]

666781

TAYLOR (DICK)
The Earl of Pembroke and the youth of
Shakespeare's Sonnets: an essay in
rehabilitation.   Reprinted from
Studies in Philology, [Vol.] 56, 1.
pp. [29].   1959.

666782

TAYLOR (DICK)

The Masque and the lance: the Earl of
Pembroke in Jacobean court entertainments
Reprinted from Tulane University. Tulane
Studies in English. Vol.8. pp.[33].
(New Orleans, La.)   1958.

666780

TAYLOR (DICK)

The Third Earl of Pembroke as a patron
of poetry. Reprinted from Tulane
University. Tulane Studies in English.
Vol.5. pp.[27]. (New Orleans La.)
1955.

666783

TAYLOR (GEORGE COFFIN)
Did Shakespeare, actor, improvise
in Every man in his humour? IN
McMANAWAY (J. G.), DAWSON (G. E.)
and WILLOUGHBY (E. E.) eds., Joseph
Quincy Adams memorial studies.
(Washington)   1948.
bibliog.

596748

Taylor (G.C.) The Modernity of
Shakespeare. From Sewanee Review,
Vol.42. pp.[16].

(Sewanee,Tenn.)   1934.

447444

TAYLOR (GEORGE COFFIN)
Montaigne-Shakespeare and the deadly
parallel. FROM Philological
Quarterly, Vol. 22.   (Iowa City)
bibliog.   1943.

563327

TAYLOR (GEORGE COFFIN)
[Review of] Shakespeare's satire,
by O. J. Campbell. IN Modern
Language Quarterly, Vol. 5.
(Seattle)   1944.

563896

Taylor (G.C.) Shakespeare's attitude
towards love and honor in Troilus
and Cressida. In Publications of the
Modern Language Association of
America, vol.45.

(Menasha,Wis.)   1930.
428365

TAYLOR (GEORGE COFFIN)
Shakespeare's use of the idea of the
beast in man. IN COFFMAN (G. R.) ed.,
Studies in language and literature.
(Chapel Hill, [N.C.])
bibliog.   1945.
University of North Carolina.
Sesquicentennial Publications

572339

TAYLOR (GEORGE COFFIN)
Two notes on Shakespeare. [1:
Shakespeare and the prognostications
in England as to the coming end of
the world; 2: The Strange case of
Du Bartas in The Taming of a Shrew.
bibliog.] IN Renaissance studies
in honor of Hardin Craig.   (Iowa)
port. bibliog.   1941.

539442

TAYLOR (GEORGE COFFIN)
William Shakespeare, thinker. FROM
University of North Carolina Exten-
sion Bulletin, Vol. 26.   2nd Series:
Lectures in the Humanities.   1945-
1946.   pp. 39-51.   (Chapel Hill,
N.C.)   1946.

610453

Taylor (H.) The Religious message
of Shakespeare. From The Congrega-
tionalist. Vol.33.

[Durban]   1933.

420466

[Taylor (John)]

A Concise history of Abington: the
abbey, park, church and parish, with
notes on the owners from the Norman
Conquest, the rectors, Shakespearean
associations, etc. Illustrated by
W.J.Rush. pp.68. (Northampton)
1897.

434975

Taylor (John)

Mrs. Siddons appears as Lady Macbeth.
In Agate (J.[E.]) ed., The English
dramatic critics.   [1932.]

399280

Taylor (John)

Mrs. Siddons's strange dress for
Rosalind. In Agate (J.[E.]) ed.,
The English dramatic critics.
[1932.]

399280

Taylor (John)

Poems on various subjects. Vol.1.
[Containing a sonnet: "Shakespeare's
Cliff".]   1827.

443705

Taylor, John
Shakespeare in film, radio, and television. IN

SPENCER, TERENCE JOHN BEW, ed.
Shakespeare: a celebration, 1564-1964.
1964.

illus. maps.   667816

TAYLOR (MARION ANSEL)
Shakespeare and Gloucestershire
(II Henry IV.)   IN The Review of
English Studies, Vol. 7.   1931.

393826

TAYLOR, NICHOLAS
Liberal & literary [: Birmingham
Reference Library and Shakespeare
Library]. FROM The Architectural
Review, Vol. 144, No. 859.   1968.
pp. 215-219, illus.
775445

TAYLOR (RUPERT)
The Date of Love's labour's lost.
(New York)   1932.

392292

TAYLOR (RUPERT)
John Shakespeare, corviser, of
Stratford-on-Avon and the Balsall
Shakespeares. [bibliog.] IN
Publications of the Modern Language
Association of America, Vol. 55.
(Menasha, Wis.) 1940.

525077

TAYLOR (RUPERT)
Shakespeare's cousin, Thomas Greene,
and his kin: possible light on the
Shakespeare family background.
IN Publications of the Modern Language
Association of America, Vol. 60.
(Menasha, Wis.) 1945.

569026

Taylor (Samuel Coleridge) see
Coleridge-Taylor (Samuel)

Taylor (W.) The Uses of Shakespeare.
From College English, Vol.2.

(Chicago) 1941.

537252

TAYLOR UNIVERSITY, Indiana.
Shakespeare festival. Programmes.
1952- . (Upland, Ind.)

Note: From 1959 onwards called Fine Arts
Festival.

771366

Tchaikovsky (P. I.) see Chaikovsky (P. I.)

Teacher's World (The) April 5, 1916:
Special Shakespeare [tercentenary]
number. pp.48. Illus.

1916.

432005

Teaching of Shakespeare *see* Study and Teaching; Tales from Shakespeare *and under the titles of the separate plays*

Tearle, Godfrey *works relating to*

—— CORNELL (KATHARINE)
Katharine Cornell [and] Godfrey
Tearle [in] Antony and Cleopatra.
pp. 20. (New York)
ports. illus. facsimile. [1947.]

593583

—— GIBBS (P.)
Our first Shakespearean actor: Godfrey
Tearle. FROM [World Review, 1947.]
port.

587307

—— MORGAN (C.)
Godfrey Tearle's Hamlet. IN AGATE
(J. [E.]) ed., The English dramatic
critics. [1932.]

399280

TEDDER (H. R.)
The Classification of Shakespeareana.
IN The Library Chronicle, Vol. 4.
1887.

96949

Teejay pseud. see Rees (T. J.)

TEETER (L.)
[Review of] The State in Shakespeare's
Greek and Roman plays, by J. E.
Phillips. IN Modern Language Notes,
Vol. 58. (Baltimore) 1943.

553688

Telbin (W.) Art in the theatre:
scenery. In The Magazine of Art,
[Vol. 12], 1889.

103127

Television Broadcasting
For television versions of Shakespeare's plays
see ENGLISH EDITIONS

—— CRANE (MILTON)
Shakespeare on television.
IN SHAKESPEARE QUARTERLY XII: 3.
pp. 323-327.
(New York) 1961.

605711

—— GRIFFIN (Mrs. ALICE)
Shakespeare through the camera's eye -
Julius Caesar in motion pictures;
Hamlet and Othello on television.
IN SHAKESPEARE QUARTERLY IV: 3.
pp. 331-336.
(New York) 1953.

605711

—— GRIFFIN (ALICE)
Shakespeare through the camera's eye
1953-1954.
IN SHAKESPEARE QUARTERLY VI.
pp. 63-66.
(New York) 1955.

605711

—— HOWARD (LEON)
Shakespeare for the family. IN The
Quarterly of Film Radio and Television,
Vol. 8. (Berkeley, Cal.) 1954.

630462/8

—— JONES (CLAUDE EDWARD)
The Imperial theme: "Macbeth" on
television. IN The Quarterly of
Film Radio and Television, Vol. 9.
(Berkeley, Cal.) 1955.

630462/9

—— JORGENSEN (PAUL ALFRED)
The Taming of the Shrew: entertainment
for television. IN The Quarterly of
Film, Radio and Television, Vol. 10.
(Berkeley, Cal.) 1956.

630462/10

— ROSENBERG (MARVIN)
Shakespeare on TV: an optimistic
survey.   IN The Quarterly of Film
Radio and Television, Vol. 9.
(Berkeley, Cal.)   1954.

630462/9

— SCHREIBER (FLORA RHETA)
Television's "Hamlet".   IN The Quarterly
of Film Radio and Television, Vol. 8.
(Berkeley, Cal.)   1953.

630462/8

— WADSWORTH (FRANK W.)
"Sound and fury" - "King Lear" on
television.   IN The Quarterly of
Film Radio and Television, Vol. 8.
(Berkeley, Cal.)   1954.

630462/8

— WALKER (ROY)
Comment no. 32: R. Walker on the
current BBC Television series of
Shakespeare's Histories "An Age of
Kings"   Broadcast 11th Aug. 1960.
ff. 4.
typescript.

666996

TELTSCHER (H. O.)
An Analysis of Sir Francis Bacon's
personality based on various specimens
of his handwriting.   IN FRANCO (J.)
The Bacon-Shakspere identities
revealed by their handwritings.
pp. 22.   (New York)
port.   facsimiles.   bibliog.
1942.

581058

Temperance *see* Drink and Drunkenness

The Tempest
General Works and Criticism

Characters

Illustrations

Music; Opera

Novels; Plays; Poems

Sources and Background

Stage History and Production

Study and Teaching; Tales

Textual History

The Tempest

— General Works and Criticism

— ABENHEIMER (K. M.)
Shakespeare's "Tempest": a psychological analysis.   IN The Psychoanalytic Review, Vol. 33.   (New York)
1946.

577280

— ALLEN (DON CAMERON)
William Shakespeare, The Tempest.
IN Allen (D. C.) Image and meaning:
metaphoric traditions in Renaissance
poetry.   (Baltimore, Md.)
bibliogs.   1960.

693797

— [ANDREWS (CONSTANCE E.)]
The Magic wand of Prospero.   FROM
The Church of the New Age Magazine,
March-May, 1931.   (Manchester)

440444

— ATKINS, S.H.
William Shakespeare: The Tempest.
1964.

Guides to English Literature
Series.   745373

— AUDEN (W. H.)
The Sea and the mirror, a commentary
on Shakespeare's "The Tempest".
IN Auden (W. H.) For the time being
[: two poems, with prose passages].
1945.

558023

— AUDEN (W. H.)
A Selection from "The Sea and the
mirror": a commentary [in dramatic
form] on Shakespeare's "The Tempest".
Produced by F. Hauser.   [Broadcast]
22nd July, 1949.   ff. [ii], 55,
6-21.
typescript.

605246

— BACON (W. A.)
A Note on "The Tempest", IV, i.
IN Notes and Queries, Vol. 192.
1947.

588005

— BAGCHI (PRIYATOSH)
A Note on "The Tempest", I.i.37-44.
IN Shakespeare commemoration volume,
edited by Taraknath Sen.   (Calcutta)
1966.

764382

— Bamborough (J.B.) Introducing
Shakespeare (6) : "The Tempest".
[Broadcast] 22nd December, 1949.
pp. [11,] 8. Typescript.

605277

— BOWEN (GWYNNETH)
Shakespeare's farewell: paper read
under the title: 'The Date and authorship of The Tempest', at a meeting of
the Shakespeare Fellowship, February,
1951.   pp. [ii], 20.   (Buxton)
                                    [1951.]
Published by the author.
                              620076

— BROWER (REUBEN ARTHUR)
The Mirror of analogy: The Tempest.
IN Brower (R. A.) The Fields of
light: an experiment in critical
reading.   (New York)   1951.

                              621904

— BUSHNELL (N. S.)
Natural supernaturalism in "The
Tempest".   pp. [15].   FROM
[Publications of the Modern Language
Association of America, Vol. 47.]
[(Menasha, Wis.)]   [1932]

                              438442

— CAMPBELL (L.)
Shakespeare's Tempest.   IN Campbell
(L.) Memorials in verse and prose.
[Edited by Frances P. Campbell].
port.   illus.   1914.
Printed for private circulation.

                              474263

— CAWLEY (R. R.)
Shakspere's use of the voyagers in
The Tempest.   IN Publications of
the Modern Language Association of
America, Vol. 41.   (Menasha, Wis.)
                              1926.

                              428361

— **Collins (J.C.) Poetry and symbolism:
a study of "The Tempest".** In The
Contemporary review, Vol. 93.

                              1908.
                              208520

— **Curry (W.C.) Sacerdotal science in
Shakespeare's 'The tempest'.** From
**Archiv für das Studium der neueren
Sprachen, Bd. 168.**

            (Berlin)   1935.
                              497542

— CURRY (W. C.)
Shakespeare's philosophical patterns
[as exhibited in "Macbeth" and "The
Tempest"].   (Baton Rouge, La.)
                    1937.   472128
_____ 2nd edn.   bibliog.
                    1959.   666437

— DAVIDSON, FRANK
The Tempest: an interpretation. IN
Journal of English and Germanic
Philology, Vol.62.   1963.

                              600780

— DOBRÉE (BONAMY)
The Tempest.   IN English Association,
Essays and studies.   New series,
Vol. 5, 1952.   Collected by A. Esdaile.
pp. [v], 89.   1952.   626849
_____ IN Shakespeare, the comedies:
a collection of critical essays.
(Englewood Cliffs, N.J.)
                    1965.   748348

— DRIVER (TOM F.)
The Shakespearian clock: time and the
vision of reality in "Romeo and Juliet"
and "The Tempest". IN Shakespeare
Quarterly XV: 4. pp.363-370. (New York)
                              1964.

                              605711

— Durning-Lawrence (Sir E.) The Shakespeare myth: Caliban and the Tempest.
From The Cambridge Magazine, May 17,
1913. pp. [4.]

                              484092

— Empson (W.) [and] Garrett (G.) Shakespeare survey: [Othello, Timon of
Athens, and the Tempest. With an
epilogue by R. Herring.]

                              [1937.]
                              472727

— ERSKINE (J.)
The Delight of great books. 1928.
Includes a chapter on "The Tempest".

                              405039

— EWEN (C. [H.] L'E.)
A Criticism of The Tempest wreck scene:
a chapter from an unpublished book.
pp. 6.   [?London]   1937.

                              469593

— FAIN, JOHN TYREE
Some notes on Ariel's song.
IN SHAKESPEARE QUARTERLY XIX: 4.
pp. 329-332.
(New York)   1968.
                              605711

— GATTY (REGINALD ARTHUR ALLIX)
Shakespeare in character and song:
As you like it; The Tempest; and,
Twelfth Night.   ff. 35.
manuscript.   [c.1925.]

                              637992

— GATTY (REGINALD ARTHUR ALLIX)
The Tempest [: a lecture].   ff. 85.
manuscript.   [c.1925.]

                              637995

— GOHN, ERNEST
The Tempest: theme and structure.
FROM: English Studies XLV: II, pp.116-
125. (Amsterdam)   1964.

                              745008

— HALES (J. W.)
Shakespeare's "Tempest".   IN The
Gentleman's Magazine. Vol. 284.
                              1898.

                              142601

— HARRISON, GEORGE BAGSHAWE
'The Tempest'.   IN Stratford Papers
on Shakespeare delivered at the
1962 Shakespeare Seminar. (Toronto)
                              1963.

                              668006

— HARRISON (T. P.)
A Note on The Tempest: a sequel.
IN Modern Language Notes, Vol. 58.
(Baltimore)   1943.

                              553688

—— HART (JOHN A.)
The Tempest.   IN Shakespeare: lectures
on five plays, by A. F. Sochatoff [and
others].   pp. xii, 83.   (Pittsburgh:
Carnegie Institute of Technology)
1958.

666185

—— HOENIGER (F. DAVID)
Prospero's storm and miracle.
IN   SHAKESPEARE QUARTERLY VII.
pp. 35-38.
(New York)   1956.

605711

—— HOLT (JOHN)
Remarks on "The Tempest" or, An Attempt
to rescue Shakespear from the many
errors falsly charged on him, by his
several editors.   [By J. Holt.] pp.92.
1750.

641444

—— HUNT, JOHN DIXON
A Critical commentary on Shakespeare's
'The Tempest'.   1968.
Macmillan critical commentaries.

773052

—— Iacuzzi (A.) The Naive theme in The
Tempest, as a link between Thomas
Shadwell and Ramón de la Cruz.
In Modern language notes, Vol.52.

(Baltimore)   1937.

479896

—— JAMES, DAVID GWILYM
The Dream of Prospero [: essay on
"The Tempest"].   (Oxford) 1967.

772370

—— JEWKES (WILFRED THOMAS)
'Excellent dumb discourse': the
limits of language in 'The Tempest'.
IN SMITH, GORDON ROSS, ed., Essays
on Shakespeare [by various authors].
(University Park, Penn.) pp. 196-210.
1965.

755528

—— KING (A. H.)
Some notes on Shakespeare's Tempest.
IN English Studies, Vol. 22.
(Amsterdam)   1940.

575606

—— KIRSCHBAUM (LEO)

Two lectures on Shakespeare: In defense
of Guildenstern and Rosencrantz; The
Tempest - apologetics or spectacle?
pp.41.   1961.

666892

—— KNIGHT (GEORGE WILSON)
"Coriolanus" and "The Tempest".
[Extract] from "The Olive and the
sword", by G. W. Knight.   FROM
The Periodical, Vol. 26.   (Oxford)
1944.
For "The Olive and the sword", see
catal. no. 550950.

552438

—— Kokeritz (H.) Thy pole-clipt vineyard,
'The Tempest', iv, 1, 68 [: an
interpretation]. In The Modern
Language Review, Vol.39

(Cambridge)   1944.

563897

—— KOTT (JAN)
Shakespeare our contemporary.
Translated by B. Taborski.   Preface
by P. Brook.   1964.   741546
_____ 2nd edn., revised.
1967.   766093
Includes "Prospero's staff".

—— LAMB (C.)
Mrs. Leicester's School and other
writings in prose and verse,
[including "On a passage in The
Tempest".   Edited] with introduction
and notes by A. Ainger.   1885.

460006

—— LAMMING (GEORGE)
The Pleasures of exile [: reflections
of a colonial writer, "a modern
Caliban", living in London]. 1960.

693150

—— [LANGFORD (J. A.)
The Tempest: three articles.]
IN Somersetshire Gazette: a newspaper issued during the voyage of
the S.S. "Somersetshire" from England
to Melbourne, Nov. 25th, 1875 -
Jan. 21st, 1876, edited by J. A.
Langford.   pp. 23.   (Melbourne)
1876.
pp. 21-22 imperfect.

536018

—— Lawrence (W.J.) The Masque in The
Tempest. In The Fortnightly
Review, Vol.113. New Series.

1920.

285541

—— Leatham (J.) "The Tempest": a criticism.
2nd edn. pp.16.

(Turriff)   [c.1920.]

[Shakespeare Studies, No.9.]

566381

—— LOWENTHAL (LEO)
Literature and the image of man
[studies of the European drama &
novel, 1600-1900].   1963.
Includes a chapter on "The Tempest".

743532

—— MASON (PHILIP) [pseud. Philip Woodruff]
Prospero's magic: some thoughts on
class and race [suggested by "Othello"
and "The Tempest"].   1962.

710708

—— MELLERS (WILFRID HOWARD)
Masque into poetic drama.
IN Mellers (W. F.) Harmonious
meeting: a study of the relationship
between English music, poetry and
theatre, c. 1500-1900.   1965.

742371

—— MERTON (STEPHEN)
"The Tempest" and "Troilus and
Cressida". FROM College English,
Vol. 7. pp. 8. (Chicago)

1945.

619467

—— MITCHELL (LEE)
Two notes on "The Tempest". FROM
Educational Theatre Journal, Vol. 2.
pp. [7.] [Ann Arbor, Mich.]

1950.

629841

—— MOORE (J. R.)
The Tempest and Robinson Crusoe.
IN The Review of English Studies,
Vol. 21. (Oxford)
bibliog.   [1945.]

570955

—— MORRIS (J. W.)
The Key-notes of Shakespere's plays:
The Tempest; [Henry V; Merchant of
Venice].   1885.   105367
_____ Another edn. 1886.   390436

—— MULLIK (B.   R.   )
Studies in Dramatists, vol.11:
Shakespeare's Tempest. 2nd edn. pp.64.
Bibliog. (Delhi)   1960.

667115

—— MUNRO (J.)
Shakespeare's "Tempest". IN The
New English Review, Vol. 12.
1946.

570944

—— NAAE (T. T.)
The Key to Shakespeare by the anatomy
of the figure on the title-page of the
Folio of 1623 of Shakespeare plays,
being an exposition of this First Folio,
with notes to The Tempest, Love's
labor's lost, and Sonnets. [Dealing
with the Bacon-Shakespeare question]
New enlarged edn.   (Boston)
ports. illus. facsimiles.   1935.

442863

—— NEILSON (FRANCIS)
Shakespeare and The Tempest. (Rindge,
N.H.)   1956.

665315

—— NORTHAM, JOHN R.
Dividing worlds. Shakespeare's "The
Tempest" and Ibsen's "Romersholm".
(Oslo)   1965.

Kristiansand Museum pamphlet, No.2.
755089

—— NUTTALL, ANTHONY DAVID
Two concepts of allegory: a study of
Shakespeare's "The Tempest" and the
logic of allegorical expression.
1967.

761470

—— OSTROWSKI, WITOLD
A Forgotten meaning of "The Tempest".
IN HELSZTYNSKI, STANISLAW, ed.,
Poland's homage to Shakespeare.
Commemorating the fourth centenary
of his birth, 1564-1964. (Warsaw)
1965.

747846

—— PALMER, DAVID JOHN, ed.
Shakespeare 'The Tempest'
a casebook.   1968.

Casebook series.   769357

—— PHILLIPS (JAMES EMERSON)
"The Tempest" and the Renaissance idea
of man. IN Shakespeare 400: essays
by American scholars on the anniversary
of the poet's birth. Published in
co-operation with the Shakespeare
Association of America.
illus.   1964.

667803

—— Reik (T.) From thirty years with
Freud. Translated from the German.
[Including a chapter entitled The
Way of all flesh, relating to the
Tempest and Hamlet, and other
Shakespeare references.]

1942.

[International Psycho-Analytical Library,
No.32.

533357

—— Robertson (J. Minto) Artistry of "The
Tempest". [From Great Thoughts,
July 1939.]

502652

—— ROBINSON, JAMES E.

Time and 'The Tempest'. FROM Journal
of English and Germanic Philology
LXIII:2, April 1964. pp.255-267.

668349

—— ROSE (BRIAN W.   )

The Tempest: a reconsideration of its
meaning. Bibliog. IN English Studies in
Africa, Vol. I. (Johannesburg)
1958.

682610/1

—ROSENHEIM (RICHARD)
The Eternal drama: a comprehensive
treatise on the syngenetic history
of humanity, dramatics, and theatre.
(New York)
 illus. bibliog.   1952.
Includes a chapter "The Mystic message
of The Tempest".

627222

— Shaaber (M.A.) "A living drollery"
(Tempest, III, iii, 21). [With
bibliographical notes.] In Modern
Language Notes, Vol.60.

(Baltimore)   1945.

571543

Shakespeare's Tempest. In All the year
round. New series, Vol.22.

1879.

38535

— Sharpe (Ella F.) From "King Lear" to
"The Tempest". Bibliog. In
Sharpe (Ella F.) Collected papers
on psycho-analysis. Edited by
Marjorie Brierley.

1950.

605922

— SISSON (CHARLES JASPER)

The Magic of Prospero. Bibliog. IN
Shakespeare Survey, [Vol.]11.
(Cambridge)   1958.

665816

— SNIDER (D. J.)
Shakespeare's "Tempest" [: an
analysis of the play].   FROM The
Journal of Speculative Philosophy,
Vol. 8.   (St. Louis)   1874.

556083

— STILL (C.)
An Interpretation of Shakespeare's
"Tempest".   IN Still (C.) The
Timeless theme: a critical theory
formulated and applied.   1936.

456789

— STOLL (E. E.)
Shakespeare and other masters [: literary
studies, including one entitled The
Tempest.   With bibliographical notes].
(Cambridge, [Mass.])
1940.
532084

— STOLL (E. E.)
"The Tempest" [: a critical essay].
pp. [28].   FROM [Publications of
the Modern Language Association of
America, vol. 47.]   [(Menasha, Wis.)]
[1932.]

438440

— TILLYARD (E. M. W.)
Shakespeare's last plays: [Cymbeline,
The Winter's tale, and The Tempest.]
pp. 85.

1938.

476626

— TRAVERSI (DEREK A.)
The Tempest.   IN Scrutiny Vol. 16.
(Cambridge)

1949.

421336/16

— Wagner ([Mrs.]Emma B.) Shakespeare's
The Tempest: an allegorical
interpretation. Edited from
manuscript and notes by H.R.Orr.

(Yellow Springs,Ohio.)
1933.
437565

— WARD (B. M.)
The Authorship of "The Tempest".
IN East Anglian magazine, Vol. 4.
(Ipswich)   1939.

510779

— WARTON (J.)
Observations on the Tempest of Shakespeare.

For editions of this work check the
main sequence under the author's name.

— WILSON (HAROLD S.)
Action and symbol in Measure for Measure
and The Tempest.
 IN SHAKESPEARE QUARTERLY IV: 4.
pp. 375-384.
(New York)   1953.

605711

— WILSON (JOHN DOVER)
The Meaning of The Tempest.   pp. 23.
(Newcastle-upon-Tyne)   1936.
 Newcastle-upon-Tyne Literary and
Philosophical Society.   Robert
Spence Watson Memorial Lecture, 1936.

460906

— WORD AND IMAGE [: Granada TV script of
readings from The Tempest, etc.,
illustrating the image of man in a
confined space, that is, an island.
Transmitted on 19th December, 1962.]
(Manchester)

667870

— ZIMBARDO (ROSE ABDELNOUR)
Form and disorder in "The Tempest".
 IN SHAKESPEARE QUARTERLY XIV: 1.
pp. 49-56.
(New York)   1963.

605711

The Tempest
— Characters

— ABENHEIMER (K. M.)
Shakespeare's "Tempest": a psychological
analysis.   IN The Psychoanalytic
Review, Vol. 33.   (New York) 1946.

577280

BENSON (A. C.)
Ariel.
IN GOLLANCZ ([Sir] I.) ed., A Book
of homage to Shakespeare.
ports. illus. facsimiles. [1916.]

264175

DURRANT (G. H.)

Prospero's wisdom. FROM Theoria, 7, 1955.
pp.[9].

667028

GARRETT (G.)
That four-flusher Prospero.
FROM Life and Letters To-day, Vol.
16]. 1937.

471786

GOWING (Mrs. A.)
The Graphic gallery of Shakespeare's
heroines. Olivia - Cleopatra -
Miranda. IN The Theatre, Vol. 12.
1888.

99108

HART (JEFFREY P.)
Prospero and Faustus. FROM Boston
University Studies in English, Vol. 2.
pp. [10]. (Boston, Mass.) 1956.

666504

JOHNSON (W. STACY)
The Genesis of Ariel.
IN SHAKESPEARE QUARTERLY II: 3.
pp. 205-210.
(New York) 1951.

605711

Koszul (A.[H.]) "Ariel" : [the source
of Shakespeare's character.] In
English studies, Vol. 19.

(Amsterdam) 1937.

485661

REED (ROBERT R.)
The Probable origin of Ariel.
IN SHAKESPEARE QUARTERLY XI: 1.
pp. 61-65.
(New York) 1960.

605711

REID (A.)
Twelve variations on the theme of
Caliban. IN Reid (A.) Steps to
a viewpoint [: poems]. pp. 48.
1947.

585309

WALLER (J. G.)
The Prospero of "The Tempest".
FROM The Gentleman's Magazine,
Aug. 1853. pp. [8.]

402707

WEST (ROBERT HUNTER)
Ariel and the outer mystery. IN
BLOOM (EDWARD A.) ed. Shakespeare
1564-1964: a collection of modern
essays by various hands. (Providence,
R.I.)
1964.
Brown University bicentennial
publications.

744437

The Tempest

— Illustrations
*The library's extensive collections of photo-
graphs and engravings are indexed but
mainly uncatalogued*

Paton (Sir J.N.) Compositions from
Shakespeare's Tempest: fifteen
engravings in outline.

1877.

421827

[QUICK (HILDA M.)
Nine woodcuts of the chief characters
in "The Tempest" as dressed and
played in Miss Dorothea Valentine's
production at Porthcurno, Cornwall,
August 1932]. [1932]

399401

The Tempest

— Music; Opera
For music scores see under the heading
Music Scores, The Tempest

CAMDEN (CARROLL)
Songs and chorusses in The Tempest.
FROM Philological Quarterly, Vol. XLI,
No. 1. 1962.

668392

DUPRÉ (H.)
Purcell [and his period, containing
references to music for The Tempest,
etc.] Translated from the French
by Catherine A. Phillips and Agnes
Bedford.
bibliog. port. facsimiles. 1928.

402858

Einstein (A.) Mozart und Shakespeare's
"Tempest". From Monatshefte fur
Deutschen Unterricht, Vol.36.

(Madison, Wis.) 1944.

578411

McMANAWAY (JAMES GILMER)
Songs and masques in "The Tempest"
[c.1674.] Edited [with a discursive
introduction]. IN Theatre Miscellany.
(Oxford) 1953.
Luttrell Society Reprints, No. 14.

637109

—— MELLERS (WILFRID HOWARD)
Purcell and the Restoration theatre.
IN Mellers (W. H.) Harmonious
meeting: a study of the relationship between English music, poetry
and theatre, c.1500-1900.   1965.

742371

—— Pearson (H.) Gilbert and Sullivan:
a biography. [With references to
Sullivan's music to "The Tempest"
and other Shakespearean plays, and
with a bibliography.] Ports.

.1935.

436434

—— POLAK (ALFRED LAURENCE)
'The Tempest' and 'The Magic flute.'
IN English, Vol. 9.   (Oxford)
1953.

481151/9

—— Squire (W.B.) The Music of Shadwell's
"Tempest" [composed by P.Humphrey].
pp. [14]. From The Musical
quarterly, Vol.7.

(New York)   1921.

523728

——STONE (GEORGE WINCHESTER)
Shakespeare's "Tempest" at Drury Lane
during Garrick's management.
IN SHAKESPEARE QUARTERLY VII.
pp. 1-7.
(New York)   1956.

605711

—— TAYLOR, ALINE MACKENZIE
Dryden's 'Enchanted isle' and
Shadwell's 'Dominion'.   FROM Studies
in philology, Extra series, no. 4.
(Chapel Hill, N.C.)   1967.
pp. 39-53.

776820

—— Ward (C.E.) The Tempest: a restoration
opera problem. [With bibliographical
notes.] In E.L.H.: a journal of
English Literary History, Vol.13.

(Baltimore, Md.)   1946.

584757

The Tempest

— Novels; Plays; Poems
see also ENGLISH EDITIONS, The
Tempest — Alterations, etc.

—— [ALDINGTON (Mrs. HILDA)]
Good frend [: a poem].   IN
[Aldington (Mrs. H.)] By Avon river
[by] H.D. [pseud.]   (New York)
1949.

602772

—— BROWNING (ROBERT)
Caliban upon Setebos [: suggested
by "The Tempest".]   IN Browning (R.)
Poetical works. Vol. 7.   1914.

473870

——[CALIBAN COMMITTEE OF GREATER BOSTON]
Program of the performances of
"Caliban: By the yellow sands": a
community drama by P. MacKaye, in
the Harvard Stadium [Boston], July 2-14,
1917. pp. 56.   [Boston, Mass.]
illus. plan.

599874

—— COOKE (G. W.)
A Guide-book to the poetic and
dramatic works of Robert Browning.
[With reference to Caliban upon
Setebos: a poem suggested by The
Tempest.]   (Boston, [Mass.])
bibliog.   1891.

529741

—— DALTON (H.) [pseud.]
The Book of drawing-room plays and
evening amusements: a comprehensive
manual of in-door recreation. Including
acting charades, proverbs, burlesques
and extravaganzas, [and, A Shakespearian
charade: scenes from The Merchant of
Venice, The Tempest and A Midsummer
night's dream.]   Illustrated by E.H.
Corbould and G. [L.P.B.] Du Maurier.
duo.[1861.]
485389

—— DAVIES (ROBERTSON)

Tempest-tost:a novel. [With references to
Shakespeare's "The Tempest".]   1952.

625841

—— GODDEN (RUMER)
A Breath of air [: a novel based on
The Tempest].
1950.

610782

—— Goodloe ([Abbie] C.) To dream again :
a comedy in one act [telling how
Shakespeare came to write "The
Tempest"]. pp. [xii] 28. Plan.

(New York)   1941.

—— Note: Originally published under the title
"Storm over Bermuda".

531790

——Hamburger (M.) "The Tempest", an
alternative [:a poem]. In
Hamburger (M.) Flowering
cactus : pp. 68.

(Aldington)   1950.

609913

—— KEYES (S. [A. K.])
Prospero [: a poem].   IN Keyes
(S. [A. K.]) Collected poems.
Edited, with a memoir and notes by
M. Meyer.   1945.

561668

—— RILKE (R. M.)
The Spirit Ariel. (After reading
Shakespeare's "Tempest".)
IN Rilke (R. M.) Requiem and other
poems. Translated by J. B. Leishman.
(Alcuin Press)   1935.   437081
————— IN Rilker (R. M.) Later poems.
1938.   482573

The Tempest

— Sources and Background

—— ALLEN (H. B.)
Shakespeare's "lay her a-hold".
IN Modern Language Notes, Vol. 52.
(Baltimore)   1937.

479896

—— Brockbank (Philip)
'The Tempest': conventions of art and empire.
IN
Stratford-upon-Avon Studies.
8: Later Shakespeare.   1966.

illus. pp.183-201.   756101

—— EBNER (DEAN)
"The Tempest": rebellion and the ideal
state.
IN SHAKESPEARE QUARTERLY XVI: 2.
pp. 161-173.
(New York)   1965.

605711

—— Garnett (R.) The Date and occasion
of 'The Tempest'. In The
Universal Review, [Vol. 3,] Jan.)
Apl. 1889.

101346

—— GESNER (CAROL)
The Tempest as pastoral romance.
IN SHAKESPEARE QUARTERLY X: 4.
pp. 531-539.
(New York)   1959.
605711

—— GRAVES (R. [R.])
The Common asphodel: collected
essays on poetry, 1922-1949.
[With references to Shakespeare,
including the essay "The Sources
of 'The Tempest'".]
frontis.   1949.

601433

—— GRAY (HENRY DAVID)
The Sources of "The Tempest".
IN Modern Language Notes, Vol. 35.
(Baltimore, Md.)   1920.

439157/35

—— Grégoire (H.) The Bulgarian origins of
"The Tempest" of Shakespeare. In
Studies in Philology. Vol.37.

(Chapel Hill, N.C.)   1940.

522312

—— HALE (EDWARD EVERETT)
Prospero's island.   With an intro-
duction by H. C. Lodge.   pp. 4.
(New York)   1919.
Columbia University.   Dramatic
Museum Publications.   Discussions of
the Drama, 3.

666337

—— HANKINS (J. E.)
Caliban, the bestial man. [bibliog.]
IN Publications of the Modern Language
Association of America, Vol. 62.
(Menasha, Wis.)   1947.

428321/62

—— HOWARTH (R. G.)
Shakespeare's Tempest.   A public
lecture delivered for the Australian
English Association on Oct. 1, 1936.
pp. 55.   (Sydney)   1936.

472072

—— HUNTER (JOSEPH)
A Disquisition on the scene, origin,
date &c. of Shakespeare's Tempest
[reviewed].   FROM The Gentleman's
Magazine, [New Series] Vol. 13.
1840.

521907

—— HUNTER (JOSEPH)
Shakespeare's Tempest and [the island
of] Lampedusa [identified with that
of Prospero]; the date of
Shakespeare's Tempest; [and the
orthography of the name of Shakespeare.]
FROM The Gentleman's Magazine, [New
Series] Vol. 13.   1840.

521907

—— JOURDAIN (S.)
A Discovery of the Barmudas (1610).
Reproduced from the copy in the Folger
Shakespeare Library.   [Edited] with
an introduction [containing references
to Shakespeare] by J. Q. Adams.
pp. x, 24.   (New York)   1940.
Scholars' Facsimiles & Reprints.

537574

—— KIPLING (RUDYARD)
The Vision of the enchanted island.
IN GOLLANCZ ([Sir] I.) ed., A Book
of homage to Shakespeare.
ports. illus. facsimiles. [1916.]

264175

—— KNOX (BERNARD M. W.)
The Tempest and the ancient comic
tradition.   IN English Institute
Essays, 1954.   (New York)

1955.

711273

KUHL, ERNEST PETER
  Shakespeare and the founders of America:
  "The Tempest". FROM Philological
  Quarterly, Vol.XLI, No.1.   1962.

668385

LAMB (CHARLES)
  On a passage in "The Tempest".   IN
  Lamb (C.) Complete correspondence
  and works. Vol. 3. 1870.   572053
  _____ IN Lamb (C.) Complete works
  in prose and verse.   Edited and
  prefaced by R. H. Shepherd.
  ports. facsimile. 1875.   552992

MAJOR (JOHN M.)
  Comus and The Tempest.
  IN SHAKESPEARE QUARTERLY X: 2.
  pp. 177-183.
  (New York)   1959.

605711

MARKLAND, MURRAY F.
  The Order of "The Knight's tale" and
  "The Tempest". [Paper read at the
  Renaissance Conference at Central
  Washington State College, Ellensburg,
  March, 1965].   FROM Research Studies,
  vol. 33, no. 1, March 1965.
  (Pullman, Wash.)   1965.
  pp. 1-10.

768345

MARX (LEO)
  Shakespeare's American fable [: the
  connections between "The Tempest" and
  America]. FROM The Massachusetts Review,
  Autumn, 1960. (University of
  Massachusetts. Amherst Mass.)
                                     1960.

667775

MORLEY (H.)
  Jacob Ayrer and "The Fair Sidea".
  IN SHAKESPEARE (W.) The Tempest.
  [Edited with an introduction by
  H. Morley.]   1887.   436519
  Cassell's National Library.
  _____ Another edn.   1896.   551137

MORRISON, HUGH WHITNEY
  Shakespeare: his daughters & his
  "Tempest". (Toronto)   1963.

668045

NOSWORTHY (J. M.)
  The Narrative sources of "The Tempest".
  [bibliog.]   IN The Review of English
  Studies, Vol. 24.   (Oxford)   1948.

318239/24

REED (ROBERT R.)
  The Probable origin of Ariel.
  IN SHAKESPEARE QUARTERLY XI: 1.
  pp. 61-65.
  (New York)   1960.

605711

STEWART (JOHN INNES MACINTOSH) [pseud.
  Michael Innes]
  "A Discovery of the Bermudas:" an
  inquiry into the sources of "The
  Tempest".   Produced by R. Heppenstall.
  [Broadcast] 29th September, 1959.
  ff. 37.
  typescript.

666285

STRACHEY, WILLIAM
  A True reportory of the wracke, and
  redempton of Sir Thomas Gates Knight;
  upon, and from the Ilands of the
  Bermudas ... July 15. 1610.   IN
  Purchas his Pilgrimes ... The Fourth
  Part ... 1625.
  pp. 1734-53.

110817

THOMPSON (J. W.)
  A Note on The Tempest.   IN Modern
  Language Notes, Vol. 52.   (Baltimore)
                                   1937.

479896

WILKINSON (H.)
  The Adventurers of Bermuda: a
  history of the island from its
  discovery until the dissolution
  of the Somers Island Company in
  1684. [With references to "The
  Tempest".]
  ports. illus. maps. facsimile.
  bibliog.   1933.

407060

The Tempest
— Stage History and Production
*Newspaper reviews, playbills, theatre pro-
grammes and theatrical illustrations — the
library's extensive collection of this material
is mainly uncatalogued but indexed
For texts of stage alterations and adaptations of the play see* **ENGLISH EDITIONS,
The Tempest** — Alterations, etc.

Adams (J.C.) The Staging of the
  Tempest, III. iii. [With biblio-
  graphical references.] In The
  Review of English Studies, Vol. 14.

1938.

495115

Back-stage at the open-air theatre [:
  a description of open-air acting at
  Finchley during Shakespeare Week,
  with photographs taken during a
  performance of "The Tempest"].   IN
  Picture Post, Vol. 20.   1943.

554750

BRERETON (A.)
  "The Tempest" on the stage.   FROM
  The Theatre, New Series, Vol. 10.
                                  1887.

530829

___ CAMDEN, CARROLL
Songs and chorusses in the Tempest.
FROM Philological Quarterly, vol.XLI,
no.1. 1962.

668392

___ CAMPBELL (O. J.)
Miss Webster and The Tempest [: a
criticism of Margaret Webster's
production of The Tempest at the
Broadway Theatre, New York]. FROM
The American Scholar, Vol. 14. (New
York) 1945.

578272

___ CRAIG (EDWARD GORDON)
On "The Tempest". IN The Mask,
Vol. 10. (Florence) 1924.

482881

___ DRYDEN [JOHN]
Albion and Albanius: an opera.
Perform'd at the Queens Theatre in
Dorset-Garden. [With a preface by
the author containing references to
his alteration of "The Tempest".]
pp. [xiv,] 34. 1691.

568320

___ HOOKER (HELENE M.)
Dryden's and Shadwell's Tempest.
IN The Huntington Library Quarterly,
Vol. 6. (San Marino)
bibliog. 1943.

549639

___ **Isaacs (H.R.) This insubstantial
pageant : The Tempest in the making
[i.e. Margaret Webster's production in New York]. Illus. In
Theatre Arts, Vol. 29.**

(New York) 1945.

567819

___ J. (A.)
Adapted from the English of William
Shakespeare. [Dryden's 'improvements'
on Shakespeare's "Tempest".] FROM
The Central Literary Magazine, Vol. 2.
[Birmingham] 1875.

558057

___ KEMP (THOMAS CHARLES)
The Stratford Festival [: 1951 productions of Henry IV Part 2 and The
Tempest]. Broadcast 28th June 1951.
ff. 5.
typescript.

617918

___ KEMP (THOMAS CHARLES)
Stratford, 1952 [: the Shakespeare
Memorial Theatre productions of
Coriolanus and The Tempest. Broad-
cast] 9th April 1952. ff. 5.
typescript.

624728

___ McMANAWAY (JAMES GILMER)
Songs and masques in "The Tempest"
[c.1674.] Edited [with a discursive
introduction]. IN Theatre Miscellany.
(Oxford) 1953.
Luttrell Society Reprints, No. 14.

637109

___ MARLE (T. B.)
Shakespeare in Budapest: "A
Midsummer night's dream" and "The
Tempest" at the Margaret Island
Open Air Theatre. IN The Hungarian
Quarterly, Vol. 5. 1939/40.

514527

___ MILTON (W. M.)
Tempest in a teapot [: discussing
whether T. Shadwell wrote an opera,
The Tempest.] IN E.L.H., Vol. 14.
(Baltimore, Md.)
bibliog. 1947.

430295/14

___ MOSS (A.)
We are such stuff [: the playing of
Prospero in The Tempest]. IN Theatre
Arts, Vol. 29. (New York) 1945.

567819

___ NEW YORK CITY SHAKESPEARE TERCENTENARY.
CELEBRATION COMMITTEE
Program of the community masque
"Caliban: By the yellow sands", by
P. MacKaye. Produced at the stadium
of the College of the City of New York,
May 23-27, 1916. pp. viii, 36. [New
York]
illus. plan.

599877

___ [Programme and illustrations of
Miss Dorothea Valentine's production
of "The Tempest" at Porthcurno,
Cornwall, August, 1932].

399402

___ PROGRAMMES OF SHAKESPEARIAN
PERFORMANCES
The Tempest

This collection, which runs from the
latter half of the nineteenth century,
is continuously augmented by the
addition of programmes of contemporary
productions.

499170

___ **Robson (W.W.) An Introduction to
"The Tempest" (the Davenant,
Dryden, Shadwell version).
[Broadcast] 6th [and] 8th
January, 1950. pp.6. Typescript.**

609487

___ **Royal Court Theatre. Souvenir of
J.H. Leigh's 50th representation
of The Tempest, Dec. 5th, 1903.
[With a note by A. Brereton.]
pp.[4.] ff [16.] Ports.**

420917

— [STEAD (W. T.)]
First impressions of the theatre.
1 – My first play: "The Tempest",
at His Majesty's. IN The Review
of Reviews, Vol. 30.   1904.

186085

— STONE (GEORGE WINCHESTER)
Shakespeare's "Tempest" at Drury Lane
during Garrick's management.
IN SHAKESPEARE QUARTERLY VII.
pp. 1–7.
(New York)   1956.

605711

— TAYLOR, ALINE MACKENZIE
Dryden's "Enchanted isle" and Shadwell's
"Dominion".   IN STUDIES IN PHILOLOGY,
Extra Series: 4.   (Chapel Hill, N.C.)
1967.
pp. 39–53.

pt. of 554520

— The Tempest [: the Broadway
production directed by Margaret
Webster]. FROM Life, Vol. 18.
[Chicago]
illus.   1945.

578276

— TREWIN (JOHN COURTENAY) and BARTON (JOHN)
"The Tempest" [at Stratford: a
discussion. Broadcast, 15th August
1957.] ff. 7.
typescript.

665666

— The Unnamed Society's 21st birthday
1915-1936 [souvenir. With an
account of the Society by N. Cardus,
and list of productions including
The Tempest.] pp. 20.   [Manchester]
illus.   [1936]

459001

— WALKER (R. S.)
The Great Globe itself [: a play
about a rehearsal of The Tempest
in 1611].   IN MARRIOTT (J. W.) [ed.]
One-act plays of to-day.   Sixth
series.
frontis.   1934.
The Harrap Library.

424087

— WILLIAM (DAVID)

"The Tempest" on the stage. IN
Stratford-upon-Avon Studies, edited by
J.R. Brown and B. Harris, Vol.1.
Jacobean theatre.   1960.

666673

— [Woodward (J.)] Some thoughts concerning
the stage in a letter to a lady.
[With reference to The Tempest.]pp. 13.

1704.

605281

The Tempest

— Study and Teaching; Tales

— BENNETT (R.)
The Story of The Tempest retold.
pp. 64.   [1941.]
The Tales that Shakespeare Told.

544917

— COLLEGE OF CAREERS, CAPE TOWN: STUDY-
AID SERIES
Notes on Shakespeare's 'The Tempest'.
(New edn. – rev. and enlarged.)
(Cape Town)   1964.

740927

— COLLEGE OF CAREERS: STUDY-AID SERIES
Notes on William Shakespeare's
"The Tempest".   1967.

764410

— FIELD (JOSEPHINE)
The Tempest, retold for young people.
[With] Act IV of the play.   pp. 56.
(Bognor Regis)
illus.   [1946.]
Crowther's "Introduction to Good
Reading" Series.

573816

— GATTY (REGINALD ARTHUR ALLIX)
The Tempest. [: the story of the
play, with notes, etc.]   ff. 51.
manuscript.   [c.1925.]

637996

— KIMBALL, ARTHUR G.
Barron's simplified approach to "The
Tempest". (Woodbury, N.Y.) 1966.

Barron's educational series.
764151

— KINGSLEY (MAUD E.)
Outline studies in literature.
No. 36: The Tempest. pp. 22.
(Boston, Mass.)   1905.

426214

— LAMB (C. and MARY A.)
The Tempest: the story of the play
told by Mary [A.] Lamb.   Simplified
by A. S. Hornby.   [English Text.]
(Tokyo)
[1948.]
"English as Speech" Series, Vol. 13.

627268

— SIMPSON (J. G.)
Commentary & questionnaire on The
Tempest.   [Reprint.] pp. 32.
1933.
Commentaries and Questionnaires in
English Literature.

547451

— SMITH (T. W.)
Shakespeare: The Tempest. pp. 52.
dgm.   [1940.]
Notes on Chosen English Texts.

601688

SMYTHE (P. E.)
The Tempest: critical notes, appreciation and exercises [on the play by
Shakespeare].   pp. 50.   (Sydney)
[1941.]

532131

STOPFORTH, L. M. D.
The Tempest, retold in modern English
prose.
illus.   [c.1963.]
Shakespeare made easier.

668208

WINDROSS (RONALD)
Three comedies [of] W. Shakespeare:
A Midsummer night's dream: The Tempest:
[and] As you like it.   Abridged and
simplified.   Illustrated by G. Irwin.
(Tales from England, 2nd Degree, No.3)
pp. 78.   (Paris)

[1952.]

631615

WOOD (S.)
The Tempest: questions and notes.
2nd edn.   pp. 46.   [c.1900.]
Dinglewood Shakespeare Manuals.

551125

The Tempest

— Textual History

GREG (W. W.)
Review [of] The Works of Shakespeare,
edited for the Syndics of the
Cambridge University Press by Sir A.
[T.] Quiller-Couch and J. D. Wilson.
Vol. 1. The Tempest. Reprinted
from the Modern Language Review,
Vol. 17.   [1922.]

554224

Pollard (A.W.) [Review of] The Works
of Shakespeare. Edited for the
Syndics of the Cambridge University
Press by Sir A.[T.] Quiller- Couch
and J.D. Wilson. [Vol.1.] The
Tempest. In The Library, 4th series,
Vol.2.

1922.

298823

Tempests

KNIGHT (GEORGE WILSON)
The Shakespearian tempest [: a study
of tempests and music in the plays].
1932.   399670
_____[2nd edn.]   (Oxford)
(The Oxford Bookshelf) 1940.   520941
_____ 3rd edn.   1953.   633720

MERCHANT, W. MOELWYN
Word and image: desert and storm [in
'Macbeth' and 'King Lear']. Produced
by Patricia Owtram. ITV script
transmitted for TV 11th February 1963.

typescript.   667869

WILLIAMS (GEORGE WALTON)
The Poetry of the storm in King Lear.
IN   SHAKESPEARE QUARTERLY II: 1.
pp. 57-71.
(New York)   1951.

605711

[TEMPLE (WILLIAM)] abp.
Poetry and science.   [With references
to Shakespeare.]   IN English
Association, Essays and studies,
Vol. 17.   (Oxford)   1932.

393436

TENISON (EVA MABEL)
Elizabethan England: being the history
of this country "in relation to all
foreign princes".   From original
manuscripts, many hitherto unpublished;
co-ordinated with XVIth century printed
matter ranging from royal proclamations
to broadside ballads.   A Survey of
life and literature.   With Portfolio
of maps.   (Leamington Spa)
illus.   12 vols.   1933-[1961].
No. 161 of an edn. limited to 325 sets
signed by the author.

442998

Tennessee Studies in Literature
THALER, ALWIN, and SANDERS, NORMAN, eds.
Shakespearean essays.   1964.

667977

TENNEY (E. A.)
Thomas Lodge [: a biography].
(Ithaca, N.Y.)
bibliog.   1935.
Cornell Studies in English.

433322

TENNIEL (Sir J.)
Cartoons.   Selected from the pages
of "Punch", [1851-1901.   Including
a cartoon of Shakespeare.]   [1901.]

517992

Tennyson, Alfred Tennyson, 1st Baron *works relating to*

___PADEN (W. D.)
Tennyson in Egypt: a study of the
imagery in his earlier work. [With
references to Shakespeare's plays.]
(Lawrence, Kansas)
bibliog. illus.   1942.
Kansas University Publications.
Humanistic Studies, No. 27.

539163

TENNYSON, HALLAM
Shakespeare translated.   Produced
by H. Tennyson.   B.B.C. radio script
broadcast 22nd November 1968.
typescript.

776829

Tercentenary 1864

—[CHAMBERS (R.)]
The Shakespeare Festival.   FROM
Chambers's Journal, 1864.   pp. [4.]

147345

— Dale (R.W.) Genius the gift of God :
a discourse on the tercentenary of
the birth of William Shakespeare.
Delivered on April 24th, 1864 in the
Independent Chapel, Stratford-on-
Avon. In Dale (R.W.) Discourses delivered on special occasions.

1866.

491337

—[FLOWER (C. E.)]
Official programme of the tercentenary
festival of the birth of Shakespeare,
to be held at Stratford-upon-Avon,
commencing on Saturday, April 23, 1864.
Also, An Account of what is known of
the poet's life, a guide to the town
and neighbourhood of Stratford-upon-
Avon, and sundrie other matters just
now of publicke interest relating thereto.
pp. 96. port. illus. plan.
                     1864.   52725
_____ Another copy.   Paper cover
wanting.   1864.   550229

—GRAVES (A. P.)
Shakespeare, April 23, 1864 [: a
poem].   FROM [The Dublin University
Magazine, Vol. 62.]   [Dublin] 1864.

561335

— Kenney (C.L.) Mr. Phelps and the
critics of his correspondence with
the Stratford Committee. pp. 8.

1864.

554142

—MAN (W. L.) and WHITE (T. A. S.)
Lecture on Shakespeare. [With, The
Tercentenary celebration of Shakespeare
at Stratford, 1864, by T. A. S. White.]
pp. 42.   (Maidstone)
ports.   illus.   1887.

419185

—MAX-MÜLLER ([Rt. Hon.] F.)
Shakespeare: speech delivered at
Stratford-on-Avon, 23rd April, 1864,
the Tercentenary of Shakespeare's
birth.   IN Max-Müller ([Rt. Hon.] F.)
Chips from a German workshop, vol. 3.
1870.

26342

— MEYNELL ([Mrs.] ALICE)
Poems, [including The Two Shakespeare
Tercentenaries, of birth, 1864; of
death, 1916; To Shakespeare.]
Complete edn.
port.   1923.   398093
_____ Another edn.   1940.   520025
_____ Another edn.   1947.   589846

— Notes drawn on the Avon bank for general
circulation. [Shakespeare Tercentary
Commemoration.] Ports. Illus. From
London Society, Vol. 5.

1864.
556283

— Official Programme of the Tercentenary
Festival of the Birth of Shakespeare...
at Stratford-upon-Avon,.. 1864.
pp. 96.

2826

— Roy (J.A.) Joseph Howe: a study in
achievement and frustration. [With
a bibliography, and reference to an
oration, by J. Howe, delivered during
the tercentenary celebrations in
Halifax, Nova Scotia]. Ports. Illus.
(Toronto)   1935.

447665

— The Shakespeare Gallery: a reproduction commemorative of the tercentenary
anniversary, 1864.   [Photographs of
engravings published by John and Josiah
Boydell.]   1867.

645040

—— Shakespeare-mad [: Shakespeare's three-hundredth birthday in London and Stratford]. *In* All the Year Round, Vol.11.

1864.

38504

—— Thom (R.W.) Coventry poems.[Containing "Shakspeare Tercentenary poem".] pp.86.

(Coventry)   [?1866].

432073

—— Trench (R.C.) Every good gift from above : a sermon preached in the parish church of Stratford-upon-Avon on Sunday, April 24, 1864 at the celebration of the tercentenary of Shakespeare's birth. 2nd edn. pp 20.

1864.

511208

—— TREWIN (JOHN COURTENAY) The Night has been unruly [: the theatre in England, 1769-1955]. Illustrated from the Raymond Mander and Joe Mitchenson Theatre Collection. ports. illus. facsimiles. bibliog.
1957.
pp. 160-181, Tercentenary Festival, Stratford-upon-Avon, 1864.

670241

—— White (T.A.S.) The Tercentenary celebration of Shakespeare at Stratford, 1864. *In* Man (W.L.) and White (T.A.S.) Lecture on Shakespeare. pp.42. Ports. Illus.

(Maidstone)   1887.

419185

—— WILLIAMS (LANGTON) How shall we honour him?   Song for the Shakespere Tercentenary Festival, written by J. T. Milne;   composed by L. Williams. pp. 5. port.
[1864.]

628459

Tercentenary 1916

—— Barnes (E.W.) William Shakespeare: a sermon preached in commemoration of the 300th anniversary of his death, May 7th, 1916, at the Temple Church. pp.14.

1916.

438656

—— CHUBB (PERCIVAL) and others, ed. The Shakespeare Tercentenary: suggestions for school and college celebrations of the Tercentenary of Shakespeare's death in 1916.   Prepared by the Drama League of America under the editorial direction of P. Chubb. With the collaboration of Mary P.Beegle, Mary W. Hinman [and] W. E. Bohn. [With a bibliography.]   pp. ii, 60. (Washington)   [1916.]

376812

—— DRINKWATER (J.) For April 23rd, 1616-1916 [: a poem]. IN GOLLANCZ ([Sir] I.) ed., A Book of homage to Shakespeare. ports. illus. facsimiles.
[1916.]   264175
_____ IN Drinkwater (J.) Olton pools [and other poems].   pp. 42.
1916.   266504
_____ Second impression.
1916.   569404
_____ Another edn.   No. 54 of edn. limited to 230 copies, signed by the author.   1923.   566422

—— HYETT ([Sir] F. A.) Why is Shakespeare our greatest poet? An address at the commemoration of the Shakespeare Tercentenary at Gloucester, May 3rd, 1916.   pp. 20. (Gloucester)   1916.

438429

—— Le Gallienne (R.) William Shakespeare and the three hundredth anniversary of his death. Illus. *From* Munsey's Magazine, April, 1916.

(New York)

516580

—— MANCHESTER, John Rylands Library Catalogue of an exhibition of the works of Shakespeare, his sources, and the writings of his principal contemporaries.   With an introductory sketch, and sixteen facsimiles. Tercentenary of the death of Shakespeare.   (Manchester)   1916.

494549

—— MANCHESTER TERCENTENARY ASSOCIATION Songs and recitations in commemoration of the Shakespeare Tercentenary by Shakespearean students and pupils in Manchester schools.   3rd edn., enlarged.   pp. 31.   (Manchester)
1916.

591416

—— A Masque setting forth the true honouring of our rare and precious poet, William Shakespeare.   pp. 45.   [1916.] "Shakespeare Memorial National Theatre, 1916", printed on cover.

494451

—— MEYNELL ([Mrs.] ALICE) Poems, [including The Two Shakespeare Tercentenaries, of birth, 1864; of death, 1916; To Shakespeare.] Complete edn. port.   1923.   398093
_____ Another edn. 1940.   520025
_____ Another edn. 1947.   589846

—— NEW YORK CITY, Shakespeare Tercentenary
Celebration Committee
Program of the community masque
"Caliban: By the yellow sands", by
P. MacKaye. Produced at the stadium
of the College of the City of New
York, May 23-27, 1916. pp. viii, 36.
[New York]
illus. plan.

599877

—— THE NEW YORK TIMES
[Ten supplements commemorating the]
Shakespeare Tercentenary, 1616-1916.
(New York)
illus. 1916.

507557

—— PACY (F.)
The Shakespeare Head Press at Stratford-
upon-Avon. A paper read, 5th May, 1916
at a meeting to commemorate the
Shakespeare tercentenary. With a note
by E. I. Fripp on the proposed publication (by the Shakespeare Head Press)
of the Chamberlains' accounts of
Stratford-upon-Avon. Reprinted from
The Library Association Record, July-
Aug. 1916. pp. 10. (Aberdeen)
1916.
545619

—— PORTER (CHARLOTTE)
A Guide to Shakespeare's stage. Prepared especially for reading circles
in connection with The Tercentennial.
pp. 18. (Chicago) 1916.

379474

—— RILEY ([Mrs.] ALICE C. D.)
Shakespeare's lovers in a garden: a
flower masque. Written for the
Drama League of America tercentenary
celebration of Shakespeare's birthday,
1915. Re-edited by the author.
Prologue and epilogue by Eleanor E.
Perkins. pp. 32.
—— Music [by various composers].
(Chicago) 1927.

407981-2

—— St. Louis Pageant Drama Association
in celebration of the Shakespeare Tercentenary. As you like it; as produced
by Margaret Anglin at St. Louis, 1916.
Preceded by a community prologue enacted
by citizens of St. Louis. Port.
[1916.]

398925

—— SCHELLING (F. E.)
The Tragedies of Shakespeare, prepared
for reading circles in connection
with the Tercentennial. pp. 20.
(Chicago) 1915.

285055

—— The Shakespeare Tercentenary meeting
held at the Mansion House, on May Day,
1916, with the general programme of
arrangements for the Tercentenary
commemoration. [With designs by
F. C. Richards.] pp. 18 [2].
(Printed at "The Sign of the Dolphin".
[1916.]

603467

—— SHERMAN (P. D.)
Outlines for the study of Shakespeare's
comedies, arranged for use in connection with the Tercentennial. pp. 20.
(Chicago) 1915.

285056

—— SKINNER (O.)
Mad folk of the theatre: ten studies
in temperament. [Containing "Will-
of-Avon's Night, April 23rd, 1916"
and other Shakespearian references.]
(Indianopolis)
ports. illus. 1928.

442504

—— Squire ([Sir] J.C.) Literary affairs
in London. [Shakespeare Tercentenary
Commemoration.] From The Dial[, Vol.
61].

[Chicago] 1916.

559990

—— The Teachers World, April 5, 1916: Special
Shakespeare [tercentenary] number. pp.
48. Illus.

1916.

432005

—— [THEATRE ROYAL, Drury Lane]
[Programme of] Shakespeare tercentenary
commemoration performance, 2nd May, 1916.

471777

—— WHIBLEY (CHARLES)
Shakespeare: the poet of England. FROM
Blackwood's Magazine, No. 1207. pp. [14.]
1916.

667278

Tercentenary Association, Manchester *see* Societies and Clubs

Tercentenary of the first Folio 1923

—— BRITISH MUSEUM SHAKESPEARE EXHIBITION 1923
Guide to the MSS. & printed books
exhibited in celebration of the
Tercentenary of the First Folio
Shakespeare. [With an introduction by
A. W. Pollard.] pp. 77.
ports. facsimiles. 1923.
Differs from 306931. Has MSS. notes,
and additional matter inserted.

531799

—Catalogue of an exhibition of early
editions of the works of Shakespeare
held in commemoration of the Tercentenary
of the First Folio, 1623, at Armstrong
College, Newcastle-upon-Tyne in the
University of Durham, February 1923.
With a preface by [E.] G. Craig.
pp. 19. [Newcastle-upon-Tyne] 1923.

414136

— Haddon (A.) Hullo playgoers :
wireless theatre talks [including
a talk on the First Folio
Tercentenary].

1924.

599788

— In commemoration of the First Folio
Tercentenary: a re-setting of the
preliminary matter of the First Folio,
with a catalogue of Shakespeariana
exhibited in the Hall of the Worshipful
Company of Stationers. Introduction
by Sir I. Gollancz. pp. 56.
(Shakespeare Association)
facsimiles. 1923.
Half tp. missing.

428768

—The Prefatory pages of the First
Folio, with a comment by Sir S. Lee.
3rd edn. pp. [19]. (London
Shakespeare League)
port. 1925.

424655

— SPIELMANN (M. H.)
[Shakespeare's portraiture: a reissue
of] The Title-page of the First Folio
of Shakespeare's plays: a comparative
study of the Droeshout portrait and
the Stratford monument. Written for
the Shakespeare Association in celebration of the First Folio Tercentenary,
1923. pp. xi, 56.
ports. illus. bibliog. genealogical
table. facsimiles. 1931.
No. 22 of edn. limited to 50 copies.
Author's signature on half tp. Date
on tp. 1924, on cover 1931.

533661

Tercentenary of the second Folio 1932

— Southwark Public Libraries and Cuming
Museum. Shakespeare Tercentenary, Second
Folio, 1632-1932; a catalogue of Shakespeare editions, playbills, broadsides,
exhibited in the Central Libraries.
Inaugurated by Sir Frank R.Benson, April
1932. pp.48.

[1932]

393886

Terriss, William (Lewin, William Charles James)
works relating to

— Smythe (A.J.) The Life of William
Terriss, actor. With an introduction by C.[W.] Scott [and containing
references to Shakespearian performances.] Ports. Illus.

1898.

420109

TERRY (D.)
British theatrical gallery: a
collection of whole-length portraits,
with biographical notices. 1825.

514264

Terry ([Dame] Ellen) The Death of
Henry Irving. Ports. From
McClure's Magazine, Vol.31.

(New York.) 1908.

516575

TERRY ([Dame] ELLEN)
Four lectures on Shakespeare. Edited,
with an introduction, by [Miss]
Christopher St. John.
port. 1932.

391411

Terry ([Dame] Ellen) Last years with
Henry Irving. Ports. From McClure's
Magazine, Vol.31.

(New York) 1908.

516574

TERRY ([Dame] ELLEN)
Memoirs, [a new edition of "Story
of my life".]. With preface, notes
and additional biographical chapters
by Edith Craig & [Miss] Christopher
St. John. 1933.

408534

TERRY (Dame ELLEN)
Signature and marginal notes.
IN FLETCHER (G.) Studies of
Shakespeare in the plays of King
John, Cymbeline, Macbeth [etc.]
1847.

621963

TERRY ([Dame] ELLEN)
Stray memories. FROM The New Review,
April 1891.

516029

Terry, Ellen Dame *works relating to*

—ADAMS (W. [H.] D.)
Miss Ellen Terry as Beatrice.   FROM
The Theatre, Nov. 1, 1882.

530826

— Aldrich (T.B.) Ellen Terry in "The
Merchant of Venice"[: a poem].
In Aldrich (T.B.) Poems [and plays].
Revised and complete Household
Edition.

(Boston, [Mass.]   1907.

544304

— BARKER, KATHLEEN M. D.
The Terrys and Godwin in Bristol.
FROM Theatre notebook, XXII, i.
pp. [1-17].   1967.

775441

— Calvert (W.) Sir Henry Irving and Miss
Ellen Terry : a record of over twenty
years at the Lyceum Theatre. pp.48.
Ports. Illus.

1897.

Note : No.60 of an edn. limited to 250 copies
printed for England and 50 for America.

499695

— Calvert (W.) Souvenir of Miss Ellen
Terry. [With references to
Shakespeare performances.]
pp.48. Ports.Illus.

[1897.]

500030

—CAMERON (AUDREY)
The Ellen Terry I knew.   Producer:
P. Stephenson.   [Broadcast] 4th
October, 1955,   ff. [11].
typescript.   1955.

665121

—COOK ([E.] D.)
Ellen Terry.   IN WARD (A. C.) [ed.]
Specimens of English dramatic
criticism, 17-20 centuries: selected
and introduced.   (Oxford)   1945.
The World's Classics.

563732

— Craig (Edith) Ellen Terry and Henry
Irving. In Souvenir of Hamlet :
six special performances in farewell
to the Lyceum Theatre, etc. pp.
xxiv. Ports. Illus.

[1939.]

502853

— Ellen Terry Memorial performances:
programmes of Shakespeare and other
performances in aid of the Ellen Terry
Memorial Fund.
port.

1929-39.

429213

—FORBES-ROBERTSON (BEATRICE)
Acting with Irving and Ellen Terry.
Producer: Leonie Cohn.   [Broadcast]
17th October, 1958.   ff. 8.
typescript.

666018

— Halstan (Margaret)Memories of Ellen
Terry and Henry Irving: a talk.
[Broadcast] 25th November, 1947.
ff.5. Typescript.

593005

— Hatton (J.) Henry Irving's impressions
of America, narrated in a series of
sketches, chronicles and conversations.
[With a preface by H.Irving, and
references to Shakespeare's plays.]
2nd edn. Ports Illus.   2 vols.

1884.

498881

— HIATT (C.)
Ellen Terry and her impersonations:
an appreciation.   [With references
to Shakespeare.]
ports.   1898.   485882
——— Another edn. 1899.   420106
——— Another edn. 1900.   553593

— HOBSON (H.)
Can actors read?   Ellen Terry's
marginal notes when studying a part.
[With references to Shakespeare.]
IN Christmas pie: pocket miscellany,
1943.   [Pie Publications]   [1943.]
Hutchinson 'Pocket' Special.

546217

— King Lear at the Lyceum, produced
Nov.10, 1892. Some extracts from
the press on the performance of
Mr. Henry Irving and Miss Ellen
Terry.

1893.

477404

— Knight (J.) Ellen Terry. In Ward (A.C.)
[ed.] Specimens of English dramatic
criticism, 17-20 centuries; selected
and introduced.

(Oxford)   1945.

(The World's Classics)

563732

— K[NIGHTS] (L. C.)
Four lectures on Shakespeare, by
Ellen Terry [: a review].   IN
The Criterion, Vol. 12, 1932.

414720

— MACKENZIE ([Sir] COMPTON)
Ellen Terry.   IN Mackenzie ([Sir] C.)
Echoes [: essays].   1954.

639463

— MANVELL, ARNOLD ROGER
Ellen Terry [: a biography]. 1968.
illus.

768747

— MANVELL, ARNOLD ROGER
Ellen Terry's Lady Macbeth.
FROM The Listener, February 2nd.
1967
pp. 159-161. illus.

771371

— Portraits, programmes etc., of
Henry Irving and Ellen Terry.
ff. 60.   [c.1850-c.1910.]

437278

— Robertson (W.G.) Time was: reminiscences [with a chapter on Ellen Terry
and Shakespeare.] Ports. Illus.

1931.

485744

— R[USSELL] (E. R. [RUSSELL, 1st Baron])
Ellen Terry as Portia. FROM The
Theatre, Jan. 1880.

516866

— ST. JOHN ([Miss] CHRISTOPHER)
Ellen Terry [: a biography]. With
Shakespearian references]. pp. 96.
ports. illus.   1907.
Stars of the Stage.

444816

— S[COTT] (C. [W.])
Miss Ellen Terry's first appearance.
FROM The Theatre, New Series, Vol. 10.
1887.

530837

— STEEN (MARGUERITE)
Ellen Terry. [With Shakespearian
references.] IN The Post Victorians.
1933.

412642

— STEVENSON-REECE (G.)
Woman's hour: I knew Ellen Terry.
[Broadcast] 25th October, 1948.
ff. 4.
typescript.

596478

— Stoker (B.) The Art of Ellen Terry.
Illus. In The Playgoer, Vol.1.

1902.

159497

— [Sturgis (J.R.)] The Shakspeare
revival in London. [Containing
references to Sir H.Irving and
Ellen Terry.] From [International
Review, Vol.6.]

[New York]   [1879.]

554169

— THEATRE ROYAL, Drury Lane
Souvenir programme given by the
theatrical & musical professions as
a tribute to Miss Ellen Terry on the
occasion of her jubilee, Tuesday
afternoon, June 12th, 1906 [including
a biographical sketch by A. Brereton].
pp. [27.]   1906.

594119

— Woolf ([Mrs.] Virginia) Ellen Terry.
In Woolf ([Mrs.] Virginia) The Moment
and other essays.

1947.

587577

TERRY (JEAN F.)
King Lear: a complete paraphrase.
2nd edn.   pp. 81.   (Farnham, Surrey)
[1961.]
The Normal Shakespeare.

666884

TERRY (JEAN F.)
Romeo and Juliet: a complete para-
phrase.   3rd edn.   pp. 64.
(Farnham, Surrey)   [1962.]
The Normal Shakespeare.

667255

Terry, Kate *works relating to*

— Miss Kate Terry in Viola.   IN Fraser's
Magazine, Vol. 72.   1865.

10672

— SPEDDING (J.)
Reviews and discussions: literary,
political and historical, not
relating to Bacon. [With a chapter:
"Twelfth Night" at the Olympic
Theatre (Miss Kate Terry in Viola.
From Frazer's Magazine, August, 1865).]
1879.

125328

Terry (W.H.) The Life and times of
John, Lord Finch. [With a bibliography and references to the authorship of works attributed to Shakespeare.] Ports. Genealogical Table.

1936.

449884

TERRY, W.N.
Abington Manor and the last of the
Shakespeares. (Northampton) 1964.

illus.   758151

TESLAR (JOSEPH ANDREW)
Shakespeare's worthy counsellor [:
influence on Shakespeare's texts
of the treatise "De optimo senatore"
by Laurentius Grimalius Goslicki
and the influence of John Zamoyski
on Goslicki].   (Rzym)
  port. illus. facsimiles. bibliog.
                                  1960.

                      666938

Tetherdown Social Circle see Muswell
Hill.

Texas Christian University
  CORDER (JIM W.) ed.
  Shakespeare 1964 [: a record of the
  celebrations of the Shakespeare Quater-
  centenary at Texas Christian
  University].   (Fort Worth, Tex.)
    illus.   1965.

                      745402

Texas University, Humanities Research
Center
  ZUKOFSKY (LOUIS) and ZUKOFSKY (Mrs.
  CELIA THAEW)
  Bottom: on Shakespeare.   Vol. 1-2.
  [Music to Shakespeare's "Pericles"
  by C. Zukofsky, Vol. 2.]   (Austin,
  Tex.)   1963.

                      741503-4

Texas University, Studies in English,
No. 5.   [Containing "A Comparison
of the characters in the Comedy of
Errors with those in the Menaechmi"
of Plautus, by E. Gill.]   (Austin,
Texas)   1925.

                      409501

Textual Emendation

*see also under titles of the separate works —
subheading:* General Works and Criticism

— BALDWIN, THOMAS WHITFIELD
  On atomizing Shakspere.
  IN SHAKESPEARE JAHRBUCH.   Bd. 91/1955.
  pp. 136-144.   (Heidelberg)

                      10531

— DEIGHTON (K.)
  The Old dramatists: conjectural
  readings. 2nd series: Shakespeare
  [etc.].   1898.

                      392885

—   Duane (W.) Shakespeariana.   From
  The Gentleman's Magazine, August 1857. pp.
  [2.]

                      402717

— ELZE (K.)
  A Letter to C. M. Ingleby, Esq.,
  containing notes and conjectural
  emendations on Shakespeare's
  "Cymbeline".   IN Anglia, Band 8.
  (Halle)   1885.

                      465552

— GREG (W. W.)
  Principles of emendation in
  Shakespeare.   IN Aspects of
  Shakespeare: British Academy
  lectures.   (Oxford)   1933.

                      401892

— HAINES (C. R.)
  Emendations to Shakespeare (Globe
  edition).   IN Notes and Queries,
  Vol. 166, January-June, 1934.

                      422514

— [Jackson (W.)] Letter 22: Passages
  in Shakespeare explained. In
  [Jackson (W.)] Thirty letters on
  various subjects. Vol.2.

                      1783.
                      546668

— Jourdain (W.C.) Some proposed emendations in the text of Shakespeare,
  and explanations of his words. From
  Philological Society. Transactions,
  1857.

                      480437

— JOURDAIN (W. C.)
  Some proposed emendations in the
  text of Shakespeare, and explanations
  of his words.   IN Transactions of
  the Philological Society, 1860-1.
  (Berlin)

                      28838

— KÖKERITZ (H.)
  Five Shakespeare notes [: textual
  criticism.   bibliog.]   IN The
  Review of English Studies, Vol. 23.
  (Oxford)   1947.

                      318239/23

— LAMBRECHTS (GUY)
  Proposed new readings in Shakespeare:
  the comedies (1).   IN
  Hommage à Shakespeare: Bulletin de
  la Faculté des Lettres de Strasbourg.
  43e année, No. 8, mai-juin 1965.
    illus.   766822

— PARSONS (H.)
  Shakespearian emendations, Nos. [I]-IX.
  [With relevant correspondence]   IN
  The Poetry Review, Vols. 37-41.
                                  1946-50.
  [No. 1.]   The History of the First
  Folio of "The Workes of William
  Shakespeare".   Nos. 2-9 [Emendations
  to "As you like it".]
                      246749/37

— PARSONS, HOWARD
  Shakespearian emendations and
    discoveries.   1953.

                      638911

— R. (W.) [of] S— Hall, Suffolk
[Commentary on Shakespeare's plays:
manuscript notes]   1780.
   A Selection from these notes was
printed in "The Gentleman's Magazine",
Vol. 50, 1780.
   On permanent deposit by Lord Cobham.

667993

— Remarks, critical, conjectural and
explanatory upon the plays of
Shakspeare [etc.], by E. H. Seymour
[: a review.]   FROM [The Monthly]
Rev[iew, Vol. 51].
   bibliog.   1806.

558070

— Shakspeare's genius justified: restora-
tions and illustrations of seven
hundred passages in Shakespeare's plays,
by Z. Jackson [: a review].   FROM
[The Eclectic Review] Vol. 12.   N[ew]
S[eries].   [1819.]

554720

— SISSON (CHARLES JASPER)
New readings in Shakespeare.
(Cambridge)
   facsimiles.   2 vols.   1956.
Shakespeare Problems, 8.

665182-3

— TANNENBAUM (S. A.)
Shaksperian scraps and other Elizabethan
fragments.   [With a foreword by
J. Q. Adams, and notes.]   (New York)
   facsimiles.   1933.

411561

— TANNENBAUM (S. A.)
Some emendations of Shakspere's
text [etc.].   Reprinted from The
Shakespeare Association Bulletin,
Vol. 6, No. 3.   pp. [8.]   1931.

413465

— TRENCH (W. F.)
A Note on five dramatic interruptions:
a contribution to the textual
criticism of Shakespeare.   FROM
Hermathena, No. 48.   pp. [8].
(Dublin)   1933.

439151

Textual History: Printing — Publishing — Editing

General Works and Early History
The Quartos
The Folios
Restoration and 18th century editions
19th century
20th century
see also Illustrations; Translation

Textual History: Printing — Publishing — Editing

— General Works and Early History

— Adams (J.Q.) Elizabethan playhouse
manuscripts and their significance
for the text of Shakespeare.
From The Johns Hopkins Alumni Magazine. Vol.21.

(Baltimore)   1932.

440787

— ALBRIGHT (EVELYN M.)
Dramatic publication in England,
1580-1640: a reply [to a review by
W. W. Greg, with his answer.]   FROM
Review of English Studies, Vol. 4.
                               1928.

497599

— ALEXANDER (PETER)
Restoring Shakespeare;   the modern
editor's task.   IN SHAKESPEARE
SURVEY 5.   (Cambridge)   1952.

623798

— Baker (H.T.) Should Shakespeare be
expurgated? From The English
Journal, vol.22.

(Chicago)   1933.

442572

— BATESON (F. [N.] W.)
Shakespeare's laundry bills: the
rationale of external evidence.
IN SHAKESPEARE JAHRBUCH.   Bd. 98
1962.   pp. 51-63.   (Heidelberg)

10531

— BATESON (F. [N.] W.)
Shakespeare's laundry bills: the
rationale of external evidence.
IN Approaches to Shakespeare [:
20th century critical essays].   (New
York)   1964.

668298

— BENNETT (ENOCH ARNOLD)
Buying Shakspere.   [From "Riceyman
Steps".]   IN Modern prose [: an
anthology] ed. by Elizabeth D'Oyley.
                               1930.

624244

— BENNETT, JOSEPHINE WATERS
Benson's alleged piracy of "Shake-
speare's Sonnets" and of some of
Jonson's works.   IN Studies in
Bibliography, Vol. 21.
(Charlottesville, Va.)   1968.
pp. 235-248.

598680

BLACK (M. W.)
Problems in the editing of Shakespeare:
interpretation.   IN English Institute
Essays, 1947.   (New York)
bibliog.   1948.

530316/1947

Block (A.) The Book collector's
vade mecum. [With a chapter on the
editions of Shakespeare's works.]
Illus.

1932.

397982

BOLTON (JOSEPH S. G.)
Worn pages in Shakespearian manuscripts.
IN SHAKESPEARE QUARTERLY VII.
pp. 177-182.
(New York)   1956.

605711

BONNARD (G. A.)
Suggestions towards an edition of
Shakespeare for French, German and
other Continental readers.
IN SHAKESPEARE SURVEY 5.   (Cambridge)
1952.

623798

BOWERS (FREDSON THAYER)
A Definitive text of Shakespeare:
problems and methods.   IN MATTHEWS
(A. D.) and EMERY (C. M.) eds.,
Studies in Shakespeare.   (Coral Gables,
Fla.)   1953.
University of Miami Publications in
English and American Literature,
Vol. 1, March 1953.

634188

BOWERS, FREDSON THAYER
Established texts and definitive
editions. FROM Philological Quarterly,
Vol.XLI, No.1.   1962.

667390

BOWERS (FREDSON THAYER)

The New textual criticism of
Shakespeare. IN Bowers (F.T.) Textual
and literary criticism. (Cambridge)
1954.

682960

BOWERS (FREDSON THAYER)
On editing Shakespeare and the Eliza-
bethan dramatists. (Philadelphia,
Pa.)   1955.
Rosenbach Fellowship in Bibliography.

665021

BOWERS (FREDSON THAYER)
Shakespeare's text and the biblio-
graphical method.   IN Studies in
Bibliography Vol. 6.   (Charlottesville,
Va.)   1953.

598680/6

BOWERS (FREDSON THAYER)
What Shakespeare wrote.   IN
SHAKESPEARE JAHRBUCH.   Bd. 98/1962.
pp. 24-50.   (Heidelberg)
10531

BOWERS, FREDSON THAYER
What Shakespeare wrote.   IN
RABKIN, NORMAN, ed., Approaches to
Shakespeare [: 20th century critical
essays].   (New York)   1964.

668298

BROWN (ARTHUR)
Editorial problems in Shakespeare:
semi-popular editions.   IN Studies
in Bibliography. Vol. 8.
(Charlottesville, Va.)   1956.

666971

BROWN, ARTHUR
'The Great variety of readers'.
IN SHAKESPEARE SURVEY 18.
(Cambridge)   1965.

749826

BROWN, ARTHUR
The Printing of books [: in Elizabethan
England].   IN SHAKESPEARE SURVEY 17.
(Cambridge)   1964.

667822

BROWN (ARTHUR)
The Rationale of old-spelling editions
of the plays of Shakespeare and his
contemporaries: a rejoinder [to John
Russell Brown].   Reprint from "Studies
in Bibliography": papers of the
Bibliographical Society of the University of Virginia, Vol. 13.   pp. 69-76.
[Charlottesville, Va.]   1960.

666972

BROWN (JOHN RUSSELL)

The Rationale of old-spelling editions
of the plays of Shakespeare and his
contemporaries. [Reprint from 'Studies
in Bibliography': papers of the
Bibliographical Society of the
University of Virginia, Vol.13.]
pp.49-67. Bibliog. [Charlottesville,
Va.]   1960.   666455

CAIRNCROSS (A. S.)
Pembroke's men and some Shakespearian
piracies.
IN SHAKESPEARE QUARTERLY XI.
pp. 335-349.
(New York)   1960.

605711

CAIRNCROSS (ANDREW SCOTT)
The Quartos and the Folio text of
"Richard III".   IN The Review of
English Studies, New Series, Vol. 8.
(Oxford)   1957.

318239/8

CAMERON (K. W.)
The Text of Othello: an analysis.
IN Publications of the Modern
Language Association of America,
vol. 49.   (Menasha, Wis.)   1934.

432218

CHANDA (S. M.)
The Text of Shakespeare.   FROM The
Calcutta Review, 1931.   pp. [14.]

389217

CHAPMAN (R. W.)
A Problem in editorial method.
[With references to editing
Shakespeare.]   IN English Association,
Essays and studies, Vol. 27, 1941.
Collected by N. C. Smith.   (Oxford)
bibliog.   1942.

533128

'Conjectural emendations on the text
of Shakspere, with observations on
the notes of the commentators.
[Incomplete.]   FROM The Gentleman's
Magazine, Aug. 1844, Feb. & June
1845.   pp. [56.]

402698

CORRIGAN (A. J.)
A Printer and his world.   [With
reference to the printing of
Shakespeare.]
illus.   1944.

553814

CROW (JOHN)
Editing and emending.   IN English
Association, Essays and studies, 1955.
New Series, Vol. 8.   1955.

649785

DAM (B. A. P. van)
Textual criticism of Shakespeare's
plays.   Offprint from English
studies, [Vol. 7.]   pp. 97-115.
(Amsterdam)   [1925.]

554209

Davis (H.) Shakespeare and copyright.
In The Atlantic Monthly, Vol.71.

(Boston,[Mass.])   1893

119144

DAWSON (G. E.)
The Copyright of Shakespeare's
dramatic works.   IN PROUTY (C. T.)
ed., Studies in honor of A. H. R.
Fairchild[, by various authors].
(Columbia, Mo.)
port.   bibliog.   1946.
University of Missouri Studies.

575822

DAWSON, GILES EDWIN
Four centuries of Shakespeare
publication. (Lawrence, Kansas)
1964.

University of Kansas Publications,
Library series.   747847

DEY (E. M.)
Notes on Shakespeare [: a criticism
of the decisions of former editors
of the plays.]   IN The Academy.
Vol. 76.   [Under the heading
"Correspondence".]   1909.

221623

DUTHIE (GEORGE IAN)
The Text of Shakespeare's "Romeo
and Juliet".   IN Studies in
Bibliography, Vol. 4.
(Charlottesville, Va.)   1951.

598680/4

FROST (DAVID)
Shakespeare in the seventeenth century.
IN SHAKESPEARE QUARTERLY XVI: 1.
pp. 81-89.
(New York)   1965.

605711

GAW (ALLISON)
Actors' names in basic Shakespearean
texts, with special reference to
Romeo and Juliet and Much ado.
FROM Publications of the Modern
Language Association of America,
Vol. 40.   (Menasha, Wis.)
bibliog.   1925.

554228

GREG (Sir WALTER WILSON)
The Date of King Lear and Shakespeare's
use of earlier versions of the story.
IN The Library.   Fourth Series.
Vol. 20.   1940.

519243

GREG (W. W.)
The Editorial problem in Shakespeare:
a survey of the foundations of the
text.   [bibliog.]   (Oxford)
1942.   536764
Clark Lectures, Trinity College,
Cambridge, 1939.
_____ 2nd edn.   1951.   614863

GREG (Sir WALTER WILSON)
The Function of bibliography in
literary criticism illustrated in
a study of the text of "King Lear".
Reprinted from Neophilologus.
pp. 22.   (Groningen)   [1933].
Allard Pierson Stichting, Afdeeling
voor Moderne Literatuurwetenschap
[Publications] No. 3.

465035

Greg (W.W.) The "Hamlet" texts
and recent work in Shakespearean
bibliography.   In The Modern Language
Review, Vol. 14.

1919.

283257

GREG (W. W.)
King Lear - mislineation and
stenography.   IN The Library, 4th
series, vol. 17.   1937.

469402

Greg (W.W.) Principles of
emendation in Shakespeare.   In   Aspects
of Shakespeare: British Academy
lectures.

1933.

401892

GREG (W. W.)
[Review of] Dramatic publication in
England, 1580-1640, by Evelyn M.
Albright.   FROM Review of English
Studies, Vol. 4.   1928.

497595

— GREG (W. W.)
Type-facsimiles and others [in] 'Facsimile'
reprints of old books, by A. W. Pollard
[and others.   With references to
Shakespeare reprints].   IN The Library,
Vol. 6.

1926.

329554

— HARDACRE, KENNETH
Shakespeare's printers [: the printing
of the text in the early 17th century].
1966.

illus.   760305

No. 145 of edition limited to
about 150.

— HASTINGS (W. T.)
To the next editor of Shakspere: notes
for his prospectus.   IN The Colophon,
Vol. 2, No. 4.   (New York) 1937.

458131

— HINMAN, CHARLTON
Shakespeare's text - then, now and
tomorrow.   IN SHAKESPEARE SURVEY 18.
(Cambridge)   1965.

749826

— HONIGMANN, E. A. J.
The Stability of Shakespeare's text.
illus.   1965.

742149

— HULME (HILDA M.)
Shakespeare's text: some notes on
linguistic procedure and its relevance
to textual criticism.   IN English
Studies, Vol. 39.   (Amsterdam)
1958.

485643/39

— INGLEBY (C. M.)
The Still lion: an essay towards
the restoration of Shakespeare's
text.   Being part of the
Shakespeare–Jahrbuch, 2.   pp. [53.]
[Berlin]   1867.

415111

— JOHNSON (SAMUEL) Preface to Shakespeare

For editions of this work check the
main sequence under the author's name.

— JUDGE (C. B.)
Elizabethan book-pirates.   [Including
references to Shakespeare.]   (Cambridge,
Mass.)
bibliog.   facsimiles.   1934.
Harvard Studies in English, 8.

416260

— KIRSCHBAUM (LEO)
Shakespeare and the Stationers.
(Ohio State University.   Graduate
School Monographs.   Contributions
in Languages and Literature, No.15:
English Series 5.)   (Columbus,
Ohio)
bibliog.   1955.

648104

— KIRSCHBAUM (L.)
Shakespeare's hypothetical marginal
additions.   IN Modern Language
Notes, Vol. 61.   (Baltimore, Md.)
1946.

579125

— KIRSCHBAUM (L.)
The True text of King Lear.   [With
bibliographical notes.]   pp. ix, 81.
(Baltimore)

1945.

621872

— MILWAUKEE PUBLIC LIBRARY, WISCONSIN
William Shakespeare, his editors and
editions: a commentary on the major
editions of Shakespeare's works,
prepared for the quatercentenary
observance of his birth in 1564.
illus.   [1964.]

668036

— MUIR, KENNETH
Shakespeare: texts and criticism.
IN SPENCER, TERENCE JOHN BEW, ed.,
Shakespeare: a celebration, 1564-
1964.
illus.   maps.   1964.

667816

— MUIR, KENNETH
The Text of Othello.   IN SHAKESPEARE
STUDIES 1.   (Cincinnati, Ohio)
1965.

750317

— MUMBY (F. A.)
The Romance of book-selling.
[Containing a chapter entitled:
"Shakespeare's publishers".]   With
a bibliography by W. H. Peet.
ports.   illus.   1910.

230091

— NOSWORTHY, JAMES MANSFIELD
Shakespeare's occasional plays:
their origin and transmission.
1965.

747250

— Notes on Shakspeare's text: [reviews
of 1.] The Text of Shakspeare vindicated
from the interpolations and corruptions
advocated by John Payne Collier, Esq.,
in his "Notes and emendations", by
S. W. Singer; [2] A Few notes on
Shakspeare, with occasional remarks on
the emendations of the manuscript-
corrector in Mr. Collier's copy of the
Folio, 1632, by A. Dyce; [3] New
illustrations of the life, studies and
writings of Shakspeare; supplementary
to all the editions, by J. Hunter;
[and 4] The Stratford Shakspeare
Specimen.   Edited by C. Knight.   IN
The Gentleman's Magazine, New Series,
Vol. 40.   1853.

18693

— ORCUTT (W. D.)
From my library walls: a kaleidoscope
of memories.   [With references to
editions of Shakespeare's works.]
port.   1946.

576555

—— PARKER, R. B.
Old books and Elizabethan printing.
IN Stratford Papers on Shakespeare
delivered at the 1961 Shakespeare
Seminar. (Toronto)   1962.

668005

—— PATRICK (D. L.)
The Textual history of Richard III.
(Stanford, Cal.)   1936.
Stanford University.   University
Series.   Language and Literature,
Vol. 6, No. 1.

463300

—— PAUL (H. N.)
Players' quartos and duodecimos of
Hamlet.   IN Modern Language Notes,
Vol. 49.   (Baltimore)   1934.

428652

—— PICKERSGILL (EDWARD H.)
On the Quarto and the Folio of
Richard III.   IN Transactions of
the New Shakespeare Society, Series 1.
No. 3.   pp. 77-124.   1875-6.

40620

—— PLOMER (H. R.)
A Short history of English printing,
1476-1900.   [With references to the
printing of Shakespeare's works,
especially the First Folio.]   2nd
edn.   1915.
Books about Books.

552471

—— POLLARD (A. W.)
A Bibliographer's praise.
IN GOLLANCZ ([Sir] I.) ed., A Book
of homage to Shakespeare.
ports. illus. facsimiles. [1916.]

264175

—— POLLARD (A. W.)
The Bibliographical approach to
Shakespeare: notes on new contributions.
IN The Library, 4th Series, Vol. 14.
1934.

422285

—— POLLARD (A. W.)
The Foundations of Shakespeare's text.
IN Aspects of Shakespeare: British
Academy lectures.   1933.

401892

—— POLLARD (A. W.)
Shakespeare's fight with the pirates
and the problems of the transmission
of his text.   2nd edn., revised with
an introduction.   (Cambridge) 1937.
Shakespeare Problems [Series No. 1.]

472130

—— POLLARD (A. W.)
Shakespeare's text.   IN GRANVILLE-
BARKER (H.) and HARRISON (G. B.) eds.,
A Companion to Shakespeare studies.
(Cambridge)
illus. bibliogs. tables. facsimiles.
            1934.   418724
_____ (New York)   1937.   479251
_____ (Cambridge) 1945.   566174

—— POLLARD (A. W.) [and others]
'Facsimile' reprints of old books, by
A. W. Pollard, G. R. Redgrave, R. W.
Chapman [and] W. W. Greg.   [With ref-
erences to Shakespeare reprints.]
IN The Library, Vol. 6.
1926.

329554

—— PRICE (H. T.)
On some peculiarities in
Shakespearean texts.   IN Essays
and studies by members of the
English department of the University
of Michigan.   1932.
University of Michigan Publications.
Language and Literature.

404800

—— Price (H.T.) Towards a scientific
method of textual criticism for the
Elizabethan drama. [With references
to Shakespeare.] Reprinted from the
Journal of English and Germanic
philology, Vol.36.

(Urbana, Ill.)   [1937.]

554218

—— REDGRAVE (G. R.)
Photographic facsimiles [in]
'Facsimile' reprints of old books,
by A. W. Pollard [and others.
With references to Shakespeare
reprints].   IN The Library, Vol. 6.
1926.

329554

—— SAMPSON (ANTONY)
The Printing of Shakespeare's plays.
IN Signature, New Series, No. 15.
facsimiles.   1952.

476085/2/15

—— SAVAGE (DEREK S.)
Hamlet & the pirates: an exercise in
literary detection.   1950.

620065

—— SHAABER (M. A.)
Problems in the editing of Shakespeare:
text.   IN English Institute Essays,
1947.   (New York)
bibliog.   1948.

530316/1947

—— Sherzer (Jane) American editions of
Shakespeare, 1753- 1866. In
Publications of the Modern Language
Association of America, Vol.22.

(Baltimore)   1907.

428342

—— SIMPSON (P.)
Proof-reading in the sixteenth,
seventeenth and eighteenth centuries.
[With Shakespearian references.]
illus.   facsimiles.   1935.
[Oxford Books on Bibliography]

434325

SISSON (CHARLES JASPER)
The Laws of Elizabethan copyright: the
Stationers' view. [Reprinted from the
Transactions of the Bibliographical
Society, The Library, March 1960.]
pp.20.

667159

TANNENBAUM (S. A.)
Shaksperian scraps and other Elizabethan
fragments. [With a foreword by
J. Q. Adams, and notes.] (New York)
facsimiles. 1933.

411561

THAYER (W. R.)
The Shakespeare hoax: a startling
prospectus. pp. 20. (Cambridge,
Mass.) 1888.

564970

THORNDIKE (A. H.)
Influence of the court-masques on
the drama, 1608-15 [: an attempt
to determine the date of The Winter's
tale.] IN Publications of the
Modern Language Association of
America, Vol. 15. (Baltimore) 1900.

428335

WALKER (ALICE)
Collateral substantive texts (with
special reference to "Hamlet".)
IN Studies in Bibliography, Vol. 7.
(Charlottesville, Va.) 1955.

598680/7

WALKER (ALICE)
Compositor determination and other
problems in Shakespearian texts.
IN Studies in Bibliography, Vol. 7.
(Charlottesville, Va.) 1955.

598680/7

WALKER (ALICE)
Principles of annotation : some
suggestions for editors of
Shakespeare. IN Studies in
Bibliography, Vol.9. (Charlottes-
-ville, Va.) 1957

598680/9

WALKER (ALICE)
The 1622 Quarto and the First Folio
texts of Othello. IN SHAKESPEARE
SURVEY 5. (Cambridge) 1952.

623798

WALKER (ALICE)
Some editorial principles (with
special reference to "Henry V").
IN Studies in Bibliography, Vol. 8.
(Charlottesville, Va.) 1956.

598680/8

WALKER (ALICE)
The Textual problem of Hamlet: a
reconsideration. IN The Review of
English Studies, New Series, Vol. 2.
(Oxford) 1951.

318239/2/2

WALKER (ALICE)
The Textual problem of 'Troilus and
Cressida'. IN The Modern Language
Review, Vol. 45. 1950.

266816/45

WALKER (ALICE)
Textual problems of the First Folio:
Richard III, King Lear, Troilus &
Cressida, 2 Henry IV, Hamlet, Othello.
(Cambridge)
bibliog. 1953.
Shakespeare Problems, 7.

633690

WALLER, FREDERICK O.
The Use of linguistic criteria in determining the copy and dates for Shakespeare's
plays.
IN Pacific coast studies in
Shakespeare. Edited by W. F. McNeir
and T. N. Greenfield. (Eugene: Ore.)
1966.

768009

WALTON (J. K.)
The Copy for the folio text of
Richard III with a note on the copy
for the folio text of King Lear.
(Auckland)
tables. bibliogs. 1955.
Auckland University College,
Monograph Series, No. 1.

665102

WALTON (J. K.)
The Quarto copy for the Folio
Richard III. IN The Review of
English Studies, New Series, Vol. 10.
bibliog. tables. 1959.

318239/10

WEBB ([T. E.])
Of the genuine text of Shakespeare.
IN The National Review, Vol. 42.
1903.

180375

WILLIAMS (P.)
Shakespeare's Troilus and Cressida:
the relationship of Quarto and
Folio. IN Virginia University
Bibliographical Society, Studies in
bibliography, Vol. 3.
(Charlottesville, Va.) 1950.

598680/3

WILLOUGHBY (E. E.)
Printed in Shakespeare's day [: a
discussion on] typical works.
IN Graphic arts and education,
Vol. 15, No. 3. pp. 20.
(Washington)
ports. illus. 1938.

485895

WILLOUGHBY (E. E.)
A Printer of Shakespeare: the books
and times of William Jaggard.
ports. facsimiles. 1934.

426107

WILSON (JOHN DOVER)
[The Living] Shakespeare [No. 5]:
The texts. [Broadcast] 29th October,
1958. ff. 8.
typescript.

666027

——Wilson (J.D.) New ideas and discoveries about Shakespeare. <u>In</u> The Virginia Quarterly Review, Vol.23.

[Charlottesville,Va.]   1947.

588089

—— WILSON (JOHN DOVER)
The New way with Shakespeare's texts: an introduction for lay readers.
1: The Foundations.
IN SHAKESPEARE SURVEY 7.   (Cambridge) 1954.

639176

—— WILSON (JOHN DOVER)
The New way with Shakespeare's texts.
2: Recent work on the text of Romeo and Juliet.   IN SHAKESPEARE SURVEY 8.
(Cambridge)   1955.

647706

—— WILSON (JOHN DOVER)
The New way with Shakespeare's texts: an introduction for lay readers.
3: In sight of Shakespeare's manuscripts.
IN SHAKESPEARE SURVEY 9.   (Cambridge) 1956.

665210

—— WILSON (JOHN DOVER)
The New way with Shakespeare's texts: an introduction for lay readers.
4: Towards the high road.   IN SHAKESPEARE SURVEY 11.   (Cambridge)
bibliog.   1958.

665816

—— WILSON (JOHN DOVER)
On editing Shakespeare, with special reference to the problems of Richard III.   IN Talking of Shakespeare [: a selection from the lectures delivered at the annual course for teachers at Stratford, 1948-1953].   1954.

641471

—WILSON (JOHN DOVER)
The Origins and development of Shakespeare's Henry IV.   IN The Library, 4th Series, Vol. 26.
(Oxford)
bibliog.   1945.

574761

—— Wilson (J.D.) The Text of the plays [of Shakespeare] : talk [broadcast] 20th July 1949. ff.9. Typescript. (Shakespeare and his world, 5).

1949.

605267

—— [WILSON (J. D.) and BLISS (W.)]
The Joy of editing Shakespeare [: a report of J. D. Wilson's broadcast talk and correspondence between J. D. Wilson and W. Bliss].   IN The Listener, Vol. 38.   1947.

589226

—— WILSON (F. P.)
Shakespeare and the "new bibliography".
IN The Bibliographical Society, 1892-1942: studies in retrospect,[by various authors].
facsimile.   1945.

565383

Textual History: Printing – Publishing – Editing

– The Quartos

—— ADAMS (J. O.)
The Quarto of King Lear and shorthand [i.e. T. Bright's system.]   FROM Modern philology, vol. 31.
(Chicago)   1931.

440600

—— ALEXANDER (P.)
Troilus and Cressida,1609.
Reprinted from the Transactions of the Bibliographical Society, 1928. 1928.
MS. letter from P. Alexander to Mr. Misleton inserted.

399895

—— BARTLETT (HENRIETTA C.)
First editions of Shakespeare's quartos.   Reprinted from The Library, Sept., 1935.   pp. 166-172.
(Bibliographical Society)   1935.

478519

—— BARTLETT (HENRIETTA C.) & POLLARD (A. W.)
A Census of Shakespeare's plays in quarto, 1594-1709.   Revised and extended [and with an introduction] by Henrietta C. Bartlett.   (New Haven, [Conn.])   1939.

511666

—— BROWN (JOHN RUSSELL)
The Compositors of "Hamlet" Q2 and "The Merchant of Venice".
IN Studies in Bibliography, Vol. 7.
(Charlottesville, Va.)   1955.

598680/7

—— CAMERON (K. W.)
"Othello", Quarto 1, reconsidered. pp. [13].   FROM [Publications of the Modern Language Association of America, vol. 47.]   [(Menasha, Wis.)]
[1932.]

438441

—— CANTRELL (PAUL L.) and WILLIAMS (GEORGE WALTON)
The Printing of the Second Quarto of "Romeo and Juliet".   IN Studies in Bibliography, Vol. 9.
(Charlottesville, Va.)   1957.

598680/9

— CRAIG (HARDIN)
A New look at Shakespeare's quartos.
(Stanford, Cal.)
bibliog.   1961.

666822

— CRAIG (HARDIN)
Revised Elizabethan quartos: an
attempt to form a class.   IN Studies
in the English Renaissance drama,
edited by Josephine W. Bennett [and
others].   1959.

684756

— DAM (B. A. P. van)
Alleyn's player's part of Greene's
Orlando Furioso, and the text of the
Q of 1594.   [Compared with the first
printed versions of Shakespeare's
plays.] FROM English Studies, Vol.
11, nos. 5-6.   (Amsterdam)
2 vols.   1929.

441439

— DANKS (KENNETH BASIL)

Decem rationes: a Shakespearean
monograph. pp.44. Bibliog.
                                  1959.

666494

— DORAN (MADELEINE)
The Quarto of King Lear and Bright's
shorthand.   FROM Modern Philology,
Vol. 33.   (Chicago, Ill.)
bibliog.   1935.

491465

— DRAPER (J. W.)
The Date of "A Midsommer nights
dreame".   IN Modern Language
Notes, Vol. 53.   (Baltimore) 1938.

493024

— FELL (H. G.)
The Connoisseur divan: a find of
'Shakespearian quartos'.   IN The
Connoisseur, Vol. 118.
illus.   1946.

581300

— FERGUSON (W. CRAIG)
The Compositors of Henry IV, Part 2,
Much ado about nothing, The Shoemakers' holiday, and The First part
of the Contention. [A reprint from
Studies in Bibliography: papers of
the Bibliographical Society of the
University of Virginia, Vol. 13]
pp. [11] [Charlottesville, Va.]
                                [1960.]

667085

— Förster (M.) Shakespeare and shorthand. [With bibliographical notes.]
From Philological quarterly, Vol.16.

(Iowa)   1937.

484071

— GRAY (H. D.)
[Reply to Hamlet Q1 and Mr. Henry
David Gray, by J. D. Wilson].
IN Publications of the Modern
Language Association of America,
Vol. 43.   1928.

428363

— GREG (W. W.)
The "Hamlet" texts and recent work
in Shakespearean bibliography.
IN The Modern Language Review,
Vol. 14.   1919.

283257

— GREG (W. W.)
[Review of] Venus and Adonis, 1593;
etc.: reproduced in facsimile from
the earliest editions, with introductions by [Sir] S. Lee.   IN The
Library, New Series, Vol. 7. 1906.

198827

— GREG (W. W.)
"Richard III" - Q5 (1612).   IN The
Library, 4th series, Vol. 17. 1937.

469402

— GREG (Sir WALTER WILSON)
The Variants in the first quarto of
"King Lear": a bibliographical and
critical enquiry.   1940.
Supplement to the Bibliographical
Society's Transactions, No. 15.
                              516912

— HART (A.)
Stolne and surreptitious copies: a
comparative study of Shakespeare's
bad quartos.   (Melbourne)
bibliog.   tables.   1942.

542219

— HINMAN (C.)
The "Copy" for the second quarto of
Othello (1630). [With bibliographical
notes.]   IN McMANAWAY (J. G.),
DAWSON (G. E.) and WILLOUGHBY (E. E.)
eds., John Quincy Adams memorial
studies.   (Washington)   1948.

596748

— [HODGSON (J. E.)]
The Remarkable story of the
Shakespearian quartos of 1619: a
brief record of the unravelling of
a puzzle in Shakespearian bibliography
and an account of the unlooked-for
discovery of a "set" of the quartos
of 1619.   pp. 12.
frontis.   facsimiles.   1946.

572406

— HOPPE (H. R.)
An Approximate printing date for
the First Quarto of Romeo and
Juliet.   IN The Library, 4th Series,
Vol. 18.   (Bibliographical Society)
                              1938.

487688

— HOPPE (H. R.)
The Bad Quarto of Romeo and Juliet:
a bibliographical and textual study.
(Ithaca, N.Y.)
tables.   bibliog.   1948.
Cornell Studies in English, Vol. 36.

596308

—— HOPPE (H. R.)
Borrowings from "Romeo and Juliet"
in the 'bad' quarto of "The Merry
Wives of Windsor".   IN The Review
of English Studies, Vol. 20.
(Oxford)   [1944.]
bibliog.

562839

—— HOPPE (H. R.)
The First Quarto of Romeo and Juliet:
a bibliographical and textual study.
IN Cornell University, Abstracts of
theses accepted in partial satis-
faction of the requirements for the
Doctor's degree, 1942.   (Ithaca,
N.Y.)   1943.

574488

—— HOPPE (H. R.)
The First Quarto version of "Romeo
and Juliet", II.vi and IV.v.43 ff.
IN The Review of English Studies,
Vol. 14.
bibliog.   1938.

495115

—— HOSLEY (RICHARD)
The Corrupting influence of the bad
quarto on the received text of
Romeo and Juliet.   IN SHAKESPEARE
QUARTERLY IV: 1.   pp. 11-33.
(New York)   1953.

605711

—— HOSLEY (RICHARD)
Quarto copy for Q2 "Romeo and Juliet".
IN Studies in Bibliography, Vol. 9.
(Charlottesville, Va.)   1957.

598680/9

—— Huth (A.H.) and Pollard (A.W.) On
the supposed false dates in
certain Shakespeare quartos.
In The Library. 3rd series,
Vol.1.

1910.

228048

—— JAGGARD (W.)
False dates in Shakespearian quartos.
IN The Library, New Series, Vol. 10.
1909.

222151

—— KABLE, WILLIAM S.
Compositor B, the Pavier quartos
and copy spellings.   IN Studies in
Bibliography, Vol. 21.
(Charlottesville, Va.)   1968.
pp. 131-161.

598680

—— Kirk (R.) Jane Bell: printer at the
East end of Chrish-Church. [With
reference to the 1655 edn. of King
Lear printed by her; and bibliographical notes.] In Craig (H.)
ed.,Essays in dramatic literature:
the Parrott presentation volume.
Port.

(Princeton)   1935

444399

—— KIRSCHBAUM (L.)
A Census of bad quartos.   IN The
Review of English Studies, Vol. 14.
bibliog.   1938.

495115

—— KIRSCHBAUM (L.)
An Hypothesis concerning the origin
of the [Shakespeare] bad quartos.
IN Publications of the Modern
Language Association of America,
Vol. 60.   (Menasha, Wis.)
bibliog.   1945.

569026

—— LAWRENCE (W. J.)
The Secret of "the bad quartos".
IN The Criterion, Vol. 10.   1930-31.

388537

—— McCLOSKEY (F. H.)
The Date of 'A Midsummer night's
dream'.   IN Modern Language Notes,
Vol. 46.   1931.

397731

—— McKENZIE (D. F.)
Compositor B's role in The Merchant
of Venice Q2 (1619).   IN Studies
in Bibliography, Vol. 12.
(Charlottesville, Va.)   1959.

598680/12

—— McMANAWAY (J. G.)
The Cancel in the quarto of 2 Henry IV.
bibliog.   IN PROUTY (C. T.) ed.,
Studies in honor of A. H. R. Fairchild
[, by various authors.]   (Columbia,
Mo.)
port.   1946.
University of Missouri Studies,
Vol. 21, No. 1.

575822

—— MATTHEWS (W.)
Peter Bales, Timothy Bright and
Shakespeare.   FROM The Journal
of English and Germanic Philology,
Vol. 34.   (Urbana, Ill.)
facsimiles.   1935.

490973

—— Matthews (W.) Shakespeare and the
reporters. In The Library, 4th
series, Vol.15.

1935.

437527

—— MATTHEWS (W.)
Shorthand and the bad Shakespeare
quartos.   IN The Modern Language
Review. Vol. 27. 1932.   (Cambridge)

410972

—— O'SULLIVAN (MARY I.)
Hamlet and Dr. Timothy Bright.
IN Publications of the Modern Language
Association of America, Vol. 41.
(Menasha, Wis.)
1926.

428361

PARTRIDGE (ASTLEY COOPER)
Shakespeare's orthography in "Venus
and Adonis" and some early Quartos.

IN SHAKESPEARE SURVEY 7.   (Cambridge)
1954.

639176

POLLARD (A. W.)
False dates in Shakespeare quartos.
IN The Library.   3rd series, Vol. 2.
1911.

235017

Pollard (A.W.) and Wilson (J.D.) What
follows if some of the good quarto
editions of Shakespeare's plays
were printed from his autograph
manuscripts. In Transactions of the
Bibliographical Society, Vol.15.

1920.

294089

PYLES (T.)
Rejected Q2 readings in the New
Shakespeare Hamlet, [edited by
J. D. Wilson: a review].   IN
ELH: a journal of English literary
history, Vol. 4.   1937.

483008

Rodd (T.) The Quarto editions of
Shakespeare's plays. From The
Gentleman's Magazine, [New Series]
Vol.13.

1840.

521907

ROSTENBERG (LEONA)
Thomas Thorpe, publisher of "Shakespeares sonnets", from the Papers of
the Bibliographical Society of
America, 1960.   pp. [22].

666962

The Shakespeare quartos [given to
Harvard University from the collection
of W. A. White] pp. [11].   FROM
Harvard Library Notes, No. 21.
(Cambridge, Mass.)   1928.

524749

SISSON (C. J.)
Shakespeare quartos as prompt-copies;
with some account of Cholmeley's
players and a new Shakespeare allusion.
[bibliog.]   IN The Review of English
Studies, Vol. 18.   (Oxford) 1942.

542539

SPALDING (THOMAS ALFRED)
On the First Quarto of Romeo and
Juliet: is there any evidence of
a second hand in it?   IN
Transactions of the New Shakespeare
Society, Series 1. No. 5.   pp. 58-87.
1877-9.

40620

STEVENSON (ALLAN H.)
Shakespearian dated watermarks.
IN Studies in Bibliography Vol. 4.
(Charlottesville, Va.)   1951.

598680/4

THOMAS (SIDNEY)
The Bibliographical links between the
first two Quartos of Romeo and Juliet.
IN The Review of English Studies,
Vol. 25.   1949.

318239/25

THOMAS (SIDNEY)
Henry Chettle and the First Quarto
of Romeo and Juliet.   IN The Review
of English Studies, New Series,
Vol. 1.   (Oxford)   1950.

318239/2/1

A Treasure restored [: the recovery
of an old volume of Shakespeare's
plays.]   IN The Times Literary
Supplement, 1946.

580183

WILLARD (O. M.)
The Survival of English books printed
before 1640: a theory and some
illustrations.   [With references
to the Shakespeare quartos.]
IN The Library, Fourth Series, Vol.
23.   (Oxford)
table.   1943.

548645

WILLIAMS (P.)
The "Second issue" of Shakespeare's
Troilus and Cressida, 1609.
IN Virginia University Bibliographical
Society, Studies in bibliography,
Vol. 2.   (Charlottesville, Va.)
1949.

598680/2

WILSON (JOHN DOVER)
Shakespeare's Richard III and The
True Tragedy of Richard the Third,
1594.   IN SHAKESPEARE QUARTERLY
III: 4.   pp. 299-306.   (New York)
1952.

605711

WILSON (J. D.)
"They sleepe all the act."   [With
references to "A Midsummer night's
dream".]   IN The Review of English
Studies, Vol. 4.   1928.

355164

WILSON (JOHN DOVER) and POLLARD (A. W.)
What follows if some of the good
quarto editions of Shakespeare's plays
were printed from his autograph
manuscripts.   IN Transactions of the
Bibliographical Society, Vol. 15.
1920.

294089

Textual History: Printing – Publishing – Editing

– The Folios

— Bald (R.C.) Bibliographical studies in the Beaumont & Fletcher folio of 1647. [With references to the Shakespeare folio, etc.] Illus. Facsimiles.

(Oxford)   1938.

(Supplement to the Bibliographical Society's Transactions, No. 13.)

495434

— BALD (R. C.)
The Shakespeare Folios. [With] Tables for the identification and collation of the Shakespeare Folio [by R. Horrox.] IN Book handbook, 1947.
facsimiles.

588086

— BALDWIN, THOMAS WHITFIELD
On act and scene division in the Shakspere first folio. (Carbondale and Edwardsville, Ill.)   1965.

745845

— BARTON (THOMAS PENNANT)
The Library's First Folio of Shakespeare. IN The Boston Public Library Quarterly Vol. 10. (Boston, Mass.)   1958.

608324/10

— BLACK (M. W.)
Shakespeare's seventeenth-century editors. IN Proceedings of the American Philosophical Society, Vol. 76. (Philadelphia) 1936.

463924

— BLACK (M. W.) and SHAABER (M. A.)
Shakespeare's seventeenth-century editors, 1632-1685. (New York)
1937.
The Modern Language Association of America, General Series.

478193

— BOWERS (FREDSON THAYER)
The Copy for the Folio Richard III. IN SHAKESPEARE QUARTERLY X: 4. pp. 541-544. (New York)   1959.

605711

— BOWERS (FREDSON THAYER)
Robert Roberts: a printer of Shakespeare's Fourth Folio.
IN SHAKESPEARE QUARTERLY II: 3. pp. 241-246.
(New York)   1951.

605711

— CASSON (L. F.)
Notes on a Shakespearean First Folio in Padua. IN Modern Language Notes. Vol. 51.   1936.

463701

— Catalogue of the first four folio editions of Shakespeare with Roger Payne's bill for binding the First Folio, from the library of H. B. H. Beaufoy, sold by order of the Beaufoy Trustees, July, 1912. pp. 7.
illus.

426551

— COLLIER (J. P.)
Notes and emendations to the text of Shakespeare's plays, from early manuscript corrections in a copy of the Folio, 1632. (Shakespeare Society)
facsimile.   1852.

420950

— COOPER (W. S.)
Fragments of Droitwich history and development: two series of essays & articles contributed [to] "The Messenger". [With references to John Heminge and the First Folio.] pp. 53. (Droitwich)
illus.   1935.

513775

— Dawbarn (C.Y.C.) Oxford and the folio plays : a supplement [to] Baconiana, Oct. 1938. pp. [80.] Facsimiles.

1938.

(Bacon Society.)

499944

— DAWSON (G. E.)
A Bibliographical problem in the First Folio of Shakespeare.
IN The Library, Fourth Series, Vol. 22.
dgm.   bibliog.   1942.

543100

— DAWSON (GILES EDWIN)
Some bibliographical irregularities in the Shakespeare Fourth Folio. A reprint from Studies in Bibliography: papers of the Bibliographical Society of the University of Virginia, Vol. 4, 1951-1952. (Charlottesville, Va.)
1951.
Signed by the author.

621177

— Description of a copy of the First Folio edition of the plays of Shakespeare, now in the collection of T. P. Barton. pp. 22. (New York)   1860.
No. 15 of a privately printed edition limited to 20 copies, signed by T. P. Barton.

555512

— Dickson (W.K.) Notes on a copy of the first folio Shakespeare in the library of the Society of Antiquaries of Scotland, Vol. 40. pp. 207-212.

[1906.]

487493

— DODD, MEAD & COMPANY
The Four Folios of Shakespeare's
plays: an account of the four
collected editions, with a census
of the known perfect copies of
the First Folio.   Offered for sale.
pp. 32.   (New York)   [1907]

506084

— FARR (H.)
Philip Chetwind and the Allott
copyrights.   [With a section
"The Shakespeare folios".]
Reprinted from The Library, Sept.
1934.   pp. [34].   (Bibliographical
Society)   1934.

425726

— FEELY (J. M.)
The Shakespearean cypher, in the
First Folio, mdcxxiii, demonstrated
and surveyed.   (Rochester, N.Y.)
1931.

419039

— The First Folio [: a review of
"Shakespeare's First Folio", by
R. C. Rhodes.]   FROM The Contemporary
Review, Literary Supplement, 1923.
pp. [3.]

389223

— FLATTER (R.)
Shakespeare's producing hand: a
study of his marks of expression
to be found in the First Folio.
port.   facsimiles.   1948.

591817

— FLATTER, RICHARD
Some instances of line-division in the
First Folio.
IN SHAKESPEARE JAHRBUCH, Bd. 92/1956.
pp. 184-196.   (Heidelberg)

10531

— FLEMING (JOHN [F.])
The Rosenbach-Bodmer Shakespeare Folios
and Quartos.
IN SHAKESPEARE QUARTERLY III: 3.
pp. 257-259.
(New York)   1952.

605711

— GRAY (HENRY DAVID)
Shakespeare or Heminge.   A rejoinder
and a surrejoinder.   By H. D. Gray
and P. Simpson.   IN The Modern
Language Review, Vol. 45.   1950.

266816/45

— G[REG] (W. W.)
The Bibliographical history of the
First Folio.   IN The Library, New
Series, Vol. 4.   1903.

180050

— GREG (W. W.)
"Richard III" - Q 5 (1612).   IN The
Library, 4th series, vol. 17.   1937.

469402

— GREG (Sir WALTER WILSON)
The Shakespeare First Folio: its
bibliographical and textual history.
(Oxford)
bibliog.   1955.

648076

— GRIFFIN (W. J.)
An Omission in the Folio text of
Richard III.   IN The Review of
English studies, Vol. 13.   [1937.]

479772

— HARRISON (F.)
A Book about books.   [Including
references to the Shakespeare First
Folio.]
illus.   dgms.   facsimiles.
1943.

545336

— HASKER (RICHARD E.)
The Copy for the First Folio
Richard II.   IN Studies in Biblio-
graphy, Vol. 5.   (Charlottesville,
Va.)   1952.

598680/5

— HINMAN (CHARLTON)
Cast-off copy for the First Folio of
Shakespeare.
IN SHAKESPEARE QUARTERLY VI:
pp. 259-273.
(New York)   1955.

605711

— HINMAN (CHARLTON)
The "Halliwell-Philipps facsimile" of
the First Folio of Shakespeare.
IN SHAKESPEARE QUARTERLY V:
pp. 395-401.
(New York)   1954.

605711

— HINMAN (CHARLTON)
Mark III: new light on the proof
reading for the First Folio of
Shakespeare.   IN Virginia University
Bibliographical Society, Studies in
bibliography, Vol. 3.   (Charlottesville,
Va.)
facsimiles.   1950.

598680/3

— HINMAN (CHARLTON)
The Prentice hand in the tragedies
of the Shakespeare First Folio:
compositor E.   IN Studies in Bibliography, Vol. 9.   (Charlottesville,
Va.)   1957.

598680/9

— HINMAN, CHARLTON
The Printing and proof-reading of
the First Folio of Shakespeare.
illus.   1963.

667542-3

— HINMAN (CHARLTON)
The Proof-reading of the First Folio
text of "Romeo and Juliet".
IN Studies in Bibliography, Vol. 6.
(Charlottesville, Va.)   1953.

598680/6

HINMAN (CHARLTON)
A Proof-sheet in the First Folio
of Shakespeare.   IN The Library,
Fourth Series, Vol. 23.   (Oxford)
facsimiles.   bibliog.   1943.

548645

HINMAN, CHARLTON
Shakespeare's text - then, now and
tomorrow.   IN SHAKESPEARE SURVEY 18.
(Cambridge)   1965.

749826

HINMAN (CHARLTON)
Six variant readings in the First
Folio of Shakespeare.   pp. 17.
(Lawrence, Kan.)   1961.
University of Kansas, Library
Series No. 13.

666933

HINMAN (CHARLTON)
Variant readings in the First Folio of
Shakespeare.
IN SHAKESPEARE QUARTERLY IV: 3.
pp. 279-288.
(New York)   1953.

605711

JAGGARD (W.)
Shakespeare once a printer and bookman:
lecture at Stationers' Hall, London,
20th Oct., 1933.   pp. 34.
(Stratford-on-Avon: Shakespeare Press)
port.   illus.   [1934.]
Printing Trade Lectures.   Twelfth
Series, 1.   Edn. limited to 450 copies.

419570

JOHNSON (E. D.)
The First Folio of Shake-speare.
frontis.   1932.

394440

JOHNSON (EDWARD DINWOODY)
Francis Bacon's maze: a demonstration of the sixth line word cipher
in the First Folio of the
"Shakespeare" plays.   (Francis
Bacon Society)   pp. viii, 68.
1961.

667055

JOHNSON (E. D.)
The Mystery of the First Folio of
the "Shakespeare" plays.   pp. 59.
(London: Bacon Society)
facsimiles.   [1946.]

576882

JOHNSON (E. D.)
Shakespearian acrostics: a
demonstration of the marginal words
in the First Folio of "Mr. William
Shakespeare's" comedies, histories
and tragedies.   2nd enlarged edn.
(London: Bacon Society)   1947.

581062

KEAST (WILLIAM R.)
The Shakespeare Folios in the Cornell
University Library, given by W. G.
Mennen, '08.   Published under the
auspices of the Cornell University
Library Associates.   pp. 16.
(Ithaca, N.Y.)   1954.

665067

LEE (Sir SIDNEY)
Notes and additions to the census of
copies of the Shakespeare First Folio.
IN The Library, New Series, Vol. 7.
1906.

198827

LEE ([Sir] S.)
Some undescribed copies of the First
Folio Shakespeare.   IN Transactions
of the Bibliographical Society,
Vol. 5.   1901.

149674

LEETE (W.)
Not of an age, but for all time:
Shakespeare folios at auction.
IN Theatre Arts Monthly, Vol. 19.
(New York)   1935.

449943

McKENZIE (D. F.)
Shakespearian punctuation - a new
beginning.   IN The Review of
English Studies, New Series,
Vol. 10.   1959.

318239/10

McMANAWAY (JAMES GILMER)
A Miscalculation in the printing of
the Third Folio.   IN The Library,
5th Series, Vol. 9.   (Oxford)
1954.
Transactions of the Bibliographical
Society, 3rd Series, Vol. 9.

99606/9/5

NAAE (T. T.)
The Key to Shakespeare by the anatomy
of the figure on the title-page of the
Folio of 1623 of Shakespeare plays,
being an exposition of this First
Folio, with notes to The Tempest,
Love's labor's lost, and Sonnets.
[Dealing with the Bacon-Shakespeare
question].   New enlarged edn. (Boston)
ports. illus. facsimiles.   1935.

442863

NEWDIGATE (B. H.)
The Printers of the First Folio
[: a review of A Printer of
Shakespeare, by E. E. Willoughby.]
IN The London Mercury, Vol. 31.
1934-5.

438778

Ordish (T.F.) The First folio Shakespeare
1623.   [From The Bookworm, Vol.1.]

[1888.]

482168

OYAMA (TOSHIKAZU)
The Folio copy of Richard III.
IN Studies in English grammar and
linguistics: a miscellany in honour
of Takanobu Otsuka.   (Tokyo)
port. dgms. tables. bibliogs.
1958.

667095

PARSONS (H.)
Shakespearian emendations [No. 1]:
the history of the First Folio of
"The Workes of William Shakespeare".
[With relevant correspondence]
IN The Poetry Review, Vol. 37-   1946-

246749/37

PEARSON (E. L.)
The Lost First Folio.   IN TARG (W.)
ed., Carrousel for bibliophiles.
(New York)
bibliog.   illus.   facsimile.
1947.

584407

Rendall (G.H.) Ben Jonson and the
First Folio edition of Shakespeare's
plays. pp. 23. Port.

(Colchester)   1939.

507045

RINDER (F.)
The Geographical distribution of the
First Folio Shakespeare.   FROM The
Burlington Magazine, Vol. 2.
[1903.]

440806

ROBINSON (ANTHONY MEREDITH LEWIN)
The Grey copy of the Shakespeare First
Folio.   IN Quarterly Bulletin of the
South African Library, Vol. 5.   (Cape
Town)   1950.

601551/5

ROSENBACH (A. S. W.)
A Description of the four folios of
Shakespeare, 1623, 1632, 1663-4,
1685 in the original bindings: gift
to the Free Library of Philadelphia.
pp. 18.
facsimiles.   1945.

559567

SECORD (A. W.)
I.M. of the First Folio Shakespeare
and other Mabbe problems.   IN
Journal of English and Germanic
Philology, Vol. 47.   (Urbana, Ill.)
bibliog.   1948.

600780/47

SHROEDER (JOHN W.)
The Great Folio of 1623: Shakespeare's
plays in the printing house.   (Ann
Arbor, Mich.)   1956.

665387

SMIDT, KRISTIAN
Injurious impostors and Richard III.
1963.
Norwegian studies in English.

668033

SMITH (C. A.)
Shakespeare's present indicative
s-endings with plural subjects: a
study in the grammar of the First
Folio.   IN Publications of the
Modern Language Association of
America, Vol. 11.   (Baltimore)
1896.

428331

SMITH (R. M.)
Fly-specks and folios, [including
the Shakespeare First Folio.]
IN The Colophon, Vol. 1, N.S.,
No. 1.
facsimiles.   1935.

438235

SMITH (R. M.)
The Pursuit of a First Folio.
IN The Colophon.   New Series,
vol. 3, no. 1.   (New York)   1938.

478439

SMITH (R. M.)
Why a First Folio Shakespeare remained
in England.   IN Review of English
Studies: a quarterly journal of
English literature and the English
language, Vol. 15.   1939.

513846

SOMER (JOHN L.)
Ralph Crane and "an olde play called
Winter's tale".   IN Four studies in
Elizabethan drama, by Roma Ball,
J. C. Pogue, J. L. Somer [and] E. J.
Kettner.   (Kansas State Teachers'
College, Emporia, Kan.)   1962.
Emporia State Research Studies,
Vol. 10, No. 4.
667737

SPIELMANN (M. H.)
[Shakespeare's portraiture: a reissue
of] The Title-page of the First Folio
of Shakespeare's plays: a comparative
study of the Droeshout portrait and
the Stratford monument.   Written for
the Shakespeare Association in celebration of the First Folio Tercentenary,
1923.   pp. xi, 56.
illus.   bibliog.   1931.
No. 22 of edn. limited to 50 copies.
Author's signature on half tp.   Date
on tp. 1924, on cover 1931.

533661

TANNENBAUM (S. A.)
Shaksperian scraps and other
Elizabethan fragments.   [Including
a chapter on Ralph Crane and The
Winter's Tale.]   (New York)
facsimiles.   1933.

411561

THOMAS (Sir D. LLEUFER)
Welshmen and the First Folio of
Shakespeare's plays (1623).   IN
Transactions of the Honourable Society
of Cymmrodorion, 1940.   1941.

530241

TODD (WILLIAM B.)
The Issues and states of the Second
Folio and Milton's epitaph on
Shakespeare.   IN Studies in Biblio-
graphy, Vol. 5.   (Charlottesville,
Va.)   1952.

598680/5

WALKER (ALICE)
Textual problems of the First Folio:
Richard III, King Lear, Troilus &
Cressida, 2 Henry IV, Hamlet, Othello.
(Cambridge)
bibliog.   1953.
Shakespeare Problems, 7.
633690

— WALTON (J. K.)
The Copy for the folio text of
Richard III with a note on the copy
for the folio text of King Lear.
(Auckland)
   tables. bibliogs.   1955.
Auckland University College,
Monograph Series, No. 1.
                 665102

— WILLOUGHBY (E. E.)
A Printer of Shakespeare: the books
and times of William Jaggard.
   ports. facsimiles.   1934.

                 426107

— WILLOUGHBY (E. E.)
The Printing of the First Folio of
Shakespeare. pp. 70.   1932.
   facsimiles.
Bibliographical Society's Transactions.
Supplement No. 8.
                 399490

Textual History: Printing – Publishing – Editing

– Restoration and 18th century Editions

— ALDEN (RAYMOND MACDONALD)
The 1710 and 1714 texts of Shakespeare's
poems. IN Modern Language Notes, Vol.
31. (Baltimore, Md.)
                      1916.

          439157/31

— BARCLAY (JAMES)
An Examination of Mr. Kenrick's review
of Mr. Johnson's edition of
Shakespeare. pp. 92.   1766.

                 113485

— BEAVER (A.)
Boydell's Shakespeare. FROM The
Magazine of Art [, Vol. 9]. [1886.]

                 564842

— BOWDLER (T.)
A Letter to the editor of the British
Critic; occasioned by the censure
pronounced in that work on [the
editions of Shakespeare by] "Johnson,
Pope, Bowdler, Warburton, Theobald,
Steevens, Reed, Malone, etc." [in
the] British Critic, April, 1822.
pp. 40.   1823.

                 537988

— BUTT (J.)
Pope's taste in Shakespeare: a paper
read before the Shakespeare
Association, March 22nd, 1935.
pp. 21.   (The Shakespeare Association)
                   1936.

                 456087

— CARTER (ELIZABETH)
On Johnson's Shakspeare [: a letter]
to Mrs. Montagu, 1766. IN PENNINGTON
(M.) Memoirs of the life of Mrs.
Elizabeth Carter.
   port.   1807.

          568218

— Catalogue of the first four folio
editions of Shakespeare with Roger
Payne's bill for binding the First
Folio, from the library of H. B. H.
Beaufoy, sold by order of the
Beaufoy Trustees, July, 1912.
pp. 7.
   illus.   [1912.]

          426551

— CHAPMAN (R. W.)
Cancels. [With a note on a cancel in
Henry V in Johnson's Shakespeare, 1765.]
(Bibliographia [No. 3.])
               1930.

           372502

— CROSSE (G.)
Charles Jennens as editor of
Shakespeare. IN The Library, Vol.
16.   (Oxford)   1936.

          454474

— DAWSON (GILES EDWIN)

Robert Walker's editions of Shakespeare.
FROM Studies in English Renaissance
Drama. [? New York]   [c.1958.]

          667866

— DAWSON (G. E.)
Three Shakespearian piracies, 1723-
1729. IN Virginia University
Bibliographical Society Papers, Vol. 1.
(Charlottesville, Va.)
   bibliog. facsimiles.   1948.

          598680/1

— DAWSON (G. E.)
Warburton, Hanmer and the 1745 edition
of Shakespeare. IN Virginia University
Bibliographical Society, Studies in
Bibliography, Vol. 2. (Charlottesville,
Va.)   1949.

          598680/2

— DIXON, P.
Pope's Shakespeare. FROM Journal of
English and Germanic Philology, LXIII:2,
April, 1964. pp.191-203.   1964.

          668350

— DOBELL (P. J. & A. E.)
A Catalogue of a remarkable collection
of publisher's agreements [etc.]
including the agreements made by
A. Pope, W. Warburton and I. Reed for
the publication of their respective
editions of Shakespeare. No. 66,
1941. pp. 12.   (Tunbridge Wells)
                 1941.

          528685

— EASTMAN (ARTHUR M.)
In defense of Dr. Johnson.
IN SHAKESPEARE QUARTERLY VIII.
pp. 493-500.   (New York)   1957.

605711

— EASTMAN (ARTHUR M.)
Johnson's Shakespeare and the laity:
a textual study.   IN PMLA:
Publications of the Modern Language
Association of America.   Vol. 65.
(New York)   1950.

428321/65

— EASTMAN (A. M.)
Johnson's Shakespearean labors in 1765.
IN Modern Language Notes, Vol. 63.
(Baltimore, Md.)
bibliog.   1948.

439157/63

— The Emphasis capitals of Shakspere
[: a review of] "The Tragedy of
Hamlet (Hamnet Edition) according to
the First Folio (spelling modernized)
with further remarks on the emphasis
capitals of Shakspere", by A. P. Paton.
FROM The Theatre, Feb. 1st, 1879.

530818

— EVANS (A. W.)
Warburton and the Warburtonians: a
study in some eighteenth-century
controversies.   [With references to
Warburton's edition of Shakespeare.]
bibliog.   port.   1932.

393202

— EVANS, GWYNNE BLAKEMORE
The Douai Manuscript - six
Shakespearean transcripts (1694-95).
FROM Philological Quarterly, Vol.XLI,
No.1.   1962.

668387

— EVANS (G. B.)
The Text of Johnson's Shakespeare
(1765).   IN Philological Quarterly,
Vol. 28.   (Iowa: University of
Iowa)   1949.

592684/28

— EWENS (ERIC)
Conversations with Dr. Johnson: No. 6.
On Shakespeare.   [B.B.C. Radio
script of programme transmitted in
Home Service, 18th October 1959.]
pp. 7.
typescript.

666444

— [FELTON (S.)]
Imperfect hints towards a new edition
of Shakespeare, written chiefly in
the year 1782.
2 vols.   1787-88.

538171

— FORD (H. L.)
Shakespeare, 1700-1740: a collation
of the editions and separate plays,
with some account of T. Johnson and
R. Walker.   (Oxford)   1935.
_____ Another copy.
This copy contains a list of addenda
and corrigenda issued after printing.
442298-9

— GREY (ZACHARY)
An Answer to certain passages in
Mr. W[arburton]'s preface to his
edition of Shakespeare, together
with some remarks on the many errors
and false criticisms in the work
itself.   [Anon.]   pp. 19.   1748.

621023

— Griffith (R.H.) Alexander Pope: a
bibliography. [With references to
his editions of Shakespeare, etc.,
and a list of bibliographical aids.]

(Austin)   1922
[University of Texas, Studies in English]

542224

— HART (C. W.)
Dr. Johnson's 1745 Shakespeare
"Proposals".   IN Modern Language
Notes, Vol. 53.   (Baltimore)   1938.

493024

— HOGAN (J. J.)
The Bicentenary of Edmond Malone,
1741-1812.   FROM Studies: an
Irish quarterly review, Vol. 30.
(Dublin)   1941.

541155

— JOHNSON (SAMUEL)
Notes to Shakespeare.   Edited, with
an introduction, by A. Sherbo.
(Los Angeles: William Andrews Clark
Memorial Library)
3 vols.   1956-58.
Augustan Reprint Society Publications,
Nos. 59-60, 65-66, 71-73.
666070

— JOHNSON (SAMUEL)
Preface to Shakespeare

For editions of this work check
the main sequence under the author's
name.

— JOHNSON (SAMUEL)
Proposals for printing the Dramatick
Works of William Shakespeare

For editions of this work check the main
sequence under the author's name.

— LANDRY (HILTON)
Malone as editor of Shakespeare's
sonnets.   IN Bulletin of the New
York Public Library, Vol. 67, No. 7.
(New York)   1963.

136894/67

— M. [pseud.]
Sketch of the life, and brief observa-
tions on the Shakespeare of the late
G. Steevens, Esq. &c.   FROM The
European Magazine, Vol. 61.
frontis.   [1812.]

564837

MacDONALD (WILBERT LORNE)
Pope and his critics: a study in
eighteenth century personalities.
ports. illus. bibliog. 1951.

615972

McKERROW (RONALD BRUNLEES)
The Treatment of Shakespeare's text
by his earlier editors, 1709-1768.
pp. 35.   [1933.]   408968
 British Academy Annual Shakespeare
Lecture, 1933.
_____ IN ALEXANDER (P.) ed., Studies
in Shakespeare: British Academy
Lecutres.   1964.   667830

[MALLET (D.)]
An Epistle to Mr. Pope, occasioned
by Theobald's Shakespear and
Bentley's Milton [: a poem.]   2nd
edn. pp. [ii], 14.   1733.
First edn. entitled "Of verbal criticism."

179160

[MALLET (D.)]
Of verbal criticism: an epistle to
Mr. Pope occasioned by Theobald's
Shakespear, and Bentley's Milton [:
a poem.]   pp. 14.   1733.   482783
 The 2nd edn. was entitled An Epistle
to Mr. Pope, etc.
_____ IN Mallet (D.) Works, New edn.
Vol. 1.   1759.   157118

MARROT (H. V.)
William Bulmer; Thomas Bensley:
a study in transition. [With
Shakespearian references.]   pp. 80.
 ports. illus. bibliog. facsimiles.
                                   1930.
Edn. limited to 200 copies.

498932

MASON (J. M.)
Comments on the plays of Beaumont
and Fletcher. With an appendix
containing some further observations
on Shakespeare, extended to the late
editions of [E.] Malone and [G.]
Steevens.
 ports.   1797.

519725

MONAGHAN (T. J.)
Johnson's additions to his "Shakespeare"
for the edition of 1773.   IN The
Review of English Studies, New Series,
Vol. 4.   (Oxford)   1953.

318239/N.S./4

MORISON (S.)
John Bell, 1745-1831, bookseller,
printer, publisher, typefounder,
journalist, &c.   [With references
to the printing and publishing of
Shakespeare's works.]   (Cambridge)
 ports. illus. facsimiles. 1930.
Printed for the author.

600906

PAUL (H. N.)
Mr. Hughs' edition of Hamlet.
IN Modern Language Notes, November,
1934. pp. 438-443.   (Baltimore)
                                   1934.

428652

PHILBRICK (N.)
Act and scene division in the first
edition of Shakespeare [1709].
IN The Theatre annual, 1944.   (New
York: Theatre Library Association)
 illus. bibliog.   1945.

563989

[Pinkerton (J.)] Remarks on the last
edition of Shakspere's Plays.   In
[Pinkerton (J.)] Letters of literature,
by R.Heron [pseud.]

1785.

78937

[Review of] The Plays of William
Shakspeare with the corrections and
illustrations of various commentators,
to which are added notes by S. Johnson
and G. Steevens.   2nd edn. revised
and augmented [by I. Reed, 1778].
IN The Monthly Review, Vol. 62.
                                   1780.

1462

[Review of] The Plays of William
Shakespeare, [with] notes by S. Johnson
and G. Steevens.   3rd edn. revised
and augmented by [I. Reed,] 1785.
IN The Monthly Review, Vol. 75.   1786.

1478

[Review of] The Plays of William
Shakespeare, in 15 volumes, with the
corrections and illustrations of
various commentators.   To which are
added notes, by S. Johnson and
G. Steevens.   The 4th edn.   Revised
and augmented; with a glossarial
index by the editor of Dodsley's
Collection of old plays [i.e. I. Reed,
1793.]   IN The British Critic, Vol.1.
                                   1793.

22191

[Review of] The Plays of William
Shakespeare, in eight volumes, with
the corrections and illustrations of
various commentators; to which are
added notes by S. Johnson.   FROM
[The] Annual Register [for the year]
1765.   [3rd edn.]   [1802.]

561329

[RITSON (J.)]
Cursory criticisms on the edition of
Shakespeare published by Malone.
                   1792.   2505
_____ IN Monthly extracts; or,
Beauties of modern authors, Vol. 3.
                   1792.   520594

SCHOLES (ROBERT E.)
Dr. Johnson and the bibliographical
criticism of Shakespeare.
IN SHAKESPEARE QUARTERLY XI.
pp. 163-171.   (New York)   1960.

605711

SEN (SAILENDRA KUMAR)
Capell and Malone, and modern critical
bibliography.   Introduction by
A. Nicoll.   (Calcutta)   1960.

667618

— SEN (SAILENDRA KUMAR)
"The Noblest Roman of them all":
Malone and Shakespearian scholarship.
IN Shakespeare commemoration volume,
edited by Taraknath Sen.   (Calcutta)
1966.

764382

— Shakespeare's Plays, as they are now
performed at the Theatre Royal in
London [: a review of Bell's edition
of Shakespeare's plays.]   IN The
Monthly Review; or, Literary Journal,
Dec. 1773–July 1774, Vol. 50.

482038

— SHERBO (ARTHUR)
Dr. Johnson's "Dictionary" and
Warburton's "Shakespeare".   IN
Philological Quarterly, Vol. 33.
(Iowa)   1954.

592684/33

— SHERBO (ARTHUR)
The Proof-sheets of Dr. Johnson's
preface to Shakespeare.   IN
Bulletin of the John Rylands Library,
Vol. 35, pp. 206–210.   (Manchester)
1952.

182129/35

— SHERBO (ARTHUR)
Samuel Johnson, editor of Shakespeare.
With an essay on "The Adventurer".
(Urbana, Ill.)
tables. bibliog.   1956.
Illinois Studies in Language and
Literature, Vol. 42.

665393

— SHERBO (ARTHUR)
Warburton and the 1745 Shakespeare.
IN The Journal of English and Germanic
Philology, Vol. 51.   (Urbana, Ill.)
1952.

600780/51

— STEVENS (G. A.)
Distress upon distress; or, Tragedy in
true taste: a heroi-comi-parodi-tragedi-
farcical burlesque in two acts.   With
annotations [etc.] by Sir Henry Humm
[i.e. G. A. Stevens] and notes by
Paulus Purgantius Pedasculus [i.e.
G. A. Stevens.   A satire on Sir T.
Hanmer's and W. Warburton's editions of
Shakespeare.]   1752.

481297

— Struble (Mildred C.) A Johnson
handbook. [With references to
Shakespeare and a bibliography.]
Ports. Illus. Facsimile.   1933.

405681

— SUMMERS ([A. J. M. A.] M.)
A Bibliography of the Restoration
drama.   (Fortune Press)   [1935].
Edn. limited to 250 copies.

436088

— SUMMERS ([A. J. M. A.] M.)
The First illustrated Shakespeare:
[Rowe's edition of 1709.]   FROM
The Connoisseur, December, 1938.
pp. [5.]
illus.

494121

— TIMPERLEY (CHARLES HENRY)
William Bulmer and the Shakespeare Press:
a biography from "A Dictionary of printers
and printing" by C.H. Timperley. With an
introductory note on the Bulmer-Martin
types, by L.B. Siegfried. Wood engravings
by J. De Pol. Published in observance of
the bicentennial of the birth of William
Bulmer, 1757-1957. pp.[iv],34[2]. Port.
(Syracuse)   1957.

666492

— WAGENKNECHT (E.)
The First editor of Shakespeare [:
N. Rowe.]   IN The Colophon, Part 8.
illus.   1931.

396607

— WALKER (ALICE)

Edward Capell and his edition of
Shakespeare.   Annual Shakespeare
Lecture of the British Academy, 1960)
pp.[15.]   [1960.]

666879

— WILLOUGHBY (EDWIN ELIOTT)
A Deadly edition of Shakespeare.
IN SHAKESPEARE QUARTERLY V.
pp. 351-357.
(New York)   1954.

605711

— WILSON (J. D.)
Malone and the upstart crow.
IN SHAKESPEARE SURVEY 4.   (Cambridge)
1951.

615854

— Winterich (J.T.) Early American books
& printing. [With reference to the
first American edition of Shakespeare]
Illus. Facsimiles.

(Boston)   1935.

490472

Textual History: Printing – Publishing – Editing

– 19th century Editions
see also **Collier**, John Payne *works relating to*

—— "Atlantic Monthly". Mr. White on
Shakespeare [: review of Comedies,
Histories, Tragedies, and Poems.
Edited by R. G. White, 1883].
1883.

62655

—— [BOWDLER (T.) the younger]
Memoir of the late John Bowdler,
Esq., to which is added some account
of the late Thomas Bowdler, editor of
the Family Shakespeare. 1825.

595374

—— BRITISH QUARTERLY REVIEW, Vol. 39
The Works of William Shakespeare,
edited by W. G. Clarke [sic] and
W. A. Wright [: a review]. 1864.

41920

—— Clapp (H.A.) Dr. Furness's Variorum
Edition of Shakespeare. In The
Atlantic Monthly, Vol.86.

(Boston) 1900.

155241

—— Distortions of the English stage:
"Macbeth" [: review of] The Works
of William Shakespeare, edited by
W. G. Clark and J. Glover, 1863.
IN The National Review, Vol. 17.
1863.

41327

—— EDINBURGH REVIEW, Vol. 136
The First collected edition of the
dramatic works of William Shakespeare.
A reproduction in exact fac-simile
of the famous First Folio, 1623, by
the newly-discovered process of photo-
lithography. Under the superintend-
ence of H. Staunton. London: 1866
[: a review]. 1872.

39006

—— F. (A. I.)
Some recent helps in the study of
Shakespeare [: a review of] 3.
The Cambridge Shakespeare, Vol. 9.
Poems, etc. FROM The Penn Monthly,
Vol. 5. (Philadelphia) 1874.

555525

—— F. (G.)
Macbeth [: Shakespearian criticism
and acting. Review of] Knight's
Cabinet Edition of Shakspere.
No. 30. IN The Westminster Review,
Vol. 41.
[1844.]

78550

—— HALL (S.)
A Letter to John Murray, Esq., upon
an aesthetic-edition of the works
of Shakespeare. pp. 37. 1841.
An autograph letter from the author
inserted in this copy.

426550

—— Harris (E.B.) The "Globe" edition
of Shakespeare: statistics
[relating to the plays and poems].
Manuscript.

1888.

531795

—— H[ENLEY] (W. E.)
The New "Romeo and Juliet" [: review
of Edition de Luxe. With Introduction by E. Dowden and illustrations
by Sir F. B. Dicksee. 1884.]
IN The Magazine of Art, Vol. 8.
1885.

78974

—— HOWARD (F.)
Drawings prepared for "The Spirit of
the plays of Shakespeare". With the
plates and references descriptive of
the plates for the large paper edition
of Hamlet and Richard II. [1827-33.]

436162

—— KITCHIN (LAURENCE)
Three on trial: an experiment in
biography. [Three plays: The Trial
of Lord Byron; The Trial of Dr.
Bowdler; and, The Trial of Machiavelli.]
With line drawings by A. Horner.
1959.

685314

—— KITCHIN (LAURENCE)
The Trial of Dr. Bowdler [: a play
relating to Bowdler's edition of
Shakespeare]. Produced by
D. Cleverdon. [Broadcast] 5th July,
1954. pp. 61.
typescript.

643708

—— KLEIN (D.)
The Case of Forman's Bocke of Plaies
[: an assertion that the notes on
Winter's tale, Cymbeline and Macbeth
were added by J. P. Collier].
Reprinted for private circulation,
from Philological Quarterly, Vol. 11.
[Iowa] [1932.]

554208

—— KNIGHT (C.)
Postscript to the sixth volume of the
pictorial edition of the works of
Shakspere; detailing the plan for the
completion of that publication, and
announcing a new library edition,
edited by C. Knight. pp. 16.
[1841.]

554722

—— M. [pseud.]
Sketch of the life, and brief observa-
tions on the Shakspeare of the late
G. Steevens, Esq. &c.   frontis.
FROM The European Magazine, Vol. 61.
[1812.]

564837

—— MORGAN (C. [L.])
The House of Macmillan (1843-1943).
[Containing references to the
'Cambridge' and 'Globe' editions of
Shakespeare.]
bibliog.   1943.

545449

—— MORLEY (H.)
The Plays of Shakespeare [: preface,
etc. to the Cassell's National
Library edition].   pp. xxxii.
1890.

Cassell's National Library.

527799

—— NEILSON (W. A.)
The Variorum Twelfth Night, [by
H. H. Furness.   A review].   IN The
Atlantic Monthly, Vol. 89.   (Cambridge,
Mass.)   1902.

170922

—— New editors - Shakespeare [: a review
of] The Works of William Shakespeare,
edited by W. G. Clark, J. Glover and
W. A. Wright.   FROM [Dublin
University Magazine,] Vol. 63.
[Dublin]   1864.

558056

—— Reasons for a new edition of
Shakspeare['s works, by J. P. Collier:
a review].   FROM [Monthly Prize
Essays, Vol. 1.]   [1846.]

560928

—— Recent Shakespearian literature
[: criticism of books published
between 1823 and 1840].   FROM The
Edinburgh Review, July, 1840.
[Edinburgh]

440301

—— REDDING (C.)
The Fac-simile Shakspeare [: on
Booth's 1862-64 reprint of the
Jaggard folio].   FROM [The New
Monthly Magazine, Vol. 133.] [1865.]

558106

—— [Review of] The Dramatic works of
W. Shakspeare, ornamented with
plates, printed for Messrs. Boydell
and G. Nicol [1802-3].   IN Review
of publications of art, Vol. 1.
1808.

524798

—— [Review of] The Dramatic works of
William Shakespeare, with notes
original and selected, by S. W. Singer;
and a Life of the poet, by C. Symmons.
FROM The Gentleman's Magazine, April
1826.   pp. [4].

402693

—— [Review of] The Works of William
Shakespeare, edited from the Folio
of 1623, by R. G. White, 1858.
IN North American Review.   1859.

41818

—— ROSENBERG (MARVIN)
Reputation, oft lost without deserving...
[Bowdler's Family Shakespeare.]
IN SHAKESPEARE QUARTERLY IX.   pp. 499-
506.   (New York)   1958.

605711

—— RUEFF (A. M.)
The Life and activities of Mr.
Thomas Bowdler.   [FROM Life and
Letters To-day, Spring, 1938.]

488919

—— RUSSELL (BERTRAND ARTHUR WILLIAM RUSSELL,
3rd Earl)
Mr. Bowdler's nightmare: family bliss.
IN Nightmares of eminent persons and
other stories.   Illustrated by
C. W. Stewart.   1954.

649737

—— SHAABER (M. A.)
The Furness Variorum Shakespeare.
IN Proceedings of the American Philo-
sophical Society, Vol. 75.
(Philadelphia)   1935.

450515

—— Shakespearian literature [: a review
of] The Plays of Shakspeare, edited
by H. Staunton, illustrations by
[Sir] J. Gilbert.   FROM [Bentley's
Quarterly Review,] Vol. 2.   [1860.]

558054

—— SPENCER (T.)
Editions of Shakespeare.   FROM The
New Republic, January 10, 1944.
(New York)

559547

—— TANNENBAUM (S. A.)
Shakspere studies.   2. An Object
lesson in Shaksperian research [:
the Collier forgery in the manuscript
of Sir Thomas More.   A reply to
W. W. Greg.]   pp. 23.   (New York)
facsimile.   1931.
Limited edn.: 250 copies.   Signed by
the author.

413467

—— TANNENBAUM (S. A.)
Textual errors in the Furness Variorum.
IN Modern Language Notes, Vol. 45,
1930.   (Baltimore)

439157

—— Text of Shakspere's plays [: a
review of] "Notes and emendations
to the text of Shakespeare's plays",
[etc.   Edited by J. P. Collier].
FROM The Gentleman's Magazine,
April 1853.

402706

—— WATTS (P.)
    Hush, there are ladies present!
    [: a radio portrait of Dr. Thomas
    Bowdler, with references to his
    expurgated edition of Shakespeare,
    broadcast] 1st June, 1945. ff. 36.
    typescript.

                                        561271

—— WATTS-DUNTON (T.)
    Note on the typographical features
    of this edition. IN SHAKESPEARE (W.)
    Comedies, tragedies, histories and
    poems. With a general introduction
    by A. C. Swinburne, introductory
    studies of the plays and poems, by
    E. Dowden, and glossaries. (Oxford)
    3 vols.   [1936]
    [Oxford Edition]

                                        449468

—— WHITE (R. G.)
    [Review of] King Lear: A New Variorum
    Edition of Shakespeare, edited by
    H. H. Furness. Vol. 5.   IN The
    Atlantic Monthly, Vols. 45 and 46.
    (Boston, [Mass.])   2 vols.   1880.

                                        19626

—— WISE (T. J.)
    Letters to John Henry Wrenn: a
    further inquiry into the guilt of
    certain nineteenth-century forgers.
    Edited [with a foreword] by Fannie
    E. Ratchford.   [With references to
    rare Shakespeare editions.]   (New
    York)
        ports.   illus.   facsimiles.
                                        1944.

                                        561530

—— WRIGHT (C.)
    Shakespeare: reprint of the first
    collected edition of the plays,
    and the "Athenaeum" of Jan. 25th,
    1862 [: a letter to the editor of
    the "Athenaeum" in answer to criticisms].
    pp. 3.   1862.

                                        535361

Textual History: Printing — Publishing — Editing

— 20th century Editions

—— BENNETT (J. O'D.)
    Much loved books: best sellers of
    the ages. [Including, "Shakespeare's
    Hamlet, and adventures in the Furness
    Variorum"; "Shakespeare's King
    Richard III".]   1928.
    bibliog.

                                        412432

—— BOWERS (FREDSON THAYER)
    McKerrow's editorial principles for
    Shakespeare reconsidered.
    IN SHAKESPEARE QUARTERLY VI.
    pp. 309-324.
    (New York) 1955.

                                        605711

—— CAMPBELL (O. J.)
    [Review of] The Tragedy of King Richard
    III, edited by H. Spencer. IN Modern
    Language Notes, December, 1934.
    (Baltimore)

                                        428652

—— Clark (A.M.) [Review of] "A New
    Variorum Edition of Shakespeare.
    Henry the Fourth, Part I; edited
    by S.B.Hemingway. 1936". In The
    Modern Language Review, Vol.33.

                                        1938.

                                        492625

—— CLUBB (M. D.)
    [Review of] "Shakespeare's Sonnets;
    edited by T. Brooke. 1936." IN
    Modern Language Notes, Vol. 53.
    (Baltimore)   1938.

                                        493024

—— CRUTTWELL (MAURICE JAMES PATRICK)
    Another part of the wood.   [Review
    of the Arden edition of the works
    of Shakespeare, new revised edn.]
    IN Essays in Criticism, Vol. 5.
    (Oxford)   1955.

                                        621866/5

—— DECKNER (ELISE)
    [Review of] The Sonnets of Shakespeare
    and Southampton, edited by W. Thomson.
    IN Beiblatt zur Anglia [Bd.] 53.
    (Halle)   1942.

                                        576459

—— Dent (J.M.) The House of Dent, 1888-1938
    [: the memoirs of J.M.Dent, 1849-1926;
    with a preface and additional chapters
    covering activities 1920-1938, by
    H.R.Dent.] Ports. Illus. Dgms.

                                        1938.

                                        490488

—— DODDS (W. M. T.)
    [Review of] King Henry V, edited by
    J. D. Wilson.   IN The Modern Language
    Review, Vol. 42.   (Cambridge)
                                        1947.

                                        266816/42

—— DUTHIE (G. I.)
    [Review of] The Merry devil of Edmonton,
    Edited by W. A. Abrams.   IN The Modern
    Language Review, Vol. 39.   (Cambridge)
                                        1944.

                                        563897

—— FARJEON (H.)
    The Text of the new Shakespeare
    [: the Limited Editions Club edition].
    IN Shakespeare: a review and a
    preview [by various authors].
    pp. [37.]   (New York)
        illus.   [c.1939.]

                                        564974

—FRICKER (ROBERT)
The New Shakespeare: "Henry VI" edited
by J. D. Wilson [: review].   IN
English Studies, Vol. 37.   (Amsterdam)
1956.

485643/37

—GREG (W. W.)
The Merry devil of Edmonton [: review
of] The Merry devil of Edmonton, 1608,
edited by W. A. Abrams.   IN The Library,
4th series, vol. 25.   (Oxford) 1945.

561404

—GREG (W. W.)
Review [of] The Works of Shakespeare,
edited for the Syndics of the
Cambridge University Press by Sir A.
[T.] Quiller-Couch and J. D. Wilson.
Vol. 1. The Tempest.   Reprinted from
the Modern Language Review. Vol. 17.
[1922.]

554224

—GREG (Sir WALTER WILSON)
[Review of] Venus and Adonis, 1593;
Lucrece, 1594; The Passionate pilgrim,
1599; Shakespeare's sonnets, 1609;
Pericles, 1609; reproduced in facsimile
from the earliest editions, with intro-
ductions by [Sir] S. Lee.   IN The
Library, New Series, Vol. 7.   1906.

198827

—GREG (W. W.)
Ronald Brunlees McKerrow, 1872-1940
[: an obituary notice.   With references to Shakespeare].   IN Proceedings
of the British Academy, 1940.
port.   [1941.]

538764

—GROOT (H. de)
Review [of] As you like it (Works of
Shakespeare, edited for the Syndics
of the Cambridge University Press,
by Sir A. [T.] Quiller-Couch and
J. D. Wilson.)   IN English studies,
Vol. 10.   (Amsterdam)   1928.

485652

—GROOT (H. de)
[Review of] The Tragedy of Hamlet:
a critical edition of the second
quarto, 1604, [edited] by T. M.
Parrott and H. Craig.   IN English
Studies, Vol. 23.   (Amsterdam) 1941.

575607

—HART (A.)
Acting versions of Elizabethan plays
[including plays of Shakespeare.]
IN Review of English Studies,
January, 1934.   pp. 1-28.

428644

—HOLSTEIN (M. G.)
Landmarks in the publishing of
Shakespeare.   IN Shakespeare: a
review and a preview [by various
authors].   pp. [37.]   (New York)
illus.   [c.1939.]
Limited Editions Club.

564974

—KOOISTRA (J.)
[Review of] The Merchant of Venice,
edited by Sir A. [T.] Quiller-Couch
and J. D. Wilson.   IN English
studies, Vol. 8.   (Amsterdam)
1926.
The New Cambridge Shakespeare.

485650

—KRANENDONK (A. G. van)
[Review of] The Works of Shakespeare,
edited for the Syndics of the
Cambridge University Press, by
Sir A. [T.] Quiller-Couch and J. D.
Wilson.   IN English Studies, Vol. 4.
(Amsterdam)   1922.

485646

—LAW (R. A.)
[Review of] Shakespeare ['s] The Life of
King Henry the Fifth, edited by
G. L. Kittredge.   IN Modern Language
Notes, Vol. 61.   (Baltimore, Md.)
1946.

579125

—LAWRENCE (W. J.)
[Reviews of] The Sonnets of Shakespeare
and Southampton, [edited] by W. Thomson;
and Shakespeare discovered, by
[Comtesse] Clara L. de Chambrun.
IN The Spectator, Vol. 160.   1938.

487969

—LEISHMAN (J. B.)
(Review of) Henry IV, Parts 1 and 2,
edited by J. D. Wilson.   IN The Review
of English Studies, Vol. 23.   (Oxford)
1947.

317239/23

—LEISHMAN (J. B.)
[Review of] The Merry devil of Edmonton,
1608.   Edited by W. A. Abrams.
IN The Review of English Studies, Vol.
20.   (Oxford)   [1944.]

562839

—LEISHMAN (J. B.)
[Review of] The Phoenix and turtle,
by W. Shakespeare and others.   1937.
IN The Review of English Studies,
Vol. 14.   1938.

495115

—LOUBIER (H.)
Die Neue Deutsche Buchkunst [including
examples of the fine printing of
Shakespeare's works].   (Stuttgart)
illus.   facsimiles.   1921.

571428

—LÜDEKE (H.)
[Review of] Shakespeare's sonnets,
edited by T. Brooke.   IN English
Studies, Vol. 22.   (Amsterdam)
1940.

575606

—McKERROW (R. B.)
Prolegomena for the Oxford Shakespeare:
a study in editorial method.
(Oxford)
1939.

498883

— McKerrow (R.B.) [Review of] "A New
Variorum Edition of Shakespeare.
Henry the Fourth, Part I. Edited
by S.B.Hemingway. 1936". In
Modern Language Notes, Vol.53.

(Baltimore) 1938.

493024

— McK[ERROW] (R. B.)
[Review of] Shakespeare's Titus
Andronicus: the First Quarto, 1594.
Reproduced in facsimile, with an
introduction by J. Q. Adams. 1936.
IN The Review of English Studies,
Vol. 14. 1938.

495115

— McMANAWAY (JAMES GILMER)
[Review of] The Complete plays and
poems of William Shakespeare. The
New Cambridge Edition. Edited by
W. A. Neilson and C. J. Hill.
IN Modern Language Notes, Vol. 58.
(Baltimore) 1943.

553688

— MACY (G.)
A Note upon a new Shakespeare [:
the Limited Editions Club edition].
IN Shakespeare: a review and a
preview [by various authors].
pp. [37.] (New York: Limited
Editions Club)
illus. [c.1939.]

564974

— MUIR (KENNETH)
Shakespeare texts for school
libraries. IN The School Library
Review, Vol. 3. (Sharnbrook)
1944.

560962

— MURRY (J. M.)
Professors and poets [: a study
of professors as critics and editors
of Shakespeare, with special reference to The New Temple Shakespeare,
edited by M. R. Ridley]. FROM The
Aryan path, Vol. 6. (Bombay) 1935.

484131

— NEILSON (W. A.)
The Variorum Twelfth Night, [by
H. H. Furness. A review].
IN The Atlantic Monthly, Vol. 89.
(Cambridge, Mass.) 1902.

170922

— NICOLL (ALLARDYCE)
A New Shakespeare [: Collins edition
of the complete works edited by
P. Alexander]. Broadcast 4th July,
1951. ff. 7.
typescript. 1951.

617919

— PARROTT (THOMAS MARC)
[Review of] The Tempest. Edited by
F. Kermode. (Arden Shakespeare) 5th
edn. IN The Journal of English and
Germanic Philology, Vol. 55.
(Urbana, Ill.) 1956.

600780/55

— POLLARD (A. W.)
[Review of] William Shakespeare. The
Tragedie of Hamlet, Prince of Denmarke.
Edited by J. D. Wilson. IN The
Library, 4th series, vol. 12. 1932.

393825

— POLLARD (A. W.)
[Review of] The Works of Shakespeare.
Edited for the Syndics of the
Cambridge University Press by Sir A.
[T.] Quiller-Couch and J. D. Wilson.
[Vol. 1.] The Tempest. IN The
Library, 4th series, Vol. 2. 1922.

298823

— POLLARD (A. W.) [and others]
'Facsimile' reprints of old books,
by A. W. Pollard, G. R. Redgrave,
R. W. Chapman [and] W. W. Greg.
[With references to Shakespeare
reprints.] IN The Library, Vol. 6.
1926.

329554

— REEVE (F. A.)
Shakespeare as a "best seller" in
France [: a review of three new
editions.] IN The Publishers'
circular and booksellers' record,
Vol. 150. 1939.

503477

— ROGERS (B.)
The Format of the new Shakespeare [:
the Limited Editions Club edition].
IN Shakespeare: a review and a
preview [by various authors].
pp. [37.] (New York: Limited
Editions Club)
illus. [c.1939.]

564974

— Shakespeare: a review and a preview
[by various authors. Including
chapters on and a prospectus of the
Limited Editions Club edition of
Shakespeare]. pp. [37.] (New
York: Limited Editions Club)
illus. [c.1939.]

564974

— SHAKESPEARE HEAD PRESS
[Prospectus of] The Works of
William Shakespeare, gathered into
one volume, pp. [4.] (Oxford)
1934.

421991

— STERN (P. Van D.)
... And William Shakespeare. IN
Ten years and William Shakespeare:
a survey of the publishing activities
of The Limited Editions Club from
Oct. 1929 to Oct. 1940 [by various
authors]. pp. 82. ([New York]:
Limited Editions Club)
port. illus. 1940.

528141

— STRATHMANN (E. A.)
[Review of] The Passionate Pilgrim,
by William Shakespeare.   The third
edn., 1612, reproduced in facsimile
from the copy in the Folger Shakespeare
Library.   IN Modern Language Quarterly,
Vol. 2.   (Seattle)   1941.

533242

— TANNENBAUM (S. A.)
How not to edit Shakspere: a review
[of "The 'New' Cambridge Shakespeare",
edited by Sir A. Quiller-Couch and
J. D. Wilson.]   FROM Philological
Quarterly, vol. 10.   (Iowa)   1931.

442561

— Tannenbaum (S.A.) Shakspere studies, 4:
The New Cambridge Shakspere and The
Two Gentlemen of Verona. Reprinted,
with additions and corrections, from
the Shakespeare Association Bulletin.
pp. 68.

(New York)   1939.

Limited edn.: 200 copies.

515136

— THOMSON (ROSAMUND D.)
[Review of] Les Sonnets de Shakespeare,
traduits en vers français [par]
F. Baldensperger.   IN Books Abroad,
Vol. 18.   (Norman, Oka.)   1944.

561400

— WALKER (ALICE)
[Review of] Antony and Cleopatra,
edited by M. R. Ridley.   Based on
the edition of R. H. Case.   (Arden
Shakespeare)   IN Review of English
Studies, New Series, Vol. 6.   1955.

318239/2/6

— [Warde (Mrs. Beatrice L.)] Some
recent editions of Shakespeare's
works by P. Beaujon.   In Signature,
[Vol.3], No. 7.

1937.

503483

— WELLS, STANLEY
Shakespeare's text on the modern stage.
IN DEUTSCHE SHAKESPEARE-GESELLSCHAFT
WEST, JAHRBUCH 1967.   pp. 175-193.
(Heidelberg)

754129

— WILSON (F. P.)
[Review of] Prolegomena for the Oxford
Shakespeare: a study in editorial
method, by R. B. McKerrow.   IN The
Library, Fourth Series, Vol. 20.
1940.

519243

— Wilson (J.D.) Thirteen volumes of
Shakespeare ["The New Shakspeare"]:
a retrospect.   In The Modern Language
Review, vol.25.

(Cambridge)   1930.

379829

THALBERG (IRVING G.)
Romeo and Juliet: a motion picture
edition, produced for Metro-Goldwyn-
Mayer by I. G. Thalberg, directed
by G. Cukor [and] arranged for the
screen by T. Jennings.
illus.   [1936]   457925
Arthur Barker Edition.
_____   Random House Edition.
[1936]   460419

Thalberg, Irving G. *works relating to*

— [Metro-Goldwyn-Mayer. A Collection
of photographs relating to Irving
G. Thalberg's production of the film
"Romeo and Juliet" as presented by
Metro-Goldwyn-Mayer.]
[1936]

468715

— [Metro-Goldwyn-Mayer. English and
American publicity material relating
to Irving G. Thalberg's film production
of "Romeo and Juliet" as presented
by Metro-Goldwyn-Mayer].

[1936]

468716

THALER (ALWIN)
Delayed exposition in Shakespeare.
IN SHAKESPEARE QUARTERLY I: 3.
pp. 140-145.
(New York)   1950.
605711

THALER (ALWIN)
"The Devil's crest" in "Measure for
measure".   IN Studies in Philology,
Vol. 50.   (Chapel Hill, N.C.)   1953.
554520/50

Thaler (A.) Faire Em (and Shakspere's
company?) in Lancashire. In
Publications of the Modern Language
Association of America, vol.46.

(Menasha,Wis.)   1931.
428366

THALER (ALWIN)
The Gods and God in King Lear.
Reprinted from Renaissance Papers,
1955.   pp. 8.   [Knoxville, Tenn.]
bibliog.   1955.

666790

THALER (ALWIN)
"In my mind's eye, Horatio".
IN   SHAKESPEARE QUARTERLY VII.
pp. 351-354.
(New York)   1956.
605711

Thaler (A.) The "Lost scenes" of
Macbeth. In Publications of the
Modern Language Association of
America, vol.49.

(Menasha,Wis.)   .1934.

432218

THALER (ALWIN)
The Man who wrote Shakespeare.
IN Tennessee Studies in Literature,
[Vol. 1].   (Knoxville)   1956.

692773/1

THALER (A.)
Mercutio and Spenser's Phantastes.
FROM Philological Quarterly, Vol.
16.   (Iowa City)   1937.

507528

THALER (ALWIN)
[Review of] Repetition in Shakespeare's
plays, by P. V. Kreider.   FROM The
Journal of English and Germanic
Philology, Vol. 42.   (Urbana, Ill.)
1943.

568674

THALER (ALWIN)
Shakespeare and democracy [: Revalua-
tions, critical and historical;
"Country" plays and strolling players;
Poets, plays and actors.]   (Knoxville,
Tenn.)
bibliog.   1941.

531788

THALER (ALWIN)

Shakespeare and our world. Reprinted
from Tennessee Studies in Literature,
vol.2. pp.[16] (Knoxville Tenn.)
1957.

666789

THALER (A.)
Shakespeare and Sir Philip Sidney:
the influence of "The Defense of
Poesy".   (Cambridge, Mass.)
bibliog.   1947.

601357

THALER (ALWIN)
Shakspere and the unhappy happy
ending.   IN Publications of the
Modern Language Association of
America, Vol. 42.   (Menasha, Wis.)
1927.

428362

THALER (A.)
Shakspere, Daniel, and Everyman.
FROM Philological quarterly, Vol.
15.   (Iowa)
bibliog.   1935.

484068

Thaler (A.) Shakespeare on style,
imagination and poetry.   In PMLA,
Publications of the Modern Language
Association of America, Vol. 53.

1938.

499373

THALER (ALWIN)
The Shaksperian element in Milton.
IN Publications of the Modern Language
Association of America, Vol. 40.
(Menasha, Wis.)   1925.

428360

Thaler (A.) Spenser and "Much Ado about
Nothing". In Studies in Philology,
Vol.37.

(Chapel Hill, N.C.)   1940.

522312

Thaler (A.) The Travelling players in
Shakspere's England. [With bibliographical notes.] Reprinted for
private circulation from Modern
philology, Vol.17. pp. [26].

[Chicago]   1920.

523732

THALER, ALWIN, and SANDERS, NORMAN, eds.
Shakespearean essays.   1964.

Tennessee studies in literature,
special no: 2.   667977

Thaler, Alwin *works relating to*

— DUTHIE (G. I.)
[Review of] Shakespeare and democracy,
by A. Thaler.   IN The Review of
English Studies, Vol. 18.   (Oxford)
1942.

542539

— STIRLING (BRENTS)
[Review of] Shakespeare and democracy,
by A. Thaler.   IN Modern Language
Quarterly, Vol. 3.   (Seattle)   1942.

544203

Thames *see* London

THAYER (WILLIAM ROSCOE)
The Shakespeare hoax: a startling
prospectus.   pp. 20.   (Cambridge,
Mass.)   1888.

564970

Theatre [: annual review of dramatic
productions and publications, with
references to Shakespeare;   edited
by] Ivor Brown.
illus.   1955–

650967

Theatre book, 1905[-1909. MS.
notebook giving details of receipts
and expenses at the Stratford-on-
Avon Memorial Theatre during the
winter seasons Oct. 1905 to Sept.
1909]. pp. 62. [1905-1909.]

539400

Theatre Exhibition (British) see
British Theatre Exhibition

Theatre Guild, New York see New York

Theatre Incorporated, New York see
New York

Theatre notebook: a quarterly of
notes and research. Vol. 1, 1945.
illus.

584117

Theatre programme [: a radio review
of the stage by Shakespearian actors.
With references to Shakespeare's
plays. Broadcast] 9th October [1946].
pp. [38.]
typescript.

579576

Theatre programme [: a radio review
of the stage: Shakespearian items,
including an introductory sketch "The
Plain man's guide to Shakespeare",
by P. Watts; a discussion "How the
plain man can appreciate Shakespeare",
by I. J. C. Brown and W. Bridges-Adams;
and a talk on "Othello", by P. Powell.
Broadcast] 2nd April [1947]. ff. 34.
typescript.

583268

Theatre today, Nos. 1-[8].
ports. illus. plans. facsimiles.
1946-[9].
All published. No. 8 entitled Film
and Theatre Today.

606680

THEATRE TODAY: Rethinking Shakespeare.
Produced by G. Hughes. I.T.V. television
script broadcast 5th April 1965.

typescript. 744156

THEATRE WORLD, Vols. 41-61. Illus.
1945-65.

1. Vols. 1-40 wanting.
2. After Vol.61, No.491 incorporated
in Plays and Players and called
"Plays and Players & Theatre
World". Catal. no. 766347.

601552

Theatres *see* **Stage History and Production**
*and under names of theatres and places where
theatres are situated*

Theatres, Elizabethan *see* **Stage History and
Production**, Elizabethan and Jacobean
Theatre

The Theatrical inquisitor and Monthly
mirror. Vols. 5, 8, 9, 11, 12.
[With references to Shakespearian
performances.]
5 vols. illus. 1814-1818.
Vols. 1-4, 6-7, 10, 13 to 16 and
N.S. Vol. 1 wanting.

485740

Theatrical observer and daily bills
of the play, No. 148, May 7, 1822-
No. 774, May 25, 1824.
3 vols. 1822-24.
Various numbers of 1822-24 and all
others wanting.

414174

Theatrical reform: the "Merchant of
Venice" at the Lyceum. In Blackwood's
Edinburgh Magazine, Vol.126, 1879.

(Edinburgh)

19628

Theatrical register, The, and general
amusement guide, No.4, Oct.22,1838.
[Including Shakespearian perform-
ances] pp.23-32.

1838.

453719

The Theatrical "World", 1893-1897,
by W. Archer. [With references to
Shakespearian plays.]
5 vols. [1894]-1898.
Vol. for 1893 has added portraits.
Vol. for 1896 has letter written by
author inserted.

503948

Theobald (B.G.) Dr.Rawley's epitaph
deciphered [to discover allusions to
the Bacon-Shakespeare question].
pp.20. Port. Facsimile.

(Bath) [1940.]

(Bacon Society)

531019

THEOBALD (BERTRAM GORDON)
Enter Francis Bacon: a sequel to
"Exit Shakspere".
port. facsimiles. bibliog.
1932.

396907

THEOBALD (B. G.)
"The Essential Shakespeare" by
[J.] D. Wilson: a commentary.
pp. 8. (Bacon Society) [1938.]

506945

THEOBALD[(LEWIS)]
The Cave of poverty: a poem, written
in imitation of Shakespeare. pp.
viii, 48. [1714.] 491342
_____ Another edn. 1715 441295

THEOBALD (LEWIS)
The Double falsehood.

For editions of this play see
ENGLISH EDITIONS: The Attributed Plays:
The Double falsehood.

THEOBALD (LEWIS)
The Forsaken maid: a new song in the
tragedy call'd Double Falsehood by
Shakespear [or rather, L. Theobald,
the music by Gouge].   pp. [2]
                         [c.1728.]

                              532160

THEOBALD, LEWIS
King Richard the Second

For editions of this play see under
English Editions: Richard the
Second: Alterations &c.

THEOBALD (LEWIS)
Preface to the works of Shakespeare
(1734) with an introduction by
H. G. Dick.   pp. 6, lxviii.   (Los
Angeles)   1949.
 Augustan Reprint Society Publication
No. [20].   Extra Series, No. 2.
(William Andrews Clark Memorial Library)

                              610858

Theobald, Lewis *works relating to*

—— The Forsaken maid: a new song in the
tragedy call'd Double Falsehood by
Shakespear [or rather, L. Theobald,
the music by Gouge].   pp. [2.]
                           [c.1728.]

                              532160

—— [MALLET (D.)]
An Epistle to Mr. Pope, occasioned
by Theobald's Shakespear and
Bentley's Milton [: a poem].
2nd edn.   pp. [ii], 14.   1733.
 First edn. entitled "Of verbal
criticism".

                              179160

—— [MALLET (D.)]
Of verbal criticism: an epistle to
Mr. Pope occasioned by Theobald's
Shakespear, and Bentley's Milton [:
a poem.]   pp. 14.   1733.   482783
 The 2nd edn. was entitled An Epistle
to Mr. Pope, etc.
          IN Mallet (D.) Works, New edn.
Vol. 1.   1759.   157118

THEOBALD (ROBERT MASTERS)
Bacon's "Promus" and Shakespeare [:
a letter] to the editor of the
"Nonconformist and Independent".
[A review of The Promus of formularies
and elegancies, by F. Bacon.   Edited
by Mrs. Constance M. Pott, 1883.]
pp. 2.   [1883.]

                              555513

THEOBALD (ROBERT MASTERS)
Shakespeare studies in Baconian light.
[Cheap edn.]   1905.

                              391949

Theosophy

—— ROGERS (L. W.)
Shakespeare and theosophy.   IN The
Theosophist, Vol. 58, Pt. 1.
(Madras)   1937.

                              469480

Thersites *see* Troilus and Cressida, Characters

Thersites Literarius, pseud. <u>see</u>
Literarius (Thersites) pseud.

Thesaurus dramaticus. Containing
celebrated passages, etc., in
the body of English plays,
antient and modern, digested
under topics. [Including passages
from Shakespeare's plays.] Frontis.
2 vols.
                         1724.

                              435158

Theses *see* Dissertations

Thewlis (G.A.) Some notes on a Bodleian
manuscript. [With an unpublished
contemporary setting of Shakespeare's
Hark, hark, the lark, from Cymbeline.]
<u>In</u> Music & Letters, Vol. 22.

                         1941.

                              532994

Thiman (E.H.) Fairy scenes from
Shakespeare: six pieces for
piano. pp.15.

[1934.]

419568

THIMAN (ERIC HARDING)
It was a lover and his lass: song
for chorus, strings, flute and piano.
[Arranged for chorus (S.A.T.B.) and
piano. Words from As you like it].
IN Thiman (E. H.) A Spring garland.
1948.

597273

THIMAN (ERIC HARDING)
O mistress mine: chorus for mixed
voices S.C.T.B. (unaccompanied).
[from Twelfth
Night]
pp. 8.   1937.

536607

THIMAN (E. H.)
Sigh no more, ladies: part-song for
S.A.T.B. [from Much ado about
nothing]. pp. 6.   1942.

536590

THIMAN (ERIC HARDING)
A Winter's song [When icicles hang by
the wall, from "Love's labour's lost"].
pp. 7.   1957.
Novello's Voice and Recorder Series.

665755

Thimm (F.[J.L.]) Shakspeare in the
British Museum. In The Library
Chronicle, Vol.4.

1887.

96949

—— Thimm (F.[J.L.]) Shakspeariana
from 1564 to 1864: an account of the
Shakspearian literature of England,
Germany, France and other European
countries during three centuries with
bibliographical introductions. 2nd edn.,
from 1864 to 1871.   1872.

402336

Thirkell (Angela) Shakespeare did not
dine out: [a conclusion based upon
internal evidence in the plays.] From
Cornhill Magazine, August, 1928.

451243

This book for him I name for Jesus'
sake, by Shakespeare's Spirit
[pseud. i.e. Sarah T. Shatford].

[New York]   [1920]

434100

THISELTON-DYER (Sir WILLIAM TURNER)
Natural history: plants. IN
Shakespeare's England, vol. 1.
(Oxford)
illus. facsimiles. bibliogs.
1917.

435745

Thom (R.W.) Coventry poems.[Containing
"Shakspeare Tercentenary poem".]
pp.86.

(Coventry)   [?1866]

432073

Thomas ([C.L.] A.) Festival of spring:
ballet divertissement from the opera
"Hamlet", [Arranged for] full
orchestra [by A.Winter.] Hawkes
Concert edn.

[1939.]

522691

Thomas ([C.L.]A.) Overture to Le
Songe d'une nuit d'été, arranged
from the full score for the organ,
by E. Evans. pp. 20.

(London)   1910.

408798

Thomas, Charles Louis Ambroise *works relating to*

—— The "Hamlet" of [C.L.] A.Thomas [: an
opera], and the Ophelia of Christine
Nilsson. From The Englishwoman's
Domestic Magazine, Aug.1, 1869.

555515

THOMAS (CLARA)
Love and work enough: the life of
Anna Jameson.
illus.   1967.
Includes a chapter "Characteristics
of women".

763439

THOMAS (Sir D. LLEUFER)
Welshmen and the First Folio of
Shakespeare's plays (1623). IN
Transactions of the Honourable Society
of Cymmrodorion, 1940   1941.

530241

THOMAS (D. VAUGHAN)
How sweet the moonlight sleeps.
(Mor felys yma y cwsg.) Words from
Shakespeare's "The Merchant of Venice".
Welsh words [and] music by D. V.
Thomas. Part song [in tonic sol-fa]
for soprano, alto, tenor and bass.
pp. 8.   1929.   405619
_____ Another edn. pp. 11.
1931.   405614

THOMAS (GILBERT)
Window in the west [: essays, mainly
literary].   1954.
  Including a chapter "Was it Bacon?"

                              643435

THOMAS (Sir HENRY)
Shakespeare in Spain.   pp. 24.
  bibliog.   1949.
British Academy.   [39th] Annual
Shakespeare Lecture.

                              604892

[THOMAS (Sir HENRY) ed.]
A Select bibliography of the writings
of Alfred W. Pollard [including
Shakespeare items.   With a brief
autobiography, My first fifty years,
by A. W. Pollard.   Edited with a
preface, and a chapter, From fifty to
seventy-five, by H. Thomas].   pp. ix,
69.   (Oxford)
port.   1938.
Edn. limited to 260 copies.

                              549399

THOMAS (M. WYNN)
The Bibliophile: the Dyce Library
and its Elizabethan plays.   [FROM
Apollo, January, 1937.]   pp. [5.]
  illus.

                              462919

THOMAS, MARY OLIVE
Cleopatra and the "mortal wretch".
IN SHAKESPEARE JAHRBUCH.   Bd 99/1963.
pp. 174-183.   (Heidelberg)

                              10531

THOMAS (MARY OLIVE)
The Repetitions in Antony's death
scene.
IN SHAKESPEARE QUARTERLY IX: 2.
pp. 153-157.
(New York) 1958.

                              605711

THOMAS (MERLIN)
The Playing of Shakespeare at Avignon:
a report with excerpts from productions
of Henry IV and Richard II, played by
the Jean Vilar Company.   Broadcast
18th November 1950.   ff. 9.
  typescript.

                              616418

THOMAS (MOY)
Hamlet's age.   FROM The Theatre,
December, 1884.

                              498968

THOMAS ([PHILIP] EDWARD)
Women, nature and poetry.   [Containing
references to the sonnets of
Shakespeare.]   IN Thomas ([P.] E.)
Feminine influence on the poets.
                              1910.

                              236222

THOMAS (RAYMOND D.)
Shakespeare's alcoholics.   pp. 15.
(White Plains, N.Y.)   1949.

                              616166

THOMAS (RICHARD HINTON) and SAMUEL
(RICHARD H.)
Expressionism in German life,
literature and the theatre (1910-
1924): studies.   [With notes and
references to Shakespeare.]
(Cambridge)
illus.   1939.

                              495269

THOMAS (SIDNEY)
The Antic Hamlet and Richard III.
(New York)
  bibliog.   1943.

                              552067

THOMAS (SIDNEY)
The Bad weather in "A Midsummer
night's dream".   IN Modern Language
Notes, Vol. 64.   (Baltimore) 1949.

                              439157/64

THOMAS (SIDNEY)
The Bibliographical links between the
first two quartos of Romeo and Juliet.
IN The Review of English Studies,
Vol. 25.   1949.

                              318239/25

THOMAS (SIDNEY)
The Date of The Comedy of Errors.
IN SHAKESPEARE QUARTERLY VII.
pp. 377-384.
(New York) 1956.

                              605711

Thomas (S.) The Elizabethan idea of
  melancholy. [With references to
  Shakespeare and bibliographical
  notes.] In Modern Language Notes,
  Vol.56.

        (Baltimore)   1941.

                              533477

THOMAS (SIDNEY)
Henry Chettle and the first quarto
of Romeo and Juliet.   IN The Review
of English Studies, New Series,
Vol. 1.   (Oxford)   1950.

                              318239/2/1

THOMAS (SIDNEY)
A Note on "The Taming of the shrew".
IN Modern Language Notes, Vol. 64.
(Baltimore)
  bibliog.   1949.

                              439157/64

Thomas (Sir W.B.) In Shakespeare's
  country. In D'Oyley (Elizabeth) ed.
  Essays past and present. With an
  introduction by Sylva Norman.

                              1936.

                              521685

THOMAS'S ROAD GUIDES
Let's go!   Where to go, what to see:
a complete guide to the Midlands,
Shakespeare's country, the Cotswolds,
The Malverns, Derbyshire, Wales, etc.,
published by Thomas's Road Guides.
pp. 72.   (Birmingham)
illus.   map.   [1939.]

499670

THOMAS-STANFORD ([Sir] CHARLES)
Who wrote Shakespeare's plays?: a
paper read before the Preston Literary
and Debating Society, Nov. 1906.
pp. 31.   1906.
Printed for private circulation.

426552

Thomasson (F.E.) The "Ireland"
   forgeries. In The Bookworm,
   3rd series, 1890.

107817

THOMPSON (ALAN REYNOLDS)
The Dry mock: a study of irony in
drama.   [With references to
Shakespeare.]   (Berkeley, Cal.)
bibliog.   1948.

594651

THOMPSON (ALEXANDER HAMILTON)
Syllabus of a course of six lectures
on Shakespeare's historical plays.
pp. 10.   (Cambridge)   1899.
Cambridge University.   Local
Lectures.

474073

Thompson (A.H.) Syllabus of a course
   of twelve lectures on Shakespeare's
 — historical plays. pp.24.

     (Cambridge)   1900.

(Cambridge University. Local Lectures.)

474074

THOMPSON (CHARLES JOHN SAMUEL)
The Hand of destiny: the folk-lore
and superstitions of everyday life.
[Including references to Shakespeare.]
illus.   1932.

446612

Thompson (C.J.S.) The Mysteries and
secrets of magic [Containing a chapter:
Magic in Shakespeare's plays.] Illus.

1927.

403349

Thompson (C.J.S.) The Mystic mandrake.
   [With quotations from Shakespeare.]
   Illus.

1934.

428182

Thompson (C.J.S.) The Witchery of
Jane Shore, the Rose of London:
the romance of a Royal mistress.
[With references to Shakespeare's
Richard the third. Ports. Illus.
Facsimiles.

1933.

417434

THOMPSON (CRAIG R.)
The Bible in English, 1525-1611.
pp. 37.   (Washington)
   ports. map. facsimiles. bibliog.
                    1959.   666179
Folger Shakespeare Library.   Folger
Booklets on Tudor and Stuart Civilization.
_____ IN Life and letters in Tudor and
Stuart England.   (Ithaca, N.Y.)
   illus.   1962.   667762
Folger Shakespeare Library.

THOMPSON (CRAIG R.)
The English Church in the sixteenth
century. pp. 57.   (Washington, D.C.)
   illus. facsimiles. bibliog.
                    1958.   666180
Folger Shakespeare Library.   Folger
Booklets on Tudor and Stuart Civilization.
_____ IN Life and letters in Tudor and
Stuart England.   (Ithaca, N.Y.)
   illus.   1962.   667762
Folger Shakespeare Library.

THOMPSON (CRAIG R.)
Schools in Tudor England.   pp. ii, 36.
(Washington, D.C.)
   illus. facsimiles. bibliog.
                    1958.   666578
Folger Shakespeare Library.   Folger
Booklets on Tudor and Stuart Civilization.
_____ IN Life and letters in Tudor
and Stuart England.   (Ithaca, N.Y.)
   illus.   1962.   667762
Folger Shakespeare Library.

THOMPSON (CRAIG R.)
Universities in Tudor England.   pp. 34.
(Washington)
   ports. illus. maps. bibliog.
                    1959.   666577
Folger Shakespeare Library.   Folger
Booklets on Tudor and Stuart Civilization.
_____ IN Life and letters in Tudor
and Stuart England.   (Ithaca, N.Y.)
   illus.   1962.   667762
Folger Shakespeare Library.

THOMPSON (D. W.)
"Full of his roperipe" and "roperipe
terms".   IN Modern Language Notes,
Vol. 53.   (Baltimore)   1938.
Romeo and Juliet II, iv, 154.

493024

Thompson, Edward *works relating to*

——STONE (G. W.)
Garrick, and an unknown operatic
version [by Captain Edward Thompson]
of "Love's labour's lost".   IN The
Review of English Studies, Vol. 15.
1939.

513846

THOMPSON (EDWARD JOHN)
Sir Walter Ralegh: the last of the
Elizabethans.   [With references to
Shakespeare.]
ports. maps. bibliog.   1935.

435812

THOMPSON (Sir EDWARD MAUNDE)
Handwriting.   IN Shakespeare's
England, vol. 1.   (Oxford)
illus. facsimiles. bibliog.
1917.

435745

THOMPSON (Sir EDWARD MAUNDE)
Two pretended autographs of
Shakespeare.   Reprinted from
"The Library", July, 1917.   pp. 27.
facsimiles.   1917.

488384

Thompson, Edward Maunde Sir *works relating to*

——KENYON (Sir F. G.)
Sir Edward Maunde Thompson, 1840-
1929: obituary notice.   IN
Proceedings of the British Academy
[Vol. 15], 1929.   [1932]

390430

THOMPSON (F.)
The Macbeth controversy.   pp. [17].
IN The Dublin Review.   Vol. [105.]
1889.

104438

THOMPSON (J. W.)
Manuscript notes on Shakespeare's
King Henry VIII.   ff. [14].
[c.1890]
The edition of the play to which these
notes refer is in the Reference Library
(Catalogue No. 463085).

463086

THOMPSON (JAMES WESTFALL)
A Note on The Tempest.   IN Modern
language notes, Vol. 52.
(Baltimore)   1937.

479896

THOMPSON (JOHN BERTRAND)
Anne Hathaway sees "Twelfth Night":
written for performance by the
Bristol Drama Club, in a Clifton
garden, June, 1936.   FROM
St. Brendan's College Magazine,
Vol. 3, No. 1.   (Bristol)
illus.   1936.

455002

THOMPSON, JOHN BERTRAND
The King's men at Stratford: "Twelfth
Night" with a difference

For editions of this play see under
English Editions: Twelfth Night:
Alterations &c.

THOMPSON (JOHN BERTRAND)
Queen Elizabeth comes to Bristol, a
pageant: an adaptation of As you
like it, by St. Brendan's College,
Bristol.   Programmes, cuttings, etc.
[Bristol]
partly typescript.   illus. [1934]

433185

THOMPSON, JOHN BERTRAND
Slaves for Bristol

For editions of this play see under
English Editions: The Tempest:
Alterations &c.

THOMPSON (KARL F.)
Richard II, martyr.
IN SHAKESPEARE QUARTERLY VIII:
pp. 159-166.
(New York)   1957.

605711

THOMPSON (KARL F.)
Shakespeare's romantic comedies.
IN P.M.L.A.: Publications of the
Modern Language Association of
America, Vol. 67.   (New York)
1952.

428321/67

THOMPSON, KARL F.
The Unknown Ulysses.
IN SHAKESPEARE QUARTERLY XIX: 2.
pp. 125-128.   (New York)
1968.

605711

THOMPSON (L.)
The Boydell Shakespeare: an English
monument to graphic arts.   IN The
Princeton University Library
Chronicle, Vol. 1, No. 2.   (Princeton)
illus.   1940.

552443

THOMS (WILLIAM JOHN)
The Folk-lore of Shakspeare, nos. 1-8.
FROM The Athenaeum [for the year
1847].
No. 9 wanting.

561774

Thomson (A.A.) The Second best bed;
or, The Truth about Shakespeare:
a comedy for broadcasting. ff.6.
Typescript.

[1934.]

422598

Thomson (C[lara] L.) A History of
Shakespearian criticism, by A.Ralli:
[a review.] In The Criterion, Vol.12,
1932.

414720

Thomson (E.[J.]) Robert Bridges
1844-1930. [With references to
Shakespeare, a bibliography and
bibliographical notes.]

(Oxford)   1944.

554790

Thomson (G.[D.]) Aeschylus and Athens:
a study in the social origins of
drama. [With a bibliography, and
references to Shakespeare.] Illus.
Maps. Dgms.

1941.

524345

THOMSON (JAMES ALEXANDER KERR)
The Classical background of English
literature. [With references to
Shakespeare.]   1948.

589818

THOMSON (JAMES ALEXANDER KERR)
Shakespeare and the classics. 1952.

622613

THOMSON, PETER W.
A Shakespearean "Method".
IN SHAKESPEARE JAHRBUCH.   Bd. 104/
1968.   pp. 192-204.   (Weimar)

10531

THOMSON (ROSAMUND D.)
[Review of] Les Sonnets de
Shakespeare, traduits en vers
français [par] F. Baldensperger.
IN Books Abroad, Vol. 18.
(Norman, Oka.)   1944.

561400

THOMSON (THEODORE RADFORD)
A Catalogue of British family histories.
With an introduction by Lord Farrer
[and a list of histories of the
Shakespeare family].   2nd edn.   1935.

443971

THOMSON, VIRGIL GARNETT
Look, how the floor of heaven. Song
for high voice. (New York)   1963.

751627

THOMSON (VIRGIL GARNETT)
Shakespeare songs for voice and
piano.   No. 1: "Was this fair
face the cause?"   Words from "All's
well that ends well".   pp. 4.
(New York)   1961.

667069

THOMSON (VIRGIL GARNETT)
Shakespeare songs for voice and piano.
No. 2: "Take, O, take those lips away".
Words by W. Shakespeare from "Measure
for measure". pp.4. (New York)
1961.

667070

THOMSON (VIRGIL GARNETT)
Shakespeare songs for voice and piano.
No. 3: "Tell me where is fancy bred".
Words from "The Merchant of Venice".
pp. 4.   (New York)   1961.

667071

THOMSON (VIRGIL GARNETT)
Shakespeare songs for voice and piano.
No. 4: "Pardon, goddess of the night".
Words by W. Shakespeare [from] "Much
ado about nothing".   pp. 4.   (New
York)   1961.

667072

THOMSON (VIRGIL GARNETT)
Shakespeare songs for voice and
piano.   No. 5: "Sigh no more,
ladies".   Words from "Much ado
about nothing".   pp. 8.   (New
York)   1961.

667073

THOMSON (WALTER) ed.
The Sonnets of William Shakespeare &
Henry Wriothesley, Third Earl of
Southampton, with A Lover's complaint
and The Phoenix & turtle.   Edited
with an introduction.   (Oxford) 1938.

480352

Thomson, Walter *works relating to*

—— DECKNER (ELISE)
[Review of] The Sonnets of Shakespeare
and Southampton, edited by W. Thomson.
IN Beiblatt zur Anglia [Bd.] 53.
(Halle)   1942.

576459

—— LAWRENCE (W. J.)
[Reviews of] The Sonnets of Shakespeare
and Southampton, [edited] by W. Thomson;
and Shakespeare discovered, by [Comtesse]
Clara L. de Chambrun.   IN The Spectator,
Vol. 160.   1938.

487969

THOMSON (WILFRID HARRY)
Shakespeare's characters: a historical
dictionary.   (Altrincham)
frontis.   genealogical tables.
1951.

616136

Thomson, William *works relating to*

—— C[LOSE] (R. C.)
Was Bacon Shakespeare? [: a review
of "On renascence drama, or History
made visible", by W. Thomson]
FROM The Victorian Review, Vol. 3.
[Melbourne]   1880.

554140

THONON, ROBERT
"Still" or "skill": a note on
Shakespeare's Sonnet CVI.
IN SHAKESPEARE JAHRBUCH.   Bd. 97/1961.
pp. 203-207.   (Heidelberg)

10531

Thornbury, George Walter *works relating to*

—— Review of "Shakspere's England; or
Sketches of our social history in
the reign of Elizabeth.   By
G. W. Thornbury".   IN Miscellaneous
reviews.   FROM The Gentleman's
Magazine, Nov. 1856.   pp. [2].

402715

—— Wood-leaves and book-leaves [: a
review of "Shakspere's England, or
Sketches of social England in the
reign of Elizabeth", by G. W. Thornbury].
FROM [Dublin University Magazine,]
Vol. 50.   [Dublin]   1857.

558099

THORNDIKE (ARTHUR RUSSELL)
Children of the Garter: memoirs of
a Windsor Castle choir-boy, during
the last years of Queen Victoria.
[With Shakespearian references.]
ports.   illus.   1937.

467159

THORNDIKE (ARTHUR RUSSELL)
In the steps of Shakespeare.   New
and revised edn.
illus.   1948.
First edn. entitled "A Wanderer with
Shakespeare".

590823

THORNDIKE (ARTHUR RUSSELL)
A Wanderer with Shakespeare.
illus.   [1939]
Later edns. entitled "In the steps of
Shakespeare".

508875

Thorndike ([A.]R.) and Thorndike (Sybil)
Lilian Baylis.   Port.

1938.

480182

THORNDIKE (ASHLEY HORACE)
Influence of the court-masques on the
drama, 1608-15 [: an attempt to
determine the date of The Winter's Tale.]
IN Publications of the Modern Language
Association of America, Vol. 15.
(Baltimore)   1900.

428335

Thorndike (A.H.) The Relations of Hamlet
to contemporary revenge plays. In
Publications of the Modern Language
Association of America, vol.17.

(Baltimore)   [1902]

428337

THORNDIKE (A. [H.])
Shakespeare in America.   IN Aspects
of Shakespeare: British Academy
lectures.   (Oxford)   1933.

401892

Thorndike (A.H.) Shakespeare's
theater, [i.e. the stage in
Shakespeare's time. With bibliographical notes]. Illus. Map. Plans.

(New York)   1925.

522855

THORNDIKE (ASHLEY HORACE)
Tragedy [: the course of English
tragedy from its beginnings to the
middle of the nineteenth century.
With chapters, "Shakespeare and his
contemporaries" and "Shakespeare",
and other references to Shakespeare.]
(Boston [Mass.])
bibliog.   1908.
The Types of English Literature.

552597

Thorndike, Sybil Dame *works relating to*

—— TREWIN (JOHN COURTENAY)

Sybil Thorndike: an illustrated study of Dame Sybil's work, with a list of her appearances on stage and screen. (Theatre World Monographs No. 4). Port. Illus.   1955.

650886

Thorndike (Sybil) and Thorndike ([A.]R.) Lilian Baylis. Port.

1938.

480182

THORNE (H. J.)
[Music specially composed for the performances of "Twelfth Night" by the John Gay Players, Barnstaple.] pp. [10.]   [Barnstaple] manuscript.   [1953.]

635426

THORNELL (J. H.) ed.
The Bill of the play: an illustrated record of the chief dramas, plays, operas bouffe, etc. produced during the year 1881 [including plays by Shakespeare].   With illustrations by H. Ludlow.   [1882.]

501364

[THORNTON (B.) and COLMAN (G.)]
Letter from Oxford on the story of Shakespeare's Merchant of Venice, [and a] copy of an original ballad from which Shakespeare is supposed to have borrowed part of his plot.   IN The Connoisseur, by Mr. Town, Critic and Censor-general. 5th edn. Vol. 1.   (Oxford)
1767.   519895
_____ IN The Connoisseur, [edited] by
A. Chalmers, [Vol. 1.] 1802.   459740
British essayists, Vol. 30.

THORNTON (G. H.)
English composition [using the subject "Shakespeare's treatment of the supernatural" as an example for essay writing.]   Edited by [Sir] J. Adams.   [1906.]
The Self Educator [Vol. 1].
528701

Thorp (Josephine) The Enchanted book-shelf: a children's play [containing an excerpt from "A Midsummer Night's dream"]. In Sanford ([Mrs.] A[nne] P.) and Schauffler (R.H.) ed[s]., The Magic of books: an anthology for Book Week.

(New York)   1941.

(Our American Holidays)

531537

THORP (JOSEPHINE)
When fairies come [: a one act play, with Shakespeare as one of the characters].   IN SANFORD ([Mrs.] A[NNE] P.) and SHAUFFLER (R. H.) eds., Little plays for little people. With an introduction by E. B. Sheldon. (New York)   1939.

531538

THORP (MARGARET FERRAND)
America at the movies.   [With references to the film versions of Shakespeare's plays.]   (New Haven [Conn.]) illus.   1940.

529969

THORP (MARGARET FARRAND)
Shakespeare and the fine arts. IN Publications of the Modern Language Association of America, Vol. 46.   (Menasha, Wis.) 1931.

428366

THORP (MARGARET FARRAND)
Shakespeare and the Movies. IN SHAKESPEARE QUARTERLY IX. pp. 357–366. (New York)   1958.

605711

THORPE (CLARENCE DeWITT)
The Aesthetic theory of Thomas Hobbes. With special reference to his contribution to the psychological approach in English literary criticism [including references to Shakespeare.] (Ann Arbor, Mich.) bibliogs.   1940.
University of Michigan Publications. Language and Literature, Vol. 18.

542577

Thorpe (C.D.) Thomas Hanmer and the anonymous essay on Hamlet. In Modern Language Notes, Vol.49.

(Baltimore)   1934.

428652

THORPE (THOMAS BANGS)
The Case of Lady Macbeth, medically considered.   IN Harper's New Monthly Magazine, Vol. 8.   (New York) 1854.

111858

Thorpe, Thomas *works relating to*

—— ROSTENBERG (LEONA)
Thomas Thorpe, publisher of "Shakespeares sonnets", from the Papers of the Bibliographical Society of America, 1960.   pp. [22]

666962

THRALL (WILLIAM FLINT)
Cymbeline, Boccaccio and the wager
story in England.   FROM Studies in
Philology, Vol. 28.   (Chapel Hill)
1931.

453873

THUMM–KINTZEL (MAGDALENE)
Shakespeare-Bacon and the Promus-
mansucript.   [English text.]
ff. 8.   (Leipzig)
facsimiles.   [1909.]

531798

THUMM–KINTZEL (MAGDALENE)
Shakespeare-Bacon study based on
handwritings.   [English text.]
pp. 16.   (Leipzig)
facsimiles.   [?1909.]

216450

THURBER (JAMES)
The Macbeth murder mystery: reprinted
from "My world and welcome to it".
FROM Senior Scholastic, Vol. 43.
(New York)   1943.

565607

THURSTON (HERBERT)
The New Baconian mare's nest [: a
reply to W. H. Mallock's article
on Mrs. Gallup's "Bi-literal
cypher".]   IN The Monthly Review,
Vol. 6.   1902.

169239

THURSTON (HERBERT)
Shakespeare's handwriting.   IN The
Month, Vol. 123.   1914.

253093

THURSTON (JOHN)
An Illustration of Shakespeare:
thirty-eight engravings on wood, by
[A. R.] Branston from new designs by
J. Thurston.   [1810]

666338

[Thurston (J.) Shakespeare illustrations:
large paper proof copies of the
engravings from drawings by J.
Thurston,.which accompanied the
edition of the works of Shakespeare
in 12 volumes printed for Thomas
Tegg, 1812-15].

431992

TICKNER (FREDERICK WINDHAM)
A Peep at Shakespeare's London.
IN Tickner (F. W.) Making the English
homeland.
illus.   1937.
Headway Histories.   Junior Series, 3.

486543

TIECK ([JOHANN] LUDWIG)
Letters hitherto unpublished, 1792-
1853; collected and edited by
E. H. Zeydel, P. Matenko [and] R. H.
Fife, with the co-operation of the
Department of Germanic Languages,
Columbia University.   [German text.
Containing Shakespearian references.]
(New York)   1937.
The Modern Language Association of
America, General Series.

484308

Tieck, Johann Ludwig *works relating to*

— **HEWETT-THAYER (H. W.)**
Tieck and the Elizabethan drama:
his marginalia.   [bibliog.]   FROM
The Journal of English and Germanic
Philology, Vol. 34.   (Urbana, Ill.)
1935.

490583

— **HORMANN (H.)**
Ludwig Tieck, theatrical reformer [:
his theories on staging, with references to various Shakespearian
productions and bibliographical notes].
FROM The Quarterly Journal of Speech,
Vol. 31.   (Detroit)   1945.

576840

— **Kahn (L.W.) Ludwig Tieck als übersetzer**
von Shakespeares sonetten. From
The Germanic Review, Vol. 9.

(Menasha)   1934.

506184

— **MARTIN (Sir T.)**
Ludwig Tieck on the English stage.
IN Martin (Sir T.) Essays on the
drama.   Second series.   1889.
Printed for private circulation.

432010

— **TOYNBEE (G.)**
Continuation to Heine [of] A. W. [von]
Schlegel's Lectures on German literature from Gottsched to Goethe given
at the University of Bonn and taken
down by G. Toynbee in 1833.   [With
references to Tieck and Shakespeare.]
Edited by H. G. Fiedler.   pp. 96.
(Oxford)
tables.   bibliogs.   1944.

552830

— **ZEYDEL (E. H.)**
Ludwig Tieck and England: a study
in the literary relations of Germany
and England during the early nineteenth century.   [With references
to Shakespeare's plays.]   1931.

390815

____ZEYDEL (E. H.)
Ludwig Tieck as a translator of
English, [including Shakespeare].
IN Publications of the Modern
Language Association of America,
Vol. 51. (Menasha, Wis.) 1936.

463431

____ZEYDEL (E. H.)
Ludwig Tieck, the German romanticist:
a critical study. [With references
to Shakespeare.] (Princeton, N.J.)
bibliog. 1935.

449035

Tiller (T.) "The Baker's daughter"
[:an excursion in literature and
mythology concerning Ophelia's
enigmatic remark in Act 4 of
"Hamlet". Broadcast] 25th April,
1950. ff. [i,] 43. Typescript.

608874

TILLER (TERENCE)
The Conscience of the king: a study
of the fool in King Lear [in dramatic
form. Broadcast] May 7th, 1952.
pp. 42.
typescript.

624733

TILLEY (MORRIS PALMER)
A Dictionary of the proverbs in
England in the sixteenth and seventeenth centuries: a collection of
the proverbs found in English
literature and the dictionaries of
the period. (Ann Arbor, Mich.)
port. bibliog. 1950.

617643

TILLEY (MORRIS PALMER)
Elizabethan proverb lore in Lyly's
Euphues and in Pettie's Petite Pallace,
with parallels from Shakespeare.
(New York) 1926.
Michigan University Pubns. Language
and Literature, Vol. 2.

399822

TILLEY (MORRIS PALMER)
The Organic unity of Twelfth Night.
IN Publications of the Modern Language
Association of America, Vol. 29.
(Baltimore) 1914.

42834

TILLEY (MORRIS P.)
A Parody of 'Euphues' in 'Romeo and
Juliet'. IN Modern Language Notes.
Vol. 41. (Baltimore, Md.) 1926.

439157/41

Tilley (M.P.) Pun and proverb as aids
to unexplained Shakespearean jests.
From Studies in Philology, Vol. 21.

(Chapel Hill, N.C.)
1924.

496552

TILLEY (MORRIS PALMER)
Some evidence in Shakespeare of contemporary efforts to refine the
language of the day. IN Publications
of the Modern Language Association of
America, Vol. 31. (Baltimore) 1916.

428351

TILLEY (MORRIS PALMER)
"'Twill be thine another day".
IN Modern Language Notes, Vol. 52.
(Baltimore) 1937.

479896

Tillotson (G.) On the poetry of Pope.
[With references to Shakespeare]

(Oxford) 1938.

476469

TILLOTSON (KATHLEEN)
"Windows" in Shakespeare.   IN The
Review of English Studies, Vol. 17.
(Oxford) 1941. 533231
_____ IN Tillotson (G.) Essays in
[English literary] criticism and
research. (Cambridge)
1942. 531163

TILLYARD (EUSTACE MANDEVILLE WETENHALL)
The Elizabethan world picture [: an
exposition of the most ordinary
beliefs about the constitution of
the world as pictured in the Elizabethan age. With references to
Shakespeare's plays.]
bibliog. 1943.

540616

TILLYARD (EUSTACE MANDEVILLE WETENHALL)
The Fairy-tale element in The Taming
of the Shrew.   IN Shakespeare 1564-
1964: a collection of modern essays
by various hands. (Providence, R.I.)
1964.

744437

TILLYARD (EUSTACE MANDEVILLE WETENHALL)
The Miltonic setting, past & present.
[With references to Shakespeare]
(Cambridge) 1938.

478351

TILLYARD (EUSTACE MANDEVILLE WETENHALL)
The Nature of comedy and Shakespeare.
pp. 15. 1958.
English Association, Presidential
Address, 1958.

665888

TILLYARD (EUSTACE MANDEVILLE WETENHALL)
Poetry, direct and oblique. [With
references to Shakespeare.]
1934. 418780
Revised [edn.] 1945. 563733

TILLYARD, EUSTACE MANDEVILLE WETENHALL
Shakespeare's early comedies. 1965.

744081

1955

TILLYARD (EUSTACE WETENHALL MANDEVILLE)
Shakespeare's historical cycle:
organism or compilation?   IN Studies
in Philology, Vol. 51.   (Chapel Hill,
N.C.)   1954.

554520/51

TILLYARD (EUSTACE MANDEVILLE WETENHALL)
Shakespeare's history plays.
 bibliog.   1944.

554244

TILLYARD (E.M.W.)
 Shakespeare's last plays: [Cymbeline,
 The Winter's tale and The Tempest.]
 pp. 85.
                          1938.

476626

TILLYARD (EUSTACE MANDEVILLE WETENHALL)
Shakespeare's problem plays [: Hamlet;
Troilus and Cressida; All's well that
ends well; and, Measure for Measure.
The Alexander Lectures at the
University of Toronto, 1948-9.]
 bibliog.   1950.

604507

TILLYARD (EUSTACE MANDEVILLE WETENHALL)
The Trial scene in 'The Merchant of
Venice'.   IN A Review of English
literature.   Vol. 2. 1961.
 bibliogs.

697306/1961

TILLYARD (EUSTACE MANDEVILLE WETENHALL)
Why did Shakespeare write "Henry the
Eighth"?   IN Essays, literary &
educational.   1962.

706890

TILLYARD (EUSTACE MANDEVILLE WETENHALL)

see also Walker (Roy), Leech (C.) and
Tillyard (E. M. W.)

Tillyard, Eustace Mandeville Wetenhall *works relating to*

— DOBREE (B.)
  [Review of] Shakespeare's last plays,
  by E. M. W. Tillyard.   IN The Criterion,
  Vol. 17.
                          1937-8

487675

  — HAWKINS (D.)
   [Review of] Shakespeare's last plays:
   [Cymbeline, The Winter's tale, and
   The Tempest,] by E. M. W. Tillyard.
   IN The Spectator, Vol. 160.   1938.

487969

— KNOX (R. S.)
  Patterns in Shakespeare [: a review
  of Shakespeare's last plays, by
  E. M. W. Tillyard, etc.].   FROM
  University of Toronto Quarterly,
  Vol. 9.   (Toronto)   1939.

530206

— LATHAM (A[GNES] M. C.)
  [Review of] Shakespeare's history plays
  [by] E. M. W. Tillyard.   IN Life and
  Letters, Vol. 46.   1945.

567808

— ROBERTS (M.)
  [Review of] Shakespeare's last plays,
  by E. M. W. Tillyard.   IN The
  London Mercury and Bookman, Vol. 38.
                            1938.

495900

— TILLOTSON (G.)
  [Review of] Shakespeare's history
  plays, by E. M. W. Tillyard.   IN
  English: the magazine of the English
  Association, Vol. 5.   (Oxford)
                            1944-45.

569018

— TRAVERSI (DEREK ANTONA)
  [A Review of] Shakespeare's last plays,
  by E. M. W. Tillyard.   IN Scrutiny,
  Vol. 6.   (Cambridge)
                            1937-38.

489751

Tillyard (E.M.W.) and Lewis (C.S.)
 The Personal heresy : a controversy
 [concerning the relation of the
 poet to his work. With references
 to Shakespeare.]

(Oxford)   1939.

498318

Tilney, Edmund *works relating to*

— BOAS (F. S.)
  Queen Elizabeth, the Revels Office and
  Edmund Tilney.   [With references to
  Shakespeare].   pp. 27.   (Oxford)
                            1938.
  Elizabeth Howland Lectures, 1937.

481919

TIMBS (JOHN)
The Boyhood of Edmund Kean.   IN
English eccentrics and eccentricities.
New edn.
 ports.   illus.   1877.

400637

Timbs (J.) The Romance of London.[With
references to Shakespeare.]
2 vols.   [1869.]

[Vol.1.]Historic sketches remarkable duels,
notorious highwaymen, rogueries,
crimes, punishments, love and marriage.

[Vol.2.]Supernatural stories, sights and
shows, strange adventures and remarkable persons.

                           410361

TIMBS (JOHN) [ed.]
A Century of anecdote from 1760 to
1860. [With anecdotes of Garrick
and his Shakespearian performances.]
                              [1869.]

Chandos Library.

                           519558

Time

— BOAS (G.)
"Troilus and Cressida" and the time
scheme.   IN The New English Review,
Vol. 13.
                              1946.

                           577268

— CLEMEN, WOLFGANG H.
Past and future in Shakespeare's
drama.   FROM Proceedings of the
British Academy, vol. 52.   1966.
pp. 231-252.   Annual Shakespeare
Lecture, 1966.
                           767672

— DANIEL (PETER AUGUSTINE)
A Note on the Rev. N. J. Halpin's time-
analysis of The Merchant of Venice.
IN Transactions of the New Shakespeare
Society, Series 1.   No. 5.   pp. 40-57.
                              1877-9.

                           40620

— DRIVER (TOM F.)
The Shakespearian clock: time and the
vision of reality in "Romeo and Juliet"
and "The Tempest". IN Shakespeare
Quarterly XV: 4. pp.363-370. (New York)
                              1964.

                           605711

— ELMEN (PAUL)
Shakespeare's gentle hours.   [Time in
the Sonnets.]
IN SHAKESPEARE QUARTERLY IV: 3.
pp. 301-309.
(New York)   1953.
                           605711

— GATTY (Mrs. [MARGARET])
The Book of sun-dials.   [With extracts
from Shakespeare.]
illus.   1872.   571644
_____ New and enlarged edn., edited
by H[oratia] K. F. Gatty and Eleanor
Lloyd.
illus.   1889.   99966

— HALPIN (N. J.)
The Dramatic unities of Shakespeare: a
letter addressed to the editor of
Blackwood's Edinburgh Magazine [i.e.
J. Wilson.   Includes a section, Time-
analysis of The Merchant of Venice].
pp. 57.   (Dublin)
                              1849.

                           57499

— JOHNSON [S.]
On dramatic unity, especially as
observed by Shakespeare; from
Mr. Johnson's preface to his edition
of Shakespeare's plays.   FROM [The]
Annual Register for the year 1765.
[3rd edn.]   [1802.]

                           561330

— JORGENSEN (PAUL A.   )
"Redeeming time" in Shakespeare's
Henry IV. IN Tennessee Studies in
Literature, Vol.5. (Knoxville)
                              1960.

                        692773/5

— LOANE (G. G.)
Time, Johnson, and Shakespeare.
IN Notes and Queries, Vol. 184.
(Oxford)   1943.

                           544211

— MILLER (D. C.)
Iago and the problem of time.   [With
bibliographical notes.]   IN English
Studies, Vol. 22.   (Amsterdam)
                              1940.

                           575606

— QUINONES, RICARDO J.
Views of time in Shakespeare. FROM
Journal of the History of Ideas, Vol.26,
No.3, July-Sept. 1965.

pp.327-352.   767204

— RAYSOR (T. M.)
The Aesthetic significance of Shakespeare's
handling of time.   [With bibliographical
notes.]   FROM Studies in philology, Vol.
32.   (Chapel Hill, N. C.)
                              1935.

                           484077

— RAYSOR (T. M.)
Intervals of time and their effect upon
dramatic values in Shakespeare's tragedies.   FROM The Journal of English and
Germanic Philology, Vol. 37.
                              1938.

                           503676

— ROSE (EDWARD)
The Inconsistency of the time in
Shakspere's plays.
IN Transactions of the New Shakespeare
Society, Series 1. Nos. 8-10. pp. 33-52.
                           1880-6.
                              99113

— SEN GUPTA (SUBODH CHANDRA)
The Whirligig of time: the problem
of duration in Shakespeare's plays.
                              1961.

                           667103

— SEWELL (A.)
Place and time in Shakespeare's plays.
IN Studies in Philology, Vol. 42.
(Chapel Hill, N.C.)
1945.

569039

— SPENCER (B. T.)
2 Henry IV and the theme of time.
FROM University of Toronto Quarterly,
Vol. 13.   (Toronto)
1944.

578419

— TANSELLE (G. THOMAS)
Time in "Romeo and Juliet". IN
Shakespeare Quarterly XV: 4. pp.349-361.
(New York)
1964.

605711

— WILSON (JOHN)
A Double-time-analysis of Macbeth and Othello.
IN Transactions of the New Shakespeare
Society, Series 1. No. 4.
pp. 351-387. and Series I   1875-8.
Nos. 6-7. pp. 21-41.

40620 11987

— WITTE (WILLIAM)
Time in 'Wallenstein' and 'Macbeth'.
IN Aberdeen University Review
Vol. 34, [No.] 3. pp. 8.
(Aberdeen)
1952.

633542

TIME [MAGAZINE]
Shakespeare, Midsummer night's box
office. [FROM Time Magazine,
July 4th, 1960.] pp. [12].
[Amsterdam]
ports.   illus.

667002

TIMMINS (SAMUEL)
Books on Shakespeare.   IN Books
for a Reference Library: lectures
on the books in the Reference
Department of the Free Public
Library, Birmingham.   1st Series.
bibliogs.   1885.
Thick paper copy.

475336

TIMMINS (S.)
A History of Warwickshire. [With references to Shakespeare and Stratford-on-
Avon, and a bibliography.]
1889.

103207

Timoleon: a tragedy [by B. Martyn].
As it is acted at the Theatre-Royal.
[Containing references to some of
Shakespeare's characters in the
prologue and epilogue.] pp. [xiv,
72.]   1730.

568321

Timon of Athens

— ADAMSON, ELGIVA, and MOORE, KATHLEEN V.
Notes on William Shakespeare's "Timon
of Athens". [Stratford, Ontario]
[1963.]

765920

— B. (A.) An Echo of the "Paragone"
in Shakespeare. [With references
to Timon of Athens.] In Journal
of the Warburg Institute, Vol. 2.

1939.

503494

—   Bond (R.W.) Lucian and Boiardo
in 'Timon of Athens'.   In The Modern
Language Review, Vol. 26.

(Cambridge.)   1931.

390362

— BOND (R. W.)
Studia otiosa: some attempts in
criticism.   [With a chapter:
Lucian and Boiardo in Timon of Athens.]
1938.

483739

— BRADBROOK, MURIEL CLARA
The Tragic pageant of 'Timon of Athens':
an inaugural lecture. (Cambridge)
1966.

759258

— BUTLER, FRANCELIA
The strange critical fortunes of
Shakespeare's "Timon of Athens".
(Ames; Iowa)   1966.

754715

— Collins (A.S.) Timon of Athens: a
reconsideration. [With bibliographical notes.] In The Review of
English Studies, Vol.22.

(Oxford)   [1946.]

579165

— COOK (DAVID)
Timon of Athens.   IN SHAKESPEARE
SURVEY 16.
illus.   1963.

667523

— CRAIG
On misanthropy and its different
species - illustration from the
characters of Hamlet, Jaques and
Timon of Athens.   IN The Lounger,
[edited] by A. Chalmers, [Vol. 3.]
1802.
British essayists, Vol. 40.

459750

— DRAPER (J. W.)
The Psychology of Shakespeare's
Timon.   IN The Modern Language
Review, Vol. 35.   (Cambridge)
bibliog.   1940.

527506

—— Draper (J.W.) The Theme of 'Timon of Athens'. pp.[2]. In The Modern Language Review, vol.29. 1934.

(Cambridge)

428653

—— DRAPER (R. P.)
Timon of Athens.
IN SHAKESPEARE QUARTERLY VIII.
pp. 195-200.
(New York)   1957.

605711

—— ELLIOTT (ROBERT C.)
The Satirist satirized.   2. Timon of Athens.   IN Elliott (R. C.) The Power of satire: magic, ritual, art.
(Princeton, N.J.)   1960.

693126

—— ELLIS-FERMOR (UNA [M.])
Timon of Athens: an unfinished play.   IN The Review of English Studies, Vol. 18.   (Oxford)
bibliog.   1942.

542539

—— EMPSON (WILLIAM)
Timon's dog [: metaphor in Shakespeare].   FROM Life and letters today. Winter 1936-7.
            [1936]   462913
_____ IN Empson (W.) The Structure of complex words.   1951.   617595

—— Empson (W.) [and] Garrett (G.) Shakespeare survey: [Othello, Timon of Athens, and the Tempest. With an epilogue by R. Herring.]

[1937.]

472727

—— FARNHAM (W. [E.])
The Beast theme in Shakespeare's "Timon".   [bibliog.]   IN Essays and studies, by members of the Department of English, University of California. (Berkeley, Cal.) 1943.
University of California Publications in English, Vol. 14.

573478

—— FARNHAM (WILLARD EDWARD)
Timon of Athens.   IN LEECH, CLIFFORD, ed., Shakespeare: the tragedies. A collection of critical essays.
(Chicago)   1965.
Gemini books.

752332

—— FLEAY (FREDERICK GARD)
On the authorship of Timon of Athens.
IN Transactions of the New Shakespeare Society, Series 1. No. 1.   pp. 130-151.
1874.
4061

—— GOLDSMITH (ROBERT HILLIS)
Did Shakespeare use the old Timon comedy?
IN SHAKESPEARE QUARTERLY IX: 1.
pp. 31-38.
(New York)   1958.

605711

—— GOMME (ANDOR)
Timon of Athens.   IN Essays in Criticism, Vol. 9.   1959.

621866/9

—— HONIGMANN (E. A. J.)
Timon of Athens.

IN SHAKESPEARE QUARTERLY XII: 1.
pp. 3-20.
(New York)   1961.
605711

—— KNIGHT (GEORGE WILSON)
Timon of Athens and its dramatic descendants.   bibliog.   IN A Review of English literature. Vol. 2. 1961.
697306/1961
_____   IN Stratford Papers on Shakespeare delivered at the 1963 Shakespeare Seminar.   (Toronto)
1964.   668007

—— Lewis ([P.]W.) A Collection of sixteen woodcuts and engravings, some coloured, illustrating Shakespeare's Timon of Athens.

[c.1921.]

465352

—— [Maginn (W.)] Shakspeare papers, No.6: Timon of Athens. In Bentley's Miscellany, Vol.3.

1838.

30953

—— Maxwell (J.C.)'Timon of Athens' [:a critical study. With bibliographical notes]. In Scrutiny, Vol.15.

(Cambridge)   1947-8.

421336/15

—— MERCHANT (WILLIAM MOELWYN)
Timon and the conceit of art.
IN SHAKESPEARE QUARTERLY VI.
pp. 249-257.
(New York)   1955.
605711

—— MUIR, KENNETH
"Timon of Athens" and the cash-nexus.
FROM The Modern quarterly miscellany, No. 1.   [1947.]
pp. 57-76.
771893

—— NOWOTTNY (WINIFRED M. T.)
Acts IV and V of Timon of Athens.
IN SHAKESPEARE QUARTERLY X: 4.
pp. 493-497.
(New York)   1959.
605711

—— PETTET (E. C.)
Timon of Athens: the disruption of feudal morality.   bibliog.   IN The Review of English Studies, Vol. 23.
(Oxford)   1947.

318239/23

—— PROGRAMMES OF SHAKESPEARIAN PERFORMANCES
Timon of Athens

This collection, which runs from the latter half of the nineteenth century, is continuously augmented by the addition of programmes of contemporary productions.
501292

—— RAMSEY (JAROLD W.)
Timon's imitation of Christ.
IN Shakespeare Studies, 2. (Cincinnati, Ohio)   1966.

761781

—— Sharp (W.) "Timon of Athens". pp.[7.]
In Harper's Monthly Magazine, Vol.116,
1907-8. Illus.

208781

—— SPENCER (TERENCE)
Shakespeare learns the value of money:
the dramatist at work on Timon of Athens.
IN SHAKESPEARE SURVEY 6.   (Cambridge)
1953.

631770

—— **Study in Shakespeare, A : Timon of**
Athens. From [The Oxford and
Cambridge Magazine,] Vol. 1.

1856.

554146

—— Timon [:   the old play, c.1600.]
IN SHAKESPEARE (W.) Timon of Athens.
[Edited with an introduction by
H. Morley.]   1888.   436520
Cassell's National Library.
——— Another edn.   1897.   527788

—— WAGGONER (G. R.)
"Timon of Athens" and the Jacobean duel.
IN SHAKESPEARE QUARTERLY XVI: 4.
pp. 303-311.
(New York) 1965.

605711

—— WECTER (D.)
Shakespere's purpose in Timon of
Athens.   IN Publications of the
Modern Language Association of
America, Vol. 43.   (Menasha, Wis.)
1928.

428363

—— Woods (A.H.) Syphilis in Shakespeare's
tragedy of Timon of Athens.   From
The American Journal of Psychiatry,
Vol. 91.

[Baltimore]   1934.

506173

TIMOTHY (H. J.) ed.
Come unto these yellow sands:
unison song.   [Words from] The
Tempest.   Music by F. H. Wood.
Tonic solfa translation by H. J.
Timothy.   pp. 4.   1936.

524583

TIMOTHY (H. J.) ed.
Full fathom five [and] While you
here do snoring lie: unison songs.
[Words from] The Tempest. Music
by F. H. Wood.   Tonic solfa translation by H. J. Timothy.   pp. 8.
1936.

524584

TIMOTHY (H. J.) ed.
Honour, riches, marriage-blessing:
unison song.   [Words from] The
Tempest.   Music by F. H. Wood.
Tonic solfa translation by H. J.
Timothy.   pp. 8.   1936.

524586

TIMOTHY (H. J.) ed.
Three Shakespeare songs.   [1.] You
spotted snakes, [from] Midsummer
night's dream [2.] The Cuckoo, [from]
Love's labour's lost [3.] The Owl,
[from] Love's labour's lost.   Tonic
solfa translation by H. J. Timothy;
music by F. H. Wood.   pp. 8.
1929.

536624

TIMOTHY (H. J.) ed.
Wedding is great Juno's crown: two-
part song.   Words from As you like
it.   Music by F. H. Wood.   Tonic
solfa translation by H. J. Timothy.
pp. 4.   1936.

524580

TIMOTHY (H. J.) ed.
What shall he have that killed the
deer?: two-part song. [Words
from As you like it.   Music by]
F. H. Wood.   Tonic solfa translation by H. J. Timothy.   pp. 4.
1936.

524582

TIMOTHY (H. J.) ed.
Where the bee sucks: unison song.
[Words from] The Tempest. [Music
by] T. [A.] Arne, arranged by
F. H. Wood.   Tonic solfa by H. J.
Timothy.   pp. 4.   1936.

524581

TIMPERLEY (CHARLES HENRY)
William Bulmer and the Shakespeare Press:
a biography from "A Dictionary of printers
and printing" by C.H. Timperley. With an
introductory note on the Bulmer-Martin
types, by L.B. Siegfried. Wood engravings
by J. De Pol. Published in observance of
the bicentennial of the birth of William
Bulmer, 1757-1957. pp.[iv],34[2]. Port.
(Syracuse)   1957.

666492

TIN ([PE] MAUNG)
Shakespeare: a Burman's appreciation.
IN GOLLANCZ ([Sir] I.) ed., A Book
of homage to Shakespeare.
ports. illus. facsimiles. [1916.]

264175

Tinker (C.B.) Painter and poet :
studies in the literary relations
of English painting. [With
bibliographical notes and references to Shakespeare.] Illus.

(Cambridge, Mass.)   1938.

(Charles Eliot Norton Lectures, 1937-38)

504571

TINKER (CHAUNCEY BREWSTER)
The Salon and English letters:
chapters on the interrelations of
literature and society in the age
of Johnson. [With references to
Mrs. Montagu's Essay on Shakespeare.]
(New York)
bibliog.   1915.

553364

Tinker (C.B.) and Lowry (H.F.) The
Poetry of Mattnew Arnold: a
commentary. [With a bibliographical
note. Including references to
Shakespeare.] Map.

1940.

525243

Tinkler (F.C.) Cymbeline. In
Scrutiny, Vol. 7.

(Cambridge)   1938.

503481

TINKLER (F. C.)
'The Winter's tale'.   IN Scrutiny,
Vol. 5.   (Cambridge)   1936-7.

469479

Tinling (Christine I.) Sidelights
from Shakespeare on the alcohol
problem. pp. 71.

[1932.]

409838

TIPPETT, MICHAEL KEMP
Songs for Ariel for voice and piano
(or harpsichord).   1964.

740240

TISON (JOHN L.   )

Shakespeare's "Consolatio" for exile.
Reprinted from Modern Language
Quarterly, 1960. pp.[17]

666965

Titania *see* A Midsummer Night's Dream, General Works and Criticism

TITCHMARSH, PETER, and others
Shakespeare country by car: a
practical guide for motorists
compiled by Peter and Helen
Titchmarsh.   (Kineton)   [1968.]

769262

TITHERLEY (ARTHUR WALSH)

Shakespeare, new side lights (overt and
covert). Ports. Illus. Tables. Bibliogs.
(Winchester)   1961.

666860

TITHERLEY (ARTHUR WALSH)
Shakespeare's identity [ascribed to]
William Stanley, 6th. Earl of Derby.
[With a glossary.]   (Winchester)
port.   genealogical table.   fac-
simile.   1952.

624595

Titherley (A.W.) Shakespeare's
sonnets as from the pen of William
Stanley, sixth Earl of Derby.
pp. 61.

(Liverpool)   1939.

502981

TITTERTON (WILLIAM RICHARD)
An Afternoon tea philosophy [: essays,
with a chapter "The Extinction of
Shakespeare".]   pp. 96.   1909.

424824

Titus Andronicus

— ADAMS (JOHN CRANFORD)
Shakespeare's revisions in "Titus
Andronicus".   IN Shakespeare 400:
essays by American scholars on the
anniversary of the poet's birth.
Published in co-operation with the
Shakespeare Association of America.
illus.   1964.

667803

— Baker (G.P.) "Tittus and Vespacia"
and "Titus and Ondronicus" in
Henslowe's Diary. In Publications
of the Modern Language Association
of America, vol.16.

(Baltimore)   1901.

428336

— BAKER (HOWARD)
Induction to tragedy: a study in
a development of form in Gorboduc,
The Spanish tragedy and Titus
Andronicus.   [Baton Rouge]
bibliog.   1939.

499784

— BOLTON (J. S. G.)
The Authentic text of Titus
Andronicus.   IN Publications of
the Modern Language Association
of America, Vol. 44.   (Menasha,
Wis.)
tables.   1929.

428364

—Bolton (J.S.G.) Titus Andronicus:
Shakespeare at thirty. From
Studies in Philology, vol.30.

(Baltimore)   1933.

441598

— Bolton (J.S.G.) Two notes on Titus
Andronicus. In Modern Language Notes,
Vol.45, March, 1930.

(Baltimore)

439157

— Bowers (F.T.) Elizabethan revenge
tragedy, 1587-1642. [With references to
Shakespeare's Hamlet and Titus
Andronicus, and with bibliographical
notes.]

(Princeton)   1940.

524602

— BROOKE (CHARLES FREDERICK TUCKER)
Titus Andronicus and Shakespeare
[: a criticism of H. D. Gray's
paper, "The Authorship of Titus
Andronicus"].   IN Modern Language
Notes, Vol. 34.   (Baltimore, Md.)
1919.

439157/34

— CANTRELL (PAUL L.) and WILLIAMS (GEORGE
WALTON)
Roberts' compositors in "Titus
Andronicus" Q2.   IN Studies in
Bibliography, Vol. 8.
(Charlottesville, Va.)   1956.

598680/8

— ENGLISH (JOHN) ed.
The Midland critics [: a B.B.C. pro-
gramme including a criticism of
Peter Brook's production of "Titus
Andronicus" at the Stratford Memorial
Theatre.   Broadcast 28th September,
1955].   ff. 30.
typescript.

665107

— FINDLATER (RICHARD)
Shakespearean atrocities [in Titus
Andronicus].   IN Twentieth Century,
Vol. 158.   1955.

14975/158

— Fuller (H. de W.) The Sources of Titus
Andronicus. In Publications of the
Modern Language Association of
America, Vol.16.

(Baltimore)   1901.

428336

— GRAY (A. K.)
Shakespeare and Titus Andronicus.
FROM Studies in Philology, Vol. 25.
[Chapel Hill, N.C.]
bibliog.   1928.

554222

— GRAY (HENRY DAVID)
"Titus Andronicus" once more [: a
reply to C. F. T. Brooke's criticism
of "The Authorship of Titus Andronicus"].
IN Modern Language Notes, Vol. 34.
(Baltimore, Md.)   1919.

439157/34

—HAMILTON (A. C.)
Titus Andronicus: the form of Shakespearian tragedy.
IN SHAKESPEARE QUARTERLY XIV: 3.
pp. 201-213.
(New York) 1963.
605711

—HILL (R. G.)
The Composition of "Titus Andronicus".
IN SHAKESPEARE SURVEY 10.   (Cambridge)
1957.

665485

—KOTT (JAN)
Shakespeare our contemporary.
Translated by B. Taborski.   Preface
by P. Brook.   1964.   741546
_____ 2nd edn., revised.
1967.   766093
Includes "Shakespeare - cruel and
true".

—The Lamentable and tragicall history
of Titus Andronicus [: a black-
letter broadside of the sixteenth
century.   A facsimile of the copy
in] the Folger Shakespeare Library,
Washington.   IN WELLS (EVELYN K.)
The Ballad tree.   (New York)
ports.   illus.   facsimiles.   bibliog.
1950.

609452

— LAW (R. A.)
The Roman background of Titus
Andronicus.   IN Studies in Philology,
Vol. 40.   (Chapel Hill N.C.)
bibliog.   1943.

549102

—McKERROW (R. B.)
A Note on Titus Andronicus.   IN
The Library, 4th series, Vol. 15.
1935.

437527

— McK[errow] (R.B.) [Review of] Shakespeare's Titus Andronicus : the
first quarto, 1594.   Reproduced
in facsimile, with an introduction
by J.Q.Adams. 1936.   In The Review
of English Studies, Vol.14.

1938.

495115

— PARROTT (THOMAS MARC)
Further observations on Titus Andronicus.
IN SHAKESPEARE QUARTERLY I: 1.
pp. 22-29.
(New York)   1950.
605711

— PARROTT (T. M.)
Shakespeare's revision of "Titus
Andronicus".   IN The Modern
Language Review, Vol. 14.   1919.

283257

PRICE (H. T.)
The Authorship of "Titus Andronicus".
FROM The Journal of English and
Germanic Philology, Vol. 42. (Urbana,
Ill.) 1943.

563270

PRICE (H. T.)
The First Quarto of Titus Andronicus.
IN English Institute Essays, 1947.
(New York)
bibliog. 1948.

530316/1947

SARGENT (R. M.)
The Source of Titus Andronicus.
IN Studies in Philology, Vol. 46,
No. 2. (Chapel Hill, N.C.)
1949.

554520/46

S[PENCER] (H.)
[Review of] "Shakespeare's Titus
Andronicus: the First Quarto, 1594.
[Edited] by J. Q. Adams. 1936."
IN Modern Language Notes, Vol. 53.
(Baltimore) 1938.

493024

SYKES (E. F.)
"Titus Andronicus" [: the production]
at the Memorial Theatre, Stratford-
upon-Avon, 1955 Festival Season.
ff. [33.]
typescript. 1955.
Journal Notes. 7th Series.

665414

TREWIN (JOHN COURTENAY)
The Night has been unruly [: the
theatre in England, 1769-1955].
Illustrated from the Raymond Mander
and Joe Mitchenson Theatre
Collection.
ports. illus. facsimiles. bibliog.
1957.
Titus Andronicus, Stratford-upon-
Avon, 1955. pp. 259-77.

670241

UNGERER (GUSTAV)

An Unrecorded Elizabethan performance
of "Titus Andronicus". IN Shakespeare
Survey, [Vol.] 14. (Cambridge)
1961.

666755

WAITH (EUGENE MERSEREAU)
The Metamorphosis of violence in
"Titus Andronicus". IN SHAKESPEARE
SURVEY 10. (Cambridge) 1957.

665485

WILSON (JOHN DOVER)
"Titus Andronicus" on the stage in
1595. bibliog. IN SHAKESPEARE
SURVEY 1. (Cambridge) 1948.

590674

Tobacco

[PHILARETES, pseud.]
Work for chimny-sweepers; or, A
Warning for tobacconists. 1601.
With an introduction by S. H.
Atkins. 1936.
Shakespeare Association Facsimiles.

452705

Tobias (Beatrice) illus.
WHITE (ANNA T.)
Three children and Shakespeare [:
the stories of A Midsummer night's
dream, A Merchant of Venice, Julius
Caesar and The Taming of the Shrew,
told mainly in Shakespeare's own
words.] (New York) 1938.

492184

Tobin (J.E.) Eighteenth century
English literature and its cultural
background : a bibliography. [With
references to Shakespeare.]

(New York) 1939.

510462

TOBIN (JAMES EDWARD)
More English plays, 1800-1850 [: a
supplement to the hand-list of plays
in A. Nicoll's A History of early
nineteenth century drama, 1800-1850].
IN Philological Quarterly, Vol. 23,
No. 4. (Iowa) 1944.
For "A History of early nineteenth
century drama" by A. Nicoll, see
catal. no. 373490.

583399

TOD (Q.)
Sadler's Wells Ballet carries on.
[With references to the ballet
Hamlet.] IN Theatre Arts, Vol.
27. (New York)
illus. 1943.

548672

TODD (MICHAEL) ed.
Maurice Evans in his new production
of Hamlet by William Shakespeare.
pp. [16.] (New York)
ports. illus. [1945.]

624736

Todd (R.) Tracks in the snow: studies
in English science and art. [Four
essays, including one entitled "The
Reputation and prejudices of Henry
Fuseli". With references to his
illustrations of Shakespeare, and
bibliographies.] Illus. Dgms.
Facsimiles.

1946.

578231

TODD (WILLIAM B.)
The Issues and states of the Second
Folio and Milton's epitaph on
Shakespeare.   IN Studies in Biblio-
graphy, Vol. 5.   (Charlottesville,
Va.)   1952.

598680/5

Tofte, Robert *works relating to*

— FOX (CHARLES ARUNDEL OVERBURY)
Notes on William Shakespeare and
Robert Tofte.   pp. 15.   (Swansea)
                    1956.   665305
Printed for the author.
_____ [2nd edn.]   pp. 60.
(Swansea)   1957.   665496
No. 18 of edn. limited to 100 copies,
printed for and signed by the author.

Toksvig (Signe) The Life of Hans
Christian Anderson. [With
Shakespearian references. Illus.

1933.

413488

TOLBERT (JAMES M.)
The Argument of Shakespeare's
"Lucrece": its sources and author-
ship.   IN The University of Texas
Studies in English, Vol. 29.   (Austin,
Tex.)   1950.

442432/29

TOLIVER (HAROLD E.)
Falstaff, the Prince, and the history
play.
IN SHAKESPEARE QUARTERLY XVI: 1.
pp. 63-80.
(New York) 1965.

605711

TOLLES (WINTON)
Tom Taylor and the Victorian drama.
[With references to Shakespeare.]
(New York)
  bibliog.   1940.
Columbia University.   Studies in
English and Comparative Literature.

520946

TOLMAN (ALBERT HARRIS)
Is Shakespeare aristocratic?   IN
Publications of the Modern Language
Association of America, Vol. 29.
(Baltimore)   1914.

428349

Tolman (A.H.) Notes on Macbeth. In
Publications of the Modern Language
Association of America, vol.11.

(Baltimore)   1896.

428331

TOLMAN (ALBERT HARRIS)
Shakespeare studies, 3: The Epic
character of Henry V [and] 4:
Drunkenness in Shakespeare.   IN
Modern Language Notes, Vol. 34.
(Baltimore, Md.)   1919.

439157/34

TOLMAN (ALBERT HARRIS)
Shakespeare's manipulation of his
sources in "As you like it".   IN
Modern Language Notes, Vol. 37.
(Baltimore, Md.)   1922.

439157/37

Tolman (A.H.) Shakespeare's part in
the "Taming of the Shrew". In
Publications of the Modern Language
Association of America, vol.5.

(Baltimore)   1890.

428325

Tolman (A.H.) A View of the views
about Hamlet. In Publications of
the Modern Language Association of
America, Vol.13.

(Baltimore)   1898.

428333

TOLMAN (ALBERT HARRIS)
The Views about Hamlet and other essays
[mostly on Shakespeare, including
Love's labour's won.   bibliog.]
(Boston [Mass.])
  illus.   1904.   544888
_____ Another edn.   1906.   450751

TOLMAN (A. H.)
Why did Shakespeare create Falstaff?
IN Publications of the Modern
Language Association of America,
Vol. 34.   (Baltimore)   1919.

428354

TOLSTOY ([Count] LEV [NIKOLAEVICH])
On Shakespeare and the drama.
Translated by V. Tchertkoff.   IN
The Fortnightly Review, Vols. 86
and 87.
  2 vols.   1906-7.

197680

Tolstoy, Lev Nikolaevich Count *works relating to*

— Craig (E.G.) Tolstoy and Shakespeare.
In Drama, vol.10.
                              1931.

409342

—— GARNETT (E.)
Tolstoy: his life and writings.
[With a selected list of Tolstoy's
writings. Including references to
Tolstoy's essay on Shakespeare and
the drama.]
port. bibliog. 1914.
Modern Biographies.

460086

—— GIBIAN (GEORGE)

Tolstoj and Shakespeare. (Musagetes:
Contributions to the History of Slavic
Literature and Culture,4) pp.47.
('s-Gravenhage) 1957.

665736

—— Harris (J.C.) Joel Chandler Harris,
editor and essayist: miscellaneous
literary, political, and social writings. Edited [with introductions] by
[Mrs.] Julia [F.] C.Harris. [With an
essay on Tolstoy's criticism of
Shakespeare, and bibliographical
notes.] Ports. Illus. Facsimiles.

(Chapel Hill, N.C.) 1931.

536323

—— KNIGHT (G. W.)
Shakespeare and Tolstoy. Pt. 1.
FROM Occult Review, 1930. pp. [5].
[1930]

389197

—— Knight (G.W.) Shakespeare and Tolstoy.
pp.27.
1934.

(The English Association Pamphlet,No.88.)

419624

—— MAYOR (J. B.)
Tolstoi as Shakespearian critic.
IN Transactions of the Royal Society
of Literature of the United Kingdom.
Second series, Vol. 27.
1907.

201930

—— ORWELL (GEORGE)
Lear, Tolstoy, and the fool [: a
discussion on Tolstoy's pamphlet
"Shakespeare and the drama"]. IN
Polemic, No. 7. 1947. 586298
For "Shakespeare and the drama" see
Catal. No. 204801.
_____ IN Orwell (G.) Shooting an
elephant, and other essays.
1950. 610432

—— Orwell (G.) Tolstoy and Shakespeare
[concerning Tolstoy's Essay on
Shakespeare. In The Listener,
Vol.25.

1941.

526583

—— SAHA (NARAYAN CHANDRA)
Tolstoy and Shakespeare.
IN Shakespeare commemoration volume,
edited by Taraknath Sen. (Calcutta)
1966.

764382

—— WINSTANLEY (L[ILIAN])
Tolstoy: [a biography. With references
to Shakespeare.] pp. 96.
port. bibliog. [1914]
People's Books.

460087

Tomb *see* Grave of Shakespeare

Tomkinson (Dudley) pseud. i.e.
Thomas Brown see Brown (T.)

Tomkis, Thomas *works relating to*

—— Boas (F.S.) 'Macbeth' and "Lingua"
[:a play in imitation of Shakespeare,
ascribed to T. Tomkis.] In The
Modern language review, Vol. 4.

(Cambridge) 1909.

266819

TOMLIN, ERIC WALTER FREDERICK
Tokyo essays. 1967.

illus. 770436

Includes four chapters on
Shakespeare.

TOMLINS (FREDERICK GUEST)
Remarks on the present state of the
English drama. [Containing references to Shakespeare.] pp. 15.
1851.

443577

TOMLINSON (T. B.)
Action and soliloquy in Macbeth.
IN Essays in Criticism, Vol. 8.
(Oxford) 1958.

621866/8

TOMLINSON, THOMAS BRIAN
A study of Elizabethan and Jacobean
tragedy. 1964.

668031

TOMLINSON (WALTER)
A Walk to Shottery from Stratford-on-
Avon.   IN Manchester Literary Club
Papers, Vol. 12.   (Manchester)
1886.

518373

TOMPKINS (JOYCE MARJORIE SANXTER)
[Review of] Sources for the biography
of Shakespeare, by [Sir] E. K. Chambers.
IN The Review of English Studies,
Vol. 23.   (Oxford)   1947.

318239/23

TOMPKINS (JOYCE MARJORIE SANXTER)
Why Pericles.   IN The Review of
English Studies, New Series, Vol. 3.
(Oxford)   1952.

318239/N.S./3

TONBRIDGE SCHOOL DRAMATIC SOCIETY
Programmes, etc. of Shakespearian
performances, 1923-1939.
illus.

431743

Tong Church

——MALONE (E.)
Autograph letter, dated 28 April 1791,
addressed to the incumbent of Tong
Church, Salop, together with a copy
of a letter in reply and a copy of an
inscription, concerning the epitaph on
the tomb of Sir Thomas Stanley in
Tong Church, said to have been written
by Shakespeare.   IN A Collection of
seventy-six original letters mainly
addressed to members of the Pakington
family.
manuscript.   [1539]-1829.
500985

——WHITE (W.)
All round the Wrekin.   [With a reference to a rhyming epitaph on the
tomb of Sir Thomas Stanley in Tong
Church, said to have been written by
Shakespeare.]   1860. 27886
———— 2nd edn.   1860. 462078

Tonge (Mildred) Black magic and miracles
in Macbeth. From The Journal of
English and Germanic philology,
vol.31.
(Illinois)   1932.

444160

[TONKS (JOSEPH WILLIAM)]
Mr. Donnelly and his disciples [: an
article on the Bacon-Shakespeare
controversy].   FROM The Central
Literary Magazine, Vol. 8.
(Birmingham)   1888.

556078

Toole (H.) Birmingham Musical Festival,
1870. Second miscellaneous concert,
including a new cantata, Ode to
Shakespeare. Words by H. Toole.
pp.15.
(Birmingham)   1870.

[Another copy.]

87760

TOOLE, WILLIAM B.
Shakespeare's problem plays: studies
in form and meaning.   (The Hague)
1966.
Studies in English literature Vol. XIX.

773660

Topical Allusions in Shakespeare

—— ALLEN (P.)
Shakespeare as a topical dramatist.
FROM Poetry and the Play, 1929.
pp. [18.]

389219

—— ALLEN (P.)
Topicalities in Shakespeare.
IN DOWNS (H.) ed., Theatre and
stage, Vol. 1.
ports.   illus.   dgms.   1934.

425661

—— LEE ([Sir] S.)
Shakespeare and public affairs.   IN
The Contemporary Review, Vol. 104.
1913.

247979

—— REESE (GERTRUDE C.)
The Question of the succession in Elizabethan drama.   [Including the plays of
Shakespeare.   With bibliographical
notes.]   IN University of Texas, Studies
in English, [Vol. 22].   (Austin, Texas)
1942.

542175

—— ROTHSCHILD (J. A. de)
Shakespeare and his day: a study
of the topical element in Shakespeare
and in the Elizabethan drama.
(Harness Prize Essay, 1901.)
bibliog.   1906.

399712

—— SIMPSON (RICHARD)
The Political use of the stage in
Shakspere's time.
IN Transactions of the New Shakespeare
Society, Series 1.   No. 2.   pp. 371-395.
1874.
4061

Topography *see* **Locality in Shakespeare**

TOPPEN (WILLEM HERMAN)
Conscience in Shakespeare's 'Macbeth'.
(Groningen) 1962.

667539

TORBARINA JOSIP
A Croat forerunner of Shakespeare.
In commemoration of the 400th
anniversary of the death of Marin
Držić (1508-1561). FROM Studia
romanica et anglica zagrabiensia, 24.
(Zagreb) pp. 5-21. 1967.

777925

TORBARINA (JOSIP)
A Minor crux in Hamlet. (Facultas
Philosophica Universitatis
Studiorum Zagrabiensis. Studia
Romanica et Anglica Zagrabiensia.
Num. 6, December 1958) pp. 13.
(Zagreb)
bibliogs. 1958.

666920

TORBARINA, JOSIP
The 'Nakedness' of the Shakespearian
tragic hero. FROM Studia romanica
et anglica zagrabiensia, no. 12.
(Zagreb) pp. 3-7. 1966.

777928

TORBARINA (JOSIP)
On rendering Shakespeare's blank
verse into other languages.
(Facultas Philosophica Universitatis
Studiorum Zagrabiensis. Studia
Romanica et Anglica Zagrabiensia,
No. 8, December 1959) pp. 12.
(Zagreb)
bibliogs.

666919

TORBARINA, JOSIP
The Setting of Shakespeare's plays.
FROM Studia Romanica et Anglica, No.17-18,
(Zagreb) pp.21-59. 1964.

755341

Toronto Shakespeare Festival

— EARLE GREY PLAYERS

[Toronto Shakespeare Festival.
Programmes, etc.] Ports. Illus.
Plans. Facsimiles. [Toronto]
[1950-1958.]

665433

— GREY (EARLE)
Shakespeare Festival, Toronto,
Canada. IN SHAKESPEARE SURVEY 10.
(Cambridge) 1957.

665485

Toronto University, Department of English
WILSON (HAROLD SOWERBY)
On the design of Shakespearian tragedy.
1957.
Studies and Texts, No. 5.

665556

Tottel, William *works relating to*

— KEEN (ALAN) [Ltd.]
The Private manuscript library of Francis
Bacon, Lord Verulam and of his law-clerk
and servant William Tottel: the history
of forty-seven Commonplace and other
written books preserved in an old country
house originally owned by Tottel, and
now discovered; the whole outlined by
A. Keen and offered for sale by private
treaty from his Gate House at Clifford's
Inn, London. [With a list of the books.]
pp. 14. .1943.
Note: Edn. limited to 50 copies.
541607

Touchstone *see* **As You Like It**, **Characters**

Tourguenef (I. S.) *see* Turgenev (I. S.)

Tourneur, Cyril *works relating to*

— TANNENBAUM (DOROTHY R.) and TANNENBAUM
(S. A.)
Cyril Tourneur (a concise bibliography).
[With references to Shakespeare.] ff.14.
(New York)
typescript. 1946.
Elizabethan Bibliographies, No. 33.

572412

TOURS (BERTHOLD)
Wedding is great Juno's crown,
arranged as a trio for two sopranos
and contralto. Words from
Shakespeare's "As you like it".
pp. 4.   1912.
Novello's Octavo Edition of Trios,
&c., for Female Voices.

594175

TOURS (BERTHOLD)
Wedding is great Juno's crown: part-
song for four voices with accompaniment.
Words from Shakespeare's "As you like
it".   pp. 4.   1913.
Novello's Part-song Book, Second
Series.

594174

TOWERS (ROBERT)
Mr. Shakespeare and the cinema.
IN Ashland Studies in Shakespeare,
1960.   (Ashland, Ore.)

666259/1960

Towndrow (F.E.) Brickwork of the
Shakespeare Memorial Theatre.
From "The Brick Builder", June,
1932. pp.[3.]

419972

TOWNSEND (CHARLES LOUIS)
The Realism of Shakespearian tragedy.
FROM The English Journal, Vol. 19.
pp. [9.]   (Chicago)   1930.

537394

TOWNSEND (CHARLES LOUIS)
Shakespeare and the wide, wide
world.   FROM The English Journal,
vol. 19.   (Chicago)   1930.

442567

TOWNSEND (FREDA L.)
Apologie for Bartholomew Fayre:
the art of Jonson's comedies.
[With references to Shakespeare.]
(New York)
bibliog.   1947.
Modern Language Association of
America, Revolving Fund Series.

580985

Toy Theatre

— Hamlet. Produced and directed by Lawrence
Olivier. A Two Cities film, 1948. [Scenes
from the film, with original set designs
by R. Furse, adapted for use in miniature
theatres.]   [1948.]

596187

— SPEAIGHT (G.)
Juvenile drama: the history of the
English toy theatre. [With lists of
publishers and plays published for the
juvenile drama, a bibliography and
references to Shakespeare.] Illus.
1946.

578246

— WILSON (A.E.) Penny plain, two pence
coloured: a history of the Juvenile drama.
With a foreword by C.B. Cochran [and a
bibliography]. Illus.   1932.

398185

Toye (F.) Rossini: a study in tragi-
comedy, [containing references to
Rossini's opera 'Otello'.] Ports.
Facsimile.

1934.

419644

TOYE (F.)
Tell me where is fancy bred? [: song,
with pianoforte accompaniment]
(Elkin) pp. 3.   1938.

515426

Toye (F.) Three songs from
Shakespeare: O Mistress mine, Come
away, death [and] Sigh no more
ladies.   pp.14.

[1919.]

515425

TOYNBEE (GEORGE)
Continuation to Heine [of] A. W. [von]
Schlegel's Lectures on German literature from Gottsched to Goethe given
at the University of Bonn and taken
down by G. Toynbee in 1833.   [With
references to Shakespeare.]   With
introduction, notes and a portrait,
edited by H. G. Fiedler.   pp. 96.
(Oxford)
bibliogs.   tables.   1944.

552830

Toyoda (M.) Shakespeare in Japan : an
historical survey. Reprinted from
the Transactions of the Japan Society
of London, Vol. 36. [With a Japanese
Shakespeare bibliography and notes.]

[1939.]

508912

The Tragedies
see also **Death in Shakespeare; Heroes and Heroism; Justice; Revenge; Villains** *and under the titles of the individual tragedies*

— ADAMS (H. H.)
English domestic or, homiletic tragedy, 1575 to 1642: an account of the development of the tragedy of the common man, showing its great dependence on religious morality, illustrated with striking examples of the interposition of Providence for the amendment of men's manners. [With references to Shakespeare.] (New York)
bibliogs.   1943.
Columbia University Studies in English and Comparative Literature.
550355

— ADAMS, ROBERT P.
Shakespeare's tragic vision.
IN Pacific coast studies in Shakespeare.
Edited by W. F. McNeir and T. N. Greenfield. (Eugene: Ore.) 1966.
768009

— BANDEL (BETTY)
The Debt of Shakespearian tragedy to early English comedy [: thesis.
With a bibliography, etc.]
microfilm.   5 vols. in 1 reel. 35 mm.
1947.
597360

— BATTENHOUSE (ROY W.)
Shakespearean tragedy: a Christian approach.   IN RABKIN (NORMAN) ed., Approaches to Shakespeare [: 20th century critical essays].   (New York)   1964.
668298

— BERKELEY (DAVID S.   )

A Guide to Shakespearean tragedy.
[Typescript.] Bibliogs. (Stillwater, Okla.)   1960.
666834

— BIRRELL (T. A.)
The Shakespearian mixture: recent approaches to Shakespeare's handling of the comic and tragic kinds.
[Offprint from "Museum", Vol. 83, 1958]   pp. [15]   [Leiden]
bibliogs.
667132

— BLACK, MATTHEW W.
Aristotle's $\mu\hat{\upsilon}\theta o\varsigma$ and the tragedies of Shakespeare.
IN DEUTSCHE SHAKESPEARE-GESELLSCHAFT WEST, JAHRBUCH 1968.   pp. 43-55.
(Heidelberg)
754129

— Blair (H.) Essays on rhetoric: abridged from lectures on that science. [With references to the tragedies of Shakespeare.] 3rd edn., with additions.

1787.

516397

— Bowers (F.T.) Elizabethan revenge tragedy, 1587-1642. [With references to Shakespeare's Hamlet and Titus Andronicus, and with bibliographical notes.]

(Princeton)   1940.

524602

— BOWRA (C. M.)
Sophoclean tragedy.   [With references to Shakespeare.]   (Oxford)
bibliog.   1944.

549175

— BRADBROOK (M[URIEL] C.)
Themes and conventions of Elizabethan tragedy.   [With references to Shakespeare's plays.]   (Cambridge)
bibliog.   1935.

431774

— BRADLEY (A. C.)
Shakespearean tragedy: lectures on Hamlet, Othello, King Lear, Macbeth.
2nd edn.   (6th impr.)
1910.   437262
_____ 2nd edn.   (20th imp.)
1932.   411976
_____ 2nd edn.   (20th imp.)
1937.   496470

— BRANAM (GEORGE C.)
Eighteenth-century adaptations of Shakespearean tragedy.   (Berkeley, Cal.)
bibliogs.   1956.
California University Publications, English Studies.
665359

— BROOKE, NICHOLAS
Shakespeare's early tragedies.
1968.

774966

— Brooke (Nicholas)
The Tragic spectacle in 'Titus Andronicus' and 'Romeo and Juliet.' IN

LEECH, CLIFFORD, ed.
Shakespeare: the tragedies.
A collection of critical essays.
(Chicago)   1965.

Gemini books.   752332

— C. (O.S.)
Notes on four tragedies: 1, Macbeth; 2, Othello; 3, King Lear; 4, Hamlet.
FROM The Parents' Review, Vol. 42.
pp. [30].   1931.

439153

— CADY (F. W.)
Motivation of the inciting force in
Shakespeare's tragedies.   IN
Elizabethan studies and other essays
[, by various authors], in honor of
George F. Reynolds.   (Boulder, Col.)
1945.
Colorado University Studies.
Series B.   Studies in the Humanities.
Vol. 2. No. 4.

569202

— CAMPBELL (LILY BESS)

Shakespeare's tragic heroes: slaves of
passion. [New edn.] Illus.
1962.

667950

— Casson (T.E.) Tragedy and the infinite,
[With references to Shakespeare's
plays]. From The Poetry Review,
August and October, 1939.

511406

— CHARLTON (H. B.)
Shakespearian tragedy.   (Cambridge)
bibliog.   1948.

595305

— Clemen (Wolfgang H.   )
The Development of imagery in Shakespeare's
great tragedies. IN

LEECH, CLIFFORD, ed.
Shakespeare: the tragedies.
A collection of critical essays.
(Chicago)   1965.

Gemini books.   752332

— CLEMEN (WOLFGANG H.   )

English tragedy before Shakespeare: the
development of dramatic speech.
Translated [from the German] by T.S.
Dorsch. Bibliog.   1961.

666756

— COGHILL (N.)
Tragedy [: broadcast talks.
Including references to Shakespeare's
tragedies.   Broadcast] 18th, 25th
February, 1944.   ff. 8, 9.
2 vols.   typescript.
Life and the Theatre, 6-7.
548002

— CUNNINGHAM (JAMES VINCENT)
Woe or wonder: the emotional effect
of Shakespearean tragedy.   (Denver,
Colo.)
bibliog.   1951.
Books of the Renaissance.
621456

— DANBY (JOHN FRANCIS)
The Living Shakespeare [No. 8]: The
Tragedies.   [Broadcast] 19th November,
1958.   pp. 15.
typescript.

666030

— DATTA, AMARESH
Shakespeare's tragic vision and art.
(Delhi)   1963.

Masters of English literature
series: 14.   746272

— DE MOOR (SIMON)

All length is torture: Shakespeare's
tragedies. (Amsterdam)   1960.

666830

— DICKEY (FRANKLIN M.)
Not wisely but too well: Shakespeare's
love tragedies.   (San Marino, Cal.)
1957.

665754

— DOBRÉE (BONAMY)
Death on the stage [: a talk on
the drama of tragedy.   With references to Macbeth].   (Forces
Educational Broadcast) [Broadcast]
15th November, 1945.   ff. 12.
typescript.

567027

— DRAPER (J. W.)
Flattery, a Shakespearean tragic
theme.   FROM Philological quarterly,
Vol. 17.   pp. 240-50.   (Iowa)
1938.

493044

— Dryden (John)
Preface containing the grounds of
criticism in tragedy. IN

LEECH, CLIFFORD, ed.
Shakespeare: the tragedies.
A collection of critical essays.
(Chicago)   1965.

Gemini books.   752332

— DYSON (HENRY VICTOR)
The Emergence of Shakespeare's
tragedy.   ([40th] Annual Shakespeare
Lecture of the British Academy, 1950)
pp. [25.]   [1950.]

630225

— FAIRCHILD (A. H. R.)
Shakespeare and the tragic theme.
(Columbia, Mo.)
bibliog.   1944.
University of Missouri Studies,
Vol. 29, No. 2.

555370

— FARNHAM (W. [E.])
The Medieval heritage of Elizabethan
tragedy.   [With notes and including
references to Shakespeare.]
(Berkeley, Cal.)
bibliog.   illus.   1936.

457045

— FARNHAM (WILLARD EDWARD)
Shakespeare's tragic frontier: the
world of his final tragedies.
(Berkeley, Cal.)   1950.

607673

— FRYE, DEAN
    Reading Shakespeare backwards. IN
    Shakespeare Quarterly XVII: 1. pp.19-24.
    (New York)   1966.

                              605711

— FRYE, NORTHROP
    Fools of time: studies in
    Shakespearian tragedy.   (Toronto)
                              1967.
    The Alexander lectures, 1966.
                              768554

— FULTON (W.)
    Tragic drama and the problem of evil.
    [With references to Shakespearean
    tragedy.]   FROM The Expository
    Times [Vol. 56].   [Edinburgh]
                              [1945.]

                              579642

— GARDNER, C. O.
    Themes of manhood in five Shakespeare
    tragedies.   FROM Theoria, Vol. XXIX.
    (Pietermaritzburg)   1967.
    pp. 1-24.

                              767908

— Green (C.C.) The Neo- classic theory
    of tragedy in England during the
    eighteenth century. [With references
    to Shakespeare, and bibliographical
    footnotes]

        (Cambridge,Mass.)   1934.

    (Harvard Studies in English, Vol.11.)

                              429627

— HANFORD (J. H.)
    Suicide in the plays of Shakespeare.
    IN Publications of the Modern
    Language Association of America,
    Vol. 27.   (Baltimore)   1912.

                              428347

— Hapgood (N.) Recent Shakespeare:
    tragedy. In Hapgood (N.) The Stage
    in America, 1897-1900.

        (New York)   1901.

                              548825

— HAPGOOD, ROBERT
    Shakespeare's maimed rites: the early
    tragedies.   FROM The Centennial
    Review, vol. 9, no. 4, Fall. 1965.
    pp. 494-508.
                              766377

— HARBAGE (ALFRED BENNETT)
    Intrigue in Elizabethan tragedy.
    IN Essays on Shakespeare and Eliza-
    bethan drama in honour of Hardin
    Craig.
    illus.   1963.

                              667532

— HARBAGE, ALFRED BENNETT, ed.
    Shakespeare, the tragedies: a
    collection of critical essays [by
    various writers]. (Englewood Cliffs,
    N.J.)   1964.

        Twentieth century views. 742273

— HARRISON (GEORGE BAGSHAWE)
    Shakespeare's tragedies.   1951.

                              619633

— HAWKES, TERRY
    Shakespeare and the reason: a study of
    the tragedies and the problem plays.
                              1964.

                              668277

— HEGEL, GEORG WILHELM FRIEDRICH
    [Shakespeare criticism from 'The
    Philosophy of fine art'.]   IN
    LEWINTER, OSWALD, ed., Shakespeare
    in Europe [by various authors].
                              1963.

                              667784

— HEILMAN (ROBERT BECHTOLD)
    Manliness in the tragedies: dramatic
    variations.   IN Shakespeare 1564-
    1964: a collection of modern essays
    by various hands.   (Providence, R.I.)
                              1964.
    Brown University bicentennial
    publications.

                              744437

— HEILMAN (ROBERT BECHTOLD)

    Shakespearian tragedy and the drama of
    disaster [by] Robert R. [sic. Heilman.
    (University of British Columbia.
    Sedgewick Memorial Lecture, 3) pp.27.
    (Vancouver)   1960.

                              667433

— HEILMAN (ROBERT BECHTOLD)
    'Twere best not know myself: Othello,
    Lear, Macbeth.   IN Shakespeare 400:
    essays by American scholars on the
    anniversary of the poet's birth.
    Published in co-operation with the
    Shakespeare Association of America.
    illus.   1964.

                              667803

— HENN (THOMAS RICE)
    The Harvest of tragedy [: aesthetics
    and ethics of the tragic form].
    illus.   dgms.   1956.
    Includes a chapter "Towards a
    Shakespearian synthesis".

                              656057

— HOLLAND, NORMAN NORWOOD
    Shakespearean tragedy and the three
    ways of psychoanalytic criticism.
    FROM The Hudson Review, 15. 1962.

                              667529

— HOLLOWAY (CHRISTOPHER JOHN)

    The Story of the night: studies in
    Shakespeare's major tragedies.
                              1961.

                              667054

— HOWARTH (ROBERT GUY)

    Shakespeare by air: broadcasts to
    schools.pp.64. (Sydney)
                              1957.

                              665865

—Introduction to Shakespeare's
tragedies. Illus. (Short Studies
in English Literature, No.12.)

[c.1920.]

415000

—KNIGHT (GEORGE WILSON)
The Imperial theme: further interpretations of Shakespeare's tragedies
including the Roman plays.   (Oxford)
1939.   499088
The Oxford Bookshelf.
_____ 3rd edn.   1951.   624617

—KNIGHT (GEORGE WILSON)
Principles of Shakespearian production,
with especial reference to the
tragedies.   1936.   450763
_____ Another edn.   [With an appendix:
Drama and the university.]
(Harmondsworth: Pelican Books)
1949.   602532

—KNIGHT (GEORGE WILSON)
The Wheel of fire: essays in interpretation of Shakespeare's sombre
tragedies.   [With an introduction
by T. S. Eliot.]   (Oxford)   1937.

465711

—KNIGHT (GEORGE WILSON)
The Wheel of fire: interpretations
of Shakespearian tragedy, with three
new essays.   4th revised and enlarged
edn.   bibliog.   1949.

599573

—LAMB (CHARLES)
On the tragedies of Shakspeare,
considered with reference to their
fitness for stage representation.
IN Lamb (C.) Complete correspondence
and works, Vol. 3.   1870.
For other editions of this work
please check the main sequence under
the author's name.

572053

—LAWLOR (JOHN)
The Tragic sense in Shakespeare.
1960.

666612

—LEAVIS (F. R.)
Tragedy and the "medium": a note
on Mr. [G.] Santayana's "Tragic
philosophy" [concerning Macbeth
and Shakespearean tragedy].   IN
Scrutiny, Vol. 12.   (Cambridge)
1943-4.
For "Tragic philosophy", see catal.
no. 463798.

564002

—LEECH (C.)
Shakespeare's tragedies and other
studies in seventeenth century
drama.   1950.

610403

—LEECH, CLIFFORD, ed.
Shakespeare: the tragedies. A Collection
of critical essays. (Chicago) 1965.

Gemini books.   752332

—LERNER, LAURENCE DAVID, ed.
Shakespeare's tragedies: a selection of
modern criticism.   1963.

Pelican original.   667948

— Lindsay (J.) A Short history of culture.
[With chapters : "William Shakespeare"
and "Shakespearian tragedy."]   Illus.

1939.

500639

—McCUTCHAN, J. WILSON
Plot outlines of Shakespeare's
tragedies, scene by scene. (New York)
1965.

Barnes & Noble focus books.
753446

—McFARLAND, THOMAS
Tragic meanings in Shakespeare.
(New York)   1966.

Studies in language and literature.
754716

—MACK (MAYNARD)
The Jacobean Shakespeare: some
observations on the construction of the
tragedies. IN Stratford-upon-Avon
Studies, edited by J.R.Brown and B.
Harris, Vol.1. Jacobean theatre.

1960.

666673

—MARTIN (A. P.)
Charles Lamb on stage representations.
[With references to his essay "On
the tragedies of Shakespeare".]
FROM [The Melbourne Review, July
1879.]   [Melbourne]

557125

—MENON (C. N.)
The Tragic trait [: tenth chapter
of the author's book "Shakespeare
criticism".]   IN BHUSHAN (V. N.)
ed., The Moving finger: anthology
of essays by Indian writers.
(Bombay)
bibliog.   1945.
Kiranavali.
Limited edn.

585059

— MICHEL (LAURENCE ANTHONY)
Shakespearean tragedy: critique of
humanism from the inside. IN The
Massachusetts Review, Summer 1961.
pp.18. (Amherst, Mass.)

667770

— MILLER (WILLIAM)
Shakespeare's tragedies: King Lear,
Macbeth, Hamlet & Othello. Port.
(Madras)   [1929.]

667279

___ MINKOV (MARKO)
   Shakespeare, Fletcher and Baroque tragedy.
   IN SHAKESPEARE SURVEY 20.   (Cambridge)
                   1967.

                          766881

___ MINKOV (MARKO)
   The Structural pattern of Shakespeare's
   tragedies.
   IN SHAKESPEARE SURVEY 3.   (Cambridge)
                   1950.

                          606026

___ MUIR (KENNETH)
   Shakespeare and the tragic pattern.
   (Annual Shakespeare Lecture of the
   British Academy, 1958)   pp. [18.]
                             [1958.]

                          666265

___ MUIR (KENNETH)

   **William Shakespeare: the great tragedies:
   Hamlet, Othello, King Lear, Macbeth.**
   (British Book News. Bibliographical
   Series of Supplements. Writers and their
   Work, No. 133). pp.46. Facsimiles.
   Bibliog.   1961.

                          666826

___ MYRICK (K. O.)
   The Theme of damnation in
   Shakespearean tragedy.   FROM
   Studies in Philology, Vol. 38.
   (Chapel Hill, N.C.)   1941.

                          529725

___ NOWOTTNY, WINIFRED M. T.
   Shakespeare's tragedies.   IN
   SUTHERLAND, JAMES, and HURSTFIELD,
   JOEL, eds., Shakespeare's world.
                   1964.

                          667808

___ NUGENT, ELIZABETH M.
   Shakespeare's Troilus and Cressida;
   Titus Andronicus; Timon of Athens;
   Pericles and Cymbeline. (New York)
                   1965.

          Monarch critiques of literature.
                   757008

___ ORNSTEIN (ROBERT)
   The Moral vision of Jacobean tragedy.
   (Madison, Wis.)
    bibliog.   1960.

                          698027

___ PHILLIPS (H. C. B.)
   Literature: its relation to life.
   [A Lecture on Shakespeare's four
   tragedies, Hamlet, Othello, Macbeth
   and King Lear.]   Bookshop practice:
   talks on books and the bookshop -
   No. 8.   FROM The Publishers' Circular,
   December 12th, 1936.   pp. [4.]

                          462918

___ PLATT (PETER)
   English and French theories of tragedy
   and comedy, based on the appreciation
   of Shakespeare in France.   Thesis
   offered for the degree of Ph.D. in
   the Faculty of Arts at the University
   of Birmingham.   [Birmingham]
   bibliog.   typescript.   1957.

                          665749

___ PRIOR (M. E.)
   The Language of tragedy [: an
   exploration into the nature of
   verse drama based on consideration
   of English verse tragedy, including
   references to Shakespeare.]   (New
   York)
    bibliog.   1947.

                          590003

___ PROSER, MATTHEW N.
   The heroic image in five Shakespearean
   tragedies. (Princeton, N.J.)   1965.

                          748405

___ Raysor (T.M.) Intervals of time and
   their effect upon dramatic values in
   Shakespeare's tragedies.   From
   The Journal of English and Germanic
   Philology, Vol. 37.

                   1938.

                          503676

___ Reed (H.) Lectures on English history
   and tragic poetry as illustrated
   by Shakspeare.   [Edited with an
   introduction and notes by W.B.
   Reed and with a bibliography.]

          (Philadelphia)   1855.

                          569831

___ RIBNER (IRVING)
   Patterns in Shakespearian tragedy.
                   1960.
   Companion volume, entitled "Jacobean
   tragedy", Catal. No. 705790.

                          666641

___ ROGERS (CARMEN)
   Heavenly justice in the tragedies
   of Shakespeare.   IN MATTHEWS (A. D.)
   and EMERY (C. M.) eds., Studies in
   Shakespeare.   (Coral Gables, Fla.)
                   1953.
   University of Miami Publications in
   English and American Literature,
   Vol. 1, March 1953.
                          634188

___ ROSEN (WILLIAM)

   Shakespeare and the craft of tragedy.
   Bibliogs. (Cambridge, Mass.)
                   1960.

                          666556

___ RUSSELL (T. W.)
   Voltaire, Dryden, & heroic tragedy.
   [With references to Shakespeare.]
   (New York)
    bibliogs.   1946.

                          575212

__ RYLANDS (G. [H. W.])
Introduction [with references to
Shakespeare]. IN Rylands (G. [H.W.])
[ed.] Elizabethan tragedy: six
representative plays (excluding
Shakespeare). 1933.

412648

__ RYMER (THOMAS)
The Tragedies of the last age; A
Short view of tragedy, with some
reflections on Shakespear. IN The
Critical works of Thomas Rymer.
Edited with an introduction and notes
by C. A. Zimansky. (New Haven [Conn.])
bibliogs. 1956.

670354

__ SAINTSBURY [G. E. B.]
The Two tragedies; a note [: the
tragic and the sentimental types of
tragedy, including references to
Shakespeare's tragedies]. IN
Blackwood's Magazine, Vol. 162.
(Edinburgh) 1897. 140338
_____ IN Saintsbury (G. [E. B.])
The Memorial volume: a new collection
of his essays and papers.
port. 1945. 563813

__ SANTAYANA (G.)
Tragic philosophy. [With references
to Shakespeare and his Macbeth.]
IN Scrutiny, Vol. 4. (Cambridge)
1935-6.
For note on this , entitled "Tragedy
and the 'medium'", by F. R. Leavis,
see catal. no. 564002.

463798

__ SCHWARTZ (ELIAS)
The Idea of the person and Shakespearian
tragedy.
IN SHAKESPEARE QUARTERLY XVI:1.
pp. 39-47.
(New York) 1965.

605711

__ SHAKESPEARE SURVEY 20 [: Shakespearian
and other tragedy]. (Cambridge)
1967.

766881

__ Shakspearean notes [on Hamlet, Antony
and Cleopatra, Troilus and Cressida,
and Macbeth]. No[s. 1 and] 2.
FROM [Dublin University Magazine,
Vol. 63.] [Dublin] 1864.

559982

__ SIEGEL (PAUL N.)
Shakespearean tragedy and the Elizabethan compromise. (New York)
bibliog. 1957.

665533

__ SIMPSON (P.)
The Theme of revenge in Elizabethan
tragedy. pp. 38. (British Academy
Annual Shakespeare Lecture, 1935)
[1935]

438945

__ SISSON (CHARLES JASPER)
Shakespeare's tragic justice.
(Ontario) [1961.]

667250

__ SOCHATOFF (A. FRED)
The Tragedies.
IN "Starre of Poets". Discussions
of Shakespeare. (Pittsburgh, Pa.:
Carnegie Institute of Technology)
1966.

766812

__ SPEAIGHT (ROBERT)
Nature in Shakespearian tragedy.
1955.

648479

__ SPRAGUE (ARTHUR COLBY)
Shakespeare and the actors: the stage
business in his plays (1660-1905).
(Cambridge, Mass.)
illus. bibliog. 1945.
The Other tragedies, pp. 281-334.

563058

__ [Stedman (J.)] Laelius and Hortensia;
or, Thoughts on the nature and
objects of taste and genius, in
a series of letters. [With
references to Shakespeare.]

(Edinburgh) 1782.

414684

__ STERNFELD (FREDERICK W.)
The Dramatic and allegorical function
of music in Shakespeare's tragedies.
IN Annales Musicologiques, Tome 3.
1955.

637889/3

__ STERNFELD (FREDERICK WILLIAM)
Music in Shakespearean tragedy.
illus. 1963.
Studies in the history of music.

667660

__ STIRLING (BRENTS)
Unity in Shakespearian tragedy: the
interplay of theme and character.
(New York) 1956.

665317

__ STOLL (ELMER EDGAR)
Reconciliation in tragedy:
Shakespeare and Sophocles. FROM
The University of Toronto Quarterly,
Vol. 4. (Toronto) 1934.

440599

__ STOLL (E. E.)
Shakespeare and other masters [:
literary studies, with special
references to Shakespeare's tragedies.]
(Cambridge [Mass.])
bibliog. 1940.

532084

—STOLL (ELMER EDGAR)
The Tragic fallacy, so-called[, in
modern drama].   Reprinted from
the University of Toronto Quarterly,
Vol. 5.   [With references to
Shakespeare.]   pp. [25.]   (Toronto)
bibliog.   1936.

568679

—THORNDIKE (A. H.)
The Relations of Hamlet to contemporary
revenge plays.   IN Publications of
the Modern Language Association of
America, vol. 17. (Baltimore) [1902]

428337

—THORNDIKE (A. H.)
Tragedy [: the course of English
tragedy from its beginnings to the
middle of the nineteenth century.
With chapters, "Shakespeare and his
contemporaries"; and "Shakespeare";
and other references to Shakespeare.]
(Boston, [Mass.])
bibliog.   1908.
The Types of English Literature.

552597

— TOMLINSON, THOMAS BRIAN
A study of Elizabethan and Jacobean
tragedy.   1964.

668031

— Townsend (C.L.) The Realism of
Shakespearian tragedy. From The
English Journal, Vol.19. pp. [9.]

(Chicago)   1930.

537394

— The Tragedies of Maddelen, Agamemnon,
Lady Macbeth, Antonia, and Clytemnestra,
by J. Galt [: a review].   FROM [The
Quarterly Review,] Vol. 11. 1814.

556071

— URE (PETER)

Shakespeare and the inward self of the
tragic hero: inaugural lecture of the
Joseph Cowen Professor of English
Language and Literature delivered at
King's College, Newcastle upon Tyne,
October, 1960. pp.22. (Durham)
1961.

666754

—VAUGHAN (C. E.)
Romantic tragedy: Shakespeare.
IN Vaughan (C. E.) Types of tragic
drama.
bibliog.   1908.   305296
_____ Another edn.   1924.   550900

—Vaughan (H.H.) New readings & new
renderings of Shakespeare's tragedies.
2nd edn. Vol.1.
1886.

All published.

466552

— Voltaire ([F.M.A.] de) Letters
concerning the English nation.
[containing a letter "On tragedy",
having references to Shakespeare.]
New edn.

1760.

519580

— WEISINGER (HERBERT)
The Myth and ritual approach to
Shakespearean tragedy.   Reprinted
from The Centennial Review of Arts
and Science, Vol. 1.   pp. 142-166.
[East Lansing, Mich.]   [1957.]

665618

— WEISINGER (HERBERT)
The Study of Shakespearian tragedy
since Bradley: a reprint from
Shakespeare Quarterly.   Vol. 6.
pp. [10].   [New York]   [1955]

665615

—WHITAKER, VIRGIL KEEBLE
The mirror up to nature: the
technique of Shakespeare's tragedies.
(San Marino, Cal.)   1965.

745405

— Whitmore (C.E.) The Elizabethan Age in
England. [With references to the
tragedies of Shakespeare.] In
Whitmore (C.E.)   The Supernatural
in tragedy.

1915.

266111

— WILSON (HAROLD SOWERBY)

On the design of Shakespearian tragedy
(University of Toronto. Department of
English. Studies and Texts, No.5).
1957.

665556

Tragedy *see* **The Tragedies**

Traill (H.D.) Plays and players. 2:
Mr. Tree's Hamlet. In The National
Review, vol.19.

1892.

115355

Transcendentalism *see* **Philosophy and
Religion**

Translation

see also under the titles of the separate works

—— BENINGTON (A.)
Translations of Shakespeare and
others.   IN North American Review,
Vol. 196.   1912.

239870

—— BRENNECKE (ERNEST and HENRY)
Shakespeare in Germany, 1590-1700;
with translations of five early
plays.
illus.   1964.
Curtain playwrights.

668171

—— DONNER, HENRY WOLFGANG
Some problems of Shakespearian
translation. (Stockholm)   1963.

Annales Academiae Regiae
Scientiarum Upsaliensis Kungl.
Vetenskapssamhållets i Uppsala Arsbok
7/1963.   740388

—— DOROSHENKO (D.)
Shakespeare in Ukrainian.   IN The
Slavonic Review, vol. 9.   1931.

382941

—— HELSZTYŃSKI (STANISŁAW)
Polish translations of Shakespeare in
the past and today.
IN SHAKESPEARE JAHRBUCH.   Bd. 100/101.
1964/1965.   pp. 284-293.   (Weimar)

10421

—— LAZENBY (MARION C.)
The Influence of Wieland and Eschenburg
on Schlegel's Shakespeare translation:
a dissertation submitted to the Board
of University Studies of The Johns
Hopkins University in conformity with
the requirements for the degree of
Doctor of Philosophy, 1941.   pp. 37.
(Baltimore)
bibliogs.   1942.

560977

—— MARK (THOMAS R.)
The First Hungarian translation of
Shakespeare's Complete Works.
IN SHAKESPEARE QUARTERLY XVI: 1.
pp. 104-115.
(New York)   1965.

605711

—— MEISNEST (F. W.)
Wieland's translation of Shakespeare.
IN The Modern Language Review, Vol.9.
(Cambridge)

1914.

266824

—— PASCAL (R.) [ed.]
Shakespeare in Germany, 1740-1815
[: German criticisms and translations,
with an introduction in English].
(Cambridge)

1937.

469784

—— PASTERNAK (B.)
Some remarks by a translator of
Shakespeare.   FROM Soviet Literature,
Sept. 1946.   (Moscow)

581952

—— PASTERNAK (BORIS)

Translating Shakespeare.[Translated
by M.Harari.] FROM Twentieth Century,
Vol.164.pp.213-228.   1958.

665934

—— PRAGER, LEONARD
Shakespeare in Yiddish.
IN SHAKESPEARE QUARTERLY XIX: 2.
pp. 149-158.   (New York)
1968.

605711

—— RILLA (W.) [ed.]
Extracts from Schlegel's translation
of Shakespeare: a reading with
introductory notes on the translation.
[Broadcast] 23rd April, 1947.   ff. 2.
typescript.
Introductory notes only.

583271

—— ROTHE (H.)
Shakespeare in German.   IN German life
and letters, Vol. 1.   (Oxford)

1937.

476079

—— SHAH (C. R.)
Shakespearean plays in Indian
languages.   [Parts] 1-2.
FROM The Aryan Path, Vol. 26.
pp. [6, 4.]   (Bombay)
2 vols.   1955.

665272-3

—— Shakespeare's plays in Turkish.   FROM
Great Britain and the East, August 1943.

(Work of the British Council: 5)

547452

—— Stamm (Rudolf) Modern 'theatrical'
translations of Shakespeare.

IN Shakespeare Survey [Vol.] 16. 1963.

illus.   667523

—— TENNYSON, HALLAM
Shakespeare translated.   Produced
by H. Tennyson.   B.B.C. radio script
broadcast 22nd November 1968.
typescript.

776829

— TORBARINA (JOSIP)
   On rendering Shakespeare's blank
   verse into other languages.
   (Facultas Philosophica Universitatis
   Studiorum Zagrabiensis.   Studia
   Romanica et Anglica Zagrabiensia,
   No. 8, December 1959)   pp. 12.
   (Zagreb)
     bibliogs.   1959.

                             666919

— UNGARETTI, GIUSEPPE
   Notes on Shakespeare's art of poetry.
   IN LEWINTER, OSWALD, ed.,
   Shakespeare in Europe [by various
   authors].   1963.

                             667784

—— WATERHOUSE (G.)
   German literature.   [With references
   to Shakespearian influence and translations, and a bibliography.]   pp. 80.
                                1928.
   Benn's Sixpenny Library [No. 55])

                             522289

— ZEYDEL (E. H.)
   Ludwig Tieck as a translator of English,
   [including Shakespeare].   IN Publications of the Modern Language Association
   of America, Vol. 51.   (Menasha, Wis.)
                                1936.

                             463431

— ZIOLECKI (Dr.)
   Shakspere in Poland, Russia, and other
   Sclavonic countries.
   IN Transactions of the New Shakespeare
   Society, Series 1.   Nos. 8-10.
   pp. 431-441.   1880-6.
                             99113

Travel in Shakespeare
see also **Voyages and Explorations**

—BAUGHAN (DENVER EWING)
   Shakespeare's attitude toward travel.
   IN Essays in honor of Walter Clyde
   Curry [by various authors].
   (Nashville, Tenn.)
     port.   bibliog.   1955.
   Vanderbilt Studies in the Humanities,
   Vol. 2.

                             671926

Travellers Guides
   JENNET (SEÁN) ed.
   The Shakespeare country and South
   Warwickshire.
     illus.   1965.

                             742102

TRAVELWISE
   Where to stay and eat in the Shakespeare
   country and the Midlands: comprehensive
   touring guide.
     map   1964.

                             667834

Travers (B.) Hamlet, retold [in
   American slang.] pp.[2.] From
   Pearson's Weekly, February 29th,
   1936.

                             450645

TRAVERSI (D. A.)
   Approach to Shakespeare.
                       1938.   492467
   _____ 2nd edition, revised and
   enlarged.   1957.   665688
   _____ 3rd edition, revised and
   enlarged.   1968-69.   773952

TRAVERSI (DEREK ANTONA)
   Commentary.   IN The Winter's tale.
   Text edited by C. J. Sisson.   (New
   York)   1960.
   The Laurel Shakespeare.   F. Fergusson,
   general editor.

                             667462

   Traversi (Derek Antona) Coriolanus.
   In Scrutiny, Vol.6.
                 (Cambridge)   1937-38.
                             489751

   Traversi (Derek Antona) Coriolanus.
   (1937). In Stallman (R.W.) [ed.]
   Critiques and essays in criticism,1920-
   1948.   (New York)   1949.

                             598617

TRAVERSI (DEREK ANTONA)
   Henry IV - Parts I & II [: an exam-
   ination].   IN Scrutiny Vol. 15.
   (Cambridge)   1947-8.

                             421336/15

TRAVERSI (DEREK ANTONA)
   "King Lear".   IN Scrutiny, Vol. 19.
   (Cambridge)   1952.

                             421336/19

TRAVERSI, DEREK ANTONA
   King Lear.   In Stratford Papers
   on Shakespeare delivered at the
   1964 Shakespeare Seminar.
   (Toronto)   1965.

                             745844

TRAVERSI (DEREK ANTONA)
   Love and war in Shakespeare's "Troilus
   and Cressida".   IN Love and violence
   [: studies by various authors.
   Translations by G. Lamb].
     illus.   1954.

                             641760

   Traversi (Derek Antona)'Measure
   for Measure' [: an essay]. In Scrutiny,
   Vol.11.   (Cambridge)   1942.

                             555576

TRAVERSI (DEREK ANTONA)
Othello. FROM The Wind and the Rain,
Vol. 6, No. 4. pp. 248-269. 1950.

639538

TRAVERSI (DEREK ANTONA)
Othello. IN LEECH, CLIFFORD, ed.,
Shakespeare: the tragedies. A
collection of critical essays.
(Chicago) 1965.
Gemini books.

752332

Traversi (Derek Antona) [A review of]
Shakespeare's last plays, by E.M.W.Tillyard.
In Scrutiny,Vol.6.
(Cambridge) 1937-38.

489751

TRAVERSI, DEREK ANTONA
'Richard II'. IN Stratford Papers
on Shakespeare delivered at the
1964 Shakespeare Seminar. (Toronto)
1965.

745844

TRAVERSI (DEREK ANTONA)
Shakespeare from "Richard II" to
"Henry V". [1958.]

665883

TRAVERSI (DEREK ANTONA)
Shakespeare: the last phase. 1954.

642461

TRAVERSI, DEREK ANTONA
Shakespeare: the Roman plays. 1963.

667658

TRAVERSI (DEREK ANTONA)
The Tempest. IN Scrutiny Vol. 16.
(Cambridge) 1949.

421336/16

Traversi (Derek Antona) Troilus and
Cressida. In Scrutiny,Vol.7.
(Cambridge) 1938.

503481

TRAVERSI (DEREK ANTONA)
William Shakespeare: the early comedies.
"The Comedy of errors"; "The Taming of
the shrew"; "The Two gentlemen of
Verona"; [and] "Love's labour's lost".
pp. 46.
port. facsimiles. bibliog. 1960.
British Book News. Bibliographical
Series of Supplements. Writers and
their Work, No. 129.

666695

TRAVERSI, DEREK ANTONA
The Winter's tale. IN MUIR, KENNETH,
ed., Shakespeare, the comedies: a
collection of critical essays.
(Englewood Cliffs, N.J.) 1965.

748348

Travesties *see* Burlesques

TREASE (GEOFFREY)
Cue for treason [: a story dealing
partly with Shakespeare and his time.]
frontis. 1940.
Tales of Two Worlds.

523002

**Tree ([Sir] H.B.) Hamlet – from an
actor's prompt book. In The Fortnightly Review. Vol. 58. New series.**

1895.

132241

Tree, Herbert Beerbohm Sir *works relating to*

—— BALL (ROBERT HAMILTON)
The Shakespeare film as record:
Sir Herbert Beerbohm Tree.
IN SHAKESPEARE QUARTERLY III: 3.
pp. 227-236.
(New York) 1952.

605711

—— BURNS (G.)
Sir Herbert Beerbohm Tree. [With
Shakespearian references.] IN
The Post Victorians. 1933.

412642

—— CRAN (Mrs. [MARION])
Herbert Beerbohm Tree [: a biography.]
1907.
Stars of the Stage.

416053

—— FORBES-ROBERTSON (BEATRICE)

In the company of Tree and Alexander.
[Script of broadcast in the Home
Service, February 1959.] (British
Broadcasting Corporation) ff.8.
Typescript.

666167

—— MAX, [pseud.]
At Her Majesty's [: a description
of Sir H. Beerbohm Tree's production
of "Midsummer night's dream".] IN
The Saturday Review, Vol. 89. 1900.

153040

—— PEARSON (HESKETH)
Beerbohm Tree: his life and laughter.
ports. illus. chronological table.
1956.

657353

——R. (E. M.)
Mr. Beerbohm Tree's Mark Antony.
IN The Westminster Review, Vol. 150.
1898.

144830

—— SCOTT (CLEMENT WILLIAM)
Some notable "Hamlets" of the present
time (Sarah Bernhardt, [Sir] H. [B.]
Irving, W. Barrett, [Sir H.] B. Tree
and [Sir J.] Forbes Robertson).
New and cheaper edn. with a new
chapter on H. B. Irving by W. L.
Courtney.   Illustrated by W. G. Mein.
ports.   1905.

540625

—— TRAILL (H. D.)
Plays and players.   2: Mr. Tree's
Hamlet.   IN The National Review,
Vol. 19.   1892.

115355

—— TRIANGLE PLAYS

Sir Herbert Tree and Constance Collier
in Macbeth. Triangle Special.
[1916.]

667956

Tree (Viola) Castles in the air: the
story of my singing days. [With
references to Shakespeare.] Ports.

1926.

544887

TREECE, HENRY
The Green man [: novel on the story of
Amleth.]   1966.

753365

Treece (H.) Speech for Hamlet. In The
New Apocalypse: an anthology of
criticism, poems and stories, by
D.Cooke [and others].

[1940.]

511389

Trees *see* Natural History

TREHERN (E. M.)
Notes on 'Hamlet'.   IN The Modern
Language Review, Vol. 40.
(Cambridge)   1945.

571545

TREMAIN (RONALD)
Come away, death: part-song for
S.A.B.   Words by Shakespeare [from
"Twelfth Night"].   pp. 4.   1958.
Novello's Choral Songs for Voices
of Limited Range.

666474

TREMAIN (RONALD)
Full fathom five: part-song for
S.A.B.   Words [from "The Tempest"].
pp. 4.   1958.
Novello's Choral Songs for Voices
of Limited Range.

666472

TREMAIN (RONALD)
Sigh no more, ladies: part-song for
S.A.B.   Words [from "Much ado about
nothing"].   pp. 4.   1958.
Novello's Choral Songs for Voices
of Limited Range.

666473

TREMAIN (RONALD)
Take, O take those lips away: part-
song for S.A.B.   Words [from
"Measure for measure"].   pp. 4.
1958.
Novello's Choral Songs for Voices
of Limited Range.

666477

TREMAIN (RONALD)

Under the greenwood tree: part-song for
S.A.B. Words by Shakespeare [from "As
You Like It"]. (Novello's Choral Songs
for Voices of Limited Range). pp.4.
1958.

666476

TREMAIN (RONALD)

When icicles hang by the wall: part-
song for S.A.B. Words by Shakespeare
[from "Love's Labour's Lost"].
(Novello's Choral Songs for Voices of
Limited Range) pp.4.   1958.

666475

TRENCH ([FREDERIC] HERBERT)
Shakespeare [: a poem].
IN GOLLANCZ ([Sir] I.) ed., A Book
of homage to Shakespeare.
ports. illus. facsimiles. [1916.]

264175

TRENCH (RICHARD CHEVENIX)
Every good gift from above: a sermon
preached in the parish church of
Stratford-upon-Avon on Sunday,
April 24, 1864 at the celebration of
the tercentenary of Shakespeare's
birth. 2nd edn. pp. 20. 1864.

511208

Trench (R.C.) Plutarch; his life, his
parallel lives and his morals: five
lectures. [With references to
Shakespeare.] 2nd edn.

1874.

68184

TRENCH (R. C.)
[Poem on Shakespeare.]   IN The
Shakespeare Tercentenary meeting
held at the Mansion House, May Day,
1916 [etc.]   pp. 18 [2].
Printed at "The Sign of the Dolphin".

603467

TRENCH (WILBRAHAM FITZJOHN)
A Note on five dramatic interruptions.
A Contribution to the textual criticism
of Shakespeare.   FROM Hermathena,
No. 48.   pp. [8].   (Dublin) 1933.

439151

TRENCH (WILBRAHAM FITZJOHN)
Shakespeare: the need for meditation.
IN GOLLANCZ ([Sir] I.) ed., A Book
of homage to Shakespeare.
ports. illus. facsimiles. [1916.]

264175

TREVELYAN (HUMPHRY)
Goethe & the Greeks [showing the
growth of his Hellenism. With
references to Shakespeare.]
(Cambridge)
bibliogs. 1941.

529389

TREVELYAN (R. C.)
Thersites [: a play on Shakespeare.]
FROM Life and Letters, Vol. 11.
pp. [9]. [1934]

428694

TREWIN (JOHN COURTENAY)
Alec Clunes: an illustrated study
of his work, with a list of his
appearances on stage and screen.
ports. illus. 1958.
Theatre World Monograph No. 12.

681247

TREWIN (JOHN COURTENAY)

Benson and the Bensonians. with a
foreword by Dorothy Green. Ports. Illus.
Bibliog. 1960.

666666

TREWIN (JOHN COURTENAY)
Edith Evans. Illustrated from the
Raymond Mander and Joe Mitchenson
Theatre Collection.
ports. illus. 1954.
[Theatre World Monograph No. 2.]

641298

TREWIN (JOHN COURTENAY)
Foreword and introductions. IN
CLEAVE (PHILIP) Shakespeare's country
in pictures.
illus. map. [1951]
[Britain Illustrated]

617494

Trewin (J.C.) I hate the films! [a
criticism of the filming of Shakespeare's plays.] In Sight & sound,
Vol. 7.

1938.

500307

TREWIN (JOHN COURTENAY)
The Night has been unruly [: the
theatre in England, 1769-1955].
Illustrated from the Raymond Mander
and Joe Mitchenson Theatre Collection.
ports. illus. facsimiles. bibliog.
1957.

670241

TREWIN (JOHN COURTENAY)
The Old Vic and Stratford-upon-Avon
1961-1962.
IN SHAKESPEARE QUARTERLY XIII: 4.
pp. 505-519.
(New York) 1962.

605711

TREWIN (JOHN COURTENAY)
Paul Scofield: an illustrated study
of his work, with a list of his
appearances on stage and screen.
ports. illus. 1956.
Theatre World Monograph No. 6.

656877

TREWIN (JOHN COURTENAY)
The Pictorial story of William
Shakespeare and Stratford upon Avon.
Foreword by L. Fox. pp. 24.
ports. illus. [1954.]

640453

TREWIN (JOHN COURTENAY)
The Pictorial story of Shakespeare
& Stratford-upon-Avon. Foreword
by L. Fox. pp. 24.
ports. illus. map. facsimile.
[1960.]
Pitkin Pictorials Ltd. "Pride of
Britain" Guides and Histories.

666649

TREWIN (J. C.)
The Post-war theatre: a survey.
[With references to Shakespearian
performances.] IN ELWIN (M.) ed.,
Pleasure ground: a miscellany of
English writing.
illus. 1947.

582769

Trewin (J.C.) [Review of] Shakespeare
criticism : an essay in synthesis, by
C. N. Menon. In Sight & sound,
Vol. 7.

1938.

500307

Trewin (J.C.) Shakespeare and the films.
[Reviews of] Shakespearian costume
for stage and screen, by F. M. Kelly.
In Sight & sound, Vol. 7.

1938.

500307

TREWIN, JOHN COURTENAY
Shakespeare on the English stage, 1900-
1964: a survey of productions,
illustrated from the Raymond Mander and
Joe Mitchenson Theatre Collection. 1964.

illus. 667799

TREWIN (JOHN COURTENAY)
The Story of Stratford upon Avon.
Photography by E. Daniels. pp. 80.
facsimile. bibliog. 1950.

607314

REWIN (JOHN COURTENAY)
Sybil Thorndike: an illustrated
study of Dame Sybil's work, with a
list of her appearances on stage and
screen.
port. illus. 1955.
Theatre World Monograph No. 4.

650886

REWIN (JOHN COURTENAY)
We'll hear a play [: a note-book of
the theatre]. With an introduction
by Sir B. Jackson. 1949.
Includes references to Shakespeare.

611287

REWIN, JOHN COURTENAY ed.
Macready, William Charles
The Journal of William Charles Macready,
1832-1851, abridged and edited by J. C.
Trewin.
illus. 1967.

764789.

Trewin, John Courtenay *works relating to*

—CRAIG (E. G.)
A Book about the Shakespeare Memorial
Theatre [: "The Shakespeare Memorial
Theatre", by Muriel C. Day and J. C.
Trewin] reviewed. 1931.

409342

TREWIN (JOHN COURTENAY) and BARTON (JOHN)
"The Tempest" [at Stratford: a
discussion. Broadcast, 15th August
1957.] ff. 7.
typescript.

665666

TREWIN (JOHN COURTENAY) and DAY
(M[URIEL] C.)
The Shakespeare Memorial Theatre.
With forewords by Sir F. [R.] Benson
and W. Bridges-Adams.
ports. illus. plan. facsimiles.
1932.

391217

TREWIN (JOHN COURTENAY) and KEMP (THOMAS
CHARLES)
The Stratford Festival: a history of
the Shakespeare Memorial Theatre.
(Birmingham)
ports. illus. 1953.

630388

TREWIN (JOHN COURTENAY) and LAMB (CHARLES
and MARY)
Tales from Shakespeare: all those told
by Charles & Mary Lamb with 12 others
newly told by J. C. Trewin.
1964.

668314

TRIANGLE PLAYS
Sir Herbert Tree and Constance Collier
in Macbeth. Triangle Special.
[1916.]

667956

TRIBE, DAVID
Freethought and humanism in Shakespeare.
1964.

744461

TRICAUD, M.-L.
Shakespeare and Claudel. FROM Theoria,
October, 1964. pp.13-20.
(Pietermaritzburg)

668360

TRIENENS (ROGER J.)
The Inception of Leontes' jealousy in
The Winter's Tale.
IN SHAKESPEARE QUARTERLY IV: 3.
pp. 321-326.
(New York) 1953.

605711

Triggs, Oscar Lovell *works relating to*

— HARRIS (JOEL CHANDLER)
Joel Chandler Harris, editor and
essayist: miscellaneous literary,
political, and social writings.
[Includes "Shakespeare of modern
business": a study of the comparison
made by O. L. Triggs between Shakespeare
and J. D. Rockefeller.] (Chapel
Hill, N.C.)
bibliog. illus. 1931.

536323

Trilling (L.) Matthew Arnold. [With
references to Shakespeare.] Port.

1939.

496463

TRINDER (WALTER)
A Fairy pastoral: part-song for
mixed voices, with piano or strings.
Words from Shakespeare's "A Midsummer Night's Dream". pp. 7.
1952.
Elkin New Choral Series, 2263.

633327

TRNKA (BOHUMIL)
Shakespeare's ethics and philosophy. IN
CHARLES UNIVERSITY ON SHAKESPEARE:
essays edited by Z. Stříbrný. (Praha)
illus. 1966.

762631

Trnka (Jiří) illus.
PETIŠKA (EDUARD)
A Midsummer night's dream: retold
for children.   Photographs of puppets
by J. Trnka.   [Translated by Jean
Layton.]   pp. 35.   1960.

666875

Trnka, Jiří *works relating to*

——   A Midsummer night's dream
[: text, with description and photographs
of the Czech puppet film made by J.
Trnka]. Edited by B. Hodek. Essays on
the film translated by S. Součková.
Illus. (Prague)   1960.

666729

Troilus and Cressida

General Works and Criticism

Characters

Music; Opera; Plays

Sources and Background

Stage History and Production

Study and Teaching; Tales

Textual History

Troilus and Cressida

– General Works and Criticism

——ALMEIDA (BARBARA HELIODORA C. de M.F. de)
"Troilus and Cressida": romantic love
revisited. IN Shakespeare Quarterly XV:
4. pp.327-332. (New York)   1964.

605711

——ARNOLD (AEROL)
The Hector-Andromache scene in
Shakespeare's "Troilus and Cressida".
IN Modern Language Quarterly, Vol.
14.   (Seattle, Wash.)

1953.

525289/14

—— Barker (E.) A Shakespeare discovery.
In The Spectator. Vol.158.

1937.

469292

—— BAYLEY, JOHN
Shakespeare's only play.   IN
Stratford Papers on Shakespeare
delivered at the 1963 Shakespeare
Seminar.   (Toronto)   1964.

668007

—— BOAS (G.)
"Troilus and Cressida" and the time
scheme.   IN The New English Review,
Vol. 13.   1946.

577268

—— BOWDEN (WILLIAM R.)
The Human Shakespeare and "Troilus and
Cressida".
IN   SHAKESPEARE QUARTERLY VIII.
pp. 167-177.
(New York)   1957.

605711

—— CAMPBELL (O. J.)
Comicall satyre and Shakespeare's
"Troilus and Cressida".   [With a
bibliography.]   (San Marino, Cal.)
1938.

495349

——Charlton (H.B.) The Dark comedies :
[Measure for Measure, All's Well that
Ends Well, Troilus and Cressida.]
Reprinted from the Bulletin of the
John Ryland's Library, Vol.21.
pp. 53.

(Manchester)   1937.

490483

—— DANIELS (F. QUINLAND)
Order and confusion in Troilus and Cressida
I.iii.
IN   SHAKESPEARE QUARTERLY XII: 3.
pp. 285-291.
(New York)   1961.

605711

——DAVIS (E.)
Troilus and Cressida.   IN English
Studies in Africa, Vol. I.
(Johannesburg)   1958.

682610/1

—— DE SELINCOURT (E.)
Troilus and Cressida.   IN De
Selincourt (E.) Oxford lectures on
poetry.   (Oxford)   1934.

421184

—— DICKEY (FRANKLIN M.)
Not wisely but too well: Shakespeare's
love tragedies.   (San Marino, Cal.)
1957.
Huntington Library.

665754

——ELLIS-FERMOR (UNA [M.])
The Frontiers of drama [: criticism
of the drama.   With a chapter
entitled "Discord in the spheres:
the universe of 'Troilus and Cressida'".]
bibliog.   1945.

563985

—EVANS (G. B.)
Pandarus' house?: Troilus and
Cressida, III, ii; IV, ii; IV, iv.
IN Modern Language Notes, Vol. 62.
(Baltimore, Md.)
bibliog.   1947.

439157/62

—FOAKES (REGINALD ANTHONY)
Troilus and Cressida reconsidered. IN
University of Toronto Quarterly, Jan.
1963. pp.13. (Toronto)

596179

—GATTY (REGINALD ARTHUR ALLIX)
Shakespeare's "Troilus and Cressida";
a structural and psychological analysis.
typescript.   [?1930.]

624887

—HARRIER (RICHARD C.)
Troilus divided.   IN Studies in the
English Renaissance drama, edited by
Josephine W. Bennett [and others].
1959.

684756

—Henderson (W.B.D.) Shakespeare's
Troilus and Cressida, yet deeper
in its tradition. In Craig (H.)
ed.,Essays in dramatic literature:
the Parrott presentation volume.
Port.
(Princeton)   1935.

444399

—KAUFMANN, RALPH JAMES
Ceremonies for chaos: the status of
'Troilus and Cressida'. FROM E.L.H.
Journal of English Literary History,
Vol. 32, No.2, June 1965. (Baltimore,
Md.)

756151

—KAULA (DAVID)
Will and reason in Troilus and Cressida.
IN SHAKESPEARE QUARTERLY XII: 3.
pp. 271-283.
(New York) 1961.

605711

—KIMBROUGH, ROBERT
Shakespeare's 'Troilus & Cressida'
and its setting.   (Cambridge, Mass.)
1964.

740459

—KNIGHT (GEORGE WILSON)
The Metaphysic of "Troilus and
Cressida".   FROM Dublin Review,
1929.   pp. [15.]   [1929]

390919

—KNIGHTS (LIONEL CHARLES)
"Troilus and Cressida" again. IN Scrutiny,
Vol. 18.

1951.

421336/18

—KNOWLAND (A. S.)
Troilus and Cressida.
IN SHAKESPEARE QUARTERLY X: 3.
pp. 353-365.
(New York) 1959.

605711

—KOTT (JAN)
Shakespeare our contemporary.
Translated by B. Taborski.   Preface
by P. Brook.   1964.   741546
_____ 2nd edn., revised.
1967.   766093
Includes "Troilus and Cressida -
amazing and modern".

—MACAULAY (ROSE)
The Critic on the air [: criticisms
of broadcasts relating to classical
themes.   Including a criticism of
"Troilus and Cressida".   Broadcast]
28th November, 1946.   ff. 7.
typescript.

582323

—MARSH, DERICK RUPERT CLEMENT
Interpretation and misinterpretation:
the problem of Troilus and Cressida.
IN SHAKESPEARE STUDIES 1.
(Cincinnati, Ohio)   1965.

750317

—MERTON (STEPHEN)
"The Tempest" and "Troilus and
Cressida".   FROM College English,
Vol. 7.   pp. 8.   (Chicago) 1945.

619467

—MORRIS (BRIAN)
The Tragic structure of Troilus and
Cressida.
IN SHAKESPEARE QUARTERLY X: 4.
pp. 481-491.
(New York) 1959.

605711

—MUIR (KENNETH)
Troilus and Cressida.   IN Shakespeare
Survey, [Vol.] 8.   (Cambridge)

1955.

647706

— A Note on Troilus and Cressida.
In The Adelphi, Vol. 15.

1938-9.

509700

—OATES, J.C.
The ambiguity of Troilus and Cressida.
IN Shakespeare Quarterly XVII: 2. pp.141-
150. (New York)   1966.

605711

— ORNSTEIN (ROBERT) ed.
Discussions of Shakespeare's problem
comedies [: All's well that ends
well; Measure for measure: Troilus
and Cressida.   Selected from various
authors].   (Boston, Mass.: D. C.
Heath and Co.)   1961.
Discussions of Literature.

667641

— RABKIN, NORMAN
Troilus and Cressida: the uses of
the double plot.   IN SHAKESPEARE
STUDIES 1.   (Cincinnati, Ohio)
1965.

750317

—— RICKEY, MARY ELLEN
'Twixt the dangerous shores: Troilus and Cressida again. IN SHAKESPEARE QUARTERLY XV: 1.   1964.

605711

—— SARGEAUNT (G. M.)
The Classical spirit.   [Containing Troilus and Cressida; The last phase; and other Shakespearian references.] [Bradford]   1936.

470852

—— SEWELL (A.)
Notes on the integrity of Troilus and Cressida. IN The Review of English Studies, Vol. 19. (Oxford) bibliog.   1943.

555539

—— **Shakespeare's Troilus and Cressida. From [The Oxford and Cambridge Magazine,] Vol. 1.**

1856.

554148

—— SLACK (ROBERT C.)
The Realms of gold and the dark comedies. IN "Starre of Poets". Discussions of Shakespeare. (Pittsburgh, Pa.: Carnegie Institute of Technology)
1966.

766812

—— SOUTHALL (RAYMOND)
"Troilus and Cressida" and the spirit of capitalism. IN KETTLE (ARNOLD) ed., Shakespeare in a changing world: essays [by various authors]. 1964.

667797

—— STEEDS (P.)
Two lesser known plays [: summary of a lecture on 'Measure for measure' and 'Troilus and Cressida'.] IN The Poetry Review, [Vol. 4.]
1914.

253079

—— SWANSTON (HAMISH F.   G.   )

The Baroque element in "Troilus and Cressida." FROM "The Durham University Journal," New Series Vol.19.pp.14-23. (Durham)   1957.

665776

—— Taylor (G.C.) Shakespeare's attitude towards love and honor in Troilus and Cressida. In Publications of the Modern Language Association of America, Vol.45.

(Menasha,Wis.)   1930.

428365

—— TILLYARD (EUSTACE MANDEVILLE WETENHALL)
Shakespeare's problem plays [: Hamlet; Troilus and Cressida; All's well that ends well; and, Measure for measure.   The Alexander Lectures at the University of Toronto. 1948-9.] bibliog.   1950.

604507

—— TRAVERSI (DEREK A.)
Love and war in Shakespeare's "Troilus and Cressida". IN Love and violence [: studies by various authors. Translations by G. Lamb]. illus.   1954.

641760

—— TRAVERSI (D. A.)
Troilus and Cressida. IN Scrutiny, Vol. 7.   (Cambridge)   1938.

503481

—— WILLIAMS (C.)
The English poetic mind. [With references to Troilus and Cressida.]
1932.

392333

Troilus and Cressida

— Characters

—— DUNKEL (WILBUR D.)
Shakespeare's Troilus.
IN SHAKESPEARE QUARTERLY II: 4. pp. 331-334.
(New York) 1951.

605711

—— DYER (FREDERICK B.)
The Destruction of Pandare. IN Shakespeare encomium, 1564-1964 [by various writers].   (New York)
1964.
City University of New York, City College Papers, 1.

747546

—— ELTON (W. R.)
Shakespeare's Ulysses and the problem of value.
IN Shakespeare Studies, 2. (Cincinnati, Ohio)   1966.

761781

—— FARNHAM (WILLARD EDWARD)
Troilus in shapes of infinite desire. IN Shakespeare 400: essays by American scholars on the anniversary of the poet's birth.   Published in co-operation with the Shakespeare Association of America. illus.   1964.

667803

GAGEN, JEAN
Hector's honor.
IN SHAKESPEARE QUARTERLY XIX: 2.
pp. 129-137.   (New York)
1968.

605711

KENNY (H.)
Shakespeare's Cressida.   IN Anglia:
Zeitschrift für englische Philologie,
Band 61.   (Halle)   1937.

479286

McCLINTOCK (M. L.)
Variations on the character of
Diomedes.   IN Ashland Studies in
Shakespeare, 1958.   (Ashland, Ore.)

666259/1958

STEHLÍKOVÁ (EVA)
Thersites, a deformed and scurrilous
Grecian.   IN
CHARLES UNIVERSITY ON SHAKESPEARE:
essays edited by Z. Stříbrný.   (Praha)
illus.   1966.

762631

SYKES (E. F.)
Segregation of the role of Diomedes.
Supplementary note to comments on
Byam Shaw's production at Stratford-
upon-Avon [of] "Troilus and Cressida".
ff. 16.
typescript.   1954.
Journal Notes.   6th Series.

665406

THOMPSON, KARL F.
The Unknown Ulysses.
IN SHAKESPEARE QUARTERLY XIX: 2.
pp. 125-128.   (New York)
1968.

605711

Troilus and Cressida

— Music; Opera; Plays

For music scores see under the heading
Music Scores, Troilus and Cressida
For texts of stage adaptations of this play
see **ENGLISH EDITIONS**, Troilus and
Cressida — Alterations, etc.

SYKES (E. F.)
"Troilus and Cressida": Sir W.
Walton's opera; libretto by C.
Hassall.   Some jottings regarding
the Covent Garden Opera Company's
performance at the Coventry Theatre,
April 1955.   ff. 15.
typescript.   [1955.]

665415

Trevelyan (R.C.) Thersites: [a play
on Shakespeare.] From Life and
Letters, Vol.11. pp.[9].

[1934]

428694

Troilus and Cressida

— Sources and Background

BRADBROOK (MURIEL CLARA)
What Shakespeare did to Chaucer's Troilus
and Criseyde.
IN SHAKESPEARE QUARTERLY IX.
pp. 311-319.
(New York)   1958.

605711

BULLOUGH (GEOFFREY)
The Lost "Troilus and Cressida".
IN English Association, Essays
and Studies, 1964.   Shakespeare
Quatercentenary ed.
illus.   1964.

667820

DENOMY (ALEXANDER JOSEPH)
The Two moralities of Chaucer's "Troilus
and Criseyde".   IN Royal Society of
Canada, Proceedings and Transactions.
3rd Series, Vol. 44.   (Ottawa)
1950.

70120/3/44

GORDON (R. K.) [ed.]
The Story of Troilus as told by Benoît
de Sainte-Maure, G. Boccaccio,
G. Chaucer, and R. Henryson.   Trans-
lations and introduction by R. K.
Gordon.   1934.

425280

KIMBROUGH (ROBERT)
The "Troilus" log: Shakespeare and
"box-office". In Shakespeare Quarterly
XV: 3. pp.201-209. (New York) 1964.

605711

LE FEVRE (R.)]
The Recuyell of the historyes of Troye.
Written in French by R. Lefevre,
translated and printed by W. Caxton
(about 1474).   The first English
printed book, now faithfully reproduced with critical introduction
[containing references to Shakespeare's
"Troilus and Cressida",] index and
glossary, by H. O. Sommer.
tables.   facsimiles.   2 vols. 1894.
No. 1 of edn. limited to 12 copies,
signed by the publisher, D. Nutt.

573703

—— POTTS (ABBIE FINDLAY)
"Cynthia's Revels", "Poetaster", and
"Troilus and Cressida".
IN SHAKESPEARE QUARTERLY V.
pp. 297-302.
(New York) 1954.

605711

—— PRESSON (ROBERT K.)
Shakespeare's "Troilus and Cressida" &
the legends of Troy.   (Madison, Wis.)
1953.

635838

—— Rollins (H.E.) The Troilus- Cressida
story from Chaucer to Shakespeare.
In Publications of the Modern
Language Association of America,
Vol.32.

(Baltimore)   1917.

428352

—— SAVAGE, JAMES E.
"Troilus and Cressida" and Elizabethan
court factions. FROM Studies in English,
Vol.5. (University, Miss.)   1964.

pp.43-66.   767187

—— Stein (Elizabeth) Caxton's Recuyell
and Shakespeare's Troilus. In
Modern Language Notes, vol.45,1930.

(Baltimore)

439157

—— TATLOCK (J. S. P.)
The Siege of Troy in Elizabethan
literature especially in Shakespeare
and Heywood.   IN Publications of
the Modern Language Association of
America, Vol. 30.   (Baltimore)
1915.

428350

—— Tatlock (J.S.P.) The Welsh 'Troilus
and Cressida' [MS. Peniarth 106,
National Library of Wales]and its
relation to the Elizabethan drama.
In The Modern Language Review, Vol.
10.

(Cambridge)   1915.

266825

—— Wagner (B.M.) Caxtons Recuyell and
Shakespeare's Troilus. In Modern
Language Notes, vol.45, March, 1930.

(Baltimore)

439157

Troilus and Cressida

— Stage History and Production
*Newspaper reviews, playbills, theatre pro-
grammes and theatrical illustrations — the
library's extensive collection of this material
is mainly uncatalogued but indexed*
*For texts of stage alterations and adaptat-
ions of the play see* **ENGLISH EDITIONS,
Troilus and Cressida** — Alterations, etc.

—— DENT (ALAN HOLMES)
Troilus and Cressida at Stratford-on-
Avon.   [Radio talk] produced by P.
Humphreys.   [Broadcast] 15th July 1954.
ff. 5.
typescript.

643700

—— GARNETT (E.)
"Troilus and Cressida" and the critics.
IN The Contemporary Review, Vol. 103.
1913.
William Poel's production.

243280

—— Kemp (T.C.) The Stratford Festival:
review of Troilus and Cressida.
[Broadcast] 9th July, 1948.ff.3.
Typescript.

593009

—— KIMBERLEY, MICHAEL EDWARD
'Troilus and Cressida' on the English
stage. Submitted for M.A. degree in
the University of Birmingham, June,
1968. (Birmingham)   1968.

Typescript.   773826

—— PLAYERS CLUB, New York
The Players eleventh annual revival:
Troilus and Cressida, by W. Shakespeare
[at] B. S. Moss' Broadway Theatre, New
York, week of June 6th 1932. [Souvenir
programme.] pp.[28.] [New York]
ports. illus. facsimile.   [1932.]

646353

—— PROGRAMMES OF SHAKESPEARIAN PERFORMANCES
Troilus and Cressida

This collection, which runs from the
latter half of the nineteenth century,
is continuously augmented by the
addition of programmes of contemporary
productions.

499171

— REYNOLDS (G. F.)
Troilus and Cressida on the Elizabethan
stage.   IN McMANAWAY (J. G.), DAWSON
(G. E.) and WILLOUGHBY (E. E.) eds.,
Joseph Quincy Adams memorial studies.
(Washington)
 bibliog.   1948.

596748

—STAMM (RUDOLF)
The Glass of Pandar's praise: the word-
scenery, mirror passages, and reported
scenes in Shakespeare's "Troilus and
Cressida".   IN English Association,
Essays and Studies, 1964: Vol. 17 of
the new series of Essays and Studies
collected by W. A. Armstrong.   Shakespeare Quatercentenary ed.
 illus.   1964.

667820

Troilus and Cressida

— Study and Teaching; Tales

—ADAMSON, ELGIVA, and MOORE, KATHLEEN V.
Notes on William Shakespeare's
"Troilus and Cressida". [Stratford,
Ontario].   [1963.]

765919

— KIMBROUGH, ROBERT
Troilus and Cressida: a scene-by-scene
analysis with critical commentary.
(New York)   1966.

Study master series. 762645

Troilus and Cressida

— Textual History

— ALEXANDER (P.)
Troilus and Cressida, 1609.
Reprinted from The Transactions of
the Bibliographical Society, 1928.
                        1928.
MS. letter from P. Alexander to
Mr. Misleton inserted.

399895

— LAVINE (ANNE RABINER)

This bow of Ulysses: Shakespeare's
"Troilus and Cressida" and its imitation
by Dryden. 1 vol. in 1 reel. 35mm. 1961.

668381

 : Microfilm negative copy made by
University Microfilms Inc., Ann Arbor,
Mich.

— NOSWORTHY, JAMES MANSFIELD
Shakespeare's occasional plays: their
origin and transmission.   1965.

747250

— WALKER (ALICE)
The Textual problem of 'Troilus and
Cressida'.   IN The Modern Language
Review, Vol. 45.
                        1950.

266816/45

— WILLIAMS (P.)
The "Second issue" of Shakespeare's
Troilus and Cressida, 1609.
 IN Virginia University Bibliographical
Society, Studies in bibliography, Vol.
2.   (Charlottesville, Va.)
                        1949.

598680/2

— WILLIAMS (P.)
Shakespeare's Troilus and Cressida:
the relationship of Quarto and Folio.
 IN Virginia University Bibliographical
Society, Studies in bibliography, Vol.
3.   (Charlottesville, Va.)
                        1950.

598680/3

Trollope, Anthony *works relating to*

—COYLE (WILLIAM)
Trollope and the bi-columned
Shakespeare.   IN Nineteenth-century
fiction, Vol. 6.   (Berkeley, Cal.)
                        1951.

612922/6

TRORY (ERNEST)
Mainly about books.   (Brighton)
 frontis.   tables.   1945.
Includes a chapter "Shakespeare in
the U.S.S.R."

564806

The Troublesome raigne of King John

For editions of this play see under
English Editions: King John:
Alterations &c.

TROUBRIDGE (St. VINCENT)
Costume in Hamlet [: the story of
the quarrel in the Kemble family,
concerning stage costumes for
Shakespeare's plays]. IN Notes
and Queries, Vol. 185. (Oxford)
1943.
Enlarging on a point made in an
article of the same title, by Madeleine
H. Dodds, also in this volume of Notes
and Queries.

549646

TROY (WILLIAM)
Commentary. IN Antony and Cleopatra.
Text edited by C. J. Sisson. (New
York) 1962.
The Laurel Shakespeare. F. Fergusson,
general editor.

667477

True and exact catalogue of all the
plays and other dramatick pieces
printed in the English tongue, contin'd
down to April 1732 [including
Shakespearian plays]. IN [JONSON] (B.)
The Three celebrated plays of Ben
Johnson. Viz. The Fox, The Alchymist,
The Silent woman.
frontis. [1732.]

527018

True Tragedy of Richard Duke of York

For editions of this play see under
ENGLISH EDITIONS OF SHAKESPEARE'S SEPARATE
PLAYS
Henry the Sixth, Part III

The True tragedie of Richard the Third

For editions of this play see under
ENGLISH EDITIONS OF SHAKESPEARE'S SEPARATE
PLAYS
Richard the Third: Alterations, &c.

TRUMAN (NEVIL P.)
Historic costuming. With a foreword
by C. B. Cochran [and a chapter
"Shakespeare's England, 1558-1625".]
port. illus. 1936.

450378

TRUMAN (N. [P.])
Historic stage costuming, 13.
Shakespeare's England. IN DOWNS (H.)
ed., Theatre and stage, Vol. 1.
ports. illus. dgms. 1934.

425661

THE TRUNK MAKER [pseud.]
Mr. Macready and Mr. Edwin Forrest.
FROM The Connoisseur, 1846. pp. [2.]

389210

THE TRUNK MAKER [pseud.]
Mr. Macready's Macbeth. FROM The
Connoisseur, 1846. pp. [2.]

389220

[TRURO CATHEDRAL SCHOOL, Shakespearian
Society
Programmes, posters, tickets, etc.
of performances.] [Truro]
[1930-39].

460001

Trussell, John *works relating to*

—— SHAABER (M. A.)
"The First rape of faire Hellen" by
John Trussell.
IN SHAKESPEARE QUARTERLY VIII.
pp. 407-448.
(New York) 1957.

605711

Truth

—— HUNTLEY, FRANK LIVINGSTONE
Macbeth and the background of Jesuitical
equivocation. FROM Publications of the
Modern Language Association of America,
LXXIX:4. (New York) 1964.

pp. 390-400. 747544

Tschaikovsky (P. I.) see Chaikovsky
(P. I.)

TSUBOUCHI (YŪZŌ)
Shakespeare and Chikamatsu.
IN GOLLANCZ ([Sir] I.) ed., A Book
of homage to Shakespeare.
ports. illus. facsimiles. [1916.]

264175

Tuan (Liu Po) see Liu Po Tuan

TUCIĆ (SRGJAN)
Shekspir i Yugosloveni. (The Homage
of the Yugoslavs.) [Servian text,
with English] by N. Forbes.

IN GOLLANCZ ([Sir] I.) ed., A Book
of homage to Shakespeare.
ports. illus. facsimiles. [1916.]

264175

TUCKER, MARY CURTIS
Towards a theory of Shakespearian
comedy: a study of the contributions
of Northrop Frye. A thesis. (Ann Arbor,
Mich.) 1963.

microfilm, positive copy.
1 vol. in 1 reel. 35mm. 745498

TUCKER (WILLIAM JOHN)
College Shakespeare: [an account of
his life and work.] (New York)
bibliog. port. 1932.

392299

TUGMAN (CECIL C.)
The Workshop: a play.   ff. [3] 12.
[Johannesburg]
  typescript.   [1952.]

630854

Tulane University Studies in English

Tulane University Studies in English
RIBNER (IRVING)
Othello and the pattern of
Shakespearean tragedy.   Reprinted
from Tulane University, Tulane Studies
in English, Vol. 5.   pp. [14].
(New Orleans, La.)
  bibliogs.   1955.

666589

Tulane University Studies in English
ROPPOLO (JOSEPH PATRICK)
American premières of two Shakespearean
plays in New Orleans: The Two
gentlemen of Verona and Antony and
Cleopatra.   Reprinted from Tulane
University, Tulane Studies in English,
Vol. 7.   pp. [8].   (New Orleans, La.)
  bibliogs.   1957.

666580

Tulane University Studies in English
ROPPOLO (JOSEPH PATRICK)
Hamlet in New Orleans.   Reprinted
from Tulane University, Tulane Studies
in English, Vol. 6.   pp. [16].
(New Orleans, La.)
  chronological table.   bibliogs.
                         1956.

666581

Tulane University Studies in English
TAYLOR (DICK)
The Masque and the lance: the Earl
of Pembroke in Jacobean court
entertainments.   Reprinted from
Tulane University, Tulane Studies in
English, Vol. 8.   pp. [33].   (New
Orleans, La.)   1958.

666780

Tulane University Studies in English
TAYLOR (DICK)
The Third Earl of Pembroke as a
patron of poetry.   Reprinted from
Tulane University, Tulane Studies
in English. Vol. 5.   pp. [27].
(New Orleans, La.)   1955.

666783

TUNBRIDGE WELLS BRANCH, BRITISH EMPIRE
SHAKESPEARE SOCIETY
  Programmes, etc., 1937-45.

547086

TUNSTALL (BEATRICE)
The Dark lady [:   a novel.]   1939.

502760

TUPPER (FREDERICK)
The Shaksperean mob.   IN Publications
of the Modern Language Association of
America, Vol. 27.   (Baltimore) 1912.

428347

Tupper, Fred S., Memorial Lectures
HARBAGE (ALFRED BENNETT)
Shakespeare & the professions.
(Washington)   1965.
  Fred S. Tupper Memorial lectures.

747852

[TUPPER (JOHN LUCAS)]
Viola and Olivia [:   a poem.   With
an etching by W. H. Deverell].   IN
The Germ, 1850.   1850.   580968
_____ A facsimile reprint.
                     1901.   157369

[TURGENEV (IVAN SERGEEVICH)]
Hamlet and Don Quixote: a lecture
[translated] from the Russian of
I. Tourgénieff by Lena Milman.
FROM The Fortnightly Review, Vol. 62.
                     1894.   148377
_____ [Broadcast] 31st March, 1951.
ff. 6.
  typescript.   1951.   620403

[TURGENEV (I. S.)]
The King Lear of the Russian steppes.
Translated from [the Russian of]
I. Tourguenef by Mrs. [Fanny] B.
Palliser.   FROM [London Society,]
Vol. 22.   [1872.]

558071

TURING, JOHN
My nephew Hamlet [: the journal of
Claudius, King of Denmark. A novel.]
Drawings by Jill McDonald.   1967.

    illus.   764131

Turkey

—— AND, METIN
  Shakespeare in Turkey.   FROM Theatre
  Research.   1964.
    pp. 75-84.   illus.

773832

—— BURIAN (ORHAN)
  Shakespeare in Turkey.
  IN SHAKESPEARE QUARTERLY II: 2.
  pp. 127-128.
  (New York) 1951.

605711

—— DRAPER (JOHN WILLIAM)
  Shakespeare and the Turk.   IN Journal
  of English and Germanic Philology,
  Vol. 55.   (Urbana, Ill.) 1956.

600780/55

—— HUMPHREYS (A. R.)
Shakespeare's plays in Turkey [: a
broadcast talk]. IN The Asiatic
Review, New Series, Vol. 41. 1945.

568954

—— Shakespeare's plays in Turkish.
FROM Great Britain and the East,
August 1943.
Work of the British Council: 5.

547452

TURNBULL (PERCY)
You spotted snakes with double tongue:
four-part [song. Words] from A
Midsummer night's dream. [Music by]
P. Turnbull. pp. 8. (Oxford)
1928.
Oxford Choral Songs, No. 721.

520362

Turner (E.F.) T leaves: a collection
of pieces for public reading.
[Including 'Shakespeare on board',
relating to the ghost scene from
Hamlet.] 3rd edn.
1885.

474962

Turner (G.[W.]) Falstaffs unknown to
fame. In The Theatre, Vol.13.

1889.

101204

TURNER (JAMES)
Shakespeare illustrated: drawings,
engravings and prints after the
first artists, including the Boydell
Gallery and other curious collections.
Culled from many sources by a member
of the Birmingham Shakespeare Reading
Club. (Birmingham)
37 vols. 1898.

665136-72

TURNER ([JULIA] CELESTE)
Anthony Mundy, an Elizabethan man of
letters. [With a list of works by
A. Mundy and references to Shakespeare.]
(Berkeley, Cal.)
bibliogs. 1928.
University of California Publications
in English, Vol. 2, No. 1.

543036

TURNER (MARGARET)
My horn-book and my top: a play in
one act. pp. [vi], 30.
1951. 621421
French's Acting Edition, No. 1597.
_____ IN MARRIOTT (J. W.) [ed.] The
Best one-act plays of 1950-51.
1952. 626661

TURNER (MARGARET)
There's rue for you: a play in one
act [on the childhood of
Shakespeare]. pp. 24. 1950.
French's Acting Edition.

605566

Turner, Muriel, illus.
NEURATH, MARIE
They lived like this in Shakespeare's
England. Artist: Muriel Turner. 1968.

illus. 774869

TURNER, ROBERT K.
The New Arden Henry VI, Parts I, II,
and III: review article.
IN SHAKESPEARE STUDIES 3. (Cincinnati,
Ohio) 1967.

771652

TURNER, ROBERT Y.
Characterization in Shakespeare's early
history plays. FROM E L H, a journal of
English Literary History, Vol. 31.
(Baltimore, Maryland) 1964.

pp. 241-258. 749531

TURNER (ROBERT Y.)
Dramatic conventions in "All's well
that ends well" IN P.M.L.A. 75 : 1960
pp. 497-502.

428321

TURNER, ROBERT Y.
Shakespeare and the public confrontation
scene in early history plays. FROM
Modern Philology, vol.62. (Chicago)
1964.

pp. 1-12. 749533

TURNER, ROBERT Y.
Significant doubling of roles in
Henry VI, part two. FROM The Library
Chronicle, Vol.30. (Philadelphia)
1964.

pp. 77-84. 749534

TURNER (WALTER JAMES REDFERN)
Berlioz: the man and his work.
[With references to Shakespeare and
a bibliography of Berlioz's works.]
ports. facsimiles. 1934.

425758

TURNER (WALTER JAMES REDFERN) [and others]
The Image of love [: a discussion
between Lucie Mannheim, M. Goring,
W. J. R. Turner, and J. Duncan; with
illustrations from Shakespeare's
"Romeo and Juliet", Schnitzler's
"Liebelei", Gogol's "Marriage", Ibsen's
"Doll's house", and Shaw's "Candida";
from the broadcast series The Living
image. Broadcast] January 25th, 1943.
ff. 20.
typescript.

539874

Turner, William *works relating to*

— WILLIAMSON (G. C.)
Shakespeare's wine-book: [A new boke
of the natures and properties of wines,
by W. Turner, 1568.]   Reprinted from
The Wine & Spirit Trade Record,
Jan. 15th 1923.   pp. 20.
illus.

408587

Tuve (Rosamund) Elizabethan and
metaphysical imagery: Renaissance
poetic and twentieth-century critics.
[With references to Shakespeare and
a bibliography.]

(Chicago)   1947.

586178

Twain, Mark *works relating to*

— LEACOCK (STEPHEN [B.])
Mark Twain.   [With references to
Shakespeare.]
port.   1932.

399208

— MASTERS (E. L.)
Mark Twain: a portrait.   [With
references to Shakespeare]   (New York)
port.   1938.

481108

— Shakespeare and the school of
assumption [: a review of 'Is
Shakespeare dead?' by M. Twain].
IN The Library, New Series. Vol. 10.
1909.

222151

TWEDDELL (GEORGE MARKHAM)
Shakspere: his times and contemporaries.   Pts. 1 [and] 3.   2nd edn.
corrected and enlarged.   pp. 40,
81-120.   (Bury & Middlesbro'-on-
Tees)
frontis.   1861-63.

399894

Twelfth Night
General Works and Criticism
Music; Opera
Novels; Plays; Poems
Sources and Background
Stage History and Production
Study and Teaching; Tales
Textual History

Twelfth Night

— General Works and Criticism

— BARNET (SYLVAN)
Charles Lamb and the tragic Malvolio.
IN Philological Quarterly, Vol. 33.
(Iowa)   1954.

592684/33

— BLISTEIN (ELMER M.   )

The Object of scorn: an aspect of the
comic antagonist. pp.[14]. Reprinted
from The Western Humanities Review,
Vol.14, No.2. (Salt Lake City)
1960.

667293

— BRADLEY (A. C.)
Feste the jester.
IN GOLLANCZ ([Sir] I.) ed., A Book
of homage to Shakespeare.
ports. illus. facsimiles. [1916.]

264175

— BRITTIN (NORMAN A.)
The Twelfth Night of Shakespeare and of
Professor Draper.
IN SHAKESPEARE QUARTERLY VII,
pp. 211-216.
(New York) 1956.

605711

— BURKE (K.)
The Philosophy of literary form:
studies in symbolic action.
[Including an essay entitled Trial
translation (from Twelfth Night).]
[Baton Rouge, La.]   1941.

531543

— BURTON (HARRY McGUIRE)

William Shakespeare: Twelfth Night.
(Guides to English Literature) pp.59.
[1962.]

667792

— COOK ([E.] D.)
Twelfth Night.   FROM Once a week,
(New Series) Vol. 1.   1866.

515797

CRANE (MILTON)
Twelfth Night and Shakespearian comedy.
IN SHAKESPEARE QUARTERLY VI.
pp. 1-8.
(New York) 1955.

605711

DRAPER (JOHN WILLIAM)
The Melancholy Duke Orsino. Reprinted
from Bulletin of the History of
Medicine, Vol. 6. pp. [12.]
bibliog. [1938.]

569109

DRAPER (J. W.)
Olivia's household. IN Publications
of the Modern Language Association
of America, Vol. 49. (Menasha, Wis.)
1934.

432218

DRAPER (JOHN WILLIAM)
Shakespeare's Illyria. IN The Review
of English Studies, Vol. 17. (Oxford)
bibliog. 1941.

533231

Draper (J.W.) Sir Toby's "Cakes and
ale". [With bibliographical references.] In English Studies, Vol.20.

(Amsterdam) 1938.

495114

DRAPER (JOHN WILLIAM)
The Twelfth Night of Shakespeare's
audience. (Stanford, Cal.)
illus. 1950.

609854

Draper (J.W.) The Wooing of Olivia.
From Neophilologus, 23e Jaargang.

(Groningen) 1937.

497780

EAGLETON, TERENCE
Language and reality in "Twelfth
night". FROM Critical Quarterly,
Autumn. 1967.
pp. 217-228.

773827

[FARJEON (H.)]
Shakespeare's characters - Orsino
[: scenes from Twelfth Night].
Arranged [with comments] by H. Farjeon.
[Broadcast 5th August, 1945.] ff. 16.
typescript.

563289

[FARJEON (H.)]
Shakespeare's characters - Sir
Toby Belch [: scenes from Twelfth
Night]. Arranged [with comments]
by H. Farjeon. [Broadcast July
16th, 1946.] ff. 18.
typescript.

573189

GARDNER (C. O.)

Some notes on the comic seriousness of
"Twelfth Night". IN Theoria, a journal
of studies, [No.] 19. pp.[8.]
[1962.]

667769

GATTY (REGINALD ARTHUR ALLIX)
Shakespeare in character and song: As
you like it: The Tempest; and, Twelfth
Night. ff. 35.
manuscript. [c.1925.]

637992

GOLLANCZ ([Sir] I.)
Bits of timber: some observations on
Shakespearian names - "Shylock";
"Polonius"; "Malvolio".
IN GOLLANCZ ([Sir] I.) ed., A Book
of homage to Shakespeare.
ports. illus. facsimiles. [1916.]

264175

GOWING (Mrs. A.)
The Graphic Gallery of Shakespeare's
heroines. Olivia - Cleopatra -
Miranda. IN The Theatre, Vol. 12.
1888.

99108

HUNT (LEIGH)
Twelfth Night. IN Essays. Edited
[with a preface] by A. Symons. With
illustrations by H. M. Brock. 1903.

519680

JENKINS (HAROLD)
Shakespeare's "Twelfth Night". IN
Shakespeare, the comedies: a collec-
tion of critical essays. (Englewood
Cliffs, N.J.) 1965.

748348

KING, WALTER N. ed.
Twentieth century interpretations
of 'Twelfth Night': a collection
of criticial essays. (Englewood
Cliffs, N.J.) 1968.
Twentieth century interpretations.

772580

KOTT (JAN)
Shakespeare our contemporary.
Translated by B. Taborski. Preface
by P. Brook. 1964. 741546
_____ 2nd edn., revised.
1967. 766093
Includes "Shakespeare's bitter
Arcadia" (in 2nd edn. only).

KUHL (E. P.)
Malvolio's "Please one, and please
all". pp. [2.] IN HEFFNER (R.)
and ALBRIGHT (EVELYN M.) Comment and
criticism. FROM [Publications of
the Modern Language Association of
America, Vol. 47.] [(Menasha, Wis.)]
[1932]

438445

—— LEATHAM (J.)
"Twelfth Night; or, What you will"
[and "A Midsummer night's dream"].
2nd edn.   pp. 16.   (Turriff)
[c.1920.]
Shakespeare Studies.
566380

—— LEECH, CLIFFORD
Twelfth Night and Shakespearian comedy
[: three lectures].   1965.
762560

—— Lewalski, Barbara K.
Thematic patterns in Twelfth Night.

IN Shakespeare Studies, 1. (Cincinnati,
Ohio)   1965.
750317

—— MACKENZIE (W. ROY)
"Standing water" [: an examination of
the term as used by Malvolio in
Twelfth Night].   IN Modern Language
Notes, Vol. 41.   (Baltimore, Md.)
1926.
439157/41

—— MANHEIM (LEONARD F.)
The Mythical joys of Shakespeare;
or, What you will.   IN Shakespeare
encomium, 1564-1964 [by various
writers].   (New York)   1964.
City University of New York, City
College Papers, 1.
747546

—— MARKELS (JULIAN)
Shakespeare's confluence of tragedy
and comedy: Twelfth Night and King
Lear.   IN Shakespeare 400: essays
by American scholars on the anniversary
of the poet's birth.   Published in
co-operation with the Shakespeare
Association of America.
illus.   1964.
667803

—— MINKOV, MARKO
Twelfth Night - an end and a beginning.
FROM Filološki pregled, 1964, 1-2.
(Beograd)

pp.117-129.   764570

—— MUESCHKE (P.) and FLEISHER (JEANNETTE)
Jonsonian elements in the comic under-
plot of "Twelfth Night".   IN
Publications of the Modern Language
Association of America, Vol. 48.
(Menasha, Wis.)   1933.
418268

—— MULLIK (B. R.)
Studies in Dramatists, vol. 9:
Shakespeare's Twelfth Night.
2nd edn.   pp. 52.   (Delhi)
bibliog.   1960.
667117

—— NAGARAJAN (S.)
"What you will": a suggestion.
IN SHAKESPEARE QUARTERLY X: 1.
pp. 61-67.
(New York)   1959.
605711

—— OYAMA (TOSHIKO)
The Language of Feste, the clown.
IN ARAKI (KAZUO) and others, eds.,
Studies in English grammar and
linguistics: a miscellany in
honour of Takanobu Otsuka.   (Tokyo)
port. dgms. tables. bibliogs.
1958.
667095

—— PALMER, D. J.
Art and nature in "Twelfth Night".
FROM The Critical Quarterly,
Autumn 1967.   pp. 201-212.
766384

—— PYLE (F.)
'Twelfth Night', 'King Lear' and
'Arcadia'.   IN The Modern
Language Review, Vol. 43.
(Cambridge)
bibliog.   1948.
266816/43

—— RAMSEY (T. W.)
On re-reading Twelfth Night.   IN
Ramsey (T. W.) Antares [: poems.]
pp. 64.   1934.
Macmillan's Contemporary Poets.
432070

—— ROYLE, E.
The Pattern of play in 'Twelfth
Night'.   FROM Theoria, October,
1964.   pp. 1-12.   (Pietermaritzburg)
668359

—— SALINGAR (L. G.)
The Design of Twelfth Night.
IN SHAKESPEARE QUARTERLY IX: 2.
pp. 117-139.
(New York)   1958.
605711

—— SEIDEN (MELVIN)
Malvolio reconsidered.   FROM The
University of Kansas City review,
Vol. XXVII, No. 2.   1961.
667735

—— SISSON (CHARLES JASPER)
Tudor intelligence tests: Malvolio
and real life.   IN Essays on
Shakespeare and Elizabethan drama
in honour of Hardin Craig.
illus.   1963.
667532

—— SOCHATOFF, A. FRED
Twelfth Night.   IN "Lovers meeting":
discussions of five plays by
Shakespeare.   (Pittsburgh, Pa.)
1964.
Carnegie series in English.
741508

—— SUMMERS (JOSEPH H.   )

The Masks of "Twelfth Night".   IN Dean
(Leonard F.) ed Shakespeare: modern
essays in criticism. pp.[10.] (New
York)   1957.
666404
_____ Revised edn. 1967.   763305

—— TANNENBAUM (S. A.)
Shaksperian scraps and other
Elizabethan fragments. [Including
a chapter on Twelfth Night.] (New
York)
  facsimiles.   1933.

411561

—— TILLEY (M. P.)
The Organic unity of Twelfth Night.
IN Publications of the Modern Language
Association of America, Vol. 29.
(Baltimore)   1914.

428349

—— Twelfth Night; or, What you will:
a study in Shakespeare.   FROM The
Oxford and Cambridge Magazine,
Vol. 1.   1856.

554147

—— Wright (L.B.) A Conduct book for
Malvolio. From Studies in philology, Vol. 31.

(Chapel Hill, N.C.)   1934.

484076

Twelfth Night

— Music; Opera
For music scores see under the heading
Music Scores, Twelfth Night

—— GORDON (P.)
Shakespeare - with music [: plans
and materials for the use of music
in the teaching of Shakespeare in
high schools, with particular reference to Twelfth Night].   FROM The
English Journal, Vol. 31. (Chicago)
                                 1942.

565601

—— HOLLANDER (JOHN)
Musica mundana and "Twelfth Night".
IN Sound and Poetry: English
Institute Essays, 1956. (New York)
                                 1957.

530316/56

—— Music shop, The.   Third series No. 8 :
"Music for a play" [: a discussion
on the music for Shakespeare's
Twelfth Night. Broadcast] 12th
June, 1941. ff. 4. Typescript.

541844

Twelfth Night

— Novels; Plays; Poems
see also **ENGLISH EDITIONS, Twelfth
Night** — Alterations, etc.

—— COURTNEY (W. L.)
Orsino to Olivia [: a poem].
IN GOLLANCZ ([Sir] I.) ed., A Book
of homage to Shakespeare.
  ports. illus. facsimiles. [1916.]

264175

——[Freeman (A.)] Malvolio's revenge:
[a sequel to Twelfth Night. Performed
by the Sheffield Educational
Settlement Players, March 10th-18th,
1939. ff. 24. Typescript.

[1939.]

500757

—— GRANT (N. F.)
Olivia and the Duke.   IN Seven new
plays: the one-act theatre, the
eighth book.   1936.   635084
_____   IN MARTIN (CONSTANCE M.) ed.,
Fifty one-act plays.   Second series.
                    1940.   511309

—— Sansom (C.) Celestial meeting: a
stage sketch for three women only
[Viola, Desdemona, Lady Macbeth.]
In Hampden (J.) [ed.] Plays without
fees. pp.96. Dgms.

[1935]

439719

——[TUPPER (J. L.)]
Viola and Olivia [: a poem.   With
an etching by W. H. Deverell].   IN
The Germ, 1850.   1850.   580968
_____ A facsimile reprint.
                       1901.   157369

—— WILLIAMS (S.)
Malvolio.   IN FULLER (M. H.) [ed.]
One-act plays for the amateur theatre.
                                 1949.

608358

Twelfth Night

— Sources and Background

—— HOTSON (JOHN LESLIE)
The First night of "Twelfth Night".
  ports.   illus.   1954.

642470

— KAUFMAN (HELEN ANDREWS)
Nicolò Secchi as a source of "Twelfth
Night".
IN SHAKESPEARE QUARTERLY V.
pp. 271-280.
(New York) 1954.

605711

— LIEVSAY (JOHN LEON)
A Word about Barnaby Rich.   IN
Journal of English and Germanic
Philology, Vol. 55. (Urbana, Ill.)
1956.

600780/55

— RICH (B.)
Apolonius and Silla.   [From Riche his
farewell to the military profession.
Possible source of incidents in Twelfth
Night.]   IN Shakespeare (W.) Twelfth-
night.   [Edited with an introduction
by H. Morley.]
1889.

Cassell's National Library

For other editions of this work check
the main sequence under the author's name.
436522

— SECCHI (NICCOLÒ)
Self-interest [: a play].   Translated by W. Reymes.   Edited by
Helen A. Kaufman. (Seattle)
bibliog.   1953.

670494

Twelfth Night

— Stage History and Production

*Newspaper reviews, playbills, theatre pro-
grammes and theatrical illustrations — the
library's extensive collection of this material
is mainly uncatalogued but indexed
For texts of stage alterations and adaptations of the play see* ENGLISH EDITIONS,
Twelfth Night *— Alterations, etc.*

— Birt (Mrs. Marie) Settings for Twelfth
Night [and] eight scenes for Twelfth
Night. ᵀn The Amateur theatre and
playwrights' journal, Vol. 3, No.
46.

1936-37.

476090

— CHESTERFIELD.   MANOR SCHOOL
Scrapbook of background material
relating to a production of "Twelfth
Night", November 1968. (Chesterfield)
illus.   2 vols.   1968.

776825-6

— COMMUNITY PLAYERS, BIRMINGHAM
Annual reports, 1st-5th (1923-24 -
1927-28) and final report, Oct., 1930.
With programmes notices and photographs of productions (including
"Twelfth Night" and "A Midsummer
night's dream".)   1923-30.

384985

— COX (TRENCHARD) and others
Twelfth Night. [Shakespeare Memorial
Theatre, Stratford, 1955]   Extract
from "Midland Critics".   [Critics:
T. Cox, Evelyn Gibbs, H. Folkes and
J. C. Moore.   Chairman: J. English.
[Broadcast] 21st April 1955. ff. 7.
typescript.

665046

— DESMOND (S.)
London nights of long ago.   [With
references to Shakespearian performances, and a chapter on Twelfth
Night.]
ports.   illus.   1927.

519055

— FORBES (LYDIA)
What you will? [on the stage production
of Twelfth Night]
IN SHAKESPEARE QUARTERLY XIII: 4.
pp. 475-485.
(New York) 1962.

605711

— GOSFORTH (J. C.)
"The First night of Twelfth Night":
a dramatic reconstruction of a
Shakespearean première.   Based on
the book by L. Hotson.   Produced
by C. Shaw. [Broadcast] 6th January,
1956.   ff. 24.
typescript.

665244

— Granville Barker's production of
Twelfth Night.   From The Morning
Post, 16 Nov. 1912.   IN WARD (A. C.)
[ed.] Specimens of English dramatic
criticism, 17-20 centuries; selected
and introduced. (Oxford) 1945.
The World's Classics.

563732

— HELLENIC DRAMATIC GROUP
Shakespeare's week, Manolidou-Aroni-
Horn present "Twelfth Night"
[Souvenir programme.   English and
Greek text.] (Alexandria) 1945.

766817

— HER MAJESTY'S THEATRE
Souvenir of "Twelfth Night" produced
by H. B. Tree, Feb. 5th, 1901.
1901.   440894
_____ Another copy.   474075

— HONOURABLE SOCIETY OF THE MIDDLE TEMPLE
Programme of Shakespeare's Twelfth
Night, acted by the Holywell Players
in the Hall of the Middle Temple
Society, June 28th, 29th and 30th,
1934.   With a note "Shakespeare
and the Middle Temple" by B. Williamson.
With photographs.]   pp. [6.]
frontis.   1934.

421992

—— INKSTER (L.)
Shakespeare and Mr. Granville Barker
[: a review of his productions of
Twelfth Night and The Winter's tale
at the Savoy]. FROM Poetry and
Drama, Vol. 1. 1913.

520180

—— King (J.C.) Twelfth Night at Stockholm.
Illus. In Theatre Today.

[1947.]

606680

—— KNIGHT (J.)
The First night of "Twelfth Night"
at the Lyceum. FROM The Theatre,
Aug. 1, 1884.

498967

—— MacCarthy (D.) Twelfth Night, or,
What You Will : [a criticism of
a production at the Phoenix Theatre.]
In The New Statesman and Nation,
Vol. 16 (New Series.)

1938.

495919

—— MARSH (NGAIO)
A Note on a production of Twelfth Night.
IN SHAKESPEARE SURVEY 8. (Cambridge)
1955.

647706

—— Meerbeck Bulletin: the official
edition of UNRRA Team 158, Nos. 33,
35, 40. [Including an account of
a performance of Shakespeare's
Twelfth Night. English and Lettish
texts.] (Meerbeck) 1946.

586202

—— Miss Kate Terry in Viola. IN Fraser's
Magazine, Vol. 72. 1865.

10672

—— [Norwich, City of, School. Programme
of a performance of 'Twelfth Night' at
the City of Norwich School, Dec.1937;
with explanatory notes on the music by
M. N. Doe. ff. 4.] [Norwich]
1937.
Note (i) Edition of 'Twelfth Night' with
MS. notes referring to the music of M.N.
Doe, catal. no. 502842. (ii) MS. of
music for 'Twelfth Night' by M.N. Doe,
catal. no. 502843.

506672

—— [Programme and illustrations of
Mr. Ernest Peirce's production of
Twelfth Night at Porthcurno, Cornwall,
August, 1933.] 1933.

412193

—— PROGRAMMES OF SHAKESPEARIAN PERFORMANCES
Twelfth Night

This collection, which runs from
the latter half of the nineteenth
century, is continuously augmented
by the addition of programmes of
contemporary productions.

499172

—— ROYAL COURT THEATRE
J. B. Fagan's production of
Shakespeare's comedy "Twelfth Night;
or, What you will". 100th performance, 16th January, 1919. Souvenir.
pp. [4.]
ports.

471793

—— SAVOY THEATRE
Twelfth Night, November 15th, 1912.
IN Play Pictorial, Vol. 21. 1913.

571883

—— SPEDDING (J.)
Reviews and discussions: literary,
political and historical, not relating
to Bacon. [With a chapter: "Twelfth
Night" at the Olympic Theatre (Miss
Kate Terry in Viola. From Frazer's
Magazine, August, 1865).] 1879.

125328

—— SWANDER, HOMER D.
Twelfth Night: critics, players, and a
script. FROM Educational Theatre Journal.
(Columbia) 1964.

pp.114-121. 747851

—— SYKES (E. F.)
"Twelfth Night": Stratford-upon-Avon
Shakespeare Memorial Theatre
[production] Festival Season 1955.
ff. 25. 1955.
Journal Notes. 7th Series.

665416

—— "Take your choice": a scene from
"Twelfth Night" in modern and in
Elizabethan speech. Shakespearean
pronounciation [sic] by F. G. Blandford.
[Adapted for broadcasting.] ff. 14.
typescript. 1937.

475848

—— [THEATRE GUILD, NEW YORK]
The Theatre Guild and Gilbert Miller
present Helen Hayes and Maurice Evans
in Shakespeare's "Twelfth Night".
Directed by Margaret Webster.
[Souvenir book.] pp. 20. [(New York)]
ports. illus. [1940.]

599879

—— THOMPSON (J. B.)
Anne Hathaway sees "Twelfth Night":
written for performance by the
Bristol Drama Club, in a Clifton
garden, June, 1936. FROM St. Brendan's
College Magazine, Vol. 3, No. 1.
(Bristol)
illus. 1936.

455002

—— Twelfth night experiment : the Questors
invite frank criticism. In The
Amateur theatre and playwrights'
journal, Vol. 40, No. 70.

1937-38.

482984

— Winter (W.) Twelfth night; Shaks-
    pere on the stage. Ports.
    In The Century Magazine, Vol. 88.

         (New York)   1914.

                   256528

— WOOLF ([Mrs.] VIRGINIA)
    The Death of the moth, and other
    essays. [Including "Twelfth Night"
    at the Old Vic. With an editorial
    note by L. S. Woolf.]   1942.

                   533636

— WOOLF ([Mrs.] VIRGINIA)
    'Twelfth Night' at the Old Vic.
    IN WARD (A. C.) [ed.] Specimens of
    English dramatic criticism, 17–20
    centuries; selected and introduced.
    (Oxford)   1945.
    The World's Classics.

                   563732

— WORTH (MARTIN)
    Twelfth Night, a Shakespearean series
    [: nine introductory scripts to a
    production of Twelfth Night for
    schools]. Televised January–March,
    1959. (Associated-Rediffusion Ltd.)
    typescript.   1959.

                   666169

— WYATT (EUPHEMIA VAN R.)
    The Drama: night's black agents.
    [Including criticism of a performance
    of Twelfth Night.] FROM The Catholic
    World, Vol. 154. (New York) 1942.

                   537250

Twelfth Night

— Study and Teaching; Tales

— ADAMSON (ELGIVA) and MOORE (KATHLEEN V.)
    Notes on William Shakespeare's
    "Twelfth Night". pp. 47.
    [Stratford, Ontario]   1957.

                   665808

— BENNETT (R.)
    The Story of Twelfth Night retold.
    pp. 64.   [1941.]
    The Tales that Shakespeare Told.

                   544918

— CARRINGTON (NORMAN THOMAS)
    Shakespeare: Twelfth Night.
    (Bath)   [1940.]   511819
    Notes on Chosen English Texts.
    _____ Another edn. 1965. 746636

— COLLEGE OF CAREERS, CAPE TOWN
    STUDY-AID SERIES
    Notes on Shakespeare's 'Twelfth night:
    or, What you will'. Rev. and enlarged
    edn. (Cape Town)   [1964.]

    typescript.   740928

— FIELD (JOSEPHINE)
    Twelfth Night, retold for young
    people. [With] Scene V, Act II
    of the play. pp. 61. (Bognor
    Regis)
    illus.   [1946.]
    Crowther's "Introduction to Good
    Reading" Series.

                   573815

— GATTY (REGINALD ARTHUR ALLIX)
    Twelfth night [: the story of the
    play, with notes, etc.] ff. 44.
    manuscript.   [c.1925.]

                   637991

— GILLIE (C.)
    Twelfth Night. IN English in educa-
    tion: a selection of articles on
    the teaching of English at different
    levels from infant school to university.
    Edited by B. Jackson & D. Thompson.
    bibliog.   1962.
    Originally published in "The Use of
    English".

                   704889

— GORDON (P.)
    Shakespeare - with music [: plans
    and materials for the use of music
    in the teaching of Shakespeare in
    high schools, with particular
    reference to Twelfth Night].
    FROM The English Journal, Vol. 31.
    (Chicago)   1942.

                   565601

— HARDY (Mrs. BARBARA GLADYS)

    Twelfth Night. (Notes on English
    Literature [Series])(Oxford: Blackwell)
                       1962.

                   667557

— KEY FACTS LTD.
    Twelfth Night [: set of 25 cards for
    revision for the General Certificate
    of Education O level examination].
                     [1967.]

     Key Facts, Shakespeare, 9.
                 763803

— Kingsley (Maud E.) Outline studies
    in literature. No.50: Twelfth
    Night. pp.35.

     (Boston, Mass.)   1906.

                   426218

— PERKINS, D. C.
    Model answers on Shakespeare's
    "Twelfth Night" [for General
    Certificate of Education].
    [Swansea]   1967.

                   763824

— STOKER (M. E.) and (STOKER (J. T.)
    Shakespeare's "Twelfth Night"; film-
    strip and notes. pp. 28.
    bibliog. 2 vols.   1954.

               646079-80

WINDROSS (RONALD)
Three Mediterranean plays: Shakespeare's
Romeo and Juliet; The Merchant of
Venice; [and,] Twelfth Night. Abridged
and simplified. Illustrated by G.
Irwin. pp. 80. (Paris)
[1952.]
Tales from England, 2nd Degree, No.4.

635256

Twelfth Night

– Textual History

Struble (G.G.) Schlegel's translation
of Twelfth Night. From The Quarterly
Journal of the University of North
Dakota. Vol.19, No.2.

(Grand Forks, N.D.)   1929.

442293

Twells (Julia H.) jun. A Visit to
Hamlet's castle. Illus. In The
Cosmopolitan, Vol.37.

(Irvington-on-Hudson,N.Y.)   1904.

187554

[Twelve scenes from Shakespeare.
Selected by G. L. Kittredge,
painted by E. A. Wilson.]

[(New York)]   [1937.]

499010

Twentieth Century Interpretations
BERMAN, RONALD, ed.
Twentieth Century interpretations
of 'Henry V': a collection of
critical essays.   (Englewood
Cliffs, N.J.)   1968.

773023

Twentieth Century Interpretations
BEVINGTON, DAVID M. ed.
Twentieth century interpretations of
'Hamlet': a collection of critical
essays. (Englewood Cliffs, N.J.) 1968.

Twentieth century interpretations.
773022

Twentieth Century Interpretations
KING, WALTER N. ed.
Twentieth century interpretations of
'Twelfth night': a collection of
critical essays. (Englewood Cliffs,
N.J.)   1968.

Twentieth century interpretations.
772580

Twentieth Century Interpretations
YOUNG, DAVID P. ed.
Twentieth century interpretations of
Henry IV part two: a collection of
critical essays.   (Englewood Cliffs,
N.J.)   1968.

775736

Twentieth Century Views
HARBAGE, ALFRED BENNETT, ed.
Shakespeare, the tragedies: a
collection of critical essays [by
various writers].   (Englewood
Cliffs, N.J.)   1964.

742273

Twentieth Century Views
MUIR, KENNETH, ed.
Shakespeare, the comedies: a
collection of critical essays.
(Englewood Cliffs, N.J.)   1965.

748348

Twentieth Century Views
WAITH, EUGENE MERSEREAU, ed.
Shakespeare, the histories: a
collection of critical essays.
(Englewood Cliffs, N.J.)   1965.

745303

Twice-told tales, 42: Was Shakespeare
ever in Scotland? (from Chambers's
Edinburgh Journal for July 18,1835).
In Chambers's Journal, 8th series,
Vol.4.
1935.

444111

TWIGG (DOUGLAS J.)
Sigh no more ladies: part song with
optional soprano solo. [Words by]
W. Shakespeare [from Much ado about
nothing.   Music by] D. J. Twigg.
pp. 8.   (York)   1936.
York Series, No. 1223.

536608

TWINE (LAURENCE)
The Patterne of painefull adventures:
containing the most excellent, pleasant
and variable historie of the strange
accidents that befell unto Prince
Apollonius, the Lady Lucina his wife
and Tharsia his daughter. [The
original of Shakespeare's Pericles,
Prince of Tyre.]   Gathered into
English by L. Twine.   pp. 77.   (New
York: Elston Press)   1903.
[Shakespeare Reprints, 3.]
Edn. limited to 170 copies.

560448

Twins

—— WALSH (G.) and POOL (R. M.)
Antithetical views on twinning
found in the Bible and Shakespeare.
FROM Southern Medicine & Surgery.
Vol. 103.   (Charlotte, N.C.)
bibliog.   1941.

565605

—— WALSH (G.) and POOL (R. M.)
Shakespeare's knowledge of twins
and twinning.   FROM Southern
Medicine & Surgery.   Vol. 102.
(Charlotte, N.C.)   1940.

565604

TWISS (HORACE)
The Patriot's progress, and Our
parodies are ended [: parodies on
Shakespeare.]   IN JERROLD (W.)
and LEONARD (R. M.) eds., A Century
of parody and imitation.
port.   [?1913]   307526
_____ Another edn. 1913.   447763

[Twiss (H.)] Posthumous parodies and
other pieces composed by celebrated
poets, but not published in their
works [Including parodies of
passages from Shakespeare].

1814.

516236

TWO CITIES FILMS, LTD.
G.C.F. presents Laurence Olivier's
Henry V by William Shakespeare
[: souvenir booklet].   pp. [16.]
[New York]
ports.   illus.   [1945.]

646355

[TWO CITIES FILMS LTD.]
Henry V: release script [by A. Dent
and L. Olivier].   ff. 87.
typescript.   [1944.]

556035

TWO CITIES FILM[S, LTD.]
Laurence Olivier presents Hamlet
by William Shakespeare.   pp. [4.]
[1948.]

596213

[TWO CITIES FILMS, LTD.]
Laurence Olivier presents Hamlet by
William Shakespeare [: photographs
from the film with a commentary in
English, French and Italian].
pp. [24].   [1949.]

600297

[TWO CITIES FILMS LTD.
Photographs of Laurence Olivier's
production of Hamlet.]   pp. [40].
[1948.]

600249

[TWO CITIES FILMS, LTD.
Photographs of Laurence Olivier's
production of Henry V.   ff. 12.]
[1944.]

555605

[Two Cities Films Ltd. Posters of
Laurence Olivier's production of
Hamlet.] 8 sheets.

[1948.]

600127

[TWO CITIES FILMS LTD.]
William Shakespeare's Henry V:
revised treatment for technicolor
film [: script] by A. Dent &
L. Olivier.   ff. 64.
typescript.   [1944.]

548730

Two Cities Films Ltd. *works relating to*

—— Cinema [: a review of Laurence
Olivier's production of Shakespeare's
Henry V, as presented by Two Cities
Films, Ltd.].   FROM Time, Vol. 47.
[Chicago]
illus.   map.   1946.

573947

—— Collectors prints Shakespearean 200-208:
Henry V.   [Coloured prints from the
film produced by Laurence Olivier and
presented by Two Cities Films, Ltd.
With an extract from the play on each
print.]   (Brownlee Nineteen-Forty-Two)
[1945.]

569085

—— Hamlet, produced and directed by Sir
Laurence Olivier for Two Cities
Films: Records of the film, No.16,
published by the British Film
Institute. pp. [8].

[1948.]

590201

—— How Henry V was designed [: the
designing of the costumes and setting
in the Two Cities Films, Ltd. presentation of Laurence Olivier's film].
IN Picture Post, Vol. 26.
illus.   1945.

565210

—— HUTTON (C. C.)
The Making of Henry V [: Laurence
Olivier's production of Henry V,
as presented by Two Cities Films,
Ltd.].   pp. 72.
ports.   illus. map. plans. [1944.]

556042

——[HUTTON (C. C.) ed.]
The Story of Shakespeare's Henry V
with illustrations from the [Two
Cities Films, Ltd.] film presentation
by Laurence Olivier [and drawings
throughout by A. W. Dean]. pp. 32.
ports. illus.   [1946.]

572074

——LEJEUNE (CAROLINE A.)
Three English films. [Includes a
review of Laurence Olivier's
production of Henry V as presented
by Two Cities Films, Ltd.]   IN
Theatre Arts, Vol. 29.   (New York)
illus.   1945.

567819

——Olivier's Hamlet [: an article on
the film, with critical letters].
pp. 4. FROM Time, Vol. 51.
[Chicago]
ports. illus.   1948.

596203

——POWELL (DILYS)
"Hamlet" on the screen [: Sir
Laurence Olivier's production].
IN Britain To-day, No. 147.
illus.   1948.

587767/147

——WILKINSON (F. W.)
Henry V [: a review of Laurence
Olivier's production as presented
by Two Cities Films, Ltd.].   IN
Sight and Sound, Vol. 13. 1944-5.

560963

Two days in Warwickshire [:
Shakespeare's country.] FROM
Chambers' Edinburgh Journal, 1845.
pp. [4.] [Edinburgh]

390781

The Two Gentlemen of Verona

——ALLEN (M. S.)
Broke's Romeus and Juliet as a
source for the Valentine-Silvia plot
in The Two Gentlemen of Verona.
IN University of Texas, Studies in
English, [No. 18.] 1938. (Austin,
Texas)

498156

—— Amicitiae Shakespearianae [No. 1:
friendship in Two Gentlemen of
Verona]. FROM [Tait's Edinburgh
Magazine,] Vol. 16. [Edinburgh]
[1849.]

554167

—— ATKINSON (DOROTHY F.)
The Source of "Two Gentlemen of
Verona".   IN Studies in Philology,
Vol. 41.   (Chapel Hill, N.C.)
bibliog.   1944.

563556

——BROOKS, HAROLD FLETCHER
Two clowns in a comedy (to say nothing
of the dog): Speed, Launce (and Crab)
in 'The Two Gentlemen of Verona'. IN
English Association. Essays and Studies.
New Series, Vol.16.   1963.

714688

—— DANBY (JOHN FRANCIS)

Shakespeare criticism and "Two
Gentlemen of Verona". Reprinted from
The Critical Quarterly. pp.[13].
1960.

667101

—— MONTEMAYOR [JORGE de]
Diana de Monte mayor.   Done out of
Spanish by [Sir] T. Wilson (1596).
Re-printed [i.e. printed from Add.
MS. 18638 in the British Museum with
an introduction, referring to
Shakespeare's "Two Gentlemen of
Verona"] by H. Thomas.   1921.

392606

—— MONTEMAYOR (JORGE DE)
The Story of the shepherdess Felismena.
From the Diana of G. de Montemayor, trans-
lated by B. Yonge. [Probable source of
incidents in Two Gentlemen of Verona.] IN
Shakespeare (W.) The Two Gentlemen of
Verona. [Edited with an introduction by
H. Morley.] (Cassell's National Library).
1889. 436523
----------Another edition 1897. 527792.

—— Parks (G.B.) The Development of The
Two Gentlemen of Verona. In Huntington
Library Bulletin, No.11.

(Cambridge,Mass.)   1937.

477589

—— PERRY (THOMAS A.)
Proteus, wry-transformed traveller.
IN SHAKESPEARE QUARTERLY V:
pp. 33-40.
(New York)   1954.

605711

—— POGUE, JIM C.
"The Two Gentlemen of Verona"
and Henry Wotton's "A Courtlie
controuersie of Cupids cautels".
IN Four Studies in Elizabethan
Drama, by Roma Ball, J. C. Pogue,
J. L. Somer [and] E. J. Kettner.
(Kansas State Teachers College,
Emporia, Kan.)   1962.

667737

—— PROGRAMMES OF SHAKESPEARIAN PERFORMANCES
The Two Gentlemen of Verona

This collection, which runs from
the latter half of the nineteenth
century, is continuously augmented
by the addition of programmes of
contemporary productions.

ROPPOLO (JOSEPH PATRICK)

American premieres of two Shakespearean plays in New Orleans: The Two gentlemen of Verona and Antony and Cleopatra. Reprinted from Tulane University. Tulane Studies in English. Vol.7. pp.[8]. Bibliogs. (New Orleans, La.)
1957.

666580

SARGENT (RALPH M.)
Sir Thomas Elyot and the integrity of The Two Gentlemen of Verona.   IN P.M.L.A.: Publications of the Modern Language Association of America, Vol. 65.   (New York)   1950.

428321/65

Scott, William O.
Proteus in Spenser and Shakespeare: the lover's identity.

IN Shakespeare Studies, 1. (Cincinnati, Ohio)   1965.

750317

Small (S.A.) The Ending of "The Two Gentlemen of Verona". In Publications of the Modern Language Association of America, Vol.48.

(Menasha, Wis.)   1933.

418268

SNIDER (D. J.)
The Two Gentlemen of Verona [: an analysis of the play].   FROM The Journal of Speculative Philosophy, Vol. 10.   (St. Louis)   1876.

556086

Stroup (T.B.) Launce and Launcelot. From The Journal of English and Germanic philology, vol.30.

(Illinois)   1931.

444158

Tannenbaum (S.A.) Shakspere studies, 4: The New Cambridge Shakspere and The Two Gentlemen of Verona. Reprinted, with additions and corrections, from the Shakespeare Association Bulletin. pp. 68.

(New York)   1939.

Limited edn.: 200 copies.

515136

The "Two Gentlemen" and the players. IN All the year round.   New series, Vol. 22.   1879.

38535

— Wales (Julia G.) Shakespeare's use of English and foreign elements in the setting of The Two Gentlemen of Verona. Reprinted from Transactions of the Wisconsin Academy of Sciences, Arts and Letters. Vol.27. pp.85-126.

[Madison]   1932.

444037

WELLS, STANLEY
The Failure of "The Two Gentlemen of Verona".
IN SHAKESPEARE JAHRBUCH.   Bd 99/1963. pp. 161-173.   (Heidelberg)

10531

The Two Noble Kinsmen

BERTRAM (PAUL)
The Date of The Two Noble Kinsmen. IN   SHAKESPEARE QUARTERLY XII: 1. pp. 21-32. (New York)   1961.

605711

BERTRAM, PAUL
Shakespeare and 'The Two noble kinsmen'. (New Brunswick)   1965.

753455

EDWARDS, PHILIP
On the design of "The Two Noble Kinsmen". IN A Review of English Literature, October 1964.   1964.

697306

HART (A.)
Shakespeare and the vocabulary of The Two noble kinsmen.   IN Hart (A.) Shakespeare and the homilies, and other pieces of research into the Elizabethan drama.   (Melbourne)
1934.   429387
_____ IN Review of English studies, July, 1934.   pp. 274-287.
[1934]   428644

HICKSON [SAMUEL]
The Shares of Shakspere and Fletcher in "The Two Noble Kinsmen".
IN Transactions of the New Shakespeare Society, Series 1. No. 1.   Appendix pp. 25-61.   1874.

4061

KÖKERITZ (H.)
The Beast-eating clown [in] The Two noble kinsmen.   bibliog. IN Modern Language Notes, Vol. 61. (Baltimore, Md.)   1946.

579125

— MUIR (KENNETH)

Shakespeare's hand in "The Two Noble
Kinsmen". Tables. Bibliog. IN
Shakespeare Survey [Vol.] 11. (Cambridge)
1958.

665816

— SPENCER (T.)
The Two Noble Kinsmen.   FROM Modern
Philology, Vol. 36.   (Chicago)
1939.

530567

— Sykes (H.D.)   The Authorship of
"The Two Noble Kinsmen".   In The
Modern Language Review, Vol. 11.

(Cambridge)   1916.

266431

Tyabji (F.B.) The Value of Shakespeare
to modern India.   From The Aryan path,
Vol. 7.

(Bombay)   1936.
484132

TYLER (J. E.)
Henry of Monmouth; or, Memoirs of
the life and character of Henry the
Fifth.
2 vols.   frontis.   1838.

79966

Tyler (J.E.) A Point in the geography
of Shakespeare, [with reference to
King John.] From Review of English
Studies, Vol.4.

1928.

497600

TYLER (P.)
Hamlet as the murdered poet.   FROM
Quarterly Review of Literature,
Vol. 3.   [New Haven, Conn.]   [1947.]

586691

Tynan (J.L.) The Influence of Greene
on Shakspere's early romance.   In
PMLA, Publications of the Modern
Language Association of America,
Vol. 27.

(Baltimore)   1912.

428347

TYNAN, KENNETH PEACOCK, ed.
Othello: the National Theatre
production.   1966.

illus.   753063

TYTLER (ERNEST J.)
As you like it: filmstrip [of the
play produced at the Old Vic Theatre,
London, March 1st, 1955];   and notes.
[Edited by] E. J. Tytler.
1 vol., 1 reel 35 mm.   [1955.]

666529-30

TYTLER (ERNEST J.)
Elizabethan theatre: filmstrip and
notes.
1 vol., 1 reel 35 mm.   1960.

666560-1

TYTLER (ERNEST J.)
Hamlet: filmstrip [of the play produced at the New Theatre, Oxford, by
Tennent Productions Ltd., Nov. 7th,
1955]; and notes.   [Edited by]
E. J. Tytler.
1 vol., 1 reel 35 mm.   [1955.]

666465-6

TYTLER (ERNEST J.)
Henry the Fourth: filmstrips [of the
plays produced at the Old Vic Theatre,
London: Part 1, April 27th 1955
and Part 2, April 28th 1955];   and
notes.   [Edited by] E. J. Tytler.
2 vols., 2 reels 35 mm.   [1955.]

666525-8

TYTLER (ERNEST J.)
King Henry the Fifth: filmstrip [of
the play produced at the Birmingham
Repertory Theatre, Feb. 12th, 1957];
and notes.   [Edited by] E. J. Tytler.
1 vol., 1 reel 35 mm.   [1957.]

666489-90

TYTLER (ERNEST J.)
Julius Caesar: filmstrip [of the
play produced at the Old Vic Theatre
on Wednesday, September 7, 1955.
With] Notes.   [Edited by] E. J. Tytler.
(Educational Productions Limited)
1 vol., 1 reel 35 mm.   1959.

666567-8

TYTLER (ERNEST J.   )

Macbeth: filmstrip [from the film made
by the Republic Pictures Corporation];
and notes.
1. vol.   1 reel 35 mm. [1949]

666691 and 666697

TYTLER (ERNEST J.)
The Merchant of Venice: filmstrip
[from the film made by Elysée-Films];
and notes.
1 vol., 1 reel 35 mm.   [?1950]

666692 and 666698

TYTLER (ERNEST J.)
The Merry Wives of Windsor: filmstrip
[of the play presented at the "Old
Vic" Theatre, May 31, 1951.   With]
Notes.   [Edited by] E. J. Tytler.
(Educational Productions Limited)
1 vol., 1 reel 35 mm.   [1959.]

666569-70

TYTLER (ERNEST J.)
A Midsummer night's dream: filmstrip
[of the play performed by the "Old
Vic" Company in the Metropolitan
Opera House, New York, on September
27, 1954. With] Notes. [Edited
by E. J. Tytler.] (Educational
Productions Limited)
  1 vol., 1 reel 35 mm.   [1959.]

                              666571-2

TYTLER (ERNEST J.)
Richard the Second: filmstrip [of
the play produced at the Theatre
Royal, Brighton, by Tennent
Productions Ltd., Dec. 8, 1952];
and notes.
  1 vol., 1 reel 35 mm.   [1952]

                     666693 and 666699

TYTLER (ERNEST J.   )

Richard the Third: filmstrip [from the
film made by London Film Productions
Ltd.].
  1. vol.   1 reel 35 mm. [1950?]

                     666694 and 666700

TYTLER (SARAH)
The American cousins: a story of
Shakespeare's country.   2nd and
cheap edn.   1899.
Digby's Popular Novel Series.

                              392895

UDNY (ERNEST)
Francis, Viscount St. Alban, commonly
but incorrectly called Lord Bacon.
2nd edn.   pp. 12.   1911.

                              549429

UHLER (JOHN EARLE)
Goethe and Shakespeare.   IN Goethe
after two centuries [: essays by
various authors].   (Baton Rouge, La.)
                             1952.
Louisiana State University Studies,
Humanities Series, No. 1.

                              623912

UHLER (JOHN EARLE)
Julius Caesar - a morality of Respublica.
IN MATTHEWS (A. D.) and EMERY (C. M.)
eds., Studies in Shakespeare.   (Coral
Gables, Fla.)   1953.
 University of Miami Publications in
English and American Literature,
Vol. 1, March 1953.

                              634188

Uhler (J.E.) Shakespeare's melancholy.
 In Caffee (N.M.) and Kirby (T.A.)
 eds. Studies for William A.Read.
 [With a bibliography.] Port.

        (Louisiana)   1940.

                              517139

Ukraine

— KURYLENKO, Y.
    William Shakespeare and the Ukraine.
                             [1964.]

           typescript. Ukrainian Society
    for Friendship and Cultural Relations
    with Foreign Countries.   740841

— VANINA, IRINA GRIGOREVNA
    Shakespeare's plays in the Ukrainian
    Soviet theatre. (Kiev)   [1964.]

           typescript. Ukrainian Society
    for Friendship and Cultural Relations
    with Foreign Countries.   740373

ULANOV (BARRY)
Shylock: the quality of justice.
IN The Bridge, Vol. 1.   (New York)
                             1955.

                              658503

ULANOV (BARRY)
Sources and resources: the literary
traditions of Christian humanism.
(Westminster, Md.)
 bibliog.   1960.
Includes a chapter "Shakespeare and
St. John of the Cross: De contemptu
mundi".

                              694579

ULEHLA, LUDMILA
Three sonnets from Shakespeare [set to
music: vocal score with piano
accompaniment].   [1966.]

                              763625

Uley Players see Societies

ULRICI (HERMANN)
Shakspeare's dramatic art: history
and character of Shakspeare's plays.
Translated from the 3rd edn. of the
German, with additions and corrections
by the author, by L. Dora Schmitz.
 2 vols.   1876-1888. 552473
_____ [Bohn's Standard Library.]
                 1892-91.   481320
_____ Another edn.   1896.   486273
_____ Another edn. 1906-08. 435329
_____ Another edn. 1911-14. 424048

Ulrici, Hermann *works relating to*

—— The Modern British Drama [: reviews
of various books on the drama
including] Shakespeare's dramatic
art, and his relation to Calderon
and Goethe, [by] H.Ulrici. From
[The North British Review,] Vol.29.

[Edinburgh]   1858.

564840

ULSTER MUSEUM, BELFAST
Shakespeare in pictures [: catalogue
of a Quatercentenary exhibition].
(Belfast)   1964.

668234

Underhill ([Sir]A.) Law. In
Shakespeare's England, vol.1.
[With bibliographies.] Illus.
Facsimiles.

(Oxford)   1917.

435745

UNDERHILL (EVELYN) [afterwards Mrs.
Stuart Moore]
William Shakespeare. Died April 23,
1616 [: a poem].
IN GOLLANCZ ([Sir] I.) ed., A Book
of homage to Shakespeare.
ports. illus. facsimiles. [1916.]

264175

Underhill Family of Warwickshire, *works relating to*

—— MORRISON (J. H.)
The Underhills of Warwickshire: an
essay in family history. [With
references to Shakespeare.]
illus. maps. facsimiles. genealogical
charts.   1932.   396911
Privately printed.
———— Another copy.   506874

UNDERWOOD (MARTIN)
William Shakespeare: a book list
newly compiled and imprinted by
St. Pancras public libraries to mark
the 400th anniversary of his birth
in 1564.   1964.

740827

UNDERWOOD (MELA)
Joe and Uta [: notes on José Ferrer
and Uta Ferrer, with special reference to their parts at the Broadway,
New York]. FROM Collier's, May 20,
1944. (New York)
illus.

578275

UNGARETTI, GIUSEPPE
Notes on Shakespeare's art of poetry.
IN LEWINTER, OSWALD, ed., Shakespeare
in Europe [by various authors].
1963.

667784

UNGER (LEONARD)
The Man in the name: essays on the
experience of poetry. (Minneapolis)
1956.
Includes a chapter "Deception and
self-deception in Shakespeare's
Henry IV".

671508

UNGERER (GUSTAV)
Two items of Spanish pronunciation in
Love's Labour's Lost.
IN SHAKESPEARE QUARTERLY XIV: 3.
pp. 245-251.
(New York) 1963.

605711

UNGERER (GUSTAV)

An Unrecorded Elizabethan performance
of "Titus Andronicus". IN Shakespeare
Survey, [Vol.] 14. (Cambridge)
1961.

666755

Unitarian Penny Library
TARRANT (W. G.)
Shakespeare and religion. pp. 24.
[c.1908.]

407941

United Artists Corporation Ltd. *works relating to*

—— KOZELKA (PAUL)
A Guide to the screen version of
Shakespeare's "Othello". Reprinted
from Audio-Visual Guide, October 1955.
pp. 16. (Maplewood, N.J.)
ports. illus. bibliog.   1955.
Photoplay Studies.

665549

—— William Shakespeare's "Othello"
starring Orson Welles: script,
publicity material and photographs.
pp. 26. (United Artists Corporation,
Ltd.)
typescript.   1954.

665294

Unities of Time and Place *see* **Locality in Shakespeare; Time**

Universe, Shakespeare's see World in Shakespeare's time.

Universities *see* **Education and Knowledge**

UNNA (JOSEPH) ed.
Children's stories from Shakespeare, by E. Nesbit, and When Shakespeare was a boy, by F. J. Furnivall. Mit Anmerkungen zum Schulgebrauch herausgegeben von J. Unna.   pp. 72. (Bielefeld)   1926.
[Velhagen & Klasings Sammlung französischer und englischer Schulausgaben]
English Authors.   Bd. 180 B.

330043

Unnamed Society's 21st Birthday 1915-1936 [Souvenir. With an account of the society by N. Cardus, and list of productions including The Tempest.]   pp. 20. [Manchester] illus.   [1936]

459001

Unwin (G.) Commerce and coinage. In Shakespeare's England, vol.1. [With bibliographies.] Illus. Facsimiles.

(Oxford)   1917.

435745

Upper Norwood Branch, British Empire Shakespeare Society. Programmes, etc. relating to Shakespearian performances.

1934-9

497015

Upton, John *works relating to*

—— Critical observations on Shakespeare, by J. Upton [: review of].   FROM The Museum: or, The Literary and Historical Register, Vol. 2.   1746.

562349

Ur Hamlet *see* **Hamlet**, Sources and Background

URBAN (SYLVANUS) [pseud.]
Table talk: The Study of Shakespeare; Judge Madden on Shakespeare; What we know concerning Shakespeare; The Shakespeare of Stratford and the Shakespeare of "Hamlet".   IN The Gentleman's Magazine, Vol. 286.
1899.

147488

URE (PETER)
Character and role from "Richard III" to "Hamlet".   IN Stratford-upon-Avon Studies, 5: Hamlet.   1963.

667698

URE (PETER)
The Looking-glass of Richard II. IN Philological Quarterly, Vol. 34. (Iowa City)   1955.

592684/34

URE (PETER)

Shakespeare and the inward self of the tragic hero: inaugural lecture of the Joseph Cowen Professor of English Language and Literature delivered at King's College, Newcastle upon Tyne, October, 1960. pp.22. (Durham)
1961.

666754

URE (PETER)

William Shakespeare: the problem plays "Troilus and Cressida"; "All's Well that Ends Well"; "Measure for Measure"; [and] "Timon of Athens". (British Book News. Bibliographical Series of Supplements. Writers and their Work, No. 140) pp.59. Illus. Bibliog.   1961.

667177

URRUTIA (ANGEL DE)
Shakespeare'n Hamlet euzkeraz. [B.B.C.] Spanish programme broadcast 12th January, 1953.   ff. 4.

634767

URRUTIA (ANGEL DE)
Shakespeare'n Mcbeth euzkeraz. [B.B.C.] Spanish programme broadcast 23rd February, 1953.   ff. 5.

634766

URWICK (Sir HENRY)
Gloves: with special reference to those of Shakespeare.   FROM The Connoisseur, 1927.   pp. [7.] illus.

389655

Urwick ([Sir]H.) Eyre (P.L.) and
Harrison (W.G.) Shylock-comic or
tragic? In The Poetry Review,
[Vol.4.]

1914.

253079

Urwin (E.C.) For love of England:
Christian citizenship lessons for
boys and girls, based on plays of
W.Shakespeare; concerning Shakespeare
and drink, Shakespeare and gambling,
Shakespeare and love of country.

1939.

504947

URWIN, G.G.
William Shakespeare: As you like it.
1964.

Guides to English Literature
Series.   745372

URWIN, G.G.
William Shakespeare: Much ado about
nothing.   1964.

Guides to English Literature
Series.   745371

USHERWOOD, STEPHEN
Shakespeare play by play. Illustrated
by R. Piper.   1967.

illus.   764809

Usill (M.) and Boas (G.) "Richard II"
at Sloane School. In School Drama,
Vol.2, No.2.

[1939.]

523131

Usury
see also The Merchant of Venice; Money

—— ASHTON (ROBERT)

Usury and high finance in the age of
Shakespeare and Jonson. Reprinted from
"Renaissance and Modern Studies", Vol.4.
(University of Nottingham) pp.[30.]
(Nottingham)   [1962.]

666966

—— SIEGEL (PAUL N.)
Shylock and the Puritan usurers.   IN
Matthews (A. D.) and Emery (C. M.) eds.
Studies in Shakespeare.   (University
of Miami Publications in English and
American literature, Vol. 1, March 1953).
(Coral Gables, Fla.)

634188

—— Wright (Celeste T.) The Usurer's sin in
Elizabethan literature. [With
bibliographical notes and containing
references to Shakespeare.] From
Studies in Philology, Vol.35.

[Chapel Hill, N.C.]

1938

503670

UTAH SHAKESPEAREAN FESTIVAL
[Programmes, etc.] (Cedar City, Utah)
1962-

illus.   668467

UTLEY (FRANCIS LEE)
The Crooked rib: an analytical index
to the argument about women in English
and Scots literature to the end of
the year 1568.   [With references to
Shakespeare.]   (Columbus: Ohio State
University)
bibliog.   1944.

559112

UTTER (ROBERT PALFREY)
In defense of Hamlet.   IN College
English Vol. 12.   (Chicago, Ill.)
1950.

598860/12

UTTER (ROBERT PALFREY)
"Wise enough to play the fool".
IN Essays in criticism by members of
the Department of English, University
of California.   [With references to
Shakespeare.]   (Berkeley, Cal.)
1934.
University of California.   Publications
in English, Vol. 4.

428119

V. (F.J.): see Vipan (F.J.)

Vagabonds *see* **Rogues and Vagabonds**

VAIL (CURTIS C. D.)
Lessing's relation to the English
language and literature.   [With
references to Shakespeare.]   (New
York)
bibliog.   1936.
Columbia University, Germanic Studies,
New Series, 3.

461806

VAILE (E. O.)
The Shakespeare–Bacon controversy.
FROM Scribner's Monthly, Vol. 9.
(New York)   1875.

555524

Val (Alfonso, Marquis de Merry del)
see Merry del Val (Alfonso, Marquis de)

VAL BAKER (DENYS)

The Minack theatre. Ports. Illus.
Chronological Table.   1960.

665856 ... 692181

Valentine *see* The Two Gentlemen of Verona

Valentine and Orson.   Translated
from the French by H. Watson.
Edited [with an introduction] by
A. Dickson.   1937.
  facsimile.
Early English Text Society, Original
Series, No. 204.
  Regarded as a source book of The
Winter's Tale and Macbeth.

467482

VALK (Mrs. DIANA)
  Shylock for a summer: one year
(1954-5) in the life of Frederick
Valk; with notes by T. Guthrie and
D. Davis.
  ports. illus.   1958.

665856

VALLINS (G. H.)
  At Stratford-on-Avon.   (Opening of
the Shakespeare Memorial Theatre,
April 23, 1932.)   [A sonnet.]
IN Vallins (G. H.) This dust, and
other poems. pp. 64.   1935.
  Macmillan's Contemporary Poets.

446623

VALLINS (GEORGE HENRY)
[Parodies of two sonnets by
Shakespeare.]   IN Vallins (G. H.)
Sincere flattery: parodies from
"Punch".
  frontis.   1954.

644413

Valpy, Abraham John *works relating to*

— [BOYDELL GALLERY]
    Illustrations to Shakspeare from
    the plates in Boydell's edn. recently
    edited and printed in 15 vols. by
    A. J. Valpy.   1834.

401056

Vamp (H.) Hamlet, the Black Prince -
  of Denmark. H. Vamp's comic dramatic
  Shakespearean scenas. pp. 6.

[c.1830.]

501623

Vamp (H.) The Merchant of Venice,
  the music arranged by J. Harroway.
  H. Vamp's comic dramatic Shakespearean scenas. pp. 8.

[c.1830.]

501622

Vamp (H.) Othello, [with music] arranged by J. Harroway. H. Vamp's
  comic dramatic Shakespearean scenas.
  pp. 6.

[c.1830.]

501620

Vamp (H.) Richard III, the music
  arranged by J. Harroway. H. Vamp's
  comic dramatic Shakespearean scenas.
  pp. 8.

[c.1830.]

501621

Vanbrugh, Violet *works relating to*

— MACLEAN (D. R.)
    Lady Macbeth (Miss Violet Vanbrugh
    recalled in 1914-1939) [: a poem].
    IN Poetry of To-Day, [New Series,
    Vol. 15].   1942.

319077/N.S./15

VAN CLEVE (CHARLES FOWLER)
The Teaching of Shakespearean plays
in American secondary schools.
pp. 9.   (Nashville, Tenn.) 1937.
  George Peabody College for Teachers.
Contribution to Education No. 213,
Abstract of.

567010

VANČURA (ZDENĚK)
  Shakespeare - whose contemporary?   IN
CHARLES UNIVERSITY ON SHAKESPEARE:
essays edited by Z. Stříbrný.   (Praha)
  illus.   1966.

762631

VAN DE WATER (JULIA C.)
  The Bastard in King John.
  IN SHAKESPEARE QUARTERLY XI.
pp. 137-146.
(New York) 1960.

605711

VANDIVER (EDWARD P.)
Simms's Border romances and Shakespeare.
IN SHAKESPEARE QUARTERLY V:
pp. 129-139.
(New York) 1954.

605711

Van Doren (C.) and Van Doren (M.)
American and British literature
since 1890. [With a bibliography
and containing references to Shakespeare.] Revised and enlarged edn.

(New York) 1939.

502982

VAN DOREN (MARK)
Shakespeare. (New York)
1939. 508433
_____ Another edn. [With a] foreword by Sir H. [S.] Walpole.
1941. 522822

Van Doren, Mark *works relating to*

—— BOWEN (ELIZABETH [D. C.])
[Review of] Shakespeare, by M. Van
Doren. IN The New Statesman and
Nation, Vol. 21, New Series. 1941.

528472

—— DOBRÉE (BONAMY)
An American's Shakespeare [: a review
of] Shakespeare, by M. Van Doren.
IN The Spectator, Vol. 166. 1941.

528481

—— JAMES (T.)
Reviews of books: Shakespeare [by]
M. Van Doren. FROM Life and Letters
Today, May, 1941. pp. [4.]

527858

—— P[LOWMAN] (M.)
[Review of] Shakespeare, by M. Van
Doren. FROM The Adelphi, Vol. 17,
New Series. 1941.

527856

Van Doren (M.) and Van Doren (C.)
American and British literature
since 1890. [With a bibliography
and containing references to
Shakespeare.] Revised and enlarged
edn.

(New York) 1939.

502982

VANINA, IRINA GRIGOREVNA
Shakespeare's plays in the Ukrainian
Soviet theatre. (Kiev) [1964.]

typescript. Ukrainian Society
for Friendship and Cultural Relations
with Foreign Countries. 740373

VAN LAAN, THOMAS F.
Ironic reversal in "Hamlet".
FROM Studies in English Literature
1500-1900, vol. 6, no. 2, Spring
1966. (Houston, Tex.) 1966.
pp. 247-262.

767903

Van Lennep (C.) see Lennep (C. van)

Van Lennep (Willem) see Lennep (Willem
van)

VANNOVSKY (ALEXANDER A.   )

The Path of Jesus from Judaism to
Christianity, as conceived by
Shakespeare: disclosure of a hidden
Jewish plot in Shakespeare's tragedy
"Hamlet". (Tokyo) 1962.

667826

VANNUCCHIO [pseud.]
To Shakespeare: a sonnet. IN The
Journal of Education, New Series,
vol. 4. 1882.

408617

VAN PATTEN (NATHAN)
An Index to bibliographies and
bibliographical contributions
relating to the work of American
and British authors, 1923-1932.
[Including Shakespeare.] (Stanford
University: [Palo Alto,] Cal.)
1934.

418638

VAN ROOSBROECK (GUSTAVE LEOPOLD)
Hamlet in France in 1663. IN
Publications of the Modern Language
Association of America, Vol. 37.
(Menasha, Wis.) 1922.

428357

VAN TROMP (HAROLD)
Halliwell-Phillipps and Hollingbury
Copse: memories of a famous
Shakespearian in Sussex. pp. [5.]
FROM Sussex County Magazine, October
1940.
bibliog.

521317

VAN WAVEREN (E.)
Commentary: an interpretation of the
Hamlet tetralogy. IN MacKAYE (PERCY)
The Mystery of Hamlet, King of
Denmark; or What we will: a tetralogy
in prologue to The Tragicall historie
of Hamlet, Prince of Denmarke, by
W. Shakespeare. (New York)
illus. 1950.

619928

[Van Winkle (E.S.)] The Spelling of
Shakespeare's name. From [Inter-
national Review,] Vol. 5.

[New York]   [1878.]

553493

Van Wyck (Jessica D.) Designing
Hamlet with Appia. Illus. In Theatre
Arts Monthly, Vol. 9.

(New York)   1925.

328359

Vardell (R.) Suite of incidental music
for Romeo & Juliet. pp.12.

(York)   1927.

(Banks Edition No.111.)

536609

Variorum Shakespeare, edited by
H. H. Furness see Furness (H. H.)
Works relating to:-

Vaughan (C.E.) Romantic tragedy :
Shakespeare. In Vaughan (C.E.)
Types of tragic drama. [With
bibliographical references.]

1924.

550900

VAUGHAN (CHARLES EDWYN) [ed.]
English literary criticism [with
references to Shakespeare].
Selected, with an introduction [and
preface] by C. E. Vaughan.
bibliog.   [1923.]

553673

Vaughan (H.H.) New readings & new
renderings of Shakespeare's tragedies.
2nd edn. Vol.1.

1886.

All published.   466552

VAUGHAN (STUART)
Commentary. IN Richard III.   Text
edited by C. J. Sisson.   (New York)
1960.
The Laurel Shakespeare.   F. Fergusson,
general editor.

667467

Vaughan Williams, Ralph *see* **Williams, Ralph Vaughan**

VAZAKAS (B.)
Midsummer night's dream [: a poem].
IN Kenyon Review, Vol. 12.
(Gambier, Ohio)   1950.

594031/12

Védel, Emile *works relating to*

—— Strachey (Marjorie) King Lear at the
Théâtre Antoine: [the French trans-
lation by P. Loti and E. Vedel.] In
The Independent review, Vol.8.

1906.

193889

VEEN (H. R. S. van der)
Jewish characters in eighteenth century
English fiction and drama. [With
Shakespearian references.] (Groningen)
1935.

440962

VEITCH (NORMAN)
The People's: a history of the
People's Theatre, Newcastle upon
Tyne, 1911-1939.   (Gateshead on
Tyne)
ports.   illus.   1950.

620792

VELIMIROVIC (NICHOLAS)
Shakespeare – the pananthropos.
IN GOLLANCZ ([Sir] I.) ed., A Book
of homage to Shakespeare.
ports.   illus.   facsimiles. [1916.]

264175

VELZ, JOHN W.
Division, confinement, and the moral
structure of King Lear. FROM Rice
University Studies 51: 1. (Houston,
Tex.)   1965.

pp.97-108.   747541

VELZ, JOHN W.
Some modern views of Shakespeare's
classicism. FROM Anglia, 81: 3/4.
(Tübingen)   1963.

pp.412-428.   747540

VENABLE (E.)
The Hamlet problem and its solution:
an interpretative study. [2nd edn.
condensed and annotated.] pp. 38.
(Cincinnati)
port.   1946.

581492

Venezky (Alice S.) see Griffin (Mrs.
Alice)

Venice

—— DRAPER (J. W.)
Shakespeare and the Doge of Venice.
IN Journal of English and Germanic
Philology, Vol. 46. (Urbana, Ill.:
University of Illinois)
bibliog. 1947.

600780/46

—— FINK (Z. S.)
The Classical republicans: an essay
in the recovery of a pattern of
thought in seventeenth century England.
[With references to the reputation of
Venice, as seen in Shakespeare's
"Othello" and "Merchant of Venice".]
(Evanston)
bibliogs. 1945.
Northwestern University Studies in the
Humanities, No. 9.

565297

—— JEFFERY (VIOLET M.)
Shakespeare's Venice. IN The
Modern Language Review, Vol. 27,
1932. (Cambridge)

410972

—— YOUNG (S.)
Shakespeare and the Venetians. IN
Theatre Arts Monthly, Vol. 14.
(New York)
illus. 1930. 379892
———— IN Theatre Arts Anthology: a
record and a prophecy. Edited by
Rosamond Gilder, H. R. Isaacs, R. M.
MacGregor [and] E. Reed. (New York)
1950. 614298

VENKATASIAH (M.) [ed.]
Longer moral quotations from
Shakespeare. 2nd edn. (Basavangudi)
1927.
Pocket Wisdom Series.

399213

VENKATASIAH (M.) [ed.]
Short moral quotations from
Shakespeare. 2nd edn. (Basavangudi)
1927.
Pocket Wisdom Series.

399212

VENTON, W. B.
Analyses of Shake-speares sonnets
using the cipher code [to prove that
Edward VI was the author]. 1968.

772619

Venus and Adonis

—— ALLEN (DON CAMERON)
On Venus and Adonis. Bibliog. IN
[Davis (H.) and Gardner (Helen L.)
eds.,] Elizabethan and Jacobean studies.
(Oxford) 1959.

687986

—— BEMROSE (J.M.)
A Critical examination of the
borrowings from "Venus and Adonis" and
"Lucrece" in Samuel Nicholson's
"Acolastus". IN Shakespeare Quarterly
XV: 1. pp.86-96. (New York) 1964.

605711

—— BRADBROOK (MURIEL C.)
Beasts and gods: Greene's 'Groatsworth
of witte' and the social purpose of
'Venus and Adonis'. IN SHAKESPEARE
SURVEY 15. (Cambridge) 1962.

667174

—— BURNAND (F. C.)
Venus and Adonis; or, The Two rivals
and the small boar [: a burlesque].
pp. 48. [Theatre Royal, Birmingham,
prompt book.] [c.1880.]
Lacy's Acting Edition No. 922.

455842

—— BUSH (D.)
Mythology and the Renaissance tradition
in English poetry. [Containing a
chapter entitled "Shakespeare: Venus
and Adonis and The Rape of Lucrece".]
(Minneapolis: University of Minnesota)
bibliog. 1933.

413283

—— BUSH (D.)
Mythology and the romantic tradition
in English poetry. [With references
to "Venus and Adonis".] (Cambridge,
Mass.)
bibliog. 1937.
Harvard Studies in English.

464426

—— BUTLER (CHRISTOPHER) and FOWLER (ALASTAIR)
Time-beguiling sport. Number
symbolism in Shakespeare's Venus and
Adonis. IN Shakespeare 1564-1964:
a collection of modern essays by
various hands. (Providence, R.I.)
1964.

Brown University bicentennial
publications.

744437

—— BUXTON (JOHN)
Elizabethan taste.
illus. 1963.
Includes a chapter "Shakespeare:
Venus and Adonis".

716219

___CANTELUPE (EUGENE B.)
An Iconographical interpretation of
"Venus and Adonis", Shakespeare's
Ovidian comedy.   IN SHAKESPEARE
QUARTERLY XIV: 2.   pp. 141-151.
(New York)   1963.

605711

___GREER, DAVID
An Early setting of lines from 'Venus
and Adonis'.   IN Music & letters,
Vol. 45, No. 2, April 1964:
Shakespeare and music.

668211

___GREG (W. W.)
[Review of] Venus and Adonis, 1593;
etc.: reproduced in facsimile from
the earliest editions, with introductions by [Sir] S. Lee.   IN The
Library, New Series, Vol. 7. 1906.

198827

___H. (T.)
Oenone and Paris [: an imitation of
Shakespeare's Venus and Adonis].
Reprinted from the unique copy in the
Folger Shakespeare Library, with [a
preface] an introduction and notes
by J. Q. Adams.   pp. xlv, 46.
(Washington, D.C.)
biblog.   facsimile.   1943.
Folger Shakespeare Library Publications.

567508

___ Hatto (A.T.) Venus and Adonis - and the
boar.[With bibliographical notes.]
In The Modern Language Review,Vol.41.

(Cambridge)   1946.

584763

___LEVER (JULIUS WALTER)
Venus and the second chance.   IN
SHAKESPEARE SURVEY 15.   (Cambridge)
1962.

667174

___MILLER (ROBERT P.   )

The Myth of Mars's hot minion in "Venus
and Adonis". IN E.L.H. Vol.26, No.4.
(Baltimore, Md.)   1959.

430295/26

___OVID
Metamorphosis. The XV books of P.
Ovidius Naso entytuled metamorphosis,
translated out of Latin into English
meeter by A. Golding. (London: W.
Serez)   1567.

447653

___PALMATIER (M. A.)
A Suggested new source in Ovid's
Metamorphoses for Shakespeare's
Venus and Adonis.   Reprinted from
The Huntington Library Quarterly,
Vol. 24, No. 2, February 1961.
pp. 9.   [San Marino, Cal.]
bibliogs.   1961.

667081

___PARSONS (J. D.)
R. Field and the first Shakespeare
poem: an essay on [E.] Arber's 40
years neglected Transcript of the
Stationers' Company's Registers'
Assignment Column disclosure of a
clerical error entry of the copyright.
pp. 12.   (Chiswick) 1935.   436336
_____ Another copy.   With MS. letter
by author.]   1935.   436337

___PARTRIDGE (ASTLEY COOPER)
Shakespeare's orthography in "Venus
and Adonis" and some early Quartos.
IN SHAKESPEARE SURVEY 7.   (Cambridge)
1954.

639176

___PRICE (H. T.)
Functions of imagery in Venus and
Adonis.   Reprinted from Papers of
the Michigan Academy of Science,
Arts and Letters, Vol. 31, 1945.
pp. [24].   [Ann Arbor, Mich.] 1947.

596024

___PUTNEY (RUFUS)
Venus Agonistes.   Reprinted from
University of Colorado Studies.
Series in Language and Literature,
No. 4, July 1953.   pp. [15].
[Boulder, Col.]   [1953.]

666115

___PUTNEY (R.)
Venus and Adonis: amour with humor.
FROM Philological Quarterly, Vol. 20.
(Iowa)   1941.

539441

___RABKIN, NORMAN
"Venus and Adonis" and the myth of love.
IN Pacific coast studies in
Shakespeare.   Edited by W. F. McNeir
and T. N. Greenfield.   (Eugene: Ore.)
1966.

768009

VERDI [GIUSEPPE]
Celebrated arias from the opera of
"Otello": Ave Maria.   [With Italian
text by A. Boito, and] English words
by P. Pinkerton.   pp. 4.   1920.

520170

Verdi ([G.]) Macbeth [from the opera
by G.] Verdi : quadrille [arranged]
by C. d'Albert. pp. 8.

[c.1850.]

501624

VERDI [GIUSEPPE]
Macbeth quadrille, on airs in Verdi's
opera arranged by C. [C.] Müller.
pp. 6.
illus.   [c.1850.]
Musical Treasury, Nos. 1139-40.

561326

Verdi, Giuseppe *works relating to*

—   Beiswanger (G.) 'From eleven to two':
Signor Verdi's Falstaff in English [at
the Metropolitan Opera House, New York].
Illus. In Theatre Arts,Vol.28.
(New York)   1944.

558366

—   B[oas] (G.) Shakespeare and
Glyndebourne [:an account of the production
of Verdi's opera Macbeth by the
Glyndebourne Opera Company]. In English,
Vol.2.   (Oxford)   1938

518293

—   Gatti (G.M.) The Two 'Macbeths'.[A
discussion on Verdi's 'Macbeth', and
Bloch's 'Macbeth'. Translated from the
Italian] by G.A.Pfister. In The Sackbut,
Vol.3.   1923.

307946

— GRAY (CECIL)
Verdi and Shakespeare.   IN Opera,
Vol. 2.   1951.

626228/2

—   Hussey (D.) Verdi [:a biography.
With references to his operas 'Otello'
and 'Falstaff']. Ports. Illus.

(Master Musicians.New Series)

1940.

514762

— KERMAN (JOSEPH)
Opera as drama.   1957.
Includes a chapter "Otello: tradi-
tional opera and the image of
Shakespeare".

676796

— KERMAN (JOSEPH)
Verdi's Otello, or Shakespeare
explained.   IN The Hudson Review,
Vol. 6.   (New York)   1953-54.

642968/6

— MARLOWE (ROGER)
Verdi and Shakespeare.   IN The
Music Review, Vol. 20.   1959.

523018/20

— MOODY (JOHN)
Verdi and Shakespeare.   Producer
R. Fiske. [Broadcast] 12th April,
1954.   ff. 11.
typescript.

643706

—   Newman (E.) Opera nights [: the
stories of 29 operas, including chapters
on Verdi's 'Falstaff' and Gounod's 'Romeo
and Juliet', with musical examples.].
Ports. Illus.   1943.

545435

—   Reynolds (E.[B.]) Verdi's 'Otello'
and Falstaff'. From The Monthly Musical
Record. Jan., 1936.

446500

—   Streatfeild (R.A.) Verdi and "King
Lear". In The Musical Times, Vol.46.
1905.

192174

—   Visetti (A.) Verdi [including an
account of Verdi's Falstaff. With a
bibliography.] pp.85. Ports. Illus.
Facsimile.

(Bell's Miniature Series
of Musicians)

1911.

495560

—   Werfel (F.) Verdi. [Including
references to his Shakespearean operas.]
Translated by Helen Jessiman. [New edn.]
[1944.]

548485

— WERFEL (F. [V.]) and STEFAN (P.)
Verdi, the man in his letters: as
edited and selected by F. [V.] Werfel
and P. Stefan.   Translated by E.
Downes.   [With references to
Shakespeare and Verdi's Shakespeare
operas.]   (New York)
ports. illus. facsimiles. 1942.

551545

—   White (E.W.) Verdi and Shakespeare.
[From 'Life and letters today",]Summer,
1938.   1938.

488926

VERNÈDE (R. E.)
"Hamlet" at a Bengal fair.   IN
Blackwood's Magazine, Vol. 188.
1910.

227926

VERNEUIL (L.)
The Fabulous life of Sarah Bernhardt.
Translated from the French by E. [A.]
Boyd.   (New York)
ports.   illus.   1942.

546688

VERNON (G.)
"As you like it" [: a criticism of
the performance at the Mansfield
Theatre, New York].   FROM The
Commonweal, Vol. 35.   (New York)
1941.

565599

VERNON (J.)
The New songs in the pantomime of
the Witches, the epilogue in Twelfth
Night, a song in Two Gentlemen of
Verona [etc.].   Adapted for the
harpsichord, violin, German flute
or guittar.   pp. [ii] 20. [c.1770.]

600303

Verplanck, Gulian Grommelin *works relating to*

— [WHIPPLE (E. P.)]
Verplanck and Hudson; Shakspeare's
plays.   IN The North American
Review, Vol. 67.   (Boston, [Mass.])
1848.

41797

Versification

— DRAPER (JOHN WILLIAM)
The Tempo-patterns of Shakespeare's
plays.   (Heidelberg)
tables.   bibliog.   1957.
Anglistische Forschungen, Heft 90.

665682

— INGRAM (JOHN K.)
On the "weak endings" of Shakspere, with
some account of the history of the verse-
tests in general.
IN Transactions of the New Shakespeare
Society, Series 1.   No. 2.   pp. 442-464.
1874.

4061

— LANGWORTHY (C. A.)
A Verse-sentence analysis of
Shakespeare's plays.   IN Publications
of the Modern Language Association of
America, Vol. 46.   (Menasha, Wis.)
1931.

428366

— Leathes (Sir S. [M.]) Rhythm in English
poetry. [With references to Shakespeare.]

1935.

439731

— MASSON (DAVID I.)
Free phonetic patterns in Shakespeare's
sonnets.   FROM Neophilologus, 38.
Jaargang.   (Groningen)   1954.

647042

— MAYOR (J. B.)
Chapters on English metre[, including
chapters on Shakespeare's blank verse
as seen in Macbeth and Hamlet].   2nd
edn. revised and enlarged.
(Cambridge)   1901.

546541

— NESS (F. W.)
The Use of rhyme in Shakespeare's
plays.   (New Haven, [Conn.])
bibliogs.   1941.
Yale Studies in English, Vol. 95.
Published on the Kingsley Trust
Association Publication Fund.

544711

— RICHARDSON (L. J.)
Repetition and rhythm in Vergil
and Shakespeare.   IN University
of California Chronicle, Vol. 32,
1930.   (Berkeley, Cal.)

400528

— Robertson (Rt. Hon. J.M.) The Scansion
of Shakespeare. In The Criterion,
Vol.8.

[1929]

361188

— SCHIPPER (J.)
A History of English versification.
[With references to the blank verse
of Shakespeare.]   (Oxford) 1910.

327526

— Smith (L.W.) Chronology and verse
in Shakespeare. From The English
Journal, vol.21.

(Chicago)   1932.

442571

— SUDDARD ([S. J.] MARY)
The Blending of prose, blank verse
and rhymed verse in "Romeo and
Juliet".   FROM The Contemporary
Review: Literary Supplement, 1910.
pp. [5.]

389209

— WAIN (JOHN BARRINGTON)
The Mind of Shakespeare.   IN GARRETT
(J.) More talking of Shakespeare.
1959.

666126

VERTUE (G.)
Note books [and autobiography.
Edited with introduction and notes
by a committee appointed by the
Walpole Society.   With index to
Vols. 1-5.   Contains references to
Shakespeare].   (Oxford)   7 vols.
ports. facsimiles. illus.   1930-
The Walpole Society.   Vols. 18, 20,
22, 24, 26, 29, 30.

376674

VERWEY (A.)
Grato m'è 'l sonno [: Dutch poem
with English paraphrase].
IN GOLLANCZ ([Sir] I.) ed., A Book
of homage to Shakespeare.
ports. illus. facsimiles. [1916.]

264175

Very heart of England, The: Shakespeare's home on the Avon. pp.[14.]
Illus From My Magazine, November,1933

414574

A Very modest club [: the Oldminster
Shakspeare Club.] FROM Chambers's
Journal, [1862.] pp. [3.]
[Edinburgh]

390783

A Very new Hamlet [: a reply to
"Hamlet", a criticism of Henry Irving:
an article in Blackwood's Magazine,
April 1879]. FROM The Theatre,
Vol. 2, New Series. 1879.
Blackwood's Magazine for April 1879
is catal. no. 12070.

530832

Vesselo (A.) Shakespeare and the films.
[A Review of] We make the movies,
edited by Nancy Naumberg. In Sight
& sound, Vol. 7.

1938.

500307

Vessie (P.R.) Psychiatry catches up
with Shakespeare. From Medical
Record, August 5, 1936.

(New York)

506180

VEST (W. E.)
William Shakespeare, therapeutist.
FROM Southern Medical Journal, Vol. 37.
(Birmingham, Ala.)
bibliog. 1944.

578416

Vest pocket Shakespearean manual of
quotations, characters, scenes and
plays. (Baltimore, Md.) 1955.

665845

Vestris, Madame *works relating to*

— WAITZKIN (L.)
The Witch of Wych Street: a study
of the theatrical reforms of Madame
Vestris. [With Shakespearian
references.] pp. 67. (Cambridge,
Mass.)
illus. bibliog. 1933.
Harvard Honors Theses in English.

423999

VIC-WELLS ASSOCIATION

[Newsletter] No.1 (March 1946)-

638014

Vicente, Gil *works relating to*

— LIVERMORE (ANN)
Gil Vicente and Shakespeare. IN
Book Handbook, Vol. 2.
facsimiles. 1951.

588086/2

VICHERT, GORDON
The Last imperialist. IN Stratford
Papers on Shakespeare delivered at
the 1964 Shakespeare Seminar.
(Toronto) 1965.

745844

Vick (H.), Castle (G.) and Awdry (Diana)
Characters from the country [:experi-
ences of Diana Awdry and H. Vick with
the Uley Players. Broadcast] 9th
May, 1938 (Midland). ff. 7. Typescript.

482433

VICK (HARRY), PHILLIPS (Mrs.) [and]
MARSH (F.)
Characters from the country: the
Uley Village Players [: a talk
between] Mrs. Phillips [and two
members of her company,] F. Marsh
[and] H. Vick. [With references
to Shakespearian productions.
Broadcast in] Midland programme,
2nd August, 1938. ff. 6.

486181

VICKERS, BRIAN
The artistry of Shakespeare's prose.
[Rev. version.] 1968.

767640

Vickers (J.) The Old Vic in photographs.
With an introduction by J.Burrell
[and references to Shakespearian
productions]. pp.[vi], 90.

1947.

588346

[VICTOR (B.?)]
Memoirs of the life of Barton Booth,
Esq.; with his character, [by B.?
Victor] poetical pieces, [by B.
Booth, and] The Case of Mr. Booth's
last illness, observ'd by A. Small.
pp. 58.
port. 1753.

422492

VICTORIA, Queen
The Training of a sovereign: an
abridged selection from "The Girlhood
of Queen Victoria", being Her Majesty's
diaries between the years 1832 and 1840.
Edited [with a preface] by Viscount
Esher. [With references to Shakespeare's
plays.] 1914.

443225

VICTORIA AND ALBERT MUSEUM, South
Kensington
Catalogue of photographs consisting
of historical and architectural
subjects and studies from nature,
chiefly contributed by Sir J. B.
Stone. [With a section "Shakespeare's
country".] pp. 24. (Board of
Education)
frontis. 1901.

424556

Victoria history of the county of
Warwick, edited by H. A. Doubleday,
W. Page, L. F. Salzman [and] P. Styles.
[With] index. [With references to
Shakespeare and Stratford-on-Avon.]
7 vols. illus. maps. 1904-55.
Victoria History of the Counties of
England.

184515

VIËTOR, WILHELM
A Shakespeare reader. In the old
spelling and with a phonetic
transcription. (New York) 1963.

749098

The View of Fraunce, by [Sir R.
Dallington.] 1604. With an intro-
duction by W. P. Barrett. 1936.
Shakespeare Association Facsimiles,
No. 13.

452707

The View of the cittye of London from
the north towards the south [c.1600.
Facsimile engraving from "Englandt's
descriptie", manuscript journal of
Abram Booth in the Library of the
University of Utrecht. With enlarge-
ment of section showing the Curtain
Theatre]. 2 sheets. [1954.]

641833-34

[Views of Stratford-on-Avon and Warwick.]
pp. [ii]. [Rock and Co.]
12 plates. [c.1855.]

573033

VIGENÈRE (BLAISE DE) Works relating to:
see Moore (W. H.) Baconian Studies.

"VIGILANT" [pseud.]
Did Shakespeare visit Denmark?
FROM The Norseman, Vol. 5. 1947.

582704

Vigny, Alfred de Le Comte *works relating to*

— LE BRETON (A.)
Le Théâtre romantique. [With a
chapter on Alfred de Vigny's translation of Othello and other references
to Shakespeare.] [c.1920.]
Bibliothèque de la Revue des Cours et
Conférences.

572306

VIHERVAARA (LYYLI) [ed.]
Elämän kudelma: Shakespearen säkeitä
kuukauden joka päivälle. Poiminut
Lyyli Vihervaara. pp. 73.
(Helsinki) 1928.
English and Finnish text.

430918

Villains

— BARNET (SYLVAN)
Coleridge on Shakespeare's villains.
IN SHAKESPEARE QUARTERLY VII.
pp. 9-20.
(New York) 1956.

605711

— BROCK (J. H. E.)
Iago & some Shakespearean villains.
pp. 48. (Cambridge)
bibliog. 1937.

475488

— COE, CHARLES NORTON
Demi-devils: the character of
Shakespeare's villains. 1963.

667723

— COE (CHARLES NORTON)
Shakespeare's villains. pp. 76.
(New York) 1957.

665578

— SPEVACK, MARVIN
Hero and villain in Shakespeare: [an
essay] on dualism and tragedy. FROM
Tennessee Studies in Literature,
Vol. XII, 1967. (Knoxville, Tenn.)

pp. 1-11. 766079

— SPIVACK (BERNARD)

Shakespeare and the allegory of evil:
the history of a metaphor in relation
to his major villains. Bibliog. (New
York) 1958.

665054

— STOLL (E. E.)
Heroes and villains: [characters of]
Shakespeare, Middleton, Byron, Dickens.
[With bibliographical notes.] IN The
Review of English Studies, Vol. 18.
(Oxford)
1942.

542539

VILLAREJO (OSCAR M.)
Shakespeare's "Romeo and Juliet": its
Spanish source.
IN SHAKESPEARE SURVEY 20. (Cambridge)
1967.

766881

VILLIERS (JACOB I. DE)
The Tragedy of 'Othello'. FROM Theoria,
[Vol.] 7. pp.[8]. [Pietermaritzburg]
[1955.]

667026

Vining, Joyce, trans.

KOZINTSEV, GRIGORII MIKHAILOVICH
Shakespeare: time and conscience.
Translated from the Russian by Joyce
Vining. 1967.

illus. 767149

VINTON (ARTHUR DUDLEY)
Those wonderful ciphers [: an account
of four Baconian ciphers]. FROM
The North American Review[, Vol. 145].
[New York] [1887.]

558104

Viola *see* **Twelfth Night,** General Works and
Criticism

VIOLI, UNICIO J.
Review notes and study guide to
Shakespeare's 'Measure for measure'.
(New York) 1964.

Monarch critiques of literature.
756288

V[IPAN] (F. J.)
Emendation of a passage in Shakspere's
"Coriolanus". FROM The Gentleman's
Magazine, March 1854. pp. [2.]

402709

V[IPAN] (F. J.)
Oversights of Schiller and Shakspere
[in "Henry the Eighth"]. FROM
The Gentleman's Magazine, June 1854.
pp. [2.]

402708

V[IPAN] (F. J.)
Undesigned imitations: Shakspere
of Erasmus [etc.]. FROM The
Gentleman's Magazine, July 1854.
pp. [4.]

402710

V[IPAN] (F. J.)
Undesigned imitations: the false
knights and the unruly brides of
Erasmus and Shakspere. FROM The
Gentleman's Magazine, Aug. 1854.
pp. [8.]

402711

Virgil *works relating to*

— KNIGHT (W. F. J.)
Roman Vergil. [With references to
Shakespeare.]
bibliog. 1944.

548212

— RICHARDSON (L. J.)
Repetition and rhythm in Vergil and
Shakespeare. IN University of
California Chronicle. (Berkeley,
Cal.) [1930]

400528

Virginia U.S.A.

— WALMSLEY (DONALD MUNRO)
Shakespeare's link with Virginia.
FROM 'History Today', Vol. 7, 1957.
pp. [8].
ports. illus. map. facsimiles.

665937

— WRIGHT (L. B.)
The First gentlemen of Virginia: intel-
lectual qualities of the early colonial
ruling class. [With references to
Shakespeare and bibliographical notes.]
(San Marino, Cal.)
1940.
Huntington Library Publications.
560820

Virginia University: Bibliographical
Society
EVANS (GWYNNE BLAKEMORE) ed.
Shakespearean prompt-books of the
seventeenth century. (Bibliographical
Society of The University of Virginia.
Charlottesville, Va.) 1960-
For setting out see under the author's
name.

Visetti (A.) Verdi [including an
account of Verdi's Falstaff. With
a bibliography.] pp. 85. Ports.
Illus. Facsimile.

1911.

(Bell's Miniature Series of Musicians)

495560

Visscher's View of London, 1616.
[Washington]
1 sheet. [1935.]
Folger Shakespeare Library Prints.

476926

VISSER (F. T.)
[Review of] Die Sprache Shakespeares
in Vers und Prosa, von W. Franz.
IN English Studies, Vol. 26.
(Amsterdam) 1944.

575610

VISSER (F. T.)
"To note" in Shakespeare's Hamlet
I, v, 178. IN English Studies,
Vol. 26. (Amsterdam) 1944.

575610

VISWANATHAM, K.
The Rejection of Falstaff: a myth.
[Waltair, India] [1965?]
pp. 6.

768976

VISWANATHAM, K.
The Sonnets of Shakespeare. FROM
"Triveni", January 1965.
(Machilipatnam, India)
pp. 16-26.

768975

VIVANTE (L.)
William Shakespeare, 1564-1616.
IN Vivante (L.) English poetry and
its contribution to the knowledge of
a creative principle. 1950.

608971

[VIZETELLY (HENRY) ed.]
Christmas with the poets: a
collection of songs, carols and
descriptive verses relating to
Christmas, from the Anglo-Norman
period to the present time.
[Including poems by Shakespeare.]
Illustrations by B. Foster. 1869.

520863

Vocabulary of Shakespeare *see* Grammar and Language

VOČADLO (OTAKAR)
Shakespeare and Bohemia.
IN SHAKESPEARE SURVEY 9. (Cambridge)
1956.

665210

Vocal Tones in Shakespeare's Works

— BERRY (FRANCIS)
Poetry and the physical voice
1962.

703839

VOCHT (HENRY de)
Shakespeare: his life, work and
after-life. pp. 40. (Turnhout,
Belgium)
ports. facsimiles. bibliog.
[1945.]

580812

VOGEL (RUTH R.)
An Evaluation of the love songs in
Shakespeare's dramatic works:
Columbia University [thesis] 1948.
IN GOLDING (NANCY L.) A Survey of
the proposed arrangements of
Shakespeare's Sonnets [etc.]
bibliog. microfilm, positive copy.
[1948.]

609350

VOGELBACK (ARTHUR L.)
Shakespeare and Melville's "Benito
Cereno". IN Modern Language Notes,
Vol. 67. (Baltimore, Md.) 1952.

439151/67

Voice, Shakespeare's *see* Vocal Tones in Shakespeare's Works

[VOIGT (F. A.)]
The Political wisdom of the English poets
[including Shakespeare] by the editor of
"The Nineteenth Century and After".
[With bibliographical notes.] FROM The
Nineteenth Century and After [Vol. 134.]
1943.

Last page typescript.

547720

VOITOLOVSKAYA (LINA)
Khadji Mukan and William Shakespeare.
[Contains description of a perform-
ance of The Taming of the Shrew in
Soviet Kazakhstan.] IN Soviet War
News, Vol. 11. 1944.

560943

VOLKMAN (R.)
Ouverture zu Shakespeare's Richard III
fur grosses Orchester. pp. 43.
[c.1870.]

579785

Volochova (Sonia) and others, trans.
SMIRNOV (A. A.)
Shakespeare: a Marxist interpretation.
Translated from the Russian by Sonia
Volochova, Sidonie Kronman, A.
Goldstein, A. Morais, Zena Rautbort
and the Editorial Committee: Angel
Flores, Charles Birchall, E. P. Greene,
Paul S. Leitner, Lola H. Sachs.   3rd
edn., revised.   pp. 93.   (New York)
1936.
Critics Group Series 2.

457904

VOLOSHIN (MAXIMILIAN)
Portia [: Russian poem with English
translation by N. Forbes.]
IN GOLLANCZ ([Sir] I.) ed., A Book
of homage to Shakespeare.
ports. illus. facsimiles. [1916.]

264175

Voltaire ([F.M.A.] de) Letters
concerning the English nation.
[Containing a letter "On tragedy",
having references to Shakespeare.]
New edn.

1760.

519580

Voltaire, François Marie Arouet de *works relating to*

— Babcock (R.W.) The English reaction
against Voltaire's criticism of
Shakespeare. pp.[18]. From Studies
in Philology, October, 1930

(Chapel Hill,N.C.)

441591

— GREEN (F. C.)
Minuet: a critical survey of French
and English literary ideas in the
eighteenth century [containing
chapters: Shakespeare and Voltaire;
Shakespeare and French dramatic
tradition; and Some comments on
T. Lounsbury's 'Shakespeare and
Voltaire'.]   1935.

431509

— HORSLEY (PHYLLIS M.)
George Keate and the Voltaire-
Shakespeare controversy.   IN
Comparative Literature Studies:
Cahiers de Littérature Comparée, Vol.
16.   (Cardiff)   1945.

579158

— Lawrenson, T.E.
Voltaire and Shakespeare. IN

OUTHIE, GEORGE IAN, ed.
Papers, mainly Shakespearian. 1964.

Aberdeen University studies,
No. 147.   668205

— LESSING [(G.E.)]
Ausgewahlte Prosa und Briefe. Edited,
with notes, by H.S. White. [Containing
"Gespenster auf der Buhne (Shakespeare
und Voltaire)" and "Weisse's Richard III".]
(New York)   1888.

(German Classics for American Students)

443693

— LESSING ([G. E.])
Voltaire and Shakespeare.   IN
Lessing [(G. E.)] Laocoon, and
other prose writings; translated
and edited by W. B. Ronnfeldt.
[1895]
Scott Library.

460153

— LOWENSTEIN (R.)
Voltaire as an historian of seventeenth-
century French drama. [With Shakespearian
references and a bibliography.]
(Baltimore)   1935.

(Johns Hopkins Studies in Romance Literatures
and Languages, Vol.25)
458110

— MAUROIS (ANDRÉ) [pseud.]
Voltaire.   Translated from the French.
port.   bibliog.   1932.

390393

— MURPHY (A.)
Against Voltaire on Shakespear.   IN The
Gray's Inn Journal, Vol. I, No. 41
(Dublin)   1756
495633.

— RUSSELL (T. W.)
Voltaire, Dryden & heroic tragedy.
[With references to Shakespeare.]
(New York)
bibliogs.   1946.

575212

— STOLL (E. E.)
Oedipus and Othello, Corneille,
Rymer and Voltaire.   [English
text.]   Extrait de la Revue Anglo-
Américaine, juin 1935.   pp. [16.]
(Paris)
bibliog.

569122

— WALPOLE (H.)
Concerning Voltaire's abuse of
Shakespeare.   IN Walpole (H.)
The Best letters of Horace Walpole.
Edited with an introduction by Anna
B. McMahan.   1909.
Laurel Crowned Letters.

493353

— [Woodhouselee (A.F. Tytler, Lord)]
Essays on the principles of
translation. [Including notes on
Voltaire's translation from Shakespeare.] 3rd edn. with additions.

(Edinburgh)   1813.

524178

Von Cossel (Louise) see Cossel (Louise von)

Vortigern *see* Ireland Forgeries

Voyages and Explorations

—Cawley (R.R.) Unpathed waters: studies in the influence of the voyagers on Elizabethan literature. [With a chapter on Shakespeare, Shakespearian references and bibliographical notes.]

(Princeton)   1940.

531287

—Cawley (R.R.) The Voyagers and Elizabethan drama. [With Shakespearian references and a bibliography.]

(Boston, [Mass.])   1938.

(Modern Language Association of America, Monograph Series, 8.)

492269

— NUTT (SARAH M.)
The Arctic voyages of William Barents in probable relation to certain of Shakespeare's plays.   IN Studies in Philology, Vol. 39.   (Chapel Hill, N.C.)
illus.   bibliog.   1942.

554520

— PENROSE (BOIES)
Tudor and early Stuart voyaging. (Washington: Folger Shakespeare Library)
illus.   maps.   1962.
Folger Booklets on Tudor and Stuart Civilization.

667843

— QUINN, DAVID BEERS
Sailors and the sea [: in Elizabethan England].   IN SHAKESPEARE SURVEY 17. (Cambridge)   1964.

667822

— ROGERS (J. D.)
Voyages and exploration: geography: maps.   IN Shakespeare's England, vol. 1.   (Oxford)
illus.   facsimiles.   bibliogs.
1917.

435745

[VREDENBURG (EDRIC WALCOTT)]
Memoir of Shakespeare.   IN The Shakespeare Birthday Book.   With 4 illustrations in colour by J. H. Bacon & others.   pp. 67.
[1921]

438184

VYVYAN (JOHN)
Shakespeare and platonic beauty.
1961.

666835

VYVYAN (JOHN)
Shakespeare and the rose of love: a study of the early plays in relation to the medieval philosophy of love.   1960.

666532

VYVYAN (JOHN)
The Shakespearean ethic.   1959.

666014

W. (J.)
Shakspeare and his native county. FROM [Fraser's Magazine,] Vol. 54. bibliog.   1856.

558098

WADDINGTON (RAYMOND B.)
Antony and Cleopatra: "what Venus did with Mars."
IN Shakespeare Studies, 2.   (Cincinnati, Ohio)   1966.

761781

WADE (JAMES EDGAR)
Mediaeval rhetoric in Shakespeare [: a dissertation submitted to the Faculty of] Saint Louis University [for the degree of Doctor of Philosophy].
microfilm copy.   1942.
University Microfilms.   Doctoral Dissertations Series.
For an abstract of this dissertation see Microfilm Abstracts Vol. 5, No. 2. Catal. No. 569025.

575680

WADE (JOSEPH HENRY)
Rambles in Shakespeare's country.
illus.   1932.

389599

Wadely (F.W.) O mistress mine: part song for male voices. T.T.B.B. Poem by Shakespeare [from Twelfth Night]; music by F.W.Wadely. pp. 7.

1929.

(Winthrop Rogers Edition of Choral Music for Festivals.)

518997

WADSWORTH, FRANK W.
Hamlet and Iago: Nineteenth-century breeches parts. IN Shakespeare Quarterly XVII: 2. pp.129-139. (New York)   1966.

605711

WADSWORTH (FRANK W.)
The Poacher from Stratford: a partial account of the controversy over the authorship of Shakespeare's plays. (Berkeley and Los Angeles)
ports.   illus.   1958.

666186

WADSWORTH (FRANK W.)
Shakespeare in action - a report.
IN College English, Vol. 16.
(Champaign, Ill.)   1955.

598860/16

WADSWORTH (FRANK W.)
"Sound and fury" - "King Lear" on
television.   IN The Quarterly of
Film Radio and Television, Vol. 8.
(Berkeley, Cal.)   1954.

630462/8

Wadsworth Guides to Literary Study
BONHEIM (HELMUT) ed.
   The King Lear perplex, [by various
   authors].   (San Francisco)
   bibliog.   1960.
   Wadsworth Guides to Literary Study.

666814

Wadsworth Guides to Literary Study
HALIO, JAY LEON, ed.
   Approaches to 'Macbeth'   (Belmont,
   Cal.)   1966.

753832

WAGENKNECHT (EDWARD CHARLES)
The First editor of Shakespeare [:
N. Rowe.]   IN The Colophon, Part 8.
(New York)
   illus.   1931.

396607

WAGENKNECHT (EDWARD)
   The Perfect revenge - Hamlet's delay:
   a reconsideration.   IN College
   English, Vol. 10.   (Chicago)
   bibliog.   1948-9.

598860/10

WAGGONER (G. R.)
   An Elizabethan attitude toward peace
   and war [: reflected in the plays of
   Shakespeare and others].   IN Philological Quarterly, Vol. 33.   (Iowa)
                          1954.

592684/33

WAGGONER (G. R.)
   "Timon of Athens" and the Jacobean duel.
   IN SHAKESPEARE QUARTERLY XVI: 4.
   pp. 303-311.
   (New York)   1965.

605711

WAGNALLS (MABEL)
   Stars of the opera: a description
   of operas & a series of interviews
   [etc.]   Revised and enlarged edn.
   (New York)
   ports.   1907.
   Includes a chapter on "Hamlet".

585260

WAGNER (BERNARD MATHIAS)
   Caxton's Recuyell and Shakespeare's
   Troilus.   IN Modern Language Notes,
   vol. 45, March, 1930.   (Baltimore)

439157

WAGNER (BERNARD MATHIAS)
London's new Mermaid Theatre at Puddle
Dock.
IN   SHAKESPEARE QUARTERLY X: 4.
   pp. 603-606.
(New York)   1959.

605711

WAGNER (BERNARD MATHIAS) ed.
   The Appreciation of Shakespeare: a
   collection of criticism, philosophic,
   literary and esthetic, by writers
   and scholar-critics of the eighteenth,
   nineteenth, and twentieth centuries.
   (Washington)   1949.

616565

WAGNER ([Mrs.] EMMA B.)
   Shakespeare's The Tempest: an
   allegorical interpretation.   Edited
   from manuscript and notes by H. R.
   Orr.   (Yellow Spring, Ohio)   1933.

437565

Wagner (H.K.) Coriolanus: review of
   Shakespeare's play. pp.21.

(Belleville.Ill.)   1934

431325

WAGNER (H. K.)
   Measure for Measure: a review of
   Shakespeare's play "Measure for
   Measure",   pp. 12.   (Belleville,
   Ill.)   1934.

431273

WAGNER (LEOPOLD)
   The Stage, with the curtain raised.
   [With references to Shakespeare.
   New, revised and enlarged edn.]
   pp. 32.   [1880]

511087

WAHR (FREDERICK BURKHART)
   Goethe's Shakespeare.   FROM
   Philological Quarterly, vol. 11.
   (Iowa)   1932.

442562

Wahr (F.B.) The Hauptmann Hamlet.
   [With bibliographical notes.] From
   Philological quarterly, Vol. 16.

(Iowa)   1937.

484072

WAIN, JOHN BARRINGTON
   Guides to Shakespeare. FROM Encounter,
   March 1964, pp.53-62.

668348

WAIN (JOHN BARRINGTON)
   The Living world of Shakespeare: a
   playgoer's guide.   1964.

668032

WAIN (JOHN BARRINGTON)
   The Mind of Shakespeare.   IN GARRETT
   (J.) More talking of Shakespeare.
                          1959.

666126

Waingrow (Marshall) see Barish
(Jonas A.) and Waingrow (Marshall)

WAINWRIGHT (JOHN WILLIAM)
   The Medical and surgical knowledge
   of William Shakspere.   With
   explanatory notes.   pp. [xii], 80.
   (New York)
   port.   1915.

666704

WAITE (VINCENT)
Will of Stratford.   IN Waite (V.)
Three costume plays [: mainly for
schoolboy players].   With a foreword by L. Banks.
   dgms.   1944.

                    553770

WAITH (EUGENE MERSEREAU)
The Herculean hero in Marlowe,
Chapman, Shakespeare and Dryden.
   illus.   1962.

                    667146

WAITH (EUGENE MERSEREAU)
Macbeth: interpretation versus adap-
tation.   IN PROUTY (CHARLES TYLER) ed.
Shakespeare: of an age and for all
time: the Yale Shakespeare Festival
Lectures.   [New Haven, Conn.] 1954.

                    640920

WAITH (EUGENE MERSEREAU)
The Metamorphosis of violence in
"Titus Andronicus".   IN SHAKESPEARE
SURVEY 10.   (Cambridge)   1957.

                    665485

WAITH, EUGENE MERSEREAU, ed.
   Shakespeare, the histories: a
   collection of critical essays.
   (Englewood Cliffs, N.J.)   1965.

        Twentieth Century Views.
                    745303

WAITZKIN (LEO)
The Witch of Wych Street: a study
of the theatrical reforms of
Madame Vestris.   [With Shakespearian
references.]   pp. 67.   (Cambridge,
Mass.)
   illus. bibliog.   1933.
Harvard Honors Theses in English.

                    423999

WAKELIN (ELLEN A.)
[Scrolls presented to Sir Fordham Flower
and L. Fox containing an account of the
events in Stratford-upon-Avon at the
Quatercentenary Birthday celebrations
with a description of the Shakespeare
Exhibition and the opening of the
Stratford canal on July 11th 1964.
With text and music of the Tercentenary
Festal Song and the Tercentenary
National Song to Shakespeare.]
   4 items in 1 reel. 35 mm.   [1964.]
Microfilm, negative copy, made at
Birmingham Reference Library, 1965. 744435

[WALBANCKE (MATTHEW) ed.]
Annalia Dubrensia [: a collection of
verses by various writers] upon the
yeerly celebration of Mr. Robert Dover's
Olimpick games upon Cotswold-Hills.
Printed by R. Raworth for M. Walbancke,
1636.   Reprint, edited [with an introduction and references to Shakespeare]
by E. R. Vyvyan.   pp. 85.   (Cheltenham)
   illus.   1878.

                    441579

WALBROOK (HENRY MACKINNON)
The Drama in Clement Scott's day.
FROM "The Fortnightly Review",
April 1934.   pp. 472-480.

                    427396

WALBROOK (H. M.)
A Playgoer's wanderings [: reminiscences of the theatre.   With references to Shakespeare.]
   ports. illus.   1926.

                    443959

WALBROOK (HENRY MACKINNON)
The Shrew that Shakespeare drew [:
Ada Rehan as Katharina.]   FROM The
Nineteenth Century, 1929.   pp. [7.]

                    389232

Walcott (F.G.) John Dryden's answer to
   Thomas Rymer's "The Tragedies of
   the last age" [With Shakespearian
   references and bibliographical notes.]
   From Philological quarterly, Vol.15.

        (Iowa)   1935.
                    484068

WALDEN (TREADWELL)
A Seat in the chair of destiny [: an
account of the Stone of Scone with
special reference to Macbeth.]   FROM
Appletons' Journal, New Series, Vol. 6.
[New York]
   bibliog.   1879.

                    558114

WALDO (TOMMY RUTH) and HERBERT (THOMAS
WALTER)
Musical terms in The Taming of the
shrew: evidence of single authorship.
IN   SHAKESPEARE QUARTERLY X: 2.
pp. 185-199.
(New York)   1959.

                    605711

WALDOCK (ARTHUR JOHN ALFRED)
"Macbeth".   IN Waldock (A. J. A.)
James, Joyce and others [: five
literary studies].   1937.

                    472629

WALES (JULIA G.)
Shakespeare's use of English and
foreign elements in the setting of
Much Ado About Nothing.   Reprinted
from Transactions of the Wisconsin
Academy of Sciences, Arts and Letters.
Vol. 28.   pp. 363-398.   [Madison]
                             1933.

                    444036

WALES (JULIA G.)
Shakespeare's use of English and
foreign elements in the setting
of The Two Gentlemen of Verona.
Reprinted from Transactions of the
Wisconsin Academy of Sciences, Arts
and Letters.   Vol. 27.   pp. 85-126.
[Madison]   1932.

                    444037

Wales and the Welsh

—— BRETT-JAMES (N. G.)
   Walking in the Welsh borders.   [With
   references to Shakespeare.]
   illus. maps.   1942.

                    535741

— Burton (P.H.) "Her Majesty commands"
[: a play, broadcast from] Cardiff,
22,Nov., 1938.ff.[1],29. Typescript.

491800

— Burton (P.H.) Master Shakespeare
and Glendower: [a play, broadcast from]
Cardiff,27 May, 1938.ff.[1] 22.Typescript.

487434

— EVANS (J. A.)
Shakespeare's Welsh characters.
FROM The Welsh Outlook, Dec., 1933.
[Newtown]

416890

—JONES, GLYN
We band of brothers.   Produced by
Myrfyn Owen.   B.B.C. television
script broadcast 29th July 1964.
(Cardiff)

668238

—LLOYD ([Sir] J. E.)
Shakespeare's Welshmen.
IN GOLLANCZ ([Sir] I.) ed., A Book
of homage to Shakespeare.
ports. illus. facsimiles. [1916.]

264175

—[REES (T. J.) ed.]
Shakespeare on Swansea men and matters:
a selection of quotations from
Shakespeare's works.   pp. 52.
(Swansea)   [1914]

555585

— TATLOCK (J. S. P.)
The Welsh 'Troilus and Cressida
[MS Peniarth 106, National Library
of Wales] and its relation to the
Elizabethan drama.   IN The Modern
Language Review, Vol. 10.
(Cambridge)   1915.

266825

—THOMAS (Sir D. LLEUFER)
Welshmen and the First Folio of
Shakespeare's plays (1623).   IN
Transactions of the Honourable Society
of Cymmrodorion, 1940.   1941.

530241

— WILLIAMS (GWYN)
Welshmen in Shakespeare's Stratford.
IN The Honourable Society of Cymmro-
dorion, Transactions, 1954.   1955.

255163/1954

— WILSON (WINIFRED G.)
Welshmen in Elizabethan London.
[With references to Shakespeare.]
FROM Life and letters today, [Vol.
41].
bibliog.   1944.

550792

WALĪ AL-DĪN YAKAN
Shakespeare [: Arabic poem, with a
summary in English.]
IN GOLLANCZ ([Sir] I.) ed., A Book
of homage to Shakespeare.
ports. illus. facsimiles. [1916.]

264175

Waliy ad-din Yeyen see Walī al-dīn
Yakan.

WALKER (ALBERT L.)
Convention in Shakespeare's description
of emotion.   FROM Philological
quarterly, Vol. 17.   (Iowa)
bibliog.   1938.

484075

WALKER (ALICE)
Collateral substantive texts (with
special reference to "Hamlet".)
IN Studies in Bibliography, Vol. 7.
(Charlottesville, Va.)   1955.

598680/7

WALKER (ALICE)
Compositor determination and other
problems in Shakespearian texts.
IN Studies in Bibliography, Vol. 7.
(Charlottesville, Va.)   1955.

598680/7

WALKER (ALICE)
Edward Capell and his edition of
Shakespeare.   pp. [15.]
[1960.]   666879
Annual Shakespeare Lecture of the
British Academy, 1960.
_____   IN Studies in Shakespeare:
British Academy lectures, selected
and introduced by P. Alexander.
1964.   667830
Oxford paperbacks.   No. 81.

WALKER (ALICE)
The Folio text of "I Henry IV".
IN Studies in Bibliography, Vol. 6.
(Charlottesville, Va.)   1953.

598680/6

WALKER (ALICE)
'Miching Malicho' and the play scene
in Hamlet.   IN The Modern Language
Review, Vol. 31.   (Cambridge)
1936.

463704

WALKER (ALICE)
The 1622 Quarto and the First Folio
texts of "Othello".   IN SHAKESPEARE
SURVEY 5.   (Cambridge)   1952.

623798

WALKER (ALICE)
Principles of annotation: some
suggestions for editors of Shakespeare.
IN Studies in Bibliography, Vol. 9.
(Charlottesville, Va.)   1957.

593680/9

WALKER (ALICE)
Quarto "copy" and the 1623 Folio:
2 Henry IV.   IN The Review of
English Studies, New Series, Vol. 2.
(Oxford)   1951.

318239/2/2

WALKER (ALICE)
[Review of] Antony and Cleopatra,
edited by M. R. Ridley.   Based on
the edition of R. H. Case.   (Arden
Shakespeare)   IN Review of English
Studies, New Series, Vol. 6.   1955.

318239/2/6

Walker (Alice) [Review of] The Textual
history of Richard III by D. L.
Patrick. 1936. In The Review of
English Studies, Vol.14.

1938.

495115

WALKER (ALICE)
Some editorial principles (with
special reference to "Henry V").
IN Studies in Bibliography, Vol. 8.
(Charlottesville, Va.)   1956.

598680/8

WALKER (ALICE)
The Textual problem of Hamlet: a
reconsideration.   IN The Review of
English Studies, New Series, Vol. 2.
(Oxford)   1951.

318239/2/2

WALKER (ALICE)
The Textual problem of "Troilus and
Cressida".   IN The Modern Language
Review, Vol. 45.   1950.

266816/45

WALKER (ALICE)
Textual problems of the First Folio:
Richard III, King Lear, Troilus &
Cressida, 2 Henry IV, Hamlet,
Othello.   (Cambridge)
bibliog.   1953.
Shakespeare Problems, 7.

633690

WALKER (DEREK)
Most things do not happen: a theatrical
comedy. [B.B.C. script, 4th November
1959.] pp. [ii], 32.
typescript.

666445

WALKER (HUGH)
The Knocking at the gate once more.
IN GOLLANCZ ([Sir] I.) ed., A Book
of homage to Shakespeare.
ports. illus. facsimiles. [1916.]

264175

WALKER (JOHN) [ed.]
A Selection of curious articles from
The Gentleman's Magazine.   [With
references to Shakespeare]   3rd
edn.
4 vols.   1814.

506797

WALKER (JOHN) the philologist
Elements of elocution: the substance
of a course of lectures on the art
of reading; delivered at several
colleges in the University of Oxford.
[With exercises and extracts from
Shakespeare.]
dgms.   1781.

521205

WALKER (JOHN) the philologist
Elements of elocution, [with] a
complete system of the passions,
showing how they affect the counten-
ance, tone of voice and gesture of
the body, exemplified by a selection
of passages of Shakspeare.   3rd edn.
port. illus.   1806.   489008
_____ 7th edr.
illus.   1825.   520869

[WALKER (JOSEPH COOPER)]
Historical memoir on Italian tragedy.
[Contains (pp. 50-62) a parallel
between L. Groto's tragedy of
Hadriana and Romeo and Juliet.]
1799.

59355

WALKER (KATHRINE SORLEY)
Robert Helpmann: a study of his
work, with a list of his appearances on stage and screen.
ports.   illus.   1957.
Theatre World Monographs.

675008

Walker (N.W.G.) Was Shakespeare a
seaman? From The P.L.A. Monthly.
No. 160.

1939.

512571

WALKER (RALPH SPENCE)
The Great Globe itself: [a play about
a rehearsal of The Tempest in 1611].
IN MARRIOTT (J. W.) [ed.] One-act
plays of to-day.   Sixth series.
frontis.   1934.
The Harrap Library.

424087

WALKER (REGINALD F.)
Companion to the study of
Shakespeare: Macbeth. pp. 72.
(Dublin)
bibliog.   1947.

592726

Walker, Robert *works relating to*

—— DAWSON (GILES EDWIN)
Robert Walker's editions of Shakespeare.
FROM Studies in English Renaissance
Drama. [? New York]   [c.1958.]

667866

—— FORD (H. L.)
Shakespeare, 1700-1740: a collation of
the editions and separate plays, with
some account of T. Johnson and R. Walker.
(Oxford)
1935.
_____ [Another copy]
Note: This copy contains a list of
addenda and corrigenda issued after
printing.

442298-9

WALKER (ROY)
The Celestial plane in Shakespeare.
IN SHAKESPEARE SURVEY 8.   (Cambridge)
1955.

647706

WALKER (ROY)
Comment no. 32: R. Walker on the
current BBC Television series of
Shakespeare's Histories, "An Age
of Kings".   Broadcast 11th Aug. 1960.
ff. 4.
typescript.

666996

WALKER, ROY
Doublet and slacks [: costume for
productions of Shakespeare].
Produced by George MacBeth.   BBC
radio script broadcast 20th April
1964.

668245

WALKER (ROY)
In fair Verona [: the importance of
scenery in the production of
Shakespeare's plays.]   IN Twentieth
Century, Vol. 156.   1954.

14975/156

WALKER (ROY)
The Northern star: an essay on the
Roman plays.
IN SHAKESPEARE QUARTERLY II: 4.
pp. 287-293.
(New York) 1951.

605711

WALKER (ROY)
The Problem of free will in
Shakespeare.   FROM The Aryan Path,
Vol. 25.   pp. [5.]   (Bombay)
1954.

638955

WALKER (R.)
The Time is free: a study of Macbeth.
bibliog.   1949.

600595

Walker (R.) The Time is out of joint:
a study of Hamlet.[With a
bibliography and bibliographical
notes.]

1948.

590826

WALKER (ROY)
Unto Caesar: a review of recent
productions.   IN SHAKESPEARE SURVEY
11.   (Cambridge)
ports.   illus.   bibliog. 1958.

665816

WALKER (ROY)
The Whirligig of time: a review of
recent productions.   IN SHAKESPEARE
SURVEY 12.   (Cambridge)
ports.   illus.   bibliog. 1959.

666150

WALKER (ROY), LEECH (CLIFFORD) and
TILLYARD (EUSTACE MANDEVILLE WETENHALL)
The Unity of "Henry IV" - a discussion.
Producer: D. S. Carne-Ross.   [Broad-
cast 22nd May 1955.]   ff. [36].
typescript.

665040

WALKER (SAXON)
Mime and heraldry in 'Henry IV,
Part 1'.   IN English, Vol. 11.
1956.

481151/11

WALKLEY (ARTHUR BINGHAM)
Frames of mind [: essays, including]
The Taming of Tragedy (in "Hamlet",
in "Richard III") [and] Sex in play-
acting (Sarah Bernhardt, her impossible
Hamlet).   1899.

544884

WALKLEY (ARTHUR BINGHAM)
A New theatrical adventure started
with King Lear.   IN AGATE (J. [E.])
ed., The English dramatic critics.
[1932.]

399280

WALKLEY (ARTHUR BINGHAM)
Playhouse impressions [: articles
reprinted chiefly from the Speaker,
National Observer and the Star.
Including articles on Shakespeare's
plays.]   1892.

460100

WALKLEY (ARTHUR BINGHAM)
The Theatre in London.   [With refer-
ences to Shakespeare]   IN
Cosmopolis, vol. 5.   1897.

137771

Walkley (A.B.) The Theatre in London.
Revival of King Richard III.   In
Cosmopolis, Vol.6.

1897.

138551

WALLACE (CHARLES WILLIAM)
The Discovery of Shakespeare [:
documentary evidence of Shakespeare's
connexion with the Globe Theatre.]
IN The Poetry Review, [Vol. 4.]
1914.

253079

Wallace (C.W.) The First London Theatre:
materials for a history, [1576-1602.]

([Lincoln, Neb.])   1913.

([Nebraska] University Studies, Vol. 13,
Nos. 1-3.)

499282

Wallace (C.W.) Shakespeare and America.
The perpetual ambassador of the
English-speaking world. In The
Poetry Review, Vol.5.

1914.

255953

WALLACE (CHARLES WILLIAM)
Shakespeare and his London associates
as revealed in recently discovered
documents.   FROM The University
Studies of the University of Nebraska,
Vol. 10.   (Lincoln, Neb.)   1910.

563272

Wallace, Charles William *works relating to*

—BASTIDE (C.)
Shakespeare and Christopher Mongoye
[Christopher Mountjoy.   With
references to the documents
discovered by C. W. Wallace.]
IN Bastide (C.) The Anglo-French
entente in the seventeenth century.
1914.

519989

WALLACE (IRVING)
The Square pegs: some characters who
dared to be different.   1958.
  Includes a chapter "The Lady who
moved Shakespeare's bones [i.e.
Delia Bacon]."

676271

Wallace (P. Hope-) see Hope-Wallace (P.)

Wallack (L.) Memories of fifty years.
  With an introduction by L. Hutton
  [and references to Shakespeare.]
  Ports. Illus. Facsimiles.

(New York)   1889.

No. 497 of an edn. of 500 copies.

499288

WALLBANK (NEWELL)
It was a lover and his lass: song
for high voice.   Words [from "As
you like it"].   pp. 7.   [1948.]

597271

WALLER, FREDERICK O.
The Use of linguistic criteria in determining the copy and dates for Shakespeare's
plays.
IN Pacific coast studies in
Shakespeare.   Edited by W. F. McNeir
and T. N. Greenfield.   (Eugene: Ore.)
1966.

768009

WALLER (JOHN GREEN)
The Prospero of "The Tempest".
FROM The Gentleman's Magazine,
Aug. 1853.   pp. [8.]

402707

Waller, Lewis *works relating to*

— Pearson (H.) 'The Last actor managers'.
   (1) H.B.Irving & Lewis Waller.
   [Broadcast] 4th October, 1949.
   ff.8. Typescript.

605259

WALLER (W. F.)
Helen Faucit [: review of "On
some of Shakespeare's female
characters," by Helena Faucit (Lady
Martin)].   IN The Theatre.   New
series.   Vol. 6.   1885.

79782

WALLERSTEIN (RUTH COONS)
Dryden and the analysis of
Shakespeare's techniques [: a study
of Dryden's imitation of Shakespeare
in "All for love".   bibliog.]   IN
The Review of English Studies, Vol.19.
(Oxford)   1943.

555539

WALLEY (HAROLD B.)
Shakespeare's portrayal of Shylock.
[bibliog.]   IN CRAIG (H.) ed.,
Essays in dramatic literature: the
Parrott presentation volume.
(Princeton)
port.   1935.

444399

WALLEY (HAROLD REINOEHL)
The Dates of Hamlet and Marston's
The Malcontent.   IN The Review of
English studies, Vol. 9.   [1933.]

414489

WALLEY (HAROLD REINOEHL)
Shakespeare's conception of Hamlet
IN Publications of the Modern
Language Association of America,
Vol. 48.   (Menasha, Wis.) 1933.

418268

WALLEY (HAROLD REINOEHL)
Shakespeare's debt to Marlowe in
"Romeo and Juliet".   IN Philological
Quarterly, Vol. 21.   (Iowa) 1942.

592684/21

Wallis (A.J.)   O Mistress mine :
   song.   [Twelfth Night].   pp. 4.

1924.

520169

Wallis (C.) Thumb prints [: a play
   for broadcasting.] ff.9. Typescript.

[1934.]

422599

WALLIS (LAWRENCE B.)
Fletcher, Beaumont & company,
entertainers to the Jacobean gentry
[including references to
Shakespeare's plays.]   (New York)
bibliog.   1947.

588580

WALLIS (NORBERT HARDY)
The Ethics of criticism, and other
essays.   [Including Two modern
plays on Shakespeare: Shakespeare,
by H. F. Rubinstein and C. Bax;
Will Shakespeare, by Clemence Dane;
and Some aspects of Shakespeare's
Richard II and Henry V.]   1924.

443990

WALLIS (NORBERT HARDY)
Literary sketches, [including essays
on Shakespeare and other Elizabethans].
1936.

458792

WALLS (ERNEST)
Shakespeare's Avon.   With sketches
by R. E. J. Bush.   1935.
The Rivers of England Series.

440880

WALMSLEY (DONALD MUNRO)

Shakespeare's link with Virginia.
FROM 'History Today', Vol. 7, 1957.
pp. [8].
ports.   illus.   map.   facsimiles.

665937

WALPOLE (HORACE)
Anecdotes of painting in England,
1760-1795, collected by H. Walpole
and now published from his original
MSS. by F. W. Hilles and P. B.
Daghlian, Vol. 5.   [With references
to Shakespeare.]   (New Haven, [Conn.])
1937.
This vol. is a continuation of the
work as first published.
484874

Walpole (H.) Concerning Voltaire's
    abuse of Shakespeare. *In* Walpole
    (H.) The Best letters of Horace Wal-
    pole.   Edited with an introduction
    by Anna B. McMahan.

1909.

(Laurel Crowned Letters)

493353

Walpole, Horace *works relating to*

— KETTON-CREMER (R. W.)
    Horace Walpole: a biography.
    [With references to Shakespeare.]
    ports.   illus.   bibliog.   1940.

514257

— MEHROTRA (K. K.)
Horace Walpole and the English novel:
a study of the influence of "The
Castle of Otranto", 1764-1820.
[With references to Shakespeare.]
(Oxford)
frontis.   bibliog.   1934.

420483

— Stein (Jess M.) Horace Walpole and
    Shakespeare. *From* Studies in
    Philology, vol.31.

(Baltimore)   1934.

441600

WALPOLE (Sir HUGH [SEYMOUR])
King Lear [: a short story].
Illustrated by F. Matania.   FROM

_____   Shakespeare's Plays as Short
Stories [1].   [1933.]   419970
_____   IN Six stories from Shakespeare.
Illustrations by F. Matania.
1934.   428744

WALPOLE (V.)
'And Cassio high in oath' ('Othello',
II, iii, 227).   IN The Modern
Language Review, Vol. 40.
(Cambridge)   1945.

571545

WALROND (HENRY)
Archery.   IN Shakespeare's England,
vol. 2.   (Oxford)
illus.   facsimiles.   bibliogs.
1917.

435746

WALSALL, Queen Mary's Grammar School,
Dramatic Society
Programmes of Shakespearian performances.   1933-
416897

WALSH (GROESBECK) and POOL (ROBERT M.)
Antithetical views on twinning
found in the Bible and Shakespeare.
FROM Southern Medicine & Surgery.
Vol. 103.   (Charlotte, N.C.)
bibliog.   1941.

565605

WALSH (GROESBECK) and POOL (ROBERT M.)
Laterality dominance in Shakespeare's
plays.   FROM Southern Medicine &
Surgery.   Vol. 104.   (Charlotte,
N.C.)   1942.

565606

WALSH (GROESBECK) and POOL (ROBERT M.)
Shakespeare's knowledge of twins and
twinning.   FROM Southern Medicine
& Surgery.   Vol. 102.   (Charlotte,
N.C.)
bibliog.   1940.

565604

WALSH, WILLIAM
Review notes and study guide to
Shakespeare's 'Antony and Cleopatra'.
(New York) 1964.

Monarch critiques of literature.
756284

WALTER (JAMES)
Shakespeare's true life: criticisms
of the leading public press [on
the book of that title]. Illustrated
by G. E. Moira. pp. 12. 1890.

396525

WALTER (JOHN HENRY)
The Dumb show and the "mouse trap"
[in "Hamlet".] IN The Modern
Language Review, Vol. 39. (Cambridge)
bibliog. 1944.

563897

WALTER (JOHN HENRY)
[Review of] Shakespeare and the tragic
theme, by A. H. R. Fairchild. IN
The Modern Language Review, Vol. 40.
(Cambridge) 1945.

571545

WALTER (JOHN HENRY)
Shakespeare in schools. IN
SHAKESPEARE SURVEY 10. (Cambridge)
1957.

665485

WALTERS (JOHN CUMING)
Knight of the pen [: an autobiography.
With a foreword by A. J. C. Walters, and
references to Shakespearean actors
and performances.] (Manchester)
ports. illus. facsimile. bibliog.
1933.

414640

Walters (J.C.) A Shakespearean
sisterhood: Imogen, Desdemona and
Hermione. In Manchester Literary
Club. Papers, Vol.32.

(Manchester) 1906.

518389

Walters (J.C.) Shakspere's "dark period":
[report on a paper]. In Manchester
Literary Club. Papers, Vol.29.

(Manchester) 1903.

518387

Walters (J.C.) Shakespeare's note
book: a new suggestion on the sonnets:
[report of a paper read by J.C. Wal-
ters]. In Manchester Literary Club.
Papers, Vol.30.

(Manchester) 1904.

518388

WALTHAMSTOW SETTLEMENT, SHAKESPEARE
GROUP
Programmes, etc., Feb. 20th 1943-57.
(Walthamstow)

547084

WALTON (J. K.)
The Copy for the folio text of
Richard III with a note on the copy
for the folio text of King Lear.
(Auckland)
tables. bibliogs. 1955.
Auckland University College,
Monograph Series, No. 1.
665102

WALTON (J.   K.   )
Lear's last speech. IN Shakespeare
Survey, [Vol.] 13. (Cambridge)
1960.

666726

WALTON (J. K.)
Macbeth. IN KETTLE (ARNOLD) ed.,
Shakespeare in a changing world:
essays [by various authors]. 1964.

667797

WALTON (J. K.)
The Quarto copy for the Folio
Richard III. IN The Review of
English Studies, New Series, Vol. 10.
tables. bibliog. 1959.

318239/10

WALTON (J.   K.   )
"Strength's abundance": a view of Othello.
IN Review of English Studies New Series,
Vol.11. (Oxford) 1960.

318239/N.S./11

WALTON (J. K.)
The Structure of Hamlet. IN
Stratford-upon-Avon Studies, 5:
Hamlet. 1963.

667698

WALTON, THOMAS
Hamlet without the buzz-buzz.
Produced by Carl Wildman. B.B.C.
radio script broadcast 15th June 1964.

668247

WALTON, Sir WILLIAM TURNER
Funeral march from [film of] "Hamlet":
full score [adapted for concert use
by Muir Mathieson.] [1963.]

667969

WALTON, Sir WILLIAM TURNER
Hamlet and Ophelia: a poem for
orchestra. [Full score.] 1968.

778223

WALTON (WILLIAM TURNER)
Passacaglia: 'Death of Falstaff'
from the film music 'Henry V'.
Arranged for organ by H. G. Ley.
pp. 4. [1949.]

600299

WALTON, Sir WILLIAM TURNER
Prelude: "Richard III". Full score.
[Adapted for concert use by M.
Mathieson]   [1964.]

668175

WALTON, Sir WILLIAM TURNER
A Shakespeare suite: "Richard III".
[Selected and adapted for concert use
by M. Mathieson. Full score.] [1964.]

668173

WALTON, Sir WILLIAM TURNER
Suite from "Henry V". Adapted for
concert use by M. Mathieson. [Full
score]   [1964.]

668174

WALTON (Sir WILLIAM TURNER)
Two pieces for strings from the
film music Henry V. 1. Passaglia:
Death of Falstaff; 2. "Touch her
soft lips and part". pp. 4,
ff. [10].   1947.

601864

WALTON (WILLIAM TURNER)
Under the greenwood tree. Set
to music by W. Walton for the film
As You Like It, produced by
Inter-Allied Film Producers Limited
(for Twentieth Century Fox).
pp. 4. (Oxford)   1937.

519018

Walton, William Turner Sir *works relating to*

—— SYKES (E. F.)
"Troilus and Cressida": Sir W. Walton's
opera; libretto by C. Hassall. Some
jottings regarding the Covent Garden
Opera Company's performance at the
Coventry Theatre, April 1955. ff. 15.
typescript.

665415

WANDSWORTH SCHOOL
Programmes of Shakespearian perform-
ances, 1925-32, 1934-8.
(Wandsworth)
Wants programme for 1933.

472595

War

—— ADCOCK (A.St. J.) The Poetry of war
[containing references to Shakes-
peare]. From The Bookman, Vol. 47.
Ports. 1914.   433739

—— DAUGHERTY (G. H.)
Shakespeare as a military critic.
FROM The Open court, Vol. 42.
pp. [20].   (Chicago)
port.   1928.

441306

—— DE MONTMORENCY (J. E. G.)
Shakespeare and war.   IN The Contemporary Review, Vol. 106.   1914.

255619

——· De M[ontmorency] (J.E.G.) Shakespeare's battle scenes. In The
Contemporary Review, Vol. 102.

1912.

239848

—— FREEMAN (J.) ed.
The Englishman at war.   "The
weather in his soul": an anthology
[containing excerpts from Shakespeare.
With a preface by the editor.]
bibliog.   1941.
Library of English Thought and Life.

533020

—— FULLER (ROSALINDE)
A Shakespeare tour in wartime.
IN Theatre arts, Vol. 24.   (New York)
1940.

525084

—— HERRING (R.)
Harlequin Mercutio, or, Plague on
your houses; a ride through raids
to resurrection [: a verse-pantomime
of present-day London. Mercutio
and Hamlet are taken as two aspects,
the spirit and conscience, of the
same person, Ego]. FROM Life and
Letters To-day, Vols. 31 and 32.

1941-2.

534897

—— JORGENSEN (PAUL ALFRED)
Divided command in Shakespeare.
IN PMLA: Publications of The Modern
Language Association of America,
Vol. 70.   (Menasha, Wis.)   1955.

428321/70

—— JORGENSEN (PAUL A.)
Shakespeare's military world.
1956.

665390

—— KNIGHT (GEORGE WILSON)
This sceptred isle: Shakespeare's
message for England at war. pp. 35.
(Oxford)
port.   1940.

520723

LAIRD (J.)
Philosophical incursions into English
literature. [With a chapter:
Shakespeare on the wars of England.]
(Cambridge)
bibliog.   1946.

576328

LANGSAM (G. GEOFFREY)
Martial books and Tudor verse.   (New
York)
bibliog.   1951.
Includes a chapter "Shakespeare and
the drama".

619330

SEMPER (I. J.)
In the steps of Dante and other
papers [including "Shakespeare and
war"].   (Dubuque)   1941.

545882

SUTTON (Sir B. E.)
Shakespeare on the art of war.
IN Journal of the Royal United
Service Institution, Vol. 89.
1944.

564001

WAGGONER (G. R.)
An Elizabethan attitude toward peace
and war [: reflected in the plays
of Shakespeare and others].   IN
Philological Quarterly, Vol. 33.
(Iowa)   1954.

592684/33

War of the Theatres *see* Boy Actors

Warburton, William *works relating to*

DAWSON (G. E.)
Warburton, Hanmer and the 1745 edition
of Shakespeare.   IN Virginia
University Bibliographical Society,
Studies in Bibliography, Vol. 2.
(Charlottesville, Va.)   1949.

598680/2

DOBELL (P. J. & A. E.)
A Catalogue of a remarkable collection
of publisher's agreements, [etc.]
including the agreements made by
A. Pope, W. Warburton and I. Reed
for the publication of their respective
editions of Shakespeare.   No. 66,
1941. pp. 12.   (Tunbridge Wells)
1941.

528685

EVANS (A. W.)
Warburton and the Warburtonians: a
study in some eighteenth-century
controversies.   [With references to
Warburton's edition of Shakespeare.]
bibliog.   port.   1932.

393202

GREY (ZACHARY)
An Answer to certain passages in
Mr. W[arburton]'s preface to his
edition of Shakespeare, together
with some remarks on the many errors
and false criticisms in the work
itself.   pp. 19.   [Anon.]   1748.

621023

SHERBO (ARTHUR)
Dr. Johnson's "Dictionary" and
Warburton's "Shakespeare".   IN
Philological Quarterly, Vol. 33.
(Iowa)   1954.

592684/33

SHERBO (ARTHUR)
Warburton and the 1745 Shakespeare.
IN The Journal of English and
Germanic Philology, Vol. 51.
(Urbana, Ill.)   1952.

600780/51

STEVENS (GEORGE ALEXANDER)
Distress upon distress; or, Tragedy
in true taste: a heroi-comi-parodi-
tragedi-farcical burlesque in two
acts.   With annotations [etc.] by
Sir Henry Humm [i.e. G. A. Stevens]
and notes by Paulus Purgantius Pedasculus
[i.e. G. A. Stevens.   A satire on
Sir T. Hanmer's and W. Warburton's
editions of Shakespeare.]   1752.

481297

WARBURTON [W.], JOHNSON [S.] and
GRIFFITH (Mrs. [ELIZABETH])
The Morality of Shakespeare's
Much ado about nothing.   FROM
Monthly Miscellany, Apr. 1776.

562345

WARD ([Sir] ADOLPHUS WILLIAM)
1616 and its centenaries.
IN GOLLANCZ ([Sir] I.) ed., A Book
of homage to Shakespeare.
ports. illus. facsimiles. [1916.]

264175

WARD (ALFRED CHARLES)
Dramatic critics and Shakespeare.
[Reprinted] from "Specimens of
English dramatic criticism, 17-20
centuries".   FROM The Periodical,
Vol. 26.   (Oxford)   1945.
For "Specimens of English dramatic
criticism, 17-20 centuries", see
catal. no. 563732.

579653

Ward (A.C.) The Frolic and the gentle:
a centenary study of Charles Lamb.
[With Shakespearian references and
a bibliography.] Port.

1934.

415864

WARD (ALFRED CHARLES)
Illustrated history of English liter-
ature.   Illustrations collected by
Elizabeth Williams, Vol. 1.
  ports. illus. facsimiles. 1953.
Includes a chapter "Shakespeare".

636908

WARD (ALFRED CHARLES)
A Literary journey through wartime
Britain [: an account of the
bombing of literary landmarks during
the War.   With references to
Shakespeare and Stratford-on-Avon.]
Illustrated by F. T. Chapman.
(Oxford)
  maps.   1943.

557332

WARD (A. C.) [ed.]
Specimens of English dramatic
criticism, 17-20 centuries; selected
and introduced.   [With articles on
Shakespearian actors and productions.]
(Oxford)
  bibliog.   1945.
The World's Classics.

563732

WARD (B. M.)
The Authorship of "The Tempest".
IN East Anglian magazine, Vol. 4.
(Ipswich)   1939.

510779

Ward (B.M.) and Allen (P.) An Enquiry
into the relations between Lord
Oxford as "Shakespeare", Queen
Elizabeth and the Fair Youth of
Shakespeare's sonnets. [With
bibliographical references.]

[1936.]

530214

WARD (BERNARD ROWLAND)
Shakespeare's Sonnets.   FROM [Poetry
and the play, 1929-30.] pp. [12.]
                               [1929]

389214

WARD ([Mrs.] CATHARINE WEED) and
WARD (H. SNOWDEN)
Shakespeare's town and times.
3rd edn. enlarged.
  illus. maps.   [1908]

452945

WARD (CHARLES EUGENE)
The Tempest: a restoration opera
problem.   IN E.L.H.: a Journal
of English Literary History, Vol.
13.   [Baltimore, Md.]
  bibliog.   1946.

584757

Ward (F.W.O.) Shakespeare [: a poem.]
From The Fireside Pictorial
Annual, 1902.

1902.

501611

Ward (Genevieve) and Whiteing (R.)
Both sides of the curtain [: a life
of Genevieve Ward, with reference
to Shakespeare performances.]
Ports. Illus.

1918.

497898

Ward, Genevieve *works relating to*

— Gustafson ([Mrs.] Zadel B.) Genevieve
Ward : a biographical sketch from
original material. [With references
to Shakespeare.] Port

(Boston)   1882.

499277

Ward (Genevieve) and Whiteing (R.)
Both sides of the curtain [: a
life of Genevieve Ward, with
reference to Shakespeare performances.] Ports   Illus.

1918.

497898

Ward (H.G.) Du Bellay and Shakespeare.
In Notes and Queries, Vol.155,
1928.

(High Wycombe)   [1928.]

354567

WARD (H. SNOWDEN)
The Shakespeare festival at Stratford-
on-Avon.   IN The Playgoer, Vol. 2.
  illus.   1902.

171877

WARD (H. SNOWDEN)
Stratford-on-Avon and the Vale of
the Red Horse.   IN The Bookman,
Vol. 25.
  illus.   1903.

181448

WARD (H. SNOWDEN) and WARD ([Mrs.]
CATHARINE WEED)
The Shakespearean guide to Stratford-
on-Avon.   With chapters on Warwick,
Kenilworth and "the Shakespeare
country" generally.   Illustrated
by W. T. Whitehead.   2nd edn.
   port.   [c.1900]

              467566

Ward (H.S.) and Ward ([Mrs.]C.W.)
Shakespeare's town and times. 3rd
edn. enlarged. Illus. Maps.

              [1908]
           452945

WARD (JOHN WILLIAM GEORGE)
Messages from master minds [: the
spiritual messages of eminent
writers].   [1922.]
   Includes a chapter "The Sublimities
of Shakespeare".

           603468

WARD (RICHARD HERON)
[Review of] Shakespeare's Coriolanus,
produced by G. Wickham in the Roman
Baths, [Bath].   [Broadcast]
28th May, 1952.   ff. 6.
typescript.

           634513

WARD, LOCK AND CO., LTD.
Guide to Stratford-upon-Avon,
Leamington, Warwick, Kenilworth
and Shakespeare's Warwickshire.
8th edn., revised.
   illus. plans. map.   [1947.]

           582168

Ward & Lock's Illustrated guide to, and
popular history of Stratford-upon-
Avon, the home of Shakespeare; with
excursions in the neighbourhood. Illus.
Maps
           [1881]
           467564

WARD, LOCK AND CO.
Illustrated guide to Kenilworth &
Coventry [Stratford etc.].
      [1887.]   438179
Imperfect.   Wants maps.
       Another ed. [1889.] 550595

WARD, LOCK & CO.
A Pictorial and descriptive guide to
Warwick, Royal Leamington Spa,
Kenilworth, Stratford-upon-Avon,
Coventry & the George Eliot country.
13th edn. revised.
   illus. maps. plans.   [1925.]

           547104

WARD, LOCK AND CO'S RED GUIDES
Stratford-upon-Avon, Leamington,
Warwick, Kenilworth and Shakespeare's
Warwickshire.   [New edn.]
   illus. maps. plans   1962.

           667322

WARD-CASEY (S.)
O mistress mine [: part-song].
Composed for the Goldthorpe Musical
Festival.   [Words by] Shakespeare
[from Twelfth Night.   Music by]
S. Ward-Casey.   pp. 8.   (York)
           1931.
York Series, No. 1079.

           536630

[Warde (Mrs. Beatrice L.)] Some
recent editions of Shakespeare's
works, by P. Beaujon. In Signature,
[Vol. 3,] No. 7.

          1937.

         503483

[WARE (JOHN R.)]
Shakespeare done into French.
[Anon.   A criticism of Le Juif de
Venise, translated by F. Dugué.]
IN The Atlantic Monthly, Vol. 6.
(Boston, Mass.)   1860.

         19352

WAREING (ALFRED [J.])
Enter Shakespeare.   IN ISAAC (WINIFRED
F. E. C.) Alfred Wareing: a biography.
With forewords by J. Bridie, I. Brown,
Rt. Hon. W. Elliot and Sir J. R.
Richmond.
   ports. illus. facsimiles.   [1950.]

         614427

WARHAFT (SIDNEY)

Anti-Semitism in "The Merchant of
Venice". FROM The Manitoba Arts Review,
Vol.10. pp.15. (Fort Garry Manitoba)
           1956.

         665738

WARHAFT (SIDNEY)

Hamlet's solid flesh resolved. IN
E.L.H., Vol.28, No.1, pp.21-30.
           1961.

        430295/28

WARHAFT, SIDNEY
The mystery of "Hamlet". IN E.L.H., a
journal of English literary history,
vol.30, no.3, 1963.

         430295

WARLOCK (PETER) [pseud. i.e. Philip
Arnold Heseltine]
A Book of songs [including "Pretty
ring time", from As you like it
and "Sigh no more, ladies", from
Much ado about nothing].   pp. 56.
   port.   [?1930.]

         596631

WARLOCK (PETER) pseud.

Mockery [: a song].   The poem by
Shakespeare [in "Love's Labour's
Lost"], pp. 4.   [1928.]

         628452

WARLOCK (PETER) pseud

Pretty ring time [: It was a lover and
his lass, from As You Like It]. (Oxford
Choral Songs) (O.U.P.)   1962.

667555

Warlock (P.) [pseud.] Sigh no more,
ladies. The poem by Shakespeare,
[from Much Ado about Nothing]; set
to music by P.Warlock [pseud.] pp.4.

(Oxford)   [1928.]

522693

Warlock (P.) [pseud.] The Sweet o'the
year: song by P.Warlock. [Words from
Winter's Tale by Shakespeare.] pp.6.

[1929.]

536619

WARNER (ALAN JOHN)
A Note on 'Antony and Cleopatra'.
IN English, Vol. 11.   1957.

481151/11

WARNER (ALAN JOHN)
Shakespeare in the tropics: an
inaugural address [at] Makerere
College, The University of East
Africa, Kampala, Uganda. pp. 26.
1954.

643973

WARNER (CHARLES DUDLEY)
The People for whom Shakespeare wrote.
[Part] 1.   FROM [The Atlantic
Monthly,] Vol. 43.   [Boston, Mass.]
1879.
Part 2 wanting.

554732

Warner (Sylvia T.) Footsteps on the
battlement [:criticisms of Hamlet]
In Theatre Today.

[1949.]

606680

[WARNER (T.)
Songs for tenor voice and pianoforte,
composed for the production of
Twelfth Night at the Swansea Little
Theatre in December, 1938]. ff. [4].
manuscript.   1938.

512988

WARNER (WILLIAM)
Albions England.   A continued historie
of the same kingdome from the originals
of the first inhabitants thereof.
[Including the story of King Lear.]
1612.

162338

Warner Brothers. A Collection of
photographs relating to Max Reinhardt's
production of [the film] "A Midsummer
Night's Dream" as presented by Warner
Brothers.

[1935]

452246

[Warner Brothers.] A Midsummer Night's
Dream: script [of the film produced
by M. Reinhardt for Warner Bros.]

(Burbank,[Cal.])   1934.

452942

WARNER BROTHERS
Press book and American and English
publicity material relating to
M. Reinhardt's production of [the
film] "A Midsummer night's dream",
as presented by Warner Brothers.
[1935]

452245

A Warning for Fair Women
"Another tragedy by Shakspere" [: a
discussion of the authorship of "A
Warning for fair women"].   FROM The
Theatre, March 1, 1879.

530819

WARNKEN (HENRY L.)
Iago as a projection of Othello.
IN PAOLUCCI (ANNE) ed., Shakespeare
encomium, 1564-1964 [by various writers].
(New York)
1964.
City University of New York, City
College Papers, 1.
747546

Warpeha (Mary J.) The Effect of the
Reformation on the English eighteenth
century critics of Shakespeare (1765-
1807): a dissertation submitted to
the Faculty of the Graduate School
of Arts and Sciences of the Catholic
University of America. [With a
bibliography.] pp.92.

(Washington)   1934.

428594

WARRELL (A.)
It was a lover and his lass.   [Words
from As you like it.]   pp. 8.
(Oxford)   1938.
Oxford Choral Songs.

522701

WARREN (CLARENCE HENRY)
Sir Philip Sidney: a study in
conflict.   [Containing references
to Shakespeare.]
ports.   illus.   [1936]

457050

Warren (Clyde T.) see Clarkson (Paul
Stephen) and Warren (Clyde T.)

WARREN (RUTH)
The Fortunes of "Henry VIII".
IN Ashland Studies in Shakespeare,
1957.   (Ashland, Ore.)   1957.

666259/1957

Warrington Literary & Philosophical
Society: see Societies and Clubs

WART (ALBERT VAN)
Studies on the character of Hamlet.
pp. 16.   (Sheffield)   1889.

647123

[WARTON (JOSEPH)]
Observations on Shakespeare's King
Lear.   IN The Adventurer, Vol. 4.
2nd edn.   1754.   494411
_____ IN The Adventurer, Vol. 4.
3rd edn.   1756.   540298
_____ IN The Adventurer, Vol. 2.
(Dublin)   1760.   533864
_____ IN The Adventurer, Vol. 4.
4th edn.   1762.   507407
_____ IN The Adventurer, Vol. 4.
New edn.   1770.   462976
_____ IN The Adventurer, Vol. 4.
New edn.   1778.   464307
_____ IN The Adventurer, Vol. 4.
New edn.   frontis.   1788.   493437
_____ IN The Adventurer, Vol. 4.
New edn.   frontis.   1793.   518119
_____ IN The Adventurer, Vol. 4.
New edn.   1797.   546224
_____ IN The Adventurer, [edited]
by A. Chalmers.   1802.   459735
British Essayists, Vol. 25.

[WARTON (JOSEPH)]
Observations on The Tempest of
Shakespeare.   IN The Adventurer,
Vol. 3.   2nd edn.   1754.   494410
_____ IN The Adventurer, Vol. 3.
3rd edn.   1756.   540297
_____ IN The Adventurer, Vol. 3.
4th edn.   1762.   507406
_____ IN The Adventurer, Vol. 3.
New edn.   1770.   462975
_____ IN The Adventurer, Vol. 3.
New edn.   1778.   464306
_____ IN The Adventurer, Vol. 3.
New edn.   frontis.   1788.   493436
_____ IN The Adventurer, Vol. 3.
New edn.   frontis.   1793.   518118
_____ IN The Adventurer, Vol. 3.
New edn.   1797.   546223
_____ IN The Adventurer, [edited]
by A. Chalmers.   1802.   459735
British Essayists, Vol. 25.

[WARTON (JOSEPH)]
Observations on The Tempest of
Shakespeare; [and] Observations on
Shakespeare's King Lear.   IN The
Adventurer, Vol. 2.   (Dublin) 1760.

533864

WARTON (THOMAS)
The History of English poetry from
the eleventh to the seventeenth
century.   [With references to
Shakespeare].   [1872]
Reprint of edn. London 1778 & 1781.

486987

**WARWICK ([FRANCES EVELYN GREVILLE],
Countess of)**
An Old English garden [at Easton
Lodge, Essex, with a description of
the Shakespeare border].   pp. 71.
illus.   1898.

449976

Warwickshire and Shakespeare's Country
see also **Arden, Forest of; Avon River;
Bidford; Charlecote; Cotswold Hills;
Gloucestershire; Henley-in-Arden; Wilmcote**

—— AUSTIN (EDWARD WILLIAM)
The Shakespeare tour: from London to
Warwick, Stratford and Oxford.
pp. ii, 89.
illus.   [1953.]
Master Guides.

633731

—— BAKER (O.)
In Shakespeare's Warwickshire and
the unknown years.
port.   illus.   dgms.   facsimiles.
1937.

475382

—— BANKS (FRANCIS RICHARD)
Warwickshire and the Shakespeare
country.   (Penguin Guides. New Series,18)
Maps. Plans. Glossary. (Harmondsworth)
1960.

666552

—— BARBER (E.)
In the heart of England: the
Warwickshire landscape [with refer-
ences to Shakespeare's country].
IN Country Life, Warwickshire Supplement.
illus.   1938.

477656

—— BARNARD (A.)
Round about Warwick, etc.   [With a
chapter on Stratford-on-Avon and
district.]   pp. 64.
ports.   illus.   1899.

179261

—— BAWDEN (W. R.) and other[s]
Warwickshire: an illustrated review
of the holiday, sporting, industrial
and commercial interests of the county.
With a foreword by Lord Leigh.   Edited
by H. E. O'Connor.   2nd edn.   [With
Shakespearian references.]
(Cheltenham: E. J. Burrow & Co. Ltd.)
map.   [1937]

469726

—— BECK ([J.])
Leamington guide; with an historical
and descriptive account of the
neighbourhood [including a chapter
on Stratford-upon-Avon and Shakespeare.]
10th edn.   (Leamington)
illus.   map.   1852.

484122

—— Black's guide to Warwickshire.
[Including a chapter on Stratford-
on-Avon.]   5th edn.   (Edinburgh)
illus.   maps.   plans.   1879.

561971

— Black's picturesque guide to Warwickshire. [With a chapter on Stratford-on-Avon.] (Edinburgh) illus. map. 1857.

283144

— Black's Warwickshire guide. [Including a chapter on Stratford-on-Avon.] 1866.

62019

— BONNEY (T. G.)
The Severn. [With references to Shakespeare and Stratford-upon-Avon.] FROM Rivers of Great Britain. pp. [47.] illus. maps. [1897.]

409849

— BRACKETT (O.)
In and around Warwick. [With references to Shakespeare and Stratford-upon-Avon.] FROM The Architectural Review, Vol. 3. 1898. pp. [4.] illus. [1898.]

409848

— BRASSINGTON (W. S.)
Picturesque Warwickshire. (Dundee) illus. [1906.] 191945
_____ Another copy. 550407

— BRIDGES-ADAMS (W.)
The Shakespeare country, with a history of the Festival Theatre and its company. pp. 48. port. illus. map. plan. 1932.

391905

— Brinkley (Matilda) Tell the bees: a Warwickshire romance [of the 16th century.]

1935.

440969

— BURGESS (A.)
Warwickshire. [With a description of Stratford-on-Avon.] illus. map. bibliog. 1950. The County Books Series.

606933

— BURGESS (JOSEPH TOM)
Historic Warwickshire. illus. [1876] 461097 Includes a chapter "The Swan of Avon".
_____ Another copy, containing 9 plates. 395828

— BURMAN (J.)
The Burman chronicle. (The story of a Warwickshire family.) [Including chapters on Shakespeare and Stratford.] pp. [xi], 99. port. illus. pedigrees.
1940. 516818
_____ Manuscript copy.
1939. 498629

— BURMAN (J.)
Gleanings from Warwickshire history [with a chapter, David Garrick at Stratford]. (Birmingham) illus. pedigrees. 1933.

411780

— BURMAN (J.)
Old Warwickshire families and houses. [With a chapter: Clopton House.] (Birmingham) illus. pedigrees. 1934. 425232
_____ Another copy. 1934. 425233

— BURROW'S Official guide to Royal Leamington Spa. [Including Stratford-on-Avon.] pp. 78. (Cheltenham) illus. map. plan. [c.1910] Burrow's 'Royal' Handbooks.

505028

— [Cassell, publisher.]Warwick and Stratford-on-Avon. pp.[20.] Illus. From Our own Country,Vol.5.

1882.

409847

— The Charm of Shakespeare's country. FROM Chambers's journal, 1907. pp. [4.] [1907]

390789

— Chichester (F.) An Illustrated map and guide [to] Shakespeare's country in the counties of Warwick, Worcester, Gloucester, and Oxford. Illustrations by A.Young. Guide book by C. [S.] St. B. Seale. pp.16, [2].

[1949.]

598126

— CLEAVE (PHILIP)
Shakespeare's country in pictures. Foreword and introductions by J. C. Trewin. illus. map. [1951.] Britain Illustrated.

617494

— COLYER (S. W.)
Shakespeare's country: a book of [33] photographs, with a foreword by Lord Willoughby de Broke. 1947. Fair Britain Series.

583360

— COOKE (H. T.) AND SON, publishers
A Guide to Warwick, Kenilworth, Stratford-on-Avon, Coventry and neighbourhood. 40th edn. (Warwick) [c.1890]

396980

— COOPER (W.)
Henley-in-Arden: an ancient market town and its surroundings. [With references to Shakespeare and Stratford-upon-Avon.] (Birmingham) port. illus. maps. bibliog. 1946.

568864

— DANIELL (D. S.)
The Time of the singing: a novel
[of Shakespeare's country.]   1941.

529726

— DELDERFIELD, ERIC RAYMOND
The visitors' brief guide to the
Shakespeare country. (Exmouth)
[1963.]

illus. map. Grey cover brief guide
series, No.19.   667949

— DE M. (S.)
Shakespeare's country [: a review
of "Things seen in Shakespeare's
country", by C. Holland.]   FROM
The Contemporary Review, Literary
Supplement, 1927.   pp. [3.]
[1927]

389230

— DIXON, J. ARTHUR, LTD.
Shakespeare's country and the
Cotswolds: a handbook for tourists.
(Newport, Isle of Wight)
illus.   map.   [1963]

667659

— ECCLES (MARK)
Shakespeare in Warwickshire.
(Madison, Wis.)
illus.   maps.   facsimiles.
bibliog.   1961.

666832

— [FIELD (W.)]
An Historical and descriptive account
of Leamington, Warwick, [Stratford-
upon-Avon,] etc.   Abridged from
["An Historical and descriptive
account of the town and castle of
Warwick and the neighbouring spa of
Leamington, etc."   By W.F.   1815].
(Warwick)   1817.

462456

— FLEMING (JOAN)
Shakespeare's country in colour: a
collection of colour photographs.
With an introductory text and notes
on the illustrations by Joan Fleming.
pp. 96.
map.   1960.
[Heritage Colour Books]

666537

— FOX (LEVI)
Shakespeare's country: an appreciation.   pp. [32.]   (Norwich)
illus.   map.   [1953.]

632969

— FOX (LEVI)

Shakespeare's town and country. pp.[48].
illus. Map. [Norwich]   [1959.]

666229

— FOX (LEVI)
Stratford-upon-Avon and the
Shakespeare country.   pp. [32.]
(Norwich)
illus.   [1955]
The Window Book Series.

646804

— FRANCIS (RAYMOND)
Looking for Elizabethan England [in
architecture].
ports.   illus.   1954.
Includes a chapter "Shakespeare country".

643324

— FRASER (MAXWELL)
Companion into Worcestershire.   [With
references to Shakespeare.]
illus.   map.   1939.
Methuen's Companion Books.

499551

— FRASER (MAXWELL)
Shakespeare's country.   (Railway
Executive, Western Region.) pp. [32].
illus.   map.   [1951.]

616296

— FURNESS (ALFRED)
The Shakespeare country including the
Peak and the Cotswolds [: photographs].
Introduction by H. J. Massingham.
illus.   1951.
Immortal Britain, 3.

622047

— GLOVER (J.) publisher
Tourist's guide, or, Rambles round
Leamington.   2nd edn.   (Leamington)
illus.   1889.   343182.
_____ Another copy.   446645

— Gover (J.E.B.) [and others], The
Place-names of Warwickshire
[including names associated with
Shakespeare. With a bibliography.]
Maps.

(Cambridge)   1936.

(English Place- name Society, vol.13.)

450451

— HAMILTON (Dom. A.) ed.
The Chronicle of the English August-
inian Canonesses Regular of the
Lateran, at St. Monica's in Louvain
(now at St. Augustine's Priory,
Newton Abbot, Devon).   [Vol. 1.]
1548 to 1625 [contains references to
Shakespeare and his Warwickshire].
(Edinburgh)   1904.

541067

— HANCOCK (CYRIL VERNON)
East and west of Severn: Midland
riches; illustrated with drawings
by D. Flanders and J. P. Wood, and
photographs by the author.
maps.   1956.
Includes a chapter "In Shakespeare's
land".

654506

— HARRIS (M[ARY] D.)
Shakespeare and Warwickshire.
IN GOLLANCZ ([Sir] I.) ed., A Book
of homage to Shakespeare.
ports.   illus.   facsimiles.   [1916.]

264175

— HARRIS (MARY D.)
Some manors, churches and villages
of Warwickshire; with an account
of certain old buildings of Coventry.
[Containing references to Stratford-
upon-Avon.] (Coventry)
port. illus. 1937. 463869
———— Another copy. 464377

— HEYWOOD (ABEL) & SON, publishers
A Guide to Royal Leamington Spa.
[With references to Shakespeare and
Stratford-upon-Avon.] pp. 28.
illus. [1913]
Abel Heywood & Son's Guide Books.

393587

— HINGELEY (J.)
Let's go to Warwickshire. With
a foreword by H. [J.] Black.
Illustrated by W. A. Green. [With
references to the Shakespeare
country.] pp. 80. (Birmingham)
illus. map. [1947.]

583419

— Hutton (W.H.) By Thames and Cotswold:
sketches of the country [and a
description of Stratford-on-Avon].
Illus. Map.

1903.

467995

— Hutton (W.H.) By Warwick ways [with
references to Shakespeare.] Illus.
From "The Treasury", Vol. 8.

([Carnarvon]) [1894.]

489542

——— Hutton (W.H.) Shakespeare's England.
Illus. In Hammerton ([Sir] J.A.) ed.,
Wonderful Britain, Vol.1.
[c.1930]

393687

— In Shakespeare's country. IN The
Gentleman's Magazine, New Series,
Vol. 14. 1875.

18735

— James (H.) English hours. [Containing
a description of a visit to Warwickshire including Stratford-upon-
Avon.] With illustrations by J.
Pennell.
1905.

569917

— JENNETT, SEÁN, ed.
The Shakespeare country and South
Warwickshire.
illus. 1965.
Travellers Guides.

742102

— Kingsley (R.G.) Shakespeare in
Warwickshire. In The Nineteenth
Century and After. Vol. 67.

1910.

224118

— KNIBB, T., publisher
Guide to Leamington and its vicinity,
including Warwick, Coventry, Stratford-
on-Avon, Kenilworth and surrounding
country. [With references to
Shakespeare.] (Leamington)
illus. map. tables. [c.1870.]
Cover-title reads: "Excursions
round Leamington".

546779

— [LALLY (GWEN) pseud.
Autobiography of a Pageant Master:
newspaper cuttings from the
Birmingham Weekly Post, February to
April, 1939. With references to
Shakespeare and Shakespeare scenes
in the Warwick Pageant, 1930.]
pp. [36.]
ports. illus. [1939.]

500724

— LEIGH (C. LEIGH, [1st Baron])
Fifth epistle to a friend in town,
Warwickshire [including references
to Shakespeare] and other poems.
1835.

438403

— Let's go! Where to go, what to see:
a complete guide to the Midlands,
Shakespeare's country, the Cotswolds,
the Malverns, Derbyshire, Wales, etc.,
published by Thomas's Road Guides.
pp. 72. (Birmingham)
illus. map. [1939.] 499670
——— Another edn. [1946.] 572746

— LIDDELL KING (CHARLES JAMES MICHAEL
ROBERTSON)
The Shakespeare country. Educational
Productions Ltd. in collaboration
with the British Travel and Holidays
Association. pp. 24.
ports. illus. slides. 1957.
[Slidebooks.] Beautiful Britain
[Series]

665982

— Lindon (S.G.) Walks and rambles in
leafy Warwickshire [Including
Stratford and Walks from Stratford].
pp.56. Plans.

(Birmingham) [1936]

450389

— Lisle (J.) Warwickshire. [With a chapter
on Stratford and Shakespearian
references.] Illus. Map.

1936.

447923

— McLEOD (T.)
The Shakespeare country, Warwick[shire
and] Worcester[shire].
bibliogs. illus. maps. [1949]
[Chambers' Illustrated Guides.
"Holiday County" Series]

599572

— MANNING (S.) and GREEN (S. G.)
English pictures, drawn with pen
and pencil. [Including a chapter
on Shakspere's country.] New edn.,
[revised.]
illus. [1889.]

403547

— MARTIN (NORAH BALDWIN)
Shakespeareland. With eight plates
in colour from paintings by
L. Squirrell. pp. 61.
illus. maps.   [1951.]
Our Beautiful Homeland.

617412

— MASSINGHAM (H. J.)
Where man belongs.
port. bibliog.   1946.
Includes a chapter "William Shakespeare
of Warwickshire".

575459

— MASSINGHAM (H. J.)
Wold without end [: reminiscences
of a year in the Cotswolds, with
references to Shakespeare.]
illus.   1932.

391397

— [MAYERS (F. S.)]
Shakespeare's country. IN Let's go!
Where to go - what to see [: a guide
to the Midlands]. 1946 edn. pp.
96. (Birmingham)
illus. map.   [1946.]

572746

— MEE (ARTHUR) ed.
Warwickshire: Shakespeare's country.
[With a description of Stratford-
upon-Avon.]
illus. maps.   1936.
The King's England.

458658

— MERCIAN [pseud.]
"Now am I in Arden", New Series [:
topographical and historical notes
relating to Warwickshire and neighbour-
ing counties. Including references to
Shakespeare and Stratford-upon-Avon.
Newspaper cuttings from the Birmingham
News, Jan.-Dec. 1942]. pp. [80.]
[Birmingham]   [1942.]
For 1st series, see files of the
Birmingham News, July 1940 - July 1941,
catal. nos. 531189-90.

544461

— MONCRIEFF (W. T.) [pseud.]
The Visitor's new guide to the spa
of Leamington Priors and its vicinity,
including [a sketch] of Stratford-
upon-Avon. With poetical illustrations serious and comic. (Leamington)
map. plan.   1818.

497708

— Morley (G.) Christmas customs of
Shakespeare's greenwood. In
Knowledge, Vol.21.

1898.

144828

— MORLEY (G.)
Customs of Shakespeare's greenwood.
IN Knowledge, Vol. 22.   1899.

150346

— MORLEY (G.)
The Language of Shakespeare's greenwood. IN Knowledge, Vol. 20.
1897.

142731

— MORLEY (G.)
Sketches of leafy Warwickshire:
rural and urban. [With references
to Stratford-on-Avon]. (Derby)
illus.   1895.
No. 48 of an edn. limited to 55 copies,
signed by the author.

448773

— MORLEY (G.)
The Superstitions of Shakespeare's
greenwood. IN Knowledge, Vol. 22.
1897.

142731

— MORTIMER (J.)
In Shakspere's country. FROM
[Transactions of the Manchester
Literary Club, Vol. 1.] [Manchester]
[1875.]

556080

— NELSON (ALEC)
The Home of Grandfather Shakespeare.
FROM Home Chimes, New Series, Vol.13.
pp.[13.]   1892.

667273

— [Newspaper cuttings relating to
Warwickshire, including Stratford-
on-Avon.]
map.   1893.

510690

— NEWTH (J. D.)
Gloucestershire. With illustrations
by G. F. Nicholls. [With references
to Shakespeare.]
map.   1927.
Black's Colour Books.

399298

— O[AKLEY] (W. H.)
Through the Shakespeare country: a
tourlet of places around the Bard's
district. FROM Cycling, Vol. 103.
illus.   1942.

534899

— Oxford and Shakespeare-land : the
world's great travel shrine. 6th
edn. pp 24. Illus. Map.

1929.

(Great Western Railway)

499902

— Page (H.E.) Rambles and walking tours
in Shakespeareland and the Cotswolds
Illus. Maps.

1933.

406184

— PEARSON (H.) and KINGSMILL (H.) [pseud.
i.e. HUGH KINGSMILL LUNN]
This blessed plot [: the record of
a tour through England in the wake
of Shakespeare]. Illustrated by
M. Weightman. 1942.

534309

— RAY (J. E.)
A Book of inns. No. 9: Around
Shakespeare's country. pp. xii, 68.
illus. 1948.

598082

— RIBTON-TURNER (C. J.)
Shakespeare's land: a description
of central and southern Warwickshire.
(Leamington)
illus. maps. plans.
[c.1895.] 557115
_____ Revised by E. Hicks.
illus. 1932. 397264

— RIDER (W.)
Views in Stratford-upon-Avon and its
vicinity. pp. [26.]
1828. 57315
_____ Large paper edn.
1828. 399820

— RUSSELL (J.)
Shakespeare's country.
illus. map. 1942.
The Face of Britain [Series].

532246

— SCARFE (NORMAN)
Shakespeare, Stratford-upon-Avon and
Warwickshire. IN SPENCER (TERENCE
JOHN BEW) ed., Shakespeare: a
celebration, 1564-1964.
illus. maps. 1964.

667816

— The Shakespeare Country. In United
Empire: the Journal of the Royal
Empire Society, Vol.30.

1939.

513335

— The Shakespeare country by Midland
"Red" from Leamington. pp. 21.
Illus. Map.

[Birmingham] [1931.]

— [Midland "Red" Motor Services]

545620

— Shakespeare-land: the world's great
travel shrine. [2nd edn.] pp. 22.
(Great Western Railway Company)
port. illus. maps. 1913.

549761

— Shakespeare's country calendar [1948.]
pp.[12.] Illus.

[1947.]

583361

— SHARP (T.)
An Epitome of the county of Warwick,
containing a brief account of the
towns, villages, and parishes.
[With a chapter, Stratford-on-Avon.]
1835. 61141
_____ Another copy. 410630

— SHOWELL (C.)
Shakespeare's Avon from source to
Severn. Illustrated with pen &
ink drawings by the author.
(Birmingham)
map. 1901 156575
_____ Another copy. Large paper edn.:
No. 61 signed by the author. 169670
_____ Another copy. No. 1 signed by
the author. 563145

— Slinn (L.A.) Guide to Warwickshire.
[With references to Shakespeare].
Illustrated by W.Green. Map.

(Worcester) [1949.]

597038

— SMITH (W.)
Evesham and neighbourhood. Revised,
extended and partially rewritten by
K. G. Smith. With an introduction
by E. A. B. Barnard. Illustrated
by E. H. New and B. C. Boulter.
[Containing references to Shakespeare.]
5th edn. (Evesham)
illus. maps. 1930.
Homeland Handbooks, No. 25.

460695

— SPOFFORD (HARRIET P.)
Woods of Warwick [: a poem]. FROM
Atalanta, Vol. 1. 1887.

515798

— Stratford-upon-Avon Scene,
incorporating Shakespeare Pictorial.
Vol. 1- (Stratford-upon-Avon)
ports. illus. 1946-
For Shakespeare Pictorial see catal.
no. 348579.

574721

— T. (S.)
Compendium of county history:
Warwickshire. [With references
to Shakespeare.] FROM The
Gentleman's Magazine, Jan. 1825.
1825.

401837

— Thomas (Sir W.B.) In Shakespeare's
country. In D'Oyley (Elizabeth) ed.
Essays past and present. With an
introduction by Sylva Norman.

1936.

521685

— THOMAS'S ROAD GUIDES
Let's go! Where to go, what to see:
a complete guide to the Midlands,
Shakespeare's country, the Cotswolds,
the Malverns, Derbyshire, Wales, etc.,
published by Thomas's Road Guides.
pp. 72. (Birmingham)
illus. map. [1939]

499670

— Through Shakespeare country by
Midland "Red". pp. 12.
[Birmingham]
port. illus. map. [1939.]   502051
_____ Another copy.   506326

— TITCHMARSH, PETER, and others
Shakespeare country by car: a
practical guide for motorists
compiled by P. and Helen Titchmarsh.
(Kineton)   [1968.]

769262

— Two days in Warwickshire [:
Shakespeare's country.] FROM
Chambers' Edinburgh Journal, 1845.
pp. [4.]   1845.

390781

— VICTORIA AND ALBERT MUSEUM, South
Kensington
Catalogue of photographs consisting
of historical and architectural
subjects and studies from nature,
chiefly contributed by Sir J. B.
Stone. [With a section
"Shakespeare's country".]   pp. 24.
(Board of Education)
frontis.   1901.

424556

— W. (J.)
Shakespeare and his native county.
FROM [Fraser's Magazine,] Vol. 54.
bibliog.   1856.

558098

— WADE (J. H.)
Rambles in Shakespeare's country.
illus.   1932.

389599

— Walls (E.) Shakespeare's Avon. With
sketches by R.E.J. Bush.

.1935.

(The Rivers of England Series, Vol.3.)

440880

— WARD (H. S.)
Stratford-on-Avon and the Vale of
the Red Horse.   IN The Bookman,
Vol. 25.
illus.   1903.

181448

— WARD (H. S.) and WARD ([Mrs.] CATHARINE W.)
The Shakespearean guide to Stratford-
on-Avon. With chapters on Warwick,
Kenilworth and "the Shakespeare
country" generally.   Illustrated by
W. T. Whitehead.   2nd edn.
port.   [c.1900]

467566

— WARD, LOCK AND CO., LTD.
Guide to Stratford-upon-Avon,
Leamington, Warwick, Kenilworth
and Shakespeare's Warwickshire.
8th edn., revised.
illus. plans. maps.   [1947.]

582168

— WARD, LOCK, AND CO.
Illustrated guide to Kenilworth &
Coventry [Stratford etc.].
[1887.]   438179
Imperfect. Wants maps.
_____ Another edn.   [1889.]   550595

— WARD, LOCK & CO.
A Pictorial and descriptive guide to
Warwick, Royal Leamington Spa,
Kenilworth, Stratford-upon-Avon,
Coventry & the George Eliot country.
13th edn. revised.
illus. map. plans.   [1925.]

547104

— WARD, LOCK AND CO'S RED GUIDES
Stratford-upon-Avon, Leamington,
Warwick, Kenilworth and Shakespeare's
Warwickshire.   [New edn.]
illus. maps. plans.   1962.

667322

— WARWICK COUNTY MUSEUM
In sweet musick is such art. An
exhibition of English music 1580-1620
arranged as the Warwickshire County
Council's contribution to the 1964
Shakespeare Festival. (Warwick)
1964.

740734

— Warwickshire. The Traditions of
Shakespeare in his own neighbourhood.
From "All the Year Round", June 27th,
1874.

1874.

489540

— Where to stay and eat in the Shakespeare
country and the Midlands: comprehensive
touring guide.   1964.

map. Travelwise.   667834

— WINDLE ([Sir] B.C.A.)
Shakespeare's country.   Illustrated
by E. H. New.   3rd edn.
map. plan.   1907.   576554
The Little Guides
_____ 4th edn.   1911.   467565
_____ 6th edn.   1923.   399299

WARWICKSHIRE & WORCESTERSHIRE MAGAZINE,
April, 1964. Shakespeare's anniversary
[: articles by various authors].
pp.35-43. (Leamington Spa)   1964.

728224

Warwickshire Journal: official
organ of the Warwickshire Rural
Community Council, Vol. 1 (1938)-
[Containing Shakespearian articles].
[Leamington Spa]   1938-

481390

WARWICKSHIRE NATURAL HISTORY AND
ARCHAEOLOGICAL SOCIETY
Catalogue of books, &c., in the
library of the Society. [Including
Shakespearian items.] pp. 61.
(Stratford-upon-Avon) 1867.

513895

Was Shakspere a Catholic? From The
Lamp [Vol.8].

[York] [1855.]

579648

WASHBURN (GEORGIA C.)
Shakespeare's ancestry. FROM The
Journal of American History, vol.
27. (New York) 1933.

442555

WASHBURN (OWEN REDINGTON)
Who are these? Writings from psychic
sources [including a communication
from Shakespeare's spirit].
(Philadelphia) 1941.

533043

Washington D.C., U.S.A.
see also Folger Shakespeare Library

—— HOROBETZ, LYNN K.
The Washington Shakespeare Summer
Festival 1968.
IN SHAKESPEARE QUARTERLY XIX: 4.
pp. 391-392.
(New York) 1968.

605711

—— THE SHAKESPEARE SOCIETY OF WASHINGTON
Programmes, 1926-54. [Washington]
1929-30; 1938-39; 1939-40; 1940-41
wanting.

645713

WASSERMAN, EARL REEVES
Shakespeare and the English romantic
movement. IN SCHUELLER, HERBERT M.,
ed., The Persistence of Shakespeare
idolatry. Essays in honour of
Robert W. Babcock. (Detroit) 1964.

668300

Waterford

—— [GARRICK (DAVID)]
The Jubilee in honour of Shakespeare:
a musical entertainment as performed
at the theatre in Waterford. With
additions. pp. 32. (Waterford)
1773.

2520

WATERHOUSE (GILBERT)
German literature. [With references
to Shakespearian influence and translations.] pp. 80.
bibliog. 1928.
Benn's Sixpenny Library [No. 55.]

522289

WATERHOUSE (RACHEL)
Shakespeare and the Birmingham Liberals
["Our Shakespeare Club"]. IN The
Central Literary magazine XXXIX:
7th April 1964. pp. 17-24.

740859

Waterloo Festival Series
KUZMICH, NATALIE
When icicles hang by the wall [set
to music for S.S.A.]. (Waterloo,
Ont.) 1966.

761162

Watermarks *see* Textual History

WATKIN (EDWARD INGRAM)
"He wanted art" [: the art and life
of Shakespeare.] IN Watkin (E. I.)
Poets and mystics.
bibliogs. 1953.

635416

WATKINS (JOHN)
Shakespeare. IN Watkins (J.) An
Universal biographical and historical
dictionary; containing a faithful
account of the lives, actions, and
characters, of the most eminent
persons of all ages and all countries.
1800.

509795

WATKINS (LESLIE)
The Story of Shakespeare's school,
1853-1953. pp. xii, 60. (Stratford-
upon-Avon)
ports. illus. 1953.

637013

WATKINS, RONALD
The Actor's task in interpreting
Shakespeare.
IN SHAKESPEARE JAHRBUCH. Bd. 91/1955.
pp. 174-181. (Heidelberg)

10531

WATKINS (RONALD)
Moonlight at the Globe: an essay in
Shakespeare production, based on
performance of A Midsummer night's
dream at Harrow School [produced on
the pattern of a supposed performance
at the Globe]. Drawings by
M. Percival; foreword by R. W. Moore.
[With musical examples.]
bibliog. 1946.

577562

WATKINS (RONALD)
On producing Shakespeare.   With
drawings by M. Percival.
    illus.   1950.

611567

Watkins, Ronald *works relating to*

—— THE HARROVIAN: LXXVII: 24.
    [Tributes to Ronald Watkins.]   1964.

668237

Watkins (V.) Ophelia [: a poem]. **In**
    Watkins (V.) The Lady with the
    unicorn [; poems].

1948.

595655

WATKINS (WALTER BARKER CRITZ)
    Absent thee from felicity [: Swift's
    satire compared with that of
    Shakespeare].   FROM The Southern
    Review, Autumn 1939.   [Baton Rouge]
                                1939.

530198

Watkins (W.B.C.) Johnson and English
    poetry before 1660. [With Shakes-
    pearian references and a biblio-
    graphy.]

    (Princeton, N.J.)   1936.

(Princeton Studies in English, 13.)

446704

WATKINS (WALTER BARKER CRITZ)
    Shakespeare & Spenser.   (Princeton,
    N.J.)
    bibliog.   1950.

611909

WATKINS (WALTER BARKER CRITZ)
    The Two techniques in King Lear.
    IN The Review of English Studies,
    Vol. 18.   (Oxford)   1942.

542539

WATSON (CURTIS BROWN)

Shakespeare and the Renaissance concept
of honor. Bibliog. (Princeton, N.J.)
                                1960.

666749

WATSON (CURTIS BROWN)
    T. S. Eliot and the interpretation of
    Shakespearean tragedy in our time.
    IN Études anglaises, XVII: 4.
    Shakespeare 1564-1964.
    illus.   1964.

742318

WATSON (EARLE MACBETH)
    Medical lore in Shakespeare.
    FROM Annals of Medical History,
    New Series, Vol. 8.   (New York)
    bibliog.   1936.

488662

WATSON (GEOFFREY) [ed.]
    The Willow song from "Othello" by
    Shakespeare.   Traditional air,
    freely arranged by G Watson.   pp. 4.
                                1949.

604298

WATSON (GEORGE)
    Three ways to Shakespeare.   Producer:
    G. MacBeth.   [Broadcast] 7 Aug. 1960.
    ff. 10.
    typescript.   1960.

666997

WATSON (HAROLD FRANCIS)
    The Sailor in English fiction and
    drama, 1550-1800.   [With references
    to Shakespeare.]   (New York)
    bibliog.   1931.
    Columbia University, Studies in English
    and Comparative Literature.

390618

WATSON (JOSEPH)
    A Lecture on Shakespeare's enigmatical
    work [i.e. Hamlet], embracing a new
    theory. Delivered before the Newport
    Lecture Association and the Newport
    Historical Society. (Newport R.I.)
                                1878.

668406

WATSON (SARA RUTH)
    Shelley and Shakespeare [by D. L.
    Clark]: an addendum, A Comparison
    of Othello and the Cenci.   IN
    Publications of the Modern Language
    Association of America, Vol. 55.
    (Menasha, Wis.)   1940.
    For "Shelley and Shakespeare" by
    D. L. Clark, see catal. no. 515058.

525077

Watson (Thomas) Works relating to:-
<u>see</u> MOORE (W. H.) Baconian studies

Watson (Sir W.) Poems, 1878-1935,
    [including a poem on Shakespeare,
    and notes.] Port.

1936.

453391

WATT (HOMER ANDREW), HOLZKNECHT (K. J.)
and ROSS (R.)
Outlines of Shakespeare's plays.
(New York)
   illus. bibliog. maps.
                   1934.   427372
College Outline Series.
_____ Another edn. 1938.   488716
_____ Another edn. 1946.   530370

WATTS (BARBARA)
Marie Ney and Shakespearian tradition.
IN The Amateur theatre and playwrights'
journal, Vol. 1, No. 6.
  port.   1934-35.

              476088

WATTS (GUY TRACEY)
Theatrical Bristol. [With references
to Shakespeare.] (Bristol)
  frontis.   1915.
Edition limited to 250 copies, of
which this is No. 204.
              491999

Watts (N.B.) Morning glory [:a
    play, including quotations from
    Shakespeare. Broadcast] 16th
    January [1950]. ff.32. Typescript.

            609483

WATTS (P. R.)
Shakespeare's "double" purchase of
New Place. FROM The Australian Law
Journal, Vol. 20. (Sydney) 1947.

           599946

WATTS (PETER)
"Hush, there are ladies present!" [:
a radio portrait of Dr. Thomas Bowdler
with references to his expurgated
edition of Shakespeare, broadcast]
1st June, 1945. ff. 36.
  typescript.

           561271

WATTS (PETER)
The Plain man's guide to Shakespeare.
IN Theatre Programme [: a radio
review of the stage: Shakespearian
items. Broadcast] 2nd April [1947.]
ff. 34.
  typescript.

           583268

WATTS (RICHARD)
Films of a moonstruck world. FROM
The Yale Review, a national quarterly,
Winter 1936. ([New Haven, Conn.])

           503866

WATTS, ROBERT A.
The Comic scenes in "Othello".
IN SHAKESPEARE QUARTERLY XIX: 4.
pp. 349-354.
(New York) 1968.
          605711

WATTS-DUNTON (THEODORE)
Christmas at the Mermaid. IN The
Coming of love, and other poems,
pp. 81-147.   1898.

          512706

WATTS-DUNTON (THEODORE)
Note on the typographical features
of this edition. IN SHAKESPEARE (W.)
Comedies, tragedies, histories and
poems. With a general introduction
by A. C. Swinburne, introductory
studies of the plays and poems, by
E. Dowden, and glossaries. (Oxford)
3 vols.   [1936]
[Oxford Edition]
          449468

WAUGH (WILLIAM TEMPLETON)
Sir John Oldcastle [: the original
of Falstaff]. IN The English
Historical Review, Vol. 20. 1905.

          191450

WAVELL (ARCHIBALD JOHN ARTHUR
2nd Earl)
Shakespeare and soldiering. IN
Essays by Divers Hands, New Series,
Vol. 27.   1955.

          647127

WAY (AGNES CALDWELL) ed.
A Shakespeare calendar. (New York)
  port.   1908.

          547690

WAY (AGNES CALDWELL) ed.
A Shakespeare calendar.
  port.   [c.1910.]

          579253

Weather *see* Meteorology

WEBB (CLEMENT CHARLES JULIEN)
Group theories of religion and the
individual. [With references to
Shakespeare.]
  bibliog.   1916.
[Wilde Lectures in Natural and
Comparative Religion, 1914]

          530692

WEBB (HENRY J.)
Falstaff's clothes. IN Modern
Language Notes, Vol. 59. (Baltimore)
  bibliog.   1944.

          563869

WEBB (HENRY J.)
The Military background in "Othello".
IN Philological Quarterly, Vol. 30.
(Iowa)   1951.

         592684/30

WEBB ([T. E.])
Of the genuine text of Shakespeare.
IN The National Review, Vol. 42.
                 1903.

          180375

WEBBE (WILLIAM) of the University of
Cambridge, Works relating to: <u>see</u>
Moore (W. H.) Baconian studies.

WEBBE (WILLIAM Y.)
Elgar's "Falstaff". FROM The New
Music Review Nov., 1929. 1929.

          516568

Weber (C.J.) Hardy of Wessex: his
life and literary career. [Including
an appendix, Hardy's debt to
Shakespeare.] Ports. Illus. Map.

(New York)   1940.

          525191

WEBER (CARL MARIA FRIEDRICH ERNST von)
Oberon: a fairy opera.   [Libretto
by J.R.Planché.]   [c.1850.]

        576513

WEBER [CARL MARIA FRIEDRICH ERNST von]
The Mermaid's song from Weber's opera
Oberon, arranged for the pianoforte
by T. Oesten.   pp. 5.   [c.1900.]

        558615

WEBER (CARL MARIA FRIEDRICH ERNST von)
Oberon.   Overture to the celebrated
romantic and fairy opera called
Oberon, performing at the Theatre
Royal, Covent Garden.   pp. 9.
            [c.1820.]
Imperfect.

        611344

WEBER (CARL MARIA FRIEDRICH ERNST von)
Overture to the grand opera of Oberon.
pp. 9.   [c.1850.]

        559572

WEBER (CARL MARIA [FRIEDRICH ERNST] von)
Overture to the opera of Oberon.
New & revised edn.   pp. 9.
            [c.1910.]

        558622

Weber, Carl Maria Friedrich von *works relating to*

—— Leduc (A.) Petite fantaisie mignonne
   sur Oberon de Weber pour piano.
   pp.5.

      (London)   [c.1880.]

        558614

WEBER-EBENHOF (ALFRED von)
Bacon-Shakespeare-Cervantes (Francis
Tudor): a criticism upon the Shaksper
and Cervantes Festivals.   [Translated,
with a note, by A. B. Cornwall.]
Leipzig, 1917.   [(Brooklyn)]
 typescript.   [1935]

        478690

WEBER[-EBENHOF] (ALFRED [von])
Farewell to European history.
          1947.
International Library of Sociology
and Social Reconstruction.
 Includes a chapter "The Loosening
of dogma and the break-through into
the depths: Shakespeare"

        585106

WEBSTER (C. M.)
Shakespeare and archery.   IN Notes
and Queries, Vol. 162.   1932.

        401808

Webster, John *works relating to*

——JENKINS (HAROLD)
   The Tragedy of revenge in Shakespeare
   and Webster.   IN SHAKESPEARE SURVEY
   14.   (Cambridge)   1961.

        666755

—— RYLANDS (G. [H. W.])
   Introductory essay [entitled] On the
   production of The Duchess of Malfi [with
   references to Shakespeare].
   IN WEBSTER (J.) The Duchess of Malfi.
   Illustrated by M. Ayrton
             1945.

        561294

——TANNENBAUM (S. A.)
   John Webster (a concise bibliography).
   [With references to Shakespeare].
   pp. x, 38.   (New York)
             1941.
   Elizabethan Bibliographies, No. 19.
   Edition limited to 300 copies.

        525230

—— WILLIAMS (C. [W. S.])
   Introductory essay [entitled] On the
   poetry of The Duchess of Malfi [with
   references to Shakespeare].
   IN WEBSTER (J.) The Duchess of Malfi.
   Illustrated by M. Ayrton.
             1945.

        561294

—— WILLIAMS (S. F.)
   Associates of Shakespeare: [1.] John
   Webster;   [2.] Ben Jonson;   [3.] Thomas
   Dekker.   [Extracts] from a lecture on
   "The Times and associates of Shakespeare",
   by S. F. Williams [, 1886].   FROM Great
   Thoughts, [Vol. 9.]
            [1888.]

        550794

—— see also MOORE (W. H.) Baconian Studies.

WEBSTER (MARGARET)
The Black Othello.   IN Paul Robeson
as Othello, the Moor of Venice [: a
souvenir book of the Margaret Webster
production of Othello at Theatre Guild,
New York].   pp. [20].   [New York]
 illus.   [1943.]

        559677

WEBSTER (MARGARET)
Commentary.   IN The Taming of the
shrew.   Text edited by C. J. Sisson.
(New York)   1961.
 The Laurel Shakespeare.   F. Fergusson,
general editor.

        667465

WEBSTER (MARGARET)
The Living Shakespeare [No. 1]:
Shakespeare in his time. [Broadcast]
1st October, 1958.   ff. 9.
    typescript.   [1958.]

666019

WEBSTER (MARGARET)
On cutting Shakespeare - and other
matters. IN The Theatre Annual, 1946.
(New York)   1946.

585797

WEBSTER (MARGARET)
On directing Shakespeare. IN
GASSNER (J. [W.]) Producing the
play. (New York)
    bibliog. illus. dgms. 1941.

536928

WEBSTER (MARGARET)
Producing Mr. Shakespeare. IN
Theatre Arts, Vol. 26. (New York)
        1942. 546127
_____ IN Theatre Arts Anthology: a
record and a prophecy. (New York)
        1950. 614298

WEBSTER (MARGARET)
Producing Othello. IN A Casebook on
'Othello', edited by L. F. Dean.
[Text and criticism by various authors.]
(New York: Thomas Y. Crowell) 1964.
Crowell Literary Casebooks.

748200

WEBSTER (MARGARET)
Shakespeare today. [With an]
introduction by M.R. Ridley.
                         1957.

665453

WEBSTER (MARGARET)
Shakespeare without tears. With an
introduction by J. M. Brown. (New
York)   1942.

536056

Webster, Margaret *works relating to*

CAMPBELL (O. J.)
Miss Webster and The Tempest [: criticism
of Margaret Webster's production of The
Tempest at the Broadway Theatre, New
York]. FROM The American Scholar, Vol.
14. (New York)
                         1945.

578272

DOWNER (A.S.)
The dark lady of Schubert Alley [:
Margaret Webster's Shakespearian
productions in America]. From The
Sewanee Review, Vol.54. (Sewanee, Tenn.)
                         1946.

586690

GILDER (ROSAMUND)
Othello and Venus: Broadway in review.
[Includes a criticism of Margaret
Webster's production of Othello under
Theatre Guild auspices, starring Paul
Robeson.] IN Theatre Arts, Vol. 27.
(New York)
    illus.   1943.

548672

HEGGIE (BARBARA)
Profiles [: a study of Margaret Webster
as a Shakespearian producer]. FROM The
New Yorker, May 20, 1944. (New York)
    port.   1944.

578278

ISAACS (H. R.)
This insubstantial pageant: The
Tempest in the making [i.e.
Margaret Webster's production
in New York.] IN Theatre Arts,
Vol. 29.   (New York)
    illus.   1945.

567819

Maurice Evans presents in New York
[at the St. James Theatre] Shakespeare's
Hamlet in its entirety. Directed by
Margaret Webster. [Souvenir book.]
pp. 16. [New York]
    ports. illus.   [1938.]

599878

The Tempest [: the Broadway production
directed by Margaret Webster]. FROM
Life, Vol. 18. [Chicago]
    illus.   1945.

578276

[THEATRE GUILD, NEW YORK]
Paul Robeson as Othello, the Moor
of Venice [: a souvenir book of
the Margaret Webster production of
Othello.] pp. [20.] [New York]
    illus.   [1943.]

559677

[THEATRE GUILD, New York]
The Theatre Guild and Gilbert Miller
present Helen Hayes and Maurice Evans
in Shakespeare's "Twelfth Night".
Directed by Margaret Webster.
[Souvenir book.] pp. 20. [New
York]
    ports. illus.   [1940.]

599879

WECTER (DIXON)
Shakespere's purpose in Timon of
Athens. IN Publications of the
Modern Language Association of
America, Vol. 43. (Menasha, Wis.)
                         1928.

428363

WEDGWOOD, CICELY V.
The Close of an epoch. IN
SUTHERLAND, JAMES, and HURSTFIELD,
JOEL, eds., Shakespeare's world.
                         1964.

667808

WEDGWOOD (C[ICELY] V.)
An Historical view of Hamlet.
[Broadcast] 6th July, 1948.   ff. 4.
typescript.

596471

WEDGWOOD, CICELY VERONICA
Shakespeare between two civil wars.
IN Shakespeare celebrated: anniversary
lectures delivered at the Folger Library
[during 1964].   (Ithaca, N.Y.)   1965.

771817

WEDMORE (Sir FREDERICK)
'Macbeth' and Irving.   IN Wedmore
(Sir F.) On books and arts.   1899.

479551

Weekes (A[gnes] R.) and Goggin (S.E.)
[eds.,] An Anthology of English
prose, for use in schools and
colleges. With introduction and
glossary. [Containing selections
from Shakespeare.]

1921

(Selected English Classics)

530166

WEEKLEY (ERNEST)
Words: ancient and modern.   [With
a chapter on Shakespeare's name and
references to his works.   Revised
edn.]   1946.

591902

WEEKLEY (ERNEST)
Words and names.   [With a chapter
on Shakespeare's name.]   1932.

398635

THE WEEKLY ORACLE: or universal library,
No. 63.   [1737.]

60561

Weer (P. A. Ter) ed.
LAMB (CHARLES and MARY ANN)
Seven tales from Shakespeare.   Anno-
tated and slightly adapted by P. A.
Ter Weer.   3rd edn.   (Zwolle)
                                1950.
Stories and Sketches, No. 34.

615444

WEGG (JERVIS)
Richard Pace, a Tudor diplomatist.
[With references to Pace in
Shakespeare's Henry the Eighth.]
                                1932.

401231

WEIDHORN (MANFRED)
Lear's schoolmasters.
IN SHAKESPEARE QUARTERLY XIII: 3.
pp. 305-316.
(New York) 1962.

605711

WEIGAND, HERMANN JOHN
Hamlet's consistent inconsistency
[and] Shakespeare in German criticism.
IN SCHUELLER, HERBERT M., ed., The
Persistence of Shakespeare idolatry.
Essays in honour of Robert W. Babcock.
(Detroit)   1964.

668300

WEIL, HERBERT, ed.
Discussions of Shakespeare's romantic
comedy [by various authors]. Edited,
with an introduction by H. Weil, Jr.
(Boston, Mass.)   1966.

Discussions of literature.
766695

WEILGART (WOLFGANG J.)
Shakespeare psychognostic: character
evolution and transformation. (Tokyo)
bibliog.   1952.

649260

WEIMANN (ROBERT)
Shakespeare on the modern stage: past
significance and present meaning.
IN SHAKESPEARE SURVEY 20.   (Cambridge)
1967.

766881

WEIMANN (ROBERT)
The Soul of the age: towards a historical approach to Shakespeare.   IN
Shakespeare in a changing world:
essays [by various authors].   1964.

667797

WEIR (S. A.)
Book Four: William Shakespeare.
IN BATEN (A. M.) The Philosophy of
Shakespeare.   (Kingsport, Tennessee)
ports.   1937.

481130

WEISINGER (HERBERT)
Iago's Iago.   FROM The University
of Kansas City Review, Vol. 20.
pp. [8.]   [Kansas City]   [1953.]

665616

WEISINGER (HERBERT)
The Myth and ritual approach to
Shakespearean tragedy.   Reprinted
from The Centennial Review of Arts
and Science, Vol. 1.   pp. 142-166.
[East Lansing, Mich.]   [1957.]

665618

WEISINGER (HERBERT)
The Study of Shakespearian tragedy
since Bradley: a reprint from
Shakespeare Quarterly.   Vol. 6.
pp. [10].   [New York]   [1955]

665615

WEISS (J.)
Romeo and Juliet, Prague, 1946.
IN Theatre Today.
illus.   1946.

606680

WEISS (SAMUEL)
"Solid", "sullied" and mutability:
a study in imagery.
IN SHAKESPEARE QUARTERLY X: 2.
pp. 220-227.
(New York)   1959.
605711

WEITZ, MORRIS
Hamlet and the philosophy of literary
criticism.   1965.

741305

WELDON (JOHN)
A Song, the words [Take, oh take
those lips away] taken out of
Shakspear.   IN [A Miscellaneous
collection of songs, set to music by
various composers.]   pp. [74].
[c.1710]

459144

Weldon's costume through the ages,
B.C. 600 to A.D. 1900 [: preface
and illustrations]. With supplementary
pages illustrating Shakespearean
costumes, etc. pp.36.

[1936]

450555

WELLCOME HISTORICAL MEDICAL MUSEUM,
LONDON
Medicine and health in Shakespeare's
England: an exhibition to commemorate
the Quatercentenary of Shakespeare's
birth. [With an introduction by F.N.L.
Poynter.]   1964.

typescript.   740733

WELLEK (RENÉ)
The Rise of English literary history.
[With references to Shakespeare and
notes.]   (Chapel Hill, N.C.)
bibliog.   1941.

531064

Welles, Orson *works relating to*

— BERNAD (MIGUEL A.)
Othello comes to town: Orson Welles
and Edmund Kean.   FROM Philippine
Studies, Vol. 4.   pp. [12].
(Manila)   1956.

665654

— KOZELKA (PAUL)
A Guide to the screen version of
Shakespeare's "Othello".   Reprinted
from Audio-Visual Guide, October 1955.
pp. 16.   (Maplewood, N.J.)
ports.   illus.   bibliog.   1955.
Photoplay Studies.

665549

— NOBLE (PETER)
The Fabulous Orson Welles.
ports.   1956.

657159

— REPUBLIC PICTURES CORPORATION
[Orson Welles' Mercury production of
"Macbeth".   Script, publicity
material and photographs.]   [1949.]

641789

— William Shakespeare's "Othello"
starring Orson Welles: script,
publicity material and photographs.
pp. 26.   (United Artists Corporation,
Ltd.)
typescript.   1954.

665294

— [WINGE (J. H.)]
Macbeth, directed by Orson Welles:
a Mercury production for Republic:
records of the film, No. 20, published
by the British Film Institute.
pp. [4.]   [1949.]

590201

Wells (H.W.) Elizabethan and Jacobean
playwrights. [With biographical and
bibliographical notes. Also] A
Supplement: A Chronological list of
extant plays produced in or about
London, 1581-1642.   2 vols.

(New York)   1939-40.

525597

WELLS (STANLEY)
Burlesques of Charles Kean's Winter's
Tale.   IN Theatre Notebook, Vol. 26,
No. 3.   pp. 78-83
illus.   1962.

584117/26

WELLS, STANLEY

The Failure of "The Two Gentlemen of
Verona".
IN SHAKESPEARE JAHRBUCH.   Bd 99/1963.
pp. 161-173.   (Heidelberg)

10531

WELLS, STANLEY
Happy endings in Shakespeare. FROM
Deutsche Shakespeare-Gesellschaft West,
Jahrbuch 1966. (Heidelberg)

pp.103-123.   756156

WELLS, STANLEY
A Reader's guide to 'Hamlet'.
IN STRATFORD-UPON-AVON STUDIES 5:
Hamlet.   1963.

667698

Wells (Stanley)
Shakespeare and romance. IN

Stratford-upon-Avon Studies.
8: Later Shakespeare.   1966.

illus. pp.49-101.   756101

WELLS, STANLEY
Shakespeare's text on the modern
stage [with special reference to
the National Theatre's "Othello".]
FROM Deutsche Shakespeare-
Gesellschaft West Jahrbuch 1967.
(Heidelberg)
pp. 175-193.   767901

WELLS, STANLEY
Shakespearian burlesques. FROM
Shakespeare Quarterly, Vol.XVI, 1.
1965.

746659

WELLS (STANLEY)
Tom O'Bedlam's song and King Lear.

IN SHAKESPEARE QUARTERLY XII: 3.
pp. 311-315.
(New York) 1961.

605711

WELLS, STANLEY, and SPENCER, TERENCE
JOHN BEW
  Shakespeare in celebration.   IN
  Spencer, T. J. B., ed., Shakespeare:
  a celebration, 1564-1964.
    illus. maps.   1964.

        667816

[WELLSTOOD (FREDERICK CHRISTIAN)]
  A Calendar of deeds relating to
  Coventry deposited in the Record
  Room at Shakespeare's Birthplace,
  Stratford-upon-Avon, by Major Charles
  H. Gregory-Hood.
    typescript.   [1943.]

        549543

Wellstood (F.C.) Catalogue of the
  books, manuscripts, works of art
  antiquities and relics exhibited in
  Shakespeare's birthplace. [With
  a preface by Sir A.D.Flower.] New
  edn. with a supplementary list of
  recent additions. Ports. Illus.
  Plans. Facsimiles.

        (Stratford-upon-Avon)
              1937.

        490699

WELLSTOOD (FREDERICK CHRISTIAN)
  Catalogue of the books, manuscripts,
  works of art, antiquities and relics
  exhibited in Shakespeare's birthplace.
  New edition, with a supplementary list
  of recent additions.   (Stratford-
  upon-Avon)
    ports. illus. plans. facsimiles.
                         1944.

        666390

WELLSTOOD (FREDERICK CHRISTIAN) [pseud.
"Saltire"]
  An Inventory of the civic insignia
  and other antiquities belonging to
  the Mayor and Corporation of Stratford-
  upon-Avon; with historical notes
  pp. 30.   (Stratford-upon-Avon)
    port. illus. facsimiles.   1940.

        642293

WELLSTOOD (FREDERICK CHRISTIAN)
  List of manorial documents preserved
  in the Record room of the Shakespeare
  Birthplace Trust, Stratford-upon-Avon.
  Reprinted from the Genealogists'
  Magazine, September, 1942.   pp. 258-
  263.   1942.

        537162

[WELLSTOOD (FREDERICK CHRISTIAN)]
  Stratford-upon-Avon races in the
  eighteenth century.   By "Saltire".
  Reprinted from the Stratford-upon-Avon
  Herald, May, 1921. pp. 32.
  [Stratford-upon-Avon]   1921.

        296928

Welsford (Enid) The Fool: his social
  and literary history. [With references
  to Shakespeare and a bibliography.]
  Ports. Illus.

              1935.

        441050

Welsford (Enid) [Review of] Frances
  A. Yates' "A Study of Love's
  Labour's Lost. 1936." In The Modern
  Language Review, Vol. 33.

              1938.

        492625

Welsh *see* Wales and the Welsh

WELTZIEN (FRITZ)
  The Elizabethan age.   [With notes
  in German.] pp. 50.   (Leipzig)
                         1927.
  Teubners Kleine Auslandtexte.
  Grossbritannien und die Vereinigten
  Staaten, 12.

        425703

WENBAN (R.)
  [Coloured drawing of the opening
  performance at the Shakespeare
  Memorial Theatre, Stratford,
  April, 1932.   With a note on]
  Shakespeare's "Prince of Wales".
  IN The National Graphic, vol. 1
  (New Series).   1932.

        397496

WENTERSDORF (KARL P.)
  The Authenticity of The Taming of the
  Shrew.
    IN SHAKESPEARE QUARTERLY V:
    pp. 11-32.
    (New York)   1954.

              605711

WENTERSDORF (KARL P.)
  The Date of Edward III.
  IN SHAKESPEARE QUARTERLY XVI: 2.
  pp. 227-231.
  (New York)   1965

              605711

WENTERSDORFF, KARL P.
  The Date of the additions in the "Booke
  of Sir Thomas More".
  IN DEUTSCHE SHAKESPEARE-GESELLSCHAFT
  WEST, JAHRBUCH 1965.   pp. 305-325.
  (Heidelberg)
              754129

Wenzel (Paul) ed.
  LAMB (CHARLES and MARY)
  Four tales from Shakespeare (condensed).
  Bearbeitet von P. Wenzel.   pp. 76.
  (Kiel und Leipzig)
    illus.   1928.
  Französische und englische Schullektüre,
  Band 75.
    English text with vocabulary, and
  German notes.

        354157

WERDER (CARL)
  The Heart of Hamlet's mystery.
  Translated from the German by
  Elizabeth Wilder.   With an intro-
  duction by W. J. Rolfe.   (New York)
              1907.   19975€
  _____ Another copy.   450752

WERFEL (FRANZ V.)
Verdi. [Including references to
his Shakespearean operas.] Translated by Helen Jessiman. [New edn.]
[1944.]

548485

WERTENBAKER (THOMAS JEFFERSON)
The Golden age of colonial culture.
[With references to performances of
Shakespeare in America.] (New York)
bibliog. 1942.
(Anson G. Phelps Lectureship on Early
American History. New York University
(Stokes Foundation) [1942])

547765

WERTHAM (FREDERIC)
Dark legend: a study in murder.
[With references to Shakespeare.]
(New York)
illus. bibliogs. 1941.

543031

WERTSCHING (PAULINE)
Fate in Elizabethan drama: Columbia
University [thesis] 1948. IN
GOLDING (NANCY L.) A Survey of the
proposed arrangements of Shakespeare's
Sonnets [etc.]
bibliog. microfilm, positive copy.
[1948.]

609350

WEST (A. LAURIE)
Shades of Shakespeare's women:
entertainment in ten scenes. pp. 32.
(New York) 1896.

395830

WEST, ALICK
The Importance of Shakespeare in the
contemporary English theatre.
IN SHAKESPEARE JAHRBUCH. Bd. 103/1967.
pp. 97-135. (Weimar)

10531

WEST (ALICK)
Shakespeare: a revaluation. [A
review of "Shakespeare: a Marxist
interpretation," by A. A. Smirnov].
IN Left review, Vol. 2. 1935[-37.]

456238

WEST, ALICK
Some current uses of 'Shakespearian'.
IN KETTLE, ARNOLD, ed., Shakespeare
in a changing world: essays [by
various authors]. 1964.

667797

WEST (EDWARD J.)
G.B.S., music and Shakespearean blank
verse. IN Elizabethan studies and
other essays[, by various authors],
in honor of George F. Reynolds.
(Boulder, Col.)
bibliog. 1945.
Colorado University Studies. Series
B. Studies in the Humanities.

569202

WEST (EDWARD J.)
G.B.S. on Shakespearean production.
IN Studies in Philology, Vol. 45.
(Chapel Hill, N.C.)
bibliog. 1948.

554520/45

WEST (EDWARD J.)
Henry Irving, 1870-1890. IN Studies
in speech and drama [by various
authors]: in honor of Alexander M.
Drummond. (Ithaca, N.Y.) 1944.
bibliog.

561280

WEST (EDWARD J.)
Irving in Shakespeare: interpretation
or creation?
IN SHAKESPEARE QUARTERLY VI:
pp. 415-422.
(New York) 1955.

605711

WEST (EDWARD J.)
Shaw, Shakespeare and Cymbeline.
IN The Theatre Annual, 1950. (New
York)

554521/1950

WEST (JOHN EBENEZER) [ed.]
O mistress mine, arranged as a duet
for female or boys' voices by J. E.
West. [Words from Twelfth Night.]
Traditional melody. School Music
Review, extra supplement, Aug. 15,
1928. pp. [4.] 1928.

516959

WEST (JOHN EBENEZER) ed.
Orpheus with his lute, by Sir Arthur
Sullivan [: three-part song. Words
from "Henry VIII". Arranged for
female voices by J. E. West]. pp. 11.
[1923.]
Novello's Octavo Edition of Trios, &c.
for Female Voices No. 48.

594161

WEST (REBECCA)
Elizabeth Montagu. IN DOBRÉE (B.)
ed., From Anne to Victoria: essays
by various hands. 1937.

463252

WEST (ROBERT HUNTER)
Ariel and the outer mystery. IN
Shakespeare 1564-1964: a collection
of modern essays by various hands.
(Providence, R.I.: Brown University)
1964.

744437

WEST (ROBERT HUNTER)
The Christianness of "Othello". IN
Shakespeare Quarterly XV: 4. pp.333-343.
(New York) 1964.

605711

WEST (ROBERT HUNTER)
Elizabethan belief in spirits and
witchcraft. IN MATTHEWS (A. D.)
and EMERY (C. M.) eds., Studies in
Shakespeare. (Coral Gables, Fla.)
1953.
University of Miami Publications in
English and American Literature,
Vol. 1, March 1953.

634188

WEST (ROBERT HUNTER)
The Invisible world: a study of
pneumatology in Elizabethan drama.
[With references to Shakespeare, and
notes.] (Athens, Georgia)
bibliog. 1939.

529590

WEST (ROBERT HUNTER)
King Hamlet's ambiguous ghost.
IN P.M.L.A.: Publications of the
Modern Language Association of America,
Vol. 70. (Menasha, Wis.) 1955.

428321/70

WEST (ROBERT HUNTER)
Sex and pessimism in King Lear.
IN SHAKESPEARE QUARTERLY XI: 1.
pp. 55-60.
(New York) 1960.

605711

WEST BROMWICH GRAMMAR SCHOOL
Programmes, etc., of Shakespeare
performances. 1930-47.

451508

WESTACOTT (CHARLES ALBERT)
The Compassionate onlooker, William
Shakespeare, 1564-1616 [: quotations
from Shakespeare's works interspersed
with notes by the compiler, showing
Shakespeare's attitude to animals].
pp. 8. [1941.]
United Humanitarian League and the
World League against Vivisection and
for the Protection of Animals.

530215

WESTACOTT (C. A.)
Shakespeare and diet. Reprinted
from The Vegetarian News, Spring
1945. pp. [4.] (Letchworth)
[1945.]

580950

WESTACOTT (CHARLES ALBERT)
Shakespeare and the animals. pp. 47.
(Letchworth)
port. [1949.]

603147

WESTBROOK (Mrs.)
[Review of] Shakespeare through
Eastern eyes, by R. G. Shahani.
IN The Asiatic Review, Vol. 29.
1933.

415141

WESTBROOK (PERRY DICKIE)
Horace's influence on Shakespeare's
Antony and Cleopatra. IN Publications
of the Modern Language Association of
America, Vol. 62. (Menasha, Wis.)
1947.

428321/62

WESTFALL (ALFRED VAN RENSSELAER)
American Shakespearean criticism,
1607-1865. (New York)
bibliogs. 1939.

507300

WESTFALL (ALFRED VAN RENSSELAER)
It started with a bullfight [: an
essay on the Bacon-Shakespeare
controversy. bibliog.] IN
PROUTY (C. T.) ed., Studies in honor
of A. H. R. Fairchild[, by various
authors]. (Columbia, Mo.)
port. 1946.
University of Missouri Studies,
Vol. 21. No. 1.

575822

WESTFALL (ALFRED VAN RENSSELAER)
A New American Shakespeare allusion.
IN Modern Language Notes, Vol. 63.
(Baltimore, Md.)
bibliog. 1948.

439157/63

WESTHAM HOUSE ADULT RESIDENTIAL COLLEGE,
Barford
Programmes of courses on Shakespeare
for adult students. [Barford, etc.]
1954-

667172

WESTLAKE, JOHN H. J.
A study of Shakespeare criticism in
the [Shakespeare] Jahrbuch 1865-1914.
M.A. [thesis] University of
Birmingham, 1966.
typescript. 1966.

768966

WESTLUND (JOSEPH)
Fancy and achievement in Love's labour's
lost.
IN SHAKESPEARE QUARTERLY XVIII: 1.
pp. 37-46.
(New York) 1967.

605711

Westminster Theatre *see* London, Westminster Theatre

WESTON (H.)
Form in literature: a theory of
technique and construction. With
a preface by John Drinkwater [and
references to Shakespeare.]
dgms. 1934.

427713

WESTRUP (Sir J. A.)
Purcell. [With references to his music
to Shakespeare's plays.] Ports. Illus.
Facsimiles. Pedigree. 1937.

(Master Musicians. New Series)

463454

WESTRUP (Sir J. A.)
Three Shakespeare songs with piano
accompaniment by J.A. Westrup.
1: Come away, death [from Twelfth Night];
2: Take, O take those lips away [from
Measure for Measure]; 3: Orpheus with his
lute [from Henry the Eighth]. pp.3,3,3.
3 vols. [1948.]

591370

WETHERBEE (LOUISE) and THURBER (S.) ed.
Life of Shakespeare, an account of
the theatre in his time, aids to the
study of As you like it. IN
SHAKESPEARE [W.] As you like it,
edited by S. Thurber, Jr. and Louise
Wetherbee. (Boston, [Mass.])
illus. bibliog. 1922.
Academy Classics.

412171

Wewitzer (R.) A Brief dramatic chronology
of actors, &c. on the London stage,
from the introduction of theatrical
entertainments into England to the
present time. New edn. [With]
miscellaneous appendix.

1817.

501291

WEY (JAMES J.)
Musical allusion and song as part of
the structure of meaning of
Shakespeare's plays: abstract of a
dissertation submitted to the Catholic
University of America. pp. viii, 17.
(Washington) 1957.

666099

Whateley, Anne *works relating to*

— Brown (I.[J.C.]) William's other
   Anne. [Broadcast] 1st March, 1940.
   ff. [2], 18.

1940.

514551

— HUTCHESON (W. J. F.)
   Shakespeare's other Anne: the life
   and works of Anne Whateley or Beck,
   who nearly married William Shakespeare
   in November 1582.A.D. (Glasgow)
   ports. illus. dqms facsimiles.
1950.

609614

— ROSS (W.)
   The Story of Anne Whateley and William
   Shaxpere, as revealed by "The Sonnets
   to Mr. W.H." and other Elizabethan
   poetry. (Glasgow)
   bibliog. 1939.

510565

"What's in a name?" [With references
to Shakespeare.] In National
Miscellany : a magazine of general
literature Vol. 4.

1855.

493348

Wheatley (H.B.) London and the life
of the town. In Shakespeare's
England, vol.2. [With bibliographies.] Illus. Facsimiles.

(Oxford) 1917.

435746

WHEATLEY (HENRY BENJAMIN)
The London stage in Elizabeth's reign.
(Royal Institution of Great Britain)
pp. 7. 1890.

665455

WHEATLEY (H. B.)
London's homage to Shakespeare.
IN GOLLANCZ ([Sir] I.) ed., A Book
of homage to Shakespeare.
ports. illus. facsimiles. [1916.]

264175

WHEATLEY (HENRY BENJAMIN)
On a contemporary drawing of the interior
of the Swan Theatre, 1596.
IN Transactions of the New Shakespeare
Society, Series 1. Nos. 11-14. 1887.
pp. 215-225.

109245

WHEATLEY (H. B.)
Prices of Shakespeare's works.
IN Wheatley (H. B.) Prices of books:
an enquiry into the changes in the
price of books which have occurred
in England at different periods.
1898.

The Library Series.

142450

Wheatley (H.B.) The Story of Romeo
and Juliet. In The Antiquary,
Vols. 5-6.

1882.

50011

WHEELER (ALFRED)
As it fell upon a day: two-part song
for equal voices with pianoforte
accompaniment. Poem by R. Barnefield
[in The Passionate Pilgrim]; music
by A. Wheeler. [Staff notation and
tonic sol-fa.]
2 vols. [1926.]

517016

[WHEELER (WILLIAM ADOLPHUS)]
Furness's Concordance to Shakespeare's
Poems. IN The North American Review,
Vol. 119. (Boston [Mass.]) 1874.

41849

Wheeling Shakespeare Club, Wheeling,
Virginia: see Societies and Clubs

[WHELER (ROBERT BELL)]
Baptisms etc., of the Shakspeare
family. FROM The Gentleman's
Magazine, Sept. 1816. pp. [6.]

402686

WHELER (ROBERT BELL)
The Bust of Shakspeare at Stratford.
FROM The Gentleman's Magazine,
Jan. and March, 1815. pp. [6.]

402865

WHELER (ROBERT BELL)
History and antiquities of Stratford-
upon-Avon: a description of the
Collegiate Church, the life of
Shakspeare, [with an] account of the
Jubilee celebrated at Stratford, in
honour of [Shakespeare, 1769].
(Stratford-upon-Avon)
illus. [1806.]

520159

Where to stay and eat in the Shakespeare
country and the Midlands: comprehensive
touring guide.   1964.

  map. Travelwise.   667834

WHETSTONE, GEORGE
Promus and Cassandra.

  For editions of this play see under
English Editions: Measure for
measure: Alterations &c.

Whetstone, George *works relating to*

— IZARD (T. C.)
  George Whetstone, mid-Elizabethan
  Gentleman of letters. [Containing
  references to the use made by
  Shakespeare of Whetstone's Promos and
  Cassandra for the plot of Measure for
  Measure. With a bibliography of
  Whetstone's works and bibliographical
  notes.] (New York)
                         1942.
  Columbia University Studies in English
  and Comparative Literature, No. 158
                         545956

— PROUTY (CHARLES TYLER)
  **George Whetstone and the sources of
  "Measure for measure". IN Shakespeare
  Quarterly XV: 2. pp.131-145. (New York)
  1964.**

                         605711

— PROUTY (CHARLES TYLER)
  George Whetstone and the sources of
  "Measure for measure".   IN
  McMANAWAY (JAMES GILMER) ed.,
  Shakespeare 400: essays by American
  scholars on the anniversary of the
  poet's birth. Published in co-
  operation with the Shakespeare
  Association of America.
    illus.   1964.

                         667803

— PROUTY (C. T.)
  George Whetstone, Peter Beverly and the
  sources of Much ado about nothing.
  FROM Studies in Philology, Vol. 38.
  (Chapel Hill, N.C.)
                         1941.

                  529724

WHIBLEY (CHARLES)
  The Aberration of a scholar [: a
  criticism of "Sous le masque de
  'William Shakespeare', William Stanley,
  VIe Comte de Derby", by A. Lefranc.]
  IN Blackwood's Magazine, Vol. 205.
                         1919.

         277013

Whibley (C.) Rogues and vagabonds. In
  Shakespeare's England, vol.2.
  [With bibliographies.] Illus.
  Facsimiles.

            (Oxford)   1917.

                  435746

WHIBLEY (CHARLES)

**Shakespeare: the poet of England. FROM
Blackwood's Magazine, No. 1207. pp.[14.]
1916.**

         667278

WHICHER (GEORGE FRISBIE)
  The Folger Shakespeare Library.
  IN Theatre arts monthly, vol. 16.
  (New York)
    illus.   1932.

                  402620

WHICHER (G. F.)
  This was a poet: a critical biography
  of Emily Dickinson. [With references to Shakespeare, and a bibliographical postscript.] (New York)
  ports. plan. facsimiles. 1938.

         548957

WHILES (WILLIAM HERBERT) and STERN (E.S.)
  Three Ganser states and Hamlet [: an
  examination of the case of Hamlet
  from a psychiatric viewpoint, giving
  reasons for believing that he suffered
  from a particular state of mind
  called the Ganser state, named after
  Dr. Ganser].   FROM The Journal of
  Mental Science, Vol. 88.   1942.
  For a reply to this article, by
  T. M. Davie, see catal. no. 552445.

                  550831

WHINCOP (T.)
  Scanderbeg; or, Love and liberty.
  To which are added, A List of all the
  dramatic authors [including
  Shakespeare], with some account of
  their lives; and of all dramatic
  pieces published in English, to the
  year 1747.
    illus.   1747.

                  484913

WHIPPLE (EDWIN PERCY)
  The Growth, limitations and toleration
  of Shakespeare's genius.   IN The
  Atlantic Monthly, Vol. 20.   (Boston,
  Mass.)   1867.

                  19366

WHIPPLE (EDWIN PERCY)
  Shakespeare, the man and the dramatist.
  IN The Atlantic Monthly, Vol. 19.
  (Boston, Mass.)   1867.

                  19365

[WHIPPLE (EDWIN PERCY)]
  Verplanck and Hudson: Shakspeare's
  plays.   IN The North American
  Review, Vol. 67.   (Boston, [Mass.])
                         1848.

                  41797

WHITAKER, VIRGIL KEEBLE
The mirror up to nature: the
technique of Shakespeare's tragedies.
(San Marino, Cal.)   1965.

745405

WHITAKER (VIRGIL KEEBLE)
Philosophy and romance in Shakespeare's
"problem" comedies.   IN JONES (R. F.)
The Seventeenth century, by R. F.
Jones and others writing in his honor.
(Stanford, Cal.)
    port.   illus.   facsimile. 1951.

622586

WHITAKER (VIRGIL KEEBLE)
Shakespeare in San Diego - the twelfth
season.
IN SHAKESPEARE QUARTERLY XII: 4.
pp. 403-408.
(New York)   1961.

605711

WHITAKER (VIRGIL KEEBLE)
Shakespeare's use of his sources.
IN MAXWELL (B.) [and others] eds.,
Renaissance studies in honor of
Hardin Craig.   (Iowa)
    port.   bibliog.   1941.
Philological Quarterly, Vol. 20,
No. 3; Iowa University [and Stanford
University].

539442

WHITAKER (VIRGIL KEEBLE)
Shakespeare's use of learning: an
inquiry into the growth of his mind
& art.   (San Marino, Cal.)
    bibliog.   1953.
Huntington Library.

637660

Whitaker, Virgil K. *works relating to*

──── NORGAARD (HOLGER)
    [Review of] Shakespeare's use of
    learning by V. K. Whitaker.   IN English
    Studies, Vol. 36.   (Amsterdam) 1955.

485643/36

WHITE (ANNE TERRY)
Three children and Shakespeare [: the
stories of A Midsummer night's dream,
The Merchant of Venice, Julius Caesar
and The Taming of the shrew, told
mainly in Shakespeare's own words.]
With drawings by Beatrice Tobias.
(New York)   1938.

492184

WHITE (ANNE TERRY)
Will Shakespeare and the Globe Theater.
Illustrated by C. W. Hodges.   1955.
World Landmark Books.

665060

WHITE (BEATRICE [MARY IRENE])
An Index to The Elizabethan stage;
and William Shakespeare: a study of
facts and problems, by Sir E. [K.]
Chambers.   (Oxford: The Shakespeare
Association)   1934.   420692
────── Another copy.   Different
imprint.   1934.   430175

WHITE (EDWARD JOSEPH)
Commentaries on the law in
Shakespeare.   2nd edn.   (St. Louis)
                             1913.

474433

WHITE (EDWIN C.)
Problems of acting and play production;
with a foreword by Flora Robson[, and
references to Shakespeare.]
    bibliog.   port.   dgms.   1939.
Theatre and Stage Series.

492656

WHITE (ERIC WALTER)
Verdi and Shakespeare.   [FROM "Life
and letters to-day",] Summer, 1938.

488926

WHITE, ERIC WALTER, ed.
[Fifteen] poems for William
Shakespeare [commissioned from
various poets to celebrate the
Quatercentenary].   With an intro-
duction.   (Stratford-upon-Avon)
                             1964.

668308

WHITE (FELIX [HAROLD])
We cobblers lead a merry life: part
song for men's voices (unaccompanied).
Poem from "The Tragedy of Locrine"
[ascribed to Shakespeare].   Music
by F. [H.] White.   pp. 8.   1933.

542327

WHITE (FELIX [HAROLD])
Where the bee sucks: unison song.
[Words by] Shakespeare [from The
Tempest; music by] F. White.
pp. 4.   1929.

586795

WHITE (HAROLD OGDEN)
Plagiarism and imitation during the
English Renaissance: a study in
critical distinctions.   [With refer-
ences to Shakspere.]   (Cambridge,
Mass.)   1935.
  Harvard Studies in English, Vol. 12.

431397

WHITE (HERBERT [MARTYN] OLIVER)
Edward Dowden, 1843-1913: an address
delivered in the Chapel of Trinity
College, Dublin, on Trinity Monday,
1943.   [With references to Dowden's
works on Shakespeare.]   pp. 22.
(Dublin)   1943.

546664

WHITE, J.W.R.
  Shakespeare's Richard III: an
  interpretation for students. (Adelaide)
                             1966.

761167

[WHITE (JAMES)]
Original letters, etc. of Sir John
Falstaff and his friends; now
first made public by a descendant
of Dame Quickly, 1796.   IN O'BRIEN
(E. J. [H.]) ed. The Guest book.
                              1935.

                         522081

WHITE (L. J.)
Two Shakespeare songs for schools:
1.   When that I was a little tiny
boy [from Twelfth Night]; 2.   Under
the greenwood tree,[from As you like
it.   Two-part or unison].   pp. 8.
                              1948.
Oxford Choral Songs.
                         595919

WHITE (MICHAEL)

Take, oh take ... [, from Measure for
Measure]. For four-part chorus of mixed
voices. (G. Schirmer. Inc.. New York)
                              1961.

                    667409

WHITE (RICHARD GRANT)
The Anatomizing of William
Shakespeare.   IN The Atlantic
Monthly,   Vols. 53 and 54.
(Boston, [Mass.])
  2 vols.   1884.

                    69457

WHITE (RICHARD GRANT)
The Bacon-Shakespeare craze [:   a
review of "The Promus of Bacon,
illustrated by passages from
Shakespeare", by Mrs. Constance M.
Pott, 1883].   IN The Atlantic
Monthly, Vol. 51, 1883.   (Boston,
Mass.)   1883.

                    60092

[WHITE (RICHARD GRANT)]
The Collier-folio Shakespeare.
Is it an imposture?   facsimiles.
FROM The Atlantic Monthly[, Vol. 4].
(Boston[, Mass.])   1859.

                    555529

White (R.G.) On the acting of Iago.   In
The Atlantic Monthly, Vol. 48.

              (Boston)   1881.

                    39574

WHITE (RICHARD GRANT)
On the confusion of time in The Merry wives.
IN Transactions of the New Shakespeare
Society, Series 1.   No. 4.
pp. 421-423.   1875-6.

                    40620

WHITE (RICHARD GRANT)
[Review of] King Lear: a New
Variorum Edition of Shakespeare,
edited by H. H. Furness.   Vol. 5.
IN The Atlantic Monthly, Vols. 45
and 46.   (Boston, [Mass.])
  2 vols.   1880.

                    19626

[WHITE (RICHARD GRANT]
The Shakespeare mystery.   FROM
The Atlantic Monthly, Vol. 8.
[Boston, Mass.]
    facsimiles.   1861.

                    554163

WHITE (RICHARD GRANT)
Stage Rosalinds.   IN The Atlantic
Monthly, Vol. 51.   (Boston, Mass.)
                              1883.

                    60092

WHITE (RICHARD GRANT)
Studies in Shakespeare.   (Boston
[Mass.])
    bibliog.   1886.   544883
_____ Another edn.   1899.   417808

White (R.G.) The Tale of the Forest of
    Arden.   From [The Galaxy,] April, 1875.

          [New York]

                    557129

White (R.G.) The Two Hamlets.   In
The Atlantic Monthly, Vol. 48.

          (Boston)   1881.

                    39574

White, Richard Grant *works relating to*

— ATLANTIC MONTHLY, vol. 57
   A Shakespearean scholar [:   a review
   of Studies in Shakespeare, by
   Richard Grant White.]   (Boston,
   [Mass.])   1886.

                    84836

— FALK (R. P.)
   Critical tendencies in Richard Grant
   White's Shakespeare commentary.
   FROM American Literature, Vol. 20.
   (Durham, N.C.)
     bibliog.   1948.

                    605683

White (T.A.S.) and Man (W.L.) Lecture
    on Shakespeare. [With The Tercenten-
    ary celebration of Shakespeare at
    Stratford, 1864, by T.A.S. White.]
    pp.42. Ports. Illus.

              (Maidstone)   1887.

                    419185

WHITE (W.) and CHAPMAN (G.)
England's royal characters in
Shakespeare's historical plays [:
genealogical table].   (Concord, N.H.)
1 sheet.   1886.

454999

WHITE (WALTER)
All round the Wrekin.   [With a reference to a rhyming epitaph on the tomb
of Sir Thomas Stanley in Tong church,
said to have been written by
Shakespeare.]   1860.   27886
_____ 2nd edn.   1860.   462078

WHITE (WILLIAM)
Francis (Bacon), Lord High Chancellor
of England.   Reprinted from "Baconiana".   pp. 23.   (London: Bacon
Society)   1900.

549419

WHITE (WILLIAM)
Osler on Shakespeare, Bacon, and
Burton.   With a reprint of his
"Creators, transmuters, and trans-
mitters as illustrated by
Shakespeare, Bacon, and Burton".
FROM Bulletin of the History of
Medicine, Vol. 7.   (Baltimore)
facsimile.   bibliog.   1939.

565596

White, William Augustus *works relating to*

— **BARTLETT (HENRIETTA C.)**
Catalogue of English books, chiefly
of the Elizabethan period.   Collected
by W. A. White and catalogued by
Henrietta C. Bartlett.   [With a
section of Shakespeare items.]   (New
York)
facsimiles.   1926.
Edition limited to 500 copies.   This
one is signed by the author.

524748

— The Shakespeare quartos [given to
Harvard University from the
collection of W.A.White. pp. [11.]
From Harvard Library Notes, No.21.

(Cambridge, Mass.)   1928.

524749

WHITEBROOK (JOHN CUDWORTH)
Fynes Moryson, Giordano Bruno and
William Shakespeare.   FROM Notes
and Queries, 1936.   1936.

462917

WHITEBROOK (JOHN CUDWORTH)
Some fresh Shakespearean facts.
IN Notes and Queries, Vol. 162.
1932.

401808

WHITEHALL (FRANK M.)
The Authorship of Shakespeare's plays.
pp. [57].
typescript.   1935.

453053

WHITEHEAD, PETER, and BEAN, ROBIN
Olivier [and] Shakespeare [: the
life of Sir Laurence Olivier, with
still photographs from his
Shakespearian films.]   French
translation by Marie-Claude Apcher,
and German translation by V. Oleram.
1966.

753020

WHITEHEAD (WILLIAM)
To Mr. Garrick.   IN [DODSLEY (R.) ed.]
A Collection of poems by several
hands.   3rd edn.,Vol. 2.
1751.   576731
_____ 4th edn., Vol. 2.
1755.   576737
_____ 5th edn., Vol. 2.
1758.   538519
_____ New edn., corrected.   Vol. 2.
1782.   99647

WHITEHOUSE (JOHN HOWARD)
The Boys of Shakespeare.   pp. [v],
30.   (Birmingham)
illus.   1953.

630843

WHITEING (R.) and WARD (GENEVIÈVE)
Both sides of the curtain [: a life
of Geneviève Ward, with reference to
Shakespeare performances.]
ports.   illus.   1918.

497898

WHITER, WALTER
A Specimen of a commentary on
Shakespeare, being the text of the
first (1794) edition, revised by
the author and never previously
published.   Edited by A. Over.
Completed by Mary Bell.   1967.

764140

Whiter, Walter *works relating to*

— **BELL (MARY)**
Walter Whiter's notes on Shakespeare.
IN SHAKESPEARE SURVEY 20.   (Cambridge)
1967.

766881

— **SEN (SAILENDRA KUMAR)**
A Neglected critic of Shakespeare:
Walter Whiter.
IN SHAKESPEARE QUARTERLY XIII: 2.
pp. 173-185.
(New York) 1962.

605711

WHITFIELD (CHRISTOPHER)
The Kinship of Thomas Combe II,
William Reynolds and William
Shakespeare.   pp. 25.   (Newnham)
genealogical tables.   1961.
One of 100 copies printed by I. Bain
at the Laverock Press.

667104

WHITFIELD (CHRISTOPHER)
Lionel Cranfield and the Rectory of
Campden. FROM Transactions of the
Bristol and Gloucestershire Archaeological
Society, Vol. 81 1962.   [1962.]

668412

WHITFIELD, CHRISTOPHER
Robert Dover and William Shakespeare.
FROM Transactions of Worcestershire
Archaeological Society, 1962.
(Worcester)   1962.

746119

WHITFIELD, CHRISTOPHER
Shakespeare's Gloucestershire
contemporaries and the Essex Rising.
FROM: Transactions of the Bristol and
Gloucestershire Archaeological Society,
Vol.82, 1963. pp.188-201.   1963.

746120

WHITFIELD, CHRISTOPHER
Sir Lewis Lewkenor and "The
Merchant of Venice": a suggested
connexion. IN Notes and Queries 11:
12, pp.123-133.   1964.

746287

WHITFIELD, CHRISTOPHER
Some of Shakespeare's contemporaries
at the Middle Temple.   FROM Notes
and Queries, N.S., vol. 13.   1966.

768971

WHITFIELD, CHRISTOPHER
Thomas Greene: Shakespeare's cousin.
A Biographical Sketch IN Notes and
Queries 11:12, pp.442-455.   1964.

746288

WHITFIELD (CHRISTOPHER) ed.
Robert Dover and the Cotswold Games
[with] "Annalia Dubrensia". [Explores
probable connection of Dover and his
friends with Shakespeare and contains
transcription of "Annalia Dubrensia":
collection of verses by various writers
in praise of Dover and his Games,
published 1636].
 port. illus. chronological tables.
facsimiles. bibliogs.   1962.

709911

WHITFIELD (J.   F.   )

[Theatrical scrapbooks, 1919-29,
including newspaper cuttings and
programmes of the Stratford-upon-Avon
Shakespeare seasons, and of productions
at Birmingham theatres. Collected by
J.F. Whitfield.] Illus.   3 vols.
                    [1919-29.]

668413-5

Whiting (B.J.) "Old maids lead apes
in hell." From Englische Studien,
Bd. 70

(Leipzig)   1936.

497796

WHITING (B. J.)
Proverbs in the earlier English
drama, with illustrations from
contemporary French plays, [and
references to Shakespeare.]
(Cambridge, Mass.)   1938.
Harvard Studies in Comparative
Literature.
                   491498

WHITING (MARY BRADFORD)
The "Open secret": a romance [relating
to the Bacon-Shakespeare controversy].
IN Comus, Nos. 10-12.   (Birmingham)
                1889.   99005
_____ Another copy.   563146

Whitley (W.T.) Thomas Gainsborough
[: a biography, containing references
to Shakespeare]. Ports. Illus. Plans.

1915.

416096

Whitman, Walt *works relating to*

— BLODGETT (H.)
Walt Whitman in England. [Including
references to Shakespeare.]
(Ithaca)
bibliog.   1934.
Cornell Studies in English.
                   418954

— Fausset (H.I'A.) Walt Whitman: poet
of democracy. [With references to
Shakespeare, and a bibliography.]
Ports.

1942.

531261

— FURNESS (C. J.)
Walt Whitman's estimate of Shakespeare.
IN Harvard Studies and notes in phil-
ology and literature, Vol. 14.
(Cambridge, Mass.)
                        1932.

398528

— HARRISON (R. C.)
Walt Whitman and Shakespeare.   IN
Publications of the Modern Language
Association of America, Vol. 44.
(Menasha, Wis.)   1929.

428364

— JOHNSON (M. O.)
Walt Whitman as a critic of liter-
ature. [Including a chapter on
Shakespeare.] pp. 73. (Lincoln,
Nebraska)
  bibliog.   1938.
University of Nebraska. Studies
in Language, Literature and Criticism.

498865

— MASTERS (E. L.)
Whitman [: a biography. With
references to Shakespeare].
  port.   1937.

463617

— STOVALL (FLOYD)
Whitman, Shakespeare, and democracy.
IN The Journal of English and Germanic
Philology, Vol. 51.   (Urbana, Ill.)
1952.

600780/51

— STOVALL (FLOYD)
Whitman's knowledge of Shakespeare.
IN Studies in Philology, Vol. 49.
(Chapel Hill, N.C.)   1952.

554520/49

Whitmore (C.E.) The Elizabethan Age in
England. [With references to the
tragedies of Shakespeare.] In
Whitmore (C.E.) The Supernatural in
tragedy.

1915.

266111

WHITNEY (LOIS)
Did Shakespeare know Leo Africanus?
FROM Publications of the Modern
Language Association of America,
Vol. 37.   (Menasha, Wis.)
  bibliog.   1922.

554235

WHITRED (GLADYS)
Adventures in music: A Midsummer
night's dream. [Script, in two
parts, of broadcast in BBC Home
Service (Schools) June, 1960].
(British Broadcasting Corporation)
ff. 13.
  typescript.

666909

WHITTAKER, HERBERT
Shakespeare in Canada before 1953.
IN Stratford Papers on Shakespeare
delivered at the 1964 Shakespeare
Seminar.   (Toronto)   1965.

745844

Whittaker (T.) Shakespeare and the world-
order. From The Hibbert Journal,
Vol.17.

1919.

474791

Whittam (Geoffrey) illus.
LAMB (CHARLES and MARY [A.])
Tales from Shakspeare.   With illus-
trations by G. Whittam.   [1955.]

649357

Whittam (Geoffrey) illus.
LAMB (CHARLES and MARY A.)
More tales from Shakespeare.
Simplified by G. Horsley.   Illustrated
by G. Whittam.   1956.
Longmans' Simplified English Series.

665361

WHITTEN (W.) [ed.]
London in song [: an anthology of
poetry, including selections from
Shakespeare].   Compiled [with an
introduction and notes by the editor].
  illus.   1898.

581350

WHITTET, T. D.
Shakespeare and his apothecaries.
FROM Proceedings of the Royal
Society of Medicine, Vol. 57,
no. 6, Oct. 1964.   pp. 899-905.
1964.

764571

Who was the Lord Hamlet?   FROM
Every Month, Vol. 1.   (Liverpool)
  bibliog.   1864.

555517

Who wrote Dickens's novels? [: a
skit on the Bacon-Shakespeare
controversy.]   IN The Cornhill
Magazine, N.S.   Vol. 11.   1888.

99469

Who wrote Shakspeare? [by R. W.
Jamieson].   IN Chambers's
Edinburgh Journal, New Series,
Vol. 18.   (Edinburgh)   1852.

42170

Who wrote Shakespeare?   FROM De
Bow's Review, Vol. 5.   [New Orleans]
1868.

558101

Who wrote the plays & poems known
as "The Works of Shakespeare"?:
an undelivered lecture, by G. H. P.
B[urne].   pp. 48.   (Leicester)
1903.

434421

WHYMARK (H. J.) ed.
The Modern reciter.   [With a parody
on Hamlet's soliloquy beginning "To
be or not to be".]   pp. 48.
[c.1880.]

547291

WHYMPER (FREDERICK)
The Sea: its stirring story of
adventure, peril & heroism. Vol.4.
[With references to Shakespeare's
allusions to the sea.]
  ports. bibliog. illus. maps.
  4 vols.   [1877-1880.]

540700

WHYTE (F.)
Actors of the century: a play-lover's
gleanings from theatrical annals.
[With references to Shakespearian
actors and performances.]
  ports. illus.   1898.

544890

WHYTE (F.)
The Victorian stage, [with
Shakespearian references.]   IN
The Pall Mall Magazine, Vol. 12.
  illus.   1897.

357026

WHYTE (SAMUEL)
Epilogue to Henry the Fourth, performed at Castletown; Occasional
epilogue to Henry the Fourth, per
formed at Drumcree, Jan. 5, 1773;
Epilogue after the tragedy of Macbeth,
performed at the Rt. Hon. L. Gardiner's
Theatre, in the Phoenix Park, 26th
and 28th Jan., 1778; [and] Occasional
address, spoken after Othello, Theatre-
Royal, Crow Street [Dublin] Aug. 3rd,
1789.   IN Whyte (S.) A Collection of
poems on various subjects.   2nd edn.
revised by E. A. Whyte.   (Dublin)
510480   1792.

WHYTE (SAMUEL) and WHYTE (E. A.)
Miscellanea nova [, with references
to Shakespeare].   (Dublin) 1801.
  Imperfect.   Wants the introductory
essay.

462972

WHYTE (SAMUEL) and WHYTE (E. A.)
A Miscellany [, with references to
Shakespeare].   (Dublin) 1799.
  Imperfect.   Wants "A Critique on
Burger's Leonora", the "Introductory
essay", etc.

60176

Whyttyngton (T.) see Phillipps (Sir T.)

WICKENS (DENNIS)
Fear no more the heat o' the sun
(dirge from Cymbeline).   Part-song
for S.A.T. or B. (unaccompanied).
pp. 6.   1955.

665337

WICKHAM, GLYNNE WILLIAM GLADSTONE
The Cockpit reconstructed.   FROM New
Theatre Magazine.   Vol. 7, no. 2,
Spring.   (Bristol)   1967.

771372

Wickham (Glynne W.G.)
'Coriolanus': Shakespeare's tragedy in
rehearsal and performance. IN
Stratford-upon-Avon Studies.
8: Later Shakespeare.   1966.

  illus. pp.167-181.   756101

WICKHAM (GLYNNE WILLIAM GLADSTONE)
General introduction.   IN The London
Shakespeare: a new annotated and
critical edition of the complete works.
Edited by J. Munro.
  glossary. bibliog. 6 vols. 1958.

665926-31

WICKHAM (GLYNNE W. G.)
Hell-castle and its door-keeper.
[Comparison with medieval drama.]
IN SHAKESPEARE SURVEY 19 [Macbeth].
pp. 69-74.   (Cambridge) 1966.

755342

WICKHAM (GLYNNE WILLIAM GLADSTONE)
Shakespeare's "small Latine and less
Greeke".   IN Talking of Shakespeare
[: a selection from the lectures
delivered at the annual course for
teachers at Stratford, 1948-1953].
                            1954.

641471

Wickham (H.) Did Shakespeare murder
  his father? From The Catholic
  World, vol.134.

                (New York)   1932.

441601

WICKHAM LEGG (J.)
Note upon the elf-locks in Romeo and Juliet
(I.iv.91 and 92).
IN Transactions of the New Shakespeare
Society, Series 1.   No. 4.   pp. 191-193.
                            1875-6.

40620

WIDDRINGTON (P. E. T.) ed.
A Spectacle, setting forth the growth
of the English drama from the tenth
century to Shakespeare.   (Oxford)
                            1931.
Includes "Merry Wives of Windsor",
Act II, Scene I.

401235

WIDMANN, JOSEPH VICTOR
The Taming of the Shrew: a comic
opera (libretto)

see under English Editions: The
Taming of the Shrew: Opera Texts

Widmann, W. *works relating to*

— Groot (H. de) [Review of] Hamlets
  Buhnenlaufbahn (1601-1877), by
  W. Widmann. In English studies,
  Vol. 15.

            (Amsterdam)   1933.

485657

Widows *see* **Women**

Wieland, Christoph Martin *works relating to*

— LAZENBY (MARION C.)
The Influence of Wieland and Eschenburg
on Schlegel's Shakespeare translation:
a dissertation submitted to the Board
of University Studies of the Johns
Hopkins University in conformity with
the requirements for the degree of
Doctor of Philosophy, 1941.
(Baltimore) pp. 37.
bibliogs.   1942.

560977

— MEISNEST (F. W.)
Wieland's translation of Shakespeare.
IN The Modern Language Review,
Vol. 9.   (Cambridge)   1914.

266824

WIGSTON (WILLIAM FRANCIS C.)
Prodromi; or, Discoveries in the
Bacon cipher problem.   pp. 10.
[c.1900.]

549417

WIKLAND (ERIK)
Elizabethan players in Sweden,
1591-92: facts and problems.
Translated by P. Hort.   Translations
from the Latin by C. E. Holm.
(Stockholm)
ports.   illus.   map.
genealogical tables.   facsimiles.
bibliog.   1962.

667260

Wilcox (J.) The Relation of Molière
to Restoration comedy. [With references to Shakespeare and a bibliography.]

(New York)   1938.

491575

WILDE (OSCAR)
The Critic as artist: a dialogue.
[With references to Shakespeare.]
IN Wilde (O.) Selected works, with
12 unpublished letters.   Edited,
with an introduction [and a chronological table] by R. Aldington.
1946.

577194

WILDE (OSCAR)
The Portrait of Mr. W.H. [Willie Hughes.]
pp. 78.   (Portland, Maine)
1901.   562744
Edition limited to 425 copies.
_____ The greatly enlarged version
prepared by the author after the
appearance of the story in 1889 but
not published.   Edited with an introduction by V. Holland.
facsimile.   1958.   665972
_____ IN HUBLER (E.) and others, The
Riddle of Shakespeare's sonnets.
1962.   667289

Wilde, Oscar *works relating to*

— BHATTACHARJEE (JYOTSNA)
Oscar Wilde as a Shakespearean critic.
IN Shakespeare commemoration volume,
edited by Taraknath Sen.   (Calcutta)
1966.

764382

— Pearson (H.) The Life of Oscar Wilde.
[With references to Shakespeare and
a bibliography.] Ports. Illus.

1946.

570763

WILDMAN, CARL, ed.
Talking of theatre [: Robert Helpmann,
Rudolf Nureyev, Lynn Seymour and
Kenneth Macmillan on Shakespeare
ballets]. B.B.C. radio script broadcast
19th April 1964.   1964.

668251

WILE (IRA SOLOMON)
Dentistry and dentists as portrayed
by Shakespere.   IN The Colophon,
Part 19.   [New York]
illus.   [1934]

438245

WILENSKI (REGINALD HOWARD)
Eric Kennington and the sculptures
at Stratford.   IN The Architectural
Review, June, 1932: Shakespeare
Memorial Theatre Number.
illus.   plans.   1932.

393576

WILEY (AUTREY N.) ed.
Rare prologues and epilogues, 1642-
1700.   [With references to prologues
and epilogues to Shakespeare's plays.]
illus.   facsimiles.   bibliog.
1940.

520137

WILEY (MARGARET LEE)
A Supplement to the bibliography of
"Shakespeare idolatry".   IN Studies
in Bibliography, Vol. 4.
(Charlottesville, Va.)   1951.

598680

WILKEN (LUBBO)
An Historical and metrical introduc-
tion into the study of Shakespeare's
Works, with particular regard to his
Julius Caesar.   FROM Königliches
Realprogymnasium zu Biedenkopf.
Osterprogramm, 1883. [and] 1889.
(Biedenkopf)   1883-9.

608840

Wilkes (Mr.) pseud. *see* Derrick (S.)

Wilkes, George *works relating to*

— Shakespeare from an American point of
view, including an inquiry as to his
religious faith and his knowledge of
law. With the Baconian theory considered. [By George Wilkes: a
review.]   IN The Nonconformist,
Vol. 38.   1877.

520508

WILKES (J.)
William Shakespeare.   IN Wilkes (J.)
Encyclopaedia Londinensis, Vol. 23.
[Edited by G. Jones.]   1828.
Portrait wanting.

537155

WILKES [T.]
A General view of the stage.   1759.

497696

WILKINS (ERNEST HATCH)
The Tale of Julia and Pruneo.
IN Harvard Library Bulletin, Vol. 8.
(Cambridge, Mass.)   1954.

586792/8

WILKINS (GEORGE)
The Painfull adventures of Pericles,
Prince of Tyre [: a novel, printed
in 1608, and founded upon
Shakespeare's play].   Edited by
K. Muir.   (Liverpool)
facsimile.   1953.
Liverpool Reprints.

637758

Wilkins, George *works relating to*

— Baker (H.T.) The Relation of Shakspere's
Pericles to George Wilkins's novel,
The Painfull adventures of Pericles,
Prince of Tyre. In Publications of
the Modern Language Association of
America, Vol.23.

(Baltimore)   1908.

428343

— BULLOUGH (GEOFFREY)
"Pericles" and the verse in Wilkins's
"Painfull adventures".   IN
Hommage à Shakespeare: Bulletin de
la Faculté des Lettres de Strasbourg.
43e année, No. 8, mai-juin 1965.
illus.   766822

WILKINS (JOHN),Bishop of Chester, works
relating to:
see Moore (W. H.) Baconian Studies.

WILKINS (LEAH W.)
Shylock's pound of flesh and Laban's
sheep.   IN Modern Language Notes,
Vol. 62.   (Baltimore, Md.)
bibliog.   1947.

439157/62

WILKINSON, ANDREW M.
A psychological approach to "Julius
Caesar." FROM A Review of English
Literature, Vol.7, no.4, Oct. 1966.
1966.

pp.65-78.   762626

WILKINSON (CYRIL HACKETT) [ed.]
More diversions: an anthology
[including quotations from
Shakespeare].   (Oxford)   1943.
For "Diversions" see catal. no.
516620.

545150

WILKINSON (FREDERICK W.)
Henry V [: a review of Laurence
Olivier's production as presented
by Two Cities films, Ltd.].   IN
Sight and Sound, Vol. 13.   1944-5.

560963

WILKINSON (H.)
The Adventurers of Bermuda: a
history of the island from its
discovery until the dissolution of
the Somers Island Company in 1684.
[With references to Shakespeare.]
ports. illus. maps. facsimile.
bibliog.   1933.

407060

WILKINSON (PHILIP)
Shakespearean suite for small orchestra:
full score.   pp. 82.   [1960]

666670

Will, Freedom of *see* Free Will and Determinism

Will, Shakespeare's *see* Life of Shakespeare, Documents

WILLARD (BARBARA)
Shakespeare in Italy. FROM Books
of to-day, Vol. 3, New series.
pp. 3.
illus.   1948.

596215

WILLARD (BRADFORD)
The Geology of Shakespeare.   FROM
The Scientific Monthly, Vol. 65.
pp. [6.]   (Baltimore, Md.) [1947]

596567

WILLARD (O. M.)
The Survival of English books printed
before 1640: a theory and some
illustrations. [With references to
the Shakespeare quartos.] IN The
Library, Fourth Series, Vol. 23.
(Oxford)
table. bibliog. 1943.

548645

WILLCOCK (GLADYS DOIDGE)
Language and poetry in Shakespeare's
early plays. ([44th] Annual
Shakespeare Lecture of the British
Academy, 1954) pp. 15. [1954.]

665023

WILLCOCK (G[LADYS] D.)
[Review of] William Shakspere's
petty school, by T. W. Baldwin.
IN The Modern Language Review,
Vol. 39. (Cambridge) 1944.

563897

WILLCOCK (G[LADYS] DOIDGE)
[Review of] William Shakspere's small
Latine and lesse Greeke, by T. W.
Baldwin. IN The Modern Language
Review, Vol. 40. (Cambridge)
1945.

571545

WILLCOCK (GLADYS DOIDGE)
Shakespeare and Elizabethan English.
IN GRANVILLE-BARKER (H.) and HARRISON
(G. B.) eds., A Companion to
Shakespeare studies. (Cambridge)
illus. bibliogs. tables. facsimiles.
1934. 418724
———— Another edn. (New York)
1937. 479251
———— Another edn. (Cambridge)
1945. 566174
———— IN Shakespeare Survey 7.
(Cambridge) 1954. 639176

WILLCOCK (GLADYS D.)
Shakespeare and rhetoric. IN English
Association, Essays and studies,
Vol. 29, 1943. Collected by
Una [M.] Ellis-Fermor. (Oxford)
1944.

553238

WILLCOCK (GLADYS DOIDGE)
Shakespeare as critic of language.
(Shakespeare Association) pp. 30.
1934.

425740

Willcock, Gladys Doidge *works relating to*

K[NIGHTS] (L. C.)
[Review of] Shakespeare as a critic
of language, by G[ladys] D. Willcock.
IN The Criterion, vol. 14, 1934-35.

440552

WILLEMENT (T.)
Banners, shields and arms for
Shakespeare's 'King Henry V';
drawings and notes by T. Willement.
pp. 16.
manuscript. 1858.

473463

Willesden Polytechnic Dramatic
Society <u>see</u> Kilburn Polytechnic
Dramatic Class

WILLETTS (ARTHUR)
Poems and sonnets, [including a sonnet
on Shakespeare.] pp. 94.
(Wolverhampton) 1896.

406875

WILLIAM, DAVID
Hamlet in the theatre. IN
STRATFORD-UPON-AVON STUDIES 5:
Hamlet. 1963.

667698

WILLIAM (DAVID)

"The Tempest" on the stage. IN
Stratford-upon-Avon Studies, edited by
J.R. Brown and B. Harris, Vol.1.
Jacobean theatre. 1960.

666673

WILLIAMS (A. FRANCON)
Kalidasa and Shakespeare [: a reply
to Kalidasa and Shakespeare, by
R. G. Shahani]. IN The Poetry
Review, Vol. 34. 1943.
For Kalidasa and Shakespeare, by
R. G. Shahani, see catal. no. 546123.

560954

WILLIAMS (ALDYTH)
Rue with a difference [: a novel,
containing a description of a
performance of Hamlet.] 1939.

502761

WILLIAMS (ARNOLD)
O mistress mine. S.A.T.B. [Words
from Twelfth Night, music by]
A. Williams. pp. 7. 1933.
York Series, No. 1127.

518996

WILLIAMS (BLANCHE COLTON)
George Eliot: a biography. [With
references to Shakespeare.] (New
York)
ports. illus. facsimiles.
1936.

456931

WILLIAMS (C. LEE)
Song of the pedlar. (The Song of
Autolycus). Words from Shakespeare's
"Winter's Tale". Music composed by
C. L. Williams. IN The Musical
Times, Vol. 48. 1907.
[Musical Times Supplement] No. 1006.

205085

WILLIAMS (C. LEE)
Song of the pedlar (the song of
Autolycus). Words from Shakespeare's
"Winter's Tale". Arranged for
female voices. pp. 7. 1922.
Novello's Octavo Edition of Trios,
&c. for Female Voices, No. 475.

594169

WILLIAMS (CHARLES [WALTER STANSBY])
Biography "of course" [: a review of]
A Life of Shakespeare,[by] H. Pearson.
IN Time and Tide, Vol. 23. 1942.

544257

WILLIAMS (CHARLES WALTER STANSBY)
The English poetic mind. [With a
chapter "The Cycle of Shakespeare"
and other Shakespearian references.]
(Oxford) 1932.

392333

WILLIAMS (CHARLES [WALTER STANSBY])
[Francis] Bacon.
frontis. 1933.

407062

WILLIAMS (CHARLES [WALTER STANSBY])
The Image of the city in English
verse. [Including references to
Shakespeare's plays.] FROM Dublin
Review, July 1940. 1940.

515963

WILLIAMS (CHARLES [WALTER STANSBY])
Introductory essay [entitled] On
the poetry of The Duchess of Malfi
[with references to Shakespeare].
IN WEBSTER (J.) The Duchess of Malfi.
Illustrated by M. Ayrton. 1945.

561294

WILLIAMS (CHARLES [WALTER STANSBY])
A Myth of Shakespeare [: a play in
verse, containing representative
scenes and speeches from Shakespeare's
plays.] (Oxford) 1936. 458510
The Oxford Bookshelf.
_____ IN The Appreciation of
Shakespeare: a collection of criticism,
philosophic, literary and esthetic, by
writers and scholar-critics of the
eighteenth, nineteenth centuries.
(Washington) 1949. 616565

WILLIAMS (CHARLES WALTER STANSBY)
Reason and beauty in the poetic mind.
[With references to Shakespeare.]
(Oxford) 1933.

412737

WILLIAMS (CHARLES [WALTER STANSBY])
Shakespeare [: review of] Shakespeare
and the popular dramatic tradition [by]
S. L. Bethell. IN Time and Tide,
Vol. 25. 1944.

562807

WILLIAMS (CHARLES WALTER STANSBY)
Shakespeare and Bacon: a scene from
an unpublished Myth of Francis Bacon.
pp. [8]. FROM This Quarter, Dec.1932.
(Paris)

401327

WILLIAMS (CHARLES [WALTER STANSBY])
Shakespeare at Stratford, April 1616
[: an imaginary monologue.] IN
This England, Vol. 1. No. 1, April 1930.
illus.

433729

WILLIAMS (CHARLES [WALTER STANSBY])
William Shakespeare. IN Williams
(C. [W. S.]) Stories of great names.
With notes by R. D. Binfield.
(Oxford)
map. 1937.

479406

WILLIAMS (CHARLES WALTER STANSBY)[ed.]
A Short life of Shakespeare, with
the sources. Abridged by C. Williams
from Sir E. [K.] Chambers's William
Shakespeare: a study of facts and
problems. (Oxford)
ports. facsimiles. genealogical
table. 1933.

401115

Williams, Charles Walter Stansby *works relating to*

── A Myth of Shakespeare: [a review of
"A Myth of Shakespeare", by C. Williams.]
FROM The Contemporary Review, Literary
Supplement, 1929. pp. [2.]

389231

WILLIAMS (D. F.) ed.
English comic characters, [including
The Gadshill adventure: a scene from
Henry IV, Part 1.] 1938.

479408

WILLIAMS (DAVID)
On producing King Lear.
IN SHAKESPEARE QUARTERLY II: 3.
pp. 247-252.
(New York) 1951.

605711

WILLIAMS, DAVID RHYS
Shakespeare, thy name is Marlowe.
(New York) 1966.

illus. 754496

WILLIAMS (EDWIN EVERITT)
Tragedy of destiny: Oedipus Tyrannus,
Macbeth, Athalie. pp. 35.
(Cambridge, Mass.)
bibliog. 1940.

527201

WILLIAMS (EMLYN)
The Light of heart: a play in three
acts. [With references to King Lear.]
1940.

512858

WILLIAMS (EMLYN)
Spring, 1600: a comedy in three
acts [relating to Richard Burbage's
company acting Shakespeare's plays
at the Globe Theatre]   1946.

569754

Williams, Emlyn *works relating to*

— FINDLATER (RICHARD)
Emlyn Williams: an illustrated study
of his work, with a list of his
appearances on stage and screen.
1956.
Theatre World Monographs.

658858

WILLIAMS (ETHEL C.)
Companion into Oxfordshire.   [With
references to Shakespeare.]
illus.   bibliog.   1935.

435922

WILLIAMS (FRANCIS)
Tell me where is fancy bred: two-part
song for equal voices with piano
accompaniment by F. Williams.   [Words
from The Merchant of Venice]; tonic
sol-fa by W. G. Glock.   pp. 4.
1936.

536620

WILLIAMS (FRANCIS)
Under the greenwood tree.   [Words
from As you like it].   pp. 4.
1937.
Oxford Choral Songs.

472997

WILLIAMS (FRANKLIN BURLEIGH)
Clarence in the malmsey-butt.   [With
special reference to Richard III.]
IN Modern Language Notes, Vol. 51.
(Baltimore)   1936.

463701

WILLIAMS (FRANKLIN BURLEIGH)
Elizabethan England [: brief text
and plates.   With references to
Shakespeare.]   (Boston, [Mass.])
ports.   illus.   bibliog.   chrono-
logical table.   facsimiles. 1939.
Illustrative Set No. 1, Museum
Extension Publications, Museum of
Fine Arts, Boston.

523012

WILLIAMS (FRANKLIN BURLEIGH)
Leicester's ghost.   IN Harvard
studies and notes in philology
and literature, Vol. 18.
(Cambridge, Mass.)   1935.

443975

WILLIAMS, FRANKLIN B., Jr.
Spenser, Shakespeare, and Zachary Jones.
IN SHAKESPEARE QUARTERLY XIX: 3.
pp. 205-212.   (New York)
1968.

605711

WILLIAMS (FRAYNE)
Mr. Shakespeare of the Globe.
(New York)
ports.   illus.   map.   facsimiles.
bibliog.   1941.

527721

WILLIAMS (GEORGE CARLL) and FOULKES
(WILLIAM ROBERTSON)
Shakespearean synopses.   (New York)
1928.

396606

WILLIAMS (GEORGE G.)
Shakespeare's basic plot situation.
IN SHAKESPEARE QUARTERLY II: 4.
pp. 313-317.
(New York)   1951.

605711

WILLIAMS (GEORGE WALTON)
The Poetry of the storm in King Lear.
IN SHAKESPEARE QUARTERLY II: 1.
pp. 57-71.
(New York)   1951.

605711

WILLIAMS (GEORGE WALTON)

see also Cantrell (Paul L.) and
Williams (G. W.)

WILLIAMS (GERRARD)
O mistress mine: short encore song.
[The words from Twelfth Night].
pp. 7.   1922.

550828

WILLIAMS (GRACE)
Three lyrics from the plays of
Shakespeare [: "Sigh no more ladies",
from "Much ado about nothing";
"Orpheus with his lute", from "Henry
the Eighth";   "Blow, blow, thou winter
wind", from "As you like it"]. S.S.A.
pp. 16.   1959.

666478

WILLIAMS, GWYN
"The Comedy of Errors" rescued from
tragedy. IN A Review of English
Literature, October 1964.

697306

WILLIAMS (GWYN)
Welshmen in Shakespeare's Stratford.
IN The Honourable Society of Cymmro-
dorion, Transactions, 1954.   1955.

255163/1954

WILLIAMS (HARCOURT)
Four years at the Old Vic, 1929-1933.
[With references to Shakespeare's
plays.]
ports.   illus.   1935.

443094

WILLIAMS (HARCOURT)
Gielgud and Hamlet.   IN The Old Vic
Company in "Hamlet" by W. Shakespeare
with John Gielgud as Hamlet.   Production by J. Richmond and J. Gielgud.
[With an introductory pamphlet
"Gielgud and Hamlet" by H. Williams.
pp. 12.
3 gramophone records. (H.M.V. ALP
1482-84)   [1957.]

665717-20

WILLIAMS (H.)
Henry Irving as Romeo.   IN Theatre
Today.
illus.   facsimile.   1946.

606680

WILLIAMS (HARCOURT)
Little Tuk's dream [: a play in
which Shakespeare appears].   IN
Williams (H.) Four fairy plays.
pp. 30.   (Samuel French, Ltd.)
1920.

534289

WILLIAMS (H.)
'Macbeth' from the producer's point
of view.   IN The Listener, Vol. 9.
illus.   1933.

407283

WILLIAMS (HARCOURT)
Old Vic saga.
ports.   illus.   facsimiles.   1949.

602439

WILLIAMS (HARCOURT)
Producing Shakespeare's plays.
IN DOWNS (H.) ed., Theatre and
stage, Vol. 1.
ports.   illus.   dgms.   1934.

425661

WILLIAMS (HARCOURT) ed.
Vic-Wells: the work of Lilian Baylis.
[A collection of appreciations by
those who knew her best.   With
references to Shakespeare.]   Photographs by A. McBean.   1938.

481118

WILLIAMS (HERBERT DARKIN)
William Shakespeare writes for the
films [: a criticism of A Midsummer
night's dream.]   FROM The Quiver,
Feb. 1936.
illus.

446225

WILLIAMS, JOHN ANTHONY
The Natural work of art: the
experience of romance in Shakespeare's
'Winter's Tale.' (Cambridge, Mass.)
1967.

LeBaron Russell Briggs Prize.
Honors essays in English, 1966.
763814

WILLIAMS (JOHN DAVID ELLIS)
Sir William Davenant's relation to
Shakespeare.   With an analysis of
the chief characters of Davenant's
plays.   Inaugural-dissertation
[für die] Kaiser-Wilhelms-Universität
Strassburg.   [Strasbourg] 1905.

608990

WILLIAMS (JOHN O.)
Y Bardd a ganodd i'r byd.   [Welsh
poem with English paraphrase.]
IN GOLLANCZ ([Sir] I.) ed., A Book
of homage to Shakespeare.
ports.   illus   facsimiles.   [1916.]

264175

WILLIAMS (LANGTON)
How shall we honour him?   Song for
the Shakespere Tercentenary Festival,
written by J. T. Milne;   composed by
L. Williams.   pp 5.
port.   [1864.]

628459

WILLIAMS (LORAINE)
Published Shakespearian music.
FROM The Quarterly Journal of Speech,
vol. 19.   (Ann Arbor)   1933.

442573

WILLIAMS (O.)
Mr. Granville Barker on Hamlet [: a
review of Prefaces to Shakespeare.
Third Series.   Hamlet, by H. Granville
Barker.   FROM National Review, vol.
108].   1937.

471788

WILLIAMS, P. C.
English Shakespearean actors: a
review.   1966.

763623

WILLIAMS (PHILIP)
The Birth and death of Falstaff reconsid-
ered.
IN SHAKESPEARE QUARTERLY VIII.
pp. 359-365.
(New York) 1957.

605711

WILLIAMS (PHILIP)
The Compositor of the 'Pied Bull'
Lear.   IN Virginia University
Bibliographical Society, Papers,
Vol. 1.   (Charlottesville, Va.)
tables.   1948.

598680/1

WILLIAMS (PHILIP)
The "Second issue" of Shakespeare's
Troilus and Cressida, 1609.   IN
Virginia University Bibliographical
Society, Studies in Bibliography,
Vol. 2.   (Charlottesville, Va.)
1949.

598680/2

WILLIAMS (PHILIP)
Shakespeare's Troilus and Cressida:
the relationship of Quarto and Folio.
IN Virginia University Bibliographical
Society, Studies in Bibliography,
Vol. 3.   (Charlottesville, Va.)
1950.

598680/3

WILLIAMS (PHILIP)
Two problems in the Folio text of King
Lear.
IN SHAKESPEARE QUARTERLY IV: 4.
pp. 451-460.
(New York) 1953.

605711

WILLIAMS (RALPH VAUGHAN)
The Cloud-capp'd towers [: four
part song.   Words from] "The Tempest".
pp. 4.   1955.
   Oxford Choral Songs.

                          665335

WILLIAMS (RALPH VAUGHAN)
Drinking song ("Back and side go bare").
Male voices (T.T.B.B.) from the cantata
"In Windsor Forest".   Music adapted
from the opera "Sir John in love"
by Ralph Vaughan Williams.   [Words
by J. Still.]   pp. 7.   [1931.]

                          405612

WILLIAMS (RALPH VAUGHAN)
Fantasia on Greensleeves.   Adapted
from the opera "Sir John in love"
[the libretto of which is based on
Shakespeare's Merry Wives of Windsor].
Arranged for pianoforte duet by
H. J. Foss.   pp. 8.   (Oxford)
                                1942.

                          544421

WILLIAMS (RALPH VAUGHAN)
In Windsor Forest: a cantata for
mixed voices.   Music adapted from
the opera "Sir John in love" [by]
Ralph Vaughan Williams.   pp. 53.
                              [1931.]

                          405618

WILLIAMS (RALPH VAUGHAN)
It was a lover: part-song for two
voices with piano accompaniment.
[Staff notation and tonic sol-fa.]
2 vols.   1922.

                          516990

WILLIAMS (RALPH VAUGHAN)
Orpheus with his lute: song.   Words
from "Henry VIII"; music by Ralph
Vaughan Williams.   pp. 4.   1903.

                          542321

WILLIAMS (RALPH VAUGHAN)
Orpheus with his lute.   Words from
"Henry VIII"; arrangement for mixed
voices by F. Tapp.   pp. [ii] 6.
                              1937.

                          601861

WILLIAMS (RALPH VAUGHAN)
Orpheus with his lute [, from Henry
VIII]. (Oxford Choral Songs) (O.U.P.)
                              [1947.]

                          667876

WILLIAMS (RALPH VAUGHAN)
Over hill, over dale: [four part
song.   Words by] Shakespeare [from]
"A Midsummer night's dream".   pp. 7.
                              1956.
Oxford Choral Songs

                          665340

WILLIAMS (RALPH VAUGHAN)
Prologue, Episode, and Interlude
from the opera Sir John in love:
the libretto based on Shakespeare's
The Merry wives of Windsor.   pp. 57.
(Oxford)   [1936.]

                          536621

WILLIAMS (RALPH VAUGHAN)
Serenade to music [: How sweet the
moonlight sleeps, etc.]   Words from
The Merchant of Venice, Act V,
Scene 1.   [Four-part song.]   pp. 20.
                              1938.

                          544420

WILLIAMS (RALPH VAUGHAN)
Sigh no more, ladies (for women's
voices) from the cantata 'In Windsor
Forest'.   Music adapted from the
opera 'Sir John in love'.   [Words
from 'Much ado about nothing'.]
pp. 8.   [1931.]

                          405613

Williams (R.V.) Sir John in love: an
   opera in four acts; the libretto
   based on Shakespeare's 'The Merry
   Wives of Windsor' (with German
   translation by A Mayer).

                     [1930.]

                          405611

WILLIAMS, RALPH VAUGHAN
   Two Shakespeare sketches from 'The
   England of Elizabeth' arranged by M.
   Mathieson.   1964.

                          745453

WILLIAMS (RAYMOND)
Drama in performance [: an examination of selected scenes from various
plays].
   illus.   plans.   bibliog.   1954.
Man and Society Series.

                          645518

WILLIAMS, RICHARD HENRY
   Tell me, where is fancy bred. Song
   for medium voice. (New York) 1963.

                          751626

[WILLIAMS (ROBERT FOLKESTONE)]
Shakespeare and his friends; or,
The Golden age of merry England
[: a novel] by the author of "The
Youth of Shakspeare"   (New York)
                              1847.

                          409504

[Williams (R.F.)] The Youth of
   Shakspeare, [a novel] by the
   author of "Shakspeare and his
   friends".

                (New York)   1847.

                          417472

Williams, Robert Folkestone *works relating to*

— The Youth of Shakspeare [: a novel by the author of "Shakspeare and his friends" i.e. R. F. Williams. A review]. FROM [The New Monthly Magazine and Humorist, Vol. 55.]
[1839.]

560925

WILLIAMS (SAMUEL FLETCHER)
Associates of Shakespeare: [1.] John Webster; [2.] Ben Jonson; [3.] Thomas Dekker. [Extracts] from a lecture on "The Times and associates of Shakespeare", by S. F. Williams[, 1886]. FROM Great Thoughts, [Vol.9.] port. [1888.]

550794

WILLIAMS (STANLEY THOMAS)
The Life of Washington Irving. [With references to Shakespeare]. (New York)
2 vols. ports. illus. facsimiles. genealogical tables. bibliog.
1935.

450173

WILLIAMS (STEPHEN)
The Immortal bard; and More bardolatry. IN Williams (S.) In the opera house.
illus. 1952.

628309

WILLIAMS (STEPHEN)
Malvolio. IN FULLER (M. H.) [ed.] One-act plays for the amateur theatre. 1949.

608358

WILLIAMS (STEPHEN)
Plays on the air: a survey of drama broadcasts. 1951.
Includes references to Shakespeare.

614870

WILLIAMS (STEPHEN) ed.

Woman: an anthology for men

[including extracts from Shakespeare relating to women]. [1942.]

538435

WILLIAMS, T. D. DUNCAN
Mr. Nahum Tate's "King Lear". FROM Studia neophilologica, vol. 38, no. 2, 1966. (Uppsala) 1967. pp. 290-300.

767900

WILLIAMS (TALCOTT)
Our great Shakspere critic: Horace Howard Furness, 1833-1912. FROM The Century Magazine, 1912-13. pp. [6.] [New York]
port. [1913]

389203

WILLIAMS (W. ALBERT)
Seals of love. (Sêl ein serch) Part-song for S.A.T.B. (Rhan-gan i S.A.T.B.) The English words by W. Shakespeare. Y Cyfieithiad Cymraeg gan H. Williams. (Llangollen) 1956.

665922

WILLIAMS (WILLIAM STANLEY GWYNN)
Two Shakespeare lyrics. 1: Spring - Gwanwyn; 2: Winter - Gaeaf. The English words [from Love's labour's lost] by Shakespeare; Y cyfieithiad Cymraeg gan T. G. Jones. [Music by] W. S. G. Williams. pp. 8. (Llangollen) 1938.
Gwynn Edition of Vocal Solos and Duets, 5010.

542320

WILLIAMSON (AUDREY)
Contemporary ballet. [With a chapter entitled "Shakespearean ballet" and references to Shakespeare.]
ports. illus. 1946.

574027

WILLIAMSON (AUDREY)
Old Vic drama: a twelve years' study of plays and players. With a foreword by Dame Sybil Thorndike.
ports. illus. 1948.

594695

WILLIAMSON (AUDREY)
Old Vic drama, 2, 1947-1957. Ports. Illus. 1957.

665668

WILLIAMSON (AUDREY)
Paul Rogers [: a study of his work for stage and screen].
port. illus. chronological table.
1956.
Theatre World Monographs No 5.

654514

WILLIAMSON (AUDREY)
Shakespeare and the Elizabethans [: productions, 1930-50]. IN Williamson (A.) Theatre of two decades [: 1930-1950].
ports. illus. 1951.

618557

WILLIAMSON (AUDREY)
Theatre of two decades [: 1930-1950]. ports. illus. 1951.
Includes a chapter "Homes of Shakespeare".

618557

Williamson (B.) Shakespeare and the Middle Temple. In [Programme of Shakespeare's Twelfth night, acted by the Holywell Players in the Hall of the Middle Temple Society, June 28th, 29th and 30th, 1934.] pp.[6.] Frontis.

1934.

421992

WILLIAMSON (CLAUDE C. H.)
Julius Caesar. FROM The Parents'
Review, Vol. 50. 1939.

523074

WILLIAMSON (CLAUDE C. H.) ed.
Readings on the character of Hamlet,
1661-1947. Compiled from over three
hundred sources. 1950.

614574

WILLIAMSON (GEORGE CHARLES)
Shakespeare's wine-book [: A New
boke of the natures and properties
of wines, by W. Turner, 1568.]
Reprinted from The Wine & Spirit
Trade Record, Jan. 15, 1923.
pp. 20.
illus.

408587

WILLIAMSON (HUGH ROSS)
The Day Shakespeare died. 1962.

666960

WILLIAMSON (HUGH ROSS)
King Claudius. IN The Best one-act
plays of 1954-55, selected by
H. Miller. 1956.

654489

WILLINK (A. H.)
Corydon. The words by Shakespeare
[from The Passionate Pilgrim]. Set
to music by A. H. Willink. pp. 4.
(Oxford) [1940.]

550829

WILLIS (N. P.)
Loiterings of travel: poems, letters
and reminiscences.] Vol. 1.
[Containing references to Stratford-
on-Avon.] 1840.

436185

WILLIS (RONALD A.)
Shakespeare in the Rockies.
IN SHAKESPEARE QUARTERLY XVII:4.
pp. 423-426.
(New York) 1966.

605711

WILLIS (WILLIAM) [ed.]
The Shakespeare-Bacon controversy:
a report of the trial of an issue
in Westminster Hall, June 20, 1627.
Read in the Inner Temple Hall,
May 29th, 1902, and prepared for
publication [with a preface] by
W. Willis. (Honourable Society of
the Inner Temple) [1902.]

499697

[WILLOBY (HENRY)]
I. Willobie's Avisa, 1594.
II. 'Apologie', 1596. III. The
Victorie of English chastitie, 1596.
IV. Penelope's complaint by Peter
Colse, 1596. Edited with intro-
duction, notes and illustrations, by
A. B. Grosart. 1880.
Edn. limited to 62 copies. Printed
for the subscribers.

495387

[Willoby (H.)] Willobie his Avisa
(in part). [Edited by H. Dorrell.]
1594. In Acheson (A.) Mistress
Davenant, the Dark Lady of Shakespeare's Sonnets. 2nd edn.

1913.

497276

[WILLOBY (HENRY)]
Willobie, his Avisa. (1594). [Edited
by H. Dorrell. Reprinted] with an
essay by G. B. Harrison. 1926.
Bodley Head Quartos, [Vol.] 15.

330265

Willoby, Henry *works relating to*

—— BROOKE ([C. F.] T.)
Willobie's Avisa. [With references
to Shakespeare.] IN PEYRE (H. M.)
ed., Essays in honor of Albert [G.]
Feuillerat [by various writers].
(New Haven [Conn.]) 1943.
Yale Romanic Studies, 22.

560305

—— GRAY (H. D.)
Shakespeare, Southampton and Avisa [: a
study on the authorship of the poem,
Willobie his Avisa, attributed to Henry
Willoby, and its references to Shakespeare
and the Earl of Southampton. With bibliographical notes]. IN Stanford Studies
in Language and Literature, 1941. Edited
by H. Craig. ([Palo Alto,] Cal.)
1941.

537291

—— see also MOORE (W. H.) Baconian studies.

WILLOUGHBY (EDWIN ELIOTT)
Cataloging and classifying the Folger
Shakespeare Library. IN The Wilson
Bulletin, Vol. 13.
illus. 1939.

503495

WILLOUGHBY (EDWIN ELIOTT)
Cataloging the early printed English
books of the Folger Shakespeare Library.
pp. 2. [Washington D.C.] 1937.

469548

WILLOUGHBY (EDWIN ELIOTT)
The Classification of the Folger
Shakespeare Library. Reprinted
from The Library Quarterly, Vol. 7.
pp. 395-400. [(Washington, D.C.)]
1937.

469587

WILLOUGHBY (EDWIN ELIOTT)
A Deadly edition of Shakespeare.
IN SHAKESPEARE QUARTERLY V:
pp. 351-357.
(New York)   1954.

605711

WILLOUGHBY (EDWIN ELIOTT)
Printed in Shakespeare's day [:   a
discussion on] typical works.   IN
Graphic arts and education, Vol. 15,
No. 3.   pp. 20.   (Washington)
ports.   illus.   1938.

485895

Willoughby (E.E.) A Printer of
Shakespeare: the books and times of
William Jaggard. Ports. Facsimiles.
1934.

426107

WILLOUGHBY (EDWIN ELIOTT)
The Printing of the First Folio of
Shakespeare.   pp. 70.
facsimiles.   1932.
Bibliographical Society's Transactions.
Supplement No. 8
399490

WILLOUGHBY (EDWIN ELIOTT)
The Reading of Shakespeare in colonial
America.   Reprinted from the papers
of the Bibliographical Society of
America, Vol. 30.   pp. 45-56.
[New York]   1936.

485893

WILLOUGHBY (E. E.)
[Review of] "Shakespeare's haunts
near Stratford", by E. I. Fripp.
IN Modern Language Notes, Vol. 46.
(Baltimore)   1931.

397731

WILLOUGHBY (EDWIN ELIOTT)
The Unfortunate Dr. Dodd: the tragedy
of an incurable optimist [:   Rev. Wm.
Dodd, who committed forgery to get
funds for publishing his edition of
Shakespeare].   IN Essays by divers
hands, New Series, Vol. 29.   1958.

678702

Willoughby, Edwin Eliott *works relating to*

— NEWDIGATE (B. H.)
The Printers of the First Folio [:   a
review of A Printer of Shakespeare,
by E. E. Willoughby.]   IN The London
Mercury, Vol. 31.   1934-5.

438778

WILLSON (LAWRENCE)
Shakespeare and the genteel tradition
in America.   FROM The New Mexico
Quarterly, Vol. 26.   pp. [20.]
(Albuquerque, N.M.)   1956.

665597

WILLY (MARGARET)
[Review of] Shakespearian comedy,
and other studies, by G. [S.]
Gordon.   IN English: the magazine
of the English Association, Vol. 5.
(Oxford)   1944-45.

569018

Wilmcote

— BROOKE ([C. F.] T.)
Shakespeare's dove-house [at Wilmcote].
IN Modern Language Notes, Vol. 59.
(Baltimore)   1944.

563869

Wilmot, James *works relating to*

— SYDENHAM OF COMBE ([G. S. CLARKE, 1st
Baron])
The First Baconian [i.e. J. Wilmot].
Reprinted from Baconiana, Feb. 1933.
pp. 8.   [Bacon Society, London]
1933.   422158
Another edn.   [1944]   549421

WILSON (ALBERT EDWARD)
Hamlet and other matters.   IN Wilson
(A. E.) Playgoer's pilgrimage.
[1948.]

596159

WILSON (A. E.)
Post-war theatre [:   plays produced
in London since June 20, 1945,
including plays of Shakespeare].
[1949.]

603205

WILSON (ALBERT EDWARD)
Prime minister of mirth: the biography
of Sir George Robey, C.B.E.
ports.   illus.   1956.
With Shakespearian references.

654604

Wilson (A.E.) Theatre guyed: the
Baedeker of Thespia. With Tittivations by Tom Titt, an Overture
by Sydney Horler. [Including a
chapter "Brighter Shakespeare",
and other references to Shakespeare.]

1935.

434180

WILSON (A. E.)
A Venetian nobleman [: a parody on
Shakespeare]. IN Wilson (A. E.)
Playwrights in aspic: some variations
upon an unoriginal theme. 1946.

573856

WILSON (ARTHUR HERMAN)
English essays and essentials [for
students of courses at Susquehanna
University. Including a section
on Shakespeare.] pp. 63.
(Selinsgrove, Pa.)
bibliog. 1941.

552436

WILSON (ARTHUR HERMAN)
The Great theme in Shakespeare.
FROM Susquehanna University Studies,
Vol. 4, pp. 62. (Selinsgrove,
Pa.) 1949.

608970

WILSON (ARTHUR HERMAN)
A History of the Philadelphia theatre,
1835 to 1855. [With Shakespearian
references.] (Philadelphia) 1935.

440184

WILSON (CECIL)
The Moscow theatre and Hamlet.
IN International Theatre Annual,
No. 1. 1956.

657618

WILSON (CORA P.)
The Shakespearean controversy [: the
seventeenth Earl of Oxford, Edward de
Vere, as the real Shakespeare.]
ff. 6.
typescript. [c.1940.]

520264

WILSON (EDMUND)
The Triple thinkers: ten essays on
literature. [With Shakespearian
references.] (Oxford) 1938.

486887

WILSON (EDMUND) [and others]
The Intent of the critic, by
E. Wilson, N. Foerster, J. C. Ransom
[and] W. H. Auden. Edited, with an
introduction, by D. A. Stauffer.
[With references to Shakespeare.]
(Princeton) 1941.
Princeton Books in the Humanities.

539455

[WILSON (EDWARD A.)
Twelve scenes from Shakespeare.
Selected by G. L. Kittredge, painted
by E. A. Wilson.] [(New York)]
[1937.]

499010

WILSON (EDWARD MERYON)
Family honour in the plays of
Shakespeare's predecessors and
contemporaries. IN English
Association Essays and Studies, 1953.
New Series, Vol. 6. 1953.

634961

WILSON (EDWARD MERYON)
Othello and the cardinal virtues.
[Broadcast] Sept. 21, 1952. pp. 5.
typescript.

630860

WILSON (EDWARD MERYON)
Othello, a tragedy of honour.
[Broadcast] May 12, 1952. ff. 6.
typescript.

630864

Wilson (Edwin) ed.
SHAW (GEORGE BERNARD)
Shaw on Shakespeare: an anthology
of Bernard Shaw's writings on the
plays and production of Shakespeare.
Edited and with an introduction by
E. Wilson. 1962.

666943

WILSON (ELKIN CALHOUN)
England's Eliza [: a study of the
idealization of Queen Elizabeth in
the poetry of her age. With
references to Shakespeare.]
(Cambridge, Mass.)
illus. facsimiles. bibliog.
1939.
Harvard Studies in English.

496481

WILSON (ELKIN CALHOUN)
Falstaff - clown and man. IN Studies
in the English Renaissance drama,
edited by Josephine W. Bennett [and
others]. 1959.

684756

WILSON (ELKIN CALHOUN)
Shakespeare's Enobarbus. IN
McMANAWAY (J. G.), DAWSON (G. E.)
and WILLOUGHBY (E. E.) eds., Joseph
Quincy Adams memorial studies.
(Washington)
bibliog. 1948.

596748

WILSON (FRANK)
Miss Alma Murray as Juliet. pp. 16.
(Chiswick Press) 1887.

415112

WILSON (FRANK PERCY)
Elizabethan and Jacobean [literature:
lectures, based on the Alexander
Lectures in English delivered in the
University of Toronto, November, 1943.
Including references to and one lecture
on Shakespeare]. (Oxford)
bibliog. 1945.

564243

WILSON (FRANK PERCY)
The Elizabethan theatre.   FROM Neophilologus, 39. Jaargang. (Groningen)
1955.

665002

WILSON (FRANK PERCY)
The English jestbooks of the sixteenth
and early seventeenth centuries [: a
paper read before the Shakespeare
Association, Nov. 26, 1937].
Reprinted from the Huntington Library
Quarterly, Vol. 2, No. 2.   pp. [38.]
[San Marino, Cal.]
bibliog.   1939.

550832

WILSON (FRANK PERCY)
English proverbs and dictionaries of
proverbs.   [With quotations from
Shakespeare.]   Reprinted from the
Transactions of the Bibliographical
Society: The Library [4th Series,
Vol. 26.]   pp. [20.]
bibliog.   1945.

565126

WILSON (FRANK PERCY)

Illustrations of social life III:
street-cries. Illus. In Shakespeare
Survey, [Vol.] 13. (Cambridge)
1960.

666726

WILSON (FRANK PERCY)
Illustrations of social life.   IV:
The Plague.   IN SHAKESPEARE SURVEY
15.   (Cambridge)   1962.

667174

WILSON (FRANK PERCY)
Marlowe and the early Shakespeare.
(The Clark Lectures, Trinity College,
Cambridge, 1951) (Oxford) 1953.

630634

WILSON (FRANK PERCY)
The Proverbial wisdom of Shakespeare:
presidential address of the Modern
Humanities Research Association,
1961.   pp. 24.   [Cambridge]

667086

WILSON (FRANK PERCY)
[Review of] Shakespeare & Jonson:
their reputations in the seventeenth
century compared, by G. E. Bentley.
IN The Library, 4th Series, Vol. 26.
(Oxford)   1945.

574761

WILSON (FRANK PERCY)
[Review of] Prolegomena for the
Oxford Shakespeare: a study in
editorial method, by R. B. McKerrow.
IN The Library.   Fourth Series.
Vol. 20.   1940.

519243

WILSON (F. P.)
Shakespeare and the diction of
common life.   pp. 33.
bibliog.   [1941.]
British Academy [31st] Annual
Shakespeare Lecture.

527000

WILSON (FRANK PERCY)
Shakespeare and the "new bibliography".
IN The Bibliographical Society,
1892-1942: studies in retrospect
[by various authors].
facsimile.   1945.

565383

WILSON (FRANK PERCY)
Shakespeare to-day [: a summary of
recent work on Shakespeare].   IN
Britain To-day, No. 131, March, 1947.

587767

WILSON (FRANK PERCY)
Shakespeare's reading.   IN
SHAKESPEARE SURVEY 3.   (Cambridge)
1950.

606026

WILSON (FRANK PERCY)

Sir Walter Wilson Greg, 1875-1959 [:
obituary notice. Reprint] from
Proceedings of the British Academy,
Vol.45. pp.307-334. Port.

[1961.]

666973

Wilson, Frank Percy *works relating to*

— McK[ERROW] (R. B.)
[Review of] The Plague in
Shakespeare's London, by F. P.
Wilson, [signed R. B. McK.]
FROM Review of English Studies,
Vol. 4.   1928.

497597

WILSON (FRANK PERCY) and
WILSON (JOHN DOVER)

Sir Edmund Kerchever Chambers, 1866-1954
[: obituary notice. Reprint] from
Proceedings of the British Academy,
Vol. 42. pp.267-285. Port.

[1956.]

665617

WILSON (HAROLD S.)
Action and symbol in Measure for Measure
and The Tempest.
IN SHAKESPEARE QUARTERLY IV: 4.
pp. 375-384.
(New York)   1953.

605711

WILSON (HAROLD S.)
Commentary.
IN SHAKESPEARE QUARTERLY IX.
pp. 307-310.
(New York) 1958.

605711

WILSON (HAROLD SOWERBY)
Dramatic emphasis in All's well that
ends well. IN The Huntington
Library Quarterly, Vol. 13. (San
Marino, Cal.) 1950.

494029/13

WILSON (HAROLD SOWERBY)
On the design of Shakespearian
tragedy. 1957.
University of Toronto. Department
of English. Studies and Texts,
No. 5.

665556

WILSON (HAROLD SOWERBY)
[Review of] Shakspere's five-act
structure, by T. W. Baldwin.
IN Modern Language Notes, Vol. 63.
(Baltimore, Md.) 1948.

439157/63

WILSON (HENRY SCHÜTZ)
The Genesis of Othello. IN The
Gentleman's Magazine, Vol. 266.
1889.

101717

WILSON (HENRY SCHÜTZ)
Guesses at Shakespeare. pp. [5.]
IN The Gentleman's Magazine, Vol.
281, 1896. 1896.

136240

WILSON (HENRY SCHÜTZ)
The Non-dramatic in Shakspeare.
FROM International Review, Vol. 4.
(New York) 1877.

553494

WILSON (HENRY SCHÜTZ)
[The Thames from] Maidenhead to
Windsor. [Including references to
"The Merry Wives of Windsor".]
IN Rivers of Great Britain: the
Thames, from source to sea.
(Cassell & Co. Ltd.)
illus. maps. table. 1891.

403543

WILSON (HENRY SCHÜTZ)
A Union with Imogen: a literary
fantasy. pp. [5.] IN The
Gentleman's Magazine, Vol. 281, 1896.

136240

— Review of "Shakespeariana" [by J.
Wilson]. FROM The Gentleman's
Magazine, Jan. 1829. pp. [4.]
1829.

402695

Wilson (J.H.) Granville's "stock-
jobbing Jew". pp.15. From Philological
Quarterly. Vol.13, 1934.

(Iowa City,[Iowa.])]

452013

WILSON (J. H.)

see also Wilson (Marion L.) and
Wilson (J. H.)

WILSON (J. S.)
Shakespeare in the interpretation of
the time [: review of] Shakespeare's
satire, by O. J. Campbell; [and]
Shakespeare and the nature of man,
by T. Spencer. FROM The Virginia
Quarterly Review, Vol. 19.
(Charlottesville, Va.) 1943.

565603

[WILSON (JAMES EDWIN)]
A Throw for a throne, or, The Prince
unmasked, [maintaining ironically
that Shakespeare's words in Hamlet
show Claudius to have been innocent
of murder, etc.] By the late
Serjeant Zinn. With introduction
and references by Chancery Lane, Esq.
[1879]

15721

[WILSON (JOHN)] [pseud. Christopher North]
Dies Boreales. No. 5. Christopher
under canvass [: conversations on
Macbeth.] IN Blackwood's Magazine,
Vol. 66. (Edinburgh) 1849.

10166

[WILSON (JOHN)] [pseud. Christopher North]
Dies Boreales Nos. 6 and 7.
Christopher under canvass [: conversa-
tions on Othello.] IN Blackwood's
Magazine, Vol. 67. (Edinburgh)
1850.

10167

WILSON (JOHN) [pseud. Christopher North]
A Double-time-analysis of Macbeth and Othello.
IN Transactions of the New Shakespeare
Society, Series 1. No. 4.
pp. 351-387 and Series I 1875-80.
Nos. 6-7. pp. 21-41.

40620 11987

WILSON [JOHN] [pseud. Christopher North]
A Few words on Shakespeare.
IN Wilson [J.] Essays critical and
imaginative, Vol. 3. Works, Vol. 7.
(Edinburgh)   1857.

34601

Wilson, John *pseud.* Christopher North *works relating to*

—— HALPIN (N. J.)
The Dramatic unities of Shakespeare:
a letter addressed to the editor of
Blackwood's Edinburgh Magazine [i.e.
J. Wilson. Includes a section, Time-
analysis of The Merchant of Venice].
pp. 57. (Dublin)
1849.

57499

—— STROUT, ALAN LANG
John Wilson (Christopher North) as a
Shakespeare critic. A study of
Shakespeare in the English Romantic
Movement.
IN SHAKESPEARE JAHRBUCH. Bd. 72/1936.
pp. 93-123. (Weimar)

10531

WILSON (JOHN) musician
Lawn as white as driven snow: Autolycus'
song from "The Winter's tale" [by]
Shakespeare; [music by] J. Wilson,
arr. [by] M. Jacobson. pp. 4.
1938.

536622

WILSON (JOHN) musician
Take, o take those lips away. From
select ayres to sing to the theorbo
or bass viol. [From] Measure for
Measure. IN BRIDGE ([Sir] J. F.)
ed., Songs from Shakespeare: the
earliest known settings. pp. 36.
[1912.]   520351
Another edn. [1924.]   474078

WILSON (JOHN) musician
Ten songs from John Wilson's "Cheerful
ayres or ballads" (1659). Arranged for
S.S.A. voices by Imogen Holst. pp.22.
(Oxford)   [1959.]

690576

WILSON (JOHN DOVER)
Ben Jonson & Julius Caesar. IN
SHAKESPEARE SURVEY 2. (Cambridge)
bibliog.   1949.

598403

WILSON (JOHN DOVER)
The Copy for 'Hamlet', 1603. IN
The Library, 3rd Series, Vol. 9.
1918.

276267

WILSON (JOHN DOVER)
The Elizabethan Shakespeare: Annual
Shakespeare Lecture, 1929. IN
Proceedings of the British Academy,
[Vol. 15] 1929.   [1932]   390430
_____ IN Aspects of Shakespeare:
British Academy lecture. (Oxford)
1933.   401892

WILSON (JOHN DOVER)
The Essential Shakespeare: a biographical adventure. (Cambridge)
port. bibliog. 1932.   391410
_____ Another edn. 1946.   574449

[WILSON (JOHN DOVER)
The Essential Shakespeare.] Personal
choice [: a radio programme in which]
D. Bower [reads] a passage from "The
Essential Shakespeare", by J. D. Wilson.
[Broadcast] 21st February, 1944.
pp. 4.
typescript.

547998

WILSON (JOHN DOVER)
The Fortunes of Falstaff [: Clark
Lectures, Cambridge, 1943.]
(Cambridge)
bibliog.   1943.

544609

Wilson (J.D.) Hamlet Q1 and Mr. Henry
David Gray. In Publications of the
Modern Language Association of
America. Vol. 43.
1928.

428363

WILSON (JOHN DOVER)
The 'Hamlet' transcript, 1593. IN
The Library, 3rd Series, Vol. 9.
1918.

276267

WILSON, JOHN DOVER
An introduction to the sonnets of
Shakespeare, for the use of historians
and others.   1963.

667945

WILSON (JOHN DOVER)
[The Living] Shakespeare [No. 5]:
The texts. [Broadcast] 29th October,
1958. ff. 8.
typescript.

666027

WILSON (JOHN DOVER)
Macbeth: a lecture. [Broadcast]
22nd April, 1947. ff. 11.
typescript.

587747

WILSON (JOHN DOVER)
Malone and the upstart crow.
IN SHAKESPEARE SURVEY 4. (Cambridge)
1951.

615854

WILSON (JOHN DOVER)
The Manuscript of Shakespeare's
Hamlet and the problems of its transmission: an essay in critical
bibliography.   (Cambridge)
  2 vols.   1934.
Shakespeare Problems, 4.

421320

WILSON (JOHN DOVER)
Martin Marprelate and Shakespeare's
Fluellen: a new theory of the
authorship of the Marprelate tracts.
IN The Library, 3rd series, Vol. 3.
                                  1912.

242076

WILSON (JOHN DOVER)
The Meaning of The Tempest.   pp. 23.
(Newcastle-upon-Tyne)   1936.
Newcastle-upon-Tyne Literary and
Philosophical Society.   Robert Spence
Watson Memorial Lecture, 1936.

460906

WILSON (JOHN DOVER)
New ideas and discoveries about
Shakespeare.   IN The Virginia
Quarterly Review, Vol. 23.
[Charlottesville, Va.]   1947.

588089

WILSON (JOHN DOVER)
The New way with Shakespeare's texts:
an introduction for lay readers.
1: The Foundations.   IN SHAKESPEARE
SURVEY 7. (Cambridge)   1954.

639176

WILSON, JOHN DOVER
The New way with Shakespeare's texts:
2. Recent work on the text of Romeo
and Juliet.   IN SHAKESPEARE SURVEY
8.   (Cambridge)   1955.

647706

WILSON (JOHN DOVER)
The New way with Shakespeare's texts:
an introduction for lay readers.
3: In sight of Shakespeare's manuscripts.   IN SHAKESPEARE SURVEY 9.
(Cambridge)   1956.

665210

WILSON (JOHN DOVER)
The New way with Shakespeare's texts:
an introduction for lay readers.
4: Towards the high road.   IN
SHAKESPEARE SURVEY 11.   (Cambridge)
                               1958.

665816

WILSON (JOHN DOVER)
On editing Shakespeare, with special
reference to the problems of
Richard III.   IN Talking of
Shakespeare [: a selection from the
lectures delivered at the annual
course for teachers at Stratford,
1948-1953].   1954.

641471

WILSON (JOHN DOVER)
The Origins and development of
Shakespeare's Henry IV.   IN The
Library, 4th Series, Vol. 26.
(Oxford)
  bibliog.   1945.

574761

WILSON (JOHN DOVER)
The Parallel plots in 'Hamlet': a
reply to Dr. W. W. Greg.   IN The
Modern Language Review, Vol. 13.
                               1918.

276260

Wilson (J.D.) The Play-scene in "Hamlet"
restored. In The Athenaeum, July-
Nov., 1918.

282311

WILSON, JOHN DOVER
The Political background of Shakespeare's
"Richard II" and "Henry IV".
IN SHAKESPEARE JAHRBUCH.   Bd 75/1939.
PP. 36-51.   (Weimar)

10531

WILSON (JOHN DOVER)
[Review of] Shakespeare's punctuation
by P. Alexander.   [With the author's
reply to the review].   IN The Review
of English Studies, Vol. 23.   (Oxford)
                               1947.

318239/23

WILSON (JOHN DOVER)
[Review of] The Genuine in Shakespeare:
a conspectus.   By J. M. Robertson.
IN The Criterion, Vol. 10.   1930-31.

388537

WILSON (J. D.)
The Scholar's contribution to the
theatre [: a broadcast talk].   ff.9.
  typescript.   1937.

465092

Wilson (J.D.) Shakespeare and
   humanity. From Les Langues
   Modernes, 41e Annee, No.3.pp.
   [7.]

1947.

598382

WILSON (JOHN DOVER)

Shakespeare's happy comedies.
                               1962.

667384

WILSON (JOHN DOVER)
Shakespeare's Richard III and The True
Tragedy of Richard the Third, 1594.
IN SHAKESPEARE QUARTERLY III: 4.
pp. 299-306.
(New York) 1952.

605711

WILSON (JOHN DOVER)
Shakespeare's 'small Latin' - how
much?   IN SHAKESPEARE SURVEY 10.
(Cambridge)   1957.

665485

Wilson (J.D.) Shakespeare's universe.
[With bibliographical notes.] pp.[18.]
From University of Edinburgh
Journal, Vol.11.

(Edinburgh)   1942.

536116

Wilson (J.D.) The Study of Shakespeare. From University of Edinburgh
Journal, Summer Number, 1936.

(Edinburgh)

515199

WILSON (JOHN DOVER)
The Text of the plays [of Shakespeare]:
talk [broadcast] 20th July 1949.
ff. 9.
typescript.
Shakespeare and his world.

605267

Wilson (J.D.) "They sleepe all the act."
From Review of English Studies, vol.4.

1928.

497598

Wilson (J.D.) Thirteen volumes of
Shakespeare ["The New Shakspeare"]:
a retrospect. In The Modern Language
Review, Vol.25.

(Cambridge)   1930.

379829

WILSON (JOHN DOVER)
"Titus Andronicus" on the stage in
1595. [bibliog.]   IN SHAKESPEARE
SURVEY 1. (Cambridge)   1948.

590674

WILSON (JOHN DOVER)
Variations on the theme of "A
Midsummer night's dream".   IN
Tribute to Walter De La Mare on
his seventy-fifth birthday [by
various authors].   1948.

594622

WILSON (JOHN DOVER)
What happens in Hamlet.   (Cambridge)
                       1935.   441025
_____ [With a letter to the author
from H. Child.]   2nd edn.
                       1937.   479404
_____ 3rd edn.   1951.   623324

WILSON (JOHN DOVER) [ed.]
Life in Shakespeare's England: a
book of Elizabethan prose.   [With
a preface, a glossary and notes by
the editor.]   2nd edn.
(Harmondsworth)
port.   illus.   facsimiles.   1944.
Pelican Books.

551817

WILSON (JOHN DOVER) [ed.]
Through Elizabethan eyes: an abridge-
ment of Life in Shakespeare's England,
for junior readers.   [An anthology.]
(Cambridge)
illus.   1939.

506256

Wilson, John Dover *works relating to*

—— ALEXANDER (P.)
[Review of] The Fortunes of Falstaff,
by J. D. Wilson.   IN The Modern
Language Review, Vol. 39.
(Cambridge)   1944.

563897

—— ALEXANDER (P.)
The Text of Hamlet.   [A Review of
the works on Hamlet by J. D. Wilson.]
IN The Review of English Studies,
Vol. 12.   1936.

463694

—— BASKERVILL (C. R.)
[Review of] The Tragedy of Hamlet,
Prince of Denmark.   Edited by
J. D. Wilson.   FROM Modern Philology,
Vol. 33.   (Cambridge, Ill.)
                       1935.

492294

—— BLISS (W.)
Hamlet, Ophelia - Mr. Wilson [: a
review of "What happens in Hamlet",
by J. D. Wilson].   FROM The Month,
March, 1936.   1936.

450641

—— CHILD (H. [H.])
[Review of] What happens in "Hamlet",
by J. D. Wilson, 1935.   IN Child
(H. [H.]) Essays and reflections.
(Cambridge)   1948.

595335

—— [DENT (A.)]
Books and authors [including a review
of Henry V, edited by J. D. Wilson,
in "The New Shakespeare"] by A. Dent.
[Broadcast] 23rd April, 1947.
ff. 14.
typescript.

583272

—— Dodds (W.M.T.) [Review of] King
Henry IV: Parts I and II, edited
by J.D.Wilson. In The Modern
Language Review, Vol.42.

(Cambridge)   1947.

266816/42

_____ EMPSON (WILLIAM)
Dover Wilson on Macbeth.   IN Kenyon
Review, Vol. 14.   (Gambier, Ohio)
1952.

594031/14

_____ EMPSON (WILLIAM)
Falstaff and Mr. Dover Wilson.
IN The Kenyon Review, Vol. 15.
(Gambier, Ohio)   1953.

594031/15

___ EMPSON (WILLIAM)
Some problems in Shakespeare, 1:
Macbeth and Professor Dover Wilson.
Produced by G. Phelps.   [Broadcast]
21st February, 1953.   ff. 12.
typescript.

634507

___ ["The Essential Shakespeare": a
review in] Memorabilia.   IN Notes
and Queries, Vol. 162, No. 18.
1932.

401808

___ FRICKER (ROBERT)
The New Shakespeare: "Henry VI"
edited by J. D. Wilson [: review].
IN English Studies, Vol. 37.
(Amsterdam)   1956.

485643/37

___ GAY (A. A.)
The Fencing match in Hamlet [: a
criticism of "What happens in Hamlet",
by J. D. Wilson.]   IN The Review of
English studies, Vol. 13.   [1937.]

479772

___ Gray (H.D.) [Reply to Hamlet Q1 and
Mr. Henry David Gray, by J. D.
Wilson]. _In_ Publications of the
Modern Language Association of
America, Vol. 43.

1928.

428363

___ GREG (W. W.)
Re-enter Ghost: a reply to J. D.
Wilson.   IN The Modern Language
Review, Vol. 14.   1919.

283257

___ GREG (W. W.)
Review [of] The Works of Shakespeare,
edited for the Syndics of the
Cambridge University Press by
Sir A. [T.] Quiller-Couch and J. D.
Wilson.   Vol. 1. The Tempest.
Reprinted from the Modern Language
Review. Vol. 17.   [1922.]

554224

___ GREG (W. W.)
What happens in "Hamlet"?: an open
letter [to J. D. Wilson].   IN The
Modern Language Review, Vol. 31.
1936.

463704

___ GRIFFITHS (G. S.)
Professor Dover Wilson's Falstaff
[: review of] The Fortunes of
Falstaff, by J. D. Wilson. IN
English: the magazine of the English
Association, Vol. 5.   (Oxford)
1944-45.

569018

___ GROOT (H. de)
[Reviews of] William Shakespeare,
by T. M. Parrott, A Companion to
Shakespeare studies, edited by
H. Granville-Barker and G. B. Harrison,
The Essential Shakespeare, by J. D.
Wilson, and On reading Shakespeare,
by L. P. Smith.   IN English studies,
Vol. 18.   (Amsterdam)   1936.

485660

___ Knight (G.W.) The Essential Shakespeare,
by J.D. Wilson: [a review]. In The
Criterion, Vol.12, 1932.

1932-33.

414720

___ KOSZUL (A. [H.])
[Review of] J. D. Wilson's "What
happens in Hamlet".   1935.   IN
English Studies, Vol. 20.   (Amsterdam)
1938.

495114

___ LEISHMAN (J. B.)
[Review of] The Fortunes of Falstaff,
by J.D. Wilson.   IN The Review of
English Studies, Vol. 20.   (Oxford)
[1944.]

562839

___ Memorabilia [including a review of
"The Essential Shakespeare", by
J. D. Wilson].   IN Notes and
Queries, Vol. 162, No. 18.   1932.

401808

___ MILLAR (J. S. L.)
Some Shakespeare doubts, addressed to
J. D. Wilson [in reply to his article,
"Treasure in an old book", published
in the Edinburgh Evening News,
5th August, 1943, concerning the finding
of a volume containing a signature
purporting to be that of Shakespeare].
pp. 12.   [Edinburgh]   [1943.]
For above article see pp. 208-9 of
Newspaper cuttings: Shakespeare
biography, 1938.   (Catal. no. 478561)

546576

___ PARROTT (T. M.)
[Review of] What happens in Hamlet,
by J. D. Wilson; Hamlet, edited by
J. D. Wilson; and The Manuscript of
Shakespeare's Hamlet and the problems
of its transmission, by J. D. Wilson.
IN Modern language notes, Vol. 52.
(Baltimore)   1937.

479896

— POLLARD (A. W.)
[Review of] William Shakespeare. The
Tragedie of Hamlet, Prince of Denmarke.
Edited by J. D. Wilson. IN The Library,
4th series, vol. 12.

1932.

393825

— POLLARD (A. W.)
[Review of] The Works of Shakespeare.
Edited for the Syndics of the Cambridge
University Press by Sir A. [T.] Quiller-
Couch and J. D. Wilson. [Vol. 1.] The
Tempest. IN The Library, 4th series,
Vol. 2.

1922.

298823

— PYLES (T.)
Rejected Q2 readings in the New
Shakespeare Hamlet, [edited by J. D.
Wilson: a review]. IN ELH: a journal
of English literary history, Vol. 4.
1937.

483008

— RYLANDS (G. [H. W.])
Shakespearian detection. [Review of]
What happens in Hamlet, by J. Dover
Wilson. IN The New Statesman and
Nation, vol. 10 (New Series). 1935.

445577

— Tannenbaum (S.A.) How not to edit
Shakspere: a review [of "The
'New' Cambridge Shakespeare",
edited by Sir A. Quiller-Couch
and J.D. Wilson.] From Philological
Quarterly, vol.10.

(Iowa)   1931.

442561

— Theobald (B.G.) "The Essential
Shakespeare" by [J.] D. Wilson : a
commentary. pp. 8.

[1938.]

(Bacon Society)

506945

[WILSON (JOHN DOVER) and BLISS (W.)]
The Joy of editing Shakespeare [: a
report of J. D. Wilson's broadcast
talk and correspondence between
J. D. Wilson and W. Bliss]. IN
The Listener, Vol. 38.   1947.

589226

WILSON (JOHN DOVER) and POLLARD (A. W.)
What follows if some of the good
quarto editions of Shakespeare's plays
were printed from his autograph
manuscripts. IN Transactions of the
Bibliographical Society, Vol. 15.
1920.

294089

WILSON (JOHN DOVER) and POLLARD (ALFRED
WILLIAM)
William Shakespeare. IN GARVIN
(KATHARINE) ed., The Great Tudors.
1935.

431775

WILSON (JOHN DOVER) and WORSLEY (THOMAS
CUTHBERT)
Shakespeare's histories at Stratford,
1951. Photographs by A. McBean.
illus.   1952.

624931

Wilson (John Dover) and Yardley (May) eds.
LAVATER (L.)
Of ghostes and spirites walking by
nyght, 1572. With introduction ["The
Ghost-scenes in Hamlet in the light of
Elizabethan spiritualism" by J. D.
Wilson] and Appendix ["The Catholic
position in the ghost controversy of
the sixteenth century with special
reference to Pierre Le Loyer's IIII
Livres des Spectres (1586)" by May
Yardley.] (Oxford)   1929.
Shakespeare Association.

362498

Wilson (L.) Six portraits from
Shakespeare, arranged with
commentary, notes and questions.
Illus.

1947.

588287

WILSON (MARION L. and J. H.)
The Tragedy of Hamlet told by Horatio;
with the full text of Shakespeare's
Hamlet. (Enschede)
ports. illus. map. plans. dgms.
facsimiles.   1956.

665634

Wilson (Molly) illus.
BRANSOM (LAURA)
Living Shakespeare: teachers'
companion [: scenes suitable for
acting by children.]   1953-
For "Living Shakespeare [: the
stories of the plays]" see Catal. no.
604746.

636356

WILSON (N. C.) Shakespeare Club: see
Societies and Clubs.

WILSON (R.)
"Macbeth" on film [: the Mercury
Theatre's production]. IN Theatre
Arts, Vol. 33. (New York)
illus.   1949.

320431/33

WILSON (RICHARD) ed.
The Approach to Shakespeare [:
selections from the plays, stories
from the plays, and sources]. With
an introduction by Mrs. A. Lang.
port. illus.   1938.
For "Approach to Shakespeare" edited
by Mrs. A. Lang see Lang (Mrs. A.)
For "A Further Approach to Shakespeare"
see Holmdahl (Freda).

476753

WILSON (ROBERT H.)
The Mariana plot of Measure for
Measure.   FROM Philological
Quarterly, vol. 9.   (Iowa) 1930.

442560

WILSON (RONALD ALFRED)
The Pre-war biographies of R. Rolland,
and their place in his work and the
period.   [With references to
Shakespeare.] (St. Andrews)
  bibliog.   1939.
St. Andrews University Publications.

507298

WILSON (STANLEY) composer
'This royal throne', for chorus,
orchestra and organ.   Words by
Shakespeare [from Richard II].
Music by S. Wilson.   To which is
added a verse of the National Anthem.
pp. 15.   1952.

631057

Wilson, Thomas Sir *works relating to*

— Craig (H.) Shakespeare and Wilson's
    "Arte of Rhetorique": an inquiry
    into the criteria for determining
    sources. From Studies in Philology,
    vol.28.
                  (Baltimore   1931.

441592

Wilson (Violet A.) Queen Elizabeth's
    maids of honour and ladies of the
    Priory Chamber [containing a chapter
    on Mary Fytton]. Ports.

                                 1923.

413618

WILSON (WINIFRED GRAHAM)
Welshmen in Elizabethan London.
[With references to Shakespeare.]
FROM Life and letters today, [Vol.
41].
  bibliog.   1944.

550792

Wimsatt (William Kurtz) ed.
JOHNSON (SAMUEL)
Samuel Johnson on Shakespeare.
Edited, with an introduction, by
W. K. Wimsatt, Jr.
  bibliog.   1960.
Dramabooks.

666718

WINCHCOMBE, GEORGE and BERNARD
Shakespeare's ghost-writer(s).
(Esher)   1968.

774419

WINCHESTER COLLEGE SHAKSPERE SOCIETY
Noctes Shaksperianae. A series of
papers by late and present members,
edited by C.H. Hawkins. Re-issue for
the Quingentenary. (Winchester) 1893.

668479

WINCOR (RICHARD)
Shakespeare's Festival Plays.
IN SHAKESPEARE QUARTERLY I: 4.
pp. 219-240.
(New York)   1950.

605711

WINDLE ([Sir] BERTRAM COGHILL ALAN)
Shakespeare's country.   Illustrated
by E. H. New.   3rd edn.
  map.   plan.   1907. 576554
The Little Guides.
_____ 4th edn.   1911. 467565
_____ 6th edn.   1923. 399299

WINDOLPH (FRANCIS LYMAN)
Reflections of the law in literature
[: Trollope, Shakespeare, Browning].
pp. 83.   (Philadelphia, Pa.)
                                 1956.

657193

Windows in Shakespeare

— TILLOTSON (KATHLEEN)
    'Windows' in Shakespeare.   IN The
    Review of English Studies, Vol. 17.
    (Oxford)
                                 1941.

533231

— TILLOTSON (KATHLEEN)
    Appendix: Windows in Shakespeare.
    IN TILLOTSON (G.) Essays in[English
    literary] criticism and research.
    (Cambridge)
                                 1942.

531163

WINDROSS (RONALD)
The Story of As you like it, abridged
and simplified.   2nd edn.   pp. 29.
[Paris]
  illus.   [1947.]
Tales from England, 2nd Degree, No.4.

588250

WINDROSS (RONALD)
The Story of Macbeth abridged and
simplified.   pp. 22.   [Paris]
  illus.   [1944.]
Tales from England, 2nd Degree, No. 3.

588249

WINDROSS (RONALD)
Two comedies: Much ado about nothing;
The Winter's tale. The stories of
these abridged and simplified.
Illustrated by M. Abauzit. (Paris:
Marcel Didier)   1962.
  Tales from England, 3rd Degree, No. 31.

                    668153

WINDROSS (RONALD)
Three comedies [of] W. Shakespeare:
A Midsummer night's dream;   The
Tempest; [and] As you like it.
Abridged and simplified.   Illus-
trated by G. Irwin.   pp. 78.
(Paris)   [1952.]
  Tales from England, 2nd Degree,
  No. 3.
                    631615

WINDROSS (RONALD)
Three Mediterranean plays:
Shakespeare's Romeo and Juliet; The
Merchant of Venice; [and,] Twelfth
Night.   Abridged and simplified.
Illustrated by G. Irwin.   pp. 80.
(Paris)   [1952.]
  Tales from England, 2nd Degree,
  No. 4.
                    635256

WINDROSS (RONALD)

Two tragedies: Othello [and] Hamlet;
abridged and simplified. Illustrated
by H. Breton. (Tales from England)
(Didier, Paris)   1961.

                    667330

Windsor

— Bolitho ([H.] H.) The Romance of
    Windsor Castle. [With references to
    Shakespeare.] Illus. Plan.

                [1946.]

                    581070

— HEDLEY, OLWEN
    Shakespeare's Windsor. FROM The
    Berkshire Archaeological Journal, Vol.61,
    (1963-4). pp.74-78. (Reading) 1964.

        illus.   746656

— Herne's Oak.   IN The Penny Magazine,
    [Vol. 11.]   New Series.
      illus.   1842.

                    132

— JESSE (E.)
    The Identity of Herne's Oak.
    FROM The Gentleman's Magazine,
    [New Series] Vol. 13.   1840.

                    521907

— M. (J.)
    Herne's Oak [: a poem].   FROM
    The Gentleman's Magazine, [New
    Series] Vol. 13.   1840.

                    521907

— PERRY (W.)
    A Treatise on the identity of
    Herne's Oak, shewing the maiden
    tree to have been the real one.
    pp. xii, 70.
      illus.   1867.
    Presentation copy bound with a panel
    of wood from the Oak on front cover.

                    474046

— PLANTAGENET [pseud.]
    Herne's Oak, Windsor Little Park.
    FROM The Gentleman's Magazine,
    [New Series] Vol. 13.
      illus.   1840.

                    521907

Wine *see* Drink and Drunkenness

[WINGE (J. H.)]
Macbeth, directed by Orson Welles,
a Mercury production for Republic:
records of the film, No. 20,
published by the British Film
Institute.   pp. [4.]   [1949.]

                    590201

Winkle (Edward S. Van) see
Van Winkle (Edward S.)

WINNER (THOMAS G.)
Chekhov's "Seagull" and Shakespeare's
"Hamlet": a study of a dramatic
device.   IN The American Slavic and
East European Review, Vol. 15. (New
York)   1956.

                    574890/15

WINNY, JAMES
The master-mistress: a study of
Shakespeare's sonnets.   1968.

                    775734

WINNY, JAMES
    The player king: a theme of
    Shakespeare's histories.   1968.

                    770967

WINSHIP (G. P.)
The First Harvard playwright: a
bibliography of the Restoration
dramatist John Crowne, with extracts
from his Prefaces and the earlier
version of the Epilogue to Sir
Courtly Nice, 1685.   [Containing
references to Crowne's alterations
of Shakespeare's Henry VI.]   pp. 22.
(Cambridge, [Mass.])   1922.

                    527318

Winslow (L.[S.] F.) Mad humanity: its
forms, apparent and obscure. [With
references to Shakespeare]. Port.
Illus.

                    1898.

                    518630

Winsor (J.) Halliwelliana: an annotated
list of publications, written or
edited by J.O. Halliwell- Phillipps.
In Harvard College Library. Bulletins,
Vols. 1-2, Nos.12-19. 2 vols.

[Cambridge,Mass.] 1879-81.

14250

Winsor (J.) Shakespeare's poems: a biblio-
graphy of the earlier editions. In
Harvard College Library. Bulletins,
Vol.1, Nos 9 and 10.

[Cambridge,Mass.] 1878-79.

14250

WINSTANLEY (L[ILIAN])
Tolstoy [: a biography. With
references to Shakespeare.] pp. 96.
port. bibliog. [1914]
People's Books.

460087

WINSTANLEY (W.)
The Life of Mr. Wil. Shakespeare.
IN England's worthies: select lives
of the most eminent persons of the
English nation.
ports. 1684.

53456

WINTER (WILLIAM)
Henry Irving [: a record of his
professional career upon the New
York stage.] (New-York)
ports. 1885.

498880

Winter (W.) Romeo and Juliet;
Shakspere on the stage. Ports.
In The Century Magazine, Vol.87.

(New York) 1914.

251086

Winter (W.) Shadows of the stage.
[With references to Shakespeare's
plays and Shakespearean actors.
First and] second series.

(Edinburgh and New York)
1892-3.

491430

WINTER (WILLIAM)
Shakespeare's England. (Boston, Mass.)
1890. 450765
_____ Author's edn. (Edinburgh)
1891. 496258
_____ Author's edn. (Edinburgh)
1894. 565610
_____ New edn. 1902. 420262
(New York)
ports. illus. 1910. 627562

Winter (W.) The Stage life of Mary
Anderson. Port.

(New York) 1886.

431985

Winter (W.) Twelfth night; Shakspere on the stage. Ports.
In The Century Magazine, Vol.88.

(New York) 1914.

256528

Winter (W.) Vagrant memories, being
further recollections of other days
[: reminiscences of American and
English actors. With references to
Shakespeare.] Ports.

1916.

449553

WINTERICH (JOHN TRACY)
Early American books & printing.
[With reference to the first American
edition of Shakespeare.] (Boston)
illus. facsimiles. 1935.

490472

WINTERS (YVOR)
Poetic style in Shakespeare's sonnets.
IN HERRNSTEIN (BARBARA) ed., Discussions
of Shakespeare's sonnets [by various
writers]. (Boston) 1964.
Discussions of literature.

748157

The Winter's Tale
General Works and Criticism
Music
Poems
Sources and Background
Stage History and Production
Study and Teaching; Tales
Textual History

The Winter's Tale
— General Works and Criticism

—— BARBER, CHARLES
'The Winter's Tale' and Jacobean
society. IN KETTLE, ARNOLD, ed.,
Shakespeare in a changing world:
essays [by various authors]. 1964.

667797

—— BETHELL (S. L.)
The Winter's Tale: a study. (New
York)
bibliog. [1947.]

584471

—— BONJOUR (ADRIEN)
The Final scene of the Winter's tale.
IN English Studies, Vol. 33.
(Amsterdam)
1952.

485643/33

—— BRYANT (J. A.)
Shakespeare's allegory: "The Winter's
tale". IN The Sewanee Review, Vol.
63. (Sewanee, Tenn.) 1955.

641628/63

—— BRYANT (JERRY H.)
The Winter's tale and the pastoral
tradition. IN SHAKESPEARE QUARTERLY
XIV: 4. pp. 387-398. (New York)
1963.

605711

—— COGHILL (NEVILL)
Six points of stage-craft in "The
Winter's tale". IN SHAKESPEARE
SURVEY 11. (Cambridge)
bibliog. 1958.

665816

—— COTTRELL (BEEKMAN W.)
The Winter's tale. IN "Lovers
meeting": discussions of five plays
by Shakespeare. (Pittsburgh:
Carnegie Institute of Technology)
1964.

741508

—— EWBANK, INGA-STINA
The Triumph of time in 'The Winter's
tale'. FROM Review of English
Literature, V, 2. pp.83-100. 1964.

745003

—— FRYE (NORTHROP)
Recognition in "The Winter's tale".
IN Essays on Shakespeare and Eliza-
bethan drama in honour of Hardin
Craig.
illus. 1963.

667532

—— GOKAK (V. K.)
The Structure of daffodils in 'The
Winter's tale'[: flower imagery in
this play]. IN The Literary
Criterion, Special number on
Shakespeare. Vol. 6, Winter, No. 1.
(Bombay) pp. 137-152. 1963.

756155

—— HALL (W. C.)
Did Shakespeare write the chorus
in "The Winter's tale"? IN
Manchester Literary Club, Papers,
Vol. 45. (Manchester) 1919.

518396

—— HART (EDWARD L.)
A Mixed consort: Leontes, Angelo, Helena.
IN Shakespeare Quarterly XV: 1.
pp.75-83. (New York) 1964.

605711

—— HOENIGER (F. DAVID)
The Meaning of The Winter's tale.
IN The University of Toronto Quarterly,
Vol. 20. (Toronto)
1950-51.

596179/20

—— HOLBROOK (DAVID)
The Quest for love [: the theme of
love in English literature, with
special reference to the work of
Chaucer, Shakespeare, and D. H.
Lawrence].
illus. 1964.
Includes a chapter "Love and continuity
in The Winter's tale".

728699

—— Jusserand (J.J.) Winter's Tale. In
Jusserand (J.J.) The School for ambassadors, and other essays. Frontis.

(New York) 1925.

485228

—— Lancaster (H.C.) Hermione's statue.
From Studies in Philology, Vol.29.

(Chapel Hill) 1932.

453874

—— MARTIN (HELENA FAUCIT [Lady])
On Hermione. pp. 70. [London]
[1890]
Privately printed. Signed by the
author.

470936

—— MUIR, KENNETH, ed.
Shakespeare, 'The Winter's tale':
a casebook. 1968.
Casebook series.

770146

—— NATHAN, NORMAN
Leontes' provocation.
IN SHAKESPEARE QUARTERLY XIX: 1.
pp. 19-24. (New York)
1968.

605711

—— NEWCASTLE (W. CAVENDISH, [1st] Duke of)
A Pleasante & merrye humor off a
roge. [Edited with a prefatory
note by F. Needham, referring to
likenesses in the play to The Winter's
tale and Much ado about nothing.]
pp. [46]. (Bungay) 1933.
Welbeck Miscellany.

431337

—— NUTTALL, A.D.
William Shakespeare "The Winter's Tale".
1966.

Studies in English Literature,
No.26.
755389

—— POGSON (BERYL)

The Winter's Tale: an esoteric
interpretation.pp.18.

[c.1955.]

665844

—— RASHBROOK (R. F.)
The Winter's tale, V, i, 58-60.
IN Notes and Queries, Vol. 192.
1947.

588005

——SCHANZER, ERNEST
The Structural pattern of 'The Winter's
tale'. From Review of English
Literature, V: 2. pp. 72-82. 1964.

744999

—— SCOTT (WILLIAM O.)
Seasons and Flowers in "The Winter's
Tale".
IN SHAKESPEARE QUARTERLY XIV: 4.
pp. 411-417.
(New York) 1963.

605711

—— SIEGEL (PAUL N.   )

Leontes, a jealous tyrant. Reprint
FROM The Review of English Studies.
N.S. Vol.1, No.4, Oct.1950.
1950.

668456

—— SMITH (HALLETT D.)
Leontes' Affectio.
IN SHAKESPEARE QUARTERLY XIV: 2.
pp. 163-166.
(New York) 1963.

605711

—— SMITH, JONATHAN
The Language of Leontes.
IN SHAKESPEARE QUARTERLY XIX: 4.
pp. 317-327.
(New York) 1968.

605711

——TILLYARD (E. M. W.)
Shakespeare's last plays: [Cymbeline,
The Winter's tale, and The Tempest.]
pp. 85.
1938.

476626

—— TINKLER (F. C.)
"The Winter's tale".   IN Scrutiny,
Vol. 5.   (Cambridge)   1936-7.

469479

—— TRAVERSI, DEREK ANTONA
The Winter's tale.   IN MUIR, KENNETH,
ed., Shakespeare, the comedies: a
collection of critical essays.
(Englewood Cliffs, N.J.)   1965.

748348

—— TRIENENS (ROGER J.)
The Inception of Leontes' jealousy in
The Winter's Tale.
IN SHAKESPEARE QUARTERLY IV: 3.
pp. 321-326.
(New York)   1953.

605711

—— Walters (J.C.) A Shakespearean
sisterhood: Imogen, Desdemona and
Hermione. In Manchester Literary
Club. Papers, Vol.32.

(Manchester)   1906.

518389

—— WILLIAMS, JOHN ANTHONY
The Natural work of art: the
experience of romance in Shakespeare's
'Winter's Tale.' (Cambridge, Mass.)
1967.

LeBaron Russell Briggs Prize.
Honors essays in English, 1966.
763814

The Winter's Tale

— Music

—— PAFFORD (J. H. P.)
Music, and the songs in The Winter's
Tale.
IN SHAKESPEARE QUARTERLY X: 2.
pp. 161-175.
(New York)   1959.

605711

The Winter's Tale

— Poems

—— MARTIN (J. S.)
A Winter's tale; and , Falstaff [:
poems].   IN Poetry of To-Day,
[New Series, Vol. 18].   1945.

319077/N.S./18

The Winter's Tale

— Sources and Background

—— BAUGHAN (D. E.)
Shakespeare's probable confusion
of the two Romanos.   FROM The
Journal of English and Germanic
Philology, Vol. 36.   (Urbana, Ill.)
1937.

488674

—— GREENE (R.)
Pandosto; or, The Triumph of time
[: abridged,   The original of
Shakespeare's Winter's tale.]   IN
SHAKESPEARE (W.) The Winter's tale.
[Edited with an introduction by
H. Morley.]   1887.   436524
Cassell's National Library.
_____ Another edn. 1894.   530845
_____ Another edn. 1898.   527776
_____ Another edn. 1901.   545593

—— HONIGMANN (E. A. J.)
Secondary sources of "The Winter's
tale".   IN Philological Quarterly,
Vol. 34.   (Iowa City)   1955.

592684/34

— JACOX (F.)
About the sea-coast of Bohemia: a
vexed question in Shakspearean
geography. FROM [Bentley's
Miscellany,] Vol. 61.
  bibliog.   [1867.]

558109

— LAWLOR, JOHN
Pandosto and the nature of dramatic
romance. FROM Philological Quarterly,
vol.XLI, no.1.   1962.

668391

— MAVEETY, S. R.
What Shakespeare did with "Pandosto":
an interpretation of "The Winter's Tale".
IN Pacific coast studies in Shakespeare.
Edited by W. F. McNeir and T. N.
Greenfield. (Eugene: Ore.) 1966.

768009

— Valentine and Orson. Translated
from the French by H. Watson.
Edited [with an introduction] by
A. Dickson.
  facsimile.   1937.
Early English Text Society, Original
Series, No. 204.
  Regarded as a source book of The
Winter's tale.

467482

The Winter's Tale

— Stage History and Production
*Newspaper reviews, playbills, theatre pro-
grammes and theatrical illustrations — the
library's extensive collection of this material
is mainly uncatalogued but indexed
For texts of stage alterations and adaptations of the play see* ENGLISH EDITIONS,
The Winter's Tale *— Alterations, etc.*

— ARCHER (W.)
"The Winter's tale": a play.
Revived at the Lyceum Theatre, Sept.
10, 1887. FROM The Theatre, New
Series, Vol. 10.   1887.

530836

— BIGGINS (DENNIS)
"Exit pursued by a Beare": a problem
in The Winter's Tale.
IN SHAKESPEARE QUARTERLY XIII: 1.
pp. 3-13.
(New York) 1962.

605711

— INKSTER (L.)
Shakespeare and Mr. Granville Barker [:
a review of his productions of
Twelfth Night and The Winter's tale
at the Savoy]. FROM Poetry and
Drama, Vol. 1.   1913.

520180

— KEMP (T. C.)
The Stratford Festival: review
of The Winter's tale. [Broadcast]
10th June, 1948. ff. 3.
  typescript.

596469

— PROGRAMMES OF SHAKESPEARIAN PERFORMANCES
The Winter's Tale

This collection, which runs from the
latter half of the nineteenth
century, is continuously augmented
by the addition of programmes of
contemporary productions.
                          499174

— THEATRE ROYAL, DRURY LANE
[Programme of performances of]
Macbeth [and] Winter's tale, Oct.-
Nov. 1878, [under the managership
of F. B. Chatterton. With an address
on Drury Lane Theatre and the story of
The Winter's tale by C. L. Kenney.]
pp. 32.   1878.

532018

— WELLS (STANLEY)
Burlesques of Charles Kean's "Winter's
tale". IN Theatre Notebook, Vol. 26.
No. 3. pp. 78-83.
  illus.   1962.

584117/26

— The Winter's tale [at His Majesty's
Theatre]. IN Play pictorial,
Vol. 8.   [1906.]

571870

The Winter's Tale

— Study and Teaching; Tales

— ADAMSON (ELGIVA) and MOORE (KATHLEEN V.)
Notes on William Shakespeare's "The
Winter's tale". pp. 47. [Stratford,
Ontario]   [1958.]

665810

— CARRINGTON (NORMAN THOMAS)
Shakespeare: The Winter's Tale.
(Notes on Chosen English Texts)
pp. 80.
                        [1956]

665240

— COX, G.P.
The Winter's tale (Shakespeare).
(Oxford)   1967.

Notes on English literature.
                        767394

—— PAGE (JOSEPHINE)
The Winter's Tale, retold by
Josephine Page.   pp. vi, 70.
(Oxford)
illus.   1941.
Tales Retold for Easy Reading, Second
Series.

539921

—— PALMER (H. E.)
Four stories from Shakespeare
[including The Winter's tale].
Adapted and rewritten with the
thousand word vocabulary.   Illustrated
by T. H. Robinson.   1937.
Thousand-Word English Senior Series.

463628

—— RANALD, MARGARET LOFTUS
Shakespeare's 'The Winter's tale'.
(New York)   1965.

Monarch critiques of literature.
756295

The Winter's Tale

— Textual History

—— KLEIN (D.)
The Case of Forman's Bocke of Plaies
[: an assertion that the notes on
Winter's tale, Cymbeline and Macbeth
were added by J. P. Collier].
Reprinted for private circulation,
from Philological Quarterly, Vol. 11.
[Iowa]   [1932.]

554208

—— NEILSON (W. A.)
The Variorum Twelfth Night, [by
H. H. Furness.   A review].   IN
The Atlantic Monthly, Vol. 89.
(Cambridge, Mass.)   1902.

170922

—— SOMER (JOHN L.)
Ralph Crane and "an olde play called
Winter's tale".   IN Four studies in
Elizabethan drama, by Roma Ball,
J. C. Pogue, J. L. Somer [and] E. J.
Kettner.   (Kansas State Teachers'
College, Emporia, Kan.)   1962.
Emporia State Research Studies,
Vol. 10, No. 4.

667737

—— TANNENBAUM (S. A.)
Shaksperian scraps and other
Elizabethan fragments.   [Including
a chapter on Ralph Crane and The
Winter's tale.]   (New York)
facsimiles.   1933.

411561

—— THORNDIKE (A. H.)
Influence of the court-masques on
the drama, 1608-15:   [an attempt
to determine the date of The Winter's
Tale.]   IN Publications of the
Modern Language Association of
America, Vol. 15.   (Baltimore)
1900.

428335

Wintringham Secondary School

see: Grimsby

WISE, ARTHUR
Weapons in the theatre [: the problems
of mounting stage fights].
illus.   1968.

777351

WISE (JOHN RICHARD [de CAPEL])
Shakspere: his birthplace and its
neighbourhood.   Illustrated by
W. J. Linton.   1861.
Differs from 63812.

513644

WISE (THOMAS JAMES)
Letters to John Henry Wrenn: a further
inquiry into the guilt of certain
nineteenth-century forgers.   Edited
[with a foreword] by Fannie E.
Ratchford.   [With references to rare
Shakespeare editions.]   (New York)
ports. illus. facsimiles. 1944.

561530

WISHART (PETER)
Two songs.   Dirge [: Fear no more
the heat of the sun, from Shakespeare's
"Cymbeline"; and, The Mountebank's
song].   pp. 7.   1953.

638093

WISTER (OWEN)
From a lover of Shakespeare and of
England.
IN GOLLANCZ ([Sir] I.) ed., A Book
of homage to Shakespeare.
ports. illus. facsimiles. [1916.]

264175

Wit and Humour
see also **Puns**

—— CAZAMIAN (LOUIS ROBERT)
The Development of English humor.
(Durham, N.C.)
1952.

633306

— Crane (W.G.) Wit and rhetoric in the Renaissance: the formal basis of Elizabethan prose style. [With a bibliography.]
(New York)   1937.

(Columbia University. Studies in English and Comparative Literature)

481097

— Starkie (W.J.M.) Wit and humour in Shakespeare. In Gollancz ([Sir]I.) ed. A Book of homage to Shakespeare. Ports. Illus. Facsimiles.
[1916.]

264175

— Tilley (M.P.) Pun and proverb as aids to unexplained Shakespearean jests. From Studies in Philology, Vol.21.
(Chapel Hill,N.C.)   1924.

496552

Witches and Witchcraft

— BRIGGS (KATHARINE MARY)
Pale Hecate's team: an examination of the beliefs on witchcraft and magic among Shakespeare's contemporaries and his immediate successors.
illus. bibliog.   1962.

667337

— Fleay (F.G.) Davenant's Macbeth and Shakespeare's witches. From Anglia, Bd. 7, pp.128-144.
[(Halle)]   [1883.]

420948

— GIFFORD (G.)
A Dialogue concerning witches and witchcraftes, 1593. With an introduction by Beatrice [M. I.] White.
bibliog.   1931.
Shakespeare Association Facsimiles, No. 1.

390117

— H[ODGSON] (G[ERALDINE E.])
Macbeth and the "sin of witchcraft". FROM Dublin Review, 1930. pp. [15.]
[1930]

390785

— HOLMES, R.
Shakespeare and witchcraft. FROM Quarterly Review, April 1967.
1967.

pp.179-188.   763355

— JEFFREYS, M.D.W.
The Weird sisters in Macbeth. IN English Studies in Africa, Vol.I. (Johannesburg)
bibliog.   1958.

682610/1

— KAULA (DAVID)
Othello possessed: notes on Shakespeare's use of magic and witchcraft. IN Shakespeare Studies, 2. (Cincinnati, Ohio)   1966.

761781

— A Lyric ode on the fairies, aerial beings and witches of Shakespeare. pp. 18.   1776.
Imperfect.

599045

— McPEEK (JAMES ANDREW SCARBOROUGH)
The "Arts inhibited" and the meaning of "Othello". FROM Boston University, Studies in English, Vol. I. pp. [19.] (Boston, Mass.)
1955.

665671

— MORLEY (G.)
Witch-finders of Shakespeare's greenwood. The last witch-hunt in rural England. IN The Quest, Vol. 9.
1918.

408730

— MOORE, J. MAVOR
Shakespeare and witchcraft. IN Stratford Papers on Shakespeare delivered at the 1961 Shakespeare Seminar. (Toronto)   1962.

668005

— OVERHOLSER (WINIFRED)
Shakespeare's psychiatry - and after. IN SHAKESPEARE QUARTERLY X: 3. pp. 335-352.
(New York)   1959.

605711

— Seaton (Ethel) Richard Galis and the Witches of Windsor. In The Library, Fourth Series, Vol. 18. pp. 268-78.
1938.

(Transactions of the Bibliographical Society, Second Series, Vol. 18)

487688

— The Shakespearan angels and devils: 1. The angels; 2. Fairies and witches. IN The Contemporary Review, Vols. 105 [and] 106. 2 vols.   1914.

251087

— SPALDING (THOMAS ALFRED)
On the witchcraft in Macbeth. IN Transactions of the New Shakespeare Society, Series 1. No. 5. pp. 27-40.
1877-9.

40620

—— THOMPSON (C. J. S.)
The Mysteries and secrets of magic.
[Containing a chapter: Magic in
Shakespeare's plays.]
illus. 1927.

403349

—— WEST (ROBERT HUNTER)
Elizabethan belief in spirits and
witchcraft. IN MATTHEWS (A. D.)
and EMERY (C. M.) eds., Studies in
Shakespeare. (Coral Gables, Fla.)
1953.
University of Miami Publications in
English and American Literature,
Vol. 1, March 1953.

634188

—— The Witches of Shakspeare. FROM
The European Magazine[, Vol. 25].
1794.

564836

WITHER (GEORGE) Works relating to:-
see Moore (W. H.) Baconian Studies.

Withington (L.) Shakespeare - the
old and the new criticism on him. In
Bibliotheca Sacra, Vol.4.
1847.

38604

Withington (R.) The Development of the
"vice" [in drama. With references to
Shakespeare.] In Essays in memory of
Barrett Wendell, by his assistants.
[With bibliographical notes.]

(Cambridge, Mass.) 1926.

524244

WITHINGTON (ROBERT)
Shakespeare and race prejudice.
IN Elizabethan studies and other
essays[, by various authors] in
honor of George F. Reynolds.
(Boulder, Col.)
bibliog. 1945.
Colorado University Studies.
Series B. Studies in the Humanities.
Vol. 2. No. 4.

569202

[WITHYCOMBE (ELIZABETH G.) and GHOSH
(J. C.)]
Annals of English literature, 1475-
1925: the principal publications
of each year, with an alphabetical
index of authors, with their works.
[Including Shakespeare's works.]
(Oxford) 1935.

444042

WITNEY (M. A.)
Francis Bacon. Published by the
Franics Bacon Society. pp. 20.
[1954.]

665279

WITT (W. H.)
Some medical references in Shakespeare.
Read before the Davidson County
Medical Society and Nashville
Academy of Medicine, November 2, 1937.
Reprinted from The Journal of the
Tennessee State Medical Association,
Vol. 31, No. 1. pp. 10. [Nashville]
. [1938.]

526119

WITTE, WILLIAM
Deus Absconditus. IN DUTHIE,
GEORGE IAN, ed., Papers, mainly
Shakespearian. 1964.
Aberdeen University studies.

668205

WITTE (WILLIAM)
Time in 'Wallenstein' and 'Macbeth'.
IN Aberdeen University Review Vol.
34, [No.] 3. pp. 8. (Aberdeen)
1952.

633542

WITTER (GILBERT)
King Henry the Seventh, [or, The
Tragedy of Perkin Warbeck]: (the
missing play). (Oxford: Shakespeare
Head Press) 1933.

435740

WIVELL (ABRAHAM)
An Inquiry into the history, authenticity and characteristics of the
Shakspere portraits. pp. 46.
frontis. facsimiles. 1848.

595514

WODEHOUSE (PELHAM GRENVILLE)
Louder and funnier [: humorous
essays. Including "An Outline
of Shakespeare".] 1932.

390607

WOEHL (ARTHUR L.)
Some plays in the repertories of the
patent houses [i.e. the playhouses
established by Thomas Killigrew and
William Davenant. With references
to plays of Shakespeare.] bibliog.
IN Studies in speech and drama [by
various authors]: in honor of
Alexander M. Drummond. (Ithaca,N.Y.)
1944.

561280

Woffington, Peg *works relating to*

—— READE (C.)
Peg Woffington: a novel.
1853. 510548
——————— With an introduction by
[H.] A. Dobson and illustrations by
H. Thomson. 1899. 387983

WOLFE (HUMBERT)
Portraits by inference. [Containing
a chapter on Sir Henry Irving.]
1934.

426961

Wolfe (Humbert) trans.
LAFOURCADE (G.)
Ode à Shakespeare, [with] an English
version by H. Wolfe.   FROM Poetry
Review, Vol. 20.   [1929.]

358825

Wolff (M.J.) Antonio Conti in seinem
Verhältnis zu Shakespeare. From
The Journal of English and Germanic
Philology, V l. 37.

1938.

503674

WOLFF (M. J.)
[Review of] Shakespeare and the homilies,
and other pieces of research into the
Elizabethan drama, by A. Hart.   FROM
Englische Studien, Bd. 71.   (Leipzig)
1936.

497800

WOLFF (TATIANA A.)
Shakespeare's influence on Pushkin's
dramatic work.   IN SHAKESPEARE
SURVEY 5.   (Cambridge)   1952.

623798

WOLFIT, Sir DONALD
The Bard and I.   Produced by David
Glencross.   B.B.C. radio script
broadcast 2nd March 1964.   1964.

668241

WOLFIT (Sir DONALD)
Hamlet: the actor's view, 2:
Producer J. Davenport. [Broadcast]
24th April, 1954. pp. 10.
   typescript.   [1954.]

643702

Wolfit, Donald Sir *works relating to*

—— Brahms (Caryl) [pscud.]
   Donald Wolfit: a profile. pp.[16.] Ports.
                              [1950.]

609054

—— DOONE (R.)
   Three Shakespearian productions
   [: Hamlet, with John Gielgud,
   Richard III, with Laurence Olivier,
   and King Lear, with Donald Wolfit].
   illus.   IN The Penguin New Writing,
   25.   (Harmondsworth)   1945.

564884

—— HALL, Sir JULIAN
   Donald Wolfit: a memoir with illustrations from his radio performances.
   Produced by C. Holme.   B.B.C. radio
   script broadcast 5th October 1968.
      typescript.   1968.

775436

—— Hope-Wallace (P.)

   Shakespeare season: Donald Wolfit [at the]
   Scala [London]. In Time and Tide, Vol.25.
                              1944.

562807

Women

—— ASQUITH (CYNTHIA) [ed.]
   She walks in beauty: descriptions
   of feminine beauty in English prose
   and poetry.   [With introduction,
   and quotations from Shakespeare.]
                              1934.

429538

—— A Baconian on Shakespeare's women.
   IN MARTIN (Sir T.) Essays on the
   drama.   Second series.   1889.
   Printed for private circulation.

432010

—— BARRIE (Sir JAMES M.)
   "The Ladies' Shakespeare": the
   substance of a speech by Sir J. M.
   Barrie, O.M., delivered at Stationers'
   Hall upon the occasion of his
   receiving the Freedom of the
   Stationers' Company, 3rd July, 1925.
   pp. 7.   1938.
    Privately printed.   Edn. limited to
   25 copies.

484135

—— BAXTER (ALICE M.) and PRIESTLEY (E.)
   Shakespearian women [: a musical
   drama, utilizing songs of Shakespeare
   and extracts from his plays].
   pp. 16.   [1949.]
    Macdonald Drama Library: Miniature
   Musical Dramas.

599925

—— BROOKS, CHARLES
   Shakespeare's heroine-actresses.
   IN SHAKESPEARE JAHRBUCH.   Bd. 96/1960.
   pp. 134-144.   (Heidelberg)

10531

—— BROOKS (CHARLES)
   Shakespeare's romantic shrews.
   IN SHAKESPEARE QUARTERLY XI.
   pp. 351-356.
   (New York) 1960.

605711

— CAMDEN (CARROLL)
 The Elizabethan woman: a panorama
 of English womanhood, 1540 to 1640.
 illus. bibliog. 1952.

 629535

— CAMDEN (C.)
 Iago on women. IN The Journal of
 English and Germanic Philology,
 Vol. 48. (Urbana, Ill.) 1949.

 600780/48

— CHESTERTON (GILBERT KEITH)
 A Handful of authors: essays on
 books and writers. Edited by
 Dorothy Collins. 1953.
 Includes a chapter "The Heroines of
 Shakespeare".

 635519

— CLARKE ([Mrs.] MARY [V.] C.)
 The Girlhood of Shakespeare's
 heroines, in a series of tales.
 2nd series. (New York)
 port. illus. 1854.
 Cover title reads, The Shakespeare
 Gift Book.

 498114

— DAVIES (M.)
 Shakespeare heroines [: poems].
 FROM [The New Monthly Magazine,]
 Vol[s]. 5[-6. New Series.] [1874.]

 558100

— Davies (W.R.) Shakespeare's boy actors
 [in the women's roles. With bibliography.] Ports. Illus.

 1939.

 493441

— GOWING (Mrs. A.)
 The Graphic Gallery of Shakespeare's
 heroines. Olivia – Cleopatra –
 Miranda. IN The Theatre, Vol. 12.
 1888.

 99108

— HARRISON (W. G.)
 Some of the women of Shakespeare: an
 essay read before the Chit Chat Club
 of San Francisco, May 9, 1898.
 pp. 38. (San Francisco) 1898.

 549093

— HAZLITT (WILLIAM)
 Shakespear's female characters.
 IN Hazlitt (W.) Complete works,
 edited by P. P. Howe, vol. 20.
 1934.
 This edition is limited to 1000 sets.

 421821

— HEATH (C.)
 The Shakspeare gallery, containing the
 principal female characters in the plays.
 Engraved from drawings by the first
 artists, under the direction of C. Heath.
 [1837]

 476424

— HEINE [H.]
 Shakespeares Mädchen und Frauen.
 IN Heines Werke, Vol. 10. (Berlin)
 [1908.]
 [Bongs] Goldene Klassiker-Bibliothek.

 575486

— HUEFFER (F. [H.] M.)
 The Critical attitude [: essays,
 including references to the women
 in Shakespeare's plays]. 1911.

 569918

— IRWIN (C. H.)
 Three of Shakespeare's heroines [:
 Volumnia, Isabella and Cordelia.]
 FROM [Girl's Own Paper, Vol. 20].
 illus. [1899.]

 550797

— JAIN (S. A.)
 Shakespeare's conception of ideal
 womanhood. (Madras) 1948.

 599166

— JAMESON (Mrs. [ANNA B.])
 Characteristics of women, moral, poetical,
 and historical. 3rd edn., corrected
 and enlarged.
 illus. 2 vols. 1835. 520870
 ——— 4th edn. 1846. 391945
 ——— Another copy. 1858. 391947
 ——— Young Lady's Library. 1 vol.
 [c.1880] 574407

— JAPP (A. H.)
 Lady Martin's Female characters of
 Shakespeare. FROM The Gentleman's
 Magazine, May, 1885. 1885.

 440304

— Kendall (L.J.) Shakespeare and
 women's place in civilized society.
 In The Poetry Review, Vol. 5.

 1914.

 255955

— LANG (G.) [ed.]
 Mirror to woman [: an anthology of
 quotations about women, including
 quotations from Shakespeare.]
 pp. 93.
 illus. [1944.]

 553054

— LEECH, CLIFFORD
 **Venus and her nun: portraits of women
 in love by Shakespeare and Marlowe.**
 FROM Studies in English literature
 1500-1900, Vol.5, No.2. (Houston, Tex.)
 1965.

 pp.247-268. 753395

— LEWES (L.)
 The Women of Shakespeare. Translated from the German [with a preface]
 by Helen Zimmern. (New York) 1895.

 473608

— McCORMICK (VIRGINIA T.)
 Women and love, as Shakespeare sees
 them. FROM The Catholic World,
 Vol. 150. (New York) 1939.

 530207

McNEAL (THOMAS H.)
Shakespeare's cruel queens.   bibliog.
IN The Huntington Library Quarterly,
Vol. 22.   1958.

494029/22

MEYNELL ([Mrs.] ALICE)
Heroines.
IN GOLLANCZ ([Sir] I.) ed., A Book
of homage to Shakespeare.
ports. illus. facsimiles. [1916.]

264175

PEARSON ([Mrs.] LU EMILY)
Elizabethan widows.   [With references
to Shakespeare.]   IN Stanford
Studies in Language and Literature,
1941.   Edited by H. Craig.   ([Palo
Alto,] Cal.)
bibliog.   1941.

537291

RUSKIN (J.)
The Queenly power of women.   [With
references to Shakespeare's
characters].   IN International
University Society's Reading Course:
text matter and biographical studies.
[Section 3.]   (Nottingham)   [1936]

465268

SPENCER, TERENCE JOHN BEW
Shakespeare and the noble woman.
IN DEUTSCHE SHAKESPEARE-GESELLSCHAFT
WEST, JAHRBUCH 1966.   pp. 49-62.
(Heidelberg)

754129

TERRY ([Dame] ELLEN)
Four lectures on Shakespeare
[including "The Triumphant women"
and "The Pathetic women".]   Edited,
with an introduction by [Miss]
Christopher St. John.
port.   1932.

391411

UTLEY (F. L.)
The Crooked rib: an analytical index
to the argument about women in English
and Scots literature to the end of the
year 1568.   [With references to
Shakespeare.]   (Columbus: Ohio State
University)   1944.

559112

WEST (A. L.)
Shades of Shakespeare's women: entertainment in ten scenes.   pp. 32.
1896.

395830

WILLIAMS (S.) ed.
Woman: an anthology for men [including
extracts from Shakespeare relating to
women.]   [1942.]

538435

The Women of Shakspeare: Portia;
Beatrice; Isabella.   FROM The
Englishwoman's Domestic Magazine[,
Aug., Sept., and Nov. 1872.]   [1872.]

557124

WOOD (B. H.)
Shakespeare [:   a poem].   IN The
Central Literary Magazine, Vol. 32,
July, 1935.   (Birmingham)
1936.   463922
_____ Another copy.   465871

WOOD (FREDERIC HERBERT)
Come unto these yellow sands: unison
song.   [Words from] The Tempest.
Music by F. H. Wood.   Tonic solfa
translation by H. J. Timothy.
pp. 4.   1936.

524583

WOOD (FREDERIC HERBERT)
Full fathom five [and] While you here
do snoring lie: unison songs.
[Words from] The Tempest.   Tonic
solfa translation by H. J. Timothy.
pp. 8.   1936.

524584

Wood (F.H.) Honour, riches, marriage-
blessing: unison song. [Words from]
The Tempest. Music by F.H.Wood. Tonic
solfa translation by H.J.Timothy.
pp.8.

1936.

524586

WOOD (FREDERIC HERBERT)
I know a bank: unison song for
schools.   [Words from A Midsummer
night's dream].   pp. 4.   1932.

518989

WOOD (FREDERIC HERBERT)
Three Shakespeare songs.   [1] You
spotted snakes, [from] A Midsummer-
night's dream.   [2] The Cuckoo,
[from] Love's labour's lost.   [3]
The Owl, [from Love's labour's lost.]
Tonic solfa translation by H. J. T
Timothy.   pp. 8.   1929.

536624

Wood (F.H.) Wedding is great Juno's
crown: two-part song. Words from As
You Like It.
Tonic solfa translation by
H.J.Timothy. pp.4.

1936.

524580

WOOD (FREDERIC HERBERT)
What shall he have that killed the
deer?:   two-part song.   [Words
from As you like it.]   Tonic solfa
translation by H. J. Timothy.
pp. 4.   1936.

524582

Wood (F.H.) ed., Where the bee sucks:
unison song. [Words from] The Tempest.
[Music by] T.[A.] Arne, arranged
by F.H.Wood. Tonic solfa
translation by H.J.Timothy. pp.4.

1936.

524581

WOOD (FREDERICK THOMAS)
The Merchant of Venice in the
eighteenth century.   FROM English
studies, Vol. 15.   (Amsterdam)
1933.

441443

Wood (F.T.) [Review of] The Genesis
of Shakespeare idolatry, 1766-
1799: a study in English criticism
of the late eighteenth century, by
R.W.Babcock.   In English studies,
Vol. 15.

(Amsterdam)   1933.

485657

Wood (F.T.) [Review of] Shakespeare
criticism, from the beginnings to
1765 : six lectures delivered at
the Presidency College under the
auspices of the University of Madras,
by V. K. A. Pillai.   From Englische
Studien, Bd. 69.   . .

(Leipzig)   1934.

497792

WOOD (F. T.)
Shakespeare and the plebs.   IN The
English Association, Essays and Studies,
Vol. 18.   (Oxford)
1933.

404182

WOOD (FREDERICK THOMAS)
Theatrical performances at Bath in
the eighteenth century.   [With
references to Shakespearian performances.]   IN Notes and Queries,
Vol. 192-   1947-

588005

[WOOD (J. S.) ed.]
Shaksperean show-book.   [Programmes
of a fancy fair, for the benefit of
the Chelsea Hospital for Women;
with original literary contributions,
illustrations and music.]   (Manchester)
[1884.]   69016
_____ Another copy, imperfect.
[1884.]   616770

WOOD (MARGARET LUCY ELIZABETH)
Instruments of darkness [: a prologue
to the murder of Duncan].   pp. [iv],
21.   plan.   1955.
French's Acting Edition, No. 340.

649352

—— WOOD (ROGER) and CLARKE (MARY)

Shakespeare at the Old Vic: the Old Vic
Five-Year First Folio Plan, 1953-4—
1957-8. Ports. Illus.   1954-8.
5 vols.

—— Note: 1956-7 and 1957-8 by Mary Clarke.

644305

WOOD (STANLEY)
The New teaching of Shakespeare in
schools.   With illustrations from
the plays of "Julius Caesar" and
"A Midsummer night's dream".
pp. 57.
bibliog.   1947.

590045

WOOD (THOMAS)
This England: a tune for massed
singing with descant.   Words taken
from Richard II, Act II, Scene 1.
pp. [6.]   1936.
Oxford Choral Songs.

457385

WOOD (W. W.)
A Comparison between Shakespeare and his
contemporaries in their use of music and
sound effects.   IN Northwestern University, Summaries of doctoral dissertations.   June-Sept. 1944, Vol. 12.
(Chicago)

1945.

586199

WOOD (WILLIAM BURKE)
Personal recollections of the stage,
embracing notices of actors, authors
and auditors during a period of
forty years.   [With Shakespearian
references.]   (Philadelphia)
port.   1855.

499279

WOODALL (HENRY)
Hamlet and Macbeth oppositely inter-
pretive.   pp. 60.   [1906.]

573423

WOODBERRY (GEORGE EDWARD)
Makers of literature: essays on
Shelley [etc.   With a chapter "Some
actors' criticisms of Othello, Iago,
and Shylock"].   (New York) 1909.

404414

WOODCOCK ([Mrs.] GWEN)
Historic haunts of England.   [With
a chapter on Stratford-on-Avon and
references to Shakespeare.]
illus.   map.   1938.

481633

WOODFORD (HUBERT G.)
Interpretations of human life -
III: Shakespeare's.   FROM [The
Inquirer, Sept. 14th, 1946.]

587299

WOODFORD COLLEGE
Programmes, etc., of Shakespeare
performances.   [1931-7]

452519

WOODFORDE (F. C.)
An Etymological index to Shakespeare's
play of Henry V.   3rd edn.   pp. 28.
(Market Drayton)
genealogical table.   [c.1890.]

484007

[Woodhouselee (A.F. Tytler, Lord)]
Essay, on the principles of translation. [Including notes on Voltaire's
translation from Shakespeare.] 3rd
edn. with additions.

(Edinburgh) 1813.

524178

WOODRUFF (NEAL)
Cymbeline. IN Shakespeare: lectures
on five plays, by A. F. Sochatoff
[and others]. pp. xii, 83.
(Pittsburgh: Carnegie Institute of
Technology) 1958.

666185

Woods (A.H.) Syphilis in Shakespeare's
tragedy of Timon of Athens. From
The American Journal of Psychiatry,
Vol. 91.

[Baltimore] 1934.

506173

WOODS, WILLIAM
The Twins; or, Which is which.

For editions of this play see under
English Editions: The Comedy of
Errors: Alterations &c.

Woodstock [or, Richard II], a moral
history [: a play]. Edited, with
a preface [containing information
on the play as a source of
Shakespeare's Richard II and on the
relations between Shakespeare and
Marlowe, notes and a glossary] by
A. P. Rossiter. 1946.

574542

Woodthorpe (R.C.) Rope for a convict
[: a novel relating to a Shakespeare
Folio.]

1939.

506255

WOODWARD (A. G.)
The Roman plays. IN Shakespeare at
400. A series of public lectures
given on the occasion of the four-
hundredth anniversary of William
Shakespeare's birth by members of
the Department of English, University
of Cape Town. (Cape Town) pp. 25-41.
typescript. 1965.

749535

WOODWARD (FRANK LEE)
Francis Bacon and the cipher story.
pp. 74. (Adyar, Madras: Theosophical
Publishing [Society]) 1932.

436312

WOODWARD (GERTRUDE L.) and McMANAWAY (J.G.)
A Check list of English plays, 1641-
1700 [including plays of Shakespeare].
(Chicago) 1945.
The Newberry Library.

572664

Woodward, Gertrude L. *and* McManaway, J. G.
works relating to

—— HARBAGE (A. [B.])
[Review of] A Check list of English
plays, 1641-1700, by Gertrude L.
Woodward and J. G. McManaway. IN
Modern Language Notes, Vol. 62.
(Baltimore, Md.) 1947.

439157/62

WOODWARD (JOHN)
Shakespeare and English painting.
(Aspects of Art in England, 1700-
1840, 8.) [With Readings from
various authors.] Broadcast
5th June, 1950. ff. 14, 18.
typescript. 2 vols.

614637

[WOODWARD (JOSIAH)]
Some thoughts concerning the stage
in a letter to a lady. pp. 13.
1704.

605281

[WOODWARD (PARKER)]
The Great Shakespeare camouflage [:
Bacon's authorship of the plays]
explained in imaginary conversations.
pp. 42. (Nottingham)
ports. facsimiles. 1918.

549416

WOOLF (VIRGINIA)
The Death of the moth, and other
essays. [Including "Twelfth Night"
at the Old Vic. With an editorial
note by L. S. Woolf.] 1942.

533636

WOOLF (VIRGINIA)
Ellen Terry. IN Woolf (Virginia)
The Moment, and other essays.
1947.

587577

WOOLF (VIRGINIA)
'Twelfth Night' at the Old Vic.
IN WARD (A. C.) [ed.] Specimens
of English dramatic criticism,
17-20 centuries; selected and
introduced. (Oxford) 1945.
The World's Classics.

563732

WOOLLCOTT (ALEXANDER)
While Rome burns [: anecdotes of
the theatre, etc., with Shakespearian
references.] 1934.

470005

Worcester (D.) The Art of satire.
[With references to Shakespeare; and
bibliographical notes.]

(Cambridge, Mass.) 1940.

526997

WORD AND IMAGE [: Granada TV script of readings from The Tempest, etc., illustrating the image of man in a confined space, that is, an island. Transmitted on 19th December, 1962.] (Manchester)

667870

Words used by Shakespeare *see* Grammar and Language

Wordsworth, Charles *works relating to*

— Shakspeare's historical plays, Roman and English [: a review.] IN The Nonconformist and Independent, Vol.4, New Series. 1883.

520514

— Shakespeare's knowledge and use of the Bible [: a review]. IN The Nonconformist and Independent, Vol. 1, New Series. 1880.

520511

WORDSWORTH (WILLIAM)
[Two] letters [relating to Shakespeare]. IN BROUGHTON (L. N.) ed., Some letters of the Wordsworth family, now first published. With a few unpublished letters of Coleridge and Southey and others. (Ithaca, N.Y.)
frontis. 1942
Cornell Studies in English, 32.

542115

Wordsworth, William *works relating to*

— BATHO (EDITH C.)
The Later Wordsworth. [With references to Shakespeare.] (Cambridge)
port. bibliog. 1933.

413487

— HAVENS (R. D.)
The Mind of a poet; a study of Wordsworth's thought with particular references to The Prelude. [With a bibliography and bibliographical notes and references to Shakespeare.] (Baltimore)
1941.

537454

— KNIGHT (W. [A.]) ed.
Wordsworthiana: a selection from papers read to the Wordsworth Society. [Containing references to Shakespeare.]
port. 1889.

429599

— MARTIN (A. D.)
The Religion of Wordsworth. [With references to Shakespeare.]
port. 1936.

458307

— SMITH (CHARLES J.)
The Effect of Shakespeare's influence on Wordsworth's "The Borderers".
IN Studies in Philology, Vol. 50. (Chapel Hill, N.C.) 1953.

554520/50

WORDSWORTH (WILLIAM and DOROTHY)
Letters, (1787-1850). Arranged and edited by E. de Selincourt. [With references to Shakespeare's plays.] (Oxford)
facsimiles. map. tables. 6 vols.
1935-1939.

437657

Work for chimny-sweepers; or, A Warning for tobacconists, [by Philaretes.] 1601. With an introduction by S. H. Atkins. 1936. Shakespeare Association Facsimiles, No. 11.

452705

WORKSOP COLLEGE
Annual Shakespearean play. A Midsummer night's dream. 1912. Signatures of actors on fly leaf.

411417

[WORKSOP COLLEGE DRAMATIC SOCIETY
Programmes of Shakespeare performances, Nov., 1931-45.] [Worksop]
[1931-45]

416898

World in Shakespeare's Time
see also **England in Shakespeare's Time**

—— TILLYARD (EUSTACE MANDEVILLE WETENHALL)
The Elizabethan world picture [: an exposition of the most ordinary beliefs about the constitution of the world as pictured in the Elizabethan age. With references to Shakespeare's plays].
bibliog.   1943.

540616

—— WILSON (JOHN DOVER)
Shakespeare's universe. bibliog.
pp. [18]. FROM University of Edinburgh Journal, Vol. 11. (Edinburgh)
1942.

536116

World Juvenile Library
LAMB (CHARLES and MARY [A.])
Tales from Shakespeare. (Cleveland)
frontis.   1937.

517222

WORLD THEATRE, Vol.XIII. Nr.2
Shakespeare 1964 [: articles by various writers in English and French]. pp.73-147. (Bruxelles)   1964.

illus.   742319

WORLD THEATRE SEASON at the Aldwych Theatre, London, March 17 - June 13, 1964. Presented by the governors of the Royal Shakespeare Company and Peter Daubeny in conjunction with the Sunday Telegraph. [Souvenir]   1964.

752257

WORMHOUDT (ARTHUR)
Hamlet's mouse trap: a psychoanalytical study of the drama. (New York)
bibliog.   1956.

665581

WORSLEY (THOMAS CUTHBERT)
The Fugitive art: dramatic comment-aries 1947-1951.
illus.   1952.

628091

WORSLEY (THOMAS CUTHBERT)
Stratford and Shakespearian production.
illus. IN Theatre in review. [By]
E. [W.] Blom [and others].
(Edinburgh)
ports. illus.   1956.

657684

WORSLEY (THOMAS CUTHBERT)
The Stratford Festival, 1949.
IN Penguin New Writing. Edited by J. Lehmann. (Harmondsworth)
illus.   1949.
Penguin Books.

586205/38

WORSLEY (THOMAS CUTHBERT)

see also WILSON (JOHN DOVER) and WORSLEY (THOMAS CUTHBERT)

WORTH (MARTIN)
Producing Macbeth [: introductory scripts to a production of Macbeth for schools]. Televised January-March, 1958. (Associated Rediffusion Ltd.). Typescript.

665945

WORTH (MARTIN)
Twelfth Night, a Shakespearean series [: nine introductory scripts to a production of Twelfth Night for schools]. Televised January-March, 1959. (Associated-Rediffusion Ltd.)
typescript.

666169

Worthing Sussex

—— ODELL (MARY T.)
The Old theatre, Worthing: the Theatre Royal, 1807-1855. [With references to Shakespearian productions.] (Aylesbury)
ports. illus. facsimiles.   1938.
(Sign of the Dolphin)

487607

—— ODELL (MARY T.)
The Theatre Royal, 1807-1855: more about the old theatre, Worthing, its plays, players and playvills, its proprietor and his playhouses. Publishing under the Worthing Art Development Scheme. [With references to Shakespearian productions.] (Worthing)
ports. illus. facsimiles.   1945.
(Sign of the Dolphin)

590855

—— ODELL (MARY T.)
The Theatre Royal, 1814-1819: Mr. [T.] Trotter of Worthing and the Brighton theatre. [With references to Shakespeare productions. Worthing pageant] published under the Worthing Art Development Scheme. (Worthing)
ports. illus. facsimiles.   1944.
Sign of the Dolphin

558632

Wotton, Henry Sir *works relating to*

—— POGUE (JIM C.)
"The Two Gentlemen of Verona" and Henry Wotton's "A Courtlie contro-versie of Cupids cautels". IN Four studies in Elizabethan drama, by Roma Ball, J.C.Pogue, J. L. Somer [and] E. J. Kettner. (Emporia: Kansas State Teachers' College)
1962.

667737

WOTTON (MABEL E.)
A Meeting-place for Shakespeare and
Drayton in the City of London [: the
Mermaid Tavern].

IN GOLLANCZ ([Sir] I.) ed., A Book
of homage to Shakespeare.
ports. illus. facsimiles. [1916.]

264175

WRAIGHT, ANNIE DORIS
In search of Christopher Marlowe: a
pictorial biography. Photography by V.F.
Stern.   1965.

illus.   744852

WRIGHT (ADAM)
As you like it: polka.   pp. 5.
illus. t.p.   [c.1850.]

501626

WRIGHT (AUSTIN)
Antony and Cleopatra.   IN Shakespeare:
lectures on five plays, by A. F.
Sochatoff [and others].   pp. xii, 83.
(Pittsburgh: Carnegie Institute of
Technology)   1958.

666185

WRIGHT (AUSTIN)
The History plays.
IN "Starre of Poets".   Discussions of
Shakespeare.   (Pittsburgh, Pa.:
Carnegie Institute of Technology)
1966.

766812

WRIGHT (B.)
Shakespeare on the screen and on
the air: substance of a lecture
delivered at a Shakespeare study-
course organized by the British
Council at Stratford-on-Avon,
April 1947.   IN Documentary News
Letter, 1947.   1947.

524257/6

WRIGHT (CELESTE T.)
The Usurer's sin in Elizabethan
literature.   [With references to
Shakespeare.]   FROM Studies in
Philology, Vol. 35.   [Chapel Hill,
N.C.]
bibliog.   1938.

503670

WRIGHT (CHARLES)
Shakespeare: reprint of the first
collected edition of the plays, and
the "Athenaeum" of Jan. 25th, 1862
[: a letter to the editor of the
"Athenaeum" in answer to criticisms.]
pp. 3.   1862.

535361

WRIGHT (FREDERIC ADAM)
Three Roman poets: Plautus, Catullus,
Ovid.   Their lives, times and works.
[With reference to Ovid's influence
on Shakespeare].
port. illus. facsimile. 1938.

479412

WRIGHT (GEORGE R.)
The English stage in the year 1638.
[With facsimile list of 24 plays
presented at Court, 1638.]   pp.
[4.]   IN The Journal of the British
Archaeological Association, vol. 16.
1860.

118739

WRIGHT (HERBERT GLADSTONE)
Boccaccio in England: from Chaucer
to Tennyson.
bibliog.   1957.

674333

Wright (J.) Shakespeare and Sussex.
From Sussex County Magazine
[Sept. 1946].

[Eastbourne]

579650

WRIGHT, LOUIS BOOKER
The Britain that Shakespeare knew.
FROM The National Geographic Magazine,
May 1964, pp.613-667. (Washington, D.C.)

illus.   744138

WRIGHT (LOUIS BOOKER)
A Conduct book for Malvolio.
FROM Studies in Philology, Vol. 31.
(Chapel Hill, N.C.)   1934.

484076

WRIGHT (L. B.)
The First gentlemen of Virginia: intel-
lectual qualities of the early colonial
ruling class.   [With references to
Shakespeare and bibliographical notes.]
(San Marino, Cal.)
1940.
Huntington Library Publications.
560820

WRIGHT, LOUIS BOOKER
The Folger Library. Two decades of
growth: an informal account.
(Charlottes-ville, Va.)   1968.

774154

WRIGHT (LOUIS BOOKER)
The Harmsworth collection and the
Folger Library.   IN The Book Collector,
Vol. 6.   1957.

649085/6

Wright (L.B.) Middle- class culture
in Elizabethan England. [With
a bibliography and references to
Shakespeare.]

(Huntington Library Publications.)
(Chapel Hill, N.C.)   1935.

444043

WRIGHT (LOUIS BOOKER)
An Obligation to Shakespeare and the
public.   IN SHAKESPEARE SURVEY 16.
illus.   1963.

667523

WRIGHT (LOUIS BOOKER)
Shakespeare's England.   By the
editors of Horizon Magazine in
consultation with L. B. Wright.
illus.   1964.
Cassell Caravel books.

743838

WRIGHT (LOUIS BOOKER)
Shakespeare's theatre and the dramatic
tradition.   pp. 36.   (Washington,D.C.)
ports. illus. maps. facsimiles.
bibliog.   1958.   666181
Folger Shakespeare Library.   Folger
Booklets on Tudor and Stuart
Civilization.
_____ IN Life and letters in Tudor
and Stuart England.   (Folger
Shakespeare Library)
illus.   1962.   667762

WRIGHT (LOUIS BOOKER)
Will Kemp and the Commedia dell'Arte.
IN Modern Language Notes, Vol. 41.
(Baltimore, Md.)   1926.

439157/41

WRIGHT (LOUIS BOOKER)
A Working library of sixteenth- and
seventeenth-century history [: the
Folger Shakespeare Library,
Washington.]   IN Libri, Vol. 10,
1960.
illus.   1960.

634661/1960

WRIGHT (LOUIS BOOKER) ed.
Advice to a son: precepts of Lord
Burghley, Sir Walter Raleigh and
Francis Osborne.   (Ithaca, N.Y.)
bibliogs.   1962.
Folger Shakespeare Library.   Folger
Documents of Tudor and Stuart
Civilization [2].

667175

WRIGHT, LOUIS BOOKER, ed.
Shakespeare celebrated: anniversary
lectures delivered at the Folger
Library [during 1964].   (Ithaca, N.Y.)
1965.

771817

WRIGHT (LOUIS BOOKER) and FREUND
(Mrs. VIRGINIA) [LA MAR] eds.
Life and letters in Tudor and Stuart
England. (Folger Shakespeare Library:
First Folger Series, [Vol.1]). Illus.
(Ithaca, N.Y.)   1962.

667762

WRIGHT (MARGOT)
A Midsummer night's dream: suite
of five pieces for piano.   pp. 9.
1938.

536625

WRIGHT, PETER
Antony and Cleopatra: an "A" level
guide.   (Stockport)   [1967]

772165

WRIGHT, PETER
Success in Shakespeare [: a guide
to 'O' and 'A' level examinations]
(Stockport)   [1968]

773078

WRIGHT (THOMAS)
On some early Latin stories imitated
at a later period by Chaucer and
Shakespeare.   Communicated to the
Society of Antiquaries by T. Wright.
[Reprinted] from The Archaeologia,
Vol. 32.   pp. 8.   1848.

554141

Wright (Ursula Kentish-) see
Kentish-Wright (Ursula)

WRIGHT (WILLIAM ALDIS)
The Bible word-book: a glossary of
archaic words and phrases in the
Authorised Version of the Bible
and the Book of Common Prayer.
[With quotations from Shakespeare.]
2nd edn. revised and enlarged. 1884.

101451

WRIGHT (WILLIAM BURNETT)
Hamlet.   IN The Atlantic Monthly,
Vol. 89.   (Cambridge, Mass.)
1902.

170922

Writers and their Work see British
Book News, Bibliographical Series
of Supplements

WROTH (LAWRENCE COUNSELMAN), LEHMANN-
HAUPT (H.) and GRANNISS (RUTH S.)
The Book in America: a history of
the making, the selling, and the
collecting of books in the United
States.   [With references to
Shakespeare collections.]   (New York)
bibliogs.   1939.
Revised and enlarged in English text
from "Das Amerikanische Buchwesen",
1937.

535232

WYATT (EUPHEMIA VAN RENSSELAER)
The Boys from Syracuse [: a review
of the stage play by G. Abbott].
FROM The Catholic World, Vol. 148.
(New York)   1939.

527854

WYATT (EUPHEMIA VAN R.)
The Drama: night's black agents.
[Including criticism of performances
of Macbeth and Twelfth Night.]
FROM The Catholic World, Vol. 154.
(New York)   1942.

537250

WYATT (E[UPHEMIA] VAN RENSSELAER)
Juliet on her toes [: Romeo and
Juliet as a ballet].   Commonweal,
Vol. 38.   (New York)   1943.

559502

WYATT (HORACE GRAHAM)
Chĕrita-Chĕrita Shakespeare.   Di-
chĕritakan sa-mula oleh H. G. Wyatt.
Di-tĕrjĕmahkan oleh A. Samad Said.
(London. Kuala Lumpur: O.U.P.)   1958.
Text in Malayan.

666153

WYATT (H. G.)
Stories from Shakespeare.   (Oxford)
illus.   1934.
Stories Retold.

421720

WYATT (H. G.)
More stories from Shakespeare.
(Oxford)
illus.   1933.
Stories Retold.

                    418059

WYATT (H. G.) and FULLERTON (D.)
The Stories of Shakespeare's plays,
Vol. 1 [: The Merchant of Venice,
Macbeth, The Tempest, Hamlet, King
Lear], retold by H. G. Wyatt and
D. Fullerton.   pp. vi, 76. (Oxford)
illus.   1939.
Tales Retold for Easy Reading,
Second Series.

                    521397

Wyck (Jessica D. Van) see Van Wyck
(Jessica D.)

WYNKOOP, WILLIAM M.
Three children of the universe:
Emerson's view of Shakespeare, Bacon,
and Milton. (The Hague)   1966.

       illus. Studies in English
Literature (Mouton)   763098

WYNTOUN (ANDREW of)
Orygynale Cronykil of Scotland,
Vol. 2 [containing the story of
Macbeth, in Book 6, Chapter 18.]
(Edinburgh)   1872.
The Historians of Scotland.

                   98037

WYNTOUN (ANDREW of)
Original Chronicle [of Scotland.]
Edited by F. J. Amours.   Vol. 4
[containing the story of Macbeth
in Book 6, Chapter 18.] (Edinburgh)
                  1906.
Scottish Text Society.

                 194374

WYSONG, J. N.
The Influence of Shakespeare's songs
on the poetry of A. E. Housman.
IN SHAKESPEARE QUARTERLY XIX: 4.
pp. 333-339.
(New York)   1968.

                 605711

WYZEWA (T. de)
[Review of] "Shakespeare's marriage
and departure from Stratford", par
J. W. Gray, [and] "Shakespearean
tragedy", par A. C. Bradley.   IN
Revue des Deux Mondes, Tome 26.
                   1905.

                 187559

YAFFE (H.) ed.
Homage to Hymen: an anthology for
the affianced and married. [With
extracts from Shakespeare.] 1940.

                 521855

Yajnik (R.K.) The Indian theatre: its
origins and its later developments
under European influence, with
special reference to Western India.
[With references to Shakespeare, and
an Indian Shakespeare bibliography.]

                 1933.

                 415878

YALE FRENCH STUDIES
Shakespeare in France. IN Yale French
Studies, Vol.33. (New Haven, Conn.)
                1964.

             746422

Yale Shakespeare Supplements

— BENTLEY (GERALD EADES)
Shakespeare, a biographical handbook.
(New Haven, Conn.)
chronological table.   bibliog.
                1961.
Yale Shakespeare Supplements.

             667051

— KÖKERITZ (HELGE)
Shakespeare's names: a pronouncing
dictionary.   (New Haven [Conn.])
tables.   1959.
Yale Shakespeare Supplements.

             666388

— NAGLER (A. M.)
Shakespeare's stage.   Translated
by R. Manheim.   (New Haven [Conn.])
facsimile.   bibliog.   1958.
Yale Shakespeare Supplements.

             666158

Yale Studies in English

— CROMWELL (OTELIA)
Thomas Heywood: a study in the
Elizabethan drama of everyday life:
a dissertation presented to the
faculty of the Graduate School of
Yale University in candidacy for the
degree of Doctor of Philosophy.
[With references to Shakespeare.]
(New Haven [Conn.])
bibliog.   1928.

             560734

— ROOT, ROBERT KILBURN
Classical mythology in Shakespeare.
(New York)   1965.

       Yale studies in English, XIX.
             754007

— SIPE, DOROTHY L.
Shakespeare's metrics.   (New Haven,
Conn.)   1968.
Yale studies in English, 167.

             773050

— YOUNG, DAVID P.
Something of great constancy: the art
of "A Midsummer night's dream".
(New Haven, Mass.)   1966.

       illus. Yale studies in English,
Vol.164.   758056

YAMAGIWA (JOSEPH KOSHIMA)
A Shakespeare allusion [in The Great
historical, geographical and poetical
dictionary, attributed to J. Collier,
1694]. IN Modern Language Notes,
Vol. 52. (Baltimore)   1937.

479896

Yankee author at Shakespeare's birthplace. (From the popular entertainment "The World and his wife"). IN
Routledge's Comic reciter, edited
and selected by J. E. Carpenter.
[1867.]

521649

YAO SHEN
Some chapters on Shakespearean
criticism: Coleridge, Hazlitt and
Stoll. A dissertation submitted for
the degree of Doctor of Education in
English, University of Michigan.
(Ann Arbor, Mich.)
bibliogs. microfilm. 35 mm. 1944.
University Microfilms Doctoral
Dissertations Series.

603942

YARRINGTON (R.) Works relating to:
see Moore (W. H.) Baconian Studies.

Yasui (Minoru) ed. see Araki (Kazuo)
and others

YATES (FRANCES AMELIA)
English actors in Paris during the
lifetime of Shakespeare. IN The
Review of English Studies, Vol. 1.
1925.

318239

Yates (Frances A.) John Florio: the
life of an Italian in Shakespeare's
England. [With a bibliography.]

(Cambridge)   1934.

421211

YATES (FRANCES A.)
Queen Elizabeth as Astraea [including
a section entitled "Shakespeare and
Astraea".] IN Journal of the
Warburg and Courtauld Institutes,
Vol. 10.
bibliog.   1947.

487462/10

YATES (FRANCES AMELIA)
Shakespeare and the Platonic tradition.
FROM University of Edinburgh Journal,
Vol. 12. (Edinburgh)
bibliog.   1942.

542806

YATES, FRANCES AMELIA
The Stage in Robert Fludd's memory system.
IN SHAKESPEARE STUDIES 3. (Cincinnati,
Ohio)   1967.

771652

YATES (FRANCES A.)
A Study of Love's labour's lost.
(Cambridge)
bibliog.   1936.
Shakespeare Problems.

450742

Yates, Frances Amelia *works relating to*

—— EMPSON (WILLIAM)
A Study of Love's labour's lost by
F. A. Yates [: a review]. IN
Life and letters today [Vol. 15.]
[1936-7]

463697

——Welsford (Enid) [Review of] Frances
A. Yates' "A Study of Love's Labour's
Lost. 1936". In The Modern Language
Review, Vol. 33.

1938.

492625

YATES (M. E. ASHTON)
Hark, hark! the lark at heaven's
gate sings, verse 2. IN SCHUBERT
(F.) Hark, hark! the lark at
heaven's gate sings; arranged for
two voices by G. Oakey. Words
[from Cymbeline]; verse 2 by M. E. A.
Yates. [Staff notation and tonic
sol-fa.]
2 vols.   [1923.]

516972

The Year's contribution to
Shakespearian study [: reviews]. In
Shakespeare survey: an annual survey of
Shakespearian study & production. [Vol.]
1 -   (Cambridge)
1948-

590674

Year's work in modern language
studies. [Including Shakespeariana.]
Vol. 1 (1929-30)- (Modern Humanities
Research Association)
378596

Yearsley (M.) The Folklore of fairy-
tale. [With references to King Lear
and a bibliography.]

1924.

524179

YEARSLEY (M.)
The Sanity of Hamlet.   1932.

401699

YEARSLEY (PERCIVAL MACLEOD)
The Death of Shakespeare. IN The
Lancet, Vol. 221.
bibliog.   1931.

389957

YEARSLEY (PERCIVAL MACLEOD)
Doctors in Elizabethan drama. [With
references to Shakespeare.] 1933.

417049

YEATMAN (JOHN PYM)
The Gentle Shakspere: a vindication.
3rd edn. (augmented). (New York:
Shakespeare Society of New York)
  ports. facsimile. 1904. 405091
——— 4th edn. (augmented). (Derby)
              1906. 467158

Yeats, William Butler *works relating to*

— CHAKRAVORTY-SPIVAK (GAYATRI)
  Shakespeare in Yeats's "Last Poems".
  IN Shakespeare commemoration volume,
  edited by Taraknath Sen. (Calcutta)
              1966.

                764382

— HONE (J. [M.])
  W. B. Yeats, 1865-1939. [With
  references to Shakespeare.]
  ports. illus. bibliog. facsimile.
             1942.

                539043

— MacNEICE ([F.] L.)
  The Poetry of W. B. Yeats. [With
  references to Shakespeare.]
  (Oxford)
  bibliog.   1941.

                522058

YELLOWLEES (HENRY)
Medicine and surgery in the 1955
season's plays. IN GARRETT (J.)
More talking of Shakespeare. 1959.

                666126

Yoder (Audrey) Animal analogy in
Shakespeare's character portrayal. [With
a bibliography and bibliographical notes.]
(New York)   1947.

               590617

YOKLAVICH (J.)
Hamlet in shammy shoes [: interpretation
of Hamlet in the eighteenth century].
IN SHAKESPEARE QUARTERLY III: 3.
pp. 208-218.
(New York) 1952.
              605711

Yolland (A.B.) 1938-1983. The Cult
of Shakespeare in Hungary. Facsimiles.
In The Hungarian Quarterly, Vol. 5.

              1939.

              514527

YORDAN, PHILIP
Joe Macbeth [film]

see under English Editions: Macbeth:
Alterations &c.

YORICK, pseud.
A Letter concerning Mr. Henry Irving
addressed to E.R.H.
  pp. 18.   1877.

                24306

Yorick's crib to the examination
paper on Shakespeare in The Real
Shakespeare by William Bliss.
pp. 36.   [1949.]

              600726

York-Lancaster tetralogy *see* History Plays

YORK SETTLEMENT COMMUNITY PLAYERS
Programmes of Shakespearian performances, 1934- (York)

              479689

YORKE (FRANCIS REGINALD STEVENS)
Inside the theatre, and Notes on the
Shakespeare Memorial Theatre. IN
The Architectural Review, June 1932:
Shakespeare Memorial Theatre Number.
  illus. plans.   1932.

              393576

Yorkshire Tragedy

— BLAYNEY (GLENN H.)
  Variants in Q1 of "A Yorkshire tragedy".
  IN The Library: Transactions of the
  Bibliographical Society, Fifth Series,
  Vol. 11, No. 4.   1956.

            99606/11

— CAWLEY, ARTHUR CLARE
  English domestic drama: "A Yorkshire
  tragedy". An inaugural lecture.
  (Leeds)
  illus.   1966.

              763620

— Friedlaender (M.) Some problems of
  "A Yorkshire tragedy" [: the question
  of Shakespeare's possible authorship.]
  From Studies in Philology, Vol. 35.

    [Chapel Hill, N.C.]   1938.

              503672

— Sykes (H.D.) The Authorship of "A
  Yorkshire tragedy". From The
  Journal of English and Germanic
  Philology, Vol. 16.

    (Urbana, Ill.)   1917.

              510468

— The Yorkshire Tragedy. Not so new,
as lamentable and true. Written
by W. Shakspeare. Printed for
T.P., 1619. [Extracts from the
text with criticism.] IN The
Retrospective Review, Vol. 9.
1824.

169

YOUNG (ARTHUR)
Six Shakespearian songs set to music
in the modern manner. pp. 16.
1947.

588779

Young (Bartholomew) [pseud. B. Giovano]
trans.
MONTEMAYOR (J. de)
The Story of the shepherdess Felismena.
From the Diana of G. de Montemayor,
translated by B. Yonge. IN
SHAKESPEARE (W.) The Two Gentlemen
of Verona. [Edited with an introduc-
tion by H. Morley.] 1889. 436523
Cassell's National Library.
_____ Another edn. 1897. 527792

Young, Charles Mayne *works relating to*

— [A Collection of letters, portraits,
etc., relating to C. M. Young.]
[1807-22.]

536369

— The Drama. [E. Kean and C. M. Young
in Othello at Drury Lane Theatre.]
FROM [The London Magazine,] Jan. 1823.
1823.

561772

YOUNG (CLEMENT CALHOUN), KURTZ (B. P.)
and GAYLEY (C. M.)
English poetry: its principles
and progress with representative
masterpieces from 1390 to 1917
and notes. [Containing references
to and quotations from Shakespeare].
New edn. revised and enlarged.
(New York) 1930.

389924

YOUNG, DAVID P.
Something of great constancy: the art
of "A Midsummer night's dream".
(New Haven, Mass.) 1966.

illus. Yale studies in English,
Vol. 164. 758056

YOUNG, DAVID P. ed.
Twentieth century interpretations of
Henry IV part two: a collection of
critical essays. (Englewood Cliffs,
N.J.) 1968.

775736

Young (F.B.) Hamlet. In Six stories
from Shakespeare Illustrations
by F. Matania.

1934.

428744

YOUNG (FRANCIS BRETT)
Hamlet. Illustrated by F. Matania.
FROM The Strand Magazine, Feb., 1934.
[1934.]
Shakespeare's Plays as Short Stories.

419970

YOUNG ([Sir]GEORGE)
Portugal and the Shakespeare
tercentenary.
IN GOLLANCZ ([Sir] I.) ed., A Book
of homage to Shakespeare.
ports. illus. facsimiles. [1916.]

264175

YOUNG (GEORGE MALCOLM)
Shakespeare and the termers [: the
supposed association of Shakespeare
with the Inns of Court]. pp. 19.
[1947.]
British Academy. [37th] Annual
Shakespeare Lecture.

586717

YOUNG (H. M.)
The Sonnets of Shakespeare: a psycho-
sexual analysis. (Columbia, Miss.)
1937.

469785

YOUNG (J. C.)
Others - and Mrs. Siddons. IN
WARD (A. C.) [ed.] Specimens of
English dramatic criticism, 17-20
centuries; selected and introduced.
(Oxford) 1945.
The World's Classics.

563732

Young (K.) The Interpretation of a
passage in 'Hamlet'. pp.[5.] In The
Modern Language Review, Vol.30, 1935.

(Cambridge) 1935.

448196

Young ([Mrs.] Louise M.) Thomas
Carlyle and the art of history.
[With notes, a bibliography, and
references to Shakespeare.]

(Philadelphia) 1939.

506409

Young (M[ary] J.) Memoirs of Mrs.
Crouch, including a retrospect of
the stage during the years she
performed. [With references to
Shakespeare.] Port. 2 vols.

1806.

536155

YOUNG (STARK)
Immortal shadows: a book of dramatic
criticism [including Shakespeariana].
1948.

598301

YOUNG (STARK)
Shakespeare and the Venetians.
IN Theatre Arts Monthly, Vol. 14.
(New York)
  illus.   1930.   379892
_____ IN Theatre Arts Anthology: a
record and a prophecy. Edited by
Rosamond Gilder, H. R. Isaacs, R. M.
MacGregor [and] E. Reed. (New York)
            1950.   614298

Young Shakespeare's Hamlet. IN All
the year round. New series.
Vol. 22.   1879.

                     38535

Younghusband (Sir F.[E.]) India
  looks at Shakespeare. From Queen's
  Quarterly, vol.41.

      (Kingston,Ont.)   1934.

            441606

The Youth of Shakspeare, by the author
of "Shakspeare and his friends", i.e.
R. F. Williams see Williams (Robert
Folkestone)

Yugoslavia

—— KLAJN (HUGO)
  Shakespeare in Yugoslavia.
  IN SHAKESPEARE QUARTERLY V.
  pp. 41-45.
  (New York) 1954.
             605711

—— POPOVIĆ (V.)
  Shakespeare in post-war Yugoslavia.
  IN SHAKESPEARE SURVEY 14. (Cambridge)
             1951.

            615854

—— Shakespeare's works among the
  Yugoslavs. FROM The Aryan Path,
  Vol. 28. pp. [5.] (Bombay)
            1957.

            665812

—— TORBARINA, JOSIP
  A Croat forerunner of Shakespeare.
  In commemoration of the 400th
  anniversary of the death of Marin
  Držić (1508-1561). FROM Studia
  romanica et anglica zagrabiensia, 24.
  (Zagreb) pp. 5-21.   1967.

            777925

Yûzô Tsubouchi see Tsubouchi (Y.)

Z. [pseud.]
On Garrick's delivery of a passage
in Shakspeare['s Richard III].
FROM [The New Monthly Magazine,
Vol. 4.]   [1822.]

           558072

ZACHRISSON (R. E.)
Shakespeare stories. Compiled and
annotated for Swedish schools, with a
Shakespeare bibliography. Fjärde
upplagan. (Stockholm)
           1926.   417273
[English and Swedish text.]
_____ Ordlista.   1928.   417285
⌊Moderna Engelska Författare, 4.

Zachrisson, Robert Eugen *works relating to*

—— Gaaf (W. van der) [Review of]
  The English pronunciation at
  Shakespeare's time as taught
  by William Bullokar, by R.E.
  Zachrisson. In English studies,
  Vol. 18.

      (Amsterdam)   1936.

           485660

ZAIDENBERG, ARTHUR
  How to draw Shakespeare's people.
  (New York)   1967.

     illus.   764483

Zamoyski, John *works relating to*

—— TESLAR (JOSEPH ANDREW)
  Shakespeare's worthy counsellor [:
  influence on Shakespeare's texts of
  the treatise "De optimo senatore"
  by Laurentius Grimalius Goslicki
  and the influence of John Zamoyski
  on Goslicki].   (Rzym)
  port. illus. facsimiles. bibliog.
              1960.

           666938

ZANDVOORT (REINARD WILLEM)
Brutus's Forum speech in "Julius
Caesar". IN Zandvoort (R. W.)
Collected papers. (Groningen)
            1954.
Groningen Studies in English.
          676242

ZANDVOORT (REINARD WILLEM)
Dramatic motivation in Macbeth.
FROM Les Langues Modernes, 45e
année. pp. [11].   1951.

          621337

ZANDVOORT (REINARD WILLEM)
Fair Portia's counterfeit.   IN
Zandvoort (R. W.) Collected papers:
a selection of notes and articles
originally published in English
Studies and other journals.
(Groningen)
   facsimiles.   bibliog.   1954.
Groningen Studies in English, 5.

676242

ZANDVOORT (REINARD WILLEM)

King Lear: the scholars and the critics.
(Koninklijke Nederlandse Akademie van
Wetenschappen,Afd. Letterkunde.Nieuwe
Reeks, Deel 19,No.7) pp.16.(Amsterdam)
1956.

665795

ZANDVOORT (REINARD WILLEM)
[Review of] Der "Hamlet" Shakespeares,
von H. H. Glunz.   IN English Studies,
Vol. 22.   (Amsterdam)   1940.

575606

Zandvoort (R.W.) [Review of] The
   Merchant of Venice, by W. Shakespeare, annotated by L.J.Guittart
   and P.J.Rijneke. (Meulenhoff's
   English Library.) In English
   studies, Vol. 1.

   (Amsterdam)   1919.

485643

ZANDVOORT (REINARD WILLEM)
[Review of] Shakespeare-Jahrbuch,
Band 77.   IN English Studies,
Vol. 25.   (Amsterdam)
   bibliog.   1943.

575609

ZANGWILL (ISRAEL)
Ghetto comedies, Vol. 2.   [Containing
The Yiddish "Hamlet".]   (Leipzig)
                           1907.

479824

ZANGWILL (ISRAEL)
The Two empires [: a sonnet.]

IN GOLLANCZ ([Sir] I.) ed., A Book
of homage to Shakespeare.
   ports.   illus.   facsimiles. [1916.]

264175

Zanoni, [pseud.] Ibsen and the drama
   [with a chapter "Shakspere vindicated".]

[1895.]

495585

ZBIERSKI (HENRYK)
Shakespeare and the "War of the
theatres": a reinterpretation.
(Poznań)
   illus.   map.   bibliog.   1957.
Poznańskie Towarzystwo Przyjaciół
Nauk.   Wydział Filologiczno-
Filozoficzny.   Prace Komisji
Filologicznej, Tom 16, Zeszyt 5.

665635

ZBIERSKI (HENRYK)
Shakespeare criticism and the influence
of George Bernard Shaw in the light of
his "Dark lady of the sonnets".   IN
Poland's homage to Shakespeare.
Commemorating the fourth centenary of
his birth, 1564-1964.   (Warsaw)
                              1965.

747846

ZEEFELD (W. GORDON)
'Coriolanus' and Jacobean politics.
IN The Modern Language Review,
Vol. 57.   1960.

266816/1960

ZEEVELD (W. GORDON)
"Food for powder" - "food for worms".
IN SHAKESPEARE QUARTERLY III: 3.
pp. 249-253.
(New York)   1952.
                              605711

ZEEVELD (W. GORDON)
The Influence of Hall on Shakespeare's
English historical plays.   A portion
of Edward Hall: a study of sixteenth
century historiography in England.
pp. [46].   (Baltimore)
   bibliog.   1937.
Reprinted from E.L.H. Vol. 3.

479555

ZEFFERTT (CHARLES)
Shakespere in Fairyland.   IN The
Fortnightly Review, Vol. 94.
                              1910.

227925

Zeffirelli, Franco *works relating to*

—— BROWN (JOHN RUSSELL)
   S. Franco Zeffirelli's "Romeo and
   Juliet".   IN SHAKESPEARE SURVEY 15.
   (Cambridge)   1962.

667174

ZEIGLER (WILBUR GLEASON)

It was Marlowe: a story of the secret
of three centuries. Illus. (Chicago)
                              1895.

668408

ZEITLIN & VERBRUGGE, booksellers
Catalogue No. 10: The Logan Clendening
collection of books about the Bacon-
Shakespeare controversy, including
most of the important discussions of
this question.   [With a prefatory
note by J. I. Zeitlin and a foreword
by L. Clendening.]   pp. 26.   (Los
Angeles)
   ports.   facsimiles.   1943.

560133

ZEYDEL (EDWIN HERMANN)
Ludwig Tieck and England: a study in
the literary relations of Germany and
England during the early nineteenth
century. [With references to
Shakespeare's plays.] (Princeton)
1931.

390815

ZEYDEL (EDWIN HERMANN)
Ludwig Tieck as a translator of English,
[including Shakespeare]. IN
Publications of the Modern Language
Association of America, Vol. 51.
(Menasha, Wis.) 1936.

463431

ZEYDEL (EDWIN HERMANN)
Ludwig Tieck, the German romanticist:
a critical study. [With references
to Shakespeare]. (Princeton, N.J.)
bibliog. 1935.

449035

ZIEGFELD THEATRE, New York
[Souvenir booklet of Vivien Leigh and
Laurence Olivier in the production of
Bernard Shaw's Caesar and Cleopatra
and Shakespeare's Antony and Cleopatra
at the Ziegfeld Theatre.] pp. [16.]
[New York]
ports. illus. [1951.]

624735

ZIMBARDO (ROSE ABDELNOUR)
Form and disorder in "The Tempest".
IN SHAKESPEARE QUARTERLY XIV: 1.
pp. 49-56.
(New York) 1963.

605711

ZINGARELLI ([N.])
Dunque il mio bene: duetto in the
opera of Romeo e Giulietta, composed
by [N.] Zingarelli. [c.1820.]

501625

ZINKEISEN (DORIS)
Designing for the stage. [With
settings for "The Taming of the
Shrew".] pp. 78.
illus. [1938.]
"How to do it" series, No. 18. The
Studio.

487004

Zinn ( ) Serjeant, pseud.

see: Wilson (James Edwin)

ZIOLECKI (Dr.)
Shakspere in Poland, Russia, and other
Sclavonic countries.
IN Transactions of the New Shakespeare
Society, Series 1. Nos. 8-10.
pp. 431-441. 1880-6.
99113

ZITNER, S. P.
Anon, anon: or, a mirror for a
magistrate. [I Henry IV Act II Scene iii]
IN SHAKESPEARE QUARTERLY XIX: 1.
pp. 63-70. (New York)
1968.

605711

ZLOTNIK (JEHUDA LEIB)
Swearing by a sword: folk-lore of
Shakespeare, with notes and illustra-
tions from Rabbinic sources. pp. 16.
(Johannesburg) 1948.

665486

ZOCCA (LOUIS RALPH)
Elizabethan narrative poetry. (New
Brunswick, N.J.)
bibliog. 1950.

612741

[ZOELLER (CARLI) ed.]
Merry Wives of Windsor [by C. O. E.]
Nicolai. [Overture, transcribed
by C. Zoeller.] [c.1910.]
Overtures arranged from the full
score for the pianoforte by
C. Zoeller, No. 5.

556812

ZOUCH (R.) Works relating to:
see Moore (W. H.) Baconian Studies.

ZUCKER (ADOLF EDWARD)
The Courtiers in "Hamlet" and "The
Wild duck", [by H. Ibsen]. IN
Modern Language Notes, Vol. 54.
(Baltimore) 1939.

509539

ZUCKER (ADOLF EDWARD)
Ibsen-Hettner-Coriolanus-Brand.
IN Modern Language Notes, Vol. 51.
(Baltimore) 1936.

463701

ZUCKER (ADOLF EDWARD)
Ibsen: the master builder. [With
references to Shakespeare].
ports. illus. bibliog. 1930.

449552

ZUKOFSKY, LOUIS, and ZUKOFSKY, Mrs.
CELIA THAEW
Bottom: on Shakespeare. Vol. 1-2.
[Music to Shakespeare's 'Pericles'
by C. Zukofsky, Vol. 2.] (Austin,
Tex.) 1963.
University of Texas, Humanities
Research Center.

741503-4